P9-DXI-164

HILLSBORO PUBLIC LIBRARIES
WITHDRAWN

Subversives

Subversives

The FBI's War on Student Radicals,

and Reagan's Rise to Power

Seth Rosenfeld

Farrar, Straus and Giroux

New York

HILLSBORO PUBLIC LIBRARIES
Hillsboro, OR
Member of Washington County
COOPERATIVE LIBRARY SERVICES

For my teachers

For my parents

For Heidi

Farrar, Straus and Giroux
18 West 18th Street, New York 10011

Copyright © 2012 by Seth Rosenfeld
Map copyright © 2012 by Dan Hubig
All rights reserved
Distributed in Canada by D&M Publishers, Inc.
Printed in the United States of America
First edition, 2012

Grateful acknowledgment is made for permission to reprint lyrics from the "I-Feel-Like-I'm-Fixin'-to-Die Rag" by Country Joe and the Fish; words and music by Joe McDonald, © 1965 (renewed 1993) by Alkatraz Corner Music Co., BMI.

Library of Congress Cataloging-in-Publication Data
Rosenfeld, Seth, 1956–
    Subversives : the FBI's war on student radicals, and Reagan's rise to power / Seth Rosenfeld. — 1st ed.
        p.   cm.
    Includes bibliographical references.
    ISBN 978-0-374-25700-2 (alk. paper)
    1. Student movements—California—Berkeley—History.   2. College students—Political activity—California—Berkeley—History.   3. University of California, Berkeley—Students—History.   4. Reagan, Ronald.   5. Subversive activities—California—Berkeley—History.   6. United States. Federal Bureau of Investigation.   7. California—Politics and government—1951–   I. Title.

LD760 .R67 2012
378.1'9810979467—dc23

4965 6894 8/12   2011041204

Designed by Jonathan D. Lippincott

www.fsgbooks.com

10   9   8   7   6   5   4   3   2   1

The most beautiful thing in the world is the freedom of speech.   —Mario Savio, quoting Diogenes

The university is not engaged in making ideas
safe for students. It is engaged in making students safe for ideas.   —Clark Kerr

Obey the prescribed rules or pack up and get out.
                                —Ronald Reagan

This presents the bureau with an opportunity . . .
                                —J. Edgar Hoover

Contents

Preface   ix
Map: Berkeley in the 1960s   x

Prologue: A Meeting at the Governor's Mansion   3

Part One: The FBI on Campus
1. Spies in the Hills   11
2. The Responsibilities Program   28
3. The Undertaker   36
4. The Rise of Clark Kerr   44
5. The Essay Question   64
6. Protest at City Hall   77
7. Communist Target—Youth   88
8. The Trial of Robert Meisenbach   100
9. An Eye-opener   112
10. The FBI Story   127

Part Two: Student Radicals
11. The Police Car   153
12. The Free Speech Movement   172
13. A Leak to the Press   198
14. Sit-in at Sproul Hall   216
15. No Evidence   232
16. An Angry Young Man   242
17. Vietnam Day   260

Part Three: The Rise of Reagan
18. The Governor's Race   291
19. The Peace Trip Dance   305

Contents

20. Sources on Campus   326
21. Landslide   347
22. Fired with Enthusiasm   368
23. Obey the Rules   379
24. A Key Activist   406
25. At Bayonet Point   418
26. People's Park   447

Epilogue: The Aftermath   489

Appendix: My Fight for the FBI Files   505
Notes   513
Selected Bibliography   677
Documents, Interviews, and Other Sources   689
Acknowledgments   703
Index   707

A photographic insert follows page 250.

Preface

This book is a work of narrative nonfiction. It is based primarily on confidential FBI files that the bureau released to the author only after a lengthy legal fight under the Freedom of Information Act. Many pages were disclosed for the first time, including those concerning the surveillance of law-abiding citizens and efforts to disrupt political organizations. Many others were reprocessed to release additional information, such as the names of people Ronald Reagan informed on. The book also draws on court records, contemporaneous news accounts, oral histories, historical works, and hundreds of interviews with activists, university administrators, politicians, present and former FBI agents, and various other officials and observers, conducted by the author over the course of three decades. There are no anonymous sources, and no fictionalized accounts. The events and dialogue recounted herein are taken directly from the record.

Berkeley in the 1960s

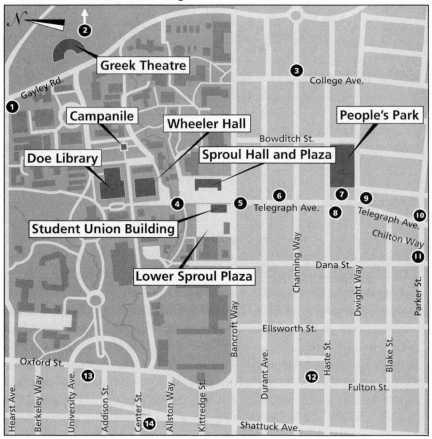

1 Founders' Rock
2 Radiation Laboratory
3 Fraternity Row
4 Sather Gate
5 Bancroft Strip
6 Robbie's Cafeteria, 2379 Telegraph Ave.
7 Caffe Mediterraneum, 2475 Telegraph Ave.
8 Cody's Books, 2454 Telegraph Ave.
9 Granma's Bookstore, 2509 Telegraph Ave.
10 Burning police car, May 15, 1969
11 William Rundle, Jr., shot May 15, 1969
12 Vietnam Day Committee headquarters, 2407 Fulton St.
13 University Hall, office of UC president Clark Kerr
14 FBI Berkeley resident agency, 2150 Shattuck Ave.

Subversives

Subterranean

Prologue: A Meeting at the Governor's Mansion

Curtis O. Lynum, the special agent in charge of the FBI's San Francisco field office, rang the bell by the front door of the governor's mansion in Sacramento. By his side stood Glenn A. Harter, who was his top domestic security agent. They had been summoned by the new governor, Ronald Reagan.

Waiting on the portico of the century-old grand Victorian that gray Monday morning in January 1967, Lynum felt some trepidation. He admired Reagan and had looked forward to meeting him, but secrecy was crucial. He was carrying confidential information about the student protests that were disrupting the University of California's Berkeley campus and making headlines across the country. He had intelligence about Mario Savio, who had been a leader of the Free Speech Movement and was Berkeley's most notorious campus agitator, and Clark Kerr, the president of the university.

Reagan had been sworn into office just two weeks earlier, and within days contacted the FBI and requested help with "the Berkeley situation." Lynum got the call at the San Francisco field office. He immediately notified J. Edgar Hoover at headquarters and recommended against meeting with Reagan—the controversy at the university was just too politically sensitive—but the director personally ordered him to go ahead. The Boss had taken a special interest in the rising conservative star who had vowed to clean up the "mess" at Berkeley.

During a fiercely contested gubernatorial campaign, Reagan had seized on the problem of campus unrest and it had become his hottest issue. Back when he was in school at Eureka College, in Illinois, he had joined in a student strike, and even helped lead it, but these Berkeley protests were different. He was disgusted with the sit-ins, the strikes, and the pickets put on by the Free Speech Movement, and the drugs and sex at the dance held by the Vietnam Day Committee in a campus gymnasium to promote antiwar protests. He declared that "beatniks, radicals, and filthy speech advocates" were proof of a "morality and decency gap" at the center of the state's Democratic Party. His message resonated: he won votes from citizens who saw the turbulence at Berkeley as a symbol of all that was ailing their country, an America facing threats from enemies abroad and rising taxes, racial strife, and generational conflict at home. Reagan defeated the incumbent Democrat, Edmund G. "Pat" Brown, in a landslide that left the state's Democratic Party a wreck and instantly made Reagan a national political figure.

Hoover welcomed Reagan's victory. For years, he had been frustrated by what classified FBI reports called "subversive" activities at the University of California's flagship campus. Berkeley had been the kind of institution that exemplified the best of American values: Here was a public university that offered a tuition-free education rivaling those offered by Harvard, Princeton, or Yale; employed a constellation of Nobel laureates; and held many millions of dollars in government research contracts. But even as the university was helping the nation win World War II by overseeing the development of the atomic bomb, Hoover's agents were investigating Berkeley students and professors suspected of spying for the Soviet Union. In the Cold War atmosphere of the late forties and early fifties, the director's concern about the school had grown when scores of faculty members refused to sign a special loyalty oath for university employees. So far, the sixties were turning out to pose an even greater challenge to authority, with the campus generating one provocation after another—that "vicious" essay question about the FBI, the protest against the House Un-American Activities Committee at San Francisco City Hall, the Free Speech Movement, the troop train protests. The old Communist Party had been bad enough, but now there was the New Left, the hippies, the Black Panthers, and Allen Ginsberg. Hoover and Clyde Tolson, his second in command at the bureau and his most intimate companion, saw Berkeley as the vortex of a youth movement fueled by "free love," drugs, and a general disrespect for authority spreading all too quickly to other campuses. Stepping up its efforts there, the bureau mounted the most extensive covert operations the FBI is known to have undertaken in any college community.

Those secret operations—and their far-ranging impact politically and culturally—are a central concern of this book.

The FBI has long denied investigating the university as an institution, and that much is true. But a legal challenge brought by this book's author pursuant to the Freedom of Information Act, over the course of twenty-seven years, forced the bureau to release more than 300,000 pages of its confidential records concerning individuals, organizations, and events on and around the campus during the Cold War, from the 1940s through the 1970s. This is the most complete record of FBI activities at any college ever released. The documents reveal that FBI agents amassed dossiers on hundreds of students and professors and on members of the Board of Regents; established informers within student groups, the faculty, and the highest levels of the university's administration; and gathered intelligence from wiretaps, mail openings, and searches of Berkeley homes and offices in the dead of night.

In court papers, the FBI maintained that its activities were lawful and intended to protect civil order and national security. But the records show bureau officials used intelligence gleaned from these clandestine operations not only to enforce the law, or to prevent violence, or to protect national security. As a federal appeals court ruled in ordering the release of the records, the bureau's activities "came to focus on political rather than law enforcement aims." And as U.S. District Judge Marilyn Hall Patel found, "The records in this case go [to] the very essence of what the government was up to during a turbulent, historic period of time."

In response to this author's prior reporting, FBI Director Robert S. Mueller III acknowledged that the bureau's surveillance and harassment of professors and students at the university during the Cold War was inappropriate. "Such investigations are wrong and anti-democratic, and past examples are a stain on the FBI's greater tradition of observing and protecting the freedom of Americans to exercise their First Amendment rights," Mueller declared. "Any repeat of such abuses will substantially reduce public confidence in the FBI and therefore undercut our ability to combat crime and protect our country against terrorism and espionage. For these reasons, I will tolerate no such undertakings in today's FBI."

FBI documents show that bureau officials misled a president by sending the White House information the bureau knew to be false; mounted a covert campaign to manipulate public opinion about campus events and embarrass university officials; collaborated with the head of the CIA to harass students; ran a secret program to fire professors whose political views were deemed unacceptable; and made common cause with Hugh Burns, the head of the state senate's un-American activities committee, instead of investigating allegations from organized crime sources in his home district of Fresno that he had taken payoffs and secretly owned a brothel.

Hoover had been trying to stifle dissent at Berkeley for years. But Governor Brown, the liberal Democrat elected in 1958 and again in 1962, had been unresponsive to Hoover's concerns about the university. Worse yet, he had betrayed Hoover's trust when the bureau sought to work with him covertly against the Free Speech Movement. In Reagan, however, the FBI director finally had an ally. Like Hoover, Reagan saw the Berkeley campus as a breeding ground for radicalism, where ungrateful students and insubordinate faculty used state resources to engage in anti-American protests. In their eyes, Savio was a "ringleader," and Kerr was, at the least, unwilling or unable to take control, and maybe a dangerous subversive himself.

Agents Lynum and Harter were surprised when the official who greeted them at the door of the governor's mansion told them Reagan would receive them upstairs in his bedroom. As they climbed the winding stairway to the master suite, Lynum hoped Reagan had picked the unusual meeting place for the sake of discretion. Lynum had warned Hoover that if reporters discovered the FBI was secretly helping Reagan stifle campus protests, it would embarrass the bureau—something Hoover hated more than anything else.

Discretion was not the only reason Reagan had chosen the unusual meeting place. As the two FBI men were admitted to the governor's bedchamber they found him propped up with pillows in a four-poster bed, suffering from a bad case of the flu. Reagan wore red pajamas, a muffler around his throat, and a robe. The covers were piled with stacks of official documents, and all around the bed stood Reagan's aides in suits and ties.

Lynum introduced himself and Harter, congratulated Reagan on his election, and held out his business card. The governor took the white rectangle, thanked them for coming, and got to the point: Reagan said he was "damned mad" that campus officials had allowed the demonstrations to continue. At one recent protest, students had even burned him in effigy. Pulling his robe closer, he said he intended to "straighten out" the university and was hoping the FBI could tell him what he was up against.

Lynum hesitated. Then, apologetically, he reminded Reagan that Hoover had agreed to the meeting on the condition that it would be just with Reagan and Lieutenant Governor Robert Finch. Lynum did not say so, but the director was concerned that other witnesses might expose the bureau's involvement.

The governor coughed and looked around the room at his aides. "Well, you heard him, boys," he said. "We'll follow the FBI's rules." Once they were gone, Lynum swore Reagan to secrecy, as Hoover had instructed, and during the next forty-five minutes the agents briefed him about the trouble at Berkeley.

Lynum had plenty of information to share. The FBI's files on Mario Savio, the brilliant philosophy student who was the spokesman for the Free Speech Movement, were especially detailed. Savio had a debilitating stutter when speaking to people in small groups, but when standing before a crowd and condemning the administration's latest injustice he spoke with divine fire. His words had inspired students to stage what was the largest campus protest in American history. Newspapers and magazines depicted him as the archetypal "angry young man," and it was true that he embodied a student movement fueled by anger at injustice, impatience for change, and a burning desire for personal freedom. Hoover ordered his agents to gather intelligence they could use to ruin his reputation or otherwise "neutralize" him, impatiently ordering them to expedite their efforts.

Hoover's agents had also compiled a bulging dossier on the man Savio saw as his enemy: Clark Kerr. As campus dissent mounted, Hoover came to blame the university president more than anyone else for not putting an end to it. Kerr had led UC to new academic heights, and he had played a key role in establishing the system that guaranteed all Californians access to higher education, a model adopted nationally and internationally. But in Hoover's eyes, Kerr confused academic freedom with academic license, coddled Communist faculty members, and failed to crack down on "young punks" like Savio. Hoover directed his agents to undermine the esteemed educator in myriad ways. He wanted Kerr removed from his post as university president. As he bluntly put it in a memo to his top aides, Kerr was "no good."

Reagan listened intently to Lynum's presentation, but he wanted more—much more. He asked for additional information on Kerr, for reports on liberal members of the Board of Regents who might oppose his policies, and for intelligence reports about any upcoming student protests. Just the week before, he had proposed charging tuition for the first time in the university's history, setting off a new wave of protests up and down the state. He told Lynum he feared subversives and liberals would attempt to misrepresent his effort to establish fiscal responsibility, and that he hoped the FBI would share information about any upcoming demonstrations against him, whether on campus or at his press conferences. It was Reagan's fear, according to Lynum's subsequent report, "that some of his press conferences could be stacked with 'left wingers' who might make an attempt to embarrass him and the state government."

Lynum said he understood his concerns, but following Hoover's instructions he made no promises. Then he and Harter wished the ailing governor a speedy recovery, departed the mansion, slipped into their dark four-door Ford, and drove back to the San Francisco field office, where Lynum sent an urgent report to the director.

The bedside meeting was extraordinary, but so was the relationship between Reagan and Hoover. It had begun decades earlier, when the actor became an informer in the FBI's investigation of Hollywood Communists. When Reagan was elected president of the Screen Actors Guild, he secretly continued to help the FBI purge fellow actors from the union's rolls. Reagan's informing proved helpful to the House Un-American Activities Committee as well, since the bureau covertly passed along information that could help HUAC hold the hearings that wracked Hollywood and led to the blacklisting and ruin of many people in the film industry. Reagan took great satisfaction from his work with the FBI, which gave him a sense of security and mission during a period when his marriage to Jane Wyman was failing, his acting career faltering, and his faith in the Democratic Party of his father crumbling. In the following years, Reagan and FBI officials courted each other through a series of confidential contacts. And after Reagan emerged as a leading conservative spokesman in the fifties, Hoover went beyond the bounds of his jurisdiction and secretly gave him personal and political help. He even lent Reagan a hand in keeping track of his own wayward children, Maureen and Michael. Now the long courtship between the FBI director and the former movie star would pay off for them both.

The FBI would become deeply involved in the clash over free speech at Berkeley between the powerful social forces represented by Reagan, Kerr, and Savio. Each of these men had a transforming vision of America and exerted extraordinary and lasting influence on the nation. By tracing the bureau's involvement with these iconic figures, this book reveals a secret history of America in the sixties. It shows how the FBI's dirty tricks at Berkeley helped fuel the student movement, damage the Democratic Party, launch Ronald Reagan's political career, and exacerbate the nation's continuing culture wars. Above all, it illustrates the dangers that the combination of secrecy and power pose to democracy, especially during turbulent times.

In his corner office at the FBI's headquarters in Washington, D.C., the director finished reviewing Lynum's report. He saw Reagan's request as a chance to finally quell demonstrations at Berkeley before they ignited even more protests at other schools all over the country.

Hoover's hand moved quickly across the report, scrawling jagged marks in blue ink.

"This," he underscored, "presents the bureau with an opportunity . . ."

Part One

The FBI on Campus

1

Spies in the Hills

On the night of November 9, 1945, two FBI agents huddled in a sedan on a dark street in the hills above the green slopes, quiet stone lecture halls, and towering Campanile of the University of California's Berkeley campus.

As fog blew through the eucalyptus trees along Grizzly Peak, obscuring the lights of San Francisco across the bay, the agents tried to stay alert and peered down the road at the front door of a bungalow at 790 Keeler Avenue. They were tailing a suspected Soviet spy named George Eltenton, who was visiting the chemist who lived there. Herve Voge was a former graduate student of J. Robert Oppenheimer, the Berkeley physicist already known as the father of the atomic bomb.

The war had ended only three months before, when the United States bombed Hiroshima and Nagasaki with two atomic devices built at the top-secret laboratories managed by the university. Uneasy allies during the war, America and the Soviet Union were becoming fierce adversaries as the Soviets imposed what Winston Churchill would soon call an "iron curtain" across Europe. The USSR seemed bent on world domination, and fear of nuclear conflict spread.

Federal officials saw the American Communist Party as the secretive arm of a foreign enemy, a Soviet-controlled organization whose members infiltrated government and private institutions, subverted official policy by fomenting unrest, and might engage in sabotage and espionage.

J. Edgar Hoover suspected that Eltenton and other Soviet spies had targeted the Berkeley campus and were using party members in their effort to obtain nuclear secrets from Oppenheimer and other Berkeley scientists. The FBI director feared that if these spies obtained those Promethean powers, the Soviet Union would use them against the United States. Urgently trying to stop this foreign plot, he opened a massive investigation of Soviet espionage at the university's atomic laboratories. On his orders, FBI agents conducted illegal break-ins, planted microphones, and tapped telephones. They kept suspects under constant surveillance, tracking them to their offices, dinner parties, and hotel rooms.

And on that cold and foggy night, they watched and waited for Eltenton outside the house on Keeler Avenue. By and by, he pulled his car to the curb and went in. Soon after, another car parked nearby, and its two occupants also entered the house. The agents took down the Washington State license number, A-24916. They soon traced the car to its owner, a young Berkeley professor named Clark Kerr.

Just below those same green hills almost a hundred years earlier, the Very Reverend Henry Durant and several other men with top hats and great expectations assembled by an outcropping. They gathered that day in May 1866 to dedicate the fields of glistening grain and grand oaks that unfurled toward the bay before them as the site for their College of California.

This land had been inhabited by Indian tribes for thousands of years, and by the late 1700s it was home to the Huichin, hunters and gatherers who were part of the Ohlone peoples. In 1769 Spanish explorers sailed into the bay, established missions, and began converting the "heathen." By the 1820s, European diseases had wiped out most of the Huichin. Around that time, the Spanish governor of California rewarded one of his loyal soldiers, Sergeant Luis Maria Peralta, with a grant of 48,000 acres along the east side of the bay. Peralta's family lost most of their land after the Gold Rush began in 1848 and, as the historian J. S. Holliday wrote, "the world rushed in." Several years later, the men in top hats acquired some of that land as the prospective grounds for their college.

The trustees gazed toward the shimmering bay, the red rocks of the Golden Gate, and the seemingly infinite horizon beyond. This western view had inspired them to name the site of their school after George Berkeley, the poet, philosopher, and Anglican bishop of Cloyne, who had posed the question: If a tree falls in the forest and no one hears it, has it really fallen? He answered, in essence: To *be* is to *be heard*. The iconoclastic Berkeley also held that entrenched bureaucracy was stifling the scholarly pursuit of truth in the Old World, and that it could be accomplished more freely in the New World. His vision of America as the "westward hope for humanity" encouraged the trustees gathered by the outcropping. One of them recited from Berkeley's poem "Verse on the Prospect of Planting Arts and Learning in America," in which he wrote, "The Muse, disgusted at an Age and Clime / Barren of every glorious Theme, / In distant Lands now waits a better Time / . . . Where men shall not impose for truth and sense / the pedantry of courts and schools . . ."

Despite their high hopes, the trustees encountered financial trouble and their private college faltered. A separate plan for a state university, meanwhile, also had stalled. But in 1862 President Lincoln signed the Morrill Land Grant College Act, which radically changed the course of higher education in America and events in Berkeley. The act gave states large tracts of federal land they could sell to fund the establishment of universities. Until then, colleges had mostly served the elite, but the act required land-grant universities to advance the national welfare by teaching practical courses in agriculture and industry and by offering instruction to the public.

Four years later, the California legislature passed the Organic Act of 1866, establishing the University of California as a land-grant college. With the Organic Act of 1868, the legislators placed the university under the authority of a largely autonomous Board of Regents and declared that the school should be free from political, partisan, or sectarian influence. Reverend Durant and his fellow trustees donated their college and land to the state, which absorbed it into the University of California. Opening in 1873 on the land dedicated to Bishop Berkeley, the university from the beginning embodied independence, civil liberties, and national security, fundamental values inherently in tension with one another.

By the 1920s, the campus was distinguished by nearly two dozen massive buildings of the classically inspired Beaux-Arts style, white stone structures with grand columns that paid homage to ancient ideals of truth and beauty and signaled the university's academic ambitions. In the center of campus, rising 303 feet and visible for miles, stood the Campanile, the great granite clock tower topped with a pyramid spire and lantern symbolizing "aspiration for enlightenment." The university's goals were furthered in 1928, when two outstanding young professors were recruited to Berkeley. Ernest O. Lawrence, an experimental physicist, soon began work on the cyclotron, or "atom smasher," a device that enabled him to separate and study the components of the atom. In 1939, he became the university's first Nobel Prize laureate. J. Robert Oppenheimer, a theoretical physicist, possessed an extraordinary capacity to synthesize different fields of knowledge. The two scientists drew other talented researchers to the university, and as World War II approached they became vitally involved in federally funded weapons research. Paramount among these efforts was the army's top-secret Manhattan Project to build the world's first atomic bomb. The university operated a vast radiation laboratory on a hill above the Berkeley campus and another at Los Alamos, New Mexico. Op-penheimer and Lawrence were soon hard at work—and so were Soviet spies.

The microphone hidden inside the Communist Party's Alameda County headquarters was identified in FBI reports only as "Confidential Infor-mant SF-631." A special team of agents had installed the bug during an illegal "black bag job," surreptitiously breaking into the party's Oakland office without a warrant. It was risky business, but the agents had become adept at these "special assignments," which Hoover rewarded with cash bonuses.

The job of monitoring the microphones and telephone taps on Com-munist Party members around the clock, however, could be numbingly dull. The "commies" seemed to be involved in every social or political cause out there, and they were always going on about some grievance, party minutia, or petty personal matter. So bored was one agent assigned to the listening post hidden in a tiny, unmarked commercial space a few miles from the Berkeley campus that he risked censure from Hoover to play a prank, placing a lipstick-smeared cigarette butt in the ashtray and leaving the next agent on duty to wonder.

The tedium was broken on the evening of October 10, 1942. The bug was picking up Steve Nelson, the head of the Communist Party in Alameda County, a member of the party's national committee, and an associate of officials at the Soviet consulate in San Francisco.

Nelson was discussing his keen interest in learning more about the secret experiments at the university's radiation lab on the hill. He was talk-ing to Giovanni Rossi Lomanitz, a Berkeley physicist and fellow Commu-nist Party member. "Rossi" was telling Nelson about his research on what was cryptically described as "a very dangerous weapon." But he added that he was thinking of quitting his research job at the lab so he could openly advocate the party's goals to workers in local shipyards.

Nelson deftly dissuaded him. He told the young scientist he was con-sidered an undercover member of the Communist Party, which needed to know about "these discoveries and research developments." His help was all the more important, Nelson said, because another scientist at the lab placed his research there above his support of the party. Though Nelson did not name this person, FBI agents believed he was J. Robert Oppenheimer.

Oppenheimer was perhaps the single most important scientist in-volved in the race to beat the Nazis in developing the bomb, and the FBI already had compiled a thick dossier on him. A New York native, he was the elder of two sons of a well-to-do textile merchant father and an artist mother. He attended Harvard, Cambridge, and Göttingen universities, and by 1929 was teaching physics at Berkeley. He spoke eight languages, was an authority on baroque music, and was well versed in art and literature. Gangly and kinetic, he sported a broad-brimmed porkpie hat and was given to jabbing the air with his pipe to emphasize a point. He seemed to vibrate with the energy of the atoms he studied and was often the nucleus of a crowd of awestruck students.

"Oppie" had been avowedly apolitical, known for his eccentricities and the strong martinis he served at his home on Shasta Road in the Berkeley Hills. But by late 1936 he had become interested in left-wing causes. He'd grown concerned about the Depression and the Nazis' treatment of German Jews. "I began to understand how deeply political and economic events could affect men's lives," he would later say. As he became involved in organizations supporting unions, better working conditions for migrant farmworkers, and the fight against fascism in Spain, he met other activists, including members of the Communist Party. Party membership grew during the Depression years, and in the 1930s about 250,000 Americans joined at least briefly, among them some 6,000 members in California, and 500 to 600 members in Alameda County.

FBI agents had spotted Oppenheimer at a social gathering in Berkeley attended by Communists in December 1940. They had obtained phone records showing he called Communists in the years before the war. They knew that his wife, Kitty, had been a Communist, and that her previous husband, Joseph Dallet, was a prominent Communist who had died fighting in the Spanish Civil War. They also knew his brother, Frank Oppenheimer, had been a member of the Communist Party as recently as 1941, and perhaps later. At least one informer claimed, in 1938, that Oppenheimer himself was a member of the Communist Party, but Oppenheimer always denied it and the FBI had been unable to prove it.

Now the bug inside the Alameda County office of the Communist Party had picked up Steve Nelson talking about his efforts to get some very dangerous secrets from him.

N.J.L. "Nat" Pieper, the special agent in charge of the San Francisco FBI office, sent an urgent report about Nelson's conversation to Hoover at headquarters.

There is, he said, a "situation" in Berkeley.

•

With his snub nose, piercing eyes, and rapid-fire speech, J. Edgar Hoover was as fearsome a figure as a Washington bureaucrat can hope to be. Close acquaintances had the privilege of addressing him as Edgar, the name by which his domineering mother summoned him. Clyde Tolson, his second in command at the FBI and his close companion, called him Eddie or Speed. Senators, who knew he collected secrets, deferred to him as Mr. Hoover. The agents who worked under his dictatorial supervision simply referred to him as the Boss.

He was driven, detail-oriented, and tough, and he adroitly administered the bureau's myriad investigations of government applicants, criminals, spies, and those he deemed subversive. He dealt deftly with the elected officials who ostensibly oversaw the bureau and he became virtually autonomous. Presidents came and went, but over the decades Hoover remained. He effectively manipulated press coverage of his operations, and used his position not only for law enforcement but to promote proper "American" values. He was, above all, suspicious of anyone who deviated from the mainstream, especially aliens.

John Edgar Hoover was born on January 1, 1895, in his parents' home at 413 Seward Square, in a predominantly white and Protestant neighborhood in southeast Washington, D.C. The government clerks and their families who lived there, like most people in the District of Columbia during the years Hoover was growing up, observed Jim Crow customs. His father, like his father's father, was a minor government functionary.

The youngest of four children, Hoover as a boy was "skinny, high strung, sickly, and excessively fearful, clinging to his mother whenever he could," according to *The Boss*, a biography by Athan G. Theoharis and John Stuart Cox. At Central High School, a public school for whites only, he never went on dates and was "known for his morality and celibacy," wrote Ovid Demaris in *The Director*. Rejected by the football team, he joined the school's ROTC program and eventually became captain of his company. He proudly wore his uniform when he taught Sunday school at his Presbyterian church. Although he would later say he had contemplated becoming a minister, as an adult he would rarely attend services.

In 1912, Hoover's senior year at Central, his father, Dickerson Hoover, suffered a psychiatric breakdown and spent time in a sanitarium. Hoover's mother, Annie, was the stronger personality, a disciplinarian "rewarding obedience and punishing disobedience with military impartiality," as she was described in a 1937 *New Yorker* profile. Hoover was afflicted with a stammer, but worked hard to overcome it by practicing elocution in his room at night. He became a leading member of the debate team, earned excellent grades, and was voted class valedictorian.

On graduating, Hoover took a job as a clerk in the Library of Congress and enrolled in night classes on law at George Washington University. In 1916 he earned a Bachelor of Law degree, without honors, and in 1917 a Master of Law degree. That April, the United States declared war on Germany, but through the help of a family friend Hoover secured a draft-exempt clerk's post at the U.S. Department of Justice. He worked in the Alien Enemy Bureau, and by war's end was the department's expert on foreign-inspired radicalism.

On June 2, 1919, a bomb exploded on the front porch of Attorney General A. Mitchell Palmer's home in northwest Washington, D.C. The bomber was killed in the blast and never identified, but anarchist literature was found in the rubble. Palmer began an antiradical campaign, promoting Hoover, now twenty-four, to be his special assistant and putting him in charge of it. Hoover studied the writings of Marx and other Communists. He built a network of informers. And he created an index of sixty thousand suspected radicals, according to *Secrecy and Power, The Life of J. Edgar Hoover*, by Richard Gid Powers. He developed the administrative techniques, theories of guilt by association, and alliances with self-styled patriotic organizations that would define his career. He also came to believe radicals not only held dangerous political theories, according to *The Boss*, but were "intellectual perverts."

Hoover oversaw a Justice Department program to round up and deport noncitizen immigrants whom he had concluded were radicals. Under immigration laws, department officials could use relatively loose administrative procedures to deport aliens who advocated anarchism or political violence, or who belonged to organizations that did. The officials were not required to meet the higher standards of evidence for criminal cases. They did not have to prove, for example, that an alien had actually resorted, or would resort, to violence. Aliens had no right to counsel while being questioned.

Based on Hoover's evidence, police and immigration agents conducted raids in twelve cities on November 7, 1919, arresting more than four hundred people. Most were poor and could not speak English. They had committed no violent crime and were guilty only of the technical charge of being aliens and members of a proscribed organization. To generate publicity, Hoover also gave special attention to the nation's most famous radical, a diminutive Russian immigrant named Emma Goldman, who wore pince-nez spectacles and high-collared blouses. He sought to deport her also on technical grounds: that she was not a citizen because her prior marriage to an American was invalid. An administrative judge agreed, and soon Goldman and 248 other foreign-born radical aliens ensnared in the raids were on a boat bound for Russia. Goldman's forced return there further disillusioned her about Soviet communism, and she moved to Britain. The deportations were Hoover's first big victory and, as he had hoped, they made front-page news.

Hoover next targeted thousands of aliens who were members of two radical organizations—the American Communist Party and the American Communist Labor Party—both of which took inspiration from the Russian Revolution. He prepared legal briefs alleging that each group had a manifesto advocating the violent overthrow of the government, and that each of their members was required to know it. On the basis of membership alone, he argued, they should all be deported. Relying on Hoover's assertions, Secretary of Labor William B. Wilson, who had jurisdiction over immigration laws, authorized arrest warrants. On January 2, 1920, Justice Department agents led raids in thirty-three cities, this time detaining some six thousand alien radicals.

At first, the so-called Palmer Raids brought Hoover and Palmer more praise, but soon they became a scandal. The detention facilities were inadequate and unsanitary. Many detainees were held incommunicado for days. The inhumane conditions of confinement sparked public outcry. Louis Post, the assistant secretary of labor who was to rule on whether each arrestee should be deported, discovered that Hoover's legal briefs blurred important differences between the two organizations. Contrary to Hoover's claims, the evidence showed that most members of the American Communist Labor Party did not know their organization professed violent overthrow of the government. Moreover, he found, the evidence showed that most of the immigrants were harmless.

Calling the raids a "gigantic and cruel hoax," Post ordered the release of about three thousand of the four thousand detainees who had been formally arrested and were facing deportation. On May 5, his boss, Secretary of Labor Wilson, also ruled against Hoover, concluding that membership in the Communist Labor Party was not cause for deportation. On June 23, a federal judge in Boston went further, finding membership in neither of the radical groups was ground for expulsion. The judge also condemned Hoover's use of informers and agents provocateurs. Ultimately, only 556 people would be deported.

Hoover fought back. He accused Post of being a Bolshevik and tried to get him impeached, but Congress instead criticized the sweeps. Hoover had hoped the raids would prompt Congress to enact a peacetime sedition law banning radical activities not only of aliens but also of citizens, but the debacle stymied his plans. By the spring of 1920, Communist revolts in Europe had fizzled and membership in domestic radical groups had fallen. The Red Scare faded. No one ever was charged for the bombing of Palmer's porch that had ostensibly triggered the dragnets.

Blamed for the disastrous raids that now bore his name, Attorney General Palmer's hopes for winning the Democratic nomination for president were ruined.

Hoover, however, suffered only a temporary setback on his continuing ascent. When the director of the Justice Department's Bureau of Investigation was fired for his part in a scandal involving bribes for government oil leases near Teapot Dome, Wyoming, Hoover got his big chance. In 1924, Attorney General Harlan Fiske Stone named him head of the bureau. Hoover boldly began to build a modern investigative agency. Firing scores of incompetent and unreliable agents, he replaced them with men trained in law or accounting. He tightened their supervision, ordering agents to report directly to him about other agents' "use of intoxicating liquors, the neglect of duties as well as other indiscretions." All agents were required to file detailed reports on their daily activities, and strict standards were set for securely handling bureau records. Using the latest technology, he established the bureau as a central clearinghouse for fingerprint-linked crime records, which helped local police track fugitives and positioned Hoover as a leader of the nation's law-enforcement community.

Hoover was still living at home with his mother. His father had died in 1921, and he was supporting her. Now slightly stocky, he had become a bit of a dandy, favoring summertime suits of white linen with a silk handkerchief tucked in the breast pocket. In 1928, he met Clyde Tolson, a Missouri native who had been confidential secretary to the secretary of war and had joined the bureau as an agent that year. Tolson was an excellent administrator, and within two years Hoover named him assistant director. They quickly became close, dining, commuting, and vacationing together.

Hoover, meanwhile, had not fully honored Attorney General Stone's admonition to refrain from engaging in domestic intelligence, and he would soon be deeply involved in political spying during the administration of President Franklin Delano Roosevelt. On taking office in 1933, FDR inherited an economic, social, and moral crisis. The Roaring Twenties had imploded. A decade of unregulated stock market speculation ended in the Great Crash of 1929 and the worst economic depression in the nation's history. Prohibition added to the national hangover. The constitutional ban on liquor from 1920 through 1933 not only failed to stop drinking but fostered widespread disrespect for the law and gave powerful mobsters such as Al Capone the opportunity to build lucrative and violent organizations running bootleg booze.

Roosevelt responded with the New Deal, the series of unprecedented federal programs intended to provide relief, recovery, and reform, and tapped Hoover to lead the New Deal's war on crime. Hoover's immediate mission was to take down the notorious gangsters—the "public enemies"—terrorizing the Midwest in a wave of sensational bank robberies, kidnappings, and shootings. In 1933 and 1934, Hoover's men caught or killed George "Machine Gun" Kelly, Charles "Pretty Boy" Floyd, and George "Baby Face" Nelson. These cases brought Hoover tremendous publicity, which he exploited with the help of newspaper editors, radio station executives, and motion picture producers hungry for heroic tales. Hoover's agents became known as G-Men—short for government men—and soon there were G-Man radio shows, G-Man comic strips, and a series of Warner Brothers' G-Man movies.

By the time the Bureau of Investigation was renamed the Federal Bureau of Investigation in 1935, Hoover had become one of the president's stars. And as Europe edged toward war, FDR turned to him to combat possible foreign espionage and sabotage at home. Although known as a great liberal, the patrician Democrat secretly expanded the FBI's domestic intelligence operations without consulting Congress or adhering to court-ordered limitations.

On August 24, 1936, Roosevelt summoned Hoover to the White House for a private discussion that would determine the course of the FBI's internal security operations far into the future. Hoover told the president that Communists were planning to "get control" of three major unions—the West Coast longshoremen's union, headed by Harry Bridges; the United Mine Workers Union; and the Newspaper Guild—"and by doing so they would be able at any time to paralyze the country." Hoover also claimed Communists had "inspired" activities in some federal agencies, including the National Labor Relations Board, which ruled on disputes between employers and unions.

Hoover had exaggerated the threat, but Roosevelt could hardly ignore such dire allegations. The president already was concerned that domestic

Communists and fascists might be acting as foreign agents. According to Hoover's memo on the meeting, FDR requested a more systematic intelligence investigation of "subversive activities in the United States, particularly Fascism and Communism."

Roosevelt subsequently issued other directives secretly expanding the FBI's internal security powers. Although the president had planned to seek funding from Congress for broader bureau operations, Hoover argued this could spark troublesome public debate, and Roosevelt instead requested a general appropriation, avoiding controversy over an intelligence expansion that went far beyond that authorized by statute. FDR also approved Hoover's request for exclusive jurisdiction over domestic intelligence investigations concerning civilians. The president was acting during a national emergency, but this exercise of executive power created what would become a permanent domestic intelligence structure centered on the FBI.

Seizing the opportunity, Hoover started several programs expanding the bureau's political surveillance. In 1940 he secured approval from the attorney general for the FBI's American Legion Contact Program, in which bureau agents would enlist more than fifty thousand members of the patriotic organization to clandestinely gather intelligence on suspected subversives.

That year, the FBI began using illegal wiretaps to gather intelligence. Roosevelt—in another secret and unilateral action—had issued a directive declaring that a U.S. Supreme Court order that banned wiretapping did not apply to national defense investigations of enemies inside the United States. Roosevelt did require that Hoover get prior approval from the attorney general for wiretaps, keep them to a minimum, "and limit them insofar as possible to aliens," but he mandated no other guidelines, no oversight of their use, and no limit on their duration.

In 1942, Hoover began a program of unauthorized break-ins of homes and offices of people suspected of "subversive activities" in order to install microphones and photograph documents. He acknowledged in internal memos that these surreptitious entries were "clearly illegal," but he deemed them an "invaluable technique." The agents called them "black bag jobs" because of the equipment kit they took along.

To supervise and conceal these activities, Hoover devised special systems of records. Sensitive communications among top FBI officials were written on pink paper "to be destroyed after action was taken." Field office memos requesting headquarters' permission to conduct break-ins were marked "Do Not File" to ensure they would not be indexed in the FBI's Central Records System, and were routed to senior bureau officials and then destroyed.

Roosevelt knew the bureau was breaking the law when agents made surreptitious entries to install telephone taps. Yet Hoover was giving him intelligence he wanted during an emergency. He was also passing along politically useful information about FDR's congressional opponents and press critics, and gossip about his friends and enemies.

Besides, Hoover was generating positive publicity for the president. FBI investigations during the war led to the convictions of several American fascists involved in German espionage. Bureau agents also captured eight German saboteurs who had landed on the East Coast by submarine. During this period, Congress exercised virtually no oversight of the FBI, even as it was growing more than tenfold from fewer than 400 agents in 1932 to 4,370 in 1945.

By this time Hoover's mother had died. He moved out of her Seward Square house and settled in a tract home closer to Tolson's house in northwest Washington. The FBI's two top officials had become more intimate, and as Richard Gid Powers put it, "The relationship was so close, so enduring, and so affectionate that it took the place of marriage for both bachelors." They could be seen three or four times each week at their reserved table at Harvey's Restaurant on Connecticut Avenue, where they were not charged for their meals and miniature cocktails. There were suspicions that the two men were homosexual, but in this era the press rarely examined the private lives of public figures and their relationship never became an issue.

Hoover had become a folk hero. With no small help from his public relations machine, he had become famous and was widely seen as impartial and incorruptible. He used this prominence as a pulpit to decry the degeneration of American institutions and to promote moral values based on church, home, and school. In a 1942 speech, he declared, "What we need is a return to God, more individually a return to the practice of religion. That is, without doubt, the greatest need in America today." In another talk that year, he contended schools were being undermined by modern teachers using "an insidious and unsound educational quackery that would rule out all the principles of discipline and control which, if carried to its illogical conclusion, would produce a generation of iconoclastic morons and criminals."

And by that fall Hoover already was focusing on another school matter: the Soviet spies at Berkeley.

•

Hoover read with great alarm Pieper's report on Steve Nelson's conversation about "a very dangerous weapon." So secret was the bomb project that not even the FBI had been officially told about it. Yet here was evidence that the Russians—with help from American Communists—were seeking to extract its secrets from the university's lab in the Berkeley hills.

FBI agents already were investigating thousands of Communist Party members as part of the bureau's routine domestic intelligence operations. Now Hoover intensified the effort, ordering FBI field offices to target party efforts to spy on the atomic research not only at Berkeley but at other labs around the country. The investigation was titled "Communist Infiltration of the Radiation Laboratory, University of California, Berkeley, California." The code name: CINRAD.

Late on March 29, 1943, FBI agents monitoring the microphone inside Steve Nelson's home at 3720 Grove Street, in Oakland, overheard another disturbing conversation.

Speaking in whispers, Nelson and a man named Joseph Weinberg were discussing "the project." Weinberg was a research physicist at the radiation lab. He worked under the supervision of Oppenheimer, who had recommended him for the job.

Nelson was saying he had talked with Oppenheimer but the physicist had been reluctant to reveal anything. He attributed Oppenheimer's reticence to his not being "politically mature," or as the FBI agents later paraphrased it, to the fact that "he was not a true and complete fanatical Marxist."

Weinberg, however, was willing. He told Nelson about the establishment of the secret laboratory at Los Alamos and gave him a scientific formula. Nelson warned him to be careful and assured him the party had people in factories all over the country gathering information for the Soviet cause.

Three days later, FBI agents watched Nelson as he walked from his home to a drugstore at MacArthur Boulevard and Grove Street and stepped into a phone booth. They traced the call he placed at 9:26 a.m. that Thursday to a house at 570 Belvedere Street in San Francisco's Cole Valley. It was the home of Peter Ivanov, vice-consul of the Soviet consulate in San Francisco.

Nelson failed to reach the Russian, but the following Tuesday agents watched as he drove to another drugstore, pushed more coins into a pay phone, and made contact. He hung up, got into his car, and drove across the Bay Bridge to San Francisco, the agents following as he erratically sped up, slowed down, and made random U-turns. He finally parked a block from St. Joseph's Hospital, at the corner of Park Hill and Buena Vista streets, not far from Ivanov's home. Setting out on foot, Nelson lost the agents on the darkened hospital grounds before climbing back into his car and speeding away.

That Saturday, agents monitoring the microphone in Nelson's home overheard another meeting, this time with Vassili Zubilin, the third secretary to the Soviet embassy in Washington, D.C. They heard Zubilin count out cash and give it to Nelson. "Jesus!" Nelson said. "You count money like a banker."

Meanwhile, FBI and army intelligence agents were investigating Lomanitz, Weinberg, and a third young scientist at the Berkeley lab. All three had been Oppenheimer's students. Suspecting they were under scrutiny, they complained to him on August 23, 1943, that they were being targeted because of their leftist political activities. He warned them to stay away from politics and "get straight" with security officials. He then advised the lab's security officer to look into a man named Eltenton.

Military officials arrived at Berkeley a few days later to question Oppenheimer. He told them three lab employees had reported being solicited to supply information to the Soviets. Eltenton, he said, had sent an intermediary to each one. Oppenheimer, however, declined to divulge the employees' names, saying they had not cooperated in the scheme and had spoken to him in confidence.

Dissatisfied, army officials again interrogated Oppenheimer on December 14, 1943. This time he named the intermediary as Haakon Maurice Chevalier, a French professor at Berkeley. He still refused to name the three men Chevalier had approached.

Three months later, General Leslie Groves, the head of the bomb project, questioned Oppenheimer and got a different story. Now he claimed Chevalier had contacted only one person—his brother, Frank, also a physicist working on the bomb project. Oppenheimer said that after his brother had told him about it, he phoned Chevalier and "gave him hell."

As FBI agents pursued their inquiry, they discovered that Chevalier was a well-known author and translator of French literary works. He had associated with prominent members of the Communist Party. He was one of Oppenheimer's close friends.

Eltenton, the agents learned, was a Briton who had worked as a senior physicist in Leningrad in the thirties and sought Soviet citizenship. In 1938 he moved to Berkeley and took a job at the Shell Development Company laboratory in nearby Emeryville. The agents investigated his contacts with Berkeley scientists, Communist Party members, and officials at the Soviet consulate in San Francisco, including Ivanov. And on that November night in the Berkeley hills, they followed him from Keeler Avenue on the twisting roads, into the fog.

Finally, the FBI struck.

Just after 2:00 p.m. on June 26, 1946, two agents entered the reception room of the Shell Development Company and asked for Eltenton. When he emerged they said they merely wanted to discuss his application for U.S. citizenship. He went with them to their office in Oakland. En route in their sedan, they asked casual questions. He acknowledged having lived in the Soviet Union but denied he had tried to become a citizen, citing the lack of freedom there and the "fear of being arrested and held on vague charges."

At the FBI office, the agents confronted him about his spying. He acknowledged he was friends with Ivanov, describing the vice-consul as a "pleasant person." He also admitted that Ivanov had asked him to get information about the Radiation Lab. Ivanov had said that without the atomic bomb, millions of Russians would needlessly die in battle against the Germans, and that Oppenheimer had the necessary data. If they brought Ivanov documents, he would photograph and return them quickly. He offered to pay them.

Eltenton insisted he had declined the offer, saying it would be absurd for him to approach Oppenheimer, because he hardly knew him. Instead, he had agreed to ask their mutual friend, Chevalier, to make the approach. Chevalier went to see Oppenheimer, but returned only to say the physicist had rebuffed him.

Even as these agents were picking up Eltenton, others were knocking on Chevalier's front door in the town of Stinson Beach, on the coast an hour north of the Golden Gate Bridge. Chevalier, too, agreed to go with them. As they drove into San Francisco, he described his work as a translator at the Nuremberg trials, praising the Allies' fairness to the Nazis. At the FBI's office at 111 Sutter Street, the agents explained he "was merely being afforded an opportunity to explain."

Chevalier admitted he knew Eltenton, that he knew Ivanov, that he was friends with Oppenheimer. Sure, he might have contacted people at the lab, but this would have been for his union work. Yes, he knew the lab was involved in "smashing atoms," but he had no idea this concerned an atomic bomb.

An agent confronted Chevalier: the bureau had reports that he had asked three different lab employees to turn over secrets about the project. A fabrication, he replied. Only after "considerable delay," the agents later wrote, did Chevalier finally admit Eltenton had asked him to procure data from Oppenheimer for the Russians. He insisted, however, that Oppenheimer had refused to participate. The interrogation over, the agents released him, as they had Eltenton.

At FBI headquarters, Hoover reviewed the Berkeley cases and concluded there was ample proof of a conspiracy to commit espionage by Eltenton, Chevalier, Nelson, Weinberg, and Ivanov. In early 1947, he sent the U.S. Department of Justice a summary of the evidence against Weinberg and Nelson. But the department did not prosecute them, according to an FBI memo that confirmed the bureau's evidence derived from an illegal bug and consequently was "not admissible" in court. The FBI's investigation of Eltenton, Chevalier, and Ivanov also had relied on black bag jobs and bugs, and when Hoover sought their prosecution the Justice Department declined. The spies escaped prosecution because of the bureau's illegal investigative methods. Hoover had placed counterintelligence above constitutional rights.

Ivanov was recalled to the Soviet Union. Eltenton returned to England, declining to comment on the matter. Chevalier moved to France and wrote in his 1965 book, *Oppenheimer, Story of a Friendship,* "If there was ever a plot in which either Eltenton or myself were even remotely involved, no trace was ever found of it." Nelson said in his autobiography, *American Radical,* "I never had any links with Soviet espionage in the United States." Weinberg denied spying, and was unsuccessfully prosecuted for perjuring himself when he denied being a member of the Communist Party, again because of the FBI's illegal investigative methods.

As for Oppenheimer, there is no doubt the brilliant Berkeley physicist was involved in causes supported by Communists in the late 1930s and early 1940s. But he was an independent liberal concerned with the cause, not the party. The government never proved he had been a Communist Party member, let alone engaged in espionage, and in 1954 a panel of the Atomic Energy Commission reached the "clear conclusion" that he was "a loyal citizen." But for reasons personal or professional, he had delayed notifying security officials that he and his associates had been asked to spy, then gave contradictory accounts about it. He paid dearly for his lapses, with the commission revoking his security clearance. As Kai Bird and

Martin Sherwin concluded in *American Prometheus: The Triumph and Tragedy of J. Robert Oppenheimer*, this was seen as a defeat not only for him but for liberalism.

The most damaging of the Soviet spies now known would not be detected for years. They operated not at Berkeley but at other Manhattan Project facilities. They were uncovered as a result of the army's top-secret Venona Project, which beginning in 1948 decoded telegrams sent between Moscow and Soviet diplomatic offices during the war. In one of the most sensationalized of these cases, Julius and Ethel Rosenberg, both Communists, were arrested in 1950, convicted of espionage, and executed. Scientists and historians have since questioned the significance of the information they might have supplied the Soviets. Although Hoover touted the case as the "Crime of the Century," he acknowledged in confidential memoranda that the Soviets likely obtained the secret of the bomb elsewhere. It is now known that evidently far more effective spies, such as the Los Alamos scientist Theodore Hall, eluded bureau agents.

As the Cold War intensified, the FBI saw its mission as nothing less than protecting the American way of life. So sweeping were the presidential directives granting the FBI domestic intelligence authority that bureau officials could investigate any person or organization they deemed "subversive."

Operating in a crisis atmosphere with little oversight, the FBI would soon begin to misuse its intelligence machinery to destroy the careers of university employees engaged in lawful dissent.

2

The Responsibilities Program

In the inner sanctum of Hoover's corner suite, on the fifth floor of the Justice Department building at Ninth Street and Pennsylvania Avenue, hung an enormous mounted sailfish that the director had caught in Florida while on vacation with Clyde Tolson. On his desk was the Bible his mother had given him. On another wall hung a framed photograph of the late attorney general Harlan Fiske Stone, the surrogate father who had helped Hoover become America's most powerful police official. Stone had warned him to refrain from political investigations that would mire the bureau in scandal and undermine democracy.

But the Cold War had intensified fears about enemies at home and abroad. By 1950, the Soviets had successfully tested an atomic bomb built partly with secrets stolen from the University of California labs. In China, Communists led by Mao Zedong had taken over. In Korea, U.S. and Chinese forces were fighting each other in an undeclared war seen not as a civil conflict between the north and the south but as a proxy battle between democracy and communism. The House Committee on Un-American Activities (commonly called the House Un-American Activities Committee, abbreviated HUAC and pronounced "*hew*-ack") was continuing a series of highly publicized hearings into alleged Communist influence in Hollywood, in government, and in education. And on February 9, 1950, a Republican senator from Wisconsin delivered a speech to the Women's Republican Club of Wheeling, West Virginia. "Today we are engaged in a final, all-out battle between Communist atheism and Christianity," Joe McCarthy declared.

While Senator McCarthy and the members of HUAC were generating controversy, however, Hoover was working behind the scenes, quietly mounting far more destructive investigations of law-abiding people he deemed "subversive," a description with no legal definition and sinister connotations.

Under his direction, FBI clerks compiled code-numbered index cards on hundreds of thousands of people engaged in constitutionally protected activities. These thin slips of cardboard, which comprised the General Index, were the essence of the bureau's power, for they were the key to the files containing agents' reports on the subject's speeches, writings, meetings, finances, family lives, medical conditions, and sometimes their sexual activity. These files, in turn, filled banks of dull metal cabinets. Their contents were gleaned not only from openly conducted FBI interviews, but from surreptitious break-ins of homes and offices, illegal electronic surveillance, pretext phone calls to unsuspecting family members, and carefully cultivated informers. The most sensitive information was locked in special safes, such as plans for the detention without judicial warrant of thousands of people in the event of a national emergency. Many of these activities, Hoover knew, were unauthorized, if not outright illegal, but he deemed them necessary to protect the nation from the enemies of democracy. And the Boss could count on the discretion of his agents, from whom he demanded absolute loyalty—and who feared his wrath.

Hoover had been growing increasingly concerned about the nation's colleges. Communists, he was convinced, were infiltrating teaching staffs and indoctrinating impressionable young people. In 1951, he initiated a secret nationwide program to remove politically suspect teachers. It was titled the Responsibilities Program, and it targeted members of the Communist Party and other subversives whom FBI officials believed would be "potentially dangerous" to "the internal security of this country" in the event of an emergency.

The program took shape after Hoover discovered that several state governors planned to meet with President Harry Truman about internal security concerns. The governors intended to ask Truman to grant them access to FBI intelligence information they could use to purge Communists employed in state agencies, including colleges and universities.

Hoover saw the governors' concern as an opportunity to mount a new attack on people he deemed subversive. But he knew the bureau's cooperation with the governors could be politically damaging if it became public. It would contradict his claim that information in the FBI's files was confidential, and expose him to charges of recklessly spreading unproven allegations of disloyalty. It would also strain his relations with President Truman, who, the FBI director was well aware, believed the threat of domestic communism was exaggerated. So with characteristic bureaucratic cunning, Hoover deceived the White House and turned the situation to his advantage.

On learning that the governors had secured an appointment with the president, Hoover sent a memo marked "Personal and Confidential" to one of Truman's top aides, Rear Admiral Sidney F. Souers. He styled this memo as a warning about the governors' agenda so the White House would not be caught off guard, and declared that he strongly opposed their request for access to FBI information. "As you know," he wrote, "we have taken a firm position in the past that the files of this Bureau are confidential and that information cannot be released outside the Executive Branch of the Federal Government." He also professed concern about the potential harm to civil liberties, saying it "might result in suffering to innocent persons."

Souers briefed Truman about Hoover's memo, and reported back that Truman appreciated Hoover's warning and would make no commitments to the governors. This was just what Hoover wanted. Having told Truman he would have nothing to do with such a program, he had successfully evaded the president's supervision of his own plan. He then arranged a private conference with the governors.

The February 12, 1951, meeting at Hoover's office lasted one hour and fifteen minutes. The governors explained that they desired FBI information to screen people seeking state and local government jobs, but that they were particularly concerned with "the matter of Communism in our colleges and universities." Hoover said he was pleased they were consulting him and explained the FBI's national security responsibilities. According to his subsequent memo on the meeting, he also described "in some detail the national picture of the Communist Party activities, pointing out that the party was now down to a hard core as a result of their own security program, and that it was necessary to keep abreast of their activities because he felt that the war, or whatever you wished to call the present situation, would eventually be won on the home front, that the home front must remain inviolate."

On a "confidential basis," Hoover briefed them on the present strength of the Communist Party, displaying a chart that showed the number of party members in each state. He discussed "the extent to which the Bureau has gone in protecting the home front," revealing that the FBI had more than twelve thousand informants in various industrial plants and more than one thousand informants inside the Communist Party. He described the FBI's secret cooperation with the American Legion, in which legionnaires acted as informers on all manner of "un-American activities." Hoover even disclosed the precise number of dangerous subversives the FBI had identified in each state, and said bureau agents kept 4,463 people considered "the most potentially dangerous" under surveillance "at all times."

Turning to the governors' concern about colleges and universities, Hoover made a proposal: They should contact the special agent in charge, or SAC, at their local FBI office whenever they had "a problem." The SAC would point them to public sources of information, such as congressional hearings and news articles about prospective professors; the bureau, of course, "could not give information from our confidential files." The governors could then use the information to identify and purge present and former members of the Communist Party and other subversive groups from their jobs.

As the meeting ended, the governors seemed satisfied and thanked Hoover. To hide their plan, he suggested they tell inquiring news reporters that they had merely discussed "how better to carry out the Presidential directive on internal security."

Five days later, without telling the attorney general, Hoover launched the Responsibilities Program, sending strict instructions to the SACs of all fifty-three FBI field offices. First, each SAC should check his field office files to identify "subversives" employed in the area. For though Hoover had told the governors that the bureau could provide only public information, the information would actually be drawn from the same kinds of confidential files the FBI had used to investigate Communist spying on the University of California's bomb project.

Hoover also directed the SACs to identify local officials whom they trusted to cooperate with the program in addition to the governors, such as police chiefs. An SAC could pass the information along only after the official promised never to reveal the FBI as the source. As an extra safeguard, the SACs were to convey the information orally, so there would be no paper trail back to the bureau. No information, he emphasized, could be provided without prior approval from headquarters.

Hoover told the agents that authority for the program came from the "responsibility of the Bureau for the internal security of the country as a whole." But he warned them to "exert the utmost judgment and discretion" so that "the Bureau's interests are protected"—in other words, to keep it secret.

The operation was soon running smoothly in nearly every state. At first, it focused on getting alleged subversives fired from their jobs at local and state agencies and public utilities. Although many of them held blue-collar positions, no job was too menial to be targeted anonymously in the name of national security. Among these employees were an electrician's helper at Pacific Gas and Electric Company in Oakland; a chef for the dining cars of the Southern Pacific Railroad Company, also in Oakland;

and a typewriter repairman at the Western Union Telegraph Company in Chicago. They also included white-collar professionals, such as the minister who worked as a clerk in a county courthouse in Detroit; the driver's license examiner at the California Department of Motor Vehicles in San Francisco; the city planner in Cincinnati; and the Oregon field director for the Boy Scouts of America.

Educators, however, quickly became the focus of the program. As Tolson noted in an April 30, 1951, memo to Hoover, "the educational field is considered a prime target by the Communist Party because it reaches the youth of our nation. A daily contact of teachers with pupils forms a close association and enables the teachers to effectively control the thinking of the pupils and thus insidiously instill into the minds of children the Communist Party line."

Tolson warned that targeting school employees under the program carried special risks of exposure because "the educational field is probably one of the most controversial and independent fields in existence." But the danger could be minimized, he suggested, by "careful selection of the responsible officials to whom this information would be given on a confidential basis."

Hoover indicated his agreement by making one of the notations he typically wrote in the margins of memos, always in a jagged hand, and always in blue ink. These curt comments were one of the main ways he managed the bureau. Here he simply scrawled, "OK-H."

Scores of elementary and high school teachers across the country were soon subjected to the program. So were nonteaching staff. In California, for example, SACs passed along allegations of subversive political activity by a librarian who had publicly criticized censorship in Los Angeles, the director of child care at the Bellflower School District, an art school judge at the state fair—even a custodian at Eagle Rock High School.

The principal goal of the program, however, was the elimination of suspect professors, lecturers, and other employees from state universities. For example, the SACs distributed allegations against faculty members and other staff at the University of Pennsylvania, the University of Michigan, the State University of New York, the University of West Virginia, the University of Wisconsin, the University of Cincinnati, the University of Oklahoma, and the University of Puerto Rico. The agents also targeted staff at private schools, including Harvard, MIT, and USC.

Allegations against at least fifteen employees at the University of California were confidentially passed to Governor Earl Warren, whom Hoover trusted. A Republican, Warren had graduated from UC Berkeley and Berkeley's Boalt Hall School of Law and gone on to a remarkable political career, winning election as Alameda County district attorney three times starting in 1926, as state attorney general in 1938, and as governor for an unprecedented three terms starting in 1942. Hoover and Warren had developed a professional relationship during Warren's days as a hard-nosed Oakland prosecutor. In 1933, Hoover provided assistance when Warren established the Anti-Racket Council of Alameda County to pursue organized crime. Warren, in turn, allowed FBI agents access to his office's well-organized files on radicals, one of the state's largest collections. By 1937, Warren and Hoover had become friendly enough that the director assigned FBI agents to chauffeur the Californian when he visited Washington, D.C. By 1948, the governor was the beneficiary of confidential FBI information about his political opponents, labor leaders, and state employees.

President Eisenhower would name Warren chief justice of the U.S. Supreme Court in 1953, and he would go on to surprise Ike and many others as he presided over some of the high court's most liberal rulings, such as *Brown v. Board of Education*, which in 1954 declared racial segregation in public schools unconstitutional and helped clear the way for the civil rights movement. The Warren Court in 1957 issued several opinions siding with people accused of being subversives, and in the ensuing years Hoover and Warren grew apart.

But in 1951, FBI officials were comfortably working with Warren under the Responsibilities Program. As one agent wrote, "Governor Warren has in the past proved himself to be reliable and discreet to receive such information."

On Hoover's orders, the SACs at the FBI's California field offices periodically phoned Warren's office and orally passed along allegations about university employees. Warren then initiated a two-pronged inquiry. His confidential secretary, Helen MacGregor, typed a summary of the FBI allegations on unmarked paper, without identifying the source. She sent one copy of this blind memo to a deputy in the state attorney general's office, who investigated the named employee and reported back to Warren. She sent a second copy to the university's president, Robert Gordon Sproul, along with a cover letter from Warren asking him to investigate the employee.

Warren had complete confidence in Sproul. The two men became fast friends when they were fellow students at Berkeley in the teens; Sproul had nominated Warren for the presidency at the 1948 Republican National

Convention. As governor, Warren was president ex officio of the university's Board of Regents, and one of Sproul's best allies in Sacramento. They were campmates at the elite Bohemian Grove.

In a typical letter, Warren wrote:

> Dear Bob,
> The enclosed information concerning Joseph Dexter Phillips, Jr., a member of the faculty of the University of California at Santa Barbara, was sent to me from a very reliable source. It makes a charge of Communist affiliations which I believe should be investigated.
> Will you please give this your serious consideration and take such actions as may be warranted . . .
> Sincerely,
> Earl Warren
> Governor

Sproul's investigation did not corroborate the FBI's allegation that Phillips, a lecturer in economics, had been a member of the Communist Party. Likewise, the deputy attorney general's inquiry discovered no evidence to substantiate the charge. The deputy found only that Phillips had signed a petition calling for the abolition of the House Un-American Activities Committee. Phillips joined the faculty of the State University of New York, meanwhile, but despite the lack of evidence, Sproul assured Warren that Phillips would never get another job at the University of California.

This happened again when Hoover targeted Thomas A. Bisson, a China scholar who had received a Rockefeller Foundation grant and was a temporary lecturer in political science at Berkeley. FBI agents prepared a lengthy report in which unnamed sources claimed Bisson had associated with alleged Communists and was himself a "radical." The report noted he had written books that "supported the Chinese Communists" and had been "critical of this country's support of the Chinese Nationalists." This information was orally given to Warren, who handled it as usual. But neither the deputy attorney general nor the university president found evidence to confirm the FBI's allegations.

Nonetheless, Sproul sent a blind memo containing the accusations to Bisson's supervisor, Frank Russell, the chairman of his department. "I am troubled," Russell replied in a note, "by the impossibility of evaluating the charges made or the inference suggested in view of the anonymous character of the charges . . . I hope that no adverse action will be taken at this time unless fairly conclusive evidence is available." Still, Sproul assured Warren the university would not renew Bisson's teaching contract.

Nor could state officials confirm the FBI's anonymous allegations that Leonie Loeb Zanger, a secretary in UCLA's Economics Department, had been a Communist Party member in 1950. Despite the absence of any verified evidence, the deputy attorney general suggested that university officials "interview" Zanger about her past. The record leaves unclear whether they did confront her, but in December 1952 she resigned.

This was how the Responsibilities Program often worked: state and local officials found the FBI's anonymous allegations inaccurate or unverifiable. But even without substantiated evidence, they pressured employees to leave their jobs or simply refused to rehire them. The covert administrative process designed by Hoover denied the accused employees the rights to test evidence and confront their accuser that were granted to defendants accused of the most heinous crimes.

Despite its widespread operation, Hoover managed to conceal the Responsibilities Program from his ostensible supervisor, the U.S. attorney general, for more than two years. He disclosed nothing about it until an aide to Attorney General Herbert Brownell, Jr., incidentally learned about his earlier meeting with the governors, and even then Hoover misled the nation's chief law enforcement officer, claiming he had merely developed an "informal" system of sharing limited information that came from reliable public sources. Hoover further portrayed the FBI's role as minor, complaining "there is an entirely erroneous impression that the FBI has the major responsibility for the internal security of the country." Based on these misrepresentations, Brownell voiced no objection.

Virtually all the governors and local officials receiving information under the Responsibilities Program kept it secret, despite obvious civil liberties concerns. But after a few of them made indiscreet comments and the FBI's role threatened to become public, Hoover ended the program. For though he wanted to rid schools and local governments of employees he deemed a threat to national security, he was more concerned with protecting the bureau's carefully cultivated image of being fair and impartial.

Over the program's four-year course, FBI officials disseminated derogatory information on at least 908 people nationwide, most of whom worked in education. According to an estimate in one FBI memo, more than half of the secretly accused were fired, quit, or otherwise left their jobs.

Hoover was pleased with the program's results. But at the University of California, rumors about anonymous charges of disloyalty were starting to trouble some professors.

3

The Undertaker

Hugh M. Burns was a convivial funeral parlor operator from Fresno who took a special interest in monitoring public morals. And as chairman of the state senate's Fact-Finding Committee on Un-American Activities, he had the means to do so. On June 9, 1951, he issued a sensational report about subversives at the University of California that heightened Hoover's concern about Berkeley.

Burns's tome, appropriately bound in red, charged that Communists were infiltrating schools all over the state. The biggest concentration was at the University of California, which was nothing less than a hotbed of spies and subversives. On top of that, his report claimed, UC officials were "aiding and abetting" the international Communist conspiracy to overthrow the United States government.

Over the course of 291 pages, Burns disinterred several incidents from the past, offering no new evidence but plenty of postmortem innuendo. Exhibit A was the Oppenheimer case. The report recounted how the Soviet vice-consul, Peter Ivanov, through George Eltenton and Haakon Chevalier, had unsuccessfully approached Oppenheimer in a quest for atomic secrets. "The facts are quite plain that these three men, Eltenton, Chevalier and Ivanov, were unanimous in picking Dr. J. Robert Oppenheimer as the most suitable man to contact," Burns's report posited. "They knew his record much better than our own security agencies, and they evaluated him as a potential traitor."

Exhibit B was the Writers' Congress held at the University of California at Los Angeles during the war. The announced goals of this conference were to discuss the craft of writing, analyze its use against fascism, and strengthen cultural understanding among allied nations. The gala opening session was to include Hollywood movie makers such as Walt Disney, famous authors and screenwriters, and representatives of Great Britain, China, and Russia. What alarmed the state un-American activities committee was the October 1943 conference's cohost, an organization called the Hollywood Writers' Mobilization. Its members included prominent authors who had been involved with communism, such as Dalton Trumbo, author of the antiwar novel *Johnny Got His Gun*. The un-American activities committee had demanded that President Sproul cancel the event but he refused, and in his opening speech he read a welcome from President Roosevelt that hailed the gathering as "a symbol, it seems to me, of our faith in the freedom of expression." Nonetheless, Burns's report now complained that the university had joined in "a traitorous enterprise."

Exhibit C was a conference held at UC Berkeley in 1945 called the Institute on Labor, Education and World Peace. Burns was outraged that the university had jointly sponsored the event with the California Labor School, another organization his committee deemed part of the Communist plot. "No person in his right mind would open his home to a gang of criminals and expose his family to peril," the report said. "Yet the trusting and uninformed heads of the university threw open the portals of the campus to persons sworn to rip apart our most trusted and sacred institutions—agents of a foreign conspiracy."

Burns concluded his exhumation with a threat: "If those to whom the parents have entrusted their children persist in airily brushing aside the terrible menace that has stared us all in the face for the past 30 years . . . this committee, at least, believes it is high time they were replaced."

Sproul was dismayed by the attack, particularly because he was a staunch anti-Communist and had been working for years to control campus radicals. During the depression years of the thirties, a small but significant number of Berkeley students had joined left-wing groups, participated in antiwar rallies, and supported the general strike of 1934 that was led by Harry Bridges. Conservative legislators complained to Sproul, and he issued regulations later known as Rule 17. One of the nation's most restrictive university rules on free speech, it prohibited students from using the campus for partisan political purposes, including distributing literature and raising funds. Sproul's stated rationale was that keeping politics off school grounds would keep politicians out of university operations, and thus help preserve academic independence. Activists responded by simply moving their protests a few feet outside Sather Gate, which at that time marked the campus's south border. Sproul, however, also directed his aides to work with local police departments, the American Legion, and District Attorney Earl Warren's office to investigate and intimidate student activists. And he later cooperated with Governor Warren in the FBI's

Responsibilities Program to purge politically suspect professors. In fact, a bureau report called him "cooperative." And—as Burns well knew—the university just two years earlier had adopted a special loyalty oath for all its employees.

Still, in an effort to be politic, Sproul issued a public statement saying that though the report's allegations were "fantastic," he was sure they were "well-intentioned." He pointed out that security measures for the bomb project had been controlled by federal agencies, not the university, and lamented that "an institution which has contributed so much to the progress and preservation of America should be thus maligned."

Several professors made their own reply to Burns. They acknowledged that during the war, when Russia was an ally, some faculty members had belonged to pro-Soviet organizations. But they argued, "It is neither fair nor honest to smear a person today for former membership in a once respectable organization." Moreover, they noted, the report failed to identify a single Communist faculty member or student organization presently on campus.

Burns's allegations made front-page headlines, particularly in the *San Francisco Examiner*, flagship of the Hearst chain and Northern California's largest newspaper. The *Examiner*'s stories carried extra weight because the Hearst family had long been involved in university affairs, both as members of the Board of Regents and as major contributors. They were militantly anti-Communist, and a Hearst representative privately told a university vice president that the school should simply fire every employee named in Burns's report.

The undertaker was surely delighted to bury the university in negative publicity; he had all but guaranteed that result by releasing the report to newspapers before letting school officials see it. His attack was part of a larger design that became clear a few weeks later in a personal letter he sent to the university's legislative liaison. "The Committee certainly has no desire to harass the University," he wrote, but until the school established a "screening unit" to help his committee eliminate politically suspect professors and students, it "creates the situation that invites these matters."

Burns was flexing his political muscle. He was a rising power, well on his way to becoming president of the state senate, California's most powerful legislator. And the legislature, of course, controlled the university's budget.

According to an early version of his official résumé, Burns was born in Chloride, Arizona, though he would later list his birthplace as the somewhat more stately-sounding Kingman, a few miles down the road. His father was a traveling salesman for the National Biscuit Company, but Burns spent most of his life in Fresno, the county seat of a vast agricultural area equidistant from Los Angeles, San Francisco, and Las Vegas. After graduating from Fresno High School, he worked as an apprentice mortician and opened his own funeral parlor. His hobby, he liked to say, was taxidermy.

Burns married in 1924 and had one daughter, but like many of the local civic leaders he spent much of his time at Fresno's finer men's clubs, joining a virtual taxonomy of them, from the Elks (Lodge No. 439) to the Fraternal Order of Eagles (Aerie No. 39) and the Loyal Order of Moose (Lodge No. 445). He was gregarious and liked to drink straight whiskey any time of day; though a Democrat, he won his first seat in the assembly in 1936 with support from Republicans.

One of his first acts on assuming office was to introduce a bill to control social diseases in California, though it stopped short of requiring the state health department to open clinics to treat syphilis, which would have smacked of socialized medicine. He won appointment to head the assembly's Committee on Public Morals, and was soon opening investigations into the state's lucrative horse racing and liquor industries. He cast himself as protector of animals and small children, but was compelled to drop a bill he carried for the medical lobby to let laboratories experiment on abandoned dogs, after the Tailwaggers' Association put up ferocious opposition. He also tried to block state funding for child care centers, arguing that children should be reared at home and "by passing this measure we're advocating one of the tenets of the Communist Party."

Elevated to the senate in 1942, Burns energetically served on California's un-American activities committee. It was one of several state versions of the House Un-American Activities Committee—all part of a network of local, state, and federal bodies dedicated to defending the nation against subversion. Their power came from their legislative authority to issue subpoenas and compel witnesses to testify—and from their immunity to libel suits that might otherwise arise from their accusatory reports. Critics contended that they operated on the basis of flimsy evidence and guilt by association.

California's version, the historian Garry Wills has written, was "the most aggressive of all the anti-Communist committees." Created by the state legislature in January 1941 as American involvement in the war loomed, it was empowered to investigate any activity that might interfere with the national defense program in California. Jack Tenney, the committee's first chairman, was a onetime radical union organizer and flamboyant former band leader who wrote the 1923 hit "Mexicali Rose." Kevin Starr, the California historian, described him as "hard-drinking, paranoid, dyspeptic— could have been played by W. C. Fields in one of that actor's grouchier moods." Tenney and his fellow committee members interpreted their mandate broadly, decreeing that "any group that attacks the Flag, institutions, traditions, Democracy and Constitution of California and the United States is un-American per se."

Tenney became so abusive of witnesses and their lawyers at the committee's public hearings, however, that the legislature eventually removed him as chairman. Taking over, Burns introduced a barrage of antisubversive laws, one of which would have required a loyalty oath for members of every state-licensed profession, from building contractors to dentists. He virtually stopped holding public hearings, on the ground that people he subpoenaed to testify were exploiting them "as a sounding board for their own ideas." Under his chairmanship, the committee instead conducted its investigations quietly, held hearings in closed session, and periodically issued red-bound reports loaded with allegations.

By now Hoover had become interested in the secretive committee making so much noise about Communists in California. FBI agents reported that its staff took elaborate security precautions out of fear that subversives might try to steal their investigative files. The material was gathered and indexed at a downtown San Francisco office in room 837 of the Mills Building, behind a door bearing a false name. All references to original sources of information were kept in a separate index, locked in a steel cabinet at the committee's Sacramento office. A duplicate set was stored in a safety deposit vault at a bank.

The agents further reported that the committee was actually run by its chief counsel, a man with bristling red eyebrows and a genial manner named Richard Ennis Combs. R. E. Combs, as he signed his documents, had dedicated his life to fighting un-Americans. Combs came from the town of Visalia, in the agricultural center of the San Joaquin Valley. According to his FBI file, he received a Bachelor of Arts degree from Berkeley and enrolled in law school there but was dismissed because of "scholastic deficiency." (He later received a law degree from the University of California's Hastings College of the Law, in San Francisco.) During the war, he worked with General Ralph Van Deman, sometimes called the father of American military intelligence.

As chief counsel to the state committee, Combs developed an extensive intelligence operation that included three staff investigators and a network of informers and amateur agents from the American Legion. Although he publicly claimed the committee never paid its informers, FBI agents reported that it paid an ex-Communist named Rena Vale, one of its main sources about Communist activities, who was "not too highly regarded as a fact purveyor." Other Combs sources, they said, also had "poor reputations."

But though Hoover's assistants warned him that the committee's reports sometimes contained "unwarranted accusations," the director deemed them of great value. Each time one was published, he ordered agents to get extra copies and incorporate them into the FBI's own files, indexing the names of everyone listed as subversive. Bureau officials then relied on this information as an authoritative basis for opening investigations of the accused, characterizing organizations as suspect, and screening federal job applicants. Besides, Combs gave the bureau information from his investigation of J. Robert Oppenheimer. FBI agents always had access to the committee's records and indexes, which ultimately included references to some 125,000 organizations and individuals.

Even as Burns was busy defending the nation against immorality and communism, the bureau was receiving allegations that he was corrupt. In the postwar boom years, Fresno developed a thriving underworld. The city of 90,000 had numerous illegal gambling operations—card games, slot and pinball machines, and horse race betting. According to one FBI report, some of them had ties to major mobsters such as Meyer "Mickey" Cohen. Civic leaders, wealthy ranchers, and law-enforcement officials were alleged to be directly involved in these criminal enterprises. And according to a previously undisclosed FBI report, "State Senator Hugh Burns has been reported to be associated with gambling interests in Fresno." He was allegedly collaborating with a crooked police official who was taking payoffs.

Prostitution was also big business in Fresno. The city's skin trade was particularly rough. "The prostitutes state that Fresno is the hardest city in California to work and if they do come here to hustle, they feel they have reached the lowest point in prostitution," according to the FBI report. One nightclub owner "is reported to have a so-called auction block to sell girls for prostitutes. There is also reported to be a needle joint between Sanger, California, and Del Rey, California, to get girls into shape for prostitution." It got to the point that military officials at nearby Castle Field Army Base complained that "numerous military personnel had received venereal diseases" at Fresno's brothels, another FBI report said. The city's busy red-light business was endangering the men defending the nation against communism. And among thirty-two known brothels was one allegedly owned by the senator. According to an FBI report, Burns was "reported to own the Dale Rooms, 847 Broadway, Fresno, which is a notorious house of prostitution."

As a result, Burns's name appeared in the confidential semiannual surveys of crime prepared by the FBI's Los Angeles field office, in both 1947 and 1948, along with those of the notorious gangsters Frank Costello, Mickey Cohen, and Abe "The Trigger" Chapman.

In Washington, Hoover and his aides took note of the reports about Burns. One headquarters memo confirmed, "Information from the Los Angeles Office has been received to the effect that he is allegedly connected with the gambling and prostitution rackets in Fresno." The reports were based on intelligence from FBI informers and, of course, do not prove the claims were true. But the released FBI records contain no indication that Hoover did anything to investigate the claims, refer them to state authorities, or otherwise try to stop Burns's alleged criminal enterprises.

Hoover, it seems, looked the other way because he and Burns were partners in the fight against the greater evil of communism. By 1949 Burns had become chairman of the state senate's Fact-Finding Committee on Un-American Activities and was perhaps the most prominent state official in California's war on radicals. He was a steadfast ally of the FBI. He promoted a state senate resolution lauding the director, and in further obeisance sent him personal copies of the committee's reports, some with "J. Edgar Hoover" embossed on the cover.

Burns's daughter, Colleen Draklich, told the author she had no knowledge of whether her father was involved in gambling and prostitution. She recalled that FBI agents often visited her father's office to use his files on un-American activities, and that when she was a child he presented her to Hoover at the Hollywood Park horse-racing track. "Daddy was very pleased to introduce me to him," Draklich said. "It was like meeting the pope."

So it was that on July 13, 1951, Burns mailed Hoover a "specially bound" copy of the report alleging that University of California officials were aiding the international Communist conspiracy, the report he hoped would pressure Sproul to establish a campus unit to screen professors and students. In a cover letter, Burns assured the director that "the Committee again pledges its entire effort in the battle against communism, and its cooperation with the Federal Bureau of Investigation and other law enforcing agencies of our country." In a cordial reply addressed to the "Honorable

Hugh M. Burns," Hoover wrote that it was "indeed a pleasure" to receive the report.

A few months later, Burns advanced an ambitious program to eliminate subversives on California campuses. It required that every college and university in the state appoint a "contact man" to help the committee.

But one contact man would refuse to cooperate.

4

The Rise of Clark Kerr

Clark Kerr had no experience running any school, let alone one of the largest in the nation. The Board of Regents unanimously chose the economics professor and labor arbitrator mainly because he had helped defuse the battle over the university loyalty oath that bitterly divided the campus community and tarnished the school's reputation.

Kerr had signed the special oath required only for university employees. He had also voted to support the school's ban on teachers who were Communists, who he felt were too ideologically biased to fairly present ideas and information contrary to their own. Nonetheless, he defended professors who had refused to sign.

In supporting the nonsigners, Kerr thought often of his childhood, and especially of his father, a fiercely independent educator. A descendant of Pennsylvania pioneers, Samuel Kerr graduated high school at age sixteen and soon began teaching at a one-room schoolhouse in the Appalachian Mountains. He attended Franklin & Marshall College, a Reformed Church school in Lancaster that Ben Franklin helped establish. Samuel Kerr became fluent in Greek and Latin and graduated with the class of 1898. A few years later, he founded Reading Classical School, a private preparatory academy, and later taught at the public Reading High School. He held that nothing should be unanimous and, though a generous man, when the principal made his annual call for teachers to donate to the Community Chest, he alone refused.

One day in Reading, Samuel Kerr met a woman who made hats embroidered with cloth flowers in the front display window of Whitner's department store. People would stop to watch her hands move deftly over the bright pieces of cloth, then step inside to order one of her creations. Samuel Kerr fell in love with the milliner and proposed to her. But Caroline Clark refused his offer until she had saved enough money to send their future children to college, for she believed as deeply as he in education.

Only after she had sold enough hats did they marry and eventually have three girls and a boy. Clark, their third child, was born on May 17, 1911.

The Kerrs lived on a three-acre farm outside of Reading, near a town called Stony Creek Mills. The poorest farms were high in the hills, the best were in the valley; the Kerr farm, tucked against a mountainside, was in between. As on all family farms, there was constant work. Young Kerr would crawl into the henhouse to collect eggs and clean them. He gathered wood, stacked it on the back porch, and stoked the Majestic cast-iron stove used for cooking, heating water, and warming the house. The space behind the stove sheltered orphaned lambs.

Kerr's parents quarreled often "over all kinds of things," he recalled, and "I was always involved in trying to keep peace between them." When he was eleven years old, his mother died of cancer. The following year his father married a woman who had an inheritance from her family's coal-mining interests, and the family moved to a 140-acre farm at nearby Jacksonwald that had abundant livestock, two apple orchards, a large vegetable garden, and a long pasture bordered by a creek. Although the Kerrs were not Amish or Mennonites like many of their neighbors, they did everything on the farm without electricity or engines, using hand and horse to produce all the food they needed, except salt, sugar, and coffee. They bartered goods and services with other community members, like the man who butchered their hogs for a share of the meat.

Kerr plowed the fields with a team of horses named Kate and Maud, whom he called "my greatest friends in the world." By age fourteen he was trapping possums and skunks and hunting birds with a single-barrel shotgun. Cutting through a neighbor's field one day, Kerr found a bull blocking the path. Realizing he had no place to hide, he suddenly charged at the beast, correctly calculating that by taking the initiative he would buy just enough time to reach the gate.

Kerr's father always let hobos sleep in the barn, after giving them a warm meal and a warning not to start a fire. He also allowed the nearby Reading Country Club to use a horse trail that ran through his property. Many years later, Kerr still recalled that some of the wealthy city folk who rode by on their thoroughbreds mocked him and his workhorses. "Look at that peasant!" they exclaimed.

Even in his own home, Kerr faced a kind of class discrimination. His stepmother and his younger half-brother, William, ate fancy store-bought foods at one end of the kitchen table, while Kerr and his sisters sat with his father at the other end and made do with cornmeal mush and tea. And while Kerr worked on the farm every night after school and on weekends,

William was spared the constant labor. Still, years later, during the Depression, Kerr and his sisters helped to finance William's college education.

Farm chores left Kerr little time for anything besides studying. Miss Elba presided over grades one through six in the one-room schoolhouse built of brick. An earnest if sometimes rebellious student, Kerr once hid a mouse in her desk drawer. And though she insisted he learn the prevailing Palmer Method of cursive writing—unless he mastered it, she warned, he would "never amount to anything"—he clung to his block letters. But with her steady encouragement he became a good pupil, did well at Reading High School, and was accepted at Swarthmore College.

A small liberal arts college with a tradition of independence, Swarthmore was founded by Quakers who had settled in Pennsylvania. Like the Pilgrims who colonized Massachussetts, they had fled religious repression under the Church of England. George Fox, an early Quaker leader, maintained that the meaning of Christ's message had been lost as the church became bureaucratized. The Society of Friends, as the Quakers called themselves, declined to worship in established churches or pay tithes. They also opposed war, refused to bear arms, and resisted mandatory oaths. In Boston, the Puritans had persecuted the Quakers, hanging several of them.

When Kerr arrived at Swarthmore in the fall of 1928, he was awestruck by the beauty of the lawns, creeks, and arboretum on the land the college occupied near Philadelphia. He would later describe his time there as "the greatest transformational experience of my life." At first he was uncomfortable being away from home, however, and his father encouraged him in a series of letters. "You are getting what I hoped for you—lectures, operas, etc. These are some of the advantages of attending college near a big city. You have had two good studies—human nature—your roommates. You can see some things to avoid. However, one can never see his own faults. Yours are unfinished or poorly finished jobs and wicked dilly-dallying when you have something on hand you do not like to do. If you want to lead a happy efficient life you *must* learn to do the unpleasant thing at once and have it off your mind. Delay only makes it harder to do. For your own sake, *Do it.*"

Although Kerr initially received poor grades, he was soon taking honors courses. Once again a teacher made the difference. "For the first time in my life," he recalled of his professor, the economist Clair Wilcox, "I ran up against a truly analytical mind applied to the understanding of current events." Kerr had planned to get a law degree and join his uncle's Wilkes-Barre law firm, but with the stock market crash in 1929 and the onset of the Great Depression he instead chose to study economics. Kerr joined the soccer, track, and basketball teams and was sports editor of the school newspaper, *The Phoenix*, where a young James Michener was editor. Kerr was elected head of Swarthmore's chapter of the Kappa Sigma fraternity and president of the men's student government.

As captain of the debate team, he discovered his power to persuade. In one debate, with the socialist Norman Thomas, Kerr questioned socialism's ability to fix the nation's economic problems. In another, he led his team to defeat their Princeton rivals by arguing "The Evils of the Machine Age Outweigh the Benefits." Kerr contended that the proliferation of machinery was morally, intellectually, and physically bad for workers, and that the drudgery of operating machines dulls the mind and the desire for self-improvement.

At Swarthmore, Kerr also found religion. His mother had been essentially nonreligious, and his father had been stymied by theological inconsistencies. "If God is all-powerful, and God is also all good, why doesn't he make a more perfect world?" Samuel Kerr had asked. "And if he is all-powerful, why doesn't he get rid of the devil?" In Quakerism, Kerr found a faith free of such contradictions. He was also drawn to its teachings of peaceful resolution to conflict and doing good in the world. He became a "convinced Friend."

Volunteering with the Quakers' nonpartisan service organization, the American Friends Service Committee, Kerr served breakfasts of donated bread, milk, and jam to hungry children in the Philadelphia ghetto. He also spent three summers on "Peace Caravans." Teams of two students from various colleges were given the use of a secondhand Model T, a weekly stipend of $12.50 each—to cover gas (22 cents per gallon), food, and lodging—and assigned to cover a wide swath of the country. Some appearances during these ten-week stints were scheduled, though most were arranged along the way at churches, schools, Rotary Clubs, and even a jail. They did not proselytize but spoke to any audience that would hear them on the dangers of militarism, the benefits of peace, and the value of the League of Nations. It was a hard sell: in the wake of the Great War most Americans were isolationist and supported a smaller role in foreign affairs and a larger military. In letters to AFSC headquarters in Philadelphia, Kerr and his partner reported constant car trouble, sometimes hostile audiences, and lots of "rah-rah" Americans.

In the spring of 1932, Kerr graduated from Swarthmore with high honors and went on his final Peace Caravan, driving cross-country and arriving that July in Southern California. Several weeks later he got a letter saying his father was ill and feared for the future of the farm. Kerr replied with concern and criticism of the institutions that had left his father so vulnerable.

"There are so many ways in which our economic system could be changed and improved so as to allow security and sufficiency for all . . . Capitalism is so cruel, so unjust and so terribly inefficient," he wrote on September 1, 1932. Suggesting his father seek support from the Society of Friends, he continued, "The Quaker religion seems so sane, reasonable and helpful. So many Churches lose their ideals . . . I get boiling mad seeing the good people in Sunday School or in Church—they pray and call themselves Christians and they seem to me to be largely hypocrites. They leave the Church and lie, steal, cheat and fight." Churches, he added, "send missionaries to give our supposedly high culture and religion to the supposedly inferior heathen—usually serving as a tool for the imperialists. The Africans say that the missionaries came and told them to look towards Heaven and when they looked down again, all their land was stolen . . . I don't mean to say that the Churches are not doing good but they are not doing nearly as much as they should or as they could."

Kerr then revealed he had made a major decision about his future. "I would never be satisfied in business," he wrote. "It may not seem advisable—but I would like to study and travel as widely as possible and prepare for some work along the line of lecturing and teaching and working for a better social and economic and political order."

Enrolling that fall at Stanford University, he began studies for a master's degree in economics, while continuing his work with the Quakers and briefly belonging to a liberal campus group called the Walrus Club. That November, he attended an antiwar meeting on the Berkeley campus and complained afterward that there were "too many Communists in it to suit me." A few months later he encountered other Communists who were trying to crash a student peace conference at the First Congregational Church in Los Angeles. Seated on the dais, Kerr found himself beside a striking, slender woman with auburn hair. She passed him a note, asking, "Are you a Communist?" "No," he replied. "Nor am I," she answered. Her name was Catherine Spaulding. She was a Stanford undergraduate, a Los Angeles native, and a Quaker. She and Kerr were married on Christmas Day of 1934.

Kerr, meanwhile, had been studying the Unemployed Cooperative League in Southern California, one of many self-help cooperatives that had sprung up around the country since the start of the Depression. People of all stations found themselves with no money and no jobs and began to swap services and goods with one another. It was similar to the bartering Kerr's family did in Stony Creek, but on a larger scale, and he saw the co-ops as "an effort by the unemployed to support themselves and do so with self-respect."

Kerr was increasingly distressed by the plight of the jobless. "There are any number of cases of babies starving to death, homes without food, gas, light or water. Families evicted. At the same time . . . food products are being left unharvested or are dumped in the ocean to keep prices up," he wrote his father. One day in March 1933 he was visiting a cooperative in Pasadena when he learned that a big finance company had evicted a pregnant mother and her sick one-year-old from their one-room shack because they were fourteen dollars behind in rent. Kerr drove co-op officials to the scene, where they found the mother and child in the street, locked out of their hovel, their paltry possessions in a heap beside them. A co-op official convened a meeting on the spot with about thirty people who voted to condemn the finance firm and smash the lock. "I helped them break the law and move the family back in," Kerr confided to his father. "This country has come to a place where one must break the law in order to insure that the people may have the privilege of 'life, liberty and the pursuit of happiness.'"

The San Joaquin Valley cotton pickers' strike of 1933 was the biggest and bloodiest agricultural strike in American history. Nearly ten thousand pickers were demanding a raise from sixty cents per hundred pounds picked to a dollar. As the *Los Angeles Times* described one of the many confrontations: "Shooing the strikers before them like so many sheep, the farmers, dominating the situation because of their bristling guns and other weapons, ran their virtual prisoners down the highway for a distance of some fifteen miles. Many of the strikers were afoot and were kept on the run." There were fights in the fields, wounded growers, and two strikers shot dead.

That fall, Kerr had transferred to UC Berkeley to continue research on self-help cooperatives and work with the economics professor Paul Taylor, who with his colleague and future wife, the photographer Dorothea Lange, would soon become known for documenting the desperate conditions of farmworkers and advocating reforms. Agribusiness interests complained that Taylor was meddling, but President Sproul declined to constrain him. Taylor dispatched Kerr to interview the adversaries in the cotton strike and "record what people said in their own words." This was the same strike that R. E. Combs of the Burns committee would later tell FBI agents had given rise to his concern about radicals in California. But where Combs saw the role of Communist strike leaders as the salient fact, Kerr saw simpler forces at work. "Strikers were living on the banks of irrigation ditches that were both sources of water and receptacles of sewage," he would write in his memoir. "There was hunger . . . There was hatred . . ."

The following summer of 1934, Kerr took a job with the California Emergency Relief Administration, which with support from the Roosevelt administration was promoting the development of co-ops in Los Angeles. Some people considered the communal effort to be un-American, and there were threats of shooting. Kerr's studies at Berkeley had thrust him into the "real world," he wrote. "Here was life in the raw as I had never seen it."

By the end of the year, Kerr had become frustrated with "arm-chair pacifists." In a letter to his father he declared, "I am getting tired of speaking on Peace to people who hear dozens of such talks each year and do nothing about the problem." He decided to take action by becoming a labor arbitrator. He would help resolve conflicts between workers and management before they turned bloody like the cotton strike. On graduating from Berkeley in 1939 with a doctoral degree in economics, he was hired as an assistant professor of economics at the University of Washington, in Seattle. He was also appointed to the federal Twelfth Regional War Labor Board there, and arbitrated hundreds of disputes in various industries over wages, hours, and working conditions. His mission was to prevent disruption of the nation's economy and to keep Seattle's factories rolling out bombers and ships to fight the Axis powers. "The American nation is involved in a war to determine whether our democratic system or Fascism shall survive," he wrote in a 1944 decision allowing only a partial wage increase to $1.25 per hour for welders. "The prosecution of this war demands sacrifices and controls . . ."

After the war, Kerr returned to UC Berkeley to teach economics and head the school's new Institute of Industrial Relations. Governor Warren had suggested the university establish the institute to find ways to prevent labor conflict that might impede the postwar economic recovery. Kerr continued to arbitrate disputes in some of the nation's biggest and roughest industries. His rulings during this period underscore a belief in nonviolence, the need for compromise, and the possibility of achieving justice within the system.

Deftly handling more than five hundred labor disputes, he became the top arbitrator on the West Coast, and some colleagues called him "the Machiavellian Quaker."

His powers of mediation, however, would soon be tested on his own campus.

•

On March 25, 1949, the regents adopted the special loyalty oath for university employees, setting off one of the most divisive conflicts in the school's history: "I do solemnly swear (or affirm) that I will support the Constitution of the United States and the Constitution of the State of California . . . that I do not believe in, and I am not a member of, nor do I support any party or organization that believes in, advocates, or teaches the overthrow of the United States Government, by force or by any illegal or unconstitutional methods."

The oath had been prompted by Senator Tenney's introduction of a bill that would have amended the state constitution to let the legislature determine the loyalty of university employees. That measure would have infringed on the university's historic autonomy and thrust the legislature deep into the school's daily operations. To forestall that, President Sproul proposed, and the regents adopted, the oath.

Neither the regents nor President Sproul consulted any professors beforehand, however, and when they first learned about it in the *Faculty Bulletin* that May, many of them were upset. Fighting communism was not what bothered them; the university had banned Communist teachers since 1940, and every faculty member already had signed the oath of allegiance required of all state employees. What disturbed them was being singled out as a politically suspect group and required to sign an additional oath. They feared this would inhibit robust campus debate necessary for free inquiry and the pursuit of truth. Moreover, the regents announced that anyone who refused to sign would be fired, even if there was no evidence that they were disloyal.

Although he opposed communism, Kerr respected the principled opposition of the nonsigners who, like his father, were "independent people who did not like to be pushed around," he later wrote. Moreover, as a Quaker, he was "particularly sympathetic to reasons of conscience for not signing an oath . . ." He joined a committee that gathered statements of support for the nonsigners from professors at other universities and from labor unions. He served on a second committee that reviewed the nonsigners' reasons and determined whether they should be retained despite their refusal to sign. This panel recommended the retention of sixty-two professors who refused to sign, while concluding it could not recommend retention of five others. Sproul urged the regents to accept the panel's findings.

The regents had agreed to review the panel's recommendations before firing anyone. But at a meeting on July 21, 1950, Regent John Francis

Neylan reneged, tipping the board toward dismissing them straightaway. A San Francisco lawyer who represented the business interests of William Randolph Hearst, Neylan was a staunch anti-Communist and oath advocate. Noting that American forces were under fire in Korea, he declared that the regents should recognize that communism posed a serious threat to democracy and fire all those who refused to sign the oath.

Kerr thought Neylan's turnabout was a breach of faith. He rose from his seat to object, but a dean sitting behind him who felt junior faculty should not address the regents tried to stop him by pulling on his coattails. Grabbing the chair in front of him, Kerr hoisted himself up and posed two questions about Neylan's refusal to consider the committee's recommendations. "First," Kerr asked, "can the regents, in good faith, close a channel which they themselves opened?" Second, Kerr asked, "Would it be proper in order to eliminate Communists to eliminate free and independent spirits?" He explained that his panel was convinced that the remaining nonsigners it had recommended for retention were "not Communist, but they are among the most independent spirits in the university." Kerr suggested the regents negotiate further with the nonsigners, adding, "It seems to me that rather than getting rid of thirty-nine people who no one wanted to get rid of a year ago, there must be a new device on which we could agree."

Governor Warren, a regent ex-officio, agreed with Kerr. But on August 25, 1950, the regents voted 12 to 10 to fire these nonsigners, even though none had been accused of being a Communist. Warren voted against firing them and later quipped that Communists would sign the oath and laugh.

Kerr's effort to persuade the board had failed. The regents had demonstrated that they—and not any group of professors—were the final authority on campus policy. There were recriminations, and some of the fired faculty sued the university to be reinstated. The American Association of University Professors censured the university administration for weakening academic freedom and denying essential rights to faculty. The controversy fueled public concern about subversives on campus.

Yet Kerr's reasoned defense of the nonsigners earned wide respect on campus. The following year, with backing from the faculty and President Sproul, the regents chose Kerr as the first chancellor of the university's Berkeley campus. They hoped his arbitrator's skills and reputation as a defender of academic independence would help heal the wounds from the oath battle.

Burns, it would turn out, had other plans for him.

•

The headline in that morning's *Daily Californian* declared, "Kerr Is U.C. 'Contact Man' for Burns State Committee."

According to the September 30, 1952, story, Senator Burns had announced that his un-American activities committee would send Kerr information about professors suspected of "subversive" activities so he could investigate them. In a separate editorial, the newspaper denounced the plan as "very much like a system of espionage."

Kerr put down his copy of the student newspaper in astonishment. Sproul had given him no inkling of such a plan. Kerr regarded the Burns committee's reports as grossly exaggerated and based on rumor and innuendo. He was convinced the committee's real targets were not spies, or even Communists, but law-abiding liberals. He feared that being identified as "contact man" for this committee would poison his relationships with professors and students and undermine him in his new mission as chancellor. Yet that was precisely what Sproul wanted. As president of the statewide university system, Sproul had run the Berkeley campus for decades without a chancellor. He did not want to relinquish control of it, even though Kerr would be reporting to him.

That was also what Burns and his chief counsel, Combs, wanted, though for different reasons. They had been pushing the university to help their committee screen professors. That was the thrust of their June 1951 report about subversive activities on campus. And at a private luncheon with Sproul the following November, they made veiled threats of issuing other sensational red-bound reports in order to get "certain needed reforms." Burns and Combs urged Sproul to assign William Wadman, the campus security officer and a former campus policeman—in fact, the first campus officer to attend the FBI's National Academy—as liaison to the committee. Wadman, they knew, had been monitoring political activity on campus for years. He had recruited students—including reporters for *The Daily Californian*—to secretly report to him about campus events. Burns considered Wadman well trained and, above all, discreet.

Sproul already feared Burns would make new charges that university officials were ignoring national security and introduce more legislation to curtail the school's autonomy. He now acceded to their request, making the University of California the first college in the state to join the contact-man program and giving Burns a powerful tool for enlisting other schools. None of these three men, however, announced their plan. They agreed that Wadman's role as the real contact man for the Berkeley campus would remain secret. Kerr's public appointment was just a cover.

Kerr knew nothing of these machinations. He understood only what he had read in *The Daily Californian*. So when his shock had given way to resolve, he responded by telling the newspaper he had no plans to communicate with the Burns committee, and moreover should problems ever arise from relations with the committee, he would consult with faculty and student leaders. And when he stepped to the podium in Dwinelle Hall's sunlit courtyard on October 1, 1952, to make his introductory remarks as the first chancellor of Berkeley, he sought to further reassure the campus community.

"I shall be eternally vigilant to preserve freedom of inquiry and freedom of expression for the students and for the faculty," he vowed. "In a world increasingly hostile to independent minds, this should always be the foremost concern of a university administration. Freedom was bought at a high price. It must not be sold at any price."

Reporting for work his first day, the new chancellor found his "office" was a chair and desk located in the hallway in the main administration building, outside Sproul's suite. Among his first assignments: responding to a petition to ban dogs from campus, and to possibly related complaints from secretaries about a flea infestation. Clearly, Sproul had a narrow view of the new chancellor's role.

But for that matter, Berkeley's three-hundred-acre campus of sixteen thousand students was calm. Fraternities and sororities were at peak popularity and dominated campus social life, athletics, and student government. That some barred blacks and Jews from membership drew little comment; there were few members of minority groups on campus anyway. Reserve Officers' Training Corps was mandatory for all freshmen and sophomore men, and the chant of uniformed students echoed across campus, "Hut, 2, 3, 4." Having emerged victorious from depression and war, the nation had a collective sense of approbation. In the early fifties, students at Berkeley and other schools were generally conformist. Simone de Beauvoir, the socialist, feminist, existentialist, and lifelong companion of Jean-Paul Sartre, spoke on campus during this period and later remarked, "I looked at the athletic-looking young people, the smiling young girls in my audience, and I thought that certainly . . . there were no more than one or two who were concerned about the news of the day."

But beneath the relentless California sun was incipient unrest. Joan

Didion, a Sacramento native who enrolled as an undergraduate in 1952, recalled, in her essay collection *The White Album,*

> At Berkeley in the Fifties no one was surprised by anything at all, a *donnée* which tended to render discourse less than spirited, and debate nonexistent . . . We simply avoided those students rumored to be FBI informers. We were that generation called "silent," but we were silent neither, as some thought, because we shared the period's official optimism nor, as others thought, because we feared its official repression. We were silent because the exhilaration of social action seemed to many of us just one more way of escaping the personal, of masking for a while that dread of the meaninglessness which was man's fate . . . The mood of Berkeley in those years was one of mild but chronic "depression" . . . I remember a teacher who drank too much one night and revealed his fright and bitterness.

Kerr worried that the faculty had become disheartened. Several professors had come to his office, timidly seeking permission to join off-campus political groups, sign petitions, or make speeches. That was up to them, Kerr replied. "I would do exactly what I wanted to do as a free American citizen."

He decided to set an example. In the fall of 1952 he joined a local group of Quakers in opposing a ballot initiative that would expand the loyalty oath for all state employees, a measure known as the Levering Act, for its author, Assemblyman Harold Levering of Los Angeles. Kerr told one newspaper that, as a private citizen, he believed it "would do little if anything to stem subversion, make possible substantial abuses of individual rights, and would do great damage to the moral precepts of individual freedom upon which our state Constitution is founded." Some regents complained about his taking a controversial public position. Edward Dickson, the board chairman, came to Kerr's office fuming and grabbed him by his lapels. "You're being looked upon as the red chancellor of the university," he said. "I hope you'll never do anything like that again." Kerr calmly explained his position; then Dickson let him loose and walked away.

The State Supreme Court, meanwhile, ruled in favor of the fired professors, holding that they could not be obliged to sign an oath not required equally of all state job holders. The opinion meant the special oath that had been precipitated by Tenney was invalid, and that the university had wrongly fired those who refused to sign it. Kerr promptly proposed rehiring them with back pay.

•

As chancellor, Kerr had access to the campus radiation labs, which meant he was subject to an FBI background inquiry. It was his second—the bureau had investigated him in 1947 when the Atomic Energy Commission wanted him to arbitrate labor disputes in the nuclear industry, a position that also involved access to classified information. During this earlier inquiry, the FBI examined the circumstances of Kerr's car being parked by the house in the Berkeley hills that November night when the suspected Soviet spy George Eltenton was visiting. Bureau agents discovered an innocent explanation: Kerr and his wife had just moved to Berkeley from Washington State and were staying with her relatives, the Voges, who owned that home and knew Eltenton. In both background inquiries, everyone described Kerr as a loyal American. FBI informers inside the Communist Party had nothing to report about him.

One confidential source, however, gave FBI agents derogatory information about Kerr. Ensconced in a nondescript office at 660 Market Street in downtown San Francisco, the Western Research Foundation was an offshoot of the numerous "Americanism Committees" that the American Legion had set up around the country to help Hoover investigate alleged subversives. It was run by Harper Knowles, an Oakland native who had worked for his father's quarry business, which supplied the stones for the university's Campanile. Knowles left the family firm for his antiradical work, and became an undercover army intelligence agent and FBI source. In the late thirties, his allegations were a basis for the federal government's first effort to deport as a Communist Harry Bridges, the Australian immigrant and leader of the 1934 San Francisco General Strike. Bridges denied being a Communist, the government failed to prove he was, and an immigration judge ruled Knowles was "neither a candid nor forthright witness."

In the 1940s, Knowles converted Western Research into a private nonprofit organization whose directors included "Nat" Pieper, the former special agent in charge of the San Francisco FBI office who had investigated Soviet espionage at Berkeley. The outfit's file cabinets were filled with newspaper clippings, transcripts of hearings before the Burns committee and HUAC, and informers' reports about Communists, socialists, liberals, union members, students, and professors. Knowles had paying contracts with businesses to screen prospective employees, but he never charged the police detectives and federal agents who routinely searched his files.

Checking Knowles's records on Kerr, an FBI agent found several items. There was a newspaper story reporting he was the contact man for the

Burns committee, and another that said he opposed the Levering Act. There was also a statement from one Louis Hicks, who had worked with him in 1942 at the War Labor Board, alleging that Kerr was then "pro-Communist." When an FBI agent subsequently questioned Hicks, however, he recanted, saying "he had no specific reason . . . to question Kerr's character, reputation or loyalty."

Kerr was granted a "Q" security clearance—the highest level.

The chancellor kept his vow and had no contact with the Burns committee about university employees. From time to time, though, President Sproul directed Kerr to examine allegations that certain professors had Communist affiliations in violation of the school's policy. Sometimes Sproul gave him a memo containing the anonymous accusations. Other times, security officer Wadman orally passed them along. Kerr had no idea some of these charges came from the FBI's Responsibilities Program.

Kerr grew increasingly disturbed about this process, telling Sproul in September 1953 that it filled him with "grave doubts." In a confidential report, he summarized six cases he'd been asked to investigate. In each instance, he had considered the available evidence and questioned the professor. In four of the cases, he found the evidence inadequate and took no action; he felt these charges caused the teachers needless anguish. In the two other cases, the professors had denied the accusations but then resigned. Kerr complained to Sproul that if they had challenged the allegations, the university would have been unable to produce any evidence because the sources were anonymous. And had they gone public, he warned, "any one of these cases might have developed into a *cause celebre* on the part of the faculty and might have exposed the University to serious legal damage." In a seventh case, a professor admitted to Kerr that he was a Communist, quietly resigned, and later committed suicide.

The campus purging operation was actually much larger than Kerr knew. This became clear when R. E. Combs traveled to Washington, D.C., and testified about the "California Plan." Appearing before the United States Senate Subcommittee on Internal Security on March 19, 1953, the chief counsel for the Burns committee described the contact-man program. Committee staff investigated professors' political activities and course content at several colleges around the state, Combs said, and "when we are in agreement on the fact that he should be discharged, that information is given to the president of the institution. He then calls the individual before him and confronts him with the documentation. And in all of the hundred-plus, I don't remember the exact number, but I do know there are more than a hundred, in not one of those cases has any individual refused to resign." Combs claimed his committee had additionally kept "at least that many if not more" professors from being hired.

This remarkable testimony—that some two hundred professors had been secretly barred from California campuses as subversives—received little notice. But in January 1954, *The Nation* magazine obtained Combs's testimony and published an article titled "G-Men on the Campus," exposing the contact-man program. The story alleged that Kerr was not really the contact man at Berkeley—it was the campus security officer, Wadman. The American Civil Liberties Union of Northern California independently confirmed this and issued a press release charging that Wadman was "engaged in the totalitarian business of policing the opinions and associations of the academic community in Berkeley."

University officials stonewalled. Sproul asserted that Wadman investigated "only personnel engaged in classified governmental research," and told the *San Francisco Chronicle* that Kerr was the only contact man. For his part, Burns told the *Chronicle* there was no system of "undercover security agents." Wadman told *The Daily Californian*, "I am not a contact man. I never have been. I never propose to be!"

All along, Kerr had believed he was the contact man, albeit an unwilling one, and he now loyally joined in dismissing the ACLU's claims as "rumours, suspicion and unfounded allegations." Based largely on the trust he had built with professors since the oath battle, the faculty's Committee on Academic Freedom declared it was satisfied with Kerr's account and there was no cause for concern.

As the ACLU pursued the matter, however, Kerr had second thoughts. One of his aides, a former navy intelligence officer named Earl Bolton, questioned Wadman, who admitted that he had been investigating "regular academic people," not just those doing classified research, and that he had been covertly working with the Burns committee. He insisted this was pursuant to Sproul's instructions.

Kerr finally realized he'd been had. His good reputation had been used as cover for a blacklisting scheme. He had been made to look like either a liar or a dupe. He feared the issue would blow up in the press, that his credibility would be destroyed, that the university would be plunged into another loyalty controversy.

He urged Sproul to arrange a meeting with Wadman, Combs, and himself. The former arbitrator wanted to get all the players in one room and resolve the matter. Throughout June he pursued the issue, but Sproul kept putting him off. On July 2, 1954, they finally met. According to Kerr's notes on the meeting that Friday, Combs came clean. He described Wadman as the "transmission belt" between the committee and the university. He said they had been working together before Kerr was named contact man, and since no one "officially" told them to stop, "they just kept on doing it."

Kerr demanded that they issue a joint statement clarifying the facts or he would put out his own. Faced with the prospect of even greater controversy, the others relented. In a statement later that day, they admitted the university had misrepresented the truth about the program, acknowledged "misunderstandings" about who the contact man was, and promised that Wadman would henceforth work only on defense contracts.

Combs was furious. The controversy convinced him Kerr was trying to sabotage the committee's efforts to eliminate subversives on campus. The episode also disturbed Hoover. From the start, he had been concerned the Responsibilities Program might be exposed. Then one day an assistant U.S. attorney general named Warren Olney III dropped by his office to relate a disturbing rumor that the FBI was giving secret reports about professors to Governor Warren. Olney had heard it from Arthur Sherry, a Berkeley law professor, who had speculated that the reports came from the FBI. Many of them, he had added, had been found to be "unsubstantiated" and had generated criticism of the bureau for "smearing" people.

Hoover dispatched an agent from the FBI's San Francisco field office to question Sherry, who confirmed his comments. Alarmed, Hoover scrawled a note instructing his aides, "Order immediate discontinuation of this project in California in view of the bad impression it is creating."

Hoover's battle against subversives in California had suffered a blow—largely because of Kerr's stubborn refusal to go along with the contact-man program. But the FBI director was determined to keep an eye on Berkeley. He told his agents to stay in close touch with Security Officer Wadman—and to be "most circumspect."

When Adlai Stevenson, the Democratic presidential contender known for his intellect, his humor, and the hole he'd worn through the sole of his shoe, addressed Berkeley students on May 8, 1956, he had to do so from a rostrum set up on the street just off campus. He had to because of Rule 17.

The rule barred students and professors from using university grounds for activities other than official school programs. It banned campus events that could "involve the University in political or sectarian religious activities in a partisan way." And it prohibited discussions of "highly controversial issues" unless "two or more aspects of the problem are to be presented by a panel of qualified speakers." President Sproul had instituted the rule in response to the rise in student activism in the thirties, hoping it would keep both student radicals and reactionary politicians at bay.

As some two thousand students sat on the sloping campus green and listened, Stevenson held forth from Oxford Street. The idealistic liberal criticized campus apathy and urged students to study the issues. "Today we live in the exciting and dangerous time of three revolutions—technological, political, and ideological," he said, gesturing toward the radiation lab on the hill behind campus. "Our need for brain power is fully as great as our need for increased water or atomic power. Our most underdeveloped resource today is the minds of our children."

And when Stevenson's opponent in the Democratic primary, Estes Kefauver, the crusading senator from Tennessee, spoke the following week, he, too, did so from the street. Kefauver criticized the Eisenhower administration for bypassing the United Nations in favor of a foreign policy that relied on threats of "massive retaliation." He condemned politicians who had signed the "southern manifesto" denouncing the U.S. Supreme Court's 1954 ruling in *Brown v. Board of Education* that desegregated the nation's public schools. He contended that the federal government's system of loyalty investigations was producing a society afraid to question authority. Then he brought up Rule 17, demanding, "Why can't a live politician get on this campus?"

Two days later, the most serious student unrest at Berkeley in decades broke out. It did not concern civil rights, national security, or foreign policy. It concerned lingerie.

The great panty raid began on the unusually warm evening of May 16, 1956. Temperatures soared above 90 degrees, distracting even diligent students from upcoming finals. By 7:00 p.m., fraternity and sorority members on the south side of campus had started a water balloon fight, and soon hundreds of students were cavorting in front of the Greek houses near Channing Way and College Avenue. Within an hour, more than two thousand students were blocking the intersection by fraternity row, opening city water taps and dousing everyone, including some police officers who diverted traffic but made no real effort to break up the revelries. By and by, the crowd dissipated on its own.

But just after 10:00 p.m. that sultry night, a phalanx of two hundred male students appeared, chanting, "We want panties!" Some of them entered a sorority house and returned with their trophies, all in good nature.

By 11:00 p.m., however, the mood had become bellicose as three thousand men methodically moved from one sorority house to the next, waiting in the street while groups of them forced their way inside, ransacked bedrooms, and grabbed undergarments. In all, twenty-six women's living quarters were invaded, and some doors and windows were broken. One woman repelled the intruders with a hot iron, and hysterical phone calls lit up the police switchboard with reports that some raiders got "quite fresh." By 12:30 a.m. the boys began drifting off, wearing slips over their clothing and panties on their heads.

The morning after, *The Daily Californian* published an outraged editorial asserting that girls had been "knocked around, assaulted, carried outside in pajamas or nude." A wire service picked it up and stories were carried in newspapers around the country and as far away as London and Beirut. Kerr vowed to investigate and a few weeks later issued a thirty-three-page "white paper" on "the riot": No women had been disrobed or injured, but there was more than $12,000 in property damage and stolen underwear. Seventy-three men took lingerie or used violence or profanity, and received discipline ranging from probation to dismissal. Police had failed to notify campus administrators about the outbreak and did little to restore order. Although there had been a rash of panty raids at colleges across the country, this was Berkeley's first.

But the school had its own history of student outbursts. "The May 16 riot was one of the worst episodes involving masses of Berkeley students which had occurred in years, but it was not unique," Kerr wrote. "On several previous occasions, notably in 1936, 1937 and 1948, large crowds of students rioted, causing substantial amounts of property damage and leading to police intervention, arrests and disciplinary action. During one of these riots, more than 80 bonfires were built in city streets, public transit service was forced to suspend for several hours and equipment was stolen from fire trucks. Another episode involved more street bonfires, serpentines of students breaking into theaters, and numerous store windows smashed because window displays contained objects of red (Stanford) color." All of these incidents were connected to football games, mainly the Big Game with Stanford.

Determinedly upbeat, Kerr concluded, "I have considerable confidence that the current generation of students at Berkeley will not again engage in such activities." But he added, "It is perhaps too idealistic to believe that there will never be another major mass disturbance by Berkeley students."

•

By the end of his six years as chancellor, Kerr had guided Berkeley toward top academic rankings—only Harvard was rated higher. He had imposed more demanding academic standards on professors, appointed close to a thousand faculty members, named new department chairmen, and won approval for construction of dormitories and a student union. As the *Oakland Tribune* reported, he had acquired a national reputation for supporting the scholar's "right of free choice, free study and free communication of ideas."

Now he would be president of the entire University of California, with eight campuses and 43,000 students. The regents had concluded he was the best man to lead the university as it prepared for a tidal wave of new students, the result of the postwar baby boom that had propelled the average birthrate to 3.6 children for women of parenting age. The regents, too, were acutely aware that the Soviet Union's successful launch of *Sputnik* in 1957, beating the United States with the first earth-orbiting satellite and beginning the space race, had underscored the importance of education to national security. The forty-seven-year-old Kerr was taking over the world's largest research university and a key defense contractor at a time of extreme Cold War tensions. Edwin Pauley, the president of the Board of Regents, announced the appointment.

Clark and Kay Kerr, and their three children, were entitled to inhabit the President's House, a stately mansion on campus for which the regent Phoebe Apperson Hearst had broken ground with a silver shovel in 1900. He instead decided they would remain in the modern one-story home he had built in neighboring El Cerrito, high on a precipice with westward views of the Golden Gate. And even after his office moved to University Hall, the new building just off campus, he would often work at home, issuing instructions in the margins of staff memos in a pinched but precise script, in green ink. "I wanted to feel independent," he said.

On September 29, 1958, Kerr was inaugurated in an elaborate ceremony at the campus's Greek Theatre. As he took his seat on the raised stage flanked by Doric columns and waited to deliver his address, the amphitheater on the hillside just above the campus filled with members of the campus community, representatives of leading universities around the world, and elected officials. Kerr thought back to Miss Elba, his teacher at the brick schoolhouse, who had helped an unruly farm boy make it to college. He thought education could change lives, that it could change the world.

Stepping to the lectern, he began a speech that echoed the westward-looking poem George Berkeley had written two centuries earlier. Once bastions of "pettifogging pedantry" and "guardians of the past," universities had evolved into "architects of progress" crucial to societies facing new challenges. "We recognize that education is more than information and that the wisdom and experience of the human condition which we have inherited are more pertinent than ever in an era of drastic change," he said. "In a century which by creating much has overthrown so much, men of intellect everywhere have an obligation which they must not betray."

Kerr's rise, however, worried some observers. Two weeks after his investiture, Richard Auerbach, special agent in charge of the FBI's San Francisco office, sent Hoover a dark memo. "Dr. Kerr," he wrote, "has always given the impression that he is a 'liberal' in the educational field, that he is not in sympathy with loyalty oaths . . . and that he is also not in complete accord with the fact that various branches of the state and local government must conduct security investigations of individuals on the various campuses." Dr. Kerr, he added, "at best is a highly controversial figure in California education."

According to Auerbach's October 16, 1958, memo, R. E. Combs had just held a two-day conclave at his home in Visalia. Present were Donald Lynn of the Alameda County District Attorney's Office intelligence unit; Inspector Charles O'Meara of the Berkeley Police Department's antisubversive squad; and William Wadman.

Combs presented a "sinister picture," according to the memo, claiming Kerr had associated with "persons of questionable loyalty" and helped "liberals and leftists get ahead." He theorized that Kerr "might be an undercover Communist." Combs vowed to investigate Kerr and said he would seek "assistance from a right wing group of University officials who would be in a position to observe Kerr close at hand."

"The ultimate aim of this plan," Combs told the group, "would be to compile a documented and convincing history of Kerr, showing him to be a dangerous radical" and "to present this to the right people"—such as sympathetic regents. "The purpose would be to try to get Kerr neutralized in his present job or even removed."

Wadman and the others present pledged to help Combs, and one of them then briefed an agent from the FBI's San Francisco office about the scheme. Auerbach was reporting Combs's plot to FBI headquarters, as he wrote, "merely for its information and in the event that the Bureau may receive some inquiry concerning Dr. Kerr."

Hoover filed the memo in a rapidly expanding dossier that reflected his growing concern about the Berkeley campus, concern that would soon turn to outrage—all because of a simple essay question.

The Essay Question

"What are the dangers to a democracy of a national police organization, like the FBI, which operates secretly and is unresponsive to criticism?"

That was optional essay question number 7 on the 1959 English aptitude test for applicants to the University of California. John R. Lechner of Los Angeles heard about the question and knew instantly what it meant. Lechner was chairman of the Americanism Committee for the 23rd District of the American Legion, and executive director of the Americanism Education League—or as one FBI memo put it, he was a "professional racketeer of Americanism." He promptly complained to an agent at the FBI's Los Angeles office that the question was "communist propaganda," and the special agent in charge reported the matter to FBI headquarters.

Hoover was livid. He viewed the question not only as subversive but as an attack on the FBI—and he took any attack on the bureau personally. His hand passed quickly across the memo as he scrawled an order in blue ink: "We really should stir up as many protests re this as possible."

Tolson assigned the matter to one of the bureau's most able men, Cartha "Deke" DeLoach, an assistant FBI director who headed the Crime Records Division. Despite its title, the division was actually the bureau's public relations arm. DeLoach's job was to promote the FBI's image, and to respond to any public criticism. He had extensive contacts among news reporters, bureau supporters, and members of the American Legion, the veterans' organization for which he happened to be director of public relations. DeLoach swiftly mounted a covert campaign intended to embarrass University of California officials and pressure them to retract the question. The operation would build Hoover's constituency and undercut Kerr's.

First, DeLoach drafted a letter for the American Legion's national commander, Martin McKneally, to send, as if he had written it himself, to

Chancellor Vern Knudsen of UCLA, protesting the question's "innuendos, false premises and downright untruths." DeLoach enlisted other Legion officials to complain to the university about the question and arranged for publication of an "exposé" about it in *Firing Line*, the newsletter sent to all Legionnaires. The article, which repeated the Burns committee's charges of Communist infiltration of the university, was titled, "The FBI—Prime Target of Attack by Pseudo Liberals and Other Left-Wing Elements."

Next, DeLoach prevailed upon David Sentner, chief of Hearst Newspapers' Washington, D.C., bureau and one of his favorite media contacts, to "attack" the university for "allowing such questions." Hearst's *Los Angeles Herald Examiner* promptly published a page-one story citing Lechner's complaints about the "vicious communist propaganda scheme," along with an editorial criticizing the university. Fulton Lewis, Jr., the nationally syndicated radio commentator, aired a negative story.

DeLoach also mobilized some of the bureau's congressional allies, including a former FBI agent who was a member of the House Un-American Activities Committee, to "make inquiries" at the university. He arranged for other former agents in private business to complain to state officials and university contributors. Assistant Director John McGuire, meanwhile, called on his contact in the Los Angeles Archdiocese to publicly condemn the question. Another assistant director, Quinn Tamm, arranged for top officials of the International Association of Chiefs of Police—representing hundreds of police chiefs and sheriffs—to complain to the university about it.

At DeLoach's direction, agents in California followed up on these efforts. When Richard Auerbach failed to respond fast enough, an irritated Hoover scrawled, "What is the matter with Auerbach? Is he afraid to tackle this?" Auerbach was ordered to meet "expeditiously" with Governor Edmund G. "Pat" Brown and make known the Boss's "extreme displeasure regarding the aptitude test question and that we feel it is a slur against the FBI and is creating a completely distorted picture in the minds of applicants for the University of California."

Auerbach met with Brown the next morning at the governor's office. Brown agreed the question was "terrible," and as the FBI agent looked on he dictated a letter instructing UCLA's chancellor to find out who authored it. Brown also had his aide tell Knudsen there was enough trouble with the university's budget without "making a mess of things in this manner."

Auerbach then enlisted a "few friendly sources" to query the governor's office, including the publishers of the *San Francisco Examiner* and the *San Francisco Chronicle*. The *Examiner* published an editorial declaring that the question wrongly equated the FBI with "political police," and assured readers the bureau did not operate secretly.

Hoover personally wrote Brown, a regent ex officio and president of the board, to complain about the "unfair and grossly misleading question." He sent letters to other regents whom his aides had determined would likely be sympathetic to the bureau's concerns. The director's February 8, 1960, letter to Edwin G. Pauley, the wealthy Los Angeles oilman and staunch anti-Communist, was typical. "I must say that I was utterly shocked by this question. The very wording of it implies as a foregone conclusion that this organization is endangering our historic and constitutionally guaranteed liberties. Students reading this question are being taught to believe something which is entirely untrue. This surely is not in the highest traditions of our academic community. I hope that you will agree that a grave injustice has been done the FBI and that steps should be taken to rectify this unfortunate error."

DeLoach soon reported back to Tolson on the steps he had taken to light a "firestorm" of protest against the university's "attack" on the bureau.

"Excellent," Hoover scrawled.

Under fire from Hoover, university officials began an internal inquiry into the offending essay question. The Subject A test, as it was known, was intended to determine whether applicants to the university had basic writing skills. They selected one of twelve topics and wrote 500 words on it. Those who failed were required to take remedial writing classes, known on campus as "bonehead English."

The officials first questioned professors at UCLA and UC Berkeley who had helped prepare the examination. The teachers explained that the questions were deliberately provocative and meant to stimulate students to go beyond the usual clichés. The topics were drawn from current events, such as recent charges by the industrialist Cyrus Eaton that America was becoming a police state. Although the professors thought many students would be interested in the FBI question, most were not. Of 5,174 students who took the test, only 157, or 3 percent, chose it.

The officials next scrutinized these essays and their grades. Had the question prompted negative comments about the FBI? Had professors rewarded anti-FBI essays with an unusual percentage of passing grades? In fact, the essays were evenly split into those for and those against the FBI.

The pass rates for the two groups were nearly identical, the scores clearly unrelated to the expressed opinion.

The regents' response to the essay question, however, was overwhelmingly negative. At a closed board meeting on February 19, 1960, Edwin Pauley took the lead in demanding that the university apologize to the FBI. With little debate, the board unanimously adopted a resolution that said, "The Regents of the University of California deeply regret that an improper question appeared in the University's Subject A examination . . . The question has, of course, been withdrawn from use in the examination, and steps are being taken to prevent a re-occurrence . . . The Regents of the University assure the Federal Bureau of Investigation of their highest respect as an essential arm of our nation's security and of the rule of law which is the keystone of our free democratic society."

In an interview, DeLoach said that he and other FBI officials had taken these actions merely to "set the record straight."

Hoover could not resist gloating. In a February 25, 1960, letter to Vice President Richard M. Nixon, he described his victory over the university as though it were the result of a spontaneous outpouring in defense of the bureau.

"Dear Dick," he wrote. "A storm of protest immediately rose in many parts of the state against this viciously misleading question . . . It was indeed most unfortunate that such a question appeared on the University aptitude test. The minds of young students were being impregnated with complete falsehood [*sic*] under the guise of truth. I was most happy to learn that the University has now withdrawn the question."

Hoover now turned to the author of the question.

Governor Brown had promised Auerbach he would determine who wrote it, but never did. So Hoover ordered his agents to identify the person responsible for "this slur against the FBI."

Webb Burke, the Los Angeles SAC, suspected the Academic Senate's Committee on Academic Freedom, a faculty group formed at Berkeley in response to the loyalty oath conflict. A year earlier, Joseph Fontenrose, a classics professor and chairman of the committee, had asked Burke, then in charge of the FBI's San Francisco office, whether FBI agents were instructed to investigate professors' political opinions. Offended, Burke reported the inquiry from the "fuzzy headed" academic to Hoover. Now Burke reminded the director that this same committee had questioned the contact-man program and "engaged in quite a bit of controversy over the so-called 'Academic Freedom.' "

The committee had played no role in preparing the English aptitude test, however, and bureau agents soon focused on a UCLA English professor named Everett L. Jones. A quiet man from South Dakota, Jones had graduated from Antioch College in Ohio and taught at Lehigh University in Pennsylvania until 1944, when he moved to San Diego. He was fascinated by Western novels and would later coauthor a book about the forgotten role of black cowboys. Jones had been serving as UCLA's supervisor for the Subject A test, meanwhile, and was quoted in the *New York Post* as denying the essay question was Communist propaganda, and in the *Los Angeles Examiner* as saying, "I must agree, however, that the question itself was unfortunately worded."

"The understatement of the year," Hoover scrawled on a memo attached to one of the stories. Just below this comment, Tolson added a note, asking, "What do files show on Jones?" Hoover wrote below that, "Let me know."

Checking the bureau's General Index at headquarters—the main index to the FBI's files in Washington, D.C.—DeLoach found allegations that a man named Everett Lee Jones had associations with two people deemed suspicious: his father, a former Unitarian minister named Harry Jones; and his wife, an alleged Communist variously known as Mrs. Everett Lee Jones, Mary Elizabeth Jones, or "Boots." There were allegations that Everett and Boots Jones had attended Communist Party meetings in San Diego. Hoover wanted to know if this was the same Everett Jones who, he suspected, had authored the question impugning the FBI.

Warning that "discretion is absolutely essential," Hoover ordered FBI agents in San Francisco, Los Angeles, and San Diego to investigate. They checked with local police departments, the University of California contact man William Wadman, and the former American Legion official Harper Knowles. Along the way they crossed paths with William Wheeler, the West Coast investigator for the House Un-American Activities Committee, who also was hunting for information about Jones. The agents confirmed that the Everett Lee Jones named in the headquarters files as the son of Harry Jones and the husband of "Boots" Jones was indeed the same Everett Lee Jones in charge of UCLA's English entrance exam.

But there was a snag: FBI agents in San Diego meanwhile had checked the membership records that they photographed during break-ins at the local Communist Party office and discovered there was actually no proof that Jones or his wife, Boots, had joined the party. The agents further determined that the allegations that the Joneses "began attending Communist Party meetings" were incorrect. Those allegations had been based on misinterpretations of fragments of discussions overheard on the FBI's bug at the party office. Moreover, informers in the party told agents they had no information about the couple. Everett and Boots Jones were clean.

"Dear Chancellor Knudsen," the anonymous letter typed on unmarked paper began,

> I feel obliged to furnish you some vital information regarding the communist connections of both Mr. Jones and his wife.
>
> By way of background, let me explain that I first became acquainted with Everett Lee and "Boots" Jones in the latter 1930's when they were attending Antioch College. During these years, they expressed views which shocked many of their friends and acquaintances . . .
>
> By the mid-1940s, however, I was to learn that Everett and "Boots" Jones, who then were living in San Diego, had become fanatical adherents to communism.
>
> Everett Jones' great sympathy for communism probably was inherited from his father, a former minister of the Unitarian Church.
>
> I hope the above facts were not previously known to you, for it is indeed impossible to believe that UCLA or any other educational institution would knowingly place a person with Everett Jones' record in a position where he can so effectively poison the minds of American youth.

The letter was dated February 19, 1960, and signed, "Sincerely yours, Antioch—Class of '38."

Copies also were mailed to Jones, Governor Brown, and three Los Angeles newspapers.

The released FBI files do not identify the letter writer, and in an interview DeLoach said he had no recollection of the episode. However, the letter contains striking similarities in both content and language to internal FBI memos. Moreover, its location within the FBI files indirectly confirms that it originated with the bureau. As a congressional investigation would later find, bureau officials during this period routinely sent such poison-pen letters in an effort to disrupt the lives of people whose lawful First Amendment activities they deemed disloyal.

The anonymous attack troubled the Jones family. At the dinner table, Jones expressed concern about the allegations, his daughter, Pam Wagner, recalled. He felt compelled to defend himself and his wife.

In a letter to Chancellor Knudsen, Jones said that as an Antioch student he actually had been a conservative and wrote editorials for the campus newspaper opposing communism. His wife's views, he said, were "no more shocking, whatever that means, than any other college fresh-man." He denied he and his wife had been fanatical Communists in San Diego. In fact, he had come to San Diego to work for the university's Division of War Research and was assigned to classified projects for the navy. He acknowledged that he and his wife had attended a lecture on the revolution in China, but denied going to Communist meetings. For the past fifteen years he had been a registered Republican, he added, and his wife was a registered Democrat. As to his father, he had been a Unitarian minister and while in the air force held a top-secret security clearance.

"I wish my accuser would identify himself," Jones concluded.

In a subsequent press statement, Knudsen said he usually ignored anonymous allegations but had questioned Jones, who denied being a Communist.

In any event, the chancellor added, Jones had "no part" in producing the essay question about the FBI. It had been prepared by other university staff at the Berkeley campus.

The FBI, it seemed, had the wrong man.

Hoover now set his sights on the entire university as the source of "the viciously misleading question."

FBI agents were ordered to search the bureau's files for any derogatory information about each of UC's six thousand faculty members and staff around the state. Thirty extra FBI employees were assigned to this special project, and on March 2, 1960, Hoover received their sixty-page report on UC's "political complexion." DeLoach, whose staff prepared the report, said in an interview that the FBI was just "sizing up" the university.

The report's first section was titled "What Is the University of Califor-nia?" It answered this question with what could have been a description of a foreign enemy. "The University of California is a mammoth, sprawling, educational empire which stretches the length and breadth of the state." It noted that UC had 5,365 faculty members.

The next section was titled "What Is the Political Complexion of the University?" It answered, "Like any other community, there is a wide range of political beliefs and theories held and expounded at the University of California. It is of interest to note, however, that there are a good many individuals who either are members of the faculty, students or employees of the University and its branches who are of considerable interest to the Federal Bureau of Investigation. They are acknowledged threats to the established, lawful, governing principles of our country."

According to the report, seventy-two university faculty members, students, and employees were on the bureau's "Security Index," a secret nationwide list of people whom FBI officials believed would be dangerous to national security during war or other major emergency and were to be arrested and held indefinitely without judicial warrant. Detainees in the San Francisco area were to be incarcerated on Angel Island, the forested mound rising from the middle of the bay. Much larger than nearby Alcatraz Island, it had been used to process prisoners of war during World War II.

The Security Index was another of Hoover's programs that employed bland administrative techniques to create powerful surveillance machinery. It harked back to the Palmer Raids, when thousands of immigrants whom the FBI listed as dangerous radicals were swept up and detained for deportation, only to be released by judges who found there was insufficient evidence against them. But though the Palmer Raids targeted aliens, the Security Index aimed at American citizens.

Hoover began the system that became the Security Index in 1939, during the run-up to U.S. involvement in World War II, when President Roosevelt had requested intelligence on the impact of communism and fascism on American life. Although there is no record Roosevelt authorized it, Hoover went beyond intelligence gathering and created the Custodial Detention Program. It was the epitome of "preventive intelligence": the FBI conducted investigations not to produce criminal prosecutions but to identify and monitor people who might engage in sabotage or espionage, or otherwise harm the homeland at some future time.

From the start, Hoover sought to evade oversight of the operation. When Attorney General Robert Jackson instructed Justice Department staff to review the program, Hoover refused to cooperate on the ground that they might leak the names of FBI informers. Jackson eventually compelled Hoover to turn over the list of prospective detainees and the evidence against them. Jackson's successor, Attorney General Francis Biddle, reviewed the material and ordered Hoover to discontinue the program, telling him there was no legal justification for it. Moreover, Biddle said, the evidence was "inadequate," the standards for inclusion on the list "defective," and the program "impractical, unwise, and dangerous."

Hoover did not abolish the custodial detention list, however. He secretly maintained it and renamed it the Security Index. He warned his agents that the Security Index was "strictly confidential, and should at no time be mentioned or alluded to in investigative reports, or discussed with agencies or individuals outside the Bureau . . ." Only as the Cold War was heating up in 1946 did Hoover reveal its existence to Biddle's successor, Attorney General Tom Clark, telling him the index listed people "who would be dangerous or potentially dangerous in the event of . . . serious crisis, involving the United States and the U.S.S.R." Clark raised no objection to what had been presented as a new operation, and Hoover proceeded to expand it.

Under the Security Index program, the FBI defined potentially dangerous people as including not only confirmed members of the Communist Party but also suspected Communists and individuals who had "shown sympathy" with Communist objectives. The index encompassed broad categories of people in labor, civil rights, education, the arts, and youth organizations.

For each person listed, FBI officials prepared a Security Index card that included his or her photograph, home and work addresses, and a characterization such as "Communist," "Socialist Workers Party," or "Miscellaneous." FBI agents could use the cards to make quick identifications and arrests. The agents regularly updated them and sought to interview the subjects, whose "refusal to cooperate" was weighed in determining their dangerousness. Subjects were removed from the list only if bureau officials concluded they no longer posed a serious threat, or if they died. To speed their roundup, the bureau stored the Security Index data on IBM cards.

Neither the FBI nor the Justice Department informed Congress about the existence of the Security Index program. Thus unaware, Congress passed its own emergency detention measure as the Korean conflict intensified domestic security concerns. The Internal Security Act of 1950, however, set higher standards for arresting and detaining people. Hoover and Justice Department officials quietly disregarded these standards, and by the mid-fifties the Security Index contained the names of 26,174 people.

•

In addition to naming the six dozen people at UC who were listed in the Security Index, DeLoach's report on the school's political complexion alleged that other professors had engaged in a panoply of improprieties.

One hundred forty-one faculty members had committed miscellaneous misdeeds such as urging the abolishment of the House Un-American Activities Committee; receiving a copy of a book by the Communist Party leader Earl Browder; and "writing a play which glorified the Chinese Communist Army and defamed Chiang Kai-shek."

Fifty-four faculty members "or their immediate relatives" subscribed or contributed to publications that bureau officials deemed subversive.

Forty current professors had protested the university's loyalty oath either by refusing to sign or by signing petitions against it.

Twenty-seven faculty members had "close relatives" who were former members of, or contributors to, the Communist Party.

Twenty-two professors had been "involved in illicit love affairs, homosexuality, sexual perversion, excessive drinking and other instances of conduct reflecting mental instability." One professor had been arrested on a complaint of "window peeping." Another "admitted that she had given birth to an illegitimate child who was subsequently given over for adoption."

Seven faculty members allegedly had admitted prior membership in the Communist Party.

The report, however, identified no faculty members as current members of the Communist Party.

And FBI agents still had found nothing in bureau files about the UC Berkeley English professor James Lynch, who, bureau officials finally discovered, had written the essay question about the dangers secret police organizations might pose to a democracy.

While Hoover was stirring up protests against the university, Kerr was trying to prevent an educational crisis, one with real implications for national security.

The biggest surge of new students in history was heading to California, the result of the baby boom, the state's growing population, and the public's heightened expectation of the right to a college education, once the preserve of the privileged elite. In fewer than ten years, officials expected, enrollments throughout the state's system of higher education would more than double to nearly 1.3 million. But that system already was at capacity. Costs were rising. And its three tiers—junior colleges, state colleges, and the university—were in disarray. There was serious doubt the state could honor its historical commitment to provide all high school students free access to a quality college education.

It fell to Kerr, as president of the University of California, to unite competing factions and produce a plan that would organize the system, contain costs, and provide access to all qualified students. "In no small measure," the historian John Aubrey Douglass wrote, "the fate of California's higher education system hung on Kerr's ability to fashion a negotiation process."

Trouble had been building for decades in a system once at the forefront of higher education. During the early 1900s, progressive reformers in the California legislature created the nation's first network of public junior colleges with guaranteed access for all high school graduates. By the late fifties, this first tier had sixty-three junior colleges around the state offering Associate of Arts degrees, vocational training, and preparation for students seeking more advanced degrees.

The state colleges, the second tier, were originally established in the late 1800s to train teachers, and by the late fifties there were fourteen colleges offering bachelor's and master's degrees.

The university, the third tier, had eight campuses staffed by the most highly qualified faculty, with exclusive authority to award doctoral degrees and conduct research.

But the system had grown piecemeal, and now the colleges and universities were fighting one another for funds and academic turf. College officials were demanding authority to offer doctoral degrees and conduct research. University officials strongly opposed this, fearing they would lose research funding to the colleges and that the quality of research and postgraduate work would suffer.

State legislators were losing patience with the bickering academics. They threatened to take over management of the system if school officials failed to agree on a coordinated plan quickly. Their concerns had been heightened when the Soviets launched *Sputnik*—as one legislative committee reported, "parents, educators and legislators were suddenly made aware that perhaps there was something lacking in the system of education as we know it in the United States."

The regents had named Kerr president partly because of his renown as a negotiator, and they directed him to resolve the matter. He saw an opportunity to create a coordinated system of higher education while protecting the university's unique role. His strategy was to move the parties toward a negotiated agreement step by step. By agreeing to support some college officials' demands, he persuaded them to join in a study of higher education that would form the basis of an overall plan for the next ten years.

Kerr convinced the legislature to pass a bill directing the colleges and the university to present a master plan at the start of the 1960 legislative session. The bill also imposed a moratorium on other legislation concerning higher education, reducing the chances for political meddling in the process. As the historian Douglass noted in *The California Idea and American Higher Education*, Kerr thus created a political context to quickly bring about major reform.

To Kerr it was a matter of defending the country. "We are not the only people searching for knowledge," he said at a March 1959 meeting between college and university representatives. "All the world, including our chief competitor, is energetically engaged in the search . . . today, high-level skill of the population is essential for the survival of the nation itself."

It was crucial, he argued, to differentiate the missions of the university and the colleges if they were to meet the needs of new students without duplication and unnecessary expense. He soon realized, however, that college officials were intent on redefining the colleges as universities. With negotiations stalled, Kerr persuaded Roy Simpson, state superintendent of education and head of the colleges, to convene a new negotiating committee that would include representatives from private colleges and a neutral arbiter. Kerr hoped the new forum and fresh players would spark a settlement.

Bit by bit, the committee members agreed on admissions standards for each of the three tiers, on maximum enrollments, and on sites for future campuses. By December 1959, with the deadline for presenting the plan to the legislature looming, the committee had agreed on everything—except whether colleges could offer doctoral programs.

Kerr was displeased that the committee members had put off deciding that key issue. In a last-minute maneuver, he rejected the partial agreement and demanded a renegotiation, throwing the entire process into question. Then he convened an emergency "summit" meeting of key players in his office at Berkeley.

There he declared that unless the colleges compromised on their demand to issue doctorates and do research, the university would withdraw its support for the colleges' request for their own board of trustees, which he had discerned as their primary goal. He then proposed a compromise: the colleges could do some research and offer a joint doctoral program with the university, although the university would maintain final control.

The parties agreed and the Master Plan for Higher Education was sent to the legislature on February 1, 1960.

It was the most comprehensive state plan for higher education ever set in law. By defining the missions of the junior colleges, the colleges, and the university, it enabled each to specialize, avoid redundancy, and save tax dollars. It maintained academic autonomy. And it preserved the historic guarantee that all of the state's high school graduates would have access to a college education. Since its adoption, the plan has been imitated by nearly every other state and several nations. *Time* magazine put Kerr on its October 17, 1960, cover, calling him the "Master Planner."

A few days after completing the plan, Kerr departed to attend a conference on higher education in Santiago, Chile, and take a vacation. He was in Argentina when the controversy over the essay question broke out. On his return to Berkeley, he was briefed about the regents' displeasure with the imbroglio and their apology to the FBI. Kerr wrote Hoover, "I should also like to add my regret over the incident." Reaching out to the FBI director, he added, "I would also ask that hereafter any objections you might have regarding the University of California in its relationship with the FBI be raised directly with me as President of the University, rather than individual members of the Board of Regents. I am sure you can appreciate why this is a more desirable method of approach." He signed his letter in his small, neat script.

Hoover's assistants, however, read Kerr's letter with jaundiced eyes. "It appears obvious that Kerr is somewhat angry at the FBI in regard to the aptitude question," Tolson wrote. "His expressions of regret are very brief and rather perfunctory. Moreover, the very fact that he suggests that in the future such incidents be called to his attention implies criticism with the way the Bureau protested over the recent question."

Hoover decided to snub Kerr's overture. "If we have any further difficulties," he scrawled, "we will deal with the regents as we recently did."

6

Protest at City Hall

Early on the morning of Thursday, May 12, 1960, scores of students walked into San Francisco's City Hall and crossed the lobby beneath a rotunda rising four stories to a windowed dome. Rays of sunlight fell on the wide marble steps of the grand staircase to the second floor. The hour rang from a clock ornamented with figures of Father Time, History, and Youth bearing the torch of the future.

The women, in skirts and blouses, and the men, in sports coats, ties, and slacks, gathered outside the thick doors of carved Manchurian oak leading to the Board of Supervisors' hearing room. Inside that coffered chamber, the House Un-American Activities Committee was about to begin three days of hearings on "subversive" activities in Northern California.

HUAC's avowed mission was to investigate Communist infiltration of society, but its spectacular charges of subversion and lack of due process had drawn mounting complaints that its real aim was the punishment of dissenters. In prior visits to California the committee had subpoenaed more than one hundred teachers, leaked their names to newspapers, and returned to Washington, D.C., without holding a hearing or otherwise affording them a chance to respond. Both the State Bar Association and the California Teachers Association had criticized its conduct.

Then, in early May, HUAC announced a new hearing in San Francisco. William Wheeler, the committee's West Coast investigator, confidentially told an FBI agent that this city was chosen because of the controversy over the English essay question at nearby Berkeley. The committee, moreover, could count on positive publicity from the *San Francisco Examiner*; Hearst representatives had obligingly put Wheeler in touch with a key witness and assigned its star investigative reporter, Ed Montgomery, to cover his testimony. Forty-eight people were subpoenaed, including two Berkeley public school teachers and—of particular interest to the students filing into City Hall—a UC Berkeley sophomore named Douglas Wachter.

Wachter was among a small but growing number of UC Berkeley students who were becoming politically active as the Cold War began to thaw on American campuses. They had huddled outside San Quentin prison across the bay in chilly night vigils against the execution of Caryl Chessman, a convicted robber and rapist whose bestselling prison writings and claims of wrongful prosecution had fueled a movement against capital punishment and won support from Billy Graham, Aldous Huxley, and Norman Mailer. They had signed petitions against the Reserve Officers' Training Corps, contending the two-year military program, which had been compulsory for undergraduate men ever since the university was founded, should be voluntary. They had picketed the local Woolworth's and Kress stores in protests organized by the campus chapter of the Congress on Racial Equality (CORE), supporting sit-ins by black students at the segregated lunch counters these variety stores operated in Greensboro, North Carolina. They were inspired by the civil rights movement, its use of nonviolent civil disobedience, and its stirring spiritual anthems.

A student organization called SLATE was in the forefront of Berkeley's nascent student movement. (The name, not an acronym, simply meant a slate of candidates.) Formed in 1958, the nonideological group challenged what its members derided as the "sandbox" politics, or child's play, of the official student government, the Associated Students of the University of California. The following year a SLATE candidate was elected ASUC president—the first time the post was wrested from the fraternities and sororities. SLATE challenged the university restrictions on campus political activity, particularly the rule that barred the ASUC from taking positions on off-campus issues.

As the date of the HUAC hearings at San Francisco City Hall approached, Mike Tigar, a Berkeley law student and SLATE leader, urged students to picket. Students for Civil Liberties, another campus group, gathered more than 1,500 signatures on a petition. "The committee punishes those who express ideas labeled by the Committee as 'un-American' by public condemnation," the group said. "The effect of this is then to create an atmosphere in which people are fearful of expressing such ideas." A headline in *The Daily Californian* declared, "Student Opposition to Hearings Grows."

•

Robert Meisenbach, tall, dark-haired, and square-jawed, wearing horn-rimmed glasses with thick lenses, stood outside the chamber doors at City Hall with the other students, one hand thrust into his suit coat pocket, the other cradling a pipe he pensively puffed. Looking at Meisenbach, one would hardly guess the Berkeley English major was about to set off a decade of student protest. Two undercover San Francisco Police Department intelligence officers posing as newspaper reporters mingled with the crowd, which they described later as "a large cross section of the populace . . . some students who appeared to be of the clean cut type, some older persons and quite a few of the Beatnik and professional demonstrator types." In response to the "reporters'" questions, one student said, "The committee is obnoxious and tries to spread fear." Another said the committee "should state some real charges rather than slandering the character of subpoenaed subjects." Many students shared these views. Celeste MacLeod, a Berkeley graduate student, would later recall that for years she had felt that Senator McCarthy unjustly branded people as Communists. She had wanted to protest before but was afraid. "Now a committee in the McCarthy tradition was not only coming to San Francisco, but it had selected a student from my own university as one of its victims. That was too much."

Meisenbach first became interested in the committee six years earlier, after his family moved into a new housing development in San Jose, where he was struck by the symmetrically laid out streets, the identical ranch houses, the dearth of trees, and the forest of television antennae. One of the biggest televised attractions that year was the 1954 U.S. Senate hearings into charges that McCarthy had pressured army officials to give preferential treatment to his former aide, G. David Schine. Joseph Welch, a Boston lawyer, presented the army's case. In a dramatic moment, a floundering McCarthy accused a young man who worked for Welch's law firm of being a Communist sympathizer, at which point Welch demanded, "Have you no sense of decency, sir, at long last? Have you left no sense of decency?" That December, the Senate voted to condemn McCarthy. Still, many Americans hesitated to openly criticize anti-Communist officials. Meisenbach recalled discussing the hearings with a friend one day when his mother interrupted to warn, "Watch what you say on the phone!"

Meisenbach served in the Marine Corps, attended junior college, and in 1959 transferred to Berkeley. He rented a room with a bed and a desk for twenty-five dollars a month. He owned two suits, one blue and one gray, which he wore to class in a different combination every day, his Oxford shirt open at the collar. He was not impressed by the Beat authors then gaining popularity; he considered their writing undisciplined, and in conversation spoofed their hipster lingo by saying "like" at the beginning of every sentence. But though he devoted himself to studying classical literature and poetry, he occasionally stopped by the large oak tree near Wheeler Hall where members of SLATE discussed issues of the day. He was impressed by SLATE because no one at his junior college had ever discussed the world beyond the campus; for that matter, few people at Berkeley did. One day by the oak tree he overheard one student tell another not to sign a petition against mandatory ROTC because "it will come back at you." When Meisenbach learned about the HUAC hearing, he resolved to protest it.

As he and the other students waited outside the chamber doors, they were surprised to see police admit a line of older people holding white passes. The committee had given the passes to members of conservative groups such as the American Legion and the Daughters of the American Revolution. Wheeler, the committee investigator, later explained to reporters, "I issued them to individuals to keep the Commies from stacking the meeting. We wanted some decent people in here." Finally officers let in some students. All the seats had been taken by then and they had to stand in the back of the chamber or crouch in the aisles.

U.S. Representative Edwin Willis, a Democrat from Louisiana, called the hearing to order and the committee's staff director, Richard Arens, summoned the first witness. Irving Fishman, an inspector with the U.S. Customs Service, testified that an increasing amount of Communist propaganda entering America was aimed at "conditioning the minds of the youth of this country." As if to prove this, Arens started to say there was picketing right outside City Hall "by people"—here he was cut off by applause from students at the back of the chamber before he continued— "by people who have been enlisted by the Communists."

Arens summoned Douglas Wachter. A slender sophomore in a gray suit and red tie, Wachter was just eighteen, a graduate of Berkeley High School. He had picketed with CORE, marched against capital punishment, and was a member of SLATE. His parents were longtime members of the Communist Party and he was a member of the party's youth group. He recently had given an interview to *The Daily Californian* about the impending hearing, which reported his comments without naming him. "I think the Committee wanted to subpoena someone on campus in order to tag Cal's political movement as un-American," he had said. "I will not be intimidated . . . I am going to fight this committee's invasion of my political freedom in every way I can."

Arens began his interrogation gently. Had he made any public statements about why he was subpoenaed? Yes, Wachter said. Had he made the statement in *The Daily Cal*? "I respectfully object to that question because it clearly violates my rights under the First Amendment to the Constitution of the United States of America," he replied. An audience member hissed at him. Arens continued, "Is there something else you have been doing that you think might be of interest to this committee?" Wachter declined to answer on the same grounds and began to say something, but Arens cut him off and demanded to know whether he was reading from a prepared statement. Wachter said yes and continued, "I feel I have an obligation as a citizen of this country to preserve the Constitution, and I do not feel that I can do so in good conscience by allowing the House Un-American Activities Committee to inquire into my beliefs or associations."

Now Arens bore down. Declaring he had information from "unimpeachable intelligence sources," he demanded, "Are you now, this instant, a member of the Communist Party?" Wachter invoked his Fifth Amendment right not to be forced to bear witness against himself, and, after refusing to answer other questions, he was excused and the hearing adjourned for lunch.

Outside the chamber doors, more students were arriving from a rally at Union Square, where hundreds of people had crammed the plaza ringed by San Francisco's finest department stores and the elegant St. Francis Hotel. Mike Tigar, the SLATE leader, had introduced Assemblyman Phil Burton, who told the crowd there, "People should be tried in a legal court of law on the basis of their actions . . . No legislative committee has the right to tell a man what he thinks and what he doesn't!"

When the hearing at City Hall reconvened after lunch, police again admitted the white card holders first. This time, even fewer students were let in. Some of them banged on the oak doors and chanted, "Open the doors!" Their voices penetrated the chamber and witnesses inside began to shout in unison with them. Chairman Willis declared, "The hearing will resume in an orderly fashion!" At his direction, police charged into the audience, grabbed several people, and started to drag them out as white card holders swatted them and yelled, "Send them back to Russia."

The unruly witnesses were finally ejected, but then students in the back rows stood up and began to sing the national anthem. The white card holders scowled and hissed. "This congressional committee will not be taken over by the Communists or those under Communist discipline,"

Willis declared. "Anyone who is engaged in disorderly conduct in this hearing room will be ejected."

By 2:00 p.m., according to the undercover police officers, people had formed a noisy mass outside the chamber and were in "an ugly mood." When the session ended they left without further conflict, but there were vows to return the next day. Many of them, an FBI agent reported, were Berkeley students.

Celeste MacLeod was among the first to arrive Friday morning. The scene had changed overnight. Police had erected a makeshift barricade, consisting of a sawhorse and rope, about fifteen feet from the chamber door. A policeman stood on either side of the door, and others patrolled the corridor. More students arrived, including Meisenbach, who had stayed the night at a friend's home in San Francisco and taken the street-car back to City Hall. The students watched as police admitted the people clutching white passes, mostly older women in hats. Their indignation grew, and student monitors urged them to stay calm. Finally police let in MacLeod and a few other students with stern warnings to be quiet. But as the hearing began, officers ejected some girls for giggling. And all morning, MacLeod heard chanting out in the hallway; the noise washed into the chamber whenever the door was opened. Judges complained that the racket was interrupting their courtrooms on the upper floors, but the committee members carried on as though they heard nothing.

During lunch recess, about three hundred students outside the chamber sang "The Star-Spangled Banner," their voices reverberating through the rotunda. Meanwhile, nearly four hundred policemen converged on City Hall. Officers in white helmets and jackboots took positions inside. Police wagons and ambulances waited at the curb.

At about 1:15, Inspector Mike Maguire opened the barricade and admitted the white-pass holders. The crowd of waiting students was livid. Fred Haines, a reporter for KPFA radio in Berkeley, was standing next to the officers behind the barricade. "For a moment the waiting crowd paused, and then an angry roar went up," Haines later wrote. "Those in the rear, who were halfway down the stairs and couldn't see what was going on, began to edge forward, and in the resulting crush began to press the flimsy saw-horse barricade toward me and the police officers, who leaped forward to hold it. Angry cries of 'Hold it! Stop pushing!' came from those in front; the barricade held and the police pushed it back into its original position."

Maguire had let in only a few students when the doorkeeper yelled, "That's all!" The crowd groaned. Monitors again urged order. The students sat down. Some resumed singing. Several minutes passed, and Haines thought the danger was over.

Just then, Vincent Hallinan crossed the lobby toward the chamber. The prominent radical lawyer had defended the labor leader Harry Bridges against perjury charges arising from one of his deportation cases. While in jail himself on contempt-of-court charges stemming from the Bridges case, Hallinan ran for president on Henry Wallace's Progressive Party ticket. Years later he would file a lawsuit challenging the authority of the Roman Catholic Church "to act as an agent of God on earth." Today he was representing two witnesses at the hearing. Approaching the doors, he saw officers unrolling fire hoses. Realizing what was about to happen, he rushed to Maguire and implored him to stop. The inspector ignored him.

The students were singing louder than ever, a hymn favored by civil rights protesters: "We shall not be moved, we shall not be moved. Like a tree standing by the water, we shall not be moved." Maguire pointed a big brass nozzle at them. "You want some water?" he shouted. "Well, you're going to get it." As Haines reported, "A trickle dripped from the nozzle, a spurt, bubbly with air—and then the hose stiffened with the full pressure of the water, which blasted into the group of seated demonstrators.

"The rotunda seemed to erupt," Haines recounted. "The singing broke up into one gigantic, horrified scream. People fled past me as I ran forward, trying to see what was going on. A huge sheet of spray, glancing off one granite pillar, flashed through the air in front of me, and I retreated. Those who stood up within ten feet or so of the hose were simply knocked down again by the force of the water, tumbling head over heels on their still seated friends. Others stood, found no place to run, their way blocked by bodies, and so sat down again. Some huddled together for protection." Burton White was one of the Berkeley students blasted broadside. "It was a shock and it hurt when it hit any vulnerable spot," he said.

Meisenbach had been standing off to the side, leaning against a marble pillar, watching the crowd and puffing his pipe. He had not been involved in the noisy sit-down. Astonished that the police had turned the hoses on the sitting students, he yelled, "You bastards!"

A second stream of water arced over the barricades and burst against faces and bodies. Several demonstrators clawed their way through the deluge, toward the barricade. When they were ten feet away they turned and linked arms, forming a human shield to protect the others.

After a while the police turned off the hoses. About 150 students remained rooted to the now flooded floor outside the chamber. There was a momentary hush, Haines reported, and then, "Somewhere in the crowd of sodden, bedraggled students a single voice began to sing, 'We shall not, we shall not be moved . . .' Another voice took it up, and another, and presently all were singing, filling the rotunda with a sound that was almost jubilant."

From the corner of his eye Haines saw movement by the police barricade. Inspector Maguire was leading a line of motorcycle officers. "There was a shout of 'Let's go,' and the phalanx of officers surged forward into the crowd of seated demonstrators, clubs swinging wildly." The singing turned into shrieks. Haines saw officers grab students, haul them to their feet, knock them down again, kicking and clubbing them. Hallinan, near the chamber door, saw two officers run toward the crowd, grab a boy, and drag him behind the barricade. They flung him to the floor, the lawyer said, and while one officer pinned him down another "commenced beating this boy upon the legs with a club."

The police drove the students off the second floor, down the steps to a wide landing on the grand staircase, a reporter for *The Daily Californian* among them. Most fled but about sixty clustered on the landing, sitting amid the streaming water. From behind, a line of helmeted officers charged up the stairs and started seizing them. Following instructions from student organizers, the protesters put their hands in their pockets and let their bodies go limp in passive resistance. The officers grabbed their arms and ankles and clothing and hauled them down the stairway, sometimes letting their heads hit the steps. Women were handled as roughly as men, their dresses riding up along the way. The police herded them outside, just beyond the larger-than-life bronze statue of a pensive Lincoln, as the water cascaded down the steps, across the main floor, and into the street.

Inside the chamber, Karl Prussion, a bankrupt building contractor, was testifying that college courses on Darwin's theory of evolution had led him to join the Communist Party. He was saying, ". . . when the spirit of man and the soul of man and the name of God are never mentioned, never discussed at the universities, a man is readily prepared to accept membership into the Communist Party." Prussion remained a party member from 1933 to 1959, when he found God and became a paid FBI informer. The Hearst Corporation had put him in touch with the committee.

At the curb in front of City Hall, police were loading vans with the last of sixty-four wet and shivering arrestees. Thirty-one were Berkeley students, including Evelyn Einstein, Albert Einstein's granddaughter. While janitors mopped up inside City Hall, officers drove the vans to police stations, where the protesters were charged with various misdemeanors. Meisenbach was the only one accused of a felony: assault. At a press conference, police claimed the English major and former marine had started the riot by grabbing a billy club from officer Ralph Schaumleffel and striking him with it. All were released after posting bail.

Mayor George Christopher had been out of town but rushed back to find City Hall still surrounded by chanting picketers. Christopher grabbed a microphone from a police car. "Please obey the law," he pleaded. "I don't want this to become a black day in the history of San Francisco." Pickets shouted back, "It already is."

The events at City Hall generated a spate of stories in San Francisco's three daily newspapers. Reporters hustled to pound out their accounts on clattering manual typewriters at cigarette-burned oak desks in the newsrooms down by Third Street, a grimy strip several blocks from the civic center. Their stories stole the lead spot from breaking news about Fidel Castro's disclosure that his ships had fired on a U.S. submarine inside Cuba's territorial waters, and President Dwight Eisenhower's tense summit with the Soviet premier, Nikita Khrushchev, on nuclear arms inspections. The *San Francisco Examiner's* headline read, "Cops Battle Student Mob at City Hall." The lead article was written by Ed Montgomery, the best-known newspaperman in the city. He claimed the students had started a "full-blown riot."

According to Montgomery: "When all the seats in the chamber were filled, Patrolman Ralph Schaumleffel, 645 Gonzales St., on duty at the door, closed it, informing the crowd there were no more seats. The mob then climbed over the barricades and stormed the door, knocking Schaumleffel down. Then, the officer said, while he was on his back, a student, Robert J. Meisenbach, 22, of 2029 Hearst St., Berkeley, an English major at UC, grabbed the policeman's nightstick and hit him over the head with it . . . Inspector Mike Maguire of the Intelligence Detail then grabbed a fire hose and ordered it turned on."

Although the other newspapers reported that Meisenbach allegedly assaulted the officer *after* police turned on the fire hoses, Montgomery claimed Meisenbach attacked him *before* police used the fire hoses, suggesting that Meisenbach leaped the barricade, struck the officer, and

ignited "the riot." Next to his article, the *Examiner* ran a mug shot of
Meisenbach captioned "nightstick swinger."

Montgomery's account was picked up by the Associated Press and wired
to newspapers across the country. It would prove crucial to the students,
the police, and the FBI.

Celeste MacLeod had left the hearing before noon Friday and returned to
campus to study. That afternoon, however, news about police hosing students down the steps of City Hall was everywhere. Although she had not
planned to do any more picketing, she joined other students in organizing
a meeting that evening. The university administration withheld permission to use a lecture hall, so some five hundred people crammed into
the basement of Barrington Hall, a student housing cooperative a few
blocks off campus, to hear firsthand reports on the confrontation. Many
resolved to return to City Hall the next day for the final hearing. Organizers urged them to dress nicely and behave.

MacLeod and about three dozen other students stayed up drinking
coffee and making picket signs. They chose messages for the signs by vote,
after agreeing that none of the placards would protest police brutality, call
the committee fascists, or attack the American Legion. Although most of
them were strangers, she would later say she had never before experienced
such "close group feelings as there was among those students between
midnight and two a.m. that night in that room."

The next morning she and hundreds of other students from Berkeley,
Stanford, and San Francisco State came together at San Francisco City
Hall. This time the building was closed and police lines blocked the entrances. About 250 people marched in a picket line around the building,
while another 1,500 gathered across Polk Street in Civic Center Plaza, listening to the hearings broadcast over large speakers. Some carried signs
that said WITCH HUNTERS GO HOME. Jessica Mitford, the radical writer,
was there and would observe drolly in an article she wrote for *The Nation*
that the episode "was for hundreds of students the first time they (literally)
got their feet wet in political action."

Inside, Police Chief Thomas Cahill was testifying about Friday's arrests. He claimed young people outside the chamber had forced officers
to use violence to restore order. Chairman Willis commended him for "a
very well done job." He also praised Inspector Maguire, saying that he
was "included among the highest of the deserving ones." The committee
then called the witnesses it had subpoenaed, including Doug Wachter's

father. Saul Wachter asked why no students were being allowed to testify about Friday's events, and Willis declared the committee already had heard from "reliable witnesses."

The crowd in the plaza was growing restive. As they listened to the broadcast hearings, the demonstrators cheered uncooperative witnesses and jeered the committee. Some gave Nazi salutes and yelled "Sieg Heil!" Throngs rushed toward City Hall when officials appeared at the doorways, and when the hearings ended police hastily escorted the committee members out a rear exit. An FBI agent reported that "serious mob violence was narrowly averted."

HUAC never returned to San Francisco. "This was probably the worst incident in the history of the committee," Willis said.

Even before the steps of City Hall had dried, angry calls were pouring into the offices of the university's president, Clark Kerr. Irate alumni and members of the public demanded the university punish students involved in the protest. Kerr, who did not think highly of HUAC and its "vague and sweeping allegations," declined to discipline them.

"Any University of California students among the demonstrators at the committee hearings were there as private individuals," he said. "They were not in any way representing the university . . ."

7

Communist Target—Youth

From his desk in the federal building, across Civic Center Plaza from City Hall, Richard Auerbach sent an urgent memo to Hoover.

"Yesterday," the special agent in charge of the FBI's San Francisco field office wrote, "we had a demonstration of Communist strength in San Francisco, the likes of which have not been seen since the infamous 1934 strike." He was comparing the City Hall protest to the strike led by Harry Bridges that shut down the West Coast maritime industry for eighty-three days and sparked a general strike that paralyzed San Francisco for four days. Scores of strikers and police were injured and two strikers died.

Auerbach may have been exaggerating, but his statement accurately reflected a growing concern among FBI officials about the University of California. He continued, "What is particularly significant, and undoubtedly of special interest to you, is the fact that much of the manpower for this riotous situation was provided by students of the University of California at Berkeley. Since Clark Kerr has become President, the situation on all campuses has deteriorated to the point where the so-called academic freedom has become academic license. The attack on the FBI in the English 'A' examination was merely one example of the deterioration of the morality and patriotism of this great university, which will have fifty thousand students in its halls."

Hoover replied swiftly, saying he was "extremely" concerned. He saw the City Hall protest not only as a radical recrudescence, but as an attack on an important ally in the war against subversion. Publicly, the FBI and the House Un-American Activities Committee were separate and independent government bodies. Covertly, they were collaborators helping each other fight common enemies and promote shared political objectives. The bureau's massive files were by law confidential, something Hoover described as sacrosanct. But at his direction senior bureau officials confidentially gave selected HUAC staff members FBI intelligence reports about people the committee was targeting. The committee then forced them to appear by subpoena and questioned them under oath, without disclosing the bureau's role. The committee, in turn, gave the FBI information it compelled these witnesses to turn over. Hoover thus used HUAC to investigate people and to discredit them as disloyal, even though he lacked sufficient evidence to charge them with any crime. In internal memos, Hoover justified this unauthorized and highly political use of confidential FBI files as necessary to protect national security.

Hoover decided to show the nation that Communists were behind the student protest against HUAC at City Hall. On May 18, 1960, he ordered Auerbach to prepare a "comprehensive analysis" of the Communist Party's role in the demonstrations. The report was to include the identities of the student groups involved and any evidence of Communist control over them. A student's participation in the protests, he said, could be ground for listing him or her in the Security Index.

Auerbach was already on it. A veteran of the FBI's investigation of Communists in Hollywood in the 1940s, he had risen through the bureau hierarchy and won the coveted post of San Francisco SAC. He assigned every agent on all three of his security squads to examine not only the Communist Party's role in the City Hall protest, but also the background of each arrestee and the "situation" at the University of California. The agents' mission was outlined in an order titled "Project: Revolution in San Francisco," which made clear the investigation's dramatic and predetermined result: a report showing that Communists had induced students to engage in "wild rioting and disorder" that "threatened the Government of the City of San Francisco and defied the authority and power of the Federal Government."

The San Francisco field office was under pressure to get the report to Hoover fast. The FBI agent supervising "Project: Revolution" told his team of agents to cut corners in "documenting" Communist involvement—that is, in supporting each allegation with citations to the underlying evidence. "We prefer not to follow the strict rules," he said. "However, we do want to have some idea of the source of the information. In describing an individual, present the most pertinent and most derogatory information available."

The agents immediately set to work on "Project: Revolution." They received secret assistance from San Francisco's three daily newspapers, which, without so much as a subpoena, confidentially turned over hundreds of unpublished photographs taken at the protest. FBI agents used them to identify people and investigate their political activities. Two weeks later the completed memo was rushed to Hoover, who deemed it well done.

He knew just how he'd use it.

On June 1, 1960, dozens of students returned to City Hall, this time to be sentenced for their roles in the disturbance. Each was charged with the misdemeanor offenses of participating in a riot, disturbing the public peace, and resisting arrest. The maximum potential penalty was one year in jail and a thousand-dollar fine.

Judge Albert Axelrod began by noting that the defendants had agreed to waive their right to a trial that would test the evidence and instead had placed their fate in his hands, allowing him to decide the case solely on the basis of police reports and on the unchallenged assumption that the reports were true. They also had agreed not to sue the city for police brutality.

The judge paused, looked over the students assembled before him, and declared that, on this basis, there was "ample grounds for a conviction." But he continued, "There is another side to the issues . . . The defendants for the most part are clean-cut American college students who will within the next few years enter into the business and professional worlds and many of them I am sure will become leaders in their respective fields. I am convinced they are not engaged in subversive activities nor in spreading subversive propaganda. They wanted to exercise their prerogative of protesting what they believed to be an undemocratic hearing. However, they chose the wrong means to accomplish their purpose and let themselves become victims of those who profit by creating unrest." The judge paused again. Then, declaring that they had been punished sufficiently, and that he hoped they had learned their lesson, he dismissed all charges "in the interest of justice."

The students were relieved, but fifty-eight of them promptly put out a statement saying, "Nobody incited us, nobody misguided us. We were led only by our own convictions and we still stand firmly by them."

This left the case of Robert Meisenbach, who faced a separate trial on the felony charge of assaulting an officer with a deadly weapon. He was the student who police had singled out as starting the riot, the one who the *San Francisco Examiner* reporter Ed Montgomery had suggested precipitated the fire hosing, the one on whom the FBI would focus.

•

One week after the charges against the other students were dismissed, bureau officials opened an investigation into Meisenbach's background. At UC Berkeley, Agent Harry Rote, Jr., reviewed his student records. They described him as having brown hair and green eyes and wearing glasses. He was six feet one and weighed 180 pounds. He was born on March 4, 1938, in Ellwood, Nebraska. His parents, John and Cordelia, lived in Oakdale, an agricultural community near Modesto on the way to Yosemite National Park.

Agent Clarence W. Dunker reviewed Meisenbach's file at Oakdale High School, including a personal questionnaire and his frequently flippant and decidedly apolitical answers: Do you intend to go to college? "Yes." Why, or why not? "Knowledge, of course." What task do you regularly have at home? "No tasks. I sponge off the parents." Do you have any special interests such as music, art, sewing, etc.? "Myself." List your hobbies and favorite amusements. "People."

There was a personal essay, too: "From the eighth grade to the end of my freshman year I was of no value to myself or the world. I was just another person who consumed three meals a day. About half way through my sophomore year in high school, the New Deal of my life began . . . For I started studying but more important than that, was that I started measuring my future . . . I consider this the most important period of my life. My idea of a successful life is becoming someone or something of value either to yourself or even better to someone else."

Dunker got more details from Meisenbach's records at Modesto Junior College. His father was a civil engineer and his mother was a housewife who had worked as a teacher before she married. Meisenbach had enrolled there in September 1956, and early on received poor grades, but by his last semester, in spring 1959, he earned two As, three Bs and one C. On a mandatory school form, the teenager described himself as friendly, patient, talented, self-confident, egotistical, tactful, cynical, and given to daydreaming. Dunker noted that Meisenbach also said he was unable to make a satisfactory religious adjustment and sometimes had difficulty understanding what he read. A psychologist's note in the file described him as an "unusual lad." Teachers had said he was "well-balanced" but held vaguely formed objectives, was little noticed, and let others take the lead. Dunker next obtained Meisenbach's Selective Service records, which showed he had joined the marines in March 1955, at age sixteen, and been honorably discharged. Local police had no records on Meisenbach or his family.

As the FBI agent completed his rounds, the local postmaster told him the Meisenbach family had recently moved to a trailer court and the father was often out of town on large construction projects.

On October 6, 1960, the agents wrapped up the investigation, reporting they had found "no subversive derogatory information concerning the subject." Nonetheless, FBI officials would take a special interest in his upcoming trial on charges of clouting Officer Schaumleffel.

Hoover and his allies on the House Un-American Activities Committee were not about to let the biggest demonstration against HUAC in its twenty-two-year history go unanswered. Nor were they content to let judge or jury determine what actually happened at City Hall. They moved swiftly to counterattack with a special report titled "Communist Target—Youth: Communist Infiltration and Agitation Tactics."

The eighteen-page booklet, signed by Hoover and illustrated with photographs of the protest, was based on the "Project: Revolution" report prepared by the San Francisco FBI field office. It claimed Communists had worked to ensure a big turnout, publicizing the protest through advertisements and petitions and transporting demonstrators from Berkeley to San Francisco City Hall. There they used "mob psychology," disrupting the hearing and getting themselves ejected in an effort to provoke the students to sing and chant. Tensions outside the carved oak doors grew and the Communists' calculations paid off: the Berkeley student Robert Meisenbach "provided the spark that touched off the flame of violence."

Worst of all, Hoover's report said, the gullible students had no idea they had been duped. "Looking at the riots and chaos Communists have created in other countries, many Americans point to the strength of our Nation and say 'It can't happen here,'" the report concluded. "The Communist success in San Francisco in May 1960 proves that it can . . ."

"Communist Target—Youth" generated alarmist news stories around the country. An Associated Press dispatch went to hundreds of daily newspapers, and *The Washington Post*, *The New York Times*, and the *New York Herald Tribune* ran stories amplifying Hoover's dire warning about American youth. He was gratified by the publicity, and took an extra step to personally thank the *San Francisco Examiner* publisher, Charles Mayer, for his editorial excoriating the students.

Others, however, had grave doubts about Hoover's account. Irving Hall and Burton White were among the Berkeley students arrested at City Hall. They felt the committee and the police had treated them poorly. Now came Hoover with a report blaming them. Hall and White joined other students in issuing a statement denying the protest was the result of a Communist plot. Bay Area newspapers interviewed them, and their rejoinder was soon on the national wires, too. "Whether the Communist Party prepared in any way for the San Francisco hearings we do not know," they said. "We do know, however, that others of Hoover's statements either are based on lack of information or are made in bad faith." They challenged Hoover to a public debate and dared him to produce his evidence.

The director did not deign to debate. Instead, FBI officials secretly drafted an "editorial" intended to counter the students' claims. The screed ignored their arguments and instead focused on Doug Wachter—the Berkeley student whom HUAC had subpoenaed—describing him as a Communist and "the son of a long-time Communist." On July 22, 1960, Hoover ordered DeLoach to feed it to the Hearst columnist George Sokolsky, who had a close relationship with the bureau.

But as Hoover's "Communist Target—Youth" gained enormous circulation, other events within and without the bureau raised questions about its truthfulness. Richard Arens, HUAC's staff director, asked his FBI contacts for details about two Communist Party youth conferences that Hoover had mentioned in the report. HUAC was considering holding hearings and Arens needed the names of the conference attendees as possible witnesses. FBI officials wanted to help, but discovered they actually had no informers at one conference, and the sole informer at the other refused to testify. The bureau's inability to produce firsthand witnesses worried Hoover. On July 22, 1960, he scrawled on a memo, "I am concerned now as to foundation for our statements in the document."

Paul Seabury, a Berkeley political science professor, meanwhile sent a pointed letter about "Communist Target—Youth" to U.S. Attorney General William P. Rogers, who was, at least nominally, Hoover's boss. Seabury was the Northern California chairman of Americans for Democratic Action, which according to the FBI's own files was a staunchly anti-Communist political organization founded by Democrats. Seabury charged that Hoover's report was "much too simple and unwarranted in fact." He disputed that the students were "led or duped" by Communists, and asserted they had been encouraged by broad public sentiment against the committee. Hoover, he concluded, had demonstrated "a profound misconception of political forces and events."

Attorney General Rogers forwarded Seabury's letter to Hoover. It was one thing to have questions raised within the bureau about a report; it was another to have them come from responsible quarters outside the bureau's control. The director began to check his facts. On August 3, 1960, he ordered Auerbach to submit "complete documentation" for the "Project: Revolution" memo on which his report was based, "paragraph by paragraph."

Auerbach rushed the documentation to FBI headquarters by overnight air express, with the assurance "All sources are regarded as reliable." There the material was reviewed by the domestic intelligence official William C. Sullivan, who had ghostwritten "Communist Target—Youth" for Hoover. On August 8, 1960, Sullivan affirmed that all the sources were "thoroughly reliable" and the director's report was "wholly factual."

Sullivan was upbeat for another reason: HUAC had just fired its own broadside at the students, a forty-two-minute documentary about the City Hall protest called *Operation Abolition*. The film featured grainy black-and-white footage subpoenaed from Bay Area television stations and a noir score. Francis E. Walter, chairman of the committee, gravely declares, "Operation Abolition—this is what the Communists call their current drive to destroy the House Committee on Un-American Activities, to weaken the Federal Bureau of Investigation, to discredit its great director, J. Edgar Hoover, and to render sterile the security laws of our government." The movie claimed the students were unwitting dupes of the Communist Party and "performed like puppets." It repeated Hoover's charge that Meisenbach leaped over a barricade, grabbed an officer's nightstick, and beat him on the head.

As the committee distributed *Operation Abolition* around the country, it provoked outrage from students. They saw that scenes had been taken out of sequence, that people were misidentified, that there was no footage of anyone leaping a barricade or attacking an officer. The documentary had been edited to make it appear that Communists directed the protest and students started the confrontation with police.

Irving Hall, one of the arrestees, told a newspaper, "Of course there were Communists there. They were subpoenaed. That doesn't mean they had anything to do with us." Hall and other students meeting at Berkeley's Plymouth Student Center decided to produce their own report in reply to

Hoover's. "The FBI and the HUAC must—and can be—shown up for what they really are!" they declared in a handbill.

Auerbach assigned two agents to investigate these activities. An informer soon obtained "by devious means" a copy of the students' line-by-line refutation of Hoover's report. The director ordered Auerbach to assess their claims, and on August 25, 1960, he reported back with some startling admissions.

Auerbach conceded it was true that Students for Civil Liberties, and not the Communist Party, had planned the protest at City Hall. It was true that HUAC had deliberately excluded the students and given most of the white passes to its friends. It was also true that this had led the students to sing and chant and sit down outside the hearing chamber.

Moreover, he continued, "Inspector Michael Maguire of the Intelligence Detail of the San Francisco Police department, who is a hot-headed and fiery Irishman, gave an order to them, which they disobeyed. He pointed to the fire hoses on the walls and threatened them . . . Some of the students yelled back, 'Go ahead.' He lost his temper and turned on the hoses." They still refused to disperse, Auerbach said, and the police resorted to inappropriate methods to arrest them.

"The students claim that it was not the Communists using mob psychology who turned the peaceful demonstration into riots, but it is their conclusion that there are two factors involved: 1) the HUAC utilized too small a hearing hall and allowed entrance by pass, and 2) the police mishandled the situation. These two points are a matter of conclusion and opinions," Auerbach said. "Maybe they are right." Still, he steadfastly assured Hoover that "the facts speak for themselves as stated in the FBI director's report."

Hoover was mollified for the moment. Besides, HUAC's *Operation Abolition* documentary was getting huge play. The Department of Defense was using the film in mandatory training. The army anticipated showing it to more than 500,000 soldiers. The navy wanted 150 copies to show sailors. Standard Oil, Pacific Gas & Electric, Pacific Telephone and Telegraph, Lockheed, and Boeing screened it for employees. It was presented at high schools, colleges, churches, Parent-Teacher Associations, police departments, and American Legion halls.

All over America, the film was making Berkeley look bad, so Kerr directed a distinguished law professor and vice-chancellor named Adrian Kragen to analyze it. After Kragen concluded the students' complaints were well-founded, Kerr dispatched him to address a forum in San Pedro, a community in Los Angeles. Only on arriving did Kragen discover it was actually a meeting of the local American Legion chapter. The nattily clad legal scholar began by trying to strike up a rapport with the audience of two hundred Legionnaires and John Birch Society members, quipping that he was "considered a conservative in everything but my dress." The evening went downhill from there, according to a report from an FBI informer who was present.

But the more the HUAC film was shown, the more questions were raised about its accuracy, and in time it proved to be the students' best weapon against the committee. It became a contemporary cult classic as students played it for overflow crowds—and pointed out error after error. Here was dramatic proof, on the order of epiphany, that the government would lie to its citizens; worse, lie about students merely trying to exercise basic constitutional rights. In a typical screening that fall, some eight hundred Berkeley students watched the movie at International House, just off campus. The crowd was overwhelmingly critical, and as an FBI report noted, each student paid 75 cents admission that went toward Meisenbach's legal defense. In a review the next day, *The Daily Californian* declared, "Seeing the film is a matter of self-preservation in our modern society. It is an education that distortion, prevarication and dishonest propaganda can come from any quarter."

The controversy spread beyond campus. Herb Caen, the *San Francisco Chronicle* columnist, commented on the movie's inaccuracies and was deluged with angry mail. He replied testily, "To sum up, what I object to most heartily is the attempt of the Committee to smear the students present as 'Communist stooges.' There is no more effective way of enforcing conformity and instilling fear . . . And few things could do more damage to what my letter writing friends like to call 'The American way of life' which, to answer their rhetorical questions, I do believe in." On November 26, 1960, *The Washington Post* ran an editorial headlined "Forgery by Film." Summarizing many of the students' complaints, the *Post* concluded that the movie "warps the truth."

J. Edgar Hoover hated the *Post*, but he couldn't ignore his hometown newspaper's assault on a film to which he was so closely linked. He set down the clipping of the *Post* editorial and scrawled on it, "What are the facts?" His aides immediately sent a teletype to Auerbach, ordering him to reassess the film's accuracy. Tolson wrote a note saying, "We should have checked on this long before now," and in his jagged hand Hoover added, "Most certainly we should have."

Auerbach soon found even more errors than the *Post* had mentioned. Most alarming were their implications for the pending Meisenbach case.

"A very particular point made by the commentator is that on Friday afternoon the students leaped barricades and that a student beat a policeman. The film does not show this at all," he said. "This point is important because it is the point at issue in a trial in the Superior Court of San Francisco, being held early next year, and it is the point that is being very vociferously denied by professors and students, even at this late date, in many of the campuses in Northern California."

Auerbach concluded that, unfortunately, "the film can be legitimately attacked." He warned Hoover that "the FBI should not become affiliated with or identified with the film."

It was too late for that. But in an effort to distance the bureau from the film, Hoover told the heads of each field office, "Under no circumstances should your comments be construed as an endorsement of the movie by the FBI." And when concerned citizens wrote Hoover asking whether they could trust the film, the FBI director dodged their questions.

A typical inquiry came from Maynard M. Wolfe, Jr., secretary of the Lucas County Council of the American Legion, in Toledo, Ohio. In his January 16, 1961, letter, Wolfe said his legion chapter had convinced a Toledo Board of Education official to show *Operation Abolition* to high school social studies classes, but that after the *Toledo Blade* published an editorial saying the film distorted the facts, the board balked. "Would it be improper to ask you for a recommendation as to its usefulness for high school people?" Wolfe asked.

Following standard procedure, Hoover's aides first checked Wolfe's name in the FBI's files—the director never responded to a citizen's inquiry without first determining whether he or she had been identified as a subversive or might be out to embarrass the bureau. If the files contained information suggesting the correspondent was less than friendly, Hoover would not answer. Finding "no derogatory information" on Wolfe, Hoover replied on January 24, 1961: "It would be improper for the FBI to endorse the activities of any legislative committee. This Bureau had no connection with the preparation of 'Operation Abolition' which, as you know, is sponsored and distributed by the House Committee. As a matter of policy, therefore, I cannot make any recommendation concerning it."

Instead, Hoover enclosed a copy of his own report on the City Hall riot.

•

"Communist Target—Youth" was becoming one of the bureau's all-time bestsellers. FBI officials were spreading copies far and wide, and making a special effort to reach students.

On August 12, 1960, an aide to Assistant Director Cartha DeLoach, who had run the FBI's campaign against the university's English essay question, proposed a scheme to get copies of the report into "the hands of every college president in the United States." The goal was to spur school administrators to take a tougher stance against subversive students. FBI agents would not send the reports directly—the bureau might then be accused of unduly pressuring the schools—so a seemingly independent intermediary would do it. Hoover read the proposal and scrawled, "Most certainly." The special agent in charge of the FBI's Cincinnati field office thus arranged to have Justin A. Rollman, a wealthy Republican activist in Cincinnati, mail several thousand copies of the report to every college president, all newspaper publishers, and "top flight industrialists" in the United States.

The FBI, meanwhile, was being flooded with requests for copies of "Communist Target—Youth" from schools, churches, police agencies, and civic groups that wanted to use it to educate citizens about the Communist threat. Hoover readily obliged, after his staff had checked the requester's name in bureau files with satisfactory results. Six thousand copies were mailed to the Calvary Baptist Church in Monrovia, California. Ten thousand copies were shipped to Detective Sergeant Stanley Olczak of the Michigan State Police. Eighteen thousand copies were delivered to the American Legion Post in Nassau County, New York, which planned to distribute them to commuters at the seventy stations along the Long Island Rail Road so they would wind up in Manhattan offices. More boxes full of the pamphlets were sent to Kiwanis, Lions, and Rotary clubs, the John Birch Society, the Daughters of the American Revolution, and Parent-Teacher Associations. The national director of the Girl Scouts of the United States of America requested three thousand copies of the report, and, finding nothing in bureau files to suggest she was a subversive, Hoover sent them along, too.

The FBI director's account of youth led astray resonated with many Americans. Their letters to Hoover reveal deep fears of a foreign threat and trust in the bureau to defend them—hopes and fears upon which Hoover was mobilizing conservatives. Mrs. Harold K. Bower of Spokane, Washington, wrote Hoover on February 13, 1961. "Believe me, I am becoming very alarmed about the Communist threat to our nation," she said. "I'm not kidding. I'm scared. When I read in the daily papers that we are to get soft with Russia; that stars of stage, screen, radio and television are against our nuclear testing . . . and Mr. Khrushchev is shown on television thundering to the American people, 'Your children will be raised under Communism'—you know, Mr. Hoover, I believe him! But it makes me mad enough to fight back! I'm glad Mr. Kennedy kept you at your post, sir. I feel safer with you there."

But as "Communist Target—Youth" circulated ever more widely, even some of Hoover's faithful came to doubt its accuracy. The Reverend Henry Gerner of the Wesley Foundation, a Methodist ministry at San Jose State College, was one of them. On March 24, 1961, he wrote Hoover to say he agreed that the report concerned "the most pressing matter, the question of how our country shall withstand internal subversion and the Communist threat to freedom." But noting that several sources had criticized it, Gerner pointedly asked Hoover whether "you still maintain to be the author and to stand behind the document which contains your name." Hoover set him straight, replying on March 24, 1961, that his report was "entirely authentic and completely documented. It does not merely represent my opinion. It is a compilation of facts accumulated during an official investigation by the FBI."

By April 17, 1961—the day before Meisenbach's trial was to begin— FBI officials had distributed more than 300,000 copies of "Communist Target—Youth," generating great anticipation about the prosecution flowing from the events beneath the gilded dome of City Hall.

That trial would not only decide the guilt or innocence of Meisenbach. It would test the students' contentions that they had been engaged in legitimate protest and were mistreated by the committee, manhandled by the police, and maligned by the FBI.

It would test the veracity of Hoover's allegations that Berkeley students had been unwitting Communist dupes, and that Meisenbach had jumped over a barricade, grabbed an officer's billy club, and started a riot.

It would be one of the first decisive battles of what would soon be called the Sixties.

8

The Trial of Robert Meisenbach

The trial of Robert Meisenbach on charges of assaulting Patrolman Ralph Schaumleffel during the City Hall protest opened April 18, 1961, in Judge Harry J. Neubarth's courtroom at 750 Kearny Street. San Francisco's Hall of Justice was just a few blocks from North Beach, the old Italian neighborhood of garlic- and espresso-scented streets that had become a haven for beatniks. The trial had been delayed by the routine court calendar, by Neubarth's attendance at the San Francisco Giants' opening game, and, above all, by Meisenbach's steadfast refusal to plea-bargain.

Nearly a year had passed since his arrest, a year of anxiety and uncertainty. From the outset, the potential consequences seemed overwhelming. If convicted of the assault charge he faced up to ten years in prison. His dream of becoming a teacher would be destroyed, his parents would be disappointed in him, and his life would be thrown into chaos. On top of that, he feared that Hoover, HUAC, and the San Francisco police would seize on his conviction as proof that the students were Communist dupes.

As his trial approached, these pressures mounted. He became distracted and unable to concentrate on his classes. He also felt tensions building within his family. His father had been displeased when he rejected the family's Catholicism, and his displeasure had grown when his son became nationally known as the man accused of starting a Communist riot at a congressional hearing. Increasingly anxious, Meisenbach had trouble sleeping and developed stomach ulcers. Once, while crossing the Bay Bridge after meeting with his lawyers in San Francisco, he saw a ship heading out to sea and wished he was on it. Another time, while trying to study on the esplanade beneath the Campanile, he found himself looking up at the clock tower, thinking one swan dive would end his agony. He had started to tremble.

Just before trial, Assistant District Attorney Walter Giubbini made Meisenbach an appealing offer: if he pleaded guilty to a minor charge the prosecution would seek only a ten-day suspended sentence, meaning no jail time. But once again Meisenbach said no. He believed in his own innocence and in the truth. So as he readied himself on the morning that his trial began, his father came to him and put a rosary in his suit coat pocket. "At least," his father told him, "it will make me feel better."

By the end of the first day, a jury of ten women and two men had been impaneled. They were mostly middle-class parents of grown children and included an elevator operator, a saleswoman, a housewife, a mailroom clerk, a typist, a telephone technician, and a plumber. Eyeing the students who filled the spectators' seats, Neubarth made clear he would tolerate no misconduct and posted six extra bailiffs around the courtroom. Burton White, a Berkeley student who had been arrested at City Hall, told a reporter he was sure the trial would be fair. Richard Auerbach, the head of the San Francisco FBI office, also was confident: Giubbini had confidentially told him he had five witnesses to support the assault charge. And he expected the *San Francisco Examiner* reporter Ed Montgomery to testify, too.

In his opening statement the next day, Giubbini focused on events outside the hearing chamber's oak doors. It was simple, he said: the demonstrators became disorderly, surged toward the door, and knocked down police barricades. Police pushed back and Meisenbach attacked Schaumleffel. In his reply, Jack Berman, one of Meisenbach's lawyers, told the jury that the charges against his client were "a fabric of lies." Meisenbach, he said, came from a respected San Joaquin Valley family and was no political activist. The Berkeley English major had gone to City Hall because he was curious about the committee. At the moment Meisenbach allegedly attacked Schaumleffel, a photograph showed, he was actually standing forty feet away, smoking his pipe. Witnesses would testify he assaulted no one and that police beat him for no reason. Angrily, Berman declared there would have been no melee if not for Inspector Michael Maguire, "the sadistic man" who had turned on the fire hose. The students in the courtroom listened intently.

Giubbini called his first witness. A stocky, blond-haired, thirty-three-year-old patrolman, Officer Ralph Schaumleffel testified he was on duty at the hearing chamber doors when the white-pass holders were admitted. Several hundred students surged once, twice, and a third time against the police barricade, shouting "Let us in!" Suddenly someone knocked him down and grabbed his billy club. "I regained my balance and looked up," he said. "Meisenbach, standing three or four feet away, had the club over my head and was starting to swing . . . I was hit on the left rear portion of my head. I grabbed Meisenbach and we fell to the floor and started wrestling, rolling back and forth." He slugged the student, subdued him, and arrested him.

On cross-examination, Berman suggested the officer was the victim not of any assault but of his own clumsiness. Schaumleffel heatedly denied he had told a fellow officer that he had slipped on the wet marble floor and struck his head. But—on a key point—he acknowledged that his encounter with Meisenbach came *after* the hoses had been turned on. Contrary to Hoover's report, and Montgomery's story, Meisenbach had not triggered a general riot and subsequent police hosing by leaping a barricade and clubbing him.

Giubbini put on two more prosecution witnesses. John Stansfield, a self-employed private investigator, testified that from a third-floor balcony he saw Meisenbach club Schaumleffel. But parts of his account contradicted the officer's story. Moreover, he acknowledged he had not come forward as a witness for ten months, and then only after running into a friend on the police force. Albert Morris, a part-time real estate agent, testified that from a fourth-floor balcony he saw Meisenbach assault Schaumleffel, but he had trouble identifying Meisenbach in the courtroom and his account diverged from both the officer's and Stansfield's.

Berman presented a series of witnesses who said they saw no violence by students before police turned the fire hoses on them. One of them, Douglas Kinney, a retired navy lieutenant who was working in the City Hall law library, testified that the commotion drew him to the fourth-floor balcony. Looking down, he saw Schaumleffel and two or three other officers beating a young man. One of them clubbed the man's head several times. "I hollered to the police to stop beating that kid," said Kinney. He ran down the stairs to the officers, jotted down the badge number on Schaumleffel's shirt, and wrote a memo about it.

Meisenbach then took the stand, wearing a gray suit. He spoke in such a low and halting voice that Charles Garry, Berman's cocounsel, repeatedly asked him to speak up. He said he had gone to City Hall to see the hearing, and just after lunch he was in the rotunda, standing by a pillar, puffing his pipe and watching the sitting, singing students. Police turned on the fire hoses and he headed toward the stairs to leave. Along the way he was doused and took cover behind another pillar, where he wiped the water off his eyeglasses. As police turned on the second hose, he again started down the slippery marble steps. He paused briefly when he saw two officers throw a man down the stairs. As he reached the landing at the head of the grand staircase, a policeman's billy club bounced at his feet. "I picked it up and tossed it away, back toward the lobby," he testified. An officer tackled him from behind, slugged him, and dragged him up the stairs to the lobby, behind some pillars, where Schaumleffel struck him across his face with a club, knocking off his glasses. Officers hauled him to an area near the oak chamber doors and beat him again. They cuffed his hands and sat him down in a puddle. He could barely see. His lip was bleeding. He was scared.

His face ashen, Meisenbach looked bleakly at Garry. The lawyer asked if anything else happened as a result of the beating. There was silence, and Meisenbach started to cry. He removed his glasses, took a neatly folded handkerchief from his breast pocket, and dabbed his eyes. "I was beaten," he said. He paused. "I was beaten and I was afraid." His voice dropped to a whisper. "I had a bowel movement, involuntary bowel movement."

Giubbini cross-examined him. Meisenbach said he had carried a picket sign protesting the committee outside City Hall that morning, but denied demonstrating inside, resisting arrest, or hitting the officer. After he stepped down from the witness box, Berman called three of his former teachers, each of whom testified that he had been a quiet and honest student.

At this point the case was scheduled to go to the jury, but the prosecutor announced he had new witnesses. Both were policemen who testified that no officer struck Meisenbach. On cross-examination, however, Officer Thomas Walsh and Assistant Inspector Cecil Pharris admitted that they did not see Meisenbach leap a barricade or club Schaumleffel.

Now Berman read the key phrase in Hoover's "Communist Target— Youth" report that accused Meisenbach of assaulting Schaumleffel: "One of the demonstrators provided the spark that touched off the flame of violence. Leaping a barricade that had been erected, he grabbed an officer's nightstick and began beating the officer over the head. The mob surged forward as if to storm the doors, and a Police Inspector ordered the fire hose turned on."

Berman asked Inspector Pharris if he'd made that statement to the FBI. He denied it.

"I am astounded," Hoover scrawled in a note to Tolson on May 2, 1961. "I have again & again been assured that our report was fool proof but . . . it certainly looks as if we didn't definitely tie down the Meisenbach incident." Tolson wrote in reply, "I think it is imperative that we get the facts

concerning this matter immediately in order to know where we stand."
Beneath that, Hoover wrote, "Yes & *at once.*"

Tolson ordered Assistant Director Belmont to get on it. Belmont, the
headquarters official who had been assigned to monitor the trial, understood the situation was serious. "This is bad," he wrote in a memo, "because
if any part of 'Communist Target—Youth' is shown to be inaccurate in the
slightest, charges can be made against its accuracy as a whole."

Belmont immediately telephoned the San Francisco FBI office and
spoke with Assistant Special Agent in Charge George Peet. "I told Mr.
Peet that, in view of the conflicting testimony at the Meisenbach trial, the
Bureau will be questioned as to the accuracy of our pamphlet," he wrote
in a memo for the record. "Bearing this in mind, we want from San Francisco a factual explanation. I told him we are going to be faced with this
very real problem."

Or as Peet put it in his own memo on the conversation, "How come
our report is wrong?"

In closing arguments the next day, Giubbini argued that the evidence
showed Meisenbach had attacked Schaumleffel. The police had merely
tried to maintain order. The student's claim that police beat him without
provocation, the prosecutor declared, was "as false as the tears he brought
out from the witness stand." The defense attorney Charles Garry then rose
to deliver the kind of impassioned remarks that had made him famous in
San Francisco legal circles. With rage in his voice, he accused the prosecution's eyewitnesses of perjury and the police of filing false reports against
Meisenbach. The student had an unblemished record, he declared, and
a guilty verdict would not only send him to prison but ruin his life. Then
the lawyer broke down in tears.

The jury took less than three hours to return a verdict of not guilty.
The students in the courtroom cheered and rushed to the defense table to
hug Meisenbach. That night, he and about 150 well-wishers celebrated in
a private room at the Old Spaghetti Factory in North Beach. They drank
the local steam beer and gathered around the scale model of City Hall used
as a trial exhibit, singing "We Shall Not Be Moved."

Hoover ordered his aides to make no comment on the verdict and to cease
distributing his report, "Communist Target—Youth."

He intensified the bureau's internal inquiry into what was beginning to look like a serious breakdown in the FBI's reporting of intelligence on activities he had publicly declared a threat to national security.

As ordered, the special agent in charge of the San Francisco office submitted his explanations for the glaring discrepancy between the Meisenbach verdict and "Project: Revolution," the supposedly comprehensive analysis by his staff that was the basis for "Communist Target—Youth."

Auerbach blamed everyone: the San Francisco Police Department had provided faulty information on Meisenbach; the prosecutor "was not well prepared"; the jury was overly sympathetic to the "handsome youth"; Neubarth was "a weak judge."

Moreover, Ed Montgomery, the *Examiner* reporter who wrote the story suggesting that Meisenbach had ignited "the riot," had mysteriously failed to testify.

Grim officials at FBI headquarters reviewed Auerbach's explanations along with the trial transcript and were compelled to reach a series of painful conclusions. As Assistant Director Belmont wrote:

> The statement that Meisenbach leaped the barricade cannot be proved.
>
> It is clear that we cannot support a statement that the hose was turned on after Meisenbach assaulted Schaumleffel.
>
> Since the jury acquitted Meisenbach, we cannot support a public position that Meisenbach assaulted Schaumleffel with his own club.

William C. Sullivan, the chief inspector in the Domestic Intelligence Division, was particularly displeased. One of Hoover's rising stars, he had ghostwritten "Communist Target—Youth" for the director, relying on Auerbach's "Project: Revolution" memo. The memo had implied that Agent Donald Kuno saw the assault. Only after the verdict did Sullivan learn that Kuno had not. Kuno had gotten the story from another FBI agent named Leo Schon. But Schon had not seen it, either—he had been at City Hall that morning, but when the violence erupted at noon he was out to lunch.

Schon, in turn, claimed he got the information verbally from Inspector Pharris of the police. But as everyone now knew, Pharris had testified he neither saw the assault nor told the FBI a demonstrator had leaped the barricade and clubbed an officer.

Now Auerbach was forced to concede his agents had failed to independently verify the allegations about Meisenbach. Facing an onslaught from headquarters, he countercharged that Sullivan, in writing "Communist Target—Youth," had misrepresented parts of his memo, added other material, and exaggerated the Communist role in the City Hall protest.

In fact, Auerbach insisted, his memo never claimed anyone leaped a barricade. It actually said, "The mob became noisier and one of them *hurtled* the barricade, knocked down a police officer, took his night stick and started beating the police officer over the head." Sullivan had confused "*hurtle*," meaning to strike against, with "*hurdle*."

Irked by this finger-pointing, Tolson wrote in the margins of a memo, "Did the San Fran Div review the pamphlet before it was issued?" Hoover scrawled alongside that, "Ask Auerbach why he didn't raise these points before."

It turned out Sullivan never had sent a draft of "Communist Target—Youth" to the San Francisco field office for review before publication, a lapse contrary to bureau procedure. To make matters worse, Assistant Director Belmont meanwhile acknowledged that he and his staff had failed to keep Hoover updated on the trial. The daily reports Auerbach sent had never reached the Boss because Belmont "had lost sight of it and apparently his boys were scared to send the material up."

Hoover had had enough. Auerbach had sent in a report without noting the source was an unproven police report. Headquarters staff had rewritten it, sensationalizing it in an effort to prove the Boss's point of view, then failed to check basic facts with the San Francisco field office. The director had been left in the dark.

"The whole matter has been grossly mishandled here & at San Francisco," Hoover told his aides. They assured him he could not be successfully sued for libel because his statements, though erroneous, had been made in an official report and were legally privileged. But he scrawled on their memo, "What is completely overlooked irrespective of liability is that all the commies want is <u>publicity</u>. By the sloppy manner this project was handled here and in S.F. we have handed such an opening to them on a platter."

Taking action, Hoover censured three San Francisco agents for errors in their initial report and five headquarters officials for delays in reporting necessary information to him. He next moved to control the damage to the FBI's reputation from Meisenbach's highly publicized acquittal. He ordered Auerbach to reinvestigate Meisenbach and his family in hope of finding derogatory information that could be used to discredit them. About all the agents could find, courtesy of a special file on Meisenbach kept by the Berkeley Police Department's intelligence unit, were reports that he had been present at a noisy party and gotten a parking ticket.

Hoover then turned to Meisenbach's defense lawyers, demanding to know whether they had solicited the job of defending Meisenbach in violation of state Bar Association regulations. They hadn't. He ordered agents to check FBI files for any derogatory information on each of the twenty defense witnesses, but this also proved fruitless. He directed Auerbach to check his files on each juror, but he found nothing negative on them.

Auerbach got clandestine help from the KCBS radio reporter Dick Leonard, a secret source for the bureau whose wife worked on the clerical staff of the San Francisco FBI office. Leonard interviewed two jurors and the judge about the case, asking questions that might elicit admissions of bias in favor of Meisenbach. He also questioned them about their stopping by the student's victory party at the Old Spaghetti Factory. Leonard then interviewed the state attorney general as to whether their visits were improper. They were not, but he gave copies of his interview tapes to the FBI.

All these efforts to discredit the verdict had failed, but Auerbach had another thought. He proposed that the bureau prepare a blurb like the ones used in "national advertising campaigns," but instead of selling soap it would praise "the good majority" of students on campus and ridicule liberal students as "Baby Beatniks," "Play Pen Revolutionaries" and "Leninists [sic] Lotharios." The item could be distributed through the FBI's "special contacts" in the National Inter-fraternity Council, the American Association of University Women, and the Hearst Corporation.

Hoover liked the idea of using the media to counter the verdict. Over the years he had formally established a secret operation, code-named the Mass Media Program. Senior bureau officials and special agents in charge cultivated special relationships with more than three hundred cooperative members of the news media, leaking them information from confidential FBI files to produce stories advancing bureau interests and in some cases even drafting the articles and editorials these journalists published under their own names. In other cases, FBI officials called on them to censor stories critical of the bureau. The journalists got "scoops" and the FBI officials clandestinely influenced public opinion and undermined their political enemies. The program had no law-enforcement purpose, and all participated with the understanding that they could never reveal the FBI's role.

DeLoach ran the program, and he'd been applying it to the City Hall problem. When he heard that United Press International was preparing a story about "the aftermath of the San Francisco youth riots," he arranged for an executive at the news service to ensure it did not embarrass the bureau.

Auerbach, meanwhile, again met with his contacts at the *San Francisco Examiner*. The publisher, Charles Mayer, and the managing editor, Lee Ettelson, readily agreed to vet Dick Nolan's columns and excise any criticism of the bureau. They also promised to kill the reporter Will Stevens's pending story about whether the FBI would retract the now discredited charges in Hoover's report.

Then Auerbach reached out to his best media contact.

Tough-talking and streetwise, Edward Samuel Montgomery operated in the nether regions inhabited by cops, criminals, private detectives, and death row convicts. A large man with dark, swept-back hair, horn-rimmed eyeglasses, and prominent front teeth, he had famously poor hearing and wore a bulky hearing aid connected to a long wire. According to local lore, he had on certain occasions lowered the device through heating ducts to eavesdrop on private conversations. He usually sported a suit and fedora, like his friends in the FBI.

In 1951 Montgomery won the Pulitzer Prize for exposing corruption involving underworld figures and officials of the Bureau of Internal Revenue, as the IRS was then named. The story began with a tip about some drunken boasting in a San Jose bar. Montgomery spent several evenings in the saloon and, according to an account in the *Examiner*, his hearing aid picked up the high-pitched voice of a woman who claimed her contacts could "fix" income tax problems. His subsequent investigation produced six front-page stories revealing that revenue officials had set up a phony Nevada mining corporation, the Mountain City Consolidated Copper Company. Criminals could avoid tax trouble by buying worthless stock in the firm as a payoff. The articles led to hearings before the California Crime Commission and U.S. Senator Estes Kefauver's special committee on crime. Ultimately, several people were convicted.

Montgomery's biggest story, however, came a few years later, during the Stephanie Bryan kidnap case. On April 28, 1955, the fourteen-year-old daughter of Charles S. Bryan, Jr., a Berkeley radiologist, disappeared while walking home from classes at Willard Junior High School in Berkeley. Detectives and FBI agents searched the grounds around the Trinity County cabin of their suspect, Burton Abbott, but found nothing and the investigation stalled. A few days later, Montgomery and the *Examiner* photographer

Bob Bryant arrived, hired a local rancher and his bloodhounds, and within hours found her decomposed body buried in a shallow grave on a manzanita-covered ridge. Montgomery phoned in the story and the *Examiner* got the scoop. Abbott was convicted and executed. The newspaper quoted law-enforcement officials in praise of Montgomery's sleuthing, and Hoover himself issued a statement. "The ingenuity and enterprise of Reporter Ed Montgomery," he said, was an "illustration of the splendid contribution which representatives of the press can make to the cause of law and order."

In 1958, Montgomery hit the big screen. His articles contending Barbara Graham was framed for the murder of a crippled Burbank widow were made into a feature film called *I Want to Live!* starring Susan Hayward, who won an Academy Award for her performance. In July 1960, he scored another coup when he exposed a journalistic hoax perpetrated by the competing *San Francisco Chronicle*. The *Chronicle* was running a widely syndicated series titled "Last Man on Earth," in which its fish-and-game reporter, Bud Boyd, and his family claimed to be living as though they were the sole survivors of a holocaust, subsisting in the California wilderness on roots, leaves, and bark. Montgomery revealed they were living in a motel, where Boyd concocted his saga poolside.

"Ed Montgomery is a one-man crusade against crime and injustice," Hearst said in one of its advertisements. "Examiner readers respect Ed Montgomery's integrity and enthusiasm. Examiner readers know they can depend on Ed Montgomery to give them the facts."

There were plenty of facts about Montgomery, and the murky worlds in which he moved, in the files of the FBI's San Francisco office. One memo said his name had been found in the personal address book of the mobster Mickey Cohen; another said that in 1959 he had informed the FBI about CIA inquiries regarding a delegation of Russians visiting the United States; another concerned the FBI's investigation into ultimately unsubstantiated allegations that he had engaged in illegal telephone tapping. Confidentially, Montgomery had been very helpful to bureau officials over the years, developing such a close relationship that he could wander around the San Francisco FBI office, chatting with agents at their desks. Above all, FBI officials knew, Montgomery was discreet.

A few weeks after Meisenbach's acquittal, Auerbach asked Montgomery why he hadn't testified at the trial. The newsman confided that his front-page story about Meisenbach was not true. According to Auerbach's subsequent report, Montgomery revealed that though he saw a man struggling with police behind the barricade at the hearing room door, he did not see him leap the barricade. Moreover, he said he had "assumed" that this man was Meisenbach, but now admitted "it couldn't possibly" have been him, because of where the altercation occurred. No, he could not identify the man he saw. Whoever that was, though, the police "liberally used their clubs on him." When Giubbini interviewed him prior to the trial and discovered all of this, he decided it was best not to call him as a witness.

But now Montgomery offered to help. He told Auerbach he was willing to give the FBI a sworn statement that would support Hoover's claim in "Communist Target—Youth" that demonstrator violence led police to hose the students.

Two days later, Montgomery submitted a personal letter to Hoover on *Examiner* stationery. "Dear Mr. Hoover," it began. "I have observed with great concern the controversy this month over the question of exactly what started the City Hall riots . . ." He continued, "Unlike the participants, I was there for the sole purpose of observing and reporting the facts in an unbiased and objective manner . . . To sum it all up, there was a fracas on the Hearing Room side of the barricade involving a young man whose identity I do not know, triggering the mob violence immediately preceding the police use of the hoses. There is no question as to this sequence of events." In a cover note, Montgomery invited Hoover to use this as he wished.

Hoover considered the reporter's statement "most helpful." He had DeLoach draft a newspaper "editorial" that excerpted Montgomery's letter supporting "Communist Target—Youth." It would be passed along to Dave Sentner of Hearst's D.C. bureau. Auerbach thought some phrases too violent and others too similar to Hoover's report, but his literary concerns were overruled; DeLoach insisted the column "was written in Dave Sentner's short, punchy style." Sentner agreed to run it, just as though he had written it.

In the wake of Meisenbach's acquittal, even more citizens wrote Hoover seeking the truth about events at San Francisco City Hall. In a typical exchange, a Pomona, California, couple asked him what they should say to friends who pointed out that Meisenbach had been acquitted. "We believe that you, sir, are one of the most trustworthy men in this nation," they added. "Our praise for your fight against Communism is unlimited. God bless you and please keep fighting." In his reply on August 24, 1961, Hoover did not answer them. Instead, he thanked them for their sentiments and quoted Montgomery's letter. "These facts speak for themselves," he said. "Despite confusing and contradictory statements which have been made about the affair, the truth is that a riot occurred and lawful authority was flouted."

"Communist Target—Youth" contributed to a bitter national controversy and widened social schisms that would surface later as the "generation gap" and the "culture wars." Yet Hoover never publicly acknowledged that his report greatly exaggerated the Communist role in a legitimate protest, contained serious errors, and wrongly accused an innocent man.

The FBI's handling of the City Hall episode was a classic intelligence failure: faulty reporting from the field about a perceived national security threat; a breakdown in the chain of command while conveying facts contrary to the official position; a study written to satisfy political biases; and a cover-up.

To citizens who continued to request copies, Hoover said only, "I am unable to furnish the publication you requested because our supply has been depleted."

But by then his report had come to the attention of an actor named Ronald Reagan.

9

An Eye-opener

One morning at his home in Hollywood, Ronald Reagan picked up the phone and had the operator place a call to FBI headquarters in Washington, D.C. When the bureau's switchboard came on the line, he asked to speak with Hoover. Told the director was out, he was instead connected to Assistant Director Cartha DeLoach. Reagan introduced himself as the host of *General Electric Theater*, the popular Sunday-night television show, and said he wanted to produce a special program based on Hoover's report, "Communist Target—Youth."

Reagan told DeLoach that the report was vitally important and "should be brought to the attention of as many of the public [*sic*] as possible." Reagan was disturbed by those "youth riots" at San Francisco City Hall. He thought the House Un-American Activities Committee had been unfairly attacked, its members slandered as "witch hunters." He would present a drama "showing how college youths could be duped by the Communist Party." It would promote Hoover's report, he said, and the director could appear at the end to warn viewers about this danger to young people.

Reagan's August 26, 1960, phone call was part of a secret and long-running relationship between the actor and the FBI. Fourteen years earlier, FBI agents had enlisted him in the bureau's battle against communism. What they told him about radicals in the movie industry, Reagan later wrote, was a revelation. He became an informer, one far more active than has been previously known. As he made fighting communism his cause, he and Hoover became lifelong allies.

Reagan's relationship with the FBI fit neatly with his evolving view of the world as an increasingly dangerous place, his penchant for dramatic conflict between good and evil, and his political and professional ambitions. His interaction with bureau agents profoundly influenced him at a key point in his life, catalyzing his transformation from liberal movie star to staunch conservative, and directly contributed to his decision to run for president of the Screen Actors Guild, which set him on the path to public office.

Ronald Wilson Reagan climbed into his Nash convertible, crossed the burning desert, and drove west to Hollywood. The Depression was deepening again, but he was twenty-six years old and had a $200-a-week contract at Warner Brothers and dreams of becoming the next matinee idol.

Reagan had come a long way from Tampico, Illinois, and the second-floor apartment above a bakery on Main Street where he was born on February 6, 1911, the same year as Clark Kerr. He was the younger of two sons born to John and Nelle Reagan. John Reagan, who went by Jack, was the child of Irish Catholic immigrants. As Reagan later recalled in *Where's the Rest of Me?*, his first autobiography, his father was a great raconteur and a "sentimental Democrat" who had no tolerance for bigotry. John Reagan believed everyone should stand on their own two feet, but he suffered from alcoholism and periodic unemployment. He could be stern: a fight in the schoolyard brought a kick in the backside; tinkering with a gas lamp got young Reagan "clobbered"; fooling with a shotgun resulted in a "licking." Nelle Reagan's ancestors came from England and Scotland. She was a housewife, a community volunteer, and "a practical do-gooder." She was also a devout member of the Christian Church (Disciples of Christ), and Reagan attended that Protestant church while growing up.

The Reagan family had little money and lived in a succession of rented homes in small towns in Illinois, and briefly in Chicago. Neither parent had graduated beyond elementary school, but every night his mother read to him, following each word with a finger as he watched. When he was five years old, one of the first stories he read aloud to her from newspapers was about the detonation by German saboteurs of a munitions depot at Black Tom, New Jersey, a terrible explosion that killed at least thirteen people, shattered hundreds of plate-glass windows in Manhattan, and damaged the Statue of Liberty. Another story was about the bombing of a Preparedness Day parade in San Francisco, in which the suspect was the radical labor leader Tom Mooney. As Reagan recalled, his youthful awareness of such events gave him "an uneasy feeling of a world outside my own."

When Reagan was nine, his family settled in Dixon, Illinois, a town of almost ten thousand people, about a hundred miles west of Chicago. He would always consider Dixon home—the place where he learned "standards and values that would guide me the rest of my life," that "America was a place that offered unlimited opportunity to those who did work hard." Reagan played on the riverbanks, watched cowboy movies at the town theater, and at a tender age assumed the role of rescuer. "I was eleven years old the first time I came home to find my father flat on his back on the front porch and no one there to lend a hand but me," he wrote.

Reagan enrolled in Dixon High School in September 1924. He joined the football, basketball, and track teams and became student body president. After portraying the villain in a school play, he concluded that "heroes are more fun." Even then he was pulled between his two main interests, sports and acting. "The fact was," he wrote, "that I just liked showing off." At fifteen he became a lifeguard at Lowell Park, on the Rock River, earning fifteen dollars a day. He held the job for seven summers and would claim he rescued seventy-seven people, though not everyone he hauled ashore appreciated it. "I got to recognize that people hate to be saved," he would write.

Reagan was neither serious about his studies nor about the idea that everyone should get a higher education. "At that time, college was far from the accepted thing," he wrote. "The notion had not yet appeared that education was a fad in which everyone should join; a Bachelor of Arts seemed very far away and a Doctor of Philosophy was revered as something almost unattainable." Graduating in June 1928, he ranked in the middle third of his class of seventy students. His date for the senior banquet was Margaret Cleaver, his minister's daughter.

Years later, an FBI agent investigating Reagan visited Dixon. A high school official told him that Reagan's father was "known to 'do a little drinking'" but his mother was well-respected. The official saw no reason to question Reagan's loyalty, saying "Reagan had good habits, good morals and a good reputation."

In the fall of 1928, Reagan enrolled at Eureka College, a small liberal arts college near Normal, Illinois, that was affiliated with the Disciples of Christ. It had red brick buildings and green lawns framed by elm trees, and about 250 students, mostly from rural areas. One of Reagan's football heroes had gone there, and Margaret Cleaver was going to go. Though he had saved up money for school, he still couldn't afford the $180 annual tuition. Only because he received financial aid from the college and got a job washing dishes could he attend.

At many campuses around the country, "flaming youth" were rebelling against the strictures of the war years, donning raccoon coats, bobbing their hair, binging on Prohibition alcohol. But as Reagan's biographer

Anne Edwards has noted, students at Eureka were especially constrained; the school's dress code, for example, prohibited skirts baring the calf. Still, that fall Reagan got his first taste of campus rebellion.

Eureka was facing a fiscal crisis, and the college president proposed a drastic cutback in faculty positions, which meant many juniors and seniors would be unable to take courses necessary for graduation. As Reagan recalled, the president "had persuaded the board of trustees to go along without any thought of consulting students or faculty," who "responded with a roar of fury." Reagan represented the freshman class on the strike committee. He would later say he was "far from a ringleader," but the ferment was centered in his frat house and he played a key role.

The students discovered that Eureka's board of trustees planned to approve the financial cuts at a meeting the night before the Thanksgiving recess. "Don't ask me about our spy system, but we had informers," Reagan wrote. So instead of heading home for the holiday, they waited for the meeting to adjourn and marched across campus to question the trustees. Reagan likened the ensuing protest to the American Revolution. "The old college bell started tolling—it was as prearranged as Paul Revere's ride," he wrote. "From dormitories and fraternity houses the students came, almost all of the faculty from their homes . . ."

Reagan's moment arrived as the protesters met at the school chapel. Student leaders asked him to announce their proposal for a campus-wide strike until all demands were met. Standing before the crowd, Reagan reviewed "the history of our patient negotiations with due emphasis on the devious manner in which the trustees had sought to take advantage of us." He realized his powers as a public speaker. "I discovered that night that an audience has a feel to it and, in the parlance of the theatre, the audience and I were together. When I came to actually presenting the motion there was no need for parliamentary procedure: they came to their feet with a roar—even the faculty members present voted by acclamation. It was heady wine."

In their revolt the students received crucial help from the faculty. "Few students attended any classes at all. All the professors attended them, marked all the absentees present, then went home. The college ground to a standstill." There were no fire hoses, no arrests, no sit-ins. The strikers went ice-skating and sledding, and every afternoon the strike committee sponsored a dance that ended in time for basketball practice. The committee enforced independent study hours and the students made up their own assignments. The youth rebellion in the heartland made national news, and after just one week the president resigned and the trustees dropped their plan for teaching cuts. "The publicity helped," Reagan wrote, "but it was our policy of polite resistance that brought victory."

The campus uprising was a powerful experience for Reagan. He recalled that the students "became the most tightly knit" and their spirit bloomed. He was proud of his role in the protest, and later wrote that it provided "an education in human nature and the rights of man to universal education that nothing could erase from our psyches."

Nonetheless, he almost dropped out the next term, despondent over his failure to become a football star and his financial straits. But school officials agreed to defer half his tuition and offered him another job washing dishes in the girls' dormitory, and Reagan reenrolled. At his fraternity, Tau Kappa Epsilon, he garnered a top-floor room with a view.

Although he remained an indifferent student, he succeeded in his main goal of starting on the football team as an offensive guard. He joined the swim team and eventually coached it. He served three years as basketball cheerleader, two years as yearbook features editor, two years on the student senate, and in his senior year was elected student body president. He joined the drama club, too, and would later joke that he majored in extracurricular activities.

Reagan and Cleaver broke up and he dated other girls, taking them to a nearby cemetery where students had favorite grave sites "usually with a large enough tombstone to provide a backrest for two and a sizable shadow." Nor were the pleasures of bootleg booze unknown to him. Still, Reagan worked hard enough to send money home to help his family buy groceries after his father was laid off. That June of 1932, he graduated with a bachelor's degree, a major in economics and sociology, and a grade point average of 1.37, or C plus.

During the FBI background investigation years later, an agent questioned people about Reagan's college days. A school clerk said his record showed no disciplinary action, the Eureka police chief had no information on him, and a former fraternity brother assured the agent that though Reagan had joined in the strike, "there was no subversive activity involved whatsoever."

Figuring Broadway and Hollywood were as accessible "as outer space," Reagan combined his interests in performing and sports and instead pursued a career in the emerging profession of radio broadcasting. That summer, he got a job with Palmer Broadcasting covering sports and used it to polish his public speaking. In a well-known anecdote, the telegraph machine went dead one day in the ninth inning of a tied game between Chicago and St. Louis. Reagan didn't want to tell the audience the station had lost contact with its reporter at the field, so he faked it. Realizing that the only action he could describe without affecting the score were foul balls, he reported one after another. "I lost count," he said. "I began to be frightened that maybe I was establishing a new world record." In reality, the batter had popped out.

By now there was more trouble at home. Jack Reagan, who campaigned for FDR in 1932, had landed a federally funded job distributing food to Dixon's needy, but his health failed and he could not work. Reagan was earning about a hundred dollars a week, more than twice what his father had ever made, and sent his parents a check every month. He also helped his brother, Neil, who had followed him to Eureka, with his college costs, and would later line up a job for him at Palmer Broadcasting.

Like Clark Kerr, Reagan loved horses, but he used them not to plow but for pleasure. In his leisure time Reagan rode courtesy of the army's nearby 14th Cavalry Regiment. He had applied for a commission as a reserve officer just to secure riding privileges, he later wrote, and exploited the army's inefficiency by stringing out the application process so he could avoid a required eye examination that he knew he'd fail and which would end his riding. Eventually forced to take the exam, he cheated on it.

Sometimes Reagan relaxed by joining coworkers for drinks, without the trouble alcohol caused his father. "Like almost every other young man," he wrote, "I had learned to drink—principally because it was against the law—and it was done out of a bottle that tasted like gasoline on the fraternity back porch or in a parked car. Now I was to discover the pleasure of more civilized drinking, in which just getting high was not the goal."

He still wanted to be a movie star, and a friend set him up with an agent in Hollywood. Inflating his résumé with what he called "little white lies," Reagan doubled his salary and described his college drama club as a professional stock company. He took a screen test at Warner Brothers and was soon easing his Nash into the studio parking lot.

Reagan would later quip that he became the Errol Flynn of the Bs, the low-budget second features on double bills. Through 1943 he would appear in thirty-one films, mostly light romantic or action movies in which he played his preferred role of a traditional hero—cavalryman, football star, government agent. While filming *Brother Rat*, a 1938 comedy set at a military academy, Reagan met the actress Jane Wyman. They were married in 1940, the same year he played his signature role of George Gipp in *Knute Rockne, All American*. Their daughter, Maureen Elizabeth, would be born in 1941, and they would adopt a son, Michael, who was born in 1945. Featured together in several films, Reagan and Wyman became an item in the Hollywood press; one newspaper dubbed them "top candidates for the title of happiest young Hollywood marrieds."

But America had been edging toward war, and in the midst of this Reagan was notified that he would be called for duty. According to the historian Stephen Vaughn, however, the actor received special treatment with help from a former FBI agent. In late 1941, Reagan was finishing his biggest film yet, a $1 million Warner Brothers production titled *Kings Row*, and was negotiating a studio contract that would nearly triple his salary. When he learned soon afterward that he would have to report for service, Warner Brothers requested a deferment on the ground that his absence would cause the studio a significant financial loss. The request was not approved, and Jack Warner deployed William Guthrie, the studio's liaison to the military. Guthrie had been with the FBI only two years when he was dismissed in 1920 "because of conduct unbecoming an Agent." An internal bureau inquiry concluded he was "entirely dishonest; was using his official position to further his own ends; [and] was not above accepting gratuities or graft." It further noted that "he depended very much on influential friends submitting communications in his behalf."

Guthrie suggested the studio send a retired military officer who was close to General Peak, commander of the U.S. Army base at the Presidio in San Francisco, to see Peak about a deferment. The studio did, and Reagan's call to duty was deferred at least twice, to April 19, 1942, four months after the attack on Pearl Harbor. Finally, Reagan was ordered to report to the cavalry reserve at Fort Mason in the Presidio, where he was eligible for limited stateside service because of his poor eyesight.

Reagan was there just five weeks. Warner and Guthrie had meanwhile convinced the Army Air Corps (the predecessor of the U.S. Air Force) to create a special movie detail. The First Motion Picture Unit was established under Warner's direction at the old Hal Roach movie studios in Culver City, twenty minutes from Reagan's home. Guthrie helped the army select some of the unit's 1,300 men and, according to Reagan's military records, arranged for his expedited transfer to it. Reagan spent the rest of the war at "Fort Roach," narrating or appearing in films that promoted the Air Corps, recruited new enlistees, or trained men for battle. He also helped produce newsreels for commercial theaters, and was promoted to captain by the end of the war. Guthrie then arranged for his prompt discharge, helping him return to civilian life and a $3,500-per-week salary (about $44,268 per week in 2012 dollars).

Not everyone in Hollywood was happy about Reagan's tour of duty. According to previously undisclosed FBI records, a movie industry source told bureau agents that Guthrie had obtained commissions and appointments to the First Motion Picture Unit "on a large scale for his friends and those of Jack Warner." Guthrie had brazenly displayed dozens of blank U.S. Army commissions and asked the source if he wanted one. Separately, a producer at Warner Brothers told FBI agents that, in his opinion, "Ronald Reagan's commission and appointment could stand investigation." The FBI opened a file on Guthrie titled "Fraud Against the Government— Bribery," but it is unclear from available records whether the bureau pursued the matter.

World War II had jolted Reagan. Before the war, he had focused on career and family. He had inherited his father's allegiance to the Democratic Party and had followed FDR "blindly," as he put it. He had not yet developed his own political philosophy. But during and after the war, he began to think more about world events. Although he never saw action, at Fort Roach he saw raw footage of Nazi death camps and of men in combat, like the film of a pilot crashing and burning to death as his comrades tried to pull him from the cockpit. Reagan also worked on top-secret training films that realistically simulated American flights over bombing targets in Japan.

Reagan had expected the Allies' victory to fix the world. He was sure all "the blood and death and confusion of World War II would result in a regeneration of mankind." Events disappointed him, however, and he determined to help. In the months after his discharge in fall 1945, he became involved in liberal causes, lending his name to fund-raising efforts and giving talks. It seemed like the right thing to do in the lingering spirit of the Popular Front, which had united Communists and liberals during the war. As he recalled, "my first evangelism came in the form of being hellbent on saving the world from neo-Fascism." But though he was taking action, Reagan still was operating on the basis of political wisdom received from his father, the FDR Democrat.

Then the Cold War set in and the national mood shifted as if from Technicolor to black and white. J. Edgar Hoover feared a Kremlin-controlled conspiracy to infiltrate Hollywood and use the world's largest producer of motion pictures to slyly manipulate public opinion against America. He had opened an investigation even before the end of the war, at about the same time he initiated the investigation of Soviet espionage in Berkeley. Code-named COMPIC—short for Communist Infiltration of the Motion-Picture Industry—the inquiry had two main goals: to determine the extent of Communist penetration of film industry unions, and to identify Communist activities by screenwriters, actors, directors, executives, and, as one FBI report put it, "the so-called intellectuals in general."

As Hoover intensified the COMPIC case, Reagan's name began showing up in reports from the bureau's Los Angeles field office alleging he had suspicious associations. An April 1946 report described him as a sponsor of the Los Angeles Committee for a Democratic Far Eastern Policy, "the latest Communist front pressure group set up for the purpose of supporting the foreign policy of Soviet Russia as it is being applied in the Orient." The report claimed the committee's sponsors and directors all had "records of Communist activity and sympathies." Besides Reagan, they included two Democratic congressmen, the muckraking author Carey McWilliams, and the actors Gregory Peck and Edward G. Robinson. Reagan had lent his name to a dinner for the committee at the Roosevelt Hotel in New York City—along with Paul Robeson, the singer and actor who criticized American racism and openly admired the Soviet Union.

A May 1946 report said Reagan recently had been elected to the executive council of the Hollywood Independent Citizens Committee of the Arts, Sciences and Professions (HICCASP). The FBI's political interest in the organization was clear. "It is a powerful political pressure group and using the motion picture industry and its prestige as a base will be the dominating factor in the coming primary elections in the State of California," the report said. "Every endorsement for public office made by this organization coincides exactly with that made by the Communist Party of the state." The group's executive council included many movie stars and, according to the report, no fewer than twenty-four Communists.

A June 1946 report said Reagan was a member of the American Veterans Committee in Los Angeles. He had served as a toastmaster at the organization's statewide convention that April, when it adopted resolutions calling for the end of racially restrictive covenants; the worldwide abolition of conscription; and United Nations control of atomic energy. This platform, the FBI reported, was "in complete conformity to that of the CP line." Some AVC members, moreover, allegedly wanted a "Communist form of government in this country."

As the COMPIC investigation continued, Hoover pressed his Los Angeles agents to develop more informers in Hollywood. Checking their files, the agents saw reports showing Reagan was well-placed in these suspect organizations. Checking further, they also saw he'd had some friendly contacts with the FBI.

One of Reagan's college fraternity brothers had become an FBI agent. On September 17, 1941, the agent, Charles Browning, Jr., told FBI headquarters that through the frat he was "intimately acquainted" with several "influential individuals" who "might be of some assistance to the Bureau," including Reagan at Warner Brothers. Hoover directed Browning to give Reagan's contact information to the head of the Los Angeles field office for future reference.

Agents called on Reagan in 1943 while investigating a suspected Nazi sympathizer, one Baron Paul Emile de Loqueyssie, also known as Paul Avalon, a French bit actor who had graced the society pages. Reagan told the agents they had met at a Beverly Hills cocktail party hosted by Arthur Lyons, the New York talent agent who represented Jack Benny, Eugene O'Neill, and Cole Porter. Reagan said "considerable drinking had been done by all persons involved," according to the agents' report, and Loqueyssie made anti-Semitic remarks that so incensed Reagan that they almost came to blows. The agents also interviewed Reagan about "other matters" not specified in their report.

In 1945, Reagan passed along some political gossip of special interest to Hoover. After Reagan's Army Air Corps basketball team played the FBI team at the Elks Club, Reagan drove home with Agent H. Rex Ellis. Reagan said he'd heard that Governor Thomas Dewey of New York, while campaigning for president several months earlier, had vowed that if elected "there would not be enough jails in the country to hold the people he was going to put into them, and that John Edgar Hoover of the FBI was going to be one of the first." Richard B. Hood, the special agent in charge of the Los Angeles office, promptly sent Hoover a report marked "Personal and Confidential" containing this hearsay and describing Reagan favorably. "Reagan is, of course, a captain in the U.S. Army," Hood wrote, and had said "he would certainly be inclined to side with Hoover."

In addition to these contacts, Reagan's brother was by now working with the FBI. Neil "Moon" Reagan had moved to Los Angeles and taken a job at the McCann Erickson advertising agency. According to a previously undisclosed FBI report, he was also serving as an informer in the bureau's investigation of alleged Communist infiltration of the radio and television industry. He was listed as "Confidential Informant T-36." Agents described him as "reliable."

"Now, in those days, I was doing little things for the FBI," he recalled during an oral history interview years later. "You know, 'Neil, we'd like you to go out and lay in the bushes and take down the car numbers off of the cars that are going to be at this little meeting in Bel-Air. Put it in a brown envelope, no return address. And always remember, if you get caught in the bushes, you can just forget about saying, well, you're doing this for the FBI, because we'll just look him right in the eye and say, 'We never saw the guy in our lives. Forget it.'"

Knowing all this, FBI officials concluded Ronald Reagan was a good prospect as an informer.

Late one night in 1946, FBI agents knocked on the front door of the eight-room house Reagan and Wyman had built at 9137 Cordell Drive, a twisting road overlooking Sunset Boulevard in Hollywood. The unexpected visitors presented official identification, and the suntanned actor, then thirty-five, invited them in. "We have some information which might be useful to you," one agent said as Reagan served coffee. "We thought you might have some information helpful to us."

"Instinctively, my old liberal reaction popped up before I could think," Reagan recalled in *Where's the Rest of Me?*, published in 1965, "and almost by rote I found myself saying, 'Now look, I don't go in for Red-baiting.' 'We don't either,' said the second one. 'It isn't a question of that. It's a question of national security. You served with the Air Corps. You know what spies and saboteurs are.' 'We thought someone the Communists hated as much as they hate you might be willing to help us,' added the third."

Reagan took the bait. "That got me," he wrote. "It's always a jolt to discover others have been talking you over. 'What do you mean?' I asked. 'Well,' he said, 'they held a meeting last night.' He described the house, gave the address, told me who was there, and what they said. I broke in. 'What did they say about me?' I demanded. 'The exact quotation,' he replied, 'was: "What are we going to do about that sonofabitching bastard Reagan?" Will that do for openers?'"

"We got to talking. I must confess that they opened my eyes to a good many things. I came to admire these men: they never accused anyone of being a Communist unless they had every last bit of evidence which would stand up against the most vicious court assault. They were extremely careful never to smear anyone or guess even on good but less than complete evidence. They were very thorough, very patient, and very accurate. We exchanged information for a few hours."

In his second autobiography, *An American Life*, published in 1990, Reagan elaborated on the agents' visit: "They confided in me that FBI investigations had shown the Party was attempting not only to gain control of the Hollywood work force but striving to influence the content of movies through the work of several prominent film writers and actors who were party members or party sympathizers. They asked if they could meet with me periodically to discuss some of the things that were going on in Hollywood. I said of course they could."

Their mission accomplished, the agents stood and bid Reagan good night. They had made what would turn out to be one of the FBI's best contacts ever.

Not long after his visit that evening from the FBI agents, Reagan attended a meeting of the board of directors of HICCASP, the star-studded political action group under bureau investigation. Reagan had recently joined the board, but what the FBI agents told him had made him wary.

A heated debate quickly erupted when James Roosevelt, FDR's son, took the floor and declared that organizations like HICCASP must be "vigilant against being used by Communist sympathizers." This was a sensitive issue. What was a "sympathizer"? And what difference did it make who supported the cause if the cause was legitimate? Other board members harshly criticized Roosevelt's proposal. Reagan was disturbed by this and mentioned it to Dore Schary, the head of MGM, who was sitting beside him. As the meeting broke up, Schary invited Reagan to stop by the home of the actress Olivia de Havilland, a board member who had starred in *Gone With the Wind* (1939).

Reagan raced over to de Havilland's apartment, to find a gathering of concerned HICCASP board members. "I was amazed when she and others in the room said they suspected Communists were trying to take over the organization," Reagan wrote in *An American Life*. "As we talked over the situation, I turned to her and whispered: 'You know, Olivia, I always thought *you* might be one of "them."' She laughed and said, 'That's funny. I thought *you* were one of them.'"

Reagan had planned only to listen during this meeting, given that he was a new board member. "But knowing a little about Communist tactics from my dealings with the FBI, I suggested that we propose a resolution to the executive committee with language that we knew a Communist couldn't accept and have Olivia submit it in the next meeting the following week and see what happened," he wrote. Reagan drafted the motion, which declared, "We reaffirm belief in free enterprise and the democratic system and repudiate Communism as desirable for the United States."

The group agreed to Reagan's plan and, as he recalled, it "proved strong enough to blow the whole organization sky-high."

On July 5, 1946, the feuding members of the full HICCASP board met at James Roosevelt's home at 623 North Bedford Drive, in Beverly Hills, this time to discuss Reagan's resolution. FBI agents hidden outside took down the license numbers of cars parked nearby, including one registered to Jane Wyman.

Inside, another argument broke out. Dalton Trumbo, the writer, and Artie Shaw, the composer, spoke against Reagan's motion. So did John Howard Lawson. The screenwriter had drawn the ire of the Tenney committee when he participated in the 1943 Writers' Congress at UCLA that Robert Gordon Sproul had refused to cancel. FBI agents had long suspected Lawson was a Communist, a suspicion they confirmed when they illegally broke into a Communist Party office in Los Angeles and photographed membership records. Waving his finger under Reagan's nose, Lawson shouted, "This organization will never adopt a statement which endorses free enterprise and repudiates communism."

Reagan's deliberately divisive measure was voted down. "It was all the proof we needed," he wrote. "HICCASP had become a Communist front organization, hiding behind a few well-intentioned Hollywood celebrities to give it credibility." Reagan, de Havilland, and their fellow plotters promptly resigned. The organization collapsed soon after.

Before quitting, though, Reagan absconded with some of HICCASP's internal records. He confided this to his brother and fellow informer during a late-night rendezvous at a Hollywood hamburger stand. As Neil Reagan recalled in his oral history interview, "One evening he calls me— evening, hell, it was about midnight—he had stopped up at the Nutburger stand (there was a Nutburger stand at the corner of Sunset and Doheny at the time, across from the drugstore). He says, 'I'm having a cup of coffee, come on up.' I said, 'Do you know what time it is?' 'Yeah.' 'Well, I've been in bed for three hours. Have your coffee and go on home and go to bed.' 'No, I want you to come up.' And I said all right; so I put a pair of trousers on and a shirt and drove up the hill. Here he is, parked. I got in, and—he's a member of the board—he says, 'You wouldn't believe it. It just came to me tonight. We have a rule that if a board member misses two meetings without being excused, you're automatically off the board.'

" 'There's a gal out at the such-and-such studio,' and he says, 'I've been a little suspicious of her. All of a sudden, we had one of these cases come up tonight, that so-and-so had missed two board meetings, and so they were off, and now we've got to find somebody else. It suddenly dawned on me that over the last several months, every time one of these cases came up, she had just the individual that would be excellent as a replacement.

"'I managed to filch the minute books before I left. I can show you the page where her board members became a majority of the board, with her replacements.'"

The 1946 minutes subsequently made their way into the FBI's possession, according to bureau records.

Reagan had successfully used the insights imparted by FBI agents to disrupt HICCASP. He soon employed similar tactics against the Hollywood chapter of the American Veterans Committee, of which he also was a board member. As he testified in a subsequent court case, the national organization of the American Veterans Committee revoked the charter of both its Hollywood and California state chapters, dismissed their officers, and placed them in trusteeship "because there had been some Communist infiltration." A lawyer asked, "Did you have any part in bringing about the revocation of that charter?" Reagan replied, "Very similar to the same activities in HICCASP." The lawyer asked, "Did you at that time, Mr. Reagan, have any special access to investigative facilities of the government, either national or state, with respect to Communist activity?" Reagan replied, "Well, unofficially someone dropped in to my living room a few times and made information available to me, but told me at the time that if I ever got in trouble from using it they would deny that they had done so."

By the fall of 1946, Reagan found himself in the midst of another battle against what he had come to see as the international Communist conspiracy in Hollywood. At this point he was third vice president on the board of directors of the Screen Actors Guild, the powerful union representing actors. He and other SAG directors conducted an inquiry so they could recommend whether guild members should support the Conference of Studio Unions. The CSU was representing movie set builders in a strike for better wages and working conditions. Although the National Labor Relations Board had recognized the CSU, the SAG directors concluded the CSU was not pursuing legitimate labor issues and was merely involved in a "jurisdictional" dispute with another union over which of them would represent the set builders. The other union, the International Alliance of Theatrical and Stage Employees, or IATSE, was headed by Roy Brewer, one of Hollywood's most militant anti-Communists.

When the Screen Actors Guild met at Hollywood Legion Stadium, the old boxing venue, Reagan presented the board's recommendation against supporting the CSU strike. A bruising debate followed in which Katharine

Hepburn and Edward G. Robinson urged support of the strike. The actor Alexander Knox stood and delivered a stinging parody of all Reagan had said. "No fighter ever bled in that ring as I did," Reagan recalled. "Alex was getting laughs, and that meant they were laughing at me." But eventually the laughter stopped and Knox was booed off the platform. In the end, the SAG voted overwhelmingly not to join the strike.

The strike wore on for months, involved violence by both employees and management, and led to what was then the largest mass arrest in California history, of some seven hundred people for violating a court order limiting the number of pickets outside film studio gates. Reagan would later say he received threats of physical harm because he opposed the CSU, and that he began to carry a gun. He saw sinister forces behind the strike. "I will say of the Communists—they were the cause of the labor strife, they used minor jurisdictional disputes as excuses for their scheme. Their aim was to gain economic control of the motion picture industry in order to finance their activities and subvert the screen for their propaganda," he wrote. "It would have been a magnificent coup for our enemies."

Reagan's views had shifted starkly since that night the FBI agents first dropped by his apartment. Bureau officials had told him there was a vast Communist plot at work behind the scenes in Hollywood. Those revelations had led him to fight Communists in HICCASP, the American Veterans Committee, and the CSU. In the process, he became convinced that some members of his own union—among them those who had opposed his position on that strike—were also subversive.

When Robert Montgomery stepped down as president of the Screen Actors Guild on March 10, 1947, the guild's board of directors elected Reagan to finish out his term. Reagan was a man with a mission.

"More than anything else," he wrote, "it was the Communists' attempted takeover of Hollywood and its worldwide weekly audience of more than five hundred million people that led me to accept a nomination to serve as a president of the SAG and, indirectly at least, set me on the road that would lead me into politics."

10

The FBI Story

One month after Reagan was elected president of the Screen Actors Guild, he welcomed FBI agents back to his home on Cordell Drive. Richard Auerbach and Fred Dupuis introduced themselves, and soon Reagan and Jane Wyman were telling them about the guild's structure and its internal politics.

They explained that the guild was run largely by its executive board, which included twelve officers plus past presidents, and had about 8,500 members. But two "cliques" of guild members had routinely opposed the board's policies and nominated their own candidates for guild offices. One clique was led by the treasurer, Anne Revere, winner of a 1944 Academy Award for Best Supporting Actress in *National Velvet*, and a direct descendant of the Revolutionary War hero Paul Revere. The other was led by Karen Morley, a civil rights activist who had played the sexy gun moll Poppy in Howard Hawks's gangster classic *Scarface* (1932). Reagan told the agents that these two actresses had opposed his recommendation that the guild not support the CSU strike. More sinister, he declared, they always "follow the Communist Party line."

Then Reagan gave the FBI agents the names of eight more actors and actresses: Howard Da Silva, who had appeared with Reagan in both *Nine Lives Are Not Enough* (1941) and *Juke Girl* (1942); Dorothy Tree, a founding member of the SAG who had appeared with Reagan in *Knute Rockne: All American* (1940); Larry Parks, who won an Oscar as Al Jolson in *The Jolson Story* (1946); Hume Cronyn, who had appeared in *The Postman Always Rings Twice* (1946) and was Jessica Tandy's husband; Howland Chamberlain, who played Thorpe in William Wyler's Oscar-winning movie about postwar adjustment, *The Best Years of Our Lives* (1946); Selena Royle, who portrayed the mother of Elizabeth Taylor's Kathie in *Courage of Lassie* (1946); Lloyd Gough, who played Roberts in Robert Rossen's *Body and Soul* (1947), which starred John Garfield and Anne Revere; and Alexander

Knox, who was nominated for an Oscar for his role as Woodrow Wilson in *Wilson* (1944), and who had ridiculed Reagan during the guild assembly at the Hollywood Legion Stadium.

When they were done, agents Auerbach and Dupuis thanked the couple for speaking with them and returned to the Los Angeles FBI office, where they prepared a report to Hoover based on Reagan's cooperation. Reagan's naming names at this April 10, 1947, meeting was contrary to his subsequent public claim that he never "pointed a finger at any individual."

The following month, Reagan again met with agent Dupuis, who asked for help identifying an actor whom he had spotted during his investigation of a liberal political organization called the Progressive Citizens of America. The PCA maintained a nonexclusionary policy that allowed people of all political persuasions to join, and was backing the former vice president Henry Wallace in his third-party bid for the presidency in 1948. Reagan recognized the man from the agent's description as the actor Richard Conte, who had played Private Rivera in the World War II drama *A Walk in the Sun* (1945) and was on his way to becoming a film noir star; just the year before, Marilyn Monroe had done her first screen test with him. According to a May 2, 1947, report, Reagan gave the agent a copy of *Movie Show* magazine containing Conte's photograph.

Reagan was turning out to be an eager aide to the FBI. He would soon prove helpful to the House Un-American Activities Committee as well.

J. Parnell Thomas, a congressman from New Jersey, arrived in Los Angeles on May 8, 1947, and checked into a suite at the Biltmore Hotel. The Republicans had wrested control of both chambers of Congress the previous November for the first time in fourteen years, and named Thomas chairman of the House Un-American Activities Committee. A fierce opponent of President Roosevelt, he believed the New Deal had sabotaged the capitalist system. Thomas himself would be indicted by a federal grand jury the following year for padding his office payroll and defrauding the government.

With Thomas was John McDowell, a Republican from Pennsylvania, and HUAC's chief counsel, a former FBI agent named Robert Stripling. They were in town to hold ten days of closed hearings. They were looking for evidence that would justify a full-scale investigation of "communistic activities and influences in the motion-picture industry." They desperately needed witnesses who would testify at a public hearing later that year in

Washington, D.C.—"friendly" witnesses who would cooperate with the
committee, affirm the dangers of communism, and produce positive publicity for their cause.

Thomas turned to Richard B. Hood, the special agent in charge, who
immediately briefed FBI headquarters officials on Thomas's request. The
COMPIC investigation had generated dossiers on the political activities
of hundreds of people in Hollywood, but no evidence of criminal activities. There was thus no legal basis for disclosing the confidential information in these records. But FBI officials knew HUAC could use it to
publicly expose alleged subversives, humiliate them, and perhaps get
them fired. So—on the strict condition that the FBI's assistance remain
secret—Hoover consented to help. "Expedite," he scrawled. "I want to
extend *every* assistance to this committee."

The next day, Assistant Director Louis Nichols phoned Hood. Nichols was Hoover's liaison to Congress and had developed close ties to conservatives such as Thomas, who could advance Hoover's political agenda.
Nichols directed Hood to search the Los Angeles field office files for information on a roster of people who might be useful to Thomas. Several hours
later, Hood sent Hoover a teletype summarizing the memos he had prepared about each of them. Reagan, he reported, could be a committee witness about "party activities among actors," and about an actress who was
alleged to be a "fellow traveler."

As president of the Screen Actors Guild, Reagan was proving to be an
especially useful source to the FBI. Jack Dales, the guild's executive secretary and Reagan's confidant, worked closely with him. On July 31, 1947,
Dales spoke with Agent Dupuis and identified as guild members a total
of fifty-four people whom the bureau suspected, but had not proved, were
Communists. FBI agents had obtained the names through an illegal break-
in of Communist Party offices in Los Angeles, and were now homing in
on them. Dales gave Agent Dupuis extensive information from guild
membership files, which contained personal details such as home addresses
and unlisted phone numbers. Given that Dales and Reagan were close
colleagues and anti-Communists, it is unlikely Dales would have turned
over such sensitive SAG data without Reagan's approval. There is no evidence that Reagan or Dales knew they were helping the FBI use illegally
obtained information, but they were an important part of making that
information useful to the bureau. And in return, they were getting FBI
information they could use against suspected subversives in their union.
As Dupuis's report put it, the names "have been verified through the Guild
as Guild members."

The names of many of those actors are now publicly known for the first time. They include Lloyd Bridges, Lee J. Cobb, J. Edward Bromberg, and Gale Sondergaard.*

Reagan—whose duty it was to protect the interests of his union members—was doing the very thing most likely to jeopardize their careers. Now Hoover could use this information from the guild's own records to investigate them and pass along leads to HUAC, which ultimately subpoenaed some of these actors and others Reagan named earlier. The actors then faced the choice of testifying about themselves and colleagues, or refusing and being blacklisted. Although they had done nothing illegal, careers and lives would be damaged.

Karen Morley and Selena Royle refused to name names and were blacklisted. Larry Parks agonized, eventually testified in tears, and was blacklisted anyway. Lee J. Cobb had been hailed as "the next Barrymore" for his portrayal of the defeated Willy Loman in the 1949 Broadway production of Arthur Miller's *Death of a Salesman*. For two years he, too, fought the committee's subpoenas, but after his career was wrecked and his wife institutionalized he relented, testifying in executive session at Hollywood's Roosevelt Hotel. "I was pretty much worn down," he told the journalist Victor Navasky for Navasky's book *Naming Names*. "I had to be employable again." Likewise, Lloyd Bridges was blacklisted for a while and eventually testified.

Joseph Bromberg, the short, stocky character actor whose films included *Cloak and Dagger* (1946) and *Guilty Bystander* (1950), was subpoenaed even though he'd explained to the committee that he suffered from a rheumatic heart. When he appeared before the panel in June 1951, he was sweating profusely and paused to take a pill as he invoked his constitutional rights, refused to testify, and accused the legislators of engaging in "witch hunts." He was blacklisted and died six months later of a heart attack, at age forty-seven.

H. Allen Smith was HUAC's chief investigator in Hollywood. He had joined the FBI in 1935 and spent five years at the bureau's Los Angeles office, becoming an assistant to the special agent in charge and overseeing internal security investigations. He had joined the HUAC staff on Hoover's recommendation. "I guess the committee must have heard that I hate any

---

*The names are listed in the endnote with the citation for this paragraph on page 560.

'ism' that isn't one hundred percent American," Smith said on taking the job. And as it turned out, he and Reagan had a personal connection: they had grown up in Dixon, Illinois. On September 2, 1947, Smith, a future California congressman, prepared a confidential report evaluating his old friend as a prospective witness.

"This individual is presently President of the Screen Actors Guild. He has no fear of any one, is a nice talker, well informed on the subject, and will make a splendid witness. He is of course reticent to testify, because he states that he is a New Deal Liberal, and does not agree with a number of individuals in the Motion Picture Alliance." The Motion Picture Alliance for the Preservation of American Ideals was the movie industry's most aggressive anti-Communist group, and included studio executives, labor leaders, and the actors John Wayne, Ward Bond, and Adolphe Menjou. Despite such disagreements, Reagan, in the coming months, would work closely with some of them, particularly Roy M. Brewer.

Smith's report continued, "I believe we straightened out a number of his differences, in that he felt Menjou and some of the others referred to him, Reagan, as a man who had been a Leftist and then reformed. Reagan resents this very much, as he states he never was a Leftist, that actually he got tangled up with a few committees that he thought were all right, but it took him some time to learn that they were not. As soon as he discovered that fact, he got out of them.

"I think that that is absolutely correct," Smith concluded. "I happen to have been raised in the same town with Reagan, and know him very well, and because of that fact he opened up and talked to me very freely, and he will go to Washington if we request him to do so. I think we should have him there."

Outside the Old House Office Building, across from the U.S. Capitol, police were turning away overflow crowds that had been drawn to the hearing's mix of celebrity, glamour, and intrigue. Forty-three actors, writers, and studio executives had been subpoenaed to appear before the House Un-American Activities Committee. Inside the marble-lined caucus room that Monday morning, J. Parnell Thomas banged his gavel and delivered a solemn statement opening the long-anticipated hearings on alleged subversive influence in Hollywood. "We all recognize that what the citizen sees and hears in his neighborhood movie house carries a powerful impact on his thoughts and behavior," he declared as the newsreel cameras whirred.

Most of the stars, however, did not appear until Wednesday, October 23, when, as the *Washington News* reported, capital police "girded for an even larger rush of feminine film fans." Robert Montgomery and George Murphy, past presidents of the Screen Actors Guild, each testified that only a tiny minority of movie actors were Communists. Then Reagan took the stand, wearing a beige suit and—forgoing his usual contact lenses—large horn-rimmed glasses of the kind he had loathed since boyhood but which bestowed greater gravitas.

Robert Stripling, the committee's chief counsel, asked a series of questions that neatly fit the statements Reagan had previously given FBI agents. Neither Stripling, nor Reagan in his restrained answers, however, gave any hint that he had ever spoken with FBI agents or had been informing on colleagues. Reagan repeated his claim that a "clique" within the Screen Actors Guild had consistently opposed the positions of the guild board and were suspected of following Communist Party tactics. He acknowledged he had no evidence, but said he had heard they were Communists from "reliable sources."

Having covered the question of Communists inside the guild, Stripling asked Reagan whether he had "ever been solicited to join" any group he considered a Communist-front organization. Stripling's light touch gave Reagan the opportunity to soft-pedal his late licentious liberalism. He had lent his name to a fund-raiser put on by the Joint Anti-Fascist Refugee Committee, which featured a recital by Paul Robeson. Reagan said he had agreed to be listed as a sponsor only because the nature of the event had been misrepresented to him, a tactic he considered typical of Communists. He also said he had "received literature" from the Committee for a Far-Eastern Democratic Policy, and though he didn't know whether it was Communist, "I only know that I didn't like their views and as a result I didn't want to have anything to do with them." He did not mention that he had been a sponsor of this group. Nor did he note his association with the American Veterans Committee or the Hollywood Independent Citizens Committee of Arts, Sciences and Professions.

Stripling then asked Reagan what steps should be taken to eliminate "Communist influences" from the movie industry. Reagan replied, ". . . I think within the bounds of our democratic rights, and never once stepping over the rights given us by democracy, we have done a pretty good job in our business of keeping those people's activities curtailed. After all, we must recognize them at present as a political party. On that basis we have exposed their lies when we came across them, we have opposed their propaganda, and I can certainly testify that in the case of the Screen

Actors Guild we have been eminently successful in preventing them from, with their usual tactics, trying to run a majority of an organization with a well-organized minority. So that fundamentally I would say in opposing those people that the best thing to do is to make democracy work. In the Screen Actors Guild we make it work by insuring everyone a vote and by keeping everyone informed. I believe that, as Thomas Jefferson put it, if all the American people know all of the facts they will never make a mistake."

It was up to the government, Reagan said, to determine whether the Communist Party should be criminalized. "As a citizen I would hesitate, or not like, to see any political party outlawed on the basis of its political ideology. We have spent one hundred and seventy years in this country on the basis that democracy is strong enough to stand up and fight against the inroads of any ideology. However, if it is proven that an organization is an agent of a power, a foreign power, or in any way not a legitimate political party, and I think the government is capable of proving that, if the proof is there, then that is another matter."

Reagan declared that he was proud of his industry's fight against Communists, adding, "I do not believe the Communists have ever at any time been able to use the motion-picture screen as a sounding board for their philosophy or ideology."

Richard Nixon, a Republican representative from California, and the other committee members posed no questions to Reagan. Chairman Thomas said he was sure that once his committee provided the American people with the facts, they would "do a job . . . to make America just as pure as we can possibly make it."

Reagan interjected: "Sir, if I might, in regard to that, say that what I was trying to express, and didn't do very well, was also this other fear. I detest, I abhor their philosophy, but I detest more than that their tactics, which are those of the fifth column, and are dishonest, but at the same time I never as a citizen want to see our country become urged by either fear or resentment of this group, that we ever compromise with any of our democratic principles through that fear or resentment. I still think that democracy can do it."

With that, A. B. Leckie, another former FBI agent on the committee's staff, led Reagan from the room.

"Quentin Reynolds: Movie Probers Let Down By Stars But Customers Love the Show."

This was the headline for a story by one of the most prominent journalists to cover the hearings. Quentin Reynolds was a war correspondent famous for his reporting on the London blitz and a frequent contributor to *Collier's Weekly*, a leading magazine of the day. Now he gave the hearings a critical review. "George Murphy, Ronald Reagan and John Garfield (who sat with the spectators) helped to make the audience happy. It is too bad that the magnificent cast was not assembled for some cause more worthy of their talents. It becomes increasingly apparent that the Committee attempts to prove that Hollywood is dominated or influenced greatly by the Communist Party is [*sic*] doomed to failure. The Committee's own witnesses are disproving the Committee's thesis." Reynolds further accused the committee of censorship. "It is using tactics which are very familiar to those of us who worked in Berlin or Moscow. The whole spirit which so obviously activates the committee is one of hatred for non-conformity. They seem to believe that non-conformity means disloyalty."

The hearings drew persons of prestige and power to a dinner in the nation's capital that week, at which Ronald Reagan chatted briefly with J. Edgar Hoover. Reagan, evidently displeased with Quentin Reynolds's article, told the director in passing that the journalist was "said to be a Communist."

Reynolds soon heard of Reagan's comment and wrote Hoover about it. "Dear Edgar," he said in his letter of October 24, 1947, "I hate to bother you with this. However, that remark Ronald Reagan made the other night at dinner has bothered me a little. I value your opinion of me, and Clyde's opinion, so much that I would like to go on record as to exactly how I feel." Reynolds proposed lunch—"a smoked shrimp or two at Harvey's"—to discuss the matter.

Jane Wyman was upset again. She did not share her husband's intense interest in politics, and they argued continually about it. He insisted that she attend meetings with him, she later complained, but her ideas "were never considered important." She had been focusing on acting, lately with more success than Reagan. She had starred opposite Ray Milland in Billy Wilder's *The Lost Weekend* in 1945, and was nominated for an Academy Award for her role opposite Gregory Peck in *The Yearling* in 1946. Their marriage had been further strained by the loss of their third child, Christine, born prematurely in June 1947. Their differences grew, Wyman later said, noting, "Finally there was nothing in common between us, nothing to sustain our marriage."

When Reagan returned home from testifying before HUAC, the woman he affectionately called "Button Nose" asked him to move out. He was, he would later say, stunned. "I suppose there had been warning signs, if only I hadn't been so busy . . ."

In his highly publicized congressional appearance, Reagan had assumed the role of civil libertarian, advocate of democratic debate, and defender of the right to hold unpopular views. By not naming names in the glare of the hearing chamber spotlights, he had avoided the shame and stigma of publicly betraying colleagues. But he already had provided names to the FBI in secret. And he soon became more deeply involved in fighting communism in Hollywood, promoting loyalty oaths, helping to blacklist actors, and informing on more colleagues. As one FBI report put it, "He was extremely active in the Guild in opposing the communists."

A few weeks after Reagan testified, members of the Screen Actors Guild extended his interim appointment by electing him president. With his support, they also voted, in January 1948, to require all guild officers to sign an oath affirming they were not affiliated with the Communist Party. The oath was in addition to a separate "voluntary statement of affirmation" presented to all guild members, which Reagan had urged and the board previously had adopted. That affirmation said:

> In support of our soldiers as they take their oath upon induction, I affirm that I will bear true faith and allegiance to the United States of America and that I will serve the United States honestly and faithfully against all its enemies. I hold Stalin and the Soviet Union responsible for the war in Korea. I support the resistance of the United States and the United Nations against this act of imperialist aggression. History having proved that Stalinism is totalitarianism, I repudiate its teachings and program, as I do those of every other form of dictatorship.

Reagan also suggested that guild members volunteer for "Americanism programs," such as those offered by the American Legion, and give speeches against communism.

Signing the affirmation was voluntary, of course, but those who refused to sign, for whatever reason, could find themselves under suspicion.

Fear permeated Hollywood—at dining tables in the faux chateaus of Beverly Hills, in chance meetings at Schwab's Pharmacy on Sunset

Boulevard, and in the arguments at the Black Watch Delicatessen across the street from the Actors' Lab Theatre, where the worn leatherette booths were occupied by Clifford Odets, Dalton Trumbo, and other left-wing intellectuals. Always edgy with studio politics, public relations concerns, and an ego-bending caste system, the film colony now faced HUAC, American Legion pickets, studio blacklists, and seemingly omnipresent FBI agents in their uniform of gray suit and fedora.

Dore Schary, an executive at Metro-Goldwyn-Mayer and a friend of Reagan's, presented himself at the office of Special Agent in Charge Richard B. Hood. Schary assured him the studio was being careful not to hire Communists or Communist sympathizers for any film production. He recounted how he had fired Betsy Blair, Gene Kelly's wife, after learning that she had participated in a meeting sponsored by HICCASP to protest the book *Red Channels*, a listing of alleged party members in the radio and television industry published by former FBI agents. She was rehired, he emphasized, only after she signed a sworn loyalty statement. Another informer, meanwhile, told an FBI agent that Gene Kelly was "greatly upset" about Blair's political activity and considered divorcing her. The actor known for his dance routines, according to a third informer, was "extremely worried about his career."

Katharine Hepburn spoke at a rally for the Progressive Citizens of America at Gilmore Stadium. Soon after, H. Allen Smith, the FBI-agent-turned-HUAC-investigator, accosted her. The committee did not want to hurt anyone, he explained, and if she had any explanation for her remarks, this was her opportunity to share it with Congress. According to an FBI report, Hepburn "drew herself up" and demanded of Smith if she did not look like an adult, declaring, furthermore, that she knew just what she was saying, was fully capable of writing her own speeches, and need make no defense of her position. James McGuiness, a writer and MGM executive, meanwhile told an FBI agent that the fact that Hepburn was living with the married Spencer Tracy showed she was "not a very high type," and her speech for the PCA just confirmed this.

Informers were everywhere. Actors, writers, talent agents, studio executives—all were reporting to the FBI on their colleagues. It got to the point that informers were informing on each other. Their reasons were not necessarily ideological. Ida Lupino, the ambitious British-born actress who later became one of Hollywood's first female directors, had made clear she wanted the FBI's help in getting her immigration application approved and was soon designated as a "Confidential National Defense Informant." In May 1947, Lupino told FBI agents she suspected the actor

Sterling Hayden was a Communist and held "questionable meetings" on his yacht. That December, she told an agent that under Reagan's leadership, the guild "appears to be waging a successful fight to keep out radical actors and actresses from executive positions." Reagan, she said, had "seen the light."

Two days later, the actor Preston Foster told an FBI agent he'd recently run into the SAG president and "Reagan mentioned that he had just been in touch with the FBI who were interested in the Screen Actors Guild activities." Foster had appeared in the 1935 movie *The Informer.* He complained that he "did not think that Reagan should disclose his connections with the FBI and wondered if Reagan was telling the truth." The agent listened but, as he noted in his report, remained carefully "non-committal."

Reagan was, according to newly released FBI records, at the center of a coterie of celebrity informers. George Murphy, the former SAG president, Democrat-turned-Republican, and future senator from California, was an informer, reporting on, among other things, colleagues at MGM studios. So were Mervyn LeRoy, the director; Sam Wood, an executive at Universal-International Studios; and Roy Brewer, who according to an FBI report has "demonstrated his reliability and his cooperation."

Olivia de Havilland also cooperated with the FBI. As of October 1947, she and her husband, the writer Marcus Goodrich, were "doing considerable work" with an FBI agent in connection with the COMPIC investigation. (This report listed Goodrich as an "informant," but did not so identify de Havilland.) Another report said Goodrich told an agent that de Havilland "is now working with Ronald Reagan, President of the Screen Actors Guild, at the latter's request, in an attempt to force Communists out of positions or [sic] control or potential control in the Guild. He said the current Congressional investigation has 'everyone jittery' in Hollywood." In correspondence with the author, de Havilland denied she was an "informant." She said her only contribution to the FBI's inquiry was one meeting with an agent, at which she discussed HICCASP and named two people she deemed suspicious. She also supported Reagan's oath position. "I was deeply concerned about the possibility that Communist forces were at work in Hollywood," she said.

On December 19, 1947, an FBI agent contacted Reagan again. In the resulting report, the agent identified Reagan as confidential informant "T-10." Several of Reagan's biographers have said this was his code number. In fact, the designation was what the FBI called a "temporary number," or "T-number," and it was another example of Hoover's mastery of the files. FBI agents assigned T-numbers to the sources they cited in a given report—whether people, illegal wiretaps, or black bag jobs—and then identified them in the text only by those numbers. Separate administrative pages, detached from the reports when they were circulated outside the bureau, listed the T-number and the identity of each source, in this case "T-10: Ronald Reagan, President, Screen Actors Guild." There is no evidence in FBI files released to date that Reagan was assigned a permanent informant number typically used to designate informers under bureau control, or that he was paid for informing; his motives clearly were not pecuniary but personal and political.

Reagan briefed the agent on his latest efforts to fight communism in Hollywood, where things were getting meaner. Although it was legal to be in the Communist Party, and though there had been no evidence that film colony Communists had otherwise broken the law, the HUAC hearings had tarnished Tinseltown. The negative publicity, an informer told the FBI, had helped drive down box office receipts by 20 percent. That November, movie magnates worried about their bottom line had met at the Waldorf-Astoria Hotel in New York City and agreed to fire the Hollywood Ten, the writers, producers, and directors who had refused to testify before HUAC and had been cited for contempt of Congress. The moguls also announced they would not knowingly employ Communists or anyone who advocated the unlawful overthrow of the government.

Reagan had been given a part in this. As the agent reported, "T-10 advised that he has been made a member of a committee headed by Louis B. Mayer the purpose of which allegedly is to 'purge' the motion picture industry of Communist Party members." Reagan also confided he had misgivings because "he did not feel it was within the authority or ability of any single man or group of men within the motion picture industry to be able to determine accurately and fairly who should be fired and who should not be fired." It was his "firm conviction," he said, that Congress should outlaw the Communist Party as a foreign-inspired conspiracy and designate organizations that were Communist-controlled. That way, membership in them would be proof of disloyalty.

This view was very different from the one he had expressed before Congress only two months earlier, when he pointedly refrained from advocating the criminalization of the Communist Party and espoused the Jeffersonian idea of tolerating dissent and trusting people to make their own decisions in the marketplace of ideas.

Reagan was growing more concerned about the Red Menace.

•

Separated from Wyman, Reagan was devoting more time to fighting communism. By November 1948, he had become chairman of the Labor League of Hollywood Voters, whose main purpose, an informer told an FBI agent, was to pressure labor unions to "get rid of Communists and to cease sponsoring candidates endorsed by Communists." Reagan also had joined the Motion Picture Industry Council, whose purpose was to oust Communists and to help innocent people who had fallen under suspicion. "We urged them to publicly declare their opposition to Communism and to volunteer to appear before the FBI and the House Un-American Activities Committee—two things no communist could agree to," he wrote in *An American Life*. "We would arrange their meetings and we would vouch for their innocence. If on the other hand someone said, 'I won't do that,' we simply said, 'We can't help you.'"

Reagan refused to help Gale Sondergaard, the character actress known for her portrayals of deliciously evil women (*The Spider Woman*, 1944) and winner of the first Academy Award for Best Supporting Actress, for her part as Faith Paleologus in *Anthony Adverse*, 1936. After Sondergaard received a subpoena to appear before HUAC in early 1951, she told the guild board that she would invoke the Fifth Amendment and refuse to testify about her political activity on the ground that as an American she had the constitutional rights of free speech and free association—even though she knew her refusal would end her career. She asked the SAG board to declare that "it will not tolerate any industry blacklist."

The board's response—approved by Reagan—was published March 20, 1951, in *The Hollywood Reporter*: "The deadly seriousness of the international situation dictates the tone of our reply. This is not the time for dialectic fencing. Like the overwhelming majority of the American people, we believe that a 'clear and present danger' to our nation exists. The Guild Board believes that all participants in the international Communist Party conspiracy against our nation should be exposed for what they are—enemies of our country and of our form of government."

It continued, "The Guild as a labor union will fight against any secret blacklist created by any group of employers. On the other hand, if any actor by his own actions outside of union activities has so offended American public opinion that he has made himself unsaleable [*sic*] at the box office, the Guild cannot and would not want to force any employer to hire him. That is the individual actor's personal responsibility and it cannot be shifted to this union."

Abandoned by her union, Sondergaard appeared before HUAC deeply tanned and defiantly turned out in a black-and-white checked suit.

Herbert Biberman, her husband, the writer and director, already had been convicted of contempt of Congress. As one of the Hollywood Ten, he had been subpoenaed by HUAC and refused to testify. Now Sondergaard also refused. Although her career was at its apex—she had just been nominated for another Academy Award for Best Supporting Actress in *Anna and the King of Siam* (1946)—she was blacklisted and moved to New York, where she played off-Broadway.

Reagan gave the same choice to Anne Revere when she was subpoenaed to testify before HUAC, also in 1951. As she recalled their exchange at her last guild meeting: " 'It's so simple,' Reagan said. 'All you've got to do is just name a couple of names that have already been named.' I said, 'That's it. I can't climb up on somebody's neck.' " Revere refused to testify and was blacklisted for more than a decade.

Neither Sondergaard nor Revere knew that Reagan already had informed on them.

Like Clark Kerr at Berkeley, Reagan in Hollywood was confronted by the issue of loyalty. Both men already had shown themselves to be strong anti-Communists. Both men had signed the oaths required of them and voted for measures declaring Communists unfit to work in their respective fields, each of which dealt with conveying ideas and values to the public. Both men had volunteered to investigate whether colleagues were Communist Party members, and to recommend whether they should keep their jobs.

But unlike Reagan, Kerr defended people he believed were loyal but who had refused to sign the oath as a matter of principle. Kerr supported those independent spirits who, like his father, refused to conform because they believed an individual's liberty was vital to the university and to democracy. Kerr distrusted Tenney, Burns, and HUAC, and their methods. Reagan would rely on Tenney's reports as proof of a Communist plot in Hollywood. He demanded that all guild members submit to HUAC's ministrations. He turned away from colleagues who would not sign the guild's loyalty oath. Kerr believed the Soviet Union posed a serious military threat abroad, but thought domestic communism never presented a serious risk to American democracy. Reagan saw imminent danger. "The Communist plan for Hollywood was remarkably simple," he wrote. "It was merely to take over the motion picture business. Not only for its profit . . . but also for a grand world-wide propaganda base."

By 1956, however, FBI officials were internally acknowledging that Communist influence in the movie industry was negligible. Hoover's fourteen-year-long COMPIC investigation had deployed scores of FBI agents, informers, black bag jobs, and illegal electronic surveillance. The inquiry confirmed that Communists worked in the film industry, and that some of them tried to hide their party membership. But as the historian Athan Theoharis found in his review of COMPIC records, the investigation produced no evidence that they engaged in espionage or violated any federal law. And according to Larry Ceplair and Steven Englund, authors of *The Inquisition in Hollywood: Politics in the Film Community, 1930–1960*, the Hollywood reds did not use movies as propaganda to undermine "any social institution."

Like the FBI's investigations at the University of California, the bureau's Hollywood inquiry came to focus on lawful First Amendment activities that Hoover deemed unpatriotic because they challenged the status quo. The investigations were premised on the belief that Americans could be easily fooled by bad ideas. And because both Hollywood and Berkeley were communities based on freedom of expression, they made convenient political targets.

But Reagan had found a cause, and through that cause he would find the love of his life.

The phone rang and Mervyn LeRoy, the producer of the *The Wizard of Oz*, told Reagan about a young actress he wanted him to meet. Wyman and Reagan had finalized their divorce in 1949, and Reagan had found himself single again, driving his Cadillac convertible by day to anti-Communist meetings and by night to the clubs where he took his dates. Reagan was promiscuous during this period, and took advantage of his position as an established older actor and guild leader who could help a starlet's career. According to *Reagan, The Hollywood Years*, by Marc Elliot, he favored one-night stands or brief affairs with women ten or fifteen years his junior.

LeRoy was telling Reagan that his actress friend needed help. She was "very much distressed because her name kept showing up on rosters of Communist front organizations." Nancy Davis, LeRoy said, had assured him that "she was violently opposed" to leftist causes. Reagan reported the call to Jack Dales at the guild office. "We did a little quick checking," Reagan wrote, "and discovered nothing detrimental to her." Satisfied that she was "in the clear," Reagan called back LeRoy and said she had nothing to worry about. The producer insisted Reagan meet with her over lunch or dinner, however, just to "quiet her fears."

Reagan knocked on her door and was soon regarding a slender, dark-haired young woman with "a wide-spaced pair of hazel eyes that looked right at you and made you look back." The adopted daughter of a Chicago neurosurgeon, Davis had majored in theater at Smith College and appeared briefly on Broadway before coming to Hollywood. On the way to La Rue's restaurant that night, she and Reagan discussed how to get her name off of "those 'bleeding hearts' lists."

Reagan's anti-Communist work may have contributed to his losing one marriage, but like Clark Kerr's Peace Caravans for the Quakers, it led him to his future wife. Reagan and Davis were married on March 4, 1952, after she became pregnant. She appeared in eleven movies, often typecast as a young mother, and played opposite Reagan in her penultimate film, *Hell Cats of the Navy*. But her career did not flourish, and after she and Reagan had two children she retired. "If you try to make two careers work, one of them has to suffer," Nancy Reagan said. "Maybe some women can do it, but not me."

Reagan's own screen career was faltering. He'd been elected president of the Screen Actors Guild five times by now and become one of the movie industry's most prominent figures. But he'd committed more and more of his time to union matters and fighting communism, spending long hours at the guild's office on the eighth floor of the Hollywood Professional Building at 7046 Hollywood Boulevard. Acting, Reagan wrote, "at times seemed to be a sideline." For a younger generation of moviegoers, he was no longer a box office magnet. By the early fifties he had been in several films he called "turkeys"; even he did not want to watch them.

The Reagans, meanwhile, had moved into a new house in Pacific Palisades. He owed taxes on income he had deferred during World War II, and in 1957 the IRS would file a lien against Reagan for back taxes of $24,911. He continued to reject scripts he deemed second-rate. Finally, he made *Prisoner of War*, playing an officer dropped behind enemy lines in North Korea to investigate the treatment of American captives. Reagan complained about unfair reviews—or, as he put it, "the reluctance of extreme liberals to enthuse about anything that upset their illusions about 'agrarian reformers.'"

Reagan began to make guest appearances on television and briefly hosted a vaudeville act at a Las Vegas casino. In 1954, he took a $125,000-a-year job doing employee and public relations for General Electric. The firm's image-conscious executives had been wary of hiring an actor for the job, according to the GE manager Earl Dunckel, but chose Reagan because he represented "good moral character."

As part of the job Reagan hosted *General Electric Theater*, a weekly television show featuring guest stars in original dramas. Most movie actors at the time looked down on television, but within six months his program became one of the most popular in its time slot, and was soon number one on Sundays at 9:00 p.m. GE vigorously promoted the show, placing stories on the cover of nearly every Sunday newspaper supplement in the country. Reagan was getting more ink than he had lately as a movie star.

Reagan's mission was not to sell appliances but the firm itself. The research-and-manufacturing conglomerate had 135 facilities and 250,000 employees around the country. Reagan visited these plants and spoke to employees with the goal of making them feel they were not just a cog in the corporate machine.

Three or four times a year, he spent several weeks on one of these demanding tours. On his arrival at a local GE plant, the managers would take him to meet employees. The assembly lines would halt as people gathered and he gave a talk, took questions, and signed autographs. He also spoke at the local Rotary Club, met the mayor, and posed for photos. He had a remarkable memory and superb timing, Dunckel said, and easily connected with his audiences. Reagan would later say the tours were "one of the most rewarding experiences of my life."

In some ways, Reagan's GE tours were his version of Kerr's Peace Caravans: he was going out into the world, meeting Americans, developing his speaking skills, spreading what he believed was an important message for the future of the country. But while Kerr had advocated world peace and international cooperation, Reagan was promoting the corporate way of life and waging his war on communism.

Along the way, Reagan developed the speech that would become his political platform, a kind of cautionary tale. At first, he focused on what he described as false perceptions of movie stars as privileged and pampered. In reality, he said, they suffered discrimination in the form of censorship, unfair tax laws, and overly aggressive reporters. He warned that "if one group of people in America could be denied fair treatment, then the freedoms and rights of all were in danger." Above all, he emphasized the threat of domestic communism. "The most dramatic part of my pitch," he later wrote, "was the account of the attempted takeover of the (film) industry by the Communists . . . a useful purpose was served in awakening many people to the threat in their own backyards."

Over time, Reagan refined this speech to reflect his evolving political philosophy, especially his concern about the "swiftly rising tide of collectivism that threatens to inundate what remains of our free economy." He

believed "the last decade has seen a quickening of tempo in our government's race toward the controlled society." He recalled, "I went out of my
way to point out that the problems of centralizing power in Washington,
with subsequent loss of freedom at the local level, were problems that
crossed party lines. I emphasized the danger of a permanent structure of
government grown so huge that it exerted power on the elected representatives and usurped their policy making functions."

The FBI had opened Reagan's eyes to the Communist threat, and he
was spreading the word.

At GE, Reagan became close to George Dalen, a former FBI agent who
had joined the corporation and was assigned to manage Reagan's operations. Dalen became Reagan's right-hand man, traveling with him on his
tours, ensuring things ran smoothly. "George Dalen has the quiet effi-
ciency that seems so typical of J. Edgar Hoover's elite corps but, in addition,
this big, rugged redhead had a sense of humor that kept the whole business
from breaking our backs," Reagan wrote in *Where's the Rest of Me?*

A fellow Midwesterner, Dalen was born in South Dakota. He flew a
bomber in World War II and joined the FBI in 1951. After graduating
from the FBI's academy in Quantico, Virginia, he and other graduates
were taken to meet Hoover. "The young agents were scared to death of
him," he recalled in an interview. Dalen did well in the bureau, working
at field offices in Philadelphia and then New York City. But he became
concerned about Hoover's mandatory requirement that each agent work
"voluntary" unpaid overtime each day—and agents' resulting systematic
falsification of time cards. His disenchantment grew after he was assigned
to a security squad in New York City. He had identified several people
suspected of being covert Communists, tracing them to an office in Brooklyn, but had been unable to find evidence to prove their party membership.
A veteran agent suggested Dalen do a "bag job."

"I knew what it was," Dalen said, "because it went on fairly frequently.
So that's what I did. I got to know the black janitor of the three-story building in Brooklyn. He let me have a key. I made a copy, and then arranged,
when nobody would be around, for a crew of four or five of us to go in
and photograph. And then one night we went in with a few people and
riffled the desks and files and took maybe five hundred to a thousand pictures of various documents. We had a little camera outfit that would hold
a roll of five hundred pieces of film, thirty-five-millimeter, with lights included." Agents developed the photographs and assigned a code number

to them so they could be cited in FBI reports as if a live source had provided them, without revealing that they were obtained illegally. The information, Dalen said, was used to monitor people and for "harassing, if that were the order of the day."

The break-ins troubled him. "Here I was, a somewhat idealistic person and doing stuff like that, just stepping all over the Constitution, but it is an easy thing to get into. You think, if you're indoctrinated sufficiently, that if it's anti-Communist, it's pro-U.S. And because we are such good guys, in quotes, it ought to be okay, whatever we do to the bad guys. And that was pretty disillusioning," he said. "I remember I wrote a note in my little pile of notes to myself, that it was strange that I should join the FBI and learn how to become an institutional liar."

Dalen left the FBI on good terms in 1954, joined GE's public relations department about a year later, and by 1956 was working with Reagan. During the many hours they spent together on trains and in cars heading to the next speech, they swapped stories about the FBI and fighting communism. Dalen did not recall telling Reagan about the bureau's illegal break-ins, which were highly secret and "still pretty fresh," but remembered Reagan had confided that he had informed on actors he suspected were Communists when he was president of the SAG. "He'd report what he saw in the meetings and in private discussions," Dalen said, and the FBI returned the favor. "I don't know how deeply it went. But they certainly were helpful to him in pointing out people that were not identified as Communists in public. He was very positive on the FBI."

The Los Angeles FBI office had Reagan's unlisted phone number on file, GRanite 3-4190, but he didn't wait for the bureau to call. He periodically contacted FBI agents to inform on people he deemed politically suspect. One was a talented young actress who said the wrong thing to him at a Hollywood garden party in May 1959. Judith Braun was a dark-haired twenty-nine-year-old who had acted off-Broadway and had recently appeared in a television adaptation of Hans Christian Andersen's fairy tale "The Nightingale." She did not like blacklisting and told Reagan so. It was a crime, she said, for someone to be denied work because he would not "tattle" on his or her colleagues for political activity years earlier. "What if they did make a mistake?" she asked. "Why should that be held against them now?" Reagan replied that he knew of no "blacklist" in Hollywood. But he added that if she meant "a group of producers banded together for the purpose of refusing employment to a Communist who was against the

U.S. during the war in Korea or during World War II, then there is a 'blacklist,'" and he was in favor of it.

In an interview, Braun recalled that she had pointed across the lawn to another guest, Lewis Milestone, who had directed *All Quiet on the Western Front,* and said, "See . . . that's Milly . . . He hasn't been able to work in a long time, because he's been blacklisted." Reagan seemed to be getting very uncomfortable, but suddenly Nancy Reagan rushed over and interposed herself, demanding, "How *dare* you question my husband!" As she glared at Braun, Reagan walked away.

Braun's remarks may have been cocktail chatter, but Reagan made sure they were noted in the FBI's files for posterity. He told an FBI agent she was being hailed as a "new discovery"—apparently someone who he thought might influence people the wrong way. Reagan told the agent where she lived and worked. As the agent noted in his report, "Mr. Reagan stated he was merely bringing this to the attention of the Los Angeles FBI for information."

Reagan was concerned about what young people thought, at least politically. In November 1960, he visited Los Angeles State College to give a speech on behalf of Democrats for Nixon. The vice president was running against John F. Kennedy, the handsome senator from Massachusetts who had wide support among younger voters. Reagan hoped his talk would win support for Nixon on campus, but during the question-and-answer period afterward a young man who identified himself as Homer Plotkin challenged some of Reagan's statements. Reagan reported the episode to his FBI contact, asserting that the student asked questions that were "right down the Commie line." Moreover, Reagan said, the "student" had a "definite group" around him who clapped at any statement he made. Perhaps this reminded Reagan of the troublesome cliques who had opposed him in the guild. Based on his tip, the FBI opened a file on Plotkin titled "Security Matter—Communist."

These episodes present a very different picture of Reagan's FBI activities than the one set out by Lou Cannon, perhaps Reagan's most influential biographer, who wrote as late as 2003 in *Governor Reagan* that "I know of no one, either publicly or privately, whom Reagan called a Communist other than those who proclaimed their own communism. He realized that such accusations often damaged the accuser, and his sense of fairness led him in the direction of scrupulous political dialogue and away from personal vilification."

In an interview, Cartha DeLoach denied that Reagan was an informer.

"He never was a close contact of ours," DeLoach said. "He was never a source of information. There was no unique relationship." Edwin Meese III, who was later one of Reagan's top aides, told the author, however, that Reagan and FBI officials had "back and forth" contact during Reagan's Hollywood years. "He felt that the contacts with the bureau were very helpful to him during that period," Meese said.

Reagan saw dramatic potential in fighting communism. In June 1958, he sought to play the part of Special Agent George Crandall in a movie to be called *The FBI Story*. The drama was based on a bestselling history of the bureau that had been written by Don Whitehead with Hoover's authorization and research assistance from the bureau's Crime Records Division. Whitehead had been required to submit his manuscript to the FBI for review before it was published, and though the book was factually accurate it presented a wholly uncritical view of the FBI.

So eager was Reagan to play the part of the valiant FBI agent killed in the line of duty that he offered to take half his normal $75,000 fee. But he didn't pass the background check. The Los Angeles FBI chief reviewed his files and saw that Reagan had been "associated with certain Communist front organizations" in the mid-forties, before he "suddenly saw the light." Senior FBI officials were wary of giving him the bureau's imprimatur. "Sounds as though Reagan would consider this another stamp to block out the past," one of them wrote. "If it reaches an issue I am just going to say 'No.'" The part of Crandall in the 1959 film instead went to Larry Pennell, while the lead role of Agent Chip Hardesty was played by James Stewart.

Reagan had failed to land the part even though the film was directed and produced by Mervyn LeRoy, the friend who had set up his first date with Nancy Davis. LeRoy subsequently revealed, to the author Ovid Demaris, Hoover's tight control over the film's production. "Everybody on that picture, from the carpenters and electricians right to the top, everybody, had to be okayed by the FBI," he said. "I had two FBI men with me all the time, for research purposes so that we did things right. He and his men controlled the movie." Likewise, Hoover would later control the *FBI* television series. Efrem Zimbalist, Jr., the show's star, recalled that the bureau reserved the right to approve every script and every actor who played an agent. "I know that Hoover's policy was that he didn't want any criminals or known Communists or subversives appearing on his show," he said, "and certainly not representing the Bureau as agents."

•

Hoover may have been unwilling to let Reagan portray an FBI agent, but he rewarded his covert assistance in Hollywood by helping him with the troubled romantic life of his disaffected daughter, Maureen. According to previously undisclosed documents, the bureau stepped forward in March of 1960, after George Murphy reached out to an FBI agent he knew in Los Angeles. Murphy was a friend of both Reagan and Hoover's.

As Murphy explained to the agent, Neil Reagan had confided that Reagan and his former wife, Jane Wyman, were "very much concerned" about Maureen. But Reagan was still hosting *General Electric Theater*, Wyman was pursuing her acting career, and they had grown distant from their eldest child. The eighteen-year-old had left Los Angeles and moved on her own to Washington, D.C. She entered the 1959 Miss Washington beauty contest (just for the chance to appear onstage, she would later say) and took work as a secretary. They heard she was living with an older man, a patrolman for the Washington Metropolitan Police Department. Supposedly the officer had told Maureen "he cannot marry her because he is already married and his wife is in some sort of an institution, possibly mental."

According to the agent's report, "Jane Wyman wishes to come to Washington to perhaps straighten out her daughter, get her back to Los Angeles, but before doing so desires to know the following: (1) Is [the man in question] employed as an officer of the Metropolitan Police Department?; (2) Is he married?; (3) Is his wife in an institution and what are the details?; and (4) Any other information which might be discreetly developed concerning the relationship."

At FBI headquarters, officials checked their files and saw that the bureau had conducted a routine investigation of Maureen Reagan a year earlier when she applied for a receptionist's job with the U.S. Immigration and Naturalization Service. That background check provided a glimpse of her traumatic family history. An official at Marymount Junior College, Arlington, Virginia, where she had dropped out, described her as personable but immature and unable to make or keep friends easily. According to the official, "Maureen was the victim of a broken home, and because she had resided in boarding schools and been away from parental contact so much of her life she was an insecure individual 'who could not make up her mind' and did not achieve goals set by herself or others."

Now she was living in Apartment A of a rooming house at 3114 Sixteenth Street, N.W., and working rather unsatisfactorily in her secretarial job.

DeLoach recommended assigning FBI agents to investigate her romantic situation, even though, as he acknowledged in a memo, "there does not appear to be any FBI jurisdiction here." Hoover scrawled "Yes," approving the investigation. Posing as an insurance salesman, one agent made a pretext phone call to neighbors; another contacted a police department source; a third interviewed the cleaning lady at her rooming house.

The inquiry quickly confirmed her parents' fears: She was living with a patrolman named John Filippone, a former marine corporal assigned to the 10th Precinct, the midnight shift. They had met one winter day when he was directing traffic near her apartment, about a year after he had made headlines for chasing and shooting a burglary suspect. He was twelve years her senior, and he was already married.

DeLoach instructed the Los Angeles FBI chief to pass the pertinent information to Murphy "on a highly confidential basis with the distinct understanding that the FBI is to be completely left out of it."

Reagan and Wyman were grateful to Hoover for the FBI's help and never revealed the bureau's assistance. It remains unclear, however, how they used this information and why they thought it appropriate to have government agents check on their daughter's personal life. The Ronald Reagan Presidential Foundation, created by President Reagan to further his legacy, declined to comment for this book. However, Edwin Meese III, who was chief of staff for Governor Reagan and Attorney General for President Reagan, said, "It's not at all unusual for citizens to question law enforcement agencies as he did in the case of Maureen." But Meese added that FBI officials "probably gave more attention to it than they might have if it were any movie actor or any citizen" because of "the fact that he had cooperated with them as president of the Screen Actors Guild." In any event, Hoover's assistance did not solve her problems. Filippone soon left his wife and, in 1961, married Maureen Reagan, but as she later wrote, he repeatedly beat her and they divorced in 1962.

Nor did it bridge the distance between Reagan and his daughter. "I still haven't spoken openly to my parents, or to anyone in my family, about the details of what I went through," she wrote twenty-seven years later in her memoir, *First Father, First Daughter.*

Reagan still wanted to join forces with the FBI in a dramatic way.

He'd been refused a role in *The FBI Story,* but after reading Hoover's "Communist Target—Youth," he was inspired to try again. Although serious questions had been raised about its accuracy, Reagan was convinced that Communists were behind the demonstration at San Francisco City Hall. He spoke with DeLoach on August 26, 1960, about his idea for a special show based on the report for *General Electric Theater*, only to have Hoover respond with a letter politely declining his proposal.

On September 8, Reagan again phoned Hoover and was told the director was unavailable. This time, Reagan declined to speak with one of Hoover's aides and said he would call back the next day. In preparation for his call, DeLoach ordered a review of the FBI's records on Reagan.

"Our files do contain numerous references to him chiefly in connection with his anti-communist activities in different Hollywood organizations," the resulting memo said. "He has been contacted on several occasions by Agents of our Los Angeles Office and in every instance has been cooperative and helpful; he in turn has visited our Los Angeles Office, and our relations with him have been cordial." Reagan is "one of Hollywood's most active political figures and considered very conservative by Hollywood standards."

FBI officials, nevertheless, feared a program based on Hoover's already troubled report might further embarrass the bureau about the City Hall debacle. As Tolson diplomatically put it, any errors in the program "would be attributable to us." Hoover concurred, scrawling beneath it "Yes."

When Reagan phoned back at 11:35 a.m. on September 9, he was again told Hoover was out and referred to DeLoach. This time, Reagan acquiesced. He told DeLoach he was disappointed in Hoover's decision that "it would be impossible to cooperate regarding this matter." He said he truly understood the "grave" threat of "communist infiltration of our youth," and wanted to do "an alarmist-type program to awaken the American public to the fact that 'it can happen here.'"

Reagan already had offered to fictionalize parts of the show, changing the location of the protest and the identities of the participants named in Hoover's report. Now, making one last pitch, he said his show would not even mention the report or the FBI in any way. He offered to let bureau officials review the script in advance, and pledged to personally narrate the program, declaring "it was high time somebody presented the true facts as to what the communists are trying to do."

DeLoach replied that the FBI "could not interpose any objection to a public service program which did not mention the name of the FBI or the Director's pamphlet 'Communist Target—Youth.'"

But he warned Reagan to be "very careful not to infer that this program is FBI sponsored." Reagan promised "this would certainly be done."

Part Two

Student Radicals

11

The Police Car

Just before noon on October 1, 1964, Jack Weinberg lugged an old door and a couple of sawhorses onto campus and set up a table in front of Sproul Hall, UC Berkeley's main administration building. Weinberg neatly stacked the literature he meant to distribute for the Congress of Racial Equality, and waited. It was the latest move in a gathering conflict over free speech on campus in which eight students already had been suspended. Soon enough, two officials from the dean's office and a campus policeman walked up and warned him he was violating university rules. Weinberg had graduated with "great distinction" in math the previous year, spent the summer doing civil rights work in Mississippi, and now represented the campus branch of CORE. He refused their order to pack up and leave and declined to identify himself. More campus policemen arrived. They told him he was under arrest and began to take him into custody. Weinberg promptly went limp, using a standard technique of nonviolent civil disobedience that forced them to pick him up. Instead of carrying him to campus police headquarters in the basement of Sproul Hall, however, they hauled him to the white police car they had driven onto the plaza. As they loaded him into the backseat, a voice from the gathering students yelled, "Sit down!" Within minutes, hundreds of students were sitting down around the police car, holding it captive in the center of sun-drenched Sproul Plaza.

As they chanted, "Let him go! Let him go!" FBI agents hidden among the bystanders watched in amazement, snapping photographs and jotting down names for the urgent teletypes they would transmit to Hoover. In all their years of surreptitiously monitoring the campus, they had never seen anything like this. The agents were astonished as the crowd of clean-cut young men and women around the car spread like ripples from a stone cast into a pond, gradually filling the plaza all the way from the student union building on one side to the impassive façade of Sproul Hall on the other.

A tall, gangly young man was the first to mount the car. An officer asked him to get down, and he did. But seconds later, the young man turned to the throng and declared with electricity in his voice, "We're staying right here until this guy is released! We will let the police car through only if he is first released from arrest!" Then he carefully removed his shoes and climbed back on top of the police car. This time the officer did not try to stop him.

The murmuring crowd was riveted by the angular figure that rose above them. He wore dark slacks and a checkered sports coat over a white Oxford shirt open at the neck. He was clean-shaven and his brown hair was cropped to medium length, though his curls were unruly. As he opened his palms and raised his arms, people joined in chanting, "Let him go! Let him go!"

The young man began to speak with a bravado that did not betray the debilitating stutter that had afflicted him much of his life. He mocked university officials for provoking the students by driving a police car onto the plaza. "We were going to hold a rally here at twelve o'clock," he declared. "And we were going to have to shout our lungs out to get people. I'm so grateful to the administration of this wonderful university. They've done it for us. Let's give them a hand."

When the clapping subsided, he chided the officers for arresting Weinberg, suggesting their exercise of authority was just another example of hypocrisy by the older generation. "We must really feel very, very sorry for these poor policemen here, you know. Good men. They're fam-i-ly men, you know. They have a job to do! That's right. They have a job to do."

Someone called out, "Just like Eichmann!"

"Yeah. Very good. It's very, you know, like Adolf Eichmann," said the man on the car roof, picking up on the comment about the Nazi officer. "He had a job to do. He fit into the machinery." People yelled their agreement. A handful of campus policemen, in tan uniforms and soft caps, stood haplessly by the car, surrounded.

With urgency gathering in his voice, he listed the students' demands to Chancellor Edward Strong, who was in charge of the Berkeley campus.

"We will not stop direct action against . . . against the administration of this university unless they accede to the following very simple and reasonable demands.

"Number one: They must immediately, that is, the chancellor—Chancellor Strong, seeing as he's the one who did it—must immediately say that no students have been suspended from the university!"

The crowd cheered.

"Number two," he continued: "Chancellor Strong must agree to meet with representatives of the . . . political organizations to discuss with them reasonable regulations governing freedom of speech on this campus, which means no arbitrary restrictions of any kind on freedom of speech on this campus. He must agree to such a meeting. That's demand number two!" he said.

"Number three: The final demand is—the chancellor must agree that no disciplinary action will be taken against anyone setting up tables or speaking here until, at the very, very least, that meeting is held!

"And I am right now publicly serving a notice of warning, and—I should say—a threat, to this administration, that they, they, they will be subject to continuous direct action by us, and it's going to be damned embarrassing for them. We're going to get foreign press, we're going to get domestic press, we're going to get all sorts of organizations against them until they accede to these legitimate demands . . ."

He explained that another student, acting on his own, was at that moment negotiating with the administration to have the charges dropped against the man in the car. "Let us suppose that does not happen, and there's a good likelihood that it won't," he said, his words quickening as he pointed to Sproul Hall.

"All right, if that does not happen, I propose that everybody at this meeting, or as many as can fit, get into that damn building, get into Dean Towle's office, into Dean Arleigh Williams's office, into the offices, and just sit at the desks, just sit right in the chairs, just sit right on the floor, and make it absolutely impossible for them to conduct their work!"

Someone shouted, "Who are you? Who appointed you?"

The man on the roof of the police car repeated the question so everyone could hear it. Many people there did not know who he was. "All right, all right," he said. "My name is Mario Savio . . . I'm one of the people who have been meeting with the deans here to see if we can have freedom of speech at the University of California."

"Are you a student?" someone asked.

"Yes, I am. A junior in philosophy."

"You *were*," a few people muttered.

Someone else asked, "Mario, how old are you?" He replied, "I'm twenty-one."

"Who was arrested and why? Is he a student?" another voice asked.

Savio explained that Weinberg had refused to identify himself to police because, the day before, students at other tables produced their registration cards for school officials, only to be singled out for citations.

The police radio inside the car crackled and a burst of static drowned him out.

"All right," Savio continued. "Now the question is, Why was he arrested? All right, we can answer that in two ways—at least! The police say he was arrested for, for violation of a trespass ordinance. All right, see?" A few people snickered at Savio's implication that the trespass charge was a pretext.

"I'll tell you why he was arrested, in my opinion," he said. "He happens to be a person . . . who has been quite outspoken in disagreement with what the administration does. Furthermore, the people that they axed the other day"—the students cited for manning the banned card tables—"were likewise people quite outspoken in their disagreement with what the administration does . . ."

The police car radio crackled again, emitting the disembodied voice of an officer: "We've got a man on the roof."

Savio continued, "They happened to pick on those people who are the most outspoken."

To illustrate his point, Savio recounted a parable from Herodotus, the Greek historian, about the best way to take over a city: "'Have you ever seen a wheat field? You see how there are some stalks of wheat that stand up above the others? It's very simple: don't cut them all down; just cut down the ones that stick up the highest. And you've won!' Well," Savio concluded, "that's precisely what they did. They're smart to that extent, at any rate."

A young man interrupted Savio and asked to speak. Savio did not recognize him but promptly ceded the makeshift podium, saying, "We believe in freedom of speech. I don't know what this fellow wants to say, but I'd like to have him say it."

Charles Powell hoisted himself onto the roof of the police car. He was president of the fraternity-dominated student government that campus activists derided as a child's "sandbox government."

Powell introduced himself and made an appeal that failed to inspire the crowd's confidence. He urged the protesters to let him represent them in negotiations with the administration. "I will go to Dean Williams and Dean Towle and ask that this one boy, here, be allowed to go free," he said, referring to Weinberg.

People demanded, What about the other eight students cited the day before? "Just a minute," Powell responded, "I'll get to the others. This one is the immediate problem, all right?"

Weinberg leaned out the car window and yelled, "I'm *not* the immediate problem. We're *all* together."

The crowd cried out in agreement, and Powell pledged that he would seek freedom for all of them. He asked the demonstrators to grant the student government one week to see "what should be done for the interest of the entire student body." They replied with a mixture of applause, laughter, and boos.

Trying to take control, Powell continued, "Now, it seems to me that my demands are reasonable enough, compared with Mario Savio's. Now I ask you . . ." but people yelled "No!"

Powell again asked the crowd to authorize him to negotiate with the administration, but someone bellowed, "Why don't you take Mario? Are you trying to divide the campus?" Powell replied, "Mario will go with me!" The students cheered.

Savio spoke again. "First, uh, there is one thing I want to announce . . . one condition I hope Mr. Powell is willing to consider," he said. "It's fine. I love to talk with people. I really do"—people chuckled at Savio's sarcasm about dealing with campus officials—"and, uh, I'll be glad to go. Well, I'll go with Charlie Powell to see these people. All right, but—I want it understood that until this person in this car is placed, you know, *out* of arrest, nobody will move from here!"

The throng roared its accord, and Savio then climbed down from the roof and went with Powell, leaving the police car in the custody of the students. The campus policemen who had been standing by the car all the while, arms folded across their chests, or hands on their hips, looked on in resignation.

The confrontation on campus had been building since students had returned to UC Berkeley that fall and discovered that school officials had begun enforcing a little-used rule barring their use of university grounds to advocate for off-campus political causes. For years, students of all political persuasions had been setting up tables, collecting contributions, and handing out leaflets for their causes along a 26-by-40-foot strip of red brick along the south entrance to campus at Bancroft Way and Telegraph Avenue. University officials had been operating on the assumption that this was city property and thus not subject to the regents' ban on political activity.

But that summer, students on the Bancroft strip had recruited people to picket the Republican National Convention under way at San Francisco's Cow Palace, where Barry Goldwater, the conservative senator from Arizona, was seeking the nomination to challenge President Lyndon Johnson. Students on the strip had also enlisted people to protest racially biased hiring at Berkeley stores and at the *Oakland Tribune*. And they had advocated against Proposition 14, a ballot measure that would reverse the state's recently enacted law prohibiting discriminatory housing practices, which was known as the Rumford Act for its author, Byron Rumford, the black state assemblyman from Berkeley. Martin Luther King, Jr., had declared the act's repeal would be "one of the most shameful developments in our nation's history." After receiving complaints about such activities on the strip, the dean's office notified student organizations that they could no longer use the area to organize for such nonuniversity causes.

This was a new generation of students, however, the baby boomers born at the dawn of the Cold War. They came of age in an era of increasing affluence, loosening social strictures, and the immediacy of televised images of shocking events such as atomic bomb tests, the assassination of President Kennedy, and civil rights marches. Some students, Savio and Weinberg among them, had spent the summer in southern states, registering black voters in the face of Ku Klux Klan violence. They had returned to Berkeley that fall, only to be told they could no longer exercise basic constitutional rights on their own campus. In contrast to the "silent generation" of the fifties, this generation was willing not only to question authority but to defy it.

Savio and other representatives of nineteen student groups, ranging from the Young Republicans to the Young Socialist Alliance, had formed the United Front, and over the course of two weeks negotiated with campus officials. On September 21, the first day of class, students picketed on the steps of Sproul Hall, and about one hundred joined an all-night vigil. When these efforts failed, some of them set up card tables in defiance of the ban.

On September 30, campus officials cited five students for putting up the prohibited tables, and events rapidly escalated. Many more students signed a "petition of complicity" on pages torn from notebooks, declaring that they, too, had manned the banned tables. That afternoon, Savio led four hundred people into Sproul Hall to present the petitions to the dean, demanding that disciplinary charges be dropped against everyone—or brought against everyone. They sat down in the hallways and remained inside until 3:00 a.m.

Savio and seven other students were indefinitely suspended as a result, but this only strengthened his resolve. When students surrounded the police car the next day, Savio was on its roof, calling for direct action and revealing Promethean powers of oratory that would inspire the nation's first major campus revolt of the 1960s.

Like Kerr as a Swarthmore college student, Savio was concerned with conditions of the poor. Like Reagan as a Eureka College student, he had great appeal to his peers. But more than either Kerr or Reagan at that stage of their lives, Savio bore an overriding sense of morality, troubling questions about authority, and a burning need to act directly against injustice.

Savio represented many of the best qualities of his generation: he was idealistic, hardworking, and brilliant. He also embodied some of his generation's most potent conflicts: the unblinking skepticism of science versus the blind faith of religion; the expectation of equality versus the experience of discrimination; the individual versus the institution; the pressure to conform versus the need to be free.

These and other battles tore at Savio. The force of these struggles, and Savio's unique gifts, would propel him to become one of the most influential and enigmatic student leaders of the sixties.

Mario Robert Savio was born in New York City on December 8, 1942. His birthday was a year and a day after the United States entered World War II. It also was the date of the Feast of the Immaculate Conception, which held special significance for his devoutly Catholic working-class family of strong Italian heritage. He was named for the holy day on which he was born, in honor of Mary.

He was the first Savio in his family to be born in America. Joseph Savio, his father, came from Santa Caterina Villarmosa, a hill town in Sicily, when he was nine years old, arriving at the Port of New York in 1929 aboard the S.S. *Providence*. Dora E. Berretti, Mario's mother, was born in New York City to a deeply religious family who came from northern Italy. Two of her sisters were nuns.

Joseph and Dora settled in a tenement apartment on Manhattan's Lower East Side, a neighborhood that had long served as a portal for immigrants seeking a better life in America. Dora, who had graduated from high school, devoted herself to keeping the family home. She had a saintly quality, loved poetry, and was a charming conversationalist. Joseph, who had quit school after completing the eleventh grade, worked in a metal fabricating factory. A large, balding, barrel-chested man with intense eyes, he exuded virility and confidence. Both Dora and Joseph were Democrats and voted for FDR, whom they saw, Savio would later say, as a "people's president." Although they were not activists, they strongly believed everyone should be treated fairly. When his mother learned that a black coworker was earning a few cents less than she did at the variety store where they worked, she protested to the boss.

Savio was born while his father was serving in the army, in Alaska, and they would not meet for more than two years. Savio's mother, meanwhile, worked at the store to pay the bills and raised Savio with help from her family, including her father, an Italian immigrant and former Fascist functionary who lived with them and was tender toward his grandson. It was a calm and nurturing household. Savio was the couple's only child so far, and his mother doted on him, dressing him like Little Lord Fauntleroy, the hero of a popular late-nineteenth-century children's novel, in velvet suits and lace collars. She spoke as much Italian to him as she did English.

Joseph, meanwhile, decided his would be "an American family." When he returned home after the war, the tranquillity Savio had known was broken. Joseph clashed with Dora over how she dressed their son. He also insisted everyone in the family speak English and "put our Italian past pretty much behind us," Savio would recall, because "that was the only way we were going to make it in America." Joseph had terrifying arguments with Dora's father, who didn't want his descendants to lose their Italian identity. Joseph ultimately prevailed and the Italian language was driven from the household. And though his baptismal certificate and birth certificate recorded his name as Mario Robert Savio, he would be listed in school records as Robert Richard Savio and known to his friends as Bob.

Amid this familial strife, Savio grew fearful of his father. He was afraid Joseph would enter his bedroom at night and kill him, and began to sleep on his back to protect himself. Not long after his father's return from the army, Savio developed a severe stammer. Stuttering may be caused by psychological factors, and Savio's may have resulted partly from his father's overbearing personality or the turmoil in his home. A few years later, when he was seven or eight, Savio was subjected to another traumatic experience at the hands of an elder when he was sexually abused by a teenage uncle, according to people he subsequently told and as first reported in *Freedom's Orator*, a biography of Savio by Robert Cohen. All this may have contributed to Savio's incipient depression.

While Savio was still a child, his family moved to Queens. The easternmost borough of New York City, it was inhabited largely by middle-class families of Jews and Catholics, many of whom had left the city in pursuit of better schools and bigger homes. The Savios lived in a two-story house at 79-22 262nd Street, in the Floral Park neighborhood. By this time his brother, Thomas, had been born. As they grew older, the boys often sat together and enjoyed the wonders of a newly popular technology, television. One of their favorite shows was *Captain Video and His Video Rangers*, which aired from 1949 to 1955 and was television's first science fiction space adventure program. The hero was a genius who traveled through time and space. In each episode he used science to do good, inventing gadgets to capture, but never kill, evildoers. The show featured "Ranger Messages" promoting themes like the Golden Rule. Savio sometimes play-acted the role of Captain Video.

Savio was exceptionally bright and curious. He scored in the 99th percentile on the Iowa Test of Basic Skills, the standard test given students in kindergarten through the eighth grade to evaluate general knowledge of language, math, and science. At the age of nine he decided to become a scientist.

His interest in science was strongly supported by his father, by now a designer and production manager at the foundry. Joseph Savio was adept at making and repairing things, and according to neighborhood myth had installed the first pizza oven on a nuclear submarine. Many evenings at the family dinner table, Savio recalled, he and his father discussed "virtually every field of science." But even as Joseph Savio encouraged Mario, he competed with him and undermined him. When they played cards, his father always had to win. When they worked together on projects, he tended to usurp them. Joseph Savio simply did not know how to relate to his eldest son, and often demeaned him. Once, Savio smashed his brother's train set in frustration over their father's monopolizing it. These interactions deepened his despair.

All the while, Savio's parents cultivated his Catholicism. By all accounts, his religious upbringing was far more rigorous than either Kerr's or Reagan's, and he was more deeply steeped in church doctrine than either of them.

Savio attended parochial school in the first and second grades, but after a nun humiliated him in front of other students, his mother transferred him to a public school. He continued to serve as an altar boy at Our Lady of the Snows Church, in Queens. Each week, the boys knelt at the altar and recited a Latin prayer called the Confiteor. In repeating the priest's phrases they confessed, "I have sinned exceedingly in thought, word, and deed." They beseeched the Virgin Mary and all the saints to intercede with God on their behalf to forgive them. Arthur Gatti, one of the altar boys, recalled that most of them rushed through the prayer so they could be done and gone, but not Savio. "Mario pronounced all the words of the Confiteor lovingly—especially those which meant 'My fault! My fault! My most grievous fault!'" Gatti sensed that these words had profound meaning for Savio, and that despite his youth he believed much was his fault.

As a child, Savio was sure he would enter the seminary and grow up to be Father Bob, intoning Latin incantations, taking confession, and administering absolution. He realized that his mother wanted him to become a priest, a martyr like his aunts in the convent. She wanted him to be like Christ, he would later say; even more, to *be* a second Christ.

He was a true believer. But early on he began to experience inner conflicts between his twin callings of science and religion. When he was about fourteen years old, he imagined a scenario in which advanced beings from another planet visited the earth and began Christianity as an experiment. He immediately felt he had committed blasphemy by having a thought in which science exceeded religion, and confided in a priest. "I felt a lot of shame about it, you know, embarrassment," he recalled. "But basically, I was questioning the historicity, the historical reliability of the Gospels and I made up this story. I said, 'Father, this is really hard for me to say. I'm worried . . .'" The priest told him it was nothing to worry about, but he couldn't stop.

In the mid-fifties, Savio attended Hillside Junior High School in the Bellerose section of Queens. Hillside was a rowdy school, according to Gatti, with student gangs and confrontations between hoodlums and teachers. Savio focused on his studies and in 1956 scored 159 on an I.Q. test, well above the average score of 100 and the starting genius level of 140. Although Gatti, a self-described class clown, hung out with other underachievers, he and Savio became friends. Once a week they were released from school early to walk the eight blocks or so to attend a Catholic discussion group called Confraternity of Church Doctrine.

In September 1957, Savio enrolled at Martin Van Buren High School in Queens Village, a middle-class neighborhood of straight streets and right angles. Recently built to accommodate swelling school rolls, Van Buren was a beige concrete building with high-ceilinged classrooms and large windows. Each day, its five thousand students, almost all of whom were white, followed a regimen replicated throughout the nation's public high schools: they reported to homeroom, sat at alphabetically arranged desks while the teacher took attendance, and recited the Pledge of Allegiance, which included the recently added words "Under God."

Savio quickly became known for being the brightest kid at Van Buren—and for his horrific stammer. Wendy Preuit, a classmate, recalled, "He would stutter, his eyes would roll, and saliva would come out of his mouth. It took him a long time to get his message out." Gatti described it as "stammering, then exploding." Once he got going, his words rushed out. Some kids made fun of him, imitating him, but Savio paid little heed.

Like the young J. Edgar Hoover, Savio struggled to overcome this speech defect. It was especially bad on the rare occasion when he challenged an authority figure. His parents arranged for speech therapy and he participated in activities that required public speaking, such as the school's drama department, where he played a lead role in its production of *Brigadoon*, a play about Americans in Scotland who stumble upon a small town outside of time. Gatti noticed with surprise that his friend did not stutter while performing.

Savio devoted most of his time, however, to his studies. His favorite classes were in science and math, especially calculus, and his grades were substantially higher than either Reagan's or Kerr's. His transcript shows he earned straight As in all subjects, never scoring below 90 and often scoring 98, 99, and 100. Everyone, Gatti recalled, thought he was the next Albert Einstein. "You always got the feeling that he was several steps ahead of you," Preuit said. "He was already onto the next thing."

Although Savio knew he was exceptionally intelligent, he was not arrogant. He volunteered as a tutor and patiently helped other students. A story in the school newspaper, *The Bee Line*, recounted how he had readily loaned a book about Emerson and Thoreau to a fellow student, even though he had forgotten his name and was too embarrassed to ask. The story ended with Savio's apologetic plea to the boy: "If you are still in the school, please return the book and forgive me for forgetting your name."

One month after Savio entered high school, the Soviet Union launched *Sputnik*, heightening fears that the Soviets were gaining technological superiority and might fire nuclear missiles at U.S. cities. Like other high school students around the country, Savio and his classmates wore "dog tags" stamped with their identities and participated in frequent nuclear attack drills. Sometimes a teacher would yell "Take cover" and students scrambled under their desks. Other times, an alarm would send them rushing to line up in the hall and march single file to a corner of the basement designated by a yellow-and-black nuclear fallout sign.

Neither Savio nor anyone else dared to challenge these exercises. Nuclear war seemed a real possibility. Earlier that year, the Atomic Energy Commission detonated the most powerful of the fifty-two atomic weapons it had tested in North America since 1945, a device developed with help from scientists at Berkeley that had four times the power of the bombs dropped on Japan. The blast, at Yucca Flat, in Nevada, released a "great red-orange fireball" and woke people sixty-five miles away, according to a *New York Times* reporter who observed it. These tests sent a message of military strength to the Russians, Savio later remarked, but "the unintended outcome was to terrify the children of the United States."

By now Savio had learned of J. Edgar Hoover's warnings about the Communist threat, and he believed them. "The commies," he recalled, "I knew, were bad." He chose to do a book report on Hoover's recently published *Masters of Deceit*. But his teacher told him, "A book by a policeman is not acceptable." Savio thought his teacher was "terribly intolerant."

Other Cold War lessons were received at home. His economics textbook mentioned Karl Marx's slogan "From each according to his ability, to each according to his need." He asked his father what this meant. As they sat in their backyard garden, Joseph Savio told a story that made clear his view. One day back in Santa Caterina, in Sicily, a Communist organizer came to see his great-grandfather Don Peppino, one of the most respected men in town, to solicit his support. After listening for a while, he asked the Communist, "You believe, then, that all men should share their wealth equally?" "That is exactly our belief, Don Peppino," the man replied. "Well, I would gladly divide my property in half and give you half," Don Peppino said to the Communist's delight. "But let me ask you one thing more. Suppose that after a year's time you have squandered your share. What are we to do then?" The Communist answered, "Oh, in that case we would need to divide the remaining property once again." At that, Don Peppino raised his walking stick and roared, "Off with you then, and be quick about it, before I hit you upside the head!"

Throughout high school, Savio was still deeply involved in his church. He continued to attend Confraternity, spending Friday evenings at the religious education meetings. Afterward, students could go to a discussion or a chaperoned dance (always prefaced by warnings about the sin of sexual attraction). Awkward around girls, Savio opted for the talks, where, Gatti recalled, he asked pointed questions about whether the church was "doing enough to realize the teachings of Jesus Christ."

In his senior year, several classmates urged Savio to run for head of the student association. Despite his stutter, he agreed. As he stood before his fellow students in the auditorium to announce his candidacy, an eternity seemed to pass before he managed to utter, "Hi, my name is Bob Savio." But Savio pressed on with his speech and his campaign. His opponent was one of the school's best-looking boys, Preuit said, but something about Savio appealed to his classmates and he won handily.

That year, Savio entered the Westinghouse Science Talent Search, the nation's oldest and most respected high school science contest. Known as the "junior Nobel Prize," the nationwide competition was founded during World War II and was intended to encourage high school seniors with the greatest potential to become creative scientists. Finalists had gone on to be awarded real Nobel Prizes. Already weary of school and increasingly depressed, Savio was reluctant to take on this additional burden, but the principal and his parents insisted. As Preuit recalled, Savio was a quiet student, and "not at all rebellious."

In his application, Savio said he planned to study physics and math in college, and if he could be doing just what he pleased in ten years he would be conducting "basic research in physics while teaching physics at a college. To help increase fund of basic knowledge [*sic*]." As part of his application, Savio submitted an experiment proving that the Thomas, Thompson, Utterback Table of Sea Water Conductivity—an established method of measuring electrical conductivity at different temperatures—"may contain errors." He stated he was competent at using a gamma-ray spectrometer, a particle-recording scaler, and a Geiger counter. He cited his father as the greatest influence on his decision to become a scientist. Although he reported having no physical defects and disabilities, in response to the question "Are you considered nervous?" he answered yes, explaining, "I speak very quickly."

Recommendations from his teachers emphasized his "scientific attitude." Bob Shupack, his eleventh-grade physics teacher, wrote that Savio had insisted on testing the explanations in his textbooks. "Refusing to accept the non-rigorous demonstration of the Universal Gas law in the college chemistry text," the teacher said in one of several examples, "he demonstrated its proof to the class on the basis of Newtonian Mechanics." Savio, he added, was unusually independent and persistent. As for his stutter, Shupack said, "Bob Savio's principal weakness is his great eagerness to communicate his ideas, with a resulting speech defect." His other defect "is the way he crowds his life by providing a free tutorship service to his struggling fellow students."

Another recommendation came from a physics professor at Manhattan College, the Christian Brothers institution in the Bronx where Savio attended a summer program sponsored by the National Science Foundation. "He is without a doubt one of the most promising young men I have met, an excellent character and warm personality," Brother Leonard wrote. "He was a real leader throughout the entire program and students sought him out for discussions . . ."

Savio told the judges he wanted nothing less than to understand the ultimate nature of the universe. "The reason that I want to make a really basic discovery in physics is that physics deals with problems so materially ultimate in nature: the properties of space and time, the structure of matter and the nature of energy. Thus, the discovery of new phenomenon—in this area much more so than in others—has, in the past, and will, I believe, in the future, radically alter in many respects our very way of thinking." But the application also revealed a nascent conflict between his interest in science and philosophy. "Subjectively speaking," he wrote, "science has always seemed much more fascinating than any other subject I have ever studied with the possible exception of philosophy . . . Objectively speaking, science seems to present one of the most philosophically satisfying methods for really 'finding things out.'"

In February 1960, he was one of 40 finalists selected from 2,900 contest applicants. As part of the program, they gathered without their parents for a five-day conference in Washington, D.C., exhibited their experiments in the rotunda of the National Science Foundation, and met with scientists and members of Congress. Although Savio would later say his project was "silly" and that he felt "fraudulent" because his exhibit had required help from his father, he found some aspects of the experience gratifying. In an evaluation of the program, he said he had enjoyed exchanging ideas with his peers, participating in a roundtable discussion on theology, and above all, "being on one's own and making one's own decisions."

That June, he graduated first in his class of 1,242, with an average grade of 96.6, and gave the valedictory speech. He faltered at first, Wendy Preuit recalled, but then his words flowed smoothly and "he gave a beautiful speech."

Savio told his fellow graduates that they were rightly proud to be Americans, for "God has certainly looked kindly upon us in giving us the freedom and prosperity we enjoy." But there was much evidence that Americans had become overly materialistic and hedonistic, "lacking ideals, vision, and conviction," and he challenged his classmates to restore America to "the land of high ideals that it has been."

"We can do something," he said.

For all his success in school and devotion in church, Savio was internally roiled by mounting questions. He had dived under his desk during the nuclear attack drills at Van Buren, but silently wondered. "I asked myself questions like 'Will it actually do the job?' And I made up these stories. Maybe it is the flash, so maybe the desk could keep me from going blind." He attended church but questioned the Bible stories he had been taught as historical fact. "Not that things couldn't have happened that way, but there seemed to be lots of reasons to think maybe they hadn't." He began to apply scientific skepticism to the world around him, with equally troubling implications. Holocaust photographs were among the empirical evidence that hit him hardest. "Heaps of bodies. Mounds of bodies. Nothing affected my consciousness more than those pictures," he recalled.

Savio was stunned by the realization that so many Germans, and so many other people, had acquiesced to mass murder. "It's like a dark, grotesque secret that people had, that at some time in the recent past people were being incinerated and piled up. I mean, how could it possibly [be]? I started to get the idea that people weren't really coming completely clean about things . . . that there was almost a conspiracy not to tell the truth to oneself, even on a mass scale." The photographs were proof of society's refusal to acknowledge blatant evil and to respond morally, "And that was the thing that started me questioning everything about reality."

While he wrestled with these questions, Savio was also struggling with his relationship to his parents. By now he had decided not to become a priest, and he felt guilt for disappointing his mother. He experienced his father as hostile and dominating, and was sometimes overwhelmed by depression.

But however quietly, Savio was increasingly questioning authority at home, at church, and at school.

In September 1960, Savio enrolled in Manhattan College, where he'd won a full four-year scholarship to study science. He focused on physics but also took courses on ancient history, classical literature, and, increasingly, philosophy. These studies both broadened his perspective and intensified his inner conflict. As he put it, "When I read the philosophers, especially, I think, it was a serious thing for me, because I was trying to do a personally serious thing. That is, I wasn't just cramming for exams. I was trying to find out what it all meant to me, and whether or not I could leave the Church." Although Savio studied hard he experienced great anxiety about taking tests, and at one point thought of quitting school. Still, he completed his first year at Manhattan College in the top 5 percent of his class and made the dean's list.

The following year he transferred to Queens College, where Gatti was a student. Like Savio, he had considered the priesthood but came to question church dogma. The two former altar boys grew closer, confiding in each other as they struggled with their religion and explored beyond ecclesiastic bounds. It was a time of profound change in the Catholic Church, which with Vatican II was reexamining its own relationship to the modern world. Some theologians were asking whether God was dead. In his influential 1961 book, *The Death of God*, Gabriel Vahanian argued that religion was failing to serve the needs of a society that, in turn, had lost touch with the sacred.

Savio withdrew from several classes, and in the spring of 1962 took a leave of absence; as he later put it, "I sort of wandered about for a year." He read, hung out with Gatti, and searched his soul. Savio urged Gatti to read several books that Gatti thought reflected his friend's turmoil over faith and family. One was *San Manuel Bueno, Martir*, a novella by Miguel de Unamuno, the great iconoclast and one of Spain's leading philosophers in the early 1900s. The book tells the story of a priest in a mountain town who endures a hellish inner conflict: he has lost his faith and would step down from the pulpit, but remains because his parishioners would be lost without him. He resolves this crisis by basing his ministry not on dogma but on the duty of love. Two of Unamuno's books had been banned as heresy by the Vatican, which decreed, "Unamuno defies the possibility of rationality showing the existence of God . . ." Unamuno himself said, "My religion is to seek for truth in life and for life in truth, even knowing I shall not find them while I live."

Some nights, Savio and Gatti would go to Greenwich Village to hang out in coffee shops or listen to folk music. They favored the Thirdside Café, at 87 West Third Street, where they heard Tiny Tim play ukulele and sing in falsetto and Phil Ochs, the "singing journalist," perform folk songs about the civil rights struggle, such as "Talking Birmingham Jam." One night, Gatti recalled, Ochs told his audience to keep an ear cocked for a new folksinger named Bob Dylan.

Wandering through Washington Square Park, they would listen to socialist firebrands holding forth from atop the benches, then head back to the living room at Gatti's parents' home in Queens to discuss religion and science and politics until dawn. Savio decried the harmful effects of automation on society. He criticized scientists as not concerned enough with the moral implications of their research. He wondered why Jesus was the son of a virgin if he was a man of the sinners, asking, Wouldn't it have been more appropriate if Jesus was the son of a whore? But Savio was neither doctrinaire nor ideological. As a result of his experience with the church, Gatti said, he was fundamentally geared toward "resisting dogma that denied the inquisitive, condemned the doubter."

Savio was losing his religion. But, even so, he had internalized Catholicism's profound sense of guilt and sin. He had absorbed the altar boy's mantra, "Mea culpa! Mea maxima culpa!" He had taken on, in some way, his mother's desire that he be a second Christ. As Gatti saw it, his friend did not have "your typical Catholic guilt about sexuality and an endless stream of venial or cardinal sins one might commit, but a personal guilt that had to have a reason." Savio's guilt was fed by his voracious curiosity about the world and his unblinking cognizance of inconvenient facts. Acknowledging evil, he felt personal responsibility for allowing evil to exist. He carried a "Christ-like acceptance of the guilt of others," Gatti said. "He took it all in."

Savio bore guilt for the acts of some of his own family members, his friend came to believe. He was ashamed that his cousin, the scientist Vincent Caleca, had worked on the Manhattan Project and helped develop the arming device for the atomic bombs dropped on Hiroshima and Nagasaki. But he felt compassion for the scientist's later anguish over the devastation his research had wrought upon Japanese civilians. Savio's grandfather had been involved in the Italian Fascist Party before immigrating to the United States, and Savio made a dark joke of this by reciting for Gatti the Fascist hymn. This connection, too, was obviously attenuated, but Gatti could see "it was there to gnaw away at him."

Although the two friends had been falling away from religious doctrine, they still were involved with Our Lady of the Snows and were influenced by the liberal movement then emerging within the Catholic Church. Attending a series of talks called the Veritas Lectures, they heard progressive priests and missionaries challenge restrictive church rules and urge young people to do good acts. Among them were Maryknoll missionaries who had lived abroad and worked to improve basic living conditions. Father Daniel Berrigan, who with his brother Philip would later be placed on the FBI's 10 Most Wanted list for destroying draft records, also spoke.

The missionaries' message moved Savio. He had rejected the rules and rituals of his religion, but had taken to heart its fundamental message of resisting evil and doing good. Now he searched for ways to make it real.

In June 1963, Savio, then twenty years old, boarded a bus for a long ride. A few months earlier, he had heard Father Felix McGowan speak at the Newman Club, a Catholic students' group at Queens College. A radical Maryknoll priest, he had reputedly fought alongside Bolivian peasants rebelling against a murderous boss. That day at the Newman Club,

McGowan told how student volunteers had traveled to Mexico to provide basic services to poor peasants. He expressed astonishment that while Americans took modern conveniences for granted, most of the world lived in relative poverty. If these people knew you could push a button on the wall and have the light of the sun pour down at night, if they knew you had a box that would display images of what people were doing thousands of miles away, they would think you lived on the moon. Get off the moon, the missionary cried, and join the world!

Savio and the other Newman Club volunteers climbed off the bus in the state of Guerrero, Mexico, where a priest directed them to Taxco. The mountain town was known for its silver jewelry and for having been a hangout for members of the Lost Generation, the disillusioned young Americans who included F. Scott Fitzgerald, John Dos Passos, and Ernest Hemingway. Taxco was full of well-preserved seventeenth-century architecture and brilliant flowers, but its great beauty only rendered more starkly its squalor and abject poverty.

A local priest boarded Savio and the other volunteers in the abbots' quarters of an old stone convent, then sent them out to see what services were needed. Learning that parts of the town had no running water, they decided to build an aqueduct. They drew up plans, dug trenches, and solicited donations from wealthy townsfolk to buy construction materials.

The mayor of Taxco abruptly halted their project, however, saying it was interfering with his own fund-raising. He promised to instead requisition government supplies for the aqueduct, but never did and the project collapsed. Savio wandered Taxco's dirt streets, giving away his pocket money to begging children, then sent home for more money and gave that away, too.

The town priest had arranged for one of Taxco's wealthy community leaders to provide meals for the volunteers, and every night this patron laid out an opulent spread. Savio was taken aback by the lavish fare and questioned his host: How could he and other people so rich neglect neighbors so poor? How could he be a good Catholic when he did not do all he could to stop such blatant suffering?

The patron replied by quoting Christ: "The Poor ye shall always have with you." Savio countered that he was twisting Jesus' words to justify his own indifference. Christ had meant not that people should accept poverty, Savio insisted, but that there would always be poor people and thus good works to be done by those better off. Savio was outraged at his host's hypocrisy, and soon the volunteers from Queens College were taking their meals in cheap cantinas.

Savio did not give up on helping the poor in Taxco, though. He met a retired local contractor named Ernesto Tapia Florez, who had once ridden with the Mexican revolutionary Emiliano Zapata. Florez and Savio started a new project using student volunteers to build a school. Gatti later took over the project and saw it through.

At the end of the summer, Savio left Taxco and headed to California. His family had recently moved to Los Angeles, where his father had work in a sheet-metal plant. His parents hoped he would attend nearby UCLA, but Savio already had set his sights on Berkeley.

12

The Free Speech Movement

Savio was in a drugstore in New York City one day in 1962 when he chanced to pick up a book called *Student*. The slim paperback, by a UC Berkeley graduate student named David Horowitz, described the beginnings of the campus movement there. "The future of this country will be decided by the courageous students who don't accept the mistakes of their elders, and who seek new solutions to the political problems which, if left unsolved, can in this decade mean the destruction of all life," the back flap declared. Leafing through amid the rows of cosmetics and candy, Savio read how Berkeley students had protested HUAC at San Francisco City Hall; how police had turned fire hoses on them; how the FBI's director had called them Communist dupes; and how the jury had acquitted Robert Meisenbach and vindicated the students.

"I knew something about Berkeley," Savio said, recalling that moment. "I just had a feeling that this was an exciting place to be, on the basis of two things: 1) that book, and therefore that reputation; and 2) the fact that there was by this time politics in the air. The Civil Rights Movement was starting to really dawn on the consciousness of America."

Savio, like many other young people, had experienced the fifties as a state of suspended animation. The Eisenhower years had offered middle-class whites greater affluence and unprecedented opportunities in consumer consumption, but as Savio recalled, "Everything was so rigid. But it was all implicitly codified. It wasn't like what we'd been told they did in Russia. There wasn't an externally imposed regimentation; there was an internally imposed regimentation." There was kind of an official sense that everything was just fine, that "nothing is going on," but in the background was always the threat of nuclear annihilation. The mood was a "strange mixture of boredom and foreboding," he said, adding, "When things feel that way, you wouldn't even mind feeling a little pain."

Savio was too young—the voting age was then twenty-one—to have cast a ballot for John F. Kennedy in November 1960, when he narrowly defeated Vice President Nixon, the former California congressman and HUAC member. But Kennedy had initially impressed him—he was young, fresh, the first Catholic elected president. He appealed to each citizen's idealism, declaring in his inaugural speech, "Ask not what your country can do for you. Ask what you can do for your country."

Savio had hoped for a leader who would mean to him what FDR had meant to his parents, but he was quickly disillusioned. With his interest in science, he closely followed Kennedy's handling of legislation to create Telstar, the world's first active communications satellite system. Congress debated whether the multinational program should be run as a public trust or as a private company for profit. Senator Wayne Morse, the Democrat from Oregon, opposed privatizing the system, calling it a giveaway to corporations. Savio thought Morse was right, and that if Kennedy were a real people's president he would back him, but he didn't. "Right with that," Savio said, "I realized that Kennedy was more flash than substance."

For Savio, the façade of the fifties was finally ripped away by the civil rights movement. At first a distant rumbling in the South, the movement had gained momentum as he was growing up. In 1954, the U.S. Supreme Court outlawed segregated public schools, prompting local integration actions across the country. In 1955, Rosa Parks refused to sit in the back of a bus in Montgomery, Alabama, and a year later the high court prohibited segregation in public transportation. In 1957, Governor Orval Faubus of Arkansas defiantly barred nine black students from a white public school in Little Rock, and President Eisenhower sent federal troops to escort them in. In 1960, black students in Greensboro, North Carolina, sat down at a segregated lunch counter at Woolworth's, inspiring similar actions.

In Queens, Savio had been impressed by the dignified manner in which blacks picketed the local Woolworth's. "I'd never seen anything like it before," he said. "So just the idea of people walking around in a little oval in front of the Woolworth's was sort of massively nonconformist for the time." It was a clear sign that "something's going on here." He was struck, too, by the televised images of Bull Connor, commissioner of public safety in Birmingham, Alabama, turning fire hoses and police dogs on peaceful black civil rights demonstrators in May 1963. Even more affecting was the marchers persevering and "holding one another against the fire hoses." As he later said, "That was so real, and what you'd been raised on was so unreal, that it was very attractive."

The black struggle affirmed Savio's sense that beneath the gleam of consumer culture there were real problems and that people could do something about them. "The Civil Rights Movement, it wasn't flash," he said later. "It wasn't a fantasy land. Kennedy was, I think, a mixed phenomenon, okay? But that's it. At crucial places, he failed to connect with reality somehow. He wasn't leading. The Civil Rights Movement was leading America."

For all of these reasons, Berkeley beckoned to Savio. "It was clear from the fact that Berkeley had been sort of at the center of the anti-HUAC demonstrations that that would be a place where you could go and become involved in that sort of thing," he said. "I just had a feeling, a good feeling, about the place, that somehow real things were going on there."

Savio arrived at Berkeley in fall 1963, moving into a boardinghouse on Hearst Avenue, the long, shady street north of campus where Robert Meisenbach had lived. The sophomore's first days were less than idyllic. His roommate was a Goldwater conservative with whom he got along "as long as we didn't discuss anything important." The building was full of raucous undergraduates who were constantly playing pranks and starting water balloon fights.

Alienated, Savio focused on his studies. At college back east, he had concentrated on science, taking a few philosophy courses as a means of examining his religious concerns. Now he set science aside altogether and declared his major as philosophy. For though he had severed his formal relationship with the church, he still was struggling with his faith. "I had to finally make the decision," he said. "Am I Catholic or not?"

The dry logic of analytical philosophy ruled the university lecture halls, but the urgency of existentialism claimed the smoky coffeehouses along Telegraph Avenue. Savio studied both branches of philosophy as he searched for his own way to think and act morally in the world. Among the existentialists, he would later say, the French novelist Albert Camus was "a serious contender for sainthood." Camus's 1942 novel *The Stranger* was in wide circulation on college campuses. The book's main character, Meursault, is alienated from his work, his girlfriend, even his own impending execution. Reading the novel was a powerful experience for Savio, who saw in Meursault's dilemma a description of his own experience of the fifties.

Savio also read two British philosophers: G. E. Moore, who espoused rigorous, commonsense analysis of philosophical problems, and J. L. Austin, who argued that speech itself was a form of action. Through his study of analytical philosophy Savio came to further question church doctrine and the justness of contemporary society. Through his study of existentialism he found an alternate system of belief—the idea that, with or without religion, individuals can make decisions and take actions that give their lives meaning. And in the campus's civil rights movement, he found the means to act on these convictions and fulfill his essential need to do good in the world.

A small number of students had started working with local branches of national civil rights organizations. The Congress of Racial Equality had organized the 1961 Freedom Rides, in which integrated groups traveled by bus through the South, defying local customs of segregated facilities. The Student Non-Violent Coordinating Committee also had been in the forefront of protests against Jim Crow laws in the South. CORE and SNCC adapted Gandhian principles of nonviolent civil disobedience to their protests. The month before Savio arrived at Berkeley these groups had joined in the March on Washington, where 250,000 people heard Martin Luther King, Jr., declare, "I have a dream."

Soon Savio began showing up at meetings of the University Friends of SNCC. He handed out leaflets on campus for SLATE, the student group that had helped organize the protest against HUAC at San Francisco City Hall. He undertook his first "direct action," picketing against Mel's Drive-In, the popular burger restaurant co-owned by Harold Dobbs, the Republican candidate for San Francisco mayor. Organized by the Ad Hoc Committee to End Discrimination, it was one of several demonstrations that fall against Bay Area firms for discriminatory hiring, and it quickly won concessions. News of these protests shared the pages of local newspapers with reports of President Kennedy's assassination that November.

Despite his increasing activism, Savio managed to get some good grades in his first semester—straight As in his three philosophy courses and a B in English. But he had been failing Elementary German and sought permission to withdraw from it. Reviewing his request, one of the deans made a confidential note suggesting Savio was having psychological problems: he was stammering and seeing a counselor at the campus's Cowell Hospital. He also had a "pattern of drops and withdrawals" that began at Queens College. Expressing concern for Savio's future and wariness about another withdrawal, he wrote, "I don't think w/d is best solution for him, though of course I should allow it if Cowell so recommends. This student's trouble is his inability to finish written assignments, though his mid-term record seems to belie this. He will become increasingly incapable of finishing anything, I think, if we aid and abet him not to finish this semester's program of studies." Savio's request to withdraw from German was denied and he received an F—the first time he had failed.

In his second semester, which started in January 1964, Savio switched his major to zoology, a move back to science that he now reasoned would better position him should he decide to attend medical school. He took a lighter load—just four courses, and only one in philosophy. But he became more and more involved in the campus's burgeoning civil rights movement, finding it irresistible for several reasons. The movement, he later said, was "the most interesting thing that one *ever* read about in the newspapers . . . the most unsullied thing, certainly . . ." It presented a clear battle between good and evil, and fit his need to fulfill a religious mission without the dogma. "This was an example of God working in the world," he said. "Allying myself in whatever way I could with that movement was an alternative to the Church . . ." The students involved in it were kindred spirits. Above all, it offered a way "to be an actor in one's own life."

Volunteering to tutor black children in reading and math, he worked closely with several children but became frustrated. Savio sensed he wasn't "preparing them for anything at all. When they'd leave the session and go back to school, whatever curiosity had been excited would just as quickly be quashed." He concluded, "It was a finger in the dike operation . . . It had the effect of convincing me personally that other, more political means of attacking the problem were what was called for . . ."

When CORE launched nightly pickets of shops in downtown Berkeley, the conservative business district just west of campus, Savio joined in. As part of this so-called Shattuck Avenue Project, CORE gave proprietors of integrated shops black-and-white placards to put in their windows. Merchants opposing the protests, meanwhile, put red, white, and blue placards in theirs.

Savio abstained, however, when other students joined CORE's "shop-in" at the Lucky's supermarket south of campus on Telegraph Avenue. After filling their carts with groceries, going through the checkout line, and being rung up, they refused to pay and walked out, leaving the clerks to restock everything and slowing the line. The idea was to interrupt business and generate negative publicity to force the management to hire more black employees, and it worked. "It just seemed a little messy," Savio said. "It seemed to lack some of the self-restraint and dignity which, at that time anyway, I hadn't completely accepted as being at least partially separated from direct actions."

•

Savio was walking by the entrance to the campus at Bancroft Way and Telegraph Avenue one day in the winter of 1964 when someone handed him a flyer for a sit-in at San Francisco's Sheraton Palace Hotel. Originally built in 1875, the Beaux-Arts hotel was one of the city's finest, and the demonstration promised to be one of the Bay Area's biggest yet. Activists had been energized by their victory over Lucky's, and the movement had acquired what Savio only half-jokingly called "moral cachet" on campus. Besides, a girl he knew was going and he wanted to impress her. Savio had met Cheryl Stevenson in a philosophy class. She, too, had broken with the Catholic Church, and she would become his girlfriend.

On March 6, Savio, Stevenson, and several other students climbed into a VW microbus, drove across the Bay Bridge, and were soon among several hundred people in the hotel's grand lobby, locking arms, holding hands, and chanting "We Shall Overcome" and "Jim Crow Must Go." An irate hotel guest leaned over a balcony and yelled, "You go back to Russia!" Savio replied, "I don't come from Russia." She said, "Well, just go back to where you belong, go back to Russia. You're a Communist!"

The twenty-two-hour sit-in stretched into the next morning and ended only after Mayor John Shelley negotiated an agreement with the hotel own-ers' association to hire more blacks in visible jobs and with equal pay at thirty-five hotels. Nearly three hundred people had been arrested for mis-demeanor trespassing. Police led Savio away just after noon. It was his first arrest.

Soon after, an FBI agent stopped by the San Francisco Police Depart-ment's intelligence unit to pick up a list of the arrestees and their photo-graphs for the bureau's dossiers. The agent's collection of misdemeanor arrest data was part of Hoover's investigation into the alleged Communist infiltration of civil rights groups. These investigations—code-named COMINFIL—ostensibly focused on Communist Party efforts to penetrate domestic groups and undermine American institutions. However, "in prac-tice the target often became the domestic groups themselves," according to the 1976 report of the U.S. Senate Select Committee to Study Govern-mental Operations with Respect to Intelligence Activities, known as the Church committee after its chairman, Senator Frank Church of Idaho. By 1964 the bureau had opened more than 441,000 "subversion" files on indi-viduals and organizations, according to the committee, and the bureau's continuing investigation of the civil rights movement would add "massive reports . . . on lawful political activity and law-abiding Americans."

Savio's part at the Sheraton Palace resulted in the first entry about him in FBI records. It would lead to encounters with both Hoover's agents and the Ku Klux Klan.

"Are you going to Mississippi?"

Savio was in San Francisco County jail following his arrest at the hotel when a cellmate asked the question. He meant Mississippi Freedom Summer, the daring and brilliant project conceived by Robert Moses, SNCC's key organizer in Mississippi. It aimed to bring hundreds of white northern students south to help register black voters who had been historically denied suffrage.

Savio liked the idea. He had been radicalized by the Sheraton Palace protest—as he would later say of getting arrested in the early sixties, "This was a big thing." He explained, "It was proving that you really were committed, that it wasn't just a matter of words." He was bonding with the movement—"People held one another. People embraced one another, sang together. It was a community." He had found this missing in school, in his own family, and he wanted to be part of it.

As a result of his increasing involvement in civil rights work, however, Savio's grades had suffered further. His second semester ended with a B in philosophy, Cs in German and physical education, and a failure to complete General Chemistry. It was painful for him. Meeting with dean's officials, he explained what he'd been doing and declared his intention to withdraw from school. Only at the last minute did he change his mind and decide to return for the fall semester.

But first he would go to Mississippi. The summer project offered not only the chance to fight discrimination, but a way for him to reaffirm his faith through action. Both the church and academics had left him wanting. "I was really on a 'doubt all things' trip in part fed by analytic philosophy," Savio recalled. "I wanted to come into contact with some reality. I had to go to Mississippi."

That June, he and two other people from Berkeley drove to SNCC's training base at the Western College for Women in Oxford, Ohio. The volunteers would soon be living in some of the South's poorest areas, in communal "Freedom Houses." And since they would be facing potential violence from police and Klansmen, they were instructed on what to do if attacked. The risks were palpable. While still at the training base, they learned that three civil rights workers—Andrew Goodman, Michael Schwerner, and James Chaney—had gone missing in Mississippi. Their disappearance gave Savio pause, but he decided to proceed and was among those volunteering for one of the most dangerous assignments.

Like Kerr on his Peace Caravans and Reagan on tour for General Electric, Savio was embarking on a demanding journey into new parts of the country to spread passionate views about freedom and democracy. In the course of their journeys, each man would gain new insights about himself and America that would shape his life and pull him inexorably toward a collision with the others. But though Savio's mission was the seemingly simple function of registering people to vote, it posed far greater risks than did either Kerr's trips promoting world peace and disarmament or Reagan's corporate excursions advancing free-market capitalism and anticommunism. Unlike Reagan and Kerr on their journeys, Savio would be challenging potentially murderous local residents in hostile territory.

Savio moved into the Freedom House in Mileston, a community of independent black farmers in Holmes County, about eighty miles from the state capital of Jackson. It was one of the less violent parts of one of the most violent states. Mississippi's deeply entrenched segregationist attitudes were made explicit in a February 1955 editorial in the Jackson *Clarion-Ledger*, the state capital's main newspaper, the year after the U.S. Supreme Court's *Brown v. Board of Education* decision: "Any white man who wants to preach integration in the South, or elsewhere in the nation, is an enemy of his own people and his own voice should be silenced . . . Call this bigotry, intolerance, or anything you please, but nobody has a right to undermine the foundations of our government." Mississippi was where, the following August, fourteen-year-old Emmett Till was tortured and murdered for allegedly flirting with a white woman at a grocery store. Savio would be astounded to learn that in Mississippi, even a house for the blind had separate entrances for whites and blacks.

Savio and the other volunteers shared the old abandoned farmhouse, with its outhouse and backyard water pump. He began to chronicle his Mississippi experiences in letters to his girlfriend back in Berkeley, Cheryl Stevenson, whom he called Cheri. The letters reveal not only his role in the fight for freedom but also his internal conflicts, and evince a mixture of hope and fear.

"It's wonderful, and I know you feel it too, to be part of such a change for good that's sweeping across our country," he wrote on July 3, just as his stint in the South was beginning. "I really believe that the history of the world is pivoting on the internal changes that are going on today in America—and we are in part the agents of that change. A breath of freedom." Savio also noted that "five Negroes" had reportedly been killed in

Amite County, in the particularly dangerous southwest part of the state where he had volunteered to work.

On a hot Sunday morning two days later, Savio sat beneath a tree outside the Freedom House and wrote to Stevenson about the latest threat. "The bomb never materialized," he noted. "And paranoia was a bit less intense than the first night spent here when we posted watches and crawled about on hands and knees to keep from standing or walking before a window." In a painful digression, Savio revealed the existential dilemma and bent for abstract thought that had partly driven him to Mississippi in search of reality. "A while ago a cow was eating grass through a fence that faces me along the right hand side of the Freedom House. As it (she!) pulled her head through the fence a loose piece of barbed wire caught on her neck. As the cow tried to disengage itself I thought of the different ways in which this could be described: in terms of sense-data; in terms of certain chemical processes; in terms of biologically determined stimulus and response—the pavlovian [*sic*] machine; or as an attempt, in the presence of frustration, of a rudimentary consciousness to deal with its environment. The poor beast seemed almost human, for after the first three explanations have been proposed, do we really understand. And then I thought—just what constitutes understanding an event? and oh how quickly it is gone—nothing lasts long enough to be understood, let alone enjoyed."

But he was becoming more involved in his work with the Council of Federated Organizations (COFO), the coalition of civil rights groups that organized the summer project. "I'm ever more feeling this is a personal fight," he wrote Stevenson on July 7, as he prepared for the perils of Amite County. "By the time I'm ready to go to the southwest, I'll feel the full personal commitment that I've desired to feel from the start." Savio had written "decided," then crossed it out and wrote "desired," adding parenthetically, "notice the significant slip: 'decided' for 'desired'!"

Savio was looking for inner freedom even as he helped others fight for their rights in the world. One day, while he and other volunteers were canvassing the homes of blacks in the town of Tchula, a deputy sheriff and members of the White Citizens' Council, which opposed desegregation, drove back and forth, blatantly trying to intimidate them. "The people at once clammed up for fear of being identified as 'uppity' Negroes," he wrote Stevenson. "These people are deathly afraid of losing their jobs. The only Negroes really active are the independent farmers who don't depend on whites' good pleasure for their livelihood." But there were encouraging moments, too. "Yesterday I spoke w/ one man who said he had been 'uplifted' by our visit," he added. "He gladly welcomed the coming freedom, and would work to hasten it. I too was 'uplifted.'"

It was a summer full of "reality." One night a strange car approached the Freedom House without giving the proper signal, and the volunteers ran through the dark woods, hearts pounding, to the homes of friendly neighbors. "We subsequently discovered that all the farms around us are armed to the teeth," he wrote. "Holmes County—as comparatively safe as it may appear—is the peaceful exterior of a dangerously live volcano. If it were not so very well known that the Negro farmers are not non-violent, I seriously doubt that a non-violent student movement would be possible in Holmes."

Hartman Turnbow, an independent black farmer and grandson of a slave, led the civil rights movement in Mileston. "Last year Mr. Turnbow's house was fired into," Savio wrote. "He fired back—he's a very fine shot! A white man was quietly buried shortly thereafter without incident and without identification, so I understand. Then they bombed Turnbow's house, setting it afire. He rebuilt it and became even stronger in the movement . . . It is men like Turnbow, and there are many in Holmes County, whose courage protects the non-violent movement . . . By contrast, the town dwellers are, as the saying goes, scared shitless. They depend for their livlihood [sic] upon employment by whites . . . Alas, these town dwellers sometimes turn us away before we can even get in the door. They have been warned by the whites not even to speak to the 'northern agitators.'"

Savio worked hard to convince people to register. As he recalled, "We'd go in teams of two, and I talked oftentimes," he recalled. "Knock, knock—person comes to the door: 'What do *you* want, sir?' It's always 'sir.' So, 'May I speak to the head of the family?' And there always was one, it was always either the father or the grandfather. (I'd) explain we're here to organize people to go down to the courthouse to vote. 'I don't want to vote.' They were afraid, obviously. Didn't want to lose his job or worse. And I got to say the following line. I couldn't believe it; I'd say,

"'Did your father vote?'

"'No sir.'

"'Did your grandfather vote?'

"'No sir.'

"'Do you want your children to vote?'

"That's all. I don't know where I got the nerve to say such a thing," Savio recalled. "I mean it was almost an effrontery to ask those questions. But I asked them."

No one said no to this approach, he added, for despite their fears, "people wanted to be on that freedom train."

Even then, they still had to face the local registrar of voters, typically a hostile white official. By law, the volunteers could observe, but not participate, in the actual registering. Savio recalled, "I brought somebody to register to vote. The guy was about sixty, seventy years old. There's the sheriff's wife behind the counter. Doffs his hat and he just stands there. Silent. She goes about her business. Finally, finally, she comes over: 'What do you want, boy?' Head down. 'Wanna reddish.' 'Boy, what do you want?' 'Wanna reddish.' 'Reddish, what's that, boy?' Here—he's obviously older than she is. He's worked all his life—such silence, such dignity, such composure. And this went on for a long time . . . Finally, she throws the thing at him, and now he has to interpret a section of the Mississippi constitution in order to qualify as a registered voter."

Savio and Robert Osman, a fellow civil rights worker, finished eating a late lunch at the Farish Street Baptist Church in Jackson. They had stopped en route from Mileston to McComb, a city in Pike County, in southwest Mississippi. Savio was to spend the rest of the summer there, instead of in Amite County, for his supervisors had decided going there would be "suicidal." It was about 3:40 p.m., on July 22, and they were walking through downtown Jackson to the COFO office on Lynch Street. With them was a local civil rights worker named John Foster, a black man whom they had met at the church. Savio was wearing a "One Man/One Vote" button. As they reached the corner of Amite and Gallatin streets, a gray 1950s Chevrolet sedan pulled up ahead of them. Two white men with cudgels got out. As Savio later recalled, "The clubs were dark wood, and appeared to be regular police billy clubs."

As the men approached, Savio saw that they were about thirty years old, thin, and wearing worn clothes. Savio and his companions ran. Foster escaped. One assailant struck Savio a glancing blow on his left shoulder. Savio darted into the middle of the intersection, turning to see one of the men trap Osman in a lot full of high grass. Following his nonviolent training, Osman dropped to the ground and covered his head. The man stood over him, swinging his club. Passersby approached and the thin white men with dark clubs climbed back into their Chevy. As they sped off, Savio sprinted after them and got the number from the light-blue-and-white Mississippi license plate.

Returning to help Osman, Savio found him badly hurt and unable to rise. Savio dashed into the nearby McKesson and Robbins Building, where employees let him use a phone to call the COFO office and the police, and Osman joined him shortly. The office workers were friendly, but when police officers arrived they told Savio and Osman they were not wanted there. Savio began to explain they were waiting for a callback from the COFO office, but the officers demanded they come along. Osman asked where they were being taken and one of them said, "Down to the station." Asked what for, an officer replied, "We'll decide when we get there." Only when Savio pointedly inquired whether they were being arrested did the officers acknowledge that they were not in custody.

Savio began to tell them about the attack on Foster, but one officer interjected, "We don't call them Negroes here—we call them niggers." On the way to the station, he cracked, "When was the last time you guys took a bath?" Arriving, the officers made a point of preceding Savio and Osman up the stairs, one of them saying, "White people first." He then suggested they "go on back where you came from and stop causing all this trouble here. Don't you have enough up there?" Another officer warned, "You'll get in a lot more trouble before you leave Mississippi." Savio feared they were about to finish the job their attackers had started. It was harrowing, but before leaving the station the civil rights workers managed to file a complaint about the assault.

Later that day, the assistant chief of the Jackson Police Department briefed local FBI agents about their complaint. The agents sent a teletype to bureau headquarters reporting that they would not be investigating the attack. This inaction was standard FBI procedure. For years, Hoover had been averse to investigating civil rights cases. He portrayed the civil rights movement as manipulated by Communists. Earlier that year, he had charged in congressional testimony that "the party is continually searching for new avenues in order to expand its influence among the Negroes." According to William C. Sullivan, one of Hoover's top aides before they had a falling out, "Hoover wasn't in favor of civil rights."

Had Savio and his colleagues been attacked several months earlier, the matter likely would have ended there. But just twenty days before the assault, President Johnson had signed the Civil Rights Act into law and called on all Americans to help "eliminate the last vestiges of injustice in America." He publicly urged Hoover to investigate civil rights violations. As a result, the director opened a permanent FBI field office in downtown Jackson, at the First Federal Building, and on July 10 appeared there with

Clyde Tolson for a press conference inaugurating it. Still, Hoover sought to soothe concerns that the federal government would impinge on local jurisdiction. He praised the state's low crime rate and downplayed the significance of the new FBI office as a minor administrative matter. When a reporter asked about the Mississippi Freedom Summer project, Hoover replied that the bureau "most certainly does not and will not give protection to civil rights workers." The director quickly repaired to Washington and the violence continued: as a headline in the Jackson *Clarion-Ledger* reported, "Hoover Leaves State/Negro Church Burned."

When officials at FBI headquarters received the teletype from the Jackson agents about the assault on Savio and his colleagues, they ordered local agents to "vigorously" investigate the attack. Two agents promptly interviewed Savio and Osman at the bureau's new Jackson office. Savio was troubled by his interaction with them, and later wrote Stevenson, "The next day we spent arguing with the FBI, who refused to accept in our signed statement anything concerning the harassment by the police, but who insisted on including the willingness of the police to take Rob to a hospital. Damned red-baiting bastards. I don't care who reads this—and, believe me, there is a good chance some one else will before you get it, Cheri. The FBI establishes a new office in Jackson and then releases its figures—unexplained—'proving' that Mississippi has the lowest crime rate of any state. Murder of Negroes isn't a crime here. And what about crimes committed by the law itself."

Not long before Savio arrived, the Freedom House in McComb had been bombed, and now a floral tapestry hung over the blown-out window in the room where the volunteers slept. It was located in a particularly poor black neighborhood, in a state whose poverty struck Savio as being every bit as dismal as what he had seen in Taxco. Still, the house was more modern than the one in Mileston, with hot and cold running water and an indoor flush toilet.

Early one morning, when Savio was on security duty at the Freedom House, he wrote to Stevenson, frequently putting down his pen to peer outside for the source of suspicious sounds. He described his hopes for the Mississippi Freedom Democratic Party, which was organized with help from SNCC to challenge the official, whites-only state Democratic organization. He believed the Republicans had turned their backs on civil rights and that the Democrats might, too. The day before, Johnson and Goldwater had agreed to avoid arousing "racial tension" during the campaign, and Savio feared that some Democrats might not push for reforms. But he had faith in Governor Edmund G. "Pat" Brown of California, who he thought would back the Freedom Party's efforts at the Democratic National Convention in Atlanta that August. "He's a key man and very friendly to our cause," Savio wrote.

As Savio finished the letter, his clock showed it was 4:40 a.m. He had a profound realization. "Mississippi was an abstraction to me before. And I could only think of what some abstract 'one' should do—namely go to Mississippi to fight—nonviolently—for freedom. But Mississippi is no longer abstract," he wrote. "The fight is mine."

At the end of the summer, Savio returned to Jackson to help law-enforcement officials identify the men who had assaulted him and his fellow civil rights workers. FBI agents had traced the license plate number of the assailants' car to the suspects and turned the case over to local prosecutors. Savio was boarded in the home of a well-to-do white couple, the Hubbards, who were sympathetic to the civil rights movement. "I reveal my weakness by writing," he wrote Stevenson. "I'm reasonably safe from myself as long as I keep busy. But this week has been one of steadily increasing loneliness . . . Most of my time has been spent in the deathly silence of this air conditioned house. I've spent so much time waiting around because there was real difficulty in observing the suspects. No arrests were made till just today. I easily picked one of the men out of a line-up this morning."

As he had in the fifties at his family home, Savio felt oppressed, guilty, and bored. "I feel returning all these fears, the feelings I've had as a member of a family in which I always felt under foot, in my father's way. I feel the same dominance and hostility of Mr. Hubbard. Mrs. Hubbard seemed hurt when I tried to arrange to spend this last night somewhere else, so I'm staying here. I almost never feel that I'm really one of the people in a room. I don't know how I affect others, nor do I regularly feel that I do—a crushing impotence."

In court a few days later, a local judge found Paul Sistrunk, a twenty-nine-year-old Klansman with prior arrests for public intoxication and assault, guilty of attacking the three civil rights workers. Savio was disgusted that Sistrunk's sentence was only thirty days in jail and a hundred-dollar fine. The *Clarion-Ledger's* headline reflected the lack of seriousness accorded the assault: "Man Found Guilty for 'Beatings.'"

The antipathy of local residents toward civil rights volunteers such as Savio also was expressed that week by one of the *Clarion-Ledger's* columnists, who complained about "those mixtures" who had been "invading" their state. The columnist frankly declared he was looking forward to their departure when the summer project ended on August 24. A news story in the same edition reported that Governor Paul Johnson had told a cheering crowd of five thousand people at the Neshoba County Fair that neither Mississippians nor their elected leaders had any obligation to enforce civil rights laws. "Segregation is the best way to peace and harmony between the races," he assured them.

Adding insult to injury, Sistrunk immediately appealed his conviction and was allowed to dispose of the entire matter by pleading guilty to simple assault and paying a fifty-dollar fine. Although FBI agents had identified a second suspect, they could not obtain sufficient evidence against him and he refused to speak with them. "He said he did not like talking to Agents of the Federal Bureau of Investigation because they are part of the Federal government which is trying to take over Mississippi," according to their report.

Still, the special agent in charge of the new Jackson office recommended that two agents be "commended for their excellent performance in this case." They had won a relatively rare conviction in the generally hostile Mississippi courts—but Hoover's aides didn't want to call attention to the bureau's role. "This does not seem desirable," one of them wrote in a memo. "I certainly agree," said another.

The violence that summer in Mississippi had been intense: at least sixty-seven black churches, businesses, and homes were bombed or burned; eighty blacks and whites were beaten by white supremacists and police; and more than a thousand volunteers were arrested. On August 4, FBI agents found the bodies of Chaney, Goodman, and Schwerner, forty-four days after they had disappeared. They had been shot and buried in an earthen dam. Chaney had been tortured before he was killed.

In the face of this brutality, the Freedom Summer project was an undeniable success. Volunteers had helped 17,000 blacks register to vote, and though only 1,600 of these applications were accepted by white county registrars, the effort helped build national support for the passage of the Voting Rights Act of 1965. They also established forty-one Freedom Schools, which introduced black students to equal education. Overall, the project promoted reform, publicized the cause, and inspired hundreds of white student volunteers who carried their commitment home to communities across the country.

Savio was asked to continue as a staff organizer in Mississippi but decided to return to Berkeley, where he had pressing matters to attend to.

He needed to find a part-time job fast; he was so broke his father had borrowed against his life insurance policy to pay his school registration fees. He intended to take Stevenson's advice and see a psychiatrist to "explore at great length" the inner conflicts that had been rending him; he told her he wanted to understand his ambiguous motivations and "aberrations" and find "wholeness." He was determined to save his imperiled academic career; the university had placed him on probation for failing to maintain the required grades. Though still unsure about which courses he'd take, he told Stevenson, "I think I shall try to prepare myself for some kind of public service, perhaps, even—tho I doubt it—politics. If there's one lesson to be learned in Mississippi, it's that there is a crying need for honest men in the service of the common good."

On July 22, 1964—the day Savio was assaulted by a Klansman in Jackson, Mississippi—Berkeley's Vice Chancellor Alex Sherriffs called a meeting with his subordinates to discuss three growing problems on campus: bicycle riding, bongo playing, and political advocacy on the Bancroft strip. Sherriffs was agitated. An *Oakland Tribune* reporter named Carl Irving had phoned the university press office, asking whether the tables and easels on the Bancroft strip were violating university rules against using the campus to engage in advocacy about off-campus issues. Looking into it, Richard Hafner, the university press officer, discovered the strip was indeed university property, even though campus officials had been operating on the basis that it was city property and city officials had been issuing permits to the students to use it. This meant activities on the strip were indeed in violation of the rules. This was a situation, Sherriffs declared, from which "we could no longer turn our heads."

Sherriffs was a forty-six-year-old psychology professor who had gone through some radical changes of his own. The son of the superintendent of schools of Santa Clara County, he had graduated from Stanford and briefly attended law school there before shifting to psychology, which he taught at Berkeley. He had signed the loyalty oath, but only with a statement of disapproval. He was a self-described liberal Democrat who had "rabidly" supported Adlai Stevenson for president and decried Joe McCarthy as "the biggest menace at that time that I'd ever known." In 1953, when Sherriffs ran for a seat on the Berkeley school board, conservatives called him a "pinko" because he had answered yes to two questions: Should fraternities and sororities be banned from the high school campus? Should Paul Robeson, the singer and avowed supporter of communism, have been allowed to perform at the high school auditorium? Sherriffs said the Greek organizations gave members a false sense of superiority and injured students they excluded. As to Robeson, he said, "In a democratic society, one should be able to hear anybody." But when he lost the election, he complained that people were afraid of communism and bitterly blamed Robeson for "raising suspicion and hatred" that contributed to his defeat.

On campus, Sherriffs became popular for teaching a "gut" psychology course that drew upwards of five hundred students to each class, and after Kerr became chancellor he named Sherriffs special liaison to the student body. He helped Kerr handle overly rowdy behavior at football games and beer blasts known as "suds at sunrise," and became chummy with members of the fraternities and sororities that dominated the student government and social life. But when Kerr became president, he did not ask Sherriffs to join his new staff. Sherriffs felt rejected and complained, but to no avail. He instead became vice chancellor for student affairs, overseeing policies on student activities at the Berkeley campus.

Sherriffs believed students were too apathetic, and he spoke with dismay about "the silent generation." He defined apathy as "not saying what you believed, if you're not sure of what the others believed, and looking to find out what the others believed before you joined them even if you didn't believe it." He blamed student apathy on overly permissive parents under the sway of Dr. Benjamin Spock, author of bestselling books on child-rearing. "This was the first generation," Sherriffs said, "who had been raised by parents in any society where the parents didn't have confidence that their feelings and their instincts or their reflex responses to their kid's behavior were appropriate. It was the era of Spock, the era of looking it up in a book." With such vacillating parents, how could students not be fearful of taking positions?

Although he decried student apathy, the vice chancellor was not happy about the activists in SLATE, the student political group that had challenged fraternity members in student elections, protested HUAC, and complained about restrictions on campus political activities that he enforced. Increasingly uneasy with their rebellious attitude, Sherriffs eventually contacted the FBI about them. Agents Donald Jones and John Hood secretly met with him at his office on March 10, 1961.

After expressing his "high personal regard" for the FBI, the psychologist presented his rather disturbing diagnosis of the Berkeley student body. He estimated that 90 percent of students on campus never spoke up, but said that since the May 1960 protest against HUAC at San Francisco City

Hall "there seems to be a rising tide among a small percentage of students of a resentment toward the government and the FBI." Which brought him to SLATE. This group, he said, was comprised of well-educated graduate students who were nothing but "office seekers and publicity hounds." Their followers were "misfits, malcontents and other politically oriented individuals who do not conform to the normal political activity in the university community."

Moreover, SLATE members had helped organize other campus groups, such as the Fair Play for Cuba Committee and the Student Civil Liberties Union. Sherriffs said he was worried because he had no way of telling whether these groups had Communist Party support. He feared that Communists might try to dominate campus groups. And if they did, "it would be very unfortunate if the majority of the student body were placed in a position where they are afraid to speak out for fear of attracting the disfavor of other students."

By law, the university could not easily deny official recognition to student groups, but Sherriffs assured the agents he believed "recognition should be denied to any organization which may have as its motive, open or secret, the discrediting of the university, the Federal Government or any other well established American ideals." Sherriffs promised to "cooperate in every way with the FBI," and vowed to "maintain the strictest of confidence in this relationship." He even agreed to not tell Kerr about this meeting, unless he first checked with Agent Jones.

To Sherriffs's further perturbation, SLATE continued to provoke controversy. Later that month, the group sponsored a campus talk by Frank Wilkinson, a Los Angeles political activist who had refused to testify before HUAC and had been sentenced to a year in prison for contempt of Congress. Assemblyman Don Mulford, the Republican whose district included the campus, demanded that Kerr cancel the speech. Kerr refused, saying the speech was permitted under the school's open forum rules. "The University is not engaged in making ideas safe for students," he said in a press statement. "It is engaged in making students safe for ideas."

Kerr's stand infuriated Regent Ed Pauley, a staunch anti-Communist, and Hugh Burns, the president of the state senate and head of the state un-American activities committee. Both were already upset with Kerr's liberalized policies, and in January 1962, they tried to get him fired. Burns claimed he had obtained a report, based on CIA intelligence, saying Kerr was acting as a Communist Party courier in Latin America. Burns told Pauley, who demanded a meeting with Kerr. In response, Kerr dispatched his trusted colleague Sherriffs to CIA headquarters in Langley, Virginia, to see Richard Bissell, the agency's deputy director in charge of covert operations, who nine months earlier had overseen the agency's failed Bay of Pigs invasion of Cuba. Bissell was a former MIT professor, and Kerr would later say he knew him "slightly." Kerr had, in fact, been friendly with the CIA. He knew that some professors had been confidentially interviewed by CIA officials about their observations during travels abroad. And on "one or two occasions" he had been interviewed "by some federal guy" about his observations of the foreign trade union movement after his tours—"What did I think of worldwide trends, how things were developing. But that was always at the high level of general policy and never in terms of reporting on any individuals and what they might have said." It was a proper function of the CIA and the State Department, Kerr told the author, adding, "I never considered myself to be part of the CIA mechanism." This was still several years before revelations about the CIA's secret involvement with American universities raised questions about academic integrity and sparked protests at Berkeley and other campuses.

Bissell gave Sherriffs a letter in which he said that according to CIA records there was no truth to Burns's charge—and in fact one component of the spy agency had been cleared to seek Kerr's cooperation on a classified matter. When Pauley, Burns, and Richard Combs confronted Kerr with the Communist courier allegation during a meeting at the Bohemian Club in San Francisco, Kerr explained that his travels had been for an educational conference. To their great surprise, he then reached into his briefcase and produced the letter. They dropped the matter. Sherriffs, however, had secretly made a copy and later gave it to Agent Don Jones of the FBI.

In the fall of 1964, Sherriffs's concern about campus activists reached new heights. SLATE published an influential student evaluation of courses that reported, "Mr. Sherriffs is rated entertaining, fun, not terribly challenging, and not at all profound. He freely wholesales his personal opinions on events of the day, both on and off campus. If you like this course, do not major in psych." This was personal criticism, but what really upset Sherriffs was a letter SLATE published calling for an "open, fierce and thoroughgoing rebellion" on the campus. The September 10, 1964, screed urged students to "organize and split this campus wide open!" It suggested they take their demands to the regents, and, if denied, "start a program of agitation, petitioning, rallies, etc., in which the final resort will be CIVIL DISOBEDIENCE." The *San Francisco Examiner*, however, reported that the letter inspired "yawns and mild laughter and little else."

Sherriffs was provoked. "It is deceitful, slanderous, and incredibly hostile toward you, and it takes on the Regents by name, and the whole University of California," he wrote Kerr a few days later. Convinced that subversives were plotting against the administration, Sherriffs searched his office for hidden microphones. "He thought somebody had posted stuff at his office so they could get all of the information they wanted from him," recalled Associate Dean of Students Arleigh Williams. "He was worried about the Communists taking over."

While Kerr was traveling in the Far East that fall, Sherriffs took action. With Chancellor Strong's concurrence, he directed Dean of Students Katherine Towle to end student political advocacy on the Bancroft strip. Towle, who had been a colonel in the U.S. Marine Corps, did not agree with this precipitous action. She believed the activities there were harmless, and served as a "safety valve" letting students say whatever they wanted so long as it complied with constitutional law. At the least, she thought, the student organizations should have been consulted first. Nonetheless, she followed orders and notified them that henceforth the ban would be strictly enforced.

Savio was outraged. As the new chairman of the University Friends of SNCC, one of the groups that had been advocating on the strip, he saw the ban not only as a denial of his First Amendment rights but as an attack on the civil rights movement itself. Only weeks before, he'd been in Mississippi, urging blacks to risk their lives by registering to vote. Now he asked himself whether he could let this stand. "Am I a Judas? I'm going to betray the people whom I endangered now that I'm back home?"

Kerr, who had returned from his trip the day after Sherriffs's edict was issued, was surprised that Savio and other students were so upset. After all, Kerr believed he had done much to open the campus to free speech: He had defended the professors who refused to sign the loyalty oath. He had revised Sproul's restrictive Rule 17 to permit political candidates to speak on campus, instead of from podiums set up across the street. He had permitted student groups to invite controversial figures such as anti-HUAC activist Frank Wilkinson to speak on campus. He had refused to punish students for participating in protests off campus. He had even convinced the regents to lift the ban on Communist speakers. Just that spring, these efforts had won Kerr an academic freedom award from the American Association of University Professors. "The blunt fact," he later wrote, "is that I had led the basic 'free speech movement' prior to 1964 . . ."

Kerr was also astonished that Sherriffs had essentially abolished the university's Sather Gate tradition. To be sure, Kerr agreed wholeheartedly with the university's long-standing ban on students using the campus to advocate for off-campus political action. In a speech that May, he had affirmed this policy: He had said that the university would not punish students arrested at the Sheraton Palace protest because they were acting as citizens, but noted at the same time, "The university will not allow students or others connected with it to use it to further their nonuniversity political or social or religious causes." The ban on campus advocacy dated to the early days of Robert Gordon Sproul's presidency, and Kerr thought it had served the school well. Keeping the university out of external politics, he believed, would keep politicians—like Hugh Burns—out of the university. That would protect the university's academic freedom. Moreover, free *speech*, as Kerr defined it, did not mean free *advocacy*. He believed that with his liberalized policies and the ban on advocacy, the campus could have robust debate and be protected from outside political pressures.

But Kerr also believed students needed a place to engage in political advocacy. Sather Gate's bronze arch, which bore the university motto, "Fiat Lux" ("Let There Be Light"), had marked the old south entrance to the university for decades. Since students were barred from engaging in political activity on campus, the city property right outside the gate had become the area where they customarily championed their causes. When the campus was expanded farther south to Bancroft and Telegraph in 1959, that area became university property off limits to activism. To preserve the Sather Gate tradition Kerr proposed, and the regents voted, to transfer the strip of land right outside the campus's new south entrance at Bancroft and Telegraph to the city, giving students a new place to speechify at will. Kerr had assumed this transfer occurred. Now he learned that it never was completed, and that Sherriffs had cracked down on the card tables there.

Kerr considered Sherriffs's action a "huge mistake." He also was disturbed that it was done while he was away and presented as a "fait accompli." As a result, the university president took the rare action of telling Chancellor Strong, to whom Sherriffs reported, that he should rescind the order. But Strong vehemently rejected Kerr's suggestion, and since the university had been decentralized and Strong was the head of the Berkeley campus, Kerr chose not to override him. Kerr would later say that he should have declared the ban null and void, or urged the regents to change the university policy on advocacy. He was president of the university, after all, and the ban was his policy. But these were unpleasant tasks, and Kerr did not follow his father's advice of long ago "to do the unpleasant thing at once and have it off your mind. Delay only makes it harder to do. For your own sake, <u>Do it</u>."

During the next two weeks, Kerr failed to take decisive action. The conflict mushroomed and now hundreds of students were surrounding a police car in the middle of Sproul Plaza.

Mario Savio and Charles Powell returned to the police car from their meeting with Strong at about 1:45 p.m., only to report that the chancellor had refused to discuss the ban until the demonstrators relinquished the car. The protest continued with new vigor.

Students took turns mounting the car roof and holding forth. Some argued that capturing the car was illegal, and therefore an inappropriate tactic. But all agreed that the university's ban on political activity was wrong. In between speeches, Barbara Dane and other local folksingers led the crowd in civil rights songs. Weinberg relaxed in the backseat, still in custody.

Declaring that Strong had rebuffed them, Savio urged the crowd to escalate the action by "taking our request back to the deans." One hundred and fifty students followed him into Sproul Hall, where they sat in outside the office of the dean of students, blocking the hallway. At the end of the day, office workers had to exit through a window.

Just past 6:00 p.m., campus police began to lock the doors to Sproul Hall. One hundred students outside the building charged the doorways and jammed them with their bodies to keep them open. In the struggle, officers trampled on several students and a girl screamed. Students pulled one officer to the floor and removed his boots, and Savio bit his leg. "He was stepping on us," he later said. At 9:00 p.m., the protesters left the building and rejoined the throng surrounding the police car.

By 11:00 p.m., a large number of fraternity men had gathered a few blocks away at Channing Circle, where the great panty raid of 1956 had begun. The "Freddies" marched to Sproul Plaza and encircled the protesters. They flicked lighted cigarettes into the crowd and demanded the car's release. One Freddie scuffled with a man speaking atop the car, which now had flat tires and a "No on 14" sticker on the bumper. Weinberg was still inside the car. The protesters chanted, "We want freedom!"

The night wore on and the debate continued from the police-car-turned-podium. A fire truck roared up and some students thought they would be hosed away. Savio began to discuss the reasons for the demonstration. People he could not see heckled him and threw eggs at him.

"Look," Savio said, "the only reason that I took part in this is that I like Cal very much. I'd like to see it better. I'm not here to destroy something! We're all here to *build* something. Why don't you help us?" Someone yelled, "Get off the car and we'll listen!"

Savio continued, telling how Thoreau had committed civil disobedience against what he thought was an unjust war. Savio asked, "Do you agree that there are times when questions of conscience exceed questions of law?" Another object whizzed by him in the dark.

As he led the crowd in "We Shall Overcome," the Freddies began to sing the theme from a children's television show, spelling out "M-I-C-K-E-Y M-O-U-S-E!" An egg splattered a policeman. At the edge of the crowd, people kicked the backs of the sitting protesters.

A man pushed his way through the throng and climbed onto the car. It was Father Fisher of Newman Hall, a Catholic campus group. The plaza grew still as he spoke: "John Kennedy once asked, 'Do not ask what your country can do for you, but what you can do for your country.' And what you can do for your countrymen is respect their differences without bloodshed."

His appeal drew lengthy applause. But no sooner had he dismounted the car than tensions flared and violence seemed imminent.

University officials, however, remained unyielding. That night, Strong issued a statement declaring, "Freedom of speech by students on campus is not the issue. The issue is one presented by deliberate violations of University rules and regulations by some students . . ."

Governor Brown, whom Savio had thought a friend of civil rights, made similar remarks. "I and President Kerr and the Regents have long fought to maintain freedom of speech," he said. "This is purely and simply an attempt on the part of the students to use the campuses of the University unlawfully by soliciting funds and recruiting students for off-campus activities. This will not be tolerated. We must have—and will continue to have—law and order on our campuses."

Kerr was worried. That Saturday was Family Day. He did not want this tableau, a symbol of the breakdown of law and order, to greet the thousands of parents due on campus for the annual open house in less than thirty-six hours.

Before retiring for the night he consulted with Sherriffs. They agreed campus officials should try to retrieve the car sometime around 4:00 a.m., when fewer people would be present. Existing records do not provide details of this plan, though it was presumably intended to minimize chances of a violent confrontation, or at least media coverage of one. Kerr had asked Brown to authorize the National Guard to help remove the demonstrators, but Brown said no because he feared bloodshed, and local police did not proceed on their own. When Kerr awoke on Friday morning, he was surprised to find the protest still going strong.

He spent much of that Friday at a conference on education in San Francisco where he delivered the keynote speech. Returning to campus in the afternoon, he learned that police chiefs from around the Bay Area had devised their own plan. Officers would advance on the plaza at 6:00 p.m. If the demonstrators failed to comply with Chancellor Strong's order to disperse, police would remove them and reclaim the car. Although aides to Kerr and Governor Brown attended the meeting, Kerr would later claim he was not consulted about this plan in advance.

Kerr was distraught. It was bad enough that officers had driven a police car into the middle of the plaza, something Kerr had never seen before. Now armed officers were streaming toward the university, an institution that was supposed to be based on reason. As a Quaker, he believed force should be the last resort. As a labor arbitrator, he recalled, "I had known how a stray shot or the thrust of a bayonet could set off a riot . . ."

By late afternoon, some five hundred police officers had marched onto campus, filling Barrow Lane behind Sproul Hall. They wore helmets and carried billy clubs. The number of protesters and onlookers on the plaza had grown to more than seven thousand. Some of them were strumming guitars and singing more civil rights songs.

As the deadline neared, Kerr received two phone calls he would later describe as "decisive." The first came from Governor Brown, who said he did not want another Alabama or Mississippi in California, ordered Kerr to step in and prevent that, and hung up.

The second call came from a group of professors who also anticipated violence. Their leader, a history and economics professor named Henry Rosovsky, told Kerr they had drafted a proposed settlement between the administration and the protesters. Rosovsky would later say he had never heard Kerr so depressed. Kerr had told him he feared "all his work over the years was going down the drain."

At 5:00 p.m., Kerr called a meeting with student representatives in a last effort to avoid a violent clash.

Savio and several other student rebels rushed across campus to University Hall. Taking the elevator to the seventh floor, the sans-culottes entered the president's office. It commanded a panoramic view of the campus and, at

its center, the Campanile clock tower. The rebels were shown to an adjoining conference room. With Savio were representatives of student groups,
including the Young Democrats, the Young Republicans, and SLATE.

Savio and Kerr regarded each other from across the room. Savio had
spent the night on the plaza and slept little. He was six feet one, 195 pounds,
and angry. Kerr, compact, bald, mild of mien, in wire-rimmed glasses and
a suit, seemed relaxed. The former labor arbitrator handed the students a
copy of a proposed agreement. Savio and the others read it and swiftly rejected it.

Savio did much of the talking and, he would later acknowledge, was
"quite impolite." A key clause would have required the students to end the
police car protest and abide by the law in any future protest of university
rules. The students were loath to make this promise, which would bar their
future use of civil disobedience, one of their strongest tactics. "If that
stays," Savio told Kerr, "I won't sign it." But Kerr rejected the students'
proposed wording. They finally agreed on a clause stating the students
would "desist from all forms of their illegal protest against University regulations." The students believed this meant only that they would end the
police car protest—not that they agreed to refrain from any future actions.

Another clause would let students distribute "information" on campus, but not "advocacy." Savio questioned Kerr about this distinction.
Would a poster urging students to attend a meeting in Oakland where
Hubert Humphrey was to speak be allowed? Yes, said Kerr. Would a poster
urging students to engage in a lawful picket outside the *Oakland Tribune*
be allowed? No, said Kerr. If both were legal action, Savio asked, why did
the university allow one and not the other? Kerr did not answer.

A third clause called for establishment of a committee composed of
students, professors, and administrators to review rules concerning political activity on campus.

As the clock ticked, the students argued among themselves. Every few
minutes, Kerr's secretary entered the room and warned that large numbers of police were on campus and she did not know how long they could
be held back.

Savio still balked at signing the agreement. He pointed out that it did
not resolve the dispute and provided only for further negotiations. They
should insist that the ban be lifted before they released the police car, he
argued.

Jackie Goldberg of the Young Democrats, however, feared the riot
squad was getting restless. "I have never known terror as I did that night,

sitting in that room trying to negotiate," she recalled. She urged the rebels to sign the agreement, and they finally did.

Kerr signed, too, but when he passed the paper to Strong the chancellor glanced at it, shook his head, and handed it back. Sherriffs also was disgusted. He felt Kerr should not have negotiated with lawbreakers. Kerr, he thought, should have told them, "Let the police car go and we'll talk; while you're around that police car, to hell with you." Instead, he had acted like an arbitrator who had no vested interest in the outcome. He had capitulated, Sherriffs believed, to students, terrorists really, who had done nothing less than hold hostage a police car for "the first time since the civil war."

With the agreement in hand, Savio and the other students rushed back across the campus to Sproul Plaza, their bodies casting long shadows in the twilight. At 7:30 p.m., he mounted the police car for the last time. He seemed to be near tears as he announced what became known as the Pact of October 2, and explained how the negotiators had arrived at each point. In doing so, he established himself as the protest's foremost spokesman. Finally, he said, "Let us agree by acclamation to accept this document. I ask you to rise quietly and with dignity and go home."

Thirty-two hours after the protest began, the students rose and departed, leaving the car with its now crushed roof and deflated tires in the middle of Sproul Plaza.

In the ensuing weeks, the students would organize themselves as the Free Speech Movement and stage ever-larger protests. And though the FSM would use nonviolent civil disobedience tactics borrowed from Mahatma Gandhi by way of the civil rights movement, the protests would shock Americans accustomed to campus conformity and make news around the world.

The FSM's growing protests would also create a crisis for Kerr—and jolt J. Edgar Hoover into action.

13

A Leak to the Press

In Washington, Hoover reviewed the reports and photographs that his agents had taken on campus. He was not pleased.

First came the university's essay question about the FBI in 1959. Then Berkeley students joined in the 1960 protest against HUAC at San Francisco City Hall and upended his report "Communist Target—Youth." Now they had captured a police car.

Hoover ordered agents around the country to investigate whether the free speech protests were part of a subversive plot.

The San Francisco field office took the lead. In the years since the City Hall protest, the office had moved two blocks to the new federal building at 450 Golden Gate Avenue, where it occupied the entire sixth floor. The special agent in charge of the new office was Curtis O. Lynum, a former gymnast and an agile administrator who'd been involved in internal security cases from the start of his career. Months after he joined the bureau in 1941 the Japanese attacked Pearl Harbor, and he helped arrest enemy aliens in Newport News, Virginia. He moved up the chain of command and was special agent in charge of the Dallas, Texas, field office when the CIA alerted the FBI that Lee Harvey Oswald had arrived there from Russia. Following standard procedure, one of Lynum's agents interviewed Oswald, but this routine matter was not brought to Lynum's attention until after Kennedy was assassinated. By then, Lynum had become head of the San Francisco office.

Like other field offices, San Francisco had a large, open "bull pen" where dozens of agents, all men, worked at gray metal desks arranged on a linoleum floor under harsh fluorescent lights. In a separate room, stenographers, all women, typed the agents' reports and transcribed their confidential interviews with informers. Supervisory agents had small offices with windows on the bull pen. Lynum had a separate suite with wood paneling, carpet, and windows overlooking the city.

In the mid-sixties the San Francisco FBI office had 300 agents, with 208 in the city and the rest in smaller offices around Northern California known as resident agencies. The agents were organized by squads that reflected Hoover's priorities. By far the largest number of agents was assigned to investigating suspected subversives, with two full squads devoted to such security cases, a total of 43 agents, or nearly 15 percent of the manpower. The squad tracking draft dodgers had 27 agents, another squad investigating espionage cases had 25 agents, and the general crimes squad had 23 agents.

Burney Threadgill, Jr., was assigned to one of the security squads. A native of Biloxi, Mississippi, he had attended public schools, where a classmate was Byron De La Beckwith, who in 1963 would assassinate the civil rights leader Medgar Evers in Mississippi. Like many agents, Threadgill had a military background. He graduated from Mississippi State University and served as a sergeant in the army's 326th Glider Infantry in Central Europe during World War II, receiving a Purple Heart. He worked briefly for the U.S. State Department before joining the FBI in 1947 and being assigned successively to the Chicago, Springfield, Seattle, and Anchorage field offices. Based in Alaska from 1950 to 1952, Threadgill worked on the FBI's "stay-behind" program, a secret Cold War operation in which agents recruited longtime local residents, or "sourdoughs," outfitted them with special FBI radios, and arranged for them to stay behind in the event the Russians invaded, so they could clandestinely report on them. At that time, he recalled, many Alaskans feared the Soviets would march from Siberia across the ice-filled Bering Strait. Threadgill received high performance reviews and in 1952 was transferred to San Francisco, where, he recalled, Hoover's men were well regarded and felt welcomed.

Like all FBI agents, those in the San Francisco field office were subject to Hoover's strict rules and the relentless administrative processes designed to enforce them. Reporting for work each morning, they removed a card with their name on it from a central rack, the resulting empty slot showing at a glance that they were in. When stepping out, they noted their destination on the card and replaced it. Agents signed for files on the individuals and organizations they were investigating, and before leaving the office returned them to clerks in wooden work trays so they could be locked up. At the end of each day, they filed a report on their activities, making notations such as "in the office for two hours dictation," "contacted so and so," and so on. The flow of paper was staggering and agents who failed to keep up were reprimanded.

The men complied with a dress code enforced as much through fear of Hoover's personal disapproval as through any written rule. They wore dark, conservative suits, white shirts, ties, and spit-polished shoes, their hair cut short and their faces closely shaved. They were subject to annual physicals and strict weight limits, though some of them complained that Hoover seemed well over the limit. "We were all taking pills to try to repress our appetite, to trim down," Threadgill recalled.

The main agents on the Free Speech Movement case were based at the FBI's small resident agency on an upper floor of the American Trust Company Building, on Shattuck Avenue in downtown Berkeley. The bureau opened this office in 1957, assigning five agents to it, including Threadgill, who found Berkeley to be a "real nice suburb." It was still run by Republicans and was de facto segregated, with more-affluent whites living around campus and in the hills and the small black population living mostly in the flats. Threadgill could still take the Key Line electric train that ran along the bottom level of the Bay Bridge into San Francisco. He and other agents sometimes played racquetball in the university's gym, and then strolled past the neat rows of shops along Telegraph Avenue and had lunch at Larry Blake's, a restaurant with sawdust on the floor and garlicky Caesar salads.

The bureau already had a larger resident agency in downtown Oakland, less than fifteen minutes away. But by the late fifties, Hoover's aides were coming to view Berkeley as the most radical city in America, with one of the highest numbers of people on the Security Index per capita. Threadgill and other security agents were kept busy meeting bureau rules that required close tracking of everyone on the index in their territory. They deployed a range of investigative techniques. A common one was the pretext phone call to gather information without revealing the FBI's interest. Threadgill was expert at this, with convincing timing and tone of voice. He sometimes posed as a postal service employee seeking forwarding information, and other times as a radical seeking a comrade's whereabouts. Informers, of course, were crucial. Each agent was under constant pressure from Hoover to maintain a minimum of two Potential Security Informants, people usually paid to provide information about "subversives" who could be developed into full-fledged informers, deep inside political groups. A panel truck outfitted with a telephoto camera was used to cover political meetings at homes and halls. "We'd park the truck close-by and try to photograph everybody going in," Threadgill said. The agents would later consult with informers to identify people in the photos and then discreetly approach them, display their photo, and try to convince them to cooperate or, failing that, to inhibit their political activity.

Among the Security Index subjects were students, professors, union members, and longtime radicals such as the lawyer Robert Treuhaft and his wife, the writer Jessica Mitford, who had become famous as the author of *The American Way of Death*, a 1963 exposé of the funeral industry. Decca, as she was known to friends, came from a politically eccentric aristocratic British family; one sister married the leader of Britain's Fascists, another became a disciple of Hitler. Mitford became a Communist. In 1947, she and Treuhaft moved to a racially integrated neighborhood in Oakland and became active in the local branch of the Communist Party. Treuhaft formed a law firm to represent unions, activists, and unpopular causes. Mitford dedicated herself to protesting racial discrimination. She would later say the party was then "the only game in town in terms of civil rights." But like many others, she and Treuhaft quit after Khrushchev's 1956 revelations of Stalin's mass executions of Soviet citizens deemed a threat to the state.

By then, Mitford and Treuhaft had become defiant targets of the Burns committee and HUAC and subjects of intense FBI scrutiny. One evening in the fifties, Threadgill and another agent named Harold Hoblit were assigned to monitor a meeting at the Treuhafts' home. They sneaked into the crawl space beneath the house to eavesdrop on Mitford and her visitors, but as the meeting wore on, Threadgill fell asleep and began to snore loudly. In a panic, Hoblit rousted him and they crept away.

Threadgill and the other security agents in Berkeley also received a stream of information from electronic surveillance. William Turner was an FBI agent who specialized in operating phone taps and bugs in Oakland and San Francisco during the early fifties. Working out of a small, unmarked office in downtown Oakland, he monitored conversations of local leftists. Years later, after he had left the bureau and become a critic of Hoover, Turner found himself at a cocktail party where he heard a mellifluous British voice that sounded oddly familiar. As Turner approached the speaker, he realized he had spent hours tapping her telephone; he even knew her favorite toothpaste (Ipana). When he explained how he had recognized her voice, Mitford, characteristically, burst into laughter.

The FBI agents relied on these intelligence methods to update their files on Security Index subjects so they could be readily rounded up in the event of a national emergency. They also used the information to disrupt their lives—sometimes with unintended consequences. In the mid-fifties, for example, a pair of agents visited the *San Francisco Chronicle*, where Mitford had begun working in the classified advertising department. After they informed her boss that she was under investigation as a suspected Communist, she was fired. Finding herself at age thirty-eight with little professional experience, no formal education, and a secure spot on a government blacklist, Mitford concluded she had no choice but to become an author, and eventually went on to famously rankle the establishment. "I figured that the only thing that requires no education and no skills," she later joked, "is writing."

By all accounts, the most ardent agent assigned to the Berkeley resident agency was Donald Edwin Jones. He was six feet tall and slightly pudgy and had established himself as the senior security agent there. After serving in the army during the war, he worked as a high school teacher and radio announcer for a fundamentalist Christian organization before joining the FBI in 1951. Jones avidly investigated those whom he suspected were godless Communists and other subversives, and even by FBI standards, Threadgill recalled, he was "gung ho." All the while, Jones remained deeply involved in evangelical activities, receiving Hoover's permission to appear on television as part of the Billy Graham Crusade, identifying himself as an FBI agent and discussing his personal faith in Jesus. Jones pressed his fellow agents to become more religious. "He was very outspoken and very dogmatic," Threadgill said.

Many nights, Jones surreptitiously entered homes and offices to rifle desks, photograph documents, and plant telephone taps and microphones. Although FBI agents informally called these illegal entries "black bag jobs," they described them in official reports euphemistically. As a supervisor put it in his performance review, Jones had "taken a leading role in the development of and contact of highly confidential sources." He "conducted numerous early-morning and late-evening surveillances in order that the sources could be contacted with the complete security necessary." Jones and other agents involved in these operations received letters of commendation from Hoover. "Dear Mr. Jones," the director wrote on one occasion. "Because of the very valuable services you rendered in the development of several highly confidential sources of information pertaining to the internal security of the United States, I have approved for you a cash award of $150.00."

Jones's main investigative targets were people involved with the campus. As his supervisor noted, he handled "delicate assignments in and about the University of California" with "excellent results." He developed confidential sources, including Security Officer William Wadman and Vice Chancellor Alex Sherriffs. Like these university officials, Jones viewed Kerr as overly permissive. Kerr happened to be the brand name of wide-mouth jam jars, and Jones once remarked sarcastically to other agents that the university president was good only for canning fruits and vegetables.

The FBI's investigation of the Free Speech Movement quickly expanded, as Jones and his colleagues collected information not only about Savio and other FSM leaders but about the students' family members, faculty supporters, and a CBS newsman who reported on the protests. Agents even scrutinized the lyrics to an extended-play album of Free Speech Movement Christmas carols titled *Joy to UC.*

FBI officials assigned a "100" classification to the FSM investigation, indicating that they viewed the protest as a potential threat to internal security. It was the same classification they gave the bureau's investigations of alleged Communist infiltration of the civil rights movement. Hoover still was operating on the secret authorization that FDR had given him twenty-five years earlier when the nation was on the brink of war. Truman, Eisenhower, and Kennedy had hardly altered the directive, which Hoover continued to cite as the basis for his investigations of "subversive activities." Nor had any president defined this term, leaving the determination of its meaning and application up to Hoover. He, of course, took the broad view and demanded that his subordinates did, too. The Church committee later found that Hoover exaggerated Communist influence in these cases and his aides then "instituted massive investigative efforts to find every possible bit of evidence of Communist links in order to substantiate the Director's preconception."

On October 20, 1964, Curtis Lynum sent Hoover a confidential fifty-five-page report that emphasized the presence of allegedly subversive influences in the Free Speech Movement. Based mainly on the work of Agent Jones, the report focused on four FSM leaders. It noted that Mario Savio had been involved in the Mississippi Freedom Summer project and was arrested at the Sheraton Palace civil rights protest; that Art Goldberg, the chairman of SLATE, had attended a meeting of the W.E.B. Du Bois Club, a self-described Marxist youth group widely believed to be a Communist Party front; and that Jackie Goldberg, his sister, was a member of the Young Democrats who in 1963 had visited Russia and Romania, where she allegedly attended a conference at the invitation of the Young Communist Movement.

Jones's report made particular note of Bettina Aptheker, the daughter of the Communist Party theoretician Herbert Aptheker and herself a member of the Communist Party. According to Jones, she mounted the police car roof several times, gave speeches encouraging the protest, and led the crowd in song. Most alarmingly, she was "observed many times in close conversation" with demonstration leaders, including Savio.

The report also described the political backgrounds of other people around Sproul Plaza the day the police car was captured: A university employee "standing in the crowd watching the demonstration" had been in the Communist Party "sometime between 1948 and 1956." A man "observed standing in the crowd" had contributed money to a left-wing school in 1947. Another man "observed standing at edge of crowd" had been a delegate to a convention of the Communist Party in 1957. Also "standing in the crowd" was a "well-known San Francisco Bay Area news commentator who has the reputation of . . . opposition to U.S. Government policies."

All told, the report named thirty-eight suspicious people as "present and/or participating in the demonstration," each personally identified by Jones, who was himself present during nearly the entire police car protest.

Hoover circulated this report to army, navy, and air force intelligence agencies, the Secret Service, and the U.S. Department of Justice, but not the detachable administrative pages that contained additional sensitive information for internal FBI use only. These pages focused on Clark Kerr and disagreements within the university administration over his handling of the police car protest. Vice Chancellor Sherriffs and Chancellor Strong had told the FBI they were "very disappointed" with Kerr. Sherriffs had added that police were "displeased with the fact that the University of California backed down and negotiated with demonstration leaders."

The students had been galvanized by their capture of the police car. It was as if they had stepped through the looking glass and emerged in a new world of their own.

Margo Adler, a freshman, later wrote: "Like many students, I wandered over to Sproul Plaza for the noon rally and arrived just after the arrest took place . . . It seemed easy and appropriate to sit down on the ground with the other students. I felt almost no fear, perhaps because the police car, usually such a powerful symbol of authority, seemed tiny and helpless in the face of our growing numbers . . . I felt a sense of exhilaration . . .

But there were moments of fear and terror as we wondered what action the authorities would take. Most of the protesters had never participated in any political demonstration before. Many cried or laughed, or were uncertain what to do . . . There was a feeling of instant community and internal power."

Bettina Aptheker, a junior, would later say her knees shook as she mounted the car and made a speech in which she quoted the abolitionist Frederick Douglass: "Power concedes nothing without a demand." The crowd cheered and she felt "suddenly grounded, strong, uplifted, and so moved I thought I would weep." The siege "marked a critical moment in my life . . . I had a sense of belonging to something, being on the inside of a community of my own making, on my own terms."

For Savio, the protest reverberated with the meaning of his work in Mississippi. "I don't know who first sat down," he recalled. "People just sat down. Then, the people being there, it was like protecting one another against the police dogs and the hoses. If you left, then they could get away with the car. If they get away with the car, they get away with murder. So just being there, helping to hold this car, just by sitting there, lying there, sleeping there (it was thirty-two hours)—that was part of the movement.

"A community was born around the car," he said, "with a real sense of all for one, and one for all. We learned that. In other words, the spirit of America after all was and increasingly for many people is again every man for himself, you know? That's not what the spirit was around that car. That's not what the spirit was in the civil rights movement, or that term at Berkeley."

On the weekend after they released the police car, Savio and other students met in Art Goldberg's apartment near campus to form an organization. They considered several names for it. Someone proposed Students for Civil Liberties, the name of a campus group that had protested HUAC at San Francisco City Hall. Someone else suggested University Rights Movement, but Savio thought the acronym—URM—lacked the appropriate dignity. Jack Weinberg, the man in the car, suggested Free Speech Movement. After much debate they approved it by one vote. Bob Starobin, a history graduate student who was there, recalled favoring that name because *FSM* could be written on walls, "like in Paris or Algiers."

On Monday, October 5, the FSM held its first rally as an organization on the steps of Sproul Hall. Despite Chancellor Strong's threat to have

him arrested, Savio proceeded with an oration that set forth the constitutional right of free speech on campus as fundamental to students being
real citizens.

"This free speech fight points up a fascinating aspect of contemporary
campus life," he said. "Students are permitted to talk all they want so long
as their speech has no consequences. One conception of the university, suggested by a classical Christian formulation, is that it be in the world but
not of the world.

"The conception of Clark Kerr by contrast is that the university is part
and parcel of this particular stage in the history of American society . . . it
is a factory that turns out a certain product needed by industry or government. Because speech does often have consequences which might alter
this perversion of higher education, the university must put itself in a position of censorship. It can permit two kinds of speech: speech which encour-
ages continuation of the status quo, and speech which advocates changes
in it so radical as to be irrelevant in the foreseeable future.

"Someone may advocate radical change in all aspects of American
society, and this I'm sure he can do with impunity. But if someone advocates sit-ins to bring about changes in discriminatory hiring practices, this
cannot be permitted because it goes against the status quo of which the
university is a part. And that is how the fight began here."

Savio was implicitly embracing ideas set forth two hundred years earlier by George Berkeley, the iconoclastic philosopher and poet for whom
the university was named. Berkeley had criticized society of yore for imposing "for truth and sense the pedantry of courts and schools." He had
argued that to *be* is to be *heard*, in essence, that being human means being able to convey ideas that other humans will hear and can act upon,
ideas that may have consequences.

Savio was explicitly attacking Kerr's description of the modern university, which he had presented in a series of speeches at Harvard that were
published in 1963 as a widely noted book, *The Uses of the University*. The
university may have started out as a single community of masters and students, Kerr argued, but was now a "multiversity"—a series of communities
that are bound together, but sometimes have competing interests: students; faculty; and public authorities such as the Board of Regents, legislators, and governors. In the middle was the multiversity president, who was
essentially a "mediator" and must be willing to compromise, but not on
"freedom and quality." "To make the multiversity work really effectively,
the moderates need to be in control of each power center and there needs
to be an attitude of tolerance," he contended. "When the extremists get in

control of the students, the faculty, or the trustees with class warfare concepts, then the 'delicate balance of interests' becomes an actual war."

Increasingly, Kerr observed, the university was "a prime instrument of national purpose" whose function was the "production" of new knowledge. Quoting another scholar (Abraham Flexner), who had described it as part of the "knowledge industry," Kerr asserted, "New knowledge is the most important factor in economic and social growth. We are just now perceiving that the university's invisible product, knowledge, may be the most powerful single element in our culture, affecting the rise and fall of professions and even of social classes, of regions and even of nations." He added, "What the railroads did for the second half of the last century and the automobile for the first half of this century may be done for the second half of this century by the knowledge industry: that is, to serve as the focal point for national growth." At another point, Kerr declared that the modern university functioned like a "mechanism held together by administrative rules and powered by money." Its product served agriculture, business and the military. However, Kerr had not called the university a "factory." And he had been describing, rather than prescribing, the university as the result of historical forces (such as those represented by the Morrill Land Grant College Act), or what he called "an imperative rather than a reasoned choice among elegant alternatives." He had, moreover, warned of serious deficiencies at sprawling modern campuses like Berkeley's, such as large classes, unavailable teachers, and little sense of community.

But Savio had made a powerful argument that the enormous institution Kerr headed was denying students fundamental rights as individuals. This message resonated with many who felt frustrated with the strictures of the fifties, and now with the university bureaucracy, and who wanted a say in the world. Mona Hutchin, a member of the campus Young Republicans, recalled, "People who had felt stifled for a long time and who were tired of standing in long lines and being handed green, pink, and orange forms for everything [they] wanted to do and having to go through all this crap every time [they] wanted to get something done were coming out. There wasn't any turning back."

The Free Speech Movement set up an executive committee representing all the student groups involved in the movement, from the Young Socialists to the Young Republicans. Members of any political group were welcome to join so long as they supported the movement's main cause. Each group had two representatives on the panel, which eventually numbered more than fifty people. This became so unwieldy that the protesters created an eleven-member steering committee to run day-to-day operations but which still had to convene the larger executive committee to make major decisions.

All that fall, FSM members seemed to be in perpetual meetings in a room on campus, at someone's apartment nearby, or on Sproul Plaza. They did not try to develop an ideology but focused on strategies to achieve the right of free speech on campus. These mass meetings became the heart of the movement. In spirit and substance, they were the antitheses of the secretive and despotic operations of both the Communist Party and Hoover's FBI.

David Goines, a member of the executive committee, recalled, "The 'participatory democracy' demanded of the evening meetings . . . meant that they went on for hours and hours; the meetings were not closed, and were often crowded with vociferous observers. People slept, did their homework, went out for dinner and came back again, but it was generally agreed that no decision could be arrived at except by consensus . . ." As Aptheker recalled, "Such a participatory process took an inordinate amount of time, but it also encouraged a confidence and trust in each other. Much of how we did things was modeled after the meetings Mario, Jack, and others had attended in Mississippi that summer."

Savio had moved from his boardinghouse on Hearst Avenue on the north side of campus to an apartment at 2536 College Avenue that became a vortex known as "FSM Central." Volunteers streamed in and out. Some worked the telephones, coordinating the rebellion. They tore several campus phone directories into sections and dialed up every student about the movement. Others organized people who could run errands, operate sound equipment, or serve as rally monitors. They worked late and often ate and slept at his place. Marilyn Noble, who had done her master's thesis on student movements, served as a self-described house mother and cooked meals with groceries they bought at the Berkeley Co-op at Telegraph and Ashby avenues, which had started as a cooperative food-buying club during the Depression. Other times they headed to Robbie's, a cheap Chinese café that offered a large plate of turkey dressing with gravy for twenty-five cents, just a few blocks down Telegraph Avenue from Larry Blake's, where Agent Jones enjoyed somewhat finer dining.

Late at night, after another exhausting meeting, Savio and others hunched over an old manual typewriter at the kitchen table, pecking out a draft of the next day's leaflet. In these days before personal computers and cell phones, the handbills were a powerful mode of communication, the latest uncensored news about the movement's positions, plans, and protests. Savio often collaborated with Suzanne Goldberg, a graduate student in philosophy and a teaching assistant who had dark eyes and long brown hair that spilled over her red corduroy dress.

Earlier that fall, Goldberg had dated Weinberg, but Savio caught her eye as she crossed campus to and from class. Listening to his speeches, she recalled, "The eloquence and honesty of Mario's words struck me for their lack of the usual manipulative rhetoric of political speeches, for his sensitivity and intelligence." He was asking the campus community to get involved in the fight for free speech, and his appeal aroused her own anger at injustice and hypocritical authority. Too many times she had heard her parents proclaim high ideals, she would later say, and then watched them act in a contrary manner. It was with some skepticism, then, that she watched Savio at FSM meetings, but she only grew more impressed. "He always took the moral stance," she would write. "He was never an opportunist." She became involved in the FSM and soon she was making speeches against the administration and working with Savio. As they fought for free speech, they grew closer. Like Kerr and Reagan, Savio would find romance through politics.

As soon as the radicals at the kitchen table had finished the leaflet, they ripped the final version from the typewriter and handed it to Goines, who was in charge of printing. Dashing through the dawn to a friend's place in Oakland, he ran off five thousand copies on a Gestetner mimeograph machine. Goines used a different color paper for each day's leaflet so people could instantly see it was the newest one. He distributed bundles to volunteers who passed out the sheets at the campus entrances. By 10:00 a.m. they had been snatched up.

All along, Savio delivered compelling speeches that seemed to express widely shared thoughts and feelings that had not yet been articulated. His words helped create a common experience and a sense of community. He had a way of drawing people into the discussion. Launching into an analysis of the administration's latest position, he would often say, "I ask you to consider . . ."

He had adopted his speaking style from civil rights leaders such as Bob Moses of SNCC, who had organized Mississippi Freedom Summer. "There was a SNCC style," Savio recalled. "You just describe things. The SNCC style was very much understated. There'd be no harangues. People would talk to you in a conversational way. That is, you weren't there to be persuaded against your will. So that in following that kind of leadership, you didn't feel dwarfed by it, you see. It was a style of leadership and quality of movement that enhanced your individuality when you joined it."

Cloaked in his herdsman's shearling coat, his hair unruly and his brow furrowed, Savio cut the figure of a romantic radical. He became a media magnet. Reporters portrayed him as the FSM's "leader," although he tried hard to avoid both the role and the image. Aptheker was struck by his disinterest in using his position for personal power and self-aggrandizement. He wanted the public to understand that the FSM represented a broad sentiment, not just a fad with students following a few Pied Pipers. Sometimes, he literally ran from reporters. Still, his picture often appeared on the front page.

He spent much time speaking with students in small groups about the importance of free speech. "The FSM owed more to Mario's genius in explicating complex issues in countless conversations than to his equal gift for charismatic oratory in a crisis," Martin Roysher, a student, recalled.

Although he still stammered when he had arrived at Berkeley the previous fall, during the Free Speech Movement Savio found his voice. Patti Iiyama had known him when he was elected chairman of SNCC's campus chapter in the spring of 1964. "He was such an ineffective speaker that we said that SNCC is just going to fall apart completely," she recalled. "But in the FSM he could explain something well and understandably . . . if he was really furious about something . . . *then* he got very eloquent."

As Savio would say years later, it was "my free speech movement."

Early on, Savio and other protesters suspected that Kerr was not dealing with them in good faith. Soon after the police car incident, the *San Francisco Examiner* and other Bay Area newspapers published stories that quoted Kerr as saying, "There is an extreme left wing element there. Forty-nine percent of the hard-core group are followers of the Castro-Mao line."

Kerr claimed the *Examiner* had misquoted him and later called the "49 percent" quote a "complete fabrication." But he acknowledged that the *San Francisco Chronicle* had correctly quoted him as stating, "I am also sorry to say that some elements have been impressed with the tactics of Fidel Castro and Mao Tse-tung. There are very few of these, but there are some . . . Many of the 'demonstrators' are not university students." He made a similar remark on October 15 at UC Davis, about an hour northeast of Berkeley, saying some demonstrators had "Communist sympathies."

Even if Kerr had been misquoted in the *Examiner*, he had implied in other statements that the FSM was unduly influenced by Communists and nonstudents. At the time, Kerr declined to name his source for these charges. He later told this author it was Vice Chancellor Alex Sherriffs.

Although he maintained that he had "little indication" Sherriffs was in contact with the FBI agent Don Jones, Kerr added, "He always claimed that he had confidential information, which I assumed was from the FBI."

Savio was disappointed that Kerr, renowned as a defender of academic freedom, had stooped to what he saw as red-baiting. But he was not inclined to be intimidated just because the FSM's ranks included some Marxists, who, in any event, had no special influence. To underscore this, Savio suggested that Aptheker make the FSM's next speech. "We should throw the only real Communist we have in Kerr's face," he said.

He and other FSM leaders also became frustrated with the committee established under the Pact of October 2 to negotiate new rules for campus political activity. They believed Kerr had packed the panel with his partisans, a strategy he had used successfully in labor negotiations and in pushing through the Master Plan for Higher Education. Some students, moreover, thought Kerr did not take them seriously. "Kerr never, at any time, realized that this was not just an exalted panty raid," David Goines said.

As the students met, rallied, and picketed, they refrained from violating campus rules against civil disobedience and political advocacy. But by early November, they had become disillusioned about negotiating with the administration. At a noon rally on Sproul Plaza on November 9, the FSM escalated the protest. Standing where the police car had been captured, Savio charged that the administration—"by its continuing acts of political oppression"—had nullified the pact that he had announced from the car roof five weeks earlier. "Accordingly," he declared, "the students have lifted the self-imposed moratorium on the exercise of the constitutionally guaranteed political rights . . . The students shall not cease in the responsible exercise of their rights."

Savio and other demonstrators immediately set up card tables on campus and resumed their political advocacy, deliberately violating the ban. Campus officials collected the names of more than seventy-five students at the outlaw tables, but took no other action. On November 16 and 17, protesters again set up tables; campus officials still held back. All the while, Sherriffs and Strong were growing more concerned.

On November 20, about three thousand people, dressed as if for church and bearing a banner that said "Free Speech," marched across campus from Sproul Plaza, under the bronze arch of Sather Gate and the university motto "Fiat Lux," to University Hall, where the regents were meeting. The board members refused to let the protesters address them and—though easing campus restrictions on student speech somewhat—rejected the FSM's central demand that the courts alone should set rules for speech on campus. The regents also decided to take disciplinary action for violations of campus rules. The protesters did not understand the extent of this punishment, however, and it seemed to many of them that campus officials were making reasonable concessions. In recent weeks, they had not attempted to remove tables set up by the FSM and other political groups. As a result, students were hesitant to commit new acts of civil disobedience.

This became painfully clear three days later, when a badly divided FSM leadership held a rally and called for an immediate sit-in at Sproul Hall. Savio and Weinberg advocated the action; Aptheker opposed it. "Mario was so strongly committed to the sit-in that at moments he shook visibly with rage," Martin Roysher recalled.

Fewer than three hundred students followed Savio into the administration building, and the November 23 protest turned out to be an utter failure. After just a few hours, the steering committee voted to abort the sit-in. Savio accepted the vote and urged everyone to leave the building, patiently arguing that the FSM would survive only by respecting the majority. But Tom Miller, a fellow protester, saw that "Mario seemed destroyed at the time."

The Free Speech Movement was faltering. Savio despaired that the students would ever win the constitutional right of free speech on campus. It appeared that Kerr had outmaneuvered the FSM with a combination of lesser concessions and leniency. Indeed, on the day of the aborted sit-in, Chancellor Strong had ordered an end to Savio's indefinite suspension, meaning he could reregister for classes.

So disheartened was Savio that he contemplated dropping out of the FSM. So did Weinberg, who thought "the movement was all over."

But J. Edgar Hoover already had set in motion events that would create new turmoil on campus. At his direction, Curtis Lynum, the special agent in charge of the San Francisco field office, slipped information about the past political activities of some of the protesters to Ed Montgomery, the *San Francisco Examiner* reporter who had falsely reported that Robert Meisenbach had triggered the 1960 riot at San Francisco City Hall. In the years since then, Montgomery and FBI agents in San Francisco had grown even closer. "He had in effect almost unlimited access to the office," Lynum recalled.

On November 25, three days after the aborted sit-in, the *Examiner* published part one of Montgomery's front-page series depicting the Free

Speech Movement as a Communist plot to disrupt colleges around the country. The stories shared the pages that week with news about the release of Warren Commission testimony on the assassination of President Kennedy; General Maxwell Taylor's plan to bomb North Vietnam; and Hoover's announcement that the FBI had identified the killers of Goodman, Schwerner, and Chaney in Mississippi. James Farmer, the head of CORE, was among the black leaders demanding Hoover's resignation because he had charged that the civil rights movement was "spearheaded at times by Communists and moral degenerates" and that Dr. Martin Luther King was "the most notorious liar in the country."

Montgomery reported: "The Marxist-dominated Free Speech Movement which has kept the UC campus at Berkeley in turmoil for weeks is destined to spread. The blueprints are drawn. The mechanics of an expansion program have begun. While planned agitation at other west coast colleges and universities may not take the operational title of Free Speech Movement, the ultimate objectives will be the same. Some cause—almost any cause—will be found or manufactured to get a show on the road."

Naming many of the same people listed a few weeks earlier in Agent Jones's confidential report, Montgomery charged that the students were "dupes, unwitting or otherwise, of trained agitators."

In an accompanying editorial, the *Examiner* demanded that campus officials expel the protesters, declaring, "Decisive use of university authority, already too long delayed, is the only course left."

Lynum reported to Hoover, "These are excellent articles. They . . . have been the subject of considerable discussion among state administrators, university administrators, students, and the general public on a statewide basis. They were extremely timely . . ."

Lynum's report to Hoover was captioned COINTELPRO, the acronym for the FBI's massive and secret Counter Intelligence Program. Under its auspices, FBI officials took techniques originally developed for use against foreign adversaries and turned them on domestic political groups whose politics they considered un-American. As the Church committee found, the goal was to prevent people from engaging in First Amendment activities that Hoover considered a threat to national security or the existing social order.

Hoover began COINTELPRO in 1956 to circumvent U.S. Supreme Court rulings that had curtailed his power to act against law-abiding domestic groups. Initially aimed at the Communist Party, the program's covert operations were eventually used to "disrupt" and "neutralize" a wide range of individuals and organizations. The Church committee found that the program was a "sophisticated vigilante operation" that violated the U.S. Constitution and broke criminal laws. "COINTELPRO," the committee concluded, "demonstrates the dangers inherent in the overbroad collection of domestic intelligence."

Montgomery's series typified one of the program's main techniques: leaks to "friendly" reporters who could be trusted to promote the bureau's goals and hide its covert role. Such leaks were meant to discredit organizations and individuals by linking them to communism.

In an interview, Lynum told the author he had helped Montgomery on some stories but could not recall having given him material for this series. In a separate interview, Montgomery acknowledged that he cooperated with the FBI. "I'm not saying I never got information from the FBI," he said. "I sure as hell did." But he denied that he had received information from the FBI for the FSM series and that he had knowingly been part of the counterintelligence program. "There's this myth . . . that's what it was, that Montgomery was a parrot for the FBI, or a funnel through which the FBI was putting this information out to the public," Montgomery said. "That's a lot of horse manure."

In what may have been an unintended consequence of the FBI's covert operations, Montgomery questioned Weinberg about who was "behind" the Free Speech Movement, and Weinberg rebuffed the reporter's implication that students were being directed by Communist Party officials, or anyone else, with a remark that became a credo for his generation: "We have a saying in the movement," he said. "'Don't trust anyone over thirty.'"

In any event, both Savio and Kerr told the author that Montgomery's series distorted public perception of campus events, increased antipathy toward the university, and hampered already difficult negotiations.

"It made it harder to operate," Kerr said. "It was a situation in which the public was certainly ill at ease anyway, and then having exaggerated press reports about what was going on on-campus—the two together create a rather explosive situation."

Savio maintained that the stories increased pressure on the administration to appear tough on students.

"They were under enormous pressure," he recalled. "The message [of the stories] was: you're dealing with a bunch of Communists whose only interest is . . . having demonstrations and disrupting the campus. You've got to get rid of them, expel them, throw them in jail."

The day Montgomery's series began, Strong signed letters initiating new disciplinary actions against Savio and three other FSM leaders. Alex Sherriffs had been pushing him to do it. Arleigh Williams, who was dean of students, recalled telling Sherriffs, "Let's call it quits. We've got enough blood right now," but Sherriffs replied, "Over my dead body." As Williams put it, "He was very, very intense about having this action happen."

Strong's letter of November 25 informed Savio that he faced disciplinary proceedings for leading the police car protest of October 1, encouraging students to sit in at Sproul Hall that day, and biting the officer's leg. In other letters bearing that date, Strong reprimanded sixty students for manning illegal tables in November.

Only days before, FSM leaders had despaired that their movement was dead. But the new disciplinary charges, and the *Examiner* series, rekindled the campus conflict.

Montgomery's stories, and other negative publicity engineered by the FBI, had a broader political effect: it cast Kerr and his key supporter, Governor Pat Brown, as not only weak on unruly students but as failing to respond to a national security threat.

This harmed Brown's reputation on an issue that would prove crucial during the next gubernatorial race.

And the trouble on campus had only just begun.

14

Sit-in at Sproul Hall

The crowd in Sproul Plaza on December 2, 1964, was unusually large and tense.

News of Chancellor Strong's decision to single out Mario Savio and his colleagues for the most severe discipline had swept the campus and the movement had surged anew.

The FSM issued an ultimatum: The demonstrators would take "direct action" in twenty-four hours—unless the administration dropped both the political ban and the disciplinary charges against protest leaders. Savio and Suzanne Goldberg drafted the letter to President Kerr. "Without the use of mass direct action we have been unable to make any substantial gains toward freedom for political activity at the University of California," they declared. "We are hereby making a final attempt to restore our political freedom without the use of mass direct action."

The administration had spurned the ultimatum, and speakers now urged the tightly packed crowd of some five thousand people to take over Sproul Hall.

Savio, in his fleece coat, stepped to the microphone and delivered what would become his most famous speech. It was not only a fiery reply to Kerr's characterization of the modern university as a part of the "knowledge industry" but a timeless rebuke of bureaucracy.

"We have an autocracy which runs this university," he said. "It's managed. We asked the following: If President Kerr actually tried to get something more liberal out of the regents in his telephone conversation, why didn't he make some public statement to that effect? And the answer we received—from a well-meaning liberal—was the following: He said, 'Would you ever imagine the manager of a firm making a statement publicly in opposition to his board of directors?' That's the answer!

"Now, I ask you to consider: If this is a firm, and if the Board of Regents are the board of directors, and if President Kerr in fact is the manager, then I'll tell you something: the faculty are a bunch of employees, and we're the raw material! But we're a bunch of raw material that don't mean to be, to have any process upon us, don't mean to be made into any product, don't mean, don't mean to end up being bought by some clients of the university, be they the government, be they industry, be they organized labor, be they anyone! We're human beings!"

The crowd cheered. Savio's voice trembled as he reached a crescendo.

"There is a time when the operation of the machine becomes so odious, makes you so sick at heart, that you can't take part; you can't even passively take part, and you've got to put your bodies upon the gears and upon the wheels, upon the levers, upon all the apparatus and you've got to make it stop.

"And you've got to indicate to the people who run it, to the people who own it, that unless you're free, the machine will be prevented from working at all!"

Savio's speech sent shivers through the crowd on the plaza. And as Joan Baez stood on the steps, strummed her guitar, and sang "We Shall Overcome," more than a thousand people filed slowly into Sproul Hall and occupied all four floors. They filled every hallway in the building, sitting against the walls to leave passageways, but campus officials soon declared the building closed and sent all employees home. By early evening, most of the protesters remained. From the windows, some lowered ropes to haul up baskets of food and supplies. They meant to hold the building until the administration capitulated.

FSM leaders designated each floor for certain activities: the first for sleeping, the second for anything, the third for studying, and the fourth for studying and sleeping. Some protesters screened Charlie Chaplin movies and *Operation Abolition*, the HUAC documentary about the 1960 protest at San Francisco City Hall. Some held Chanukah services, others danced and sang or put on impromptu classes about theology, mathematics, and Spanish. Joan Baez, who was about the same age as the protesters and had been active in the civil rights movement, and Ira Sandperl, a Gandhian scholar and her mentor, led a class on music and nonviolence. Gary Snyder discussed poetry. In the basement, students stretched out atop drums containing emergency food and water stockpiled in case of nuclear war.

Savio and other FSM leaders met in a women's restroom to discuss their next step in what was the nation's biggest campus sit-in ever. With bullhorn in hand, he walked the floors, urging people to remain orderly. That evening, he gave a speech connecting the struggles in the South and on the campus with a larger fight against an expanding culture of consumerism and bureaucracy, a talk he later called "An End to History."

Last summer I went to Mississippi to join the struggle there for civil rights. This fall I am engaged in another phase of the same struggle, this time in Berkeley. The two battlefields may seem quite different to some observers, but this is not the case. The same rights are at stake in both places—the right to participate as citizens in democratic society and the right to due process of law. Further, it is a struggle against the same enemy. In Mississippi an autocratic and powerful minority rules, through organized violence, to suppress the vast, virtually powerless majority. In California, the privileged minority manipulates the university bureaucracy to suppress the students' political expression. That "respectable" bureaucracy masks the financial plutocrats; that impersonal bureaucracy is the efficient enemy in a "Brave New World."

In our free-speech fight at the University of California, we have come up against what may emerge as the greatest problem of our nation—depersonalized, unresponsive bureaucracy. We have encountered the organized status quo in Mississippi, but it is the same in Berkeley. Here we find it impossible usually to meet with anyone but secretaries. Beyond that, we find functionaries who cannot make policy but can only hide behind the rules. We have discovered total lack of response on the part of the policy makers. To grasp a situation which is truly Kafkaesque, it is necessary to understand the bureaucratic mentality. And we have learned quite a bit about it this fall, more outside the classroom than in.

As bureaucrat, an administrator believes that nothing new happens. He occupies an ahistorical point of view . . .

The same is true of all bureaucracies. They begin as tools, means to certain legitimate goals, and they end up feeding their own existence. The conception that bureaucrats have is that history has in fact come to an end. No events can occur now that the Second World War is over which can change American society substantially. We proceed by standard procedures as we are.

The most crucial problems facing the United States today are the problem of automation and the problem of racial injustice. Most people who will be put out of jobs by machines will not accept an end to events, this historical plateau, as the point beyond which no change occurs. Negroes will not accept an end to history here. All of us must refuse to accept history's final judgment that in America there is no place in society for people whose skins are dark. On campus students are not about to accept it as fact that the university has ceased evolving and is in its final state of perfection, that students and faculty are respectively raw material and employees, or that the university is to be autocratically run by unresponsive bureaucrats.

Here is the real contradiction: the bureaucrats hold history as ended. As a result significant parts of the population both on campus and off are dispossessed and these dispossessed are not about to accept this ahistorical point of view. It is out of this that the conflict has occurred with the university bureaucracy and will continue to occur until that bureaucracy becomes responsive or until it is clear the university cannot function.

The things we are asking for in our civil rights protests have a deceptively quaint ring. We are asking for the due process of law. We are asking for our actions to be judged by committees of our peers. We are asking that regulations ought to be considered as arrived at legitimately only from the consensus of the governed. These phrases are all pretty old, but they are not being taken seriously in America today, nor are they being taken seriously on the Berkeley campus.

The university is the place where people begin seriously to question the conditions of their existence and raise the issue of whether they can be committed to the society they have been born into. After a long period of apathy during the fifties, students have begun not only to question but, having arrived at answers, to act on those answers. This is part of a growing understanding among many people in America that history has not ended, that a better society is possible, and that it is worth dying for . . .

Hundreds of officers from nearby police departments were converging on the campus. They set up a command center in the university police headquarters, which happened to be at the south end of the basement of Sproul Hall. Edwin Meese III, an Alameda County deputy district attorney, was there coordinating them. Outside Sproul Hall, Agent Don Jones, wearing casual clothes to better blend in, watched for passing protesters and took down their names. The bureaucracy may have been faceless, but it knew who its enemies were. Jones filed "urgent" reports that were sent via the bureau's internal teletype system to Hoover. In one summary, he reported that protesters had scaled the façade of Sproul Hall and from an upper balcony unfurled large banners spelling out *F.S.M.*

At his office across campus on the seventh floor of University Hall, Kerr worried about violence between the police and unarmed students. He called an emergency meeting with key members of the Board of Regents at the Hilton Inn near the San Francisco Airport. There he proposed a simple process: no one else would be allowed into the building but anyone could leave with impunity. Lights and water would remain on. At 10:00 the next morning, the situation would be reassessed. The regents agreed and the meeting ended at 9:15 p.m. Kerr contacted Governor Brown, who was at a banquet in Los Angeles, and he concurred. Brown and Kerr planned to visit Sproul Hall the next morning and try to persuade the protesters to leave peacefully before they were removed by force. Kerr then withdrew for the evening to his home in El Cerrito, on the precipice.

At 11:05 p.m. Kerr's phone rang and an aide on campus told him that Brown had changed his mind. Alex Sherriffs had intervened. Ever since the police car was captured, the vice chancellor had been seething at both the protesters and Kerr. Now, he thought, Kerr's lax policies had led to the student occupation of the administration building. As Kerr was heading home that evening, Sherriffs phoned one of Brown's Sacramento aides and reported that a photographer friend of his had just complained of being roughed up by protesters inside Sproul Hall. The aide phoned Brown, Brown spoke with Meese, and plans were made to arrest everyone.

Midnight passed. Some protesters studied, some slept. A few discreetly smoked marijuana and, as one student later recalled, on the roof of the administration building two young women caught up in the passions of the moment lost their virginity. At about 3 a.m. Chancellor Strong appeared. "May I have your attention?" Strong said through a megahorn as he moved through the crowd, a policeman at his side. "This assemblage has developed to such a point that the purpose and work of the university have been materially impaired." Students cheered. "It is clear that there have been acts of disobedience and illegality which cannot be tolerated," he continued. "The university has shown great restraint and patience in exercising its legitimate authority in order to allow every opportunity for expressing differing points of view. The university always stands ready to engage in the established and accepted procedures for resolving differences of opinion . . . I request that you immediately disperse . . . Please go."

Savio followed Strong as he went floor to floor and repeated the order. Glaring at Strong, he hoped to catch his eye. He was surging with anger. He believed the chancellor was a hypocrite, that the university never had been willing to seriously discuss lifting the restrictions on free speech. Strong did not meet his gaze.

When the chancellor and his police escort had left, Savio returned to each floor, warning juveniles and anyone on probation to leave. He and other protest leaders urged everyone else to move to the upper floors and go limp when arrested, to slow police in removing them. They wanted students arriving for class in the morning to see the continuing arrests in the hope that this would inspire them to join the protest.

Some 635 police officers had assembled outside Sproul Hall. Detachments entered the building and prepared to arrest demonstrators and bring them to the police station in the basement for booking. The first person arrested, however, was Jessica Mitford's husband, Bob Treuhaft, who had been inside serving as one of the FSM's volunteer lawyers. He had been speaking with news reporters in the press room when Meese spotted him and told an officer, "There's somebody here who is not a member of the press." Treuhaft replied, "Well, that makes three of us." As the radical lawyer was taken into custody for trespassing, John Sparrow, an associate counsel to the Board of Regents and ally of Vice Chancellor Sherriffs, could not resist remarking, "Bob, what are you doing here?"

Savio walked downstairs to the basement to ask Lieutenant Merle Chandler to let in another FSM attorney. He repeated the request several times but Chandler did not answer. Their exchange became hostile. "God damn you!" Savio yelled, and turning his back on the officer started up the stairway to the first floor. He had not gotten far before another officer blocked his path. Savio tried to pass on the side but the officer pushed him back with his billy club. Savio, responding with passive resistance, collapsed on the stairway. Police officers grabbed his arms and legs and dragged him down the rest of the stairs and carried him into the basement hallway. He swore, struggled, struck at a billy club one was holding, and berated their "machinelike" behavior. They deposited him in the hallway, and though he lay limply he was raging inside. Furious that the university was using police to end the demonstration, he began to yell, "Am I under arrest? What are the charges?" The officers did not answer.

The law-enforcement machinery functioned efficiently as officers arrested the leaders first and then everyone else, starting with the fourth floor and working their way down. The protesters were charged with trespassing, failure to disperse, and resisting arrest, taken to the basement, photographed, fingerprinted, loaded onto buses, and sent off to Santa Rita Jail. Still, it took police twelve hours to arrest 773 people, the largest mass arrest in California since that of movie set workers in the 1946 strike opposed by the Screen Actors Guild leader Ronald Reagan. The limp demonstrators had forced officers to drag or carry them, slowing the process enough that the arrests were not completed until late the next afternoon. As Savio had hoped, students passing Sproul Hall saw cordons of police inside and heard occasional screams. Some of the arrestees later complained that officers used excessive force, twisting their arms or bouncing their bodies on the long stone stairway.

The shock of the massive police action on campus drew more than five thousand closely packed people to a rally on Sproul Plaza the next day. Two young state legislators, Willie Brown and John Burton, spoke in support of the protesters. Savio, who had been released on bail, called on students to picket and mount a strike to shut the university. In the following days, several thousand picketed the campus and many more boycotted classes. Steve Weissman, chairman of the Graduate Coordinating Council, the graduate students' arm of the FSM, helped organize the strike. By one estimate, nearly half of all classes were closed as students demonstrated on campus and outside Governor Brown's office at the state capitol in Sacramento. Pinned to their clothing were IBM punch cards that read, "I am a student: Do Not Fold, Spindle or Mutilate."

Kerr was in despair. He had failed to stop the use of police force. Now the campus was in chaos. As the crisis had built all that fall, he sometimes sought to calm himself by silently contemplating in the Quaker tradition or by working in the garden at his El Cerrito home, an activity that harked back to his youth on his father's farm. Pulling weeds, he imagined the small ones as students, the large ones as faculty, and the biggest ones as regents.

In an urgent effort to reestablish order, he canceled all classes and called an unprecedented campus-wide meeting at the Greek Theatre for December 7. On that Monday morning, sixteen thousand people filled the amphitheater in the hills just above the central campus. The administration had carefully planned the event, seating fraternity and sorority members considered supportive of the administration in the front rows, in easy view of television cameras. Instead of the usual uniformed police, ushers were employed for crowd control. Kerr sat onstage in a high-backed chair, flanked by all the department chairmen, gazing out at the assembly. Only six years earlier he had been welcomed here as president, in an elaborate ceremony that included the staging of a Greek tragedy. At the time he gave no thought to the play's augury. Now he began his remarks by noting the amphitheater had been the scene of many dramatic performances, drawing sniggers from the audience.

Kerr proceeded to propose a settlement to the controversy that, he declared, would "inaugurate a new era of freedom under law." He had worked hard for the proposal, which was drafted by the department chairmen and supported by the governor and regents. The university administration would take no disciplinary action against students for protest activities up to and including the big sit-in at Sproul Hall. It would accept the court's pending judgment on the arrests as full discipline. And it would adopt liberalized rules for student political activity on campus. The proposal, however, stopped short of permitting students to advocate on campus for off-campus political activities, such as civil rights sit-ins. It still denied them full constitutional rights of free speech on campus.

Some people in the crowd hissed. Nonetheless, Kerr's earnest presentation, his appeal for campus unity, and his offer of amnesty drew a standing ovation from many. Just maybe, he thought, the conflict was finally over.

But no sooner had Kerr concluded his remarks than Savio entered stage left. Wearing a dark suit and tie, he strode slowly past the seated department heads toward the podium. In one hand was a scroll. He and other FSM leaders had decided he would attempt a brief reply. They considered Kerr's proposal an administration effort to preempt a more liberal proposal already under consideration in the faculty's Academic Senate. Earlier, Savio had asked Kerr if he could address the assembly and was told no, because it was a "structured meeting." Now, as the former high school valedictorian with the debilitating stutter moved toward center stage, he had to find the words to persuade everyone that Kerr was wrong and the FSM was right.

Savio placed his hands on the lectern as if to collect his thoughts and took a breath. Two campus police officers rushed at him, nearly knocking over Kerr on their way. One officer grabbed Savio around the throat, snapping his head back. The other officer twisted his arm behind his back. Savio went limp as they pulled him away from the podium by his coat and tie. The audience gasped and booed as Savio was dragged backstage. They began to chant, "Let him speak!" and "We want Mario!"

Kerr was shaken and walked backstage to see what was happening. On the way he encountered the university policeman in charge, Sergeant Robert Ludden, whom he recalled as the officer who had overreacted and drawn his gun on students during the great panty raid of 1956. Ludden was breathing heavily, standing there as though he expected Kerr to thank him for saving his life, but Kerr already was thinking the police action "looked like fascism" and that his efforts to craft a settlement had just been destroyed.

Officers finally allowed Savio to get up from the floor where they had been holding him prone. His suit was dirty and wrinkled, his brow furrowed. After several minutes of confusion, Kerr relented and let him return to the lectern. At this moment Savio probably could have said almost anything and had the crowd with him. Eschewing his scroll, he tersely announced a rally at noon in Sproul Plaza: "Please leave here. Clear this disastrous scene, and get down to discussing the issues."

Minutes later, the largest rally yet in the course of the Free Speech Movement jammed Sproul Plaza and the adjacent pathways. More than ten thousand people heard Savio call Kerr's proposal "totally unacceptable," and many of them roared in agreement.

The drama at the Greek Theatre generated more national media attention for the Free Speech Movement. *The New York Times* played the story on page one with a photo of the officers grabbing Savio. With characteristic understatement, the *Times* reported, "It was one of the most unusual events ever to occur in the theater, the scene last spring of speeches by U Thant, the Secretary General of the United Nations, and Ambassador Adlai E. Stevenson."

The next day, the Academic Senate, the body representing faculty members, met to consider the university policy on student political activity. Once again, severe official action had energized the movement for free speech. Many professors who had been undecided about the FSM were outraged by the manhandling of Savio. Some of them bitterly recalled the loyalty oath controversy, when the administration and the regents had fired faculty members who refused to sign the oath on principle. They saw their impending vote as a way to reaffirm not only free speech but also academic autonomy.

As the faculty debated inside Wheeler Hall, crowds of students waited outside, listening via loudspeakers. They knew their fate was in the faculty's hands. Finally, the professors voted 824 to 115 to support the FSM's position that students on campus should have full rights under the U.S. Constitution. This vote dramatically shifted the balance of power in the campus struggle: the administration was now up against not only the students but an overwhelming majority of the faculty. Leaving Wheeler, the professors passed through throngs of students clapping, cheering, and crying tears of joy.

At a press conference afterward, Savio appeared in a fresh suit and tie. It was his twenty-second birthday that day and a crowd of supporters sang

"Happy Birthday, Mario!" In response to a reporter's question, Savio acknowledged that he had been suspended from school and that his grades had suffered because of his activism. But at this moment he was jubilant. When asked what all the turmoil meant to him, Savio borrowed a religious reference from the ninth chapter of Melville's *Moby-Dick*, saying, "Woe to him who would try to pour oil on the waters when God has brewed them into a gale."

That night, recalled Rob Hurwitt, a graduate student in English and an FSM organizer, turned into a "succession of parties, a blur of champagne and dancing and wine and more dancing and talking and beer and romance."

But it wasn't over. The matter still had to go to the regents, and pressure was mounting on all sides. Ralph Gleason, the *San Francisco Chronicle's* music and culture critic, praised the students for speaking plainly, if clamorously. "Literature, poetry and history are not made by smooth jowl and blue suit," he wrote. "They are made with sweat and passion and dedication to truth and honor."

Governor Brown, however, called for order. Don Mulford, the Republican assemblyman whose district included the campus, declared that Communists were behind the FSM. And J. Edgar Hoover took steps to discredit the protesters.

Mario Savio disembarked the plane at New York's JFK International Airport, cut across the tarmac, and headed for the terminal. With him were Suzanne Goldberg, Bettina Aptheker, and Steve Weissman. They were on a speaking tour of college campuses to promote student rights and raise funds for their legal defense in the upcoming sit-in trial. Five FBI agents surreptitiously watched as they held a press conference at the terminal that Thursday, December 10, 1964, then tailed them as they rode into Manhattan to tape a television interview on *The Les Crane Show*. ABC's answer to Johnny Carson, Crane that June had hosted the first American television appearance of the Rolling Stones, then on their maiden U.S. tour. After Savio finished at ABC, FBI agents continued their surveillance as he stopped for a late dinner and was driven to his aunt's home on Long Island. An agent already had phoned her under a pretext: pretending to be a friend from the Mississippi Freedom Summer project, he casually questioned her about Savio's plans.

At 10:00 the next morning, bureau agents, now posing as newspaper reporters, attended a press conference that the FSM leaders held at the

Overseas Press Club in Manhattan. Savio called for full freedom of speech on college campuses and reform of universities, which had become more focused on serving business interests than on educating people. He urged students to protest in Times Square should the regents reject the FSM's demand for constitutional rights.

The FBI agents posing as reporters asked Savio what he thought of Hoover's prediction that there would be "organized" and "bogus" attempts to "divert the energies of our universities using such slogans as 'Free Speech' and 'Civil Rights.'" Savio replied, "I don't think intelligent men take Mr. Hoover's statements seriously." The agents asked if there were Communists in the Free Speech Movement. Savio said there were fifty people on the FSM's steering committee, four of whom considered themselves revolutionary socialists. The agent-reporters then asked if he was being "directed by outside influences." The Communist Party, Savio said, was getting a lot of credit for matters it was not involved in. As for outside influences, he charged that Assemblyman Don Mulford and the *Oakland Tribune*'s publisher, William Knowland, were the ones who had meddled in university affairs and caused trouble between the administration and the students.

Later that day, four FBI agents surveilled the student leaders during their appearances at Savio's old school, Queens College, and at Columbia University. They followed Savio and Aptheker to LaGuardia Airport, where they boarded a plane for Boston. Other agents picked up the coverage there, attending the press conference at Harvard, where Savio was asked similarly loaded questions about alleged foreign manipulation of the FSM. "Savio," they reported, "reacted sharply to press questions re communist infiltration of FSM."

In fact, the FBI had no evidence Savio was involved with a Communist plot. Even as the bureau was covertly planting news reports that suggested he was subversive, Lynum, the special agent in charge of the San Francisco office, was telling Hoover, "To date investigation has not developed any information indicating that Savio has been affiliated with any subversive groups."

Nonetheless, the "press" questions planted by the FBI agents had their intended effect of poisoning the well of public opinion. As the protesters flew back to Berkeley, newspapers around the country carried accounts of Savio's denial that he and the Free Speech Movement were under Communist influence.

"Results widely reported," the agents noted.

•

Governor Brown was on his private home phone, talking to Curtis Lynum. It was the day after the Academic Senate had voted to back the FSM's demands, and Brown now confided to the FBI agent that he was worried. He said he had received more mail about the FSM protests than he had about any other issue in his two terms as governor. He feared the Board of Regents was losing control of the university. Brown and other regents had read Ed Montgomery's series in the *Examiner* alleging subversives were behind the protest, and they were alarmed. Lynum assured him the stories were "very factual."

Brown said that if the FBI could give him information on the demonstrators, he would use it to make "the proper suggestions" at the next regents' meeting. As Lynum noted in a subsequent memo for his records, "The Governor requested that any information I furnished to him be given to him personally since he found that he could not trust some of his closest advisors, stating, 'I have quite a few liberals around me.'"

Hoover swiftly agreed to Brown's request for confidential information, but as always he demanded secrecy. "In view of the highly explosive situation," he warned Lynum, "this matter must be personally handled by you in such a manner as to preclude the FBI from becoming involved."

Lynum's staff promptly prepared the material for Brown. It was based on Agent Don Jones's earlier memo purporting to document subversive influence on the Free Speech Movement, and focused on nineteen students and faculty members who were "observed at" FSM demonstrations and were listed in the bureau's Security Index. Most of them had played minor parts in the protest, but Hoover's objective was to create the impression that Communists were running the show.

Leon Wofsy, a professor of bacteriology, was featured prominently. Wofsy had been deeply, and publicly, involved in the Communist Party. But he quit in 1957, telling FBI agents in a confidential interview that he had concluded he made "many mistakes" and regretted his past statements about communism. Since that interview, the FBI had investigated Wofsy and found no evidence of continued party membership. Moreover, although Wofsy had supported the Free Speech Movement, he'd had little to do with it. Lynum told Hoover earlier that week that no less a source than Alex Sherriffs had reported Wofsy "had only a minor part, if any, in promoting the unrest." He was just one of some 1,500 faculty members in the Academic Senate, Sherriffs said, and exerted no more influence on final decisions than had anyone else. But Hoover knew better. "How naïve can the vice chancellor get?" he scrawled. Tolson and his other assistants concurred. "This is an example of the harm that a dedicated communist can accomplish when he is not exposed and is allowed to operate," one aide wrote.

On December 14, Lynum confidentially met with Brown and delivered the FBI memo about the "communist affiliations" of fourteen students and five faculty members who had been "present" during the demonstrations. Although Lynum gave Brown information about Wofsy's past involvement with the Communist Party, he did not mention that his role in the FSM was reportedly insignificant.

Brown told Lynum he was "most appreciative" and promised to never reveal the FBI's role.

Hoover had cooperated with Brown for naught. Four days later, at a tense meeting in Los Angeles, Kerr urged the regents to vote that university rules should comply with the First and Fourteenth Amendments of the U.S. Constitution, and they did so unanimously. Savio and the FSM had finally forced them to concede that students had the right to free speech on campus.

The regents also voted to replace Chancellor Strong, but Sherriffs, who had led the crackdown on the Bancroft strip, remained as vice chancellor for now, angrier than ever at the activists and at Kerr.

Hoover's efforts to rein in the Free Speech Movement had failed. "This whole affair points to the need for the bureau to take all action within its jurisdiction to protect over 26,000 students at the University from a few hundred students containing within their ranks a handful of communists that [sic] would mislead, confuse and bewilder a great many students to their own detriment," he told his aides.

"While this memorandum concerns only the University of California at Berkeley, the same thing could happen at other colleges across the land. We need to and will give continuous attention to this matter."

To make sure, Hoover ordered Lynum to "go beyond the usual steps." Then he got the request from the White House.

President Johnson was waiting in the Oval Office with Vice President Humphrey when Clark Kerr walked in. Three weeks earlier, Johnson had handed Barry Goldwater a devastating defeat. The Arizona senator represented the most conservative wing of his party. He had opposed the Civil Rights Act of 1964, advocated the use of nuclear weapons in Vietnam, and proudly declared that "extremism in defense of liberty is no vice." Johnson's campaign had effectively portrayed him as a far-right extremist. One of his television ads showed a little girl plucking petals from a daisy as a man's voice ominously counts down a missile launch, the camera closes in on her, and, at zero, her image dissolves into a mushrooming nuclear blast. "Vote for President Johnson on November 3," another voice says. "The stakes are too high for you to stay home."

Johnson had assumed the presidency less than a year earlier, after Kennedy was assassinated, and won reelection by one of the widest margins of the popular vote ever. Now he was selecting members of his cabinet. Kerr had served on presidential commissions under Eisenhower and Kennedy, and JFK had offered him the post of secretary of labor, though he turned it down because he was working on the Master Plan for Higher Education. Johnson had been considering him for several spots—he had been mentioned as a possibility for ambassador to South Vietnam and even for director of the CIA.

In early December 1964, Kerr was at the White House for a meeting of the president's Labor-Management Advisory Committee when he was summoned to the Oval Office. Johnson told Kerr he wanted to name him secretary for Health, Education, and Welfare, a position that would give him tremendous influence on national educational policy.

"I've looked from the Pacific to the Atlantic and from Mexico to Canada, and you're the man I want," the Texan drawled. "You'll have more money to work with than anybody else has had in American history."

"Mr. President, I will have to think about that," Kerr replied.

"What is there to think about?" Johnson said. "I have asked you as president of the United States and commander of the armed forces."

Kerr explained that he would have to consider his responsibility to the university.

Johnson turned, took Humphrey by the arm, and walked away, saying, "You just go ahead and think."

Kerr was at a crossroads. Although the conflict at Berkeley had been overwhelming for him and others on the ground, its significance as the portent of a national student movement had not yet widely registered with those at some remove, and clearly not with the president. Yet even as Johnson was handing him a way out of the crisis, Kerr hesitated to take it.

Before Kerr had returned to California to mull over the offer, however, an impatient Johnson ordered Hoover to conduct a routine background investigation of Kerr's character, associates, and loyalty. But as a federal appeals court would later rule in a Freedom of Information Act lawsuit brought by the author, FBI records "strongly" suggest that Hoover investigated Kerr for the purposes of sabotaging his career.

On December 31, 1964, the director sent Johnson a summary of the bureau's findings on Kerr. It noted his prior presidential appointments. It reported that most of the people interviewed were overwhelmingly positive—more than a dozen recommended him for the cabinet post, including Governor Brown; Edward Carter, chairman of the Board of Regents; and U.S. Senator Pierre Salinger. It stated, moreover, that FBI informers inside the Communist Party had no information on him.

But Hoover slanted the twelve-page report by including damaging allegations against Kerr—without telling Johnson that the bureau had investigated each of the charges and found them baseless.

Nearly three pages were devoted to allegations made by Richard Combs, the Burns committee legal counsel who had held the secret meeting in 1958 to plot Kerr's firing.

Combs asserted that a man named Louis Hicks, who had worked with Kerr at the federal War Labor Board in San Francisco in the 1940s, had claimed Kerr was "pro-Communist." Hoover's report failed to note, however, that when FBI agents interviewed Hicks he denied making the charge.

Combs claimed that when Kerr worked for the War Labor Board, he had been a close associate of Sam Kagel, a renowned labor arbitrator who was allegedly pro-Communist. This charge was first reported in 1958 by William Wadman, the UC security officer and FBI contact who had pledged to help Combs get Kerr fired. Hoover's report did not say that bureau agents had found no evidence that Kerr and Kagel had more than a professional relationship, and that the Communist charge against Kagel was itself not credible. Moreover, the report did not mention that the person who originally made the charge was an informer who had been arrested many times for burglary.

Finally, Combs claimed that Kerr, while chancellor of Berkeley, had employed two women who were later dismissed as security risks. That charge also had originated with Wadman. The report omitted the fact that FBI agents found that the women "have never been dismissed for security reasons."

Hoover's report to the White House also included a page of comments from Don Mulford, the Berkeley assemblyman who had sharply criticized Kerr for easing university restrictions on student political activity and for letting Communists speak on campus. In these remarks, Mulford said he was so disturbed about Kerr's operations as university president that, in all fairness, he would not comment one way or another on his suitability for a federal post.

But Hoover, employing one of his administrative artifices, sent the White House a separate letter containing other, more sinister allegations from Mulford. The letter said Mulford had confidentially made these comments, "which he requested not be included in any report concerning Dr. Kerr for fear that Dr. Kerr might eventually learn that he furnished such information."

Here Mulford portrayed Kerr as part of a Communist conspiracy. He claimed that a source—whose identity he could not recall—had told him Kerr had "some connections with the Communist Party during World War II."

Mulford also cited the incident at the Greek Theatre, complaining that Savio "had taken over the meeting from Dr. Kerr and humiliated him." Mulford had been present and asked Kerr why he did not "take action." Kerr replied, "What can I do?" Mulford angrily answered, "This is where you and I part company."

Hoover's letter to the White House continued, "Mr. Mulford stated he is convinced there has been a decided increase of persons representing the 'left-wing' element who are members of the faculty of the University of California. He stated that due to this and the 'cowardly' way with which Dr. Kerr has dealt with the student demonstrations it would appear that someone has a hold over him."

In an interview, Cartha DeLoach denied that the FBI had tried to damage Kerr's reputation. Kerr told the author that he had not known Hoover sent falsehoods about him to the White House when Johnson was considering him for secretary of HEW.

Early one morning after his meeting with Johnson in the Oval Office, Kerr phoned the White House to discuss the HEW post. In the interim, however, the president had decided to withdraw the offer. Kerr was unaware of this; he would later say he had planned to turn down the job on the ground that he was committed to seeing Berkeley through its troubles.

But before Kerr could tell Johnson his decision, the president, clearly irritated, cut him off and grumbled that word of Kerr's possible appointment had leaked to the press, embarrassing both the current HEW secretary and himself.

Then Johnson abruptly hung up. It was the last time Kerr would be offered a cabinet post.

15

No Evidence

Hoover was still determined to turn public sentiment against the Free Speech Movement.

He decided to publish a new report linking the student protest to Communists, similar to "Communist Target—Youth." That highly publicized pamphlet had been disproved in court and created controversy that drew activists like Savio to Berkeley, but as far as the director was concerned it served its purpose: his charge that Communists had duped the students at San Francisco City Hall was now widely accepted as gospel by many conservatives, including Ronald Reagan.

F. J. Baumgardner, the supervisor at bureau headquarters who had been censured for errors in "Communist Target—Youth," took charge of the new project. On December 16, 1964, he phoned Lynum at the San Francisco office to relay Hoover's orders.

A cautious bureaucrat who had been burned before, Baumgardner summarized their conversation in a memo for his files. This time, he noted, Hoover wanted everything nailed down. "I told Lynum he should set out the names of individual Communists or other subversives who took part in the demonstrations, that he should give complete identification and subversive background concerning each," he wrote. "I instructed that the summary must be documented in detail . . ."

Lynum was a savvy bureaucrat, too, and he sensed trouble. It looked like Hoover was dictating the conclusion, despite facts to the contrary. Such a report might well be publicly disproved, and he would be blamed for it.

In a memo dated December 18, he tried to dissuade Hoover from pursuing a project intended to tie the Free Speech Movement to Communists. He astutely assured the director that his agents were "preparing a further summary as requested," but warned:

"It would appear from the information available to date that although there were subversives who took part in the demonstrations that the demonstrations would have taken place any way and no information has been received or developed to date that these demonstrations were suggested, operated, or controlled by the Communist Party."

Headquarters was insistent, however, so as the deadline for submitting the report loomed, Lynum again wrote Hoover and reiterated his message.

"For the Bureau's information," he stated on January 8, 1965, "it will not be possible to submit a summary similar to Communist Target Youth, as suggested by Mr. Baumgardner, inasmuch as sufficient information has not been developed to show a degree of influence by the Communist Party, either before or during the demonstrations. It is the opinion of this office that subversive participation in the demonstrations did not have any bearing on the measure of success achieved."

Some Communists and socialists were among the tens of thousands of participants, Lynum reported, but "the demonstrations would have taken place with or without any participation by subversives, because of basic grievances."

Eleven days later, on January 19, 1965, he sent Hoover a third memo affirming this finding.

It was as of this date, a federal appeals court would later rule in the author's Freedom of Information Act lawsuit, that the FBI's investigation of the Free Speech Movement ceased to have any legitimate purpose and instead "came to focus on political rather than law enforcement aims."

The FBI never published a report on the Free Speech Movement. But Hoover wasn't going to let a lack of evidence deter him from punishing protesters such as Savio, or university administrators such as Kerr—"bleeding hearts," he had called them—who had failed to do the job themselves.

Kerr, he had concluded, was "no good."

At 9:00 a.m. on January 28, 1965, John McCone, the director of the Central Intelligence Agency, attended the daily intelligence briefing. Vietnam was on the verge of "the most violent war in its history," and within weeks the first battalions of U.S. Marines would land in Da Nang.

At 10:00 a.m. McCone briefed members of the Joint Committee on Atomic Energy about foreign nuclear weapons developments. That October, China had conducted its first atomic test, becoming the fifth nation, after the United States, the Soviet Union, Britain, and France, to have the bomb, and heightening concerns about nuclear proliferation.

Afterward, McCone headed to a lunch meeting at the State Department, which was confronting turmoil in Africa and the Middle East.

Then he made his way to FBI headquarters, where he had an appointment with J. Edgar Hoover about another crisis—the protests at Berkeley.

McCone wore an immaculate suit, his white hair combed back neatly, and rimless spectacles through which his brown eyes directed a level gaze. As the journalist Mary McGrory once observed, "No one looking at Mr. McCone's open face . . . would ever suspect him of trying to decipher invisible handwriting or following someone down a dark street."

But McCone's mild countenance and manicured mien belied his ability to navigate the deepest waters of business and government. He was a conservative Republican, a hard-line anti-Communist, and a wealthy industrialist. He was shrewd, tough, and bold, and in serving his country he had served himself.

John Alex McCone was born in San Francisco, and decades later could still recall, as a four-year-old, standing with his father atop a hill by the Fairmont Hotel, watching the city in flames after the great earthquake of 1906. His father's family had been in the mining and machinery businesses in Nevada in the late 1800s, and after graduating Lowell High School in San Francisco he enrolled at UC Berkeley, where he earned a Bachelor of Science degree cum laude in engineering in 1922. During the next decade he worked in the steel industry as a riveter, a foreman, and, finally, an executive.

In 1937, he joined with Stephen D. Bechtel to form a company that designed and built oil refineries and power plants for installations in the United States and abroad. During the war, he became involved in the arms industry and made millions of dollars building ships, outfitting B-29 bombers for combat, and operating oil tankers for the navy throughout the Pacific. After the war his fortune grew as he concentrated on overseas shipping, especially of ore and oil.

McCone and his wife lived in San Marino, a small city in Los Angeles County known for its elegant mansions and the old-money families who inhabited them. He was a member of the most exclusive social clubs, a philanthropist and a golfer. He was also a devout Catholic, deeply involved with his church at the highest levels. Pope Pius XII bestowed upon him the Grand Cross of the Order of St. Sylvester.

McCone held a series of top-level defense posts, and in 1956 served as President Eisenhower's personal representative to the Vatican at the pope's eightieth-birthday celebration. Two years later Ike named him chairman of the Atomic Energy Commission, and in 1961 President Kennedy nominated him as head of the Central Intelligence Agency in what proved to be one of his most controversial appointments.

In a series of his syndicated "The Washington Merry-Go-Round" columns, the muckraker Drew Pearson delved into McCone's business background. According to Pearson, McCone had engaged in a conflict of interest when he was undersecretary of the air force: he had awarded a contract for C-119 cargo "Flying Boxcar" planes to a firm run by Henry J. Kaiser, in which the Bechtel family, who were McCone's partners at the time, held a stake. Pearson claimed that McCone "made more money out of Uncle Sam on war contracts than perhaps any other man now working for the Government."

Other press accounts alleged that McCone, as a trustee of the California Institute of Technology in 1956, had tried to fire ten professors because they publicly supported the presidential candidate Adlai Stevenson's call for a nuclear test ban. McCone, who was then campaigning for Stevenson's opponent, President Eisenhower, charged that the teachers had "used their position as professors of distinction . . . to inject themselves into a political discussion . . . using the university as a platform."

During his confirmation hearing, McCone denied he had engaged in wartime profiteering and conflicts of interest. As to the professors, McCone said he had brought no "formal" charges against them, but added, "I would be less than frank . . . if I did not say that there were a few people who knew I was quite disturbed and annoyed by the position that had been taken by them." In 1962 the Senate approved McCone's nomination by a vote of 71 to 12.

As CIA director, McCone inherited an agency reeling from the disastrous U.S.-backed invasion of Cuba at the Bay of Pigs in April 1961. But when he'd been in office only a few months, he played a central role in guiding the nation through one of its greatest Cold War crises, the Cuban Missile Crisis. The Soviet Union placed nuclear missiles on the island that were far more powerful than the bombs dropped on Japan and could strike nearly every major U.S. city. McCone was the only one of Kennedy's advisers to foresee the presence of the missiles. And he proposed blockading Cuba, which ended the crisis without a military strike that could have rapidly turned into nuclear war.

Cuba would come back to haunt McCone, however. He would later deny he had known that during his tenure as director, agency officials had plotted to assassinate the Cuban leader, Fidel Castro. He would insist that he never would have authorized such operations. According to one of his

aides, he considered assassination to be "morally reprehensible." Mc-
Cone had once remarked, "If I got myself involved in something like this,
I might end up getting myself excommunicated."

Yet he had looked the other way when presented with evidence that
the CIA had pursued a plan to assassinate Castro only a few months before
he became director. That evidence emerged after the *Chicago Sun-Times*
published a story on August 16, 1963, asserting that the CIA had ties to the
Mafia boss Salvatore "Sam" Giancana. McCone asked Richard Helms, the
deputy director in charge of covert operations, for a report on the article's
allegations.

Helms came to McCone's office at CIA headquarters and handed
him a document confirming that, between August 1960 and May 1961,
the CIA had planned to pay a mobster named Johnny Rosselli $150,000 to
kill Castro. Walter Elder, McCone's executive assistant, was in the room
and later testified that McCone read the paper and handed it back to
Helms, saying only, "Well, this did not happen during my tenure." McCone
did not inquire then, or at any other point, as to whether other assassination plans were continuing. Nor did he issue any written order prohibiting
assassinations.

Had he asked, the CIA chief might have learned that plots to kill Castro were not only under consideration but being carried out on his watch.
As the Church committee later found, one scheme involved using Rosselli to deliver poison pills to an assassin in Cuba. A second involved planting an exploding seashell in an area where Castro went scuba diving. A
third involved having an intermediary present Castro with a contaminated
diving suit. A fourth called for arming an assassin with a ballpoint pen
rigged with a poison hypodermic needle, which was delivered to a Cuban
working with the CIA whose code name was AM/LASH, on November 22, 1963, the day President Kennedy was assassinated. Ultimately,
none of these plots against Castro was fully executed.

Appearing before the Church committee on June 6, 1975, to give
three hours of closed-door testimony, McCone explained the rationale for
his striking disinterest. He summarized his testimony in previously unre-
leased memos he prepared for his private files. "I said I took no action with
respect to other assassinations because my position was clearly known," he
wrote. "I said I thought it was understood that I didn't think it was proper
for the United States government or the CIA to involve itself in assassinations on moral grounds . . . I did not issue a written order and it would
have been a strange thing for a Director to do, not knowing that anything
was afoot in this area."

Ultimately, the Church committee found no evidence that McCone had known the CIA plotted assassinations during his tenure. The committee faulted McCone for not having issued a written ban on assassinations, but was unable to determine who had authorized the plots, partly because of the agency's doctrine of "plausible deniability."

McCone was upset to learn about them years later. "I was distressed I didn't know about these things," he wrote, "because it gave credibility to the statements that the CIA is a free-wheeling and undisciplined organization . . ."

McCone arrived for his meeting at Hoover's office in the Justice Department building at 3:30 p.m. on January 28, and the nation's two most powerful intelligence officials got down to a blunt discussion about Berkeley.

McCone told Hoover he took a personal interest in his alma mater and was disturbed about the Free Speech Movement protests. Hoover complained about the FBI's past "difficulties" with Kerr. In fact, he declared, much of the problem was that Kerr—and his key supporter, Governor Brown—"have given in on everything these young punks causing the trouble have wanted." McCone agreed that it was necessary to take "corrective action."

Both men were aware of the delicate nature of their meeting. The National Security Act of 1947, which created the CIA, prohibited the agency from engaging in domestic intelligence activities. R. James Woolsey, CIA director from 1993 to 1995, later told the author, "It's entirely inappropriate for a director of Central Intelligence to be involved in anything dealing with political views or investigations of Americans."

Or as McCone warned Hoover, "Any action taken against subversive types must be handled in a very prudent manner," especially given "the general sensitivity of people in the academic world."

McCone, however, had just the man to handle it.

Coconut Island was twenty-eight acres of Hawaiian heaven, a personal paradise on the windward side of Oahu, replete with luxurious accommodations, pools, tennis courts, and a skeet range. One of its owners was Edwin Wendell Pauley, the wealthy UC regent, and he liked to play host there to businessmen and politicians such as Harry Truman, Lyndon Johnson, and Richard Nixon. Clark Kerr once stayed over between planes on the way to Tokyo, and spent the night drinking whiskey with Pauley. At

6:00 a.m. Pauley suggested they take a swim in one of his lagoons, and encouraged Kerr to jump in first. As Kerr smacked the water he saw the flash of a dorsal fin coming at him fast and thought for sure it was a shark. It was one of Pauley's pet porpoises, but years later Kerr would recall thinking, however fleetingly, that Pauley had taken advantage of him.

A large man with a bad back that sent chronic pain shooting through his body, Pauley walked stiffly to the meetings of the University of California Board of Regents, on which he was the senior member.

He had donated millions of dollars to the university, which named both the Pauley Pavilion, at UCLA, and the Pauley Ballroom, in the student union building at UC Berkeley, in his honor. A regent since 1940, he was by far the board's harshest critic of both student protesters and Kerr's handling of them. More than once he had urged the board to fire Kerr.

Pauley and McCone had been close friends since childhood and were classmates at UC Berkeley, where they both graduated in 1922.

After going into the oil business with his father, Pauley in 1927 set out on his own and became one of the country's leading independent oilmen. He also became a major donor to the Democratic Party, serving as secretary and then treasurer for the Democratic National Committee.

Like McCone, he held a succession of high-level government appointments that drew on his business acumen. During World War II he coordinated the lend-lease program supplying fuel to the Soviet Union and Britain, and after the fighting he served as U.S. Representative to the Allied Commission on Reparations.

And like McCone, he faced charges of profiteering that he vehemently denied. President Truman in 1945 nominated Pauley to be undersecretary of the navy, but withdrew his name after Secretary of the Interior Harold Ickes claimed Pauley had offered to raise $300,000 in campaign funds if the federal government dropped its claim to potentially profitable tidal oil lands. Pauley was later named special assistant to the secretary of the army, but the Senate refused to confirm him after Harold Stassen, former governor of Minnesota, claimed he had used inside information to make nearly $1 million speculating on scarce postwar commodities such as wheat.

Returning to Los Angeles, Pauley ran his oil firm and developed shopping centers and housing tracts. For a while he was part owner of the Los Angeles Rams football team. In the early fifties, the FBI received allegations against him ranging from rumors that he and other industrialists went on hunting trips that were "a guise for wild parties," to claims that he "shook down" executives of the Minnesota Mining and Manufacturing

Company for an interest in a Torrance, California, rubber plant. The claims were not proved.

FBI agents conducted a routine background investigation of Pauley in the mid-sixties, when President Johnson was considering him for a federal post. Most of his business associates, and friends including Art Linkletter, recommended him. But one oilman said Pauley had taken to having as many as three martinis before lunch. Dorothy Buffum Chandler, a fellow regent and a director of the Times-Mirror Company, which owned the *Los Angeles Times*, told agents Pauley seemed "ill or aged beyond his years" and that he often slept at regents' meetings. But she added, "Pauley is a strong-willed person who can be almost ruthless in order to make his point or accomplish his purpose."

And as McCone now told Hoover at his office, Pauley was very upset about the "situation at Berkeley." He'd been infuriated by the spectacle of Savio and other students holding a police car hostage in front of the student union, for which he'd donated millions.

Pauley, McCone continued, was "anxious to get a line on any persons who are communists or have communist associations, either on the faculty or in the student body." He would then use the information—without disclosing his source, of course—to convince the Board of Regents to take action.

Hoover agreed to give Pauley information from FBI files. It was part of what the federal appeals court in a Freedom of Information Act lawsuit brought by the author would later rule was the FBI's unlawful campaign "to have Kerr fired from the presidency."

Once their meeting had ended and McCone had departed, Hoover phoned Wesley M. Grapp, the special agent in charge of the Los Angeles field office.

A trusted lieutenant, Grapp had joined the bureau in 1946 after serving as a navy officer during the war. A tall, craggy man with a dark pompadour, he had started out as an agent and ran the FBI's Miami office before taking over the Los Angeles office in March 1964. Inside the bureau, Grapp was feared and hated by subordinates who found him to be a harsh and sometimes abusive disciplinarian. He would eventually be caught electronically bugging his own staff.

Since arriving in Los Angeles, Grapp had scored positive press for arresting draft dodgers, check kiters, and bank robbers, as well as for his theory that the city's balmy weather attracted criminals. On Hoover's behalf, he received an award from the Americanism Education League praising the director for "preserving the integrity of this federal law enforcement agency."

Hoover instructed Grapp to give Pauley untraceable memos on students and faculty members who were "causing trouble at Berkeley." They were to be prepared using "plain paper and not identified with the FBI." Although Hoover described them as consisting only of "public source" information, all of the data came from the FBI's confidential files.

Pauley could use the material to discredit the demonstrators and persuade the regents to get tough on them—and on Kerr.

But Hoover admonished Grapp, "It must be impressed upon Mr. Pauley that this data is being furnished in strict confidence."

Five days later, Grapp met with Pauley at his wood-paneled office in the Pauley Petroleum Building, a five-story, glass-walled structure on Santa Monica Boulevard. Pauley began the conference of February 2, 1965, by recalling that "obnoxious question"—the one on the English entrance exam—"concerning the FBI being secret police." He had demanded that the regents apologize to Hoover for it.

Pauley confided that he was "deeply disturbed" about the Free Speech Movement and how Kerr had handled it. He assured Grapp he had "no use for Kerr," and had previously accused him of being a "communist or a communist follower." The twenty-four-member Board of Regents was split into three factions, he explained, and his faction wanted "strong positive action taken immediately to clean up the mess." The problem was that so far he'd been unable to muster the votes to fire Kerr. He blamed the impasse on three "ultra-liberal" regents who staunchly backed Kerr.

All were prominent Northern California Democrats whom Brown had named to the board: William Coblentz, a San Francisco lawyer who was formerly special counsel to Governor Brown; Elinor Haas Heller, who had been a member of the Democratic National Committee; and William Matson Roth, a shipping executive and member of the ACLU executive committee.

Pauley told Grapp he had heard that during the 1950s the FBI secretly gave university officials background reports on professors. Unknown to him, this procedure had been part of the bureau's Responsibilities Program, which Hoover had since discontinued for fear it was becoming too widely known and would embarrass the bureau.

Pauley said he already had amassed his own files on Mario Savio and other demonstrators. But he wanted the FBI to screen professors, and said he would personally pay someone to check bureau files.

Grapp gave the bureau's stock answer, saying the FBI depended on "the confidence the American public has in us, which is due in part to the fact that our files are confidential."

But after obtaining Pauley's promise not to reveal the bureau as his source, Grapp handed him Hoover's blind memos about students and faculty involved in the Free Speech Movement.

Pauley quickly read one. "This is perfect," he said. "This is just what I need."

It was a four-page report on the UC Berkeley immunology professor Leon Wofsy. Like the report Lynum had given Brown, it noted Wofsy had been a self-avowed Communist Party official as late as 1956, but failed to say the FBI had found no evidence he had been involved with the party since and that he reportedly exerted no special influence on the FSM.

Two days later, Grapp reported to Hoover that Pauley would be "an excellent source of information" about internal university affairs. Moreover, Pauley could "use his influence to curtail, harass and at times eliminate communists and ultra-liberal members on the faculty"—and on the Board of Regents.

Two weeks after that, Grapp verbally gave Pauley additional reports containing information from confidential bureau files about Coblentz, Roth, and Heller, the regents who had opposed Pauley's efforts to fire Kerr.

The reports described their minor involvement with liberal groups in prior decades—all of which they had disclosed to the FBI as part of the background checks they underwent as regents overseeing the university's nuclear research programs. Hoover had lifted the information from the confidential Personnel Security Questionnaires they had filed and was using it against them—even though each of them held top-level security clearances.

In an interview, Cartha DeLoach, assistant FBI director at the time, denied that the bureau had attempted to remove Kerr, professors, or students from the university. But Grapp, in a separate interview, confirmed that he leaked the information to Pauley.

Pauley was deeply grateful to have the FBI information about his opponents on the board, for he was determined to oust Kerr.

As he told Grapp, the university would remain in turmoil "as long as the current officials were in power at the university."

16

An Angry Young Man

One afternoon in March 1965 a pot-smoking, pill-popping poetaster searching for "experience" wandered onto campus and pulled out a red felt-tip pen.

John J. Thompson had come from New York City, where he lived in a cold-water flat on the Lower East Side, worked part-time as a messenger, and hung out with civil rights activists and radicals. His interests, however, were more literary and social. His heroes were the comic Lenny Bruce and the poet Allen Ginsberg. He identified with their illicit use of drugs, their flagrant use of obscenity, and their railings against the confines of conformity.

Fueled by marijuana and Benzedrine, Thompson wrote poems and short stories that he relentlessly submitted to magazines despite unremitting rejection. The only thing he wanted as much as getting published was losing his virginity. Thompson already had been intrigued by news reports about the Free Speech Movement when a friend returned from Berkeley and regaled him with tales of willing women. Soon after he turned twenty-two, Thompson grabbed his last paycheck, hoisted a borrowed knapsack, and hitchhiked to Berkeley.

Arriving on campus that winter, Thompson was intoxicated by the palpable sense of change. Sproul Plaza was the scene of young people freely advocating causes of all kinds. As Thomas Pynchon described it in *The Crying of Lot 49*, one came "downslope from Wheeler Hall, through Sather Gate into a plaza teeming with corduroy, denim, bare legs, blonde hair, hornrims, bicycle spokes in the sun, bookbags, swaying card tables, long paper petitions dangling to earth, posters for undecipherable FSM's, YAF's, BCDC's, suds in the fountain, students in nose-to-nose dialogue." Calvin Trillin, the *New Yorker* writer, visited the campus that winter and reported "the leaders of the Free Speech Movement find themselves in a perhaps unexpected position—that of revolutionaries whose revolution has succeeded." Or as John Thompson put it, "Walking the streets in the days of the Free Speech Movement got you higher than a handfulla bennies."

Thompson was painfully aware that he had missed the chance to go to Mississippi for Freedom Summer. "I wanted to do my part for the revolution, but I was disorganized, depressed, painfully shy and mad at the world . . ." He had also admitted to himself that he'd been too scared to go south, for which he was ashamed. Now, in Berkeley, he felt, "here was a second chance to be part of something bigger than myself."

Thompson moved in with some people whom he had met through the Progressive Labor Party, a Maoist political group. He started manning the organization's table on campus. He marched in picket lines, smoked more pot, took LSD, thumbed rides around California, had lots of sex, and joined the growing community of young people who had been drawn to Berkeley in the wake of the FSM.

On Wednesday, March 3, 1965, the writer manqué found himself hanging around the strip at Bancroft and Telegraph, thinking once again about his appalling lack of experience.

"Nothing was happening in my life worth writing about (or so I thought), and what's a writer without a story to tell?" he told David Goines for his book *The Free Speech Movement: Coming of Age in the 1960s.* "Well, maybe if I got put in jail overnight, or for a few days, I'd have a story." With that in mind, he borrowed a piece of notebook paper from a student at the Cal Conservatives for Political Action table, folded it in half, and in large letters, with his red felt-tip pen, wrote what *The Daily Californian* later reported was "a four-letter word for sexual intercourse." Then he sat down with his sign in front of the student union built with a donation from the regent Ed Pauley, and waited.

A young man with a crew cut stormed over, ripped the paper from Thompson's hands, and crumpled it up. "What are you, some kind of degenerate? If you're still sittin' here when I get back I'm gonna break your neck," he said and stalked off. Thompson promptly made another sign and sat down again.

Mario Savio walked by, did a double take, and paused. He remarked on the versatility of the word—"it could be a noun, verb, adverb, adjective, gerund." Thompson nodded, wrote "(verb)" under it, and waited some more.

The crew-cut man returned with a policeman, who arrested Thompson and marched him off to the police station in the basement of Sproul Hall.

On Thursday, some of Thompson's friends put up a large sign reading FUCK DEFENSE FUND above a table on the strip. They were collecting contributions for his legal defense and trying to advance the obscenity issue by further provoking the authorities.

It worked. Campus police arrested two more students and led them to the police station. A third was arrested after following them while reading aloud passages that contained the offending word from D. H. Lawrence's novel *Lady Chatterley's Lover*, which the U.S. Supreme Court had recently ruled was not obscene. A fourth, who held up a sign saying, SUPPORT THE FUCK CAUSE, also was arrested and released.

On Friday, Thompson gave a speech in front of the student union building that featured words beginning with "f." He began each word by drawing out the initial fricative, titillating the crowd and goading the police, as in "ffffffffffffffffflower." They were all, however, "clean" words.

Other speakers were less demure. Dan Rosenthal, chairman of the Cal Conservatives for Political Action, defended Thompson, announcing that he had ordered one thousand "Fuck Communism" signs. Someone else led the crowd in a cheer: "Give me an F, Give me a U, Give me a C, Give me a K—What's that spell?" Charlie Artman, a nonstudent member of the campus community, pointed out that a fraternity had named its entrant in the campus's annual Ugly Man Contest "Pussy Galore." It was a reference to the femme fatale in the risqué James Bond movie *Goldfinger*, based on Ian Fleming's novel, then playing in theaters alongside *Mary Poppins*. Artman noted indignantly that the frat was selling "I like Pussy" buttons, but no frat boys had been arrested for their thinly veiled vulgarities. He asked, "Is not this the height of obscenity, of hypocrisy, of filth and deceit?"

After the rally, Thompson was arrested along with the other speakers on misdemeanor charges of uttering obscenities in public. *The Daily Cal* aptly dubbed the protests the "Filthy Speech Movement," and that was how the latest outrage at Berkeley was soon described in newspapers across the country.

These events divided the leaders of the Free Speech Movement. They had risked their academic standing and jail to establish basic constitutional rights on campus, only to have Thompson come along and stick everyone's face in what was, even if you agreed with him on principle, plain old profanity. A few FSM leaders, most notably Art Goldberg, joined the new protest with the intention of expanding free speech rights beyond politics. The word at issue, Goldberg contended, was so commonplace that it was unfair to arrest Thompson, who had simply brought it into the open. Others saw the controversy as a trivialization of their cause by those whom David

Goines called the "barbarian horde to which we had inadvertently opened the gates."

Savio was particularly put off. "I was very dismayed," he recalled. "On the one hand, there were people who wanted to drop the whole thing as something we ought not to deal with. On the other hand, Jack [Weinberg] presented the position that this was something we ought to defend as an abridgement of the content of speech. My position was that we should take a stand on the issue of due process"—to ensure the university treated the protesters fairly. "But somehow the issue seemed too abstract to people. People didn't want to associate themselves with the problem of obscenity."

Ultimately, several FSM leaders issued a statement in which they distanced their movement from the brouhaha and affirmed their position that the courts, and not the university administration, should define permissible speech. "The FSM did not initiate or support this controversy," they said. "We regret both that the students involved acted in an unfortunate manner and that the police and some administrators chose to escalate the issue and endanger campus peace rather than permit student interest to wane."

But other students inflamed the controversy by publishing a new campus magazine called *Spider*, a forerunner of what would soon become known as the underground press. Its editors included Jackie Goldberg, the FSM leader. The fortnightly's title was an acronym that stood for Sex, Politics, International Communism, Drugs, Extremism, and Rock 'n' Roll, and it was only partly satirical.

Spider was a blunt declaration that students were going to discuss doing things they were not supposed to discuss, let alone do. Its early issues were laden with profanity, but beneath the bravado the magazine was an earnest effort to more accurately reflect certain aspects of student life ignored elsewhere. The second issue, for example, critiqued an article about reading trends on campus that had appeared in *The New York Times Book Review*. *Spider* challenged the *Times*'s claim that J. D. Salinger's *The Catcher in the Rye* (1951) and William Golding's *Lord of the Flies* (1954)— both fundamentally apolitical works whose protagonists are adolescents— had the greatest following among college students. This was out-of-date, according to *Spider*, which suggested that readership of Joseph Heller's antibureaucracy novel, *Catch-22* (1961), and James Baldwin's tale of Greenwich Village bohemians, *Another Country* (1962), provided a more accurate gauge of current student interests. For that matter, the magazine said, Ian Fleming's James Bond series outsold them all and was perhaps even more revealing about society's values. The point was that despite establishment decrees about what people *should* like to read, young people, and Americans in general, were besotted with Bondian themes of Cold War survival, sexual adventure, and living outside the rules with "a license to kill."

This issue of *Spider* also featured an interview with Mike Meyerson, the former chairman of SLATE who had helped lead the Bay Area civil rights movement and was now a member of the Marxist W.E.B. Du Bois Club. There were poems by John Thompson, who was, finally, getting published. And there was a detailed article about using morning glory seeds to take LSD-like trips. "Almost everybody knows that you can get high on morning glory seeds; although few people know how to do so, it is really quite simple (and quite legal)," the story began.

The university administration quickly banned *Spider*'s sale on campus. Curtis Lynum sent FBI headquarters a report about the "Filthy Speech Movement" along with a copy of *Spider* in a sealed "evidence" envelope, and Hoover reported the matter to the White House. "This movement," he informed the president, "concerned the flagrant public use of a four-letter word not utilized by people of good taste in mixed company."

The Filthy Speech Movement and *Spider* were signs that the nascent sixties counterculture was seeping from the margins of society onto the nation's college campuses. This was most manifest at Berkeley, with its proximity to San Francisco, a defiant avant-garde outpost. As *The New York Times* noted in 1957, "a good deal of the writing, the poetry and the painting of this generation (to say nothing of its deep interest in modern jazz) has emerged in the so-called 'San Francisco Renaissance' . . ."

Allen Ginsberg, the poet, Jack Kerouac, the author of *On the Road*, and Lawrence Ferlinghetti, the poet, publisher, and proprietor of the City Lights bookstore, were among the East Coast refugees who made San Francisco what another critic called "the Beat Generation's capital." The movement had crystallized around the October 7, 1955, poetry reading at the Six Gallery at 3119 Fillmore Street, where Ginsberg premiered his poem "Howl," a searing Walt Whitman–via–John Coltrane blast at conformity. Two years later, San Francisco police officers who deemed "Howl" obscene arrested Ferlinghetti, the poem's publisher, but he was acquitted when a court found that "Howl" had "redeeming social value" and was protected speech under the First Amendment.

Lenny Bruce was another target of the San Francisco police. He had been a nightclub headliner in North Beach, the hilly neighborhood that became a beat base in the fifties. The police busted the Long Island native for obscenity during a performance at the Jazz Workshop, at 471 Broadway, in 1961, an arrest he successfully challenged in court. Though acquitted, he became a target for obscenity and drug arrests everywhere he performed. But as the critic Charles Champlin wrote in the *Los Angeles Times*, his profanities "were only the side effects of Bruce's whole attitude of scathing irreverence toward the settled, the right, the proper, the mealy-mouthed and the hypocritical." Or as Bruce put it, "People should be taught what is, not what should be. All my humor is based on destruction and despair. If the whole world were tranquil, without disease and violence, I'd be standing in the breadline—right back of J. Edgar Hoover."

Like Bruce, Ginsberg had experimented with mind-expanding drugs and his work reflected it. As early as 1959 he had tried LSD, the most powerful psychomimetic drug known, a molecule that altered the nervous system's normal transmission of sensory data, chemically defying the body's neural censors: just micrograms of the colorless, odorless, tasteless substance induced vivid hallucinations and synesthesia, in which users reported feeling sounds and hearing colors.

A Swiss scientist named Albert Hofmann first synthesized LSD while studying medicinal plants in 1938. By the early fifties, some psychiatrists were using it to treat alcoholism and study schizophrenia. The CIA, meanwhile, initiated secret studies of its potential use in covert warfare under a program code-named MK-ULTRA that included testing it on unsuspecting people. In 1955, Aldous Huxley, the intrepid British intellectual, tried LSD and wrote about the hallucinogenic experience in a book published the following year, *Heaven and Hell*.

Timothy Leary, a clinical psychologist at Harvard, had begun to study LSD and similar substances, which he called "psychedelic," or mind-manifesting. He was sure they could help society by opening doors to psychological insights, mystical experiences, and expanded consciousness. Federal law restricted distribution of the drugs to legitimate researchers, but Leary believed the government was interfering with freedom of consciousness, which he considered a right as fundamental as freedom of speech. In 1963, Harvard terminated his employment amid concerns that he had given the drugs to undergraduates. By then, a small psychedelic subculture had taken root in Cambridge.

Another had sprouted on Perry Lane, in Palo Alto, home of a young author named Ken Kesey. Raised on an Oregon farm, Kesey in 1958 enrolled in Stanford University's creative writing program, where one of his professors was Malcolm Cowley, the legendary editor of Jack Kerouac's books. Kesey was working on a novel about the beatniks of North Beach, and to help pay his bills volunteered as a drug test subject receiving seventy-five dollars a session in a federally funded program at the Veterans Administration Hospital in Menlo Park. He and his friends soon began trying LSD and other psychedelic drugs at home. These experiences inspired his 1962 bestselling novel, *One Flew Over the Cuckoo's Nest*, which *Time* called "a roar of protest against middlebrow society's Rules and the invisible Rulers who enforce them."

In the summer of 1964, while Savio was in Mississippi and Goldwater was at the Cow Palace, Kesey and his cohorts, who called themselves the Merry Pranksters, were heading cross-country in an old school bus, luridly painted in Day-Glo, that they had named "Further," sowing the seeds of psychedelia. By February 1965, the first large quantities of LSD were hitting the streets in pastel-colored pills known as "acid." Much of it was made by Augustus Owsley Stanley III, the grandson of a U.S. senator from Kentucky, who had enrolled at Berkeley in 1963, dropped out, and begun brewing batches of it in the bathroom of a house near the campus, at 1647 Virginia Street. He was soon supplying massive amounts of pure LSD to Kesey, the rock band later known as the Grateful Dead, and young seekers like John Thompson.

The Beats, the Free Speech Movement, the Merry Pranksters—all this fed the ferment at Berkeley, attracting students and nonstudents. Several months after John Thompson was arrested for profanity, the journalist Hunter S. Thompson (no relation) wrote an article for *The Nation* about the campus's changing culture and reported, "There is no longer the sharp division that used to exist between the beatnik and the square: too many radicals wear ties and sport coats; too many engineering students wear boots and Levis. Some of the most bohemian-looking girls around the campus are Left-puritans, while some of the sweetest-looking sorority types are confirmed pot smokers and wear diaphragms on all occasions."

Thompson concluded, "The climate is easy, the people are congenial, and the action never dies."

The Filthy Speech Movement never did attract much support among students or faculty, but it infuriated a clique of campus conservatives led by Professor Hardin Blair Jones.

Six feet three, balding and gray, Jones seemed much older than his fifty-one years. An avid collector of butterflies and rare Japanese furniture, he struck some acquaintances as a trifle self-important. He was assistant director of the university's Donner Radiation Laboratory, the world's first research center devoted to nuclear medicine, where John Lawrence, the brother of Ernest O. Lawrence, was director. In the fifties, Jones became one of the earliest scientists to warn that cigarette smoking could cause cancer, but he sought to calm public fears about fallout from atomic bomb tests, telling one newspaper that people were in "more danger waiting for a bus." An amino acid called cystine would double a person's resistance to the radiation, the medical physicist assured people—just so long as they injected it immediately before the blast. He also studied the biomedical causes of aging, but what worried him of late were the causes of youth.

Jones was often seen at student rallies on Sproul Plaza, furiously taking notes. After the convocation at the Greek Theatre, where Savio was dragged from the podium, Jones had followed the excited crowd to the rally on the plaza, where he demanded to be heard. Ignored at first, he raised his voice louder and louder and condemned them for damaging the university. He warned students to steer clear of the FSM, and organized some of his colleagues to oppose what he saw as nothing less than revolution.

Increasingly, Jones blamed Kerr for campus demonstrations. He complained bitterly about Kerr's handling of them to conservative regents, exacerbating their concerns about the Filthy Speech Movement. Martin Meyerson, the acting chancellor who replaced Strong, already had brought administrative charges against the filthy few for using obscenities on campus. But some regents privately pressured Kerr to expel them immediately. Kerr felt these regents were not only asking him to circumvent established procedures for student discipline, but were intruding on his presidential prerogatives.

In protest, Kerr and Meyerson on March 10, 1965, abruptly announced their resignations. Kerr criticized the students for making an issue of obscenity, the faculty for failing to help restore student discipline, and the regents for exceeding their bounds. "I have joined in a dramatic step, which is not my inclination," he said in a statement. "I have done so to try to stop, to the extent I can be helpful, the continuing and destructive degradation of freedom into license and a new confrontation at Berkeley which could only damage the campus even more. The university must not drift further into license and disunity."

It was a bold gambit: Kerr was publicly forcing the regents to either support his handling of campus affairs—or let him go in the midst of a crisis. The former arbitrator known as the Machiavellian Quaker had successfully used the ploy before, when as a new chancellor he told the regents he would quit unless Sproul gave him more authority. Once again, he felt he was in an untenable position and needed to break out. It was like the time he was caught in the field near his father's farm and realized the only way he could get to safety was to charge the bull.

Kerr's proffered resignation came as a shock, but not everyone was saddened. Assemblyman Don Mulford greeted the prospect of his departure with glee. Declaring it would close "one of the most unfortunate periods" in the university's history, he promptly called for a "strong" new president who would "restore discipline." Hugh Burns, president of the state senate, told reporters that Kerr's failure to screen out subversives on campus had caused "a state of anarchy" at Berkeley. Ed Pauley said it was high time Kerr left.

But Governor Brown prevailed upon the regents to support Kerr, faculty groups passed resolutions backing him, and students rallied in his defense. Three days after they had announced their resignations, Kerr and Meyerson withdrew them.

Kerr's stratagem had worked. But the filthy-speech episode had heightened tensions between Kerr and his critics. Mulford introduced a measure making it illegal for nonstudents to refuse orders to leave university grounds when it appeared they were doing anything "likely to interfere with the peaceful conduct of the campus."

"This disgraceful conduct," the author of the so-called Mulford Act declared, "must be dealt with immediately . . ."

All along, Hoover had been exploiting the turmoil on campus, tapping into the university's internal divisions to develop informers and gain intelligence he could use against Savio and Kerr.

On January 27, 1965, Professor Hardin Jones secretly contacted Agent Perry Moothart of the FBI. Jones told Moothart that he was calling at the suggestion of R. E. Combs, the chief counsel for the Burns committee, and proceeded to make sinister charges. He claimed Kerr had hired staff members with "questionable" backgrounds and had "lied" about campus events. And according to Moothart's memo on the conversation, "Prof. Jones went on to relate that he was working towards . . . selling the Regents with the idea that Pres. Kerr should be removed."

Jones offered to funnel more information to the FBI, and a few weeks later bureau officials formally designated him as a "Potential Security Informant" and began paying him. Jones helped them set up a network of university officials to inform on students, faculty, and Kerr.

(*Top*) Ronald Reagan and J. Edgar Hoover at FBI headquarters in 1968 after a secret meeting about the protests at the University of California, in a photograph released as a result of the author's Freedom of Information Act lawsuits. Reagan, who had been an FBI informer in Hollywood, could count on covert political and personal help from the FBI. (*Bottom*) The Vietnam Day Committee marches to the Oakland Army Terminal in October 1965. (Top: *The Investigator*, Federal Bureau of Investigation; bottom: Lonnie Wilson, The *Oakland Tribune* Collection, The Oakland Museum of California. Gift of ANG Newspapers)

Clark Kerr was inaugurated as president of the University of California in 1958 and fathered the Master Plan, a model for universal access to higher education (*top*). His liberal policies angered state senator Hugh Burns (*bottom left*, with fellow senator Jack Tenney, center, and aide R. E. Combs, left, in 1944). FBI director J. Edgar Hoover (*bottom right*, with his second-in-command, Clyde Tolson, in 1939) secretly sought to oust Kerr. (Top: The *San Francisco News-Call Bulletin* Collection, San Francisco History Center, San Francisco Public Library; bottom left: The *San Francisco Examiner* Collection, The Bancroft Library, University of California, Berkeley; bottom right: *Los Angeles Daily News*)

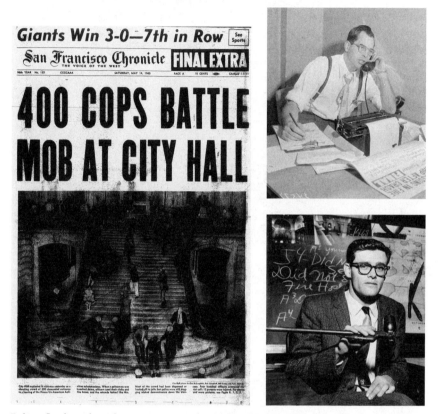

Police fire-hosed students protesting the House Un-American Activities Committee at San Francisco City Hall in May 1960 (*left*). Hoover charged that Communists manipulated the unsuspecting youths, and Ed Montgomery (*top right*, in 1951) of the *San Francisco Examiner*, a secret FBI contact, reported that English major Robert Meisenbach (*bottom right*, in 1961) had clubbed an officer during the protest. (Left: The *San Francisco Chronicle*; top right: The *San Francisco Examiner* Collection, The Bancroft Library, University of California, Berkeley; bottom right: The *San Francisco News-Call Bulletin* Collection, San Francisco History Center, San Francisco Public Library)

Ronald Reagan married Jane Wyman (*top*) in 1940, the year they costarred in *Brother Rat and a Baby*. But as she focused on acting, he became more involved in fighting communism, and they divorced. (*Bottom*) Reagan testifies before HUAC in 1947. (Top: Warner Brothers/Associated Press; bottom: Ronald Reagan Library)

(*Clockwise from top*) In the fall of 1964, Mario Savio emerged as a leader of the Free Speech Movement at Berkeley and a symbol of student defiance. The FSM marched through Sather Gate to University Hall that November. Savio and his fiancée, Suzanne Goldberg, arrived at their trial on charges stemming from the Sproul Hall sit-in that December. (Top: Steven Marcus, The Bancroft Library, University of California, Berkeley; bottom right: Don Kechely, The Bancroft Library, University of California, Berkeley; bottom left: The *San Francisco News-Call Bulletin* Collection, San Francisco History Center, San Francisco Public Library)

FBI agent Donald Jones and his colleagues conducting surveillance of protesters in 1964 (*top*). Richard Aoki (*bottom*, in 1970) became one of the FBI's key informers in Berkeley, gave guns to the Black Panthers, and helped lead the Third World Liberation Front strike. (Top: Courtesy of Howard Harawitz; bottom: Nikki Arai, courtesy of Shoshana Arai)

(*Clockwise from top*) Protesters and police clashed in May 1969 when university administrators reclaimed a vacant lot used as People's Park. Alameda County deputy sheriffs opened fire, killing James Rector and blinding Alan Blanchard. A National Guard helicopter dropped tear gas over Sproul Plaza, and it wafted through the city. (Top: Courtesy of Ron Stinnett; bottom, right and left: The *San Francisco Examiner* Collection, The Bancroft Library, University of California, Berkeley)

After campaigning for the governorship, vowing to crack down on protests at Berkeley, Reagan and his wife, Nancy, celebrated a landslide victory on November 8, 1966, at the Biltmore Hotel in Los Angeles. The secret alliance he forged with J. Edgar Hoover's FBI over the decades helped set Reagan on the path to the White House. (Ronald Reagan Library)

One month later, Hardin Jones and John Lawrence visited the regent Catherine Hearst at her mansion in the exclusive San Francisco suburb of Hillsborough for what turned into a five-hour discussion about campus problems. She was the wife of Randolph A. Hearst, president of the *San Francisco Examiner*, chairman of the Hearst Corporation, and son of William Randolph Hearst, who had been the subject of Orson Welles's scathing movie *Citizen Kane*. A wealthy debutante from Atlanta, Catherine Wood Campbell married Hearst in 1938 and became a San Francisco socialite and a philanthropist. After Governor Goodwin Knight named her to the Board of Regents in 1956, she and Kerr became friendly. At his request, the conservative Republican even made the motion that led the Board of Regents in 1963 to lift the ban against Communist speakers on campus. Kerr and Hearst had flown back to San Francisco together from that board meeting in Los Angeles, and all the way she complained that her family would take turns "spanking" her for her vote. As Kerr recalled, from that point on their friendship waned. Now, as Hearst concluded the conversation with Jones and Lawrence at her home, she asked them to set up a secret meeting between her and FBI agents.

Jones decided to enlist other members of his campus intelligence network in this effort. He called on William Wadman, the campus security officer who had served as the Burns committee's contact man until Kerr effectively severed that relationship, infuriating both Burns and Combs. Jones also contacted John Sparrow, the associate counsel to the Board of Regents, who had become close to Vice Chancellor Alex Sherriffs in their mutual opposition to Kerr's handling of the Free Speech Movement. Wadman and Sparrow, in turn, arranged for FBI agents to interview Hearst.

On March 5, just as the Filthy Speech Movement was in full fester, Hearst received Glenn Harter, a supervisor in the FBI's San Francisco office, and Roland Finley, a senior agent, at her home. She reminded them that in December she had heartily recommended Kerr when agents interviewed her during his background investigation for possible appointment as HEW secretary. Now, Hearst said, she had "changed her mind completely."

She proceeded to give the FBI agents a lengthy statement. "Mrs. Hearst stated that her eyes have now been opened regarding Clark Kerr," according to their report. "She has given the activities of Kerr a careful scrutiny and she now feels that he is a complete tyrant and a liar; that he has told different stories at different times and will give an answer to suit the occasion. She has stated that he is very devious and does not feel that he is honest with the Board of Regents."

Kerr had mistreated Strong, who had merely tried to enforce the rules, she said. Moreover, Kerr wanted to end the university's contracts with the Atomic Energy Commission because they focused on weapons production and not academic research. She added that when she was hospitalized recently, Mrs. Kerr had the audacity to intrude on her privacy by inviting her to stay at the Kerr home to recuperate, which she felt was "very poor manners."

As the interview ended, Hearst asked the agents not to disseminate her remarks outside the FBI, saying she feared it would get back to Kerr and be "very embarrassing." But at FBI headquarters her comments were seized upon. That December, Hoover had sent President Johnson the background report loaded with false allegations and unfounded claims that Kerr was "pro-communist" and "probably a fellow traveler." Her new statements presented another opportunity to discredit him.

Disregarding her request, Hoover on March 19 ordered that a report based on her remarks be sent to the White House. He did so even though there was no pending investigation of Kerr for any federal post. It was "absolutely necessary," he declared, that the president know Kerr allegedly wanted to end the university's work for the Atomic Energy Commission, especially "in view of information . . . indicating he was responsible for removal of restrictions against communist speakers on the university campus."

The report, delivered to the White House by Assistant Director DeLoach, also contained Hearst's charge that Kerr was "a complete tyrant and a liar."

Lewis F. Powell, Jr., the Virginia lawyer and president of the American Bar Association whom President Nixon would name to the U.S. Supreme Court in 1971, was preparing a speech to San Francisco lawyers about the Free Speech Movement and turned to the FBI for help.

"Powell asks if it would be possible for us to furnish him the facts regarding the demonstrations, particularly with regard to the role of communists and their sympathizers," bureau officials said in a February 25, 1965, memo to Hoover. Noting that Powell was "a close and trusted friend of the Bureau," they proposed cooperating with him "in the strictest confidence."

Hoover agreed, and they gave Powell a five-page report emphasizing that "there was a subversive element involved" in the FSM. It further suggested the protests resulted from Kerr's "questionable interpretation of academic freedom" and "permissiveness." In his talk to the Bar Association of

San Francisco at the Sheraton Palace Hotel the following month, Powell duly criticized campus protesters and called for a revival of public morality.

Hoover, meanwhile, appeared before a closed session of the House Appropriations Subcommittee on March 4, 1965, and testified that five faculty members and thirty-eight students or people otherwise "connected" with the university had "subversive backgrounds." He singled out Savio, insinuating that he was romantically involved with Bettina Aptheker, his fellow FSM leader and daughter of the Communist Party official Herbert Aptheker. Bettina Aptheker, he said, accompanied Savio on a speaking tour and was his "close advisor." Communists had managed to "mislead, confuse and bewilder" students involved in the Free Speech Movement, Hoover claimed, and planned to likewise "exploit" student demonstrations on other campuses.

Although the FBI director was suggesting that the nation's college students were in peril, there is no indication in the record that any congressman at the hearing questioned his assertions. But by then Hoover had developed a cozy relationship with John J. Rooney, the Democratic congressman from Brooklyn and head of the subcommittee, which controlled funding for the FBI. Rooney never had turned down Hoover's requests for appropriations. Hoover, in turn, had slipped Rooney confidential FBI information he could use against political opponents.

Even as Hoover was testifying, however, he knew there was no evidence that Savio or the Free Speech Movement was under the influence of any group plotting to overthrow the U.S. government. He knew the FSM was a nonviolent protest against a university rule. He knew Savio had broken no federal law. He knew all this because his agents had repeatedly told him so.

On March 12, 1965, Lynum sent Hoover a thirty-three-page report stamped "SECRET" that Agent Don Jones had prepared on nearly every aspect of Savio's life. Describing him physically, it noted he had no scars but "has slight speech impediment at times." It recapped his academic history, noting he'd been high school valedictorian and Westinghouse finalist. It said his health was listed as excellent in confidential university records, but that Alex Sherriffs had reported Savio "could be suffering from Petit Mal Epilepsy," a mild form of epilepsy caused by a brain disorder and characterized by sudden lapses of conscious activity, fluttering eyelids, and twitching facial muscles. (Sherriffs was mistaken.)

Jones's report also noted that as a leader of the Free Speech Movement, Savio had been quoted extensively in the press. It excerpted a wide-ranging interview he had given to the popular photojournalism magazine *Life*.

On politics: "I am not a political person. My involvement in the Free Speech Movement is religious and moral . . . I don't know what made me get up and give that first speech. I only know I had to. What was it Kierkegaard said about free acts? They're the ones that, looking back, you realize you couldn't help doing?"

On civil disobedience: "If you accept that societies can be run by rules, as I do, then you necessarily accept as a consequence that you can't disobey the rules every time you disapprove. However, when you're considering something that constitutes an extreme abridgement of your rights, conscience is the court of last resort."

On the nation: "America may be the most poverty-stricken country in the world. Not materially. But intellectually it is bankrupt. And morally it's poverty-stricken. But in such a way that it's not clear to you that you're poor. It's very hard to know you're poor if you're eating well."

On modern education: "Clark Kerr is the ideologist for a kind of 'brave new world' conception of education. The multiversity serves many publics at once, he says . . . But Kerr's public . . . is the corporate establishment of California, plus a lot of national firms, the government, especially the Pentagon."

The report concluded by reviewing Savio's alleged "contacts" with "subversive" groups: He had spoken twice at meetings of the Socialist Workers Party and once at the W.E.B. Du Bois Club. During the FSM he had frequently—and publicly—associated with Bettina Aptheker.

It was all guilt by association: None of the FBI's informers in the Communist Party could provide any information on Savio. Nonetheless, based on this report, Lynum proposed putting Savio on one of the bureau's secret, unauthorized lists of subversives to be arrested, without judicial warrant, in the event of a national emergency.

FBI officials had created the Reserve Index for people they deemed not quite dangerous enough for the Security Index. As of 1962, the Reserve Index included approximately 10,969 names. Section A of the Reserve Index listed people whom agents believed "in a time of national emergency, are in a position to influence others against the national interest . . . due to their subversive associations and ideology." They included professors, union leaders, lawyers, doctors, journalists, and writers such as Norman Mailer. Section B of the index listed people considered a lesser threat, to be detained after those on the A list were rounded up.

Lynum recommended Savio for Section B "in view of his leadership in the Free Speech Movement (FSM) and the national news coverage of the FSM, his contacts with known Communist Party members, his contemptuous attitude, and other miscellaneous activities."

In response, Hoover admonished Lynum for not putting Savio's name on the detention list sooner. He feared Savio was emerging as a charismatic national figure who would inspire other students to rebel.

Savio was back on the steps of Sproul Hall.

It was April 26, 1965, and he was denouncing the university's punishment of four students who had joined in John Thompson's "Filthy Speech Movement." One had been dismissed, the other three suspended.

Savio thought the Filthy Speech Movement was "silly" and that the students had not acted "in line with the true function of the university." Nonetheless, he now charged that university officials had denied them "even rudimentary demands of due process." It was the kind of argument the campus community had come to expect from Savio: even if he disagreed with someone's speech, he believed they should be treated fairly.

Then he abruptly announced he was quitting as a student leader. He feared the Free Speech Movement was becoming "undemocratic," he said, and that he was guilty of "Bonapartism."

A hush fell over the crowd as Savio decried the growing gap between FSM leaders and the student body. The dominance of those leaders was depriving other students of their chance to come forward as leaders, he said.

"I've thought a long time about it," he continued in a quavering voice. "Good luck and goodbye."

People stood in stunned silence, but gradually their applause rose in acclamation as Savio slipped away.

It was more than the incessant incandescent intensity of having been the FSM's main spokesman every waking hour for the last six months. That would burn out anyone.

Savio had been struggling—with misgivings about leadership, with his own internal conflicts, with the difficulty of balancing the personal and the political. He had neglected his studies and wanted more time for his relationship with Suzanne Goldberg, to whom he had only lately become engaged. He elaborated on some of these concerns in a letter to *The Daily Californian*, implying that students had become too dependent on him.

"The campus must organize itself," he wrote. "If the student rights movement at Berkeley must inevitably fail without my leadership, then it were best that it fail. I should do a great disservice to our community if I were to make myself indispensable; and in recent weeks I have become very nearly indispensable."

Suzanne Goldberg recalled, "He didn't want to be in the position of being the leader and he felt that everybody was looking to him . . . to give all the answers." Goldberg, who would become a psychotherapist, concluded that Savio's ambivalence stemmed partly from his political and philosophical convictions. His mixed feelings about being a leader also seemed to reflect the conflicting psychological forces that hindered him in private life yet helped him become a powerful public figure. She theorized that his religious background drove him to be a moral leader, while at the same time creating an impossible standard for him to live up to. As a result, he was often disappointed in himself and "he struggled with it."

Savio's dilemma was magnified by the media's focus on him. To be sure, he and other FSM members had found journalistic coverage useful in promoting their cause. This was especially true with larger news organizations, he said later, "because with big press we had a lever. In other words, it was embarrassing to the university."

At the same time, all the publicity intensified his inner turmoil. "For me, it was hard," Savio recalled. "Because movements sometimes need powers of oratory. It's a resource. I had that particular ability. That fact in itself separates you from most people, and the press made it worse, because the press tended to really glom on to me." *The New York Times*, for example, had published profiles of Savio headlined "A Rebel on Campus" and "His Friends Look on Savio as a 'Genius.'"

Even though the FSM took pains to operate democratically, Savio lamented that, as portrayed in the media, "it would be like I was some 'maximum leader' or something like that. Then I would feel real shame facing people in the movement." Even more troubling, "after a while, it's possible to become seduced by your own press image. It's like living in a house of mirrors. All you see is your own image." As a result, "They make you the very thing they accuse you of being, you see? I say 'they'; I mean it's the press. That is, this is not, in other words, some plan that's cooked up by the FBI. That's the way the press covers these things."

Savio had no idea of the extent to which bureau officials were manipulating news coverage of the student protests. But whatever prompted him to step down from the FSM, he told *The Daily Californian*, "This does not preclude . . . my participation in campus political activity at sometime in the future."

A few weeks after Savio quit the movement, the FBI agents Don Jones and Harold Hoblit summoned him to their downtown Berkeley office.

Jones was one of the agents who specialized in conducting black bag jobs. Hoblit was one of the agents who had crawled under Jessica Mitford's house to eavesdrop.

Arriving with his attorney for the May 12, 1965, meeting, Savio was sarcastic from the start, remarking, "So this is the Federal Bureau of *Inquisition*."

Agents Jones and Hoblit, according to their subsequent report, "immediately advised that he was in the Berkeley resident agency of the Federal Bureau of *Investigation*." They told him the FBI had received letters threatening him with physical harm and that they were investigating this matter.

The agents balked at the presence of his attorney, however, saying they "could not vouch for the confidential matter of information if a third party is present and therefore, preferred not to discuss the matter."

Savio refused to dispatch his lawyer, Alex Hoffman, a friend who had accompanied him in case he needed legal advice. And he took the occasion to criticize what he called the FBI's "failure to make arrests and take action in the South where human rights are being violated every day."

The FBI, the agents replied, always fulfills its duty. Nonetheless, Savio declined to cooperate with their inquiry. They said they saw no reason to prolong the meeting, and he agreed.

On the way out Savio apologized for his remark about the "Federal Bureau of Inquisition."

Five days later, on May 17, 1965, Congressman Rooney's subcommittee publicly released the director's secret testimony alleging that Communists had exploited the FSM in a plot to disrupt the nation's campuses and that Savio was under the sway of Bettina Aptheker.

The next day, newspapers reported his charges with headlines like, "Hoover Links Reds to Campus Rioting" (*Chicago Tribune*); "Hoover says Reds Aided Coast Riots" (*The New York Times*); and "Subversives in FSM, FBI Chief Contends" (*Berkeley Daily Gazette*).

Albeit unwittingly, the press had served Hoover's counterintelligence aims. The stories once again put Savio and Kerr on the defensive. Neil

Smelser, a sociology professor and assistant to Acting Chancellor Meyerson, denied that the Communist Party had a significant role in the protest. "If there was any dominant ideology in the FSM," he told the *Los Angeles Times*, "it was the ideology of the civil rights movement."

In reply to Hoover's remarks, Savio told reporters, "I don't know what kind of answer can be intelligently given to such a ridiculous statement." He refused to be red-baited, and freely stated that he'd met Herbert Aptheker once after he gave a speech on campus, joining him and Bettina Aptheker for lunch. "But the point is, if I had known Herbert Aptheker daily for weeks or months, I wouldn't want to deny it," he said. "I found him a very congenial gentleman."

Bettina Aptheker later recalled that some press accounts insinuated that she and Savio were romantically involved. "In fact, Mario and I were never lovers," she wrote in her 2006 memoir. "We did have a wonderful friendship. For me it was one of the best, most rewarding and closest friendships I had ever had."

She and Savio issued a joint reply to Hoover's testimony. "We find Mr. Hoover's statements . . . patently absurd," they said. "It once again indicates Mr. Hoover's inability to grapple with and understand that there were real issues confronting the students at the University of California."

The regents William Roth and Fred Dutton, however, were very concerned about Hoover's allegations. Both men were staunch allies of Kerr and Brown. Roth had developed Ghirardelli Square at Fisherman's Wharf in San Francisco. Dutton had won a Purple Heart medal at the Battle of the Bulge and served in 1958 as Governor Brown's campaign manager and later as President Kennedy's cabinet secretary.

The day after Hoover's testimony made national headlines, the two liberal Democrats requested an FBI briefing on "communist participation in the student riots." Assistant Director DeLoach told Hoover it would be a "mistake." Bureau officials already had leaked such information to Ed Pauley, Ed Montgomery, Lewis Powell, and Governor Brown as part of the FBI's efforts to discredit the Free Speech Movement and unseat Kerr. But now DeLoach phoned Dutton and demurred, writing in a memo, "I told him of the confidential nature of our files." Hoover scrawled in the margin, "Right—H."

A few days later, the *New York Herald Tribune* published a special guest article by Governor Brown that responded to the import of Hoover's charge about the FSM: that his administration had failed to properly deal with a foreign conspiracy on campus.

First, Brown acknowledged the FSM had "real grievances" that most students supported and the university needed to correct. Second, he criticized students for engaging in civil disobedience. Third, he noted, "Some people—even some people in high places—have charged that the Free Speech Movement was all a Communist plot. This is a nice, easy explanation for a very complicated situation. But it just isn't true."

Then Brown dropped a bomb.

"The Federal Bureau of Investigation turned over to me their confidential file on the Berkeley situation with respect to subversive activities," he wrote. "Unquestionably, there were some Communists involved, but the FBI's file shows the Free Speech Movement was not instigated by the Communist party or any of its front organizations."

Hoover's leak to the governor had backfired. Brown had betrayed his pledge of secrecy and exposed the bureau's disclosure of confidential information. Clearly, he could no longer be trusted as an ally in the fight against subversion.

Appalled, the director told the heads of each FBI field office in California, "In view of Governor Brown's remarks he should be furnished no information by your offices in the future."

Hoover still believed that Kerr and Savio posed threats to social order, however, and he meant to do something about it.

17

Vietnam Day

"Hot damn, Vietnam!" Norman Mailer was saying as the adrenaline and alcohol pounded in his temples. "Hot damn, Vietnam!"

Mailer surveyed the crowd that had come to the lower athletic field of the Berkeley campus for Vietnam Day and plunged into a satirical rant about Lyndon Johnson and why the United States was in Vietnam.

Blue-eyed, jug-eared, and barrel-chested, the maverick author ripped the president's manners, moral inconsistencies, and, most of all, his war. Mailer knew something about war—he'd served in World War II and written about it in his acclaimed 1948 novel, *The Naked and the Dead*. Now he was more than a little intoxicated, and so profane that KPFA, Berkeley's community radio station, pulled its live broadcast for fear of losing its license.

Mailer poked mercilessly at what he called "the recesses of that mysterious and explosive personality" in the White House: "Johnson had compromised too many contradictions. And now the contradictions were in his face. When he smiled the corners of his mouth squeezed gloom. When he was pious, his eyes twinkled irony. When he spoke in a righteous tone, he looked corrupt . . . Roaring, smarting, bellowing, stabbing fingers on advisers' chests, hugging his daughters, enjoying his food, belching, burping, mean and unforgiving, vindictive, generous, ebullient, vain, suddenly depressed, then roguish, then overbearing, suddenly modest again, only to bellow and fart once more."

Mailer challenged the conventional Cold War view of global geopolitics. "And I would argue," he said, "that neither capitalism nor communism is the defense of civilization, but that they are rather each in their own way malignancies upon the spirit of honest adventure and open inquiry which developed across the centuries from the primitive man to the Renaissance." He charged that Johnson had cynically escalated the war to boost his own political power, coldly calculating that "if there was one thing better than Harlem in the summer, it was air raids on rice paddies and napalm on red gooks. *Now* we had a game."

Mailer concluded with a curse: "Only listen, Lyndon Johnson, you've gone too far this time. You are a bully with an air force, and since you will not call off your air force, there are young people who will persecute you back. It is a little thing, but it will hound you into nightmares and endless corridors of night without sleep. It will hound you. For listen, this is only one of the thousand things they will do. They will go on marches and they will make demonstrations, and they will begin a war of public protest against you which will never cease. It will go on and on, and it will get stronger and stronger."

Young people, he said, might just print photographs of the president and post them everywhere—only upside down.

"Vietnam! Hot damn! You, Lyndon Johnson, will see those pictures everywhere . . . Everywhere, upside down! Upside down!"

Vietnam Day was one of the nation's earliest teach-ins on the war in Vietnam, and to that point the largest, running thirty-six continuous hours on May 20 and 21, 1965. More than ten thousand people came to the field behind the student union building to hear some of the nation's leading social and political critics discuss not only the war but those aspects of American politics that had made possible, even inevitable, the country's descent into a conflict they warned would end in military and moral defeat.

The event had been prompted by Johnson's sharp escalation of the undeclared war in Southeast Asia; that March, he had begun massive bombing of North Vietnam with Operation Rolling Thunder. For though the war had been on the margins of public consciousness, its history was starting to emerge in a smattering of teach-ins and protests around the country: how the U.S. government had been financially supporting South Vietnam's fight against North Vietnam since at least 1954, when the French withdrew after a failed nine-year military campaign against the Chinese-backed North Vietnamese; how President Kennedy had refused to send uniformed troops to Vietnam but increased the number of "military advisers" from the seven hundred Eisenhower had sent to twelve thousand, deploying helicopters, U.S. fighter pilots, and Green Berets; how Johnson had further intensified the conflict.

LBJ had campaigned as a peaceful alternative to Goldwater. But in August 1964 he announced that North Vietnamese torpedo boats had attacked two U.S. Navy ships in international waters of the Gulf of Tonkin. Historians have since questioned the veracity of the government's claims, but Johnson asked for authority to take all necessary steps to protect American armed forces and Congress swiftly approved the Gulf of Tonkin Resolution, allowing the president to use military force in Vietnam without formally declaring war. Johnson sent in troops and the aerial bombing began. Polls showed that Americans overwhelmingly supported the war.

Like Kennedy and Eisenhower, Johnson subscribed to that article of Cold War faith, the Domino Theory: the conflict in Vietnam was not just a local battle over self-determination but part of a global, Manichean struggle between democracy and communism, God and godlessness, good and evil. If South Vietnam fell, the theory went, other countries would topple one after the other in a cascade, until the United States and its allies were surrounded and it was game over.

Jerry Rubin and Barbara Gullahorn had come up with the idea for Vietnam Day to challenge Johnson's claims that the war was necessary and right. A Cincinnati native who had attended Oberlin College, Rubin worked as a newspaper sportswriter before coming to Berkeley in January 1964 for graduate studies in sociology. He dropped out, joined in the civil rights movement, and that summer visited Cuba, where he was impressed by speeches of Fidel Castro and Che Guevara. He was involved only on the fringes of the Free Speech Movement and was not arrested in it. Gullahorn was a political science major who had planned to join the Peace Corps. The couple enlisted the help of Stephen Smale, a brilliant UC Berkeley math professor and supporter of the Free Speech Movement who had publicly called for an end to the bombing. Rubin, Gullahorn, and Smale wanted to put on the biggest teach-in yet. In Smale's words, they wanted to "make Johnson cringe."

Working out of Rubin's tiny apartment in a run-down rooming house at 2502 Telegraph Avenue, four blocks from Sproul Plaza, they sought out famous and provocative speakers. Among those they enlisted besides Mailer were the independent journalist I. F. Stone, the child psychologist Benjamin Spock, the Mississippi Freedom Summer organizer Robert Moses, the San Francisco poet Kenneth Rexroth, the folksinger Phil Ochs, the hipster-satirist Paul Krassner, the iconoclastic San Francisco Mime Troupe, the comedian Dick Gregory, and Mario Savio.

Vietnam Day represented a confluence of the currents coursing through Berkeley. The civil rights movement had inspired the Free Speech Movement; the FSM, having affirmed students' right to engage in political advocacy on campus, had cleared the way for Vietnam Day. Already, these forces were coming together in what would become known as the New Left, a brash, independent reform movement that broke not only with conservatives but with liberals. The unifying theme was that, contrary to the Norman Rockwell images of America that graced the covers of *The Saturday Evening Post*, things were terribly wrong and young people could change them.

The speakers had no one point of view, but all displayed deep disillusionment with Democrats who had bought into Cold War politics, appeased Joseph McCarthy, acted slowly on civil rights, and now, overwhelmingly, supported the war. The U.S. State Department had declined invitations to send a speaker, saying the program was "not balanced." The government's refusal to participate was symbolized by an empty chair onstage.

I. F. Stone, the journalist known for poring over official documents and exposing government deceits in his self-published *I. F. Stone's Weekly*, drew the teach-in's greatest applause. Short, owlish, with wire-rimmed glasses balanced on his nose, "Izzy" Stone gave the crowd a history lesson. He focused on a fundamental contradiction in post–World War II American foreign policy: the United States' willingness to support corrupt politicians and dictators around the world because they were anti-Communist. He argued that America had undermined governments engaged in democratic social reform because their programs conflicted with the financial interests of U.S. corporations such as United Fruit and Standard Oil. This foreign policy, Stone said, violated the best American principles and perversely promoted misery, revolution, and communism. "We are," he declared, "our own worst enemies!"

Benjamin Spock called on parents and students to stop the war. Author of the postwar era's most popular books on child care, the pediatrician had departed sharply from traditional child-rearing doctrine. His theories vexed conservative psychologists like Alex Sherriffs, who deemed them overly permissive. "It has been particularly parents who have been able to visualize the danger to their children of fallout and of nuclear destruction," Spock told the crowd. "And I think it is students, those who realize that they will be asked to fight the wars, who also have been able to avoid the denial that affects at least ninety percent of our population." Americans mistakenly assumed, he added, that "all the difficulties the United States gets into in international affairs is due to the malevolence of our adversaries and that the United States has had no responsibility in creating these difficulties."

Now Savio rose to speak. The student who had overcome a stutter and electrified the campus from atop a police car took the stage with some of the nation's most famous social critics. As he had done so often during the

Free Speech Movement days, he drew people in to consider the issue with him. "So, all I really have are a lot of questions, and I hope they are questions similar to ones that have been troubling other people who are here. Maybe if we can at least get our questions out in the open, we can begin to talk about the answers."

He asked: How had the United States gone from rebelling against its imperial oppressor in 1776 to opposing revolts of other nations oppressed by imperialism in 1965? "I have been trying to figure out why it is that we ended up on the other side," he said. "I try to think of the bad things that our leaders say about those people who now are on the other side. One of the things they say is, 'They don't believe in God. See, the Communists officially don't believe in God.' And it seemed to me awfully peculiar that we should be in the situation of declared or undeclared war against people, at least in part, because they claim not to believe in God. I don't believe in God . . .

"Let's consider a very radical suggestion," he continued. "What if, for example, the president of the United States announced tomorrow that over a period of five years the United States would totally disarm? Not just nuclear weapons, but all weapons. Put them away slowly so as not to destroy the American economy. And the president would extend an invitation to the Russians and the Chinese to do likewise . . .

"But no solution such as this could be seriously considered or discussed by any of the responsible people formulating our foreign policy . . . And that brings me to what I think is the important question.

"If an idea like that couldn't be seriously entertained before a responsible audience, then in what sense is decision-making in America democratic? In what sense? What about the consent of the governed?"

Stepping to the microphone, Dick Gregory, the civil rights activist and comedian, riffed on his new book *Nigger*. "And don't act like you never heard that word before," he said. "The book's dedicated to my mother. Just like to read the dedication page to you: it says, 'Dear Mom, wherever you are, if ever you hear the word *nigger* again, remember, they're just advertising my book.'" Gregory had even mailed a copy to President Johnson. "I wasn't that stuck on him having my book," he explained. "I was just determined to get me a *Nigger* in the White House."

Gregory urged civil disobedience. "When the law starts upholding bad laws and enforcing poverty on people, then the law becomes the criminal and must be broke." Noting that the state's voters had recently passed Proposition 14 to overturn the Rumford Fair Housing Act, he disparaged California as "Mississippi with palm trees."

"And for the benefit of you FBI agents that might still be in the house," he said, "tell Hoover to give you all better flashbulbs because you cats is making my picture a little bit too black. And also, you FBI agents in the house, I'd like for you to take this message to J. Edgar Hoover who called Martin Luther King 'the most notorious liar in the country.' King is so upset by it, he's crying all the way to the front of the bus."

Gregory continued, "Hoover just blasted your Free Speech Movement out here as being Communist-controlled. He's called SNCC Communist-controlled. But I want you FBI agents to go back and ask Hoover for me, why is it he's never called Lincoln Rockwell [founder of the American Nazi Party, and no relation to Norman Rockwell] Communist? Or the Ku Klux Klan? Hoover, to me, is probably the most vicious, dangerous man in this country. Yeah, good old J. Edgar Hoover is so damn quick to call anything that happens for good 'Communist.'"

FBI agents *were* in the house. Special Agent Don Jones and four more were monitoring the teach-in, taking down names. Even before Vietnam Day began, Curtis Lynum, the head of the San Francisco office, had taken steps to undermine the event. He and other FBI officials believed the teach-in would not present the proper perspective on the war, so they covertly arranged for the distribution of five thousand copies of a *San Francisco Examiner* editorial linking it to subversives. "The Berkeley technique is one the Communists have long used," it read. "They seek out protest issues that have legitimate overtones. Then, through the skillful manipulation of loyal citizens they are able to mask their own divisive and alien purposes."

As proof of these charges, the *Examiner* cited Hoover's recently released congressional testimony about Savio, as well as Ed Montgomery's November series about the FSM that, in turn, had been based on information the FBI leaked to him under the bureau's counterintelligence program. The editorial concluded, "Before you tear up your draft card . . . before you condemn the military . . . before you march in peace parades . . . ask yourself: Does this serve freedom . . . or slavery?"

Lynum told Hoover that his distribution of this editorial was "the only organized effort to present a rational defense of United States foreign policy at this 'teach-in.'" But the FBI's editorializing had little apparent effect. The teach-in vastly exceeded its organizers' expectations, generating huge crowds, contributions, and a list of volunteers eager to establish a permanent Vietnam Day Committee, which became, for a while, the nation's largest, most effective, and most provocative antiwar group.

•

In July 1965, the Vietnam Day Committee moved its office a few blocks from Rubin's apartment to a run-down two-story Victorian house with an overgrown garden at 2407 Fulton Street. The front door was always unlocked. The living room had a broken-down couch and walls adorned with a STOP THE WAR banner, a psychedelic peace sign, and a large poster of the Latin American revolutionary Che Guevara. There was an aquarium containing a live turtle beneath a sign warning, "Sex Lesson Number One: Don't Fuck with a Turtle." An adjacent room was lined with books on Southeast Asia and foreign policy, and a refrigerator in the dingy kitchen was usually loaded with beer. Drug use was discouraged, but the smell of burning marijuana sometimes laced the air.

All kinds of people showed up. Allen Ginsberg, his dome bald, his black beard long, often dropped in. Joe McDonald, a Berkeley folksinger, stopped by. So did Phil Ochs, the protest singer out of Greenwich Village's folk music scene who had played the 1963 Newport Folk Festival along with Peter, Paul, and Mary, Joan Baez, and Bob Dylan. Savio sometimes showed up, too, though he sought no special status and deliberately acted like any other of the students, dropouts, professors, housewives, and octogenarian members of Grandmothers for Peace who made up the VDC's rank and file.

The place was frenetic. With donations pouring in, the committee soon had ten staff members, paid a hundred dollars a month each, and twelve incessantly ringing phones. Volunteer subcommittees were established to write leaflets, plan protests, and correspond with other antiwar groups.

At first, Jerry Rubin and Steve Smale cochaired the VDC. Although Rubin was a dropout and could be bombastic, he and the soft-spoken math genius worked well together. Eventually, the VDC elected a steering committee that also included Robert Scheer, a UC Berkeley graduate student who had written a widely cited history of American involvement in Vietnam; the UC Berkeley math professor Morris Hirsch; and the Free Speech Movement veterans Jack Weinberg, Steve Weissman, Bettina Aptheker, and Rob Hurwitt.

Like the FSM, the VDC was nonideological, nonexclusionary, and operated to an extraordinary degree on the basis of participatory democracy. "You could go in there most any time. It was a place where a lot of discussion went on . . . a lot of debate, a lot of learning. People were still trying to find things," recalled Joe Blum, a VDC volunteer. "It didn't have a party line. People had to think for themselves."

There were frequent mass meetings at headquarters or in some large room on campus. Anyone could speak, and the meetings could go on for hours before consensus was reached. Members of the Communist Party, the Socialist Workers Party, the Progressive Labor Party, and pacifist groups such as the War Resisters League participated, but the vast majority of people who showed up were political independents. Ginsberg's frequent attendance, for example, drew long-haired young people, more interested in peace than politics, who were becoming known as hippies.

Ginsberg's presence also drew the FBI's interest. Bureau agents described the pacifist poet in an April 26, 1965, form letter to the Secret Service as "potentially dangerous." According to the form's check-marked boxes, Ginsberg fell under the rather broad category that included "subversives, ultrarightists, racists and fascists who meet one or more of the following criteria: (a) Evidence of emotional instability (including unstable residence and employment record) or irrational or suicidal behavior; (b) Expressions of strong or violent anti-U.S. sentiment; (c) Prior acts (including arrests or convictions) or conduct or statements indicating a propensity for violence and antipathy toward good order and government."

In fact, Ginsberg was a steadfast proponent of nonviolent tactics and would repeatedly steer the VDC away from potentially violent confrontations.

Michael O'Hanlon was one of the many people who seemed to connect with the committee through happenstance. Raised in a blue-collar Bronx household, O'Hanlon had a conservative background. His parents were Republicans and so was he in the early sixties when he enrolled at Orange Coast College, near Los Angeles, to study petroleum technology. He became involved with the Young Republicans and the Young Americans for Freedom, and in a campus debate defended the war. Though judged the winner, he began to wonder, and after researching the Geneva Accords he concluded his opponent had been correct.

O'Hanlon quit school, traveled around the country, and woke up in a Haight-Ashbury crash pad. Visiting Berkeley, he found himself on Sproul Plaza watching a fierce argument about the war between a young man with bushy hair and a mustache manning the VDC's table and five members of the ROTC. O'Hanlon jumped into the debate on the antiwar side. When it was over, the mustached man introduced himself as Jerry Rubin, and asked him to watch the table for a while.

O'Hanlon quickly became a key VDC member. He staffed the table on Sproul Plaza by day, and slept on the couch at headquarters by night.

He became the group's main man on campus, handing out leaflets, recruiting new members, debating all comers. He kept a large bulletin board
beside the table and posted articles about the war, whether pro or con. "I
believed in as much openness as possible," he recalled. "Trying to hide
the unpleasant side was always a bad idea." Only later would it come out
that he had his own secrets.

Despite their diversity, the VDC's members agreed that they needed
to stage media-grabbing spectacles to focus public attention on what they
saw as an unjust war. As the *VDC News* declared:

"Vietnam, like Mississippi, is not an aberration—it is a mirror of
America . . . Vietnam reduces to absurdity the fifth grade civics class
rhetoric about American democracy and American morality, and lays bare
the reality: a white nation bombing a colored people; a Christian country
bombing a non-Christian country; a rich, highly developed nation laying
waste the resources of an underdeveloped land.

"We must say to Johnson, Inc.: 'If you want to go on killing Vietnamese, you must jail Americans.' . . . We will invoke a law higher than that of
the state, as the United States and its allies did at the Nuremberg Trials:
When the state acts immorally, it is the duty of the individuals to refuse to
participate in its immorality . . .

"Our massive civil disobedience, aimed at blocking the war machine
of the United States, will send shock waves from Maine to California, and
from the United States to all parts of the world."

On July 29, members of the VDC and the FSM led a march of about five
hundred people from Sproul Plaza to Berkeley's Civic Center Park to protest the war and the unexpectedly stiff sentences recently given Savio and
others arrested in the FSM's Sproul Hall sit-in. At the rally, Thomas Parkinson, a UC Berkeley English professor, spoke in support of the defendants.
A poet and proponent of the Beats, he had been shot in the face at his
campus office in 1961 by a religious zealot who claimed God had ordered
him to kill "Communist" teachers. Parkinson urged the students not to
be discouraged by their sentences and to keep protesting "to make a better
world." Steve Smale condemned the war. And—as Norman Mailer had
vowed—VDC members passed out flyers featuring a photograph of President Johnson, upside down. Upside down! Ginsberg chanted a Tibetan
mantra while clinking little silver cymbals, which he said would calm the
judge.

Savio had just been sentenced to 120 days in jail for his role in the sit-in—the stiffest penalty handed down yet. He now urged more demonstrations against the court proceedings, which he termed patently unfair. He also called for the formation of a new political party, criticizing both Democrats and Republicans as too beholden to business interests. "We must construct our own community of protest to take back our self-government," he said.

Bettina Aptheker, her dirty-blond hair tied back, stepped forward to deliver her remarks, but instead pointed to a middle-aged man in suit and tie who was taking notes at the periphery. "There's someone here in the crowd today I would like to introduce you to," Aptheker said, pausing so people could turn to look. "His name is Donald Jones, and he is an FBI agent."

Jones had been investigating the twenty-two-year-old history major and self-avowed Communist for months. One day she had answered the door at her North Oakland cottage to find a stocky man in a suit, a red tie, and a crew cut. "Good morning," he said. "My name is Donald Jones. I'm with the FBI." Holding out his badge, he asked to come in. Aptheker said no. Jones persisted. "You would make it a lot easier on yourself if you cooperated with us," he said. Shutting the door, she replied, "I will never cooperate with you." A few weeks later, she came home early to find another man in a suit in her living room, rifling her desk files. She screamed and he fled. On another occasion, she discovered two other men in suits as they were breaking into the home of friends who had recently put her up. She saw all of this as political harassment and had publicly called for Hoover's resignation.

"There he is!" she said, now pointing at Jones. "Come up here, Mr. Jones! Come up and speak to us! We believe in freedom of speech!"

People chuckled and stared. Jones acted nonchalant, as if she meant someone else, and after a while slipped away.

But the FBI agent was upset. He'd been caught snooping, red-handed as it were, and that could embarrass the bureau, a violation of Hoover's cardinal rule. Returning to the FBI office in the Wells Fargo Building a few blocks away, he submitted a detailed report to Lynum, trying to put the best light on it.

Jones explained that the FBI now had 161 Berkeley residents on its Security Index. It was his job to track them and to periodically try to interview them, as he had Aptheker. During the fifties most Communists had kept quiet about the FBI's approaches to avoid a stigma, but she had gleefully gone public and taken him along.

"As a consequence," Jones wrote, "other unidentified individuals who were in sympathy with the anti-American purpose of the rally harangued me and took my picture. At all times I maintained dignified silence and conducted myself in a most gentlemanly manner. I believe that this tactic was employed by them in order to harass the FBI and hinder it in carrying out its investigative responsibilities."

One of Hoover's aides ordered Jones reassigned, but Lynum appealed to Hoover and he was spared.

Aptheker had nearly caused Jones serious trouble—and he would not forget it.

One day Mike O'Hanlon noticed a small article in the *Berkeley Daily Gazette* about the Santa Fe Railroad's plans to reopen a stretch of track running through the Berkeley flats. The train would transport troops to the Oakland Army Terminal, where they would board ships bound for Vietnam. O'Hanlon showed the story to Jerry Rubin, he recalled, and "the next thing I know I'm in the Central Valley, waiting for a train to come by so I could alert them it was on the way."

When the troop train approached University Avenue in Berkeley on the morning of August 5, 1965, about a hundred pickets were waiting. They carried signs reading, DON'T FIGHT FOR A DICTATORSHIP and MAKE LOVE NOT WAR. As the locomotive neared, the engineer blasted his horn. The train slowed, but it kept coming and three young men holding a banner that said "STOP!" jumped away at the last moment.

The next afternoon, the crowd awaiting the troop train had grown to four hundred. This time they tried to block it as it rolled through Emeryville, just south of Berkeley. Alameda County sheriff's deputies formed a flying wedge in front of the engine and escorted the train and its cargo of soldiers past them.

Led by Rubin and Smale, the VDC responded with its most aggressive protest yet. Just before noon on August 12 the largest crowd to date tried to block a troop train as it passed through Berkeley. About five hundred demonstrators gathered as counterdemonstrators heckled them. Police again tried to contain the protesters, but they scattered. Several of them sat down on the tracks as the locomotive chugged toward them. Fearing some would be crushed, O'Hanlon ran to them and shoved them aside.

Rubin leaped onto the train. Other demonstrators grabbed the steel handgrips on the cars and hoisted themselves aboard to hand antiwar leaflets to the soldiers. Police yanked one woman off the train twice but she clambered up a third time, hanging from its side for nearly a mile. Four people were injured in falls from the cars, and two were arrested, but the protesters ultimately succeeded in momentarily halting the train. From behind closed windows, most of the soldiers regarded the demonstrators blankly, but one held up his fingers in a peace sign.

Rubin and Smale were ecstatic. As they had hoped, the troop train protests generated dramatic headlines and photographs in newspapers from the *Berkeley Daily Gazette* to *The New York Times*.

FBI agents who had mixed in with the spectators took their own photographs and identified the demonstrators for their reports to Hoover.

VDC leaders, however, already were planning their next action.

Perched high atop Nob Hill, the Fairmont was one of San Francisco's most elegant hotels and commanded a stunning view of downtown. The massive Beaux-Arts structure had been built with a mining fortune, and until they burned in the great earthquake, it was surrounded by mansions belonging to the "big four" railroad magnates, Stanford, Crocker, Hopkins, and Huntington. Every president since Taft had made the Fairmont his San Francisco residence, and the United Nations Charter was drafted in its Garden Room.

On the sidewalk in front, Jerry Rubin and his band of scruffy protesters, some of whom carried placards that asked, MUST WE KILL MOTHERS AND KIDS? took a position. And as cable cars full of tourists rattled by, Rubin scanned the traffic for General Maxwell Taylor, who, the VDC had learned, would soon be checking in.

Taylor had been chairman of the Joint Chiefs of Staff and U.S. ambassador to Vietnam, and was now a special adviser to President Johnson on Vietnam. In the words of one VDC leaflet, he was "one of the chief architects" of the war: he had authored the "Taylor Plan," which first committed American troops; conceived the idea of turning Vietnamese villages into "strategic hamlets"; and supported the bombing of North Vietnam. "Gen. Taylor has blood on his hands!" another flyer said. "We intend to stand witness to this fact as long as he remains in this city."

When the general's limousine pulled up at about 6:00 p.m., the demonstrators swarmed it and one of them sprawled across its hood. They screamed epithets as he pushed his way out of the car, and followed him into the hotel, across the plush mezzanine carpets, past the Corinthian columns, and into the elevator. Hotel guests gaped as he fled across the lobby and ducked into a hotel office, only to have his tormentors mass outside the door, trapping him inside for more than an hour as they stomped their feet and sang, "We Shall Not Be Moved."

Rubin, Barbara Gullahorn, and Steve Weissman were among those arrested and carried away by police, but other protesters kept vigil outside the hotel all night, rallying the next afternoon when Robert Scheer, a VDC leader and foreign editor of the radical magazine *Ramparts,* made a speech condemning the war.

The Fairmont protest generated more headlines for the VDC—and more reports from the FBI agents who had staked it out.

Taylor would only tell a reporter, "I have no real comment to make on this unpleasantness."

Emboldened by these successes, Rubin and Smale vowed to mount nothing less than the nation's largest-ever antiwar protest.

As announced by the VDC, the International Days of Protest would be "one massive internationally coordinated action" to bring "the full impact of world opinion . . . against the policy of the American government."

With the protests set for October 15 and 16, VDC volunteers began organizing at home and abroad. They contacted antiwar groups in Argentina, Uruguay, Mexico, Great Britain, Canada, and Japan. VDC members also joined with Students for a Democratic Society to form the National Coordinating Committee to End the War in Vietnam, based in Madison, Wisconsin, and began planning protests in sixty U.S. cities, including Atlanta, Boston, Chicago, and New York.

The biggest and most dramatic action would be in Berkeley. There would be another teach-in on campus followed by a nighttime march to the Oakland Army Terminal, where the committee threatened "massive civil disobedience"—or what Smale called a "peace invasion." In the *VDC News,* committee leaders suggested that "if thousands of students and others block the gates of the Oakland Army Terminal where munitions are shipped to Vietnam, and are arrested . . . scenes of thousands of middle class youths being carried away by military police will be in every American living room . . . The issue will be opened."

The VDC's plans caused new concerns for the bureau. Back on August 3, 1965, Lynum informed Hoover that his initial inquiry had determined the antiwar group was not part of a Communist plot and that further investigation of the organization "does not appear warranted at this time." That was not enough for the Boss. On August 12, he ordered

Lynum to intensify the investigation on the ground that the VDC "has been very active in organizing and participating in demonstrations protesting U.S. policy toward Vietnam." Hoover's explicit rationale for the investigation had thus shifted from trying to ferret out Communists to spying on citizens because they were dissenting from government policy. As the Church committee would later report, the bureau's investigations wound up "targeting almost every anti-war group, and spread to students demonstrating against anything."

More than a dozen agents were soon investigating the VDC, using increasingly intrusive methods of surveillance. They obtained lists of the numbers dialed on the phones at VDC headquarters, and the phone company, without a legally required subpoena, traced them and identified the people called. They obtained the organization's bank records, again without a subpoena, including lists of deposits and the payees on each check. A bank employee tipped off Rubin, however, and he held a press conference and accused the FBI of prying. An FBI spokesman falsely denied it.

Other agents tracked down the company that made the VDC's antiwar buttons and dropped in on the owner. He revealed that the committee had ordered thousands of pins reading HOT DAMN! VIETNAM DAY COMMITTEE, displaying President Johnson's picture upside down. The buttons were of particular interest, according to an agent's report, because "President Johnson has now become aware that his picture has been displayed in VDC demonstrations in an upside down manner. He is provoked about this."

The agents continued to secretly receive information from their special contacts in the media. Dick Leonard, the KCBS radio reporter whose wife worked for the bureau, provided unaired tapes of interviews in which he questioned VDC members about committee operations. A *San Francisco Examiner* employee supplied unpublished photographs taken at a rally. Ed Montgomery, the *Examiner* reporter, passed along information from his interview with the VDC leader Morris Hirsch.

Alex Sherriffs had by now been dismissed as vice chancellor but continued to teach psychology and serve as an FBI source. He slipped Agent Don Jones confidential university records concerning students and faculty involved in the antiwar group, disclosing, among other things, Steve Weissman's medical history.

Informers recruited by the agents took information from VDC headquarters, including lists of members, contributors, subscribers to the *VDC News*, and people forming a legal defense committee in case of arrests. At least two infiltrators became involved in planning protests. One was elected to the VDC steering committee and helped direct its activities even as he reported on them to the FBI.

Jerry Rubin and other VDC leaders suspected there were informers in their midst and were wary of anyone proposing violent activity. Mike O'Hanlon recalled that one man suggested blowing up the tracks to block the troop trains. Rob Hurwitt, a graduate student in English who was in charge of training the VDC monitors for the upcoming march to the Oakland Army Terminal, recalled that two men volunteered to use force against policemen who tried to stop the protest. One of them whispered that he had access to guns. Hurwitt and O'Hanlon figured these people were either crazy or agents provocateurs trying to entrap them.

FBI agents took particular interest in the VDC's communications systems. Having learned through informers that parade monitors would use walkie-talkies, agents canvassed local electronics stores and identified the gear they had purchased. They looked into whether the VDC's use of the walkie-talkies would be illegal, which could provide an opportunity to arrest the leaders or otherwise interfere with the march, but the Federal Communications Commission said no license was necessary. Agents also told U.S. Department of Justice officials that VDC members had discussed using the devices to monitor and jam police radios. Assistant U.S. Attorney Jerrold Ladar assured the bureau he would "definitely" prosecute any protesters interfering with police communications.

"Such tactics," Ladar declared, "are not only in violation of the law, but could cause a terrible situation in the event of an emergency . . ."

Edwin Meese III, the deputy district attorney who had helped prosecute Savio and the other Sproul Hall sit-ins, was a graduate of UC Berkeley's Boalt Hall School of Law and a reserve army intelligence official. He also was the point man on campus protests for District Attorney Frank Coakley, a Republican whose office had jurisdiction over Berkeley and Oakland and secretly maintained one of the oldest and most aggressive political intelligence units in the state. Meese worked with the intelligence unit and other police agencies investigating the VDC, including the University of California Police Department, the Berkeley Police Department, and the Oakland Police Department, which had three rookie officers working full-time as undercover agents inside the committee.

Meese also collaborated with the FBI. He produced a confidential report on sixteen VDC leaders that was sent to the bureau under the heading "Subject: Key Personnel of 'Vietnam Day Committee.'" In early October, he and Don Lynn, of the DA's intelligence unit, met with FBI agents at their Oakland office to discuss the upcoming march. He told the agents that police might block the marchers if they tried to enter Oakland, and that if they sat down in the street and refused to disperse, police would give a secret signal and make mass arrests. The agencies favored a plan, he said, to arrest the leaders first, as they had during the big sit-in at Sproul Hall, on the theory that the remaining protesters would then be easier to handle. Police officials also discussed deploying a substance called "instant banana peel" to disable protesters by making them slip and fall.

With the big march less than two weeks off, a frustrated Frank Coakley convened a conference of concerned law-enforcement officials. The university, the district attorney told them, was helping the VDC illegally interfere with the armed forces. He had asked Governor Brown to order President Kerr to bar the committee from using the Berkeley campus to mount the protest. But Brown had merely forwarded Coakley's request to Kerr, who passed it along to the new chancellor, Roger Heyns. And since the VDC had meanwhile announced it would abstain from civil disobedience during the march, Heyns had ruled the committee could hold its teach-in on campus.

Lieutenant Colonel Schroy of the U.S. Army had other worries. Warning the police officials that he was about to reveal very sensitive information, he said the Oakland Army Terminal was extremely vulnerable to trespass, "that even a two or three year old child could get in." Moreover, the base had stockpiled critical materials bound for Vietnam, and if the demonstrators damaged them "it would be a serious blow."

Agent Albert Clark gave a "rundown" on the FBI's investigation of the committee, saying "this was not a communist-sponsored operation, although there were some individual subversives connected with the VDC."

But neither Clark nor any other FBI official mentioned that the bureau was in the midst of a secret campaign to disrupt the peace group. Hoover had initiated the COINTELPRO operation with a memo declaring that the VDC was "the moving force in organizing an international demonstration . . . in protest of United States policy toward Vietnam." His directive noted, "Due to the loose organizational structure of this group, it appears to lend itself to our taking effective counterintelligence action." He ordered Lynum to consider the use of false mailings under the committee's name changing the date of the demonstrations; bogus letters to other activist groups such as Students for a Democratic Society "to create animosity between the two organizations"; and a phony document criticizing the North Vietnamese for atrocities against U.S. troops. Noting that a group of UC Berkeley professors had written an open letter criticizing the VDC, Hoover also ordered, "Consider whether this situation can be exploited . . ."

Lynum assured Hoover, "This matter has not been overlooked. Such actions as have been practical have been taken. These include close cooperation with civilian law enforcement agencies and military authorities often leading to unforeseen problems for the VDC in their demonstrations; selected anonymous mailings of appropriate news articles and editorials to VDC headquarters and VDC leaders; and the removal of material from VDC headquarters which handicapped their operations."

Further, Lynum suggested tipping off local authorities that VDC headquarters was filthy, that the committee was "selling" liquor without a license (the help-yourself beer for twenty-five cents a can in the refrigerator), and that marijuana cigarettes had been seen on the premises. He proposed that the bureau make an anonymous donation to the professors opposing the VDC and recruit South Vietnamese speakers to attend rallies and counter the VDC's speakers.

But Lynum warned, "Any approach to the matter of counterintelligence here must bear in mind that the VDC is, for the most part, composed of highly educated young people (many of whom hold doctorates), who have boundless energy and apparently more money and manpower than the Bureau would have for counter measures."

Coakley called it treason.

But as people gathered for the teach-in at Lower Sproul Plaza, Paul Goodman, the author of *Growing Up Absurd*, and other speakers affirmed it was right to protest the war. Brigadier General Hugh B. Hester, a retired army veteran, said, "I never knew protests and marching to express opinion was treason. You are not opposing those in the military service. You are helping them by bringing to an end an immoral, illegal, and totally unnecessary war." Franz Schurmann, an Asia expert and UC Berkeley professor, criticized both China and the United States for using the war for their own purposes. Neither nation cared how many Vietnamese died, he declared, warning that such official cynicism was costing America international respect. Allen Ginsberg, ever the pacifist provocateur, read what one FBI agent at the scene would only describe in his report as "a very obscene poem that was anti-war in nature."

The most peculiar presentation was made by Ken Kesey, who saun-
tered onto the speakers' stage wearing an orange jumpsuit and a Day-Glo
orange army helmet ornamented with Soviet hammers and sickles, Nazi
swastikas, and American flags. This was the result of elaborate preparation
undertaken by Kesey and his entourage of Merry Pranksters at his spread
in La Honda, where he now lived, about half an hour southwest of Palo
Alto in the Santa Cruz Mountains. Deep in the redwoods, Kesey had a
cabin where he wrote beneath the filtered sunlight as discarded marijuana
seeds sprouted from the decaying carpet. As his friend and fellow Prankster
Robert Stone would write, "Witchy fingers of morning glory vine wound
in every shelf and corner of that cabin like illuminations in some hoary
manuscript."

The Pranksters had repainted their bus specially for the rally in a bizarre montage that featured nationalist symbols against a background the
color of dried blood. They rigged it with fake cannons and a gun turret on
the roof. And, as usual, they wired the bus with loudspeakers, microphones,
tape recorders, and cameras to create their own instantaneous, interactive,
multimedia Möbius strip recording their experience. On the day of the
protest, Neal Cassady, a Prankster who had been Jack Kerouac's buddy
and was the model for the hero of his book *On the Road*, took the wheel
and they headed north toward Berkeley.

Kesey's crew hadn't gotten far before local police stopped the bus,
questioned its occupants, and figured they'd better notify the FBI. According to one officer's summary, Lee Quarnstrom politely explained that
he and Kesey had organized a caravan of cars to follow the bus from the
Stanford Shopping Center to Berkeley. "The vehicles will be decorated
in a number of ways," the report said. "One of the cars has the Stars and
Stripes painted on it with a replica of a machine gun on top and on the
back of it is a sign saying 'Bomb the World.' Others of the cars will have
the swastika painted on them."

Kesey and Quarnstrom, it added, "were arrested a couple months ago
in Kesey's cabin in La Honda and charged with possession of narcotics,
and are now out on bail. They say their organization is called Intrepid Trips,
Inc., and that the address of the organization is the same as Kesey's . . .
They say they are against the war, but are not necessarily in sympathy
with the pacifists; however, if they are arrested they will not resist. They
stated specifically, 'We are looking for publicity.'"

Arriving at campus near dusk, Cassady parked the bus near Sproul
Plaza and the Pranksters were soon onstage with Kesey. But instead of delivering the rousing antiwar speech that might have been expected from

the author of *One Flew Over the Cuckoo's Nest*, Kesey, in his soft Oregon drawl, imparted a cosmic view of the situation. He suggested the antiwar protesters were unwittingly part of the establishment's game, a centuries-old syndrome of war and protest. Then he pulled out a harmonica and began to wheeze out a dirgelike version of "Home on the Range." The Pranksters joined in with a cacophony of electric guitars and horns, as Tom Wolfe described it, "all crazed aglow at sundown." Then Kesey concluded, "There's only one thing to do . . . there's only one thing's gonna do any good at all . . . And that's everybody just look at it, look at the war, and turn your backs and say . . . Fuck it . . ."

Even as protesters from all over the country were streaming into Berkeley, lawyers for the Vietnam Day Committee were in court, making feverish last-minute legal challenges to a refusal by the city of Oakland to grant a parade permit. Coakley argued that a large march through rough neighborhoods in Oakland posed too much risk to people and property. Peter Franck, a VDC attorney, countered that the refusal violated the protesters' constitutional rights of free speech and free assembly. The Ninth Circuit U.S. Court of Appeals ruled in favor of Oakland: there would be no permit.

Nonetheless, as night fell on October 15, several thousand marchers departed from the campus entrance at Bancroft Way and Telegraph Avenue, crossed the Bancroft strip, and surged south down Telegraph Avenue toward the Oakland Army Terminal, where they intended to hold an all-night rally and hand soldiers leaflets calling for an end to the war.

First came a line of demonstrators displaying a black-and-white banner reading, NATIONAL, INTERNATIONAL DAYS OF PROTEST. Next came the VDC's battered red flatbed truck, equipped with loudspeakers and walkie-talkies to communicate with more than a hundred parade monitors wearing special armbands, whom Rob Hurwitt had trained to maintain safety. Aboard the truck were VDC leaders, including Robert Scheer, Jack Weinberg, and Steve Weissman. Allen Ginsberg and his fellow poet Gary Snyder chanted mantras to calm the crowd. Stretching behind them for more than a mile were rows and rows of protesters in a march the *Los Angeles Times* described as peaceful, if sometimes chaotic.

FBI agents in cars and on foot followed along, identifying participants, recording speeches, and noting Kesey's bus "had numerous small flags on it and a large U.S. flag on the back." Lawrence Cott, an operative with Harper Knowles's Western Research Foundation, helped the agents, photographing marchers and writing down license numbers of cars and messages on bumper stickers he deemed suspicious, such as "Make Love Not War."

As the forefront of the march reached the Oakland border along Woolsey Street, it was met by a phalanx of nearly three hundred Oakland policemen who formed two V-shaped rows blocking the road. They wore helmets and carried clubs. At the center stood Chief Edward Toothman of the Oakland police. Behind him were motorcycle squads and trucks loaded with barricades, sandbags, and rope. Six hundred National Guard troops were on alert.

The marchers lurched to a halt on the opposite side of the intersection of Telegraph and Woolsey. They had come only three-fourths of a mile, far short of their destination nearly seven miles away. The rhomboid of asphalt between them and the police line was a no-man's-land eerily illuminated with shards of light from cars, streetlamps, and neon signs. Hecklers lined the sidewalks, yelling, "Kill, kill, kill in Vietnam" and "We want war." Some threw eggs and harder objects. The mood was tense, the police were jumpy.

Jack Weinberg dismounted the platform on the VDC's red truck and walked toward the police line. A year earlier, he had been held inside the police car on Sproul Plaza for more than thirty hours. Now he crossed the barricade and met with Chief Toothman inside a police truck.

Although the Berkeley Police Department had let the parade proceed without a permit, Oakland authorities refused. Weinberg could not convince Toothman otherwise and soon walked back through the police line, across the asphalt to the red truck. The VDC leaders fiercely debated whether to confront the cops, ultimately voting 5–4 to turn back, a decision Weinberg announced from atop the truck. It took forty-seven minutes for the entire march to pass through the intersection and arc toward downtown Berkeley.

They regrouped at Civic Center Park, across from the Veterans Memorial Building, where Savio and the other Sproul Hall sit-ins had been sentenced. VDC leaders vowed to march again on Saturday, and a jug band featuring Joe McDonald and Barry Melton, who later formed Country Joe and the Fish, took the stage. Their performance was interrupted shortly after midnight, when someone lobbed an olive-green tear-gas canister into the crowd, scattering people. "I got it right in the face," O'Hanlon recalled.

A City of Berkeley police officer found the head monitor, Rob Hurwitt, in the park and summoned him to a squad car. Hurwitt climbed inside and Chief William Beall gave him a friendly warning: If the marchers tried to cross the city line the next day, Oakland police might respond with violence. Beall drove Hurwitt to the border to show him where the police would take positions. "We'll be right here," he said, "but we won't be able to control the OPD." The cruiser returned Hurwitt to the rally. By 3:00 a.m. most of the demonstrators had dispersed. Some slept in the park, only to be awakened early when the city gardener turned on the lawn sprinklers.

Five thousand people set out down Grove Street on Saturday afternoon and again marched toward Oakland. The VDC's battered red truck again led the parade with a chanting, cymbal-clanging Ginsberg. FBI agents again drove on parallel streets, listening in on the parade monitors' walkie-talkies. Oakland police again blocked the protesters' path at the city line.

But instead of turning back, this time people at the front of the march sat down and held a rally in the road. The VDC monitors trained by Hurwitt formed a protective line around them. Hundreds of spectators jammed the sidewalks, cheering or jeering.

Tucked behind the Oakland police line were members of the Hell's Angels, the motorcycle gang known for terrorizing small towns. The Angels were at the height of their infamy as outlaw bikers that fall, following a series of highly publicized arrests for rape, robbery, and rioting. FBI agents noticed the Angels' ominous behavior that day. "Some of the members began wrapping their hands very obviously in leather belts," an agent later reported, and one Angel muttered, "They aren't coming into Oakland."

Suddenly the Oakland police line parted. Out burst the Hell's Angels, snarling men in sunglasses, jackboots, and black leather jackets emblazoned with a winged skull. Conn "Ringo" Hallinan was one of the first VDC monitors to spot the bikers. Figuring they were there to bust up the march, he grabbed his walkie-talkie to warn the other monitors. "I tried to get back to Bob [Hurwitt] to tell him," Hallinan recalled, "but the damned thing didn't work." Hurwitt was back by the truck and had seen the Angels advance and grabbed his walkie-talkie to alert the marchers, but it, too, was jammed. "All of a sudden we were getting unexplained interference," he said. "We lost contact."

Eighteen Hell's Angels charged. One Angel slugged Hallinan. Two others grabbed an antiwar banner and tore it up, flinging the shreds into the air, yelling, "America first! America for Americans!" Two other Angels crashed through a line of VDC monitors, punching demonstrators, yelling, "Why don't you go home!"

Ralph H. "Sonny" Barger, president of the Hell's Angels Oakland chapter, came around the side, ran at Hurwitt, and swung a metal pipe against his head. For an instant Barger seemed stunned that Hurwitt was still standing. Then he ripped the bullhorn from Hurwitt's hands, smashed it on the road, and ran back behind the Oakland police line.

At this point, a writer for *The Daily Californian* reported, "Pandemonium broke out." Berkeley policemen who had been patrolling their side of the city line under Chief Beall's command rushed into the throng to grab the bikers. The Angels resisted and the officers clubbed them. Oakland police advanced in lockstep, closing the space between their line and the front of the march. Spectators screamed and fled. Several Angels ran to the red truck and ripped away its peace signs. Michael "Tiny" Walter, an Angel who stood six feet seven and weighed 270 pounds, was arrested on charges that he scuffled with the Berkeley police officer Claude D. Glenn, breaking his leg.

Chief Toothman of the Oakland police would later deny the VDC's charges that his men had permitted the Angels to attack the peace march. Asked why they didn't arrest the Angels before the assault, Toothman protested, "The Hell's Angels also have civil rights. You can't just arrest people unless they violate the law, even though they are a bunch of persons of bad repute."

Hunter Thompson, then working on his book *Hell's Angels*, had a different view. He had been behind the Oakland police line and found it near impenetrable even as a journalist. "So it is still beyond my understanding," he wrote, "how a dozen Hell's Angels, obviously intent on causing trouble, managed to filter through and attack the leaders of the protest march . . ." Robert Stone, who had become a friend of Kesey's at Stanford while working on his first novel, *Hall of Mirrors*, also was at the march. He later wrote that "the Oakland cops let the Hell's Angels attack the demonstrators."

Berkeley officers finally clubbed "Tiny" Walter into submission and arrested him and several other Angels. The demonstrators cheered the police and then finished their rally in the middle of the road. Robert Scheer gave a speech. "It is impossible for the United States to wage war of this brutality and duration without affecting our institutions," he said. "See what has already happened to them in California."

Sonny Barger would later say he thought no one expected the Hell's Angels to show up. They simply went to watch the march but were enraged by the antiwar message. "Something inside me snapped," he wrote in his autobiography, "and I responded the only way I knew how, violently."

FBI agents had known the Angels might show up. As Lynum reported to Hoover, "It had been rumored among police circles that these individuals, who have had numerous encounters with law enforcement, wanted to improve their image by attacking the VDC and thus showing their patriotism."

But FBI agents did not warn VDC members. Instead, they took steps that heightened the danger to the protesters, the police, and the public. In the weeks before the march, the agents had secured the parade monitors' communication codes: 10-1—situation normal; 10-6—parade stopped; 10-2—serious disturbance; and "May Day"—death, shooting, or serious accident. And though they knew from their inquiries at the Federal Communications Commission that it was illegal, they jammed the walkie-talkies by taking turns calling one another all afternoon on their radios. "This effectively prevented the VDC monitors from getting any real use out of the walkie-talkies," Lynum reported.

The director's aides replied, "You should be alert for future opportunities to initiate similar counterintelligence action."

Despite harassment from FBI agents and Hell's Angels, the International Days of Protest was another smashing success for the Vietnam Day Committee.

VDC leaders had instigated three days of protest against the war, with more than 100,000 people demonstrating in dozens of cities. They had drawn an estimated 10,000 people to each of the two biggest marches, in Manhattan and Berkeley. They had inspired demonstrations in London, Rome, Copenhagen, Stockholm, Brussels, and Tokyo. And now they were vowing to mount a new march and go all the way to the Oakland Army Terminal—with or without a parade permit.

Assemblyman Don Mulford was infuriated. He saw the VDC's latest escapades as further proof of Kerr's mismanagement of the university. In a speech to the Berkeley City Breakfast Club, the part-time insurance salesman declared that "in spite of announcements by U.C. President Clark Kerr that a new era has begun at the university, the cold fact remains that the protest is organized at the university and we find that university professors are once again involved. I'm tired of hearing bleating excuses for professors' illegal activities as their right under 'academic freedom' or 'free speech.'"

District Attorney Coakley demanded that university officials stop the VDC from using the campus as a "staging area" for unpermitted marches. And U.S. Senator George Murphy, Ronald Reagan's close friend from their days at the Screen Actors Guild, released a letter in which he urged Governor Brown to take firm action and "reassure the nation that a handful of leotard clad, bearded beatnicks [sic] do not speak for the majority of Californians."

Conservative anger over Kerr's handling of student unrest had been fired that summer by yet another red-bound report from Hugh Burns, the former undertaker and chairman of the senate's subcommittee on Un-American Activities. As usual, it was authored by the subcommittee's counsel and Kerr foe, R. E. Combs. "The Thirteenth Report on Un-American Activities in California," as it was officially titled, purported to impartially address subversive activities throughout the state. Just five pages were devoted to the John Birch Society, however, and the report essentially defended the burgeoning far-right group that claimed President Eisenhower had been a "dedicated, conscious agent of the Communist conspiracy" and that had recently doubled in size with chapters across the country.

By contrast, 156 of the report's 177 pages were devoted to alleged subversion at UC Berkeley and such subjects as SLATE, the Free Speech Movement, the Filthy Speech Movement, and the university's president. The report reviewed Kerr's career as far back as 1933, when he was a graduate student doing field research near Combs's hometown of Visalia for a study of the San Joaquin County cotton pickers' strike. It reiterated complaints that he had supported measures letting Communists speak on campus, failed to adequately discipline students, and opposed campus security measures such as the contact-man program. It claimed that over the decades he had come into "close contact" with Communists and some of his "most intimate colleagues" were participants in "Pro-Communist activities."

The report also charged that Kerr had lied to the regents by telling them he did not need a security officer to investigate "subversive activities" on campus because "arrangements had been made to get the information from the FBI." Both Combs and the FBI knew this allegation against Kerr was untrue: An agent had questioned Combs about the claim while he was preparing the report, and Combs acknowledged it was baseless. Yet Hoover gave tacit approval to Combs's accusation, permitting him to proceed without objection.

Only months earlier Kerr had been excoriated by students for denying them free speech. Now the latest Burns report sparked a new round of inflammatory headlines, such as the *San Francisco Examiner*'s "Probers

Blame Kerr and Reds." Kerr indignantly denied the charges and defended his policies. "When I came into office . . . people who were running for state office—in California elections—were not even allowed to speak," he told reporters. "I am proud that I am the chief proponent of the open forum, allowing people from the left, the center and the right to speak on campus." Claiming the report was full of "distortions, inaccuracies and false conclusions," Kerr challenged Burns to relinquish his legislative immunity so he could sue him and Combs for defamation. Burns declined.

With impeccable timing, Burns had released the report just as the Board of Regents was meeting in San Francisco, and Senior Regent Ed Pauley seized on it in his long-burning effort to fire Kerr, declaring it "brings up matters . . . which should be corrected." For months, Pauley had been trying to assemble the necessary votes. Alex Sherriffs had kept Agent Don Jones posted on Pauley's efforts. Sherriffs had become a confidant of Catherine Hearst, one of Pauley's allies, and she briefed him on the board's internal deliberations, saying she planned to second the motion to fire Kerr.

As of late June, Pauley still lacked the votes. But as he assured Wesley Grapp, he was not giving up.

Hardin Jones, the assistant director of the Donner Radiation Lab at UC Berkeley, had been growing more and more upset. He had worked briefly as a paid FBI informer and had kept in touch with bureau agents. And on September 28, 1965, he traveled from his home in the Berkeley hills to see Grapp personally.

Meeting at the Los Angeles FBI office, Jones told Grapp he had come at Pauley's suggestion and proceeded to tell a tale that even agents would find remarkable. Jones made the by now usual charge that Kerr was under Communist control. But he went on to claim that the Communist Party line was being espoused in classes on anthropology, speech, English, political science, history, and even zoology. Despite the fact that the party had been waning for years, Jones now declared "UCB was a Communist university, run by Communists for the benefit of Communists . . ." If this continued, he said, the university would indoctrinate generations of Communists who would eventually take over the state.

The next day, Jones appeared at the San Francisco FBI office and made even more allegations in a meeting with Agent Don Jones and Special Agent in Charge Curtis Lynum. Although the professor acknowledged he could not prove there was a single Communist on campus, he insisted this was only further evidence of the nefarious plot. He was so concerned, he said, that he was going to Washington, D.C., to personally brief the FBI director.

Lynum immediately alerted Hoover. While describing Jones as a good American and a man of "considerable influence," he recommended against the meeting. "This situation is highly controversial and highly political," he said, "and it is felt that the Bureau should be extremely careful and not be involved in any way."

A few weeks later, on October 7, Hardin Jones approached the receptionist at FBI headquarters in Washington and asked for Hoover. Told the director was unavailable, he instead met with a veteran agent named Fern Stukenbroeker. Jones now expressed his concern with even greater intensity. There had been nothing less than a Communist revolution at the university, he said, and most people, perhaps even FBI officials, did not understand the danger.

Kerr was to blame. Kerr had packed the university with more than two hundred "liberal-type" professors. They were the hard-core troublemakers. They had supported the FSM and the VDC, and they used their classrooms to promote "anarchism." This Jones described as "the intellectual attitude which denounced the United States, the institutions of a free society and the values of integrity and honesty which form the backbone not only of the free university but of Western culture." The Filthy Speech Movement was just one result of this, Jones said, adding that students had even formed "Sexual Freedom" clubs.

All the tumult was scaring away good students. Families were afraid to send their children to Berkeley. Fraternities were having trouble recruiting members from the influx of "beatniks, scoffers and 'free thinkers.'" In short, Jones said, under Clark Kerr, Berkeley had become the "biggest subversive thinking machine in the country."

And Kerr—he was a manipulator, a "liar," and "as much a danger as Hitler." Moreover, Jones said, pausing to note that he was a scientist, and thus indicating he was qualified to make the diagnosis, Kerr "is probably suffering from emotional illness." In fact, he said, "Kerr displays every symptom of being paranoid." Only one thing could stop the conspiracy, Jones declared—Kerr's removal.

As the meeting ended, Jones handed Stukenbroeker a draft of a letter he had written to President Johnson setting out his concerns. Attached was a copy of a Vietnam Day Committee flyer picturing Johnson, upside down. The agent thanked him and promised to bring his information to Hoover's attention. Then he prepared a ten-page report for the director, describing Jones as "sincere" but adding, "At times, he seemed to be carried away . . ."

Ed Pauley eagerly received Wesley Grapp at his office in the Pauley Petroleum Building two weeks later, and shared startling news.

The regent revealed that he recently had met with his close friend, the former CIA director John McCone, about the continuing unrest at their old school. Then he displayed a letter that McCone had written to President Johnson and read it aloud:

"I have gone over the confidential FBI reports sent to Mr. Edwin Pauley," McCone had written, "and it appears to me to be more or less perfunctory name checks and did not reveal serious communist influence, except in one or two instances . . . but I can assume there is enough going on to recommend a searching and penetrative investigation by the FBI." He added, "This should be done immediately . . ."

McCone, Pauley continued, had suggested Johnson order the FBI "to clean out the communists and to get rid of Clark Kerr."

Grapp was stunned. He had given Pauley those FBI reports on students and faculty on the express condition that he never disclose the source.

So when Pauley had finished speaking, the question arose as to why he had let McCone see FBI reports given him in the strictest confidence. Pauley brushed it off, saying he just "took the liberty." Grapp diplomatically decided not to make an issue of it.

Pauley then told Grapp that he and McCone wanted nothing less than an intensive investigation of "the influence of the communists on Clark Kerr and his activities, as well as [on] the faculty and the other key figures at the university."

The oil tycoon instructed Grapp to give him the resulting reports, which he would then use in his efforts to fire Kerr. If that were not possible, he said, Grapp should give them to President Johnson and he would pass the information along to Pauley.

When Hoover read Grapp's report about this October 20 meeting, he was concerned. Here was a potential debacle: He had tried to use Pauley to stifle dissent on campus but had undeniably lost control of the counterintelligence operation. Pauley had violated his promise to keep the FBI's unlawful assistance to him secret. McCone had then exposed Hoover's hand to President Johnson. Even worse, the CIA director had disparaged the FBI's reports as "perfunctory," suggesting the bureau had been lax in dealing with a security problem at the nation's largest university.

Clearly, Pauley was a loose cannon. In his zeal to oust Kerr, he might even reveal Hoover's activities to the public. Hoover had to act swiftly.

With a jagged scrawl in the margins of the report, he ordered his aides, "We are to give Pauley *nothing* henceforth."

And to preempt McCone's request for a new investigation, he ordered them to expedite a report on "the Berkeley situation," demanding, "When will this be completed?"

Under the circumstances, the director could not afford to ignore Hardin Jones's claims about a massive campus conspiracy. Jones was, after all, close to Pauley. And Pauley was close to McCone. So Hoover emphasized in his order, "Allegations have been received that the hard core of the revolt on the UCB campus is under the direction of President Clark Kerr of the University of California and 200 professors on the UCB campus."

The resulting report was titled "Subversive Activities at the University of California, Berkeley." It fell far short of substantiating Hardin Jones's charges of a sinister intellectual plot masterminded by Clark Kerr. In fact, it did not find a single professor who was a member of any Communist or socialist organization, or was in violation of the security oath or any criminal law.

But it emphasized that during Kerr's tenure as president student unrest had increased. And it made clear that—based on the thousands of dossiers the bureau had opened as a result—FBI officials had sharply increased the number of people on campus to be rounded up in the event of a national emergency.

The memorandum listed a total of 95 people at the Berkeley campus—16 professors, 27 university employees, and 52 students—who were on the bureau's Security Index or Reserve Index. Only four years earlier, the FBI had listed 72 people on the Security Index throughout the entire *statewide* university.

The seemingly endless turmoil emanating from Clark Kerr's campus, the report declared, represented nothing less than an "attack on . . . the American way of life."

By the end of October 1965, a frustrated Pauley conceded to Grapp he was still "short two votes to fire Clark Kerr."

FBI officials had come to realize that the problem was not in Berkeley but in Sacramento. "Governor Pat Brown has injected himself into the move on the part of some of the Regents to oust Kerr," an aide to Hoover wrote on October 28, 1965. "He regards the issue as a political one and would do everything in his power to retain Kerr as President."

Kerr would remain in charge of the university, it seemed, as long as Brown remained governor.

Part Three

The Rise of Reagan

18

The Governor's Race

With a fire crackling in the hearth behind him, Ronald Reagan fixed his gaze on the television camera set up at his home in Pacific Palisades and announced that he was entering the race for governor of California.

To Hoover and other FBI officials, who had become increasingly frustrated with Clark Kerr's failure to end the protests at Berkeley, Reagan's announcement on January 4, 1966, was a breath of fresh air. Over the years, bureau officials had approvingly taken note as the actor who wanted to star in *The FBI Story* transformed himself into a leading conservative spokesman.

Along the way, they compiled a thick dossier—several dossiers, actually—on the man who would become known around the world as the citizen politician who took on big government and fiercely defended democracy. The confidential files contained hundreds of pages of field reports, news clippings, congressional testimony, and memos bearing Hoover's fateful scrawled orders. Like snapshots, they are fragmentary, but taken together they present a grainy montage of Reagan on his way to becoming president, and beyond that, a folk hero, meticulously documenting many of his activities as actor, informer, and, increasingly, politician.

In 1960, one record noted, Reagan campaigned as a Democrat for Nixon against John F. Kennedy. Although he was a lifelong Democrat, Reagan charged that the party was going socialist. "I feel no Democrat can ignore that the party has been taken over by a faction which seeks to pattern the Democratic Party and its policies after those of the Labor-Socialist government of England [*sic*]," he declared.

In an address to a conference of food executives in Chicago the following year, he warned that the Communist Party "has ordered once again the infiltration" of the movie industry. And liberals were once again aiding and abetting the reds. "They are crawling out from under the rocks," he told the twenty-fourth annual meeting of the Super Market Institute on May 8, 1961. Specifically, he claimed Communists had tried to consolidate control of film industry unions "under the umbrella of Harry Bridges's maritime union." He added ominously, "We in Hollywood broke their power once but it was only an isolated battle. Memories being as short as they are, there are plenty of well-meaning but misguided people willing to give them a hand."

Hoover saw a news story about Reagan's allegations and dispatched a pair of agents to question him at his home at 1669 San Onofre Drive. Reagan and his wife, Nancy, welcomed them in. But when the agents asked what his assertions were based on, he reversed course and claimed he had been misquoted. "Mr. Reagan said he had no specific confidential sources or any first-hand information," the agents reported afterward. "However, he feels that one who has been actively following and combating the Communist movement in Hollywood over the years, such as himself, can acquire a nose for these matters; that one can 'smell' a situation when it starts to develop."

Reagan also told the agents that powerful Hollywood figures—whom he did not name—had blacklisted him because of his anti-Communist work. As the agents reported, "He also believes it is not popular to be an active or outspoken anti-Communist; that those who are, or have been, just do not seem to get the picture assignments they once did. Reagan said he himself has felt this, although it is something difficult to prove." As the interview ended, Reagan promised that, as he had in the past, he would give the FBI any "pertinent" information he came across concerning subversives.

Reagan soon made other exaggerated charges about Communists that also came to Hoover's attention. On October 26, 1961, Senator Frank Church, a member of the Senate Foreign Relations Committee, wrote Hoover concerning a newspaper report about another of Reagan's speeches. In the seventies the Idaho Democrat would lead a congressional investigation into abuses of power by the FBI, CIA, and other intelligence agencies. Now he asked Hoover, "Do you have any information that would support Mr. Reagan's charges as made in this article that Communists are infiltrating all phases of the government?"

Hoover rebuffed the senator's inquiry. "In view of your concern," he wrote, "may I point out that the communists have tried to infiltrate every part of our society, but they have not achieved substantial success . . ." He did not discuss Reagan's claims but commented generally, "This is no time for rumors, unfounded suspicion, gossip and the hurling of false accusations." An internal note on Hoover's copy of the letter suggests why the director was defensive. "Ronald Reagan has been very active in anti-communist activities in several Hollywood organizations," it said. "He has been contacted on several occasions by Agents of the Los Angeles Office and has been cooperative and helpful."

The following year, Reagan raised money for John Rousselot, the Southern California Republican congressman and prominent John Birch Society member. Reagan gave the keynote speech at a fifty-dollar-a-plate fund-raiser in which he insinuated that President Kennedy was leading America toward socialism. Kennedy administration officials, he charged, believed "the old-fashioned idea of individuality is inadequate in modern day problems and seeks to establish government control of the economy and society."

In March 1962, Reagan, as host of *General Electric Theater*, presented a television special about Marion Miller, who had infiltrated the Communist Party for the FBI and told all in a book, *I Was a Spy: The Story of a Brave Housewife*. Miller agreed to let Reagan produce the show only after she was unable to interest any studio in making a feature movie about her experiences as an informer, she confidentially told the FBI. Reagan snapped it up, and guest-starred as Miller's husband.

Later that year, however, General Electric executives dropped Reagan from his $125,000-per-year job as host of the show and company representative after concluding that his speeches had become too politically extreme. They had received complaints, for example, about Reagan's assertions that the Tennessee Valley Authority was an example of overgrown government. A New Deal program to aid the blighted Southeast, the TVA was engaged in enterprises that traditionally were the province of private business, such as building dams, producing fertilizer, and operating power plants. The TVA also was one of GE's biggest customers. "They got pretty up in arms," recalled George Dalen, who worked with Reagan at GE. "We got some heat from that."

Reagan was disappointed, but getting fired didn't change his views. Nineteen sixty-two was the year that he finally registered as a Republican. He again backed Richard Nixon, this time in the former vice president's unsuccessful bid for governor against Pat Brown.

All along, Reagan continued to cultivate his relationship with FBI officials. He was a guest at the steak barbecues and "firearms sessions" put on by the Los Angeles FBI office in the early sixties at the Pasadena Firearms Range—Walt Disney was there, and George Murphy helped with the cooking.

Hoover's aides, meanwhile, noted that Reagan was extending his political activities beyond California. In January 1964 they circulated a memo saying he was one of several "active anticommunists" who had lent their names to Project Prayer, a nationwide organization promoting an amendment to the U.S. Constitution that would permit prayer in public schools. John Wayne and Roy Rogers also supported this ultimately unsuccessful effort.

That spring, Reagan helped raise money for the Young Americans for Freedom, the national organization of conservative college students. He became a member of the YAF's advisory board, and wrote a fund-raising letter declaring, "I know of no other group in the nation which is going to be more effective in preserving and extending our cherished goals."

The YAF was not focusing its energies on the fight against racial discrimination, or joining in Mississippi Freedom Summer. YAFers saw international communism as the greatest threat to America's liberties, pledged to support the House Un-American Activities Committee, and decried liberalism as "stemming from socialist thought and often serving as an unwitting handmaiden of Communist subversion."

YAF literature quoted J. Edgar Hoover's exhortations to American youth: "Do not hesitate to speak out and bring public pressure to bear upon negative influences within your communities . . . May you always protect America's heritage of freedom. May you, with God's holy guidance, preserve and strengthen that priceless heritage for the generations yet to come."

In fact, the FBI and the YAF had a special relationship that dated to at least 1961, when the New York FBI field office suggested the bureau "explore the possibilities of discreetly aiding this organization of youth who apparently are militantly fighting communism . . ." At various colleges, for example, the FBI could "anonymously provide the Young Americans for Freedom chapter with ammunition, e.g., background of the C.P. [Communist Party] speaker, 'loaded' questions, prior embarrassing public statements, etc."

Later in 1964, Reagan, John Wayne, and Senator Barry Goldwater headlined a program at the San Diego Patriotic Society that bestowed an "American Patriot Award" upon Hoover, who accepted in absentia.

But it was "A Time for Choosing," Reagan's hugely successful television fund-raising speech on behalf of Goldwater's presidential bid, that thrust him into the national spotlight. The half-hour prerecorded talk was the culmination of Reagan's political development, a logical outgrowth of his postwar experience in secretly working with the FBI, fighting Communists as president of the Screen Actors Guild, and serving as a corporate spokesman.

The speech first aired on October 27, 1964, just as the Free Speech Movement was building at Berkeley. In the talk, Reagan spoke in avuncular tones and apocalyptic terms, striking at Soviet repression abroad and at big government, regulation, welfare, and taxes as evidence of creeping socialism at home.

Like Savio's talks that fall at Berkeley, Reagan's address was an impassioned dissent against what he saw as a complacent, if not morally corrupt, status quo. Like Savio, Reagan attacked bureaucracy, elitism, and the loss of individual freedom. And like the student radical, he took inspiration from the Founding Fathers and called for participatory democracy.

"This is the issue of this election," Reagan declared,

> whether we believe in our capacity for self-government or whether we abandon the American Revolution and confess that a little intellectual elite in a far-distant capital can plan our lives for us better than we can plan them ourselves . . .
>
> There's only an up or down—[up to] man's age-old dream—the ultimate in individual freedom consistent with law and order—or down to the ant heap of totalitarianism. And, regardless of their sincerity, their humanitarian motives, those who would trade our freedom for security have embarked on this downward course . . .
>
> Federal employees number two and a half million. These proliferating bureaus with their thousands of regulations have cost us many of our Constitutional safeguards. How many of us realize that today federal agents can invade a man's property without a warrant?

Both Reagan and Savio were complaining about certain side effects of the nation's explosive postwar growth. Savio's dissent, however, sprang from the civil rights movement, which he saw as posing the defining issue facing America. In Mississippi he had seen firsthand the effects of deregulation, or more precisely, *no* regulation: rampant racism; systemic denial of basic rights; bullying, beatings, and bombings.

Reagan's dissent, by contrast, stemmed from what he perceived as government intrusions on the free market, on property rights, on profit. The civil rights movement was mounting, it was front-page news, but in this major address Reagan did not mention it. Rather, he defended what he believed were traditional American values. To Reagan, the single biggest threat to America was communism, with socialism and liberals close behind.

But both Reagan and Savio called for direct confrontation with what they saw as evil. "We're at war with the most dangerous enemy that has ever faced mankind in his long climb from the swamp to the stars," Reagan declared in the speech.

And that is the issue of this campaign that makes all of the other problems that I've discussed academic, unless we realize that we're in a war that must be won. Those who would trade our freedom for the soup kitchen of the welfare state have told us they have a utopian solution of peace without victory. They call their policy "accommodation." And they say if we'll only avoid any direct confrontation with the enemy, he'll forget his evil ways and learn to love us. All who oppose them are indicted as war mongers . . .

Admittedly there's a risk in any course we follow . . . but every lesson of history tells us that the greater risk lies in appeasement and this is the specter our well-meaning liberal friends refuse to face—that their policy of accommodation is appeasement, and it gives no choice between peace and war, only between fight or surrender. If we continue to accommodate, continue to back and retreat, eventually we have to face the final demand—the ultimatum . . .

You and I know and do not believe that life is so dear and peace so sweet as to be purchased at the price of chains and slavery. If nothing in life is worth dying for, when did this begin—just in the face of this enemy? Or should Moses have told the children of Israel to live in slavery under the pharaohs? Should Christ have refused the cross? Should the patriots at Concord Bridge have thrown down their guns and refused to fire the shot heard 'round the world? . . .

You and I have a rendezvous with destiny. We'll preserve for our children this, the last best hope of man on earth, or we'll sentence them to take the last step into a thousand years of darkness.

The speech was widely seen as a successful national political debut. Although Goldwater lost to Johnson that November, Reagan became the new hope of the nation's conservatives, some of whom were soon urging him to challenge Brown for the governorship.

Reagan was reluctant to run. He would later say he liked his life as it was. He recently had become the master of ceremonies on *Death Valley Days*, a job his brother had suggested. But Neil Reagan was urging him to enter the race, as was a group of wealthy Southern Californians who became known as Reagan's "kitchen cabinet." In early 1965, Reagan was seriously considering it. But just then his name surfaced in a major federal organized crime investigation.

In January 1965, FBI agents were closing in on Joseph "Joe Bananas" Bonanno, the fearsome head of one of New York's five Mafia families. Bonanno's soldiers had long been involved in gambling, extortion, and murder, and partly as a result of his rivalry with other dons, he had moved to Arizona, where he continued to direct his far-flung criminal enterprises.

Hoover had long expressed skepticism about the existence of the Mafia—he was more intent on investigating alleged subversives in the film industry and the educational field—but in 1957 New York State police discovered undeniable evidence of mob leaders meeting in Apalachin, New York. A few years later, Robert F. Kennedy, the brash young attorney general, with the blessing of his brother the president, made organized crime his top priority and, much to Hoover's annoyance, pressed him to act. The former mob soldier Joe Valachi's explosive congressional testimony in 1963 generated more heat, and the Manhattan federal prosecutor Robert Morgenthau opened a sensational grand jury investigation of Bonanno.

So it was that FBI agents in Phoenix were intensively investigating the Bonanno operation when they made an unexpected discovery: According to previously undisclosed FBI records, "the son of Ronald Reagan was associating with the son of Joe Bonnano [*sic*]." That is, Michael Reagan, the adopted son of Reagan and Jane Wyman, was consorting with Bonanno's son, Joseph. Both of the eighteen-year-olds were estranged from their parents and had bonded over their shared love of driving fast cars, chasing girls, and acting tough. As Joseph's older brother Salvatore recalled in Gay Talese's *Honor Thy Father*, "He was the wild one of the family, a drag racer, a bronco rider, a nonconformist . . ." Michael Reagan, one FBI report said, "has been observed in company of Joseph Bonanno, Jr., recently on numerous occasions."

Joe Bonanno, Jr., or Joseph, as he was known, was not then involved in organized crime, but he was spending time at his father's home, the inner sanctum. In October 1964 Joseph had been arrested in connection with the beating of a Scottsdale, Arizona, coffee shop owner, breaking his nose and cheekbone. In January 1965, *The New York Times* reported that he was being subpoenaed to appear before Morgenthau's grand jury to testify about his father. Moreover, according to one of the FBI records, Joseph and Michael were involved in unspecified activity that is the "subject of growing concern among residents of that particular neighborhood."

Following routine procedure, the Phoenix agents asked their counterparts in Los Angeles to interview Ronald Reagan for any information he might have gleaned from his son. It is also possible that they hoped to develop Michael as an informer like his dad; in fact, agents soon sought to develop as an informer another teenage friend of Joseph's, David Hill, Jr., who lived with the Bonanno family for a while. The investigation, after all, was a top priority.

But Hoover interceded. The day after he met with the CIA director, John McCone, to discuss Governor Brown's lack of backbone in handling protests at Berkeley, Hoover blocked agents from questioning Reagan, thus sparing him potentially adverse publicity that could have damaged his political chances. Declaring "it is unlikely that Ronald Reagan would have any information of significance," Hoover instead directed agents from the Los Angeles office, with whom Reagan had established a "cordial" relationship, to confidentially warn him about his son's dangerous dalliance.

Reagan was very grateful for Hoover's help. News that his son was hanging out with the son of one of America's most notorious Mafia bosses might have damaged his first foray into electoral politics, or at least raised questions about his parenting. The gubernatorial race would be hotly contested: Governor Brown, the incumbent Democrat, had even publicized a minor conviction from 1939 for milk price fixing against the Republican contender George Christopher, a dairyman and former San Francisco mayor. Brown's supporters also sought to link Reagan to the John Birch Society and other right-wing extremists during the contest. William Roth, who had been a member of Brown's election team in 1962, told the author that had campaign staff acquired information about Reagan's son palling around with Joe Bonanno's boy, they "sure as hell" would have used it.

Indeed. Reagan on February 1, 1965, told Special Agent William L. Byrne, Jr., that he "was most appreciative and stated he realized that such an association and actions on the part of his son might well jeopardize any political aspirations he might have. Reagan stated he would telephone his son and instruct him to disassociate himself gracefully and in a manner which would cause no trouble or speculation. He stated that the Bureau's courtesy in this matter will be kept absolutely confidential. Reagan commented that he realizes that it would be improper to express his appreciation in writing and requested that SA Byrne convey the great admiration he has for the Director and the Bureau and to express his thanks for the Bureau's cooperation."

Here was Ronald Reagan, avowed opponent of big government and people's overdependence on it, once again taking personal and political assistance from the FBI at taxpayer expense. Only this time, Reagan was accepting aid that gave him an advantage in an electoral race. Moreover, he seems to have been unaware, or unconcerned, that in doing so he was becoming beholden to the Boss. For Hoover now had two things on Reagan: his son's unsavory friendship with Joe Jr., and Reagan's effort to hide it with secret help from the FBI. If this came out, it would embarrass both Reagan and the bureau. They were becoming partners in a secret alliance, one less than democratic.

The FBI tried to suppress the fact that it was Reagan's son, Michael, who was involved with Joseph Bonanno, Jr., deleting his identity in the documents released in response to the author's FOIA request. The bureau and the Justice Department claimed this information was exempt from release on the ground that it concerned "law enforcement" activities. However, U.S. District Court Judge Marilyn Hall Patel in September 2010 ordered the FBI to release this information, ruling it concerned not legitimate law enforcement but the FBI's effort "to protect or promote Reagan's political career."

Edwin Meese III, who was Governor Reagan's top legal aide, told the author, "I don't see that as being political. It's more somebody trying to help out personally, which is not at all unusual when law-enforcement officers see something happening, to try to prevent the bad things from occurring." According to Meese, the FBI's assistance to Reagan with Michael Reagan, and Maureen Reagan, was neither contrary to the bureau's proper role or inconsistent with Reagan's stated principles.

Neither Reagan nor any of his biographers has ever mentioned the Bonanno affair. Only Michael Reagan noted it, albeit briefly, in his 1988 autobiography, *On the Outside Looking In*. "One night when I was at The Library, a short, thin Italian who was about my age introduced himself as Joe Bonanno, Jr. The name didn't mean a thing to me. He probably befriended me because he knew who I was. I soon learned that his father was a celebrity of sorts, too—a famous Mafioso reputed to be the 'boss of bosses.' . . . I liked being in Joe's company because he was the epitome of macho. When we'd go out, people would clear space for us as we walked by. I felt important and tough just being a part of his retinue," he wrote.

"Then, out of the blue, Dad telephoned me. He said that the FBI had seen my car parked in front of Joe's house and had traced the license plates to me. 'I don't want you to see that young man again, he's trouble,' Dad said. I didn't know that Dad was considering running for governor of California and my friendship with Joe Jr. might prove to be embarrassing to his campaign, so I got angry. I told Dad that the only time he ever called me was when he thought I did something wrong; he never called when things were going right."

Michael hung up. He and Joseph laughed about the call and went drag racing.

Newspapers continued to carry stories about the FBI's investigation of the Bonannos, but the teenagers' worrisome relationship never came up.

That December, Savio had urged students to put their bodies on the gears and the students had occupied Sproul Hall. When Reagan first heard about the Free Speech Movement, he recalled, "I was angry." Now, as he tested the political waters, it seemed someone always brought up Berkeley.

"Wherever I went in the state," Reagan recalled in an oral history interview, "the first question and literally the first half-dozen questions were about what I would do about the University of California at Berkeley . . . wherever it was, mountain, desert, seashore, the situation at Berkeley and the university came up. This is how it became an issue. You knew that this was the number one thing on the people's minds."

He quickly warmed to it. Speaking at the Greater Los Angeles Press Club that January of 1965, Reagan said he approved of the arrests of Savio and the other demonstrators, adding, "I'm sorry they did away with paddles in fraternities." He took other positions at odds with Berkeley activists like Savio that day. He said he would have voted against the federal Civil Rights Act of 1964, which prohibited discrimination in public accommodations, because "I don't think you can protect one individual's rights by infringing on another's right." As to Vietnam, he said, "We've got to realize we're in a war and we've got to decide whether this is the best place to halt the enemy. If it is, we've got to throw everything into it. If it isn't, we've got to decide where we will draw the line." Reagan subscribed wholeheartedly to the Domino Theory and was sure the Communist threat was all too near. "Sometimes," he said, "I feel the line runs from San Diego to Seattle."

As to why conservatives were badly defeated in the 1964 elections, he told the press club it wasn't because their ideas had been rejected—it was because they had failed to stage a clear confrontation with liberals. And he meant to do just that.

On March 17, 1965, Hoover read a column about Reagan in *The Washington Post* that called his pitch for Goldwater "by far" the best speech of the 1964 presidential campaign. Referring to the Free Speech Movement as those "recent campus riots," the article said, "At this juncture in California affairs, un-American activities are an important issue."

Reagan was on the rise. He was making political news in Hoover's hometown paper, about his special subject. Hoover scrawled in the margin, "Let me have a summary on Ronald Reagan." The next day, Assistant Director DeLoach gave him a three-page précis of information in FBI files on Reagan that emphasized he might challenge Brown for the governorship.

In the following months, FBI officials took note as Reagan began to take on the Vietnam Day Committee. On October 11, 1965, just before the VDC's first attempt to march to the Oakland Army Terminal, he told a crowd at Coalinga College, in Fresno County, that Congress should declare war on Vietnam so that "the anti-Vietnam demonstrations and the act of burning draft cards would be treasonable." Several days later he elaborated in a talk to the Republican Alliance in San Francisco, saying that one advantage of declaring war is that people blocking troop trains could then be prosecuted for lending aid and comfort to the enemy. He took the occasion to charge that top officers of some Democratic volunteer groups "are members of known Communistic front organizations," although he provided no proof of this allegation.

A few days after the Hell's Angels attacked the VDC march, Reagan was in Oakland, telling a convention of the California Apartment House Owners Association that the antiwar demonstration was "the fruit of appeasement." He had previously used the word *appeasement* to portray liberals as bowing to Soviet aggression. His use of it now implied that Kerr—and Brown—were likewise bowing to a foreign plot and echoed Hoover's insinuations that Communists were behind the campus unrest.

"The time to have stopped it," Reagan said, "was when the students first blocked a police car on the campus. The administration should have taken the leaders by the scruff of their necks and kicked them out, and it should have put the rest of them back to work doing their homework."

On December 8, 1965, a few days after VDC members picketed Vice

President Hubert H. Humphrey in San Francisco, Reagan told a Republican political dinner in nearby Hayward that university officials had been too weak in handling "a few loud-mouthed dissidents who used the campus for vulgarity."

By now, Berkeley had emerged as what Reagan's biographer Lou Cannon would call "the most potent issue of the campaign." Reagan was tapping into anger and resentment that Americans felt about the disruption of their lives by conflicts over civil rights, sexual freedom, and the war in Vietnam. The turmoil on campus symbolized this upheaval and provided a prime political target.

That January, 1966, Reagan formally entered the governor's race with his prerecorded address by the hearth. The talk was screened for news reporters at the Statler Hilton in Los Angeles, then simultaneously broadcast on fifteen television stations around the state.

Reagan outlined his by then familiar themes—big government, taxes, welfare freeloaders, and "ever-decreasing individual freedom." Democratic leaders, he said, had embarked on a course of "more and more control and regulation of the economy and of our lives" that would lead only to "the ant heap of totalitarianism." The Republican Party, by contrast, "is the party of limited government, individual freedom, and adherence to the Constitution."

This speech drew upon his fund-raising pitch for Goldwater, in which he had not addressed civil rights. This time he did broach the subject—though without uttering that phrase. "There must be no lack of equal opportunity, no inequality before the law, no differing standards with regards to constitutional rights for any American, and we are all Americans," he said. He quickly qualified his statement, however, adding that "there is a limit to what can be accomplished by laws and regulations, and I seriously question whether anything additional is needed in that line."

And he emphasized that he would be focusing on Berkeley. "Will we allow a great university to be brought to its knees by a noisy, dissident minority? Will we meet their neurotic vulgarities with vacillation and weakness?" he asked.

"Or will we tell those entrusted with administering the university we expect them to enforce a code based on decency, common sense, and dedication to the high and noble purpose of the university?"

•

Hoover's aides watched with special interest a few days later when Reagan appeared on NBC's *Meet the Press*, the nation's premier television interview program.

The questions that Sunday morning were a test, in effect, of whether the fifty-four-year-old rookie politician from California could handle himself in the major leagues. Lawrence Spivak, one of the show's reporters, began by asking Reagan to respond to the comment that his campaign "is an attempt to turn an actor into a believable candidate for governor and to make voters forget your right-wing views."

Brushing it off, Reagan replied that "this is a false image that is being created, or that they are attempting to create with regard to me." In fact, Reagan said, his views had not changed much since his days as a Democrat. He still believed "that anything . . . that imposed unfairly on the individual or the freedom of the individual was tyranny and should be opposed."

He was pressed to explain his previous statement, that had he been a member of Congress he would have opposed the 1964 Civil Rights Act. Reagan had said he disagreed with the law because it infringed on private property rights. Now he said that—though he fully supported aims of the act—he opposed it because it was "a badly written piece of legislation." He added, "I am just incapable of prejudice; I believe this."

At a tense point in the January 9, 1966, show, Reagan was asked why he hadn't disavowed the John Birch Society, a group associated with far-right conspiracy theories. Robert Welch, the society's founder, had charged that President Franklin Roosevelt, Chief Justice Earl Warren, and President Dwight Eisenhower were Communists and traitors. Reagan had backed the congressional campaign of one of the society's more prominent members, John Rousselot, in 1962. Under pressure for months to clarify his stand on the group, Reagan recently had issued a press release saying he never was a member of the group and disagreed with Welch's "reckless and imprudent statements."

Now Reagan said, "I have been quite critical of many statements of their founder, Mr. Welch, and I think some of them have approached the ridiculous, but I am going to appeal in the campaign to individuals." He was espousing a nonexclusionary philosophy similar to the one Savio had touted for the Free Speech Movement. Reagan added, "I figure that any individual who elects to go along with me and vote for me has bought my philosophy, and I haven't bought his."

Besides, he said, the Burns committee had looked into the group and found "nothing of a subversive nature." And so had Hoover. "He said they had found no occasion to investigate because they only investigated subversive organizations," Reagan said. "I am only going by his word, and so far I just happen to be a naïve enough soul that I can't ever recall finding J. Edgar Hoover being dishonest or making a statement that was irresponsible."

It was true that the FBI had not conducted a "formal" investigation of the John Birch Society like its investigations of the Free Speech Movement and the Vietnam Day Committee. But the bureau had collected thousands of pages of records on the society, its members, and its activities. In internal memoranda, FBI officials spoke harshly of the organization. Assistant Director Cartha DeLoach had described the JBS in 1961 as a "fanatical right-wing" group with "utterly absurd viewpoints." He had suggested prohibiting the organization from distributing FBI literature because its members were attempting to "capitalize on the bureau's prestige." He added that "in view of the extremist position taken by this group . . . we should not, of course, have anything to do with them." Hoover had agreed.

In fact, bureau officials watching *Meet the Press* knew that their files contained a potentially explosive memo about Reagan and the John Birch Society. In June 1960, an informer, whom the FBI memo described as "reliable," reported that Reagan secretly belonged to the organization's Beverly Hills chapter. This chapter, the informer had alleged, included the actors John Wayne, Adolphe Menjou, and Zasu Pitts, the screenwriter Morrie Ryskind, and the columnist Hedda Hopper.

The FBI files released to the author do not show whether the bureau investigated the claim, or whether it is true. In an interview, John F. McManus, the president of the John Birch Society, said Reagan never was a member of the group. Menjou, Ryskind, and Wayne were involved with the society, he said, adding he did not know whether Hopper and Pitts were. None of the major Reagan biographers has concluded he was a member of the society.

Hoover and his aides knew the informer's allegation—although entirely unproven—could damage Reagan's campaign if it became public. It was precisely the kind of uncorroborated information that they had leaked to tarnish Savio, Kerr, and Brown. But they kept this memo safely locked away.

"Over all," FBI executives said about the *Meet the Press* show, "Reagan made a good appearance and was quite quick and witty in answering the numerous questions put to him which could have been considerably embarrassing to his future political ambitions."

19

The Peace Trip Dance

Jerry Rubin and company had been keeping FBI agents busy ever since the big march.

Right away the VDC had started preparing for a new foray into Oakland. And right away Oakland officials announced they would again stop the marchers at the city line. This time, however, the VDC won a federal court order allowing them to proceed 4.7 miles from campus to DeFremery Park, just west of downtown Oakland. That, of course, meant little to the Hell's Angels, rumored to be planning another attack. The Angels, like the VDC, were nonconformists. But as Hunter Thompson wrote, "Their political views are limited to the same kind of retrograde patriotism that motivates the John Birch Society, the Ku Klux Klan and the American Nazi Party."

At a mass meeting to plan the march, anxious antiwar activists discussed the potential attack. Someone suggested the marchers carry batons for self-defense. Allen Ginsberg proposed just the opposite. He called for a nonthreatening march that would disarm the Angels, and distributed a plan for a festive protest "OUTSIDE the war psychology." Those at the mass meeting adopted this concept, according to Ginsberg's biographer Michael Schumacher, planting the seeds for a strategy of peaceful opposition that would become known as "flower power."

Hunter Thompson had introduced Kesey to some of the Angels earlier that summer, and Kesey now invited members of the Angels' San Francisco chapter down to La Honda for a full-blown Prankster party. There the Angels met the acid avatar Richard Alpert, the Harvard psychology professor soon to become known as Baba Ram Dass, and Ginsberg, who would later memorialize the meeting in his poem "First Party at Ken Kesey's with Hell's Angels." Ginsberg wrote: ". . . 3 A.M. the blast of loudspeakers hi-fi Rolling Stones Ray Charles Beatles . . . twenty youths dancing to the vibration thru the floor, a little weed . . . beer cans bent . . .

police cars parked outside . . ." Or as Thompson put it, the soiree was a "roaring success."

Still, the party at Kesey's had not settled things. As the day of the VDC's proposed march approached, Ginsberg desperately tried to avert another violent clash with the savage bikers. He arranged a public forum on November 12 in the student cafeteria at San Jose State College, about fifty miles south of San Francisco. Wearing a long robe, the bearded poet began the summit meeting by ringing a tiny silver Buddhist bell and chanting for five minutes "to protect everybody from evil." Then he made his remarks in the form of a 200-line poem called "To the Angels." It began:

> These are the thoughts—anxieties—of anxious marchers
> That the Angels will attack them
> for kicks, or to get publicity, to take the heat off
> themselves
> or to get goodwill of police & press &/or
> right wing Money

Only one Angel appeared at the forum, however. Giving his name as "Louie," he told the *San Francisco Chronicle* that the Angels would not break the law. "I got a lot of respect for Uncle Sam and for my mother and my brothers and sisters and for my own two little kids," he explained. "If I catch my two little kids ever marching I'll break their heads in."

The meeting also failed to allay the activists' fear that the bikers would assault unarmed students, professors, and Grandmothers for Peace. So in a last effort a few days before the march, Ginsberg, Kesey, and several Pranksters visited the Hell's Angels leader Sonny Barger at his Oakland home. At first the mood was tense. But after everyone except Ginsberg ingested large doses of LSD, the poet led them in chanting "Om" and told Barger he loved him. The tête-à-tête ended hopefully. Ginsberg's efforts inspired Norman Mailer to send the poet his own poem, titled "Ode to Allen Ginsberg":

> I sometimes think
> that little Jew bastard
> that queer ugly kike
> is the bravest man in America.

Eight days later, on November 20, 1965, VDC leaders armed with the court order led the march of some eight thousand people from Sproul Plaza to DeFremery Park in Oakland for a rally. John Burton, a Democratic assemblyman from San Francisco, was one of several people who spoke against the war. Dan Healy, a member of the Young Democrats, told how he had refused the draft and asked, "Why should I be made to fight for a cause that is not mine?" Donald Duncan, a former Green Beret master sergeant in Vietnam, declared, "I was marching for eighteen months in Vietnam. It's a pleasure to march today for something that makes sense."

Young Americans for Freedom staged a counterdemonstration. And once again, the VDC's walkie-talkies were mysteriously jammed. But this time, perhaps due to the ministrations of Messrs. Ginsberg and Kesey, the Hell's Angels did not materialize.

"Hey, hey, LBJ, how many kids did you kill today?"

The VDC was back at the Fairmont, this time picketing Vice President Hubert H. Humphrey, who was inside at a Democratic Party fund-raiser. FBI agents again were back too, and recorded the presence of Allen Ginsberg, Rob Hurwitt, Mike O'Hanlon, Bettina Aptheker, and other committee members that Friday, December 3, 1965. Then, as night fell, Ginsberg and some of the others set off for Bob Dylan's opening show at the Berkeley Community Theater, where they were joined in the front row by Lawrence Ferlinghetti, Ken Kesey, and a handful of Hell's Angels.

Dylan was twenty-four years old, about eighteen months older than Savio. The native of Hibbing, Minnesota, already had become one of the most popular folksingers in America and an international star. His songs had climbed the *Billboard* charts alongside the Beatles' and the Beach Boys'. But the mercurial musician was trying something new. Earlier that year, he'd gone electric at the Newport Folk Festival and some of his fans thought he had sold out. After plugging in his sunburst Fender Stratocaster, he'd been booed at concerts around the country.

No one booed Dylan in Berkeley. He took the stage in a suit with large houndstooth checks, his hair standing on end like 100,000 electric wires. He played a solo acoustic set, accompanying himself with guitar and harmonica on "Mr. Tambourine Man," "Baby Blue," and "Desolation Row." After a break, he returned with his electric group, the Hawks, who would become known as the Band. Turning it up, they tore through "Like a Rolling Stone," "Tombstone Blues," and "Ballad of a Thin Man." Dylan sang, "Something is happening, and you don't know what it is, do you, Mr. Jones?"

Reviews of Dylan's shows ran in Bay Area newspapers along with news reports that the Johnson administration was seeking to double the budget for the war. Ralph Gleason, the *San Francisco Chronicle*'s cultural columnist, was a self-described member of the older generation but was keenly attuned to youth culture. Headlining his piece "In Berkeley They Dig Bob Dylan," he described a "curious rapport" between the crowd and the electrified former folkie. Noting that Phil Ochs once described Dylan as "LSD on stage," Gleason remarked, "I wouldn't know. But I do know it is a powerful experience in more than musical terms to dig his concerts. The audience's relationship to the singer is possibly the most direct and powerful I have ever witnessed. He moves them in a deep and sometimes disturbing way . . . Something most certainly IS happening here . . ."

But if Dylan captured the zeitgeist at Berkeley, he pointedly refrained from joining the VDC's protests. During a press conference at San Francisco's public television station KQED just before that show, he was characteristically cryptic when a reporter asked if he would protest Humphrey.

"No, I'll be busy tonight," he said, smiling, chain-smoking, alluding to his concert but also hinting that he operated in a different realm. Dylan had written early "protest songs" and in 1963 performed in support of civil rights workers in Mississippi. But like Kesey's, Dylan's revolution was more personal and social than political. Another journalist asked if he was planning any demonstrations.

"I thought of one," Dylan said softly, exhaling smoke. "A group of protesters here, perhaps carrying cards with pictures of a Jack of Diamonds on them, an Ace of Spades on them, pictures of mules. Maybe words. Oh, maybe about twenty-five or thirty thousand of these things printed up, and just picket. Carry the signs and picket. In front of the post office." Someone asked what words he'd put on his signs, and Dylan's eyes played lambently on the reporters who filled the room. "Oh, words. 'Camera.' 'Microphone.' 'Loose.' Just words. Names of some famous people."

Puzzled, a reporter asked if he considered himself a politician. "Well, I guess so," Dylan said, smiling and lighting another cigarette. "I have my own party, though. There's no presidents in the party . . . or vice presidents or secretaries, so it makes it kinda hard to get in . . . I don't think my party would ever be approved by the White House."

Even he didn't know who was in his party, he said, but added, "Oh, you can recognize the people in it when you see them."

In January 1966, the VDC picketed Congressman Jeffrey Cohelan's Oakland office, protesting the liberal Democrat's support of the war and demanding that he call for Johnson's impeachment. He did not. In February, Bettina Aptheker led three hundred women in a march that stayed on the sidewalks and thus required no permit, finally reaching the Oakland Army Terminal to hold the VDC's first rally there. On March 25, VDC members protested the U.N. ambassador Arthur Goldberg's address at the Greek Theatre, in which he defended U.S. intervention in Vietnam. As he rose to accept his honorary degree, audience members booed, prompting President Kerr to interject, "May I suggest that if those individuals who asked for protection of their free speech would be willing to grant it to others, we would be able to proceed." About a thousand people walked out, but the convocation continued. In his speech that afternoon, Kerr called for ensuring that young people have access to education. "Instead of closing doors we should open them wider," he declared. "Instead of concentrating on the rising costs of education we should concentrate on the benefits of it."

And in his remarks, Governor Brown praised the new chancellor of Berkeley, Roger Heyns, for finding the right balance between order and free speech on campus.

"With his help," Brown declared somewhat prematurely, "we have survived the crisis."

All the while, a secret unit of the Vietnam Day Committee who called themselves the Peace Commandos had been mounting their own covert operations.

The commandos had discovered that the U.S. Army was training dogs in a remote part of nearby Tilden Park for use in Vietnam. They made official-looking signs and strategically posted them throughout the grounds. "CAUTION," the signs read, "Army War Dogs in This Area. Do Not Leave Raw Meat Exposed. Keep Children and Pets Within Sight. If Dog Approaches DO NOT MOVE. Wait For Handler—VDC Public Service—FN2017-J." Rob Hurwitt recalled, "It took less than a week and that base and those dogs were gone."

The commandos also learned that the army was transporting napalm along city streets to the Oakland Army Terminal for shipment to Vietnam. They began following the convoys in a van displaying a large NAPALM sign. Several towns along the route soon banned trucks carrying the incendiary gel.

Then there was the "VDC Air Force"—a handful of commandos who launched "peace bombing" sorties up and down the state. Taking to the air in a tiny Cessna plane, they dropped hundreds of thousands of leaflets that winter over Disneyland in Anaheim, the Rose Bowl in Pasadena, Long Beach Naval Air Station, and downtown San Francisco. The red, white, and blue leaflets looked like patriotic confetti as they fluttered to the ground. But when curious people picked them up, they found an antiwar message and a startling photograph: the napalm-charred bodies of a Vietnamese mother and child.

These "peace bombings" generated more publicity for the VDC's antiwar cause—and more heat from the feds and Ed Meese of the Alameda County District Attorney's Office. As the prosecutor in charge of "special investigations," Meese focused on political dissidents. He worked with Don Lynn, of the office's intelligence unit, which dated its operations to the days when Earl Warren was district attorney. A former U.S. Army colonel who served in the tank corps during World War II, Lynn had attended the FBI's National Academy and, according to a bureau memo, was "very close" to the San Francisco office.

Lynn's unit had been giving extra attention to Berkeley activists ever since the 1960 protest against HUAC at San Francisco City Hall. He gathered intelligence about them through full-time undercover agents, free-lance investigators, and informers. Much of this information was sent to the FBI in a stream of confidential reports. San Francisco FBI officials considered this information so sensitive they assigned the DA's unit a permanent source code number, CSSF-40-S.

The district attorney's intelligence unit had inserted an undercover operative deep inside the VDC. His name was Glenn D. Fowler, and he was a twenty-one-year-old student at San Jose State College. Fowler "volunteered" to work at VDC headquarters, got to know Jerry Rubin and other VDC leaders, and helped handle public relations for the antiwar group. Meanwhile, he secretly tape-recorded conversations with VDC members, took committee records, and phoned in reports to his controller, a mysterious, hard-driven woman named Patricia Atthowe. Eventually, he managed to penetrate the furtive Peace Commandos.

On the night of January 14, 1966, Fowler helped the VDC Air Force carry out what would be their final peace bombing. Flying at low altitude with lights off, the red-and-silver Cessna 180 made a wide loop over Oakland, San Francisco, and the Alameda Naval Air Station, dropping fifty thousand leaflets. Fowler and another commando were working as the airplane's ground support, and Fowler surreptitiously phoned Alameda County law-enforcement officials, who sent up three light planes to track the

Cessna. When it touched down at an airstrip in San Carlos, a half hour south of San Francisco, they arrested four people, including Fowler.

Meese's office sent reports on the case to the FBI, but he was disappointed to learn that the Peace Commandos had broken no federal law. They were charged only with misdemeanors in Alameda County Court. The pilot and copilot were convicted for littering and fined all of $110 each. Charges against Fowler and his ground-crew partner were dropped on the pretext that they had played minor parts, and his undercover role never was revealed.

Hoover had been pushing Lynum to take more aggressive action to expose, disrupt, and neutralize the Berkeley activists. "The number and quality of counterintelligence recommendations submitted by your office during recent months fall below the standards set by other major offices," he warned. "You are instructed to . . . insure appropriate and imaginative counterintelligence operations are instituted on a continuing basis in the future."

Lynum replied, "It is respectfully pointed out that the Counterintelligence Program is well on the mind of every agent working security cases in the San Francisco office and each Bureau communication in this subject is brought to the attention of all concerned. A tremendous amount of time and discussion on various possibilities has taken place in this office . . ." He assured Hoover that his agents were examining their investigative files "with a view towards digging out that information which could in any way be used in the Counterintelligence Program."

Leaking information about the sexual activity of some radicals, he added, might not be effective because they "do not have the same moral standards as a Bureau employee." Nonetheless, on November 2, 1965, San Francisco agents took steps to expose the "immorality" of a VDC activist who was "the father of a son born out of wedlock." They typed an anonymous letter on commercially purchased stationery detailing his sexual activity and mailed it to *Tocsin*, which billed itself as "The West's Leading Anti-Communist Weekly."

A four-page black-and-white newsletter available by subscription only, *Tocsin*'s stated goal was to expose Communists, but its targets included liberals and student activists. It was published by Charles Fox, a graduate student in Romance languages at Berkeley. Fox had practically no assets, and with nothing to lose in a libel suit he made increasingly vicious verbal attacks on his opponents. According to an FBI report, however, he had a secret financial angel: Patrick Frawley, Jr., a Southern California million-aire who was chairman of the Schick Safety Razor Company and had become an ardent supporter of conservative causes after the Communist takeover of one of his factories in Cuba. He reportedly gave Fox about a thousand dollars a month.

Each issue of *Tocsin* served up excerpts of HUAC transcripts, Burns committee reports, and other allegations of subversive activity among pro-fessors and students, often printed alongside pictures taken surreptitiously on campus. But *Tocsin* also was used by law-enforcement agencies to anony-mously brand people as un-American. According to an FBI memo, "the Subversive Details of the East Bay Police Departments and the Alameda County Sheriff's Office feed information to Fox to aid him in document-ing his articles through the use of the many cross references in their files. He receives similar cooperation from Harper Knowles of the Western Research Foundation." FBI agents also found the newsletter useful, anony-mously sending in derogatory information about people and organizations, then quoting *Tocsin* articles in their reports as though they were indepen-dent documentation of subversion.

Even as Fox and his editor, George H. Keith, busily accused other people of engaging in nonconformist activities, they were involved in what was then considered to be one of society's greatest transgressions. They were homosexual lovers. An FBI agent discovered their secret inadvertently when he dropped in on them during an assignment and found them in flagrante delicto. This revelation did not dissuade Hoover from continuing to use *Tocsin* to discredit people. As he had with allegations that State Senator Hugh Burns owned a whorehouse, Hoover readily overlooked the indiscre-tions of his fellow anti-Communists.

One student whom Hoover harassed with *Tocsin* was Bettina Ap-theker, who was an appealing target because she was the daughter of the Communist Party theoretician Herbert Aptheker. By publicizing her role in campus protests, bureau officials hoped to taint the organizations and people she worked with, particularly Mario Savio.

FBI agents anonymously sent *Tocsin* a notice from *People's World* about an upcoming wedding reception for Aptheker and her groom, Jack Kurzweil. The reception was a fund-raiser for the Communist Party news-paper and for the Free Speech Movement defendants. *Tocsin* ran a story emphasizing that the reception was attended by John Searle, an assistant professor of philosophy and a special assistant to the chancellor who had served on a campus rules committee with Aptheker. Although Lynum was pleased with this result, he reported the matter in the passive voice that semantically obscured the author's responsibility and typified bureau memos. "It is felt that the Tocsin article is especially beneficial for future use," he wrote. "This information will help to document Searle as far as subversive activities are concerned."

FBI agents again took aim at Aptheker in another COINTELPRO operation that used the *San Francisco Examiner*. Although many of her colleagues in the FSM and the VDC already knew she was a Communist, she decided to make it a matter of public record. On November 9, 1965, she wrote an open letter to *The Daily Californian* disclosing her party membership. She explained her hope that this openness would help prevent red-baiting of the antiwar movement. FBI agents, however, seized on her letter in what they termed a "splendid opportunity" to discredit the student movement and influence university policy.

The morning her letter appeared in the campus paper, agents alerted the *Examiner*, which rushed a story about her "confession" onto that afternoon's front page under the banner headline "Bettina Admits It: She's a Red!"

"This is a real accomplishment," Lynum told Hoover, "because it brings to the attention of thousands of people the fact that a present active communist has been prominent in the Free Speech Movement and in the current Vietnam Day Committee movement at the University."

Lynum hoped the negative publicity would prod President Kerr and Governor Brown to deal with student protesters more severely. "On a long-range basis," he wrote, "it may possibly bolster the spines of the politicians and administrators of the University who are now confronted with the fact that communists are active in the various movements at the University." Just to be sure, a few months later FBI agents fed similar information about Aptheker to the *Examiner* columnist Guy Wright, who used it in a January 1966 article presenting her in what Lynum called "an unfavorable light."

Later that year, Agent Don Jones proposed a somewhat different operation against Aptheker. She had exposed him at a rally, embarrassing the bureau and nearly forcing his transfer. Now he suggested discrediting her with bumper stickers that showed a Batman symbol and read "Battina Craptalker for Governor."

Hoover liked the idea. "Since communists are extremely sensitive to ridicule and because this caption so accurately describes Aptheker's propaganda efforts, San Francisco is authorized to place these stickers on the bumpers of appropriate communist-owned automobiles," he said, though warning, "This must be handled in such a way as to completely protect the Bureau's interest. San Francisco should use all appropriate security measures in carrying out this operation so that this effort cannot be traced in any way to this Bureau."

Mike O'Hanlon had become a prominent part of the Vietnam Day Committee's operations, manning its table on campus, serving on the steering committee, and tirelessly helping to organize large protests. For the first time in his life he felt good about himself and what he was doing. But in February 1966, FBI agents discovered the dark secret in his past.

O'Hanlon's given name was Francis Medaille and he was one of nine children born to a troubled Bronx couple. The family was poor, their apartment was overcrowded, and Medaille would later say his parents physically abused him. When he was fifteen years old he ran away to Florida, got caught, and was sent home. Soon after, he was suspended from Cardinal Hayes High School in the Bronx, where a school official recommended he get psychiatric care. Several weeks later, he committed a terrible crime. He threw a seven-year-old neighborhood girl from the roof of his apartment building to her death.

Medaille readily confessed. He told police he had lured her to the roof with promises of a dime and a lollipop, and was then overcome with a compulsion to choke her. A court found the adolescent mentally ill, and after he pleaded guilty to a reduced charge of first-degree manslaughter he was sentenced to the Matteawan State Hospital for the Criminally Insane, in Beacon, New York. Released in 1963, he was placed on five years probation. But in 1965 his family moved to Garden Grove, California, and he failed to keep appointments with his probation officer. New York City officials issued a local warrant for his arrest for violating the terms of his probation. Meanwhile, he started going by the alias of Mike O'Hanlon, moved to Berkeley, and fell in with the Vietnam Day Committee.

Lynum was delighted with this discovery. "Due to Subject's involvement in VDC, Berkeley, and the nature of the crime committed, it is believed this case possesses outstanding possibilities under the Bureau's Counterintelligence Program," he reported to Hoover. "It is believed an apprehension of Subject by Bureau personnel would receive wide-spread news coverage and could possibly provide nation-wide embarrassment to the anti-Vietnam movement."

Still, Lynum emphasized his concern for public safety and urged a speedy arrest. "Aside from the counterintelligence aspect," he continued, "it is believed that the nature of Subject's crime, his probable present mental condition, and his extensive traveling, would dictate that he be brought before proper authorities at an early date." He recommended that Hoover "urgently" press New York City officials to obtain an extradition order for Medaille. If New York City officials could not afford it, he suggested, the FBI should pay for it.

Hoover's priority was not protecting public safety, however, but influencing public opinion. When New York City officials said they lacked funds for extradition, he refused to cover the costs, though this was well within his power. Instead, he ordered Lynum to confidentially give information from FBI intelligence files on Medaille to Ed Montgomery of the *San Francisco Examiner* with the suggestion that he "utilize the information furnished as the basis for a feature article discrediting the VDC."

Montgomery, Hoover noted, was someone "who has been successfully used in similar counterintelligence techniques and who can be relied upon not to reveal the Bureau's interest."

Lynum again urged that the bureau first ensure Medaille's arrest, but Hoover was adamant. On March 9, 1966, he ordered Lynum to "immediately contact Montgomery."

N.Y. SEX CASE, GRIM PAST OF VDC LEADER

Under that front page headline Montgomery's story began:

A paid non-student functionary of the Vietnam Day Committee in Berkeley and recent speaker at Mills College is wanted in New York, where he was adjudged a sexual psychopath and killer, The Examiner learned yesterday.

He is Frances [*sic*] Michael Medaille, 23, alias Michael J. O'Hanlon, who lives at VDC headquarters at 2407 Fulton St., Berkeley. As O'Hanlon, he played an active role in recent campus demonstrations.

In February 1958, Medaille lured a seven-year-old girl to the roof of a New York apartment house. He molested the girl and hurled her to her death in the street 12 floors below.

Montgomery was happy to get another "scoop" from his secret sources at the FBI. He not only wrote the article but got the *Examiner* to hold it for publication until March 20, the Sunday before nationwide antiwar demonstrations, when it would have greater potential for undermining the protest.

The reporter had emphasized in his story that Medaille spoke at Mills, a women's college in Oakland, but according to Medaille, Montgomery did not bother to contact either him or his family for their side of the story. Had he done so, Medaille said, Montgomery might have learned that he did not in fact molest the girl.

Other newspapers around the country picked up Montgomery's story. So did the *National Review*, the conservative magazine edited by William F. Buckley, Jr., a cofounder of Young Americans for Freedom. Tens of thousands of people had marched against the war that week, but Buckley's magazine declared, "The biggest story developed a few days before the protest when reporter Ed Montgomery of the San Francisco Examiner uncovered the history of demonstration leader Francis Medaille."

Even after the *Examiner* story ran, the FBI took no steps to arrest Medaille, and he remained at large. He had every chance to flee, which may have been Hoover's hope, as that would have heightened the scandal. Instead, Medaille wrote *The Daily Californian* a letter in which he expressed his remorse and tried to explain what he had done as an adolescent.

"It was anger and fear that drove me to my actions," he said, "anger and fear of others and of myself."

He continued, "After I was first put on probation, I decided that I would be respectable, that I would be a regular member of the regular community. To accomplish this, I attended college, took Petroleum Technology, joined the Young Republicans, and the YAF, and went out into the fine world of America, where I found fear, anger, and frustration everywhere, and myself inescapably joined in the madness. Fear of China, fear of the 'commies,' of the Bomb, of Civil Rights, a lack of understanding, the inability to perceive a fellow human as a fellow human . . ."

In the face of this, he decided to join the antiwar movement and work for peace. He should have told his colleagues about his past, he acknowledged, but had been too afraid. He declared that he was proud of his work with the VDC, and closed his letter, "Yours in sadness, Francis Medaille."

Medaille continued to work openly with the VDC. Eventually, New York City authorities obtained an extradition warrant and only then did FBI agents arrest him—some nine weeks after the bureau learned he was wanted for probation violation—as he was demonstrating against the war in front of the Federal Building in San Francisco. Continuing its coverage of the story, the *Examiner* reported the arrest of "the bearded Medaille." Returned to New York City, he was found guilty of violating the terms of his probation.

Years later, Medaille told the author he still struggled with the awful memory of killing the girl. "I take full responsibility," he said. "There's not a day I don't think about it."

He added that he had not known about the FBI's role in his case, and said agents should have arrested him promptly.

But Hoover's aides were content with the counterintelligence operation.

"It has resulted in lessened activity of the VDC," Lynum reported.

With Medaille knocked out of the picture, Jerry Rubin arranged for another VDC volunteer to man the group's campus table. Stew Albert had come to San Francisco from New York City, where he graduated from Pace University, participated in an antinuclear demonstration organized by the Catholic Worker, and followed his father into the city's civil service, working as an investigator for the New York Department of Welfare. In the summer of 1965, he rode a Greyhound bus to San Francisco and visited Ferlinghetti's City Lights bookstore in North Beach, where an employee suggested he check out the Vietnam Day Committee.

Albert soon became a VDC regular and a close friend of Jerry Rubin. With long blond curls and mustache, a barrel chest, and leather boots, Albert had the good-natured air of a Kentucky colonel. He proved to be a charismatic campus spokesman for the VDC, a job that put him on the path to becoming a nationally prominent activist. He would later become involved with the Yippies, the political provocateurs who included Rubin, Abbie Hoffman, and Paul Krassner, and were known for surreal pranks such as sprinkling dollar bills from the balcony of the New York Stock Exchange, attempting to levitate the Pentagon, and running a pig for president.

The FBI's counterintelligence operation against Medaille, it turned out, helped create the opportunity for Albert's even more attention-grabbing protests.

When the bomb went off at the VDC offices at 12:09 a.m. on April 9, 1966, Stew Albert was drinking coffee at Caffe Mediterraneum on Telegraph Avenue, two blocks away. He heard the blast and rushed to the Fulton Street headquarters. As the *Berkeley Daily Gazette* would note, the VDC had been plagued by burglaries that year, and its members had received death letters and bomb threats. Several of these came from the Minutemen, a right-wing vigilante group, while others were unsigned. Rob Hurwitt had filed a report with the FBI claiming an air force enlistee had mailed him a bullet, and though agents confirmed it they took no action.

Police had not yet cordoned off the house, and Albert went inside. The rear of the building was badly damaged. "The place was a shambles," he recalled. "It's amazing how close we came to a tragedy." Had the bomb been placed differently, authorities later said, the house would have been demolished. As it was, the explosion below the back stairs created a vacuum, sucking the windows into the house and sending several committee members who were working in the front rooms to the hospital with minor lacerations. The explosion also damaged a neighboring house and broke windows for blocks.

The Berkeley Police Department began what Chief Addison Fording described in a letter to frightened neighbors as an "intensive" investigation utilizing "all resources of this department." Because the building was well-lit and obviously inhabited at the time, the potential criminal charge was raised from bombing to attempted murder. It was what one former Berkeley policeman described as "the first politically inspired bombing in Berkeley."

Even the conservative *Berkeley Daily Gazette*, no friend of the protesters, was outraged. "The bombing may have been intended only [as] a protest against the views of the VDC. As such it was a shameful attack on free speech and the fabric of our democracy," the paper editorialized. "The police consider that there is a would-be murderer loose in Berkeley. And we agree."

Shortly after the blast, Berkeley police notified the San Francisco FBI office, where the night supervisor sent a teletype alert to headquarters. This was standard procedure. Although the FBI could have assumed jurisdiction under federal civil rights laws, the U.S. Department of Justice instructed the bureau not to investigate the bombing. Nonetheless, FBI headquarters officials took a keen interest in it and sought to influence the Berkeley police investigation. As in the Medaille matter, bureau records show, the FBI's main goal was not the pursuit of criminal justice but covert action.

Right away, bureau officials told Berkeley police the explosion might be connected to the bombing one month earlier of the W.E.B. Du Bois Clubs of America office in San Francisco. The Du Bois Club was the Marxist youth group active on the Berkeley campus whose most prominent member was Bettina Aptheker. In the Du Bois Club bombing, the FBI similarly did not assume jurisdiction but sought to shape how the public saw the political organization.

The Du Bois Club had been bombed on March 6. Two days later, FBI officials working under the counterintelligence program drafted an editorial suggesting that Terence and Matthew Hallinan, members of the Du Bois Club and sons of the radical lawyer Vincent Hallinan, had blown up their own office to avoid complying with a federal subpoena for the organization's records. It was an absurd notion, but Hoover's aides gave the draft to Fulton Lewis, Jr., and he used the FBI's item in his nationally syndicated column. "There is speculation," Lewis wrote, "that the explosion may have been an 'inside job' designed to win sympathy for the organization."

FBI officials then gave San Francisco police another story: that one of its confidential sources had claimed the Du Bois Club might have been bombed by a rival left-wing political group active on the Berkeley campus called the Progressive Labor Party. Bureau officials made this source available to the police. An internal FBI memo explained their motives. "If, in fact, the Progressive Labor Party was responsible for the bombing, a successful prosecution could lead to convictions of leading figures in the Progressive Labor Party and at the same time expose the wild and unfounded charges of the Du Bois Clubs leaders and other left wing groups that the explosion was the work of right wing extremists," an aide to Hoover wrote. "This situation represents an excellent opportunity to expose and disrupt two separate communist elements."

Soon after the VDC bombing, FBI headquarters officials ordered San Francisco agents to make the same source available to Berkeley police. The bureau's purpose was once again to show that the Progressive Labor Party "or other subversive groups" were responsible for the attack. Over the next few months, FBI agents closely followed the progress of both the Berkeley and San Francisco police probes.

San Francisco police, however, found that the FBI's confidential source led nowhere. "We had no real substantial leads to go on," said Robert McClennan, a San Francisco bomb squad detective. "There was never any real thread to tie the two together." Neither case was solved, and after the police closed their investigations the FBI lost interest.

By the time of the bombing, the VDC already had begun to fade as its leaders turned to other pursuits, such as Robert Scheer's run for Congress against the incumbent Democrat, Jeffrey Cohelan, on a platform of ending the war in Vietnam. Jerry Rubin managed the campaign for a while, and more than a thousand people worked on it, including Alice Waters, who would later become renowned for her restaurant, Chez Panisse. Although Scheer lost in the primary, he carried Berkeley by 54 percent and in the district won 45 percent.

Dynamite helped end the VDC's days as the nation's leading antiwar group, but its latest activities already had pushed conservatives to new levels of outrage at Clark Kerr. Indeed, they were still riled up about that loud, lewd, lysergic dance in the men's gym, an outburst that exceeded even the excesses of the great panty raid of 1956.

To the hip, the small advertisement in the back pages of *The Daily Californian* left little doubt about the nature of the dance to be held on March 25, 1966: "Peace Trip VDC Benefit Dance. The Jefferson Airplane, the Mystery Trend, The Morning Fog & The Great Surprise. Psychedelic Lights. Harmon Gym. Donation $1.50."

President Kerr and other university administrators were apparently clueless. They certainly did not anticipate a scene bearing the unmistakable influence of Ken Kesey's psychedelic parties, which had grown into a public phenomenon known as "Acid Tests." Only a handful of campus cops were on duty that night at the gym, and their confidential reports record what they saw in bug-eyed detail.

According to the officers, the dance was out of control from the start, when some four thousand students and nonstudents pushed and shoved to buy tickets at the door. "This crowd was very unruly, loud, dirty," one officer wrote, "and the body odor was terrible." The policemen entered the darkened gym and squeezed onto the jammed dance floor. In the center on a raised platform the Jefferson Airplane and two other bands were playing simultaneously at floor-vibrating volume.

The policemen were awash in sound, light, and color as people around them danced with abandon, stroboscopic bursts capturing their movements in infinite freeze frames. "I observed one female who was holding her skirt above her waist exposing her lower extremities, writhing in an erotic manner contorting her body [as if] in an act of intercourse," a sergeant reported. "She appeared to be in some type of trance and was oblivious to anyone on the dance floor . . . I observed another female . . . the front of her blouse was completely unbuttoned exposing her chest area . . . Many of the couples were dancing in such a manner as to leave nothing to the imagination as to their inner most feelings and desires." In the bleachers some people appeared to be having sex. "One couple was lying in prone position on top of the bleacher seat with the female on the bottom and the male astride her. The girl's skirt was up around her hips."

The officers noticed young people staggering about drunk. Others seemed to be high on drugs. "There was a strong sweet, sickening odor which I immediately detected as marijuana," an officer reported. "This odor was prevalent throughout the gymnasium and especially underneath the main floor bleachers . . . Many couples on the dance floor were wreathing [sic] and swaying under the influence of drugs . . . There were people laying [sic] on the floor in a dazed condition . . . just walking around in a somewhat dazed condition." In fact, many were stoned on large doses of still-legal LSD. Or as a janitor put it in his affidavit, "The people on the dance floor were acting very funny . . ."

A sergeant was transfixed by the light show projected on screens at each end of the gym, describing it as "Pop Art Movies . . . colored fluids being dripped on the lenses of the camera which in turn mushroomed . . . followed by another colored drop . . . When this sequence of colors was completed then movies of males and females, sometimes clothed and sometimes nude, were projected onto the screen . . . a type of erotic dance in which the male would run his hands over the nude female's body and at times they would girate [sic] their bodies in such a fashion to indicate sexual relations and ecstasy . . ." In the hot, close room, another officer unexpectedly experienced an altered state of consciousness: ". . . they had mounted overhead some sort of a ray-like very bright light and when a person stood in the light . . . it gave you a very weird feeling like you were in a trance-like state, and it scared me, it actually upset me . . ."

At 2:15 a.m. it was clear the musicians had no intention of quitting anytime soon, and police cut the power. The crowd dispersed, leaving the gym littered with empty bottles and puddles of vomit. Sergeant Robert Ludden, one of the officers who had grabbed Savio at the Greek Theatre, was on the scene. "The conduct at this dance is totally inexcusable," he wrote in his report.

Several days later, District Attorney Frank Coakley announced that he had reviewed the campus police reports and, though there was insufficient evidence to file criminal charges, he would confer with university officials about preventing "such incidents" in the future.

This was not enough for Hugh Burns, chairman of the Fact-Finding Subcommittee on Un-American Activities. On May 6, 1966, his committee released another of its red-bound reports blaming events on Kerr.

Dwelling on the lurid details, the report charged that the dance was the logical result of his "consistently retreating before the demands of rebelling students" and "fostering an anything goes atmosphere." Kerr quickly held a press conference and declared the report was full of "distortions, half-truths, inaccuracies, and statements on situations taken out of context."

Burns still had failed to identify a single Communist professor, but his latest charges sparked more bad press for the university with headlines like "Senators Zero in on 'Filth.'"

And they gave new ammunition to Reagan.

The crowd at San Francisco's Cow Palace was the biggest yet of Reagan's campaign. This was the same venue where Barry Goldwater had his finest hour two years earlier, winning his party's presidential endorsement while Berkeley students picketed outside. Reagan already was well ahead of his opponents in the race for the Republican nomination to oppose Governor Brown that November. Now, rows and rows of cheering people voiced new hope for advancing the conservative cause.

The "Reagan Roundup," as the May 12, 1966, rally was billed, was decidedly different from the VDC's "Peace Trip" dance. There were no strobe lights, no pot, and no hippies here. As *The New York Times* observed, this crowd was well-groomed, well-fed, and well-to-do. A huge American flag borrowed from the Shriners—one newspaper said it was the biggest in the world—hung behind the stage. Miles of red, white, and blue bunting festooned the walls of the cavernous arena originally built for agricultural events as one of FDR's New Deal projects. Country-and-western bands played while men dressed as cowboys and Indians strolled the grounds. Chuck wagons dispensed box lunches of cold fried chicken, potato salad, and apple pie.

Smiling, fresh-faced young women in uniforms greeted the guests. These were the "Reagan Girls." Their job was to "add charm and sparkle" to the candidate's events. As the campaign's "Reagan Girls Manual" suggested, "Whenever there is a parade or car caravan, make sure a carful of attractive Reagan Girls are a part of it. Have the Reagan Girls attend all your meetings—their presence is an added attraction for the males in your group!"

Each Reagan Girl was carefully chosen by county campaign aides. The manual specified the necessary physical attributes: She must be "attractive, friendly, and charming"; between the ages of sixteen and twenty-five; and have "a 25 (twenty-five) inch waist maximum."

"The REAGAN GIRL is a young, wholesome, vivacious, natural, all-American girl. Repeat, YOUNG, NATURAL!!" the manual said. "She recognizes that politics is not meant to be a social free-for-all and has chosen to contribute to better government by becoming a Reagan Girl."

Nancy Reagan personally picked their mandatory uniform: a red wool beret worn on the left side of the head over hair worn down; a white double-knit turtleneck top with long sleeves that completely covered the upper body; and a red stain-resistant, crease-resistant, synthetic drop-waist box-pleated skirt "hemmed to the *top* of the knee and *not* one inch above." (Emphasis in original.) The outfit was completed by white tennis sneakers, white gloves, and, across the front of the blouse, a red, white, and blue Reagan emblem.

The manual specified an equally strict code of conduct. No gum chewing, smoking, or alcoholic drinks. No giving out phone numbers and addresses, meeting boyfriends, or making dates. "It must be remembered," an internal campaign memo said, "that the Reagan Girls, as they represent Mr. Reagan in public, must be the acme of attractiveness, charm, and good behavior."

As the Reagan Girls sparkled and charmed, the crowd of about 4,500 people at the Cow Palace was entertained by some of Reagan's Hollywood friends. There were remarks by Buddy Ebsen, who played Jed Clampett in the television series *The Beverly Hillbillies*, and Don DeFore, who costarred in *The Adventures of Ozzie and Harriet*. Chuck Connors, hero of the Western series *The Rifleman*, introduced Reagan as "a man in a state that needs a man."

With Nancy on his arm, Reagan emerged from beneath the giant flag to deafening cheers. The couple strode up and down the aisles, one honor guard of Reagan Girls preceding them and another following. Finally, the Reagans ascended the stage. Nancy sat to Reagan's side and fixed an adoring gaze on him as he stepped to the rostrum and began what had been billed as a major campaign speech. He attacked bureaucracy, rising taxes, and welfare recipients. Then he turned to Berkeley:

> There is a leadership gap, and a morality and decency gap, in Sacramento. And there is no better illustration of that than what has been perpetrated . . . at the University of California at Berkeley, where a small minority of beatniks, radicals, and filthy speech advocates have brought such shame to . . . a great university.

The giant hall reverberated with foot-stomping as Reagan declared that the latest report from the Burns committee was further proof that President Kerr and Governor Brown had to go—and Mario Savio, too.

Focusing on the VDC dance, Reagan continued:

The report tells us that many of those attending were clearly of high school age. The hall was entirely dark except for the light from two movie screens. On these screens the nude torsos of men and women were portrayed, from time to time, in suggestive positions and movements.

Three rock and roll bands played simultaneously. The smell of marijuana was thick throughout the hall. There were signs that some of those present had taken dope. There were indications of other happenings that cannot be mentioned here.

How could this happen on the campus of a great university? It happened because those responsible abdicated their responsibilities . . .

It began a year ago when so-called free speech advocates, who in truth have no appreciation of freedom, were allowed to assault and humiliate an officer of the law. This was the moment when the ringleaders should have been taken by the scruff of the neck and thrown off the campus permanently.

It continued through the filthy speech movement, through activities of the Vietnam Day Committee, and this has been allowed to go on in the name of academic freedom. What in heaven's name does "academic freedom" have to do with rioting, with anarchy, with attempts to destroy the primary purpose of the university, which is to educate our young people?

Proclaiming that taxpayers had a right to know what was going on at the university, Reagan accused Governor Brown of a "cover-up." He called for legislative hearings "into the charges of communism and blatant sexual misconduct on the campus."

He demanded that the university impose a "code of conduct" on faculty "that would force them to serve as examples of good behavior and decency for the young people in their charge":

When those who advocate an open mind keep it open at both ends with no thought process in the middle, the open mind becomes a hose for any idea that comes along. If scholars are to be recognized as having a right to press their particular value judgments, perhaps the time has come also for institutions of higher learning to assert themselves as positive forces in the battles for men's minds.

This could mean they would insist upon mature, responsible conduct and respect for the individual from their faculty members and might even call on them to be proponents of those ethical and moral standards demanded by the great majority of our society.

These things could be done and should be done. The people not only have a right to know what is going on at their universities, they have a right to expect the best from those responsible for it.

Claiming that he had independently verified some of the allegations in the Burns report—he had his sources—Reagan demanded the dismissal of "those responsible for the degradation of a great university."

The hall trembled with applause.

20

Sources on Campus

Reagan's car pulled up outside the Piedmont home of the Republican assemblyman Don Mulford and the candidate was ushered inside for a secret
meeting. Having easily defeated George Christopher in the June 7, 1966,
GOP primary two months before, Reagan was now running all-out against
Governor Brown. His campaign schedule was intense, but he stole time
for this meeting in the small, affluent suburb five miles from the Berkeley
campus.

Reagan had been promised important inside information about his
hottest election issue, student unrest at Berkeley. His campaign already
had benefited from the exaggerated claims of a Communist conspiracy on
campus that were widely publicized by Ed Montgomery of the *San Francisco Examiner*, other conservative journalists, and R. E. Combs of the
Burns committee, all of whom had received covert help from the FBI.

Public concern about subversion at the university was also stoked that
summer by the House Un-American Activities Committee's hearings in
Washington, D.C. Humiliated by students at San Francisco City Hall
back in 1960, the crusading committee members were now revisiting the
matter of Berkeley activists from a safer distance. They summoned Deputy District Attorney Edwin Meese III to testify that university officials
had allowed the Vietnam Day Committee to use the campus to mount
illegal protests.

Meese's outrage was unmistakable despite his matter-of-fact recount-
ing of the antiwar group's antics—the marches, the interference with troop
trains, the harassment of army dog trainers, the "peace bombings." These
activities were especially serious, he testified, because they involved highly
organized violations of the law. He noted, for example, that VDC organizers used "an elaborate communications system, often with walkie-talkie
radios, to direct various portions of the demonstrations." All this disrupted routine business, Meese said, and cost more than $100,000 in

public funds for extra police protection. Worse yet, it gave "aid and comfort to the enemy."

So excitedly was the thirty-four-year-old prosecutor describing the VDC's provocations that U.S. Representative Joe Pool, the Texas Democrat chairing the session, asked him to "go just a little more slowly." Meese calmed down, only to be interrupted again—this time by the VDC leader Jerry Rubin. Rubin had been subpoenaed to appear before the committee for what promised to be a ritual drubbing, but had preempted his interrogators by arriving in full Revolutionary War regalia, complete with tri-cornered hat.

Piping up from his seat in the gallery, Rubin demanded that he be allowed to cross-examine Meese. A confused Pool asked, "What is it you want to say?" Rubin replied, "First, I want to introduce myself. My name is Jerry Rubin. I would like to make an explanation as to why I am wearing the uniform of the American Revolution of 1776." Pool cut him off, saying, "I don't care to hear that," but Rubin continued. "I am wearing it because America is degrading its 1776 ideals," he said, and again demanded the opportunity to interrogate Meese. The congressman ordered him to sit down. "This is quite a courtroom," Rubin retorted. Meese resumed his testimony, and when he was done Pool praised him as "a great American." But perhaps recalling HUAC's last unpleasant encounter with Berkeley activists, Pool dismissed Rubin without giving him the chance to testify and turn the hearing into full-blown street theater. Back in California, the HUAC hearings produced more headlines about the incorrigibles on campus.

Reagan had certainly had his adventures—helping to lead a strike at Eureka College, enjoying bootleg booze, engaging in promiscuous sex in Hollywood, impregnating Nancy Davis out of wedlock—but these antiwar antics were different. In the months since his appearance at the Cow Palace, the former actor had been pounding Governor Brown about Berkeley, and especially about the VDC dance. He fired off telegrams to the state legislature demanding an investigation of Burns's allegations of campus misconduct. He issued a position paper titled "Academic Freedom," declaring, "Preservation of free speech does not justify letting beatniks and advocates of sexual orgies, drug usage and 'filthy speech' disrupt the academic community and interfere with our universities' purpose."

Governor Brown announced that he had asked the Board of Regents to investigate Burns's charges, but Reagan called this a "cover-up." He claimed a regents' inquiry would be biased because President Kerr was an ex officio member of the board. Shooting off more telegrams, Reagan urged the regents to instead hold public hearings and require university officials to testify about campus protests. At a press conference, he released copies of the telegrams and again described the VDC dance as "something in the nature of an orgy." Brown replied that Reagan's comments were "an effort by a self-seeking politician to get headlines at the expense of the university." Reagan maintained that Berkeley was an issue "because the people have chosen it."

Reagan was on a roll. At a Memorial Day picnic in San Diego, he called for a "moral crusade" to close the "decency gap." To the delight of his Republican audience, he demanded that Brown get tough on "the small minority" of students responsible for the "shameful things that have been going on" at Berkeley. "And if that means kicking them out," he declared to wild applause, "kick 'em out!"

At the National Press Club in Washington, D.C., on June 16, Reagan again played to the crowd, joking that some things that went on at the university were simply too shocking to mention to such an audience. He belittled Brown's call for advances in higher education—a "space-age education for a space-age generation," the governor had said—cracking, "If he means some of the goings-on at Berkeley are 'way out,' no argument." He repeated what had become his main talking point: that "a vacillating administration has permitted a fractional minority of beatniks, filthy speech advocates, and malcontents to interfere . . ."

Two days later, Reagan again evoked the image of fornicating radicals at the VDC dance. "Even if the governor does not term this type of event an orgy, I do, as do many other outraged Californians," he told the *Los Angeles Times*. "If this was not an orgy, why is the governor afraid to call public hearings?"

Don Mulford took a proprietary interest in the university that occupied a large part of his district. An Oakland native, he had graduated from UC Berkeley in 1939 with a bachelor's degree in political science. He enlisted in the ROTC program and then served four years in the army during World War II. In 1953 he took over his father's insurance firm, and in 1959 he was first elected to the state assembly.

Mulford had assiduously cultivated FBI officials. In 1960, he applauded Hoover's "Communist Target—Youth," writing the director to say "thank you for rendering once again a real service to every American. I am anxious to serve in any way possible." In 1962 he wrote Hoover again to request an autographed photo for his office at the state legislature. Mulford also prevailed upon the director to send a letter congratulating his son on becoming an Eagle Scout. "I want to extend my congratulations on your accomplishment in receiving the Eagle Badge Award of the Boy Scouts of America," Hoover wrote. "You can take deep pride in this achievement which clearly indicates your devotion to the highest principles of Scouting. The youth of today who make every effort to do their best for God and Country are insuring our Nation of leaders who will guide it to new heights of progress."

If Hoover was obliging, Mulford was on the right side. In 1961 the special agent in charge of the San Francisco FBI office wrote, "He is very anti-Clark Kerr and is much concerned about the future of the University and . . . the charges of subversion therein . . . In essence, he feels that Kerr is a self-seeker and an opportunist who is more interested in his personal public image than in the good of the University. He has indicated that in the near future he will help spearhead some sort of drive in the Legislature to counteract the policies of Kerr and his group."

In 1963, FBI officials formally designated Mulford as an "SAC Contact"—a person whom the special agent in charge of the San Francisco FBI office could confidentially call on for help. Under the heading "Services This Contact Can Provide," Lynum wrote, "Mr. Mulford, in view of his position as a State Assemblyman, could be of great assistance to this office as an SAC Contact. He would be able to provide general intelligence type of information that would be helpful on matters before the Legislature having a bearing on law enforcement, racial matters, fair housing ordinance, etc." In the following years, Mulford was especially helpful in regard to the university, secretly providing the FBI with derogatory statements about Clark Kerr.

For Reagan's visit, Mulford had summoned to his home several university officials who also despised Kerr and had been serving as FBI informers. Each had been giving bureau agents internal university information that, they believed, showed Kerr not only had tolerated subversive activities on campus but might well be part of the plot. They would turn out to be some of Reagan's best sources about Berkeley.

Among those present were Hardin Jones, assistant director of UC's radiation lab; John Sparrow, assistant general counsel to the regents; and Alex Sherriffs, the former vice chancellor at Berkeley. Several months after the FSM won the right of free speech on campus, Sherriffs was demoted from his position as vice chancellor. Angry and resentful, the psychology professor had continued to supply Agent Don Jones with information from confidential university files about students, professors, and Kerr.

Professor Hardin Jones had been a paid FBI informer and helped the bureau set up a network of campus sources. And, as he had confided to one agent, he was also working with Richard Combs of the Burns committee "towards removing President Kerr." By late 1965 FBI officials had become skeptical of Jones's claims, however, and the bureau stopped paying him. Agents nonetheless continued to rely on him as "an established source."

Sparrow had contacted the FBI at Professor Jones's suggestion after becoming upset about Kerr's failure to more severely punish Mario Savio and other FSM activists. By virtue of his position as a lawyer for the regents, Sparrow was privy to the most sensitive and confidential university matters. Yet he had violated that fiduciary trust by giving internal information about campus operations to Combs and to FBI agents. Among other things, he gave agents a copy of a private letter in which Kerr assured a worried professor that he supported academic freedom on campus. In Sparrow's eyes, the letter showed Kerr might be subversive. Sparrow also had helped FBI agents arrange their secret meeting with Catherine Hearst, in which she alleged that Kerr appeared to be under someone's "control."

In an interview, Sparrow confirmed that he was at the Mulford meeting. He also acknowledged that he was engaging in partisan political activity against Kerr, a member of the board he represented. He took these "extraordinary" actions, he said, because he was concerned about the university's "welfare."

At Mulford's home, these disaffected campus officials briefed Reagan about "communist efforts to influence the students" at Berkeley, according to the assemblyman's account to an FBI agent. They also told Reagan that Kerr's removal was "vital" to the university's future.

Reagan listened in astonishment to Sherriffs, Jones, and Sparrow. The situation at Berkeley was as bad as, if not worse than, what these men had been telling his campaign operatives about the campus.

Reagan's operatives were with BASICO, a Los Angeles research firm that had been retained to help him discuss campaign issues. Behavior

Science Corporation, as the outfit was also known, was headed by two behavioral psychologists. Stanley Plog had been a professional trombonist who earned his Ph.D. at Harvard with a dissertation analyzing letters from congressional constituents in response to the McCarthy hearings. Ken Holden had been a professional pilot. Plog and Holden met at UCLA in the early 1960s and bonded over their mutual disdain of therapy and shared conviction that the campus was overpopulated by professors with liberal views. (Plog by now was writing position papers for the Republican State Central Committee.) They started BASICO, providing psychological assessments of prospective executive employees for corporations. Job candidates would jokingly ask each other if they had been "Plogged."

Reagan's campaign hired BASICO soon after the candidate made a glaring error in his January 1966 campaign kickoff speech. He had declared that 15.1 percent of Californians were on welfare; the figure was actually 5.1. As Plog and Holden recalled, when they came aboard Reagan had a clear political philosophy but little grasp of state operations and issues. With their staff of about two dozen researchers, they soon identified the top seventeen or eighteen campaign subjects and prepared summaries about each on five-by-eight-inch cards kept securely in a set of black three-ring binders. Reagan carried the binders as he crisscrossed the state, relying on them as he prepared his speeches.

Plog, Holden, or their associate, Jim Gibson, always traveled with Reagan so they could monitor audience reaction to his talks and immediately call BASICO headquarters for research assistance if necessary. This regimen helped Reagan avoid politically costly gaffes and gave him a superior command of the issues. "I don't want to say we molded him," Holden told the author. "But we certainly did help him become operationally more effective." He added—only partly in jest—that "the Berlin Wall wouldn't have come down unless it had been for Stan and I [sic]."

Like Reagan, Plog and Holden recognized Berkeley as a pivotal topic and conducted extensive research for him about the university. Some of their most important information—Holden would call it crucial—came from the FBI's campus informers who gathered at Mulford's house.

The secret contacts between these informers and BASICO began when Hardin Jones phoned the Reagan campaign during the primary and arranged a meeting in Los Angeles. "Jones and one or two of his Berkeley colleagues traveled to BASICO's offices and offered whatever encouragement or data they could give us to help Reagan get elected because they could see . . . the Communists were taking over Berkeley and they were afraid what this was going to do for academic freedom," Holden said. Sherriffs also visited BASICO's office, though mostly they spoke on the phone. "We were passing information back and forth," Holden said. "It was mainly, I think, coming from him, because we were looking for information and data and so on that Reagan might use." Sparrow, meanwhile, provided information to the Reagan campaign in telephone conversations and letters. "They were working through us," Holden added, "and we were the conduit." As Sparrow wrote in one letter to Reagan, "I address this to you in care of Ken Holden in order to preserve the confidential nature of this communication."

Hardin Jones and his colleagues provided the Reagan campaign with sweeping allegations about Kerr and Communist conspiracies on campus, similar to those Jones had been giving the FBI. For example, Jones told Agent Don Jones, "I have recently witnessed a massive indoctrination of freshmen in New Left politics during the freshmen orientation program." Likewise, Holden recalled, "They were telling us how the indoctrination was taking place. That the graduate students, and the Communist-oriented ones is all I can say, they would have this big meeting of all the new students. The first thing they would tell the entering freshmen on the first day is to 'absolutely forget everything your parents ever told you about anything. You're going to learn what's really going on now.' It was pure, left-wing, Communist propaganda." Even if the graduate students were not actual members of the Communist Party, Holden added, they were still subversive. "Let's face it," he said, "it didn't make any difference. They were spouting the Communist line and undermining parental controls."

Hardin Jones and his compatriots leveled even more alarming charges at Kerr. "These professors related that Clark Kerr was not only indorsing [sic] these 'orientations' but that his wife was a card-carrying Communist," Holden said. These charges, of course, were false.

At one point, Reagan's campus contacts supplied advance intelligence that helped him avoid a debacle during a campaign appearance at Berkeley's Boalt Hall School of Law. Reagan was scheduled to speak there about contemporary legal issues. At the last minute, Holden recalled, "We got an inside tip that they were going to ask him about some obscure paragraph or two in the labor laws." BASICO staff briefed Reagan on his way to Boalt, however, and he was ready for the question. "They couldn't believe this man was so well versed in labor law in California," Holden said. "It was a tour de force. And that was the essence of what we were trying to do in the campaign."

The FBI's campus informers also had a broader impact: they encouraged Reagan to push the Berkeley issue hard. According to Holden, Hardin Jones's initial visit to the BASICO office "was the prelude, particularly, to getting Ron to really take care of the whole question of Berkeley in a really powerful way." As the campaign continued, Plog and Holden could quote Sherriffs, Jones, and Sparrow with authority when briefing Reagan on Berkeley. "They were very helpful," Holden said. "When talking with Reagan we could give him a lot of confidence . . . when we had this kind of information he took it as gold-plated."

Indeed, after the meeting at Mulford's, Reagan wrote the assemblyman to express his gratitude. "Just a note of thanks for a most interesting meeting in your home," he said in the August 17 letter. "While the pressures are arising from all sides to abandon the Berkeley issue, I very much appreciate the help of yourself and your associates in providing the true facts on this matter.

"We shall be counting on you for continuing help," he said.

Soon after Reagan's meeting with the FBI's campus informers, J. Edgar Hoover personally gave his campaign a boost when he publicly endorsed the candidate's proposal to set up a new police training academy.

Reagan had announced his plan for a new anticrime academy on August 20, 1966. The institute would teach "police, sheriff's deputies and other law officers the newest methods in crime prevention and solution." It would be located in Berkeley, he said, and "with Mr. Hoover's help such a school could become a sort of FBI academy of California."

Reagan already had written to the director about it. "Because of your long record, not only of successfully fighting crime, but also of developing new techniques and methods, and because you have given the United States a crime-fighting force second to none in the world, we are eager to have your aid and advice in this project," Reagan said. "I would be grateful, indeed, if you could give serious consideration to aiding in this effort."

After reviewing Reagan's letter, Hoover's aides noted in an internal memo, "Mr. Reagan is the Republican candidate for Governor of California. He has visited our Los Angeles Office and relations with him have been cordial. He is well known for his anti-communist activities in various Hollywood organizations and has been considered one of Hollywood's most active conservative political leaders."

There was, however, a problem: only a few months earlier Hoover had issued a statement saying, "It is and always has been my firm policy to refrain from lending support to any candidate in campaigns for political office."

In Reagan's case, however, the director made an exception. "I can assure you that this Bureau is always willing to extend its cooperative services to any and all local, state and federal agencies in order to more effectively combat crime," he said in an August 24, 1966, letter to the candidate. "I hope you will not hesitate to call upon the FBI for assistance in all matters of mutual interest."

In an interview, Cartha DeLoach denied the FBI helped Reagan's campaign. "Heavens no," he said. "We stayed ten miles away from political campaigns. Why should a fact-finding investigative agency involve themselves in political campaigns?"

William F. Buckley, Jr., was one of many conservatives who recognized that events at the university could be decisive in the governor's race. He was editor of the *National Review*, a right-wing rhetorician, and a founder of the Young Americans for Freedom, whose advisory board included Reagan.

It was summer break and the campus was calm. But in a column for the *Los Angeles Times*, Buckley saw fit to liken the Free Speech Movement to the bloody race riots that broke out in the Watts section of Los Angeles in August 1965. "A big issue of the campaign is the arrant, unrepentant indiscipline of the students at Berkeley who two years ago succeeded in grinding education to a halt there and turning the campus into a sort of ivy-covered Watts presided over by a young satrap, Mario Savio, who would occasionally vouchsafe a little released time for schooling between riots," Buckley wrote.

"A preternatural silence reigns at the University of California in Berkeley. But school opens soon, and the eyes of all of California will be on the re-assembled students whose activities could have a lot to do with whether Mr. Brown has any chance at all to succeed himself as governor of California."

Just after Labor Day, Reagan opened the final two months of his campaign with a new attack on Berkeley—this time vowing to conduct a formal investigation of the university with help from John McCone.

McCone had resigned as CIA director in April 1965, weeks after arranging for Hoover to leak confidential FBI reports about students, faculty, and liberal regents to Ed Pauley. Since then, McCone had been busy.

Governor Brown had named him to lead an investigation into the cause of the Watts riots, which had instantly symbolized the nation's deepening urban unrest. Lasting six days, the disorders resulted in 34 deaths, 1,032 injuries, 3,952 arrests, and $40 million in property damage. Marauders had chanted, "Burn, baby, burn."

The McCone Commission concluded that the August 1965 riot was sparked by the arrest of Marquette Frye, a twenty-one-year-old black man, for reckless driving on the evening of Wednesday, August 7. A large mob drawn by word of police brutality gathered, and some people began stoning passing motorists. The next night an estimated 10,000 black residents took to the streets. Some tossed rocks and Molotov cocktails, others fired guns and looted as the violence spread to a 46.5-square-mile area. The riots continued until late Saturday night, when more than 1,600 police officers and sheriffs' deputies and 13,900 National Guardsmen were called out.

According to the commission, a complex of factors had contributed to the outbreak: the passage of Proposition 14, which repealed the state's Rumford Fair Housing Act; antipoverty programs that failed to meet promises; and the growing use of civil disobedience as a means of redress. Above all, the riots reflected decades of inner-city discrimination, deprivation, and desperation. The commission's December 1965 report recommended vigorous investigation into citizen claims of police abuse, improved housing, more job training, and better educational services, beginning with preschool.

McCone also ran his businesses, golfed at exclusive clubs, and socialized with some of the richest and most powerful members of Southern California society. He had supported George Christopher in the Republican gubernatorial primary race as a moderate, but after Reagan easily won, McCone threw his support behind him and in August 1966 joined the campaign as head of an executive policy advice committee.

Now Reagan would have the man who had stared down the Soviets and probed race riots investigate Berkeley.

He announced the plan in a telecast address marking the last stretch of the gubernatorial race. In the September 9 speech at the Biltmore Bowl in Los Angeles, Reagan declared that Kerr and Brown had failed to impose discipline, and as a result the university was "threatened by the irresponsible and destructive conduct of a small radical minority."

In remarks that echoed Hardin Jones's earlier statements to FBI officials, Reagan asserted that the "so-called New Left" had used the university, "even in the classrooms, as a political propaganda base with no pretense of allowing balanced discussion and divergent points of view."

He claimed undergraduate applications had dropped and professors were leaving UC "at a rate of three times as great as the normal turnover."

He also contended that Brown had falsely accused him of having extremist connections—of having collaborated with members of the John Birch Society—while Brown and his administration had been commandeered by "militant left-wing radicals":

> I charge that there has been political interference which has resulted in the appeasement of campus malcontents and filthy-speech advocates under the pretense of preserving academic freedom.
>
> Actually, this policy of appeasement has been dictated by political expediency in this election year in the hope of sweeping the problem under the rug. This will, of course, be denied.
>
> The governor, aided by his well-oiled and heavily financed machine, will charge instead that I would impose political control on the university. He remains deafeningly silent about how the problem should be solved . . .
>
> We must have a fair and open inquiry and we must maintain academic freedom for the university and keep it isolated from political influence.
>
> As governor, I will ask the most qualified man in California and the nation—John McCone—to conduct such an inquiry.

Brown denied Reagan's charges and accused his opponent of using the university as "the football for his campaign kickoff."

Kerr meanwhile sought to counter Reagan's claim that the Berkeley campus was in ruins and enrollment was dropping. He told the regents at a board meeting in San Diego that undergraduate applications for 1966–67 were actually up 36 percent over the previous year. Besides, Berkeley had recently been rated above Harvard and Yale as "the best balanced distinguished university in the nation."

But Reagan did not let up. A few days later, he claimed he had "evidence" that UC officials had avoided a drop in enrollment only by lowering admissions standards and accepting students who were previously unqualified. A university official replied that admissions standards had not changed since adoption of the Master Plan for Education in 1960.

Reagan refused to name his sources for the allegation, but he assured the *Los Angeles Times* it came from concerned professors at Berkeley.

•

As Reagan railed against the Peace Trip dance in the gym, FBI agents hunted for Ken Kesey, whose Acid Tests had inspired the offending event. Since his strange, harmonica-humming appearance at the VDC teach-in the previous October, Kesey had been buzzing like a honeybee in a field of spring flowers, psychedelically pollinating the West Coast. He and his Merry Pranksters had put on Acid Tests in Santa Cruz, San Jose, Palo Alto, Muir Beach, San Francisco, and Portland, LSD-infused multi-media events that were half party and half quest for higher consciousness. At their headquarters in the La Honda redwoods, the Pranksters had also been planning the Trips Festival, a three-day affair to be held in late January 1966 at the Longshoremen's Hall in San Francisco, which promised to be the biggest Acid Test yet.

On the evening of January 19, Kesey dropped in for a planning session at the North Beach apartment of Stewart Brand, a fellow Prankster who would later produce the *Whole Earth Catalog*. At about 2 a.m., Kesey was up on the roof with Carolyn Adams, a Prankster better known as Mountain Girl, taking in the city lights, when police, responding to a neighbor's complaint, climbed the stairs, found them with a small amount of marijuana, and arrested them. It was Kesey's second pot bust in recent months, and if convicted he faced three years in jail. But he was released on bail and resumed preparations for the Trips Festival, which was held on January 23 and 24, complete with live music by the Grateful Dead, light shows, and plenty of acid courtesy of the former Berkeley student known as Owsley. As Tom Wolfe would write, "The Haight-Ashbury era began that weekend."

Kesey, however, failed to materialize in court for hearings on his marijuana arrest on February 3 and again on February 7. Then, on February 13, police disclosed that his pink, green, and lavender VW microbus had been found abandoned on a desolate stretch of Highway 1 by the cliffs high above the roaring Humboldt County coast. Inside the bus was a rambling sixteen-page letter, an apparent suicide note reading in part, "Ocean, Ocean, Ocean, I'll beat you in the end."

Police searched for Kesey to no avail. The head Prankster had pulled another prank. He already was sipping cold *cervezas* on a beach in Mexico, where he would spend the next several months writing poetry, playing an Appalachian mountain harp, and getting high. Joined by his wife and children and other Pranksters, he soon reestablished a facsimile of his old La Honda scene near the port of Manzanillo.

As word of the outlaw author's whereabouts filtered back to the States, his status as a counterculture hero grew and the East Coast literary establishment arched an eyebrow. *Esquire* magazine dispatched Robert Stone to find him and write the story of his hallucinatory hegira, but Stone went native and wound up staying on in Mexico with his old Perry Lane pal. *Esquire* then dispatched Tom Wolfe, who tracked Kesey to Mexico but arrived after the fugitive had already returned to the States. Wolfe would eventually catch up with Kesey and tell his psychedelic saga in *The Electric Kool-Aid Acid Test*. Wolfe's novelistic approach proved to be a perfect match for his subject; the 1968 book would become a bestseller, help usher in a revolutionary style of literary reportage known as the New Journalism, and serve as a neon billboard for the dilating hippie culture. For now, though, Kesey faded, like a chimera, from the public's consciousness.

But not from J. Edgar Hoover's. The FBI had obtained a warrant for his arrest on charges of unlawful flight to avoid state prosecution. Curtis Lynum, the special agent in charge of the San Francisco office, supervised the investigation. Lynum found today's youth rather odd—"a generation . . . different than any other," he would say—and Kesey and his clan downright weird. And though the former gymnast respected Kesey as an athlete and a successful author, he was nonplussed by his counterculture behavior. He assigned two agents to track him down, cautioning them about his physical prowess.

They'd had little luck in the seven months since he disappeared, but on October 6, 1966, the *San Francisco Chronicle* published an astonishing article. According to the page-one story, Kesey had sneaked back to the Bay Area. He even had attended a Trips Festival at San Francisco State College, lectured to a creative writing class at Stanford, and held a clandestine conference at which he revealed his plan for an "acid graduation ceremony." Kesey had softly drawled, "I think it's time we graduated out of acid. LSD has reached a stature where Babbitt begins to take it. It used to be Hell's Angels and Bohemians, but now the son of the hardware store owner in Des Moines is taking it. We're here to save them." Elaborating later, Kesey said the graduation was meant to help young people who had confused getting high on psychedelic drugs with attaining higher consciousness.

"I felt that acid, meaning LSD, is a door that can be used to go into another room . . . People I saw going through that door and going through that door and going through that door, and not into this room." Getting stuck in that doorway is dangerous, he declared, noting that psychedelic drug use is "increasing faster than people can keep up with it." As Kesey envisioned the graduation ceremony, he would bestow diplomas on Jerry Garcia, a Hell's Angel, and other acid veterans to symbolize moving beyond the doors of perception.

Yet most remarkable, the *Chronicle* noted, was Kesey's defiant declaration: "I intend to stay in this country as a fugitive, and as salt in J. Edgar Hoover's wounds." The thirty-one-year-old author repeated the taunt to the seventy-one-year-old FBI director verbatim in a secretly prerecorded television interview that aired on October 20.

Lynum was not happy to see the fugitive's twinkling eyes on the evening news. "The FBI was not looking good," he recalled. "Kesey was effectively 'thumbing his nose' at the law enforcement community."

About twenty-five minutes after Kesey's insubordinate interview aired on KGO-TV's six o'clock news that Thursday, Kesey and a friend were driving south from San Francisco on Highway 101, just past Candlestick Park. As their red panel van cruised along in the anonymous commuter traffic, Kesey, in the passenger seat, removed the cowboy hat and glasses he had been wearing as a disguise.

A few car lengths away, four FBI agents were carpooling home. One was the lead agent on the Kesey case. As their car came abreast of the van, the agent happened to glance over. "There's Ken Kesey—one of my fugitives—he's beside the driver of the old van in the next lane!" he said. He pulled out a mug shot of Kesey, looked at it, and looked back at Kesey. He waved at Kesey. Kesey waved back. Yes, it was him!

In the red truck, Kesey looked again and now saw men in crew cuts and suits motioning furiously at him. One of them was thrusting out a badge.

Kesey's friend tried to speed away but the sedan full of FBI agents easily overtook them. The van swerved to the shoulder, screeched to a stop, and Kesey jumped out, bounded the guardrail, and streaked across a field, past playing children.

The FBI car pulled over and the lead agent, a former football player, gave chase and eventually caught the fugitive, who surrendered without a struggle. Kesey would later say the two agents who took him to city jail had read his books and treated him well. "The FBI are good guys," he said. "The best of the cops."

Kesey's marijuana cases were subsequently resolved when he was sentenced to six months in a San Mateo County honor camp, not far from his La Honda redoubt. He appeared for one court hearing in a bright green shirt with orange sleeves, prompting the judge to scold, "Join the human race and conform a little . . ."

•

An outraged mother of five walked into another courtroom in Alameda County that month to press her lawsuit against Clark Kerr and the University of California. Patricia Atthowe claimed the UC Berkeley dean's office had refused to let her review records listing the officers, faculty advisers, and stated purposes of officially registered student organizations. Declaring that she was merely a concerned taxpayer, Atthowe said she wanted to know who was behind groups like the University Friends of SNCC, the campus Vietnam Day Committee, and the Campus Sexual Freedom Forum, which had "no place in an institution of higher learning." Soon newspapers across the state were carrying stories about the "Oakland housewife" taking on UC. Some articles noted that she was associated with the Reagan campaign, though she claimed her research was unrelated. But no one knew she also worked with the Alameda County District Attorney's intelligence unit, covertly collecting information that was funneled to the FBI.

Reagan had vowed he would "never oppose the right of students to hear divergent political and social views." But as he intensified his criticism of Berkeley in the final weeks of the campaign, he objected to upcoming campus speeches by both Robert F. Kennedy, the New York senator and former U.S. attorney general, and Stokely Carmichael, the civil rights advocate.

At a Republican rally near Los Angeles on October 20, Reagan declared that Kennedy's appearance would be proof that Brown "is injecting the campus again directly into politics." He added, "I am told that the university's public relations staff has been devoting full time in recent days to making this meeting a success. Now this is a flagrant misuse of the public relations staff."

Kennedy had indeed come to California to campaign for Brown, but not at Berkeley. According to university officials, his visit there had received no special planning and would be nonpartisan. His speech, on civil rights, had been arranged months earlier by the Inter-Fraternity Council.

On that Sunday, October 23, Kennedy began his address at the Greek Theatre with a warm embrace. "You are the first college to become a major political issue since George III attacked Harvard for being a center of political rebellion and subversion," he said. "As for me, I am glad of Berkeley . . . I welcome the passionate concern with the condition and future of the American nation which can be found on this campus."

Declaring that he understood black frustration, Kennedy called for greater progress in civil rights. At the same time, he condemned the riots in Watts, Oakland, and other urban areas. Even worse than these acts of violence, he said, were the words of a "very few Negro spokesmen . . . who have called for hatred to fight prejudice, racism to meet racism, violence to destroy oppression."

He also assailed "white backlash" that "masks hostility to the swift and complete fulfillment of equal opportunity." He said that "any leader who seeks to exploit this feeling for the momentary advantage of office fails his duty to the people of this country."

Kennedy concluded: "You are a generation which is coming of age at one of the rarest moments in history—a time when the old order of things is crumbling and a new world society is painfully struggling to take shape. You can use your enormous privilege and opportunity to seek purely private pleasure and gain. But history will judge you, and, as the years pass, you will ultimately judge yourself, on the extent to which you have used your gifts to lighten and enrich the lives of your fellow men."

After his talk, people in the audience asked Kennedy about his position on the war in Vietnam. He gamely replied, "I'd probably agree with a slogan that I've heard from this campus—'I'd rather make love than war.' From then on, it becomes more difficult." Pressed for a more specific answer, he disappointed antiwar activists by stating he had no moral objection to the U.S. bombing of North Vietnam.

Stokely Carmichael had been scheduled to speak at the Greek one week later. In recent months, the tall, thin twenty-five-year-old had become known as the nation's leading advocate of "Black Power."

Born on June 21, 1941, the year before Savio, in Port-of-Spain, Trinidad and Tobago, Carmichael received a formal British education. When he was eleven years old he immigrated to Harlem, but his father, a carpenter and taxi driver, soon moved the family to a neighborhood of Italians and Jews in the East Bronx where they were the only blacks. As a teenager, he initially opposed student sit-ins at segregated lunch counters in the South. But after seeing televised images of young blacks impassively climbing back onto their stools after whites had pushed them off and poured ketchup and sugar on them, he became a dedicated civil rights activist.

As a Howard University freshman in 1960, he joined CORE's Freedom Rides, in which whites and blacks rode buses through the South to challenge segregation of travel facilities. They were repeatedly arrested, and he spent forty-nine days in Mississippi's notorious Parchman Penitentiary, where he was beaten. Upon graduating with a bachelor's degree in philosophy in 1964, he joined the Student Nonviolent Coordinating Committee, which that summer sent Savio and other white volunteers south. Carmichael helped register thousands of blacks to vote in Lowndes County, Alabama. When the established white parties rejected these new voters, he organized an all-black party called the Lowndes County Freedom Organization. In May 1966, he was elected chairman of SNCC over the more moderate John Lewis in a vote that signaled young black activists' growing impatience with Martin Luther King's doctrine of nonviolent civil disobedience.

Over and over, Carmichael had seen southern whites assault nonviolent blacks. He had seen the complicity of local law enforcement. He had been arrested more than two dozen times during nonviolent protests. Then, in June 1966, James Meredith embarked on a fateful 220-mile solo march from Memphis, Tennessee, to Jackson, Mississippi. Four years earlier, Meredith had won a federal court order overturning Mississippi State University's exclusion of blacks; now he wanted to encourage blacks to overcome their fear of white reprisal and register to vote. As he walked along the side of Highway 51 near Hernando, Mississippi, on June 6, an unemployed white man stepped from the adjacent woods, called Meredith's name, and fired two shotgun blasts at his back.

While Meredith was hospitalized, Carmichael and other civil rights activists took up his march. On June 16, near Greenwood, Mississippi, Carmichael was setting up a rest camp on the grounds of a black elementary school when he was arrested for trespassing on public property. Released after several hours, he rejoined the marchers at a rally and told them with disgust that this was his twenty-seventh arrest and it was time to stop asking for freedom. "What we are going to start saying now is 'Black Power,'" he declared. Soon young blacks across the country had taken up the call.

Martin Luther King, Jr., called the phrase "unfortunate." Other critics said the term smacked of "reverse racism" and "black nationalism." Carmichael explained that he meant "blacks coming together to gain social, political, and economic power." But potential violence worried some observers. Gene Roberts, the *New York Times* reporter covering the civil rights movement, wrote that "there is something intoxicating about the chant 'black power.' It leads Stokely Carmichael . . . to talk of tearing down courthouses. And it leads . . . an aide to Mr. Carmichael, to mutter that 'white blood will flow.'"

At Berkeley on October 29, Carmichael was to deliver the keynote address for a Black Power conference sponsored by Students for a Democratic Society. Michael Lerner, a campus SDS leader and veteran of the Free Speech Movement, told a reporter he hoped the event would encourage Governor Brown and Ronald Reagan to address "Negro problems."

Reagan's campaign operatives at BASICO saw Carmichael's upcoming talk as another opportunity to score political points using the university. In a confidential memo captioned "Berkeley," they set out a strategy by which Reagan could capitalize on Carmichael's appearance. They wrote:

Evidence from our contacts with professors at Berkeley indicate that trouble is building up and there will be more noisy demonstrations before the election.

If the disorders boil into public prominence again, before the election, on balance it would be good for our campaign. However, since Brown got more favorable mail on his action cleaning out Sproul Hall during the previous demonstrations than on anything he's ever done, he probably will make political hay by taking some definitive action which will place him in a favorable leadership role, and in all the newspaper headlines, during the final crucial weeks of the campaign.

Suggestion: Some prediction of these disorders before they happened and emphasis on Brown's ineptitude in dealing with higher education at Berkeley, and revelation that his statements that "Nothing is wrong at Berkeley" are false, may put him in a defensive position so he cannot capitalize on any action he may be forced to take in the next several weeks.

Since Berkeley and Higher Education are one of the public's greatest concerns, Brown cannot be allowed to, at this late date, preempt the role of saving the University from the radicals and the dissidents.

Further information on this situation is being developed . . .

Cunning or cynical, practical or paranoid, Plog and Holden's reasoning evidently impressed Reagan.

On October 18, the candidate sent Carmichael a telegram urging him to cancel his appearance, saying it "could possibly cause trouble and do damage to both our state and a great university."

"It is imperative that our elections November 8 be held in an atmosphere of calm and goodwill," Reagan wrote. "Your appearance on the Berkeley campus so soon before the election will stir strong emotions and could possibly do damage to both parties. I ask you to hold off your appearance until a later date when any proposals you may have to offer can be considered calmly and rationally."

The Greek Theatre, after all, was where, just one year earlier, Mario Savio had been dragged offstage by police, turning the campus against the administration and speeding the Free Speech Movement toward victory.

But despite his stated purpose of maintaining calm, Reagan simultaneously issued an inflammatory press release asking Carmichael not to speak. He further politicized the issue by calling on Brown to join him in urging Carmichael to stay away. "California must not become a hotbed of racial riots," Reagan said at a Republican rally. "We cannot have the university campus used as a base from which to foment riots." Brown declined Reagan's invitation, saying it was up to university officials to decide who was allowed to speak on the campus.

In suit, tie, and close-cut hair, a large banner reading "Black Power" stretched behind him, Carmichael took the stage before some ten thousand people at the Greek Theatre as planned. His speech was by turns bitter, angry, hip, funny, and provocative.

Like Kennedy the week before, Carmichael urged change. But he saw little hope within existing institutions. In his eyes, white Americans had failed to make democracy work. America—all of Western civilization—was corrupt and racist.

The missionaries came with the Bible, and we had the land. When they left, they had the land, and we still have the Bible. And that has been the rationalization for Western civilization as it moves across the world, . . . stealing and plundering and raping everybody in its path. Their one rationalization is that the rest of the world is uncivilized and they are in fact civilized.

In order to understand white supremacy we must dismiss the fallacious notion that white people can give anybody their freedom. No man can give anybody his freedom. A man is born free.

You may enslave a man after he is born free, and that is in fact what this country does. It enslaves black people after they're born, so that the only acts that white people can do is [sic] to stop denying black people their freedom . . .

I maintain that every civil rights bill in this country was passed for white people, not for black people. For example, I am black. I know that. I also know that while I am black I am a human being, and therefore I have the right to go into any public place. White people didn't know that. Every time I tried to go into a place they stopped me. So some boys had to write a bill to tell that white man, "He's a human being; don't stop him."

I knew that I could vote and that that wasn't a privilege; it was my right. Every time I tried I was shot, killed, or jailed, beaten or economically deprived. So somebody had to write a bill for white people to tell them, "When a black man comes to vote, don't bother him." That bill, again, was for white people, not for black people.

So that when you talk about open occupancy, I know I can live any place I want to live. It is white people across this country who are incapable of allowing me to live where I want to live. You need a civil rights bill, not me. I know I can live where I want to live.

Carmichael told how SNCC workers had helped form the Lowndes County Freedom Organization after the white-dominated Democratic Party shunned newly registered black voters. Alabama law required each political party to have an emblem, and Carmichael's organization chose the panther, "a beautiful black animal which symbolizes the strength and dignity of black people, an animal that never strikes back until he's back so far into the wall, he's got nothing to do but spring out." The symbol of the white Alabama Democratic Party was a white rooster, he noted, adding rather wryly that though the press called his party the "Black Panther Party" they never called the Alabama Democratic Party the "White Cock Party." He quipped, "That just points out America's problem with sex and color."

Carmichael called for the creation of new political institutions based on moral values. But whites and blacks should work separately for change, he said, because white leadership diminished the power of black organizations. "The fact is that all black people often question whether or not they are equal to whites, because every time they start to do something, white people are around showing them how to do it. If we are going to eliminate that for the generation that comes after us, then black people must be seen in positions of power, doing and articulating for themselves."

White activists should instead fight racism within white society. "The question," he continued, "is can the white activist not try to be a Pepsi Generation who comes alive in the black community, but can he be a man who's willing to move into the white community and start organizing where the organization is needed?"

Referring to Reagan and Brown, Carmichael asked, "Can the white society or the white activist disassociate himself with [sic] two clowns who waste time parrying with each other rather than talking about the problems that are facing people in this state? Can you dissociate yourself with those clowns and start to build new institutions . . ."

Unlike Kennedy in his talk at the Greek, Carmichael unconditionally condemned the war in Vietnam, calling it illegal, immoral, and another example of American racism. "And the question is, what can we do to stop that war? What can we do to stop the people who, in the name of our country, are killing babies, women, and children? And I maintain . . . the only power we have is the power to say, 'Hell no!' to the draft."

Although he expressed great frustration at the slow pace of civil rights reforms, Carmichael did not call for civil disobedience. But he made very clear his belief that violence was warranted in certain situations.

"If South Africa today were to rebel, and black people were to shoot the hell out of all the white people there," he said, it would be "as they should." And in the United States, "if you play like Nazis, we playing back [sic] with you this time around: Get hip to that."

"We are on the move for our liberation . . . We are concerned with getting the things we want, the things that we have to have to be able to function. The question is, will white people overcome their racism and allow for that to happen in this country? If that does not happen, brothers and sisters, we have no choice but to say very clearly, 'Move over, or we're going to move on over you.'"

Despite Reagan's well-publicized concerns, the Black Power conference ended without incident. Carmichael's speech did, however, underscore the arrival of a new branch of the civil rights movement based on a separate black identity, articulated anger, and greater militancy. When two students at Merritt College in Oakland, Huey Newton and Bobby Seale, formed a black activist organization that month, they borrowed their name from Carmichael's Lowndes County Freedom Organization, calling themselves the Black Panther Party for Self Defense.

Both Reagan and Brown denounced Carmichael's comments at Berkeley. Reagan also declared that he saw no white backlash in the gubernatorial race—"except in the mind of someone who wants to use it in a political sense."

21

Landslide

Mario Savio and Suzanne Goldberg were married in the spring following the FSM's victory. Suzanne had long brown hair and brown eyes and freckles, and at five feet two and 110 pounds she was petite, especially beside his lanky frame. But she was three and a half years older than him, and every bit his equal. The two philosophy students could spend hours talking about everything from community organizing to Freud. Although she was born in Brooklyn, her family had moved to Scarsdale and then Westport, Connecticut, where she graduated from high school as a valedictorian in 1957. Her father, Charles, was a lawyer, an insurance broker, and the president of a necktie manufacturing firm. Her mother, Nettie, was a housewife and helped run his businesses.

Goldberg earned a bachelor's degree in philosophy from Cornell University in 1961, where she was in a sorority, and a master's degree from the City College of New York. She had participated in a few peace rallies on the East Coast, but did not think of herself as a political activist. She enrolled at Berkeley in the fall of 1963 because she had heard it was a beautiful place to study and was intent on earning a doctoral degree in philosophy.

But though she was a serious student, she had stopped to hear Savio talk about free speech as she cut through the sun-dappled crowds on campus, and his words had drawn her in. "I found the moral imperative so passionately and compellingly enunciated by Mario that I would have felt I was betraying my own moral integrity to go on about my business just because I didn't want to risk hurting my career," she would say. She got involved in the Graduate Coordinating Council, the graduate students' arm of the FSM, and became a delegate to the FSM Steering Committee, where she emerged as a militant. She agreed with Savio when he argued for continuing the aborted Sproul Hall sit-in back in November. At the big sit-in that December, she was captain of the monitors on the fourth floor of Sproul Hall, instructing other students on how to "pack in" and helping to ready fire extinguishers to douse possible police tear-gas bombs. She had dropped out of school to devote herself to the FSM, and was now being prosecuted in the mass trial at the Veterans Memorial Building in downtown Berkeley.

Through it all, Savio and Goldberg had grown closer and fallen in love, until one day that spring they were excused from the trial to attend their wedding. They were radiant, one observer remarked, full of joy and hope. "We believed the world to be wide-open to us," she would say. The couple declared their intention to complete their studies and have children. "Marriage is a way the community can share in the joy of two people," Savio said, though adding, "two people getting married outside the religious context."

It was a small civil ceremony at the home of Municipal Court Judge Jerome Pacht in Los Angeles on May 23, 1965. Savio wore a carnation in his suit coat lapel. Goldberg wore a beige dress and her hair in a French twist. The only attendees were Savio's parents, Joseph and Dora, Savio's brother Tom, his friend and lawyer Alex Hoffman, and Hoffman's companion, Elsa Knight Thompson, the KPFA news director. Goldberg's parents, who disapproved of Savio, did not attend. ("My mother read the *New York Post* and thought Mario was a troublemaker," Suzanne recalled.) When a reporter interviewed him about their marriage, Savio took the opportunity to make a political statement. "There's one thing we'd really like to have as a wedding present," he said. "We would like President Johnson to withdraw all our troops from Vietnam . . . very little would make us happier."

An FBI agent discreetly obtained a copy of the Savios' marriage license and questioned the county clerk who had issued it to them a few days earlier. "Mario was very evasive to all questions. Suzanne did all the talking," the clerk readily reported. "They are both going to go back to Cal in September . . . they both needed haircuts and they were both a mess."

Savio had applied for readmission to Berkeley, this time changing his major from philosophy to physics. "Revival of old interests," he wrote on his application, the terse explanation giving little hint that the switch reflected a deepening existential crisis. The university approved his application to return in the fall of 1965.

But the couple did not return that fall. "We both felt that Mario needed to be away from Berkeley, where everyone seemed to need something from him and constantly pressured him to be something for them," Goldberg said. He was also struggling with his internal conflicts. "There were signs from the beginning of our relationship that something disturbing lurked deep inside Mario," Goldberg wrote. "He even warned me that something was wrong. In the winter following the FSM, Mario had had very intense and, as he described them, frightening and repulsive hallucinations under the influence of marijuana in a social situation where his friends were quietly enjoying themselves." Still, she wrote, "I was twenty-five (Mario was twenty-two) and naïve and thought that as long as we loved each other all would be well . . ."

In September 1965, they boarded a ship, bound for Italy and England. They planned to stay abroad as long as a year. Savio had told Goldberg that, more than anything, he wanted to study physics, and the best place to do that was at the University of Oxford. With help from friends, they arranged for him to begin studies at St. Catherine's College there later that year on a scholarship. Goldberg was pregnant with their first child. The *San Francisco Chronicle* reported, "Friends say Savio is uncertain about what he wants to do and feels a period abroad may help him make a decision."

The FBI also was uncertain. Agent Don Jones interviewed the Savios' neighbors in Berkeley to ascertain their travel plans. Other agents reviewed their passport files at the State Department. FBI headquarters alerted bureau offices in London, Paris, and Rome that the Savios were afoot. In a classified bulletin, Hoover requested that the CIA report "any pertinent information" about them. They were among several thousand American antiwar activists, the Church committee later found, whom the agency tracked for the FBI by contacting foreign intelligence services.

In January 1966, the FBI's London office reported that the CIA had found no evidence the Savios were involved in "security" matters. A bureau agent nonetheless placed an unlimited "lookout notice" for the couple with the Immigration and Naturalization Service. The lookout system worked like a modern "no-fly" list, except that instead of blocking their travel, any INS agent who encountered them would alert the FBI immediately.

Oxford must have been a dream come true for the high school valedictorian who wanted to make a fundamental discovery about the nature of the universe. Alan Louis Charles Bullock, the Master of St. Catherine's, was so impressed by Savio that he admitted him to the honors program in physics. The Right Honourable Lord Bullock of Leafield got to know the couple and later wrote, "I came to have considerable respect for these two young people and their motives."

Savio's work was clearly up to Oxford's standards. But though he initially did well there, he began to have trouble concentrating on his studies. Goldberg became aware that he suffered from a compulsive think-ing disorder. "I remember after a bus ride with Mario his incredible intel-ligence focused on a problem he described having to do with passing telephone poles on the road. He spent hours analyzing such problems in-stead of working on problems assigned at St. Catherine's. When he worked on the latter he would get lost in one small part of a problem and never get to the others—so much so that even he was disturbed," she would write years later. "This compulsive focus might be seen as Mario's desperate need to get at the truth of something he perceived to be unexplained. This was harmless in some contexts and at times even led to brilliant in-sights. In other situations, however, this compulsiveness became crippling to him . . ."

Savio, moreover, was still thinking about Berkeley. In December, he wrote to the campus registrar inquiring about the deadlines for readmission. Savio also asked, "What is my status with the University of California? (The irony in this last question is unavoidable but not intended.)" The registrar replied with a letter noting that he had withdrawn as a student "in good standing" and supplying the requested application dates.

Savio confided to Bullock that he might leave Oxford. The professors there would have liked Savio to stay. As Bullock later wrote, "There is no doubt that if he had wished to continue we should have been glad to allow him to do so." But after wrestling with it Savio told Bullock he had de-cided "he should return to California and face the situation there." After only a few months at Oxford, Goldberg recalled, "We had to leave . . . because Mario's internal pressures became too great for him."

On February 16, 1966, an INS inspector at Kennedy International Airport in New York notified FBI agents that the Savios and their infant son, Ste-fan, had just arrived from London on Icelandic Airlines. Their stated desti-nation, the INS agent reported, was Berkeley.

FBI agents on both coasts began to search for the Savios as though they were fugitives. In Berkeley, Agent Don Jones reported on March 21, 1966, that "confidential sources and informants have been alerted to notify this office . . . if and when they arrive." He also checked with his contacts at local phone and utilities companies for billing records that would show their new address. At Jones's request, agents in New York, Los Angeles, and New Haven contacted local police and postal officials seeking any evidence that the Savios were visiting relatives.

All to no avail. The Savios had been driving back to California with his parents. On May 20, 1966, their new landlord in Berkeley reported their arrival to Agent Jones. The Savios moved into an apartment at 2106 McGee Street, several blocks below campus. Posing as a member of UC Berkeley's Philosophy Department who was considering hiring him, Jones phoned Savio and learned that he planned to return to school to study math or physics. The agent promptly updated Savio's address on the FBI's detention list.

Savio had planned to refrain from politics and quietly focus on his studies. He would, after all, be rather old for a junior, and he did have family responsibilities. Within days of his arrival, though, the mere fact that he had returned to Berkeley became national news. On May 23, 1966, newspapers published stories stating that he had applied for readmission to Berkeley. The articles about Savio's school plans shared the pages with reports about a mob in Saigon burning U.S. cars and chanting "Down with Americans," Jack Ruby's sanity hearing in his trial for shooting Lee Harvey Oswald, and Governor Brown's accusation that Reagan was on a "headline hunt" at the university's expense.

A few weeks later, Max Rafferty, a member of the university's Board of Regents and the state superintendent of schools, publicly released an irate letter he had sent other regents about reports that "the ineffable Mr. Savio" was about to be readmitted to Berkeley. "In view of the farcical manner in which he changed the respected image of the university a few months ago to that of a baggy-pants slapstick comedian, I suggest that we regents submit ourselves forthwith to group psychotherapy," Rafferty wrote. "If we let this character back in, we've got to be nuts." This, of course, made for more headlines.

Savio had sought none of this publicity. In fact, he had yet to apply for readmission. He had remained largely in seclusion, struggling to take care of his family and make ends meet. He had been working odd jobs, such as painting houses with former members of the Vietnam Day Committee and bartending part-time at the Steppenwolf. The bar took its name from Hermann Hesse's 1927 novel, which described a protagonist torn between noble and savage impulses against a backdrop of free love and drug use. Max Scherr, a former lawyer from Baltimore who served as an infantryman during World War II and upon discharge studied sociology at UC Berkeley, had acquired the Steppenwolf in 1958. He sold it in early 1965, using the proceeds to start the *Berkeley Barb* underground newspaper, which in just a few years would attain a circulation of 85,000. The

Steppenwolf's new owners hired Big Bill Miller, the VDC activist and disaffected nephew of Bing Crosby, to run the place, and Miller hired Rob Hurwitt, another VDC veteran, and Savio to tend bar.

Located in the warehouse wasteland of the flats, at 2136 San Pablo Avenue, the Steppenwolf became a center of Berkeley's incipient counterculture—or, as one FBI report put it, "a typical 'hangout' for the bohemian element." By day it was a coffeehouse, but in early evening the music shifted from folk to R&B, and at night it segued into psychedelic rock 'n' roll. The hot, narrow space was jammed with students, activists, hippies, and the occasional biker and enlisted man. "Everybody in it, cheek to jowl, butt to belly, thigh to thigh, hand to crotch, and front to backside, was jumping and dancing to the thundering music," wrote Suzanne Lipsett, an author who sometimes joined the other patrons boogying atop the tables. One night, as Savio was bending to pull a draft, a candle on the bar ignited his famously bushy hair with a whoosh. The flames were quickly doused with beer and Savio laughed.

Hurwitt was friends with Savio and sometimes gave him a lift home after the bar closed. Occasionally they sat awhile in Hurwitt's black Peugeot, smoking marijuana and talking. "Compared to a lot of people around, Mario did not seem very trippy," Hurwitt recalled. "Mario was one of the brightest people I've ever known. He had a mind that could really analyze things. And he could explain things to you. Like the mathematical formula for getting wrinkles out of a plane. He explained to me in great detail, so clearly, what Steve Smale's great contribution to mathematics was. I completely understood it. And the next day I could not recall it." (Smale, a topologist, had proved one of mathematics's oldest and most difficult problems, Poincaré's conjecture for the fifth dimension, showing that it is possible to determine whether a hypothetical surface in a five-dimensional universe is a sphere.)

Savio struck Hurwitt as possessing an unusual combination of great charisma and great shyness, although his charisma seemed to conceal just how shy he was. "I thought Mario could be a huge success at anything," said Hurwitt, adding, "There were clearly things holding him back."

In the wake of the news reports that he had reapplied to Berkeley, Savio reluctantly granted a wide-ranging and unusually revealing interview to Lynn Ludlow, who had joined the *San Francisco Examiner* in 1963, was its youngest reporter, and had sympathetically covered campus protests.

In the resulting story, Ludlow noted that since returning from England Savio had refrained from making public appearances even for causes he supported. Yet many students continued to regard him, as one of them had put it, as "Mario, our Savio." Playing the hero may have been tempting to many public figures, including Ronald Reagan, but Savio told Ludlow he abhorred that role and blamed the media for foisting it on him. "To focus on personalities rather than on issues is to obscure the issues and encourage the least democratic sentiments of the public," he said. Leaders could be seduced, he added, into "confusing their personal destinies with their political role—and therefore into using the political arena to act out solutions to their personal psychological quirks."

As to his new responsibilities as a parent, the twenty-three-year-old Savio, perhaps thinking back to his own childhood, said, "Becoming a father doesn't make me less angry at how society harms growing children through their families, but it makes me much more sensitive to how very difficult it is to avoid hurting one's children in some way—just by being a parent. This helps me to regard with greater sympathy those whom I consider political enemies because they, too, were little children at one time and are no less victims of an ill society."

Looking tired, thin, and sometimes uneasy during the interview, Savio said he had developed doubts about whether civil disobedience tactics such as mass sit-ins and mass arrests were still effective means of reform. He questioned whether acts of moral principle would move established interests to share power. He also expressed frustration with both the Republicans and the Democrats. Citing the efforts of Stokely Carmichael's Lowndes County Freedom Organization to secure power for black voters, he called for a new independent party in California to seek radical change through the political process.

"The naïveté," Savio said, "is gone."

Several days after Ludlow's story appeared, Agent Don Jones reviewed the FBI's dossier on Savio. "It was determined that although the file has a considerable amount of information therein no subversive-type information is contained in this file," Jones wrote on July 21, 1966. But he noted, "Savio continues to be a figure who attracts newsmen and other news media and is therefore given publicity . . ." As a result, Jones recommended keeping both Savio and his wife, Suzanne, on the Reserve Index for further investigation and possible detention.

Although the reports that Savio had sought readmission were wrong—he still had not reapplied—the attendant publicity jolted jittery campus officials into defensive action against him. Only a year earlier, they had approved his application to return for the fall 1965 semester. Now they feared having to admit him. In a memorandum marked "Most Confidential," Admissions Officer F. T. Malm wrote that "as it stands," the admissions office would be "obliged" to approve his application for readmission, unless the chancellor or the dean of students blocked it. Malm concluded his June 20, 1966, memo by unequivocally stating, "My personal recommendation would be: READMIT."

Chancellor Roger Heyns thought otherwise. Since coming to Berkeley from the University of Michigan in the wake of the Filthy Speech Movement, Heyns had been taking a tougher stance toward student protesters. He began looking for ways to keep Savio off campus in the event he did seek readmission. Heyns got help from Thomas Cunningham, the general counsel to the Board of Regents. Cunningham worked closely with Associate Counsel John Sparrow, who had been slipping the FBI information about campus protests. Like Sparrow, Cunningham was deeply troubled by what he saw as Kerr's failure to properly discipline student protesters, especially Savio.

On June 29, 1966, Cunningham wrote Heyns's assistant, Vice Chancellor Earl Cheit, a letter that began, "You have asked whether the University can lawfully refuse to readmit Mario Savio . . ." He went on to explain that the courts would likely allow the university to bar Savio if he engaged in misconduct that university officials had reasonably determined "warrants a denial." Heyns sent Kerr a copy of the lawyer's memo, making the president aware of his efforts to exclude Savio. There is no indication in Savio's student records that Kerr objected.

Savio finally applied on August 12, 1966, sparking another round of headlines. (*The New York Times*'s read "Savio Seeks Readmission.") In support of his application, Savio submitted a letter in which he revealed some of his travails. He wrote, in part:

Sir,
 I had not wanted to apply before having saved enough money to be able to attend full-time, as well as to support my wife and eight-month old child. (My wife is unable to work at present because she is breast-feeding the baby.) . . . Unfortunately it has been impossible to secure full-time employment: I am registered with the State Employment Office, and with the Student Placement Office (for temporary, full-time work), but about two months have gone by without either finding me anything. I have, of course, looked for work on my own, but have succeeded, thus far,

in obtaining only part time work and odd jobs. I presently am employed as a bartender, four nights a week, at the Steppenwolf . . . With the limited employments I have obtained we have managed to keep in food and rent money.

In addition to this problem of finance, we arrived back in Berkeley quite late, at a time when apartments were not easy to find—no easier than work. This late arrival was the result of a decision to live in New York with my parents until they had earned enough money to come back to California, which the five of us did in my parents' car. Our staying with them in New York enabled us to help my parents financially—but mostly in terms of moral support, my grandmother having recently died. At all events, as a result of our late arrival we had to live a long time in a friend's living room here in Berkeley until we could find an apartment we could afford. The great uncertainty of all these arrangements has further added to the great general contingency of our circumstances, and has served as a further disincentive to undertaking the responsibility of a University program at this time.

On top of all this, Savio said he had been faced with "certain considerably more personal matters which had been preventing me from applying sooner." He did not specify these problems, but since the end of the FSM he had been increasingly beset by depression. Also, his son, Stefan, was suffering from what only years later would be diagnosed as Fragile X syndrome, a form of inherited intellectual and developmental disabilities. ("He was very difficult from the start," Suzanne Goldberg later wrote. "He would cry inconsolably with what we thought was colic but turned out never to go away, later taking the form of frequent tantrums.") Savio concluded his letter, "In view of the above I respectfully request your favorable action on my petition."

Four days later, Dean William B. Fretter wrote Savio to say the university had denied his application for the fall term on the ground that it was submitted six days past the last deadline. "Exceptions to the deadline are made only when the late application is due to causes beyond the student's control," Fretter wrote. In an indication of the intense public interest in Savio's activities and the political pressure on the university to stifle campus unrest, campus officials took the unusual step of issuing a press release that announced the denial, triggering another wave of news reports. ("Savio Readmission Denied at Berkeley" said *The New York Times*'s headline.)

Savio promptly resubmitted his application for the following winter quarter, inevitably sparking more media coverage. Cunningham just as promptly suggested to Heyns other possible grounds for excluding the former Free Speech Movement leader. In preparing his brief, the general counsel reached all the way back to Savio's unauthorized attempt to speak at the Greek Theatre in December 1964 and to his contempt citation for having called the judge presiding over his subsequent sit-in trial a hypocrite.

But these incidents had occurred before May 1965, when the university approved his readmission for that fall, and Savio had broken no campus rules since then. It thus appeared that the university had no valid reason to deny readmission to the former student rebel. It was just bad timing for school officials already under fire from Reagan as he intensified his campaign attacks on Berkeley. Speaking in Stockton that September, Reagan allowed that it was up to UC officials to decide whether to readmit Savio, but said, "My own inclination would be that he should not be readmitted."

Then Savio gave them a reason.

On November 4, 1966, Savio was back on the steps of Sproul Hall for the first time since he resigned from the FSM in April 1965, once again calling the university administration to account.

It had been nearly two years since the FSM established the right of students to engage in political activity on campus. Student organizations had been holding rallies on the Sproul steps and the adjoining plaza nearly every school day at noon. For several months, however, Chancellor Heyns had been mulling a proposal to banish rallies there and permit them only in the lower plaza behind the student union, about 135 yards away and out of the main flow of foot traffic. Heyns contended that rallies on Sproul Plaza clogged the area, created captive audiences, and too often devolved from what was supposed to be democratic discourse into demagogic diatribe.

Savio saw Heyns's proposal as nothing less than a direct assault on rights won by the Free Speech Movement on those very steps. He and other activists now mustered a new movement to "Save Our Steps." As in 1964, they formed a broad coalition to oppose the administration, which they named the Council of Campus Organizations. On November 3, the CCO convened at Westminster House, a Christian residence hall directly across from campus, where the FSM executive committee had met. Savio joined in this strategy session, all the while bouncing eleven-month-old Stefan on his lap.

When Savio stepped to the microphone at noon the next day, the throng in Sproul Plaza cheered him as a homecoming hero. His hair was bushier than when he last stood there, the furrows in his brow perhaps deeper, his oratory still potent.

"Greetings, friends," he said that Friday, and he quickly got to the point. Heyns's proposal to move the rallies, he declared, was a "flagrant violation of student civil liberties." Moreover, it violated the Academic Senate's resolution of December 8, 1964, which decisively swung faculty support behind the students' demand for constitutional rights on campus. Savio argued that the resolution meant speech on campus should be regulated only to the extent necessary to protect the university's normal functioning from interference. Rallies on the Sproul steps, he asserted, constituted no such hindrance.

As Savio spoke, his remarks were nearly drowned out by a jazz band playing on the terrace of the adjacent student union. Continuing nonetheless, he recalled that during the FSM Kerr sought to move all rallies to the lower plaza. The FSM had resisted because that location would have isolated speakers from many students who might become interested in their cause only if they happened to hear them while crossing Sproul Plaza. Free speech, Savio declared, meant effective speech. And effective speech, as Bishop Berkeley had posited, meant being heard.

Once again Savio threw himself on the gears of the machine. He noted that a man had been arrested for violating a rule that barred nonstudents from handing out leaflets on campus. Such activity did not interfere with university operations, Savio argued, and the prohibition therefore was an unconstitutional infringement on free speech "more befitting a prison than a university." The nonstudent then passed out copies of what he called "a damn good leaflet which I had a good part in writing." It was titled "Traditional Liberties."

As he completed his symbolic act of defiance, Savio explained that the violation was meant to spark a court test of the rule's constitutionality. "What I just did in no way interferes with the normal functioning of the university," he said. "And for this sort of act we can expect Hugh 'The Inquisitor' Burns, and Maxwell Rafferty and [Regent John] Canaday and others to get upset. And then *they* will interfere with the normal functioning of the university."

Savio vowed to defend the steps and threatened to bring a new sit-in or strike. The crowd cheered, and he declared, "We mean business!"

That evening, Lynum sent an urgent teletype to Hoover: Savio was back.

Chancellor Heyns and other campus officials made no immediate response to Savio's bold challenge.

On the following Monday, however, they sent him a notice stating that because of his "deliberate violation" of campus rules against nonstudents handing out literature on campus without permission, they had denied his application for readmission.

William Boyd, the vice chancellor for student affairs, wrote, "In admissions cases where conduct is an issue, the practice of this University has been to favor admission or readmission where the applicant shows reasonable promise that he will obey the rules and regulations.

"The evidence of recent days, far from suggesting such an assumption in your case, strongly supports the conclusion that if readmitted you would not comply with University regulations with which you did not agree."

Boyd's November 7 letter offered Savio an administrative hearing before the denial was finalized, but only on "the facts upon which this decision is based," not on the constitutionality of the rule.

University officials released this letter to news reporters. (This time *The New York Times* headlined its story "Savio Readmission Denied in Berkeley After New Protest.")

On Tuesday, November 8, as Californians went to the polls to vote in the gubernatorial race, Heyns followed up by announcing new restrictions on rallies. He agreed to let them continue on the Sproul steps on a "trial" basis, but only if they did not exceed forty minutes, were at a lower volume, and speakers did not engage in what he called "slander, intimidation and deliberate misrepresentation." If there were more actions like Savio's "public, deliberate and provocative rule violation," Heyns warned, he would ban rallies there. "The days of doing business in this campus by coercion or the threat of coercion are over," he declared. "The days of influencing opinion or administration policy by such means are over. Where there is coercion there is neither freedom of expression or action."

Later on Election Day, Savio announced he would fight the denial of his readmission as well as any move to ban rallies on the steps. He demanded a hearing that would test the legality of the campus rule against nonstudents distributing leaflets.

Savio accused Heyns of cracking down in an effort to preempt Reagan's threat to have John McCone investigate the university. "I'm only speculating," he told reporters, "but maybe the chancellor is fearful that Ronnie Reagan will win the election and he wants to indicate that he doesn't need an investigation, that the university can provide internal protection."

If the administration banned rallies on the steps, Savio warned, "the turmoil this issue will generate will rival that of the FSM."

As the returns rolled in on election night, Reagan took an early lead and steadily advanced it. Brown was once known as the "Giant Killer" for his upset defeats of the former U.S. senator and *Oakland Tribune* heir William Knowland in 1958 and Richard Nixon in 1962. But after two terms in office Brown, age sixty-two, was tired and ran a lackluster campaign.

In contrast, Reagan successfully appealed to voter concerns about big government, high taxes, rising crime, and social upheaval. Political analysts concluded that "white backlash"—voters' negative reaction not only to urban riots but to the enactment of the Rumford Fair Housing Act, passage of the Civil Rights Act of 1964, and growing black demands for equal opportunity—had significant impact. The phenomenon hurt Brown, who had championed civil rights laws, and helped Reagan, who had opposed them.

No doubt many voters were unhappy with Brown's handling of protests at Berkeley. Yet in relentlessly making it a major theme, Reagan had found one issue, one institution, one place that symbolized their broader concerns. He had reduced the complex and unsettling changes sweeping America to the ostensibly simple matter of giving those ungrateful college kids and egghead administrators a little old-fashioned discipline, just like his dad gave him when he was a boy back in Dixon.

When Brown conceded on election night, the crowd at Reagan campaign headquarters in the Biltmore Hotel in Los Angeles exulted. A band played, Reagan Girls sparkled, and hundreds of supporters stomped and cheered until 10:47 p.m., when Reagan and his wife finally emerged to greet them. "I pledge a government of all the people of California," he declared. "Partisanship ended as of today."

It was a landslide. Reagan had defeated Brown by nearly one million votes. He had led a Republican sweep that left the California Democratic Party a wreck, spearheaded a conservative resurgence, and instantly made him a national political figure.

The next day, Hoover wrote to Reagan. "Heartiest congratulations upon your election as Governor of California," his November 9 letter said.

"Your many friends in this Bureau join me in the hope that your term in office will meet with every success, and we want you to feel free to call on us whenever we can be of service."

Curtis Lynum wrote to Reagan five days later. "May I convey my heartiest congratulations to you on your election as Governor. If we can be of any service in matters of mutual interest . . . please feel free to call on me."

Three days after that, Wesley Grapp, the special agent in charge of the Los Angeles office, wrote to Reagan: "This is to convey my sincere congratulations upon your election as Governor of California. My associates in the Los Angeles Division of the FBI join me in extending to you best wishes for continued success and want you to know of our desire to assist you in any way possible."

Reagan replied, "I assure you that I accept with the greatest of pleasure."

H. R. Haldeman was having a dinner party. He was hosting the fête for the governor-elect and the university regents at his Los Angeles home. Harry Robbins Haldeman was president of the Alumni Association of UCLA, a position that made him a regent ex officio. He had served in the Naval Reserve during World War II, graduated from UCLA in 1948, and was a vice president of the J. Walter Thompson Company. A resolute conservative, the advertising executive had managed Nixon's unsuccessful 1962 campaign against Brown for governor. Upon being elected president in 1968, Nixon would make Haldeman his chief of staff. Tall and thin, with a crew cut that seemed to bristle with the arrogance for which he was known, Haldeman would later describe himself as "the president's son-of-a-bitch." Ultimately, he would be convicted of conspiracy and obstruction of justice for his role in engineering the break-in at Democratic National Committee headquarters that led to the Watergate scandal. On the night of the regents' dinner, however, Haldeman had just turned forty and he hoped to ingratiate himself with Reagan, to whom he had written during the campaign, offering his assistance on "one of the strongest present issues, the University of California."

The soiree chez Haldeman that Thursday, November 17, was meant to welcome Reagan to the regents, but the mood was tense. It was Kerr's first meeting with Reagan, and the man who had so often excoriated his handling of campus affairs during the campaign was decidedly cold. "He barely greeted me," Kerr later told the author Bill Boyarsky.

For Kerr, the board meeting preceding the dinner had been overshadowed by another matter, one involving the Vietnam Day Committee.

Stephen Smale had recently won the Fields Medal, the world's highest honor for mathematicians. Awarded by the International Mathematical Union, the gold medal is often described as "the Nobel Prize of mathematics." Berkeley campus officials accordingly proposed giving Smale a raise. But he had been in the headlines the previous year as an arrant leader of the VDC and its efforts to stop troop trains. Reagan had criticized these protests as aiding and abetting the enemy. Even worse, perhaps, when Smale received the Fields Award in Moscow, where the mathematics association was convening, he held a press conference denouncing both Soviet restrictions on academic freedom and U.S. involvement in Vietnam. His August 1966 speech made international news, alarmed FBI officials, and further angered Reagan.

Kerr knew that even though Smale's academic achievement was extraordinary, rewarding him would be controversial because of his antiwar activities. Kerr had discussed the proposed raise with the chancellors, most of whom recommended not bringing it before the regents at this time because it was bound to be divisive. Kerr disagreed, telling them, "If I were not willing to support the Smale nomination, I did not deserve to be president." He put the proposed raise on the regents' agenda and won the board's approval only by a 9–6 vote with three abstentions.

At Haldeman's dinner table a few hours later, one of the regents rose to toast Reagan as "the man who will bring a big breath of fresh air into the university." Edwin Pauley then brought up Smale's raise, commenting,"It was treasonable to think of rewarding a faculty member who, in the midst of a war, was trying to sabotage the federal government's policies." Turning to Reagan, Pauley asked what he thought. Reagan replied that once he was inaugurated and became a member of the board, he would "see to it that no person was appointed to the faculty or promoted within it whose moral standards did not conform to those of the surrounding community."

Kerr sat silently as he regarded Reagan and Pauley and the other regents around the table, but he was thoroughly appalled. "There we were at the house of Bob Haldeman, located within a few blocks of Hollywood and Vine, which I then considered one of the moral cesspools of the United States," he recalled. "I put my head in my hands and thought to myself, 'Are we going to fall to a level so low?'"

The evening went downhill from there. After dinner, Ed Carter, the regents' chairman, sidled up to Kerr and softly warned, "You better stay out of sight and not say a word." A little later, Norton Simon, another regent, whispered to him, "Before this is all over, you're going to be covered in blood."

•

While the regents were dining at Haldeman's, Don Mulford was returning from FBI headquarters in Washington, D.C. The assemblyman had
been furious with Kerr for years. He had arranged the meeting between
the FBI's campus informers and Reagan at his home during the campaign, and was now a member of the governor-elect's transition team. Sitting down with one of Hoover's assistants that Thursday, Mulford made a
proposition.

Would the bureau provide information "to assist Governor Reagan in
identifying communists and other left-wing extremists"? he asked. "The
purpose will be either to eliminate them from the state government or to
prevent their receiving an appointment." Specifically, he said, "Reagan is
planning to clean up the University of California at Berkeley."

The FBI agent told Mulford "his position was well-understood." He did
not say so, but the proposed arrangement would be similar to the bureau's
Responsibilities Program. For that matter, it would be like the understanding the bureau had with Reagan when he was head of the Screen Actors
Guild. However, the agent replied that "the FBI could not be placed in
the position of 'clearing' appointees to state positions." He suggested Mulford instead contact the Burns committee, which, he explained, served as
a clearinghouse for information concerning "communists and liberal personalities."

Persisting, Mulford said he appreciated the bureau's position but
thought "it would be well to place on record . . . the attitude of the incom-
ing administration of his state regarding these matters." The agent still
demurred, saying the bureau was "precluded from the action he suggested."

But Hoover quickly alerted all California FBI offices to Mulford's
proposal. "In the event that you, or another of the California offices is
contacted by Reagan or one of his assistants regarding this matter," he ordered, "the Bureau should be immediately advised . . ."

FBI officials were having problems with Reagan's own political past.
As governor, Reagan would have access to UC's atomic research data.
As a result, the Atomic Energy Act required a comprehensive background
investigation of him, just as it had of Kerr. Hoover had abused this process
to deliberately spread false allegations and damaging comments about
Kerr, and he now abused it to help Reagan.

The process began on December 18, 1966, when the governor-elect filled out, under penalty of perjury, a mandatory Personnel Security Questionnaire that asked, among other questions:

Are you now, or have you ever been, a member of any organization which has been designated by the United States Attorney General as required under the provisions of Executive Order 10450?

Are you now, or have you ever been, a member of any foreign or domestic organization, association, movement, group, or combination of persons which is totalitarian, fascist, communist, or subversive . . . ?

Applicants were required to list any such groups and the dates they were involved with them.

Reagan answered "no" to both questions and signed an acknowledgment that "any false statement herein may be punished as a felony."

From the start, FBI officials took steps to shield Reagan from potential criticism during the background inquiry. They ordered agents to conduct no investigation in Sacramento, though there might have been knowledgeable sources there. They directed them not to interview Reagan's ex-wife, the actress Jane Wyman, according to a memo that noted, "Under ordinary circumstances, the divorced spouse of an applicant is interviewed for their comments concerning the applicant." And they told them to do no interviews concerning Reagan "on any university campus."

Everyone whom agents did interview gave Reagan shining recommendations.

But files at the Los Angeles FBI office contained troubling details from his Hollywood days. The dossiers showed that in 1946 he had been a sponsor of the Committee for a Democratic Far Eastern Policy, which had been designated as subversive by the U.S. attorney general in 1953 under Executive Order 10450.

The records also showed that in 1946 Reagan had been a member of the American Veterans Committee, whose California section had been cited in a 1948 report by the predecessor of the Burns committee as "communist dominated" and "a vociferous, decadent minority in national AVC affairs."

But Wesley Grapp, the special agent in charge of the Los Angeles FBI office, approved a background report that omitted Reagan's association with the two groups officially deemed subversive.

When officials at FBI headquarters read Grapp's report, they were concerned. Reagan was by now a staunch anti-Communist, but the bureau could not risk such blatant omissions. Hundreds of people in the late 1940s and early 1950s had been dismissed from federal employment for failing to disclose the same kind of activity. They ordered Grapp to revise the report to include Reagan's role in the organizations.

Yet the bureau's final report to the Atomic Energy Commission did not mention Reagan's false statement that he had never belonged to a subversive organization, which, by law, could itself be reason to deny a security clearance.

Perhaps Reagan thought it was just a matter of "little white lies," like those he used to embellish his résumé when he first applied at Warner Brothers. Phil Battaglia, a Los Angeles lawyer who was Reagan's chief of staff at the time, told the author he did not recall the security clearance application. Edwin Meese III, who joined the administration after Reagan had signed the form, said he did not know why Reagan denied his past association with the groups.

Assistant Director Cartha DeLoach denied that the FBI gave Reagan special treatment in preparing the report. But Grapp and another former agent acknowledged in interviews that it was standard procedure for the FBI to point out discrepancies between an applicant's sworn statement and the bureau's investigative findings.

"Yeah, sure, they'd put that in," Grapp said.

Savio was leading the biggest protest against the university administration since the Free Speech Movement.

On Wednesday morning, November 30, 1966, two navy lieutenant commanders and a marine lieutenant entered the basement of the student union building, set up a table in the hall near the school store, and began recruiting students for the Reserve Officers' Training Corps.

Soon after, a man and a woman with the Berkeley Draft Information Committee set up their own table nearby, offering antiwar information. Campus officials ordered them to leave because their off-campus group did not have permission to distribute literature on campus. By midday several hundred students jammed the hallway in protest. Vice Chancellor William Boyd arrived and pleaded with the protesters to leave before he declared the sit-in an unlawful assembly.

Suddenly Savio appeared. He had not meant to get involved in a new dispute with campus officials, certainly not on that day, his son's first birthday. In fact, Savio was due at home for Stefan's party. But some students had urgently summoned him to the student union building, and he now was exhorting the protesters to defy Boyd, the same campus official who had signed the letter denying him readmission because he had distributed handbills on campus. Savio demanded that the university allow the antiwar table alongside the military recruiting table. The military was an off-campus group, he argued, why should it be allowed a table if the antiwar group was not? Unmoved, Boyd gave everyone ten minutes to clear out before he called in police.

At about 5:45 p.m., some thirty police officers and Alameda County Sheriff's deputies marched into the packed basement. Armed with clubs and warrants for the arrest of six nonstudents who had been identified as "outside agitators," they pushed their way into the jeering throng. One officer was knocked down, a second bitten on the hand, and a third punched. The officers plucked five suspects from the crowd, including the Vietnam Day Committee veterans Jerry Rubin, Stew Albert, Steve Hamilton, Mike Smith, and Big Bill Miller, and trundled them off to a waiting bus. It was blocked by more protesters, including Savio, outside agitator number six. At Santa Rita County Jail all were charged with trespassing and released after posting four hundred dollars' bail.

Savio had missed his son's birthday party, but he made his way back from Santa Rita and around midnight joined a mass meeting in the student union's Pauley Ballroom. There he called for a strike, declaring, "The university pays no attention unless they are confronted by a show of force."

The strike plan was ratified the next day at a ninety-minute noon rally on Sproul Plaza attended by more than five thousand people despite intermittent rain. Savio set forth their demands: no police called to campus to solve political problems; no punishment for the ROTC protesters; campus disciplinary procedures must conform with the U.S. Constitution; nonstudents must have the same rights as government agencies to set up tables and distribute information on campus. Pickets immediately appeared at campus entrances, and by day's end strike leaders claimed dozens of classes had been canceled.

Chancellor Heyns responded at a press conference twenty-four hours later. He agreed to reconsider the policy that allowed military recruiters in the student union. But he said he approved of calling in police to make arrests, vowed to do it again if necessary, and declined to seek amnesty for the six arrestees. He refused, moreover, to negotiate with nonstudents like Savio.

The latest Berkeley protests sparked more outrage around the state. Meeting in Fresno, the California Young Republicans voted to offer Savio five dollars to get a haircut, a shave, and a bar of soap. In Sacramento, Assemblyman Mulford asked the regents to fire any professors involved in the new disorders, declaring, "The people of California are demanding action."

Reagan spoke at the Ambassador Hotel in Los Angeles. "In all the sound and fury at Berkeley one voice is missing. And since it is the voice of those who built the university and pay the entire cost of its operation it's time that voice was heard," he said.

"The people of California provide free access to an education unmatched anywhere in the world. They have a right to lay down rules and a code of conduct for those who accept that gift of a free education.

"No one is compelled to attend the university. Those who do attend should accept and obey the prescribed rules or pack up and get out."

Reagan blamed university officials for not enforcing the rules, and vowed that on taking office in January, "I'll certainly make my views known as a regent."

Meanwhile, the board met in emergency session on Tuesday, December 6, at the Edgewater Inn, near the Oakland Airport. Ed Pauley demanded that the university fire all teaching assistants involved in the strike. Kerr argued this would be unfair, because the regents never had adopted a policy of dismissing employees who went on strike. The former labor arbitrator thought it "the greater cause of justice to make our position clear to people before we begin penalizing people."

This time, the board backed Kerr, voting 13–2 to warn the teaching assistants that if they failed to return to work the next day they would be fired. Pauley and Catherine Hearst were against the measure, which the oilman called "a lovely little handout." The protesters, however, decided to suspend their strike, which already had lost momentum. The faculty's Academic Senate had overwhelmingly backed Heyns's enforcement of the rules, and most students were focusing on finals.

As the week of turmoil ended, the campus exuded relief. At a noon rally on Sproul Plaza the next day, several hundred students sang the Beatles' "Yellow Submarine." Released that fall as a 45 r.p.m. single and on the album *Revolver*, it was written as a child's song by Paul McCartney, then twenty-four, and John Lennon, then twenty-six. But the tune's lyrics—"beneath the waves . . . we all live in a yellow submarine . . . our friends are all aboard . . . every one of us has all we need"—were at once silly, psychedelic, and subversive.

With the students smiling and singing on Sproul Plaza, Kerr thought the crisis had passed. But Savio had once again rallied them to demand a greater voice on the campus.

"We'll be back next term because our demands haven't been met," he swore. "The chancellor has to understand that. The Board of Regents has to understand it. And Ronald Reagan has to understand it."

22

Fired with Enthusiasm

Just before midnight, Ronald Reagan and six members of the official gubernatorial party took their places on a dais in the grand rotunda of the state capitol. Behind them was a white marble statue of Queen Isabella of Spain pledging support to Christopher Columbus for his voyage to the New World. Turning to his old friend George Murphy, the U.S. senator and former Screen Actors Guild president, Reagan remarked, "Well, George, here we are on the late show again." Widely varying reasons have been given for Reagan's decision to proceed at the odd hour—that he believed doing it as soon as possible would prevent Governor Brown from making last-minute appointments, that he thought later in the day television crews would be busy covering New Year's parades, and that Nancy Reagan's astrologer had revealed it as the most propitious moment. In any event, at 12:16 a.m. on January 2, 1967, as a bank of television cameras whirred and 150 special guests looked on, Reagan took the oath of office as California's thirty-third governor, placing his hand on the oldest Bible his staff could find in the state, the one Father Junipero Serra had brought from Spain almost two centuries earlier as the missionaries were beginning to convert Native Americans such as the Huichin, who inhabited the land that became Berkeley.

So began the glitziest gubernatorial gala Sacramento had ever seen, a week of events that led one Democrat to complain it was "Hollywood at its best." There were marching bands and color guards, the San Francisco Symphony performed with Jack Benny (on violin), and movie stars graced the Inaugural Ball. At the $500-a-couple champagne reception, held in the ballroom of the El Dorado Hotel, Nancy Reagan wore a bouffant hairdo, diamond-and-emerald pendant earrings, and a floor-length white James Galanos gown, baring one shoulder.

On the morning of the traditional inauguration address, Reagan attended a prayer breakfast at the Sacramento Memorial Auditorium, where he declared, "Belief in and dependence on God is absolutely essential. It will be an integral part of our public life as long as I am governor. No one could think of carrying on with our problems without the help of God." Motorcycle officers then led Reagan's motorcade along streets lined with cheering crowds to the capitol's west plaza, where, under heightened security, he delivered his debut speech.

Setting forth his administration's agenda, Reagan pledged to crack down on crime, trim welfare programs that undermined "self-reliance," cut back bureaucracy, and reduce the state's huge deficit. He vowed to swiftly put down any civil unrest, declaring, "Lawlessness by the mob, as with the individual, will not be tolerated." He admonished University of California students to abide by the rules or "get their education elsewhere." And he warned professors, "It does not constitute political interference with intellectual freedom for the tax-paying citizens—who support the college and university systems—to ask that, in addition to teaching, they build character on accepted moral and ethical standards."

Nine days later, the new governor was furious with Clark Kerr. Reagan's plan to cut the budget for higher education and impose tuition for the first time in the university's ninety-nine-year history had leaked to the press and caused a furor. Reagan was seeking a 10 percent reduction for all state agencies, but Kerr calculated that state funding for the university would be cut at least 20 percent. Moreover, the proposed $400 annual tuition would be on top of the $275 already charged for incidental fees, making UC one of the most expensive public universities in the nation. As a student at Eureka, Reagan had protested cutbacks proposed by the college president, but now many observers saw him as either oblivious to the university's booming enrollments or intent on punishing the school he had castigated during his campaign.

Kerr was appalled. The University of California never had turned away a qualified student. He warned the regents that Reagan's proposal would force the school to reduce enrollment at its nine campuses that fall by 22,400 students, and sent a private telegram to each chancellor freezing admissions until the budget situation was clarified. The press got hold of it, and the tuition controversy was on the front page for days. It dominated the new governor's first major press conference, and the *Los Angeles Times* called his performance "not exactly 'Oscar' caliber." Reagan angrily denied he was planning massive cuts in the university and college budgets. He accused Kerr of acting like Chicken Little, exaggerating the reductions and needlessly frightening parents and students with the "unwarranted" admission freezes. He complained that his administration had been portrayed as "an opponent of educational ideas engaged in total warfare against the academic community—sole defender of cultural and intellectual progress."

In retaliation, Reagan declared, "Right at the moment I'm tempted to cut the university's approximately $700,000-a-year public relations budget, since it would seem a good share of it is being spent publicizing me." Asked if he would support Kerr's dismissal, Reagan replied, "I'd rather keep that with the Board of Regents," but added he "certainly will participate in such a discussion." *The New York Times* observed that Reagan had "in effect declared war on the university's president."

Concerned, Kerr phoned Reagan's office and requested an appointment. He wanted to discuss the history of the university and its constitutional autonomy. He hoped this might help Reagan appreciate some of the academic community's interests. Reagan agreed to meet with Kerr— and then had Lieutenant Governor Robert Finch phone Curtis Lynum at the San Francisco FBI office. Finch told him Reagan was scheduled to meet with Kerr about "the Berkeley situation" in forty-eight hours, but first wanted to confer with FBI agents.

Lynum immediately contacted FBI headquarters, per Hoover's orders. The agent urged bureau officials to avoid a potentially controversial meeting with Reagan and instead refer him to "former university officials and others who are fully aware of the Berkeley situation."

But the Boss ordered Lynum to see Reagan, and two days later, on January 16, he and Glenn Harter, his security supervisor, were briefing him in his bedroom at the governor's mansion. They told the flu-stricken Reagan that subversives had been involved in the Free Speech Movement, the Filthy Speech Movement, and the Vietnam Day Committee. They discussed Mario Savio's recent reappearance and his vow to lead more demonstrations. They addressed what they deemed Kerr's repeated failure to take control. As Lynum put it in an interview, Kerr "just appeased the students. He didn't take any action. You can't have students stopping trains, for crying out loud, and not be disciplined."

Reagan sat upright in bed, tightening his robe across his chest, taking it all in. He seemed to be hard of hearing, Lynum recalled, and "I had to talk to him fairly loud." Reagan expressed great anger at Kerr. And he requested a wide range of additional intelligence from the bureau—on Kerr, on liberal regents, and on upcoming protests at the university and at his press conferences. Any information, he said, "would be very helpful."

Lynum, again following Hoover's orders, made no commitments. He told Reagan the FBI had not investigated the university and referred him to the Burns committee's reports about subversive activities on campus. Reagan, of course, already had cited one of those reports as evidence of an orgy at the VDC dance and a leadership gap in the state Democratic Party.

As the bedside meeting ended, Reagan again thanked the agents for coming and expressed his admiration for Hoover.

Hoover seized the chance to help Reagan clean up Berkeley.

In a memo circulated among his top aides the next day, he noted that Reagan was clearly determined to take appropriate action at Berkeley. "This presents the Bureau with an opportunity to take positive steps to thwart the ever increasing agitation by subversive elements on the campuses," the director said. "Agitators on other campuses take their lead from activities which occur at Berkeley. If agitational activity at Berkeley can be effectively curtailed, this could set up a chain reaction which will result in the curtailment of such activities on other campuses throughout the United States."

Hoover wanted to help Reagan. The former actor had been useful to the FBI as a Hollywood informer and a staunch public supporter of the bureau. Now he could be a powerful political ally. He could finally get rid of Kerr and what Hoover saw as his "palliative attitude toward campus agitation."

As Cartha DeLoach said in an interview, "Mr. Hoover obviously felt that Governor Brown was not putting up a strong stand" against the campus unrest because of his "being friendly with Kerr." He added, "Consequently, later on, [Hoover] felt friendly towards Reagan and dealt with him . . ."

Still, Hoover feared the FBI's assistance to Reagan might be publicly exposed and embarrass the bureau. So in his distinctive blue ink he outlined a plan to help Reagan that employed some of his administrative artifices and would leave no incriminating paper trail that could be traced back to the bureau.

According to the plan, Lynum would agree to warn Reagan about any future protests at Berkeley or at his press conferences.

But—for the record—Lynum would tell Reagan the FBI had "no pertinent information" about Kerr or the regents.

Instead, the senior FBI official Charles Brennan, who "has the quali-

fications and ability to handle this sensitive matter," would confidentially
brief Reagan.

"We cannot furnish the governor anything else," Hoover scrawled.
"We do not know him well enough and we would possibly be involved in
an academic war."

Just after high noon on January 20, 1967, Reagan's limousine pulled up at
University Hall across from the Berkeley campus for his first meeting of
the Board of Regents.

The monthly meeting had begun rather inauspiciously the day before,
as more than three thousand students demonstrated directly across the
street against Reagan's proposal for tuition. Students had debated how to
conduct the protest. Savio spoke against hanging Reagan in effigy as "being
in rather poor taste"; *The Daily Cal* editorialized in favor of protesting "in
the most civil manner"; and the official student government proposed a
silent vigil. But the hippie scene was blooming—Timothy Leary would soon
give a talk billed on campus as a "Psychedelic Celebration entitled the
Death of the Mind." And when several thousand students marched from
Sproul Plaza to the grassy slope across from University Hall, they found
an acid rock band called the Loading Zone set up on a flatbed truck, blaring away. Some students wore Yellow Submarine buttons, representing
what Lynn Ludlow of the *San Francisco Examiner* described as the "hipster-
political merger." A banner with psychedelic-style lettering read, "Turn on,
Tuition, Drop Out." Despite Savio's plea, the governor was hung in effigy
with a placard that said REDUCE REAGAN BY 10%.

Awaiting Reagan inside University Hall, in their windowless, sound-
proof meeting room, the new Board of Regents was more sympathetic to
his view of Berkeley. Reagan's election had dramatically shifted the balance of power on the board. Brown and two other staunch defenders of
Kerr had been supplanted by Reagan, Lieutenant Governor Finch, and
Allan Grant, who was Reagan's new president of the State Agriculture
Board and a critic of Kerr.

Kerr's walk to the boardroom on the first floor was much shorter than
Reagan's drive from Sacramento. He had only to take the elevator down
from his seventh-floor office, where, just over two years ago, he had negotiated with Savio and other student leaders, as riot squads stood ready, over
the release of the police car. But Kerr's journey must have felt infinitely
longer. All through the campaign Reagan had vilified him, and in the
weeks since the election Kerr had been faced with sign after sign that the

governor would quickly deliver on his campaign promise to clean up Berkeley and seek his dismissal.

There had been the disturbing dinner at Haldeman's house. Then Phil Boyd, a Republican regent from Riverside, had approached Kerr on behalf of Reagan and asked him to resign, saying that the new governor wanted a new university president and Kerr should oblige him. Theodore Meyer, the chairman of the board, also asked him to step down.

Kerr could understand that the board would want a president who could work well with the governor; that would be in the university's best interest. And he would have been willing to resign at the end of the academic year, or even take a sabbatical and not return. Over the years he had fought many battles, and he felt he had accomplished most of what he set out to do. By this point, he said, "I was tired and downhearted."

But the stubborn son of an independent Pennsylvania farmer was not inclined to bend his knee. An immediate resignation would be an indignity, he thought—worse, an "abject subservience." Moreover, Kerr was concerned that it would undermine the university's historic autonomy. "I would not have my last act as president appear to endorse the view that a new governor had the right to immediately dismiss the head of a constitutionally independent institution," he recalled; ". . . this would be a bad precedent for the University of California . . ." No previous governor had demanded the right to replace the president of the university. Why, he wondered, should Reagan, the first governor to campaign against the school, have this "special consideration"?

Still, he sought a rapprochement. Twice Kerr made appointments to meet with Reagan, only to have Reagan cancel, once to go to Los Angeles, and again when, confined to his bed in the governor's mansion, he met with FBI agents.

As the date of the regents' meeting in Berkeley neared, rumors of Kerr's imminent demise swirled around him. The day before the meeting, the *Los Angeles Times* had reported that "all indications" were that Reagan would seek his dismissal in February. The *San Francisco Examiner* reported that "sources close to Governor Reagan" said Kerr would be fired "in about a month."

Kerr grew anxious to clarify his future as university president. On the morning of the regents' meeting, he met privately with Theodore Meyer, a San Francisco lawyer, and the vice chair, Dorothy Chandler, whose son, Otis Chandler, was publisher of the *Los Angeles Times*.

Kerr told them that if the board was going to fire him they should do it now, since as a lame duck he would be ineffective in negotiating the budget with the state legislature. He would later say he was asking not for a vote of confidence but for a "quick execution." Yet his request was similar to his threatened resignations of years past, gambits by which he had consolidated his independence as chancellor and president. He was telling the regents to either let him go—or back him. As he had as a boy on his father's farm, he was once again charging the bull.

Meyer and Chandler promised to bring his concerns to the rest of the board.

Reagan emerged from his limousine and entered University Hall at noon. Lyn Nofziger, his press secretary, would later say the governor had planned to wait several months before asking the board to terminate Kerr, so the dismissal would not look purely political. Kerr's refusal to resign, however, had forced a showdown.

Reagan looked nervous as he joined the regents' meeting and took his seat at the large polished conference table. To his immediate right sat Ed Pauley, the oil tycoon. To his left sat Theodore Meyer, then Kerr. Reagan wore a black suit, white shirt, and dark tie, and a white handkerchief in his breast pocket. He said little and fidgeted with paper clips and his reading glasses. According to one newspaper account, "His face was a shifting pattern of reaction—eyebrows in motion, lips pursed and the corners of his mouth angling downward. He was dressed as for a funeral."

Soon after Reagan's arrival, Kerr was asked to leave the meeting room. Convening in executive session for the next two hours, Reagan and the regents discussed Kerr's fate. Finally, Allan Grant moved to fire Kerr. When other regents pointed out that the new Reagan appointee's motion might appear to be politically motivated, Laurence Kennedy, Jr., a Redding attorney who had been appointed by Brown, made the motion.

Thirteen votes were needed.

The vote was 14–8.

Immediately after the still unannounced decision, Meyer and Chandler met privately with Kerr a second time and again asked him to resign. Meyer, according to Kerr, said that if he stepped down, the board would "take very good care of you." Kerr saw this as an "attempted bribe" so the onus of his departure would be on him, rather than on the board for firing him. Once again, he refused.

Reagan, meanwhile, left the boardroom to catch a plane for Los Angeles, avoiding contact with Kerr. As he exited University Hall and climbed back into his limousine, he flashed a smile at the spectators who had gathered in the rain, the first major storm of the year. "It's been a most interesting and somewhat tiring experience," he said, "and I look forward to future meetings." Only after he had departed was Kerr allowed back into the meeting room. Meyer then announced, "Clark Kerr has been dismissed as president of the university effective immediately."

The words fell "like a whip across my face," Kerr would later say. He was momentarily stunned. Then a wave of indignation washed over him. He asked himself, "Had I been so morally corrupt or so financially irresponsible or so criminally involved that I warranted instant dismissal . . . ?" But though he was seething inside, Kerr stolidly asked if he could continue to serve as president through the end of the meeting, as he was the only person prepared to present the lengthy agenda. The regents agreed.

At the press conference afterward, Kerr spoke in a calm voice as he made parting comments to a hushed crowd of reporters, university employees, and students who had rushed to the meeting room. He proclaimed his gratitude for the opportunity to have led the nation's biggest and best public university. In nearly fifteen years as chancellor and president, he said, the university had achieved unprecedented accessibility, academic distinction, and freedom of expression on campus. He recommended giving students a greater role in governing the university, and praised the new generation as "abler than before, better motivated than before." He emphasized the importance of independent scholarship, declaring "the quality of a university is its faculty."

He had harsh words for the regents, whom he criticized as failing to provide "a buffer against the winds of politics" to protect the university's autonomy. As to those who had accused him of coddling campus protesters, he said, "there are some individuals around the state who have suggested that the heavy hand of the police would have been more helpful in solving the problems of the university if it had been used. I personally don't believe in that. I think a university ought to be run on other grounds." The man behind the Master Plan for Higher Education also criticized Reagan's proposed tuition as a barrier to advancement. "The best investment that any society makes," he said, "is in the education of its young people."

Even as he spoke, Kerr began to feel relief after months of turmoil and uncertainty. When the press conference ended, the crowd gave him a lengthy standing ovation. It was the only time that day he came close to tears. As *California Monthly*, the university's alumni magazine, reported, "Kerr seemed surprised, bewildered, as he slowly rose from his chair and walked out of the room, down the corridor, briefcase still in hand."

Later, when he had regained his sense of humor, Kerr would say, "I left the presidency as I entered it—fired with enthusiasm."

Three days after the firing, Theodore Meyer released a statement saying Kerr's relations with the regents had been "adversely affected by his handling of the Berkeley campus disorders in the fall of 1964 . . . Some subsequent events did not improve the relationship." Meyer made no reference to Reagan but added, "The resulting uncertainty and controversy has been harmful to the university in many ways."

Kerr's dismissal hardened attitudes on all sides of the campus conflict. At Berkeley, students flew the flag at half mast. The ASUC, the official student government there, declared shock and anger at his firing. The Inter-Fraternity Council condemned the "hypocrisy" of the governor and his administration for turning the university into a political football. Hundreds of professors at campuses around the state signed letters of protest and peacefully demonstrated, and ten thousand teachers and students rallied outside the state capitol. There were national repercussions as well. William Trombley, the *Los Angeles Times*'s education reporter, wrote,"Kerr's ouster is being viewed on campuses across the country as a political hatchet job." Nathan Pusey, president of Harvard, called it "a misfortune" and "an affront to higher education generally."

Others were glad to see Kerr go. Edwin Pauley said rather coyly, "Obviously, I think everything the regents do is for the good of the university." Hugh Burns declared his firing "inevitable" and called on the campus community to "act with restraint during the critical period just ahead." Don Mulford said, "I hope this is the beginning of a new era at the university. I also hope this restores some discipline so that students can have an education free from turmoil. I think this is the end of the Mario Savios . . ."

Savio cheered Kerr's fall. Kerr's liberalizations of campus rules on political activity never went far enough for Savio and other campus activists who saw him as a faceless bureaucrat and hypocritical liberal. "Good riddance to bad rubbish," Savio and several colleagues told *The Daily Californian*. "The multiversity is dead; long live the university. The new governor's administration has started auspiciously."

A few days later, Savio and his colleagues tempered their statement, somewhat. "We do not think Clark Kerr is rubbish," they said. "We would like to know what he is but he's never once let us find out." They said their remarks were made in "hatred of an educational system which has dehumanized both those who operate it and those who live within it . . . To a great extent Clark Kerr has built this gangrenous and amoral bureaucracy—it would be hard to forget that. Nor is it easy (or desirable) to forget the past forty months—the short victories but long disillusionments."

And a few days after that, Savio et al. elaborated in another round of denunciation. Affirming that they were "not at all sorry to see Kerr go," they criticized him as a contemptible establishment liberal whose efforts to accommodate conservatives at the expense of moral ideals had brought about his own demise.

"Where he should have explained and publicly defended the legitimate goals of the Berkeley students, he has instead resisted only the grossest atavisms of Regents and politicians," they said in a letter to the student newspaper. "With a liberal flourish, he has cooperated with a policy of suppressing rebellion and ignoring its causes. This could only lead to more rebellion; and more rebellion has provided an excuse for reaction."

They bitterly recalled that Kerr early on tainted the Free Speech Movement as harboring admirers of Castro and Mao, in effect telling people that "the students could not be taken seriously because they were subversives." Turning to his 1963 book analyzing the modern university, they contended, "The bureaucratic amorality of Kerr's multiversity is symbolized by the character of its chief administrator. In 'Uses of the University' Kerr depicts the plight of the lonely university president who must serve many 'publics': in commerce, in industry, and in government. He tells how he must be not two-faced, but many-faced, one for each 'public.' The image evokes cold pity. Before our eyes Kerr becomes a ghost: the ghost behind the face with a smile for everyone."

Then—echoing Reagan's allegations that Kerr had "appeased" student protesters—they issued a call to arms: "From Kerr's firing we must draw a political lesson. Attempts to preserve the university's freedom by appeasing its enemies can only result in defeat. We must all now—faculty as well as students—publicly and openly resist the power of the Board of Regents."

Savio added that Kerr's dismissal might well lead to a new strike "against the tyrannical authority represented by Ronald Reagan."

At first, Reagan denied having any idea that the question of Kerr's discharge would come up at the regents' meeting. "It's all a big surprise to me," he said when a reporter caught up with him in Los Angeles after the vote. Reagan also denied he had sought the board's removal of Kerr. "The inference of politics or partisanship in the action is not borne out," he added. "None was involved."

Several days later, though, Reagan admitted at a press conference that he had discussed the possibility of Kerr's resignation with some regents before the meeting. "The regents had come to me," Reagan said. "I told them what my own feeling was with regard to the possible need for a change, but that I would not initiate such a procedure, and certainly did not feel that in my first meeting as a regent this was something that was properly on the agenda." He still maintained that he had not maneuvered behind the scenes to remove Kerr. And he made no mention of his secret bedroom meeting with the FBI agents.

Hoover and his agents had closely followed Kerr's termination.

Minutes after the board voted, John Sparrow, the associate general counsel to the regents, gleefully phoned the news to Alex Sherriffs and Hardin Jones, the other campus informers who had helped the FBI and the Reagan campaign undermine Kerr. Then Sparrow phoned Agent Don Jones and told him, too.

Three days later, another FBI agent confidentially spoke with Laurence Kennedy, Jr., the regent who made the motion to fire Kerr. "Regent Kennedy mentioned that the Board of Regents felt that some of the faculty members at the University were CP sympathizers," the agent reported, "and he understood that the Governor . . . had received information in this regard."

Not long after Kerr's firing, Reagan wrote to Hoover saying he was pleased to learn that the FBI was opening a Sacramento office. "This will more ably assist all of us in our continuing fight against crime and subversion," Reagan said in his letter of February 27, 1967. "Please accept my personal assurance that your agency will have the most complete cooperation possible from my office." In a handwritten note he added, "P.S. I've just always felt better knowing your men are around."

Hoover replied on March 7, "I do hope you will not hesitate to call on us whenever we can be of service . . . I share your confidence that a great deal can be accomplished by working together."

23

Obey the Rules

Reagan had made a campaign pledge to clean up the "mess" at Berkeley, and he meant to keep it.

From the start, he took a more hands-on approach than Governor Brown had toward the university. Brown had refrained from attending most regents' meetings on the principle that the board could function more freely without the political overtones inherent in the presence of the state's highest elected official. Reagan made a point of appearing and often held press conferences that turned the meetings into a media spectacle. He thrust the governor's office into areas traditionally left to campus officials, such as monitoring student activities, checking teachers' classroom conduct, and screening faculty appointments. He cut the university's budget and pushed the regents to impose fees that were, in effect, the first tuition in the school's history. Although some cuts were surely inevitable, he continued his campaign practice of making broad charges of campus misconduct, heightening public outrage, damaging morale on campus, and undermining support for the institution. He would claim that professors generally did not teach enough, that too much of what they did teach was left-wing propaganda, and that some gave better grades to liberal students (though he provided no evidence of this). He complained about "subsidizing intellectual curiosity," and his auditors suggested the university sell its rare book collection to generate state revenue.

But all this, and the firing of Clark Kerr, did not quell unrest on the Berkeley campus or anywhere else. Hippies, black militants, and antiwar protesters were challenging the establishment as never before. Nineteen sixty-seven, Reagan's first year in office, was transmogrifying into the long hot summer, the Vietnam Summer, the Summer of Love.

•

Allen Ginsberg, in white cotton kurta and flowered garland, opened the proceedings that sunny Saturday in San Francisco's Golden Gate Park with a Buddhist chant. Timothy Leary, clutching a daffodil as though it were a scepter, mounted the incense-shrouded stage and exhorted the crowd to "Turn on, tune in, drop out." The Grateful Dead and Jefferson Airplane played, some of the lately psychedelicized Hell's Angels provided security services, and Owsley distributed free samples of his latest batch of LSD, which he dubbed "White Lightning."

The Human Be-In drew several thousand people together on January 14, 1967, the week before Reagan would attend his first regents' meeting and Clark Kerr would be fired. Organized by Berkeley radicals such as Jerry Rubin, late of the Vietnam Day Committee, and Haight-Ashbury heavies such as Allen Cohen, editor of the *Oracle* underground newspaper, the "happening" was intended to unite the parallel universes of antiwar activists and hippies in one cosmic force for peace and love. Word of the new scene spread, and tens of thousands of young people were soon converging on San Francisco and Berkeley for the Summer of Love. Haight-Ashbury became the hippie capital of the world, and Telegraph Avenue, which not too long before had been a neat shopping district where the FBI agents Don Jones and Burney Threadgill enjoyed strolling to Larry Blake's for burgers, teemed with long-haired young people wearing bell-bottoms, brocade, and beads.

The politico-psychedelic phenomenon that had manifested itself at the VDC dance and so angered Reagan had dilated like the pupils of someone tripping on 400 micrograms of acid. Hunter Thompson observed that many Berkeley radicals had joined the drug culture in disillusion; they saw Reagan's election, the Republican sweep, and Kerr's firing as "brutal confirmation of the futility of fighting the establishment on its own terms." But as the *Ramparts* editor Warren Hinckle noted, "all hippies *ipso facto* have a political posture—one of unremitting opposition to the Establishment . . ." To Joan Didion, the hippies were further indicia of a disintegrating society. "We were seeing the desperate attempt of a handful of pathetically unequipped children to create a community in a social vacuum. Once we had seen these children, we could no longer overlook the vacuum, no longer pretend that the society's atomization could be reversed," she wrote.

"The center was not holding."

Bobby Seale, chairman of the Black Panther Party, ascended the steps of Sproul Hall, flanked by other black men with equally solemn expressions, and recounted the Panthers' by now notorious field trip to Sacramento.

On a warm May morning a few days before, Seale and about thirty other young men and women wearing black leather blazers and berets and brandishing loaded guns strode toward the state capitol. Gliding by a class of eighth-grade students waiting on the west lawn for a picnic with Governor Reagan, the Panthers entered the domed neoclassical building that housed the state legislature and the governor's office. They breezed by startled bureaucrats, climbed the stairs to the second floor, and pushed past the swinging wooden doors to the Assembly hearing room. Legislators in the midst of debating a bill on public safety looked up in shock at the armed men standing in the rear of the chamber.

Before much else could happen, state police escorted the interlopers out, citing an assembly rule that barred weapons there. The officers led them to a police station downstairs, where they took their guns, jacked out the ammunition, and returned them as a crowd watched. Seale explained that they were protesting Assemblyman Don Mulford's bill, which would reverse the current law and prohibit carrying loaded firearms within Oakland city limits—a measure "aimed at keeping the black people disarmed and powerless at the very same time that racist agencies throughout the country are intensifying the terror, brutality, murder, and repression of black people."

Seale and the other Panthers marched away from the capitol just as Reagan emerged on the upper steps. His picnic with the eighth graders was hastily moved from the lawn to his office, where the children sat on the red carpet and ate fried chicken. The Panthers, meanwhile, were arrested and charged with conspiracy to disrupt the state assembly. Speaking at a press conference, Reagan dismissed the Panther protest as "absurd." But in the days following what a *Los Angeles Times* story called the "startling intrusion by a band of armed Negroes," security measures were heightened. Reagan sent State Senator Hugh Burns, whose office was in another part of the capitol, a toy cannon with a note that would prove only partly in jest.

"Be assured," he wrote, "that the full 'military might' of the Southeast corner will be mobilized to instantly help you resist aggression, and preserve your self determination . . ."

One week later, Martin Luther King, Jr., stood in Seale's place on the Sproul Hall steps and delivered a different message.

King had been continuing to work for racial equality through nonviolent means. He believed blacks had made important gains through civil disobedience, but was urging them to concentrate more on political organizing, union activism, and economic boycotts. For though they had achieved legal and legislative victories, he told the people who filled the plaza on May 17, they still faced "backlashing." He called for an end to racism, poverty, and the "evil" war in Vietnam. He urged students to participate in Vietnam Summer, in which young people across the country would knock on doors, give people the facts about the war, and "build a powerful peace block that can really have influence in the 1968 election." Yet when professors and students presented a petition asking him to run for president on a peace ticket with Benjamin Spock, King demurred, saying, "I've never thought of myself as a politician." He praised them for their role in the civil rights movement, proclaiming, "Berkeley is the conscience of the academic community." And he declared that many Americans are committed to justice. "This is why I can still say without reluctance, black and white together—we shall overcome!"

King still was the nation's preeminent civil rights leader. But though the Panthers' extreme militancy was endorsed by a minority of black Americans, it reflected a general frustration with the slow pace of reform, lingering fear of whites, and fraying relations with police. These tensions ignited in "the long hot summer" of urban riots. The worst were in Newark and Detroit, where police officers and National Guardsmen were called in. By year's end there had been 160 disorders around the nation and at least $55 million in damage, 83 deaths, and many more injuries, mostly of black residents.

Reagan saw a plot. "It would be pretty naïve to believe these riots are just spontaneous," he said at a July 25 press conference. "I believe there is a plan." But like the allegation he'd made in 1961 that Communists were again trying to take over Hollywood, this one was fantastic. U.S. Department of Justice officials told the *Los Angeles Times* that FBI agents had been continuously investigating whether the racial disorders were centrally directed, and based on close surveillance of black militants, campus activists, and Communist Party members they had found no such evidence. A bipartisan panel appointed by President Johnson to investigate the causes of racial unrest would confirm there was no plot. Rather, the National Advisory Commission on Civil Disorders said ingrained white racism created the conditions that fueled the riots, namely pervasive discrimination in housing, employment, and education. And though the commission condemned rioters for breaking the law, it found that black violence had been greatly exaggerated by the police and the press. In fact, it said, "most reported sniping incidents were demonstrated to be gunfire by either police or National Guardsmen."

There was a grave danger, the commission warned, that "in their anxiety to control disorders, some law enforcement agencies may resort to indiscriminate, repressive use of force against wholly innocent elements . . ."

The biggest organized protests that summer were against the war.

Mario Savio and other men who were married and had children qualified for a deferment from military service. So did students making satisfactory progress in college. But unless they had powerful friends who could secure preferential treatment, as the studio chief Jack Warner had done for Reagan during World War II, all other able-bodied males between the ages of eighteen and thirty-five were deployed as the government saw fit. By now there were more than 448,000 U.S. troops in Vietnam. Deferments were down, and draft calls were up. Some students tried to "beat the draft" with the advice of a pamphlet circulated at the card tables on Sproul Plaza—for example, "Be an epileptic . . . Arrive drunk . . . Be an undesirable. Go for a couple of weeks without a shower. Really look dirty. Stink." Other men burned their draft cards, fled to Canada, or simply refused to report for induction, all of which made them subject to FBI investigation. Berkeley's Country Joe and the Fish expressed the dread and contempt many on campus felt in the "I-Feel-Like-I'm-Fixin'-to-Die Rag":

> Come on all of you big strong men,
> Uncle Sam needs your help again.
> He's got himself in a terrible jam
> Way down yonder in Vietnam
> So put down your books and pick up a gun,
> We're gonna have a whole lotta fun.
>
> And it's one, two, three,
> What are we fighting for?
> Don't ask me, I don't give a damn,
> Next stop is Viet Nam;
> And it's five, six, seven,
> Open up the Pearly Gates,
> Well there ain't no time to wonder why,
> Whoopee! we're all gonna die.

The most militant of the antiwar demonstrations that year, "Stop the Draft Week," began on October 16 in several major cities across the country. In Oakland, the target was the Army Induction Center. The protests there started on Monday with peaceful pickets and the arrest of Joan Baez and about 140 other pacifists who tried to block the entrances. But Berkeley students already were preparing a more aggressive protest for Tuesday. They had intended to hold a teach-in on campus on Monday night at Pauley Ballroom, across the plaza from Sproul Hall. The official student government was sponsoring it and Chancellor Roger Heyns had granted a permit allowing it to begin at 11:00 p.m. Afterward, students planned to go to Oakland, where they would "shut down" access to the induction center. It was an arrant application of the rights established by the Free Speech Movement.

Reagan disapproved. "The announced objective is to disrupt the operations of the Oakland Induction Center, stop buses loaded with draftees, and actively resist police efforts to maintain law and order," he declared at a press conference, calling such conduct "totally foreign to our way of life." He claimed that some professors were planning to cancel classes during the protest in "a perversion of the function of our universities and colleges" and "a flagrant violation of academic freedom." He offered no evidence of this, however, nor did he identify the source of his allegations.

As they had with the Vietnam Day Committee's march, Alameda County officials sought to stop the action, this time through a legal motion that would bar use of the campus for the teach-in and other actions that amounted to "on-campus advocacy of off-campus violations." University officials opposed this effort to halt the teach-in on the ground that it was an improper constraint on "an educational affair." The county judge, however, granted the injunction, and Chancellor Heyns enforced it, locking the doors to Pauley Ballroom.

In defiance, some five thousand people rallied on Sproul Plaza that Monday night, and at 5:00 a.m. Tuesday they descended on the induction center. Though nonviolent, they aggressively blocked doorways and busloads of inductees, chanting, "Hell no! Nobody goes!" Five hundred Oakland policemen assembled in a V-shaped line, as they had when they stopped the VDC march at the Oakland border. Police directed the demonstrators to disperse, but many would later say they never heard the orders. With boot-thud on asphalt the line of officers advanced, swinging two-foot billy clubs "like scythes," according to the *San Francisco Chronicle*, and squirting canisters of a new crowd-control chemical called Mace that caused temporary blindness and nausea. According to eyewitnesses, the officers indiscriminately struck and sprayed protesters, doctors, clergymen, and news reporters. "An officer said this was an unlawful assembly," Reverend Mark Sullivan said. "Then I was hit in the stomach and knocked to the ground." Twenty-seven people required hospital treatment. Jack Weinberg later observed, "It was suicide on Tuesday to sit down in front of advancing police officers."

Chief Charles Gain defended the performance of his men in what students were calling "Bloody Tuesday." But later that day a federal judge issued an order restraining police from interfering with news reporters. Several Northern California law-enforcement officials criticized the use of force. "Wading in swinging to end a peaceable if unlawful activity is not right," U.S. Attorney Cecil Poole said. "Punishment is generally reserved for the courts." Or as Sheriff Earl Whitmore of San Mateo County put it, "This running around swinging nightsticks is in bad taste." Reagan, however, declared that the police had acted "in the finest tradition of California's law enforcement agencies."

The demonstrations on Wednesday and Thursday were more civil. But on Friday, Berkeley students joined in the largest and most disruptive protest at the induction center yet, as six thousand people delayed busloads of inductees and stalled morning traffic in downtown Oakland for hours. Repaying the police for Tuesday's abuse, protesters deployed themselves as mobile squads in the streets around the center. Wearing helmets and carrying homemade plywood shields, some blocked intersections by deflating car and truck tires, or by erecting "barricades" of potted trees, newspaper racks, garbage cans, and anything else they could drag into the road. They overturned a car, threw bottles and rocks at police, and spray-painted buildings with peace signs. Eight officers and ten demonstrators were injured, and twenty-eight people were arrested on charges ranging from failure to disperse to assaulting an officer. Extreme action had generated extreme reaction. The clash, said Todd Gitlin, who joined in the protest and later wrote about it in his book *The Sixties: Years of Hope, Days of Rage*, was a turning point in the antiwar movement, from protest to resistance.

The next day in Washington, D.C., Stop the Draft Week ended ominously. Fifty-five thousand people marched peacefully from the Lincoln Memorial to the Pentagon, but at the end several thousand tried to storm the building. U.S. marshals and soldiers repelled them with clubs and rifle butts. That night, groups of protesters occupied the Pentagon lawn, wrapped in blankets and huddled around eerily flickering bonfires. Among those arrested were Daniel Berrigan, Jerry Rubin, and Norman Mailer, who chronicled the event in his Pulitzer Prize–winning book *The Armies of the*

Night. The demonstration, Mailer wrote, "spoke of a vitality in nature which no number of bombings in space nor inner-space might ever subdue . . ."

Reagan was not so uplifted. "There is absolutely nothing that justifies this kind of conduct," he said at a press conference. "This is trying to force your will upon the people by violence and law breaking, and I just don't think it should be tolerated at any time, any place in our country." He had called earlier for declaring war on North Vietnam, saying it would be a mistake to rule out the use of nuclear weapons. Now he renewed his call for a declaration of war so authorities on that basis could prosecute protesters for giving "aid and comfort to the enemy."

Some days Agent Donald Jones took a position on the balcony of Pauley Ballroom, joining the cluster of newsmen, campus officials, and plainclothes police observing the rallies on Sproul Plaza. The FBI still was operating on Hoover's broad interpretation of the bureau's authority to investigate "subversive" activities, which had come to mean students protesting virtually anything. Jones and his fellow agents collected information on campus organizations ranging from the Young Socialist Alliance to Students for a Democratic Society, to the Campus Sexual Rights Forum, the Psychedelic Information and Service, and the Recall Ronald Reagan Campaign. ("So far," an informer reported, "there are 5,000 petitions being circulated.")

Jones religiously followed Hoover's edict—Don't embarrass the bureau! He'd already gotten into trouble because Bettina Aptheker fingered him at a rally, and he didn't want any more. But Stew Albert's wife, Joann, worked in the registrar's office, and she discovered that campus officials were letting FBI and CIA agents review student records. Soon Jerry Rubin went public with it, and campus administrators eventually admitted that government agents on average examined 10 student files a day, or roughly 2,500 a year. Chancellor Heyns publicly promised to restrict access to the files, but he privately told Agent Jones not to worry. Or as Jones put it in his malaprop report, Heyns promised "he would bend every effort to make available to the FBI any required document or record at UCB."

In addition, Jones continued to receive information from informers at the university, including Alex Sherriffs, John Sparrow, and, of course, Professor Hardin Jones, who was now urging FBI officials to establish a "truth agency" to warn students that subversives were infiltrating the faculty and the administration.

But when a reporter for *The Daily Californian* phoned and said he wanted to write an article about the FBI in Berkeley, Agent Jones told him the bureau had "no particular interest . . . in the faculty or students." Nor, he added, was the FBI interested in "the current administrative and political problems at UCB."

Three days before Christmas, Reagan reached out again for Hoover's help. One of his assistants phoned to say the governor was planning an eastern speaking tour and hoped to meet with the director. He wanted to discuss "the crime problem and the situation at the University of California." The aide emphasized that "there would be absolutely no publicity" about the meeting. Hoover swiftly scrawled his approval: "At 10 a.m. Jan. 18—H."

Reagan kicked off the tour in Tulsa on a Tuesday. He had been in office just a year, but his highly publicized speaking trip was widely seen as a testing of the presidential waters. At each stop, he offered what the *New York Times* correspondent Gladwin Hill called "carefully crafted rhetoric, alternately amusing and hortatory." He still espoused his anti-big-government philosophy. And much as he had accused Governor Brown of coddling the Free Speech Movement and fostering a morality gap, he now accused the Johnson administration of being too easy on antiwar protesters and presiding over an "erosion of morality." In a talk to the Economic Club of New York at the Waldorf-Astoria Hotel, where two decades earlier movie moguls adopted a Hollywood blacklist that Reagan helped enforce, he now decried government's "inch-by-inch encroachment" upon rights "traditionally held to be the proper possession of the people." Then he set off to Washington for his meeting with Hoover.

Hoover's aides had carefully prepared for it. Charles Brennan, a supervisor with the Internal Security Section, ordered San Francisco agents to assemble a special report on "the subversive picture at UC, as well as anything involving political relations, that is, how politics influences action or failure to take action at UC, such items as President Kerr being dismissed, and any other pertinent things which the Governor might pose to the Director." But as Curtis Lynum had before, Charles Bates, the new special agent in charge of the San Francisco FBI office, told Hoover there was scant evidence of a Communist plot on campus.

The day before the meeting, Hoover's aides sent him news stories about Reagan being touted as a possible presidential candidate. They noted the articles made no mention of his imminent conference with

Hoover—a disclosure that would have embarrassed an FBI director ostensibly involved neither in spying on campus nor in partisan politics.

At 10:00 a.m. the next day, Hoover warmly welcomed the rising political star he had secretly helped over the years, and Reagan responded in kind to the man he revered as a national hero. The governor then introduced Edwin Meese III, his top legal adviser. Meese recalled that the meeting ran a full hour as they shared intelligence information about Berkeley activists. Or, as Hoover put it in his terse memo for the record, "The Governor called to pay his respects and renew his friendship . . . We discussed generally some of the problems which the Governor has had to face up to at the University of California and his determination that law and order are maintained there."

After the meeting, Reagan wrapped up his tour with stops in Pittsburgh and St. Louis, where he made more charges that members of the Johnson administration maintained a "permissive attitude" and "don't look too unkindly on taking to the streets in violence." Heading back to California, the presidential aspirant could count his journey a major success. He had boosted his national profile, rallied Republicans, and raised some $2 million for the GOP—more than any individual had collected for the party in years. And behind the scenes he had affirmed his alliance with Hoover, who could help handle one of his biggest problems, protests at Berkeley.

Several days later in Sacramento, Reagan received a package from Hoover. It was a commemorative photograph taken of the two men at FBI headquarters, clasping hands. Reagan replied, "Thank you so much for the picture. Nancy is having it framed, and I shall be very proud to have it here in the office for all to see. It was good of you to give me so much time, and both Mr. Meese and I are very grateful. It was a most productive morning for us."

Reagan had long appreciated the value of secret sources to gain an advantage over his opponents. Back when he was a student at Eureka College, an informer had tipped him and his fellow protesters to the administration's plans. In Hollywood, Reagan had been an informer against colleagues whom the FBI deemed a threat to national security, and the bureau gave him information he could use against his opponents in the Screen Actors Guild. During his gubernatorial campaign, he had used informers to gather information against Clark Kerr. In office a few weeks, he had asked Hoover for intelligence about students and professors. By the end of his first year as governor, he had hired two top aides who were fierce foes of Mario Savio and were deeply involved in political spying.

Alex Sherriffs had been largely responsible for the decision to crack down on Savio and other student activists on the Bancroft strip that gave rise to the Free Speech Movement. Sherriffs blamed Kerr for thwarting his efforts to rein in the impertinent students, and resented faculty members who had overwhelmingly supported them. Demoted from the prestigious post of vice chancellor in the wake of the protest, he embarked on a speaking tour during which he decried "confusion of freedom with license, confusion of democracy with anarchy, and spoiled children and spoiled adults who take the law into their own hands." The psychology professor would recall these dark months as a time of "my own little crusade, when my little academic world was crumbling." Meanwhile, he continued to serve as an informer, providing the FBI with information on students and colleagues. He never disclosed this—or his having provided campus intelligence to Reagan during the gubernatorial race. Instead, he falsely suggested in an official State of California oral history that he never met Reagan during the campaign. "I didn't do anything for anybody in the Reagan campaign—period," he said.

Sherriffs would later say he initially saw Reagan as "a right-wing kook." But as Reagan took on the Free Speech Movement and the Vietnam Day Committee, Sherriffs grew to admire him and switched his registration to Republican so he could vote for him. He exulted in Kerr's ouster and began to privately advise the new governor's administration on campus affairs. On December 19, 1967, Reagan named him his special assistant for education.

Sherriffs's office was a few doors down the hall from the governor's corner suite in the state capitol. A sign on his wall displayed Reagan's motto, "Obey the rules or get out." Like Reagan, Sherriffs opposed lowering the voting age from twenty-one to eighteen, even though eighteen-year-olds were being drafted and dying for their country. "Why reward idiocy?" the former psychology professor said. "Why give them the vote when they show little responsibility on the campuses?" And like Reagan, he believed in firm discipline for student protesters. "Action should be with the least amount of force necessary, with a minimum of punitive effort and with firmness, rapidity and explanation," he said, adding, "The least amount of force necessary may be quite a bit."

Sherriffs quickly became Reagan's most important aide on higher education. He attended regents' meetings, joined in cabinet conferences, screened legislative proposals, and gave speeches. He also worked with the

Board of Regents to toughen policy on campus protests. He answered letters and drafted public statements for Reagan on student unrest. Sherriffs,
moreover, gathered intelligence about university affairs to give the governor an inside edge. Conservative professors funneled information to him
about colleagues they deemed suspect, and he sent Reagan reports like the
one beginning, "Ron, my spies tell me . . ."

Edwin Meese III came to Reagan's attention largely as a result of his prosecution of Savio and the other Sproul Hall sit-ins, and soon after taking
office the governor named him extradition and clemency secretary.

Like Reagan, the thirty-five-year-old former assistant district attorney
believed the death penalty was a deterrent to crime, Russia was bent on
world domination, and campus unrest was part of a Communist plot. His
passions were law enforcement and military operations. To relax at home
he listened to the police scanner, and in homage to the officers at whom
students hurled the epithet he collected figurines of pigs.

His great-grandfather had immigrated from Germany in 1850, came
west by covered wagon during the Gold Rush, and settled in the Oakland
Hills. The family was active in civic affairs and had become part of the
local establishment: Meese's grandfather was the treasurer of Oakland; his
father was a clerk in police court and Alameda county tax collector. Each
night when Meese was a boy, his family members joined in standing to
recite the Pledge of Allegiance and kneeling to pray. Like Oakland itself,
the Lutheran church where they worshiped on Sundays had been mostly
white. But as southern blacks migrated to the city during World War II to
work in local shipyards, some of them began to attend the church, which
accommodated the new congregants by holding segregated services and
airing out the pews before whites arrived for their communion. Meese attended public schools and won a scholarship to Yale, where he majored in
political science, joined the debate team, managed the track team, enlisted in ROTC, and earned a bachelor's degree in 1953. He then enrolled
at UC Berkeley's Boalt Hall School of Law but took two years off to serve
in the army. He would remain in the military reserves for nearly thirty
years, specializing in intelligence operations.

Graduating from Boalt in 1958, Meese married his high school sweet-
heart and joined District Attorney Frank Coakley's office. Meese prosecuted pot smokers, worked with the FBI to gather intelligence on Berkeley
activists, and coordinated police responses to demonstrations. His strategy
was to marshal officers from multiple law-enforcement agencies under

mutual-aid pacts in an overwhelming show of force intended to discourage unlawful protests and, if necessary, subdue them. When Savio led the big sit-in at Sproul Hall in December 1964, Meese was in the basement of the building, at the operations post in the campus police station. He took the call when Governor Brown phoned long after nightfall seeking advice on the situation.

"I gave a rundown on the situation to Pat Brown," Meese recalled. "I told him that it was the unanimous recommendation [of the various law-enforcement officers on the scene] that the people in the building should be arrested and taken out of there. I told him that if they were allowed to stay there would be another mob scene, even bigger, the next day." Following Meese's advice, Brown ordered police to clear the building, reneging on his promise to Kerr that he would try persuasion before using force against the nonviolent students.

Meese deployed a tactic that would become standard procedure at subsequent demonstrations: he directed officers to first arrest and remove leaders such as Savio on the theory that the remaining demonstrators would be disorganized, disheartened, and easier to dominate.

When he prosecuted Savio in 1965, Meese was about ten years older than the Free Speech Movement protesters. He was a major in the Army Reserve. That year he was named an Outstanding Young Man of America by the U.S. Junior Chamber of Commerce. During the trial he showed no empathy for the defendants. Suzanne Goldberg recalled that while the coprosecutor D. Lowell Jensen would greet the student defendants in court, "Meese would never respond to us if we'd smile or say hello to him in the halls. He'd walk by without speaking."

The Free Speech Movement and the Vietnam Day Committee's marches to the border of his native Oakland disturbed Meese. He saw no justification for their civil disobedience, their deliberate violations of the law, their disrupting business. Like Sherriffs, he believed a handful of radicals had manipulated their "gullible and naïve" peers into a rabble. And like Reagan, he believed antiwar protests prolonged the Vietnam conflict and cost American lives. Meese was angry that activists had been able to use the Berkeley campus to mount one protest after another. He soon took the title of legal affairs secretary and assumed broad responsibility for criminal justice matters, liaison to law enforcement, and—increasingly—organizing the state response to disorders at Berkeley.

Installing a sophisticated radio communications system, Meese turned his office into a war room from which he commanded a counteroffensive. He outlined his efforts in reports to Reagan. "We have the model mutual aid plan for the nation," he said in one. "We have inventoried necessary supplies, given to local agencies a half-million dollars worth of riot equipment, prepositioned [sic] vital emergency gear, upheld the communications system and worked out a plan with the federal government for additional immediate resources." In another report he told the governor, "In cooperation with the FBI, the California Highway Patrol established the nation's first computer-to-computer crime information hookup." He noted that "information banks have been established to store and exchange data" on Black Panthers, activists, and "anarchists."

Although it was highly questionable, Meese sought to open a secret intelligence pipeline from the U.S. Army directly to Reagan's office. He reached out to Lieutenant General Stanley R. Larsen, Commanding General of the Sixth United States Army, based at the Presidio in San Francisco.

"Dear General Larsen," Meese wrote on October 16, 1968. "Governor Reagan has expressed a personal interest concerning the extent of dissident and unlawful activities occurring on school campuses in California. He has directed his staff to gather information upon which he might base appropriate future plans."

Meese noted that another aide to Reagan recently had visited the army base, had "inquired as to the availability of information pertaining to dissident activities of a general nature upon major college campuses in California," and was told "detailed information could be made available upon formal request."

Meese continued, "It is requested that intelligence information be provided to me relative to incidents and/or activities adversely affecting ROTC training at both college and high school level, and that any other information which you feel should be brought to the Governor's attention, pertaining to dissident or unlawful activities be included.

"I am most interested in incidents, proposed dissident plans, names of individuals and organizations, both student and faculty, either participating in or supporting these activities, and any current campus policies which are not in the best interest of the ROTC program."

Like Reagan's earlier request to the FBI for information about Kerr and campus protests, Meese's was sweeping: He sought not only information about potentially illegal acts, but also about perfectly legal activity. Moreover, his appeal for information about school "policies" that the military found a hindrance to ROTC programs implied that the governor's office would use this intelligence to press college administrators to better accommodate armed forces recruiting.

And like Reagan's request, Meese's was sensitive: Although he was an officer in the Army Reserve, he was not entitled to army intelligence reports for unofficial use, and certainly not for spying on citizens for political purposes. And though the army had amassed dossiers on the political activities of more than 100,000 civilians, and on "virtually every group engaged in dissent in the United States," it lacked the authority to do so, as a congressional investigation would conclude.

Larsen was thus wary. His chief of staff replied to Meese on October 28, 1968, with a proposal that would insulate the general from potential allegations of misusing military intelligence. "The information you requested is available," he wrote. "However, we would prefer to furnish it orally to General Ames." Glenn C. Ames was the Army officer who served as Adjutant General of the State of California, head of the state's National Guard units. Meese could attend the oral briefing if Ames agreed, Larsen's aide suggested. This way there would be no record that the Army channeled unauthorized political intelligence directly to Reagan's top civilian aide.

In an interview, the author asked Meese whether it was appropriate for the military to provide the requested information. "Well, I don't know. But I don't think there was anything inappropriate about it. And I assume that it may be that there was information that they just felt they wanted to keep within the military or have that as the military channel, so that nobody could claim that they were cooperating in anything that had to do with political activity."

Meese's office was directly across the hall from Reagan's suite. He soon became Reagan's chief of staff and legal adviser, while retaining overall responsibility for the administration's response to student protests and crimes like "starting fires on the campus."

As Meese carried out Reagan's directive to gather intelligence on campus activists, he received assistance from several shadowy private operatives.

One of them was Patricia Atthowe, the mysterious "Oakland housewife" who had sued the University of California to release student records and campaigned for Reagan, and who would go on to establish a private intelligence firm that worked with utility companies, corporations, and government agencies. Like Meese, Atthowe was an Oakland native whose family had a history of government service. Her grandfather, Henry P. Meehan, had been a state assemblyman. Her father, Emmett Sylvester Meehan, was an investigator for the State Board of Equalization. Growing up in North Oakland, near the Berkeley border, she attended the College of the Holy Names, married Harold L. Atthowe, an Alameda County sheriff's deputy, had five children, and became active in the local Republican clubs.

Atthowe was deeply disturbed by challenges to the local establishment emanating from the Berkeley campus, like the Free Speech Movement. Her husband had helped arrest Savio and the other students during the big sit-in at Sproul Hall. The protests so upset her that she wrote Governor Brown complaining that "this kind of activity is being initiated with the tacit approval of the University administration." She demanded, "Do you feel in your considered opinion that a change in administration is advisable at the University? Specifically, would you be in favor of the resignation of Clark Kerr?" Brown replied curtly, "Thank you for your recent letter asking if I think a change in the administration at the University of California is desirable. I do not."

She was resolute. The winter of the Free Speech Movement's victory, Atthowe, then thirty-one, ran for a seat on the Oakland School Board. "We must rededicate ourselves to the ideals of responsible citizenship," she said in a campaign statement published in the *Oakland Tribune* alongside a photograph in which she gazed confidently from beneath a dark bouffant. She garnered just 15,510 votes in the primary that May, but in defeat issued a call to arms. "Our city is plagued by destructive philosophies, which thrive on voter apathy," she declared. "It is amazing how much destruction is being wrought in the name of social justice, freedom and humanitarianism. We must remain a solid force against coercion, threats, and petty politics, and stand firmly committed to quality education undiluted by social intercourse."

In a speech the next year, she assailed what she called "tremendous subversive pressures being exercised against official bodies." Her talk was sponsored by Berkeley Citizens United, a group of local conservatives aligned with Assemblyman Don Mulford. BCU members met at the office of the Berkeley Realty Board, a reflection of their landed interests and opposition to the Rumford Fair Housing Act. At one meeting, the BCU screened *The Truth About Communism*, a film narrated by Reagan. At another, the *San Francisco Examiner* reporter Ed Montgomery gave a talk titled, "Berkeley: Radical Capital of the West." In their monthly newsletter, BCU members lamented that "substantial citizens" were being forced to flee the increasingly noisome protests of Berkeley. With bitter humor they published a mock university catalog listing courses such as "Riot 101," "Draft Dodging," "Introduction to Free Love," "Communism," and "Personal Hygiene (Optional)."

Throughout 1966, Atthowe grew increasingly agitated about Berkeley activists. She worked with the district attorney's intelligence unit to investigate the Vietnam Day Committee, acting as the controller for the undercover agent who infiltrated the Peace Commandos; combed student records for evidence of radical activity; and worked hard for Reagan's gubernatorial campaign. After his victory, she continued her research on campus activists, telling a meeting of the United Republicans of California, "The university is a political weapon."

She elaborated in a report published in 1968 under the name California Information Council. "The Free Speech Movement opened a Pandora's political box," it said. "The university had adopted a perverted definition of free speech which embraced subversion, treason and violence. License was enshrined as an absolute right thereby assuring the future of Berkeley as the avante garde [*sic*] of national student disruption." Meese retained a copy in the files of his Legal Affairs Unit.

The following year, Atthowe and her husband bought Western Research Foundation, the private dossier service founded by Harper Knowles, the American Legion official who had tried to get Harry Bridges deported. She renamed it Research West and to help run it hired Don Lynn, the inspector with the Alameda County district attorney's intelligence unit who had worked closely with Meese and FBI agents investigating student protests. Like Atthowe, Lynn had grown increasingly agitated by campus unrest.

Atthowe also hired an amiable man named Robert Lamborn who had his own connections to the FBI. Born in 1923, he attended Berkeley High and studied journalism at Oregon State College (now Oregon State University). After the United States entered World War II, he joined the Army Air Force and served as an aerial photographer, manning a camera in the tail section of a B-24 airplane that trailed American bombers to document damage to their targets. After several harrowing missions, he transferred to his unit's newspaper and, under a reporter's guise, worked in an intelligence capacity, making contacts at the nearby Soviet military mission. Lamborn later recalled offering chocolate to a Soviet guard there, only to hear him reply that he preferred soap. Returning with a bar, he was astonished to see the Russian, famished for lard, rip off the wrapper and bite into it.

Returning to Berkeley in 1946, Lamborn married Mary Louise Dalziel, the granddaughter of an original owner of the Clorox Company. He dabbled as a custom furniture maker, working out of a shop on College Avenue, a few miles from campus. But, wealthy through marriage, he spent much of his time tooling around in his sports cars and delving into conservative politics. One afternoon in 1961, Agent Burney Threadgill of the FBI knocked on Lamborn's door in the Berkeley hills and asked him to help investigate student activists. Threadgill explained that Hoover feared embarrassment if agents were discovered on campus. Soon Lamborn was again posing as a reporter, wandering Berkeley with his Nikon camera, snapping shots of students and professors. Among the protests he photographed for the FBI were the Free Speech Movement, the Vietnam Day Committee's troop-train demonstrations, and Stop the Draft Week. Some of his photos wound up in *Tocsin*, the anti-Communist newsletter the FBI used in its COINTELPRO operations.

Lamborn began to work with the intelligence unit at the Alameda County District Attorney's Office, where he met Don Lynn and Ed Meese. Along the way, he became friendly with Hardin Jones, Ed Montgomery, and Patricia Atthowe, loaning her some of his inherited Clorox money to buy Western Research.

The "Oakland housewife" brought great enterprise to her intelligence operation. Ranks of women had served in civil defense campaigns, federal programs during the Cold War that enabled them to step beyond the confines of traditional female roles in the name of patriotism. But in a perhaps inadvertent boost for women's liberation, Atthowe became formidable in the male-dominated world of domestic intelligence, largely through sheer force of personality.

As Lamborn recalled, she was a "very devout Catholic . . . a very combative person. She was very strong. St. Thomas Aquinas was her hero, and she extremely patriotic." Charles Fox, the *Tocsin* editor and a closeted homosexual, sounded downright liberal when he grumbled that "her conservative philosophy drags religion and morality into the issue." Perhaps out of professional jealousy, Richard Combs disparaged Atthowe and her staff as "sensationalists." Harper Knowles simply referred to her as "the dictator," complaining, "She obviously wears the pants in the office." He added that she "boasts quite a bit about the work she did on campus."

Moving the firm's already voluminous files from the old Western Research office on Market Street, Atthowe set up Research West's new office across the bay in room 501 of a flatiron building at 1419 Broadway in downtown Oakland. She merged the files with her own dossiers, which filled four huge rotating file cabinets. The frosted glass on the office door gave up little, bearing only the black stenciled words "Trust Department."

Atthowe took pains to keep a low profile, but over the next decade she had several brushes with unwanted publicity. The first came in 1972, after the *San Francisco Examiner* published a two-part exposé headlined "Synanon: Racket of the Century." Founded as a self-help drug rehabilitation program, Synanon had grown into an alternative community of some 1,700 residents, mostly living in Marin County, California. The articles alleged that Synanon violated tax laws, urged clients to steal, prevented people from leaving its facilities, and probably followed a Communist ideology.

Synanon brought two lawsuits against the *Examiner* and its owner, the Hearst Corporation, the first for libel, the second for conspiracy and "dirty tricks." The defendants denied the charges but paid $600,000 to settle the libel case—at that time the largest libel settlement ever paid—and $2 million to settle the other case. Although Research West and its personnel were not defendants, the litigation revealed that Lamborn had proposed the story and contributed to it by introducing a former Synanon member to Ed Montgomery. The suit also uncovered evidence that the *Examiner* had paid Research West and its predecessor, Western Research, an annual retainer for providing information on alleged subversives—Montgomery was the newspaper's liaison to the firm. Randolph Hearst testified that his wife, Catherine Hearst, one of the university regents most upset by campus protests, had met several times with Atthowe, whom he described as a "bright gal."

Atthowe's next brush with exposure came when Congressman John Moss summoned her to appear before his Subcommittee on Oversight and Investigations. Pacific Gas & Electric, a California utility company, had paid nearly $90,000 to Research West between 1971 and 1976, according to federal records, and Georgia Power had paid more than $7,000. A staunch advocate of open government who authored the federal Freedom of Information Act, Moss was concerned that Research West was spying on antinuclear activists and that the FBI might be sharing its files with the firm.

On February 7, 1978, he subpoenaed Atthowe to appear before his committee with all Research West records concerning critics of nuclear power, including Ralph Nader, the Natural Resources Defense Council, and the Union of Concerned Scientists. Moss also ordered her to bring all records concerning the methods her firm used to obtain such information.

Several weeks later, Atthowe stood before the subcommittee in the Rayburn House Office Building in Washington. She now felt the weight of a congressional inquiry bearing down upon her, as had Doug Wachter and Jerry Rubin years earlier when they stood before the House Un-American Activities Committee. And like the radicals, she was defiant. Atthowe claimed her firm was involved in investigative reporting and told

Moss she would not comply with the subpoena on constitutional grounds of "free speech."

That June, Moss's panel approved a resolution finding Atthowe in contempt of Congress. In response, she told reporters that nuclear utilities received inadequate protection from law enforcement and needed private firms like hers to help prevent terrorist attacks against them. She charged that legal restrictions on government spying had "castrated" police agencies and that the Freedom of Information Act impeded the flow of information between them. The FOIA, she said, was a "terrorist support mechanism." Moss retired later that year and the new Congress did not pursue contempt proceedings. She would boast that she had thwarted Congress.

Since then, documents have been released under the FOIA that show Research West did serve as a clandestine exchange for intelligence about people engaged in lawful First Amendment activities. A 1969 FBI report stated the firm "operates as an investigative agency and a clearing house of information regarding all types of subversive activities." Research West, another bureau report said, provided information to businesses, police departments, and security agencies, including the FBI.

There were other spooky aspects to Research West. The CIA was legally barred from engaging in domestic surveillance, but Lamborn said in an interview that he was paid as a "security consultant" for the CIA, and, as he had for the FBI, he collected information on the Berkeley campus for the agency. In this way, he explained, he provided the CIA with "plausible deniability" that it was spying. However, at another point he declared, "As far as I'm concerned, the agency wasn't involved in any of that because they had no legal jurisdiction." Harold E. Chipman, an undercover CIA operative who had ostensibly retired from the agency, also worked with Atthowe. They were partners in a firm called Market Analysis, Inc., which claimed to be involved in international commodities brokering, and shared a floor with Research West. Chipman's wife testified in their divorce case that he gave money to Atthowe to invest in the Bahamas, a claim Chipman denied. "Needless to say," she said of her husband and his associates, "these people are tough and professional, and are capable of almost anything." Chipman apparently had some sense of humor: He drove an old Checker cab, and in official state records used the alias "Orwell." In response to a FOIA request for CIA records on Research West, the agency asserted that the "CIA can neither confirm nor deny the existence or nonexistence of records responsive to your request. The fact of the existence or nonexistence of requested records is currently and properly classified." The CIA declined further comment.

Research West meanwhile sold its services to private business. As Atthowe put it in one solicitation, "The *counter-corporate culture* has become a major force in the US and around the world; and Research West has tracked its component groups, its leaders, its sources of funding." The firm also offered "projections" for corporations worried about possible protests, letting them know in advance about the size, intensity, and tactics they might expect. It also vetted prospective employees. But while Atthowe portrayed her firm's mission as protecting business from terrorists, internal records from one client show that it functioned as a blacklisting service.

Mother's Cake & Cookie Company, of Oakland, retained Research West to screen applicants for jobs at its factories. According to a former secretary at the bakery, Mother's sent copies of job applications to Research West, which checked their names with its sources and sent back a list of those deemed not "clear" along with a brief explanation. Apparently, it did not take much to be found too dangerous to work in a cookie factory: one applicant in the late seventies was found not clear because his mother-in-law had been listed as an emergency contact by someone arrested in a civil rights protest at Mel's Drive-In back in 1963. As with the targets of the FBI's Responsibilities Program, the rejected bakers never were given a chance to rebut the anonymous allegations against them.

Research West's client list expanded to include Dow Chemical Co., Kaiser Aluminum, Standard Oil, utility and telephone companies, and high-technology firms, according to Robert Lamborn. Richard Mellon Scaife, the billionaire backer of conservative causes, also was a client. Atthowe moved Research West to a luxury building overlooking the bay at 2200 Powell Street in neighboring Emeryville. The firm occupied the entire fourth floor, along with Market Analysis, Inc. The suite had thirty-six offices, fifty-one parking spaces, and a monthly rent of nearly $19,000.

But by 1981 Atthowe's businesses had imploded. She failed to pay employees, office-supply vendors, and her landlord, resulting in several lawsuits and court judgments against her. She was evicted from her offices, the furnishings seized and sold at auction. The Internal Revenue Service filed liens against her and her companies for back taxes. Moreover, Atthowe and her companies defaulted on more than $1 million in bank loans to Research West, forcing several prominent people who had privately guaranteed them to pay out of pocket. Catherine Hearst shelled out $200,000; Richard Mellon Scaife, $75,000; and Richard K. Miller, a vice president of Pacific Gas & Electric, $175,000. They, in turn, sued Research West for reimbursement. Miller's suit further accused Atthowe of fraud: he claimed she had promised to secure his loan guarantee with "valuable research files" but instead hid them to "defeat the creditors of Research West." Atthowe did not respond to his suit or to the others—her attorney said she had gone to Europe and was unavailable—and the location of the files remains secret. (Nor did Atthowe respond to the author's subsequent requests for comment.) The intelligence operation she created to protect business from Berkeley radicals, it seems, had fallen victim to the free market.

By then Research West had long served as a confidential source for Governor Reagan and his aide Edwin Meese III, supplying reports on students, professors, and administrators. As Lamborn, one of the firm's investigators, bluntly recalled, "I was reporting to the governor's office." Meese confirmed that Research West supplied information to the governor's office. Not long after the firm's demise, two detectives from the Los Angeles Police Department interviewed Richard Miller, the Pacific Gas & Electric executive who had guaranteed a loan to Atthowe. They were investigating allegations that officers in the LAPD intelligence unit had shared police files with private intelligence organizations such as Research West. According to their official notes, Miller told them, "Atthowe and [her organization] provided good information. Ronald Reagan could verify Atthowe's reliability."

Perhaps the strangest informer to pass through Berkeley and supply Governor Reagan with intelligence reports about campus activists was John Herbert Rees, an alleged con man, womanizer, police informer, and sometime priest impersonator.

The Briton first achieved notoriety in America when Grace Metalious, author of the bestseller *Peyton Place*, died in 1964 and left everything to him and nothing to her three children in a will executed the day before her death. Metalious had achieved wealth and fame for her 1953 novel about the dark side of small-town life, but like some of her characters she had succumbed to drink, despair, and dissolution. Rees had known her only six months, and the Boston papers made much of it, reporting that he had deserted his wife and five children in England. According to FBI reports, Rees was born in 1926; served in the Royal Air Force as a military policeman; worked for London's *Daily Mirror*, where he repeatedly misused his position to procure free meals and other benefits and was eventually fired; and engaged in "numerous" affairs. He renounced Metalious's bequest, the reports asserted, after learning her estate was in debt.

In an interview with the author, Rees deflected some questions and denied some allegations. He said he had left his family, but had not deserted them. He called accounts of his romantic activities "greatly exaggerated" and said he was merely Metalious's "business manager." He relinquished his interest in her estate, he insisted, so it would benefit her husband and children. His business activities at the *Daily Mirror* were always proper, he said, adding he had no inkling why federal reports alleged that in Britain he had been a "known con-man." Asked if he disputed the claim, he replied, "I'd want the definition."

By 1968 Rees had relocated to Newark, New Jersey, where he ran a company called National Goals, Inc., described in its literature as a "nonprofit organization specializing in areas of education, training and law enforcement." He and an investigator for the House Un-American Activities Committee named Herbert Romerstein visited the FBI office there with an offer from Rees. As FBI agents wrote in their report, "He stated he had information of a racial and criminal nature which he and the investigator from HUAC believed was of an interest to the FBI . . . He attempted to sell himself and his services to the FBI."

But the bureau wasn't buying—at least not yet. "Rees talked in generalities . . . and furnished no information of value," the report continued. "The interviewing agents believed his interests were self-serving and that he came to the FBI thinking this would enhance his credentials in contacting other potential clients." Hoover ordered his assistants to warn HUAC about him.

Rees—and HUAC—were undaunted. In the fall of 1968, he was working undercover in Chicago for the committee, collecting information about the protests against the Democratic National Convention that August. Antiwar demonstrators had clashed with police, which led to televised images of police brutality and eventually the indictment on riot charges of the activists who became known as the Chicago Seven. Again a HUAC investigator offered the FBI the fruits of Rees's labors. Again agents shied away. "We should not initiate any interview with this unscrupulous, unethical individual concerning his knowledge of the disturbances in Chicago," an agent wrote, "as to do so would be a waste of time."

Yet Rees had found his niche. He'd made several cameo appearances before HUAC. He was peddling intelligence information on leftist groups to various police departments, picking up new information from them that he could sell elsewhere. He was circulating to selected government agencies, intelligence units, and conservative politicians his self-published periodical, *Information Digest*, which purported to focus on "the background . . . operations and real capabilities of social movements and protest groups."

Rees also had found a new spouse. John and Sheila Rees arrived in Washington, D.C., in 1970 and quickly infiltrated the activist community. Rotund, bearded, and long-haired, John was an articulate pamphleteer who at this point sported the collar of an Anglican priest and identified himself as "Reverend John Seely of the United Reform Church of America." Big-boned and over six feet tall, Sheila was a whiz at office work. She told people her name was Sheila Louise O'Connor.

The couple moved into a commune at 1616 Longfellow Street, N.W. They joined in many of the district's protests. He opened a bookstore and meeting place called the Red House Collective at 1247 Twentieth Street, N.W., ten blocks from the White House.

That July, Secret Service agents spotted him in a demonstration at the South Vietnamese embassy. Running a computer check on him, they got several surprising hits, according to the resulting report: The Washington Metropolitan Police Department disclosed that it employed him as an informer. The Chicago Police Department reported that "subject is unreliable and known to make a profession of providing intelligence to police departments." The Secret Service report said that "subject was a known con man in England" and used several aliases, including John Sealy, S. L. O'Connor, and Jonathan Goldstein. It also said he "possibly carries a gun."

Rees was involved in several intelligence operations for the Washington Metropolitan Police Department, which had helped finance Rees's bookstore with the intention of using it to collect intelligence on activists who gathered there, according to FBI reports.

He also began informing for the FBI. In 1971, the bureau assigned him the code number WF-3796 and the code name "Lepron" to conceal his identity in reports. FBI supervisors ordered their agents to be "discreet and circumspect" in dealing with him.

One day at the commune, his roommate Pat Richartz stumbled upon a bizarre cache in Rees's usually locked room—several guns, boxes of bullets, and a black suitcase containing what seemed to be wiretapping equipment, according to an affidavit she signed under penalty of perjury. In the midst of her discovery the couple walked in and confronted her. Sheila beat her while John held back her two young daughters, according to the affidavit. Stew Albert, the Vietnam Day Committee leader, was then living in Washington and saw Richartz soon afterward. "She came up to my apartment looking very messed up," he recalled.

Richartz accused the couple of being informers, but no one believed her. She was seen as an outsider; they were seen as valuable volunteers. They proceeded to work with the Institute for Policy Studies, a progressive think tank opposed to the war in Vietnam. Sheila Rees became an office manager for the local chapter of the National Lawyers Guild, which was providing legal counsel to antiwar activists. All along, John Rees was sending the FBI reports on the two organizations, as well as copies of their internal records, including a letter about the guild's plan to investigate unlawful government surveillance.

Richartz's suspicions were not confirmed until 1975, however, when New York State Assembly staff investigating *Information Digest* contacted the organization. The assembly's report concluded that Rees's newsletter contained "raw, unevaluated, editorialized and frequently derogatory information" that was being used to "develop dossiers on thousands of patriotic and decent Americans."

In the interview, Rees admitted that he and his wife had collected information on political activists. He acknowledged using false names and posing as a radical. He affirmed that the Washington Metropolitan Police Department had paid the rent for the Red House bookstore he used to gather intelligence on visitors. But he denied that any government agency ever paid him for informing and, moreover, that he'd ever been an informer. He claimed the incident with Pat Richartz never occurred. FBI agents, he added, had been mistaken in deeming him an unethical, unscrupulous opportunist.

By now, Rees had been busy in Berkeley. "Rees has been furnishing information to the California Department of Justice Bureau of Criminal Identification and Investigation (CII)," said a February 10, 1972, FBI report.

Governor Reagan and his staff also received Rees's newsletter, which contained reports on Jessica Mitford, Jerry Rubin, the Black Panthers, and campus political groups. Rees told the author that Reagan "had my material, and he made use of my material . . . And that goes back years. That goes back to the time he was governor of California." Rees insisted he was merely a reporter who favored stories about "what I like to call the further shores of political thought," ranging from the far left to the far right. In the following years, Rees wrote for *The Review of the News*, a publication of the John Birch Society, and his wife worked on the staff of the Georgia congressman Larry McDonald, the president of the society. When questioned about Rees in 1983, President Reagan's spokesmen, and FBI officials, declined to comment. More recently, Edwin Meese III told the author that he did not recall Rees.

Rees was also sending information to Research West, according to Robert Lamborn, the self-described FBI and CIA consultant who worked there. He recalled that Rees and his wife specialized in "penetration jobs," adding, "They were sort of political prostitutes, but very clever."

In one of those jobs, Rees infiltrated a Berkeley commune on Ashby Avenue where Tom Hayden, the former president of Students for a Democratic Society, was spending time. "He was staying at Tom Hayden's over there on Ashby, and the guys were sitting around smoking dope and drinking Red Mountain," recalled Lamborn. "Tom kept looking at John and trying to figure out . . . he thought he had seen him before.

"So in his haze, he decided that after John had gone upstairs and gone to bed he'd go up and take a look at him again. So he went in the bedroom. John was a big fat slob, and he was lying there half nude on the bed. He heard Tom come in. Tom snuck in and kind of pulled back the sheet a little bit and was looking at John's face.

"And John reached up, threw his arms around Tom, and pulled him down into the bed, and said, 'I've had the hots for you, too!' He said Tom Hayden almost shit."

J. Edgar Hoover meanwhile continued to help the fledgling governor, sending him information about students, professors, and prospective university employees. In June 1968, for example, Meese told John Williams, the special agent in charge of the FBI's Sacramento office, that the new UC president, Charles Hitch, was considering naming the political scientist Mark F. Ferber to be in charge of university relations for urban affairs.

"Governor's office is concerned about possible 'left wing' associates of applicant," Williams said in a teletype to Hoover. "Governor's office has requested any information available which will be held in absolute confidence by the governor's office, both as to content and source. As bureau is aware, Governor Reagan's office has been most cooperative with this office and has been most discreet in all contacts."

Hoover authorized Williams to tell Meese that a check of FBI files and criminal-history records had found no information on Ferber. He was hired, and in later years served on the staff of President Ford's Privacy Protection Study Commission.

Over brunch with Assistant Director Cartha DeLoach, Reagan sought FBI information about another scholar he suspected of being subversive. Nearly ten years earlier, Reagan had pitched DeLoach his idea for a television show based on "Communist Target—Youth," only to be turned down. Now Reagan told him in "strict confidence" that the UC regents were considering hiring the Columbia University math professor Serge Lang.

"Governor Reagan stated he was most suspicious of this individual inasmuch as he had heard rumors that this man was mixed up in various student uprisings," DeLoach later reported. "Governor Reagan indicated he would appreciate being furnished on a confidential basis any information that the FBI could give him. He stressed that the source of this information would not be revealed."

With Hoover's approval, FBI agents conducted a discreet inquiry at Columbia. John Williams, the special agent in charge of the Sacramento office, then gave Reagan a blind memo stating that Lang was independent but "has always been known as a political radical" and had supported student protesters. Lang went on to teach at Berkeley but never became a tenured professor there. He later joined the faculty at Yale.

In an interview, Meese said it "would not be unusual" for the governor to confidentially request FBI information about prospective university and state employees. This was done only to protect "public safety," he said, and was not political screening.

Meese even asked the FBI to investigate the background of a woman he was considering hiring as his secretary. Forwarding this request to Hoover, Williams noted she would "have access to confidential information regarding racial agitation, and other matters" and emphasized that Meese was one of his special "contacts."

Nonetheless, it was clearly outside the bureau's jurisdiction to screen state employees not involved in federal matters. Tolson recommended against doing the personal favor. Hoover overrode him with a memo noting, "Governor Reagan's Office has been extremely cooperative."

24

A Key Activist

Mario and Suzanne Savio loaded their seventeen-month-old son, Stefan, and their bags into their secondhand station wagon and drove away from Berkeley.

Savio had been struggling to get by, bartending at the Steppenwolf, doing odd jobs. He had been convicted of causing a public nuisance for his part in the protest against the navy recruiters the previous November, along with Jerry Rubin, Stew Albert, Steve Hamilton, and Mike Smith, and had drawn the stiffest sentence: ninety days in county jail and a $350 fine. That conviction and the one for the Sproul Hall sit-in were on appeal, but still they weighed on him. And, finally, he had given up his fight for readmission, saying he was too broke to go to school.

He was, moreover, worried about his boy, who remained inexplicably difficult and required constant attention. Although Savio was coping with his own travails, Suzanne said, he was "always kind to Stefan." Much as Savio's mother had doted on him, he doted on Stefan. Recalling his own traumatic experience at the hands of a domineering father, he deliberately dealt with the child on a democratic basis, consulting him as to his wishes with the same meticulous care as when he was debating an adult about an important political point. The civil rights activist was determined to avoid "the concentration of authority" that went with the traditional family. Just the thought of Stefan being dominated, he wrote to a friend, made Savio "fearful to the point of panic." But the young couple would not learn until much later that Stefan had severe developmental disabilities, and as Suzanne recalled, her husband's efforts only left Stefan "anxious and confused" and Savio disappointed in himself.

On top of all this, he was still fighting the depression that had afflicted him since he was a teenager.

"Things were too difficult here," Suzanne told the *Berkeley Barb* as they prepared to leave town in early May 1967. "We're just going to get in the car and go."

Savio may have thought he was leaving Berkeley behind, but he would soon find that he was still caught up in radical politics—and in the gears and levers of the FBI's surveillance machinery. All along, Hoover had been intensifying the bureau's investigation of the man he and Reagan blamed for starting so much of the trouble at Berkeley.

A few weeks after Reagan's inauguration, Agent Don Jones had reported an informer's claim that Savio had attended two "educational classes" of the Berkeley branch of the Communist Party back in August 1966. Jones's report of January 23, 1967, suggested that Savio was more involved with Communists than previously known. The bureau repeated the allegation in other internal communications and forwarded it to army intelligence. Here, it seemed, was the proof Hoover had been looking for all along.

But it was wrong. According to a subsequent FBI report, the informer's statement had been incorrectly transcribed: Savio was not present. His name had been merely mentioned. Nonetheless, FBI officials continued to circulate the erroneous allegation. There is no evidence in Savio's dossier that they told army intelligence about the mistake. And on the basis of that unfounded report, bureau officials on February 23, 1967, ordered San Francisco agents to upgrade Savio from the Reserve Index to the Security Index, the list of people whom the bureau deemed most dangerous to national security in the event of a national emergency, to be detained indefinitely without judicial warrant.

FBI agents also issued a "Security Flash" for Savio, entering a notice in the bureau's main crime computer to alert field offices whenever a police agency inquired about him. The Security Flash listed Savio as having the "alias" of "José Martí." Martí was a nineteenth-century Cuban poet, exile, and revolutionary leader killed in battle against the Spanish colonialists. Savio had listed his phone under the obscure young revolutionary's name to avoid unwanted calls. Later he changed it to "Alfredo Joe Marti" as a joke. The bureau promptly updated his file to reflect the new "alias." But something was happening, and Mr. Jones did not know what it was.

For weeks FBI agents searched for Savio and his family. On June 7, an agent contacted the property manager of their old apartment on McGee Street, who said the couple had bought a used station wagon and planned to visit Savio's relatives in Southern California, then drive east to Massachusetts, where he might enroll at Amherst College. FBI agents in Los

Angeles, New York, and Massachusetts quickly contacted local police and college officials who might have some leads, but to no avail.

The Savios had driven to Los Angeles and on to Nogales, Mexico, on the Arizona border, where their car broke down and they were stranded without money. Desperate, Savio went to the U.S. consulate and asked for financial help. For three hours he pleaded with the resident bureaucrats, but they were reluctant to help the bedraggled family and kept referring them to the Red Cross in Tucson. "Why should I go to Tucson when I have a direct representative of the president of the United States here?" he implored them. Finally, the consulate arranged a twenty-five-dollar loan and they went away in the stifling heat. Reporting the episode to the FBI, the consul would describe them as part of the "California hippie tribe."

For a while the family settled near Los Angeles, renting an apartment in El Monte, closer to Savio's parents, but within weeks the owner discovered Savio was the infamous Free Speech Movement leader and ordered them to vacate the premises.

FBI agents ended their hunt for Savio only when he appeared in Alameda County Municipal Court in Berkeley on June 30, 1967, as scheduled, to be sentenced to 120 days at Santa Rita County Jail for the Sproul Hall sit-in. Savio was resolute. "I would do it again," he told reporters. "I think it is the best thing that ever happened for American education."

Jail was an unexpected relief. In July he wrote Lynne Hollander, his friend and fellow FSM arrestee, that incarceration "has been good for me. I've long needed to be free of obligation, to be alone, to take stock. This place is a strange combination of monastery and boys' camp, and less regimented than the high school I went to." In a later letter to her, he lamented the loss of the loving community that had united around the civil rights movement and the Free Speech Movement. "What we once called 'the Movement' has changed, it seems to me, quite out of existence," he wrote in August. "People are really moving in different ways. Some people . . . are talking about beginning political work in the factories again, others are moving in the direction, roughly, of the Haight Ashbury. Neither direction is quite mine." He still felt an "obligation" to help create a new political force, he said, "Yet I don't feel I'm ready to try." He wanted to first resolve his psychological struggles, get his family well settled, and find "stability and permanence."

When Suzanne visited Mario in jail, the sheriff's deputies seemed to cut their meetings short, and she complained to them about it. They arrested her, claiming that she had refused to leave. She was jailed for several hours until Savio's father bailed her out. (She denied that she had refused to leave, and a charge of resisting arrest was dropped when she pleaded no contest to disturbing the peace and was placed on probation.) At another point while her husband was in jail, Agent Don Jones phoned Suzanne at home. Posing as an author hoping to collaborate with Savio on a book about "the current new left movement," Jones asked about his plans. "She stated Mario is not interested in writing any books or articles at the present time and, in fact, has welcomed the opportunity to do reading and some research while he is in jail," Jones reported. "She stated Mario does not want to become involved in any further political activity upon his release from jail but hopes to obtain a job and 'settle down and live a normal life.'"

At 6:00 p.m. on October 24, 1967, Savio was released from Santa Rita jail. FBI agents had been anticipating his release and took down the license number of the white Plymouth Valiant that picked him up. (It was registered, they noted, to Reginald Zelnik, an assistant history professor at Berkeley who had supported the FSM.) Judge Floyd Talbott had suspended Suzanne Savio's forty-five-day sentence for the Sproul Hall sit-in so she could care for Stefan. The judge also cut eighty days off Savio's combined two-hundred-day sentence for the sit-in and the ROTC protest, declaring, "Mario was a model prisoner and it appears Mario has reformed."

Hoover thought otherwise.

On January 30, 1968, twelve days after he met with Reagan and Meese, the FBI director initiated a nationwide covert action program that would home in on Savio.

In a directive, Hoover designated him as one of several "Key Activists." The order defined these targets as members of the "New Left" who were "extremely active and most vocal in their statements denouncing the United States and calling for civil disobedience and other forms of unlawful and disruptive acts."

The Church committee would find, however, that FBI officials had selected people as Key Activists not because they were suspected of criminal activity but because of their effective First Amendment activities. Hoover's order named fourteen other people involved in the antiwar movement around the country, including Jerry Rubin, Tom Hayden, and Robert Scheer. Within three years the program would expand to target seventy-three people.

Agents assigned to investigate the Key Activists were required to maintain "high-level informant coverage." They were to deploy electronic and physical surveillance. They were to identify the activists' sources of funds and supposed "foreign contacts." Hoover wanted "detailed and complete information regarding their day-to-day activities" as well as their "future plans for staging demonstrations and disruptive acts directed against the Government."

In San Francisco, Don Jones and at least three other FBI agents investigated Savio. A mortgage company gave the agents confidential financial information about the Savios' purchase of a home at 1607 Ninth Street in the low-income West Berkeley flats. Banks gave the agents figures on the couple's meager accounts. One account had a balance of $2.20, another of $5.00, a third of $33.40. The Pacific Telephone and Telegraph Company's security officer provided Savio's subscriber data, noting the phone company had instituted a collection action against him for delinquent bills. To avoid constant unwanted calls, Savio had continued to list his phone under the names of famous people he evidently admired—the poet Wallace Stevens, the artist Käthe Kollwitz, the physicist David Bohm. Agent Jones listed these names as additional "aliases" in his dossier.

It was all a violation of the reclusive radical's privacy. As if to prove Savio's thesis that individuals are inherently at odds with bureaucracies, every commercial institution readily complied with the FBI's requests for personal information about him and his wife, without requiring any subpoena. Although subsequent laws would bar businesses from releasing personal information to the government, the Patriot Act, passed in 2001 to help prevent terrorism, greatly eased those restrictions.

Discovering that Savio had a new job, Agent Jones interviewed his boss at an electrical parts firm called Berkeley Tanometer, at 1214 Fifth Street, where the former Westinghouse Science Competition finalist worked for a while on an assembly line. According to Jones's report, Eugene Ellerbush said Savio was hired in November 1967 through the state employment agency after having had "great difficulty" finding work. Ellerbush had tried to "orient him to the free enterprise system and the American way of life," he said, and Savio had confided that he had "personal emotional problems" stemming from his childhood. Savio had told him that as a small boy he was keenly interested in science and spent all his time reading scientific publications. But his parents were constantly "badgering" him to be more of "a typical American boy" who built model airplanes, went on hikes, and read comic books.

Ellerbush told Jones he had ordered other employees to give Savio extra help. But though Savio learned quickly, he became disillusioned and complained that his job was "too repetitious." Savio came to his office and said he was having trouble remembering from one day to the next how to assemble a particular electronics device. Savio theorized that because he detested assembly line work, he blocked it out of his mind each night and had to relearn it the next day. He felt, he said, like he was "losing his memory." Resigning after only six weeks, Savio told his boss he needed time to "think through his personal problems."

Agent Jones continued to track Savio, making periodic "spot checks" of his residence and developing a neighbor as a source. But despite such efforts, Jones and other FBI agents found no evidence that he was involved with any violent or subversive group. On February 15, 1968, Jones reported that he might not qualify as a Key Activist. But—just to be sure— the agents would "keep up with Savio's day-to-day activities."

Savio stood before a packed auditorium at Berkeley's Garfield Junior High School on March 10, 1968, and announced that he had decided to join the political establishment.

He wanted to run for the office of state senator from Alameda County on the Peace and Freedom Party ticket. A third-party forerunner of Barry Commoner's Citizens Party and the Green Party, the Peace and Freedom Party sought to unite disaffected liberals, peace activists, and Black Power advocates behind its platform opposing racism and the war in Vietnam. The PFP slate included Eldridge Cleaver, the Black Panther leader, for president; Huey Newton, for Congress; and Bobby Seale and Kathleen Cleaver, Eldridge's wife, for state assembly. Robert Scheer, of the Vietnam Day Committee, was one of the main party organizers. So was Jack Weinberg, of the Free Speech Movement.

In his speech seeking the party's endorsement that Wednesday night, Savio called for far-reaching reform. Like Reagan in his gubernatorial campaign, he attacked big government and called for greater local control. The New Deal, Savio said, had done much good but "did a good bit of mischief, too. It began a process of runaway growth in the central government: a maze of agencies and commissions and bureaucracies."

But while Reagan believed the profit motive would naturally provide for society's needs if unobstructed by government regulation, Savio was convinced unbridled capitalism would ensure that large parts of the population remained in poverty. And while Reagan saw the economy mainly from the businessman's point of view, Savio looked at it more from the employee's perspective, with an eye toward race and class. "Most white working people have the good jobs they have, make the good money they do, only because a full fifth of the population (the largest part of which is black) get the least interesting, least desirable jobs at the lowest rates of pay," he said. This income gap, moreover, was growing. "The poorest fifth of the population has a smaller share of American wealth today than it did at the end of the war," he said. And on a global basis, "the minority of white people in the world benefits from the impoverishment of the millions who starve."

Savio declared that America must reorganize itself along lines of common economic interest. "All those who gain least from war and poverty—the working people, the small farmers, the small businessmen, the professionals . . . must join together now against the minority in big business and finance who own and run this country, and whose lust for power and profit and whose utter disregard for human suffering threatens now to bring the world to a final catastrophe," he said.

"Our great task is to organize the people into a new majority. Americans are practical people . . . we must convince them that it is essential that our economy be dominated by production to satisfy human needs, not to swell profits; that this production can be planned publicly and democratically and that it should be, and that administration of the economy should be highly decentralized so that the decisions are really made by the people rather than by private or public bureaucrats."

"America has the unique opportunity to help usher in a Golden Age of peace and freedom," he concluded. "We can begin in this election year a great turning in America away from an empire of disaster, towards peace."

In the following weeks, the candidate attacked the Democratic Party as failing to adequately address poverty, racism, and the war. He called for cutting military spending and raising income taxes, saying, "We must take from the rich and help the poor."

Martin Luther King, Jr., meanwhile, was in Memphis, preparing to lead a march of sanitation workers protesting poor wages and working conditions. On April 4 he was assassinated there while standing on the balcony of the Lorraine Motel. Riots broke out in cities across the nation and U.S. troops were dispatched to quell them. In Oakland, a shootout with police on April 6 left the Black Panther "L'il Bobby" Hutton dead and Eldridge Cleaver wounded.

Two days later, Savio led a peaceful march of five thousand people from the Berkeley campus through the white neighborhood of Piedmont, where Assemblyman Don Mulford lived, to the Alameda County Courthouse in downtown Oakland. Huey Newton was being held there on charges of shooting the Oakland police officer John Frey in a separate incident. Massing outside the courthouse, the demonstrators chanted "Free Huey" and "Don't Kill Blacks."

As Savio campaigned, the FBI investigated. Agents scrutinized his official campaign registration papers. Noting that he had listed his occupation as freelance writer, Jones updated his Security Index card to show he worked at home, just in case the bureau needed to pick him up.

All the while, Savio was struggling. He confided in a letter to his old friend and fellow altar boy Arthur Gatti that he had little energy for the campaign mainly because of "my own tendency to fall apart from internal chaos." He also had reservations about the Peace and Freedom Party, which he had come to see as too sectarian. He believed its leaders "should be trying to build a broad-base opposition party. Instead they seem content— gleeful!—about confining their activities to addressing only the committed." In addition, he was concerned that the party had put itself "under the lash of a troubled alliance with the Panthers," whose violent rhetoric he disliked. At one party meeting, he opposed a motion to demand the freeing of Huey Newton "by any means necessary," declaring, "I don't think the revolution in America depends on burning down half the city of Oakland to free one man. Almost all are in jail unfairly."

He was deeply divided over his public role. "I hate being in politics, having to manipulate lives," he told the *Berkeley Barb* reporter Gar Smith, who visited his office, a garage cluttered with paint cans, cast-off furniture, and other debris that, Smith said, lent the place "an atmosphere of honest poverty and quiet desperation."

Savio spoke of his campaign goals: to improve public education; to set up a lending library of tools for people who could not afford their own; to assemble legal services that employed attorneys and law students to help indigent criminal defendants. He spoke against excessive government control and urged a larger citizen role in public policy.

But he told Smith he hoped "I will not have to continue to be a very public person after the campaign . . . If this speech making and public activity after the campaign becomes one of the major focuses . . . it would be very unhealthy."

Hoover already was planning to help him get out of politics.

•

The bureau was taking steps to not only spy on Savio but to sabotage him. In an urgent memo on May 10, 1968, the director had authorized a highly sensitive operation called "Counterintelligence Program—New Left."

"The purpose of this program is to expose, disrupt, and otherwise neutralize the activities of the various New Left organizations, their leadership and adherents," Hoover said in a May 10, 1968, memo.

> The Bureau has been very closely following the activities of the New Left and the Key Activists and is highly concerned that the anarchistic activities of a few can paralyze institutions of learning, induction centers, cripple traffic, and tie the arms of law enforcement officials all to the detriment of our society.
>
> The organizations and activists who spout revolution and unlawfully challenge society to obtain their demands must not only be contained, but must be neutralized. Law and order is mandatory for any civilized society to survive.

COINTELPRO–New Left was the last of five formal FBI counterintelligence programs. Beginning in 1956, Hoover had set up four COINTELPRO programs respectively aimed at the Communist Party, the Socialist Workers Party, "White Hate Groups," and "Black Nationalist Hate Groups." He would abruptly end these programs in 1971, only after persons unknown broke into the FBI office in Media, Pennsylvania, stole documents revealing them, and anonymously distributed copies to news organizations.

Congress would later find that though bureau officials undertook COINTELPRO in the name of national security, its purpose was "preventing or disrupting the exercise of First Amendment rights." The program took tactics developed for use against foreign adversaries during war and applied them to citizens: leaking phony allegations, sending anonymous poison-pen letters, interfering with jobs, having people arrested on drug charges, distributing misinformation, and encouraging violence. "In essence, the Bureau took the law into its own hands, conducting a sophisticated vigilante operation against domestic enemies," the committee said. "Many of the techniques used would be intolerable in a democratic society even if all of the targets had been involved in violent activity, but COINTELPRO went far beyond that. The unexpressed major premise of the programs was a law enforcement agency has the duty to do whatever is necessary to combat perceived threats to the existing social and political order."

FBI officials deployed the program against a "staggering range" of people and organizations, the committee found, including Martin Luther King, Jr., Black Panthers, almost every antiwar group, college administrators, and "students demonstrating against anything."

On May 17, 1968, Hoover ordered San Francisco agents to turn the program against three Bay Area men: John Gerassi, a journalist and professor at San Francisco State College; Robert Scheer, the former Berkeley graduate student, Vietnam Day Committee leader, and congressional candidate who was now an editor of *Ramparts*; and Mario Savio.

As to the former Free Speech Movement leader, Hoover was clear: "You should bear in mind that one of the prime objectives should be to neutralize him in the new left movement," he ordered. "You will be expected to pursue this investigation aggressively and with imagination."

However, Charles Bates, who had taken over as special agent in charge of the San Francisco office after Lynum retired, replied that the three targets were "not members of any known subversive organizations such as the CP, SWP, et cetera. They are independent free thinkers and do not appear to be answerable to any one person or any group or organization."

Besides, there was a practical problem in trying to intimidate New Left activists by using the media to expose their unconventional lifestyle. "They are not embarrassed by this coverage," Bates said. "In fact, they seem to enjoy it and thrive on it." Nonetheless, Bates made sure his agents remained alert for opportunities to otherwise neutralize them.

On May 31, 1968, headquarters officials asked the Internal Revenue Service for copies of the Savios' 1966 and 1967 tax returns. According to the Church committee, FBI officials requested tax returns for at least 120 people under COINTELPRO. They had no legitimate basis to request the returns, and the IRS turned them over in violation of federal regulations, the committee said. The bureau illegally used the returns to gather intelligence, to prompt audits, and to otherwise harass people because of their political activities.

The Savios' joint returns showed they had earned all of $2,106.31 in 1966 and $2,046.00 in 1967.

If they were getting money from Moscow, it wasn't listed on their Form 1040.

Savio drew only 4,292 votes, less than 2 percent of the total cast, in the primary election on June 4, 1968.

Shortly after midnight of that day, Robert F. Kennedy was assassinated as he walked through the kitchen of the Ambassador Hotel in Los

Angeles, just after he had proclaimed victory in the California Democratic primary. Since his speech at the Greek Theatre, Kennedy had come
out against the war and had drawn wide support among young people.
His murder, so soon after King's, left many disillusioned with the prospects
for change through the political system.

In Sacramento, Alex Sherriffs, Reagan's top education adviser, drafted
a letter that the governor sent to the UC regents and released to the public
over his signature. In the letter, Reagan blamed Kennedy's death on campus violence that he traced to the Free Speech Movement.

"We have just experienced a terrible tragedy in the assassination of
Senator Robert F. Kennedy," Reagan said.

> The ramifications of this violent and destructive act extend be-
> yond the death of one of the significant figures of our time and
> the deep hurt to loved ones. The confidence of millions of people
> in their society, in justice, and in orderly processes as the only
> civilized means to obtain human goals has been shaken.
>
> But here we come to the critical point—it was the erosion
> over recent years of just such confidence that has led to today's
> climate of violence. We do not need to be reminded that our edu-
> cational institutions are among the most valued and the most in-
> fluential of all the institutions which make up our society and
> which represent it to our youth.
>
> I must ask you, then, do you believe for one minute that a
> captured police car and an imprisoned representative of law at
> Berkeley has had no effect on our citizens? This was an act of vio-
> lence which was claimed as a victory by those who broke the law,
> and which was for them a victory in fact.
>
> Do you believe that breaking and entering campus buildings
> by force and stopping the processes of an institution of American
> society has had no effect on our youth?
>
> Do you see the constant resistance on the part of members of
> the faculty and of the administration to the rightful place of law
> enforcement in a democratic society as insignificant?
>
> Is freedom of speech, but only for some, what America is re-
> ally all about? On some campuses faculty members and students
> tell us over and over again that that is the way it is.
>
> A sick campus community in California in many ways is re-
> sponsible for a sick community around those campuses. Long
> have we heard that we should yield to the ideas and the leadership

of these institutions. Let these campuses then be models for what is good for our society. It is our responsibility, and we have it in our authority to see to it that they are.

Wednesday at noon, while Robert Kennedy was fighting for his life, I penned the statement I enclose; today as I reread these words I am even more convinced that I am describing where our problems lie.

Sincerely,
Ronald Reagan
Governor

About two weeks later, officials at FBI headquarters sent the Secret Service a confidential form letter alleging that Savio posed a potential threat to the safety of the president. The June 21, 1968, notice was an example of what the Church committee called "imprecise and over-inclusive criteria" that improperly ensnared student activists like Savio.

The same day, Agent Don Jones coincidentally reported—in a memo titled "COUNTERINTELLIGENCE PROGRAM . . . Mario Robert Savio . . . Key Activist"—that there was still no evidence that Savio was under the influence of any subversive group. He also noted Savio had continued to have trouble finding employment after his failed campaign for state senator.

Savio did have a little luck: he had been hired only recently as a ship's clerk through the International Longshore & Warehouse Union at San Francisco's Pier 9. But not long after, an FBI agent contacted an ILWU dispatcher who was secretly a bureau source. The dispatcher promised he "would do everything in his power to keep Savio from getting anywhere through the hiring hall," according to Agent Jones's report. His job on the pier lasted only through August and soon he was looking for work again.

By now, Savio was barely involved in politics. FBI officials finally took his name off their list of Key Activists. But he was not free of the bureau's surveillance apparatus.

25

At Bayonet Point

The strikers stood shoulder to shoulder, blocking the path beneath the wrought-iron arch of Sather Gate. They were mostly Black, Latino, and Asian, and many wore olive-green army surplus jackets, combat boots, and black gloves. Some gripped heavy wooden stakes.

A blond-haired student hurrying to class tried to cut through. The pickets shoved him back, knocking his volume of Cicero's *Orations* to the ground. Other students and professors tried to pass and fists flew. There was a clunk and a hiss, and a tear-gas canister spewed white fumes as police charged and the pickets scattered. Some ran down the corridors of Dwinelle Hall, smashing classroom windows and sweeping books off desks. A fire alarm rang in nearby Barrows Hall, and a stink bomb forced the evacuation of Sproul Hall. Regrouping later at the student union building, strike leaders vowed to "close this goddamn place down."

It was January 28, 1969, and this was the latest action of the Third World Liberation Front, an extraordinary coalition of militant minority student groups demanding that the administration establish an ethnic studies college. Some TWLF leaders had been inspired by Mario Savio and the Free Speech Movement. But where the FSM had used nonviolent sit-ins to affirm the right to advocate on campus for off-campus causes such as civil rights, the TWLF was accusing the university itself of discriminatory hiring and biased teaching that perpetuated racism throughout society. And whereas Savio never suggested protesters use violence against property or people, the TWLF was mounting what would become the campus's most violent protest to date.

Hoover ordered his agents to investigate the TWLF on the ground that it potentially threatened internal security and civil order. But one of the strike's most militant leaders had a long—and until now secret—history of working as a paid FBI informer. His name was Richard Aoki, and at the bureau's direction he had infiltrated a succession of Bay Area radical organizations. He had given the Black Panthers some of their first guns and weapons training, encouraging them on a course that would contribute to shootouts with police and the organization's demise. And during the Third World Strike, he encouraged physical confrontations that prompted Governor Reagan to take the most severe law-enforcement measures against the Berkeley campus yet—ones that ultimately would have fatal consequences.

Richard Masato Aoki had slicked-back hair, wore sunglasses even at night, and carried himself with a swagger that intimidated and intrigued even his fellow radicals. A thirty-year-old graduate student with a military background, Aoki cut a mysterious figure on campus. He spoke in such a heavy ghetto patois that people who only heard his voice assumed he was black. His identity, in fact, had been defined by dualities: he was American and he was Japanese; he was an outstanding student and he was a hoodlum; he was a revolutionary and he worked for J. Edgar Hoover.

The double standard of discrimination had forged his family's fate. At the turn of the century, his grandfather, Jitsuji Aoki, emigrated from the Hiroshima area of Japan and settled in West Oakland, in a large Japanese community known as Little Yokohama. He established a successful noodle factory, but in 1909 his brother caused a scandal by marrying Helen Gladys Emery, the daughter of Archdeacon John Emery of the Episcopal Diocese of California. Intermarriage of Caucasians and "Orientals" was barred by state law. The *San Francisco Chronicle* ran stories about Helen's "wild infatuation" with her "yellow lover," and in her Marin County town of Corte Madera people threw rocks at her.

Shozo Aoki, Jitsuji's son, was born in Oakland in 1914. He studied engineering at UC Berkeley, enlisted in the campus ROTC program, married, and on November 20, 1938, had the first of two sons, Richard. But after Japan attacked Pearl Harbor the family was packed onto a heavily guarded train with blackened windows and sent to Topaz, Utah, one of ten "relocation centers" used to imprison more than 110,000 Japanese Americans living on the West Coast during the war. Richard was just four years old, and would always remember the desert barracks ringed by barbed wire and gun turrets. He was internee number 13711-C.

The internment destroyed the family. While at Topaz, Richard's parents separated. Upon their release in 1945, the boys and their father moved to his family's home in West Oakland, which had been looted but at least not confiscated as many others had been. Disillusioned, Shozo became a small-time gangster, served time in jail, and eventually deserted his family. It was part of the great upheaval throughout Little Yokohama: Japanese residents had been uprooted, southern blacks had moved in to work at wartime shipyards, and whites had fled to Piedmont and other neighborhoods where real estate covenants excluded minorities.

Growing up in the poor black neighborhood, hearing neighbors' accounts of southern lynchings, witnessing police abuse of his friends, recalling his internment, Richard became convinced early on that "people of color in this country really get unequal treatment." He joined a gang and despite his diminutive size became known as a fierce street fighter who would boast, with characteristic bravado, "I was the baddest Oriental come out of West Oakland." He shoplifted, burgled homes, and stole car parts for "the midnight auto supply business," he recalled, and was repeatedly arrested by Oakland police for "mostly petty-type stuff." Still, he managed to graduate from Herbert Hoover Junior High School as co-valedictorian.

Despite the stigma against divorce, Richard's mother, Toshiko, left Shozo and won custody of her sons and moved the family to the Berkeley flats. At Berkeley High School, Richard became president of the Stamp and Coin Club and did well academically—he had "career ambitions," he would say. But he got into trouble again when he assaulted another student in the hall and, as he recalled, "beat him half to death." Three days after graduating in January 1957, Richard reported for duty at Fort Ord, near Monterey. He had enlisted in the U.S. Army the prior year, at age seventeen. He gave friends various explanations for his decision, but would later tell this author that he had "cut a deal" in which authorities agreed to seal his juvenile record.

Aoki harbored ambitions of becoming the army's first Asian American general. He served about a year of active duty as an infantryman and a medic and seven more in the reserves. Although he never saw combat he became a firearms expert. "I got to play with all the toys I wanted to play with when I was growing up. Pistols, rifles, machine guns, mortars, rocket launchers," he said. "Sometimes they let me play with the tank." In 1964, however, he took an honorable discharge as a sergeant. As Aoki told it, in his last years of service he began to question the war in Vietnam and turned down the army's offer of a commission. So it was only natural that the following year he became involved with the Vietnam Day Committee, he claimed, and at this point began to explore left-wing political groups. "I methodically went through the organizations, went to their meetings, talked to their people, and started getting an idea of where they were at politically, before

I made the decision to join the SWP," or Socialist Workers Party, he told the author.

In fact, Aoki had been deeply involved in left-wing political organizations for years at the behest of the FBI. He had been recruited as an informer in the late 1950s by Burney Threadgill, one of the agents who worked with Don Jones at the bureau's Berkeley office. Threadgill approached Aoki after an FBI wiretap on the home phone of Saul and Billie Wachter, local members of the Communist Party, picked up his conversation with his fellow Berkeley High classmate Doug Wachter, who in a few years would be subpoenaed to testify before HUAC at San Francisco City Hall. Soft-spoken and sympathetic, Threadgill asked Aoki how he felt about the Soviet Union, and the young man replied that he had no interest in communism. "I said, 'Well, why don't you just go to some of the meetings and tell me who's there and what they talked about?' Very pleasant little guy. He always wore dark glasses. I got to know him," the retired agent recalled in an interview. "I developed him." According to Threadgill, it was at the bureau's direction that Aoki began to attend meetings of political organizations. "The activities he got involved in," he said, "was because of us using him as an informant."

Aoki's undercover activities followed a pattern similar to that of other FBI informers, in which they established credentials in a left-wing organization and used them as entrée to other groups. Initially, he gathered information about the Communist Party, Threadgill said. (Aoki had what he called a "personal beef" with the Communist Party because it had supported the Japanese internment; J. Edgar Hoover, on the other hand, had opposed the internment.) But Aoki soon focused on the Socialist Workers Party and the Young Socialist Alliance. The FBI was in the midst of a massive investigation of the SWP and, according to a subsequent court ruling, one in ten of its members was actually an FBI informer. Aoki met regularly with Threadgill. As Threadgill recalled, "I'd call him and say, 'When do you want to get together?' I'd say, 'I'll meet you on the street corner at so-and-so and so on.' I would park a couple of blocks away and get out and go and sit down and talk to him." Other times, Aoki filed reports by phone. Threadgill worked with Aoki through mid-1965, when he transferred to a different FBI office and turned him over to a fellow agent. Aoki was well positioned to inform on a wide range of activists in Berkeley—and especially on their connections to foreign students and organizations, a subject of special interest to the FBI. "He was one of the best sources we had," Threadgill said. "Oh yeah, he was a character."

FBI records trace Aoki's political steps: In the fifties he was associated with the Labor Youth League, the youth organization created by the Communist Party. On October 1, 1961, he was officially accepted as a member of the Berkeley branch of the Young Socialist Alliance. The following spring he was elected to the group's executive council. By December 1962, he also had become a member of the Oakland-Berkeley Branch of the SWP. Aoki served as the socialists' liaison to Bay Area civil rights groups, including the Committee to Uphold the Right to Travel, which was formed to support students who traveled to Cuba in defiance of the State Department's ban.

Although he was a student at Merritt College, Aoki was spending a lot of time around the Berkeley campus. He was there when Savio and other students captured the police car in October 1964, he would say, but chose not to get involved. The following year, however, he joined the Vietnam Day Committee and worked on its international committee, handling correspondence from antiwar groups in Asia, Africa, and Latin America. As a result, he recalled, "I had networked with a lot of people overseas and a lot of the foreign students at UC Berkeley who were radical." Now Aoki was perfectly positioned to inform on a wide range of organizations and people in Berkeley.

When this author asked Aoki whether he had been an FBI informer, during a lengthy interview about his life in 2007, Aoki's first response was a long silence. After a while he replied, " 'Oh' is all I can say." When this author asked if he was wrong in understanding that Aoki had been an informer, he replied, "I think you are." But Aoki added, as if by way of explanation, "People change. It is complex. Layer upon layer." When pressed further for a yes or a no, Aoki again replied indirectly, saying, "I'm denying it. Or 'no comment' is the standard response, I think."

Aoki's role as an informer is especially significant in light of events then unfolding at Merritt College. There he met Huey Newton, a prelaw student who was the younger brother of an old friend from West Oakland, Melvin Newton. "We prowled the streets a lot together. Got into a lot of trouble," he said of Huey Newton. He also connected with Bobby Seale, a Merritt engineering student. Newton and Seale were involved in a student group called the Soul Students Advisory Council. Aoki talked politics with them and arranged for Seale to speak at a socialist meeting.

In the fall of 1966, Aoki enrolled at UC Berkeley as a junior in sociology. Meanwhile, Newton and Seale were conceptualizing the organization that would become the Black Panther Party for Self Defense. One night that October they took a draft of their ten-point political program to Aoki's Berkeley apartment to discuss it over beer and wine. Aoki soon gave the Panthers some of their first guns. As Seale recounted in his autobiography, *Seize the Time*:

> Late in November 1966, we went to a Third World brother we knew, a Japanese radical cat. He had guns for a motherfucker: .357 Magnums, 22's, 9mm's, what have you. We told him that we wanted these guns to begin to institutionalize and let black people know that we have to defend ourselves as Malcolm X said we must. We didn't have any money to buy guns. We told him that if he was a real revolutionary he better go on and give them up to us because we needed them now to begin educating the people to wage a revolutionary struggle. So he gave us an M-1 and a 9mm.

Sometime after the first of the New Year, Aoki joined the Black Panther Party and gave them more guns, according to Seale. As Aoki said, "I had a little collection and Bobby and Huey knew about it, and so when the Party was formed, I decided to turn it over to the group . . . They were planning to do shotgun patrols on the police, and they needed to be armed in order to do that . . . And so when you see the guys out there marching and everything, I'm somewhat responsible for the military slant to the organization's public image." Or as the historian Curtis Austin, author of *Up Against the Wall: Violence in the Making and Unmaking of the Black Panther Party*, commented on Aoki's arming of the Panthers, "Regardless of his motivation, he played a role in setting in motion a series of events that placed the Bay Area under worldwide scrutiny."

The following spring, the Panthers displayed guns during their "community patrols" of the police and their visit to the state capitol. The action generated wide publicity and new recruits and Black Panther chapters around the country. But though carrying unconcealed weapons was legal at the time, there is little doubt that their presence contributed to confrontations between the Panthers and the police. In October 1967, Newton was in a shootout that left him and the Oakland police officer Herbert Heanes wounded and Officer John Frey dead. In April 1968, Eldridge Cleaver and five other Panthers were involved in a firefight with Oakland police that wounded him and two officers, and killed the Black Panther Bobby Hutton. The Panthers denied the resulting criminal charges but several were convicted. Seale would later acknowledge that in other instances some Panther members broke party rules and used guns for crimes. Aoki confirmed this, adding, "I'm not exactly proud of that." By any reckoning, the use of guns brought violence, legal trouble, and discredit to the Panthers, all goals of the FBI's COINTELPRO to destroy the organization. Did Aoki help the Panthers fight for justice, or did he set them up?

During the same period Aoki was arming the Panthers, he was informing for the FBI. An FBI report on the Black Panther Party dated November 16, 1967, lists him as informant T-2. According to this report, in May 1967 he told an FBI agent that earlier in the year Newton and Seale had named him the party's minister of education. He explained that they had been fellow students at Oakland City College (which had been renamed Merritt College) and they knew he had studied the revolutionary writings of Frantz Fanon, Marcus Garvey, Malcolm X, and W.E.B. Du Bois. Newton and Seale selected him for a leadership role, he said, because of his experience in serving as chairman of a civil rights organization at UC Berkeley that had been started by the Socialist Workers Party.

But at the time Aoki told few people on campus he was a Black Panther. "I played it low-key while I was a student at Berkeley," he said, "until things started moving with the various radical and ethnic groups up there, which became the Third World Liberation Front."

In the spring of 1968, while Savio was campaigning for state senate and Hoover was targeting him for disruption, Reagan embarked on another national fund-raising tour, while still maintaining he was a "non-candidate" for the Republican presidential nomination. The fifty-seven-year-old governor declared that "the nation is totally out of control"; that if the Paris peace talks with the North Vietnamese failed, the United States should "kick the devil out of them"; and that Democratic leaders were permitting America to lose the arms race. All the while he attacked campus unrest. University administrators had "abdicated their authority," he charged, to "rabblerousers and hatemongers, members of the New Left who are really unwashed members of the old right, practicing stormtrooper tactics." Their protests, he said, "have nothing to do with civil rights or equal treatment." Everywhere he was met by cheers and REAGAN FOR PRESIDENT placards, but he did not officially announce his candidacy until the Republican National Convention that August in Miami Beach, Florida. Although he lost the nomination to Richard Nixon, he further established himself as a national contender and once again delivered his message to college students: "Obey the rules or get out."

So in September he was extremely disturbed to learn that UC Berkeley administrators had approved a course titled "Social Analysis 139X—Dehumanization and Regeneration in the American Social Order." It had been proposed by students and was being offered by the university's Board of Educational Development, created following the Free Speech Movement to promote experimental courses relevant to current events. The topic was to be problems of race, poverty, and justice; the principal lecturer, Eldridge Cleaver, minister of information, the Black Panther Party.

Cleaver already was notorious. He had served time in Folsom Prison and after being paroled published *Soul on Ice*, a memoir in which he said he had raped as "an insurrectionary act" but realized upon reflection in prison that it was morally wrong. Critically acclaimed, the book became a bestseller in 1968. But that April the thirty-three-year-old Cleaver was involved in the fatal shootout with Oakland police. While Cleaver was free on bail and awaiting trial, plans were made for his lectures at Berkeley.

Reagan denounced the university administration and threatened an investigation of the school from "top to bottom." He declared, "If Eldridge Cleaver is allowed to teach our children, they may come home one night and slit our throats." For his part, Cleaver gleefully led students in chants of "Fuck Reagan." In one speech he proclaimed, "Ronald Reagan is a punk, a sissy, and a coward, and I challenge him to a duel to the death or until he says Uncle Eldridge. I give him a choice of weapons—a gun, a knife, a baseball bat, or marshmallows." Hoover heightened the conflict: on his orders, FBI agents transcribed one of Cleaver's speeches criticizing Reagan in obscene terms and anonymously mailed one hundred copies to school officials, clergymen, alumni associations, and Rotarians. As one agent wrote, "Objective is to bring pressure to bear upon academic administrators to deny Cleaver a forum for future diatribes."

University officials hastened to explain that Cleaver would merely be a guest speaker, not a salaried professor. But the regents denied credit for the course and censured the staff who had approved it. This prompted the Academic Senate to rebuke the regents for infringing on academic freedom and sparked a sit-in at Sproul Hall, where 122 people were arrested. The next day, 1,500 protesters marched from Sproul Plaza to Moses Hall, where some barged into offices, temporarily trapping a dean and barricading the doors with furniture. Edwin Meese III, Reagan's aide, led police into the building to arrest 77 demonstrators.

But after all that, the Panther's first talk was noteworthy mainly for its dearth of obscenities. Moreover, he never finished the course: in November 1968, he absconded while on bail in the shooting case. He took sanctuary in Algeria, where he would later welcome another man wanted by the FBI, Timothy Leary, who had escaped from a minimum-security California state prison where he was serving time for possession of marijuana. Leary's North African sojourn had been facilitated by Stew Albert, the former Vietnam Day Committee leader, who would recall it as a bizarre interlude involving guns, LSD, and sunburn.

Reagan was still fuming about the Cleaver course when he arrived in Berkeley for the monthly regents' meeting on January 17, 1969. He found the students upset, too, though for different reasons. Peering through the plate-glass windows on the ground floor of University Hall that Friday morning, Reagan could see hundreds of demonstrators outside the building. They were protesting what they called racist university policies and demanding more courses in ethnic studies. Some carried signs showing their solidarity with strikers at San Francisco State College who were making similar demands there.

By now Berkeley was ripe for racial conflict. When Roger Heyns became chancellor in 1965, he was astonished to find so few minority students, so few programs to help them, and so few courses addressing the minority experience. He launched several reforms, including an Educational Opportunity Program that offered financial and academic aid. But the statistics remained stark: of some 26,000 UC Berkeley students who responded to an official survey, roughly 800 identified themselves as Afro-American, 315 as Chicano, and 40 as Native American. Together they comprised less than 5 percent of the student body, a proportion far lower than their combined share of the state population.

Students began to organize. In May 1968, the Afro-American Students Union, led by Charles Brown and Jim Nabors, sent Heyns a detailed proposal for a black studies program. They charged that the university furthered racial discrimination through curriculums that denigrated black history and culture. They called for a program that would offer an undergraduate degree in black studies, with courses such as Introduction to Black Anthropology, Economics and Racism, and Police in the Black Community. Minority students would be preferred, but whites would not be excluded. "We demand a program of 'Black Studies,'" they declared, "a program which will be of, by and for black people." Heyns took it under consideration.

Meanwhile, other students at Berkeley formed the Asian American Political Alliance. One of the nation's first Asian activist student groups, its driving forces were Yuji Ichioka, a UC Berkeley graduate student who had been interned, and his wife, Emma Gee, who had participated in Mississippi Freedom Summer. Ichioka coined the term "Asian American" to emphasize the group's pan-Asian nature and to unite Japanese, Chinese, Filipinos, and Koreans—whom whites tended to lump together but who had disparate histories and rarely cooperated with one another. Ichioka and other AAPA members despised the label "Oriental" as the equivalent of "nigger." They rejected the stereotype of Asians as the hardworking and submissive "model minority." The AAPA aligned itself with all minority groups, declaring, "We believe that American society is historically racist . . . exploiting all non-white people in the process of building up their affluent society."

At about the same time, the Mexican-American Student Confederation formed a campus chapter. Ysidro Macias, an undergraduate from Salinas, in California's Central Valley, placed an ad in *The Daily Californian* and a handful of students responded. Macias became the chapter's president and Manuel Delgado its vice president. The new MASC members debated what it meant to be "Chicano"—Were you Mexican because of your heritage? American because of your birthplace? Concluding that a Chicano was neither one but some of both, they embraced their unique identity. Their threat of a picket prompted the owner of a Telegraph Avenue taqueria to abandon his logo, a stereotypically fat, happy Mexican in serape and sombrero. They convinced campus officials to expand the Educational Opportunity Program to include more Chicanos. They sat in at the office of President Charles Hitch to protest the university's purchase of grapes being boycotted by Cesar Chavez's United Farm Workers. Eleven students were arrested, and when some refused bail and began a hunger strike in jail, about five hundred students marched across campus in support. In October 1968, the university agreed to stop serving grapes in its cafeterias and to establish a Chicano studies center.

Racial tension at Berkeley had been further heightened by an acute awareness of the violent student strike across the bay at San Francisco State College, where minority students already had formed a separate Third World Liberation Front and were demanding their own ethnic studies school. The most prominent of several protests for ethnic studies at colleges around the country, it had begun in early November and led to continuous confrontations between police and students, numerous arrests, and the school's closing for more than a week. On January 5, 1969, Reagan declared he would use force to keep San Francisco State open. "Those who want to get an education, those who want to teach, should be

protected in that at the point of a bayonet if necessary," he said in an impromptu interview at a Sacramento airport. "It has to be kept open if you
have to surround the college with whatever force is necessary. I don't care
what force it takes. That force must be applied."

Reagan's remarks instantly drew criticism as being needlessly provocative. The governor's press officer sought to soften his point. Reagan himself
noted he had used the "bayonet" phrase during his gubernatorial campaign to explain his position on civil rights. He had said then that—
though he would have voted against the U.S. Civil Rights Act of 1964 because he believed it contained unconstitutional measures—he opposed
racial prejudice: "I think that the position of government should be that
there are no hyphenated citizens and that every citizen is exactly equal
before the law and entitled to everything that the Constitution guarantees
any citizen, and it is the responsibility of government, at the point of bayonet if necessary, to see that every citizen gets those constitutional rights."

He was alluding to President Eisenhower's historic 1957 decision to
send U.S. Army troops to Little Rock, Arkansas, to enforce a court order,
over the objections of local whites led by Governor Orval Faubus, affirming that blacks had the right to attend a public high school there. But
Reagan's reference to bayonets now had a twist: it not only emphasized his
tough stance against campus protests, but appealed to white resentment of
civil rights laws.

By mid-January 1969, members of the Afro-American Student Union at
Berkeley had become frustrated. Nine months had passed since the AASU
submitted its proposal, and though the campus administration finally
agreed to establish a black studies program, the students believed the result
was greatly diluted. In an angry letter published in *The Daily Californian*,
AASU members declared, "We are asking for a completely autonomous
department of black studies to be wholly controlled by black people. Masters (managers) know that the slaves will wait no longer!"

The AASU decided to mount a strike and sought to enlist the Mexican-
American Student Confederation and the Asian American Political Alliance. In closed meetings, the black students argued that it served the other
groups' interests to join in. But the groups were suspicious of one another.
The Asians and Chicanos questioned whether the blacks would share
power. The Chicanos complained that the blacks had not supported their
grape protest. Some of the blacks and Chicanos doubted the Asian students
were tough enough to be good allies.

The discussions were an awakening. Delgado, for one, realized that he had held racist attitudes. He recalled growing up thinking that "blacks were bad off because they didn't work hard enough." He was struck by the fact that this was the first time he had spoken with any Asian person other than the shopkeeper in his childhood barrio. He had always seen Asians as passive and conservative. Yet here was Richard Aoki of the AAPA boldly arguing that banding together was the only hope minority groups had for achieving equality.

Despite their differences, the students found common cause in their conviction that the university wrongly excluded minority students and faculty and that the curriculum failed to reflect the experience of their people. They voted to form a single organization in which they would share power equally and were soon joined by the Native American Student Union. They set up a central committee to direct their new organization, naming it, like the strike organization at San Francisco State, the Third World Liberation Front.

In contrast to most white student radicals at Berkeley, Aoki and the other TWLF leaders were older and had personally experienced discrimination, poverty, and the criminal justice system. Charles Brown, of the Afro-American Student Union, came from a poor part of Los Angeles and had served in the Coast Guard. Don Davis, also with AASU, had served in the navy. LaNada Means, of the Native American Student Union, was a member of the Shoshone-Bannock tribe and had grown up on an Indian reservation in Idaho and in government boarding schools. Ysidro Macias, of MASC, had served with the army in Korea.

Manuel Delgado sported a Pancho Villa mustache, but as one reporter noted, he looked "more like a matinee idol than a desperado." The cofounder of the campus MASC chapter had grown up in San Bernardino and run with violent gangs in the barrio, where he was known as "Mad Dog." As a teenager he stabbed a man at a dance and spent time in juvenile hall for shooting at a car full of other gang members. He served briefly in the National Guard. Dropping out of San Bernardino High School, he planned to live in the barrio and work as a carpenter. But he contracted Valley Fever and during rehabilitation attended the local community college, earning grades that qualified him for a transfer to the University of California to study architecture. It was the kind of upward opportunity envisioned in Clark Kerr's Master Plan for Higher Education, but Delgado was as much drawn to Berkeley because he had read about the Free Speech Movement and admired Mario Savio.

Arriving for winter term 1968, he wrote in his memoir, *The Last*

Chicano: A Mexican American Experience, was like "entering a three ring circus." He stepped off the bus at Bancroft and Telegraph and onto the strip, teeming with students carrying books. Young people were engaged in vehement political arguments around the folding tables that offered radical leaflets and lined Sproul Plaza all the way to Sather Gate. Looking around, he saw posters lionizing Mao, Castro, and Ho Chi Minh. Activists in costumes satirized the Selective Service director, General Hershey, as "General Hershey Bar" and General Westmoreland as "General Waste-more-land." Peter Camejo, a leader of the Young Socialists Alliance, stood atop a wall, denouncing U.S. imperialism. A Christian evangelist displayed a sign urging students to "Win with Jesus." Gone were the horn-rimmed spectacles and crew cuts of the early sixties; the students now favored wire-rimmed "granny glasses," loose, flowing clothes, and long, uncombed hair. Women, he noticed, went braless.

Delgado attended an orientation session for new students, then made his way down Telegraph Avenue, past curbside vendors offering macramé, tie-died T-shirts, and Buddhist literature. The kids were mostly white and more than a few were panhandling. Black men and white women were hanging out together, something he'd never seen before. He rented a furnished room for $75 above Sandwiches-a-Go-Go, across Bancroft Way from the student union building, and by day attended large lecture classes and by night parties where pot smoke and political talk filled the room. That term, the campus chapter of Students for a Democratic Society screened *The Battle of Algiers,* a dramatization of the Algerian guerillas' terrorist campaign to oust the French colonialists in the late fifties, which he took as a "textbook" for student radicals. In the following months, the political mood on campus got edgier as the war escalated, King and Kennedy were assassinated, and police brutality outside the 1968 Democratic National Convention in Chicago was televised for all to see. Soon Delgado was a leader of the Third World Liberation Front.

"The politically charged Berkeley atmosphere," he would say, "made everything seem possible."

Outside University Hall that Friday, the crowd had been restrained until some students saw the governor inside and yelled, "Look, it's Ronnie!" Soon the throng had taken up Cleaver's chant of "Fuck Reagan." Reagan smiled and, according to an account in *The Daily Californian,* outstretched his middle finger. Several minutes later, protesters on the other side of the building surged toward an entrance and shattered the glass doors. Calm was soon restored, but after the meeting students threw eggs at Reagan as he climbed into his limousine. A young blond girl in a miniskirt was poised to heave another as he drove off.

Two days later, the central committee of the Third World Liberation Front held a mass meeting in Dwinelle Hall where a capacity crowd voted to strike. The TWLF leaders had upped the ante: they now demanded not just an ethnic studies department but creation of a Third World College on campus by next fall, with separate departments of Asian, Afro-American, Mexican-American, and Native American studies. They also asked that more Third World people be placed in positions of power throughout the university; that Third World programs be put under control of Third World people; and that the university guarantee admission and financial aid for all Third World applicants.

Chancellor Heyns himself was frustrated with the slow pace of reform. His anguish was visible at a press conference where he acknowledged that the TWLF's demands reflected worthy goals but insisted there was no need for a strike. With gray hair and eyes framed by horn-rimmed glasses, the chancellor painstakingly detailed his administration's efforts to meet minority needs. The Educational Opportunity Program he had started in 1965 now served 800 minority and disadvantaged students, constituting one of the nation's best rates. A program to help prepare high school students for the university enrolled 165 students. The number of minority graduate students had increased from 158 in 1966 to more than 300. Moreover, at the request of the Afro-American Student Union, eight black studies courses had been added to the curriculum.

As to the AASU's earlier demands, Heyns said the administration had approved a program that would offer a bachelor's degree starting in the fall of 1969. Campus officials, moreover, had recommended creating a formal Department of Afro-American Studies with the same autonomy as other departments. While conceding there was much more to be done, Heyns said, "The point should be clear . . . the campus has been working vigorously to make the institution more responsive to the needs of the minority students." Troublemakers were just trying to mimic San Francisco State's protests, he claimed, warning that he would not hesitate to call in police to keep the campus open. He pleaded with students not to strike.

On the eve of the strike deadline, TWLF leaders rejected Heyns's entreaty. At a mass meeting inside Pauley Ballroom, Delgado asserted that all of these accomplishments were "meaningless" because they had not changed the structure of the university as an institution that had perpetuated discrimination. "What we're asking for is control," he said at the January 21 gathering. "We want our own college, which we control, books, courses, faculty, and admissions requirements." At stake was nothing less than the right to self-determination, "the right to write history." He urged the predominantly white audience to support the strike, warning, "The longer you wait to come into the strike, the more possibility that the strike will become something that we don't want it to be."

The strike lurched to a shaky start the next morning. The protesters picked up statements of support from officials of four unions representing campus employees and from several dozen faculty members. Nonetheless, classroom attendance that Wednesday was barely affected. At most, some three hundred students and supporters picketed at noon, mainly at Sather Gate. Undercover intelligence officers from the Alameda County District Attorney's Office circulated through the crowd and identified Jack Weinberg, Tom Hayden, Stew Albert, and Assemblyman Willie Brown. They also noted there were a few scuffles between strikers and "fraternity types."

That night, a fire erupted in the main auditorium inside Wheeler Hall, just beyond Sather Gate, filling the stately granite structure with flames that could be seen from Oakland. Among those forced to flee the four-story building were students in a poetry class taught by Professor Peter Dale Scott, an antiwar activist. The fire gutted the grand auditorium but spared surrounding classrooms because it burned upward through the coffered wooden ceiling and huge skylight.

Heyns called it arson. A TWLF spokesman deplored the fire and disavowed any role in it, saying the group's intent was not to destroy but "to open public property to all people." Strikers suggested the fire could have been set to discredit them. Years later, Richard Aoki told the author, "Our official version is there was some mishap or something, and it caught fire." He added, "That's the one we stuck to." He said he did not know who set the fire, but "if I knew, I'd give 'em a medal."

The next day fewer people joined the picket lines, and during the following week support for the strike dwindled, which was attributed partly to student disgust about the fire and partly to the inclement weather.

Despairing, Aoki and the other strike leaders met at their makeshift headquarters in the university's Chicano Center, a house on Channing Way near Telegraph Avenue, a few blocks from campus, where a Mexican flag hung above the front door. They were chagrined at the low turnout, even by minority students. They knew they needed strong support from white students for the strike to be effective—but few whites seemed ready to strike for ethnic studies.

Delgado proposed changing tactics from informational picket lines to physically blocking pathways to classes: protesters would lock arms and force confrontations with students who tried to pass. This, he argued, would provoke police to make arrests, which would generate broader student support.

Someone voiced concern that many people would get hurt, but Aoki promptly backed the idea. "Yeah, I'll do it," he said, "and I'll direct the action on the street." When strike leaders met a few days later at the student union to review their plan, Delgado said the pickets should apply "militant, nonviolent resistance." But Aoki, carrying a long stick, and wearing a leather jacket and dark sunglasses, declared, "I'm ready to kick jock ass."

On signal, the pickets at the main campus entrance at Bancroft and Telegraph locked arms, blocking the path. As they had expected, clean-cut fraternity types tried to crash through the line, some muttering racial epithets. The pickets repelled them. One striker knocked down a professor who tried to pass. A squad of campus and City of Berkeley police arrived and used their clubs to push the strikers back toward Ludwig's Fountain in the middle of the plaza. "Pigs off campus!" the pickets yelled.

As the strikers had hoped, the police response attracted more protesters. The next day, about a hundred pickets blocked access at the Bancroft and Telegraph entry while another hundred blocked Sather Gate. Some wore army surplus helmets and carried sticks. The mood was tense. They shouted, "On strike! Shut it down!"

Mario Savio suddenly appeared on the picket line. No longer a student, he had kept away from campus controversies. He had taken a job at Cody's, one of the city's best-known bookstores, a few blocks down Telegraph Avenue from campus, working thirty hours a week to leave himself some badly needed personal time. A poem he published in *The Daily Californian* that week reflected the internal conflicts that continued to roil him—and his concern for racial justice. Titled "Baby Talk," it began,

What I would say is not for clapping made—nor for a grade,
But only for a god obeyed.
Demonstrators in a dream are brothers,
Demons black,
White and perfect others,

Perfect whites are traitors to their brothers,
Traitors for the pay of others . . .
The child unto the parent-monster talks,
The monster-parent breaks its run, The Parent walks.

But though he stopped by to show his support for the cause, as he had at the Navy ROTC protest two years earlier, when he wound up getting arrested and missed his baby boy's birthday party, this time he stayed only briefly and hurried off to work.

Within hours the conflict escalated. As he had warned, Heyns summoned more police under the mutual-aid plan, and some sixty officers from the Alameda County Sheriff's Office, the California Highway Patrol, and local police departments marched down Bancroft Avenue, batons in hand. They ordered the pickets at Bancroft and Telegraph to disperse, then waded into the crowd. Retreating, the protesters joined the other line at Sather Gate, where officers again dispersed them.

The demonstrators regrouped into a long serpentine line, eventually numbering more than a thousand people, and marched four abreast around the campus. Again protesters swept through Dwinelle Hall, disrupting classes and breaking windows. There was an arson attempt that morning at Girton Hall, the senior women's building, where seven gasoline-filled bottles stopped with rags were ignited with little damage. Around noon someone phoned in a fire threat to Wheeler Hall, but it was a false alarm.

This pattern continued in the following days, as the weather turned so uncharacteristically cold that snow fell on the hills east of campus. As soon as police dispersed people on the picket lines, they regrouped into "snake dances," winding around campus, chanting "Power to the People!" Grim-faced police lined either side of Sather Gate to keep the passage open. Strikers and nonstrikers sporadically scuffled. Sheriff's deputies—employing Edwin Meese III's technique of singling out protest leaders—made the first two arrests of the strike, on charges of blocking a thoroughfare.

Aoki, speaking at a January 30 press conference, charged that "there was no illegal activities [sic] that necessitated the invasion of police on the campus Tuesday." Delgado claimed the strike was now "very successful." Support had, in fact, grown. The student senate voted to back the strike demands. *The Daily Californian* deplored the violence but editorialized in support of the TWLF's goals. In a letter to the editor, one student contended the blockades were invaluable if only for showing white students "what the black man has faced for centuries: the denial of his rights as a member of the community." But many students resented the strike. In their letters they complained that strikers had shoved them for no reason; that they had paid their fees and had a right to attend class; that minority students "nurtured too long by a Welfare Society" were again demanding special treatment. "If you truly want your own school then go build it," said a coed calling herself a "true WASP." The picket lines grew longer, but classes were still largely unaffected.

Appearing before the Academic Senate, Heyns made his strongest criticism of the strike to date. He bitterly complained that since it began, the campus had been riven by "the predictable pattern of disruption and provocation." There had been seven arson attempts, vandalism to fourteen buildings, at least four charges of battery, and several bomb threats. "Let there be no mistake about the phenomenon we are dealing with, or the intentions of those making some of the operating decisions," he said, vowing, "We will continue to seek warrants for the arrest of anyone who violates the law."

Dissatisfied, Sheriff Frank Madigan sent an angry letter to Reagan and the regents accusing the chancellor of failing to control the protests. Madigan complained that activists continued to use the Berkeley campus as a "staging ground" for demonstrations that had exhausted local police resources.

In the midst of it all, Manuel Delgado received a phone call saying that some of the black strike leaders had "kidnapped" Richard Rodriguez and were holding him in an apartment on Shattuck Avenue. Rodriguez was on the staff of the university's YMCA at Stiles Hall, Delgado's trusted colleague, and one of the more moderate strike leaders. Rushing over, Delgado found Rodriguez seated in the middle of a room as if being interrogated, as several blacks looked on and Aoki hovered over him. "We're going to kill this motherfucking snitch," Aoki said, slapping Rodriguez across the face.

Delgado stepped between them, took Rodriguez, and left. Aoki later explained, "Some of us felt that he was a mole for the administration, because he was constantly throwing water on our plans. Rodriguez was perceived as being one of the soft people." Afterward, Aoki sought to assuage Delgado, revealing that he was secretly a member of the Black Panthers and it was his "job" to stay close to the black strikers to make sure they weren't unduly influenced by black nationalists who were rivals of the Panthers. "That's why it looks like I'm on their side all the time," he said. Delgado remained suspicious of Aoki, however, because he "seemed to be playing two sides on the Central Committee."

On Tuesday, February 4, pickets beat several nonstrikers with sticks and umbrellas as they tried to walk through a stationary picket line at the Bancroft and Telegraph entrance. Campus police moved in to break it up, and about four hundred pickets regrouped at Sather Gate.

Sheriff Madigan deployed a new version of Meese's selective-arrest technique. With a sudden blast of an air horn, two plainclothes officers who had slipped in among the strikers grabbed a leader and tried to arrest him. The crowd contracted and strikers started beating the officers. They fought back with blackjacks but were outnumbered. One officer lost control of his pistol, and students gaped as it skidded across Sproul Plaza.

A squad of sheriff's deputies in blue jumpsuits and riot gear charged into the crowd and rescued their colleagues amid a hail of tomatoes, cans, and rocks. Glenn Dyer, one of Madigan's aides, later acknowledged that this was a "highly hazardous tactic." "Obviously, when tension is high the risks of plainclothes officers making arrests within a mob are great," he said at a police conference. "Officers were injured, stitches and casts were required, but the gains more than offset the losses." The technique "softened up the hard core opposition," he said. "Psychologically, this tactic has an obvious effect on the dissidents, they don't know who amongst them in the mob is a peace officer."

Strikers and nonstrikers meanwhile fought at Dwinelle Hall. Winding through Doe Library, demonstrators shouted and dumped card catalogs on the floor, while others snaked through Wheeler Hall, overturning large ceramic ashtrays and smashing windows. Deputies chased them onto Sproul Plaza, swinging clubs. About a hundred people spilled off campus and into the intersection at Bancroft and Telegraph, where they blocked traffic and started a bonfire.

By day's end twenty people were arrested. At least five students were treated for injuries, and two deputies were hospitalized. During the melee, strikers began calling the sheriff's deputies "Blue Meanies," borrowing the name from "Yellow Submarine," the recently released, animated movie based on the Beatles' songs, in which the music-hating Blue Meanies attack a paradise called Pepperland.

In his Sacramento office the next day, Reagan proclaimed a "state of extreme emergency" on the Berkeley campus, authorizing officers of the California Highway Patrol to help maintain order there "as long as may be necessary." He had invoked the state disaster code, which defines "state of extreme emergency" as "conditions of extreme peril to the safety of persons and property . . . caused by an enemy attack or threatened attack or other cause."

The extraordinary measure placed all state and local law-enforcement officials in the area under the direct control of the governor. Reagan, in turn, delegated their day-to-day control to Sheriff Madigan, empowering him to request as many officers as needed. Fifty CHP patrolmen were immediately dispatched to the campus. Edwin Meese III, in charge of planning the governor's response, told reporters the officers could remain there indefinitely.

At a press conference, Reagan said he was acting with the concurrence of university officials. "I just feel we have come to the end of the road in depending on local law enforcement on campuses," Reagan said. "It isn't good enough anymore to wait until the rocks are flying and the beatings start. The campus must be free of violence, threats, and intimidation."

Five days later, Reagan addressed a meeting of nearly five hundred law-enforcement officers, military officials, and intelligence agents from throughout California. They had quietly gathered at the El Dorado Hotel in Sacramento, where, just two years earlier, Reagan and his wife, Nancy, had danced at a gala ball to celebrate his election. Now the governor was inaugurating a secretive training session for putting down civil disturbances like the TWLF.

The February 10, 1969, conference was meant to improve coordination between local police agencies and the state's Military Department. In the wake of riots and antiwar protests spreading throughout the nation, President Johnson had ordered the U.S. Army to develop a centralized contingency plan for military intervention and to fund state planning efforts. Code-named "Cable Splicer," the California operation called for a series of "paper exercises" in which police and state military officials responded to hypothetical civil disturbances, one of which involved minority protesters setting fire to school buildings. In each scenario, local police departments responded to an incident, set up a command post, collected intelligence, and dispatched officers. As the "disturbance" escalated, they summoned outside help and coordinated with other agencies. Ultimately, some scenarios required deployment of the California National Guard.

The meeting at the El Dorado was conducted circumspectly. Military officials were instructed to wear civilian clothing "to prevent adverse publicity or misleading psychological effects." Participants were told to destroy exercise directives "in accordance with current regulations pertaining to documents identified 'For Official Use Only.'" There was no advance publicity, and selected reporters were permitted to cover Reagan's presentation only. Even then, the scope of the operation was downplayed. "No mention of Cable Splicer . . . to be made during any portion of the orientation," said a terse directive to conference participants. As a result, the operation received scant public attention.

Reagan was present in his capacity as commander in chief of the state's police agencies and its Military Department, which consisted of the California contingents of the National Guard. As governor, he had authority to proclaim emergencies, impose curfews, and deploy these forces. With him were Edwin Meese III and Major General Glenn C. Ames, commander of the State Military Department. Reagan had hoped J. Edgar Hoover would join them, but though the ever-cautious FBI director was listed in the tentative agenda as the main speaker, he did not appear. So after everyone stood for the Pledge of Allegiance and the state military chaplain gave the invocation, Reagan delivered the keynote speech in his place.

"You know there are some people in the state who, if they could see this gathering right now, and my presence here, would decide their worst fears and convictions had been realized—I was planning a military takeover," he joked as he began.

"I am supposed to say a few words of welcome and perhaps mention the subject that has brought you together. If I hesitate to do that, to use the term *emergency* in discussing law and order and crime, I hope you will understand I am a little fed up with emergencies lately. I have thought that it would be nice if we could lump some of our 'emergencies' together—like certain people in certain academic circles who have been of trouble lately—if we could mix them with the oil and then have the flood."

Reagan was making the same religious reference that Savio had made after the FSM's victory when he said, "Woe to him who would try to pour oil on the waters when God has brewed them into a gale"—but Reagan was using it to opposite effect.

The governor praised police and military officials for safeguarding citizens and declared that "protecting the rights of even the least individual among us is basically the only excuse government has for even existing." He noted he had been quoted recently as vowing to keep San Francisco State College open at "bayonet point." He now claimed a reporter had misquoted him, but his thrust was the same. "Some days ago I used . . . the word *bayonet* and it caused a certain reaction among a number of people. I will admit that the manner in which it was reported was somewhat distorted . . . It was done in the context of keeping our campuses open at the point of bayonets, if necessary, and I will admit that this does bring a somewhat harsh picture to mind.

"Actually, the context in which I used it, I would reaffirm, because I used it in the context of the government's responsibility to protect the people. And in answer to the question, 'Was there any limit to the force that government should use in the protection of the rights of the individual?' I used the illustration of saying, 'No, that government was obliged, at the point of a bayonet, if necessary, to preserve these rights.'" Reagan added, "I mean that."

Sheriff Madigan had done an excellent job in responding to the TWLF strike in Berkeley, the governor said, but his resources had been stretched to the limit. So Reagan declared a state of emergency on the Berkeley campus and sent in the California Highway Patrol. This had restored order, and if similar situations arise, he vowed, "there will be no delay in declaring a state of emergency on that campus . . ."

In apocalyptic terms, Reagan echoed "the speech" that had launched his political career, his 1964 talk on behalf of Barry Goldwater, in which he said in reference to the Soviet Union, "We are faced with the most evil enemy mankind has known in his long climb from the swamp to the stars." Now referring to Berkeley, he said, "You are gathered here . . . to further the kinds of plans that we have started, and to make sure that the process in the six-thousand-year history of man, of pushing the jungle back, creating a clearing where men can live in peace and go about their business with some measure of safety for themselves and for their family. You are on the firing line for that at the local and at the international level. I commend you for it, and again pledge you the all out support that we can give you in achieving your purpose. Because of late the jungle has been creeping in again a little closer to our boundaries, the boundaries of those clearings that man has created over these centuries and these thousands of years. And so I wish you Godspeed and great success . . ."

Although Hoover hadn't made it to Reagan's law-enforcement luncheon, his agents had been busy on campus. President Johnson had pushed Hoover for more intelligence on domestic dissent, and that winter President Nixon was demanding even more reporting on student activists and antiwar demonstrators. Hoover launched a new nationwide program to monitor "student agitation" that was code-named STAG, and he would soon order inquiries into every black college organization in the country.

In Berkeley, Don Jones and more than a dozen other FBI agents were investigating the TWLF strike. They continued to receive information from their longtime campus sources: Alex Sherriffs, now Reagan's top education aide, provided information about the regents' deliberations; the

San Francisco Examiner reporter Ed Montgomery passed along information on the strikers; Patricia Atthowe, the Oakland-housewife-turned-private-intelligence operative, arranged for the covert filming of protesters and gave agents copies of the footage.

Professor Hardin Jones, meanwhile, was near apoplectic. He told agents that Chancellor Heyns was doing nothing to counter propaganda promoting dangerous drugs and "illicit acts of sexuality." He complained, in vivid detail, about a "pornographic . . . brutal, sadistic, inhuman and insane" political satire put on by Berkeley's Drama Department called *Ergo.* "The sex acts appeared actual," the medical physicist declared, while opining, "Probably they were simulated because of the difficulty of having performers with sufficient anatomical and responsive sexuality for the circumstances."

Don Jones and his colleagues also operated informers involved at different levels of strike activity. One informer submitted detailed reports about the picket lines. A second attended rallies and meetings of organizations supporting the strike, including the campus chapter of the nation's largest teachers' union, the American Federation of Teachers, Local 1570, which represented teaching assistants.

A third informer—whose identity the FBI also withheld in documents released under the FOIA—was active at the highest levels of the Third World Liberation Front. This informer reported on the small, closed meetings and planning sessions of the TWLF's Steering Committee; its efforts to build support with other organizations, including the Black Panthers; its private negotiations with Chancellor Heyns; and its internal discussions about tactics, including whether to intensify picketing and use violence.

Yet nothing in released FBI files shows that FBI agents ever queried any of their informers about who might have set fire to Wheeler Auditorium— even though university officials requested "any possible" help from the bureau—and the cause of the blaze was never determined.

The week after Reagan's inspirational talk to law-enforcement officers at the El Dorado Hotel, police cracked down on campus.

Thursday, February 13, 1969, began peacefully, if noisily. There was a picket line at Bancroft and Telegraph, and at the noon rally TWLF leaders excoriated Heyns, the "Blue Meanies," and Reagan. Some three hundred strikers marched in a circular picket line near Sather Gate. Within this circle was a smaller one formed by teaching assistants with AFT Local 1570.

Sheriff's deputies and highway patrolmen swept into the pickets and arrested the teaching assistants. New picket lines formed and swirled through Sproul Plaza. Police and pickets scuffled. A line of protesters snaked through the Bear's Lair student cafeteria on Lower Sproul Plaza, upending tables, throwing chairs, and knocking a student to the ground. Others charged into Doe Library and emptied card catalog trays.

Thirty-six people were arrested, most for blocking a pathway, but at least one for assaulting an officer. Madigan, who sported a natty business suit and a red feather in his hat, surveyed the scene and assured a reporter, "I have complete control of the campus as far as police functions go."

In the basement of Sproul Hall, meanwhile, sheriff's deputies delivered summary punishment to several arrestees, according to university employees who worked in offices near the police station there. They shoved one man to his knees and struck him. A few minutes later, two plainclothes officers dragged a student to a corner where an officer beat him. "Please don't hit me anymore!" the boy cried. "Won't somebody help me?" As two deputies held a black man against a wall and frisked him, a third came from behind, clubbed him, and muttered sarcastically, "Sorry about that, kid."

In the next few days, accounts of police brutality, along with the arrests of the peacefully picketing teaching assistants, triggered new support for the strike and anger at the deputies. A faculty union, Local 1474 of the American Federation of Teachers, condemned the arrests of the teaching assistants as lawless. The librarians' and clerks' unions also denounced the "unprovoked" police assaults on pickets and innocent bystanders. Professors joined the picket line for the first time, as about thirty of them carried signs that read PICKETING IS LEGAL. The Daily Californian, while condemning striker violence, declared, "The police must go. Now. They are out of control, attacking without either reason or provocation." Madigan defended his men, insisting that the teaching assistants failed to comply with orders to disperse.

As the next regents' meeting approached, strike leaders escalated their protests. On February 17, several hundred strikers marched through campus, with some of them again disrupting the library and the cafeteria. The next morning, there was more picketing and fighting. During a particularly violent episode, a squad of Alameda County sheriff's deputies surrounded Richard Aoki on the picket line. Sergeant Louis Santucci grabbed Aoki, who is shown in a photo trying to twist free. "It wasn't your civil rights thing of going limp," Aoki recalled. "I mean, we were fighting every inch of the way." He was charged with interfering with an officer but was later acquitted.

There was more violence on Wednesday, February 19. Peaceful morning pickets gave way to an unauthorized rally on Sproul Plaza. Sheriff's deputies—again employing Meese's selective-arrest tactic—plunged into the crowd. Again this tactic provoked violent reaction. As officers responded with clubs, the throng swelled to more than a thousand people. Some pelted police with rocks, bottles, and cherry bombs.

Strikers marched across campus, smashing windows. On their return to Sproul Plaza, officers charged. According to *The Daily Californian*, officers also chased some students for no apparent reason. The *San Francisco Chronicle* reported that police pursued students "like rabbits, to balconies, rooftops and into buildings, where they were trapped." There they fought hand to hand. For the first time police used Mace on campus. At one point, a protester threw a firebomb. TWLF leaders urged protesters to go home but they blocked traffic at Bancroft and Telegraph, dispersing only in mid-afternoon. Five people were injured and twenty-five were arrested. Yet despite some drop in attendance, most classes continued normally.

When the regents convened at University Hall the next day, the violence escalated. After a noon rally at Sproul Plaza about two thousand people marched to University Hall, shouting, "We want Reagan!" The mass then withdrew to Sproul Plaza, still mostly calm. Chief Thomas Houchins of the Alameda County Sheriff's Office, in charge of the police, would later claim a student threw the first tear-gas canister; others disputed this. In any event, deputies proceeded to hurl scores of tear-gas canisters, many of which students threw back. As Agent Don Jones reported, "At times, a cloud of tear gas covered a great portion of the Sproul Plaza and surrounding areas." Police forced the crowd off campus but this led to more trouble: demonstrators built a bonfire at the intersection of Bancroft and Telegraph, smashed store windows, and tipped over two police vans.

Madigan summoned backup under the mutual-aid plan and some four hundred officers from police departments around Northern California converged on the campus. By 8:00 p.m. the streets were quieted, but the university canceled night classes and locked all buildings. Twenty-six officers had been injured and seventeen people arrested in the most violent day of protest in the university's history.

That night, Reagan announced that he had directed the California National Guard to "make whatever preparations may be necessary" to help police maintain order when he attended the regents' meeting the next day.

•

At dawn the police massed at University Hall. More than seven hundred law-enforcement officers from throughout Northern California had been summoned. Alameda County sheriff's deputies took positions on rooftops overlooking the streets around University Hall. The National Guard set up a command post in a parking garage directly across the street. One thousand troops waited nearby.

Reagan's limousine approached University Hall shortly before 10:00 a.m. amid great anticipation, as it had two years earlier on the day the regents voted to fire Clark Kerr. This time, Reagan's driver passed double lines of helmeted riot police at either end of the block before pulling to a stop. Emerging from the car, Reagan paused to speak with reporters and again suggested that liberal faculty members were to blame for the student protests. He vowed to stop the demonstrations at Berkeley—"whatever it takes."

Inside University Hall that Friday, February 21, the regents considered emergency measures to quell the mounting protests. One proposal called for immediate suspension of any student upon "reasonable cause to believe" that he or she had disrupted a campus at which the governor had declared a state of emergency. Several regents objected on the ground that the measure was likely unconstitutional, but Reagan was insistent. "This is a revolution," he said. "The FBI made public a report that the tactics of the revolutionaries had been changed and that now they would participate in destruction of property, physical violence, and burn campuses if necessary." William Coblentz and William Roth, the regents about whom Hoover had earlier leaked FBI reports to Edwin Pauley, voted no, but the measure passed.

Across Oxford Street from University Hall, about three thousand students held an orderly rally. Strike monitors urged, "Keep it cool. No rocks, no cherry bombs. No confrontation with the pigs." Ysidro Macias claimed the previous day's violence had been provoked by police and "street people not connected with the strike." Ominously, he declared, "Today we are showing control of the strike. Monday it may be different." Jim Nabors of the Afro-American Student Union was more threatening. "We want the college and we'll have it. If necessary, we'll destroy this university and even the state administration because we will not compromise on our goals." The crowd roared obscenities at Reagan, but the National Guard was not deployed and the rally ended when it began to rain.

In the following days the campus remained tense. Nabors declared in a *Daily Californian* column that the strikers would never drop their demand for a Third World College. They would prevail, he vowed, "by any means necessary." The political science student was quoting Malcolm X's maxim that blacks must achieve justice—whatever it takes. The late militant leader had meant that in the face of white violence, and a government that had failed to stop it, blacks should arm themselves for self-defense as they pursued their rights. Nabors's allusion reflected the growing militancy not only of black activists but of antiwar protesters, feminists, and other movement members who also quoted the imperative. Conservatives were uttering similar oaths, albeit toward their own ends. Reagan had said, "I don't care what force it takes."

Professors and students, meanwhile, condemned excesses of both police and protesters. In one letter to *The Daily Californian*, a teaching assistant complained that strike leaders seemed to "turn violence on and off." In another letter, an activist complained that—with their "you are either for us or against us" stance—strikers used intimidation instead of intellect on their followers. "One of the reasons the FSM was successful," he wrote, "was that the leadership was careful not to exceed the radicalism of their constituency."

There were more attempted arsons of unknown origin. Strikers again locked arms, blocking Sather Gate. Sheriff's deputies again arrested strike leaders in the midst of unruly crowds, courting violent clashes. On February 28, campus police tried to arrest a striker for assaulting a student and were themselves attacked. Another campus policeman was ambushed and severely beaten. When police tried to open paths through the picket lines, demonstrators threw fruit and rocks. By late afternoon a surly mob of some seven hundred people had gathered on Sproul Plaza.

For the first time, the National Guard was deployed on campus. Eight armed troops helped sheriff's deputies and highway patrolmen sweep the plaza. Two of them were outfitted with tear-gas-dispensing backpacks; the other six carried rifles tipped with bayonets.

Soon the only people left on the rain-drenched plaza were police officers wearing gas masks.

Vandals had poured glue on all 310 seats in the Academic Senate's chamber in Lewis Hall, forcing the crucial meeting of March 4 to convene in the Physical Sciences Building.

This was the faculty body that had decisively supported the Free Speech Movement, but now it just as decisively backed the campus administration. Chancellor Heyns told the 550 professors present that he would not agree to the TWLF's demands for student control of an ethnic studies department, special admissions standards, and a "community action" unit. And in near-unanimous accord, the senate called for creating an ethnic studies department subject to regular campus rules, while recommending that its chairman report directly to Heyns and that it be structured for potential growth into a college of ethnic studies.

The strike subsided. FBI agents noted the appearance of several Black Panthers on the picket lines, but determined through a phone tap on the Panthers' Berkeley headquarters that they were there only as "extras" for a movie called *Zabriskie Point* being filmed on campus by Michelangelo Antonioni.

On March 14, the TWLF central committee debated whether to end the strike. Richard Aoki argued for escalating the violence. "I was willing to risk everything for keeping the struggle going," he told the author. "We'd have taken on the National Guard. Then it would have gotten real violent. I figured we would have gotten more if we continued it just a bit, even though the threat of massive escalation, because of bringing in of the National Guard, would've really resulted in some stuff. But we had plans. I had plans."

The plan was to steal guns from National Guard armories. "We'd have had their weapons," he said. At that time, Aoki recalled, there were "National Guard armories all over this area, stocked with that stuff, and we knew where they were. My faction was willing to take the strike to a higher level." At a meeting in Stiles Hall, however, weary strikers voted overwhelmingly to end the strike.

Strike leaders and their supporters would later say their protest hastened the establishment of the ethnic studies department and spurred other schools across the country to adopt similar curricula now accepted as a vital part of higher education. Undoubtedly, these programs have drawn more minorities to college and produced more professors of diverse ethnic backgrounds. Moreover, they have prompted people to examine human experience from a wider range of ethnic viewpoints, better preparing America to succeed as a democracy in a changing world.

But there was much violence. Although the vast majority of students never were involved in the strike, scores of protesters and police were injured. Vandalism damages totaled $125,000, according to a university estimate, and the fire at Wheeler Auditorium another $750,000. Police arrested at least 115 people, some several times. The university disciplined 195 students. Aoki would later boast that it was the longest, bloodiest, costliest student strike in the history of the university.

The FBI never has accounted for the role that its longtime informer Richard Aoki played in arming the Black Panthers and in encouraging violence during the strike. (In response to the author's inquiry and his Freedom of Information Act lawsuit, FBI officials refused to confirm or deny whether Aoki was an informant or reveal whether the bureau was withholding additional records about him.) Aoki earned a master's degree in social work at Berkeley and became an early coordinator of the Asian American Studies program there but left to join Peralta Community College in Oakland, where he taught and counseled students until retiring in 1998. In later years, he continued to advocate for racial justice and granted several interviews about his past as a militant radical. Aoki suffered from kidney disease, and on March 15, 2009, he committed suicide at age seventy by shooting himself in the stomach with a Smith & Wesson .38 Special revolver at his Berkeley home. Aoki's fellow activists, unaware that he had been an informer, honored him with a memorial held in Wheeler Hall, where he was extolled as a fearless leader and servant of the people.

The TWLF episode heightened the long-running conflict between Reagan and Berkeley. As Agent Don Jones noted in a lengthy FBI report on the strike, "considerable controversy" had arisen over the governor's charges that university administrators failed to adequately discipline students and faculty during the strike. "This is guerilla warfare," Reagan had said at one point, and "the only thing that can win in campus guerilla warfare is . . . you eliminate them by firing the faculty members or expelling the students." But according to Jones, "Almost all of the faculty members at UCB have expressed opposition to student agitational activities which result in violence, damage or terror, while expressing sympathy with constructive change in the usual process, social and political reform and orderly descent [sic]." Only two of two thousand faculty had refused to teach during the strike, Jones reported, and only one had been arrested. Moreover, the agent said, "much of the violence and damage to buildings . . . can be attributed to the 'street people'"—not students but "nomads, anarchists, unaffiliated with any formal organizations, flower children, drug users and addicts and other riffraff."

However inflammatory Reagan's allegations were during the strike, a poll showed the conflict had boosted his popularity to an all-time high.

The state of emergency remained in effect through the winter.

The National Guard was poised for action.

26

People's Park

The park was Mike Delacour's idea. He wanted to put on a free rock concert for the students, activists, and hippies who had made Telegraph Avenue and the narrow side streets just south of the campus their home. The neighborhood was crammed with bookstores, record shops, coffeehouses, cheap restaurants, and low-rent, brown-shingle apartment houses—a room with a shared kitchen and bath went for fifty dollars a month—and had become a counterculture center. Here, the *Ramparts* editor Robert Scheer remarked wryly, young people freely "practiced fornication, smoked marijuana, wrote leaflets, mobilized protests and read sinister revolutionary tracts."

Delacour, who ran the Red Square Dress Shop on Telegraph, reflected certain essential attributes of the neighborhood. He was thirty-one years old, had shoulder-length brown hair, and wore a crinkled white Indian shirt embroidered with bits of mirror. Although he'd always been an upstart, he'd tried to make it in the "straight" world. As a teenager, he was put on probation after wrecking a car in which officers found a hundred cans of beer. He dropped out of high school, got married, and fathered a child. After completing night school at eighteen, he became a mechanic's helper at General Dynamics in San Diego. During his next eight years with the defense contractor, Delacour was promoted to research and mechanical technician and helped build missile sites at Vandenberg Air Force Base. He made good money and bought a tract home in a San Diego suburb where he lived with his wife and their children, three in all. It was supposed to be the American Dream, he later said, but he wasn't happy. He worked fifty weeks a year, didn't know his neighbors, and felt no sense of community. Still only twenty-six, he divorced his wife, quit his job, and bummed around Europe, where he heard about the Free Speech Movement and decided to move to Berkeley. He became a volunteer in the Vietnam Day Committee and the voter registration drive for the Peace and Freedom Party in 1968, the year Mario Savio ran for state assembly.

But he tired of politics and turned to running the dress shop, hanging out at the Caffe Mediterraneum, and grooving on Telegraph Avenue's hippie scene.

To play at the concert, Delacour enlisted Joy of Cooking, a Berkeley rock band led by Terry Garthwaite and Toni Brown. Then he strolled around the corner from his shop to survey the large vacant lot behind the Caffe Med where he thought they could play. The site was worse than he remembered—three acres of mud holes and dust strewn with old foundations, abandoned cars, and broken glass. This is where—six months before the violence at Altamont and a year before the killings at Kent State—the end of the sixties would begin.

Lot number 1875-2, as the 270-by-450-foot parcel was officially known, was owned by the university. In 1956, Clark Kerr, then chancellor, had convinced the regents to adopt a development plan that would expand the campus by acquiring private properties around the campus, including this one. The university would exercise its power of eminent domain and raze the old two-story single-family homes and rooming houses adjacent to Telegraph Avenue, then use the land to build sports fields, auditoriums, and dormitory towers. The university's stated goal was to make the campus more hospitable for the influx of baby-boom students expected during the next decade.

The regents approved Kerr's plan but the university ran out of funds and the project stalled. The area south of campus meanwhile attracted more and more students, radicals, and disaffected young people. In reaction, the City of Berkeley's Republican administration sought to develop the locale under a federal urban renewal program for "blighted" areas and sought to show that the property amply met the criteria. A city study concluded it was "environmentally deficient . . . because of an obsolete and inefficient subdivision pattern." Police department statistics purported to show it was plagued by crime. Above all, as the *Berkeley Daily Gazette* reported, the plan's supporters were aghast "at the intrusion of the nationwide Beatnik element into their part of town, and the resulting image of Telegraph Avenue as 'America's Left Bank.'"

The redevelopment plan, however, was defeated by a coalition of merchants who feared their rents would soar, students who relied on the cheap housing, and longtime residents who wanted to keep their homes. Chancellor Roger Heyns then suggested that the university acquire lot 1875-2 to build what he publicly said was an urgently needed soccer field. But as the regent Fred Dutton later told *Ramparts* magazine, Heyns privately pitched his proposal to the regents as a way to abate a troublesome population—as "an act against the hippie culture." The board approved purchasing the lot for $1.3 million in 1967, demolished the rooming houses there, and in the following ten months the parcel fell into desuetude.

Finding the lot in such poor condition, Delacour canceled the concert. But the former aerospace mechanic was convinced the land should be made into a park for the Telegraph Avenue community and called a meeting at his dress shop on April 13, 1969. Present were Wendy Schlessinger, who had graduated from college at age nineteen and taught in the Long Island public schools before coming to Berkeley for graduate school and dropping out; Paul Glusman, an undergraduate student who had been arrested in the Moses Hall sit-in arising from the Cleaver course controversy and was known for his absurdist sense of humor (he started a campus group called "Concerned Stalinists for Peace"); and Stew Albert, who rose to prominence in the Vietnam Day Committee after the FBI sabotaged Francis Medaille. Others soon got involved, including Art Goldberg, a former Free Speech Movement leader; Jon Read, a landscape architect who had been involved in the VDC; Big Bill Miller, who ran the Steppenwolf Bar; and Frank Bardacke, a graduate student in political science at Berkeley until he was dismissed for helping to organize Stop the Draft Week. All agreed to Delacour's proposal: "Let's build a park!"

Schlessinger collected contributions from local merchants while Read gathered gardening tools, Delacour rebooked Joy of Cooking, and Albert wrote the announcement for the April 18 edition of the *Berkeley Barb*. It was an open invitation. "Hear ye, hear ye," it said. "A park will be built this Sunday between Dwight Way and Haste Street. The land is owned by the university, which tore down a lot of beautiful houses in order to build a swamp . . . We want the park to be a cultural, political freak-out and rap center for the Western world . . . The university has no right to create ugliness as a way of life . . . Nobody supervises, and the trip belongs to whoever dreams." It was signed, "Robin Hood's Park Commissioner."

On April 20, about two hundred people showed up and on a corner of the lot put down sod, planted flowers, installed children's swings and picnic tables, and built a fire pit. Joy of Cooking inaugurated the park with a concert. From a tree someone hung a sign reading POWER TO THE PEOPLE PARK, and soon everyone called the place "People's Park." Art Goldberg told *The Daily Californian* the park was a protest against "the university's effort to destroy the Telegraph Avenue community." He added, "This is the beginning of resistance. After a couple of weeks, the kids won't let anybody take away their park." Sergeant R. E. Hull of the university's police department agreed. "It is my feeling," he wrote, "the longer they are there, the harder it is going to be to dislodge them."

In that spring before Woodstock, People's Park grew. In the following days the park attracted thousands of visitors: students, hippies, sunbathing sorority girls, mothers with children, and elderly neighbors. Soon there were flower beds, saplings, shrubs, and a plot marked "People's Revolutionary Corn Garden." Anyone could bring a plant, grab a shovel, and join in; there was no formal structure and participants worked out the design as they went along. It was a return to nature, a communal act, a condemnation of bureaucracy. Here, with their own hands, people could do something positive in the face of an implacable establishment. Savio, who had grown a thick beard, was still working as a salesclerk at Cody's, just down the street, and stopped by. He liked what he saw.

Chancellor Heyns and other campus officials did not share his enthusiasm for the park just three and a half blocks from Sproul Plaza. Some neighbors had complained about the crowds and the noise—there was bongo drumming late into the night. Then there was the prosaic problem of liability: the university's acquiescence to the unauthorized use of its land would pose a major insurance risk. On April 27, exactly one week after the park opened, Heyns announced the school would proceed with plans to build a soccer field there.

That day, park supporters circulated a leaflet written by Frank Bardacke. Entitled "Who Owns the Park" and printed over the image of Geronimo cradling a long gun, the manifesto declared:

> Someday a petty official will appear with a piece of paper, called a land title, which states that the University of California owns the land of the People's Park. Where did that piece of paper come from? What is its worth?
>
> A long time ago the Costanoan Indians lived in the area now called Berkeley. They had no concept of land ownership. They believed that the land was under the care and guardianship of the people who used it and lived on it.
>
> Catholic missionaries took the land away from the Indians . . . They ripped it off in the name of God.
>
> The Mexican Government took the land away from the Church. The Mexican Government had guns and an army. God's word was not as strong . . .

The Americans . . . had a stronger army . . . and took the land. . . . All this time there were still some Indians around who claimed the land. The American army killed most of them . . .

Finally, some very rich men, who run the University of California, bought the land.

Immediately these men destroyed the houses that had been built on the land. The land went the way of so much other land in America—it became a parking lot.

We are building a park on the land. We will take care of it and guard it, in the spirit of the Costanoan Indians. When the University comes with its land title we will tell them: "Your land title is covered with blood. We won't touch it. Your people ripped off the land from the Indians a long time ago. If you want it back now, you will have to fight for it . . ."

In Sacramento, Governor Reagan's aides took note of the park at the May 9 conference of the Emergency Planning Council, a little-known committee charged with ensuring that state officials were prepared to respond to natural disasters and civil disturbances. Gathered around the conference table in the governor's chambers were representatives of the state Department of Justice, the California Highway Patrol, and the State Military Department. Edwin Meese III presided. It was his duty to oversee the administration's handling of campus protests, and the conference began by reviewing the recently completed Cable Splicer training exercise, in which police and military officials responded to a hypothetical demonstration that turned violent. The exercise had covered topics such as the deployment of police and military forces, "the fair treatment of civilians," the proper handling of prisoners, and the use of force, particularly shotguns. Training materials warned police to take extra care when pursuing snipers and other suspects who were "intermingled with innocent civilians." A report on the exercise, dated May 1, had concluded the training went well but identified several key "problem areas," including a "communications gap" between military and law-enforcement officials; delays in mobilizing military forces to support local police; and the need to ensure availability of sufficient antiriot equipment.

Meese and his colleagues at the meeting moved on to review the latest intelligence reports about potential trouble spots around the state: an antiwar rally in Chico; the Hell's Angels' possible disruption of the annual Frog Jumping Jubilee in rural Angels Camp; and antidraft protests at Stanford University. At Berkeley, Meese noted, university officials were planning to reclaim the plot of land that hippies, students, and radicals had turned into a community park. There was, according to meeting minutes, "the possibility of a demonstration in retaliation."

In the early-morning darkness of May 15, several dozen law-enforcement officers approached People's Park. A police helicopter hovered as officers pierced the interior of the park with searchlights. The occupants sounded a bugle and cried, "The pigs are gathering!"

Within minutes the park was ringed by California Highway Patrol officers and Alameda County sheriff's deputies. One of the deputies was Lawrence Riche, a twenty-four-year-old Oakland native who had joined the sheriff's department in June 1968 soon after he was discharged from the army. Like nearly a sixth of the forty-four deputies who had received urgent phone calls at their homes ordering them to report for duty that morning in full riot gear, Riche still was a probationary employee, or rookie. But though he never had been on riot control duty, he did have combat experience. He had volunteered for service in Vietnam after dropping out of New Mexico State University, where he studied music with the hope of becoming a teacher. He played trombone in the army's Ninth Division Band—he was attached to the band the whole year he was in Vietnam— and manned a helicopter machine gun during the Tet Offensive. "We couldn't see what it was that we were firing at," he later said, "but it was just any time before you came in to land you'd clear the area around your landing strip."

Riche peered into the jangle of light and shadow in People's Park. Dozens of men and women were rising from sleeping bags, scurrying past newly planted bushes, or huddling around the flames of the fire pit. Some wore helmets and carried sticks. By 5:10 a.m. everyone had left the park except for three men—two who had assumed the lotus position and one who simply said he preferred to be arrested. All three were taken into custody without incident. At 5:50 a construction crew hired by the university arrived, and while Riche and other deputies stood guard or lounged on the swing sets, the workers began erecting an eight-foot-high Cyclone fence around the park. Sergeant R. E. Hull of the university police told a fellow officer, "Everything went awfully easily."

Word that police had seized People's Park in the dead of night spread quickly, and by noon about two thousand people crammed Sproul Plaza. The Sproul Hall steps had been reserved for a rally celebrating Israel's Independence Day by the New Left Forum, a student group led by the former

Free Speech Movement activist (and later editor of *Tikkun*) Michael Lerner, but he ceded the podium to park supporters. People had been provoked by the university's act of stealth, and the crowd was large and agitated. On the steps where Mario Savio had delivered his ardent addresses almost five years earlier, several park supporters made impassioned remarks. The last was Dan Siegel, a law student and president-elect of the campus's official student government, who according to police logs began his talk at 12:36 p.m.

"Now, we have not yet exactly decided what we are going to do. But there is [*sic*] some plans. I have a suggestion, let's go down to the People's Park, because we are the people. But a couple of things, a couple of points I would like to make. If we are to win this thing, it is because we are making it more costly for the university to put up its fence than it is for them to take down their fence. What we have to do then, is maximize the cost to them, minimize the cost to us. So what that means is people be careful. Don't let those pigs beat the shit out of you. Don't let yourselves get arrested on felonies. Go down there and take the park."

Siegel would later say the microphone was disconnected and he was cut off in mid-sentence. In any event, as his last words reverberated, the crowd surged from the plaza and down Telegraph Avenue. William Donovan Rundle, Jr., felt the throng pressing around him. The son of a conservative Los Angeles insurance executive, Rundle had enrolled at UC Berkeley at age seventeen that April, and the freshman now wore striped bell-bottom pants, wire-rimmed glasses with tinted lenses, and shoulder-length hair. Like others in the crowd, he saw the park as a creative endeavor and the university's action as unfair. This was the first demonstration Rundle had joined at Berkeley, and he thought it would be "just another march . . . against injustice." But events were cascading toward what would become the most violent clash between police and protesters in Berkeley's history, and Rundle would be swept along. Ronald Reagan would finally have his showdown.

For years, Reagan had been describing demonstrators as the enemy, declaring at press conferences that they threatened the nation's security, vowing to use whatever force was necessary to suppress them. But today the law-enforcement officials acting under his authority in Berkeley would make a response that was tragically flawed.

It is clear from a wide range of evidence, including court testimony, police records, and FBI files, that despite years of escalating campus protests, and despite warnings about a conflict over the park, Reagan and his top law-enforcement aide, Meese, were poorly prepared for the events of

May 15. So was Sheriff Frank Madigan, who—under the state of emergency Reagan had declared during the Third World Strike but never
rescinded—remained supreme commander of all forces in Berkeley.

For all their planning, Reagan and his aides failed to have a sufficient
number of law-enforcement officers on duty that day. As a result, the officers relied on tear gas and birdshot to disperse crowds. When they quickly
ran out of these essential nonlethal weapons, they turned to the use of
deadly ones. Reagan's forces did precisely what the National Advisory
Commission on Civil Disorders had warned against a year earlier—that
"in their anxiety to control disorders, some law enforcement agencies may
resort to indiscriminate, repressive use of force against wholly innocent
elements . . ."

In an interview, Meese conceded that he and other responsible officials did not anticipate the intensity of the park conflict, and that as a result police on the scene "lacked the number of people and they didn't
have all the equipment." He also acknowledged there were problems
about "who exactly was in charge of particular sectors of the operation."
However, he said police used appropriate levels of force, and that he
doubted they shot bystanders. He blamed the situation on unexpected violence, mainly from "street people," adding, "People's Park was a particularly violent thing where the people who were involved there were trying
to kill police officers. They were throwing sharpened spikes from rooftops
down onto the police."

Chanting "We want the park!" the mass of students, hippies, and activists marched three blocks down Telegraph to Haste Street. There they
would turn left and march the half block up Haste to the park. Although
people were angry that the university had seized the park, the crowd's
overall mood was upbeat. Several marchers even carried young children.
But at Haste they were blocked by a line of seventy-five California Highway Patrolmen in riot gear. Some people in the crowd broke the plate-
glass windows of the Bank of America office. Others uncapped a fire
hydrant, dousing officers. It remains unclear which came first, but police
threw tear-gas canisters into the crowd, and people hurled bottles and
rocks at police. One highway patrolman received a minor knife wound,
though it is not known whether this was connected with the protest or an
unrelated crime. Trapped in the crowd near the corner of Telegraph and
Haste, William Donovan Rundle, Jr., felt a wave of apprehension as several Berkeley city policemen rushed forward to shut off the hydrant.

Several blocks away, Riche and the other sheriff's deputies were fin-

ishing lunch at their staging area, a parking garage beneath the campus
tennis courts on Bancroft Way near Bowditch Street, when they received
orders to assist the police. In their blue jumpsuits and helmets, and black
boots and gloves, two squads of about ten deputies each trooped single-file
down Bancroft Way and turned onto Telegraph Avenue. Riche was the
eighth man in his squad. At Haste Street they faced a barrage of bottles
and rocks and pieces of pipe and took cover by pressing close to the buildings. Riche was hit but not injured by a dirt clod, the only time that day
he would be struck. Another deputy was hit on his face shield by a piece
of pipe. There was a tremendous din—people clapping and yelling obscenities and chanting "Kill the pigs!" and "Take the park!" The deputies
reached into their leather shoulder pouches, withdrew tear-gas grenades,
pulled the pins, and lobbed them at the protesters. Soon the area was thick
with noxious white vapor. Still caught in the crowd, Rundle noticed that
some protesters wearing gas masks and gloves picked up the hissing gas
canisters and threw them back. His eyes were burning, and as soon as he
could he fled down a side street, where a neighbor lent him a garden hose
to rinse his face. He recovered well enough to return to campus, where he
sat under a tree and studied Shakespeare's last play, *The Tempest.*

Like Rundle, Deputy Riche was apprehensive. Remarkably, in planning for a possible protest Sheriff Madigan and other police officials never
even considered the possibility that the crowds would become too large to
handle. Nor, Madigan would also testify, did these planning sessions address the proper level of force officers should apply.

Greatly outnumbered, Riche and the other deputies were ordered
to withdraw to the parking garage on Bancroft Way. Thomas Houchins,
chief sheriff's deputy, then phoned Madigan, who was at the Jack London
hotel in downtown Oakland for a previously scheduled conference on
civil defense (it was unrelated to the park conflict). Houchins told him
they were "losing the riot . . . this was the worst he had ever seen." At
Houchins's request, Madigan authorized the use of riot guns. Each deputy then took from a white equipment van a Remington or Winchester
riot gun, a short-barreled shotgun that fires more widely dispersed shot. As
discussed with Madigan, they were issued two kinds of shells, one loaded
with birdshot, one with buckshot. Birdshot is about the size of a BB and is
usually nonfatal to humans. Buckshot—about a third of an inch in diam-
eter, slightly larger than a .30-caliber bullet—is used to kill deer and can
kill people. Two rounds of buckshot were loaded first and then two rounds
of birdshot; this way, the birdshot would be fired first. There simply was

not enough birdshot on hand. As Madigan later testified, "It wasn't anticipated that more than a few rounds would be fired, and therefore the buckshot would not be used."

At 1:15 p.m., according to police logs, the deputies marched out of the parking garage, helmets gleaming, and headed south on Bowditch Street, then west on Haste, where the crowd had massed, chanting and yelling. Some people were throwing bottles, rocks, pieces of metal bar, and chunks of concrete at the highway patrol officers. Captain Glenn Dyer fired two warning shots and—following their orders—other deputies fired at will. They discharged at least five rounds. Riche, however, held his fire.

The deputies pursued a group of about fifty people west on Haste Street, crossing Telegraph Avenue. This cluster kept about a half block ahead as the deputies threw tear-gas grenades and continuously sprayed the area with a pepper-fogger machine strapped on one deputy's back. More debris was thrown and some deputies fired into a parking lot on Haste Street, hitting uninvolved students who had just come out of their dormitory to go to class. Michael W. Beavers, a freshman in political science who had never been involved in a protest and was on his way to hand in a paper, was shot and suffered a collapsed lung. "It felt like I had been hit in the chest with a sledgehammer," he recalled.

The pattern would be repeated throughout the south-of-campus area that afternoon as the deputies dispersed demonstrators and tear-gassed and shot bystanders.

Marching in single file, the deputies turned south on Dana Street. A small crowd at the corner of Dwight Way fled before them. Sergeant Louis Santucci leveled his riot gun and allegedly shot Christopher D. Venn in the back, knocking him to the gutter with birdshot injuries. Santucci would later say Venn had thrown a rock and hit him; Venn would deny it. Three bystanders later said Venn had done nothing to provoke the deputies. The deputies neither arrested Venn nor summoned medical help for him, as with many other people they shot that day.

Several blocks away at the corner of Telegraph and Parker, protesters overturned an unoccupied police car. At about 1:20 p.m. they cornered two Berkeley reserve police officers who had retreated under a hail of rocks to a parking lot at the Cunha Pontiac body shop, a half block from the overturned car. One of the officers drew his revolver and pointed it at an advancing protester, but he and his fellow officer escaped into the shop without firing.

The upended car was set afire, sending up a thick column of black smoke and attracting a crowd of spectators. At about 2:15 p.m. the deputies

in blue approached. Marching up Parker toward the car, some fired warning shots into the street, ricocheting pellets. The deputies sprayed more
tear gas and discharged their riot guns into the crowd. They later said protesters had thrown rocks at them, though witnesses said the officers fired
without cause. A man walking on Telegraph was struck and fell to the
street screaming and clutching his back. Another man was struck and fell
onto a lawn bleeding.

Vincent Ferrari, a freelance photographer, had been walking south on
Telegraph toward the smoking car. He saw a police car zigzagging on
Dwight Way, veering toward pedestrians while an officer in the passenger
seat launched tear-gas canisters out the open window. As Ferrari reached
Parker, the crowd there already was fleeing. He turned and ran back up
Telegraph, then west on Blake, but was hit with forty-eight birdshot pellets
in the legs, arms, and face. Daryl Lembke, a *Los Angeles Times* reporter,
also was shot by a deputy as he retreated on Blake. "The area was like a war
zone," Lembke later said.

Scores of people were watching from windows and rooftops as the
deputies trooped north on Telegraph below, still in single file, back toward campus. Much of the avenue was clear, but a crowd had gathered
about two blocks north at Dwight Way. By now some deputies had fired
their loads of birdshot and were down to buckshot.

Perched on the roof of the pale three-story building that housed
Granma's Bookstore at 2509 Telegraph were about half a dozen spectators,
including James Bennett Rector, a twenty-six-year-old laborer from San
Jose who wore a black leather motorcycle jacket and a white cloth in his
right rear pocket. On the roof of a pink two-story building next door,
about two dozen people stood outside the penthouse office of the Berkeley Repertory Cinema, including George Pauley, the theater's owner, and
Alan Blanchard, a carpenter who worked for him who was an artist and
the father of a three-month-old boy. Atop the roof of a building farther
south a red-haired youth clutched a rock in each hand.

Pauley and Blanchard yelled at him to stop, but the rocks sailed through
the air and thudded on the road without hitting anyone. Immediately, several deputies wheeled, raised their shotguns, and fired at least nine rounds
toward the roofs. Riche looked toward the cinema roof, saw people standing on it, and decided to clear the area. He squeezed his trigger and the
edge of the roof blew apart in a spray of stucco.

Blanchard had been watching from above, and the last thing he ever
saw was a deputy's shotgun pointing toward him. Birdshot struck both of
his eyes, blinding him forever. Buckshot hit Rector, doubling him over and

knocking him to the roof. A photo taken minutes later shows Rector lying on his back as bystanders attend to him and his blood stains the shingles.

The deputies turned east on Dwight Way, stopping to rest and get re-supplied with tear gas. It was about 3:00 p.m., and some of them had run out more than an hour before. By now Madigan had summoned help from other Bay Area police departments, and a tactical squad from the San Francisco Police Department armed with riot guns was clearing crowds on Sproul Plaza. Members of that squad fired at least twelve rounds. An internal San Francisco Police Department inquiry would find they had been following Chief Deputy Houchins's orders that "if our gas supply became exhausted to use bird shot."

An army jeep carrying a tear-gas dispenser and a police officer armed with a shotgun meanwhile drove through the area south of campus. According to witnesses, the officer fired randomly at people on the sidewalks. Dan Porter, eighteen, and his friend Fred Campbell were walk-ing to pick up Campbell's sister from high school when a jeep came toward them spraying tear gas. They ran into an alley to avoid the fumes. The of-ficer in the jeep shot Porter in the back of his legs with buckshot. "They just pulled up and started spraying gas and shooting," Porter told the *Los Angeles Times*. "They just shot and left."

Nearby at Berkeley High School East Campus, officials had locked the gates to keep out troublemakers, but tear gas wafted onto school grounds. As students and teachers scrambled inside, a sheriff's deputy fired his riot gun toward the school yard, striking a sixteen-year-old student.

The excessive and arbitrary use of gas and guns stunned Berkeley residents. The vast majority of them had engaged in no violence, but some became so outraged at the police conduct that they, too, picked up rocks.

Mario Savio was one of them. He never advocated violence, but he believed in the right of self-defense. In Mississippi, he had seen evidence of racist violence and he respected the black farmers such as Hartman Turnbow who took up arms to protect themselves and their property. Savio was not a leader in the People's Park protest, but he believed the deputies were unjustly hurting innocent people. In anger, he later confided, he grabbed a rock and threw it.

The squad of deputies continued up Dwight Way and turned south on Regent Street toward Parker Street. Near that corner at least one of them fired his riot gun at a suspected rock-thrower but struck three pass-ersby. Clarence Edson, a painting contractor who had just alighted from his truck, was hit in the leg. Richard Ehrenberger, an architect who had been walking along Regent Street to his Porsche, was struck in his leg. Allan Francke, who was walking home from the campus's Cowell Hospital, where he was fulfilling his duty as a conscientious objector by assisting quadriplegic students, had parts of three fingers blown off his left hand. "I heard a shot. I looked down at my left hand and saw that it was all bloody," he said.

The deputies gathered at the Standard Oil gas station at the corner of Parker Street and Telegraph Avenue for a break. It was about 3:30 p.m. and the initial riotous behavior had subsided. Police had reopened traffic on Telegraph south of Dwight, and the deputies relaxed, some sitting on a short wall with their legs outstretched.

Nearby, the overturned police car continued to smolder and draw spectators, including William Donovan Rundle, Jr. He had finished reading *The Tempest* on campus and was headed toward his dormitory. He stopped to eat at a hot dog stand and then walked down to check out the car.

Riche was ordered to accompany another deputy with a pepper fogger and disperse the crowd of some twenty-five onlookers. As the deputies approached, Rundle and the others retreated west on Parker to Chilton. Suddenly, the pepper fogger sputtered and died. The crowd applauded. The deputy with the broken machine turned and began walking back to the gas station. Riche stayed behind.

Slowly he raised his riot gun, leveled it, and squeezed the trigger. As he did, a photographer named Robert Altman, inside a home at the corner, photographed him.

Buckshot tore through Rundle's intestines, causing injuries that would require multiple surgeries, including two colostomies.

Riche saw a man crumpled on the sidewalk, then turned and walked back to the gas station.

Witnesses would say Rundle had done nothing to provoke the shooting. But Riche claimed that someone—he was not sure who—had thrown a rock that landed near him. He claimed other rocks and debris were thrown at him, and he feared for his safety. He had fired his machine gun to clear helicopter landing zones in Vietnam, and now he had fired his riot gun to clear the street in Berkeley.

Savio, too, had nearly been shot. He was walking home when he crossed paths with the crowd at Chilton and Parker. He was standing near Rundle and saw Riche raise his gun. He ducked behind a car, then rushed over to the fallen student and helped him into a neighbor's home. Later, people wondered whether the deputy had been aiming at Savio. Savio would say he saw no reason for the deputy to fire. And even though it never became publicly known that Savio had thrown a rock in another area earlier that day, and even though that admission could have gotten him in trouble and brought unwanted publicity, he volunteered to be a witness for Rundle. Paramedics came and loaded Rundle into an ambulance. A passerby in a suit stopped and yelled, "I hope you die, you goddamned hippie."

It was the last shooting of the day. At least 169 people had been injured, including 111 police officers of whom 19 required medical treatment. No officer had been shot or seriously hurt. More than 58 civilians were injured, 51 by police birdshot and buckshot, although some estimates were twice that number. Many were shot in the back.

Police had arrested 48 people on charges ranging from failure to disperse to assaulting an officer.

By 6:00 p.m. that Thursday, Riche and the other deputies were off duty.

In Sacramento, Reagan grimly reviewed the situation reports and conferred with Meese. This was precisely the kind of disturbance they were supposed to have been prepared for under the Cable Splicer program and their other anti-subversion plans. Now events had overtaken the governor and his top aide. That evening, Reagan activated three battalions of the California National Guard, some 2,500 troops from the 49th Infantry Brigade. The military would back up local police on the streets of Berkeley. All forces would be under the command of Sheriff Madigan.

As troops mobilized at the Oakland Army Terminal, a police helicopter cut the night sky above Berkeley, its loudspeaker blaring in a mechanical voice Reagan's proclamation:

"No person shall loiter in or about any public street or other public place in the city of Berkeley, including the campus of the University of California between the hours of ten p.m. and six a.m. of the following day.

"No person shall conduct or participate in a meeting, assembly, or parade or use a sound or voice amplifier in or upon the public streets or other public place in the City of Berkeley, including the campus of the University of California."

Reagan had imposed martial law on the entire city. Any violation of these sweeping rules could lead to an arrest.

The sun burned through the morning fog the next day, glinting off the bayonets affixed to the M1 rifles of Reagan's forces, who formed corus-

cated lines around People's Park and down Telegraph Avenue, past Robbie's, the Caffe Med, and Cody's.

The National Guard troops made camp in People's Park, pitching green
army tents by the swing sets. The main staging area was several miles away
in the Berkeley Marina, a strip of land at the foot of University Avenue, the
main road from the highway to the campus. This arsenal included bales of
barbed wire, tear-gas launchers, and four tanks. Troops in olive-green jeeps
and transport trucks rumbled toward campus, past Savio's neighborhood in
the Berkeley flats. For the next twenty days, they would occupy Berkeley.

At the regents' meeting in Los Angeles that Friday, Reagan praised
university officials for having fenced off the park. He assured everyone
that police had acted only after "the heaviest provocation."

Even as he spoke, demonstrators were mounting the first of several
protests in defiance of his emergency orders. Several hundred people gathered peacefully at Sproul Plaza for a noon rally, but advancing police and
highway patrol officers forced them to regroup on the esplanade at the base
of the Campanile, a short walk away. Among those who spoke there was
Allan Temko, the *San Francisco Chronicle*'s architecture critic and an instructor at the university, who defended the park as "the greatest innova-
tion in recreational design since our great nineteenth-century parks . . . the
beginning of a new era in democratic city planning."

Agent Harold Hoblit of the FBI, who years earlier had crawled under
Jessica Mitford's house to spy on her, was on campus, and at 12:25 p.m. he
phoned university police to warn that another group of protesters was gathering. Troops formed a line at Fulton Street, at the west edge of campus,
but three thousand demonstrators managed to mass in front of Berkeley
City Hall, where they remained until 3:00 p.m. A few rocks were thrown,
and police fired at least one tear-gas canister, but it was relatively calm.

Savio was deeply disturbed by Reagan's actions, and that evening he
joined a meeting to plan protests. It was held at Merritt College in Oakland to circumvent Reagan's ban on public gatherings in Berkeley. According to an FBI report, Savio opposed a suggested strike at the university,
arguing, "We've tried that a number of times and it hasn't worked." His
view held sway and the group instead decided to employ nonviolent civil
disobedience tactics based on those used in the civil rights movement.
On Saturday, he and Suzanne joined about three hundred people
who marched in downtown Berkeley. Their goal was to peacefully clog
streets and stores, disrupting business and prompting shop owners
concerned about lost sales to press City Hall for the National Guard's
withdrawal.

In a lookout post atop the Bank of America building, Sergeant R. E. Hull and other university police officers scanned the clapping and chanting crowd. They noted the presence of the Savios, Mike Delacour, Frank Bardacke, Art Goldberg, and Paul Glusman. They also noted people distributing leaflets, one of which paraphrased Dylan's defiant song "Maggie's Farm" to suggest a merchant might not like that "the National Guard stands around his door." A phalanx of soldiers advanced and herded the protesters away from downtown and onto the campus.

To many demonstrators, the National Guardsmen were different from the Blue Meanies. They were younger, and some opposed the war and had joined the guard to beat the draft. Troops occasionally flashed a smile, discreetly raised two fingers in a peace sign, or flirted with young women. But they still were an occupying force and that day, according to army records, fifteen soldiers were temporarily incapacitated after "hippie-type females" gave them cookies and oranges laced with LSD. On campus, meanwhile, demonstrators flew kites to impede helicopter surveillance.

Sunday also saw little violence: park supporters with pickaxes and potted plants began work on another vacant lot they dubbed "People's Park Annex." Four thousand marchers then tried to reach the original park but troops turned them away.

Tension mounted on Monday after university officials disclosed that police bullets had entered an occupied room at Doe Library on what was now being called Bloody Thursday. Nearly a thousand people gathered for a rally on Sproul Plaza. For the first time, large numbers of troops moved onto campus to disperse the crowd, bayonets bristling.

That night, James Rector, the San Jose youth shot on the roof of Granma's Bookstore, died at Herrick Hospital. Madigan had personally authorized the loading and firing of buckshot, but publicly claimed deputies were issued only birdshot. Now doctors disclosed that they had removed buckshot pellets from Rector's chest cavity. The sheriff had been less than forthright about his deputies' use of deadly force.

In anger and sorrow, protesters called for a silent memorial march to downtown Berkeley, again defying Reagan's ban. About three thousand of them massed at noon the next day on Sproul Plaza. Wearing black armbands, they marched through Sather Gate to the Campanile, then headed west toward downtown. At Oxford Street troops turned them back toward the campus, and soon many found themselves trapped on Sproul Plaza.

A tight line of soldiers and policemen in gas masks blocked the path at Sather Gate. At the other end of the plaza, another line blocked the main entrance at Bancroft and Telegraph. For more than half an hour, the soldiers let people enter but not leave the plaza, capturing hundreds of people who milled about in passive confusion.

The beat of helicopter rotors grew louder. Above the Berkeley hills a dark Sikorsky U-19 appeared, then arced over the plaza and released a white plume that fell toward the upturned heads below. The chopper circled by the Campanile and dropped more of the caustic stuff.

People on the plaza panicked and tried to flee, but soldiers and police still blocked the exits. Police chased them, hurling tear-gas canisters in a chemical barrage that lasted ninety minutes.

Spring breezes spread the gas. It drifted into classrooms and the campus's Cowell Hospital. It wafted into residential areas, a nursery school, a junior high school, and the university's Strawberry Canyon recreational facility, where it sickened mothers and children.

At a press conference in Sacramento, Commanding General Glenn Ames, Reagan's military chief, claimed the helicopter had dropped tear gas to protect troops. He denied that the plaza had been sealed off, and said the five hundred to six hundred people there had been given eight minutes to leave. At first a guard spokesman told reporters the substance was conventional tear gas, or CN gas, the kind typically used by police. But the following day the officer disclosed that it was actually much stronger CS gas, a version of which was developed for use in Vietnam.

The helicopter tear-gassing of the city prompted further outrage among Berkeley residents. Paul Halvonik, an attorney with the American Civil Liberties Union, filed a federal lawsuit challenging the constitutionality of Reagan's emergency regulations banning meetings of more than two people in Berkeley. U.S. District Court Judge Robert F. Peckham ordered Reagan's representatives to appear at a hearing the following Monday to show why he should not reverse the decree. The judge said, "On its face, the regulations appear to be extremely broad. It appears to make serious inroads on the First Amendment rights of Berkeley citizens. There are problems in respect to a serious constitutional infringement."

Reagan was unfazed. That same day, he met with several Berkeley professors upset about the military occupation of the city. Attuned to potential publicity, he invited news reporters to attend the session in his cabinet meeting room. With cameras rolling, Reagan blamed university administrators and teachers for letting student protests get out of hand. One professor accused the governor of creating such a tense atmosphere at the university that the chancellors overreacted to incidents in order to keep Reagan from seeking their dismissal. "You are a liar!" Reagan shouted, angrily pounding his desk. He demanded the professor's name, and after Leon Wofsy, the former Communist who had supported the Free Speech Movement, identified himself, Reagan smugly replied, "You can bet I won't be surprised at anything you say."

Reagan refused the professors' request to withdraw the troops from Berkeley. He defended the deputies' use of shotguns. He likened the conflict to war. "We seem to be getting down to the situation that occurs between two nations—of who started the war," he said. And while he allowed that the helicopter gassing may have been a "tactical mistake," he declared, "once the dogs of war have been unleashed you must expect things will happen."

Still, Berkeleyans defied Reagan's ban on public meetings. At noon on Thursday, May 22, some 1,500 people set out from Sproul Plaza to downtown Berkeley to demonstrate peaceably. But the troops and police were waiting for them, ready to spring a trap identified in Cable Splicer records as "Operation Box."

As the professors leading the march reached the intersection of Shattuck Avenue and Center Street, police ordered them to disperse but did not try to enforce the order. Instead, the guard and police diverted their path. Then, at Allston Way, the march was stopped by a tight line of National Guardsmen. Many people who did try to leave found their path blocked by a second line of soldiers, who had come up behind them. Troop transport trucks roared up with more soldiers, who closed all other exits and boxed them in.

A combined force of police, deputies, and highway patrolmen herded the marchers—and everyone else—into a parking lot by the Bank of America. There Captain Charles Plummer of the Berkeley Police announced that they were all under arrest for unlawful assembly. Once again, scores of innocent bystanders were caught up as a result of overly aggressive police tactics. A mother who had run to a drugstore for a quick purchase pleaded with a soldier to release her, but he refused, even after she hysterically explained that she had left her young children waiting in her car. Two young women who had been clothes shopping were directed by police to go to the corner, only to be arrested there. So was a young man who had been buying stamps. Tim Findley, a *San Francisco Chronicle* reporter covering the protest, was caught in the maneuver and arrested. So was Robert Scheer, editor of *Ramparts*.

In the bank parking lot the arrestees were loaded onto yellow buses and driven thirty miles southeast to the Santa Rita Rehabilitation Center, a route now familiar to Berkeley protesters. The county prison farm was operated by the sheriff's department, and many of the deputies who had been assigned to the shotgun squads on Bloody Thursday were back on regular duty as guards there, including Riche.

The abuse began as soon as the buses pulled inside the jail gates. It was later detailed in affidavits filed in court and in first-person accounts published by Findley and Scheer. Deputies ordered their wards to hustle off the buses and used batons to hit those who did not move fast enough. All male arrestees were ordered to lie facedown on the gravel-covered cement prison yard in neat rows.

"Get down on your face, turn your head to the left, and line up to the man to your left's head," a deputy barked. "Now get hands down at your sides. Don't move. Don't talk." Every twenty minutes they were ordered to turn their heads in the opposite direction en masse. Deputies stalked the aisles, striking or kicking anyone slightly out of order, or even chewing gum. From the flat angle afforded by his prone position, Findley had a terrifying view of the guards' shiny black boots and swinging batons. "Don't none of you move," one of them said. "We shoot to kill here."

For as long as seven hours, the men were forced to lie there as gravel pressed into their cheeks. Periodically, a deputy called groups of eight to the intake building for booking. A white-haired clerk at a table took fingerprints. "These have to be right for the FBI," he told one arrestee. "What's the FBI's interest?" the prisoner asked. "We're gonna keep track of you troublemakers," the clerk replied, "and put all you troublemakers in concentration camps."

Around 10:00 p.m. the deputies marched the men into cold barracks for the night but would not permit sleep, randomly ordering them to perform military drills or to squat for prolonged periods. Calling them "filthy hippies," "assholes," and "motherfuckers," deputies threatened and beat some of them for no reason.

At 4:45 a.m. they were rousted for a breakfast of cereal and watery milk. "Super Joel" Tornabene, a People's Park organizer, refused to eat. Riche and another deputy allegedly ordered him to stand up, lean forward, and rest his forehead and nose against a wooden pole. Several deputies took turns whacking their nightsticks against the opposite side of the pole. After a while blood ran from Tornabene's nose.

Deputies returned their prisoners to the barracks. They were denied the right to make a phone call, and many were unaware friends had posted bail for their release. Finally, a deputy burst in at 8:00 a.m. and ordered them to line up outside for a final drill. "Awright you creeps!" another deputy yelled.

"When I shout 'Who do we love?' you shout back 'The Blue Meanies!'"
Only after they had complied to his satisfaction were they marched back to
the intake building and allowed to be bailed out.

On May 25, U.S. District Court Judge Peckham issued a temporary
restraining order prohibiting physical and verbal abuse of prisoners at
Santa Rita. He acted in response to a lawsuit brought by a former federal
prosecutor named James J. Brosnahan and several other lawyers who presented sworn affidavits of prisoners alleging brutality there.

Reagan meanwhile relaxed—but did not rescind—the curfew he had
imposed on Berkeley. He announced this just a few hours after military
and police forces finished the Operation Box roundup downtown, citing
improved conditions. By so acting before the hearing Judge Peckham had
set for the following Monday on his sweeping curfew, the governor avoided
a potentially embarrassing ruling that he had violated the constitutional
rights of an entire city.

Eventually, Alameda County judges dismissed all 482 arrests made
during Operation Box. The judges found that officers under Sheriff Madigan's command had used generic arrest warrants that lacked constitutionally required evidence that individuals had committed specific crimes.

At a press conference, Madigan promised to discipline his men for any
misconduct at Santa Rita.

Some of his young deputies were Vietnam veterans, he explained, and
"they have a feeling that these prisoners should be treated like Viet Cong."

The mass arrests downtown and the reports of brutality at Santa Rita fueled protests that spread far beyond the original park supporters and took
many forms. In the largest student vote to date at UC Berkeley, 85 percent
of 14,969 students approved a referendum that endorsed using the vacant
lot as a community-developed People's Park. Students at every UC campus except the San Francisco Medical Center called for class boycotts
in solidarity with Berkeley students. Seven thousand students from colleges throughout the state marched peaceably in Sacramento to show
their concern about Reagan's use of force in Berkeley.

More Berkeley faculty refused to teach than had during any prior controversy, on the ground that martial law stifled the spirit of free inquiry.
The campus's Academic Senate demanded the immediate withdrawal of
outside police and military forces. Several professors declared that "Berkeley has been under a reign of terror."

Inspired by the conflict over the use of the park land, two thousand students and faculty gathered in Lower Sproul Plaza on May 28 to hold one of the nation's first teach-ins on ecology. Sim Van der Ryn, the pioneering architecture professor, and other experts discussed the use of public space and man's relationship to the environment. Gary Snyder read his "Smokey the Bear Sutra," a poem in which the Great Sun Buddha of the Jurassic Age returns in the form of Smokey the Bear to save humankind from modern ills such as "advertising, air pollution, television, or the police" and protect "those who love the woods and rivers, Gods and animals, hobos and madmen, prisoners and sick people, musicians, playful women, and hopeful children . . ."

At Winterland Auditorium in San Francisco, Santana, Creedence Clearwater Revival, the Jefferson Airplane, and the Grateful Dead played a benefit, complete with psychedelic light shows, organized by Bill Graham to help defray the legal costs of people arrested in the Berkeley dragnet. The hometown bands would perform a few months later at Max Yasgur's farm, with Jerry Garcia squeezing notes from his guitar in "rainbow spirals round and round."

The Episcopal bishop of California denounced what he called Reagan's "strong-armed and brutal methods," while representatives of other denominations joined in asking the governor to ease "the policy of military repression in Berkeley." Wallace Johnson, Berkeley's Republican mayor, criticized the law-enforcement operations as "clumsy and inefficient." The City Council asked Reagan to rescind his proclamation of extreme emergency in the city. Democrats at the national and state levels condemned excessive police force. Assemblyman John Burton charged that Reagan had turned Berkeley into "his own Vietnam."

Reagan steadfastly defended the forces occupying Berkeley. He also used the park conflict to further his long-running campaign against "Berkeley"—that is, the counterculture, liberals, and Democrats—and to build support among conservatives. In an appearance before the Italian Federation in San Francisco's North Beach on May 19, Reagan declared, "What is going on in Berkeley is not only a threat to our youth but a menace to our whole land." He charged that "anarchists" were behind the disturbances and were making false claims of "academic freedom." "The taxpayer is not going to stand for this," Reagan added. "It's immoral to ask him to."

At a Sacramento press conference the next day, Reagan made new and greatly exaggerated allegations. As he had in years past in regard to Communists, urban riots, and the antiwar movement, he saw a nefarious plot behind events. He charged that "police took a tremendous and unprovoked beating from a well-prepared and well-armed mass of people who had stock-piled all kinds of weapons and missiles. They include pieces of steel rods, as well as bricks, large rocks, chunks of cement, iron pipes, and so on. Only after the riot erupted, and only after police officers and citizens were seriously hurt, did the police find themselves forced to defend themselves and to contain the mob with tear gas and in some cases—when all other police methods were insufficient—with shotguns loaded with birdshot. This was done only to protect life and property and in response to felonious assaults with deadly weapons . . ."

Reagan linked Rector's death to those of a janitor killed by a bomb blast at UC Santa Barbara and two men shot on the UCLA campus in the feud between the Black Panthers and the United Slaves. It was unknown that the FBI was in the midst of a counterintelligence operation using false letters, offensive cartoons, and informers that was intended to foment violence between the rival Black Power groups—or, as one FBI official put it, "to grant nature the opportunity to take her due course."

"The tragedy of this entire attempt at revolution is that a fourth person is now dead as a result of violence at or near our college and university campuses," Reagan said of Rector's death. "It should be obvious to every Californian that there are those in our midst who are bent on destroying our society and our democracy and they will go to any ends to achieve their purpose—whether it be a so-called park or a college curriculum. I now urge—more deeply than ever before and more fervently than it is possible to express—that those relative few who are seeking to destroy us by turning one against the other must be dealt with firmly, swiftly, and with the justice they deserve."

The governor told reporters he was convinced there was a conspiracy behind Bloody Thursday because of the presence at Berkeley of people associated with earlier disturbances there and elsewhere. Pressed for names, Reagan said his list would include Mario Savio.

Reagan was reaching. As heinous as the deaths on the campuses at Santa Barbara and Los Angeles were, they were not connected to each other or to events at Berkeley. But it was rhetorically effective for the governor to lump them together, just as he had previously linked the assassination of Bobby Kennedy to campus protests.

A review of FBI and police reports does not support Reagan's claim that the conflict was the result of a massive plot. Further, these records contain no claims that protesters attacked citizens or looted. According to an FBI report, police said that other than the burning of the City of Berkeley police car, the disturbance "did not produce a great deal of property damage." As for Savio, Reagan was unfairly trying to taint the man who symbolized the student movement. The free-speech spokesman had no role in organizing the park's development before the conflict, acted only as an individual on Bloody Thursday, and played a limited part in protests afterward.

Reagan's lengthy statement did not address certain salient but inconvenient facts, such as the deputies' use of buckshot, Madigan's false denials that they had fired the lethal load, and the police gassing and shooting of many bystanders.

At a $100-a-plate Republican fund-raiser on May 22, Reagan further sought to downplay the death of James Rector. In an apparent effort to discredit the youth and imply that deputies were justified in shooting him, Reagan disclosed that after he was shot, police found a rifle and electronic surveillance equipment in the trunk of his car. (This sounded sinister, but Berkeley police later said the rifle was disassembled and possession of the items was legal; Rector's landlord separately told a reporter that Rector had used electronic gear to make bootleg long-distance phone calls.) To the glee of his Orange County audience, Reagan blamed Rector's death on university officials, and by inference Clark Kerr. "The police didn't kill the young man," he declared. "He was killed by the first college administrator who said some time ago it was all right to break the laws in the name of dissent." Several days later, Reagan told reporters he could not imagine police handling things otherwise. "I don't see where anything different was possible other than surrender . . . complete surrender . . ."

Reagan successfully communicated a narrative that played well with most Californians, galvanized conservatives, and boosted his political ratings. He refused to lift the state of emergency or recall the National Guard. And when park organizers announced their biggest protest yet—a Memorial Day march through Berkeley—he vowed that "whatever force is necessary will be on hand."

At a press conference the day before the march, an angry Sheriff Madigan echoed the governor. He finally admitted he had issued buckshot to his deputies on Bloody Thursday, and as his hands trembled he warned that his men would continue to use the lethal ammunition.

People's Park had made international news, and on the day of the march John Lennon, in Montreal with his new bride, Yoko Ono, phoned the Berkeley radio station KPFA. "Keep it up," Lennon said. "If you're doing it peaceful, we're with you. No piece of grass is worth losing your life for."

•

Reverend Richard York, pastor of the Berkeley Free Church, gave the invocation: "Our leader, Jesus, the Prophet who resisted the Establishment, march here beside us." Then the mass set out from the lot at Grant Street and Hearst Avenue west of campus, dubbed "People's Park Annex," on their two-mile trek. They quickly noticed that all side streets were closed by coils of concertina wire and deputies with shotguns. It was the end of May and it was bright, and the twenty thousand marchers were packed tight for blocks. There were antiwar protesters, Hell's Angels, senior citizens, Black Panthers, Free Speech Movement veterans, hippies, women's liberation advocates, rich people from the hills, poor people from the flats, and student delegations from all over. Many waved American flags, green ecology banners, or peace signs. They clapped and sang to the tune of "We Shall Overcome." When they reached People's Park, a yellow truck pulled up and young men unrolled a blanket of sod the width of Haste Street and planted flowers in it. A rock band jammed and women danced topless. Then the symbolic park was rolled up, the women put on their shirts, and the marchers returned to their starting point, leaving the fence around the park adorned with daisies. Despite concern about more violence, all was orderly, and there was a carnival air—a sense of relief, of coming together—in the face of it all. Pat Cody, who owned Cody's Books with her husband, Fred, recalled, "People were very emotional, very close to each other, always very close to tears or laughter. It was hot, and at times the streets were so packed that it was impossible to keep moving. Residents along the march route got garden hoses and sprayed us, and everyone raised their arms and opened their mouths . . ."

The march, however, did not resolve the fate of lot 1875-2. At a public meeting several weeks later, the Berkeley City Council voted to lease the lot from the university to continue the park. Among those supporting the idea was Thomas P. F. Hoving, director of the Metropolitan Museum of Art in New York City and former director of parks and recreation there, who likened it to "pocket parks" created on bits of vacant land in Manhattan. And at the regents' meeting on June 20, a now more sympathetic Chancellor Heyns proposed using the western part of the lot for a playing field and leasing the eastern part to the city for a nominal fee, until the university built student apartments there. The city would be responsible for regulating the "experimental user-developed and maintained community park." It was belated acknowledgment of the broad community support for the park. But Reagan was adamant. He led the board to vote 16–7 to reject the proposal and instead use the site for a temporary soccer field and parking lot. The governor simply was not going to cede any ground—not even a few acres of rubble—in his battle with Berkeley.

After the meeting, Dorothy Walker, a Berkeley city planning commissioner, told the governor, "The blood of the people of Berkeley will be on your hands." "Fine," Reagan replied, and referring to the soap company that had sponsored his television series *Death Valley Days*, he added, "I'll wash it off with Boraxo."

A few days after Reagan and the regents blocked the park plan, Mario Savio returned to Sproul Plaza to make his first speech there in almost two years. He had been steering clear of trouble on campus and focusing on his family. He still harbored hopes of reenrolling at Berkeley and finally getting his bachelor's degree. Yet he had been powerfully affected by the conflict over the park. It was less than a block from his job at Cody's, at Telegraph and Haste. He had seen William Rundle, Jr., shot, and was almost shot himself. Every day in the three weeks since, he had walked past the soldiers occupying the city. He was compelled to join the protest downtown in defiance of Reagan's curfew. Although Savio could not have foreseen the park conflict back in the days of the big sit-in at Sproul Hall, in the city that gave birth to the Free Speech Movement he had seen just how fragile constitutional rights could be in the face of governmental decree and army bayonets. He'd also seen the community's resilience.

Now Savio stood on the steps of Sproul Hall, once again waiting his turn to speak. It was June 26, 1969, and he was among several prominent activists who had come to share their insights on the meaning of the cataclysm over the scrap of land called People's Park. Two FBI informers were there and filed reports. Tom Hayden, a Chicago Seven defendant, told the crowd that the fight represented "something new and distinctive" in the movement. Frank Bardacke, a park instigator, urged everyone to work together systematically and build alternative institutions to improve society. "We must not only be capable of going into the streets," he said, "but we must be organized . . ." Dan Siegel, the student body president-elect whose speech preceded the shootings, agreed that protest alone was not enough and emphasized working for change through the political system. "Our militancy," said Siegel, "has to be controlled by our programs and not vice versa."

Savio did not deliver an incendiary call for people to throw their bodies on the gears and levers as he had when he stood in that same spot five years earlier. His wiry hair piled atop his furrowed brow like a thunder-head, he instead explicated what the park meant in the battle against the machine. For years, he had viewed hippies as too apolitical and somewhat anti-intellectual. He thought LSD could provide useful insights and people could form positive bonds by passing the marijuana pipe, but that too many had used these drugs to escape and "got blown away." He saw Leary's exhortation to "Turn on, tune in, drop out" as "the most irresponsible slogan of the era." But while critical of the counterculture, he believed it offered hope for making "a new society." And he now described People's Park as representing a war over fundamental social values.

"Some of the good brothers and sisters started building a park on land they'd ripped off," he said, "and though it was far better for people to have a park there—and what a park!—nonetheless everyone from the governor down to [Berkeley City Council member] John de Bonnis had apoplexy. They even murdered one of our people."

He did not dwell on the shootings, however, but sought to move people forward. "We are here," he said, "because some of our people sensed in the air that we'd all had vacation enough, that just sitting on our butts smoking dope wasn't getting us any closer to the Aquarian Age. Not to say that smoking dope isn't just fine! So ready or not, it was time to proclaim the social revolution by seizing the means of leisure."

It was a twist on the Marxian dictum that workers must seize the means of production—factories, raw materials, et cetera—to create a more equitable society. "We are the first postindustrial generation . . . the first generation with time on its hands," he said. "Try to remember back to the distant nineteen fifties—the period which functions in our mythology much as the Dark Ages did for the men of the Enlightenment. In the Dark Fifties one of the things which used to worry what they call 'social commentators' was this: Whatever would people in the future age of automation do with so much free time? Just imagine such a problem! Why, people might go quite mad with the boredom, now that American capitalism had solved all the major problems, and was fast doing away with much of the 'worthwhile' work. And there would always follow the sense that some super messianic camp director—like Clark Kerr or Daniel Bell—would have to figure out things for all the poor, beleisured souls to do. Well, the future is here right now. We are those very same poor souls. So what do we do with all our free time? As I see it, the great hope of People's Park is that in our leisure time—so to speak—we will make the social revolution."

The industrial society of the fifties had created the affluence of the sixties, which freed a generation to question the received reality. Finding a lucrative market in the baby boomers, big business, in turn, had become a prime purveyor of insurgent youth culture. This paradox reflected an inherently democratic aspect of capitalism, Savio seemed to be saying, but one that could lure consumers into accepting commercial facsimiles in lieu of authentic experience.

"The last hope of the ruling class was that they could buy us off by selling us enough of our records, and paisley ties and shirts, and bell-bottom trousers," he declared. "Buy us off nothing! Well, it hasn't worked quite that way. They made bread on our records—but the music turned out to be pretty subversive. Then People's Park—we started seizing their property."

Yes, Reagan, Meese, and the Blue Meanies had taught a harsh lesson to the dreamers of People's Park, Savio said, and for the moment "they might have even won." But he saw a more positive lesson in the conflict: the inescapable realization that even privileged white kids could be subject to official brutality when challenging powerful vested interests. And having realized this, white and black activists should work with each other to seek justice. "That is the great strategic hope implicit in People's Park, and the most important reason the establishment (if it knows its own interests) should fear it," he said.

"We in the postindustrial sector cannot be bought off, because in order to do our thing we must challenge on as fundamental a level as our black brothers and sisters the property relations of this society. It is thus a deeply revolutionary cry which is raised by People's Park in postindustrial capitalism: Seize the means of leisure!"

The question now, he said, is whether the new generation will escape being subverted by commercialism and authoritarian social pressures.

"Will enough New Men," he asked, "come up fast enough to make the difference between liberation and disaster?"

While Reagan defended the actions of law-enforcement officials on Bloody Thursday, the American Civil Liberties Union gathered witness statements documenting dozens of beatings and shootings, mostly by Alameda County sheriff's deputies. *Ramparts* magazine retained the renowned San Francisco private investigator Hal Lipset and the former FBI agent William Turner and published their findings that deputies had gone on a "bloody rampage through the streets of Berkeley." The *Los Angeles Times* detailed police shootings of bystanders, including news reporters, and concluded that officials had deployed techniques "more familiar to a war zone than to an American college campus."

Gradually a series of official investigations also unfolded, but each was compromised by conflicts of interest and raised more questions than it answered.

Sheriff Frank Madigan, who had been caught making false statements that his men fired only birdshot, announced an inquiry into their use of shotguns and treatment of prisoners. He put Thomas J. Houchins, his chief deputy, in charge. Houchins had urged the use of shotguns and was on record as saying it was inevitable that people in neighborhoods where there was fighting might be mistaken for rioters and get shot. ACLU officials feared that assigning a deputy involved in the shootings to the investigation would render it of "questionable objectivity." The results of the inquiry, disclosed on July 2, appeared to justify these concerns: No one was punished for any shooting. Four supervisors and six deputies received recommended suspensions of up to fifteen days without pay, and in some cases demotions, for mistreatment of prisoners at Santa Rita. Lawrence Riche, the probationary deputy, received five days' suspension for his misconduct at the jail. The county civil service commission, however, reversed most of this meager discipline.

The Alameda County Coroner conducted an inquest into the time, place, and circumstances of James Rector's death. The coroner assembled a panel that heard two days of testimony during which several witnesses swore that Rector was merely watching when he was shot. And though officers testified that the riot was uncontrollable and they feared for their lives, none claimed he saw Rector throw anything from the roof. One deputy said he fired in that direction because he saw an unidentified person raise his arm and throw a rock. This inquiry, however, was not an adversary proceeding and there was no cross-examination. The coroner would later acknowledge he and his staff had handpicked the middle-aged panel members from a group of familiar people. They deliberated thirty-eight minutes before finding that Rector's death was "justifiable homicide by an unknown and unidentifiable Alameda County sheriff's deputy."

By contrast, the Alameda County grand jury faulted everyone: University administrators had vacillated between negotiating with park supporters and taking a hard line; city officials had failed to enforce health codes at the park; "revolutionaries" had fomented the violent confrontation on May 15, and some of them had stockpiled objects to throw at police. Law-enforcement agencies were unprepared, the helicopter gassing of Sproul Plaza was "inadvisable," and police failed to give sufficient warning about the imminent use of gas and guns. Deputies were justified in resorting to shotguns, but in isolated cases they fired "indiscriminately." Yet even this report did not mention Blanchard's blinding or Rector's death, and recommended only misdemeanor criminal charges against the deputies Lawrence Riche and Gary Nelson for using undue force on prisoners at Santa Rita. The inquiry was conducted under the authority of D. Lowell Jensen, who with Edwin Meese III had prosecuted the Free Speech Movement protesters and who had succeeded Frank Coakley as district attorney. Nonetheless, the report was in effect a rebuke not only of Sheriff Madigan but also of Governor Reagan, whose office was responsible for responding to states of emergency.

By now Reagan had released his own report. Entitled "The 'People's Park': A Report on a Confrontation at Berkeley, California, Submitted to Governor Ronald Reagan," the thirty-eight-page "white paper" assumed a stance of objectivity. Reagan's office refused to comment on the document or name the staff members who prepared it, but records indicate it was under the authority of Meese, who had close ties to Alameda County law enforcement and was in charge of coordinating the state's preparedness for campus unrest. It was another instance of an interested agency investigating itself. Meese made clear his predisposition in an interview with Robert Scheer several years later when—even though it never was proved that Rector threw anything from the roof—he declared, "James Rector deserved to die."

Predictably, Reagan's study blamed the park conflict on "dangerous militants." While saying the report accused no one of a crime, its anonymous author named several park activists and listed their arrests at past demonstrations, including Stew Albert, Art Goldberg, and Frank Bardacke. Although Mario Savio had not been in the forefront of the protest, the report emphasized that the "principal leader of the 1964 'Free Speech Movement'" had spoken at a rally in support of the park.

The document discounted the widespread support for a community park, declaring, "The participation of citizens who were motivated by a simple desire to improve the environment was eagerly sought and exploited by those who used People's Park as an issue for confrontation." The logic could have come straight from Hoover's report "Communist Target—Youth."

The study pointed out that Dan Siegel, who gave the speech declaring, "Let's go down and take the park," had been accused of inciting the riot. A jury, however, would soon acquit him of the misdemeanor charge.

The report repeated allegations that some protesters had "stockpiled" rocks, sticks, and pieces of metal on the roofs and bombarded police on the streets. It said deputies fired their shotguns only in self-defense. Although it noted Rector had been killed, the report sought to further diminish his death by pointing out the twenty-five-year-old had prior arrests for burglary and possession of marijuana. The study did not mention Alan Blanchard.

While allowing that "some of the wounded said they were not demonstrating," the report did not address salient issues such as the deputies' use of buckshot, the mass arrests in downtown Berkeley, and the National Guard's helicopter tear-gas attack. The latter incident by now had become a sore point even among law-enforcement officials. Back in June, Thomas Houchins, the sheriff's chief deputy who had authorized the gassing, publicly declared he would not have done so if National Guard officials "hadn't lied to me" about how the gas would spread. This drew an angry response from General Glenn Ames, Reagan's military commander and head of the California National Guard, that smacked of cover-up. In a confidential letter to Sheriff Madigan, Ames said he had warned Houchins that "delivery of chemical agents from a helicopter is not a very precise form of delivery but is intended to cover a large area with a large volume of gas on a quick basis." Ames complained that he had gone out of his way to publicly defend "the use of deadly force by your department and the activities of your personnel at the Santa Rita Prison Farm." He added, "It is my firm belief that whenever law enforcement or the military become involved in a problem of this sort they must maintain a united front as far as the news media and the public are concerned."

That, essentially, is what Reagan's report did. In an interview, Meese denied that the "white paper" failed to fully and fairly examine events. "Well, no, this wasn't an investigation," he explained. "This was a description of an incident."

With such conflicts of interest undermining local and state inquiries, it fell to the federal government to thoroughly investigate the deputies' alleged use of excessive force, but that inquiry would also be compromised.

As United States Attorney for the Northern District of California, Cecil Poole was the top federal prosecutor in that part of the state. His appointment by President Kennedy in 1961 had made the Alabama native the first black to hold such a post in the fifty states. Poole had angered conservatives, including Senator George Murphy, Reagan's friend, when he criticized the unauthorized arrest of five people for not having their draft cards with them. Fiercely independent, he initiated an FBI investigation based on the scores of complaints his office had received about the deputies' conduct during the People's Park conflict.

The FBI's assignment in Berkeley was complicated, as it had been in Mississippi when the bureau investigated the beatings of Mario Savio and other voting rights activists. The FBI had authority to probe allegations of federal civil rights violations and police brutality, yet agents were being asked to investigate, and potentially harm, Alameda County sheriff's deputies, members of the Bay Area law-enforcement community who for years had worked with them against Berkeley activists.

From the start, this situation worried Justice Department officials assigned to the case. Jeffrey L. Smith, the department's top civil rights attorney on the West Coast, was well aware that San Francisco FBI agents believed Sheriff Madigan had handled things properly and were not sympathetic to the investigation. As of early August 1969, Smith pointed out in a memo, agents had interviewed only two people present during the alleged abuses at Santa Rita; they had not even obtained the addresses of witnesses who had filed sworn affidavits in court. "It is doubtful these people would cooperate with the FBI even if they were located," Smith added. "Most students and street people in Berkeley are refusing to talk to the FBI. This in large part stems from their general distrust of the FBI and the feeling of many witnesses that the FBI is investigating them rather than taking statements."

These fears were heightened when FBI agents arrested Christopher Venn, the twenty-two-year-old part-time longshoreman who had been shot in the back on Dwight Way. The incident was notorious because the *San Francisco Chronicle* had published a stunning photograph taken as a deputy aimed his shotgun at the fleeing Venn from a distance of less than fifty feet. Venn's case offered a potentially strong prosecution, and he granted agents an interview. But several days later, the bureau learned that a judge in El Paso had issued a warrant for him for violating probation in a drug case. San Francisco FBI agents quickly arrested the bearded and beaded Venn. "In the eyes of all students and street people in Berkeley, Mr. Venn's probation was revoked because he complained to and cooperated with the federal government," Smith wrote. "The arrest of Venn has destroyed any hopes of cooperation from the students."

Nonetheless, during the next several months agents interviewed more than 250 people. And though Sheriff Madigan refused to turn over official documents to the agents, U.S. Attorney Poole obtained a subpoena forcing him to do so. Poole presented the evidence to a federal grand jury in San Francisco, and on February 2, 1970, the panel returned indictments against twelve current or former sheriff's deputies for conspiracy and imposing summary punishment in violation of federal civil rights laws during the park protests. They were among the last indictments obtained by Poole. President Nixon and John Mitchell, his attorney general and former campaign manager, were in the process of naming their own U.S. attorneys around the country, and Poole would leave office in a few days to teach at UC Berkeley's Boalt Hall School of Law.

The indictments charged ten deputies with conspiring to injure or intimidate prisoners at Santa Rita. Six of those same deputies, and two others, also were indicted for beating prisoners at Santa Rita or for wrongly shooting people on Bloody Thursday. Deputy Riche was charged in the most incidents: the former army trombonist was accused of shooting William D. Rundle, Jr., Allan Francke, Clarence Edson, and Richard Ehrenberger. He and a second deputy were accused of firing their shotguns toward James Rector and Alan Blanchard. He also was charged with beating Joel Tornabene at Santa Rita. A conviction on the conspiracy charge alone carried a maximum penalty of ten years in jail and a ten-thousand-dollar fine.

Madigan was appalled. Denouncing the indictments as "one of the sickest operations of government I have ever seen," he complained bitterly to reporters that Poole had always stood aside when radicals trying to "bring down the government" violated the civil rights of other citizens. "We have tried to defend the government and we have tried to get the federal government to assist us and we never got the cooperation. This is the draft boards, the train stop at Berkeley, the Third World Revolution . . . the whole bit." The sheriff accused the U.S. Justice Department of conducting a "witch hunt" and giving "aid and comfort to our enemies."

Other members of the local establishment in which Meese had come up were likewise enraged. Assemblyman Don Mulford, the Alameda County Mayors Conference, and the county Board of Supervisors all condemned the indictments. The Oakland Police Officers Association charged that the grand jury investigation was biased. And the Alameda County Deputy Sheriffs' Association mounted a letter-writing campaign to dismiss the charges. In an appeal to President Nixon, the association asked him to block the prosecution in "the interest of justice," adding, "We know that you are committed to reversing the trend of lawlessness in our nation." The organization also wrote directly to U.S. Attorney General John Mitchell at his residence in the Watergate Apartments.

The indictments posed political trouble for local officials—and for the governor. In large part, Reagan had built his political career on fighting student protesters. He had campaigned long and loud to clean up Berkeley. People's Park had been his apocalypse. A criminal conviction against any of his forces would be a wounding reversal, much as Robert Meisenbach's acquittal had been for J. Edgar Hoover.

Declaring that he was "shocked" by the indictments, Reagan charged at a press conference that the federal government was stepping in "and superseding local authority and autonomy" even though state and county agencies had conducted thorough investigations. "There just seems to be lately a concerted effort always in trying to find if possible where did the officials of law enforcement go wrong, and we don't seem to have the same attitude with regard to those who precipitated the violence and the rioting in the first place," he said.

Two weeks later, the governor seized the initiative in the wake of new violence. On February 13, 1970, two pipe bombs exploded in the parking lot of the Berkeley police headquarters, injuring two men. No one claimed responsibility for the attacks, and the perpetrators were not identified. Three days later, protests broke out in New York and San Francisco in reaction to the contempt-of-court sentences against Jerry Rubin, his codefendants, and their lawyers in the Chicago Seven conspiracy trial. In Berkeley, bands of protesters marched downtown, smashing bank windows and knocking a policeman unconscious. In another attack, a pipe bomb exploded that night outside a police station in the Haight-Ashbury district, injuring several officers and killing one.

In a letter to U.S. Attorney General Mitchell that he immediately released to reporters, Reagan wrote of Berkeley, "This city has suffered from a long series of violent confrontations planned by mindless revolutionaries who are dedicated to the overthrow of our democratic system of government and free way of life. State government and local law enforcement agencies in California are doing all in their power to bring a halt to these violent confrontations. We intend to continue in these efforts. However, to enhance the effectiveness of our own actions at the state and local levels, I am requesting that the Department of Justice immediately convene a federal grand jury, and that your agency begin an investigation as soon as possible to determine whether there have been any violations of federal laws by those persons fomenting and participating in these riots . . . I strongly believe that the recent violence by the mob in Berkeley . . . willfully violated the civil rights of literally hundreds of law-abiding citizens." Mitchell promptly complied by ordering an FBI investigation into the disturbances and promising to dispatch Justice Department attorneys to California "for consultation" with the governor.

With the first trial of the sheriff's deputies still months off, Reagan again appealed to Mitchell, this time privately inviting him to be the keynote speaker at the next Cable Splicer conference on responding to civil disorders. "Dear John," Reagan wrote on April 28, "You are aware, I am sure, that I attach the greatest importance to the readiness of California state and local governments to meet any emergency situation that might arise. The conference will be the culmination of five months of intensive planning and training of civil and state military staffs. It is my pleasure to cordially invite you, on behalf of the people of the State of California, to be our honored guest."

By the time the Cable Splicer conference convened in May 1970, more blood had been shed. It was now after People's Park, after the massive protests against Nixon's secret bombing of Cambodia, after National Guard soldiers killed four students at Kent State University in Ohio and police killed two students at Jackson State College in Mississippi. It was after scores of bombings around the country that were attributed to a tiny minority of left-wing extremists. Telegraph Avenue was still drawing swarms of long-haired young people. Jimi Hendrix, wearing a fringed shirt and gripping a Stratocaster, performed that month at the Berkeley Community Theatre. "Give us about a minute to get tuned up and get rid of these joints and everything . . . Forget about yesterday, or tomorrow, whatever you say. This is our own little world tonight," he said as he opened the second set. The sound waves from his stacks of Marshall amplifiers looped back into his guitar until his riffs exceeded themselves and were transformed into electronically supersaturated howls and cries. He played "Stone Free," "Purple Haze," and an incandescent version of the "Star-Spangled Banner" that, he said, was "the way it really is, in the air that you breathe every day, the way it really sounds." He closed with "Voodoo Child (Slight Return)," dedicating it to the Black Panthers and People's Park.

At their own gathering, the police and military officials who had helped put down the People's Park protest, and others since then, shared their likewise candid views. "Hello 'pigs,' " said Captain Charles Plummer of the Berkeley Police Department in his opening remarks. "I bring you greetings from Moscow USA, also known as Berkeley. It certainly is a unique city. It has been branded as the laboratory of revolution and certainly you can't argue with that too much." Thomas Houchins, who had been promoted to undersheriff, followed Plummer. "I think he meant lavatory, because that is just about what it is out there," he said. "It has been the breeding and proving ground for all the revolutionary tactics. They try it out in Berkeley and take it elsewhere." Lieutenant General

Stanley R. Larsen, the commanding general of the Sixth Army, who had arranged for Edwin Meese III to receive army intelligence reports about protesters, spoke urgently of the need for joint military and police operations, saying, "We are both heading in the same direction . . . the salvation of the greatest country in the world."

In comments even more dire, Major General Glenn Ames, the head of the governor's military department, declared, "Until reason returns, until these hard-core revolutionaries are separated from the American campuses and immobilized, until the unwholesome and pernicious influence of radical professors on the formative minds of our young can be broken, until someone discovers that burning a building or breaking a window is not a very relevant way to peace, until our college administrators step back into reality and realize that the management of the personnel of a factory, a city, or a club . . . can be accomplished only through rules, regulations, and laws, until the anti-military, anti-American doomsday voices in our Congress can be stilled at the ballot box, until that silent majority becomes articulate, until that day, there stands between the American public and the forces of anarchy and destruction only that thin blue line of law enforcement. And thin it is."

The federal trial of Lawrence Riche, Alameda County sheriff's deputy, for shooting William Rundle, Jr., opened in Judge Stanley A. Weigel's courtroom in San Francisco on August 31, 1970. It would prove to be the first of several doomed prosecutions.

In his opening statement, Assistant U.S. Attorney Jerry Cimmet said evidence would show Riche had fired without justification into a crowd that was not creating a disturbance. Cimmet put on prosecution witnesses who testified that Riche shot as demonstrators were retreating and there was no serious threat to him. Taking the stand in his own defense, Riche, a twenty-five-year-old described in press accounts as "baby-faced," said he and other deputies were "ill-equipped" that day but did their best. Events frightened him, and, the former army man said, "I felt like I was back in Vietnam again." He fired because rocks were landing near the officer carrying the pepper fogger. Donning gas mask and riot helmet to complete his testimony, he said in a voice that seemed disembodied, "I was not shooting indiscriminately. I was shooting where the rocks were coming from." Innocent bystanders, he added, "shouldn't have been there."

When Riche was acquitted on September 16, the foreman told the

San Francisco Chronicle that jurors lacked the certainty necessary to convict him for shooting maliciously. "We had no doubt he did shoot Rundle, and with buckshot. Our trouble was over his intent. We had reasonable doubt about Riche's intent. There was a riot that day." One month later, another jury acquitted Riche in the shootings of the painting contractor Clarence Edson and the architect Richard Ehrenberger, and deadlocked on whether he illegally shot the hospital aide Allan Francke. Riche's retrial in the Francke shooting would also end in a hung jury.

With most of the trials still ahead, Reagan again appealed to Attorney General John Mitchell, this time urging him to meet with Robert Donovan, president of the Deputy Sheriffs' Association, which had been lobbying to get the prosecutions dropped. "The matters which would be the subject of conversation are of great importance to Alameda County officials and to the law enforcement profession across the state," Reagan wrote on October 20, 1970.

Replying ten days later, Mitchell confided to Reagan that the head of the department's civil rights division, his appointee Jerris Leonard, had met with Donovan. Mitchell also revealed that the department would drop key charges against the deputies. "I am sure you will be pleased to know that reconsideration has been given to some of the pending cases that resulted from the Berkeley 'People's Park' riot and the subsequent activities at the Santa Rita Jail, which will result in the dismissal of some of the charges," he said. "I have directed Mr. Leonard to continue to carefully review each case in light of evidence produced during the trial of these matters and he assures me that he is in close touch with United States Attorney James Browning, so that you may be assured that every consideration is being given to these matters."

In an interview, Meese said the idea that Reagan was trying to politically influence the federal prosecutions of the deputies was "silly."

During a confidential meeting in Judge Weigel's chambers a few days later, Browning, the Nixon appointee who had replaced Cecil Poole, made a startling announcement: he wanted to delay the trials on the shooting of Rector and Francke and outright dismiss three other shooting cases. The prosecutors assigned to the cases—Jerry Cimmet and Arthur Chotin—were "amazed," according to an internal Justice Department memo. "They had not expected any suggestion of dismissing the shooting cases . . ." The judge also was stunned. He told Browning there were "serious matters of public policy involved and he could not understand why the United States Attorney was taking this position." Browning replied that he was following instructions from his superiors in Washington.

Several more trials ended in acquittals or hung juries. Then, on December 18, Browning moved to dismiss seven of the remaining indictments that charged deputies with shootings and beatings. An irritated Judge Weigel agreed to dismiss only four, saying the government had not provided appropriate notice concerning the other three.

The remaining prosecutions fared just as poorly. The following February, Lawrence Riche and Leonard Johnson were acquitted in the killing of Rector and the blinding of Blanchard. Having thus far tried six cases and achieved only acquittals or deadlocked juries, the Justice Department moved to dismiss all remaining charges. "We think we would just be wasting everyone's time," Browning said.

No deputy was convicted of any crime arising from the shootings on Bloody Thursday or the treatment of prisoners at Santa Rita.

With the federal prosecutions having come to naught, people who had been falsely arrested, tear-gassed, beaten, or shot during the park conflict turned to private lawyers to file civil suits seeking compensation for their damages.

William Rundle, Jr., shot in the stomach by Riche, was among them. Ronald M. Greenberg, a young Los Angeles lawyer, pursued his case vigorously. He had been retained by Rundle's father. Greenberg alleged in court papers that Deputy Riche had shot the freshman without justification on the afternoon of May 15, well after riotous activities had subsided. He claimed Madigan, Houchins, and other sheriff's officials had engaged in a conspiracy to deprive Rundle and others of their civil rights by using excessive force. Greenberg gathered evidence showing that—despite years of student demonstrations and warnings about the imminent park protest—the sheriff's department had failed to properly prepare for it, assigned deputies who were "essentially untrained," issued riot guns and lethal buckshot to them, and failed to provide "adequate leadership or control." Sheriff's officials should have foreseen, he charged, that the deputies would indiscriminately shoot people who were lawfully on the streets like Rundle.

Madigan and his codefendants denied all this and filed evidence in their defense, including a copy of Reagan's white paper on the park conflict. They asked the court to throw out Rundle's lawsuit, but Judge Peckham ruled that Greenberg had presented sufficient evidence of his claims to proceed with his case. Greenberg uncovered evidence FBI agents had missed. He found photographs that showed a man with a movie camera standing near Riche at the time of the shooting. Agents never located this potentially crucial witness even though he had been sitting in court as a spectator during Rundle's criminal trial. His name was Steve Dane and he had filmed events during the People's Park protest and the incident in which Riche was accused of shooting Rundle. His film, which Greenberg played for the author, showed that contrary to Riche's claim of flying rocks and debris and combat conditions, the area was calm at the time of the shooting. It shows an officer slowly and deliberately firing. Greenberg was convinced that the film would be powerful evidence.

This never was proved, however, because the county agreed to settle the case before trial by paying Rundle an out-of-court settlement. The county denied any wrongdoing, as it did when it similarly settled other civil suits alleging police abuse during the People's Park protests. The total cost to taxpayers of these lawsuits, never made public, was at least $1,005,050, according to the author's survey of people involved in the cases. While the amount may seem low in terms of more modern settlements, at the time it was a large sum for police misconduct lawsuits. Governor Reagan and his staff often complained about taxpayers having to foot the bill for police responses to protests, but the deputies' alleged misconduct cost well more than the $764,000 his finance chief Caspar Weinberger reported as the price of deploying the National Guard in Berkeley during People's Park.

To be sure, the standard of proof necessary to prevail in civil court is substantially lower than in criminal court. Jurors must be convinced that a case is proved only by a preponderance of the evidence, rather than beyond a reasonable doubt. Moreover, in criminal court prosecutors must overcome jurors' historical reluctance to convict police officers for actions taken in the line of duty. And, as noted, witnesses and victims had been reluctant to cooperate with the FBI.

But it is also true that no one in the White House pressed Hoover to ensure FBI agents aggressively investigated the civil rights cases in Berkeley, as President Johnson had pushed the director in the Mississippi cases. Nixon was not so ardent a supporter of civil rights as was Johnson. Neither was his attorney general, John Mitchell. Nor, for that matter, was Jerris Leonard, the assistant attorney general in charge of the Justice Department's Civil Rights Division, whom *The Washington Post* called "a Mitchell man to the core." Even as Leonard was overseeing the FBI investigation of the deputies, he was secretly arranging for CIA officials to copy intelligence files that the Justice Department had compiled from FBI reports on twelve thousand people involved in lawful dissent nationwide, in an effort to determine whether they had "engaged in foreign travel" or "received foreign assistance or funding." (The CIA concluded in 1971 that there was no foreign control and direction of the American New Left, which is "basically self-sufficient and moves under its own impetus.")

Hoover had been putting his efforts into expanding the FBI's domestic intelligence operations. He had begun yet another program to investigate activist professors at Berkeley and other campuses across the nation, this one titled "Faculty Involvement in New Left Activities." He had continued to pressure the special agents in charge of FBI field offices to aggressively pursue COINTELPRO, the program that Congress would find unlawfully interfered with the constitutional rights of people dissenting from government policy. Angela Davis was one of COINTELPRO's targets. In July 1969, a UCLA student named William Divale, a self-described sex "swinger" whom the FBI had paid $15,000 for informing, wrote a letter to the campus newspaper revealing that Davis was being allowed to teach a philosophy course at UCLA even though she was a member of the Communist Party. Ed Montgomery, the FBI's man at the *San Francisco Examiner*, then publicized the allegation, leading to a major controversy over academic freedom. At Governor Reagan's urging, the regents fired her. FBI officials hoped the case would strengthen the university's ban on Communist professors and "deal a severe setback" to the party, but the U.S. Supreme Court ultimately upheld a ruling that the ban was unconstitutional and Davis was reinstated.

Hoover did not similarly push his agents to investigate the sheriff's deputies for their alleged civil rights violations during the People's Park protest. According to FBI records, he ordered agents to conduct "limited" investigations. This meant that agents' inquiries were circumscribed, that they did not have the opportunity to gather as much evidence as they might have in a full field investigation, and that there was less chance the jury deliberations would end in convictions. More rigorous FBI investigations, though, might also have embarrassed the bureau's close allies in the battle against subversives, especially the governor with presidential aspirations.

Soon after the Justice Department opened the FBI investigation of the deputies' conduct, Reagan dispatched two emissaries to FBI headquarters in Washington, D.C., to meet with his longtime contact, Assistant Director Cartha "Deke" DeLoach.

DeLoach received Herb Ellingwood and his aide, Theodore Baier, at

9:15 a.m. on July 17, 1969. Ellingwood was one of Meese's top assistants. Like Meese, he had been a prosecutor in the Alameda County District Attorney's Office under Frank Coakley. When Meese became Governor Reagan's executive assistant, Ellingwood took over his post as legal affairs secretary. And like Meese, Ellingwood was a secret contact of the FBI's Sacramento office.

In his subsequent memo on the meeting, DeLoach did not mention the federal investigation of the deputies. Instead, he described Ellingwood's frank account of the Reagan administration's great frustration with campus protests and the established governmental procedures for handling them. Ellingwood explained that the governor, as one member of the Board of Regents, could not outright fire the eight chancellors of the state university campuses whom he considered "more or less palliative" toward student activists. Reagan had considered asking friendly state legislators to carry bills to dismiss the chancellors, but concluded this was "politically unwise."

Moreover, Ellingwood complained, the California Supreme Court "has been worse than the U.S. Supreme Court insofar as favoritism towards these groups is concerned." He noted, however, that several justices would be retiring and that Reagan planned to appoint new ones, "which will cause a better balance towards conservatism."

Despite these difficulties, he said, "Governor Reagan is dedicated to the destruction of disruptive elements on California college campuses" and his administration "will attack these groups" through several methods.

These included "hounding the groups as much as possible by bringing any form of violation available against them." For example, he said, "if any of these groups has a bookstore on campus they will bring building code violations against them."

Reagan officials would also consider "referring tax violations to the Internal Revenue Service of the State of California and to the Federal Internal Revenue Service" to cause trouble for dissenters.

Finally, the administration would mount a "psychological warfare campaign" against them, said Ellingwood, adding that he would "confer with Department of Defense officials today to get ideas from those individuals as to how to conduct campaigns of that nature."

DeLoach replied that FBI officials "were well aware of such potentials."

When the author asked Meese about this, he replied, "I have no recollection at all of us planning to do these things . . . There was never any concentrated strategy to do these things."

As Ellingwood ended the meeting with DeLoach, he asked the FBI to give Reagan more intelligence reports for "the California fight against these groups."

He then handed DeLoach a copy of Reagan's white paper on People's Park, conveyed the governor's great admiration for Hoover, and thanked DeLoach for his time.

DeLoach passed Reagan's request for confidential information to Hoover.

"It is suggested that each request be handled on an individual and confidential basis," DeLoach wrote. "This has been done in the past and has worked quite successfully."

Hoover scrawled, in blue ink, "O.K.—H."

Epilogue: The Aftermath

On the morning of May 2, 1972, J. Edgar Hoover was found dead on the floor of his bedroom. Helen Gandy, his longtime secretary, quickly executed one of his final orders: to destroy his personal office files.

Thirty-five file cabinet drawers full of records were removed from his office and shredded. Gandy would later testify that none of them involved bureau business, that they were all private. But some documents survived, having been recently transferred to other files. They concerned illegal black bag jobs and other highly sensitive matters, such as the bureau's investigation into the 1971 bombing of the U.S. Capitol, during which agents bugged the home of Stew Albert, the former Vietnam Day Committee activist turned Yippie, and his wife, Judy Clavir, who would sue the FBI for unlawful surveillance and win a twenty-thousand-dollar settlement.

At 11:00 a.m. that day, Attorney General Richard Kleindienst told the world: J. Edgar Hoover, the FBI's first and only director, was dead at seventy-seven. The cause was given as "hypertensive cardio-vascular disease," a complication of high blood pressure, and possibly a heart attack. Hoover had served forty-eight years as head of the bureau, through eight presidents and sixteen attorneys general. Politicians of both parties were quick to praise him, and Congress voted to let his body lie in state in the Capitol rotunda, an honor that had been bestowed on few presidents. In Sacramento, Ronald Reagan declared that no man had meant more to America in the twentieth century.

Certainly, Hoover had meant a lot to him. Their special relationship had continued to grow through the last years of the director's life, in ways large and small. In September 1970, the FBI inspector Edward S. Miller sought out Reagan while auditing the Sacramento field office, as Mark Felt had three years before. The governor was "extremely cordial," Miller reported, and, as always, expressed his "highest regard for the Director." A few months later, Hoover met with Robert Mardian, the newly named assistant attorney general in charge of internal security for the U.S. Department of Justice. They discussed Soviet espionage and the need to more aggressively prosecute members of the Black Panthers, the Students for a Democratic Society, and the Weather Underground. Then they turned to another matter of mutual concern: Governor Reagan's recent association with Frank Sinatra and its potential harm to his political prospects.

That July, Sinatra, an erstwhile liberal, had announced he was backing Reagan's bid for reelection against the assembly speaker, Jesse Unruh. Reagan embraced his support, and Ol' Blue Eyes became chairman of Democrats for Reagan. But the suave singer had recently made some troubling headlines: while gambling at Caesars Palace in Las Vegas he scuffled with a casino executive, grabbed him by the throat, and vowed, "The mob will take care of you." An aroused local district attorney told reporters he wanted to question Sinatra about his "friendships with members of the underworld." It was the latest bad press about his Mafia associations. In 1963, for example, authorities revoked his gambling operator's license because he had entertained the Chicago mob boss Salvatore "Sam" Giancana at his Lake Tahoe casino, the Cal-Neva Lodge. Now Sinatra was performing around California, raising thousands for Reagan and enthralling Nancy. Mardian complained that his own efforts to convince the governor of "Sinatra's unsavory background" had been met with disbelief. Hoover assured Mardian he was "well acquainted" with Reagan and "will brief him concerning Sinatra." Reagan's FBI files do not indicate whether the director did, but Reagan continued to publicly associate with Sinatra, who continued to raise money for him.

Hoover sought to protect Reagan in other ways. In March 1971, one of the governor's assistants told his FBI contact there were "indications" that students were planning "disruptive activities" during Reagan's upcoming speech at the Los Angeles Trade Technical School. Hoover's aides ordered agents to investigate and pass the findings to Reagan's staff. A few days later, Reagan wrote Hoover to say, "I have just learned of your latest generosity where I am concerned . . . Once again, I am in your debt and just wanted you to know how very grateful I am. Here in California, the great cooperation we've always had with the Bureau continues and is a source of great comfort to me and, indeed, to all of us."

The director also loaned Reagan an armored Cadillac for his visit to a Los Angeles neighborhood that one bureau official described as a "ghetto area." Hoover kept several bulletproof limousines garaged at field offices in areas he frequented, such as Southern California, where he and Tolson liked to visit the horse racing tracks. And when Reagan inquired about buying the car, bureau executives proposed rigging the bid to ensure he got it. "If for some reason the Governor's office was not the high bidder and the high bidder was somebody unacceptable to us, we of course could withdraw the vehicle from the bidding process," one of them wrote. Hoover scrawled, "OK—H." The FBI had paid $19,377 for the 1967 car, and sold it to Reagan four years later for $3,000.

Reagan, meanwhile, defended Hoover. That spring, the nation's number one G-Man was caught in a cross fire: Sam Irvin, a senator from North Carolina, was pressing the Justice Department to turn over records on FBI surveillance activities. Senator Hale Boggs of Louisiana, the house majority leader, charged that the bureau had tapped the telephones of congressmen and adopted "the tactics of the Soviet Union and Hitler's Gestapo." The Citizens Commission to Investigate the FBI broke into the FBI's resident agency in Media, Pennsylvania, and was mailing stolen documents to selected politicians and newspapers, exposing the bureau's widespread spying on student and black activists and giving the public its first glimpse of COINTELPRO.

Reagan decided to counter all this in a speech to the California Peace Officers Association. But first, one of his assistants, Herb Ellingwood, confidentially asked bureau officials to give Reagan material "assailing the critics of the FBI and showing the FBI's accomplishments." They promptly provided a memo. "Critics accuse the FBI of being a 'secret police' and invading the privacy of citizens," it said. "Nothing could be more wrong. Mr. Hoover's whole career has been one of opposing a national police in this country." Reagan incorporated portions of it in his talk, without disclosing the bureau's editorial assistance. "Some critics make a mockery of the facts by suggesting that the FBI seeks to become some sort of secret police," he declared. "Unlike some who criticize him, J. Edgar Hoover's entire career has been devoted to keeping government the servant of the people rather than making government the master." In a note, Hoover thanked Reagan for "your effort to set the record straight."

Reagan was at a Republican governors' conference in White Sulphur Springs, West Virginia, when he learned of the memorial for Hoover. He immediately made plans to attend, and at his request two FBI agents met his party at Washington National Airport and escorted them to the Capitol. It was pouring rain as the grand rotunda filled with congressmen, cabinet members, and Supreme Court justices, including Lewis Powell, the recent appointee who had received Hoover's help several years earlier in preparing his speech criticizing the Free Speech Movement. Standing front and center were Hoover's top assistants, now serving as honorary pallbearers. A military honor guard unloaded the hearse and carried in the Boss's lead-lined casket. Chief Justice Warren Burger then spoke, lauding Hoover as "a man of high principles" who was "ready and able to deal with crisis after crisis." He lay in state for twenty-four hours as thousands of people filed by his closed coffin, at rest on the same black catafalque that once cradled Lincoln's body.

Hoover had been present at the birth of Reagan's political career, and Reagan was present at the end of Hoover's. The director was buried the next day in the Congressional Cemetery, after President Nixon eulogized him at National Presbyterian Church. "The American people today are tired of disorder, disruption, and disrespect for law," Nixon said. "America wants to come back to the law as a way of life, and as we do come back to the law, the memory of this great man, who never left the law as a way of life, will be accorded even more honor . . ." The casket was lowered and the flag shrouding it folded and presented to Tolson, who looked weak and confused. He had resigned the day after his companion's death, and on inheriting nearly all of his estate lived in Hoover's house among his antiques until his own death three years later.

Reagan's alliance with the FBI continued, with all the niceties. On February 27, 1973, Nancy Reagan and several of her friends were given "a very special tour" of headquarters. The governor was invited to more shoot-and-barbecues hosted by Los Angeles FBI agents. But the bureau's spying was about to be exposed as never before. Carl Stern, a reporter with NBC, had noticed the code name COINTELPRO in dossiers distributed from the break-in at the Pennsylvania FBI field office and filed a Freedom of Information Act request for records about it. Bureau officials refused, but in late 1973 a federal court ordered their release. Senator Frank Church's committee held its groundbreaking hearings and issued reports revealing the CIA's plots to assassinate foreign leaders and its testing of LSD on unwitting citizens, as well as the FBI's unconstitutional and unlawful intelligence operations. On April 7, 1977, a federal grand jury indicted John Kearney, a retired supervisor in the FBI's New York field office, for overseeing illegal mail opening and wiretapping in Manhattan during the Weather Underground investigation. It was the first of several anticipated indictments resulting from a Justice Department inquiry, and the charges rattled the bureau. In an unprecedented protest, some three hundred agents picketed outside the courthouse.

Once again Reagan came to the bureau's defense. Now in private life after two terms as governor, he was continuing his political evangelism through speeches, editorials, and a syndicated radio show. In a May 23, 1977, broadcast, he charged that proposed intelligence reforms would hamper the bureau's effectiveness. He contended that wiretapping and mail openings were necessary for FBI agents to uncover terrorist attacks in advance. He had urged the Justice Department to drop the prosecution of Alameda County sheriff's deputies who shot bystanders during the People's Park protests. Now he urged the department to drop the case against Kearney.

Justice officials dismissed the charges the following year but obtained new indictments against Mark Felt and Ed Miller, who as FBI inspectors had stopped by Governor Reagan's office to pay their respects. They were accused of authorizing illegal break-ins at the homes of relatives and acquaintances of Weather Underground fugitives who had claimed responsibility for bombings at the Capitol, the Pentagon, and other federal offices. Felt, age sixty-four, had become the FBI's second-highest official. Miller, fifty-four, had become head of the bureau's domestic intelligence division. The highest-ranking FBI officials ever prosecuted for misconduct, they insisted they authorized the warrantless searches in the interest of their country. The jury, however, found them guilty of conspiracy to violate civil rights. The judge dispensed lenient sentences—fines of $5,000 for Felt and $3,000 for Miller—which were stayed pending their appeals.

In one of his first acts as governor, Reagan had called on the FBI for help with the situation at Berkeley. In one of his first acts as president, he unconditionally pardoned agents Felt and Miller. Ten days after being sworn in on January 20, 1981, Reagan went outside the Justice Department's standard procedures and initiated the pardons with the assistance of Edwin Meese III, now his counselor. Reagan said, "The record demonstrates that they acted not with criminal intent but in the belief that they had grants of authority reaching to the highest levels of government." In a private note to Miller, he added, "I had made myself a campaign promise that I would reward you for what you had done for your country if I had the opportunity and if it became necessary. I'm sorry it took so long, but I couldn't push bureaucracy into a higher speed."

Reagan's action was extraordinary. Normally, a convict must apply for a pardon. Justice Department procedure specified they should wait at least three years. Most pardons, moreover, were granted only after the applicant had served time in jail or paid a fine. No one from the White House had even consulted the prosecutors, who were not pleased. One of them, Francis J. Martin, disputed Reagan's statement that Felt and Miller had no criminal intent in authorizing the break-ins. "That assertion is false," Martin wrote in an opinion piece published in *The New York Times*. "The FBI's own documents attest to the fact that it is false. After an eight-week trial, 12 jurors unanimously found it to be false." He added, "The American people fought a revolution to put a stop to just such official lawlessness—a lawlessness denounced in the days of the Founding Fathers as an exercise of arbitrary power that 'would put the liberty of every man in the hands of every petty officer.'"

The pardons signaled what was to come. In late 1982, a grassroots movement for a nuclear freeze was sweeping America, as more than three hundred city and county councils, seventeen state legislatures, and eleven million voters in eight states endorsed measures calling for an end to the arms race between the United States and the Soviet Union. As it became an issue in congressional elections that October, Reagan asserted the movement was "inspired not by the sincere and honest people who want peace but by some who want the weakening of America, and so are manipulating many honest and sincere people." He repeated the charge in November, saying "plenty of evidence" proved there were "foreign agents that were sent to help instigate and help create and keep such a movement going." This evidence, the White House added, included a story in *Reader's Digest* titled "The K.G.B.'s Magical War for Peace" by the senior editor John Barron, which claimed the freeze campaign was a Soviet scheme to secure military superiority. The *Reader's Digest* piece, it turned out, was based partly on articles by John Rees, the police informer who had supplied reports on Berkeley activists to Reagan's staff when he was governor, and who FBI officials had once described as "an unscrupulous, unethical individual" whose information "cannot be considered reliable."

Reagan's contention that foreign agents were behind the freeze movement recalled claims he had made years earlier that Communists were again taking over Hollywood, that reds had manipulated students protesting HUAC at San Francisco City Hall, and that there was a grand plot behind the urban riots of 1967. And like each of those assertions, his charges about the nuclear disarmament movement would eventually be disproved by the FBI's own reports. Though bureau officials initially backed Reagan, Director William Webster told *Face the Nation* in April 1983 that "the overall freeze effort does not seem to us to have been dominated . . . or successfully manipulated" by the Soviets.

By then President Reagan had signed an executive order that for the first time allowed the CIA to engage in domestic covert operations. He had relaxed restrictions on FBI investigations of domestic political groups, broadening their scope and the use of informers. William French Smith, Reagan's attorney general, assured the public that FBI guidelines would protect lawful political dissent and help prevent terrorist attacks.

But it was revealed in ensuing years that the FBI investigated Physicians for Social Responsibility, which advocated a bilateral nuclear freeze; questioned scores of American travelers to Nicaragua who opposed Reagan's support of the contras' efforts to violently overthrow the elected Sandinista government; and ran a "library awareness" program in which agents purportedly hunting Soviet agents pressured librarians across the nation to provide confidential information on patrons' book borrowing.

The FBI also mounted a massive inquiry into the activities of citizens challenging Reagan's policies in Central America. Fifty-nine field offices investigated the Committee in Solidarity with the People of El Salvador, or CISPES, collecting information on more than two thousand people and hundreds of organizations, including the Quakers' Friends Religious Society, the Southern Christian Leadership Conference, and the National Education Association. As they had in their investigation of the Vietnam Day Committee nearly twenty years earlier, agents photographed rallies, took down license plate numbers, and deployed informers. And like the VDC case, this one produced no charges of wrongdoing. The investigation stemmed from allegations, later proved false, that CISPES was funding terrorist groups in El Salvador. An internal FBI review found no proper basis for the probe and resulted in discipline for six supervisors. The Senate Select Committee on Intelligence called the CISPES inquiry a "serious failure in FBI management."

President Reagan also curtailed the Freedom of Information Act, expanded the kinds of information that could be withheld in the name of national security, and successfully urged Congress to pass a law that barred naming covert intelligence agents.

At a congressional hearing, Floyd Abrams, the renowned First Amendment lawyer, testified that Reagan's policies were consistently at odds with the free flow of information, which after all is the basis of free speech. "It is almost as if information were in the nature of a potentially disabling, contagious disease, which must be feared, controlled, and ultimately quarantined," he said.

On March 26, 1975, a bomb exploded in the women's restroom on the eleventh floor of the Great Western Bank Building in downtown Berkeley, above the FBI's resident agency, the offices of Don Jones and the other agents who covered the campus community. A group calling itself the Red Guerrilla Family, previously unknown to authorities, claimed credit for the attack, saying it was meant "to help defend the people from Fascist intimidation and harassment." There were no injuries, but broken water pipes flooded not only the FBI office, but also the tenth-floor office of Clark Kerr.

Within hours of being summarily fired by the Board of Regents, Kerr had been hired as chairman of the Carnegie Commission on the Future of Higher Education, the prestigious privately funded think tank. But while highly regarded nationally, he was shunned by the academic establishment in California. University associates refused to acknowledge him in public. He was warned that if he accepted an invitation to speak at the funeral of the football star Cort Majors, captain of UC Berkeley's "Wonder Teams" of the 1920s, other mourners would boycott it. He was asked not to attend the university's centennial celebration in 1968. And when he resumed his tenured position as an economics professor at Berkeley, Reagan told reporters, "It doesn't make sense to dismiss a coach and hire him back as an assistant coach." Six years later, Kerr had taught just one seminar and had been invited to visit other UC campuses only twice. Some students continued to see him as their enemy. While delivering a lecture at Indiana University, Kerr was "pied" by a graduate student wearing a Halloween mask. He calmly drew out a handkerchief, wiped the lemon meringue from his face, remarked that it was tasty, and completed his talk.

Kerr and his family still lived in the home he had built not far from campus on a precipice with a sweeping view of the Golden Gate Bridge and the western horizon, and he remained dedicated to public service. He became the leader of a group of distinguished scholars, businessmen, and clergymen calling for an end to the war in Vietnam. The National Committee for a Political Settlement in Vietnam lobbied politicians, held press conferences, and placed full-page ads in *The New York Times* calling for an immediate cease-fire, free elections, and full freedom for all political groups in South Vietnam. "I have the impression," he told a reporter, "that opportunities for negotiation were not fully exploited . . ."

After his dismissal as UC president and the FBI's false background report to President Johnson about him, Kerr never received another cabinet-level appointment. But in 1982, he was part of an official U.S. delegation monitoring elections in El Salvador. And in 1984 he chaired a panel that arbitrated a contract between the U.S. Postal Service and its two largest unions, ending a five-month deadlock with a contract for 500,000 employees in what was the nation's largest labor mediation.

However, it was with the Carnegie Commission that Kerr did his most important work during this period. From his office in downtown Berkeley, Kerr directed a series of studies that constitute the most exhaustive examination of the purpose and performance of higher education in America. These reports had a major impact on national policy and advanced the cause of universal access to quality higher education embodied in California's 1960 Master Plan: they directly contributed to the creation of the Basic Opportunity Grant Program, better known as the Pell Grant program, which provides federal grants to college students in financial need; the federal Fund for the Improvement of Post-Secondary Education, which supports innovative teaching programs; and the Health Manpower Act, which alleviated a potentially severe shortage of doctors and other health care professionals by making federal grants to medical schools and establishing regional Health Education Centers. Kerr also criticized schools for pursuing federal aid to grow the institution rather than benefit students. And he warned that higher education was entering an "age of survivalism," a time of less funding and public support.

On leaving Carnegie in 1980, he continued to promote educational reform. He called on colleges to expand programs for black and Hispanic studies. He urged the nation to prepare for "Tidal Wave II," the arrival of the children of the baby boomers who had themselves flooded the campuses in the sixties. Meanwhile, he produced a two-volume memoir, *The Gold and the Blue*. And the Pennsylvania farmer's son pursued his lifelong hobby of gardening, though he no longer assigned to weeds the names of troublesome students, faculty, and regents. The Board of Regents eventually appointed him president emeritus, and now buildings on four campuses are named for him, including the Clark Kerr Campus, a student housing complex at Berkeley.

Kerr died in 2003, at age ninety-two. In the late 1970s he requested his FBI files under the FOIA, but, according to Kerr, an FBI official told him "they couldn't send me anything." Until shown FBI records obtained during research for this book, Kerr said, he was unaware of the FBI's unlawful spying on campus or its campaign to fire him. He called the FBI's conduct "despicable." In a 2002 interview at his El Cerrito home, he said, "I always had a high opinion of the FBI, so it came to me as quite a shock that they would step outside their boundaries the way they did. I think they did me some damage." The FBI also harmed the integrity of the school by exacerbating internal disputes, he said, adding, "What bothers me is that the FBI would want to go so far outside its proper jurisdiction and get involved in the internal affairs of the university."

•

Mario Savio and his wife, Suzanne Goldberg, were still living in Berkeley when their second son, Nadav, was born in 1970. Savio was twenty-seven, and according to an FBI report had become unemployed earlier that year. He was tending to his family, shunning publicity, staying out of politics. "It's not so easy for myself to get busted at the drop of a hat when I've got two children I'm responsible for," he explained to a reporter for *The New York Times* in a short and reluctant interview. But that September, when he was readmitted to UC Berkeley as a junior in biological sciences, he again drew unwanted attention from newsmen and politicians. Asked about Savio's reappearance, Governor Reagan said, "Mr. Savio has been working on a job in Berkeley the last several years and he claims he simply wants to go back and get an education. If he reveals that he deceived us, then I think appropriate action will be taken."

There were signs, however, that Savio still was torn between school and politics. Less than three months later, he and his wife both filed as candidates for mayor in the upcoming Berkeley election. "Only one of us will eventually run, and we'll decide which one next week," he told a reporter. Neither of them entered the race, though, and after supporting a Berkeley city measure for community control of the police they dropped from sight.

In May a source at the phone company informed the FBI that the Savios were moving to Venice, a beach community west of Los Angeles. An agent staked out their new address to verify the tip. Savio had listed his phone number under "Alfredo Joe Marti," a play on his earlier use of the name of the Cuban poet José Martí, but again the humor was lost on the FBI. Another agent duly checked bureau files for any information on Alfredo Joe and notified the Secret Service of his new "alias."

Savio had all but disappeared. He was entering a new period of difficulty, turning sharply inward. His education was again on hold. He was scraping by financially. He was increasingly depressed and wracked by self-doubt. His marriage was disintegrating. In April 1972, newspapers reported that Suzanne Goldberg had sued for divorce, citing irreconcilable differences. An FBI agent examined the court case and verified it. She was an unemployed schoolteacher, allowed to file *in forma pauperis* without paying the usual forty-four-dollar court fee. Goldberg would later say their union failed not because she and Savio fought but because he had been waylaid by his psychological problems and felt wholly inadequate as husband and father. For a while she remained in Venice, according to a bureau report, living at the odd address of 924½ Mario Place. She won custody of their sons and returned with them to Berkeley, where she studied health sciences. Savio despaired. At one point he appeared at the Los Angeles home of Jackie Goldberg, a fellow Free Speech Movement leader. "He showed up homeless on my doorstep," she recalled. "He was in a very bad emotional state, and he just needed a place to stay."

Hoover died that May of 1972 and the Watergate burglars were arrested in June, an event that would eventually lead to the impeachment of President Nixon. The FBI continued to track Savio, but in July agents suddenly lost him. Posing as a former acquaintance, one agent phoned the home of Savio's parents, but the woman who answered said she had no idea where he was. For seven months agents could not locate him. The space on his Administrative Index card for his home address was stamped "unknown." Finally a confidential source tipped off the FBI that he was receiving psychiatric care at the Neuropsychiatric Institute at UCLA. Richard Schmoerlitz, another student involved in the FSM, was also being treated there and recalled, "I really couldn't talk to him much about it but I thought it was really crazy that Mario and I, who had both fought [the] University of California, flipped out at the same time and wound up committed inside the system." The FBI promptly updated its detention list to show the hospital as Savio's residence, in case agents needed to arrest him as a security threat during a national emergency.

Savio had been overcome by internal pressures, compulsive thinking, and panic attacks. He was unable to function at jobs. He worried about money and about his disabled son. He sank deeper into depression. In the midst of all this, his mother died from cancer. Devastated, he attempted suicide. The Free Speech Movement had given Savio's conflicting inner forces an external focus, a constructive outlet, and a loving and supportive community. But as the movement faded, he found himself more and more alone against his demons. When his marriage broke up, he was admitted to the psychiatric hospital and spent long periods there as an inpatient. In unpublished poems, he wrote of patients in restraints, on "sleep dep" and "behavior-mod," of "poison working in my soul," and of having "the prettiest room in hell."

By early 1974, Savio had returned to Venice, where he lived alone, in seclusion. Bearded and thin, he rented a small one-room apartment with a bed, a desk, a chair, and a chest of drawers. On it stood a statue of the Virgin Mary, for whom he had been named. He taught mathematics at Mar Vista Elementary, an alternative school in Venice. Sometimes he attended meetings of the Venice Town Council, at which he requested the installation of street signals for the safety of the children. He took no leadership positions.

Still, he was so disturbed by the May 1974 shootout between the Los Angeles Police and members of the Symbionese Liberation Army—in which thousands of bullets were fired, the house caught fire, and six SLA members inside died—that he wrote an op-ed piece about it for the *Los Angeles Times*. Without endorsing the SLA's criminal activities, he argued that the police had used "brutal and excessive" force, administering summary execution when they should have cordoned off the area, waited out the suspects, and let the criminal justice system decide their fate. The police actions, he argued, had endangered the public and the democratic process. The FBI added a copy of the editorial to his dossier.

Savio was nearly inactive politically, yet he remained enmeshed in the gears of government surveillance until January 21, 1975, when the FBI finally closed his file and rescinded its "lookout" notice for him. That very day, Congress created the Church committee to investigate FBI abuses of power. The committee soon revealed an astonishing array of improper bureau activities, such as anonymously mailing Martin Luther King, Jr., an audiotape of his personal activities recorded through microphones secreted in his hotel rooms, along with a note suggesting he commit suicide before it became public. The committee's findings prompted calls for a legislative charter defining the FBI's powers. Congress backed down, however, after President Gerald Ford's administration agreed to adopt internal guidelines for FBI activities, which, unlike a charter, could be revised at the president's discretion.

The year Reagan was elected as the fortieth president, Savio married Lynne Hollander, who had been arrested in the big sit-in at Sproul Hall. She had transferred to Cal from Bryn Mawr partly because she was taken with Allen Ginsberg's poem "A Strange New Cottage in Berkeley," and was a senior in English when she sat down in the crowd around the police car that fall of 1964. She admired Savio—she would later say she was immediately attracted to his "whole being"—and they became friends. He smoked marijuana for the first time with her and Michael Rossman, and the summer after the FSM, she drove cross-country with a group that included him and Suzanne; when the Savios went off to England, she went to Mississippi to do civil rights work. She returned to school and became a clinical psychologist, but during Savio's troubled years she stayed in close touch with him. They lived in an apartment on Greenwich Street in San Francisco in the late seventies, married in 1980, and had a son named Daniel. Savio finally returned to school—not to Berkeley, but to San

Francisco State University, where he graduated summa cum laude with a bachelor's degree in 1984, and a master's degree in 1989, both in physics. He taught at San Francisco State and Modesto Junior College, and eventually resumed political activity, albeit in a more measured manner.

In 1984, he revisited Berkeley to join in commemorating the twentieth anniversary of the Free Speech Movement. It was during the same period that Kerr served as an official observer of the elections in El Salvador and Reagan was helping fund the contras' effort to overthrow Nicaragua's democratically elected Sandinista government. Looking older than his forty-one years, with a bald pate and a gray ponytail, Savio once again spoke from the Sproul steps. He condemned Reagan's policies in Central America and urged students to protest them before they caused "another Vietnam." He wept as the large crowd sang a civil rights song. The following year, Savio returned, this time to support students protesting the university's ties to investments in apartheid South Africa. Scores of them had been arrested, and he urged them to persevere, saying activists at other campuses looked to those at Berkeley for inspiration.

In 1990, Savio and his family moved to Sebastopol, a bucolic town in Sonoma County not far from the coast. He became an instructor at Sonoma State University, teaching physics, math, and logic to remedial students. In the ensuing years, he fought against Proposition 187, the ballot measure that denied public health and educational services to illegal immigrants, which he called scapegoating. (It was passed by voters but ruled unconstitutional in federal court.) He opposed Proposition 209, which rolled back affirmative action programs in state employment, education, and contracting. (Passed by voters, it was upheld in federal court.) And he became feverishly involved in fighting a proposal to raise student fees on the ground that it would unfairly harm poor students, and participated in a charged debate with the president of Sonoma State. (The fee hike was successfully challenged.) The latter effort strained him physically. Since the early 1980s he had been having health problems related to a condition called mitral valve prolapse, in which one of the heart valves does not close properly. He had several bouts of endocarditis, an associated infection, three of which had required hospitalization. He had recently experienced an episode of atrial fibrillation, or irregular heartbeat. Not long after the debate, while helping his son move an amplifier, he had a cardiac arrest, went into a coma, and never regained consciousness. He died on November 6, 1996. He was fifty-three years old.

University of California officials had resisted prior efforts to honor the school's most famous student protester, but after his death they permitted a small bronze plaque to be embedded in the Sproul Hall steps, reading MARIO SAVIO STEPS, DEDICATED 1997. And with funding from a sympathetic alumnus, the Free Speech Movement Café was opened in the undergraduate library at Berkeley.

Savio gave one of his last speeches at Berkeley when the Free Speech Movement turned thirty, as even this generational revolt crossed that inevitable threshold. It was late 1994 and the world was again in turmoil.

"We are moving right now in a direction which one could call creeping barbarism," Savio declared, as he crystallized the philosophy that had guided him throughout his life. "We have to be prepared, on the basis of our moral insight, to struggle even if we do not know that we are going to win."

Appendix: My Fight for the FBI Files

Notes

Selected Bibliography

Documents, Interviews, and Other Sources

Acknowledgments

Index

Appendix: My Fight for the FBI Files

This book began when my phone rang one afternoon in the summer of 1981. I was a senior at UC Berkeley, living in an apartment above the Berkeley Co-op's grocery store on University Avenue, and my editor at *The Daily Californian*, Ken Weiss, was on the line. The student newspaper had obtained about nine thousand pages of previously secret FBI files concerning the campus during the sixties. Would I see if there was a story?

I already knew UC Berkeley had been an epicenter of student protests, which Ronald Reagan had made a top issue in his 1966 campaign for governor. I also knew that congressional hearings in the seventies had revealed widespread FBI surveillance and harassment of citizens engaged in dissent elsewhere. Now I had a chance to see what the FBI had been up to at Berkeley.

A few days later I was pushing a hand truck loaded with FBI files across campus to my apartment, wondering what they might reveal. I had no idea I was embarking on a thirty-one-year odyssey into the FBI's covert campus activities; that I would bring five lawsuits under the Freedom of Information Act in a precedent-setting legal fight that would reach the steps of the U.S. Supreme Court; that the FBI would spend more than $1 million trying to withhold public information in these cases; and that ultimately the story would involve not only FBI operations on campus but a CIA director, the Board of Regents, a plot to fire UC president Clark Kerr, and the man who would become the nation's fortieth president.

Back in 1977, *The Daily Cal* had sent the FBI a "massive" FOIA request and declared on its front page, "The public has a right to know the extent of FBI surveillance activities in Berkeley during the 60's and early 70's." Over the following years, some documents trickled into the newspaper's office at 2490 Channing Way. Then Weiss called, and soon the files, the subject of my senior project, were spread across the old door propped up on milk crates that I used as a desk. The next year, *The Daily Cal* published my stories based on those records. They disclosed that the FBI had tried to "disrupt" the 1964 Free Speech Movement, which challenged the university's unconstitutional rule against on-campus political activity, as well as the Vietnam Day Committee, which in 1965 organized some of the nation's largest antiwar protests.

Reading those files, I suspected there was more to the story of the FBI in Berkeley. Many pages had been heavily excised. Others seemed to be missing. Still others hinted at files not yet requested. One memo in particular intrigued me because J. Edgar Hoover himself had scrawled in the margin, "I know Kerr is no good." What did this mean? Why was America's most powerful law-enforcement official demonizing one of its most respected educators? When I asked Kerr about it at his office at the Institute for Industrial Relations, a few blocks off campus, the president emeritus shrugged. With typical reserve, Kerr told me he had no idea, but would like to know if I ever found out. He added that he had requested his own FBI files years earlier, with little success. I asked Kerr to sign a waiver permitting me to request his otherwise private files and he did, as did Mario Savio and several other activists during the course of my research.

In November 1981, I hunkered down over the cast-iron Royal I'd bought second-hand at a nearby typewriter shop and banged out the first in a series of FOIA requests for "any and all" records on Kerr, Savio, and more than a hundred other people, organizations, and events. With some anticipation, I mailed it at the downtown Berkeley post office. I figured I'd receive the new files within a year or so, write up my findings, and move on to the next story. Two and a half years later, I was still waiting for the files. Meanwhile, I took a job as a cub reporter with the *San Francisco Examiner*, covering cops and courts in suburban Redwood City. I continued to pursue the FBI file project independently, and consulted with Lowell Bergman, Dan Noyes, and David Weir, founders of the Center for Investigative Reporting, the independent nonprofit news organization. The Center referred me to the San Francisco civil rights lawyer Thomas Steel, who took my case pro bono and over the next several years filed three lawsuits to pry loose the files.

The Freedom of Information Act is the law that established the public's right to records of federal agencies. Before the FOIA was passed, federal officials had wide discretion to withhold information on such vague ground as "for good cause found." The law says all records of executive-branch agencies are presumed to be public and must be released upon request, unless the contents fall into nine exempt categories, such as national security, law enforcement, and personal privacy. A key measure allows requesters to challenge agency denials of information in federal court. Thus, while the Constitution guarantees free speech, the FOIA ensures that people have access to data that can be crucial for informed speech. Yet no presidential administration has fully embraced the act: President Johnson threatened to veto it before it was passed in 1966, and President Ford did veto the 1974 amendments that Congress nonetheless approved to strengthen it. Generally, Republicans have been less supportive of the FOIA and Democrats more, but in my experience the FBI consistently withholds far too much public information.

The FOIA (pronounced *foy*-ah) requires agencies to waive processing fees when releasing records would "primarily benefit the general public." But the FBI determined there was little public interest in releasing the records I had requested and demanded that I pay thousands of dollars before they would process them. In 1985, Steel filed a lawsuit seeking a fee waiver. In an affidavit, I explained that releasing the records would benefit the public because they would shed light on how the FBI had secretly affected the nation's largest public university. I explained that not only the contents of the records, but also the bureau's internal administrative markings and handwritten notations—like Hoover's remark that Kerr was "no good"—were necessary for fully understanding FBI operations. Later that year, U.S. District Judge Marilyn Hall Patel ruled that the bureau had "abused its discretion in failing to conform to its own guidelines" and ordered it to waive all fees, saying, "Plaintiff has persuasively demonstrated in his affidavit that his research requires meticulous examination of records that may not on their face indicate much to an untrained observer."

The FBI released several thousand pages of records but heavily excised them, sometimes blacking out whole pages. I wondered whether the bureau was America's biggest consumer of Magic Markers. The FBI variously claimed the information had to be withheld to protect the privacy of people named in the records, law enforcement operations, and national security. What lay behind the impenetrable darkness of the FBI's black felt-tip pen? If I couldn't see the information, how could I persuade the court to order its release? I spent evenings and weekends analyzing the records. My initial research relied on UC Berkeley libraries, especially the government document, newspaper, and periodical libraries. There I found evidence that cast doubt on the secrecy claims. And while browsing at Shakespeare & Co., a used book store on Telegraph Avenue, I stumbled upon *I Lived Inside the Campus Revolution,* in which one of the FBI's student informers recounted his undercover exploits—about which the FBI was nonetheless withholding information. My research filled a growing number of file cabinets in my second-story apartment on San Francisco's Telegraph Hill, causing my landlord concern about the strength of his floors.

In a second lawsuit, Tom Steel and his staff challenged the deletions. In an effort to convince the government to release the information, David Golove, the main attorney on this part of the case, and I flew to Washington, D.C. An agent assigned to the case met us in the lobby of the J. Edgar Hoover Building and escorted us to our meeting, remarking en route that he'd rather be kicking down doors and making arrests. We sat at one end of a long conference table in a windowless room, while representatives of the FBI, the army, the air force, and several other federal agencies that had deleted parts of the records clustered at the other end. Each time we questioned a deletion, these officials got up en masse and went outside to confer. This process, unfortunately, proved fruitless.

Ultimately, five federal judges would order the FBI to release information. In 1988, then–U.S. Magistrate Claudia Wilken concluded that the FBI was wrongly withholding information on the Free Speech Movement and Kerr. In 1991, Judge Patel adopted the magistrate's findings with few changes. Patel ruled that I had presented "highly persuasive" evidence, consisting mostly of the FBI's own documents, that showed that the bureau's initially lawful investigation of the Free Speech Movement—undertaken to determine whether the protests violated federal laws or threatened national security— had turned into political spying. The judge also found that FBI records showed that the bureau had investigated Kerr unlawfully. Information deleted from these records, therefore, could not be withheld on law-enforcement grounds. Moreover, the FBI in several instances had fought to keep secret information that already was public, Patel said, adding, "These circumstances raise serious doubt about the care and good faith in which defendants have processed these requests."

Ten years had passed since I mailed off my initial request, and I thought I'd finally get to the records, but the FBI asked Patel to reconsider. She declined, noting there was a strong public interest in disclosure because "the records in this case go [to] the very essence of what the government was up to during a turbulent, historic period of time." The FBI appealed to the Ninth Circuit U.S. Court of Appeals. But in a 1995 decision written by Judge Melvin Brunetti, the appeals court affirmed virtually all of Patel's ruling. Having reviewed the uncensored FBI records in chambers, the appeals panel concluded that the documents "strongly suggest" that the bureau's investigation of the FSM became an effort to "harass political opponents of the FBI's allies among the Regents, not to investigate subversion and civil disorder." The court also found that "Rosenfeld introduced evidence showing that the FBI waged a concerted effort in the late 1950s and 1960s to have Kerr fired from the presidency of UC." These bureau records, it said, "strongly support the suspicion that the FBI was investigating Kerr to have him removed from the UC administration, because FBI officials disagreed with his politics or his handling of administrative matters."

Now, I thought, I will at last see the records—but the FBI asked the three-judge appeals court to reconsider. When it declined, the FBI asked the entire Ninth Circuit, comprised of judges throughout the western states, to review the decision. No judge voted to take the case. Nonetheless, in late 1995 the FBI filed a petition for review with the U.S. Supreme Court. This posed several possibilities: I might well prevail, but the court might further delay the records' release and overturn the Ninth Circuit's decision in favor of open government. For its part, the FBI risked the possibility of another adverse ruling, especially since its own documents were so damning.

Before the Supreme Court decided whether to review the case, Steel's office crafted a settlement that kept the Ninth Circuit's precedent on the books and required the FBI to release the records with fewer redactions. In addition, the bureau paid Steel more than $600,000 under a provision of the FOIA—intended to promote government accountability—that requires federal agencies to pay the legal fees of plaintiffs who have substantially prevailed. That sum was in addition to the bureau's own legal costs and the $900,000 it said it had spent processing records that it now had to reprocess.

The settlement also resolved the third suit, which I had filed in 1990 to force the FBI to release the rest of the records in a timely way. The bureau claimed it was diligently handling the request, but Patel found it had "deliberately and unlawfully" delayed the records' release. "At the FBI's current rate," she said, "processing of plaintiff's FOIA request will take forty years."

Finally, the FBI began to release information it had been withholding for more than fifteen years. In 1997 I took a year's unpaid leave from the *Examiner's* investigative team to start researching the files, which at this point totaled more than 200,000 pages. Here at last was the secret history of the FBI's role in some of the most dramatic events of the sixties. A note scrawled by Hoover in 1971 reflected the bureau's institutional reticence. "I sense *utter fright* as to the Freedom of Information Act. It doesn't open up the flood gates to every 'kook,' 'jackal' and 'coyote' to all our publications, files & records.—H." I had not finished reviewing the records by the time I was due to return to the newspaper. Then, in 2000, the Hearst Corporation sold the *Examiner* and bought the *San Francisco Chronicle*, and I moved to the morning paper along with most of my colleagues. I proposed a story based on the FBI records, and on June 9, 2002, the *Chronicle* published "The Campus Files: Reagan, Hoover and the UC Red Scare." The article revealed how Hoover and other FBI officials had campaigned to get Kerr fired, which he was, in January of 1967, at the first meeting attended by the newly elected Governor Reagan.

I was glad to get the story out after so many years. The Associated Press picked it up, and accounts appeared in newspapers around the country and on radio and television. The article also prompted editorials, including one in *The New York Times* that said "These accounts of the F.B.I.'s malfeasance are a powerful reminder of how easily intelligence organizations deployed to protect freedom can become its worst enemy." The FBI refused to respond to the *Chronicle's* findings, but the newspaper received more than five hundred e-mails and letters from readers. Senator Patrick Leahy of Vermont, the chairman of the Senate Judiciary Committee, said at a hearing that the bureau's efforts to get Kerr fired were "outrageous and some would even say criminal conduct on the part of the FBI . . ." Senator Dianne Feinstein of California wrote the FBI director, Robert S. Mueller III, two letters expressing her "deep concern" about the *Chronicle's* disclosures and asking him to outline steps taken to prevent the FBI from again misusing its power. She also asked if the FBI had deliberately tried to cover up embarrassing information in FBI documents, adding, "As we have seen from this *Chronicle* article, FOIA is often the only way the American people can be assured of government accountability."

The FBI sent two replies to Feinstein. In a September 26, 2002, letter, Eleni P. Kalisch, section chief of the bureau's Government Relations office, addressed some of her questions and assured her that "the FBI did not deliberately seek to prevent Mr. Rosenfeld from obtaining the information he requested." Three months later, Director Mueller made a more complete response: "First, I want to state clearly my personal opinion about the extralegal investigations cited in your first letter," he wrote on December 23. "As a citizen of this country, I abhor any investigative activity that targets or punishes individuals for the constitutional expression of their views. Such investigations are wrong and anti-democratic, and past examples are a stain on the FBI's greater tradition of observing and protecting the freedom of Americans to exercise their First Amendment rights. Any repeat of such abuses will substantially reduce public confidence in the FBI and therefore undercut our ability to combat crime and protect our country against terrorism and espionage. For these reasons, I will tolerate no such undertakings in today's FBI. Second, I would like to explain why I am confident that we will not see a return to the investigative excesses you cited in your letter. Those investigations all took place prior to the establishment of the comprehensive oversight apparatus and the legal limitations that currently govern the conduct of domestic intelligence operations."

Mueller said he had asked the FBI's general counsel to examine the record of my FOIA cases to determine whether the bureau "pursued litigation as a means to prevent or delay Mr. Rosenfeld from obtaining information to which he was entitled under the FOIA." Mueller also instructed the Records Management Division to "determine whether the FBI redacted information in order to shield the FBI from embarrassment or to cover up unlawful activities." He declared, "To the extent that the FBI's conduct regarding this case is proven to have been inappropriate or ill-motivated, I will take steps to make sure such conduct is not repeated."

In July 2005 I requested a copy of the general counsel's inquiry under the FOIA. Sixteen months later, in November 2006, the FBI released a memorandum—but deleted all the findings. However, the memo still contained a quote from Howard Shapiro, then the FBI's general counsel, complaining that in the bureau's failed appeal to the Ninth Circuit, "it appears that we were advancing arguments that bordered on the frivolous in order to cover our own previous misconduct."

I had hoped that after all the litigation the FBI would swiftly release the rest of the files concerning UC during the Cold War. The settlement agreement required all records to be produced by May 1997. But though the bureau released most of the records by then, it did not release what it claimed were the last 43,704 pages until February 2006. Even then, it was clear that other information should have been released as well. By now, Tom Steel had sadly passed away. David Greene and James Wheaton, attorneys with the nonprofit First Amendment Project in Oakland, took on my FOIA cases and filed the first of many court motions seeking the remaining records.

At a hearing before Magistrate Judge Elizabeth D. Laporte, a Justice Department attorney contended that the FBI had made "unprecedented" efforts to respond to my requests and had "substantially" complied with the settlement agreement. He urged her to reject my motion. But after considering the evidence, Laporte, in February 2007, ordered the FBI to conduct new searches. As a result, the bureau released another 41,373 pages. They included 4,650 pages on the FBI's counterintelligence program (COINTELPRO), which, among other things, showed that the bureau sought to covertly damage the careers of several UC faculty members.

The settlement agreement also required the FBI to release all records concerning Ronald Reagan from the earliest document up to January 1, 1979. The FBI released 2,894 pages, and closed this request. But it seemed the bureau was again improperly withholding information about its activities concerning an important public figure.

I tried to resolve the Reagan matter before Judge Laporte, since we were already before her on other parts of the settlement agreement, but the FBI insisted I file a new lawsuit in order to pursue it. I did, in June 2007, and the case was assigned to Judge Patel—but now the bureau claimed I had waited too long to challenge its processing of my original Reagan request. So I filed a new FOIA request for them, but then the FBI failed to respond within the statutory period. I amended my complaint to include this new request, as well as several others on subjects related to Reagan.

The FBI again denied my claims and sought to have them dismissed. One of the bureau's arguments was that I had failed to file administrative appeals for partial releases of records. But Judge Patel noted that I had filed several such appeals—and that the FBI had not responded to them for months. "Defendants are attempting to shield the disclosure of information by marshaling administrative technicalities," she said, ruling the case could proceed. "Indeed, it is the agency's delayed responses that purportedly made Rosenfeld's claims unexhausted."

Only after this fourth lawsuit did the FBI release records I had been seeking for years. In 2004 I had requested records on Alex Sherriffs, the UC Berkeley vice chancellor, Free Speech Movement foe, and bureau informer who became Governor Reagan's top education aide; the FBI had claimed it found no responsive records but now released twenty-two pages. The bureau had released nothing in response to my May 2006 request for records on Herbert Ellingwood, who became Governor Reagan's legal affairs secretary and was an FBI contact; now it released 1,381 pages. The FBI had released three pages in response to my 2005 request for records on Neil Reagan, Ronald Reagan's late brother and an FBI informer; now it released ninety-seven pages.

There was yet another battle over the Reagan records. First the FBI released more documents on the former governor, but most were not for the years I had requested. Then it released thirty-five pages and said there were no additional records. But the court found "numerous deficiencies" in the bureau's account of its searches, and FBI officials admitted they had misinterpreted my request. Eventually, the FBI released 6,398 pages for the correct period, along with another 1,073 pages on the Screen Actors Guild, of which Reagan had been president.

Then there were the mysterious "summary memoranda." I had noticed in the released files a series of memos that neatly listed dozens of records concerning Reagan, along with their file and serial numbers, which the FBI still had not processed. The bureau claimed they were not indexed under Reagan's name and therefore it had no obligation to produce them. But Patel ruled that "the fact remains that the non-released records pertain to the subject of the search and specifically inform the readers as to where to find additional information." As a result, the FBI released another 743 pages.

The documents reveal new details about Ronald Reagan's decades-long relationship with the FBI. They show he was a much more aggressive informer in Hollywood than previously thought and identify additional people he had reported to the FBI. For example, one document, about a meeting between Reagan, his wife, Jane Wyman, and FBI agents at Reagan's home on April 10, 1947, had been previously released in a censored form that identified three people whom the Reagans named as suspected Communists. The uncensored version identifies ten actors they named at this meeting. Another part of this document had been so heavily excised that it was incomprehensible. The unredacted pages, also released in response to my fourth lawsuit, show that while Reagan was president of the Screen Actors Guild, FBI agents had wide access to confidential guild personnel records on dozens of actors, including Lloyd Bridges, Lee J. Cobb, J. Edward Bromberg, and Gale Sondergaard.

Yet it appeared that the bureau was still making unfounded exemptions. David Greene, my attorney, and I tried to resolve these issues informally in conferences with members of the FBI's FOIA unit. For example, I brought up a document that read "On his 'General Electric Theater' series, Reagan has produced a two-part program concerning the activities of"—with the rest of the sentence deleted. I suspected the excised information concerned Marion Miller, an FBI informer who had surfaced to publicly testify before Congress about her undercover work, wrote a book called *I Was a Spy: The Story of a Brave Housewife*, and then let Reagan dramatize her story on his television show. I also noted that the bureau had previously released Miller's identity in another document. Yet FBI officials insisted the deletion was necessary to protect "law-enforcement information." Only when we challenged the document in court did the bureau release this information.

This unwarranted secrecy claim was significant for another reason: in the course of the lawsuit, we discovered that the FBI's FOIA unit maintains what it calls an "institutional knowledge" database of previously disclosed informers and deceased people. This and other deletions suggest the bureau does not consistently update the database or apply it to FOIA requests, and as a result, the FBI routinely withholds public information.

The newly released records also show that Hoover returned the favor of Reagan's assistance to bureau agents in Hollywood by helping him in his personal and political life. In records released to me in 1996, the FBI had deleted information about an investigation concerning Maureen Reagan, the daughter of Reagan and Jane Wyman. After the fourth lawsuit, the bureau released less heavily redacted records showing FBI agents had helped her concerned parents by investigating her turbulent romantic life, even while noting that this was clearly outside bureau jurisdiction.

The FBI still sought to withhold information about its special help to Reagan. Another document appeared to show Hoover warning Reagan that one of his close associates was consorting with the son of Mafia boss Joseph "Joe Bananas" Bonanno. The FBI had deleted this associate's identity on the ground that it was law-enforcement information. However, Judge Patel later ordered the bureau to release Michael Reagan's identity. "Information regarding acts taken to protect or promote Reagan's political career, or acts done as political favors to Reagan[,] serve no legitimate law enforcement purpose," she found. "Such activities fall outside of the FBI's statutory mandate. . . ."

Judge Patel also ruled that public figures and public officials have diminished privacy rights, and this weighs in favor of releasing information about them. This is especially true when they have voluntarily placed themselves in the public light, for example through political activity. She ordered the FBI to reprocess 1,300 pages and release additional information consistent with her findings.

Judge Patel assumed senior status, and in 2011 the case was transferred to Judge Edward M. Chen. In response to new challenges I filed, the FBI released the name of the Washington, D.C., police officer who was dating Maureen Reagan and whom the FBI had investigated on Ronald Reagan's behalf. The FBI also released Michael Reagan's name in a report saying he had been repeatedly seen with Joseph Bonanno, Jr. Benjamin Wolf Stein brought a fifth lawsuit on my behalf before Magistrate Judge Maria-Elena James, seeking records on Richard Aoki, who had boasted of arming the Black Panthers and whom I had learned was an FBI informant.

My fight for the files resulted in the release of the most extensive record of FBI activities concerning a university during J. Edgar Hoover's tenure, and the most complete release of bureau records on Ronald Reagan's pre-presidential years. These documents show that during the Cold War, FBI officials sought to change the course of history by secretly interceding in events, manipulating public opinion, and taking sides in partisan politics. The bureau's efforts, decades later, to improperly withhold information about those activities under the FOIA are, in effect, another attempt to shape history, this time by obscuring the past.

Reagan's long association with the FBI meant a great deal to him, and when Hoover sent a photograph of himself and Reagan posing together at FBI headquarters, Mrs. Reagan had it framed so her husband could display it in his office. During my fourth lawsuit, the bureau said it had searched all logical indexes and could not find the photo. In fact, the FBI revealed that it could not locate more than fifty-eight files on Reagan, and had destroyed forty-eight others pursuant to its record-keeping procedures.

FBI officials eventually found a copy of the photograph—in the bureau's public affairs office.

Notes

Abbreviations Used in Notes

Newspapers

BDG	*Berkeley Daily Gazette*
DC	*Daily Californian*
LAT	*Los Angeles Times*
NYT	*New York Times*
OT	*Oakland Tribune*
SFC	*San Francisco Chronicle*
SFX	*San Francisco Examiner*
SJM	*San Jose Mercury*
SJN	*San Jose News*
SJMN	*San Jose Mercury News*
SFBG	*San Francisco Bay Guardian*
SFNCB	*San Francisco News-Call Bulletin*
WP	*Washington Post* (also used for *Washington Post and Times Herald*)
LED	Letter to the Editor

Organizations, Institutions, and Individuals

ACS	Alex C. Sherriffs
ADA	Americans for Democratic Action
Bancroft	Bancroft Library, University of California at Berkeley
Church	U.S. Senate Select Committee to Study Governmental Operations with Respect to Intelligence Activities, chaired by the senator Frank Church
CIA	Central Intelligence Agency
CORE	Congress of Racial Equality
CP	Communist Party
FBI	Federal Bureau of Investigation
FSM	Free Speech Movement
HUAC	House Un-American Activities Committee (formally called House Committee on Un-American Activities or HCUA)
RR	Ronald Reagan
RRPL	Ronald Reagan Presidential Library
SAG	Screen Actors Guild
SNCC	Student Non-Violent Coordinating Committee
SWP	Socialist Workers Party
UC	University of California

UCB   University of California at Berkeley
VDC   Vietnam Day Committee

FBI Investigations and Programs
COINTELPRO   FBI's counterintelligence program
CINRAD   Communist Infiltration of the University of California Radiation
                 Laboratory, FBI investigation into
COMPIC   Communist Infiltration—Motion Picture Industry, FBI
                 investigation into
NR   Not Recorded (an FBI record that was not given a serial number)
SAC   Special Agent in Charge

A note on citations to FBI records and publications: For newspaper references, the first few words of the headline are included to identify the article. Complete book titles are listed in the Bibliography. For FBI records, in most instances documents are cited by their serial number, in which the first group of digits indicates the kind of investigation, the second group indicates the subject of the investigation, and the third group specifies the document within that file. (For example, 100-54060-1 is the first document in Mario Savio's internal security file.) The document date is included if there is more than one document with the same serial number in the file, or if the document has an incomplete or illegible serial number. The FBI had a practice of not assigning serial numbers to some documents, and instead marking them NR, for "Not Recorded."

Epigraph
vii   *The most beautiful*: Savio made the statement in an interview with Doug Gilles. An excerpt is at the Free Speech Movement Archives, www.fsm-a.org/stacks/mario /savio_gilles.htm.
vii   *The university*: Kerr's quote is in *Turning Points and Ironies*, 31.
vii   *Obey the prescribed*: Reagan is quoted in *LAT* 12/3/66, "Reagan UC Edict."
vii   *This presents the bureau*: Hoover made the point in 100-151646-218, 1/17/67.

Prologue: A Meeting at the Governor's Mansion
3   *Curtis O. Lynum*: The account of the meeting in Reagan's bedroom, and the events immediately leading to it, is based on 100-151646-216; 100-151646-218, 1/17/67; 100-151646-218, 1/19/67; 100-446740-14; *LAT* 12/21/72, "The New Governor's Mansion"; author interviews with Curtis O. Lynum and Glenn Harter.
3   *Reagan had been sworn*: He took the oath at 12:16 a.m., January 2, 1967, *NYT* 1/2/67, "Reagan Sworn"; *NYT* 12/4/66, "Reagan Starts"; *NYT* 1/6/67, "The Inauguration"; *SFC* 1/2/67, "Reagan Takes Oath."
3   *The Boss had taken*: The relationship between Hoover and Reagan is detailed and noted throughout the book as it develops.
3   *During a fiercely*: On the intensity of the 1966 gubernatorial race, see *Reagan*, 109; *Ronnie & Jesse*, 76, 78; *LAT* 5/28/66, "Reagan vs. Christopher"; *Reagan*, 116; *Ronnie & Jesse*, 80–82; *LAT* 8/12/66, "Coate Says Report Proves." On Berkeley becoming Reagan's hottest issue, see *Reagan*, 110, 113–14, 148; *Governor Reagan*, 9, 150, 157, 271.
3   *Back when he*: Where, 26–30; *Early Reagan*, 88–94.
3   *He was disgusted*: For examples of Reagan's expressions of extreme displeasure with Berkeley protests, see *LAT* 1/22/65, "Reagan to Decide Soon"; *OT* 10/22/65, "Reagan Critical of UC Officialdom"; *OT* 5/13/66, "U.C. Probe Demanded by Reagan";

BDG 5/13/66, "Reagan Urges UC Quiz"; *SFX* 5/13/66, "4,500 Hear S.F. Talk by Reagan"; *SFC* 5/13/66, "Reagan Lashes"; *LAT* 5/13/66, "Reagan Demands"; *NYT* 5/14/66, "Reagan Demands Berkeley Inquiry."

4   *He declared that "beatniks . . .":* The quote is from Reagan's May 1966 speech at the Cow Palace, described in Chapter 19.

4   *His message resonated: Governor Reagan,* 157, 271.

4   *Reagan defeated:* Reagan was elected governor on November 8, 1966, by nearly one million votes, *LAT* 11/9/66, "Reagan Triumphs"; *LAT* 11/9/66, "Government of All"; *NYT* 11/10/66, "Reagan Emerging"; *Governor Reagan,* 160.

4   *Hoover welcomed:* 100-382196-11; 100-151646-218, 1/17/67; author interview with Cartha DeLoach.

4   *For years:* Hoover's concern about allegedly subversive activities at UC Berkeley are documented in the FBI's files on the university, particularly 100-151646 and 100-34204. Former FBI agents also described it in author interviews with Cartha De-Loach, Curtis O. Lynum, Glenn Harter, Burney Threadgill, Jr., and Wesley Grapp.

4   *Berkeley had been:* UC Berkeley's rise to become the nation's largest and best public research university, its historical commitment to no tuition, and its key government contracts are discussed in Clark Kerr's memoirs, *The Gold and the Blue,* volumes 1 and 2, hereafter "Kerr." When Kerr became UC president in 1958, the university had seven Nobel laureates, *NYT* 11/26/57, "University of California Names Urey"; *LAT* 11/29/57, "UC Faculty Is Growing Stronger."

4   *But even as:* The FBI's investigation of suspected Soviet spies at the UC-run radiation labs that helped develop the atomic bomb is documented in 100-190625. This investigation, code-named CINRAD, is discussed in *American Prometheus* and *Brotherhood of the Bomb.*

4   *In the Cold War:* Hoover and other FBI officials' general suspicion of professors who refused to sign the loyalty oath is expressed throughout FBI files concerning the university. See, for example, indexed newspaper clippings in 100-34204-35, 100-34204-36, 100-34204-37, 100-34204-38, and the 1960 FBI report on UC's "political complexion," which lists professors who opposed the oath, 62-103031-87.

4   *So far, the sixties . . . to other campuses:* The bureau's mounting concern about protests emanating from UC Berkeley in the sixties is documented in bureau files, including those on the university, the Free Speech Movement, the Vietnam Day Committee, Stop the Draft Week, the Third World Liberation Front, People's Park, and other protests, and the people and organizations involved with them, as described in the following chapters.

4   *Stepping up its efforts:* Several excellent books have examined FBI activities at various colleges. See, for example, Theoharis, *Chasing Spies;* Schrecker, *No Ivory Tower;* Diamond, *Compromised Campus.* In addition, the U.S. Senate Select Committee to Study Governmental Operations with Respect to Intelligence Activities, known as the Church committee for its chairman, Senator Frank Church, and hereafter called "Church," revealed FBI activities on campuses, such as the bureau's effort in 1968 to tarnish the reputation of Antioch University in Ohio because it was a "center for New Left activity," Church, book III, 5; Church, vol. 6, 434–39. The Church committee also reported that the FBI sought to undermine the Free University of New Mexico and "other alternative schools," Church, book III, 5. Moreover, "in 1970 the FBI ordered investigations of every member of the Students for a Democratic Society and of 'every Black Student Union and similar group regardless of their past or present involvement in disorders,' " Church, book II, 8. The FBI targeted "almost every" antiwar group and "students demonstrating against anything," Church, book III, 26. However, none of the foregoing works exhaustively examined the FBI's

long-term activities in a single campus community. UC's unique roles in both the production of atomic weapons and in social and political protest attracted intense scrutiny from the FBI, and the documents released to the author provide an unprecedented view of the bureau's operations in the campus community.

4   *The FBI has long*: See SFC 6/9/02, "Reagan, Hoover and the UC Red Scare." In a 1965 memo on allegedly subversive activities at the university, for example, a top FBI official wrote, "We have never conducted an investigation of that university or of any other university as such. Information of a subversive nature concerning activities on any college campus has been developed through investigations we have conducted of specific individuals and organizations . . ." See 100-151646-185. But as the Church committee found, the FBI's investigation of alleged Communist infiltration of organizations often exaggerated that threat and used it as a basis for the investigations, which came to focus on completely lawful First Amendment activities. See Church, book II, 48, 49, 67–68, 81, 175–82.

4   *But a legal challenge*: Starting in 1985, the author brought four lawsuits under the FOIA in the U.S. District Court for Northern California that resulted in the release of the records. See C-85-1709 MHP, C-85-2247 MHP, C-90-3576 MHP, and C-07-03240 MHP, each captioned *Seth Rosenfeld v. United States Department of Justice and Federal Bureau of Investigation*. The author's legal fight for the files is described in the Appendix.

5   *In court papers*: The FBI asserted that its activities were lawful in the course of defending its withholding of information from the released records. See Declaration of Special Agent Angus B. Llewellyn, a supervisor in the FBI's FOIA Section, in *Seth Rosenfeld v. U.S. Department of Justice and Federal Bureau of Investigation*, C-85-2247 MHP and C-85-1709 MHP. In regard to the Free Speech Movement, for example, Llewellyn stated, "The investigation was conducted in order to ascertain the influence or involvement in the Free Speech Movement by individuals affiliated or associated with subversive groups, such as the Communist Party of the United States of America (CPUSA), the Young Socialist Alliance (YSA), Progressive Labor Party (PLP), the Socialist Workers Party (SWP), or of CPUSA-front groups, such as the W.E.B. Dubois Club." Llewellyn further stated the FBI had a responsibility to investigate matters of espionage, insurrection, seditious conspiracy, and civil disorders, riots, and civil rights. In regard to Clark Kerr, Llewellyn stated that the FBI's investigations were conducted pursuant to its duties to conduct background and applicant inquiries at the request of various federal agencies and the White House.

5   *But the records show . . . protect national security*: As a result of the author's lawsuits under the FOIA, both the U.S. District Court and the Ninth Circuit U.S. Court of Appeals ruled that certain FBI activities concerning the Free Speech Movement and Clark Kerr had no legitimate law-enforcement purpose and were conducted for political purposes. See *Seth Rosenfeld v. United States Department of Justice*, Ninth Circuit U.S. Court of Appeals, Decision, 57 F3d 803; *Seth Rosenfeld v. United States Department of Justice*, C-85-1709 MHP and C-85-2247 MHP, Consolidated, opinion entered 3/29/91. In addition, as a result of another FOIA lawsuit brought by the author, the court found that certain FBI activities involving Ronald Reagan had no legitimate law-enforcement purpose and were political in nature; see *Seth Rosenfeld v. United States Department of Justice*, C-07-3240 MHP Memorandum & Order, filed 9/1/10. Other FBI activities described in this book are consistent with those that the U.S. Senate Select Committee to Study Governmental Operations with Respect to Intelligence Activities, popularly known as the Church committee, found to be unlawful or unconstitutional. See *Intelligence Activities and the Rights*

of Americans, Final Report, book II, 1976, and *Supplemental Detailed Staff Reports on Intelligence Activities and the Rights of Americans*, book III, 1976.

5   *As a federal appeals*: Seth Rosenfeld v. *United States Department of Justice*, Ninth Circuit U.S. Court of Appeals, Decision, 57 F3d 803.

5   *And as U.S. District*: Seth Rosenfeld v. *United States Department of Justice*, C-85-1709 MHP and C-85-2247 MHP, Consolidated, opinion entered 9/23/91.

5   *In response to this*: Mueller made his comments in a letter dated December 23, 2002, to Senator Dianne Feinstein, in response to the author's June 9, 2002, article in the *San Francisco Chronicle*, "Reagan, Hoover and the UC Red Scare." Some of his comments were reported in *SFC* 2/16/03, "FBI Chief Admits '60s Spying on UC 'Wrong.'"

5   *FBI documents show*: The FBI's misleading report about Clark Kerr is discussed in Chapter 14.

5   *. . . mounted a covert campaign*: The FBI's media campaign about the university's English essay question is described in Chapter 5.

5   *. . . collaborated with*: Hoover's secret plan with the CIA director John McCone is recounted in Chapter 15.

5   *. . . ran a secret program*: The bureau's Responsibilities Program is examined in Chapter 2.

5   *. . . made common cause with*: Hoover's interactions with State Senator Hugh Burns and the director's handling of reports of Burns's alleged corruption are revealed in Chapter 3.

5   *Hoover had been trying*: Hoover's efforts to quash dissent at the university date to at least the early 1950s, as seen in the Responsibilities Program, and many other examples are discussed in the book, such as the bureau's responses to the protest against HUAC at San Francisco City Hall in 1960 and the Free Speech Movement in 1964.

5   *But Governor Brown . . . Free Speech Movement*: Brown's reaction to FBI charges of subversion in the Free Speech Movement is described in Chapters 14 and 16.

6   *In Reagan*: Hoover noted his optimism about working with Reagan against dissent at Berkeley in 100-151646-218, 1/17/67, a hope that was well founded, as detailed in Chapter 22 and elsewhere in the text.

6   *Like Hoover . . . subversive himself*: Reagan made his views of Savio, Kerr, and protests at Berkeley clear before and after his election as governor in November 1966, as recounted in the text. See, for example, his speech at the Cow Palace that May, described in Chapter 19. Reagan's concern that Kerr might be a subversive is noted in 100-151646-218, 1/17/67. Hoover's view of Savio as a ringleader is documented in Savio FBI file 100-54060, and his opinions of Kerr as lacking sufficient backbone, and his unfounded implications that Kerr was potentially subversive, emerge from bureau files on Kerr and the university, also described in the text. See, for example, his handling of the background report on Kerr in Chapter 14.

7   *Lynum had plenty*: This paragraph is based on FBI files on Mario Savio, including 100-54060; 100-154189; 157-984; 44-26027. The classification "100" denotes domestic security. The classification "157" denotes civil unrest.

7   *Hoover's agents had also*: This paragraph is based on FBI files on Clark Kerr, including 77-7764; 116-34; 116-325; 161-3037; 77-79655; 116-210; and from FBI files on UC, including 100-151646; 100-34204.

8   *The bedside meeting*: This paragraph is drawn from FBI files on Reagan, including 100-382196; 116-460320; 161-10803; 80-579; 116-70463; 261-2715; 80-990; and files on UC, including 100-151646; 100-34204. This paragraph is also drawn from FBI files on Maureen Reagan, including 77-81528-8; 77-81528-9, 3/10/60; 77-81528-10, 3/15/60; and Jane Wyman cross-reference 100-338892-124. These activities are more fully described throughout the book.

8   *The FBI would become*: The extent of the FBI's involvement in the campus community at Berkeley and the seminal conflict there is documented in the staggering volume of records the bureau compiled. A selected list of FBI files consulted for this book is in the Appendix.

8   *In his corner office: The FBI: A Comprehensive Reference Guide*, 250.

8   *He saw Reagan's*: 100-151646-218, 1/17/67.

8   *Hoover's hand*: The director's jagged scrawl appears on many headquarters documents, and his characteristic use of blue ink is noted in several sources, including Cartha "Deke" DeLoach's *Hoover's FBI*, 17.

8   *"This," he underscored*: The quote is from 100-151646-218, 1/17/67.

1: Spies in the Hills

11   *On the night*: This and other details of the FBI espionage investigation are in FBI HQ file 100-19065, captioned, "Communist Infiltration of Radiation Laboratory, University of California, Berkeley, California," code-named CINRAD. For more on CINRAD, see *American Prometheus*; *Brotherhood of the Bomb*; *The Quest for Absolute Security*; *Chasing Spies*.

11   *As fog blew . . . the atomic bomb*: 116-325-4, n.d.; 116-325-20, 2/25/47; 116-325-21, 5/17/47; 100-5113-151, 2/21/46; *American Prometheus*, 174–75, 199–201, 323.

11   *Uneasy allies*: Churchill gave his speech at Westminster College, Fulton, Missouri, March 5, 1946.

11   *Federal officials: Chasing Spies*, 10–11, 15–33; *The FBI: A Comprehensive Reference Guide*, 24; Church, book III, 414, 427–28, which notes: "During the Cold War period the domestic intelligence activities of the Federal Government were rooted in a firm national consensus regarding the danger to the United States from international Communism. No distinction was made between the threats posed by the Soviet Union and by Communists within this country." However, "the degree of consensus in favor of repression of the Communist Party should not be overstated. In contrast to the Congressional enthusiasm, President Truman was concerned about the risks to constitutional government. According to one White House staff member's notes during the debate over the Internal Security Act of 1950, 'The President said that the situation . . . was the worst it had been since the Alien and Sedition Laws of 1789, that a lot of people on the Hill should know better but had been stampeded into running with their tails between their legs.'"

11   *J. Edgar Hoover . . . hotel rooms*: The FBI's investigation, code-named CINRAD, and its techniques, are detailed in 100-190625. CINRAD is discussed in *American Prometheus*, *Brotherhood of the Bomb*, and *Chasing Spies*. The FBI's investigative methods are also described in *The FBI: A Comprehensive Reference Guide*, 21–22.

12   *And on that cold . . . named Clark Kerr*: HQ 116-325-4, n.d.; 116-325-20, 2/25/47; 116-325-21, 5/17/47; 100-5113-151, 2/21/46.

12   *Just below those*: In this and the next four paragraphs, the account of the origins of UC Berkeley is from *Berkeley: A City in History*, 1–28; *The California Idea and American Higher Education*, 19–46; *Berkeley: A Literary Tribute*, xi–xii; *The Campus Guide*, 1–4, 120–22. The phrase "westward hope for humanity" is from *The Campus Guide*, 122. On Bishop Berkeley and his axiom *esse est percipi*, see www.iep.utm .edu/berkeley/, accessed 7/5/10. Although the literal translation is "To be is to be perceived," the colloquial expression "to be heard" is used here.

13   *By the 1920s*: On the development of the campus and its architecture, see *The Campus Guide*; *Berkeley: A City in History*, 58–61; *Teachers & Scholars*, 23–27.

13   *In the center: The Campus Guide*, pp. 44–47. The quote is Helfand's.

13   *The university's goals . . . hard at work*: On Oppenheimer, see *Berkeley: A City in History*, 63, 116–19. On Oppenheimer, Lawrence, and the University of California's role in the Manhattan Project, see *Brotherhood of the Bomb*; *American Prometheus*; *The Making of the Atomic Bomb*, 451; *LAT* 7/17/05, "Power and Money in Los Alamos Contract." On Oppenheimer and Lawrence attracting other talented researchers to Berkeley, see *American Prometheus*, 82–86. On Lawrence, see *Nobel Lectures, Physics 1922–1941*, nobelprize.org/nobel_prizes/physics/laureates/1939/lawrence-bio.html, accessed 7/6/10.

14   *The microphone*: 100-190625-2648, vol. 52, p. 26.

14   *A special team . . . with cash bonuses*: Hoover's *FBI*, 317.

14   *The job of . . . to wonder*: This description is based on *Brotherhood of the Bomb*, 56; Hoover's *FBI*, 315–16; author interview with Burney Threadgill, Jr., who recounted the prank.

14   *The tedium*: The conversation is described in 100-190625-2648, vol. 52, p. 26; 100-190625-2648, vol. 53, pp. 207, 229. More on Nelson's background is in 100-190625-2648, vol. 52, pp. 2, 22–31; 100-190625-59. See also *Steve Nelson, American Radical*.

14   *Oppenheimer was perhaps*: 100-190625-1, 2/25/43; 100-190625-2648, vol. 53, p. 226; *American Prometheus*, 179–88, 323; *Brotherhood of the Bomb*, 63, 71; *WP* 8/12/45, "Bomb Test Just Highlight for Oppenheimer"; *LAT* 10/17/45, "Award Discloses A-Bomb Built in U.C. Laboratory."

15   *A New York native . . . awestruck students*: *Brotherhood of the Bomb*, 11–15, 60–63; *NYT* 2/19/67, "J. Robert Oppenheimer"; 100-190625-2648, vol. 53, pp. 226–27; *American Prometheus*, 82–85, 171.

15   *"Oppie" . . . would later say*: *NYT* 2/19/67, "J. Robert Oppenheimer"; *American Prometheus*, 96–97, 104, 114–17, 121–24, 135–36.

15   *As he became . . . Alameda County*: *American Prometheus*, 115, 123, 135–36; *Brotherhood of the Bomb*, 55, 57.

15   *FBI agents . . . before the war*: 100-190625-2648, vol. 53, pp. 226–36; *Brotherhood of the Bomb*, 55, 30; *American Prometheus*, 137.

15   *They knew that*: 100-190625-2648, vol. 53, pp. 237–38.

15   *They also knew*: 100-190625-2648, vol. 53, pp. 217–25, and 100-190625-2733, p. 22; *American Prometheus*, 134.

15   *At least*: 100-190625-2648, vol. 53, pp. 226–36; *American Prometheus*, 136, 142.

15   *N.J.L. "Nat" Pieper . . . in Berkeley*: 100-190625-1, 2/25/43; 100-190625-2X, 3/31/43.

16   *With his snub*: Information about Hoover's life and career has been drawn principally from *The Boss*; *Secrecy and Power*; *J. Edgar Hoover*; *The Director*. Jack Alexander's three-part *New Yorker* profile of Hoover, published 9/25/37, 10/2/37, and 10/9/37, remains a seminal source.

16   *John Edgar Hoover was born . . . Jim Crow customs*: *The Boss*, 19, 24; *Secrecy and Power*, 6, 9–10, 13–17; *The Director*, 3; *J. Edgar Hoover*, 63–64.
      On discriminatory customs in Washington, D.C., during this era, see *The Secret City*, pp. 161–72.
      On the race and occupation of Hoover's neighbors, see U.S. Census data, year 1900; Census Place: Washington, Washington, District of Columbia; Roll: T623_164; Page: 8B; Enumeration District: 127, at search.ancestry.com/cgi-bin/sse.dll?h =375616&db=1900usfedcen&indiv=try, accessed 5/18/11.
      See also U.S. Census data, year 1910; Census Place: Precinct 5, Washington, District of Columbia; Roll: T624_152; Page: 7B; Enumeration District: 0098; Image: 42; FHL Number: 1374165, at search.ancestry.com/cgi-bin/sse.dll?h=151848446&db =1910USCenIndex&indiv=try, accessed 5/18/11.

16   *His father: Secrecy and Power,* 127, 128.
16   *The youngest: The Boss,* 19, 26.
16   *At Central: The Director,* 3–4; *Secrecy and Power,* 25–27.
16   *Rejected by . . . attend services: The Director,* 3–4; *The Boss,* 16, 25–32, 328; *Secrecy and Power,* 15–16, 28.
16   *In 1912: The Boss,* 34.
16   *Hoover's mother: New Yorker* profile, op. cit.
16   *Hoover was afflicted: The Boss,* 34; *The Director,* 7; *Secrecy and Power,* 28–30, 159.
17   *On graduating . . . Master of Law degree: The Boss,* 35–36; *Secrecy and Power,* 40.
17   *That April: Young J. Edgar,* 3–4.
17   *He worked: Secrecy and Power,* 48–55; *The Boss,* 54.
17   *On June 2, 1919 . . . charge of it: The Boss,* 55–56; *Secrecy and Power,* 62–63.
17   *Hoover studied: Secrecy and Power,* 68.
17   *He built . . . Richard Gid Powers: The Director,* 53–54; *Secrecy and Power,* 66–69, 91, 127–29.
17   *He developed: The Director,* 51–52.
17   *He also came: The Boss,* 62.
17   *Hoover oversaw . . . being questioned: Secrecy and Power,* 66–72, 105; *The FBI: A Comprehensive Reference Guide,* 9.
17   *Based on . . . front-page news: Secrecy and Power,* 74–87; *The Boss,* 61–63. On Goldman, see the Emma Goldman Papers, UC Berkeley, sunsite.berkeley.edu/goldman/, accessed 10/28/11.
18   *Hoover next . . . alien radicals: Secrecy and Power,* 96–104; *The Boss,* 63–64.
18   *At first:* This paragraph and the next are based on *Secrecy and Power,* 112–19; *The Boss,* 63–65.
19   *Hoover fought back . . . the dragnets: Secrecy and Power,* 119–26; *The Boss,* 64–67.
19   *Blamed for:* This paragraph and the next are based on *Secrecy and Power,* 120–55; *The Boss,* 80–90, 102–105; *The FBI: A Comprehensive Reference Guide,* 10–12.
19   *Hoover was still: Secrecy and Power,* 131.
19   *His father: The Boss,* 74.
19   *Now slightly: Secrecy and Power,* 159.
19   *In 1928 . . . vacationing together: Secrecy and Power,* 169–73, 313–15; *The Boss,* 107–108; *The FBI: A Comprehensive Reference Guide,* 357; *The Director,* 11–14, 18, 19, 30–32, 87–88.
19   *Hoover, meanwhile: Secrecy and Power,* 147, 161, 162, 216, 179–80, 228–30; *The Boss,* 151.
19   *On taking office . . . the nation's history: Don't Know Much About History,* 345; *Secrecy and Power,* 179–80.
20   *Prohibition . . . bootleg booze: Secrecy and Power,* 173, 176; *The FBI: A Comprehensive Reference Guide,* 51.
20   *Roosevelt responded . . . G-Man movies: Secrecy and Power,* 186–96, 201–208; *The FBI: A Comprehensive Reference Guide,* 12–14; *The Director,* 53–54; *The Boss,* 117–32.
20   *By the time: Secrecy and Power,* 196, 201; *The FBI: A Comprehensive Reference Guide,* 364.
20   *On August 24, 1936:* This paragraph and the next are based on Church, book III, 392–94; Church, book II, 25; *Secrecy and Power,* 229; *The Boss,* 150–51; *The FBI: A Comprehensive Reference Guide,* 15–18. Note that Roosevelt never *formally* authorized the FBI to conduct domestic intelligence investigations of "subversive activities," except for this 1936 oral instruction and another oral instruction in 1938. His written directives were limited to investigations of espionage, sabotage, and violations of neutrality regulations, Church, book III, 405.

21 *Roosevelt subsequently*: The FBI: A Comprehensive Reference Guide, 16–18.

21 *Although the president had . . . centered on the FBI*: Church, book III, 398–403; *The Boss*, 178–85. Roosevelt revealed part of the FBI's mission in September 1939, after Germany invaded Poland. At Hoover's request, he issued a press release saying he had asked the FBI to take charge of "matters relating to espionage, sabotage and violations of the neutrality regulations." Other law-enforcement agencies were directed to turn over all relevant information to the bureau. On the foregoing, see Church, book III, 404–405; *The Boss*, 180–81; *The FBI: A Comprehensive Reference Guide*, 15–32.

21 *Seizing . . . suspected subversives*: The FBI: A Comprehensive Reference Guide, 366.

21 *That year . . . on their duration*: Church, book III, 279; *The FBI: A Comprehensive Reference Guide*, 21, 31; *The Boss*, 171.

21 *In 1942, Hoover . . . an "invaluable technique"*: The FBI: A Comprehensive Reference Guide, 22.

21 *The agents called*: Hoover's FBI (Turner), 317; author interviews with Burney Threadgill, Jr., and Bob Lamborn.

21 *To supervise . . . then destroyed*: The FBI: A Comprehensive Reference Guide, 22; *The Boss*, 174–75.

22 *Roosevelt knew*: The FBI: A Comprehensive Reference Guide, 21–22; author correspondence with Athan Theoharis.

22 *Yet Hoover . . . friends and enemies*: The FBI: A Comprehensive Reference Guide, 18–19; *Secrecy and Power*, 216; *The Boss*, 186.

22 *Besides, Hoover . . . by submarine*: The FBI: A Comprehensive Reference Guide, 22, 23.

22 *During this period*: The FBI: A Comprehensive Reference Guide, 4, 23.

22 *By this time . . . northwest Washington*: Secrecy and Power, 259–60.

22 *The FBI's two top*: Ibid., 171.

22 *They could be*: The Director, 17–18, and 13–19 on Hoover's other freeloading; *Lost Washington*, greatergreaterwashington.org/post/2655/lost-washington-harveys -restaurant/, accessed 2/14/11.

22 *There were suspicions*: Secrecy and Power, 171–73. It should be noted that some authors, most notably Anthony Summers in his 1993 book, *Official and Confidential: The Secret Life of J. Edgar Hoover*, have reported that Hoover and Tolson were sexually involved. Summers reports unconfirmed allegations that Hoover on one occasion wore "a fluffy black dress." He further writes that organized crime figures claimed to have obtained proof of Hoover's homosexuality and used it to blackmail him so the FBI would not investigate them. However, no one has ever found the evidence documenting such charges—the smoking tutu, as it were. Athan Theoharis makes the salient point in *J. Edgar Hoover, Sex, and Crime*: Such unproven claims, while perhaps intriguing, divert attention from the more dangerous and complex Cold War circumstances that allowed Hoover to operate with excessive power and inadequate oversight.

22 *Hoover had become . . . "morons and criminals"*: Secrecy and Power, 196–214, 251, 253–54, 257–58, 263; *The FBI: A Comprehensive Reference Guide*, 262–72, 282.

23 *Hoover read*: 100-190625-1, 3/9/43; 100-190625-2, 3/22/43; 100-190625-5, 4/7/43.

23 *So secret*: Brotherhood of the Bomb, 72, 99.

23 *FBI agents already*: Church, book III, 413, 417, 421; *Chasing Spies*, 60; *The Quest for Absolute Security*, 65.

23 *Now Hoover intensified . . . CINRAD*: 100-190625-6 through 100-190625-17, 4/8/43 and 4/9/43.

23 *Late on March 29 . . . Soviet cause*: The overheard conversation is described in 100-190625-2668, 1/24/47, p. 6; 100-190625-2005, 8/20/45. This conversation is discussed in *Brotherhood of the Bomb*, 96–98, and *American Prometheus*, 188–93.

23 *Weinberg was a research . . . for the job*: 100-190625-2648, pp. 9, 12–14.

23   *Three days later*: This paragraph and the next are based on 100-190625-3, 4/7/43; 100-190625-2005, 8/20/45.
24   *That Saturday . . . "like a banker"*: 100-190625-2005, 8/20/45, pp. 29–30.
24   *Meanwhile, FBI and army . . . a man named Eltenton*: *Brotherhood of the Bomb*, 107. The third young scientist was David Joseph Bohm. A summary of the investigation to this point is in 100-190625-2648, vols. 52 and 53.
24   *Military officials arrived . . . in confidence*: 100-190625-2648, vol. 53, pp. 231–32; 100-190625-2005, 8/20/45, p. 34; 100-190625-2668, 1/24/47, p. 14 et seq.
24   *Dissatisfied . . . Chevalier had approached*: 100-190625-2668, 1/24/47, p. 14.
24   *Three months later . . . "gave him hell"*: Ibid., pp. 14–15.
24   *As FBI agents . . . close friends*: 100-190625-2648, vol. 52, pp. 43–50.
24   *Eltenton, the agents . . . including Ivanov*: 100-190625-2668, 1/24/47, pp. 14, 37–43; 100-190625-2648, vol. 52, pp. 34–40; 100-190625-2005, 8/20/45; 116-12283-4, in Robert Gordon Sproul cross-references.
25   *And on that November*: 100-5113-151, "Clark Kerr, Fund for the Republic," 10/9/53 or 10/9/55, behind serial 116-325-36; author interview with Clark Kerr. The home being staked out was that of Herve Voge, who, by coincidence, was related to Clark Kerr's wife. However, this detail did not figure significantly in the FBI's investigations of Kerr during the 1960s, a fact that underscores that the FBI's interest in Kerr was primarily political.
25   *Just after 2:00 p.m. . . . rebuffed him*: The account of the FBI's interrogation of Eltenton is in S.F. 100-214312-115 (Kerr cross-references), 6/28/46.
25   *Even as these agents . . . they had Eltenton*: The account of the FBI's interrogation of Chevalier is in ibid.
26   *He insisted, however*: 100-190625-2648, vol. 52, p. 50.
26   *At FBI headquarters . . . methods*: 100-190625-2683, 3/14/47. It should be noted, however, that according to FBI files, Weinberg was removed from the atomic bomb project on March 31, 1944, 100-190625-2648, vol. 52, p. 21; 100-190625-2668, 1/24/47, p. 14. So was Lomanitz, after officials declined to support his draft deferment, 100-190625-2668, 1/24/47, p. 12; 100-190625-2648, vol. 53, pp. 206, 208. Bohm was considered too important to the bomb project to be let go, but was kept under heightened scrutiny, 100-190625-2648, vol. 52, p. 155. The Justice Department later prosecuted Weinberg for perjury in denying that he was a member of the Communist Party or that he knew Nelson. The prosecutor, however, could not document the charge because Hoover would not reveal the bureau's microphone evidence against him at trial. As a result, the jury acquitted Weinberg, *American Prometheus*, 455, 459; *Brotherhood of the Bomb*, 263–64. Disclosing the evidence would have revealed the FBI's illegal investigative techniques and possibly disrupted its continuing electronic surveillance of Bay Area Communists and their associates.
26   *Ivanov was recalled*: 100-190625-2648, vol. 52, p. 35.
26   *Eltenton returned*: *Brotherhood of the Bomb*, 189; *American Prometheus*, 544; NYT 11/1/47, "Eltenton Refuses Comment."
26   *Chevalier moved*: LAT 7/18/65, "Writer Haakon Chevalier Dies"; LAT 11/1/47, "Teacher Denies Seeking Secret Data"; WP 5/28/54, "Oppenheimer Is Defended"; NYT 12/3/54, "Oppenheimer Case Held"; *Oppenheimer, Story of a Friendship*, 169.
26   *Nelson said*: *American Radical*, 292–95.
26   *Weinberg denied*: LAT 5/10/50, "Witness Links Top." Weinberg also denied engaging in espionage when questioned by FBI agents, 100-190625-2648, vol. 52, p. 22.
26   *As for Oppenheimer . . . for liberalism*: Oppenheimer's security clearance ordeal is detailed in *American Prometheus* and *Brotherhood of the Bomb*. See also NYT 2/20/67, "Oppenheimer, the 'Father of the Atomic Bomb.'" On his association with Commu-

nists and the government's failure to prove Communist Party membership, *American Prometheus*, 119–24, 135–42, 144–46, 150–52, 234. On the lack of evidence that Oppenheimer engaged in espionage, see *Chasing Spies*, 254, n. 16; *American Prometheus*, 550, wherein the authors conclude, "Oppenheimer's defeat was also a defeat for American liberalism."

27 *The most damaging . . . during the war*: *Chasing Spies*, 17, 81–83; see also *The FBI, A Comprehensive Reference Guide*; *Bombshell*; National Security Agency website at www.nsa.gov/about/_files/cryptologic_heritage/publications/coldwar/venona_story .pdf, accessed 7/6/10.

27 *In one of the most . . . the bomb elsewhere*: *The FBI: A Comprehensive Reference Guide*, 64–66.

27 *It is now known*: *Bombshell*; *Chasing Spies*, 17, 81–83; *The Quest for Absolute Security*, 65–70; *Venona, Decoding Soviet Espionage in America*, 10–13, 16, 314–317.

27 *As the Cold War*: On the FBI's authority and operations during the Cold War period, see Church, book III, 427–64; *The FBI: A Comprehensive Reference Guide*, 24–32.

27 *So sweeping*: *The Boss*, 150–54, 180–81, 314; author interview with Athan Theoharis. Further, the Church committee noted that Presidents Truman, Eisenhower, and Kennedy hardly changed FDR's original directive, which Hoover continued to cite as the basis for his investigations of "subversive activities," Church, book III, 463–64. No president ever defined this term, leaving the determination of its meaning and scope to Hoover's discretion, Church, book II, 45–46; Church, book III, 463–64. The Church committee also noted, "The breadth of the FBI's investigations of 'subversive activity' led to massive collection of information on law abiding citizens . . . the FBI's concept of 'subversive infiltration' was so broad that (for instance) it permitted the investigation for decades of peaceful protest groups such as the National Association for the Advancement of Colored People (NAACP)," Church, book II, 46–47. This lack of a clear legal standard continued to be a problem: "The 1960 FBI manual did not define 'subversive' groups in terms of their links to a foreign government, only as 'Marxist revolutionary-type' organizations 'seeking the overthrow of the U.S. government,'" Church, book II, 47–48. By way of further context, the Church committee noted, "There is no question that both Congress and the public expected the FBI to gather domestic intelligence about Communists. But the broad scope of FBI investigations, its specific programs . . . and its use of intrusive techniques and disruptive counterintelligence measures against domestic 'subversives' were not fully known by anyone outside the Bureau," Church, book III, 429.

2: The Responsibilities Program

28 *In the inner*: This paragraph is based on Jack Alexander's *New Yorker* profile of Hoover, published 9/25/37, 10/2/37, and 10/9/37; *The Boss*, 82–85; *Secrecy and Power*, 146–47; Church, book III, 388; *J. Edgar Hoover: The Man and the Secrets*, 617–18; *The FBI: A Comprehensive Reference Guide*, 250–51; *Hoover's FBI: The Inside Story*, 11–13. On the Department of Justice Building, see www.gsa.gov/portal/ext/html /site/hb/category/25431/actionParameter/exploreByBuilding/buildingId/321, accessed 1/12/11. In 2001 it was renamed for Robert F. Kennedy, attorney general 1961–1964.

28 *By 1950, the Soviets*: On the Soviets' successful espionage at the atomic labs overseen by the University of California, see *Bombshell*, *Chasing Spies*, and *The Quest for Absolute Security*.

28 *The House Un-American*: On HUAC, see *The Committee*.

28   *And on February 9, 1950:* Speech of Joseph McCarthy, Wheeling, West Virginia,
     February 9, 1950, *History Matters: The U.S. Survey Course on the Web,* historymatters
     .gmu.edu/d/6456/, accessed 1/11/11. Over the following months, he would make
     wildly varying claims about the number of Communists in government, *Many Are
     the Crimes,* 241–43; *The Age of McCarthyism,* 1, 63; *The Life and Times of I. F. Stone,*
     254–55.
28   *While Senator McCarthy:* Regarding the definition of *subversive,* or lack thereof, see
     Church, book II, 46–49, 176. McCarthy's Wheeling, West Virginia, speech is in
     The Age of McCarthyism, 211.
28   *Under his direction: The Boss,* 10, 256–61; *The FBI: A Comprehensive Reference
     Guide,* 31–32; Church, book II, 5–14, 19, 46–49; Church, book III, 448–51.
29   *These thin slips . . . national emergency:* On the FBI's filing systems and administra-
     tive operations, see generally, *The Boss; The FBI: A Comprehensive Reference Guide;
     Are You Now or Have You Ever Been in the FBI Files; Unlocking the Files of the FBI.*
     This description is also based on author interviews with agents Lynum and Thread-
     gill and review of FBI records cited as sources for this book.
29   *Many of these:* Hoover's attitudes, including those toward ends and means, negative
     publicity that embarrassed the bureau, criticism of the bureau, and dissension
     within the ranks, are well documented in FBI records and in secondary sources.
     See, for example, *The Boss* and *J. Edgar Hoover: The Man and the Secrets.* For an
     example of an FBI memo acknowledging the illegality of surreptitious entries, see
     The FBI: A Comprehensive Reference Guide, 184–86. On Hoover's dictatorial ad-
     ministration, see *Secrecy and Power,* 220–27, 381–83. Lynum and Threadgill dis-
     cussed these subjects in interviews with the author. Since 1941, FBI employees were
     under the federal government's Excepted Service and thus not protected by Civil
     Service procedures, *The FBI: A Comprehensive Reference Guide,* 212. They labored
     under Hoover's authoritarian rule, *Secrecy and Power,* 218–20, 222–27.
29   *Hoover had been growing:* On the Responsibilities Program in general, see *The FBI:
     A Comprehensive Reference Guide,* 30, 369; *The Boss,* 217, 217n; *Chasing Spies,* 223–
     30; *The Quest for Absolute Security,* 154; *Many Are the Crimes,* 212–13, 220, 221,
     222, 272, 273, 363; FBI HQ Responsibilities Program file 62-93875. The program is
     also discussed in *Compromised Campus,* wherein Sigmund Diamond concludes
     that it amounted to a political blacklist. "If the purpose of the effort was to provide
     evidence of criminality, it failed. But that was not its purpose—it was to intimidate,
     and in that it succeeded," *Compromised Campus,* 274.
29   *The program took:* 62-93875-1; 62-93875-57; 62-93875-2663, vol. 46.
29   *Hoover saw:* 62-93875-1; 62-93875-57; 62-93875-2663, vol. 46.
29   *On learning:* This and the next paragraph are based on 62-93875-1; 62-93875-57;
     62-93875-91; 62-93875-2663, vol. 46.
30   *The February 12, 1951, meeting:* The description of the meeting in this and the fol-
     lowing paragraphs is from 62-93875-88, 2/12/51. The delegation of seven governors
     included Frank Lausche of Ohio; Elbert Carvel of Delaware; Gordon Browning of
     Tennessee; Frederick Payne of Maine; Sherman Adams of New Hampshire; Walter
     Kohler, Jr., of Wisconsin; and Adlai Stevenson of Illinois. On the American Legion
     Contact Program, see *The Boss,* 193–98.
31   *Five days later:* Hoover's February 17, 1951, orders are summarized in 62-93875-2663,
     vol. 46; *Chasing Spies,* 223–30. See also SAC letter no. 19, 2/17/51, 62-93875-NR,
     vol. 3.
31   *Hoover also directed . . . from headquarters:* 62-93875-2663, vol. 46; SAC letter no. 19,
     2/17/51, 62-93875-NR, vol. 3.
31   *Hoover told the agents:* 62-93875-2663, vol. 46, p. 3.

31 *But he warned*: SAC letter no. 19, 2/17/51, 62-93875-NR, vol. 3, before 62-93875-87.
31 *The operation*: The program is described in the voluminous HQ file 62-93875.
    Among its targets were an electrician's helper at Pacific Gas and Electric Company
    in Oakland, 62-93875-286, vol. 7; a chef for the dining cars of the Southern Pacific
    Railroad Company, also in Oakland, and a typewriter repairman at the Western
    Union Telegraph Company in Chicago, NR, 5/15/51, behind 62-93875-277, and
    62-93875-NR, 5/25/51, before 62-93875-282, vol. 7; a minister who worked as a
    clerk in the probate department of the county courthouse in Detroit, Michigan,
    62-93875-NR, before 62-93875-537, vol. 10; a driver's license examiner at the Cali-
    fornia Department of Motor Vehicles in San Francisco, 62-93875-710, vol. 14; the
    city planner in Cincinnati, 62-93875-1823, vol. 31; the Oregon field director for the
    Boy Scouts of America, 62-93875-887 and 62-93875-889, vol. 17. Other examples
    include an assistant city solicitor in Baltimore, Maryland, 62-93875-508; a clerk in
    the law department of the City of New York, 62-93875-498; a nurse in the San Fran-
    cisco Department of Public Health, 62-93875-NR, 6/25/52, before 62-93875-864,
    vol. 17; and an applicant for a narcotics agent's job with the federal Bureau of Nar-
    cotics, 62-93875-NR, 8/15/52, after 62-93875-907, vol. 17.
32 *Educators, however*: This and the next two paragraphs are based on 62-93875-204,
    4/30/51, vol. 6; 62-93875-2663, vol. 46.
32 *Scores of elementary . . . High School*: As to scores of teaching and nonteaching staff,
    see Responsibilities Program 62-938755, vols. 1–46; by a librarian, 62-93875-NR,
    7/20/51, before 458, vol. 9; the director of child care, 62-93875-NR, 9/18/51, vol. 11; a
    custodian at Eagle Rock High School in California, 62-93875-NY, 9/19/51, before
    62-93875-545, vol. 11; even an art school judge at the California state fair, 62-93875-NR,
    7/18/51, vol. 9.
32 *The principal goal . . . Puerto Rico*: University of Pennsylvania, 62-93875-299, vol. 7,
    and 62-93875-2542, vol. 44; University of Michigan, 62-93875-NR, 7/26/51, vol. 9;
    State University of New York, 62-93875-NR, 7/26/51, vol. 9; New York University,
    62-93875-2259 and 62-93875-2260, vol. 37; University of West Virginia, 62-93875-870,
    vol. 17; University of Cincinnati, 62-93875-2254, vol. 37; University of Oklahoma,
    62-93875-529, vol. 10; University of Puerto Rico, 62-93875-537, vol. 10. On the Uni-
    versity of Wisconsin, see *Chasing Spies*, 226.
32 *The agents also targeted*: On USC, see 62-93875-562, vol. 11; *Chasing Spies*, 226.
32 *Allegations against*: 100-151646-NR, 3/31/54, behind 100-151646-10, vol. 1. For ex-
    ample, Hoover sent Warren allegations concerning Thomas Arthur Bisson, a lecturer
    in political science at the University of California, 62-93875-545 and subsequent
    62-93875-NR, 8/16/51, 62-93875-NR, 9/20/51, all in vol. 11; Thomas Charles Hall,
    Jr., a staff member in the Chemistry Department at UCLA, 62-93875-561, vol. 11;
    Joseph Dexter Phillips, Jr., an instructor at the University of California at Santa Bar-
    bara, 62-93875-564, vol. 11; Walter Herbert Miller, an employee of UCLA,
    62-93875-565, vol. 11; John Young Gilbert, an employee of the Physics Department at
    UCLA, 62-93875-566, vol. 11; Wade Cuthbert Rollins, Jr., an associate professor in
    the Division of Animal Husbandry at UC Davis, 62-93875-830 and preceding
    62-93875-NR, 3/21/52, and 62-93875-NR, 4/10/52, vol. 16; and Professor Harry Stein-
    metz at San Diego State College, 62-93875-NR, 8/27/52, after 62-93875-907, vol. 17.
33 *A Republican*: Warren is described at the websites of the Supreme Court Historical
    Society, www.supremecourthistory.org/history/supremecourthistory_history_chief
    _014warren.htm, accessed 7/27/10; and the website of Earl Warren College, warren
    .ucsd.edu/about/biography.html, accessed 7/27/10.
33 *Hoover and Warren . . . largest collections*: *Cloak and Gavel*, 47–48; *Justice for All*, 56,
    63; author interviews with Burney Threadgill, Jr., and Bob Lamborn.

33   *By 1937, Warren . . . state employees: Cloak and Gavel*, 47–49, 156 n. 16; *Justice for All*, 56, 214–16.

33   *President Eisenhower . . . grew apart*: On the cooling of relations between Hoover and Warren, see *Justice for All*, 351–54, 442. Jim Newton notes the 1957 rulings that upset Hoover involved setbacks for legislative committees investigating alleged subversives, *Watkins v. United States* and *Sweezy v. New Hampshire*; the reinstatement of a State Department official fired for security concerns, *Service v. Dulles et al.*; and the reversal of the convictions of fourteen Communists under the Smith Act, *Yates v. United States*.

33   *But in 1951 . . . "such information"*: 62-93875-NR, 8/16/52, vol. 17.

33   *On Hoover's orders . . . investigate the employee*: 100-151646-NR, 3/30/54, behind 100-151646-9; 100-151646-10; 100-151646-NR, 4/7/54, behind 100-151646-10; 100-151646-NR, 3/31/54, behind 100-151646-10.

33   *Warren had complete . . . Bohemian Grove: The California Oath Controversy*, 86; *The California Idea and American Higher Education*, 142, 175; *Justice for All*, 119, 209–10, 218.

34   *"Dear Bob . . . Sincerely, Earl Warren, Governor"*: The text of this letter and the records describing its upshot are from the Bancroft Library, UC Berkeley, President's Papers, CU-5 serial 4, box 38, folder 16. See also 62-93875-564, vol. 11.

34   *This happened again*: The Bisson episode is drawn from 62-93875-NR, 9/20/51, vol. 11; 62-93875-NR, 8/16/51, after 62-93875-545, vol. 11; President's Papers, CU-5 serial 4, box 38, folder 15, Bancroft.

35   *Nor could state*: The Zanger matter is drawn from 62-93875-NR, 9/29/52 (both), 62-93875-NR, 9/16/52, all in vol. 18, after 62-93875-926; President's Papers, CU-5 serial 4, box 38, folder 9, Bancroft.

35   *This was how*: 62-93875-2172, vol. 36; 100-151646-NR, 3/30/54, before 100-151646-10, vol. 1; 62-93875-2663, vol. 46; *Many Are the Crimes*, 273.

35   *Despite its widespread . . . civil liberties concerns*: This paragraph is based on 62-93875-1275, vol. 22; 62-93875-2663, vol. 46, p. 16, which notes Hoover so described it to the attorney general on April 28, 1953, more than two years after he started the program. According to this bureau history of the program, in December 1953 Hoover made an additional disclosure to the attorney general, but it was not until after bad publicity about the operation the following October that he more fully described it. The attorney general then agreed to continue the program but urged Hoover to keep it secret to avoid more negative press. Ibid., pp. 16–18.

35   *Virtually all*: This paragraph is based on 62-93875-2663, vol. 46; *Chasing Spies*, 223–30.

35   *Over the program's . . . left their jobs*: The 908 figure is in 62-93875-2532, 11/10/54, vol. 43, which notes it includes 47 people in Chicago, 50 in Minneapolis, 52 in Detroit, 110 in Philadelphia, 161 in New York City, and 206 in California, more than in any other state. Another report, based on 794 cases, estimated that 55.9 percent of those accused left their jobs. It also notes that 429 of the 794 worked in education, 62-93875-2650, vol. 45.

35   *Hoover was pleased*: As an FBI memo noted, bureau officials saw the Responsibilities Program as "a weapon with which the FBI can continue to apply economic pressure on members of the Communist Party and other subversive organizations thereby deterring the actions of these organizations," 62-93875-2205, vol. 37. See also *Chasing Spies*, 228–30.

3: The Undertaker

36   *Hugh M. Burns*: Burns and his legislative interests are described in articles covering his tenure in the state legislature from 1937 to 1970, which appeared in the *San Francisco Chronicle, San Francisco Examiner,* and *Los Angeles Times,* and in reports of the state legislature's Fact-Finding Committee on Un-American Activities. His gregarious nature is also described in "Inside the Senate Fact-Finding Committee on Un-American Activities," by Burton H. Wolfe, in *The Californian,* March 1962; *LAT* 11/29/88, "Former State Senate Leader Hugh Burns Dies"; *Fresno Bee* 11/28/98, "Hugh Burns, Former Senator, Dies"; Richard Combs's introduction to Burns's oral history interview, "Hugh M. Burns, Legislative and Political Concerns of the Senate Pro Tem, 1957–1970," p. 54, in *Government History Documentation Project: Goodwin Knight/Edmund Brown, Sr., Era,* conducted by Amelia R. Fry, Gabrielle Morris, and James H. Rowland, Regional Oral History Office, Bancroft Library, UC Berkeley, hereinafter Oral History.

36   *Burns's tome*: This 1951 report was titled *Sixth Report of the Senate Fact-Finding Committee on Un-American Activities.* The copy relied on is in 100-15252-Bulky 56, hereinafter *Sixth Report.*

36   *On top of*: Sixth Report, 64.

36   *Over the course . . . "potential traitor"*: The cited parts on Oppenheimer are *Sixth Report,* 238, 242–43.

36   *Exhibit B*: The Writers Congress is discussed at *Sixth Report,* 51. The "traitorous enterprise" quote is at *Sixth Report,* 55. Other information on the conference is drawn from Robert Gordon Sproul FBI cross-reference, 100-7322-57; *LAT* 10/2/43, "Sproul Welcomes Writers Congress."

37   *Exhibit C was*: The discussion of the Berkeley conference is at *Sixth Report,* 63.

37   *Burns concluded*: Sixth Report, 65.

37   *Sproul was dismayed . . . politically suspect professors*: This part is drawn from *When the Old Left Was Young,* 4, 100–102; *Berkeley: A City in History,* 100, 102; *Berkeley at War,* 14–15; Kerr, vol. 2, 122–26; *The Campus Guide,* 40; *American Prometheus,* 105–106.

38   *In fact*: Memorandum for the Director, 3/28/42, serial 1-10-1672, in Sproul cross-references.

38   *And—as Burns well knew*: The California Oath Controversy, 26. *Resisting McCarthyism,* 194, 204, 213; "The Loyalty Oath Controversy," University of California, sunsite.berkeley.edu/~ucalhist/archives_exhibits/loyaltyoath/timelinesummary .html, accessed 6/13/11.

38   *Still, in an effort*: Statement by Dr. Robert G. Sproul, president of the University of California, 6/11/51, President's Papers, series CU-5, box 37, folder 13, Bancroft.

38   *Several professors made*: Statement by UC Faculty on the Burns Report, n.d., President's Papers, series CU-5, box 37, folder 13, Bancroft.

38   *Burns's allegations*: Copies of the news articles are contained in 100-34204, serials 1–5, vol. 1, for example: *S.F. Call-Bulletin* 6/9/51, "Say Campus Spy"; No Publication, n.d., "Report Claims Reds Infiltrate"; No Publication, n.d., "California Warned Reds on Campuses"; *S.F. Call-Bulletin* 6/10/51, "Red Housecleaning at U.C. Demanded"; *SFX* 6/9/51, "Report Hits U.C. Staff." See also *LAT* 6/9/51, "Red Drive Charged"; *NYT* 6/9/51, "California Campus"; *SFC* 3/13/51, "Fifth Column in Schools."

38   *The Examiner's*: Hearst family members donated great amounts of time and money to the university, and they or their representatives were a near-continuous presence on the Board of Regents for almost eighty years. Phoebe Apperson Hearst, the widow of Senator George Hearst and the mother of William Randolph Hearst, the basis of

the newspaper tycoon portrayed in the Orson Welles movie *Citizen Kane*, served from 1897 to 1919. John Francis Neylan, the Hearst Corporation's lead lawyer on the West Coast, served from 1928 to 1955. Catherine C. Hearst, the wife of *Examiner* president and Hearst Corp. chairman Randolph Apperson Hearst, the son of William Randolph Hearst, would serve from 1956 to 1976. See "The Regents of the University of California," UC Regents website, www.universityofcalifornia.edu/regents/regentslistb.pdf, accessed 7/27/10. On the Hearsts, see *LAT* 8/15/51, "Hearst Ruled"; *NYT* 8/15/51, "Career of Hearst"; *NYT* 4/14/19, "Mrs. Phoebe Hearst"; *NYT* 12/19/00, "Randolph A. Hearst"; *LAT* 1/1/99, "Catherine Campbell Hearst."

38 *. . . a Hearst representative*: Corley to Sproul, 6/6/51, President's Papers, series CU-5, box 37, folder 13, Bancroft.

38 *The undertaker*: Hill to Sproul, 6/13/51, "1943 Hollywood Writers' Congress and the Hollywood Quarterly," President's Papers, series CU-5, box 37, folder 13, Bancroft.

38 *His attack was . . . "invites these matters"*: Burns to Corley, 7/17/51, President's Papers, series CU-5, box 37, folder 13, Bancroft.

38 *Burns was flexing*: Burns was a savvy backroom wheeler-dealer who would serve as president pro tempore of the California Senate from 1957 to 1969. He co-authored or sponsored key measures for California's massive water and freeway projects. *LAT* 11/29/88, "Former State Senate Leader"; *Fresno Bee* 11/28/88, "Hugh Burns, Former Senator, Dies."

38 *According to an early*: This paragraph and the next are based on Burns's résumés from 1938 and 1959, which are in the *San Francisco Examiner*'s clip files on Burns. Burns's statement that his father worked for the National Biscuit Company is in "Hugh M. Burns, Legislative and Political Concerns of the Senate Pro Tem, 1957–1970," interview conducted by Amelia R. Fry, Gabrielle Morris, and James H. Rowland in 1977, 1978 ("Burns oral history"), 89. His taste for whiskey is from the February 6, no year listed, but apparently 1952, memo GC to Kerr, "DR. KERR, Wadman brought me . . . ," in Kerr Presidential Papers, CU-302, carton 1, folder 32, Bancroft. Burns also liked brandy, *LAT* 11/29/88, "Former State Senate Leader."

39 *One of his first*: This account of his legislative efforts is drawn from contemporaneous articles in the *San Francisco Examiner* and *San Francisco Chronicle*.

39 *Elevated to the senate*: The role of the committee is described in the *Sixth Report*, 1–7, and in FBI records and other sources cited below. The committee's legislative immunity is noted in "Inside the Senate Fact-Finding Committee on Un-American Activities," by Burton H. Wolfe, *The Californian*, March 1962.

39 *It was one*: *The Great Fear*, 70–81, states that California's was "an agency of misery" that was "foremost among the state 'un-American' legislative committees," 77.

39 *California's version*: Wills's quote is in *Ronald Reagan's America*, 243. The descriptions of the state committee and chairmen Tenney and Burns are drawn from *The Tenney Committee*; *Embattled Dreams*, chapter 10; "Inside the Senate Fact-Finding Committee on Un-American Activities," by Burton H. Wolfe, *The Californian*, March 1962; *LAT* 4/2/67, *West Magazine*, "California's Lonely Secret Agent," by Mary Ellen Leary; testimony of the committee's chief counsel Richard E. Combs before the U.S. Senate Subcommittee to Investigate the Administration of the Internal Security Act and Other Internal Security Laws of the Committee on the Judiciary, 3/19/53 ("Combs Testimony"). Material on the committee and its operations was also drawn from the FBI files on the committee, Combs, Burns, and Tenney. The committee's origin and aims are discussed in 100-15252-29, vol. 2. Over the years the committee had several iterations and titles, starting in 1940 as the Assembly Relief Investigating Committee headed by Sam Yorty, *The Tenney Committee*, 3 *et seq.* Combs was counsel to that committee and its subsequent versions, 100-15252-7X.

40   *Kevin Starr: Embattled Dreams*, 301.

40   *Tenney and his fellow*: 100-15252-29, vol. 2.

40   *Tenney became*: This paragraph is based on the aforementioned materials on the committee, and on *Embattled Dreams*, 303, 307; *LAT* 4/2/67, *West Magazine*, "California's Lonely Secret Agent." *The Great Fear*, 78; Burns's quote is from his oral history, op. cit., 54.

40   *By now Hoover had*: Some of the committee's elaborate security measures are described in 100-15252-7.

40   *The agents further*: The FBI's relationship with the committee is detailed in bureau files on the committee, Burns, Tenney, and Combs. The allegations about Combs's academic deficiencies are in 77-71425-17. On the origins of Combs's fight against radicals, see HQ cross-ref 9-HQ-6057-2, 4/3/40; HQ cross-ref 39-915-852, 10/24/40; 39-915-463X1, 10/28/40; Combs Testimony, 606–607; 100-15252-29; *LAT* 4/2/67, *West Magazine*, "California's Lonely Secret Agent." On Combs and General Van Deman, see 100-17959-27, p. 2, in SF-190-25; 77-71425-13, p. 3; 100-15252-14; *LAT* 4/2/67, *West Magazine*, "California's Lonely Secret Agent." On Van Deman, see Military Intelligence, Lineage Series, Center of Military History, U.S. Army, Washington, D.C., 1998, John Patrick Finnegan, www.history.army.mil/books/Lineage /mi/mi-fm.htm., accessed 7/3/10. On Combs's intelligence operation, in addition to the foregoing, see file 77-71425 on him. Combs's physical description is from *LAT* 4/2/67, *West Magazine*, "California's Lonely Secret Agent."

41   *Although he publicly*: Combs's claim that the committee never paid an informer is in *LAT* 4/2/67, *West Magazine*, "California's Lonely Secret Agent."

41   *. . . FBI agents reported*: 100-15252-23.

41   *. . . "not too highly regarded"*: The quote is in 100-15252-17. Further, an agent reported, "Rena Vale is supplying most of the information to form the basis of the Committee hearings. Most of her history concerning activities of the Communist party is superficial and relates to old history," 100-15252-7X. On Vale, see also *The Tenney Committee*, 49, 96, 128.

41   *Other Combs sources*: 100-15252-7, which states: "In evaluating the Committee's investigative files from the indices, it is apparent that the greater part of the information they contain has been acquired from several well-known professional witnesses on Communist activities in this state, including Arthur Kent, John Leech and Rena Vale." It adds, "all these witnesses have poor reputations."

41   *But though Hoover's*: The quote is in 100-15252-25, 4/25/43. See also 100-15252-6, 3/27/41; 100-15252-29 and enclosure.

41   *Each time*: For example, see 100-15252-25; 100-15252-27, 5/26/43; 100-15252-60; 100-15252-62; 100-15252-64.

41   *Bureau officials*: In addition to the records cited immediately above, see 100-15252-8, 8/14/41; 100-15252-43; 100-15252-NR, 5/17/50, behind 100-15252-43.

41   *FBI agents always*: 100-15252-6, 3/27/41; 100-15252-2; 100-15252-5; 100-15252-6X, 7/10/41; 100-15252-7; 100-15252-25; 121-15820-5. The figure of 125,000 index cards is from an executive summary of the files produced in 1998 by the California Senate Rules Committee, and Associated Press, 11/8/99, "California Ordered to Open." In addition, Combs arranged for FBI agents to interview committee witnesses, 100-15252-43, 7/27/50. He gave the bureau testimony the committee had taken in closed hearings, vol. 4, 100-15252-96; 100-15252-102; 100-15252-NR, 3/6/58, behind 100-15252-102. And he offered to subpoena people and question them under oath at the bureau's request, 100-15252-7X, 7/26/41. Further, FBI records state that Combs provided notes and interviews from his investigation of J. Robert Oppenheimer, 100-17828-1488, 5/13/54. An FBI memo noted: ". . . we have interviewed Combs on a

number of occasions in the Weinberg and Oppenheimer cases . . . We have obtained his notes and the results of his interviews. We have also reviewed his files and obtained pertinent photographs and sketches from his files." FBI officials described Combs as "an established contact of the Los Angeles Office," 100-17828-1483, 5/13/54. He had been cooperating with FBI agents since at least 1942, 65-HQ-2682-243, 5/23/42.

41 *Even as Burns:* The unproven allegations and the quotes about Burns's role in Fresno corruption in this paragraph and the next are described in 62-75147, sub 26, serial 243, vols. 22, 23 and 24, dated 4/15/48; 62-75147, sub 26, bulky exhibit, serial 208, dated 10/15/47; 62-75147, sub 26, section 21, serial 208, dated 10/15/47.

42 *As a result:* 62-75147, sub 26, serial 243, vols. 22, 23, 24, dated 4/15/48; 62-75147, sub 26, bulky exhibit, serial 208, dated 10/15/47; 62-75147, sub 26, section 21, serial 208, dated 10/15/47.

42 *In Washington . . . claims were true:* 100-15252-97, vol. 4, 8/2/57.

42 *But the released:* The author requested any and all records concerning Burns from FBI HQ and the S.F., Sacramento, L.A., and Washington, D.C., field offices.

42 *Hoover, it seems, looked:* Burns became head of the state un-American activities committee in 1949, *The Tenney Committee,* 15. Tenney had been in decline for some time by then. Burns was previously vice-chair, *SFC* 6/21/49, "Tenney Steps Out." The committee and its chairmen were big boosters of Hoover. The Hoover resolution, introduced by Tenney, commended the director and his FBI agents for their "excellent work" and "the diligence, courage and foresight which have been demonstrated," 100-15252-49, 9/21/50. The secretary of the state senate sent Hoover a framed copy, and Hoover replied, "It is heartening to my associates and to me personally to realize that we have the support and encouragement of the Senate of California. It is indeed true that these days are fraught with national peril . . . ," 100-15252-49, 9/27/50.

42 *. . . in further obeisance:* Under both Burns and Tenney, the committee sent copies of its reports to Hoover personally, 100-15252-26, 4/24/45; 100-15252-31, 5/22/45; 100-15252-36, 4/23/47; 100-15252-97, 8/2/57; 100-15252-111, 10/19/61. Some were embossed with Hoover's name, 100-15252-36, 5/16/47; 100-15252-39X, 7/7/49.

42 *Burns's daughter:* This paragraph is based on an author interview with Colleen Draklich.

42 *So it was that:* This paragraph is based on 100-15252-55, 7/13/51, and 100-15252-55, 7/27/51.

4: The Rise of Clark Kerr

44 *Clark Kerr had:* The account of the loyalty oath controversy, Kerr's role in it, and his subsequent ascendancy as a result of it, is drawn mainly from Kerr's memoir, *The Gold and the Blue,* vols. 1 and 2; *The California Oath Controversy; Resisting Mc-Carthyism;* author interview with Kerr; *The Loyalty Oath Controversy, University of California,* ucblibrary3.berkeley.edu/uchistory/archives_exhibits/loyaltyoath/, accessed 8/4/10.

44 *Kerr had signed:* Kerr, vol. 1, 138; Kerr, vol. 2, 22, 40–42.

44 *In supporting:* Kerr, vol. 1, 138; author interview with Kerr.

44 *A descendant of . . . he alone refused:* Kerr, vol. 1, 10–14, 138; author interviews with Kerr and his half-brother, William Kerr; author correspondence with William Kerr; author interview with Clark E. Kerr (Clark Kerr's son).

44 *One day in Reading . . . May 17, 1911:* Kerr, vol. 1, 12; author interview with Kerr and William Kerr; author correspondence with William Kerr.

45 *The Kerrs lived . . . orphaned lambs:* Kerr, vol. 1, 10; author interview with Kerr.

45 *Kerr's parents quarreled . . . share of the meat*: Kerr, vol. 1, 10; author interviews with Kerr and William Kerr; author correspondence with William Kerr.

45 *Kerr plowed . . . reach the gate*: Kerr, vol. 1, 10; author interviews with Kerr and William Kerr; author interview with Clark E. Kerr.

45 *Kerr's father . . . they exclaimed*: Kerr, vol. 1, 138; author interview with Kerr and Clark E. Kerr.

45 *Even in his own . . . college education*: Author interviews with Kerr and William Kerr. It should be noted, however, that in an interview William Kerr recalled that he worked on the farm, and did not recall eating separately.

46 *Farm chores . . . Swarthmore College*: The account of Kerr's early school days is from Kerr, vol. 1, 12, and author interview with Kerr. Miss Elba also recounted the mouse prank in *SFC* 9/30/58, "Kerr's Teacher Recalls."

46 *A small liberal arts*: On Swarthmore College and its Quaker roots, see www .swarthmore.edu/x18.xml, accessed 8/4/10.

46 *Like the Pilgrims . . . hanging several of them*: On Quakerism, see www.qis.net /~daruma/index.html, especially "Facts About Friends," by Ted Hoare, accessed 8/3/10. On the hangings, see *Puritans and Puritanism in Europe and America: A Comprehensive Encyclopedia*, Francis J. Bremer and Tom Webster, editors, timeline, pp. xl–xli; "America's True History of Religious Tolerance," by Kenneth C. Davis, *Smithsonian*, October 2010, www.smithsonianmag.com/history-archaeology /Americas-True-History-of-Religious-Tolerance.html, accessed 11/11/11.

46 *When Kerr arrived*: Kerr, vol. 1, 12–13; Swarthmore College website, op. cit.

46 *He would later describe*: Kerr, vol. 1, 12–13.

46 *At first . . . "Do it"*: Letters between Kerr and his father and other family members span the years 1928 and 1935 and are in President's Personal Papers, CU-302, carton 70, folders 7, 13, 14, and 15, Bancroft. Quoted here is Samuel to Clark, 9/23/28.

46 *Although Kerr initially . . . to study economics*: Kerr's college transcript is in President's Personal Papers, CU-302, carton 70, folder 29, Bancroft; Kerr, vol. 1, 13. Kerr's quote about Clair Wilcox, and his initial plan to become a lawyer, are from *Swarthmore College Bulletin*, Alumni Issue, May 1968. That he lived in a dormitory is from Kay Kerr's 12/6/03 letter to Dan West of Swarthmore College, courtesy of Alisa Giardinelli, associate director, News & Information, Swarthmore College.

46 *Kerr joined the soccer . . . self-improvement*: The description of Kerr's extracurricular activities and debating are from Kerr, vol. 1, 13, 383; articles in Swarthmore's student newspaper, *The Phoenix*, editions dated 4/16/29, 11/5/29, 1/14/30, 10/14/30, 1/20/31, 3/3/31, 4/28/31, 1/19/32, 2/16/32, 2/23/32, and 6/6/32; summary prepared by Alisa Giardinelli, associate director, News & Information, Swarthmore College. On the Norman Thomas debate, see also Kerr, vol. 1, 134.

47 *At Swarthmore, Kerr also*: Kerr, vol. 1, 13; author interview with Kerr. A "convinced friend" is someone who decides to join the faith, as opposed to a "birthright friend," who is born into it.

47 *Volunteering . . . a larger military*: Kerr, vol. 1, 4, 13. The correspondence with Kerr and his fellow Peace Caravan volunteers is lodged with the American Friends Service Committee headquarters in Philadelphia, whose staff provided copies to the author, along with other records on Kerr's Peace Caravan work. Among the letters used for this account of his activities are those dated 6/24/29, 7/1/29, 7/11/29, 7/12/29, 7/16/29, 7/22/29, 7/29/29, 8/5/29, 8/13/29, 8/16/29, 8/21/29, 8/27/29, 9/4/29, 3/23/30, 5/8/30, 6/28/30, 7/6/30, 7/16/30, 7/21/30, 7/22/30, 7/23/30, 7/25/30, 8/1/30, 8/2/30, 8/5/30, 8/9/30, 8/19/30, 8/20/30, 8/23/30, 9/4/30, 9/12/30, and 9/1/32. The account is also drawn from the Peace Caravan newsletters from 1930 and the Peace Caravan

application of Kerr's fellow caravaner, Neville Gee, which AFSC headquarters also provided to the author.

47   *In letters*: Examples of reported car trouble are in Kerr to Ray Newton, 7/16/29 and 8/27/29. Kerr noted the sometimes hostile audiences in his commencement address at Bryn Mawr College, published in the *Bryn Mawr Alumnae Bulletin*, Summer 1970. The "rah rah" quote is from Don Stickney to Ray Newton, 8/21/29.

47   *In the spring*: The description of Kerr's trips is based on his above-mentioned correspondence with the AFSC and with his family members, lodged respectively at AFSC headquarters, and in President's Personal Papers, CU-302, carton 70, folders 7, 13, 14, 15, Bancroft.

47   *Several weeks later . . . father so vulnerable*: Kerr letter to his father, 9/1/32, President's Personal Papers, CU-302, carton 70, folder 15, Bancroft.

48   *"There are so many"*: The quotes are from the 9/1/32 letter.

48   *Enrolling*: Kerr, vol. 1, 4, 134–35; Kerr letter to his father, 11/12/32, op. cit., Bancroft; author interview with Kerr. Kerr writes that he was a member of the Walrus Club when it petitioned to be affiliated with the League for Industrial Democracy, which was associated with Norman Thomas's Socialist Party.

48   *That November*: Kerr letter to his father, 11/12/32, op. cit., Bancroft.

48   *A few months . . . Christmas Day of 1934*: LAT 5/18/59, "She Thrives on Pioneering"; Kerr letter to his father, 6/10/34, op. cit., folder 15, Bancroft; Kerr, vol. 2, 123–24; *Time* 10/17/60, "Master Planner"; author interview with Kerr.

48   *Kerr, meanwhile . . . one another*: On the Ground in the Thirties, vii; Kerr, vol. 1, 105; author interview with Kerr.

48   *It was similar*: The quote is from On the Ground in the Thirties, vii.

49   *Kerr was increasingly*: This paragraph is drawn from Kerr letter to his father, 3/11/33, op. cit., folder 14, Bancroft.

49   *The San Joaquin Valley . . . shot dead*: On the Ground in the Thirties, x; Kerr, vol. 1, 4–5; LAT 1/15/34, "Red Strike Aim Fails"; LAT 10/9/33, "Strike War Flares Up"; LAT 2/2/34, "Eight Acquitted."

49   *That fall . . . "own words"*: Kerr, vol. 1, 4–5; On the Ground in the Thirties, vii (with Kerr's quote); *Berkeley: A City in History*, 100–101, in which Charles Wollenberg notes that though powerful agribusiness interests pressed President Sproul to curtail Taylor's work, Taylor reported his academic freedom was not affected. Taylor writes in On the Ground in the Thirties that Lange worked with him in 1935 and later became his wife, xi.

49   *This was the same*: Combs described his views on radical involvement in the cotton strike to an FBI agent, as reported in 39-915-413X4 HRBIM, 10/24/40.

49   *"Strikers were living . . ."*: Kerr, vol. 1, 4–5.

50   *The following summer*: Kerr's job was through the State Relief Administration, May 1934–January 1935, according to his Personnel Security Questionnaire, 116-325-12; 116-325-24; 116-325-19, p. 3; On the Ground in the Thirties, 242, n. 9.

50   *Some people*: Kerr letter to his father, 6/10/34, op. cit., folder 15, Bancroft.

50   *Kerr's studies . . . "never seen it"*: Kerr, vol. 1, 4.

50   *By the end*: Kerr letters to his father, 11/20/33 and 11/12/33, Bancroft, op. cit., folder 14.

50   *He decided to . . . cotton strike*: Kerr, vol. 1, 14.

50   *On graduating*: Ibid.

50   *He was also*: Ibid.; author interview with Kerr; 116-325-15.

50   *His mission*: Kerr's mission is illustrated in his arbitration rulings published in *War Labor Reports*. For example, see *New Service Laundries, Inc., Eugene, Oregon, and Laundry Workers International Union, Local 206 (AFL)*, 10 WLR 626, 8/5/43; *Pacific Northwest Foundry Operators, Washington and Oregon, and International Molders*

and *Foundry Workers Union of North America, Locals 139, 180, 311 (AFL), 14 WLR 46*, 1/17/43. Author interview with Kerr.

50 *"The American nation . . . ."*: "Washington Metal Trades, Inc., Pacific Northwest Foundry Operators, 17," *War Labor Reports* 481, 7/13/44.

50 *After the war*: Kerr, vol. 1, 6–7; 116-325-3.

50 *Kerr continued*: Kerr, vol. 1, 47.

50 *His rulings*: In a case involving the steam schooner industry, he ruled that union members could refuse to cross a legitimate picket line because the "sanctity of picket lines" was key to American unionism, *Waterfront Employers Assn. of the Pacific Coast and ILWU, No. 67, 786, American Labor Arbitration Awards*, 8/12/47. In a decision on the meatpacking industry, he upheld the union's right to strike but said employees could be fired for engaging in violence on the picket line. "Regardless of how just the cause, the means of pursuing it must be proper also," he wrote. *Cudahy Packing Co. and United Packinghouse Workers of America, CIO, American Labor Arbitration Awards 68, 160*, 11/7/48. He condemned worker violence in a case concerning a Hawaiian sugarcane plantation. "This cannot be condoned," he ruled. "The essence of free collective bargaining is the resort to persuasion and reason, and to withdrawal of effort as a last resort, but not to physical violence. Abraham Lincoln once stated: 'There is no grievance which is a fit object of redress by mob law.' This is a basic principle of democratic society." *Pioneer Mill Co., Ltd., and ILWU, Local 144, Unit 9, American Labor Arbitration* reports *67, 638*, 2/24/47. Kerr remained a practicing Quaker, author interview with Kerr; e-mail to author from Stephen McNeil, AFSC, San Francisco, 5/8/07.

50 *Deftly handling*: *Time* 10/17/60, "Master Planner"; Kerr, vol. 1, 14.

51 *On March 25, 1949*: The version of the oath quoted in the text is from *The California Oath Controversy*, 26, and Kerr, vol. 2, 30. The regents revised this version on June 24, 1949. The revised version was substantially the same and stated in pertinent part, "I do solemnly swear (or affirm) that I will support the Constitution of the United States and the Constitution of the State of California . . . that I am not a member of the Communist Party or under any oath, or a party to any agreement, or under any commitment that is in conflict with my obligation under oath," *The California Oath Controversy*, 45–47.

51 *The oath had been*: This paragraph is based on Kerr, vol. 2, 29. There is no doubt Tenney's bill was a precipitating factor, but see *The California Oath Controversy*, in which David Gardner discusses the complexities around the university's adoption of the oath.

51 *Neither the regents*: *The California Oath Controversy*, 29–30; Kerr, vol. 2, 30.

51 *Fighting communism . . . pursuit of truth*: Kerr, vol. 1, 8–9; Kerr, vol. 2, 38, 39–40, 42; *The California Oath Controversy*, 28–29; author interview with Kerr.

51 *Moreover, the regents*: *The California Oath Controversy*, 116–17.

51 *Although he opposed . . . "not signing an oath . . ."*: Kerr, vol. 1, 8–9, 138.

51 *He joined . . . refusal to sign*: Kerr's role in the oath controversy is described in *The California Oath Controversy*, 156; Kerr, vol. 1, 9; Kerr, vol. 2, 34–36; *Resisting McCarthyism*, 127, 134.

51 *This panel recommended . . . the panel's findings*: The sixty-two was subsequently reduced to thirty-nine, since twenty-two signed and one resigned. The figures are from *The California Oath Controversy*, 177, 179, 185–86, 300. The five professors failed to win recommendations not because they were found to be disloyal, but because they would not cooperate with Kerr's committee, which could thus make no recommendation. Kerr's committee reviewed only professors who were members of the Academic Senate. In addition to these, some non–Academic Senate professors and members of the nonacademic staff also refused to sign.

51 *The regents had agreed . . . sign the oath*: The board's decision and Neylan's vote are recounted in Kerr, vol. 2, 32–33; *The California Oath Controversy*, 185–90; *Resisting McCarthyism*, 177.

52 *Kerr thought Neylan's*: Kerr, vol. 1, 9, 138–39; Kerr, vol. 2, 35; *The California Oath Controversy*, 187–89.

52 *He rose*: The anecdote is in *The California Oath Controversy*, 188–89; *Resisting McCarthyism*, 176; Kerr, vol. 1, 35. Kerr's language is from the regents' minutes in Kerr, vol. 2, 35. As to the 39 figure, see the above note for the key words "The panel recommended . . ."

52 *Governor Warren*: *The California Oath Controversy*, 189.

52 *But on August 25*: *The California Oath Controversy*, 197–202.

52 *Warren voted against*: Kerr, vol. 1, 8; Kerr, vol. 2, 35; Kerr interview with author; *The California Oath Controversy*, 125.

52 *Kerr's effort*: The aftermath of the oath battle is discussed in the aforementioned books on the oath. In particular, see Kerr, vol. 1, 8–9, 138–39, 140–42; Kerr, vol. 2, 28; *The California Oath Controversy*, 208–10 (on the AAUP censure), and 245–51 (in which, *inter alia*, Gardner speculates that the conflict later contributed to faculty support for the Free Speech Movement); *Resisting McCarthyism*, 220–42. The faculty lawsuits are described in *The California Oath Controversy*, 204, 242–44, 253–54; Kerr, vol. 2, 36.

52 *Yet Kerr's reasoned*: This paragraph is based on *Resisting McCarthyism*, 213; Kerr, vol. 1, 9, 47; Kerr, vol. 2, 36; SFC 1/26/52, "Appointment Announced by Regents"; NYT 1/26/52, "Dr. Kerr Promoted"; author interview with Kerr.

53 *The headline . . . in astonishment*: DC 9/30/52; author interview with Kerr.

53 *Sproul had given him*: The remainder of this paragraph is based on Kerr, vol. 2, 48–53; *Documentary Supplements to the Gold and the Blue*, 131–40; author interview with Kerr.

53 *That was also*: Burns and Combs were proponents of the loyalty oath and would neither have appreciated Kerr's efforts on behalf of the nonsigners nor wanted him in any position to oppose their plans. Publicly naming him the contact man could only have caused some members of the academic community to be suspicious of him and thus undermined his credibility. A story in the *San Francisco Examiner* on October 1, 1952, the day after the surprise announcement, was headlined, "Kerr to Watch for Reds at U.C.," and stated he would act as a "clearing house" for reports of subversive activities on campus.

53 *They had been pushing*: On Burns and Combs's June 1951 report calling for screening professors, see Chapter 3.

53 *And at a private*: Sproul memorialized the November 13, 1951, luncheon in his private office diary, portions of which are in Robert Gordon Sproul President's Papers, CU-5, series 4, carton 37, folder 15, Bancroft. The relevant entry is dated 11/13/51.

53 *Burns and Combs urged . . . discreet*: Kerr Personal Papers, Bancroft, CU-302, carton 1, folder 2, Bud to Clark, 11/30/53, "Confidential." Combs also used students as campus informers, see H. E. Stone to Sproul, 3/27/52, President's Papers, CU-5, series 4, box 37, folder 14, Bancroft. On Captain Wadman attending the National Academy, see "UCPD History," police.berkeley.edu/about_UCPD/ucpdhistory.html, accessed 8/1/11.

53 *Sproul already feared*: Sproul to McCarthy, 6/15/51, Robert Gordon Sproul President's Papers, CU-5, series 4, carton 37, folder 14, Bancroft.

53 *He now acceded . . . just a cover*: The confidential agreement is described in Sproul's office diary, 11/13/51, Robert Gordon Sproul President's Papers, CU-5, series 4, car-

ton 37, folder 15, Bancroft. Note that Sproul did not announce that Wadman was the "actual" liaison to the Burns committee, Sproul office diary, 1/7/53; Sproul office diary, 1/26/52. Once Burns and Combs had enlisted Sproul, they used this to sign up colleges around the state, a process Sproul described in his office diary. Burns and Combs arranged a private meeting with the heads of nearly every college in Southern California, including USC, Claremont Men's College, Occidental College, Pomona, Whittier, Redlands, and the California Institute of Technology. As Sproul recounted this March 24, 1952, gathering, "Senator Burns presented the Problem of Communist Infiltration of Colleges and Universities by Communists [*sic*], and asked the cooperation of the group in handling the problem. He said that the Committee had in mind no blacklist or 'gestapo' but merely an exchange of information for the protection of all. He asked me to describe the University of California plan, and I did so. He then asked for similar contact men in other institutions, and the assembled presidents each gave him a name," Sproul office diary, 3/24/52. They held a similar meeting in June 1952 with heads of Northern California schools, who also joined the program, Sproul office diary, 7/9/52. Kerr was the only contact man named publicly, Kerr, vol. 2, 51.

54 *Kerr knew nothing*: Author interview with Kerr; Kerr, vol. 2, 49–53.

54 *So when his shock*: Kerr to Sproul, 6/9/54, Kerr Personal Papers, Bancroft, CU-302, carton 1, folder 2; DC 10/3/52, "Kerr States 'Contact Man' Job Policy"; Kerr interview with author.

54 *And when he stepped*: "Chancellor Kerr's Remarks at University Meeting, October 1, 1952," in Kerr Personal Papers, CU-302, carton 11, folder 34, Bancroft.

54 *Reporting for work*: Author interview with Kerr; Kerr, vol. 1, 24–25, in which Kerr dryly notes that the *Oxford English Dictionary* defines *chancellor* as an "honorary" position, "Keeper of His Majesty's conscience" and "guardian of infants, lunatics, and idiots."

54 *Among his first*: Kerr, vol. 1, 41.

54 *But for that matter . . . generally conformist*: On campus life and Kerr's tenure in the fifties, see Kerr, vol. 1, 16–107, 109, 132–33, 146, 237, 380, 382–83. David Goines notes the "silent generation" in *The Free Speech Movement: Coming of Age in the Sixties*, 39. Alex Sherriffs, a psychology professor and administration liaison to fraternities and sororities, described the fifties' students as being deeply apathetic. "Alex C. Sherriffs, the University of California and the Free Speech Movement," oral history interview by James Rowland, 1978, Regional Oral History, Bancroft, 15–16, 32; author interview with Michael Rossman.

54 *Simone de Beauvoir*: de Beauvoir is quoted in *Berkeley! A Literary Tribute*, 72–73.

54 *But beneath . . . fright and bitterness"*: Joan Didion, "On the Morning After the Sixties," in *The White Album*, 329–31.

55 *Kerr worried*: Kerr, vol. 1, 130.

55 *He decided to . . . "Constitution is founded"*: Ibid., 130; 116-325-30; SFC 11/1/52, "UC's Kerr Opposes Loyalty Oaths." The ballot initiative, known as Proposition 6, would replace the Levering Act loyalty oath that had been passed by the legislature. Proposition 6 was also known as the Levering oath because Levering had proposed it. *LAT* 10/21/53, "The Levering Act"; *LAT* 11/5/52, "State-wide Returns"; *LAT* 3/27/51, "State Employee Loyalty Oath."

55 *Some regents complained . . . walked away*: Kerr, vol. 1, 130–31; author interview with Kerr. The Levering oath measure passed easily, *The California Oath Controversy*, 250.

55 *The State Supreme Court*: The decision was issued October 17, 1952, *The California Oath Controversy*, 242–43.

55 *Kerr promptly proposed*: In a memo to Sproul he wrote, "In a situation in which the legal rights of the nonsigners to back pay appear to be so clear, it seems to me a mistake to force them to take legal action (which will be expensive both for them and the University) to obtain back pay. Faculty-Regents relationships and general faculty morale would be greatly improved if The Regents would act voluntarily . . . ," Kerr to Sproul, 5/13/53, President's Papers, CU-5, series 4, carton 39, folder 1, Bancroft. See also Kerr, vol. 1, 131.

56 *As chancellor . . . report about him*: The 1947 background investigation is FBI HQ file 116-325. The 1952 investigation is in 116-325.

56 *During this earlier*: 116-325-4, n.d., behind 116-325-4, 3/10/47; 116-325-21, 5/17/47; 100-5113-157.

56 *Bureau agents discovered*: 116-325-23; 116-325-30.

56 *One confidential source*: 116-325-40, pp. 2, 14. CSSF-33X is variously identified as Western Research Foundation or its proprietor, Harper Knowles, in 100-36985-1460; 100-54060-1009; 100-36985-429; and other records.

56 *Ensconced in*: The sketch of Knowles and the Western Research Foundation is drawn from FBI files on Knowles; *Harry Bridges: The Rise and Fall of Radical Labor in the U.S.*; *Many Are the Crimes*, 68; Synanon investigative report, 5/9/75, interview of Harper Knowles, *Synanon v. Hearst*, S.F. Superior Court No. 651-749; author interview with Burney Threadgill, Jr. It is also based upon FBI files on Harper Knowles: 39-915-171X, 9/5/40; 138-1335-20, 8/19/53; 100-39577-3X14, 2/5/47; 100-39577-3X18, 1/25/54; 100-39577-8; 100-39577-9; 100-39577-10, 4/30/54; 100-39577-11; 100-39577-15, 2/23/67; 39-915-619; 39-915-202, 10/1/40; 39-915-1, 8/27/40. It also draws on *S.F. Examiner* articles dated 9/15/31, "Second Suit"; 9/26/31, "Knowles Divorce"; 8/28/39, "Bridges Will Call"; 8/29/39, "More Witnesses"; 8/31/39, "Theft of Legion Data"; 8/31/39, "Legion Data"; 9/1/39, "Legion Evidence"; 10/18/63, "The 'Inside' View"; 2/19/77, "Harper Knowles"; *SFC* 8/29/39, "Knowles Questioned." Further information comes from an "inter-office correspondence," dated 4/25/57, contained in the *S.F. Examiner's* "morgue" that was prepared by a research librarian of the newspaper, whose management retained Western Research Foundation. "There is an outfit in San Francisco called 'Western Research Foundation' that specializes in indexing all types of papers and publications (private, state, county, and federal) for data relative to Communists and Communist organizations. There is an almost complete file of all types of congressional reports on communist activities in this foundation. The outfit services the Federal Bureau of Investigation and other agencies . . . They specialize in confidential research." A handwritten note on the memo says, "The FBI told us of its existence."

56 *It was run by*: SFX 12/23/75, "Targets Were UFW"; SFX 2/19/77, "Harper L. Knowles."

56 *In the late thirties*: NYT 12/31/39, "Case on Bridges Scored."

56 *Bridges denied*: Ibid.; *Many Are the Crimes*, 94.

56 *In the 1940s*: "Articles of Incorporation of Western Research Foundation," 9/18/46, filed with the California Secretary of State; *The Nation*, 5/6/78, "The Intelligence Laundry."

56 *Checking Knowles's records*: 116-325-30.

57 *Kerr was granted*: 161-3037-27; author interview with Kerr.

57 *The chancellor kept*: "Academic Freedom at Berkeley," Report to Representative Assembly, May 16, 1955, by Clark Kerr, President's Papers, CU-5, series 4, carton 37, folder 14, Bancroft.

57 *From time to time . . . passed them along*: Ibid.; Kerr to Sproul, 9/23/53, "Confidential," President's Papers, CU-5, series 4, carton 37, folder 14, Bancroft; author interview with Kerr.

57 *Kerr had no idea*: Author interview with Kerr.

57 *Kerr grew increasingly . . . "serious legal damage"*: Kerr to Sproul, 9/23/53, "Confidential," op. cit.

57 *In a seventh*: Kerr, vol. 2, 57–58; author interview with Kerr.

57 *The campus purging operation*: This paragraph is based on the testimony of Richard E. Combs, chief counsel for the California Senate Committee on Un-American Activities before the U.S. Senate Subcommittee to Investigate the Administration of the Internal Security Act and Other Internal Security Laws of the Committee on the Judiciary, Washington, D.C., 3/19/53.

58 *This remarkable . . . Wadman: The Nation*, 1/30/54, "G-Men on the Campus," by Walter Gerstel.

58 *The American Civil Liberties Union*: Kerr Personal Papers, CU-302, carton 1, folder 35; ACLU press release, 7/2/54, Bancroft; NYT 7/5/54, "Faculty 'Checker' in West Assailed."

58 *University officials . . . "classified governmental research"*: Sproul to Besig of the ACLU, 4/5/54, Kerr Personal Papers, CU-302, carton 1, folder 2, Bancroft; *DC* 3/31/54, "Kerr the Only 'Contact Man' He Says at Gripe Session," in Kerr Personal Papers, CU-302, carton 1, folder 36, Bancroft; NYT 7/5/54, "Faculty 'Checker' in West Assailed."

58 *. . . told the* San Francisco Chronicle: Sproul memo, "Questions and Answers for San Francisco Chronicle," 5/14/54, and *SFC* 5/19/54, "UC Quashes Rumor," both in Kerr Personal Papers, CU-302, carton 1, folder 2, Bancroft.

58 *For his part, Burns*: DC 5/19/53, "Campus Counter-spies Report," Kerr Personal Papers, CU-302, carton 1, folder 2, Bancroft.

58 *Wadman told*: DC 4/16/54, "Wadman Clears"; Kerr Personal Papers, CU-302, carton 1, folder 36.

58 *All along, Kerr*: Kerr's initial reaction and public statement are described in several records, including *SFC* 5/19/54, "UC Quashes Rumor"; *DC* 5/24/54, "A Danger to Academic Freedom"; *DC* 5/19/53, "Campus Counter-spies Report"; Kerr to Besig, 6/7/54; Kerr to Sproul, 6/7/54, "Confidential and Urgent"; Kerr to Virginia and Bud, 6/7/54, "Extremely Confidential"; all in Kerr Personal Papers, CU-302, carton 1, folder 2, Bancroft. Bud is Eugene Burdick, one of Kerr's assistants, a political-science professor and coauthor of the 1958 novel *The Ugly American*. Virginia is Virginia Taylor (later Norris), a key assistant to Kerr. Kerr, vol. 2, also discusses the contact-man episode, 49–58.

58 *Based largely on*: DC 5/20/54, "'No Spies' States Academic Senate," Kerr Personal Papers, CU-302, carton 1, folder 2, Bancroft.

58 *As the ACLU pursued*: Burdick to Sproul, 2/20/54, Kerr Personal Papers, CU-302, carton 1, folder 2, Bancroft.

58 *One of his aides*: On the investigation by Kerr and his staff, see Bolton Memo to Confidential File, 6/11/54; Kerr to Virginia and Bud, 6/7/54, "Extremely Confidential"; Kerr memo 6/7/54, "Ernie Besig," all in Kerr Personal Papers, CU-302, carton 1, folder 2, Bancroft.

58 *Kerr finally realized*: "I am not the real contact man for the Berkeley campus," he wrote in a memo to his staff in early June. "My name was publicly announced as contact man but the name given to Combs and Burns was Wadman's." Kerr to Virginia and Bud, 6/7/54, "Extremely Confidential," op. cit.

58 *He feared*: Ibid.; Kerr to Besig, 6/7/54; Kerr letter to Sproul, "Draft—not sent, sat. breakfast," 5/13/54; all in Kerr Personal Papers, CU-302, carton 1, folder 2, Bancroft; author interview with Kerr.

58 *He urged Sproul*: Kerr memo, "Pres. Sproul," 6/11/54; Kerr to Sproul, 6/8/54, "Confidential—Urgent"; Kerr to Besig, 6/7/54; Kerr memo, 6/7/54, "Ernest Besig—Phone"; Kerr Personal Papers, CU-302, carton 1, folder 2, Bancroft.

58 *Throughout June*: "Summary of Events on and following June 7" (1954), Kerr Personal Papers, CU-302, carton 1, folder 35, Bancroft.

59 *On July 2, 1954 . . . put out his own*: Kerr memo, "Alice Heyneman, Mrs. Stewart, et al. re ACLU," 7/2-3/54, five pages, Kerr Personal Papers, CU-302, carton 1, folder 5, Bancroft.

59 *In a statement*: The joint statement was also signed by Vice President James Corley. Security Officer William Wadman slipped a copy to the FBI, 100-34204-68. See also "Summary of Events on and following June 7" (1954), Kerr Personal Papers, CU-302, carton 1, folder 5, Bancroft.

59 *Combs was furious . . . subversives on campus*: Bud to Clark, "Confidential," 7/8/54, Kerr Personal Papers, CU-302, carton 1, folder 5, Bancroft, which states Combs "reacted very negatively." In addition, Combs sent Sproul a letter that did not name but clearly referred to Kerr and complained of "conciliation and weakness." See Combs to Sproul, 9/9/54, Kerr Personal Papers, CU-302, carton 1, folder 4, Bancroft.

59 *The episode also*: The anecdote about Warren Olney III and Hoover is in 100-151646-10.

59 *Hoover dispatched . . . "it is creating"*: 100-151646-NR, 3/30/54, before 100-151646-10.

59 *He told his agents*: 100-151646-14-X1, 10/8/54; 100-151646-14X, 9/29/54.

59 *When Adlai Stevenson . . . Rule 17*: Kerr, vol. 1, 95; Kerr, vol. 2, 123; DC 5/9/56, "Guttural Sounds."

59 *The rule barred*: Kerr, vol. 1, 95–96, 166; Kerr, vol. 2, 122–28. The text of Rule 17 is in *Documentary Supplements to the Gold and the Blue.*

60 *As some two thousand students*: This paragraph is based on BDG 5/9/56, "Demo Urges Federal Aid for Education"; DC 5/7/56, "Adlai to Talk at West Gate Tomorrow"; DC 5/9/56, "Adlai Stevenson Stresses"; DC 5/9/56, "Guttural Sounds."

60 *And when Stevenson's opponent*: This paragraph is based on DC 5/15/56, "Kefauver Hits Rule 17"; NYT 5/15/56, "Kefauver Scorns."

60 *Two days later*: The account of the panty raid is drawn from the report of Acting Lieutenant W. H. Garratt, 5/17/56, Kerr Personal Papers, CU-302, carton 4, folder 29, Bancroft; Kerr's report on the episode, DC 6/5/56, "Chancellor's Office Releases White Paper on Panty Raid"; DC 5/17/56, "Students Go Wild"; DC 5/18/56, "Confusion Follows U.C. Rioting."

61 *The morning after*: DC 5/17/56, "The Masses Are Asses."

61 *A wire service*: See, for example, WP 5/18/56, "3000 Take Part"; LAT 5/18/56, "Berkeley Panty Raiders"; *Philadelphia Inquirer* 5/18/56, "Panty Raids?"; *Plain Dealer* (Cleveland) 5/19/56.

61 *Kerr vowed*: DC 5/18/56, "Confusion Follows U.C. Rioting."

61 *. . . "white paper" on "the riot"*: The findings are from Kerr's report in DC 6/5/56, "Chancellor's Office Releases White Paper on Panty Raid." Ultimately, several students were suspended, DC 5/29/56, "Rioters Receive Suspensions."

62 *By the end*: Kerr, vol. 1, 56.

62 *He had imposed*: Ibid., 63.

62 *. . . appointed close to*: Ibid., 62.

62 *. . . named new department chairmen*: Ibid., 64–65.

62 *. . . won approval for construction*: Ibid., 93–94, 102–105.

62 *As the* Oakland Tribune: OT 10/19/57, "Clark Kerr New President of UC," in Kerr Personal Papers, CU-302, carton 4, folder 9, Bancroft.

62 *Now he would*: NYT 9/27/58, "Kerr Installed"; LAT 6/30/58, "Dr. Sproul Bows Out"; the Nobel laureate Glenn Seaborg became the new chancellor of the university's Berkeley campus, LAT 7/19/58, "Seaborg New."

62 *The regents had concluded*: This paragraph is based on Kerr, vol. 1; BDG 10/19/57, "Clark Kerr New UC President." The birthrate is in Kerr, vol. 1, 72.

62 *Edwin Pauley*: OT 10/20/57, "Home of New U.C. Prexy"; *SFX* 10/19/57, "UC Gets a Fine New President"; *DC* 10/21/57, "A Liberal Triumph"; *OT* 10/19/57, "Clark Kerr New President"; *DC* 10/21/57, "Berkeley Chancellor Chosen," all in Kerr Personal Papers, CU-302, carton 4, folder 9, Bancroft; *LAT* 10/24/57, "Dr. Kerr Will Head"; *LAT* 2/20/58, "President-Designate."

62 *Clark and Kay . . . he said: The Campus Guide*, 137–39; Kerr, vol. 2, 33–34, 167; author interview with Clark E. Kerr. On Kerr working at home and his handwriting, see *NYT* 2/14/65, "The Berkeley Affair."

62 *On September 29, 1958*: The account of Kerr's inauguration, and his thoughts onstage, are drawn from Kerr, vol. 1, 160; "Master Plan for Inauguration," "Performances Celebrating the Inauguration," and "The Inauguration of Clark Kerr" program, all in Kerr Personal Papers, CU-302, carton 26, folder 10, Bancroft; *SFC* 9/30/58, "Kerr Tells Aims at UC Inauguration"; *BDG* 9/20/58, "Kerr Inauguration to Draw Scholars," in 100-34204-114; *LAT* 9/11/58, "Dr. Kerr's Inaugural"; *LAT* 9/15/58, "Kerr Inaugural"; *LAT* 9/25/58, "UCLA Will Install"; author interview with Kerr.

62 *Stepping to*: "The Worth of Intellect," inaugural address, Clark Kerr, UC Berkeley, 9/29/58, Kerr Personal Papers, CU-302, box 28, folder 16, Bancroft.

63 *Kerr's rise, however*: Auerbach's memo describing Combs's conclave, and Hoover's placing it in the FBI file on the university, are in 100-34204-118 and 100-34204-119.

5: The Essay Question

64 *"What are the dangers . . ."*: The descriptions of the question and Lechner are from 62-103031-24; 62-103031-32; 62-103031-16, 2/4/60; 62-103031-28; 62-103031-27. See also Chronology of Subject "A" Problem, "Confidential," 2/23/60, Kerr Personal Papers, CU-302, carton 4, folder 21, Bancroft, which provides a detailed account of the essay episode from the perspective of university administrators.

64 *Hoover was livid*: His quote is from 62-103031-15, 2/1/60. His use of handwritten notations to communicate his thoughts and decisions to subordinates is illustrated by the many examples in bureau records reviewed by the author. See also *From the Secret Files of J. Edgar Hoover*, which offers others. That Hoover favored blue ink is based on interviews with former FBI agents, including Curtis O. Lynum, former special agent in charge of the San Francisco field office; *J. Edgar Hoover: The Man and the Secrets*, 533; *Secrecy and Power*, 218; *Hoover's FBI*, 17. His attitude toward criticism of the bureau is well documented in biographies of him, including *The Director*; *J. Edgar Hoover: The Man and the Secrets*; *Secrecy and Power*; *The Boss*.

64 *Tolson assigned*: 62-103031-17. DeLoach's role in the bureau's response to the essay question is detailed in subsequently cited FBI records. His biographical data is from *The FBI: A Comprehensive Reference Guide*, 228–29; 322; *Secrecy and Power*, 397–98; *The Boss*, 216.

64 *First, DeLoach*: 62-103031-34.

65 *DeLoach enlisted*: 62-103031-16, 2/4/60; 62-103031-28; 62-103031-93.

65 *The article*: 62-103031-17; 62-103031-93.

65 *Next, DeLoach*: 62-103031-17; 62-103031-31; 62-103031-34.

65 *Hearst's Los Angeles*: 62-103031-16; 62-103031-93.

65 *Fulton Lewis, Jr.*: 62-103031-17.

65 *DeLoach also mobilized*: Ibid.

65 *He arranged*: 62-103031-NR, 3/1/60, behind 62-103031-52; 62-103031-38 and 62-103031-39; 62-103031-47X1; 62-103031-48.

65   *Assistant Director John McGuire*: 62-103031-17.
65   *Another assistant director*: 62-103031-17; 62-103031-40; 62-103031-NR, behind 62-103031-51.
65   *At DeLoach's direction*: 62-103031-17; 62-103031-19; 62-103031-20.
65   *When Richard Auerbach*: 62-103031-20.
65   *Auerbach was ordered*: The Auerbach-Brown anecdote is from 62-103031-21; 62-103031-22; 62-103031-23.
65   *Auerbach then enlisted*: 62-103031-23; 62-103031-68.
66   *The* Examiner *published*: 62-103031-37; 62-103031-68; 62-103031-93.
66   *Hoover personally*: 62-103031-NR, behind 62-103031-29.
66   *He sent letters*: 62-103031-13; 62-103031-14; 62-103031-19; 62-103031-35; 62-103031-36.
66   *The director's February 8, 1960 . . . "this unfortunate error"*: 62-103031-14.
66   *DeLoach soon reported back*: 62-103031-17.
66   *"Excellent"*: 62-103031-34.
66   *Under fire*: Details of the university's internal investigation concerning the essay question are drawn from Chronology of Subject "A" Problem, "Confidential," 2/23/60, op. cit.; *Chancellor at Berkeley*, 355 et seq.; Hart to Wellman, 2/15/60, Chancellor's Papers, Archives, CU-149, box 39, folder 25, Bancroft. On Cyrus Eaton, see *LAT* 5/5/58, "U.S. Becoming a Police State, Eaton Charges."
67   *The regents' response*: 62-103031-45; 62-103031-63; Chronology of Subject "A" Problem, 2/23/60, op. cit.; minutes of regents' meeting, Riverside, California, 2/19/60, Kerr Personal Papers, CU-302, carton 4, folder 21, Bancroft.
67   *In an interview*: DeLoach interview with author.
67   *Hoover could not . . . "withdrawn the question"*: Hoover's letter to Nixon is in 62-103031-49.
67   *Governor Brown had promised*: 62-103031-45; 62-103031-NR, behind 62-103031-29; 62-103031-23.
67   *So Hoover ordered*: 62-103031-23.
67   *Webb Burke*: 62-103031-46, 2/8/60.
67   *A year earlier . . . academic to Hoover*: 100-34204-105. As to formation of the Committee on Academic Freedom, see *The Loyalty Oath Controversy: University of California, 1949–1951*, expanded timeline, sunsite.berkeley.edu/~ucalhist/archives _exhibits/loyaltyoath/timeline1950_3.html, accessed 8/8/10.
67   *Now Burke*: 62-103031-46, 2/8/60.
68   *The committee*: This paragraph is based on 62-103031-46; 62-103031-29; author interview with Jones's daughter, Pam Wagner; author interview with Jones's grandson, Jon Tigar; *LAT* 7/5/82, "Everett Jones, UCLA's Arbiter of English, 'Retires.'" On *The Negro Cowboys*, see *NYT* 2/4/65, "Books of the Times"; *LAT* 10/25/70, "Black Frontiersmen in American West"; *Chicago Tribune* 2/7/65, "Negro Cowhands Gain Their Due."
68   *. . . and was quoted*: In addition to the February 11, 1960, *New York Post* story cited in the text, this part is based on 62-103036-46; 62-103036-47X3; 62-103036-59, which contains *Los Angeles Herald Examiner* 2/11/60, "UC Test Called Red-Tinged."
68   *"The understatement . . ."*: 62-103036-47X3.
68   *Checking the bureau's . . . impugning the FBI*: 62-103031-28. On Harry Jones, see 62-103031-28; 62-103031-30. On Mary Elizabeth Jones, see 62-103031-79; 62-103031-28; 62-103031-46; 62-103031-46, 2/8/60.
68   *Warning that . . . English entrance exam*: 62-103031-46, 2/12/60. The agents' inquiry is described in 62-103031-54; 62-103031-30. Wheeler's interest—he wanted names—is also noted in Chronology of Subject "A" Problem, "Confidential," 2/23/60, op. cit.

68   *But there was . . . at the party office:* 62-103031-60, 2/29/60.
69   *Moreover, informers:* 62-103031-61, 3/1/60.
69   *"Dear Chancellor Knudsen":* The letter is in 62-103031-69.
69   *Copies also were:* 62-103031-69.
69   *The released FBI files . . . with the bureau:* Author's review of the FBI files and inter-
     views with Athan Theoharis and Cartha DeLoach.
69   *As a congressional:* Church, book III, 1–79, "COINTELPRO: The FBI's Covert Ac-
     tion Programs Against American Citizens," especially 8, 43–44, 60.
70   *The anonymous attack . . . and his wife:* Author interview with Pam Wagner.
70   *In a letter:* Jones's letter is in 62-103031-69.
70   *In a subsequent:* Knudsen's statement is in 62-103031-69.
70   *Hoover now set:* 62-103031-49; 62-103031-87.
70   *FBI agents were ordered:* This paragraph is based on 62-103031-47X; the March 2,
     1960, report, titled "University of California," in 62-103030-87; author interview
     with DeLoach.
70   *The report's first section:* The description of the report in this and the following para-
     graphs is based on the author's review of the report in 62-103030-87.
71   *Detainees:* Author interview with Burney Threadgill, Jr. On the history of Angel
     Island, see the Angel Island Association website, angelisland.org/history/, accessed
     8/8/10.
71   *The Security Index:* The description of the Security Index and its history is based
     primarily on the final reports of the U.S. Senate Select Committee to Study Gov-
     ernmental Operations with Respect to Intelligence Activities, 1976. In particular,
     see book III, "The Development of FBI Domestic Intelligence Investigations," 417
     et seq.; author interview with Athan Theoharis.
71   *But though the Palmer:* That the Security Index included U.S. citizens is clear from
     the aforementioned discussion in the Church committee and numerous FBI Secu-
     rity Index records listing citizens. See, for example, Church, book III, 412–21, 441.
     See also *Spying on Americans,* 46.
71   *Hoover began the system . . . at some future time:* Church, book III, 412–22. Roose-
     velt's 1936 and 1938 requests are noted in Church, book III, 394, 397–98, 399, 405.
     Athan Theoharis notes there is no record of Roosevelt having approved it, *Spying on
     Americans,* 42–43, 45.
71   *From the start . . . "unwise, and dangerous":* Church, book III, 417–22.
72   *Hoover did not abolish . . . "outside the Bureau . . .":* Ibid., 420–21.
72   *Only as the Cold . . . to expand it:* Ibid., 436–38.
72   *Under the Security Index . . . youth organizations:* Ibid., 437, 438.
72   *For each person:* The description of the mechanics of the Security Index is based on the
     author's review of FBI records and interviews with former FBI agent Burney Thread-
     gill, Jr., former FBI special agent in charge Curtis O. Lynum, and Athan Theoharis.
72   *Subjects were removed:* Church, book III, 440, 446; author interviews with Thread-
     gill and Lynum.
72   *To speed: Spying on Americans,* 46.
72   *Neither the FBI nor:* This paragraph is based on Church, book III, 436–46.
72   *The Internal Security Act:* The conflict was with Title II (the Emergency Detention
     Program) of the Act, *Spying on Americans,* 48. Some of the FBI's concerns about the
     Internal Security Act and the problems its higher standards posed for the FBI's Se-
     curity Index program were outlined in an internal memo by Milton "Mickey" Ladd,
     then the FBI's number three official. According to Ladd's memo, the FBI's Security
     Index criteria for listing people to be detained greatly overstepped the limits of the law.
     Ladd wrote that the bureau's Security Index included "the names of many persons

who we consider dangerous but who do not fall within the standards set forth in the Internal Security Act of 1950." In addition, he noted, the Act did not permit the FBI to suspend the writ of habeas corpus, the fundamental power of the courts to determine whether a person is being unlawfully imprisoned and should be released. In Ladd's view, this "would prove a definite hindrance to the execution of necessary measures . . ." Moreover, the Internal Security Act required an individual warrant for each arrest, meaning the FBI would have to submit a sworn affidavit setting forth specific evidence against each person, instead of using one master warrant to sweep up all targets. This, Ladd complained, would be "a detrimental, time-consuming procedure," Church, book III, 445.

72 *Hoover and Justice*: Ibid., 442–46, 545–46. The Security Index was renamed the Administrative Index, or ADEX, in 1971, and was continued to 1973, when FBI officials quietly ended it in the wake of the Watergate scandal and the changing political climate. Although the program never was used to make mass arrests, the bureau did use it to gather information on thousands of law-abiding people and to interfere with the rights of many of them simply because bureau officials disagreed with their First Amendment activities. For an insightful discussion of the Security Index, see *Spying on Americans*, 40–64.

73 *In addition*: The FBI's report on the University of California is in 62-103030-87. Among the renowned professors it cited (though not as being on the Security Index) were Woodrow Wilson Borah, a history professor who had done groundbreaking work in documenting the decimation of Mexico's native population as a result of the Spanish conquest; Arthur G. Brodeur, a professor of English known for his book *The Art of Beowulf*; and Israel L. Chaikoff, a professor of physiology credited with being the first to learn precisely how the body forms thyroid hormones. Also listed was Philip E. Lilienthal, associate director of the University of California Press. *NYT* 12/28/99, "Woodrow Borah"; *NYT* 9/15/71, "Arthur G. Brodeur"; *NYT* 1/27/66, "Dr. I. L. Chaikoff"; *LAT* 10/29/06, "Sally Lilienthal, 87."

73 *While Hoover*: The discussion of California's crisis in higher education, the Master Plan, and Kerr's role in the plan is primarily based on Kerr, vol. 1, 172–90, and on John A. Douglass's comprehensive book *The California Idea and American Higher Education*.

73 *The biggest surge*: Kerr, vol. 1, 72, 173, 174. Kerr writes that from 1960 to 1968 enrollment in the University of California system (including UC Berkeley and UCLA) rose from 50,000 to 100,000; in the state colleges from 95,000 to 210,000; and in the community colleges from 485,000 to 975,000.

74 *It fell to Kerr . . . "negotiation process"*: *The California Idea*, 251.

74 *Trouble had been*: *The California Idea*; *LAT* 2/6/59, "College Future to Be Weighed."

74 *The state colleges*: Ibid.

74 *The university*: *LAT* 6/30/58, "Dr. Sproul Bows Out"; Kerr, vol. 1, 174.

74 *But the system . . . would suffer*: *NYT* 12/20/59, "Educators Near Accord on Coast"; Kerr, vol. 1, 174, 175.

74 *State legislators . . . "United States"*: Kerr, vol. 1, 174; *The California Idea*, 235, 246–47.

74 *The regents had named . . . ten years*: *The California Idea*, 248, 257–58.

75 *Kerr convinced . . . bring about major reform*: *The California Idea*, 259, 264.

75 *To Kerr . . . "the nation itself"*: *The California Idea*, 261.

75 *It was crucial . . . spark a settlement*: *The California Idea*, 262–71; Kerr, vol. 1, 172–90.

75 *Bit by bit . . . February 1, 1960*: This account of the final negotiations ending in the approval of the Master Plan is drawn from *The California Idea*, 289–96, 301; Kerr, vol. 1, 180–81.

76 *It was the most*: The description of the plan and its impact is drawn from Kerr, vol. 1, 186–90; *The California Idea*, 15, 297, 308–25; *Time* 10/17/60, "Master Planner." As Kerr notes and Douglass discusses in detail, the Master Plan built on the vision of public education articulated by California's Progressive movement between 1900 and 1920. Kerr, vol. 1, 186–87; *The California Idea*, 15, 81–113, 312–13.

76 *A few days after*: Kerr's calendar is in Kerr Personal Papers, CU-302, carton 12, folder 46, Bancroft. His absence is also noted in Chronology of Subject "A" Problem, 2/23/60, Kerr Personal Papers, CU-302, carton 4, folder 21, Bancroft; 62-103031-77. *LAT* 2/18/60, "UC President Kerr in Buenos Aires," notes he was to attend a meeting of the American Republics Superior Council of Education.

76 *Kerr wrote*: Kerr's 3/28/60 letter is in 62-103031-NR, after 62-103031-92.

76 *Hoover's assistants . . . "recent question"*: 62-105057-2, 4/4/60.

76 *Hoover decided*: Ibid.

6: Protest at City Hall

77 *Early on*: The account of the City Hall protest is drawn mainly from news reports in the *S.F. Examiner*, *S.F. Chronicle*, *S.F. News-Call Bulletin*, *Berkeley Daily Gazette*, *Oakland Tribune*, *The Daily Californian* student newspaper, *The Californian* magazine edited by Burton H. Wolfe (especially the "Black Friday" article in the July–August 1960 issue, which includes eyewitness accounts by Burton White and others); *Student* by David Horowitz; the lengthy and vivid eyewitness account of the KPFA radio reporter Fred Haines, which appears in *Student*; FBI records, interviews, and other sources, as referenced below. The description of the students' dress is based on newspaper photographs, interviews with participants, and *Operation Abolition*, the documentary film about the protest produced by HUAC.

77 *Rays of sunlight*: The description of City Hall architecture is from *City Guides Training Material, City Hall Architectural Drawings*, by Trudie Douglas, 1979; *S.F. Sunday Examiner and Chronicle*, 5/22/66, "Retrospective of the Brown Period"; "City Hall Renovation," by John Barbey, Liberty Hill Neighborhood Association; and "The Civic Center of San Francisco, a Dream Come True, in the Municipal Record," November, no year noted, all at the San Francisco History Center, San Francisco Public Library, folders "SF Buildings—Tour Materials" and "SF Buildings—City Hall (New)."

77 *HUAC's avowed mission*: *The Age of McCarthyism*, 12, 29, 54–61, 248. No less than Earl Warren, the chief justice of the U.S. Supreme Court, former California governor, and a staunch anti-Communist, declared in 1959 that "exposure and punishment is the aim of this committee and the reason for its existence." Warren's comment was in a dissenting opinion by Justice Hugo Black in a ruling that upheld the contempt conviction of Professor Lloyd Barenblatt, *NYT* 6/14/59, "The Nation." 100-36985-360. On HUAC, see *The Age of McCarthyism*, 12, 29, 57.

77 *In prior visits*: 100-36985-231; 100-36985-232; 100-36985-236; 100-36985-208; 100-36985-338; 100-36985-339; 100-36985-317. See also *The Committee*, 423, 432.

77 *Then, in early May*: DC 5/2/60, "Teachers Called by Committee"; SFX 5/7/60, "3 Groups Protest Red Quiz," in 100-36985-412; SJM 5/12/60, "S.J. Church Blasts House Red Probers," in 100-36985-414; SJN 5/7/60, "Denunciations of House Hearing Keep Mounting," in 100-36985-415; *The Committee*, 428.

77 *William Wheeler*: 100-36985-272; 100-36985-385; 100-36985-386; 62-103031-54.

77 *The committee, moreover*: 100-36985-272, which identifies the witness as Karl Prussion. Hearst newspapers had a record of sensationally covering allegations of communism and working closely with anti-Communist organizations. See also Chapter 5,

"The Essay Question"; *Many Are the Crimes*, 44, 78, 127, 256, 345; *Hoover and the Un-Americans*, 35, 37, 80, 90; *Spying on Americans*, 163–65.

77 *Forty-eight people*: DC 5/2/60, "Teachers Called by Committee"; *SJN* 5/7/60, "Denunciations of House Hearing Keep Mounting," in 100-36985-415.

78 *Wachter was among . . . spiritual anthems*: The description of the budding student activism at Berkeley is drawn from *Student*, 17–46; *The Wedding Within the War*, 30–71; DC 4/6/60, "City Council Opposes Picketing"; DC 4/19/60, "Legality of Store Picketing Assured"; DC 4/19/60, "Regents May Decide on ROTC"; author interviews with Michael Rossman, Irving Hall, Burton White, Burton Wolfe, and Douglas Wachter. On Chessman, see also the University of Southern California Libraries Archives, www.usc.edu/libraries/archives/la/scandals/chessman.html, accessed 8/13/10. On the black student sit-in movement, see *In Struggle*, 9–30; *Parting the Waters*, 271–303.

78 *A small student organization . . . on off-campus issues*: On SLATE, see *The Free Speech Movement*, 65–82, 541; *Student*, 17–22; *Berkeley at War*, 15–16, 88; *The Wedding Within the War*, 30–99; *Chancellor at Berkeley*; *Turning Points and Ironies*, 12–16, 27–45; *First Amendment Felon*, 204–205, 224–28, 264–65; DC 4/5/60, "Sherriffs Defends Directives"; DC 5/3/60, "Slate Rally Today"; DC 5/4/60, "Directives Challenged by Ex Com"; DC 5/5/60, "Committee Called 'Un-American,'" in 100-36985-417; DC 5/5/60, "ASUC: Reps-at-Large"; DC 5/9/60, "Slate Rally Discusses"; DC 5/12/60, LED "Protest." See also Kerr, vol. 2, 131–32, 150–53; *Thirteenth Report, Un-American Activities in California*, 22–32; SLATE website at www .slatearchives.org/biblio.htm, accessed 8/13/10.

78 *As the date*: DC 5/5/60, "Committee Called 'Un-American'"; DC 5/11/60, "Petition Opposes Acts of House Committee"; DC 5/12/60, "Picketing, Protest Rallies."

78 *Students for Civil Liberties . . . "Opposition to Hearings Grows"*: DC 5/3/60, "Student Opposition to Hearing Grows."

79 *Robert Meisenbach . . . student protest*: Author interview with Robert Meisenbach; accounts of the protest and his trial in *S.F. Examiner*, *S.F. Chronicle*, *S.F. News-Call Bulletin*, and *The Californian*; 100-46140-5; 100-46140-6.

79 *Two undercover . . . "subpoenaed subjects"*: SF 100-36985-1158 with SFPD report of Pharris, 5/17/60.

79 *Many students*: Author interview with Michael Rossman.

79 *Celeste MacLeod . . . "too much"*: Celeste MacLeod, Meiklejohn Civil Liberties Institute Archives, carton 14, folder "Notes on HUAC Hearing," Bancroft.

79 *Meisenbach first became*: Author interview with Meisenbach.

79 *One of the biggest . . . condemn McCarthy*: On the Army-McCarthy hearings, see *Many Are the Crimes*, 259–65; *The Age of McCarthyism*, 64–65; *The Age of Anxiety*, 379–431; *Time* 10/4/54, "The Censure of Joe McCarthy"; author interview with Meisenbach.

79 *Still, many Americans . . . "the phone!"*: Author interview with Meisenbach.

79 *Meisenbach served . . . protest it*: Author interview with Meisenbach; 100-46140-5; 100-46140-6.

80 *As he and . . . in the aisles*: Author interviews with Meisenbach, Hall, and White; SFC 5/13/60, "City Hall Crowd in Angry Protest of Red Probe"; *The Californian*, July–August 1960, "Black Friday."

80 *U.S. Representative Edwin Willis*: The description of the committee proceeding in this and the following paragraphs is from the transcript, Hearings before the Committee on Un-American Activities, House of Representatives, Eighty-sixth Congress, Second Session, Part 1, May 12, 1960, "The Northern California District of

the Communist Party, Structure-Objectives-Leadership" (denoted in the notes for this chapter as "Hearings"); 100-36895-539.

80   *Arens summoned Douglas Wachter*: The account of Wachter and his testimony is from *DC* 5/4/60, "Subpoenaed Student Tells Why"; *The Californian*, July–August 1960, "Black Friday"; 100-151646-22; *The Wedding Within the War*, 51–52; author interviews with Burney Threadgill, Jr., and Douglas Wachter; Hearings. On Billie Wachter's alleged membership in the Communist Party, see 100-36985-758. On Saul and Doug Wachter's alleged membership, see Hearings, op. cit., 1924, 1928, 2174. For Saul Wachter's response to the committee's questions, see Hearings, op. cit., 2148–51. For Doug Wachter's response, see Hearings, op. cit., 1966–69.

81   *Outside the chamber doors . . . "doesn't!"*: *The Californian*, July–August 1960, "Black Friday"; *Student*, 69; *SFX* 5/13/60, "150 U.C. Students March on Union Square"; *DC* 5/13/60, "Committee's Tactics Protested at Rally."

81   *When the hearing . . . "back to Russia"*: *DC* 5/13/60, "Committee Hearings Marked by Violence"; *Student*, 69; Hearings; *The Californian*, July–August 1960, "Black Friday."

81   *The unruly witnesses . . . "will be ejected"*: Hearings; *The Californian*, July–August 1960, "Black Friday"; *Student*, 69; *SFX* 5/13/60, "Mob Storms Un-American Hearing Here."

82   *By 2:00 p.m. . . . Berkeley students*: 100-36985-1158 with SFPD report of Pharris, 5/17/60. Details of Thursday's events also were drawn from *OT* 5/12/60, "Jeering Students Ring Red Probe"; *DC* 5/13/60, "Committee Hearings Marked by Violence"; *DC* 5/13/60, "Un-American Activity Hearings"; *BDG* 5/12/60, "Hundreds Open S.F. Red Quiz"; *BDG* 5/13/60, "UC Student Refuses Answers"; *SFX* 5/13/60, "Mob Storms Un-American Hearing Here"; *SFC* 5/13/60, "City Hall Crowd in Angry Protest of Red Probe"; *SFC* 5/13/60, "1000 at Union Square for Protest"; *SFNCB* 5/12/60, "Cops Battle Angry Crowds at Red Quiz"; 100-36985-1158.

82   *Celeste MacLeod . . . heard nothing*: Celeste MacLeod, Meiklejohn Civil Liberties Institute Archives, carton 14, folder "Notes on HUAC Hearing," Bancroft; author interview with Meisenbach; *SFC* 5/14/60, "400 Policemen Rush to City Hall—64 Arrested"; *OT* 5/13/60, "General Riot Breaks Out at Red Quiz"; *SFX* 5/14/60, "Cops Battle Student Mob at City Hall"; Hearings.

82   *During lunch recess . . . at the curb*: *The Californian*, July–August 1960, "Black Friday"; Haines in *Student*, 71; *SFC* 5/14/60, "400 Policemen Rush to City Hall—64 Arrested"; *OT* 5/13/60, "General Riot Breaks Out at Red Quiz"; *SFX* 5/14/60, "Cops Battle Student Mob at City Hall."

82   *At about 1:15 . . . danger was over*: *The Californian*, July–August 1960, "Black Friday"; Haines in *Student*, 70–81; 100-36985-1158 with SFPD report of Pharris, 5/17/60.

83   *Just then, Vincent Hallinan . . . ignored him*: Affidavit of Vincent Hallinan in 100-36985-1201. On Hallinan, see *NYT* 10/4/92, "Vincent Hallinan Is Dead at 95"; *NYT* 12/19/61, "Church Is Challenged."

83   *The students were singing . . . seated demonstrators*: Haines in *Student*, 73.

83   *"The rotunda seemed . . . for protection"*: Ibid.

83   *Burton White . . . he said*: *The Californian*, July–August 1960, "Black Friday."

83   *Meisenbach had been . . . "You bastards!"*: Author interview with Meisenbach; Meisenbach testimony in *People v. Robert Meisenbach*, No. 57454, San Francisco Superior Court, Thursday, April 27, 1961, in 100-434714-EBF 72.

83   *A second stream*: The description of the melee is based on Haines's account in *Student*, 73–81; *The Californian*, July–August 1960, "Black Friday"; *DC* 5/16/60, "Eyewitness Account of 'Battle.' "

84 *Hallinan, near the chamber*: Vincent Hallinan, sworn affidavit, 5/20/60, behind 100-434714-56.
84 *Inside the chamber . . . "Communist Party"*: Hearings, op. cit.
84 *Prussion remained*: Ibid.
84 *The Hearst Corporation*: 100-36985-272.
84 *At the curb . . . posting bail*: Author interview with Meisenbach; BDG 5/16/60, "Trial by Jury Asked by UC Coed in Riot"; SFC 5/14/60, "Names of the 64 Arrested"; BDG 5/14/60, "31 Berkeleyans Arrested"; DC 5/16/60, "Eyewitness Account of 'Battle'"; SFX 5/16/60, "63 Rioters Face Court Today"; SFX 5/16/60, "63 in Court Today on Riot Charges"; OT 5/16/60, "Red Probe 'Rioters' Win Delay"; *The Californian*, July–August 1960, "Black Friday."
85 *Mayor George Christopher*: SFNCB 5/13/60, "Mayor Booed, Cheered"; SFC 5/14/60, "Mayor Appalled"; *The Californian*, July–August 1960, "Black Friday."
85 *The events at*: Among those stories which have provided details for this account are SFX 5/14/60, "Cops Battle Student Mob at City Hall"; SFX 5/14/60, "Shouts of 'Sadists' at Red Probe"; SFX 5/14/60, "The Student Riot," editorial on events of 5/13/60; SFX 5/14/60, "Worst Ever, Says Head of Probers"; SFX 5/14/60, "Justice Took Holiday"; SFX 5/14/60, "62 Arrested in S.F. Riots Listed"; SFX 5/14/60, "$1,000 in Water Damage"; SFC 5/14/60, "400 Cops Battle Mob at City Hall"; SFC 5/14/60, "Police, Crowd Battle Outside Red Hearing"; SFC 5/14/60, "400 Policemen Rush to City Hall—64 Arrested"; SFC 5/14/60, "How Police Clubs Drove Crowd Out"; SFC 5/14/60, "Lawyer Is Drenched, Jailed for Protest"; SFC 5/14/60, "List of the Injured"; OT 5/13/60, "General Riot Breaks Out at Red Quiz"; SFNCB 5/13/60, "Wild City Hall Riot!"; SFNCB 5/13/60, "6 Thrown Out for Taunts at Red Hearing"; SFNCB 5/13/60, "Rioting at City Hall!"; SFNCB 5/14/60, "Police 'Fortify' City Hall"; SFNCB 5/14/60, "City Hall 'Jungle'—Emotion Reigned"; DC 5/16/60, "Eyewitness Account of 'Battle'"; DC 5/16/60, "Students Are 'Dupes' Says HUAC"; DC 5/16/60, "House Committee Hearings Continue Through 'Rioting.'" See also Mel Wax's report in the *New York Post*, 5/15/60.
85 *Reporters hustled*: Author interviews with former *S.F. Examiner* reporters Lynn Ludlow and Gerald D. Adams about the history of San Francisco newspapers.
85 *Their stories stole*: Front pages, SFX, final edition, and SFC, 5/14/60.
85 *The San Francisco Examiner's*: Montgomery's article, SFX 5/14/60, "Cops Battle Student Mob at City Hall"; *The Californian*, June 1961, "How the Examiner's Pulitzer Prize Winner Reported 'Black Friday.'"
85 *According to Montgomery . . . "nightstick swinger"*: SFX 5/14/60, "Cops Battle Student Mob at City Hall."
86 *Montgomery's account was picked*: *The Californian*, July–August 1960, "Black Friday"; *The Californian*, June 1961, "How the Examiner's Pulitzer Prize Winner Reported 'Black Friday.'"
86 *Celeste MacLeod had left . . . nicely and behave*: Celeste MacLeod, Meiklejohn Civil Liberties Institute Archives, carton 14, folder "Notes on HUAC Hearing," Bancroft; BDG 5/14/60, "31 Berkeleyans Arrested."
86 *MacLeod and about three . . . "in that room"*: Celeste MacLeod, Meiklejohn Civil Liberties Institute Archives, carton 14, folder "Notes on HUAC Hearing," Bancroft.
86 *The next morning . . . "Go Home"*: Celeste MacLeod, Meiklejohn Civil Liberties Institute Archives, carton 14, folder "Notes on HUAC Hearing," Bancroft. Details of events on Saturday also were drawn from SFX 5/15/60, "4,000 Mass at Red Quiz: No Violence"; SFX 5/15/60, "Red Probers Booed by Crowd When They Appear on

Balcony"; *SFX* 5/15/60, "Cahill, Carberry Commended for Police Work at Hearings"; *SFX* 5/15/60, "Einstein Kin Booked"; *SFC* 5/15/60, "5000 Gather at City Hall for Red Hearing Protest"; *OT* 5/14/60, "1,500 Gather Outside Probe at S.F. City Hall"; *OT* 5/14/60, "Ex-Red Says Party Still Peril"; *OT* 5/15/60, "Prober Says S.F. Riots Inspired by Commies"; *OT* 5/15/60, "More Hostile Witnesses Defy Red Probers"; *BDG* 5/14/60, "Hearing Is Under Heavy Police Guard"; *SFNCB* 5/14/60, "5000 Mass at City Hall."

86 *Jessica Mitford*: Mitford, "The Indignant Generation," *The Nation*, 5/27/61. In a letter to her daughter, Constancia "Dinky" Romilly, Mitford wrote somewhat more somberly, "My impression in these parts is that the students are about now coming up with a bang against forces they hardly knew existed, let alone knew the strength of—FBI etc. How they'll react is an interesting question," *Decca*, 241.

86 *Inside, Police Chief . . . "reliable witnesses"*: Hearings, op. cit.

87 *The crowd . . . rear exit*: Celeste MacLeod, Meiklejohn Civil Liberties Institute Archives, carton 14, folder "Notes on HUAC Hearing," Bancroft; 100-36985-445; *DC* 5/16/60, "Students Orderly Saturday as Hundreds Picket Hearing."

87 *An FBI agent*: 100-36985-445.

87 *HUAC never*: *SFC* 5/13/10, " 'Black Friday,' Birth of U.S. Protest Movement"; author interview with Irving Hall.

87 *"This was probably . . ."*: *BDG* 5/14/60, "Hearing Is Under Heavy Guard"; *SFC* 5/14/60, "Chairman Says 'Worst Incident.' "

87 *Even before the steps*: *Chancellor at Berkeley*, 462; author interview with Clark Kerr.

87 *Kerr, who did not*: Kerr, vol. 2, 48.

87 *"Any University of California . . ."*: *DC* 5/16/60, "Kerr Also Issues Statement"; *SFC* 5/14/60, "UC Students Plan Orderly Protest."

7: Communist Target—Youth

88 *From his desk . . . "1934 strike"*: 100-151646-22.

88 *He was comparing*: On Bridges and the 1934 strike, see *J. Edgar Hoover: The Man and the Secrets*, 245–46; *Endangered Dreams*, 102–107, 108–20, 221–22; *American Prometheus*, 105–106.

88 *Auerbach may have*: 100-151646-22.

88 *Hoover replied*: 61-7582-4496.

88 *Covertly, they were . . . protect national security*: For examples documented in one of the FBI's several files on HUAC, see 100-36985-28; 100-36985-35; 100-36985-101; 100-36985-148; 100-36985-201; 100-36985-204; 100-36985-240; 100-36985-268; 100-36985-284; 100-36985-285; 100-36985-395. Bureau officials routinely misled the public about the FBI's true relationship with the committee; in 1957, for example, an FBI official in San Francisco told an inquiring citizen, "the FBI has no connection with the HCUA," 100-36985-222. On confidentiality of FBI files, Hoover assured *Newsweek* that year that FBI files were confidential and could not be disclosed, see *J. Edgar Hoover Speaks Concerning Communism*, 130. See also *Spying on Americans*, 134, 136; *The FBI: A Comprehensive Reference Guide*, 116, 147, 151–52, 157, 367, 368, 370. Other examples are cited in the text.

89 *Hoover decided . . . the Security Index*: Hoover's orders are in 61-7582-4496.

89 *Auerbach was already . . . "Federal Government"*: 100-36985-460; 100-36985-no serial, behind 100-36985-1187, Clifford to all agents, 5/17/60; 100-36985-no serial, behind 100-36985-1187, Clifford to all agents, 5/20/60.

89 *The San Francisco field office . . . "available"*: 100-36985-460; 100-36985-no serial, behind 100-36985-1187, Clifford to all agents, 5/17/60; 100-36985-no serial, behind 100-36985-1187, Clifford to all agents, 5/20/60.
89 *They received secret*: 100-36985-593.
90 *Two weeks later*: 61-7582-4530. The memo is 61-7582-4522, vol. 139 EBF and 100-36985-548.
90 *On June 1, 1960*: The account of the hearing is drawn from Judge Axelrod's ruling in *People of the State of California v. Christopher Bacon et al.*, in 100-36985-519, vol. 6; SFC 6/2/60, "Judge Clears Students; 'Riot' Charges Dismissed"; SFNCB 6/1/60, "61 Students Freed in City Hall Riots," in 100-36985-530; SFX 5/28/60, "60 in Riot," in 100-36985-528.
90 *The students were relieved*: SFC 6/2/60, "Judge Clears Students; 'Riot' Charges Dismissed."
90 *This left the case*: SFC 6/9/60, "Student Given Delay in City Hall Riot Assault."
91 *One week after . . . Yosemite National Park*: 100-46140-2; 100-46140-4.
91 *Agent Clarence*: Dunker's inquiries and the material he gathered in this and the following paragraphs are detailed in 100-46140-6; 100-46140 1-A(2).
92 *On October 6, 1960*: 100-46140-11.
92 *The eighteen-page booklet*: "Communist Target—Youth: Communist Infiltration and Agitation Tactics" was prepared by the FBI and published by HUAC. It was subtitled "A Report by J. Edgar Hoover, Director of the Federal Bureau of Investigation, Illustrating Communist Strategy and Tactics in the Rioting Which Occurred During House Committee on Un-American Activities Hearings, San Francisco, May 12–14, 1960," copy in 61-7582-4538.
92 *"Communist Target—Youth" generated*: NYT 7/18/60, "F.B.I. Chief Says Reds Incite Youth"; LAT 7/18/60, "S.F. Student Riots"; WP 7/19/60, "Hoover Says Reds"; SFC 7/19/60, "'Reds Boast of Riots,'" in 100-36985-654; SFNCB 7/18/60, "City Hall Riot Blueprint for Reds: Hoover," in 100-36985-647; BDG 7/19/60, "FBI Chief Blames Reds in S.F. Riot," in 100-36985-649; SFX 7/18/60, "FBI Lists Reds in S.F. Riot, How Students were Duped," in 100-36985-646.
92 *An Associated Press*: An example of the AP dispatch is in 61-7582-4547.
92 *He was gratified*: 100-36985-676, 7/28/60.
93 *Others, however*: This paragraph is based on SFC 7/20/60, "21 in S.F. Riots Deny Hoover's Version"; BDG 7/2/60, "UC Students Deny Reds Led S.F. Riot," in 100-36985-657; OT 7/21/60, "U.C. Student Calls Hoover Report Lie," in 100-36985-668; New York Post 7/20/60, "Students to Hoover," in 61-7582-4542; Washington Evening Star 7/21/60, "Hoover's Charge on Riot Disputed," in 61-7582-4542.
93 *The director did not . . . with the bureau*: 62-7582-4542. On Sokolsky, see *The Boss*, 247, 277, 293n; *The Secret Life of J. Edgar Hoover*, 216.
93 *Richard Arens*: The Arens anecdote is from 61-7582-4550; 61-7582-4563.
93 *Paul Seabury . . . "forces and events"*: 100-36985-663; 100-36985-688; BDG date illegible, "Riot Report Criticized," in 100-36985-678; SFC 7/22/60, "ADA Calls Hoover's Report on Riot False." On the ADA, see *The Age of McCarthyism*, 88.
94 *Attorney General Rogers . . . "paragraph by paragraph"*: 100-36985-688; 100-36985-682; 100-36985-691.
94 *Auerbach rushed*: 100-36985-683.
94 *There the material . . . "wholly factual"*: 61-7582-4530X; 61-7582-4573X, 8/8/60.
94 *Sullivan was upbeat*: 100-36985-636.
94 *The film featured . . . on the head*: Operation Abolition DVD, Quality Information Publishers, Inc.
94 *As the committee*: For example, see SFX 8/7/60, "Church Row over S.F. Riot Film," in

100-36985-697; *SFX* 8/8/60, "Row over Riot Film," in 100-36985-707; 100-36985-709; *BDG* 3/2/61, "Students Continue Fight," in 100-36985-996. See also *The Committee*, 431–32.

94 *Irving Hall*: *SFX* 8/8/60, "Row over Riot Film," in 100-36985-707.

94 *Hall and other . . . in a handbill*: 100-36985-736.

95 *Auerbach assigned*: 100-36985-704, with note: "Handle . . ."

95 *An informer*: 100-36985-716; 100-36985-715.

95 *The director ordered*: Hoover's order is 100-36985-754; Auerbach's assessment is 100-36985-755.

95 *Auerbach conceded*: This and the following paragraphs summarizing Auerbach's assessment are from 100-36985-755.

95 *Besides, HUAC's . . . show sailors*: The military's use of the film is described in 61-7582-NR, 7/26/60, behind 61-7582-4545; 61-7582-4626.

95 *Standard Oil*: Some of the corporations showing the film are identified in *The Reporter* magazine article "A Movie with a Message," 11/24/60; 100-36985-773; 100-36985-788; *SJM* 3/3/61, "Lockheed Halts Showings," in 100-36985-998; news article 2/11/60 (name of newspaper illegible), in 100-36985-950. Other firms were planning to screen it, including General Electric and the Halliburton Company, 61-7582-4618; 61-7582-NR, 12/1/60 behind 61-7582-4629. On industry's use of it generally, see 61-7582-NR behind 61-7582-4629.

95 *It was presented*: For example, see 100-36985-844; 100-36985-907; 61-7582-4554; 100-36985-771; 100-36985-773; 100-36985-775; 100-36985-778.

95 *All over America . . . who was present*: Kragen's analysis is in Kerr Personal Papers CU-302, carton 4, folder 21, Kragen report to Kerr and Kerr cover letter, 12/16/60, Bancroft. Kragen's talk and the informer's report are in 100-36985-856, 9/6/60; 100-36985-858.

96 *But the more . . . constitutional rights*: 100-36985-798, in which the HUAC investigator Wheeler concedes errors to the student activist Burton White; *The National Guardian* 1/16/61, "Walter Declares War," in 100-36985-907; *Stanford Daily* 11/30/60, "'Operation Abolition,'" in 100-36985-837; *Stanford Daily* 1/13/60, "A Lively Show at Stanford," in 100-36985-909; *BDG* 3/2/61, "Students Continue Fight," in 100-36985-996; *Time* 3/17/61, "Operation Abolition: The Investigation." See also *The Committee*, 431–32.

96 *In a typical screening . . . legal defense*: *OT* 9/30/60, "U.C. Students Sit Quietly," in 100-36985-794; article 10/8/60 (newspaper name illegible), "Students Hoot," in 100-36985-796.

96 *In a review*: News article 10/8/60 (newspaper name illegible), "Students Hoot," in 100-36985-796, which discusses the *Daily Californian* review.

96 *Herb Caen*: *SFC* 11/20/60, Caen column, "I Am in Receipt," in 100-36985-831.

96 *On November 26, 1960*: Editorial in 61-7582-4646.

96 *J. Edgar Hoover hated*: *The Director*, 192, 208.

96 *He set down . . . the film's accuracy*: 61-7582-4646, 11/29/60.

96 *Tolson wrote*: 61-7582-4645.

96 *Auerbach soon found . . . "in Northern California"*: 61-7582-4688, 1/4/61; 100-36985-853, 12/9/60.

97 *Auerbach concluded*: 100-36985-853, 12/9/60.

97 *But in an effort*: 100-36985-863.

97 *A typical inquiry*: The Wolfe anecdote is based on 62-106289-158, which contains the correspondence and the background check on Wolfe. This is one of many such exchanges recorded in file 62-106289.

98 *On August 12, 1960 . . . "Most certainly"*: 62-106289-2.

98   *The special agent . . . the United States*: 62-106289-10; 62-106289-100; 62-106289-128.
98   *The FBI, meanwhile*: Many examples of the FBI's wide distribution of the report are
     found in file 62-106289, some cited below.
98   *Hoover readily obliged*: In a typical reply to one curious college student at Louisiana
     State University, Hoover wrote, "The cancerous growth of communism poses a most
     serious challenge to our heritage, and it is most encouraging to learn of the endeav-
     ors of our youth to alert the students in our colleges and universities to the evils of
     this menace." See 62-106289-182.
98   *Six thousand*: 62-106289-199.
98   *Ten thousand*: 62-106289-135; 62-106289-253.
98   *Eighteen thousand*: 62-106289-205; 62-106289-207.
98   *More boxes*: For a PTA example, see 62-106289-151.
98   *The national director*: 62-106289-177.
98   *The FBI director's*: There are many examples of this correspondence in file 62-106289.
     For instance, R. G. Rydin, vice president of the Atchison, Topeka and Santa Fe Rail-
     way System, based in Chicago, wrote Hoover in November 1960 to commend his
     report, remarking, "One shudders at times in seeing how gullible some of our young
     people are." See 62-106289-114. Reverend William J. McDonald, the rector of Catho-
     lic University in Washington, D.C., on September 29, 1960, congratulated Hoover
     on "Communist Target—Youth" and shared some divine inspiration. Hoover re-
     plied, "The remarks of His Holiness Pope Pius XI are certainly apropos. The com-
     munist movement has, of course, historically sought the minds of youth." See
     62-106289-87.
98   *Mrs. Harold K. Bower . . . "with you there"*: 62-106289-187.
99   *But as "Communist Target"*: There are many examples of skeptical correspondence
     in file 62-106289 as well. For one, Gordon Shull, a professor at the College of
     Wooster, in Ohio, wrote Hoover on April 17, 1961, noting that the Bay Area Students
     Committee for the Abolition of HCUA had challenged police claims that a student
     started the City Hall fracas by jumping over a barrier and attacking an officer. Shull
     asked "whether you have sources other than police reports concerning the events
     immediately leading up to the violent episode. Did a student actually leap a barri-
     cade, grab an officer's night stick and beat him over the head?" Replying on April
     26, 1961, Hoover reaffirmed his findings in the "Communist Target—Youth" report.
     See 62-106289-286.
99   *The Reverend Henry Gerner . . . "by the FBI"*: 62-106289-233.
99   *By April 17, 1961*: The 300,000 figure is a tally of various shipments cited in 62-
     106289. The anticipation of the upcoming Meisenbach trial is reflected in news-
     paper articles and student literature about it. See, for example, *SFX* 1/15/61, Dick
     Nolan column, "The City."
99   *It would be*: This has been noted. For example, see *SFC* 5/17/80, "The Radicalism";
     The Free Speech Movement, 71–73; *The Sixties: Years of Hope, Days of Rage*, 81–85;
     Student, 160, in which David Horowitz concludes, "The fight that the students are
     putting up is just the preliminary struggle."

8: The Trial of Robert Meisenbach

100 *The trial*: The account of Meisenbach's trial was drawn from articles in *S.F. Exam-
     iner*, *S.F. News-Call Bulletin*, and *S.F. Chronicle*; *The Californian*, June 1961, "The
     Meisenbach Case," by Irving Hall; *Streetfighter in the Courtroom: The People's Ad-
     vocate*, by Charles Garry and Art Goldberg, 70–96; trial records; FBI documents on
     Meisenbach and the trial; author interview with Meisenbach.

100 *The trial had been*: SFX 11/5/60, "Trial Date Set"; SFX 1/25/61, "City Hall Riot Trial Postponed"; SFX 3/1/61, "City Hall Riots Trial Postponed"; SFX 3/9/61, "Riot Trial Delayed Again"; SFC 3/16/61, "City Hall Riot Trial Postponed"; SFX 3/29/61, Dick Nolan column, "Hall of Justice"; SFX 4/6/61, "Now, Giants Game Delays Riot Trial"; SFX 4/11/61, "Meisenbach Trial Delayed"; SFX 4/17/61, "Oft-Delayed City Hall Riot Trial Tomorrow"; SFC 4/17/61, "City Hall Riot Trial Tomorrow." Meisenbach's refusal to plea-bargain is described in SFX 4/10/61, "Riot Trial on Wednesday," and author interview with Meisenbach.
100 *Nearly a year . . . Communist dupes*: Author interview with Meisenbach.
100 *As his trial approached . . . started to tremble*: Ibid.
100 *Just before trial . . . "feel better"*: Ibid.; SFC 4/26/61, Herb Caen, "Pocketful of Notes."
101 *By the end*: SFC 4/19/61, "Quick Start in City Hall Riot Trial."
101 *Eyeing the students*: Ibid.
101 *Burton White*: SFX 4/19/61, "Who's at the Trial—and Why?"
101 *Richard Auerbach . . . the assault charge*: 100-434714-22.
101 *And he expected*: Auerbach's belief that Montgomery would provide key testimony is made clear in 100-36985-1165, 5/4/61; 100-46140-160, 5/16/61; 100-434714-67, 5/17/61; 100-434714-68, 5/16/61.
101 *In his opening . . . listened intently*: 100-434714-6; SFC 4/20/61, "Cop's Story Shaken at Riot Trial."
101 *Giubbini called . . . arrested him*: 100-434714-6; SFC 4/20/61, "Cop's Story Shaken at Riot Trial."
102 *On cross-examination . . . clubbing him*: 100-434714-6; 100-434714-11; SFC 4/21/61, "New Version of Riot Cop's Story"; SFX 4/21/61, "Riot Trial Defense Rips Cop."
102 *Giubbini put on two . . . and Stansfield's*: The account of Stansfield's and Morris's testimony is from 100-434714-11; 100-434714-18; SFC 4/21/61, "New Version of Riot Cop's Story—Eyewitness"; SFC 4/22/61, "New Story by City Hall Riot Eyewitness"; SFX 4/22/61, "A Diagram of Confusion"; SFX 4/22/61, "3 Versions in Riot 'Slugging'"; SFX 4/24/61, "Riot Trial of State Near End."
102 *Berman presented . . . memo about it*: 100-434714-19; SFX 4/25/61, "'I Saw No Riot Attack on Police'"; SFX 4/26/61, "Prof's Story of City Hall Riot"; SFC 4/24/61, "Riot Trial Defense Today"; SFC 4/27/61, "Meisenbach Called a 'Victim'"; SFX 4/27/61, "'Student Victim of Riot Cops.'"
102 *Meisenbach then took*: The account of Meisenbach's testimony is based on 100-434714-21; 100-434714-23; 100-434714-24; SFX 4/28/61, "Says He Was Victim of Three Beatings"; SFX 4/28/61, "Close-Up of Student's City Hall Riot Story"; SFC 4/23/61, "Meisenbach Tells of Riot—In Tears"; author interview with Meisenbach.
103 *At this point . . . club Schaumleffel*: 100-434714-28; 100-434714-52, p. 5; SFX 5/1/61, "Riot Trial Arguments on Today"; SFC 5/2/61, "Parade of Cops vs. Meisenbach"; SFX 5/2/61, "Riot Trial Riddle."
103 *Now Berman . . . He denied it*: 100-434714-52, p. 5.
103 *"I am astounded . . ."*: Hoover and Tolson's comments are in 100-434714-NR, 5/2/60, behind 100-434714-39.
104 *Tolson ordered*: Ibid.
104 *"This is bad . . ."*: 100-434714-43.
104 *Belmont immediately . . . "very real problem"*: 100-434714-NR, 5/2/60, Belmont to Parsons, before 100-434714-40.
104 *Or as Peet*: 100-46140-139.
104 *In closing arguments . . . broke down in tears*: 100-434714-33; SFX 5/3/61, "Who Lied? Riot Trial's Big Question"; SFC 5/3/61, "Both Sides Charge Lies"; SFNCB

5/3/61, "Riot Case in Hands of Jury"; *OT* 5/3/61, "Jurors Begin Deliberations in Riot Case."

104 *The jury took*: SFX 5/4/61, "Verdict Never in Doubt"; *SFC* 5/4/61, "Meisenbach Freed in S.F. Riot Trial."

104 *The students*: 100-434714-25, p. 2.

104 *That night . . . "We Shall Not Be Moved"*: SFX 5/4/61, "Verdict Is Reached in Less Than Three Hours" and "Meisenbach, Jurors in N. Beach Victory Fling"; 100-434714-25, p. 5. Additional news reports on Meisenbach's victory party are attached to 100-434714-46, 5/4/61, including *SFNCB* 5/4/61, "Riot Trial Fete Held 'Shocking'" and "4 Jurors Sing Jolly Fellow at Party"; *OT* 5/4/61, "Jury Comes In, Barrel Rolls Out" and "Meisenbach Cleared, Back to University."

104 *Hoover ordered*: 100-434714-41, 5/3/61.

105 *He intensified*: Hoover's internal inquiry is detailed in the citations for the following paragraphs.

105 *As ordered . . . failed to testify*: Auerbach's explanations are in 100-434714-32, 5/2/61, p. 7; 100-434714-25, 5/4/61; 100-36985-1165, vol. 13, 5/4/61, Auerbach memo to file.

105 *Grim officials . . . "his own club"*: Belmont's assessment is in 100-434714-52.

105 *William C. Sullivan*: 100-434714-29.

105 *One of Hoover's*: 62-106298-327; *The FBI: A Comprehensive Reference Guide*, 354.

105 *The memo had implied . . . clubbed an officer*: That neither Kuno nor Schon saw the events is drawn from 100-434714-29; 100-434714-52, p. 5; 100-434714-28.

106 *Now Auerbach was forced . . . "hurdle"*: Hoover's demands and Auerbach's defiant responses are in 100-36985-1185; 100-434714-NR, 5/10/61, behind 100-434714-52; 100-36985-1064, 4/6/61; 100-36985-1153, 4/28/61.

106 *Sullivan had confused*: In addition to the above citations, see *The Life and Times of an FBI Agent* by Donald W. Kuno, 181–84, in which Kuno, the agent who wrote the troublesome report using the word *hurtle*, asserts that Auerbach became aware of this semantic problem while the Meisenbach trial was pending and pressured Kuno to falsely testify that he saw Meisenbach leap the barricade. Kuno writes that he angrily told Auerbach, "I wouldn't perjure myself under any circumstance." Kuno reiterated his contentions in an interview with the author.

106 *Irked by this . . . "points before"*: 62-106289-350, 5/12/61.

106 *It turned out*: 62-106289-348; 100-36985-1193; 62-106289-327.

106 *To make matters . . . "material up"*: Belmont to Parsons, 100-434714-41, 5/3/61; 100-46140-151; 100-434714-30; 100-434714-37.

106 *Hoover had had enough*: 100-434714-30, 5/5/61; 100-46140-151, 5/10/61.

106 *Headquarters staff*: 100-434714-41, 5/3/61; 100-434714-47, 5/11/61; 100-434714-30, 5/5/61.

106 *"The whole matter . . ."*: 100-434714-47, 5/11/61.

106 *They assured him*: 62-106289-333, 5/13/61.

106 *Taking action*: 100-434714-31, 5/10/61; *The Life and Times of an FBI Agent*, 182–83.

106 *He ordered Auerbach*: 100-36985-1165.

106 *About all the agents*: 100-434714-26; 100-434714-46.

107 *Hoover then turned*: 100-36985-1165.

107 *They hadn't*: 100-434714-46.

107 *He ordered agents*: 100-434714-38.

107 *He directed Auerbach*: 100-36985-1165; 100-434714-26 and 100-434714-46; 100-434714-59; 100-434714-60.

107 *Auerbach got clandestine . . . tapes to the FBI*: 100-434714-34; 100-434714-53; 100-46140-71; 100-434714-72; 100-434714-79; author interview with Burney Threadgill, Jr.

107 *All these efforts . . . Hearst Corporation*: 100-46149-143, 5/3/61.

107 *Hoover liked*: The description of the FBI's Mass Media Program is based on *Spying on Americans*, 133–34, 163–65; *Racial Matters*, 198–99, 207, 215, 275; *The FBI: A Comprehensive Reference Guide*, 29–30; author interview with Athan Theoharis. Among the bureau's friendly journalists were Fulton Lewis, Jr., the radio commentator; Walter Winchell, the gossip reporter; Lyle Wilson, a UPI executive; Ray McHugh, the chief of the Copley News Service; the Hearst columnist George Sokolsky; and the *San Francisco Examiner* reporter Ed Montgomery.

107 *DeLoach ran*: *Racial Matters*, 198–99; the UPI example is in 100-434714-NR, behind 100-434714-53, 5/17/61.

108 *Auerbach, meanwhile . . . in Hoover's report*: 100-36985-1085, 4/26/61.

108 *Tough-talking*: The sketch of Montgomery is drawn from *SFBG* 7/23/76, "The Adventures of Ed Montgomery," by Burton H. Wolfe; *Decathlon of Death*, by Jack Leslie; *SFX* 7/17/75, "Montgomery Ends 30 Years"; *LAT* 4/11/92, "Ed Montgomery, Award-Winning Journalist"; Montgomery's file of articles in the *San Francisco Examiner's* library; author interviews with Lynn Ludlow, Burney Threadgill, Jr., and Curtis O. Lynum.

108 *In 1951 Montgomery . . . tax problems*: *NYT* 5/8/51, "Winners of the 1951 Pulitzer Prizes"; *NYT* 5/8/51, "Richter Is Pulitzer Novelist"; *SFX* 5/8/51, "Bared Crime, Tax Link"; *SFX* 9/28/51, "Chronology of Expose"; *SFX* 7/17/75, "Montgomery Ends 30 Years"; *Editor and Publisher* 5/26/51, *Examiner* advertisement; *S.F. Bay Guardian* 7/23/76, "The Adventures of Ed Montgomery"; *Napa County Record* 10/1/75, "Pulitzer-Winning Gumshoe"; *NYT* 3/21/51, "3 Crime Inquiry Figures"; *NYT* 3/29/52, "3 Sentenced in Tax Case."

108 *Montgomery's biggest*: On the Bryan story, see *SFX* 1/24/57, "Abbott Case on TV"; *SFX*, 7/21/55, "Expected It"; *SFX* 7/21/65, "Date-by-Date Account"; *SFX* 7/21/65, "Arrested Student"; *SFX* 7/22/55, "Examiner Men"; *LAT* 7/22/55, "UC Student to Face Trial in Girl's Slaying." See also *For the People*, 190–200. Burton W. Abbott was prosecuted by District Attorney Coakley, convicted, and executed in 1957. *LAT* 3/17/57, "Abbott Execution Spurs Drive to Ban Death Term." Governor Goodwin Knight decided to grant a stay of execution so Abbott could file a new court appeal, but his phone call to the gas chamber at San Quentin came two minutes too late, *NYT* 3/16/57, "Stay of Execution."

109 *The newspaper quoted*: *SFX* 7/22/55, "FBI Chief Hoover Lauds Examiner Feat."

109 *In 1958, Montgomery*: On the Graham story, see *SFX* 3/28/58, Dick Nolan column; *SFX* 11/3/58, "Ed Montgomery Off"; *SFX* 11/23/58, "Susan Tells of Role"; *SFX*, n.d., "Death in the Morning Air"; *Decathlon of Death*, Internet Movie Database, www .imdb.com/title/tt0051758/, accessed 8/18/2010.

109 *In July 1960*: *SFX* 7/22/60, "$1,500,000 Lawsuit Filed"; *SFX* 7/27/60, "Last Man Hunt"; *SFBG* 7/23/76, "The Adventures of Ed Montgomery," by Burton H. Wolfe.

109 *"Ed Montgomery is . . ."*: *SFX*, newspaper ad, 9/15/66.

109 *There were plenty . . . illegal telephone tapping*: For San Francisco FBI field office records on Montgomery, see 100-434714-57; 139-18; 100-434714-55; 100-434714-71. Also on Montgomery and the FBI, see *SFBG* 7/23/76, *feed/back, The Journalism Report & Review of Northern California*, Spring 1978, "Hoover's FBI, The Media and the Myth," by Harold Kruger, and Summer/Fall 1978, "The Ex and Chron Everybody Knows . . . Now"; *SFBG* 7/23/76, "The Adventures of Ed Montgomery," and court record in the case of *Montgomery v. Bay Guardian Co., Inc.*, S.F. Superior Court No. 722-487, in which the *Bay Guardian* successfully defended itself against Montgomery's libel suit stemming from its story concerning his relationship with the FBI.

109 *Confidentially, Montgomery*: 100-434714-57; 100-434714-71; author interviews with former SAC Curtis O. Lynum and former FBI agent Burney Threadgill, Jr.
109 *Above all*: 100-434714-55; 100-434714-71; author interviews with Lynum and Threadgill.
109 *A few weeks*: This paragraph is based on 100-46140-160, 5/16/61; 100-434714-67, 5/16/61.
110 *But now Montgomery*: Montgomery's offer is described in 100-46140-160, 5/16/61; 100-434714-67, 5/16/61; 100-434714-68, 5/16/61; 100-434714-73, 6/1/61.
110 *Two days later*: Montgomery's letter and note are in 100-434714-64.
110 *Hoover considered*: 100-434714-64, 5/25/61; 100-434714-71, 5/24/61; 100-434714-74, 5/24/61.
110 *He had DeLoach*: 100-46140-168; 100-434714-55, 5/24/61, vol. 2.
110 *Sentner agreed*: 100-434714-61, 5/24/61. However, FBI officials chose not to include Montgomery's name in the editorial. As Belmont explained, the excerpt of his letter would still influence public opinion because it described Montgomery sufficiently "to identify him to persons in the newspaper field," 100-434714-55, 5/24/61, vol. 2.
110 *In the wake*: Some of their correspondence is in file 62-106289.
110 *In a typical . . . "authority was flouted"*: 100-434714-80.
111 *To citizens*: 62-106289-421, 9/13/61.

9: An Eye-opener
112 *One morning at his home*: This paragraph and the next are based on 100-382196-2; 100-382196-3; *Where's the Rest of Me?*, 200, wherein Reagan writes, "The Committee was—and still is—the target of Communists . . . Anyone who took the Committee's side was a 'crackpot' or 'Fascist.' The congressmen themselves were 'witch hunters and Gestapo.'" On *General Electric Theater*, see the Museum of Broadcast Communications website, www.museum.tv/eotvsection.php?entrycode=generalelect, accessed 2/24/11.
112 *Reagan's August 26 . . . path to public office*: Reagan alluded to his secret relationship with the FBI in his two autobiographies, *Where's the Rest of Me? The Ronald Reagan Story*, written with Richard Hubler and published in 1965, and *An American Life: The Autobiography*, written with Robert Lindsey and published in 1990. Not until 1985, in his second term as president, were the first FBI records on Reagan released, in response to an FOIA request by Jack Sirica, a *San Jose Mercury-News* reporter and the son of the Watergate judge John Sirica. Totaling fewer than 200 pages, these documents showed Reagan had been an informer, but they were heavily redacted. A Reagan administration spokesman at that time downplayed Reagan's role, saying FBI officials had described his involvement with the bureau as "very minor." (In fact, subsequently released records show that the White House previewed these documents and approved their release.)
    This same batch of FBI files was subsequently relied upon by Reagan biographers, all of whom were constrained by the limited number of pages and their deletions. Garry Wills wrote in *Reagan's America: Innocents at Home* (1987), "The records released in his file are incomplete—there is a notice of pages omitted, and many are blacked out entirely except for dates and case numbers" (249). In *Early Reagan* (1987), Anne Edwards likewise lamented the "numerous missing pages" and "blackened paragraphs" (306). For *Ronald Reagan in Hollywood* (1994), Stephen Vaughn was confronted by similarly censored records, and in *Dutch: A Memoir of Ronald Reagan*, Edmund Morris said he was troubled by "those blotted-out names" (289). Lou Cannon has been perhaps Reagan's primary biographer and had the

most prolonged access to his subject, and with multiple biographies has had perhaps the widest readership, but of Reagan's major biographers he has evinced the least interest in his subject's secret relationship with the FBI. Cannon wrote in his first book on Reagan, *Ronnie & Jesse* (1969), that Reagan had "cooperated with the FBI" in Hollywood (38), but in his widely circulated subsequent books hardly went beyond this. In *Reagan* (1982), he did not examine Reagan's informing on Hollywood colleagues. In *President Reagan: The Role of a Lifetime* (1991), he cited the same records released to the *San Jose Mercury News* and again noted only that Reagan "cooperated." Finally, in *Governor Reagan: His Rise to Power* (2003), Cannon reiterated almost verbatim the conclusion he had reached twenty-one years earlier in *Reagan* (1986), writing, "I know of no one, either publicly or privately, whom Reagan called a Communist other than those who proclaimed their own communism" (101). Had the FBI made a more timely and complete disclosure of the records on Reagan, Cannon might well have come to a different conclusion—or not—but at least he would have had the opportunity to consider it.

Only at this late stage does a more comprehensive picture of Reagan's involvement with the FBI emerge. As set out in this text, it is based on Reagan's court testimony; author interviews with his former associates, George Dalen and Edwin Meese III, and with former bureau agents; FBI records released to the author as the result of FOIA requests for records not only on Ronald Reagan but on Neil Reagan, Maureen Reagan, Jane Wyman, the Screen Actors Guild, and the University of California; and four lawsuits brought by the author to compel the FBI to comply with these requests. See *Rosenfeld v. Federal Bureau of Investigation and U.S. Department of Justice*, Case Nos. 85-1709 MHP; 85-2247 MHP; 90-3576 MHP; and 3:07-cv-03240 MHP, all in the U.S. District Court, Northern District of California. The author has also gratefully drawn on biographies of Reagan by Garry Wills, Anne Edwards, Marc Eliot, Bill Boyarsky, Stephen Vaughn, and, of course, Lou Cannon.

113 *Ronald Wilson Reagan*: The material about Reagan's life up to his arrival in Hollywood is drawn mostly from *Where's the Rest of Me?* (hereafter *Where*); *An American Life: The Autobiography* (hereafter *American Life*); *Early Reagan*, by Anne Edwards; and the RRPL website at www.reagan.utexas.edu/archives/reference/reference.html (hereafter RRPL website), accessed 8/20/10. Reagan's salary of $200 a week and arrival in Hollywood in 1937 is in *Where*, 74–76. His Nash is noted in *American Life*, 116, and *Ronald Reagan: Fate, Freedom, and the Making of History*, by John Patrick Diggins, 71.

113 *Reagan had come*: *Where*, 3.

113 *He was the younger*: Ibid., 10.

113 *John Reagan . . . for bigotry*: Ibid., 7–9.

113 *John Reagan believed everyone*: Ibid., 7–10, 40–42, 54, 59, 84, 97–98.

113 *He could be*: Ibid., 8, 11, 14.

113 *Nelle Reagan's ancestors*: *American Life*, 22.

113 *She was a housewife*: *Where*, 9–16.

113 *She was also*: *American Life*, 22. On the Disciples of Christ, see the website of the Christian Church (Disciples of Christ), www.disciples.org/, accessed 8/20/10.

113 *The Reagan family*: This paragraph is based on *Where*, 9–13. On the Black Tom explosion of July 30, 1916, see *NYT* 7/31/16, "Glass Damage Exceeds a Million"; *NYT* 7/31/16, "First Explosion Terrific"; *LAT* 7/30/16, "Thirty-three Firemen Killed"; website of the New Jersey Department of Environmental Protection, www.state.nj .us/dep/parksandforests/parks/liberty_state_park/liberty_blacktomexplosion.html, accessed 8/20/10. On the San Francisco bombing of July 22, 1916, see *LAT* 7/23/16, "Six Are Killed"; *NYT* 7/24/16, "Bomb Plot"; Dartmouth College Library Bulletin,

www.dartmouth.edu/~library/Library_Bulletin/Nov1989/LB-N89-VClose2.html, accessed 8/20/10.

113 *When Reagan was nine . . . the role of rescuer*: *Where*, 17–18; *American Life*, 27.

114 *"I was eleven . . .":* The anecdote about finding his father drunk is in *Where*, 7–8.

114 *Reagan enrolled*: This paragraph is based on *Where*, 18–21; *American Life*, 38–43; RRPL website, op. cit.

114 *Reagan was neither*: His comments on college are from *Where*, 22.

114 *Graduating in June*: 116-460320-13.

114 *His date*: *Where*, 22.

114 *Years later*: This paragraph is based on 116-460320-15.

114 *In the fall*: This paragraph is based on *Where*, 23–24; *Early Reagan*, 83. On Eureka College, see www.eureka.edu/, accessed 8/20/10.

114 *At many campuses*: *Early Reagan*, 84–85.

115 *Eureka was facing*: The description of Eureka's cutbacks and Reagan's role in the ensuing student strike in this and the following paragraphs is based on *Where*, 26–30; *Early Reagan*, 88–94.

116 *Nonetheless, he almost*: This and the next two paragraphs are based on *Where*, 30–44; *American Life*, 49; *Early Reagan*, 99.

116 *That June*: According to his 1967 FBI background investigation, the Eureka College registrar's office told an FBI agent that Reagan had a 1.37 overall grade point average, which was equivalent to a C plus. See 116-460320-13.

116 *During the FBI background*: This paragraph is based on 116-460320-13.

116 *Figuring Broadway*: This paragraph is drawn from *Where*, 44–51, 58–59, 66–67.

117 *By now . . . could not work*: Ibid., 52–54, 59.

117 *Reagan was earning*: Ibid., 40, 54.

117 *He also helped*: Ibid., 55, 31, 41, 61.

117 *Like Clark Kerr . . . cheated on it*: Ibid., 67–68.

117 *Sometimes Reagan relaxed . . . "not the goal"*: Ibid., 56.

117 *He still wanted . . . studio parking lot*: Ibid., 70–74.

117 *Reagan would later*: Ibid., 81.

117 *Through 1943*: *Early Reagan*, 495–512.

117 *While filming*: *Where*, 87, 201; *American Life*, 92.

117 *They were married*: Wyman and Reagan were wed on January 24, 1940, according to RRPL website, op. cit. However, *Early Reagan* has the date as January 26, 1940, as does *LAT* 1/27/40, "Screen Couple Wed in Kirk."

117 *Their daughter*: Maureen Reagan was born on January 4, 1941, RRPL website, op. cit.; Wyman is quoted as saying Michael Reagan was adopted the day he was born, March 18, 1945, *Early Reagan*, 282. Michael Reagan writes that he was three days old when adopted, *On the Outside Looking In*, 15.

118 *Featured together*: During this period Reagan and Wyman appeared together in *Brother Rat* (1938), *Brother Rat and a Baby* (1940), *An Angel from Texas* (1940), and *Tugboat Annie Sails Again* (1940), according to *Early Reagan*, 495. The quote is from *LAT* 6/8/41, "Those Happy Reagans."

118 *But America . . . (in 2012 dollars)*: The account of Reagan's military service in this and the following two paragraphs is based on Stephen L. Vaughn's *Ronald Reagan in Hollywood: Movies and Politics*, 104–18. As Vaughn writes, "Strings had been pulled, although there was no hint of such maneuvering in Reagan's version of his war service." The account also draws upon FBI records on William Guthrie as released to Vaughn and lodged with the Wisconsin Historical Society Archives, which provided copies to the author, particularly 67-1077-2 and 67-1077-3. The account also draws on *Where*; *American Life*; *Reagan, the Hollywood Years*; *Early Reagan*; and on

Reagan's military service summary, provided to me by the National Personnel Records Center, and his military records at the RRPL. The latter contains a May 5, 1942, letter from Guthrie to Major General George C. Kenney, U.S. Air Force, requesting Reagan's transfer to the air force, so he could play the lead in an air force movie. Guthrie, who signed the letter as location manager for Warner Brothers, added, "General Arnold indicated a desire that this be accomplished and he instructed me to contact you so that you could make the necessary request from Reagan's immediate superior . . . If this is in line with regulations I will appreciate anything you could do to expedite Reagan's transfer . . ." Reagan Military Records, Record Group 407, RRPL. Reagan's $3,500-a-week salary is in *Where*, 140.

119 *Not everyone*: This paragraph is based on 80-579-2.

119 *World War II*: The description of the postwar change in Reagan's perspective is based on *Where*. As Reagan writes, "The story of my disillusionment with big government is linked fundamentally with the ideals that suddenly sprouted and put forth in the war years," *Where*, 139.

119 *He had inherited*: Reagan described his Democratic allegiance in *Where*, 139; *American Life*, 119.

119 *Although he never . . . targets in Japan*: *Where*, 117–20; *American Life*, 97–99.

119 *Reagan had expected . . . "mankind"*: *Where*, 139.

119 *Events disappointed*: Ibid., 140.

119 *In the months . . . FDR Democrat*: Ibid., 139–41.

119 *J. Edgar Hoover feared*: 100-138754-4, pp. 1–2, foia.fbi.gov/compic.htm, accessed 1/24/02. This document was among the COMPIC records the FBI posted on its electronic reading room, but which it then removed.

119 *He had opened*: Hoover opened the COMPIC investigation in 1942, *The Quest for Absolute Security*, 72. The FBI opened the CINRAD investigation in 1943, ibid., 63.

119 *Code-named COMPIC*: 100-138754-4.

120 *An April 1946 . . . Edward G. Robinson*: 100-138754-124.

120 *Reagan had lent*: 100-64700-684 EBF HQ cross-reference. On Robeson, see *LAT* 1/24/76, "Paul Robeson, Singer"; *NYT* 1/24/76, "Paul Robeson Dead."

120 *A May 1946 . . . twenty-four Communists*: 100-138754-125.

120 *A June 1946 . . . "in this country"*: HQ 100-339008-31.

120 *As the COMPIC investigation*: Hoover continually pressed agents to develop informers in major investigations, author interview with Burney Threadgill, Jr.

121 *One of Reagan's college . . . for future reference*: 66-2542-7560; 100-382196-1.

121 *Agents called on . . . in their report*: The Nazi sympathizer anecdote is in 100-146517-33; 100-382196-1, p. 7; 80-579-2, p. 9. On de Loqueyssie, see *LAT* 11/21/46, "Try for Phone Number"; *LAT* 2/21/46, "Movie Dillinger"; *LAT* 6/14/42, "Titled Polish Couple." On Arthur Lyons, see *LAT* 4/3/88, "The World's Youngest"; *LAT* 5/22/30, "Judgment Given"; *NYT* 7/13/30, "A Get-Together"; *LAT* 12/20/31, "Hobnobbing"; *NYT* 9/3/42, "U.S. to Get."

121 *In 1945, Reagan . . . "side with Hoover"*: The Dewey anecdote is from HQ 62-116607-1; *The Boss*, 264.

121 *In addition to . . . as "reliable"*: 100-340922-20, "Communist Infiltration of the Radio-Television Industry," pp. 23, 24, 82. As David Caute notes, hundreds of people were blacklisted in the radio and television industry, *The Great Fear*, 521, 530. Neil Reagan was well positioned to inform because he was, according to an FBI document, a member of the board of directors of the Radio Directors Guild, search slip 1/23/67, behind 116-70463-1.

121 *"Now, in those days . . ."*: Neil Reagan described his work for the FBI in an oral history interview, *Neil Reagan, Private Dimensions and Public Images: The Early Political*

Campaigns of Ronald Reagan, An Interview Conducted by Stephen Stern, 1981, University of California, Regional Oral History Project, 30 et seq., cited hereafter as *Neil Reagan Oral History*. Neil Reagan's boast was recounted in Garry Wills's 1986 biography, *Reagan's America*.

122 *Late one night . . . "a few hours"*: Reagan recounted the FBI's nighttime visit in *Where*, 169–70, and *American Life*, 111. On Reagan's home at 9137 Cordell Drive, see *Early Reagan*, 231, 244; "The Residences of Ronald Reagan," RRPL, www.rea gan.utexas.edu/archives/reference/residences.html, accessed 2/4/11; *The Ultimate Hollywood Tour Book*, www.nrbooks.com/sample_chapter.htm, accessed 2/4/11.

122 *In his second autobiography . . . "of course they could"*: *American Life*, 111. In addition, and as described in the subsequent text, Reagan confirmed years later in sworn court testimony that such meetings occurred. See Ronald Reagan testimony, 7/1/55, *Michael D. Jeffers v. Screen Extras Guild*, Civ. 21698, Appeal from the Superior Court of Los Angeles County, Reporter's Transcript on Appeal, vol. 12, 3396–415, on file with the California State Archives, hereafter cited as *Jeffers*.

123 *Not long after . . . "whole organization sky-high"*: This account of the HICCASP episode is from *American Life*, 112–13, and *Where*, 166–68. Reagan also refers to the meeting and his resolution in his testimony in *Jeffers*, 3396–3400. On de Havilland, see NYT 3/14/47, "Olivia de Havilland Wins"; LAT 11/5/76, "TV's 'GWTW' Galls."

124 *On July 5, 1946*: The FBI surveillance is noted in 100-338892-63.

124 *Inside, another argument . . . John Howard Lawson*: *Where*, 168; *Jeffers*, 3396–3400.

124 *The screenwriter had drawn*: 100-24499-276, 10/25/43.

124 *FBI agents had long*: Author's exchange with Athan Theoharis, 2008.

124 *Waving his finger*: *Where*, 168; 100-338892-124.

124 *Reagan's deliberately . . . collapsed soon after*: *American Life*, 113. Stephen Vaughn discusses this episode in *Ronald Reagan in Hollywood*, 130–31, 278 n. 49, n. 50.

124 *Before quitting*: Neil Reagan's account is from *Neil Reagan Oral History*, op. cit., 30 et seq.

125 *The 1946 minutes*: The FBI received the 1946 minutes and other records of HIC-CASP in 1949, according to an FBI report that deleted the identity of the source, LA 80-579-2, pp. 27–29.

125 *He soon employed . . . "had done so"*: Reagan's account of disrupting the American Veterans Committee is from his testimony in *Jeffers*, 3400–3401. See also *Ronald Reagan in Hollywood* on Reagan's involvement with the AVC.

125 *By the fall*: On the CSU strike and Reagan's role in the SAG debate about whether to support it, see *Where*, 135–38, 142–64; *Reagan's America*, 228–58; *Early Reagan*, 308–17; *Dark Victory*, 65–73; *Governor Reagan*, 86–90, 94; SAG website, www.sag .org/ronald-reagan, accessed 2/1/11.

125 *When the Screen*: The account of the meeting is from *Where*, 182–83.

126 *The strike wore*: LAT 9/27/46, "Violence Opens Studio Strike"; NYT 10/2/46, "37 Hurt"; LAT 11/16/46, "700 Film Strike Pickets Arrested"; *Where*, 155.

126 *Reagan would later*: *Where*, 174; *Early Reagan*, 320–21, 331. Reagan's statements suggest he suspected the threat might have come from Communists. See his comments about the "group" in *Where*, 173, 174.

126 *He saw sinister*: Reagan's quote is from *Where*, 136, 159, 162.

126 *Reagan's views*: This conclusion is based on the author's analysis of Reagan's autobiographies, FBI records, and the other cited materials concerning the FBI and Reagan. Garry Wills notes that Reagan's involvement with the FBI was an important part of his political development. As to the FBI agents' nighttime visit to Reagan's home, Wills writes, "It was from this period, if not from this session, that Reagan hardened forever his belief that the CSU strike was part of a Communist plot,"

Reagan's America, 247. More broadly, Wills argues that from 1947 on Reagan was in "essential sympathy" with Hoover's view that naïve Americans were being threatened by subversives, ibid., 283. Wills further comments, "Those who say Reagan's career suffered, or his marriage did, because he was wrapped up in union affairs in the late forties underestimate the urgency of his mission. He was busy at saving the nation. This was more important than the movies. In fact it was the reality the movies could only hint at. He had been a T-Man in his Bancroft series. Now he was really T-10, a servant of his government against the most dangerous kind of conspiracy. He had not been with Neil during his period of ambush from the Bel-Air shrubbery. But now he, too, was helping the FBI. Both Reagans were once again G-Men," *Reagan's America*, 250.

126 *In the process*: *Where*, 159.

126 *When Robert Montgomery*: *Early Reagan*, 494; SAG website, timeline, www.sag.org /sag-timeline, accessed 8/22/10.

126 *"More than anything . . ."*: *American Life*, 114.

10: The FBI Story

127 *One month after*: The account of the meeting is based on 100-338892-124; 100-38754-188. Reagan's claim of never pointing the finger is in *Where*, 158. Information about the actors is from *NYT* 12/19/90, "Anne Revere"; *NYT* 4/27/03, "Karen Morley"; Internet Movie Database, www.imdb.com/, accessed 8/23/10. On the Reagans' home at 9137 Cordell Drive, see *Early Reagan*, 231, 244; "The Residences of Ronald Reagan," RRPL, www.reagan.utexas.edu/archives/reference/residences.html, accessed 2/4/11; *The Ultimate Hollywood Tour Book*, www.nrbooks.com/sample _chapter.htm, accessed 2/4/11.

128 *When they were done*: 100-138754-188. In response to the author's FOIA request, the FBI reprocessed this document to release the names of all the actors named in it by Reagan.

128 *The following month*: This anecdote is from LA 80-579-2, p. 29; 100-138754-308. On the PCA, see *WP* 1/6/47, "Rejecting the Reds"; *WP* 1/19/47, "Third Party Chances Slim in '48"; *NYT* 9/20/47, "Wallace Condemns Anti-Red 'Hysteria'"; *NYT* 1/19/48, "PCA Votes 74-Point Platform"; *Governor Reagan*, 95; *Naming Names*, 54. On Conte, see *NYT* 4/16/75, "Richard Conte, Actor"; *LAT* 4/16/75, "Richard Conte, Cold-Eyed"; *LAT* 3/31/10, "Classic Hollywood"; www.imdb.com/, accessed 2/2/11. Conte later joined Humphrey Bogart and other actors in supporting the "un-friendly witnesses" called before HUAC in October 1947, *WP* 10/25/47, "Reds Tried." In response to the author's FOIA request, the FBI reprocessed this document to release Conte's name.

128 *J. Parnell Thomas . . . defrauding the government*: *LAT* 1/23/47, "Hollywood Radicals Face Congress Quiz"; *LAT* 5/9/47, "Rep. Thomas Tells Goals." On Thomas, see *Time* 11/15/48, "Thomas in Reverse," www.time.com/time/magazine/article /0,9171,853405,00.html, accessed 8/25/10. See also *Early Reagan*, 338–39, 349, 349n; *Governor Reagan*, 90, 96; *Chasing Spies*, 159n.

128 *With Thomas was . . . for their cause*: On Thomas's Los Angeles visit, see *LAT* 5/9/47, "Rep. Thomas Tells Goals"; *LAT* 5/10/47, "U.S. Officials to Figure in Hollywood Red Inquiry"; *LAT* 5/16/47, "Former Russian Official"; *LAT* 5/17/47, "Wider Inquiry on Hollywood 'Reds' Urged"; *Early Reagan*, 339; *Chasing Spies*, 151–69.

129 *Thomas turned*: 61-7582-1463, 5/13/47; *The Boss*, 253–54; *Chasing Spies*, 158–59.

129 *The COMPIC investigation . . . in these records*: *Chasing Spies*, 151–69. The FBI's online "reading room" listed parts of the COMPIC files totaling 13,533 pages, foia .fbi.gov/foiaindex/foiaindex.htm, accessed 8/27/10, before their removal.

129 *But FBI officials knew:* The Boss, 215; Chasing Spies, 158–59.

129 *So—on the strict* . . . *"to this committee":* The Boss, 254–55; Chasing Spies, 158–59.

129 *The next day:* The account of Nichols and his call is based on Chasing Spies, 158–59. On Nichols, see The FBI: A Comprehensive Reference Guide, 346.

129 *Several hours* . . . *"fellow traveler":* 61-7582-1463, 5/13/47.

129 *As president:* This paragraph is based on 100-138754-188, pp. 157–60, and 100-138754-188, pp. 157–60. On FBI agents illegally obtaining the names through break-ins in the first place, see Chasing Spies, 34, 154, 155, 163. On Dales and his relationship with Reagan, see Jack Dales, Pragmatic Leadership: Ronald Reagan as President of the Screen Actors Guild, An Interview Conducted by Michael Tuchman in 1981, Oral History Program, UCLA, Introduction, 8, 18, 19–20, 33, 35, 42. That SAG president Reagan exchanged information with the FBI about guild members is further evidenced by statements of his close associates. See the statements of George Dalen, page 145, and Edwin Meese III, page 147.

130 *The names of many:* FBI records list 42 of the 54 actors who were "currently in good standing with the Screen Actors Guild," and on whom Dales turned over SAG information to the FBI. According to FBI records, they are Georgia Backus, Helen Beverly, Roman Bohnen, Lloyd Bridges, Joseph Bromberg, Morris Carnovsky, Howland Chamberlain, Lee Cobb, Howard Da Silva, Mary Jo Ellis, Virginia Farmer, June Foray, Julie Gibson, Jody Gilbert, Lloyd Gough, Freddy Graff, Alvin Hammer, Tom Holland, Victoria Horne, Victor Killian, Mark Lawrence, Canada Lee, Norman Lloyd, Ray Mayer, John "Skins" Miller, Patricia Miller, Karen Morley, Ruth Nelson, Larry Parks, Stanley Prager, Lucien Prival, Anne Revere, Amelia Romano, Shimen Ruskin, Robin Short, Art Smith, Gale Sondergaard, Dorothy Tree, Peter Virgo, Ernest Whitman, Lynn Whitney, and Buddy Yarus, 100-138754-188, pp. 157–60.

130 *Now Hoover could:* Chasing Spies, 158–59, 161–63; author interview with Athan Theoharis.

130 *The actors then faced:* Naming Names, ix–x, and in general for an excellent discussion of the ethics of Hollywood blacklists. On specific subpoenaed actors, see also www.imdb.com/, accessed 8/27/10.

130 *Although they had done:* See discussion on legality of Communist Party membership below.

130 *Karen Morley:* NYT 4/27/03, "Karen Morley"; LAT 4/23/03, "Karen Morley"; Tender Comrades, 470–80; NYT 4/30/83, "Selena Royle"; LAT 5/6/83, "Selena Royle."

130 *Larry Parks:* LAT 3/22/51, "Larry Parks Says"; NYT 3/22/51, "Larry Parks Says"; NYT 3/23/51, "Ex-Red Parks"; LAT 3/23/51, "Larry Parks Out"; NYT 3/23/51, "Columbia Cancels"; Naming Names, 147, 371–73.

130 *Lee J. Cobb* . . . *"employable again":* Naming Names, 268–73, 305; LAT 2/12/76, "Lee J. Cobb"; NYT 2/12/76, "Lee J. Cobb."

130 *Likewise, Lloyd Bridges:* NYT 3/11/88, "Lloyd Bridges"; Naming Names, 98, 102–103.

130 *Joseph Bromberg* . . . *at age forty-seven:* Naming Names, 219–20, 340–42, 347, 363–64; NYT 12/7/51, "J. E. Bromberg"; NYT 6/27/51, "Bromberg Silent"; LAT 6/27/51, "Bromberg Refuses"; LAT 12/7/51, "J. E. Bromberg."

130 *H. Allen Smith:* The biographical material on Smith is from H. A. Smith testimony, 10/20/47, before HCUA, "Hearings Regarding the Communist Infiltration of the Motion Picture Industry" (hereafter cited as HUAC Hollywood Hearings), 4–5; LAT 7/24/47, "Former G-Man Will Complete Film Red Inquiry"; Chasing Spies, 160, 162; 61-7582-1471, 8/12/47. Smith served in the California legislature and then eight terms as a congressman, see Biographical Director of the United States Congress, bioguide.congress.gov/scripts/biodisplay.pl?index=S000545, accessed 2/25/11.

131 *On September 2, 1947 . . . "have him there"*: Smith Report of September 2, 1947, HUAC records, NARA Legislative Records, "Exhibits, Evidence and Other Records," box 6, Reagan folder, RG233, Records of the U.S. House of Representatives.
131 *Outside the Old*: This paragraph is based on *Washington Star*, 10/23/47, "Parade of Stars Continues"; *Washington News*, 10/23/47, "Star-Studded Cast." Thomas's remarks are from *HUAC Hollywood Hearings*, 1–3; *Early Reagan*, 339–40.
132 *Most of the stars . . . were Communists*: *Washington News* 10/23/47, "Star-Studded Cast"; *Washington Star* 10/23/47, "Parade of Stars Continues"; *Early Reagan*, 341.
132 *Then Reagan took*: *Early Reagan*, 341; *Where*, 19.
132 *Robert Stripling*: The account of Reagan's testimony is from *HUAC Hollywood Hearings*, op. cit., 213–18. The correct name of the group is Committee for a Democratic Far Eastern Policy, per its literature. On Reagan sponsoring a dinner for it, see 100-38754-124; 100-64700-684 EBF, HQ cross-reference.
133 *With that, A. B. Leckie*: HUAC Hollywood Hearings, 5, 218; LAT 7/24/47, "Former G-Man."
133 *"Quentin Reynolds . . ."*: The account of the dinner, the Hoover-Reagan exchange, and Reynolds's reaction is from 94-34419-1; 100-138754-A, behind 94-34419-1. On Reynolds, see *SFC* 3/18/65, "Reynolds Dies at 62"; *NYT* 3/18/65, "Quentin Reynolds Is Dead at 62."
134 *Jane Wyman was*: This paragraph is based on *Early Reagan*, 353–55; *LAT* 6/29/48, "Jane Wyman Divorced, Blames Rift on Politics"; *Chicago Daily Tribune* 7/2/48, Hedda Hopper, "Looking at Hollywood." Christine Reagan was born on June 26, 1947, and died nine hours later, *Reagan, The Hollywood Years*, 202. See also *Early Reagan*, 325. Jane Wyman would win the Academy Award for Best Actress for her role in the 1948 movie *Johnny Belinda*.
135 *When Reagan returned*: *Where*, 200–201. They were divorced in 1948, *Early Reagan*, 355.
135 *In his highly*: As Garry Wills noted in *Reagan's America*, 255, "It is true that Reagan did not publicly name names in his testimony—a ritual of humiliation that was intended not for investigative purposes but penitential ones."
135 *As one FBI report*: 100-382196-7, p. 2.
135 *A few weeks*: *Washington Evening Star* 11/17/47, "Screen Actors Guild Votes," in 100-138754-A.
135 *With his support . . . October 9, 1950*: *Reagan's America*, 254; *Early Reagan*, 350; *Washington Evening Star* 11/17/47, "Screen Actors Guild Votes," in 100-138754-A; *L.A. Herald Express* 11/17/47, "Red Ban by Film Actors," in 100-138754-A; *NYT* 11/18/47, "Actors Elect Reagan"; author correspondence with Valerie Yaros, SAG historian. The affirmation is quoted in *Early Reagan*, 333–34, though the given date is off.
135 *Fear permeated . . . left-wing intellectuals*: On the pervasive mood during the blacklist days, see *Naming Names*; *Tender Comrades*; *The Inquisition in Hollywood*; *The Memory of All That*; *Refugee from Hollywood*.
136 *Always edgy*: The caste system is noted in *Nancy Reagan*, 116, and *Early Reagan*, 227. The description of the agents is from *The Inquisition in Hollywood*, 409. American Legion pickets and blacklisting are noted in *Report on Blacklisting*; blacklisting is noted in *Naming Names*.
136 *Dore Schary . . . sworn loyalty statement*: The Gene Kelly–Betsy Blair anecdote is from 100-138754-695, 1/2/51. The FBI reprocessed this document in response to the author's request to release the names of Kelly and Blair.
136 *Another informer*: 100-138754-691, 2/14/50, p. 30.

136 *The actor known*: 100-138754-367, 12/19/47, p. 6.

136 *Katharine Hepburn*: The anecdote is from 100-138754-367, 12/19/47, p. 35.

136 *James McGuiness*: 100-15732-537, 9/4/47, pp. 3–4. The FBI reprocessed this document in response to the author's request to release McGuiness's name.

136 *Informers were everywhere . . . not necessarily ideological*: The widespread informing is documented in the FBI's files on COMPIC and the SAG.

136 *Ida Lupino*: On her informing, see 66-2542-3-26-1988, 6/3/47 and 5/15/47; 80-579-2, pp. 5–6, 29. Lupino says Reagan had seen the light, 100-138754-367, pp. 22 and 40. The latter report lists her as Confidential Informant T-9. The FBI reprocessed these documents to release Lupino's and Hayden's names. On Lupino, see *NYT* 11/23/97, "A Woman Forgotten"; *LAT* 8/5/95, "Ida Lupino."

137 *Two days later*: The Foster anecdote is from LA 80-579-2, p. 15. The FBI reprocessed this document to release Foster's name. On Foster, see *LAT* 7/15/70, "Film, Television Star Preston Foster." Still another informer said Reagan was nefariously involved with Americans for Democratic Action, even though it was staunchly anti-Communist, and that he had "helped the Communist movement," 100-138754-461, pp. 5–6. Other informers reporting on Reagan are noted in LA 80-579-2, pp. 15, 16–17, 32.

137 *Reagan was . . . "and his cooperation"*: On Murphy informing, see the search slips on him in LA 116-70463, which list him as an informant. Murphy was close enough to FBI agents to be made an honorary member of the Los Angeles chapter of the Society of Former Special Agents, ibid. As Garry Wills noted, Murphy was a trusted friend of both J. Edgar Hoover and Reagan's, *Reagan's America*, 245, citing Robert Scheer's report in the *Los Angeles Times* on June 25, 1980. Reagan himself wrote that Murphy "was equally aware of the strange creatures crawling from under the make-believe rocks . . . I owe a great deal to this cool, dapper guy who had to deal with me in my early white-eyed liberal daze," *Where*, 179. Murphy was a strong influence on Reagan, who would later join him in switching to the Republican Party, *Early Reagan*, 273, 294. Wood is listed as a producer at Universal-International Studios and a "confidential informant" in 100-138754-367, p. 40. He was a friend of Reagan's, the first president of the Motion Picture Alliance for the Preservation of American Ideals, and had directed Reagan in *Kings Row*, as noted in *Reagan's America*, 244. Reagan trusted him deeply as a director, *Where*, 103. LeRoy and Brewer are each listed as a "confidential informant" in 100-138754-367, p. 40. Brewer is further identified as an informer in 100-360657-3, 7/18/49, pp. 1–3, and is listed with a Permanent Symbol Number informer number, LA 3226, in 100-138754-481, 8/6/48. (See second following note as to FBI source numbers.) In response to the author's FOIA request, the FBI reprocessed these records to release the names of Murphy, LeRoy, Wood, and Brewer.

137 *Olivia de Havilland*: On de Havilland and her husband, the writer Marcus Goodrich, see LA 80-579-2, p. 2; 100-15732-537, 9/4/47, p. 4; 100-138754-667, p. 41; *American Life*, 115. In response to the author's FOIA request, the FBI reprocessed these records to release the names of Goodrich and de Havilland. Correspondence, de Havilland to Rosenfeld, 3/15/12, 3/19/12. Goodrich is deceased.

137 *On December 19, 1947*: The account of this contact between Reagan and the FBI is from 100-138754-367. There has been some misunderstanding in the literature on Reagan as informer as to the meaning of his being designated "T-10." Several authors have written that the FBI assigned Reagan this as his informant number. Others have counted the eighteen "T" numbers listed on page 40 of this particular report, 100-138754-367, under the heading "Confidential Informants," and concluded that the FBI had eighteen informants in Hollywood. These assumptions are incorrect.

First, FBI records show that the bureau developed many more informers in the course of its COMPIC investigation. Second, Reagan was not "Informant T-10." This "T" number was merely assigned to him within this particular report. In another report, in which Reagan informed on the actor Lloyd Gough, he was listed as T-6. See 100-382196-1, p. 8.

A useful description of "T" numbers comes from the reference book *Are You Now or Have You Ever Been in the FBI Files*, p. 211, which states a "T" number "Indicates confidential informant or source; a 'T' number is temporary, and applies only to the document in which it appears; for example, the same source may be T-1 in one document and T-5 in another. The identity of the 'T' sources used in a report is usually provided on an 'Administrative' page attached to the report; however, these identifications are generally deleted by the FBI when the reports are released." This explanation is consistent with the FBI's: that a "Temporary source symbol number," or "T-symbol," is used to disguise the identity of a source within a document so that the document can be circulated outside the FBI to other agencies. See Declaration of FBI agent Angus Llewellyn, in *Seth Rosenfeld v. U.S. Department of Justice and Federal Bureau of Investigation*, C-85-2247 MHP and C-85-1709MHP. The FBI does assign "Permanent Symbol Numbers," which consist of a two-letter abbreviation for the FBI field office where the informer is operating, followed by a sequentially assigned number, Declaration of FBI Agent Angus B. Llewellyn, ibid. In many cases, informers with a Permanent Symbol Number are paid. Author interviews with former FBI agent Burney Threadgill, Jr.

There is no indication in FBI records released on Reagan that he had a Permanent Symbol Number, or that he was paid. This diminishes neither the fact that the FBI considered him a confidential informer nor the fact that Reagan, largely by virtue of his position as president of an important Hollywood union, was a valuable one.

138 *Reagan briefed*: 100-138754-367.

138 *Although it was*: The U.S. Justice Department in June 1948 obtained indictments of twelve top party leaders, and they were convicted in October 1949 of violating the Smith Act by conspiring to promote the violent overthrow of the government. The U.S. Supreme Court upheld the convictions in 1951 in the *Dennis* case. The Justice Department then prosecuted ninety-three second-tier party leaders and again won convictions. But in 1957, the high court, ruling in the *Yates* case, overturned those convictions and effectively reversed the *Dennis* case, holding that the government must show the defendants advocated "action and not merely abstract doctrine." *The FBI: A Comprehensive Reference Guide*, 27–28, 64; *Many Are the Crimes*, 126, 190–200, 295. While other laws and regulations restricted Communist activity, no law outlawed the party or made membership illegal, *Many Are the Crimes*, 190. Further, the COMPIC inquiry had found no criminal activity, *Chasing Spies*, 156; NYT 11/23/47, "Legality of Communism."

138 *The negative publicity*: 100-138754-367.

138 *That November*: The meeting of the magnates and the resulting "Waldorf Statement" established formal, if unofficial, blacklisting in Hollywood. They vowed, "We will not knowingly employ a Communist or a member of any party or group which advocates the overthrow of the Government of the United States by force or by illegal or unconstitutional methods," *The Age of McCarthyism*, 215; *The Inquisition in Hollywood*, 328–31, 445; see also NYT 11/25/47, "Ten Film Men Cited"; LAT 11/26/47, "Film Heads to Fire Reds."

138 *Reagan had been*: This paragraph is based on 100-138754-367.

138 *This view*: On the change in Reagan's stance, see *Reagan's America*, 256, and *Ronald Reagan in Hollywood*, 155.

139 *By November 1948:* 100-138754-503, 1/18/49, citing *Hollywood Reporter* 11/11/48;
     100-138754-513. On the League, see *Reagan's America,* 253.
139 *Reagan also had joined:* 100-138754-472, 7/19/48; 100-138754-842, pp. 22 and 23;
     100-382196-1. On MPIC, see *Report on Blacklisting 1) Movies,* 82; Ronald Reagan in
     Hollywood, 184, 188–89.
139 *"We urged them . . .":* The quote is from *American Life,* 115.
139 *Reagan refused:* The Sondergaard episode is based on *Early Reagan,* 427–28; *Reagan's
     America,* 254; *Governor Reagan,* 101; *Where,* 158. On Hollywood blacklisting, see *Re-
     port on Blacklisting 1) Movies,* 162–63. On Sondergaard, see *NYT* 8/16/85, "Gale
     Sondergaard"; *LAT* 8/16/85, "Gale Sondergaard"; *LAT* 3/27/51, "Actress Gale Sonder-
     gaard"; *LAT* 3/22/51, "Larry Parks Says"; *NYT* 3/22/51, "Larry Parks Says"; *LAT* 3/17/51,
     "Actress Assails"; *NYT* 3/1/51, "Film Trio"; *NYT* 3/21/51, "Union Refuses to Back."
139 *The board's response: Early Reagan,* 427–28.
140 *Reagan gave the same . . . "'somebody's neck'": Early Reagan,* 350.
140 *Revere refused: NYT* 12/19/90, "Anne Revere"; *NYT* 5/31/51, "Anne Revere Quits";
     LAT 8/17/80, "Ronald Reagan in Hollywood: The Making of a Saga."
140 *Neither Sondergaard:* There is no indication they knew in either published materials
     or in FBI records released to the author.
140 *Like Clark Kerr:* In addition to the oath and affirmation, the SAG membership in
     1953 unanimously recommended adoption of an additional loyalty oath for all new
     SAG members. This had been proposed by a special committee of the SAG board that
     included Reagan and George Murphy. Since most studios hired only guild mem-
     bers, a refusal to sign the oath meant losing not only guild membership but also
     employment. See *NYT* 7/1/53, "Screen Actors Ask for Loyalty Oath"; *WP* 7/2/53,
     "Screen Actors' Guild Adopts Loyalty Oath"; *Early Reagan,* 334. On Hollywood
     blacklisting, see *Report on Blacklisting 1) Movies,* 163–64.
140 *But unlike Reagan:* For Kerr's views on the oaths, see Chapter 4: "The Rise of Clark
     Kerr."
140 *Kerr distrusted Tenney:* Kerr's views on HUAC, Tenney, and Burns are from Kerr,
     vol. 2, 48–49; author interview with Kerr.
140 *Reagan would rely:* Reagan cited the Tenney committee's report as proof of a Com-
     munist plot in Hollywood in *Where,* 162.
140 *Kerr believed the Soviet:* Kerr, vol. 2, 68–69.
140 *Reagan saw imminent:* Reagan's views are in *Where* and *American Life;* his quote is
     from *Where,* 162.
140 *By 1956: Chasing Spies,* 151. As early as September 1951 an FBI report concluded,
     "Current information from confidential sources indicates no important Communist
     influence in principal motion picture guilds in Hollywood at present, with excep-
     tion of a numerically small but vocal clique in the Screen Writers Guild . . . ,"
     100-138754-667. In December 1951, another FBI report said "guilds and crafts gen-
     erally free of any real communist influence at present time," 100-138754-691.
140 *Hoover's fourteen-year-long:* 100-138754-481; *Chasing Spies,* 151–56, 161.
141 *The inquiry confirmed: Chasing Spies,* 155.
141 *But as the historian:* Ibid., 154–55.
141 *And according to:* Ceplair and Englund write, "There is no evidence to indicate that
     the Hollywood Reds ever, in any way, conspired, or tried to conspire, against the
     United States Government, spied for the Soviet Union, or even undermined any
     social institution in this country," *The Inquisition in Hollywood,* 243. Theoharis's
     review of FBI records supports this conclusion. He notes that in October 1944,
     Hoover sent a report of his findings on alleged Communist influence in movies to
     Attorney General Francis Biddle, who took no action. The FBI's allegations were

"primarily ideological" and based on dubious sources, Theoharis found. "Given the ideological tenor of Hoover's report and its failure to cite any instance of illegal conduct, an unimpressed attorney general did not even respond," *Chasing Spies*, 151–56.

141 *Like the FBI's: The Inquisition in Hollywood*, 254. The FBI's political investigations and harassment of students, professors, and administrators at the University of California are documented in the text. On other FBI intrusions into the academic community, see *No Ivory Tower*, especially 257; *Compromised Campus*, particularly Chapter 10, "The FBI Dissemination Program"; *The Boss*, 217; *Chasing Spies*, 156, 164, 167.

141 *The phone rang*: The LeRoy anecdote is in *Where*, 233–34. There are different accounts of how they met, but Nancy and Ronald Reagan both note the political connection. See *My Turn*, by Nancy Reagan, pp. 93–94.

141 *Wyman and Reagan: Early Reagan*, 355.

141 *. . . and Reagan had found himself: Where*, 203.

141 *Reagan was promiscuous . . . his junior: Reagan: The Hollywood Years*, 222–23, 233–36, 238, 243.

141 *LeRoy was telling*: The account and Reagan's quotes are from *Where*, 233–34.

142 *Reagan knocked*: Ibid.

142 *The adopted daughter*: Davis's background is from *Nancy Reagan: The Unauthorized Biography*; "Biography of Nancy Reagan," RRPL website, www.reagan.utexas .edu/archives/reference/reference.html#Ronald_Reagan, accessed 8/29/10.

142 *Reagan and Davis: Nancy Reagan: The Unauthorized Biography*, 86, 101; *Ronnie & Nancy*, 264–65; *Reagan: The Hollywood Years*, 249, 253.

142 *She appeared: Where*, 237; "Nancy Reagan Films and Release Dates," RRPL website, www.reagan.utexas.edu/archives/reference/nrfilms.html, accessed 8/29/10.

142 *But her career*: Her professional decline is described in *Early Reagan*, 379, 430. Patricia Ann Reagan was born on October 22, 1952, according to Ronald Reagan's Pre-Presidential Time Line, 1911–1980, at the RRPL website, www.reagan.utexas .edu/archives/reference/prepreschrono.html, accessed 2/5/11. Ronald Prescott Reagan was born May 20, 1958, according to his Facebook entry, www.facebook.com/ pages/Ronald-Prescott-Reagan/115358438479105, accessed 2/5/11.

142 *"If you try . . .": Where*, 241.

142 *Reagan's own screen*: Reagan discusses his flagging film career in ibid., 241, 242, 244, 245.

142 *He'd been elected*: SAG website, history, SAG presidents, www.sag.org/ronald-reagan, accessed 6/22/11.

142 *. . . spending long hours*: SAG website, history, guild headquarters, www.sag.org/guild -headquarters, accessed 6/22/11.

142 *Acting, Reagan wrote: Where*, 191, 244.

142 *For a younger generation*: Ibid., 186.

142 *By the early fifties*: Ibid., 245, 246–47.

142 *The Reagans, meanwhile: Governor Reagan*, 79; *Where*, 242; "Residences of Ronald Reagan," RRPL website, www.reagan.utexas.edu/archives/reference/residences .html, accessed 8/29/10.

142 *He owed taxes . . . of $24,911*: 116-460320-10, 2/1/67.

142 *He continued to reject . . . "'agrarian reformers'": Where*, 245–47, 248.

142 *Reagan began to make*: Ibid., 247–51.

142 *In 1954*: Ibid., 251–73; *Governor Reagan*, 107–13, in which Cannon notes GE soon raised Reagan's salary to $150,000 a year.

142 *The firm's*: Earl B. Dunckel, "Ronald Reagan and the General Electric Theater,

1954–1955," Oral History by Gabrielle Morris, Regional Oral History Office, Bancroft, 2, 3, hereafter cited as *Dunckel Oral History.*

143 *As part of the job: Dunckel Oral History,* 4–5; *Where,* 253–55; *Governor Reagan,* 107, 109; *Reagan's America,* 268; *Early Reagan,* 461.

143 *Most movie actors: Dunckel Oral History,* 2, 5. Reagan himself was initially averse to doing a TV series, *Where,* 247, 248, 251.

143 *GE vigorously promoted: Dunckel Oral History,* 5.

143 *Reagan's mission:* Ibid., 5, 6.

143 *The research-and-manufacturing: Where,* 257, 259; *Governor Reagan,* 108.

143 *Reagan visited: Where,* 251, 257.

143 *Three or four:* The description of Reagan's GE tours is based on *Where,* 257–73; *Dunckel Oral History,* 9–21; *Governor Reagan,* 108; author interview with George Dalen.

143 *He had a remarkable: Dunckel Oral History,* 7, 14, 19–21.

143 *Reagan would later: Where,* 259–61.

143 *Along the way:* For discussions about the evolution of Reagan's speech, see ibid., 266, 273; *Governor Reagan,* 121–25; *Reagan's America,* 283–88.

143 *At first . . . aggressive reporters: Where,* 263–64.

143 *He warned that:* Ibid., 265.

143 *Above all . . . "own backyards":* Ibid., 264.

143 *Over time: Governor Reagan,* 109–10; Reagan's quotes are from *Where,* 266, 267.

144 *At GE, Reagan:* Reagan described Dalen in *Where,* 265, 266.

144 *A fellow Midwesterner:* The description of Dalen, his work with Reagan and the FBI, his concerns about his FBI assignments, and his quotes in this and the following paragraphs are from the author's interview with Dalen.

145 *The Los Angeles:* The anecdote about Reagan informing on Braun and the quotes are from LA 80-579-2, p. 35; 100-55965-12; author interview with Braun. On Braun's acting career, see *NYT* 2/20/58, "A Serious Berle"; *NYT* 11/5/57, "Well-Acted Shocker"; *NYT* 5/10/57, "Books by Cozzens"; *LAT* 5/8/57, "Magnani to Do Comedy"; Internet Movie Database, www.imdb.com/search/name, accessed 8/30/10. Reagan publicly denied there was a blacklist, *Reagan's America,* 253, 254; *Reagan,* 85; *Governor Reagan,* 100; *The Committee,* 300; *Early Reagan,* 427.

146 *Reagan was concerned:* The anecdote about Reagan informing on Plotkin and the quotes are from LA 80-579-3, p. 6.

146 *These episodes present: Governor Reagan,* 101.

146 *In an interview . . . Meese said:* Author interviews with DeLoach and Meese, 2002. Jane Wyman did not respond to a request for comment, made in 2002 through her Hollywood representative Jan Stern, on FBI records concerning her and Reagan. Wyman died in 2007.

147 *Reagan saw dramatic:* The account of Reagan's attempt to play the part of George Crandall in *The FBI Story* is from LA 80-579-2, p. 7.

147 *The drama was based:* The FBI's role in producing the book is from *The FBI: A Comprehensive Reference Guide,* 284, 370; *The Boss,* 16, 310–11.

147 *The part of Crandall:* Internet Movie Database, www.imdb.com/search/name, accessed 8/30/10.

147 *Reagan had failed:* This paragraph is based on *The Director,* 67, 68. *The FBI* television series aired between 1965 and 1974, according to the Internet Movie Database, www.imdb.com/search/name, accessed 8/30/10.

148 *Hoover may have:* The account of the FBI helping Reagan secretly check on Maureen Reagan's romantic relationship with Filippone is based on 100-382196-7; FBI HQ files on Maureen Reagan, including 77-81528-8; 77-81528-9, 3/10/60; 77-81528-10,

3/15/60; WP 9/1/50, "Ten Police Added"; WP 2/7/56, "New Dispatch Center"; WP 6/25/58, "100 Thefts Laid to Man Police Shot"; *First Father, First Daughter*; NYT 8/9/01, "Maureen Reagan"; NYT 4/26/81, "Daughter of President." Filippone died in 2006. George Murphy was elected U.S. senator from California in 1964.

148 *Murphy was a friend*: *Reagan's America*, 245; "Say . . . Didn't You Used to Be George Murphy?," 281.

148 *She entered*: *First Father, First Daughter*, 115.

148 *At FBI headquarters*: This paragraph is based on 77-81528-7.

149 *The Ronald Reagan*: Author e-mail and phone calls to Allison Borio, for Joanne Drake, Deputy Chief of Staff, Ronald Reagan Presidential Foundation, 11/14/11. Drake referred the author to Meese.

149 *In any event . . .* First Father, First Daughter: *First Father, First Daughter*, 120–34; LAT 8/9/01, "Maureen Reagan, 60, Dies of Cancer."

149 *He'd been refused*: Reagan's further efforts to win Hoover's approval to do a show on "Communist Target—Youth," and the FBI's response, are described in 100-382196-4; 100-382196-5; 100-382196-3.

11: The Police Car

153 *Just before noon*: The account of the start of the police car protest is based on *California Rising*, 298–300; *The Free Speech Movement: Coming of Age in the 1960s*, 161–75. On Weinberg, see *The Spiral of Conflict*, 148; *The Free Speech Movement: Coming of Age in the 1960s*, 161–62, 664.

153 *As they chanted*: The presence of the agents and their reaction are from 100-151646-35 and author interview with Burney Threadgill, Jr.

154 *A tall, gangly*: The description of the police car protest, ending with the paragraph beginning "The throng roared . . . ," is based on *The Beginning*; *The Spiral of Conflict*; *The Free Speech Movement: Coming of Age in the 1960s*, 161–75; 100-151646-35; and "Mario Savio Discusses the FSM and Its Roots," audio recording, date and interviewer unknown, courtesy Lynne Hollander and Michael Rossman, UC Berkeley Library, Social Activism Sound Recording Project: *The Free Speech Movement and Its Legacy*, Tapes 1–4, www.lib.berkeley.edu/MRC/pacificafsm.html #saviointerview, accessed 9/3/10. (Author's note: a comparison of this tape with *The Free Speech Movement: Coming of Age in the 1960s*, 93–99, and the source cited at p. 626 n. 1, under "Freedom Summer," indicates this interview of Savio was made by Marston Schultz and Burton White in 1965.) The dialogue is from *The Spiral of Conflict: Berkeley 1964*. The description of Savio is from photographs in *Freedom's Orator*, FBI records, and his December 1960 Selective Service System registration card, released to the author under the FOIA, which also notes he was six feet one, weighed about 190 pounds, and had a birthmark on his left calf.

154 *A handful*: On the mild response of the campus policemen who had tried to arrest Weinberg, see *The Free Speech Movement: Coming of Age in the 1960s*, 202, and the photos at 168, 169, 176, 180.

157 *The confrontation*: This paragraph is based on *California Monthly*, February 1965, "Three Months of Crisis, Chronology of Events," Bancroft, bancroft.berkeley.edu /FSM/chron.html, accessed 6/23/11; *The Free Speech Movement: Coming of Age in the 1960s*, 103–59; *The Beginning*, 1–97; Kerr, vol. 2, 130, 137–200; "Mario Savio Discusses the FSM and Its Roots," audio recording, op. cit. The dimensions of the Bancroft strip are from Kerr, vol. 2, 144.

157 *For years*: Kerr, vol. 2, 127, 130–31, 137, 145.

157 *But that summer . . . "our nation's history"*: The student picketing of the Republican

convention and the *Oakland Tribune* is noted in "Statement Concerning the Application of University Policies and Berkeley Campus Regulations at the Bancroft-Telegraph Entrance," Katherine Towle, 10/9/64, in *Documentary Supplements to the Gold and the Blue*, 87. On student opposition to Proposition 14, see *LAT* 12/9/64, "Berkeley Peace Plan"; *LAT* 2/17/64, "Dr. King Blasts Move"; *LAT* 2/17/64, "Move to Repeal Rumford Act"; *LAT* 2/26/64, "Initiative on Housing"; *NYT* 8/18/64, "Parties on Coast"; *LAT* 11/1/64, "Propositions: Nation's Eyes Are on California."

158 *After receiving*: There is much discussion in the literature of the FSM about whether William F. Knowland, editor-in-chief of the *Oakland Tribune* and California manager of the Goldwater for President campaign, pressured the university to impose the ban. Although many students at the time assumed this was true, there has been no proof of it. It is established, however, that the *Tribune* dispatched the reporter Carl Irving to make inquiries about whether political activity on the strip violated university policy. See *The Spiral of Conflict*, 92–97, 106–107, 201, 225; *The Free Speech Movement: Coming of Age in the 1960s*, 103–10, 114–15; Kerr, vol. 2, 187. Katherine Towle, dean of students, said the *Tribune* inquiry "was really the question . . . that put everybody's mind on this." See *The Spiral of Conflict*, 97. She also wrote a memo noting that in July 1964 there had been "complaints" to the university about the recruiting of pickets against both the convention and the *Tribune* and that they "really brought the matter to a head." See "Statement Concerning the Application of University Policies and Berkeley Campus Regulations at the Bancroft-Telegraph Entrance," Katherine Towle, 10/9/64, in *Documentary Supplements to the Gold and the Blue*, 87. Towle did not specify the source of the complaints. For his part, Vice Chancellor Alex Sherriffs denied there was pressure from the *Tribune*, but acknowledged repeated complaints from "some lady extremists in the community." See Alex C. Sherriffs, "The University of California and the Free Speech Movement: Perspective from a Faculty Member and an Administrator," an oral history conducted in 1978 by James Rowland, Regional Oral History Office, Bancroft, 27–29.

158 *This was a new*: Savio discussed these influences on his generation in "The Reminiscences of Mario Savio," Columbia University Center for Oral History Collection, 3/5/85, 10–24, 42–47, 57–58; and in "Thirty Years Later, Reflections on the FSM," by Mario Savio, in *The Free Speech Movement: Reflections on Berkeley in the 1960s*. See also *The Free Speech Movement: Coming of Age in the 1960s*, 19–26, and *The Sixties: Years of Hope, Days of Rage*. Author interview with Michael Rossman.

158 *Some students*: W. J. Rorabough reports in *Berkeley at War*, 19, that "over the summer thirty to sixty students had worked for civil rights in Mississippi . . ." Others worked elsewhere, such as Rob Hurwitt, who discussed coming to campus after dodging bullets in Louisiana that summer in "Present at the Birth: A Free Speech Movement Journal," first published in the *East Bay Express* and available at the Free Speech Movement Archives, www.fsm-a.org/pres_birth.html, accessed 6/23/11.

158 *Savio and other representatives*: These events leading to the police car protest are recounted in *The Free Speech Movement: Coming of Age in the 1960s*, 117–59; *The Spiral of Conflict*, 103–39; *California Monthly*, February 1965, "Three Months of Crisis, Chronology of Events," Bancroft, bancroft.berkeley.edu/FSM/chron.html, accessed 6/23/11.

159 *The force*: Savio's influence has been widely acknowledged in the literature of the sixties. As Taylor Branch wrote, Savio was "arguably the first nationally known white student of the civil rights era," *At Canaan's Edge*, 79–80. On Savio generally, see *Freedom's Orator*.

159 *Mario Robert Savio*: Savio's biographical information is from Mario Savio survey, 4/21/65, by Professor John Leggett, Sproul Hall Incident Reports, CU-560, box 8, Bancroft, 48–52; "Mario Savio's Religious Influences and Origins," by Arthur Gatti, *Radical History Review*, Spring 1998; "The Reminiscences of Mario Savio," op. cit., 1–4, 15.

159 *Joseph Savio*: Joseph's birthplace is from Savio's questionnaire for the Westinghouse Science Talent Search, now known as the Intel Science Talent Search, which provided the author with a copy of his records there.

Ferdinando Savio, Mario's grandfather, first came from Sicily to America in 1923, arriving in the Port of New York aboard the S.S. *Conte Rosse*. In 1929, he was joined by his family—wife Visentza, daughter Margherita, son Tony, and the eldest child, Giuseppe, later called Joseph, father of Mario. See "Passenger and Crew Lists of Vessels Arriving at New York, New York, 1897–1957," National Archives Publication T715, and 1930 U.S. Federal Census Records for Manhattan, Roll 1554, p. 19A, Enumeration District 204, Image 1076.0, National Archives Publication T626. This information was provided through AncestryInstitution.com at NARA's Archives I Research Support Branch, Washington, D.C.

159 *Dora E. Berretti . . . were nuns*: Mario Savio survey, 4/21/65, by Professor John Leggett, Sproul Hall Incident Reports, CU-560, box 8, Bancroft, 48–52; "Mario Savio's Religious Influences and Origins," by Arthur Gatti, *Radical History Review*, Spring 1998; "The Reminiscences of Mario Savio," op. cit., 1–3; *Freedom's Orator*, 19.

159 *Joseph and Dora*: Author interview with Arthur Gatti; "The Reminiscences of Mario Savio," op. cit., 2.

159 *Dora . . . a charming conversationalist*: Mario Savio survey, 4/21/65, by Professor John Leggett, Sproul Hall Incident Reports, CU-560, box 8, Bancroft, 48–52; "Mario Savio's Religious Influences and Origins," by Arthur Gatti, *Radical History Review*, Spring 1998; author interview with Arthur Gatti.

159 *A large, balding*: Mario Savio survey, 4/21/65, by Professor John Leggett, Sproul Hall Incident Reports, CU-560, box 8, Bancroft, 48–52; "Mario Savio's Religious Influences and Origins," by Arthur Gatti, *Radical History Review*, Spring 1998; author interview with Arthur Gatti; author interview with Suzanne Goldberg.

159 *Both Dora and Joseph . . . to the boss*: This paragraph is based on Mario Savio survey, 4/21/65, by Professor John Leggett, Sproul Hall Incident Reports, CU-560, box 8, Bancroft, 48–52; "The Reminiscences of Mario Savio," op. cit., 4, 15.

160 *Savio was born*: Author interview with Suzanne Goldberg; "The Reminiscences of Mario Savio," op. cit., 41.

160 *Savio's mother*: Author interview with Arthur Gatti; "The Reminiscences of Mario Savio," op. cit., 2; *Freedom's Orator*, 19.

160 *. . . former Fascist functionary*: *Freedom's Orator*, 19.

160 *It was a calm*: Ibid.

160 *Savio was the couple's*: Author interview with Suzanne Goldberg. In *Little Lord Fauntleroy*, written by Frances Hodgson Burnett and published in 1886, a boy named Cedric learns he is heir to a British earldom and leaves New York to live in the family castle. His grandfather, the earl, tries to teach him to be an aristocrat who dresses as such, but through Cedric the old man learns about kindness and justice. The book was the basis for eponymous movies in 1921 and 1936 and influenced children's fashions in America before World War II, Internet Movie Database, www.imdb.com/, accessed 2/7/11.

160 *She spoke*: "The Reminiscences of Mario Savio," op. cit., 2.

160 *Joseph, meanwhile . . . "make it in America"*: "The Reminiscences of Mario Savio," op. cit., 2.

160 *Joseph had terrifying*: Ibid.; *Freedom's Orator*, 25.
160 *Joseph ultimately prevailed*: "The Reminiscences of Mario Savio," op. cit., 2.
160 *And though*: Savio birth certificate; Savio testimony about his baptismal certificate, transcript, *The State of California v. Mario Savio, et al.*, Nos. C-7468 to C-7547, 5/13/65, p. 22, and 5/19/65, pp. 22–24, BANC MSS 99/281, carton 34, Alexander Meiklejohn Collection, Bancroft; Savio questionnaire for the Westinghouse Science Talent Search; "Mario Savio's Religious Influences and Origins," by Arthur Gatti, *Radical History Review*, Spring 1998; author interview with Wendy Preuit, nee Wendy Kagan.
160 *Amid this familial*: *Freedom's Orator*, 25.
160 *Not long after . . . in his home*: Ibid., 20.
160 *A few years later . . . incipient depression*: Robert Cohen reports the sexual abuse in ibid., 25. He writes that Savio never discussed the incident publicly but confided it to friends and relatives, and in an autobiographical tape described it as a key event in his childhood and a cause of long-term depression. Cohen comments, "Serious as the abuse was, it may have been less central to Mario's psychological problems than was his tense relationship with his father." In her essay, Suzanne Goldberg, while not explicitly referring to sexual abuse, notes that Savio had "early childhood experiences, which were deeply disturbing and unresolved." See "Mario, Personal and Political," by Suzanne Goldberg, 560, in *The Free Speech Movement: Reflections on Berkeley in the 1960s*. In interviews with Cheryl Stevenson, Suzanne Goldberg, and Lynne Hollander, this author confirmed that Savio had said he was sexually abused. Goldberg stated that the reported abuse occurred when Savio was nine years old.
160 *While Savio was still . . . bigger homes*: "The Reminiscences of Mario Savio," op. cit., 1; author interview with Arthur Gatti; "Thirty Years Later, Reflections on the FSM," by Mario Savio, in *The Free Speech Movement: Reflections on Berkeley in the 1960s*.
160 *The Savios lived*: Author interview with Arthur Gatti; Savio questionnaire for Westinghouse Science Talent Search; Scholastic Transfer Record, attached to "Personal Data Blank," in Savio Talent Search file.
160 *As they grew*: On television, see "Television History—The First 75 Years," www .tvhistory.tv/index.html, accessed 6/24/11.
161 *One of their favorite*: "The Reminiscences of Mario Savio," op. cit., 16. On *Captain Video*, see Museum of Broadcast Communications, www.museum.tv/eotvsection .php?entrycode=captainvideo, accessed 9/7/10.
161 *Savio was exceptionally*: This paragraph is based on the "Personal Data Blank" and "Questions to be used for news purposes" form that Savio submitted to the Westinghouse Science Talent Search.
161 *His interest*: "Personal Data Blank" that Savio submitted to the Westinghouse Science Talent Search.
161 *Joseph Savio was adept . . . "field of science"*: "Mario Savio's Religious Influences and Origins," by Arthur Gatti, *Radical History Review*, Spring 1998; author interview with Suzanne Goldberg.
161 *But even as Joseph*: Author interview with Suzanne Goldberg.
161 *When they played*: *Freedom's Orator*, 25.
161 *When they worked . . . humiliated him*: Author interview with Suzanne Goldberg.
161 *Once, Savio smashed*: *Freedom's Orator*, 25.
161 *These interactions*: In *Freedom's Orator*, Cohen discusses Savio's depression at several points, including pp. 24–25. He cites Lynne Hollander, Savio's widow, as saying his depression was not diagnosed during his childhood, 426 n. 30.
161 *All the while . . . either of them*: "Mario Savio's Religious Influences and Origins," by Arthur Gatti, *Radical History Review*, Spring 1998; author interview with Arthur

Gatti; *Freedom's Orator*; *The Free Speech Movement: Reflections on Berkeley in the 1960s*; "The Reminiscences of Mario Savio," op. cit., 3, 5, 6, 8, 9, 10, 32.

161 *Savio attended*: This paragraph is based on "Mario Savio's Religious Influences and Origins," by Arthur Gatti, *Radical History Review*, Spring 1998; author interviews with Arthur Gatti and Lynne Hollander.

162 *As a child . . . a second Christ*: "Mario Savio's Religious Influences and Origins," by Arthur Gatti, *Radical History Review*, Spring 1998; "Thirty Years Later, Reflections on the FSM," by Mario Savio, 59, and "Mario, Personal and Political," by Suzanne Goldberg, 560, both in *The Free Speech Movement: Reflections on Berkeley in the 1960s*; "The Reminiscences of Mario Savio," op. cit., 3; author interviews with Arthur Gatti and Suzanne Goldberg.

162 *He was a true*: This paragraph is based on "The Reminiscences of Mario Savio," op. cit., 8–9; "Mario Savio's Religious Influences and Origins," by Arthur Gatti, *Radical History Review*, Spring 1998; author interview with Arthur Gatti.

162 *In the mid-fifties*: This paragraph is based on "Mario Savio's Religious Influences and Origins," by Arthur Gatti, *Radical History Review*, Spring 1998; author interview with Arthur Gatti; Scholastic Transfer Record, attached to "Personal Data Blank" that Savio submitted to the Westinghouse Science Talent Search.

162 *In September 1957*: This paragraph is based on Scholastic Transfer Record, attached to "Personal Data Blank" that Savio submitted to the Westinghouse Science Talent Search; author interview with Arthur Gatti; author interview with Wendy Preuit (nee Kagan). On the pledge, see *NYT* 6/15/54, "President Hails Revised Pledge."

162 *Savio quickly*: This paragraph is based on author interviews with Wendy Preuit and Arthur Gatti; "Mario Savio's Religious Influences and Origins," by Arthur Gatti, *Radical History Review*, Spring 1998.

163 *Like the young . . . stutter while performing*: *Freedom's Orator*, 20; author interview with Arthur Gatti.

163 *Savio devoted . . . "the next thing"*: Scholastic Transfer Record and "Personal Data Blank" that Savio submitted to the Westinghouse Science Talent Search; "Mario Savio's Religious Influences and Origins," by Arthur Gatti, *Radical History Review*, Spring 1998; author interviews with Arthur Gatti and Wendy Preuit.

163 *Although Savio knew . . . "your name"*: Author interviews with Arthur Gatti and Wendy Preuit; *The Bee Line*, vol. IV, no. 8, 4/8/60, " 'Wanted: Book,' Pleads Bob Savio," Martin Van Buren High School.

163 *One month after . . . nuclear fallout sign*: Wendy Preuit described Van Buren's nuclear attack drills in an interview with the author. Savio discussed them in "Thirty Years Later, Reflections on the FSM," by Mario Savio, in *The Free Speech Movement: Reflections on Berkeley in the 1960s*.

163 *Neither Savio nor*: "Thirty Years Later, Reflections on the FSM," by Mario Savio, in *The Free Speech Movement: Reflections on Berkeley in the 1960s*.

163 *Earlier that year*: *NYT* 7/6/57, "A.E.C. Sets off Greatest Blast."

164 *These tests sent*: "Mario Savio graduation speech, Sidwell Friends School, June 10, 1988," www.fsm-a.org/mariolinks.html, accessed 9/7/10.

164 *By now Savio . . . "were bad"*: "Thirty Years Later, Reflections on the FSM," by Mario Savio, in *The Free Speech Movement: Reflections on Berkeley in the 1960s*.

164 *He chose to*: The anecdote is from "The Reminiscences of Mario Savio," op. cit., 7–8. On *Masters of Deceit*, see *The FBI: A Comprehensive Reference Guide*, 229; *Hoover's FBI: The Men and the Myth*, 122; *The Boss*, 311.

164 *Other Cold War*: The Don Peppino story is from "Mario Savio graduation speech, Sidwell Friends School, June 10, 1988," www.fsm-a.org/mariolinks.html, accessed 9/7/10.

164 *Throughout high school . . . "Jesus Christ"*: "Mario Savio's Religious Influences and Origins," by Arthur Gatti, *Radical History Review*, Spring 1998; author interviews with Arthur Gatti and Wendy Preuit.

164 *In his senior year*: The account of Savio running for class president is from author interview with Wendy Preuit; "Mario Savio's Religious Influences and Origins," by Arthur Gatti, *Radical History Review*, Spring 1998.

164 *That year, Savio*: Savio application to the Westinghouse Science Talent Search, December 1959. Copies of this and related materials from his Science Talent Search file were provided to the author courtesy of the Science Service, Washington, D.C., which administers the competition, now known as the Intel Science Talent Search for its current sponsor. On the Science Talent Search, see *Celebrating 60 Years of Science*, Glynnis Thompson Kaye, published by the Intel Corp., 2001.

165 *Already weary*: *Freedom's Orator*, 23–25.

165 *As Preuit recalled*: Author interview with Wendy Preuit.

165 *In his application . . . "very quickly"*: Savio application to the Westinghouse Science Talent Search, op. cit.

165 *Recommendations . . . "struggling fellow students"*: Ibid.

165 *Another recommendation . . . "for discussions . . ."*: Ibid.

165 *Savio told . . . 'finding things out'"*: Ibid.

166 *In February 1960 . . . members of Congress*: NYT 2/3/60, "Science 'Search' Names Finalists"; "STI-60 Evaluation Questionnaire"; Savio to Davis, 4/23/60; Savio to Schriver, 4/23/60; U.S. Senator Jacob Javits letter to Savio 2/3/60, all in Savio Science Talent Search File.

166 *Although Savio . . . from his father*: *Freedom's Orator*, 24.

166 *. . . he found some . . . "one's own decisions"*: Savio described parts of the program as very worthwhile and wrote that meeting with other student scientists was "a highly rewarding experience." He cited the "incalculable value" of being on one's own. See "STI-60 Evaluation Questionnaire"; Savio to Davis, 4/23/60; Savio to Schriver, 4/23/60, all in Savio Science Talent Search file, op. cit.

166 *That June*: Scholastic Transfer Record, attached to "Personal Data Blank," in Savio Talent Search file, op. cit.

166 *He faltered*: The description of Savio's valedictory speech is from author interview with Wendy Preuit.

166 *Savio told*: The text of Savio's valedictory speech is in *Freedom's Orator*, 323.

166 *For all his success*: This paragraph is drawn from "Thirty Years Later, Reflections on the FSM," by Mario Savio, in *The Free Speech Movement: Reflections on Berkeley in the 1960s*.

167 *Savio was stunned . . . "everything about reality"*: Ibid.

167 *While he wrestled*: This paragraph is based on "Mario Savio's Religious Influences and Origins," by Arthur Gatti, *Radical History Review*, Spring 1998; Savio letter to Cheri Stevenson, 8/12/64, in "Mario Savio Correspondence: Mississippi, to Cheri Stevenson, Berkeley, Calif.," BANC MSS 2006/110, vol. 1, Bancroft; *Freedom's Orator*, 24–26; author interviews with Arthur Gatti and Suzanne Goldberg.

167 *In September 1960*: The description of Savio's studies at Manhattan College is from his college transcript, Chancellor's Records, CU-149, box 72, folder 14, Bancroft, and 100-54060-137. His four-year scholarship is noted in *LAT* 12/9/64, "His Friends Look on Savio as a 'Genius'"; "The Reminiscences of Mario Savio," op. cit., 9, 18.

167 *As he put it*: "The Reminiscences of Mario Savio," op. cit., 10.

167 *Although Savio studied*: Author interview with Arthur Gatti.

167 *Still, he completed*: Manhattan College transcript, Chancellor's Records, CU-149, box 72, folder 14, Bancroft. His class rank is in 100-54060-137, p. 4.

167 *The following year*: Queens College Transcript, Chancellor's Records, CU-149, box 72, folder 14, Bancroft.

167 *Like Savio . . . ecclesiastic bounds*: Author interview with Arthur Gatti; "Mario Savio's Religious Influences and Origins," by Arthur Gatti, *Radical History Review*, Spring 1998.

168 *It was a time*: The Columbia Encyclopedia, fifth edition, p. 2864.

168 *Some theologians . . . with the sacred*: NYT, 8/6/61, "A Fierce but Eloquent Prophet of the Lord"; *Time* 10/22/65, "The God Is Dead Movement."

168 *Savio withdrew*: Queens College Transcript, Chancellor's Records, CU-149, box 72, folder 14, Bancroft; "The Reminiscences of Mario Savio," op. cit., 10.

168 *He read, hung out*: The rest of this paragraph is from author interview with Arthur Gatti; "Mario Savio's Religious Influences and Origins," by Arthur Gatti, *Radical History Review*, Spring 1998. On Unamuno, see *NYT* 1/2/37, "De Unamuno Dies"; *NYT* 1/31/57, "Vatican Bans 2 Books."

168 *Some nights*: This paragraph is based on author interview with Arthur Gatti; "Mario Savio's Religious Influences and Origins," by Arthur Gatti, *Radical History Review*, Spring 1998.

168 *Wandering through*: This paragraph is based on author interview with Arthur Gatti; "Mario Savio's Religious Influences and Origins," by Arthur Gatti, *Radical History Review*, Spring 1998.

169 *Savio was losing*: This paragraph is based on author interview with Arthur Gatti; "Mario Savio's Religious Influences and Origins," by Arthur Gatti, *Radical History Review*, Spring 1998; "The Reminiscences of Mario Savio," 9–10; "Thirty Years Later, Reflections on the FSM," by Mario Savio, in *The Free Speech Movement: Reflections on Berkeley in the 1960s*, 59–62.

169 *Savio bore guilt*: This paragraph is based on author interview with Arthur Gatti; "Mario Savio's Religious Influences and Origins," by Arthur Gatti, *Radical History Review*, Spring 1998. Savio states in his Westinghouse Talent Search application that Caleca, his second cousin on his father's side, worked on the Manhattan Project.

169 *Although the two*: This paragraph is based on author interview with Arthur Gatti; "Mario Savio's Religious Influences and Origins," by Arthur Gatti, *Radical History Review*, Spring 1998. On the Maryknoll missionaries, see home.maryknoll.org /maryknoll/, accessed 2/7/11.

169 *The missionaries' message*: Author interview with Arthur Gatti; "Mario Savio's Religious Influences and Origins," by Arthur Gatti, *Radical History Review*, Spring 1998.

169 *In June 1963*: McGowan's talk and how it inspired Savio and Gatti to do volunteer work in Mexico are described in the sources immediately above. On McGowan, see *NYT* 8/2/63, "Cuba Evolves a Marxist Ideology."

170 *Savio and the other*: The account of Savio in Mexico is based on author interview with Arthur Gatti; "Mario Savio's Religious Influences and Origins," by Arthur Gatti, *Radical History Review*, Spring 1998.

171 *At the end . . . sheet-metal plant*: Savio letter, 6/7/63, to Office of Admissions, Chancellor's Records, CU-149, box 72, folder 14, Bancroft; Mario Savio survey, 4/21/65, by Professor John Leggett, Sproul Hall Incident Reports, CU-560, box 8, Bancroft, 50; author interview with Suzanne Goldberg; *LAT* 12/9/64, "His Friends Look on Savio as a 'Genius.'"

171 *His parents*: "The Reminiscences of Mario Savio," op. cit., 10.

12: The Free Speech Movement

172 *Savio was in*: This anecdote is based on "The Reminiscences of Mario Savio," op. cit., 10–11; Kerr, vol. 2, 120–21; *Student.*

172 *"I knew something . . .":* Savio's quotes are from "The Reminiscences of Mario Savio," op. cit., 10.

172 *Savio, like many:* This paragraph is based on "The Reminiscences of Mario Savio," op. cit., 11–14.

173 *Savio was too young:* The voting age was then twenty-one; Savio was seventeen when Kennedy was elected president in November 1960, "The Reminiscences of Mario Savio," 14, 15, 16.

173 *But Kennedy:* Ibid., 15, 16.

173 *Savio had hoped for:* This paragraph is based on ibid., 14–17. On Telstar, see *LAT* 8/4/62, "Satellite Bill Safeguards"; *LAT* 8/20/62, "Readers Defend, Denounce Morse"; *WP* 8/3/62, "The Rain Dance of Rebel Morse."

173 *For Savio:* "The Reminiscences of Mario Savio," op. cit., 17–18.

173 *In 1954 . . . inspiring similar actions:* Many fine books have been written on the civil rights events cited here. For examples of contemporaneous news accounts, see *LAT* 5/18/54, "High Court Bans Segregation in Schools"; *NYT* 12/6/55, "Buses Boycotted over Race Issue"; *WP* 11/14/56, "Top Tribunal Outlaws Bus Segregation"; *LAT* 9/25/57, "1000 U.S. Paratroops Patrol in Little Rock"; *NYT* 2/11/60, "Negroes Extend Store Picketing."

173 *In Queens . . . "going on here":* "The Reminiscences of Mario Savio," op. cit., 13.

173 *He was struck . . . "very attractive":* *Pillar of Fire*, 77; "The Reminiscences of Mario Savio," op. cit., 12; *LAT* 5/4/63, "New Alabama Riot, Police Dogs, Fire Hoses"; *LAT* 5/5/63, "Birmingham Police clash with 1,000."

174 *The black struggle . . . "leading America":* "The Reminiscences of Mario Savio," op. cit., 18.

174 *For all of these . . . "on there":* Ibid., 11.

174 *Savio arrived . . . water balloon fights:* Savio's matriculation date and address are in Savio's UC Berkeley records, Chancellor's Records, CU-149, box 72, folder 14, Bancroft. Savio described his initial accommodations in "Mario Savio Discusses the FSM and Its Roots," date and interviewer unknown, courtesy Lynne Hollander and Michael Rossman, UC Berkeley Library, Social Activism Sound Recording Project: *The Free Speech Movement and Its Legacy*, Tape 4, www.lib.berkeley.edu/MRC /pacificafsm.html#saviointerview, accessed 9/3/10.

174 *Alienated, Savio:* His courses are in Savio's UC Berkeley records, op. cit.

174 *Now he set . . . "Catholic or not?":* "Thirty Years Later, Reflections on the FSM," by Mario Savio, in *The Free Speech Movement: Reflections on Berkeley in the 1960s*, 62.

174 *The dry logic . . . "contender for sainthood":* Ibid., 62–63.

174 *Camus's 1942 novel:* "The Reminiscences of Mario Savio," op. cit., 34.

174 *Savio also read:* "Thirty Years Later, Reflections on the FSM," by Mario Savio, in *The Free Speech Movement: Reflections on Berkeley in the 1960s*, 62.

175 *Through his study . . . do good in the world:* Ibid., 62–64; "The Reminiscences of Mario Savio," op. cit., 33–35.

175 *A small number:* "Thirty Years Later, Reflections on the FSM," by Mario Savio, in *The Free Speech Movement: Reflections on Berkeley in the 1960s*, 63; *The Free Speech Movement: Coming of Age in the 1960s*, 93; "The Reminiscences of Mario Savio," op. cit., 20–21.

175 *The Congress of Racial:* CORE website, www.core-online.org/, accessed 9/13/10.

175 *The Student Non-Violent: In Struggle*, 1–2.

175 *CORE and SNCC:* Ibid., CORE website, op. cit.

175 *The month before*: In *Struggle*, 92–95; CORE website, op. cit.

175 *Soon Savio*: *The Free Speech Movement: Coming of Age in the 1960s*, 93; *Berkeley Daily Planet*, 7/7–13/06, "Mel's Drive-In Saw Birth of Civil Rights Movement," www.berkeleydailyplanet.com/pdfs/h-07–07–06.pdf, accessed 3/4/11.

175 *He handed out*: Author interview with Allan Solomonow.

175 *He undertook . . . quickly won concessions*: *The Free Speech Movement: Coming of Age in the 1960s*, 98, 644; *Berkeley at War*, 72; "Mario Savio Discusses the FSM," UC Berkeley Library, Social Activism Sound Recording Project: *The Free Speech Movement and Its Legacy*, Tape 4, www.lib.berkeley.edu/MRC/pacificafsm .html#saviointerview, accessed 9/3/10. Early 1960s Bay Area civil rights activity is summarized in 100-442529-269. The Mel's protest was in November 1963.

175 *News of these*: For example, see *BDG* 11/22/63.

175 *Despite his increasing*: This paragraph is based on records from Savio's academic file at UC Berkeley, Chancellor's Records, CU-149, box 72, folder 14, Bancroft.

176 *In his second semester . . . philosophy*: Ibid.

176 *But he became more . . . "unsullied thing, certainly . . ."*: *The Free Speech Movement: Coming of Age in the 1960s*, 93–94.

176 *It presented . . . "to the Church . . ."*: "Thirty Years Later, Reflections on the FSM," by Mario Savio, in *The Free Speech Movement: Reflections on Berkeley in the 1960s*, 61.

176 *The students . . . "one's own life"*: *The Free Speech Movement: Coming of Age in the 1960s*, 93–94.

176 *Volunteering . . . "called for . . ."*: Ibid., 98.

176 *When CORE launched*: This paragraph and the next are based on ibid., 99; "Mario Savio Discusses the FSM and Its Roots," UC Berkeley Library, Social Activism Sound Recording Project: *The Free Speech Movement and Its Legacy*, Tape 4, www .lib.berkeley.edu/MRC/pacificafsm.html#saviointerview, accessed 9/3/10; *Berkeley at War*, 72–73; author interview with Kate Coleman.

177 *Savio was walking*: "Thirty Years Later, Reflections on the FSM," by Mario Savio, in *The Free Speech Movement: Reflections on Berkeley in the 1960s*, 63.

177 *Originally built . . . become his girlfriend*: Ibid., 63–64. On the Sheraton Palace, see www.sfpalace.com/History, accessed 9/13/10. On Cheri Stevenson, see *Freedom's Orator*, 42.

177 *On March 6*: "Mario Savio Discusses the FSM and Its Roots," UC Berkeley Library, Social Activism Sound Recording Project: The Free Speech Movement and Its Legacy, Tape 4, www.lib.berkeley.edu/MRC/pacificafsm.html#saviointerview, accessed 9/3/10.

177 *An irate hotel guest*: The dialogue is from "Thirty Years Later, Reflections on the FSM," by Mario Savio, in *The Free Speech Movement: Reflections on Berkeley in the 1960s*, 64.

177 *The twenty-two-hour sit-in . . . misdemeanor trespassing*: "The Reminiscences of Mario Savio," op. cit., 21; *LAT* 3/8/64, "Pact on Racial Hiring"; *The Shadow of the Panther*, 57–60; 100-442529-269.

177 *Police led Savio away*: "The Reminiscences of Mario Savio," op. cit., 21; 100-54060-115. Savio was charged with disturbing the peace but was acquitted, 100-54060-116.

177 *Soon after, an FBI*: 100-54060-115.

177 *The agent's collection . . . "law-abiding Americans"*: Church, book III, 448–51, 481.

178 *Savio's part*: Savio's San Francisco Police Department arrest sheet and the resulting FBI entry dated 3/15/64 are behind 100-54060-115.

178 *"Are you going . . ."*: Savio recounts the exchange in "Thirty Years Later, Reflections on the FSM," by Mario Savio, in *The Free Speech Movement: Reflections on Berkeley in the 1960s*, 64.

178 *He meant Mississippi . . . suffrage*: In *Struggle*, 96, 46; *We Are Not Afraid*, 35–42, 263–66; *Like a Holy Crusade*, 17–24.

178 *Savio liked . . . be part of it*: "The Reminiscences of Mario Savio," op. cit., 21, 23.

178 *As a result*: This paragraph is based on Savio's UC Berkeley records, Chancellor's Records, CU-149, box 72, folder 14, Bancroft. On the pain of schoolwork, see Savio-Stevenson letters, op. cit., 7/25/64.

178 *But first*: This paragraph is based on "Thirty Years Later, Reflections on the FSM," by Mario Savio, in *The Free Speech Movement: Reflections on Berkeley in the 1960s*, 64.

178 *That June*: Virginia Steele entry at Veterans of the Civil Rights Movement website, crmvet.org, accessed 9/15/10.

178 *The volunteers would . . . dangerous assignments*: "The Reminiscences of Mario Savio," op. cit., 28–30; *We Are Not Afraid*, 34–42, 263–66, 385–88; author interview with Sam Walker.

179 *Like Kerr . . . in hostile territory*: To be sure, Kerr faced potential physical violence from people angry about his message. It could be argued that Reagan's journey extended to Hollywood, where he sometimes encountered hostility as a result of his fight against communism and received threats of bodily harm because of his opposition to the CSU labor strike. Still, the danger Savio and other Summer Project volunteers faced in Mississippi from Klan violence and police brutality was of another order, as the number of beatings, bombings, and killings there that summer vividly attests.

179 *Savio moved*: Savio letters, both dated 7/3/64, to Cheri Stevenson, in "Mario Savio Correspondence: Mississippi, to Cheri Stevenson, Berkeley, Calif.," BANC MSS 2006/110, vol. 1, Bancroft, hereafter "Stevenson letters." On Mileston, see Veterans of the Civil Rights Movement website, crmvet.org, accessed 9/15/10.

179 *It was one of*: Stevenson letters, op. cit., 7/3/64, marked "later"; *June 1964*, by Jim Kates, entry at Veterans of the Civil Rights Movement website, crmvet.org, accessed 9/15/10.

179 *Mississippi's deeply*: The editorial quoted is in "The Undiscovered Country: The Civil Rights Movement in Holmes County, Mississippi, 1954–1968," Master's Dissertation of Jeffrey Brian Howell, Mississippi State University, May 2005, p. 7.

179 *Mississippi was where*: Ibid., 13.

179 *Savio would be astounded*: Stevenson letters, op. cit., 8/1/64.

179 *Savio and the other*: Stevenson letters, both dated 7/3/64.

179 *He began to chronicle*: Stevenson letters, op. cit.

179 *"It's wonderful . . ."*: This paragraph is from Stevenson letters, op. cit., 7/3/64, marked "later." Robert Cohen notes the dangers of southwest Mississippi in *Freedom's Orator*, 53–54.

180 *On a hot*: This paragraph is from Stevenson letters, op. cit., 7/5/64.

180 *But he was becoming*: This paragraph is from Stevenson letters, op. cit., 7/7/64. On COFO, see Council of Federated Organization Records, Mississippi Department of Archives & History, http://zed.mdah.state.ms.us/cgi-bin/koha/opac-detail.pl?biblio number=25676, accessed 4/26/12. This collection includes statements from Freedom Summer participants, including Savio.

180 *Savio was looking*: This paragraph is from Stevenson letters, 7/7/64.

181 *It was a summer*: This paragraph is from Stevenson letters, 7/25/64.

181 *Hartman Turnbow*: This paragraph is from Stevenson letters, 7/25/64. On Turnbow, see *In Struggle*, 89, 123; *NYT* 9/14/80, "Looking at America." In *Pillar of Fire*, Taylor Branch notes that Turnbow was "the first Holmes County Negro of the century to present himself as a voter."

181 *Savio worked hard*: Savio's account of registering black voters is from "Thirty Years

Later, Reflections on the FSM," by Mario Savio, in *The Free Speech Movement: Reflections on Berkeley in the 1960s*, 65.

182 *Even then, they still*: Savio's further account of voter registering is from "Thirty Years Later, Reflections on the FSM," by Mario Savio, in *The Free Speech Movement: Reflections on Berkeley in the 1960s*, 64, 65.

182 *Savio and Robert Osman*: The account of the attack on Savio and Osman and their interactions with the police is from Savio deposition in *Council of Federation Organizations et al. v. L. A. Rainey, et al.*, USDC Civil Action No. 3599 (J)(M), lodged with the Mississippi Department of Archives & History, Collection Z/1867.000/S; FBI file 44-26027 on the bureau's investigation of the attack; "The Reminiscences of Mario Savio," op. cit., 36–37; Stevenson letters, 7/25/64. On Savio not going to Amite County, see Stevenson letters, 7/25/64.

183 *Later that day . . . the attack*: 44-26027-1.

183 *This inaction . . . manipulated by Communists*: *The FBI: A Comprehensive Reference Guide*, 69–72.

183 *Earlier that year*: NYT 4/22/64, "Hoover Says Reds Exploit Negroes."

183 *According to William C. Sullivan*: *The Director*, 204.

183 *Had Savio and his*: The material in this paragraph on President Johnson's signing of the Civil Rights Act, Hoover's visit to Jackson, and the opening of the new FBI office there is drawn from *Pillar of Fire*, 387–88, 397–98; *The FBI: A Comprehensive Reference Guide*, 71; NYT 7/3/64, "Johnson's Address on Civil Rights Bill."

184 *When officials*: General Investigative Division note, 7/23/63, behind 44–26027-1, op. cit.

184 *Two agents promptly*: 44–26027-18.

184 *Savio was troubled . . . "the law itself"*: Stevenson letters, 7/25/64.

184 *Not long before*: This paragraph is based on Stevenson letters, 7/25/64.

184 *Early one morning*: This paragraph is based on Stevenson letters, 7/25/64; NYT 7/25/64, "Goldwater Joins Johnson in a Ban on Inciting Riots."

185 *As Savio finished*: This paragraph is based on Stevenson letters, 7/25/64.

185 *At the end*: Stevenson letters, 8/12/64.

185 *FBI agents had traced*: 44-26027-9; 44-26027-7.

185 *Savio was boarded . . . "line-up this morning"*: Stevenson letters, 8/12/64.

185 *As he had*: This paragraph is based on Stevenson letters, 8/12/64.

185 *In court: Jackson Clarion-Ledger* 8/14/64, "Man Found Guilty for 'Beatings'"; 44-26027.

185 *Savio was disgusted*: Stevenson letters, 8/16/64; "The Reminiscences of Mario Savio," op. cit., 37.

185 *The* Clarion-Ledger's: *Jackson Clarion-Ledger* 8/14/64, "Man Found Guilty for 'Beatings.'"

185 *The antipathy . . . on August 24*: *Jackson Clarion-Ledger* 8/13/64, "Affairs of State," by Charles M. Hills.

186 *A news story . . . he assured them*: *Jackson Clarion-Ledger* 8/13/64, "LBJ Attacks CR Attempts."

186 *Adding insult*: 44-26027-25; 44-26027-26.

186 *Although FBI agents . . . their report*: 44-26027-21.

186 *Still, the special agent*: 44-26027-22.

186 *"This does not seem" . . . said another*: 44-26027-17.

186 *The violence . . . arrested*: *Freedom Summer*, 96.

186 *On August 4 . . . earthen dam*: In *Struggle*, 114–15; NYT 10/3/64, "2 Indicted by U.S. in Rights Murders."

186 *Chaney had been*: *Jackson Clarion-Ledger* 6/4/00, "Experts: Autopsy Reveals Beating," by Jerry Mitchell.

186 *In the face*: This paragraph is based on information from the website of the Dr. Martin Luther King, Jr., Papers Project, Encyclopedia, "Mississippi Freedom Summer," mlk-kpp01.stanford.edu/index.php/encyclopedia/encyclopedia/enc_freedom _summer_1964/, accessed 6/25/11. On the summer project as a source of energy and inspiration, see "Holding One Another," by Waldo Martin, in *The Free Speech Movement: Reflections on Berkeley in the 1960s*, 83; "The Reminiscences of Mario Savio," op. cit., 44, in which Savio says of Mississippi Freedom Summer, "It was the trigger for very deep change . . . There was, at that point, as there had never been in America, a determination on the part of a significant number of young white Americans that racism had to go."

186 *Savio was asked*: Stevenson letters, 8/16/64.

187 *He needed*: Stevenson letters, 8/1/64; Savio's UC Berkeley records, Chancellor's Records, CU-149, box 72, folder 14, Bancroft.

187 *He intended*: Stevenson letters, 7/25/64.

187 *He was determined*: Stevenson letters, 8/1/64.

187 *Though still unsure . . . "common good"*: Stevenson letters, 8/4/64 and 7/25/64.

187 *On July 22, 1964 . . . Sherriffs was agitated*: Alex C. Sherriffs, "The University of California and the Free Speech Movement: Perspective from a Faculty Member and an Administrator," an oral history conducted in 1978 by James Rowland, Regional Oral History Office, Bancroft, 23, 23a, hereafter "Rowland interview with Sherriffs"; *The Free Speech Movement: Coming of Age in the 1960s*, 107–11, including notes.

187 *An* Oakland Tribune *. . . violation of the rules: U.S. Constitution: The Spiral of Conflict*, 91–93; *Freedom's Orator*, 79–80; Kerr, vol. 2, 145, 182–87. There are varying accounts about which university officials knew the strip was university property, when they knew it, and what they did about it. In all cases, it is clear that after the *Oakland Tribune* inquiry, Sherriffs took a lead role in precipitously cracking down on student political activities there.

187 *This was a situation*: Rowland interview with Sherriffs, 23.

187 *Sherriffs was . . . "I'd ever known"*: Rowland interview with Sherriffs, including Interview History, 1, 5, 6, 8, 10, 64. Sherriffs had signed the university loyalty oath, but appended a statement of his disapproval of it, ibid., 5. Sherriffs was born on December 14, 1917.

187 *In 1953, when . . . "to hear anybody"*: LAT 1/8/68, "Reagan's New Education Aide"; *Life* 6/15/53, "Citizen Runs for School Board."

188 *But when he lost: Life* 6/15/53, "Citizen Runs for School Board."

188 *On campus . . . social life*: Rowland interview with Sherriffs, 1–2, 13–16; Kerr, vol. 2, 169–70.

188 *But when Kerr . . . Berkeley campus*: Rowland interview with Sherriffs, 14, 19, 17; Kerr, vol. 2, 170.

188 *Sherriffs believed*: This paragraph is based on Rowland interview with Sherriffs, 15–17, 31–33, 67–69.

188 *Although he decried . . . enforced by Sherriffs: The Free Speech Movement: Coming of Age in the 1960s*, 65–82, 650; Kerr, vol. 2, 150–53, 186–87, and 383 n. 29, which is the text of a memo Sherriffs wrote Kerr about his SLATE concerns.

188 *Increasingly uneasy*: The account of Sherriffs's subsequent meeting with the FBI agents and the quotes in the following paragraphs are from 100-34204-286.

189 *To Sherriffs's further*: This paragraph is based on 100-151646-NR, 3/20/61, behind 100-151646-27; Chronology, Slate website, www.slatearchives.org/chronology.htm, accessed 2/18/11. Kerr's quote is in *Turning Points and Ironies*, 31.

189 *Kerr's stand*: This and the next paragraph are based on Kerr, vol. 2, 53–56; Rowland interview with Sherriffs, 57–61; author interview with Kerr; Bissell's letter in 77-7764-83. Kerr wrote that he was one of several educators in CHEAR (Conference on Higher Education in American Republics) trying to influence educational development in Latin America, Kerr, vol. 2, 55–56. He further writes that the CIA had not previously told him he had been cleared to work as an agent on its behalf, and that he never did, Kerr, vol. 2, 54. But though Kerr writes that the Bissell letter says "the CIA had cleared me in case it ever needed me as an agent," the letter does not indicate that the CIA investigated him or "cleared" him. The letter actually says "one component of this Agency was granted clearance to seek your cooperation and to consult with you on a classified activity." It adds, "I can assure that there is no information of a derogatory nature concerning you in our records." On Bissell, see *NYT* 2/8/94, "Richard M. Bissell"; *Legacy of Ashes*, 186.

190 *Kerr had, in fact . . . other campuses*: Author interview with Kerr. On the CIA and academia, see *NYT* 2/15/67, "C.I.A. Aid on Campus"; *LAT* 2/16/67, "Johnson Orders Investigation"; *LAT* 11/7/67, "UC Protesters Fail"; *LAT* 11/15/67, "CIA Recalls Recruiters"; *NYT* 11/19/69, "Notre Dame Expels"; *LAT* 2/19/78, "CIA Papers Show."

190 *Sherriffs, however*: 77-7764-83.

190 *In the fall*: Kerr, vol. 2, 383 n. 29; Bolton to Kerr, 9/27/65, "Strictly Confidential," Kerr Personal Papers CU-302, box 66, folder 21, Bancroft; Statement Concerning the Application of University Policies and Berkeley Campus Regulations at the Bancroft-Telegraph Entrance, Katherine Towle, 10/9/64, in *Documentary Supplements to the Gold and the Blue*, 87. Towle did not specify the source of the complaints, however.

190 *SLATE published . . . "major in psych"*: *The Free Speech Movement: Coming of Age in the 1960s*, 107, 621; SLATE Archives, archive.slatearchives.org/gs/HASH331a.dir /ncse251.pdf, accessed 3/5/11.

190 *The September 10, 1964*: *The Free Speech Movement: Coming of Age in the 1960s*, 79–80.

190 *The San Francisco Examiner*: *Turning Points and Ironies*, 61.

190 *Sherriffs was provoked . . . a few days later*: Sherriffs to Kerr, 9/15/64, President's Personal Papers, CU-302, carton 4, folder 23, Bancroft.

191 *Convinced that subversives . . . "taking over"*: Arleigh Williams, dean of students, "The Free Speech Movement and the Six Years' War, 1964–1970," interviews conducted by Germaine LaBerge, 1988 and 1989, Regional Oral History Office, Bancroft, as quoted in *The Free Speech Movement: Coming of Age in the 1960s*, 111; Kerr, vol. 2, 171, 173, 186.

191 *While Kerr was . . . the Bancroft strip*: Rowland interview with Sherriffs, 23–26; Kerr, vol. 2, 182, 183, 190, 192, 209, 211, 241; *The Free Speech Movement: Coming of Age in the 1960s*, 621; Bolton to Kerr, 9/27/65, "Strictly Confidential," Kerr Personal Papers, CU-302, box 66, folder 21, Bancroft, in which Sherriffs reportedly states he "alone was responsible for directing Towle to issue the memo."

191 *Towle, who had . . . consulted first*: Kerr, vol. 2, 182, 183, 190–92, 209, 211, 241; *The Free Speech Movement: Coming of Age in the 1960s*, 664; Bolton to Kerr, 9/27/65, "Strictly Confidential," Kerr Personal Papers, CU-302, box 66, folder 21, Bancroft.

191 *Nonetheless, she followed*: Towle's letter is in *Documentary Supplements to the Gold and the Blue*, edited by Clark Kerr, Institute of Government Studies, UC Berkeley, 79.

191 *Savio was outraged . . . "I'm back home?"*: "Thirty Years Later, Reflections on the FSM," by Mario Savio, in *The Free Speech Movement: Reflections on Berkeley in the 1960s*, 65–66.

191 *Kerr, who had*: This paragraph is based on Kerr, vol. 2, 126–28, 134–35, 155, 163.
191 *Kerr was also astonished*: Ibid., 161, 179–80, 185.
192 *To be sure . . . academic freedom*: Ibid., 122–26 (re Rule 17), 129, 125–26, 138–39, 177 (re. Kerr's May 1964 speech at UC Davis), 186.
192 *Moreover, free speech . . . political pressures*: Ibid., 142–43; author interview with Kerr.
192 *But Kerr also believed*: Kerr, vol. 2, 154, 161, 179–80, 185; *Freedom's Orator*, 77–82.
192 *Sather Gate's bronze arch*: The history of the free speech zone is from Kerr, vol. 2, 130–31, 145, 154, 161, 176, 182, 183–84, 187; *The Campus Guide, University of California, Berkeley*, 36–50; *The Free Speech Movement: Coming of Age in the 1960s*, 40, 107–110; *Berkeley at War*, 14, 18–19; *Freedom's Orator*, 77–82.
192 *Kerr considered . . . his policy*: Kerr, vol. 2, 161, 176, 179–81, 185, 188.
192 *But these were*: Samuel Kerr to Clark Kerr, 9/23/28, President's Personal Papers, CU-302, carton 70, folders 7, 13, 14, and 15, Bancroft.
193 *Mario Savio*: *The Beginning*, 119–20.
193 *Students took turns . . . civil rights songs*: Ibid., 119, 120. Author interview with Barbara Dane.
193 *Weinberg relaxed*: *The Free Speech Movement: Coming of Age in the 1960s*, 198–99, 204.
193 *Declaring that Strong*: *The Beginning*, 120.
193 *One hundred and fifty*: Ibid., 120–23.
193 *Just past 6:00 p.m.*: This paragraph is based on ibid., 122; *The Free Speech Movement: Coming of Age in the 1960s*, 177–88. Savio's quote is from transcript, *State of California v. Mario Savio, et al.*, nos. C-7468–C-7547, 5/18/65, p. 46, BANC MSS 99/281, carton 34, Alexander Meiklejohn Collection, Bancroft.
193 *By 11:00 p.m.*: This paragraph is based on *The Beginning*, 123–25; *The Free Speech Movement: Coming of Age in the 1960s*, 167, 172 (the bumper sticker), 191, 199; author interview with Michael Rossman.
193 *The night wore . . . His appeal drew . . .*: These paragraphs are based on *The Beginning*, 126–32; *The Free Speech Movement: Coming of Age in the 1960s*, 191–97; author interview with Michael Rossman.
194 *University officials . . . "by some students . . ."*: This paragraph is based on *The Beginning*, 133.
194 *Governor Brown . . . "on our campuses"*: Ibid.
194 *Kerr was worried . . . thirty-six hours*: Kerr, vol. 2, 196.
194 *Before retiring*: This paragraph is based on Kerr, vol. 2, 196–97; *The Beginning*, 135; Kerr to Forbes, 4/14/65, "Confidential," *Documentary Supplements to the Gold and the Blue*, 229; *California Rising*, 300, 441 n. 25. As Ethan Rarick writes in the latter, although Kerr's memoir does not mention it, Kerr recalled in an early oral history that he asked Brown to deploy the National Guard and Brown said no. Rarick notes, however, that Brown was not asked about this in his oral history. Separately, Vice Chancellor Sherriffs and Chancellor Strong stated that Kerr, at the least, had been trying to reach Brown about sending in the Guard. See Bolton to Kerr, 9/27/65, "Strictly Confidential," Kerr Personal Papers, CU-302, box 66, folder 21, Bancroft; *California Monthly*, February 1965, "Three Months of Crisis, Chronology of Events," Bancroft, bancroft.berkeley.edu/FSM/chron.html, accessed 6/23/11.
195 *He spent*: This paragraph is based on Kerr, vol. 2, 197; *The Beginning*, 136–37.
195 *Kerr was distraught*: This paragraph is based on Kerr, vol. 2, 199.
195 *By late afternoon . . . more than seven thousand*: *The Beginning*, 140–41.
195 *Some of them*: *The Free Speech Movement: Coming of Age in the 1960s*, 179.
195 *As the deadline . . . and hung up*: Kerr, vol. 2, 197.

195 *The second call . . . "down the drain"*: Ibid.; *The Beginning*, 139–40.
195 *At 5:00 p.m.*: Kerr, vol. 2, 197; *The Beginning*, 140.
195 *Savio and several . . . and SLATE*: Kerr, vol. 2, 197–98; *The Beginning*, 141–44; *The Campus Guide*, 322–23.
196 *Savio and Kerr*: This paragraph is based on *The Free Speech Movement: Coming of Age in the 1960s*, 98, 213–19; "Mario Savio Discusses the FSM and Its Roots," UC Berkeley Library, Social Activism Sound Recording Project: *The Free Speech Movement and Its Legacy*, Tape 2, www.lib.berkeley.edu/MRC/pacificafsm.html#saviointerview, accessed 9/3/10; author interview with Kerr.
196 *The former labor . . . swiftly rejected it*: *The Beginning*, 141–43.
196 *Savio did much*: *The Free Speech Movement: Coming of Age in the 1960s*, 214, 216, 218.
196 *A key clause . . . any future actions*: *The Beginning*, 141–42; *The Free Speech Movement: Coming of Age in the 1960s*, 214, 217.
196 *Another clause*: This paragraph is based on *The Free Speech Movement: Coming of Age in the 1960s*, 214–15.
196 *A third clause*: *The Beginning*, 143.
196 *As the clock . . . held back*: Ibid., 141–42; *The Free Speech Movement: Coming of Age in the 1960s*, 215–20, 228.
196 *Savio still balked . . . he argued*: *The Beginning*, 142; *The Free Speech Movement: Coming of Age in the 1960s*, 221.
196 *Jackie Goldberg . . . they finally did*: *The Beginning*, 142–43.
197 *Kerr signed*: Kerr, vol. 2, 198.
197 *Sherriffs also was disgusted . . . "civil war"*: Rowland interview with Sherriffs, 33–35, 60.
197 *With the agreement*: This paragraph is based on *The Free Speech Movement: Coming of Age in the 1960s*, 219, 230–32; Kerr, vol. 2, 198; *The Beginning*, 144.
197 *Thirty-two hours*: The thirty-two-hour figure is based on both *The Beginning*, 144–45, and *California Monthly*, February 1965, "Three Months of Crisis, Chronology of Events," Bancroft, bancroft.berkeley.edu/FSM/chron.html, accessed 6/23/11.
197 *In the ensuing*: On Gandhi's influence on the civil rights movement, see *In Struggle*, 2, 16, 21, 298. For a critical view of the Free Speech Movement's use of civil disobedience as diverging from Gandhi's principles, see Kerr, vol. 2, 205.

13: A Leak to the Press

198 *In Washington*: FBI informative note, 10/2/64, behind 62-103031-163, vol. 4; 100-151646-35.
198 *Hoover ordered*: The FBI stated in court papers filed in the author's FOIA cases that the FSM investigation was conducted "in order to ascertain the influence or involvement in the Free Speech Movement by individuals affiliated or associated with subversive groups." These groups included the Communist Party and its "front group," the W.E.B. Du Bois Club, the Socialist Workers Party, and the Young Socialist Alliance; Declaration of Agent Angus B. Llewellyn, *Seth Rosenfeld v. U.S. Department of Justice and Federal Bureau of Investigation*, C-85-2247 MHP and C-85-1709 MHP. The FBI's investigation of the FSM is detailed in several FBI files, including 100-151646, 100-34204, 100-66367, and 100-54086; and in bureau files on Mario Savio and other people involved in the FSM. These files all carry the "100" classification, which denotes investigation of allegedly Communist or subversive individuals and organizations, or their alleged infiltration or influence on organizations. The Church committee later found that in such inquiries FBI officials "greatly exaggerated" the alleged influence of subversives and gathered vast amounts of

intelligence on law-abiding citizens simply because they were challenging the existing social order or government policy, Church, book II, 46–49, 67–68, 175–78, 240–
41. On the FBI's "100" classification, see *Are You Now or Have You Ever Been in the
FBI Files*, 28.

198 *The San Francisco field office*: The S.F. Field Office was designated as the "Office of
Origin."

198 *In the years*: The remainder of this paragraph is based on the author's interviews
with Curtis O. Lynum and on his books, *The FBI and I* and *The FBI Wife*.

198 *Like other field*: This paragraph is based on author interviews with Curtis O. Lynum
and Burney Threadgill, Jr.

199 *In the mid-sixties*: Detailed descriptions of the office staffing were provided by Curtis O. Lynum.

199 *Burney Threadgill, Jr.*: This paragraph is based on author interview with Burney
Threadgill, Jr.; Threadgill's FBI personnel file, 67-420376.

199 *Like all FBI agents*: This paragraph and the next are based on author interviews with
Lynum and Threadgill; FBI personnel files of agents Threadgill, 67-420376, and
Donald E. Jones, 67-455005.

200 *The main agents . . . salads*: *Berkeley at War*, 3–7, 18; *Berkeley: A City in Time*, 50–54,
94, 95, 113, 123, 129, 130; author interview with Threadgill.

200 *The bureau already . . . per capita*: Author interview with Threadgill.

200 *Threadgill and other . . . their political activity*: Author interviews with Lynum and
Threadgill; FBI personnel files of Threadgill and Jones, op. cit. Lynum recalled
Threadgill as being especially adept at pretext calls.

201 *Among the Security Index*: Treuhaft's FBI HQ file is 100-421790; 100-421790-82
notes he is on the Security Index. Mitford's FBI HQ file is 77-27703; 77-27703-152
notes she is on the Security Index. See Chapter 5 for a discussion of the Security
Index, which notes people listed on it at UC. See also Church, book III, 417–27,
which notes categories of people on the Security Index, including "education" and
"labor."

201 *Jessica Mitford . . . threat to the state*: On Mitford, see *Decca: The Letters of Jessica
Mitford*, ix–xvi, 47, 97, 101–109, 145, 162; *Intimate Politics*, 105–106; NYT 7/24/96,
"Jessica Mitford, Incisive Critic." On Treuhaft, see *LAT* 11/16/01, "Robert Treuhaft,
89; Crusading Attorney"; *NYT* 12/2/01, "Robert Treuhaft, Lawyer Who Inspired."

201 *By then, Mitford*: *Decca: The Letters of Jessica Mitford*; Mitford FBI file 77-27703,
NR, 9/9/51, in front of serial 60; Mitford and Treuhaft FBI files, op. cit.

201 *One evening . . . crept away*: Author interview with Threadgill.

201 *Threadgill and the other*: Author interview with Threadgill; *Rearview Mirror*, 4. FBI
wiretapping and bugging is discussed in *The FBI: A Comprehensive Reference Guide*,
The Boss, and other works.

201 *William Turner was . . . burst into laughter*: *Rearview Mirror*, 4; *Decca: The Letters of
Jessica Mitford*, 104–105. Turner was by then a writer for the radical magazine *Ramparts*. He had quit the bureau after becoming disenchanted with Hoover's despo-
tism, his overemphasis on the Communist Party, and his failure to aggressively
pursue organized crime. In an interview with the author, Turner later described the
CP as "a bunch of do-gooders who had no other place to go. They never did have
much of a following."

201 *The FBI agents relied*: Author interview with Threadgill; author review of FBI files
on Security Index subjects, including Mario Savio. On the Security Index, see
Chapter 5.

201 *They also used*: According to the historian Athan Theoharis and the author's review
of files from the FBI's Responsibilities Program, the FBI under that program sought

to oust Security Index subjects from their jobs. FBI records show that the bureau also conducted COINTELPRO-type actions against Security Index subjects.

201 *In the mid-fifties*: The anecdote about the FBI getting Mitford fired from the *San Francisco Chronicle* is from *Decca: The Letters of Jessica Mitford*, 108–109.

202 *"I figured that"*: NYT 7/24/96, "Jessica Mitford, Incisive."

202 *By all accounts*: This paragraph is based on author interviews with Lynum and Threadgill; Hoover's permission is recorded in Jones's FBI file, 67-455005-no serial, 430-58, in front of 67-455005-67.

202 *Many nights*: This paragraph is based on Jones's FBI personnel file 67-455005-53; 67-455005-52; 67-455005-55, "Addendum."

202 *Jones's main investigative*: Author interviews with Lynum and Threadgill; 67-455005-46; 67-455005-63; 67-455005-55, "Addendum." On Jones and Sherriffs, see, for example, 100-151646-35; 100-151646-49; 100-34204-286; 62-101031-166. On Wadman's ties to the FBI, see 100-151646-14X1, 10/8/54; 100-151646-14X, 9/29/54; 100-151646-87; 77-7764-50 and 77-7764-51.

203 *Like these university officials . . . fruits and vegetables*: Author interview with Threadgill, who recalled Jones's remark about Kerr. When I phoned Jones years before his death he declined to comment, told me he would report my inquiry to the San Francisco FBI office, and hung up.

203 *The FBI's investigation*: The FBI investigation of the FSM is documented in 100-151646; 100-34204; 100-66367; 100-54086; as well as in bureau files on Mario Savio, Suzanne Goldberg, Jackie Goldberg, Arthur Goldberg, Steve Weissman, and Jack Weinberg. The FBI entered into its indexes the names of professors who signed a petition supporting the FSM, 100-151646-122, and those of professors who otherwise backed the FSM, 100-151646-59. The FBI collected information on the CBS newsman Arthur S. Baron because of his reporting on the FSM, 100-66367-175. The FBI examined a parents' committee that raised funds for FSM arrestees, 100-151646-87. Agents filed the Christmas carol lyrics in 100-54086-1A.

203 *FBI officials assigned . . . civil rights movement*: The FBI's various files on the FSM are all classified as "100" investigations. On the "100" classification and internal security investigations, see *Are You Now or Have You Ever Been in the FBI Files*, 28; *Unlocking the Files of the FBI*, 99–102; Church, book II, 46–49, 67–68, 175–78, 240–41.

203 *Hoover still was operating . . . up to Hoover*: Church, book II, 46; Church, book III, 469; author interview with Athan Theoharis.

203 *He, of course . . ."preconception"*: Church, book III, 480–81.

203 *On October 20, 1964*: The description of the report and its circulation in this and the following paragraphs is based on 100-151646-35.

204 *The students*: Author interview with Michael Rossman.

204 *Margo Adler*: This paragraph is based on *Heretic's Heart*, 68, 82–83.

205 *Bettina Aptheker*: This paragraph is based on *Intimate Politics*, 131, 133. The length of the siege is put at thirty-two hours in both *The Beginning*, 144–45, and *California Monthly*, February 1965, "Three Months of Crisis, Chronology of Events," Bancroft, bancroft.berkeley.edu/FSM/chron.html, accessed 6/23/11.

205 *For Savio*: This paragraph and the next are based on "The Reminiscences of Mario Savio," op. cit., 59.

205 *On the weekend*: This paragraph is based on *The Free Speech Movement: Coming of Age in the 1960s*, 237–39, 695.

205 *On Monday, October 5*: This paragraph is based on ibid., 282.

206 *"This free speech . . ."*: Savio's remarks in this and the following paragraphs are from ibid., 237.

206 *Savio was implicitly*: Bishop George Berkeley, "Verses on the Prospect of Planting Arts and Learning in America," in *Berkeley: A Literary Tribute*, 3.

206 *Savio was explicitly*: This paragraph and the next are based on Kerr's *The Uses of the University*, first edition, 1963. Quotes, in order, are from pp. 6, 36, 37, 39, 87, 88, vi, 88 (again), 20, 6 (again).

207 *But Savio had made*: This paragraph is based on *The Free Speech Movement: Coming of Age in the 1960s*, 248, which contains the parentheses.

207 *The Free Speech Movement*: This paragraph is based on "Recollections of the FSM," by Martin Roysher, 146–47, in *The Free Speech Movement: Reflections on Berkeley in the 1960s*; *Berkeley, 1964: The Spiral of Conflict*, 218; *The Free Speech Movement: Coming of Age in the 1960s*, 647.

208 *All that fall*: Author interview with Michael Rossman. On the FSM and its operations in general, see *The Free Speech Movement: Coming of Age in the 1960s*; *The Free Speech Movement: Reflections on Berkeley in the 1960s*; *Heretic's Heart*; *Intimate Politics*; and *The Wedding Within the War*, all of which provide participant accounts.

208 *David Goines . . . "except by consensus . . ."*: *The Free Speech Movement: Coming of Age in the 1960s*, 245.

208 *As Aptheker recalled*: *Intimate Politics*, 135.

208 *Savio had moved*: This paragraph is based on *The Free Speech Movement: Coming of Age in the 1960s*, 207, 252–56, 266. On the Berkeley Co-op, see *Berkeley: A City in History*, 101; *The Free Speech Movement: Coming of Age in the 1960s*, 207.

208 *Late at night*: This paragraph is based on *The Free Speech Movement: Coming of Age in the 1960s*, 254; *Intimate Politics*, 135; "Mario, Personal and Political," by Suzanne Goldberg, 559, in *The Free Speech Movement: Reflections on Berkeley in the 1960s*.

209 *Earlier that fall . . . "never an opportunist"*: Author interview with Suzanne Goldberg; "Mario, Personal and Political," by Suzanne Goldberg, 557–59, in *The Free Speech Movement: Reflections on Berkeley in the 1960s*.

209 *As soon as*: *The Free Speech Movement: Coming of Age in the 1960s*, 256–57; *Intimate Politics*, 135.

209 *All along, Savio*: This paragraph is based on "Recollections of the FSM," by Martin Roysher, op. cit., 148–49; *The Free Speech Movement: Coming of Age in the 1960s*, 241; author interviews with Michael Rossman and Eleanor Bertino.

209 *He had adopted*: This paragraph is based on "The Reminiscences of Mario Savio," op. cit., 51, 52.

210 *Cloaked in*: This paragraph is based on "Recollections of the FSM," by Martin Roysher, 148–49; *Intimate Politics*, 134–35; "The Reminiscences of Mario Savio," op. cit., 61–66; author interview with Michael Rossman. For photographs of Savio in his shearling coat, see *The Free Speech Movement: Coming of Age in the 1960s*, 360, 366.

210 *He spent much*: "Recollections of the FSM," by Martin Roysher, 148–49.

210 *Although he still*: David Goines recalled Savio as still stuttering unless he was impassioned, as did Patti Iiyama, in *The Free Speech Movement: Coming of Age in the 1960s*, 172, 172n.

210 *As Savio would*: www.fsm-a.org/stacks/mario/savio_gilles.htm.

210 *Early on, Savio*: *The Beginning*, 150; *The Free Speech Movement: Coming of Age in the 1960s*, 279; SFNCB 10/3/64, "Kerr Cites Element of Castro-Mao Reds"; SFC 10/3/64, "Kerr Ruled Out Compromise."

210 *Kerr claimed*: This paragraph is based on Kerr, vol. 2, 275–76; *The Beginning*, 196–97; *The Free Speech Movement: Coming of Age in the 1960s*, 279; SFNCB 10/3/64, "Kerr Cites Element"; SFC 10/3/64, "Kerr Ruled Out Compromise."

210 *At the time . . . "from the FBI"*: Author interview with Kerr.

211 *Savio was disappointed*: This paragraph is based on *Intimate Politics*, 133–34; *The Free Speech Movement: Coming of Age in the 1960s*, 280.

211 *He and other FSM*: This paragraph is based on "Recollections of the FSM," by Martin Roysher, 143; *The Free Speech Movement: Coming of Age in the 1960s*, 284–93, 272 (quote); *The Spiral of Conflict*, 219–46.

211 *As the students met . . . escalated the protest*: This paragraph is based on *The Free Speech Movement: Coming of Age in the 1960s*, 298, 303, 325–27; *The Beginning*, 155, 156, 162, 165, 169, 170–71, 172; *Intimate Politics*, 137.

211 *Standing where the police . . . "exercise of their rights"*: *The Free Speech Movement: Coming of Age in the 1960s*, 327.

211 *Savio and other . . . still held back*: Ibid., 327–29, 334.

211 *All the while*: Rowland interview with Sherriffs, Bancroft, 34–35, 39 (regarding Strong's role), 46, 51; *The Spiral of Conflict*, 231, 237–41.

211 *On November 20*: *The Free Speech Movement: Coming of Age in the 1960s*, 336, 337; *The Beginning*, 178–84.

211 *The board members refused*: *The Free Speech Movement: Coming of Age in the 1960s*, 341; *The Beginning*, 178–84.

212 *The regents also*: Kerr, vol. 2, 206–208; *The Beginning*, 181–83, 193.

212 *The protesters*: *The Beginning*, 181–83, 186, 193; *The Free Speech Movement: Coming of Age in the 1960s*, 348–54.

212 *In recent weeks . . . disobedience*: *The Free Speech Movement: Coming of Age in the 1960s*, 327, 329, 334; "Recollections of the FSM," by Martin Roysher, 149; *The Beginning*, 172, 174, 175, 178, 186.

212 *This became painfully*: *The Spiral of Conflict*, 259–60; "Recollections of the FSM," by Martin Roysher, 149; *The Free Speech Movement: Coming of Age in the 1960s*, 343.

212 *Savio and Weinberg*: *The Spiral of Conflict*, 260–61.

212 *"Mario was so . . ."*: "Recollections of the FSM," by Martin Roysher, 149.

212 *Fewer than*: This paragraph is based on *The Spiral of Conflict*, 260–62; "Recollections of the FSM," by Martin Roysher, 149; *The Free Speech Movement: Coming of Age in the 1960s*, 343, 345.

212 *The Free Speech Movement . . . free speech on campus*: "Recollections of the FSM," by Martin Roysher, 149–50; *The Free Speech Movement: Coming of Age in the 1960s*, 345, 347, 354.

212 *Indeed, on the day*: Strong to Savio, 11/23/64, Chancellor's Records, CU-149, box 72, folder 14, Bancroft.

212 *So disheartened*: *The Free Speech Movement: Coming of Age in the 1960s*, 345.

212 *But J. Edgar Hoover already . . . City Hall*: 100-151646-NR, 12/9/64, behind 151646-36X; 100-151646-61X.

212 *In the years since . . . Lynum recalled*: Author interview with Curtis O. Lynum.

212 *On November 25 . . . "in the country"*: Montgomery's series ran on 11/25/64, 11/26/64, and 11/27/64. Hoover called King a "notorious liar" at a press conference after King complained about how the FBI assigned agents to civil rights investigations, Church, book III, 156. Hoover's charge came amid the bureau's massive COINTELPRO campaign to destroy King personally and politically, Church, book III, 79–184.

213 *Montgomery reported*: The quote is from *SFX* 11/27/64, "UC Free Speech Unrest May Spread."

213 *Naming many*: *SFX* 11/27/64, "UC Free Speech Unrest May Spread"; *SFX* 11/26/64, "A Guide to UC Free Speechers"; *SFX* 11/26/64, "Behind the Scenes at UC."

213 *In an accompanying*: *SFX* 11/25/64, "UC's Growing Disorders."

213 *Lynum reported . . . "extremely timely . . ."*: 100-151646-61X.

213 *Lynum's report*: 100-151646-61X.
213 *Under its auspices . . . existing social order*: Church, book III, 1–79.
213 *Hoover began*: This paragraph is based on Church, book III, 3–16.
214 *Montgomery's series*: Church, book III, 16; author correspondence with Athan Theoharis.
214 *In an interview*: Author interview with Curtis O. Lynum.
214 *In a separate*: Author interview with Ed Montgomery.
214 *In what may*: The anecdote is from the *Berkeley Daily Planet*, 4/6/00, "Don't trust anyone over 30"; *Berkeley Daily Planet*, 8/3/11, "FSM Vet Jack Weinberg"; *The Free Speech Movement: Coming of Age in the 1960s*, 266.
214 *In any event*: Author interviews with Kerr and Savio.
214 *"It made it . . ."*: Author interview with Kerr.
214 *Savio maintained*: Author interview with Savio.
214 *"They were under . . ."*: Author interview with Savio.
214 *The day Montgomery's*: Strong to Savio, 11/25/64, Savio academic records, Bancroft. Heirich writes in *The Spiral of Conflict*, 265, that it was mailed November 28, which would be the day after Montgomery's series ended. Goines reports in *The Free Speech Movement: Coming of Age in the 1960s*, 354, that Savio, Jackie Goldberg, Brian Turner, and Art Goldberg received their letters on November 28.
214 *Alex Sherriffs had*: *The Free Speech Movement: Coming of Age in the 1960s*, 355, quoting Germaine LaBerge's oral history interview with Arleigh Williams, 114–15; Reginald Zelnik, "On the Side of the Angels," 298, in *The Free Speech Movement: Reflections on Berkeley in the 1960s*.
215 *Strong's letter*: Strong to Savio, 11/25/64, Chancellor's Records, CU-149, box 72, folder 14, Bancroft.
215 *In other letters*: "A Faculty Chronology," Free Speech Movement Archives website, www.fsm-a.org/, accessed 6/26/11.
215 *Only days before . . . the campus conflict*: *The Free Speech Movement: Coming of Age in the 1960s*, 354–56; *The Spiral of Conflict*, 264–70.

14: Sit-in at Sproul Hall
216 *The crowd*: *The Beginning*, 198–99.
216 *News of Chancellor*: Ibid., 193, 194.
216 *The FSM issued*: Ibid., 195, 197, 198.
216 *Savio and Suzanne Goldberg*: Mario Savio and Suzanne Goldberg, for the FSM Steering Committee, to Clark Kerr, 12/1/64, copy provided to the author by Suzanne Goldberg.
216 *The administration*: *The Beginning*, 198.
216 *Savio, in his fleece*: For a video clip of Savio's December 2, 1964 speech, see Free Speech Movement Archives, www.fsm-a.org/videogalleryindex.html, accessed 9/27/10.
216 *"We have an autocracy . . ."*: The text of the conclusion of Savio's speech is at the Free Speech Movement Archives, www.fsm-a.org/stacks/mario/mario_speech.html, accessed 9/27/10.
217 *Savio's speech sent*: Author interview with Michael Rossman. See also comments of Margot Adler in "My Life in the FSM," 119, and "Recollections of the FSM," by Martin Roysher, 144, both in *The Free Speech Movement: Reflections on Berkeley in the 1960s*; *Intimate Politics*, 142.
217 *And as Joan Baez . . . food and supplies*: *The Free Speech Movement: Coming of Age in the 1960s*, 361–67; *The Spiral of Conflict*, 272–73. Baez, already a star, was just

under two years older than Savio and already had been active in the civil rights movement, www.joanbaez.com/chronology.html, accessed 9/28/10. For a photo of Baez at the rally, see *The Beginning*, after the table of contents.

217 *They meant to hold: The State of California v. Mario Savio, et al.*, nos. C-7468–C-7547, 5/19/65, p. 32, BANC MSS 99/281, carton 34, Alexander Meiklejohn Collection, Bancroft.

217 *FSM leaders . . . case of nuclear war: The Free Speech Movement: Coming of Age in the 1960s*, 364–66; *The Beginning*, 201–202; *Heretic's Heart*, 90–91; *Berkeley at War*, 31–34; *Intimate Politics*, 142; *Freedom's Orator*, 194; NYT 9/3/05, "Bookstore Writes 'The End' to an Era."

217 *Savio and other FSM: The Free Speech Movement: Coming of Age in the 1960s*, 367. Other times they met in a stairwell, *The State of California v. Mario Savio, et al.*, nos. C-7468–C-7547, 5/19/65, p. 33, BANC MSS 99/281, carton 34, Alexander Meiklejohn Collection, Bancroft. On the sit-in being the largest, see *Freedom's Orator*, 198.

217 *With bullhorn in hand: The State of California v. Mario Savio, et al.*, nos. C-7468–C-7547, 5/19/65, pp. 40, 43, BANC MSS 99/281, carton 34, Alexander Meiklejohn Collection, Bancroft.

217 *That evening . . . "An End to History"*: The text of the talk and a brief explanation by Savio are at the Free Speech Movement Archives, www.fsm-a.org/stacks/end historysavio.html, accessed 9/28/10.

218 *"Last summer . . ."*: Ibid.

219 *Hundreds of officers: The Beginning*, 204.

219 *They set up*: Author interview with John Sparrow; *California Rising*, 307.

219 *Edwin Meese III: With Reagan*, 29; *Ronald Reagan: His Life and Rise to the Presidency*, 187; *California Rising*, 306; author interview with John Sparrow.

219 *Outside Sproul Hall*: Author interview with John Sparrow, an attorney for the regents, who knew Agent Jones.

220 *Jones filed*: Author interview with Threadgill.

220 *In one summary*: 100-151646-45. However, Rob Hurwitt recalled that protesters simply climbed the stairs to hang the banners.

220 *At his office*: This paragraph is based on *The Beginning*, 202–203; Kerr, vol. 2, 212; *California Rising*, 303–304.

220 *At 11:05 p.m.: The Beginning*, 202–203. But note that Kerr later recalled that Brown phoned him directly at home, Kerr, vol. 2, 212–13.

220 *Alex Sherriffs*: Kerr, vol. 2, 213; Rowland interview of Sherriffs, op. cit., 35–37, 48–49.

220 *Ever since the police . . . inside Sproul Hall*: Rowland interview with Sherriffs, op. cit., 34–38, 44–51.

220 *The aide phoned Brown*: Rowland interview with Sherriffs, 35–37, 48–49; Kerr, vol. 2, 212–13; *The Free Speech Movement: Coming of Age in the 1960s*, 367–68; *Berkeley at War*, 32; Ethan Rarick reports that Supervising Inspector Daniel O'Connell of the California Highway Patrol phoned Brown to urge arrests, and O'Connell then put Meese on the line, *California Rising*, 304–307.

220 *Midnight passed . . . virginity: The Wedding Within the War*, 122; *The Free Speech Movement: Coming of Age in the 1960s*, 365–66.

220 *At about 3 a.m. . . . "Please go": The Free Speech Movement: Coming of Age in the 1960s*, 369; Kerr, vol. 2, 213.

221 *Savio followed Strong . . . meet his gaze: The State of California v. Mario Savio, et al.*, nos. C-7468–C-7547, 5/19/65, p. 61, BANC MSS 99/281, carton 34, Alexander Meiklejohn Collection, Bancroft.

221 *When the chancellor*: Ibid., 53–57.

221 *He and other*: Ibid.; *The Beginning*, 204.
221 *They wanted students*: Ibid.
221 *Some 635 police*: Ibid.
221 *Detachments entered*: Ibid., 204–205.
221 *The first person*: Ibid., 204.
221 *He had been speaking . . . "three of us"*: Decca: *The Letters of Jessica Mitford*, 334, which notes Treuhaft's trespassing charge was dropped after he dismissed his suit against Meese for false arrest.
221 *As the radical lawyer . . . "doing here?"*: Author interview with John Sparrow.
221 *Savio walked*: This anecdote is based on *The State of California v. Mario Savio, et al.*, nos. C-7468–C-7547, 5/19/65, 70–73, and 5/17/65, 58–88, BANC MSS 99/281, carton 34, Alexander Meiklejohn Collection, Bancroft; Mario Savio survey, 4/21/65, by Professor John Leggett, Sproul Hall Incident Reports, CU-560, box 8, Bancroft, pp. 1–5.
221 *The law-enforcement machinery*: This account of the arrests is based on *The Free Speech Movement: Coming of Age in the 1960s*, 374–95; *The Beginning*, 204–206, 216; *Heretic's Heart*, 92–93; *Berkeley at War*, 33; *Intimate Politics*, 143–44; *LAT* 12/4/64, "801 UC Arrests"; *LAT* 12/5/64, "1000 UC Pickets Urge Students"; *NYT* 12/4/65, "796 Students Arrested." The literature varies on both the number of police present and the number of arrests. *The New York Times* reported that officials variously said 761, 801, and 814 were arrested, *NYT* 12/5/64, "Students Picket." By all accounts, the number arrested was more than the seven hundred or so arrested in the Conference of Studio Unions strike on November 15, 1946, described then as the largest mass arrest in California history, *LAT* 11/16/46, "700 Film Strike Pickets Arrested." Reagan was a third vice president of the SAG at the time, and had been chosen by secret ballot of the board to replace Robert Montgomery as president, *Early Reagan*, 494; SAG Timeline, www.sag.org/sag-timeline, accessed 6/27/11; SAG Presidents, Ronald Reagan, www.sag.org/ronald-reagan, accessed 6/27/11.
222 *The shock*: *The Beginning*, 206–207, estimates five thousand to ten thousand at the rally.
222 *Two young state*: *The Free Speech Movement: Coming of Age in the 1960s*, 397.
222 *Savio, who had been*: *NYT* 12/5/64, "Students Picket on Coast Campus."
222 *In the following . . . "or Mutilate"*: *NYT* 12/5/64, "Students Picket on Coast Campus"; *The Free Speech Movement: Coming of Age in the 1960s*, 395–415; Kerr, vol. 2, 213.
222 *Kerr was in despair . . . as regents*: Author interview with Kerr; Kerr, vol. 2, 317.
222 *In an urgent . . . central campus*: *The Free Speech Movement: Coming of Age in the 1960s*, 421–22; Kerr, vol. 2, 214–15; *The Beginning*, 219.
222 *The administration . . . crowd control*: *The Beginning*, 219, 221; Kerr, vol. 2, 214.
222 *Kerr sat onstage*: *The Beginning*, 222.
222 *Only six years . . . augury*: Kerr, vol. 1, 160.
223 *Now he began*: *The Free Speech Movement: Coming of Age in the 1960s*, 422.
223 *Kerr proceeded*: The paragraph is based on *The Beginning*, 219–24; Kerr, vol. 2, 214–15.
223 *Some people . . . finally over*: Kerr, vol. 2, 214; *The Beginning*, 224; *NYT* 12/8/64, "Berkeley Free Speech Parley."
223 *But no sooner*: This and the following four paragraphs are drawn from *The Free Speech Movement: Coming of Age in the 1960s*, 423–29; *The Beginning*, 222–25; Kerr, vol. 2, 214–15.
224 *Minutes later*: This paragraph is drawn from *The Free Speech Movement: Coming of Age in the 1960s*, 427–29; *The Beginning*, 228; Kerr, vol. 2, 214–15.
224 *The drama*: This paragraph is based on *Turning Points and Ironies*, 86–93; *NYT* 12/8/64, "Berkeley Peace Parley Upset as Police Grab Student."

224 *The next day*: This paragraph is based on *The Beginning*, 228–45; Kerr, vol. 2, 44, 115, 215–18; *The Free Speech Movement: Coming of Age in the 1960s*, 439–42; *East Bay Express* 9/28/84, "Present at Birth: A Free Speech Movement Journal," by Rob Hurwitt; author interview with Clark Kerr. For a discussion of the complex motives behind the faculty vote, see "On the Side of the Angels," by Reginald Zelnik, in *The Free Speech Movement: Reflections on Berkeley in the 1960s*, 312–14.

224 *As the faculty debated*: This paragraph is based on *The Beginning*, 228–45; Kerr, vol. 2, 215–18; *The Free Speech Movement: Coming of Age in the 1960s*, 439–44; *East Bay Express*, 9/28/84, "Present at Birth: A Free Speech Movement Journal," by Rob Hurwitt; "On the Side of the Angels," by Reginald Zelnik, in *The Free Speech Movement: Reflections on Berkeley in the 1960s*, 318–19.

224 *At a press conference . . . "into a gale"*: NYT 12/9/64, "A Rebel on Campus."

225 *That night*: East Bay Express 9/28/84, "Present at Birth: A Free Speech Movement Journal," by Rob Hurwitt.

225 *Ralph Gleason*: SFC 12/9/64, "The Tragedy at the Greek Theatre."

225 *Governor Brown*: WP 12/9/64, "Gov. Brown Pleads."

225 *Don Mulford*: Ibid.

225 *Mario Savio disembarked*: The FBI's surveillance of Savio's cross-country trip in this and the following paragraphs is based on FBI files on Savio and the FSM, including 100-151646-43; 100-151646-47; 100-151646-50X1; 100-151646-50X2; 100-151646-53X; 100-151646-53X2; 100-151646-53X3; 100-151646-56X; 100-151646-56X1; 100-151646-56X2; 100-151646-58; 100-151646-59X; 100-151646-59X1; 100-151646-63; 100-34204-855; 100-54086-100; 100-154189-30; 100-154189-31; 100-154189-36; 100-154189-51; 100-154189-62; 100-154189-63. On Crane, see NYT 7/15/08, "Les Crane, Talk-Show Host." FBI files also show that during the investigation of Savio in New York, FBI agents conducted surveillance of the home of Savio's aunt in Floral Park on Long Island and traced the license plates of cars parked nearby, 100-154189-62. Agents also searched bureau files for information on Savio's parents and found nothing on them, 100-154189-26; 100-154189-27. The pretext call to his aunt is noted in 100-1511646-47.

226 *In fact, the FBI*: This paragraph and the next are based on 100-151646-51; 100-151646-61X; 100-151646-50X1; 100-54086-100; 100-151646-56X2; 100-151646-47, cover pages and report, both dated 12/16/64; *The Harvard Crimson*'s story noted Savio's denial of Communist influence, 100-151646-59X1. See also *Chicago Tribune*, Table of Contents, 12/12/64; NYT 12/12/64, "Berkeley Youth Leader"; WP 12/12/64, "Movement Support by Foreign Money Is Denied."

226 *"Results widely"*: 100-151646-56X2.

227 *Governor Brown*: The account of the phone conversation is from 100-34204-815; 100-34204-840.

227 *Brown said that*: 100-34204-815.

227 *As Lynum*: 100-34204-815.

227 *Hoover swiftly . . . "from becoming involved"*: 100-34204-822.

227 *Lynum's staff promptly*: This paragraph is based on 100-151646-50X, SF to HQ, 6:36 p.m., 12/9/64; 100-151646-50X, SF to HQ, 10:53 p.m., 12/9/64; 100-151646-51 and attachment with same serial number. Although this memo purported to list fourteen students and five "faculty members" on the bureau's Security Index, three of the five faculty members were actually graduate students working as teaching assistants or researchers. One person's identity was excised in the released records. The only actual faculty member thus identified is Leon Wofsy, whose background and limited role are discussed in the text. Named in the memo are Bettina Aptheker, John A. Belisle, Jr., Kenneth Cloke, Susan Cloke, Celia Anne Cohen, Barbara

Garson, Eda Toni Godel, Arthur Lee Goldberg, Conn Hallinan, Eleanor Harawitz, Robert Paul Kaufman, Jack Kurzweill, Margaret Lima, James Petras, Myra Riskin, Stephen Salaff, Helen Schiff, Leon Wofsy, and (name deleted). It must be noted that there is no evidence that any of them had engaged in any improper activity.

227 *Leon Wofsy . . . continued party membership*: 100-151646-51, memo and attachment; 100-151646-52; 100-151646-59. Note that though these memos convey the claim that in 1957 Communist Party leaders and Wofsy agreed to circulate a false story that he had left the party, they provide no attribution or basis for this assertion. Further, the memos note that Wofsy told the FBI in 1957 that he had quit the party, and that since then the bureau had found no evidence to the contrary, including from its informers in the party.

227 *Moreover, although Wofsy . . . than had anyone else*: 100-151646-56.
228 *But Hoover knew better . . . scrawled*: 100-151646-51.
228 *Tolson and his other*: 100-151646-52.
228 *On December 14*: This paragraph is based on 100-151646-51 and 100-151646-46.
228 *Brown told Lynum*: 100-151646-46.
228 *Hoover had cooperated*: The regents' vote is described in Kerr, vol. 2, 230–35; *The Beginning*, 249.
228 *The regents also voted*: Kerr, vol. 2, 235, 241; Rowland interview with Sherriffs, op. cit., 46.
228 *"This whole affair . . . to this matter"*: 100-151646-51.
228 *To make sure*: 100-32404-873.
228 *President Johnson*: On Goldwater, his defeat, and Johnson's television ad, see *LAT* 5/30/98, "Barry Goldwater"; *NYT* 5/30/98, "Barry Goldwater Is Dead." The ad was viewed at ushistorygirl.webs.com/apps/videos/videos/show/9769322-lyndon-johnson -campaign-ad-peace-little-girl-daisy-1964, accessed 2/9/11.
229 *Johnson had assumed*: Before the Storm, 513.
229 *Kerr had served*: 161-3037-27; Kerr, vol. 1, 137; Kerr, vol. 2, 278–79. They included the President's Commission on National Goals, 1960, and the Board of Visitors of the U.S. Military Academy, 1959–1960, both under Eisenhower; and the President's Advisory Committee on Labor-Management Policy, 1961–1964, under Kennedy and Johnson.
229 *. . . and JFK had offered*: Kerr, vol. 2, 279.
229 *Johnson had been considering*: On Johnson's apparently rather preliminary consideration of Kerr for various posts, see these recordings of President Johnson in discussion with the named party, available at the LBJ Library: WH6406.05 Richard Russell, 6/11/64, 12:26 p.m., Citation 3680 (Kerr as ambassador to South Vietnam); WH6406.19 Orville Freeman, 6/30/64, 12 p.m., Citation 3960 (Kerr as chairman of the National Food Marketing Commission); WH6411.22 Robert McNamara, 11/17/64, 7 p.m., Citation 6389 (Kerr as CIA head); WH6411.23 Don Cook, 11/18/64, 9:25 a.m., Citation 6390 (Kerr as HEW head or CIA head); WH6412.01 Robert Mc-Namara, 12/4/64, 2:30 p.m., Citation 6604 (Kerr for a post that is unclear).
229 *In early December*: The descriptions of LBJ's Oval Office offer is from 77-7764-40; Kerr, vol. 2, 278–79; Kerr oral history with LBJ Library, 8/12/85, by Janet Kerr-Tener, 11–15; author interview with Kerr. Kerr's accounts of the meeting have varied slightly over the years as to dialogue but are substantially consistent. The dialogue quoted here is from his interview with Kerr-Tener.
229 *Before Kerr*: 161-3037-1.
229 *But as a federal*: "The later documents all strongly support the suspicion that the FBI was investigating Kerr to have him removed from the UC administration, because FBI officials disagreed with his politics or his handling of administrative mat-

ters." 57 F3d 803 *Rosenfeld v. United States Department of Justice*, U.S. Court of Appeals, Ninth Circuit, June 12, 1995.

230 *On December 31, 1964 . . . information on him*: The summary is 161-3037-27, dated 12/30/64; the FBI's internal note, 161-3037-26, states it was sent 12/31/64.

230 *But Hoover slanted*: The FBI's bias is revealed in comparing the report with earlier FBI records that discussed the allegations.

230 *Nearly three pages*: 161-3037-27, pp. 4–6.

230 *Combs asserted*: 161-3037-27, p. 4.

230 *Hoover's report failed*: 116-325-30, p. 3.

230 *Combs claimed*: 161-3037-27, p. 4.

230 *This charge was*: 77-7764-15; 77-7764-17.

230 *Hoover's report did not say*: 77-7764-15; 77-7764-17. In an interview with the author, Kagel denied he had been a Communist.

230 *Moreover, the report*: 77-7764-15.

230 *Finally, Combs claimed*: 161-3037-27, pp. 5–6.

230 *That charge also . . . "for security reasons"*: 77-7764-11; 77-7764-15.

230 *Hoover's report . . . for a federal post*: 161-3037-27, pp. 8–9.

231 *But Hoover, employing . . . "a hold over him"*: Hoover's letter containing Mulford's additional comments is also marked 161-3037-27, but is dated 12/31/64.

231 *In an interview . . . secretary of HEW*: Author interviews with DeLoach and Kerr.

231 *Early one morning*: This and the following paragraphs are based on the author's interviews with Kerr. However, it should be noted that apparently prior to this final phone conversation there was another one between Kerr and Johnson that is partially captured in LBJ White House Tape WH6412.01, Clark Kerr, 12/11/64, 3:05 p.m., Citation 6608. From this tape, it is unclear who initiated the call just after noon PST. Kerr tells Johnson he is ready to take the HEW job, saying, "Well, the chairman of the board said he wanted to wait until the regents could meet so he could talk with them next week. But I'm prepared to do whatever you want anytime." Johnson replies, "Well, it seems to me that if you're prepared to act regardless of what they do," to which Kerr says, "Yeah." Johnson continues, "I think, then, that it's a question of timing," and tells Kerr not to publicly deny the job has been offered to him "in light of the fact that we may come along pretty soon." Johnson asks, "But how long is it going to take you to extricate yourself?" Kerr answers, "Well, you know that the university is in a bit of trouble at one of our campuses at Berkeley." Johnson says, "Yeah," and Kerr continues, "Which has of late seemed a bit difficult. But that's going to go on for quite some time. So there's no point waiting for that." Clearly, at this point the offer was still open and Kerr was willing to take it. The author questioned LBJ's former aide Bill Moyers, but he said he could not recall the matter.

15: No Evidence

232 *He decided to*: 100-151646-77, p. 2.

232 *F. J. Baumgardner*: This and the following paragraphs about Baumgardner's call are based on 62-103031-188; 100-151646-61X.

232 *Lynum was*: Author interview with Lynum; *The FBI and I*.

232 *In a memo . . . "the Communist Party"*: 100-151646-61X.

233 *Headquarters was insistent . . . "basic grievances"*: 100-151646-77.

233 *Eleven days later*: 100-151646-87, p. 2.

233 *It was as*: 57 F3d 803 *Rosenfeld v. United States Department of Justice*, U.S. Court of Appeals, Ninth Circuit, June 12, 1995.

233 *But Hoover:* 100-151646, no serial number, behind 100-151646-27, dated 3/20/61.
233 *At 9:00 a.m.:* McCone's black leather appointment book, John A. McCone Papers, Bancroft, BANC MSS 95/20 c, carton 39.
233 *Vietnam was on: A Bright Shining Lie,* 501 (the quote is Neil Sheehan's); *Legacy of Ashes,* 247; *WP* 3/8/65, "Marines in Viet-Nam"; *LAT* 3/7/65, "Marines Serve Political Warning"; *LAT* 3/7/65, "Troop Move Represents"; *LAT* 3/7/65, "3,500 U.S. Marines."
233 *At 10:00 a.m. . . . nuclear proliferation:* Transcript, Joint Committee on Atomic Energy, Congress of the United States, Meeting No. 89-1-5, Thursday, January 28, 1965, Executive Session, in John A. McCone Papers, Bancroft, BANC MSS 95/20 c, carton 7, folder 35; *NYT* 10/25/64, "China and Nuclear Spread"; *NYT* 10/18/64, "China's Bomb."
234 *Afterward . . . the Middle East:* McCone's black leather appointment book, John A. McCone Papers, Bancroft, BANC MSS 95/20 c, carton 39; *LAT* 1/22/65, "Johnson Gives Leaders"; *NYT* 1/22/65, "Johnson Briefs Congress."
234 *Then he made:* 100-151646-83.
234 *McCone wore . . . "a dark street":* *LAT* 2/16/91, "John A. McCone"; *Washington Star* 1/19/62, "New CIA Chief Has Little to Tell Senators," John A. McCone Papers, Bancroft, BANC MSS 95/20 c, carton 7, folder 41.
234 *But McCone's mild . . . served himself:* *NYT* 2/16/91, "John A. McCone"; *LAT* 2/16/91, "John A. McCone." On McCone, see *Legacy of Ashes,* 180–248.
234 *John Alex McCone:* McCone to Peterson, outgoing telegram, 5/21/59, John A. McCone Papers, Bancroft, BANC MSS 95/20 c, carton 34, folder 1.
234 *His father's family . . . an executive:* Biography, "John Alex McCone," John A. McCone Papers, Bancroft, BANC MSS 95/20 c, carton 34, folder 2.
234 *In 1937:* This paragraph is based on ibid.; *NYT* 3/15/89, "Stephen D. Bechtel"; *Legacy of Ashes,* 180.
234 *McCone and his . . . St. Sylvester:* "Background Information, John A. McCone," 9/16/58, John A. McCone Papers, Bancroft, BANC MSS 95/20 c, carton 34, folder 1; *LAT* 12/3/64, "CIA Director McCone." Rosemary McCone died in 1961, and the following year McCone married Theiline Pigott, Biography, "John Alex McCone," John A. McCone Papers, Bancroft, BANC MSS 95/20 c, carton 34, folder 2.
234 *McCone held . . . controversial appointments:* "Background Information, John A. McCone," op. cit.; *WP* 10/23/61, "McCone Selection."
235 *In a series . . . "working for the Government":* Examples of Pearson's McCone columns are *LAT* 1/10/62, "Senate Committee May Review"; *LAT* 1/11/62, "Both Parties Urged"; *LAT* 1/12/62, "McCone's Appearances"; *LAT* 1/17/62, "McCone Seen"; *LAT* 1/19/62, "McCone Accused of Profiting"; *LAT* 1/26/62, "Senate Probe"; *WP* 1/25/62, "McCone Withheld."
235 *Other press accounts . . . "as a platform":* *Akron Beacon Journal* 10/27/61, "Choice of McCone"; *St. Louis Post Dispatch* 1/18/62, "McCone Gives Qualified"; *Washington Star* 1/18/62, "McCone Denies Effort"; *New Republic* 2/12/62, "They Said 'No' to McCone," all in John A. McCone Papers, Bancroft, BANC MSS 95/20 c, carton 7, folders 41 and 42.
235 *During his confirmation:* *Baltimore Sun* 1/19/62, "Senate Unit Gives"; *WP* 1/19/62, "McCone Pictures," John A. McCone Papers, Bancroft, BANC MSS 95/20 c, carton 7, folder 41.
235 *As to the professors:* *St. Louis Post Dispatch* 1/18/62, "McCone Gives Qualified"; *St. Louis Post Dispatch* 1/19/62, "Senate Group Is Expected"; *New Republic* 1/29/62, "McCone's Confirmation," in John A. McCone Papers, Bancroft Library, BANC MSS 95/20 c, carton 7, folder 41.
235 *In 1962 the Senate:* *NYT* 2/9/62, "In the Nation."

235 *As CIA director*: International Journal of Intelligence and Counterintelligence, vol. 2, no. 4, "John McCone and the Cuban Missile Crisis," in John A. McCone Papers, Bancroft, BANC MSS 95/20 c, carton 7, folder 39; *Legacy of Ashes*, 174, 187, 191, 202, 207.

235 *But when he'd*: *Legacy of Ashes*, 207.

235 *The Soviet Union*: Ibid., 196.

235 *McCone was the only*: Ibid., 194, 195, 196, 197, 203.

235 *And he proposed*: Ibid., 202, 203–205.

235 *Cuba would come back*: This paragraph is based on ibid., 92, 99, 100, 101, 105, 106; Church committee, "Alleged Assassination Plots Involving Foreign Leaders," Report No. 94-465, 1975, pp. 101, 105, 106. On McCone's view of assassinations as "abhorrent," see *Legacy of Ashes*, 190.

236 *Yet he had looked . . . "during my tenure"*: Church Committee, "Alleged Assassination Plots Involving Foreign Leaders," Report No. 94-465, 1975, pp. 107–108; McCone, "Confidential, Memorandum of Discussion with Mr. David W. Belin and Mr. Mason Cargill on Thursday, April 17, 1975, Washington, D.C.—10:00 a.m. to 5:30 p.m.," in John A. McCone Papers, Bancroft, BANC MSS 95/20 c, carton 8, folder 7. On the CIA-mob plot to kill Castro, see also *Legacy of Ashes*.

236 *McCone did not*: Church Committee, "Alleged Assassination Plots Involving Foreign Leaders," Report No. 94-465, 1975, pp. 100, 105, 108.

236 *Nor did he*: Ibid., pp. 276, 277; McCone, "Memorandum for File, Testimony before the Church Committee was Friday, June 6, 1975," in John A. McCone Papers, Bancroft, BANC MSS 95/20 c, carton 8, folder 8.

236 *Had he asked*: This paragraph is based on Church Committee, "Alleged Assassination Plots Involving Foreign Leaders," Report No. 94-465, 1975, pp. 71–72, 83–89, 99. It should be noted, however, that the committee found evidence Helms and other CIA officials kept information about the assassination schemes from McCone, ibid., 91–180. But note, too, Helms's testimony regarding McCone: "I have no reason to impugn his integrity. On the other hand, I don't understand how it was he didn't hear about some of these things that he claims that he didn't," ibid., 100–101. See also *Legacy of Ashes*, 181, 187, 190, 217.

236 *Appearing before*: McCone, "Memorandum for File, Testimony before the Church Committee was Friday, June 6, 1975," in John A. McCone Papers, Bancroft, BANC MSS 95/20 c, carton 8, folder 8; WP 6/7/75, "Plotting on Castro Confirmed."

236 *He summarized . . . "in this area"*: McCone, "Memorandum for File, Testimony before the Church Committee was Friday, June 6, 1975," in John A. McCone Papers, Bancroft, BANC MSS 95/20 c, carton 8, folder 8.

237 *Ultimately, the Church . . . "plausible deniability"*: Church Committee, "Alleged Assassination Plots Involving Foreign Leaders," Report No. 94-465, 1975, pp. 264, 261, 276, 273, 277. The committee concluded, "A firm written order against engaging in assassination should also have been issued by McCone if, as he testified, he had exhibited strong aversion to assassination," ibid., 277.

237 *McCone was upset . . . "organization . . ."*: McCone, "Memorandum for File, Testimony before the Church Committee was Friday, June 6, 1975," in John A. McCone Papers, Bancroft, BANC MSS 95/20 c, carton 8, folder 8.

237 *McCone arrived*: The account of the Hoover and McCone meeting is based on 100-151646-83; 100-151646-95; 100-151646-128.

237 *R. James Woolsey*: Author interview with Woolsey.

237 *Coconut Island . . . Richard Nixon*: LAT 9/5/65, "A Traveler"; WP 1/13/48, "Washington Calling"; NYT 12/2/48, "Pacific Resort Planned"; NYT 3/23/53, "Truman to Work"; LAT 5/4/53, "Truman's Back"; WP 2/16/47, "Cost Quarter Million"; NYT

8/30/47, "Anderson Heads"; *LAT* 2/16/47, "Pacific Island"; *A Brief History of Coconut Island*, Hawai'i Institute of Marine Biology, www.hawaii.edu/himb/about.html, accessed 3/12/11.

237 *Clark Kerr once stayed*: This anecdote is from Kerr, vol. 2, 56–57.
238 *A large man*: Author interviews with Kerr and John Sparrow.
238 *He had donated*: This paragraph is based on *LAT* 7/29/81, "Edwin W. Pauley"; *NYT* 7/29/81, "Edwin Wendell Pauley Sr., 78"; Kerr, vol. 2, 39, 65, 67, 69–72, 284, 295–97; author interview with Kerr.
238 *Pauley and McCone*: McCone 77-40957-116, p. 18; 77-40957-1; Pauley 161-4895-22, p. 55.
238 *After going into*: This and the next two paragraphs are based on *LAT* 7/29/81, "Edwin W. Pauley"; *NYT* 7/29/81, "Edwin Wendell Pauley Sr., 78"; *LAT* 3/14/46, "Truman Calls Back"; *LAT* 2/8/48, "Pauley Resigns"; 161-4895-22 and attached résumé.
238 *Returning to . . . Rams football team*: *LAT* 7/29/81, "Edwin W. Pauley."
238 *In the early . . . not proved*: 62-103031-14.
239 *FBI agents conducted*: This paragraph is based on 161-4895-22.
239 *And as McCone*: This paragraph and the next are based on 100-151646-95 and author's interview with Kerr.
239 *Hoover agreed*: 100-151646-95.
239 *It was part*: 57 F3d 803 *Rosenfeld v. United States Department of Justice*, U.S. Court of Appeals, Ninth Circuit, June 12, 1995.
239 *Once their*: 100-151646-95.
239 *A trusted lieutenant*: This paragraph and the next are based on *LAT* 2/7/64, "Simon to Retire"; *LAT* 3/22/64, "L.A. Climate Boosts"; *LAT* 6/3/64, "Draft Evasion Suspect"; *LAT* 10/29/64, "FBI's Hoover Named"; *LAT* 10/13/64, "Man Charged"; *LAT* 12/8/64, "Bud Suhl Surrenders"; *LAT* 12/15/64, "Jockey Held"; *Hoover's FBI: The Men and the Myth*, 29–34; *Rearview Mirror*, 15, 16, 27–28. Grapp was protected by Hoover, but after the director died Grapp was demoted and abruptly retired, whereon he was excluded from the Society of Former Special Agents of the FBI, the retired agents' fraternal organization, *Rearview Mirror*, 27–28.
240 *Hoover instructed . . . "with the FBI"*: 100-151646-95. The FBI's internal copies of the blind memos given to Pauley, retained in FBI 100-151646-93, concerned nineteen people. Eight of them had been the subject of the FBI's earlier leak to Governor Brown. The Pauley memos named Bettina Aptheker, Harold Draper, Elena Flemming, Barbara Garson, Arthur Lee Goldberg, Jackie Goldberg, Lee F. Goldblatt, Conn Hallinan, Joseph Amos Harris, Robert Paul Kaufman, Margaret Lima, Richard Jeffrey Lustig, Edward Jerry Rosenfeld (no relation to the author), Sydney R. Stapleton, Alan B. Steinberg, Joseph Tussman, David Wellman, Ann Ginger Wood, and, of course, Leon Wofsy. Again, it must be noted that there is no evidence any of them had engaged in any improper activity.
240 *Although Hoover*: 100-151646-93; 100-151646-95; 100-151646-99.
240 *Pauley could use*: 100-151646-95.
240 *But Hoover admonished*: 100-151646-93.
240 *Five days later*: The account of the meeting in this and the next paragraph is based on 100-151646-98; 100-151646-99; 100-151646-97; *LAT* 6/4/61, "Architect Completes"; *LAT* 3/10/61, "Becket Opens"; *LAT* 4/6/71, "Exchange Offer."
240 *All were prominent*: 100-151646-100, 2/9/65; 100-151646-100, 2/11/65. On Roth and Ghirardelli, see *LAT* 9/7/85, "Ship Heiress."
240 *Unknown to him*: On the Responsibilities Program and Hoover's ending it in California, see Chapter 4.

241 *It was a four-page*: 100-151646-93.
241 *Like the report*: 100-151646-93.
241 *Two days later*: This paragraph is based on 100-151646-98.
241 *Two weeks after*: 100-151646-100, 2/9/65; 100-151646-100, 2/11/65; 100-151646-101.
241 *The reports . . . security clearances*: 100-151646-100, 2/9/65; 100-151646-100, 2/11/65; 62-103031-195.
241 *In an interview*: Author interview with DeLoach.
241 *But Grapp*: Author interview with Grapp.
241 *Pauley was deeply*: 100-151646-101, 2/17/65.
241 *As he told Grapp*: 100-151646-101, 2/17/65.

16: An Angry Young Man

242 *One afternoon*: The saga of John Thompson and the Filthy Speech Movement is based on *The Free Speech Movement: Coming of Age in the 1960s*, 480–508, except as otherwise noted. It also draws on Kerr, vol. 2, 260–64; *LAT* 4/22/65, "UC Expels"; *LAT* 4/23/65, "4 Students Punished"; *LAT* 5/12/65, "Judge Convicts 9"; and other material as noted.
242 *John J. Thompson . . . confines of conformity*: *The Free Speech Movement: Coming of Age in the 1960s*, 480–508.
242 *Fueled by marijuana . . . hitchhiked to Berkeley*: Ibid.
242 *Arriving on campus*: Ibid.
242 *As Thomas Pynchon*: *The Crying of Lot 49*, as excerpted in *Berkeley! A Literary Tribute*, 102.
242 *Calvin Trillin*: *The New Yorker* 3/13/65, "Letter from Berkeley."
243 *Or as John Thompson*: *The Free Speech Movement: Coming of Age in the 1960s*, 485.
243 *Thompson was painfully . . . of the FSM*: Ibid., 484, 485, 486.
243 *On Wednesday*: Ibid., 486.
243 *"Nothing was happening" . . . and waited*: Ibid., 486–87.
243 *A young man . . . sat down again*: Ibid., 487.
243 *Mario Savio walked*: Ibid. The quote is Thompson's.
243 *The crew-cut man returned*: DC 3/4/65, "Obscene Sign Causes Arrest"; *The Free Speech Movement: Coming of Age in the 1960s*, 487.
244 *On Thursday*: DC 3/5/65, "More Arrested for Obscenity."
244 *It worked*: Ibid.
244 *On Friday*: *The Free Speech Movement: Coming of Age in the 1960s*, 492–96.
244 *Other speakers*: Ibid.
244 *After the rally*: DC 3/8/65, "Student Signs Complaints"; *The Free Speech Movement: Coming of Age in the 1960s*, 492–96.
244 *The Daily Cal*: DC 3/11/65, "Freedom and Responsibility," an opinion piece in which Kerr writes that *The Daily Cal* so-named it; *LAT* 3/10/65, "UC President Clark Kerr Resigns Post"; *NYT* 3/11/65, "Kerr's Resignation," which notes *The Daily Cal* dubbed it the "filthy speech movement"; *Chicago Tribune* 4/14/65, "Vote U. of Cal."
244 *These events divided . . . "opened the gates"*: *The Free Speech Movement: Coming of Age in the 1960s*, 489–91.
245 *Savio was particularly . . . "problem of obscenity"*: Ibid., 490.
245 *Ultimately, several FSM . . . "to wane"*: Ibid., 489–90.
245 *But other students . . . partly satirical*: The *Spider* episode is based on ibid., 496–508, which notes the first issue of the fortnightly appeared March 1, 1965; *LAT* 3/19/65, "Magazine Obscenity"; DC 3/19/65, "Meyerson Orders Ban"; DC 3/19/65, editorial,

"Why?"; *DC* 3/22/65, "Meyerson Bans 'Spider'"; *DC* 3/22/65, "Students Blast Ban"; *DC* 3/24/65, "'Spider' Ban Upheld"; 100-151646-124.

245 Spider *was . . . "license to kill"*: The FBI obtained a copy of the March 15, 1965, issue of *Spider*, secured it in a manila envelope marked "Evidence," and placed it in the bureau's files on UC, 100-151646-124.

246 *This issue . . . the story began: Spider*, in 100-151646-124.

246 *The university administration: Spider* was banned on March 19, 1965, and permitted back on campus on April 1, 1965, under more liberal rules for selling literature on campus, *The Free Speech Movement: Coming of Age in the 1960s*, 497, 698; *DC* 3/19/65, "Meyerson Orders Ban"; *DC* 3/19/65, editorial, "Why?"; *DC* 3/22/65, "'Meyerson Bans 'Spider'"; *DC* 3/22/65, "Students Blast Ban"; *DC* 3/24/65, "'Spider' Ban Upheld."

246 *Curtis Lynum sent*: 100-151646-124; 100-151646-137, 5/3/65.

246 *The Filthy Speech*: For a discussion of the San Francisco Bay Area's developing counterculture and activism and its influence on the Berkeley campus, see "The Fatal Attractions of the Berkeley Campus," Kerr, vol. 2, 111–21.

246 As The New York Times: *NYT* 9/5/57, "Books of the Times."

246 *Allen Ginsberg . . . "Generation's capital"*: The quote is from *NYT* 10/2/58, "Books of the Times." On Beat writers in San Francisco, see also *NYT* 9/5/57, "Books of the Times"; *NYT* 9/2/56, "West Coast Rhythms"; *WP* 9/8/57, "Vocal, the Frantic Fringe"; *LAT* 9/28/58, "Good-by to the Beatniks!" Ginsberg was born in Newark, N.J.; Kerouac in Lowell, Mass.; Ferlinghetti in Yonkers, N.Y., see Literary Kicks, www.litkicks.com/, accessed 6/28/11.

246 *The movement . . . blast at conformity: The Fifties*, 306–307; *The Beat Generation in San Francisco: A Literary Tour*, 109–10; *Dharma Lion*, 200–202, 215–16; *Ginsberg: A Biography*, 187–91, 195–97; *The Trials of Lenny Bruce*, 39-41; *"Howl" Fifty Years Later*; Literary Kicks, "Six Gallery," www.litkicks.com/Places/SixGallery.html, accessed 6/28/11. Note that some works give the date of the Six Gallery reading as October 13, 1955.

246 *Two years later: The Fifties*, 307.

246 *Lenny Bruce*: This paragraph is based on *LAT* 8/5/66, "Death of Lenny Bruce"; *NYT* 8/4/66, "Lenny Bruce." His San Francisco performance, arrest, trial, and acquittal are recounted in *The Trials of Lenny Bruce*, 47–78.

247 *Like Bruce . . . hearing colors: The Trials of Lenny Bruce*, 41–46; *Ginsberg: A Biography*, 260–83; *Acid Dreams*, 58–61, 77–81, 110–11. On LSD, see *Life* 3/25/66, "LSD, The Exploding Threat of the Mind Drug That Got Out of Control"; *Look* 11/5/63, "The Strange Case of the Harvard Drug Scandal."

247 *A Swiss scientist*: This paragraph is based on *NYT* 1/7/06, "Nearly 100, LSD's Father Ponders"; *Acid Dreams* timeline, www.levity.com/aciddreams/timeline.html, accessed 6/8/11.

247 *The CIA, meanwhile*: On the history of LSD, including the CIA's deep involvement with it, see *Acid Dreams*.

247 *In 1955, Aldous Huxley: Acid Dreams*, 48; *NYT* 3/29/56, "Books of the Times," on *Heaven and Hell*.

247 *Timothy Leary*: This paragraph is based on *Look* 11/5/63, "The Strange Case of the Harvard Drug Scandal"; *Acid Dreams*, 73–89.

247 *Another had sprouted*: This paragraph is based on *Stanford Magazine*, January/February 2002, "What a Trip"; *The Electric Kool-Aid Acid Test*, 33–49; *Prime Green*, 89–95; *Acid Dreams*, 119; *NYT* 11/11/01, "Ken Kesey, Author of 'Cuckoo's Nest'"; *LAT* 11/11/01, "Ken Kesey, Novelist"; *Time* 2/16/62, "Books: Life in a Loony Bin."

248 *In the summer*: Kesey's cross-country adventure is recounted in *The Electric Kool-Aid Acid Test*. See also *Prime Green*, 121–23.

248 *By February 1965*: Acid Dreams, 146.
248 *Much of it . . . John Thompson*: On Owsley, see *The Electric Kool-Aid Acid Test*, 210–13; *The Haight-Ashbury: A History*; *LAT* 10/3/66, "'Mr. LSD'"; *NYT* 6/28/67, "A Drug More Potent"; *LAT* 12/22/67, "Reported 'Mr. LSD'"; *LAT* 2/22/68, "2 San Francisco Men"; *LAT* 6/21/86, "Summer of Love."
248 *Several months after*: *The Nation* 9/27/65, "The Nonstudent Left," by Hunter S. Thompson.
248 *Thompson concluded*: Ibid.
248 *The Filthy Speech*: *The Spiral of Conflict*, 360–68; *NYT* 3/11/65, "Kerr's Resignation at Berkeley."
248 *Six feet three*: This paragraph is based on Jones's informant file, 134-deleted; his Personnel Security Questionnaire, Hardin Jones Collection, Bancroft, 79 112/c, carton 5, folder, Personal-Biography; *NYT* 2/18/78, "Dr. Hardin Jones"; *SFX* 8/18/50, "Radiation Ray Tests Studied"; *SFX* 5/7/58, "Atomic Fallout Held Negligible"; *Lafayette Sun* 5/17/63, "Want to See Butterflies"; author interview with Ken Holden; author interview with Jones's wife, Helen Jones. On John Lawrence, see *NYT* 9/9/91, "John H. Lawrence"; *SFC* 9/12/91, "Berkeley's 'Rad Lab Gang.'"
249 *Jones was often seen*: Author interview with John Sparrow.
249 *After the convocation*: The anecdote is from "Alexander Grendon: Research with Hardin Jones at Donner Laboratory, 1957–1978," by Sally Smith Hughes, Bancroft, 87/163 c, pp. 43–45.
249 *He warned students*: Ibid.
249 *Increasingly, Jones blamed*: Kerr, vol. 2, 72, 166; author interviews with John Sparrow and Clark Kerr.
249 *He complained*: Author interview with John Sparrow. Jones's contacts with regents are further noted in 77-7764-48 ("Regents"); 77-7764-50 (Hearst); 100-151646-172 ("members of the Board of Regents"); 100-151646-177 (Pauley); 100-151646-174X, enclosure to attached letter Jones to Mr. President, 10/4/65 (Hearst); Jones to Max Rafferty, 12/13/65, Hardin Jones Papers, 79/112c, box 12, folder "Letters by Jones," Bancroft.
249 *Martin Meyerson*: The account of the events surrounding the proffered resignations of Kerr and Meyerson in this paragraph and the next are drawn from Kerr, vol. 2, 260–64; *The Free Speech Movement: Coming of Age in the 1960s*, 505; *The Spiral of Conflict*, 360–67; *SFX* 3/11/65, "Kerr's Case"; *SFC* 3/11/65, "Why Kerr Quit"; *SFNCB* 3/10/65, "Why UC's Kerr Resigned"; *OT* 3/10/65, "Turmoil at UC"; *SFX* 3/10/65, "Crisis at U.C."; *SFC* 3/10/65, "Kerr, Meyerson Quit." Kerr's quote is from *SFX* 3/11/65, "Full Text of Kerr's Statement," all in 100-34204, vol. 13. Also *LAT* 3/10/65, "UC President Kerr Resigns"; *LAT* 3/11/65, "Ultimatum as Factor"; *NYT* 3/11/65, "Kerr's Resignation."
250 *Assemblyman Don Mulford . . . "restore discipline"*: *SFC* 3/10/65, "Reactions to the UC Resignations," in 100-34204, vol. 13.
250 *Hugh Burns*: *SFNCB* 3/11/65, "Senate Chief Rips," in 100-34204-1325, vol. 13.
250 *Ed Pauley*: *SFX* 3/1/65, "A Wide Reaction," in 100-34204, vol. 13.
250 *But Governor Brown . . . withdrew them*: *SFC* 3/10/65 "Swift Move Startles Governor"; *OT* 3/10/65, "Turmoil at UC"; *SFNCB* 3/10/65, "Student Paper Asks"; *SFNCB* 3/10/65, "Expressions of Support"; *LAT* 3/12/65, "Campus Striving"; *SFX* 3/13/65, "Brown's Plea"; *SFX* 3/15/65, "Kerr's Scant."
250 *Mulford introduced*: This paragraph and the next are from *The Nation* 9/27/65, "The Nonstudent Left," by Hunter S. Thompson; *LAT* 3/18/65, "Expulsions at UC Asked."
250 *On January 27, 1965*: This paragraph is based on 77-7764-48.
250 *Jones offered*: This paragraph is based on 77-7764-48 and Hardin Jones Informant File, 134-deleted, which shows the FBI had designated him as a Potential Security

Informant as of 2/18/65, and that he supplied information about Kerr, other administrators, faculty, and student protesters. A Potential Security Informant, or PSI, may be very active as an informer but must establish his or her credibility before being designated as a Security Informant. PSIs are usually paid, *Are You Now or Have You Ever Been in the FBI Files*, 201; author interview with Burney Threadgill, Jr.

250 *Jones helped them*: Details are set out in the following text. See also plaintiffs' interview of Richard Combs, 3/3/75, investigative report in *Synanon v. Hearst*, S. F. Superior Court No. 651-749.

251 *One month later*: This paragraph is based on 77-7764-50; *LAT* 1/1/99, "Catherine Campbell Hearst"; Kerr, vol. 2, 134.

251 *Jones decided*: This paragraph is based on 77-7764-51.

251 *On March 5*: The account of the Catherine Hearst–FBI meeting is based on 77-7764-50.

252 *Disregarding her request*: 77-7764-55, 3/19/65.

252 *The report*: 161-3037-30, 3/25/65; 161-3037-31, with enclosure; 77-7764-55, 3/22/65.

252 *Lewis F. Powell, Jr.*: The Powell anecdote is based on 62-103031-200, 2/25/65; 62-103031-200, 3/2/65; *SFX* 3/24/65, "Lawyer's Plea for Morality." Powell later gave similar speeches decrying campus unrest, *NYT* 5/2/65, "Civil Disobedience Scored"; *WP* 2/26/66, "Extremists of 'New Left.'" On Powell, see also *NYT* 10/22/71, "Lewis Franklin Powell, Jr."

253 *Hoover, meanwhile*: This paragraph is based on *J. Edgar Hoover Speaks Concerning Communism*, 45–46, citing FBI appropriations hearings 1966; *NYT* 5/18/65, "Hoover Links Reds to Berkeley Strife"; *Chicago Tribune* 5/18/65, "Hoover Links Reds"; *LAT* 5/18/65, "Hoover Links Subversives"; *LAT* 5/19/65, "Red Influence at Berkeley Denied."

253 *But by then . . . political opponents*: *The Boss*, 213, 306–307, 308n; *The Bureau: The Secret History of the FBI*, 131; *The Secret Life of J. Edgar Hoover*, 223. The author conducted research in the John J. Rooney Collection, Brooklyn College Archive and Special Collections, Brooklyn College of the City University of New York, Accession No. 89-005. Those records contain a "Biographical Note" that states, "As a good friend of FBI Director J. Edgar Hoover, Rooney and several other Congressmen were charged with having received sensitive material on their political opponents, although these charges were never proven."

253 *Even as Hoover . . . told him so*: See, for example, 100-151646-51; 100-151646-61X; 100-151646-50X1; 100-54086-100; 100-54060-102.

253 *On March 12, 1965*: The report is 100-54060-137.

253 *(Sherriffs was mistaken.)*: Suzanne Goldberg told the author that Savio did not have petit mal epilepsy.

254 *It was all guilt . . . on Savio*: 100-54060-137.

254 *Nonetheless*: 100-54060-137.

254 *FBI officials*: The description of the Reserve Index is from Church, book III, 447; the number of names on it is noted at p. 468.

254 *Lynum recommended Savio*: 100-54060-137.

255 *In response*: 100-54060-184.

255 *Savio was back*: The account of Savio's speech is drawn from *DC* 4/27/65, "Mario Resigns"; *OT* 4/27/65, "Savio Quits"; *SFNCB* 4/27/65, "Savio Bows Out"; *SFC* 4/27/65, "Savio Retires"; *SFX* 4/27/65, "Savio Quits," all in 100-54060, vol. 2.

255 *One had been*: *DC* 4/22/65, "Meyerson Ousts."

255 *Savio thought*: *SFC* 3/12/65, "Savio Lashes Kerr," in 100-54060-156.

255 *Savio had been struggling*: *Freedom's Orator*, 237–42, 245–46; see also 227, 250.

255 *He elaborated*: DC 4/28/65, "To the Berkeley Students and Faculty," in 100-54060-193.

256 *Suzanne Goldberg recalled*: Goldberg shared her insights in an interview with the author and in her essay, "Mario, Personal and Political," in *The Free Speech Movement: Reflections on Berkeley in the 1960s*, 557.

256 *Savio's dilemma*: Savio discussed his paradoxical relationship with the media in "The Reminiscences of Mario Savio," op. cit., 60–66.

256 *The New York Times*: NYT 12/9/64, "His Friends Look on Savio as a 'Genius'"; NYT 12/9/64, "A Rebel on Campus, Mario Savio."

256 *Savio had no*: Author interview with Savio.

256 *But whatever prompted*: DC, 4/28/65, "To the Berkeley Students and Faculty," in 100-54060-193.

257 *A few weeks*: Savio's visit to the FBI is described in 100-54060-210; author interview with Alex Hoffman.

257 *Five days later*: This paragraph and the next are based on NYT 5/18/65, "Hoover Links Reds"; *Chicago Tribune* 5/18/65, "Hoover Links Reds"; LAT 5/18/65, "Hoover Links Subversives"; LAT 5/19/65, "Red Influence at Berkeley Denied"; SFNCB 5/18/65, "Reds Linked"; BDG 5/18/65, "Subversives in FSM"; SFX 5/18/65, "Reds Involved" and "Reds Blamed."

257 *Neil Smelser . . . "civil rights movement"*: LAT 5/19/65, "Red Influence at Berkeley Denied."

258 *In reply to Hoover's . . . "gentleman"*: Ibid.

258 *Bettina Aptheker*: Intimate Politics, 134.

258 *She and Savio . . . "University of California"*: 100-151646-145.

258 *The regents William Roth . . . cabinet secretary*: LAT 9/7/85, "Philanthropist Developed Ghirardelli"; LAT 6/27/05, "Fred Dutton"; author interviews with Dutton, Roth, and William Coblentz.

258 *The day after*: This paragraph is based on 100-151646-143. In separate interviews, Roth and Dutton denied seeking information from the FBI.

258 *A few days*: New York Herald Tribune 5/23/65, "New Breed of Student," in 100-151646-NR, before 100-151646-150.

259 *Appalled*: 100-151646-NR, 5/25/65, before 100-151646-150.

17: Vietnam Day

260 *"Hot damn, Vietnam!"*: Transcripts of the Vietnam Day speeches by Mailer and other speakers were published as *We Accuse*, copy in VDC file 100-55462-A. Vietnam Day was also the subject of a documentary, *Vietnam Day, Berkeley*, directed by Ernest Callenbach et al., Pacifica Film Archive, UC Berkeley.

260 *Blue-eyed*: On Mailer, see NYT 11/11/07, "Norman Mailer, Towering Writer." *Berkeley at War*, 92, states Mailer was drunk and that KPFA cut its broadcast because of his profanities.

261 *Vietnam Day was*: This paragraph is based on *Out Now!*, 45–61; *Stephen Smale: The Mathematician Who Broke the Dimension Barrier*, 93–127; NYT 5/23/65, "33-Hour Teach-In"; *Berkeley at War*, 91–92; author interviews with Jerry Rubin, Stew Albert, Steve Smale, Morris Hirsch, and Paul Montauk.

261 *The event*: For this and the next two paragraphs, on the Vietnam War and the U.S. antiwar movement, see *A People's History of the United States*, 469–501; *Stephen Smale*, 94–97. On the advent of teach-ins, which originated at the University of Michigan, see *Out Now!*, 45–61.

262 *Jerry Rubin*: This paragraph and the next are based on *Stephen Smale*, 93–104; *Out Now!*, 57–61; *Berkeley at War*, 92; *Do It!*; *Growing (Up) at 37*; NYT 11/30/94, "Jerry Rubin"; LAT 5/14/69, "Jerry Rubin"; WP 4/27/69, "Profile of a Revolutionary"; NYT 9/12/65, "New Vietnam Protest"; 100-55462-2; author interviews with Rubin, Albert, and Hurwitt. Although Rubin claims in *Growing (Up) at 37* that he attended "every" FSM activity, Gullahorn recalled in *Stephen Smale* that he was much less involved, a recollection supported by the author's interview with Stew Albert.

262 *Vietnam Day represented*: On the New Left, see also *The Sixties: Years of Hope, Days of Rage*.

263 *The speakers had*: For the speakers' statements, see *We Accuse*, copy in VDC file 100-55462-A; NYT 5/23/65, "33-Hour Teach-In"; audio recordings of Vietnam Day speeches, Pacifica Radio Archives, North Hollywood, Calif.

263 *The U.S. State Department*: The empty chair is noted in *Berkeley at War*, 92.

263 *I. F. Stone*: NYT 6/19/89, "I. F. Stone"; *Berkeley at War*, 92.

263 *Benjamin Spock*: On Spock, see NYT 3/17/98, "Benjamin Spock, World's Pediatrician."

263 *His theories vexed*: Sherriffs discussed Spock and overly permissive parents in Rowland interview with Sherriffs, op. cit., 31–32; *Alex Sherriffs, Education Advisor to Ronald Reagan and State University Administrator, 1969–1982*, an oral history conducted by Gabrielle Morris and Sara Sharp in 1981 and 1982, Bancroft, 12, 15, 59–60, 74; LAT 1/8/68, "Reagan's New Education Aide."

263 *Now Savio*: *We Accuse*, copy in 100-55462-A; Pacifica Radio Archives.

264 *Stepping to*: On Gregory and *Nigger*, see LAT 9/12/65, "Best-selling Hardbacks"; NYT 11/1/64, "First of All a Man." George Lincoln Rockwell founded the American Nazi Party, NYT 8/26/67, "Rockwell, U.S. Nazi."

265 *FBI agents* were: 100-444372-16; 105-138315-139.

265 *Even before Vietnam Day*: 100-151646-NR, Baumgardner to Sullivan, 5/21/65, and 100-151646-NR, Director to San Francisco, 5/21/65, both behind 100-151646-146; 100-3-104-47-illegible, 6/10/65, in CP USA COINTELPRO files, reproduced by Scholarly Resources, Inc., 1978.

265 *"The Berkeley technique"*: SFX 5/19/65, "The Disruptions from the Left," copy enclosed with 100-3-104-47-illegible, 6/10/65, CP USA COINTELPRO files, reproduced by Scholarly Resources, Inc., 1978.

265 *Lynum told Hoover*: 100-3-104-47-illegible, 6/10/65, CP USA COINTELPRO files, reproduced by Scholarly Resources, Inc.

265 *But the FBI's editorializing . . . Vietnam Day Committee*: *Stephen Smale*, 103–106; *Out Now!*, 54, 69, 70, 75, 84–89; author interviews with Paul Montauk, Jerry Rubin, Joe Blum, and Stew Albert. The VDC and the FBI's surveillance and harassment of it are discussed in DC 6/4/82, "Of Spies & Radicals," by Seth Rosenfeld.

266 *In July 1965*: The description of the VDC is based on author interviews with Paul Montauk, Jerry Rubin, Stew Albert, Rob Hurwitt, Stephen Smale, Morris Hirsch, Joe Blum, and Mike O'Hanlon (Francis Medaille). The VDC is also described in *Stephen Smale*; *Out Now!*; *Berkeley at War*; *Who the Hell Is Stew Albert?*, 32–52; *Do It!*, 32–46; *Growing (Up) at 37*, 79–82; SFX 8/23/65, "Berkeley Pickets' Nerve Center," in 100-55462-134.

266 *Allen Ginsberg*: Ginsberg's involvement with the VDC is described in *Dharma Lion* and *Berkeley at War*.

267 *Ginsberg's presence*: This paragraph is based on FBI memo concerning Allen Ginsberg 105-137059-6, in Allen Ginsberg Correspondence Collection, Stanford University, Special Collections, MO733.

267 *In fact, Ginsberg*: *Dharma Lion*, 452–55; *Who the Hell Is Stew Albert?*, 44; author interview with Rob Hurwitt.

267 *Michael O'Hanlon*: This and the next two paragraphs are based on author interviews with O'Hanlon (Francis Medaille) and Albert; *Who the Hell Is Stew Albert?*, 35; *DC* 3/23/66, O'Hanlon/Medaille letter in "Letters to the Ice Box." Further source material on him is in the notes for Chapter 19.
268 *Despite their diversity*: For an explicit statement, see the VDC leaflet "International Days of Protest" in 100-55462-200.
268 *"Vietnam, like Mississippi . . ."*: The quotes are excerpted from *Vietnam Day Committee News*, vol. 1, no. 2, July–August 1965, in 100-55462-11.
268 *On July 29*: The account of the rally is based on 100-55462-39; 100-444372-16; 100-51646-166, 7/29/65; 100-151646-166, 8/3/65; 100-151646-169, 8/2/65; 100-151646-169, 8/3/65; 100-151646-170; 100-34204-1667; 100-34204-1698; *LAT* 7/27/65, "Savio Given"; *SFC* 7/30/65, "UC Rallies Protest"; *SFX* 7/30/65, "UC Sit-Ins Shy Bail Money" (with photo of Aptheker); *LAT* 7/30/65, "1,500 Protest Terms"; *OT* 7/30/65, "Jail Term for Sit-In"; *NYT* 9/2/56, "West Coast Rhythms"; *LAT* 3/7/61, "Another Look at the Beatniks"; *NYT* 1/18/92, "Thomas Parkinson"; *Berkeley at War*, 43–44; *Intimate Politics*, 160–61. Both *Intimate Politics* and FBI files discuss this incident. The American Trust Building had been renamed Wells Fargo.
269 *Jones had been*: This paragraph is based on *Intimate Politics*, 108, 116, 117–18, 120–21; 100-151646-169, 8/2/65.
269 *But the FBI agent*: The account of Jones's and other FBI officials' reactions to Aptheker exposing him is based on 100-151646-166, 7/29/65; 100-151646-166, 8/3/65; 100-151646-169, 8/2/65; 100-151646-169, 8/3/65; 100-151646-170.
270 *One day Mike O'Hanlon*: This paragraph is based on author interview with O'Hanlon.
270 *When the troop train*: The account of the troop train protests in this and the following paragraphs is drawn from 105-138315-2984, pp. 114–20; *SFX* 8/6/65, "Pacifists Try to Ambush," in 100-55462-31; 100-55462-32; 100-55462-33; *BDG* 8/5/65, "Pickets with Banner Leap," in 100-55462-35; 100-55462-43; 100-55462-50; *SFC* 8/13/65, "Battle over Train," in 100-55462-53; *SFX* 8/13/65, "6 Anti-Viet War," in 100-55462-54; 100-55462-60; *OT* 8/12/65, "Protesters Warned," in 100-55462-62; 100-55462-63; *OT* 8/13/65, "Protesters Halt Train," in 100-55462-69; 100-55462-78; 100-55462-79; *NYT* 8/7/65, "Demonstrators Try"; 100-444372-10; Vietnam Day Committee, Summary Report, 12/10/65, Berkeley Chief of Police A. H. Fording, series 2003/326, box C, Heirich Papers, Bancroft; *Stephen Smale*, 104–13; *Do It!*, 32–37; *Berkeley at War*, 93–94; *Growing (Up) at* 37, 80; author interview with O'Hanlon.
271 *FBI agents who had*: 100-55462-32; 100-55462-33; 100-55462-34; 100-55462-43; 100-55462-49; 100-55462-50; 100-55462-63; 100-55462-78; 100-55462-79; 100-444372-10; author interview with O'Hanlon.
271 *Perched high atop*: The account of the Fairmont protest and the FBI surveillance of it is based on *Stephen Smale*, 113; *SFNCB* 8/25/65, "Demonstrators Infiltrate," in 100-55462-135; 100-55462-138; *SFX* 8/25/65, "A Rude Welcome," in 100-55462-138; 100-55462-139; 100-55462-140; 100-55462-141; *SFNCB* 8/27/65, "Jury Trial Set," in 100-55462-148; *OT* 8/25/65, "Gen. Taylor Target," in 100-55462-150; 105-138315-2984, pp. 120–22; 100-55462-194; 100-55462-214; 100-55462-371; 100-444372-NR after serial 13; author interviews with Threadgill and O'Hanlon. On the Fairmont, see www.fairmont.com/sanfrancisco/AboutUs/HotelHistory.htm, accessed 1/4/11.
271 *Taylor had been*: On Taylor, see *NYT* 4/21/87, "Maxwell D. Taylor"; *LAT* 4/21/87, "Gen. Maxwell Taylor"; *NYT* 8/26/65, "Taylor Says Communists." The VDC leaflets on Taylor are in 100-55462-125 and 100-55462-126.
272 *Emboldened*: *SFC* 9/10/65, "Big Peace March," in 100-55462-204; *NYT* 9/12/65, "New Vietnam Protest"; VDC leaflets in 100-55462-14; 100-444372-15; 100-444372-21, with flyer "Oct. 15–16"; *Out Now!*, 89.

272 *As announced by*: The leaflet "News from the Vietnam Day Committee" is in 100-55462-14.
272 *With the protests*: This paragraph and the next are based on 100-444372-15; 100-444372-21; *National Guardian* 9/4/65, in 100-55462-206; VDC leaflet, "Vietnam Day Committee Oct. 15–16," in 100-55462-210; *VDC News*, in 100-55462-11; 105-138315-2984, pp. 125–26; *NYT* 9/12/65, "New Vietnam Protest"; *NYT* 10/16/65, "Policy in Vietnam Scored"; *SFX* 10/17/65, "Melee at Oakland Border"; *Stephen Smale*, 113–20; author interviews with O'Hanlon and Hurwitt.
272 *The VDC's plans . . . "at this time"*: 100-55462-13.
272 *On August 12*: 100-444372-1.
273 *As the Church committee*: Church, book III, 26.
273 *More than a dozen*: The agents are noted throughout 100-55462 and 100-444372.
273 *They obtained lists*: 100-55462-481; 100-55462-570; 100-55462-122.
273 *They obtained the organization's . . . denied it*: 100-55462-218; 100-55462-929.
273 *Other agents tracked . . . upside down*: 100-55462-617.
273 *The buttons were*: 100-55462-551.
273 *Dick Leonard*: 100-444372-16; 100-55462-169; 100-55462-195; 100-55462-14; 100-55462-1A Section 7; author interview with Curtis O. Lynum.
273 *A San Francisco Examiner*: 100-55462-195; 100-55462-1A(1).
273 *Ed Montgomery*: 100-55462-84.
273 *Alex Sherriffs . . . medical history*: 100-444372-NR after 100-444372-13 dated 8/26/65 (Weissman medical record); 100-55462-34; 100-55462-137; 100-55462-151; 100-55462-202. Sherriffs states he was forced to resign as vice chancellor for student affairs soon after Roger Heyns became chancellor in July 1965, but continued to teach. See Rowland interview with Sherriffs, op. cit., 62–64. On Sherriffs's replacement by John Searle, see *LAT* 9/16/65, ". . . And FSM Leader Sees Calm." By mid-September 1965 Sherriffs was on sabbatical, 100-55462-215.
273 *Informers recruited*: See 100-55462-686; 100-55462-688; 100-55462-1022; 100-55462-222; 100-55462-373; 100-55462-418; 100-55462-438; 100-55462-429; 100-55462-420; 100-55462-440; 100-55462-442; 100-55462-443; 100-55462-461; 100-555462-222; 100-55642-774; 100-55462-783.
273 *At least two infiltrators . . . to the FBI*: Author interview with Hurwitt.
274 *Jerry Rubin and other*: Author interviews with Rubin, Albert, Hurwitt, Weissman, and O'Hanlon.
274 *Mike O'Hanlon recalled*: Author interview with O'Hanlon.
274 *Rob Hurwitt*: Author interview with Hurwitt.
274 *Hurwitt and O'Hanlon*: Author interviews with Hurwitt and O'Hanlon.
274 *FBI agents took*: 100-55462-404; 100-55462-512; 100-55462-584; 100-55462-571; 100-55462-568; 100-55462-936.
274 *Agents also told . . . "event of an emergency . . ."*: 100-55462-512.
274 *Edwin Meese III*: This paragraph is based on 100-55462-379; *With Reagan*, 28–29; *For the People*, 74, 160–61, 244, 229; author interview with Burney Threadgill, Jr.; Testimony of Edwin Meese III, Investigative Hearings, Committee on Un-American Activities, House of Representatives, 89th Congress, August 17 and 18, 1965. It should be noted that the district attorney's intelligence unit dated at least to the 1930s tenure of District Attorney Earl Warren, *Cloak and Gavel*, 48.
274 *Meese also collaborated*: In addition to the instances cited in the text, see 100-55462-529, in which he alerted the FBI to the VDC's application for a parade permit that was filed by Mike O'Hanlon.
274 *He produced*: 100-55462-355.
275 *In early October . . . easier to handle*: 100-55462-569.

275 *Police officials:* The discussion re "instant banana peel" is based on the author's interview with William Beall, former chief of both UC Berkeley police and City of
Berkeley police.

275 *With the big march:* This paragraph is based on 100-55462-379; Stephen Smale,
118–19.

275 *Lieutenant Colonel Schroy:* This paragraph is based on 100-55462-379.

275 *Agent Albert Clark:* 100-55462-379.

275 *But neither Clark nor:* Neither the FBI memo on this meeting, 100-55462-379, nor
other bureau records released to the author, indicate FBI officials advised other law-
enforcement and military agencies coping with the VDC's protests about the bureau's COINTELPRO campaign to disrupt the VDC. As the Church committee
noted, COINTELPRO operations were "not directed at obtaining evidence for use
in possible criminal prosecutions" arising from student and antiwar protests.
"Rather, they were secret programs—'under no circumstances' to be 'made known
outside the Bureau'—which used unlawful or improper acts to 'disrupt' or 'neutralize' the activities of groups and individuals on the basis of imprecise criteria,"
Church, book II, 86. The committee found that some COINTELPRO actions were
illegal or dangerous, and others "can only be described as 'abhorrent in a free society,'" Church, book III, 8. COINTELPRO targeted people involved in lawful dissent, Church, book II, 211–13.

275 *Hoover had initiated . . . "can be exploited . . .":* This paragraph is based on
100-444372-19.

276 *Lynum assured:* This paragraph and the next two are based on 100-444372-76.

276 *Coakley called it:* OT 10/14/65, "Coakley Warning"; OT 10/15/65, "Protesters Vow to
Defy Parade Ban"; OT 10/14/65, "Oakland Bans Viet Day Parade."

276 *But as people gathered:* This paragraph is based on LAT 10/16/65, "UC March
Avoids Showdown"; 100-55462-564; 100-55462-1057.

277 *The most peculiar:* The Electric Kool-Aid Acid Test, 216–20.

277 *This was the result:* Ibid.

277 *Deep in the redwoods . . . "manuscript":* Prime Green, 89–90.

277 *The Pranksters had repainted . . . north toward Berkeley:* The Electric Kool-Aid Acid
Test, 216–20.

277 *Kesey's crew:* The account of the police stop is from 100-55462-564; The Electric
Kool-Aid Acid Test, 219; author interview with Lee Quarnstrom.

277 *Arriving at campus . . . "Fuck it . . .":* The Electric Kool-Aid Acid Test, 220–25.

278 *Even as protesters:* This paragraph is based on OT 10/15/65, "Protesters Vow to Defy
Parade Ban"; OT 10/16/65, "2 Federal Courts Uphold Denial of March Permits";
LAT 10/16/65, "UC March Avoids Showdown"; The Electric Kool-Aid Acid Test, 217;
author interview with Rob Hurwitt.

278 *Nonetheless, as night:* LAT 10/16/65, "UC March Avoids Showdown"; OT 10/15/65,
"Protesters Vow to Defy Parade Ban"; OT 10/14/65, "Oakland Bans Viet Day Parade."

278 *First came:* This paragraph is based on LAT 10/16/65, "UC March Avoids Showdown"; OT 10/16/65, "Police Lines"; Dharma Lion, 452; author interviews with
Hurwitt, Weissman, and O'Hanlon.

278 *FBI agents in cars:* 100-55462-1057; 100-55462-936.

278 *Lawrence Cott:* 100-55462-1009.

279 *As the forefront:* The account of the march to the Oakland border, the police block-
ade, and the encampment at Civic Center Plaza is based on 100-444372-53;
100-444372-54; 100-444372-56; 100-444372-57; 100-444372-61; 100-444372-62;
100-444372-65; 100-444372-69; NYT 10/16/65, "10,000 Turn Back in a Coast
March"; OT 10/16/65, "Police Lines Turn Back"; LAT 10/16/65, "UC March Avoids

Showdown"; *DC* 10/18/65, "7000 March Down Telegraph"; *OT* 10/17/65, "Hell's Angels Attack"; *OT* 10/28/65, "Hell's Angel Hearing Set"; *Do It!* 39–43; *The Electric Kool-Aid Acid Test*, 225–26; author interviews with Hurwitt, O'Hanlon, and Melton.

280 *Five thousand people*: The account of the second march and the Hell's Angels attack on it is based on 100-444372-52; 100-444372-55; 100-444372-58; 100-444372-60; 100-444372-69; 100-444372-47; *OT* 10/17/65, "Hell's Angels Attack"; *LAT* 10/17/65, "Hell's Angels Attack"; *NYT* 10/17/65, "Cyclists Break Up"; *SFX* 10/17/65, "Melee at Oakland Border"; *DC* 10/18/65, "Hell's Angels Attack March"; *"Do It!* 43–44; *Hell's Angels, A Strange and Terrible Saga*, 244–46; author interviews with Hurwitt, O'Hanlon, and Conn "Ringo" Hallinan.

280 *Tucked behind . . . rioting*: *LAT* 3/16/65, "Hell's Angels Called Threat"; *LAT* 6/22/65, "32 Arraigned"; *LAT* 7/6/65, "Eight Suspects Held"; *LAT* 6/20/65, "Police, Troops Quell Resort"; *Hell's Angels*.

280 *FBI agents noticed . . . "coming into Oakland"*: 100-44372-60.

280 *Conn "Ringo" Hallinan . . . "We lost contact"*: Author interviews with Hurwitt and Hallinan.

281 *Ralph H. "Sonny" Barger . . . Oakland police line*: Author interview with Hurwitt.

281 *At this point*: *DC* 10/18/65, "Hell's Angels Attack."

281 *Chief Toothman . . . "bad repute"*: *OT* 10/20/65, "Heyns Bars Organizing on Campus"; *SFX* 10/19/65, "Chief Defends."

281 *Hunter Thompson . . . "protest march . . ."*: *Hell's Angels*, 245.

281 *Robert Stone . . . "attack the demonstrators"*: *Prime Green*, 207.

281 *Robert Scheer gave . . . "in California"*: *DC* 10/18/65, "Hell's Angels Attack."

281 *Sonny Barger would*: *Hell's Angel: The Life and Times of Sonny Barger and the Hell's Angels Motorcycle Club*, pp. 120–21.

282 *FBI agents had known . . . "showing their patriotism"*: 100-444372-60.

282 *But FBI agents*: Author interviews with Hurwitt and O'Hanlon.

282 *In the weeks before*: 100-55462-584.

282 *And though they . . . Lynum reported*: 100-3-104-47-368, 11/16/65.

282 *The director's aides*: 100-3-104-47-368, 12/1/65.

282 *VDC leaders had instigated . . . a parade permit*: *WP* 10/18/65, "Viet War Protests End on West Coast"; *NYT* 10/18/65, "Vietnam Protest Called a Success"; *LAT* 10/17/65, "Nationwide Protest Rallies Plagued by Hecklers"; *Stephen Smale*, 121, 123; *Growing (Up)* at 37, 81.

282 *Assemblyman Don Mulford*: This paragraph is based on *OT* 10/15/65, "Protesters Vow to Defy Parade Ban."

283 *District Attorney Coakley*: *OT* 10/27/65, "UC Given a Warning by Unruh."

283 *And U.S. Senator*: *LAT* 10/24/65, "Perspective"; *LAT* 10/13/65, "Avert UC Disorder."

283 *Conservative anger*: This paragraph and the next are based on Thirteenth Report, Un-American Activities in California, 1965, Senate Factfinding Subcommittee on Un-American Activities, California Legislature.

283 *The report also charged*: Ibid., 145–46.

283 *Both Combs and the FBI*: 100-151646-89; 100-151646-90; 100-151646-91; 100-151646-80, 1/27/65.

283 *Now the latest Burns report*: *SFNCB* 6/18/65, "Report on UC Rebellion—Kerr Is Called Too Tolerant," in 100-151646-153; *SFX* 6/19/65, "Probers Blame," in 100-34204-1603; *SFX* 6/19/65, "Teale Calls It," in 100-34204-1599.

284 *Kerr indignantly denied . . . "on campus"*: *SFNCB* 6/18/65, "Kerr Charges Report," in 100-151646-153.

284 *Claiming the report . . . Burns declined*: *LAT* 10/6/65, "Brown Joins Attack on UC Report"; *LAT* 10/5/65, "Kerr Challenges"; Kerr, vol. 2, 62–64.

284 *With impeccable*: SFNCB 6/18/65, "Kerr Charges Report," in 100-151646-153; SFX 6/19/65, "President's Defense," in 100-34204-1602.

284 *Alex Sherriffs had kept*: 100-151642-152; 100-151642-154.

284 *Sherriffs had become*: 100-151642-152; 100-55462-551; author interview with John Sparrow.

284 *As of late June . . . not giving up*: 100-151642-154; 100-151642-155; 100-151642-168.

284 *Hardin Jones*: Jones informant file 134-deleted shows that he was a Potential Security Informant, someone who is paid for information, but that as of October 28, 1965, the FBI agent handling him concluded his information was not worth money. "A review of the file and personal contact with PSI," the agent wrote, "fails to reflect that he is in a position to furnish information of continuing value. It is suggested that PSI be utilized as an Established [*sic*] source at the University of California in the future and this case be closed." Jones continued to supply the FBI with information in that capacity, as recorded in bureau files.

284 *Meeting at*: This meeting is described in 100-151646-174.

284 *The next day*: This meeting is in 100-151646-172.

285 *Lynum immediately*: Lynum's report is in 100-151646-172 and 100-151646-173.

285 *A few weeks later*: Jones's October 5, 1965, visit to FBI HQ is described in 100-151646-174X.

286 *Ed Pauley eagerly*: This October 20, 1965, meeting and Grapp's reaction are described in 100-151646-178; author interview with Grapp.

287 *With a jagged scrawl*: 100-151646-179.

287 *And to preempt*: 100-151646-184; 100-151646-185.

287 *So Hoover emphasized*: 100-151646-176.

287 *The resulting report*: The report and cover memo are in 100-151646-183. The memorandum, dated 11/1/65, does not distinguish between the number of people on the Security Index and the number on the Reserve Index. The Reserve Index was created in June 1960, three months after the March 1960 report that listed 72 people on the Security Index. Church, book III, 446, 447, 468.

287 *By the end*: 100-151646-178.

287 *FBI officials*: 100-151646-179.

18: The Governor's Race

291 *With a fire*: LAT 1/5/66, "Reagan Announces"; NYT 1/5/66, "Reagan Enters"; *Governor Reagan*, 141.

291 *To Hoover*: This paragraph is based on the author's review of Reagan FBI file 100-382196 and interviews with former FBI officials, including Cartha DeLoach, Curtis O. Lynum, Glenn Harter, and Burney Threadgill, Jr.

291 *Along the way*: The FBI compiled several politically oriented files on Reagan in his prepresidential years, including HQ 100-382196, field office files LA 80-579 and SF 80-990, and numerous cross-references concerning him in files on other subjects. When he became governor of California, the FBI also conducted background investigations of him because he would have access to classified information at the University of California's nuclear facilities. In response to the author's lawsuit under the FOIA, the FBI by letter dated September 3, 2010, stated it had processed 7,474 pages on Reagan from FBI HQ and the San Francisco, Los Angeles, San Diego, Sacramento, and Washington field offices, and was releasing 6,398 pages. The FBI claimed these were all responsive nonexempt records covering the earliest documents in its files up to January 1, 1979. By letter dated September 28, 2010, the FBI stated it had reviewed an additional 829 pages of which it was releasing 743 pages

from documents listed in "summary memos" concerning Reagan within the same time frame.

291 *In 1960 . . . he declared*: 80-579-3; LAT 10/2/60, "40 Section Chairmen for Nixon Drive Named."

291 *In an address . . . "them a hand"*: Chicago Daily News 5/8/61, "Warns Reds," in 100-138754-1216.

292 *Hoover saw*: This anecdote is based on 100-138754-1220. A reprint of Reagan's talk by the Super Market Institute, titled "Encroachments of Our Freedom," shows the newspaper report that said he had claimed the Communist Party "has ordered once again the infiltration" of the movie and television industry and "they are crawling out from under the rocks" was accurate. Reprint provided to the author by the Food Marketing Institute.

292 *Reagan soon made*: This paragraph and the next are based on 100-382196 NR, 10/26/61, and 100-382196 NR, 11/9/1961. On Church, see NYT 4/8/84, "Frank Church of Idaho."

293 *The following year . . . "and society"*: LAT 8/31/62, "Rousselot Criticizes Kennedy's Cuba Policy."

293 *In March 1962 . . . Miller's husband*: 100-375582-152; 100-340922-480; the show on Marion Miller was called *My Dark Days*, www.tvrage.com/shows/id-3652/episode _guide/, accessed 5/12/11.

293 *Later that year*: This paragraph is based on *Reagan's America*, 284; *Governor Reagan*, 109–14; *Don't Know Much About History*, 352; "From the New Deal to the New Century," TVA website, www.tva.gov/abouttva/history.htm, accessed 5/12/11; author interview with George Dalen.

293 *Reagan was disappointed*: Governor Reagan, 109–14.

293 *Nineteen sixty-two*: Ronald Reagan Pre-presidential Biographical Sketch, RRPL, www.reagan.utexas.edu/archives/reference/prepresbio.html, accessed 5/12/11.

293 *He again backed*: LAT 8/30/62, "Republican Clubs Sponsor"; "RN and RR," the New Nixon Blog, the Richard Nixon Foundation, blog.nixonfoundation.org/2011/02 /rn-and-rr/, accessed 5/12/11.

293 *All along, Reagan*: Reagan's periodic contacts with FBI officials are noted in his FBI files, particularly HQ 100-382196, field office files LA 80-579 and SF 80-990, and cross-references.

293 *He was a guest*: 80-579-3; William G. Simon to President Reagan, 4/17/81, President Reagan Records, RRPL, Felt/Miller Pardon File, released in response to author's FOIA request, FOIA F04-113 and FOIA F05-117.

293 *Hoover's aides*: This paragraph is based on HQ 62-108049-40.

294 *That spring*: This and the next two paragraphs are based on 100-434516-143 EBF; 100-434516-63, 5/28/62, YAF fundraising letter, Reagan to Hoover.

294 *In fact*: 100-434516- NR, 5/11/61, before 100-434516-13, in HQ file on YAF. Hoover at the time was wary of the FBI becoming involved with the YAF because of the group's possible ties to the John Birch Society. Nonetheless, HQ authorized the New York FBI field office to submit proposals for using the YAF in COINTELPRO operations. In 1964, the YAF's executive director told FBI agents the organization's records were open to the FBI and that he hoped the bureau would warn the YAF if it discovered that any of its members were doing anything that would embarrass the group. See 100-434516-NR, 4/13/61; 100-434516-NR, 4/10/61, after 100-434516-11; 100-434516-143; 100-434516-147. In 1965, HQ officials approved the S.F. FBI field office covertly using the YAF to distribute leaflets attacking the W.E.B. Du Bois Club that were prepared by the FBI. See 100-3-104-47-509, 6/11/65; 100-3-104-47-NR,

6/14/65; 100-3-104-47-NR, 6/16/65; 100-3-104-illegible; all in Scholarly Resources microfilm COINTELPRO collection, Doe Library, UC Berkeley.

294 *Later in 1964*: 100-382196-7.

294 *But it was*: The excerpts of the speech are from the text of "A Time for Choosing," given on October 27, 1964. It is available at www.reagan.utexas.edu/archives/reference /timechoosing.html, accessed 5/12/11. A video of the talk was viewed at www.you tube.com/watch?v=qXBswFfh6AY, accessed 5/12/11.

296 *The speech was widely*: According to the political journalists David Broder and Steven Hess, Reagan's pitch for Goldwater was "the most successful national political debut since William Jennings Bryan electrified the 1896 Democratic Convention with the 'Cross of Gold' speech," quoted in *Before the Storm*, 504. See also NYT 1/23/65, "Reagan Weighing New Role."

296 *Reagan was reluctant*: This paragraph is based on "Neil Reagan, Private Dimensions and Public Images: The Early Political Campaigns of Ronald Reagan," An Interview Conducted by Stephen Stern, 1981, UCLA, 20–22, 23, 35–36; "On Becoming Governor," Ronald Reagan Oral History, by Sarah Sharp and Gabrielle Morris, in *Governor Reagan and His Cabinet: An Introduction*, Bancroft, 3, 4; NYT 6/18/89, "Holmes Tuttle"; NYT 8/13/64, "Reagan to Be New Host"; LAT 1/22/65, "Reagan to Decide Soon on Running for Office"; *Ronnie & Jesse*, 71–72, 73, 74; *Governor Reagan*, 133–34, 136; *Early Reagan*, 479, 489–90.

297 *In January 1965, FBI*: The FBI investigation of the Bonanno crime family is described in *Honor Thy Father* and *A Man of Honor*. See also LAT 10/21/64, "N.Y. Gang Kidnap"; NYT 10/21/64, "'Joe Bananas'"; NYT 12/30/64, "Son of Bonanno."

297 *Hoover had long*: This paragraph is based on *A Man of Honor*, 220, 224, 225, 230, 232, 259; *Kennedy Justice*, 45, 46, 48, 49, 51, 55, 61, 63, 65, 67, 77; *J. Edgar Hoover: The Man and the Secrets*, 452–53, 454, 456, 474, 532–33; *Honor Thy Father*, 97, 105–106, 108, 109; *Rearview Mirror*, 9; *The Bureau: The Secret History of the FBI*, 112–15; NYT 8/7/63, "Crime Syndicate Is Seeking Revenge"; NYT 9/29/63, "Mafia Wields Sinister Power"; NYT 2/13/64, "Grand Jury Calls"; NYT 12/22/64, "Jury Waits"; NYT 12/23/64, "More Questioned"; NYT 1/1/65, "U.S. Jury Told Bonanno Heads"; NYT 1/5/65, "Three Children of Bonanno"; NYT 1/6/65, "1,500 in 5 Crime"; NYT 1/15/65, "Reputed Chieftain"; NYT 1/20/65, "Bonanno Jury"; NYT 2/14/65, "Mafia Steps Up"; NYT 3/3/65, "Bonanno Son Gets."

297 *So it was that . . . "numerous occasions"*: LA 80-579-3, pp. 4, 5, 6.

297 *As his older brother*: Honor Thy Father, 27.

297 *Joe Bonanno, Jr.*: On Joe Jr., see *Honor Thy Father*, 27, 100–101, 109, 364–71, 366, 367; *A Man of Honor*, 193, 230, 315, 317, 319, 328. On his later criminal problems, see *A Man of Honor*, 320, 343, 344.

297 *In October 1964*: Chicago Tribune 2/19/65, "Bonanno's Son"; Chicago Tribune 3/12/65, "Bonanno's Son." The booking log made available to the author by the Scottsdale Police Department public information officer Sergeant Mark Clark shows Bonanno's arrest on October 6, 1964.

297 *In January 1965, The New York Times*: NYT 1/5/65, "Three Children of Bonanno"; NYT 1/6/65, "1,500 in 5 Crime."

298 *Moreover, according to*: LA 80-579-3, pp. 4, 5, 6.

298 *Following routine procedure*: LA 80-579-3, pp. 4–5. It is standard procedure for one FBI field office to ask another field office to handle such "leads" in the latter's geographic area. Author interview with Curtis O. Lynum.

298 *It is also possible*: The FBI's attempt to use David Hill, Jr., as an informer is described

in *A Man of Honor*, 330, 331, 332, which states Hill was briefly an informer but then quit and told Joe Bonanno about it; *Honor Thy Father*, 368, 369, which states Hill refused the FBI's entreaties; *Time* 8/22/69, which also reports that Hill refused.

298 *But Hoover interceded*: This paragraph is based on LA 80-579-3, p. 5. Reagan's "cordial" relationship with the Los Angeles FBI office is noted in 100-382196-7.

298 *Reagan was very*: LA 80-579-3, pp. 5–6.

298 *The gubernatorial race*: *Reagan*, 109; *Ronnie & Jesse*, 76, 78; *LAT* 5/28/66, "Reagan vs. Christopher."

298 *Brown's supporters also*: *Reagan*, 116; *Ronnie & Jesse*, 80–82; *LAT* 8/12/66, "Coate Says Report Proves."

298 *William Roth*: Author interview with William Roth.

298 *Indeed*: This paragraph is based on LA 80-579-3, pp. 5–6.

299 *Here was*: Reagan's anti-big-government stance is discussed in many works, including *Reagan*, 98–100, 108.

299 *The FBI tried*: This paragraph is based on Memorandum & Order, Re: Second set of Cross-Motions for Summary Judgment, *Seth Rosenfeld v. U.S. Department of Justice and Federal Bureau of Investigation*, C-07-3240 MHP, 9/1/10.

299 *In an interview*: Author interview with Edwin Meese III.

299 *Only Michael Reagan*: Michael Reagan's account is from *On the Outside Looking In*, 102–103. Joe Bonanno, Jr., died in 2005.

300 *Newspapers continued*: *The New York Times*, the *Chicago Tribune*, the *Los Angeles Times*, and *The Washington Post* each continued to cover the Bonanno story.

300 *When Reagan first heard*: "On Becoming Governor," Ronald Reagan Oral History, by Sarah Sharp and Gabrielle Morris, in *Governor Reagan and His Cabinet: An Introduction*, Bancroft, 29, 20–21.

300 *Speaking at the Greater*: His comments at the press club are from *LAT* 1/22/65, "Reagan to Decide Soon."

301 *On March 17, 1965*: This paragraph and the next are based on 100-382196-7.

301 *In the following*: This paragraph is based on *LAT* 10/12/65, "Statement by Reagan on Viet War Criticized"; *LAT* 10/14/65, "Politicians Periling Peaceful"; *LAT* 10/21/65, "Reagan Urges Johnson to Tell Vietnam Facts"; "Announcement Day Press Conference . . . Statler Hilton, Pacific Ballroom, Jan. 4, 1966," Reagan Gubernatorial Papers, RRPL, folder: 66 Campaign Speeches, book 1; "On Becoming Governor," op. cit., 18; author interviews with Curtis O. Lynum and Burney Threadgill, Jr.

301 *A few days after . . . "their homework"*: OT 10/22/65, "Reagan Critical of UC Officialdom." On Reagan's use of the word *appeasement*, see *LAT* 2/16/64, "Young GOP Refuses"; *NYT* 1/23/65, "Reagan Weighing"; *NYT* 11/14/65, "The Ronald Reagan Story"; "Time for Choosing Speech, October 27, 1964," RRPL, www.reagan.utexas.edu /archives/reference/reference.html#Ronald_Reagan, accessed 5/13/11.

301 *On December 8, 1965*: OT 12/9/65, "Reagan on Verge of Declaring," RRPL, Reagan Gubernatorial Papers, folder "66 ED University of California 1 of 2."

302 *By now, Berkeley*: *Reagan*, 113–14.

302 *Reagan was tapping . . . political target*: *Reagan*, 108, 110, 148; *Governor Reagan*, 9, 150, 157.

302 *That January, 1966, Reagan*: The description of Reagan's opening talk is based on *LAT* 1/5/66, "Reagan Announces"; *NYT* 1/5/66, "Reagan Enters"; "A Plan for Action: An Address by Ronald Reagan," 1/4/66, RRPL, Reagan Gubernatorial Papers; *Governor Reagan*, 141.

303 *Hoover's aides watched*: 100-382196-8.

303 *The questions . . . "should be opposed"*: Meet the Press, NBC, 1/9/66, transcript; *LAT* 1/22/65, "Reagan to Decide Soon."

303 *At a tense point*: On Robert Welch and the JBS, Thirteenth Report, Un-American Activities in California, 1965, Senate Factfinding Subcommittee on Un-American Activities, 171–75.

303 *Reagan had backed*: LAT 8/24/62, "$50-a-Plate Dinner"; LAT 4/4/61, "Rep. Rousselot Defends"; LAT 8/31/62, "Rousselot Criticizes"; NYT 1/23/65, "Reagan Weighing." In July 1964, Rousselot became the national director of public relations for the JBS, Thirteenth Report, op. cit., 173.

303 *Under pressure*: "Reagan's Stand on the John Birch Society," 9/24/65, in "Where Ronald Reagan Stands," '66 Campaign, RR, folder three of four, box C-32, '66 Campaign Subject Files, RRPL; "Announcement Day Press Conference . . . Statler Hilton, Pacific Ballroom, Jan. 4, 1966," Reagan Gubernatorial Papers, RRPL, folder: 66 Campaign Speeches, Book 1; *Ronnie & Jesse*, 80–82; NYT 11/14/65, "The Ronald Reagan Story."

304 *It was true*: NYT 11/19/64, "Hoover Assails Warren Findings."

304 *But the bureau . . . Hoover had agreed*: This paragraph is based on information from "FBI Files and Documents Pertaining to Extreme Right Individuals, Groups, and Their Assertions," by Ernie Lazar, ernie1241.googlepages.com/home, and sites.google .com/site/ernie124102/jbs-1, accessed 5/13/11. Lazar has done extensive research using the FOIA to obtain FBI files on right-wing extremism, and was the first person to receive the entire FBI HQ main file on the JBS, totaling some 12,000 pages. Lazar quotes DeLoach's comments as being from 62-104401-789; 62-104401-851.

304 *In fact, bureau*: This paragraph is based on 100-59001-21; 116-70463-11.

304 *The FBI files*: Author review of Reagan FBI files; author interview with McManus.

304 *Hoover and his*: Author review of FBI files on Reagan; author interview with Burney Threadgill, Jr.

304 *"Over all . . ."*: 100-382196-8.

19: The Peace Trip Dance

305 *Right away . . . another attack*: NYT 11/4/65, "Hell's Angels Will Picket Viet Marchers"; LAT 11/21/65, "5,800 Protest Vietnam in Quiet Oakland March."

305 *But as Hunter*: Hell's Angels: A Strange and Terrible Saga, 246.

305 *At a mass meeting . . . "flower power"*: Dharma Lion, 453, wherein Michael Schumacher writes, "Flower Power—the affirmation of group opposition, stated gently and peacefully—was born."

305 *Hunter Thompson . . . "roaring success"*: Hell's Angels, 230; www.poemhunter.com /poem/first-party-at-ken-kesey-s-with-hell-s-angels/, accessed 5/15/11.

306 *As the day*: The description of the San Jose State meeting and poem excerpt are from SFC 11/13/65, "The Hells Angels,'" in 100-55462-1147; Hell's Angels, 247–52.

306 *The meeting also . . . ended hopefully*: Hell's Angels, 246; Dharma Lion, 454–55.

306 *Ginsberg's efforts*: Mailer's poem is from Allen Ginsberg Papers, Stanford University, Manuscripts Division, M0733.

306 *Eight days later . . . "makes sense"*: NYT 11/21/65, "8,000 War Critics March."

307 *Young Americans*: This paragraph is based on SFX 11/21/65, "Viet Day March," in 100-55462-1244; BDG 11/22/65, "Protest March," in 100-55462-1265; 100-444372-88; 100-444372-93.

307 *"Hey, hey, LBJ . . ."*: The account of the protest is from 100-55462-1402, 12/13/65; DC 12/6/65, "VDC Pickets VP Humphrey."

307 *Then, as night fell*: Dharma Lion, 455; DC 12/1/65, Concert Advertisement; SFC 12/6/65, "In Berkeley They Dig Bob Dylan." On Dylan in Berkeley, see also "Beat

Generation Gallery," photos and captions by Larry Keenan, www.emptymirror
books.com/keenan/b1965-7.html, accessed 5/15/11.

307 *Dylan was*: This paragraph is based on *NYT* 8/30/65, "Dylan Conquers"; *LAT*
9/3/65, "Brenda Lee"; *OT* 12/4/65, "Singer Bob Dylan"; *LAT* 9/6/65, "Folks Pay
Homage to Dylan"; *LAT* 10/11/65, "Winds of Change"; *LAT* 8/1/65, "American
Sounds"; *NYT* 8/11/65, "The Beatles Will"; *NYT* 8/27/65, "Pop Singers"; *DC*
12/10/65, "Dylan 'Sellout'?" In 1965 Dylan had three songs on the *Billboard* "Hot 100"
chart: "Like a Rolling Stone," "Positively 4th Street," and "Subterranean Homesick
Blues," see Billboard "Bob Dylan Album & Song Chart History," www.billboard.com
/artist/bob-dylan/chart-history/4511?sort=timeon#/artist/bob-dylan/chart-history
/4511?sort=timeon, accessed 5/15/11.

307 *No one booed*: This paragraph and the next are based on *SFX* 12/4/65, "Bob Dylan's
Concert"; *OT* 12/4/65, "Singer Bob Dylan"; *SFC* 12/6/65, "In Berkeley They Dig
Bob Dylan."

308 *But if Dylan*: The account of the press conference is based on "Dylan Speaks, The
Legendary 1965 Press Conference in San Francisco," DVD recording of December
3, 1965, press conference at KQED; *SFC* 12/4/65, "'It's Lonely.'"

308 *In January 1966 . . . "survived the crisis"*: 100-444372-154; *DC* 3/25/66, "Charter
Day"; *DC* 3/28/66, "Charter Day Protests"; *WP* 3/26/66, "1000 Protest"; *NYT*
3/26/66, "Berkeley Hears Goldberg."

309 *All the while*: Author interviews with Rob Hurwitt and Stew Albert; Meese recounts
some of the Peace Commandos' exploits in Testimony of Edwin Meese III, Hearings, Committee on Un-American Activities, House of Representatives, 89th Congress, August 17–19, 1966.

309 *The commandos had discovered*: This paragraph is based on 100-55462-209;
100-55462-228; 100-55462-248; 100-55462-279; 100-444372-29; *OT* 9/20/65, "Viet
Protest"; *OT* 9/25/65, "Parks Rule"; *OT* 9/29/65, "Army Ends"; *DC* date illegible,
"VDC Wins Out," in 100-55462-307; *DC* 6/4/82, "Of Spies & Radicals," by Seth
Rosenfeld; author interview with Rob Hurwitt.

309 *The commandos also . . . the incendiary gel*: "Of Spies & Radicals," by Seth Rosenfeld.

309 *Then there was*: This paragraph is based on *NYT* 1/11/66, "Antiwar Leaflets"; *OT*
1/15/66, "Eastbay Lawmen Track"; *OT* 1/16/66, "4 Freed on Bail"; *OT* 1/18/66,
"Leaflet 'Bomb'"; *OT* 1/28/66, "Littering Charge"; *OT* 2/14/66, "Innocent Pleas";
OT 5/14/66, "'Bombers' of Leaflets Fined"; *DC* 6/4/82, "Of Spies & Radicals," by
Seth Rosenfeld; author interview with Rob Hurwitt.

310 *These "peace bombings"*: 100-55462-1538; 100-55462-1539; 100-55462-1542;
100-55462-1543; 100-55462-1546; 100-44372-121; 100-44372-122.

310 *As the prosecutor*: Testimony of Edwin Meese III, Hearings, Committee on Un-
American Activities, House of Representatives, 89th Congress, August 17–19, 1966,
p. 1075; *With Reagan*, 28, 29.

310 *He worked with*: Testimony of Edwin Meese III, Hearings, Committee on Un-
American Activities, House of Representatives, 89th Congress, August 17–19, 1966,
p. 1109.

310 *. . . dated its operations*: For the People, 74, 160–61, 244, 229; *Cloak and Gavel*, 48–
49; *Justice for All*, 56; author interviews with Curtis O. Lynum and Burney Threadgill, Jr.

310 *A former U.S. Army . . . World War II*: Synanon interview of Harper Knowles, 5/9/75,
Synanon v. Hearst libel case, S.F. Superior Court No. 651-749.

310 *. . . attended the FBI's National*: 100-55462-379, p. 4; 100-39577-NR, 4/18/69, before
100-39577-17.

310   . . . *and, according to*: 100-55462-379.

310   *Lynn's unit*: *For the People*, 244, 251.

310   *He gathered*: Testimony of Edwin Meese III, Hearings, Committee on Un-American Activities, House of Representatives, 89th Congress, August 17–19, 1966, pp. 1094, 1095; author interviews with Burney Threadgill, Jr., and Bob Lamborn.

310   *Much of this information*: For example, see 100-34204-118; 100-34204-119; 100-55462-1542; 100-55462-1543; 100-55462-1573; 100-444372-121; 100-444372-128; 77-7764-23; 77-7764-24; 157-9295-19.

310   *San Francisco FBI*: Author interview with Burney Threadgill, Jr. For example, see 100-55462-1732; 100-55462-1595; 100-55462-1596; 100-55462-1617; 100-55462-1630; 100-55462-1631; 100-55462-1638. Permanent Symbol Numbers are used to conceal the identity of sources supplying the FBI with information on a routine basis, Declaration of FBI Agent Angus B. Llewellyn in *Seth Rosenfeld v. U.S. Department of Justice and Federal Bureau of Investigation*, C-85-2247 MHP and C-85-1709 MHP.

310   *The district attorney's*: The account of the infiltration, capture, and fining of the VDC "peace bombers" is based on 100-55462-1732; OT 1/15/66, "Eastbay Lawmen Track"; OT 1/16/66, "4 Freed on Bail"; OT 1/18/66, "Leaflet 'Bomb'"; OT 1/28/66, "Littering Charge"; OT 2/14/66, "Innocent Pleas"; OT 5/14/66, "'Bombers' of Leaflets Fined." Fowler died in 2001. Meese testified that the district attorney's inquiry was unable to prove the four arrestees were members of the VDC, see Testimony of Edwin Meese III, Hearings, Committee on Un-American Activities, House of Representatives, 89th Congress, August 17–19, 1966, p. 1100.

311   *Meese's office sent . . . never was revealed*: 100-55462-1732; OT 1/15/66, "Eastbay Lawmen Track"; Testimony of Edwin Meese III, Hearings, Committee on Un-American Activities, House of Representatives, 89th Congress, August 17–19, 1966, pp. 1100, 1256–60.

311   *Hoover had been*: This paragraph is based on 100-3-104-47-306, 6/15/65, CP USA COINTELPRO files, reproduced by Scholarly Resources, Inc., 1978.

311   *Lynum replied*: This paragraph is based on 100-3-104-47-340, 9/15/65, CP USA COINTELPRO files, reproduced by Scholarly Resources, Inc., 1978.

311   *Leaking information*: 100-3-104-47-344, 9/30/65, CP USA COINTELPRO files, reproduced by Scholarly Resources, Inc., 1978.

311   *Nonetheless . . . "Anti-Communist Weekly"*: 100-3-104-47-340; 100-3-104-47-illegible, 11/11/65, both in CP USA COINTELPRO files, reproduced by Scholarly Resources, Inc., 1978.

311   *A four-page*: This paragraph is based on 100-49796-162; 100-436291-161. On Frawley, see NYT 11/9/98, "Patrick Frawley, Jr."

312   *Each issue*: Copies of *Tocsin* in 100-49796; *The Berkeley Review* 1/11/62, "Tocsin or Toxin?" in 100-63453-7.

312   *But* Tocsin *also . . . "Foundation"*: 100-49796-162; 100-49796-231.

312   *FBI agents also*: 100-436291-161, which states, "Counterintelligence information has previously been furnished anonymously to 'Tocsin' by the San Francisco Office"; 100-3-104-47-illegible, 10/26/65, in CP USA COINTELPRO files, reproduced by Scholarly Resources, Inc., 1978, which states, "'Tocsin' is a leading anticommunist newspaper on the West Coast which we have successfully used through anonymous techniques to expose communist activities"; 100-49796-231, which states, "The bureau has advised that inasmuch as 'Tocsin' is public source information, that this information should be used in Bureau reports." On the FBI indexing names in Tocsin, see 100-63453-12.

312   *Even as Fox*: This paragraph is based on author interview with Burney Threadgill, Jr.

312   *This revelation*: The FBI continued to use *Tocsin* in counterintelligence operations

and to cite its articles as authority that people were subversive until a libel suit drove it out of business. A Bay Area minister named Edward Peet retained the radical lawyer Vincent Hallinan and sued *Tocsin* for $2 million, SFC 2/2/66, "Notes of a Newsnik," by Herb Caen, in 100-49796-244. By the end of the next year, *Tocsin's* voluminous files had been bought by the Church League of America, in Wheaton, Illinois. In a February 1, 1967, letter to "Dear Fellow American," Edgar Bundy, the league's executive secretary, boasted his organization will "give the Conservative cause the largest research library in the United States on subversive activities with the single exception of the Federal Bureau of Investigation," 100-49796-273. FBI officials, however, viewed Bundy askance and warned him not to claim he had access to FBI files. Bundy, an FBI memo said, "is typical of irresponsible professional anti-Communists," 100-49796-275.

312 *One student whom*: The Aptheker/*Tocsin* anecdote is based on 100-3-104-47-358, 10/21/65, CP USA COINTELPRO files, reproduced by Scholarly Resources, Inc., 1978.

313 *FBI agents again*: The Aptheker/*Examiner* anecdote is based on 100-3-104-47-473, 11/10/65, CP USA COINTELPRO files, reproduced by Scholarly Resources, Inc., 1978; *Intimate Politics*, pp. 164, 165.

313 *Just to be sure*: 100-3-104-47-386, 1/11/66, CP USA COINTELPRO files, reproduced by Scholarly Resources, Inc., 1978.

313 *Later that year*: The Aptheker/bumper sticker anecdote is based on 100-3-104-47-454, 9/16/66, CP USA COINTELPRO files, reproduced by Scholarly Resources, Inc., 1978.

314 *Mike O'Hanlon*: The O'Hanlon/Medaille story is based on 100-3-104-47-403, 2/18/66; 100-3-104-47-403, 3/1/66; 100-3-104-47-401, 3/3/66; 100-3-104-47-401, 3/9/66; 100-3-104-47-illegible, 4/14/66; 100-3-104-47-illegible, 4/15/66; 100-3-104-47-413, 3/25/66; SFX 3/20/66, "N.Y. Sex Case, Grim Past of VDC Leader"; SFX 4/13/66, "Medaille, N.Y. Parolee"; DC 3/23/66, "Letters to the Ice Box"; NYT 2/12/58, NYT 2/13/58, "Parents Stand By"; "Suspended Pupil, 15, Held in Killing"; NYT 2/26/58, "Boy Indicted in Murder"; NYT 4/19/58, "Girl Slayer, 15, Committed"; NYT 4/22/66, "Man Sought Here Arrested on Coast"; *Nashville Banner* 4/22/66, "FBI Arrests Noted Leftist"; *National Review* 4/12/66, "On the Left"; N.Y. *Post* 2/12/58, "On the Roof"; N.Y. *Post* 2/13/58, "A Mother's Agony"; N.Y. *Post* 2/26/58, "Boy, 15, Must Stand"; N.Y. *Post* 2/25/58, "Indict Boy"; N.Y. *Post* 3/4/58, "Matteawan Due"; N.Y. *Post* 4/3/58, "Doctors Call Medaille Boy Insane"; N.Y. *Post* 4/22/66, " '58 Rooftop Slayer"; N.Y. *Daily Mirror* 2/26/58, "If Boy's Guilty"; N.Y. *Daily Mirror* 2/26/58, "Boy Indicted"; N.Y. *Herald Tribune* 2/12/58, "Boy Pushes Girl"; N.Y. *Herald Tribune* 2/13/58, "2 Families Stunned"; N.Y. *Herald Tribune* 4/4/58, "Boy Who Threw"; N.Y. *Herald Tribune* 4/19/58, "Boy Held"; N.Y. *Daily News* 2/12/58, "Boy Pushes Girl"; N.Y. *Daily News* 2/13/58, "Order Mental Tests"; N.Y. *Daily News*, 6/5/66, "Calif. Pacifist Held"; author interview with Francis Medaille.

317 *With Medaille knocked*: This and the next two paragraphs are based on *Who the Hell Is Stew Albert?*; *Do It!*; NYT 2/1/06, "Stew Albert"; LAT 2/2/06, "Stew Albert"; author interview with Stew Albert; www.stewalbert.com/, accessed 5/15/11.

317 *When the bomb*: This and the following three paragraphs describing the bombing and some of the initial reaction are based on 100-55462-1793; BDG 4/12/66, "Bomber of VDC Must Be Found," in 100-55462-B-121; BDG 4/9/66, "VDC HQ Here Bombed," in 100-55462-B-123; BDG 4/11/66, "VDC Bombing," in 100-55462-B-124; NYT 4/10/66, "Blast Rocks"; WP 4/10/66, "Explosion Rips"; DC 6/4/82, "Of Spies & Radicals," by Seth Rosenfeld; author interviews with Rob Hurwitt, Joe Blum, Stew Albert.

318 *Shortly after . . . Berkeley police investigation*: 100-55462-1791; 100-55462-1792; 100-444372-158.
318 *Right away . . . Bettina Aptheker*: 100-55462-1792; 100-55462-1815; 100-55462-1818; 100-444372-152; DC 6/4/82, "Of Spies & Radicals," by Seth Rosenfeld. On the DCA, see 100-441164-412.
319 *In the Du Bois Club*: 100-441164-273; 100-441164-NR, 3/8/66; 100-441164-267; 100-441164-47-180.
319 *The Du Bois Club had . . . organization*: 100-3-104-3962, 3/8/66; 100-441164-155; 100-441164-278 (Lewis's column); author interview with T. Hallinan.
319 *FBI officials then . . . to the police*: 100-441164-273, 3/18/66; 100-441164-267, 3/21/66. See also 100-3-104-47, serial illegible, 4/14/66, CP USA COINTELPRO files, reproduced by Scholarly Resources, Inc., 1978.
319 *An internal FBI . . . "communist elements"*: 100-441164-273, 3/18/66.
319 *Soon after . . . for the attack*: 100-55462-1792, 4/9/66.
319 *Over the next*: 100-444372-NR, 5/11/66; 100-444372-173; 100-444372-190.
319 *San Francisco police*: Author interview with McClennan; *DC* 6/4/82, "Of Spies & Radicals," by Seth Rosenfeld.
319 *By the time*: This paragraph is based on author interviews with Rob Hurwitt, Stew Albert, and Joe Blum. On the Scheer campaign, see *Berkeley at War*, 99–106. On Alice Waters, see *The Free Speech Movement*, 615.
320 *Dynamite*: This paragraph is based on Senate Factfinding Subcommittee on Un-American Activities, Thirteenth Report Supplement, 1966, 133–34; *BDG* 4/11/66, "Berkeley Is My Beat."
320 *To the hip*: A copy of the ad that ran March 23, 24, and 25, 1966, is in "Confidential—Re Berkeley Campus File on V.D.C. Dance," 9/12/66, Shephard to Kerr, with attachments, Kerr Personal Papers, folder 26, "Student Protests," CU-302, carton 4, Bancroft.
320 *President Kerr*: This paragraph and the officers' following description of the dance are based on "Confidential—Re Berkeley Campus File on V.D.C. Dance," Ibid.
321 *Several days later*: OT 4/6/66, "VDC Dance 'Orgy.'"
321 *This was not enough*: The description of Burns's report is based on Senate Factfinding Subcommittee on Un-American Activities, Thirteenth Report Supplement, 1966; NYT 5/7/66, "Berkeley Called Red Infiltrated."
322 *The crowd*: The description of the rally is based on OT 5/13/66, "U.C. Probe Demanded by Reagan"; *BDG* 5/13/66, "Reagan Urges UC Quiz"; *SFX* 5/13/66, "4,500 Hear S.F. Talk by Reagan"; *SFC* 5/13/66, "Reagan Lashes"; *LAT* 5/13/66, "Reagan Demands"; *NYT* 5/14/66, "Reagan Demands Berkeley Inquiry." On the Cow Palace, see www.cowpalace.com/, accessed 5/16/11.
322 *Reagan already*: Governor Reagan, 147, 148.
322 *Smiling, fresh-faced*: The description of the Reagan Girls in this and the following paragraphs is based on "Reagan Girls, Information Sheet," box C-33, folder: "RR—Staff Inter-Office Memos 3 of 4"; "Reagan Girls Manual" and "Reagan Girls Organization," in box C-33, folder: "RR Committee 1 of 4"; and "Memo—To: All Youth for Reagan County," 5/12/66, box C-33, folder: "Staff Inter-Office Memos, 2 of 4," all in Campaign Subject Files, Ronald Reagan Gubernatorial Papers, RRPL.
323 *"There is a leadership"*: The quotes are from "Excerpts from Ronald Reagan Speech at Cow Palace," Reagan Gubernatorial Papers, box C-30, Speeches and Statements, folder: "Book II (5)," RRPL.

20: Sources on Campus

326 *Reagan's car*: Reagan's meeting and its purpose are described in Sparrow to Reagan, 1/5/66, and Reagan to Sparrow (Sparrow is incorrectly called Spaun), 11/30/66, both in box C-29, 1966 Campaign, Governor's Personal Correspondence, folder: Letters of Particular Interest, M-Z, RRPL; author interview with Sparrow.

326 *Having easily*: *Governor Reagan*, 148.

326 *His campaign*: The FBI's assistance to Ed Montgomery, Fulton Lewis, Jr., Richard Combs, and Hugh Burns are discussed in the text.

326 *Public concern*: The account of the hearing is based on Testimony of Edwin Meese III, Hearings, Committee on Un-American Activities, U.S. House of Representatives, 89th Congress, August 16–19, 1966, pp. 1074–1159, 1260.

327 *Back in California*: NYT 8/18/66, "Lawyer Ejected"; LAT 8/19/66, "Vietnam Hearing"; NYT 8/19/66, "Leftists Object"; LAT 8/20/66, "House Probe Finds"; OT 8/5/66, "Bay Area's VDC Members on HCUA's"; OT 8/18/66, "Protesters Aid Enemy, Says Meese"; OT 8/18/66, "HCUA Told of 'Criminal' VDC."

327 *He fired off*: "News Release, Citizens Committee to Elect Ronald Reagan Governor," 5/18/66, box C-34, RR '66 Campaign Subject Files, folder: "66 Ed: University of California 1 of 2," Reagan Gubernatorial Papers, RRPL.

327 *He issued*: "Ronald Reagan Speaks Out on the Issues, #4 Academic Freedom," box C-33, RR Campaign Subject Files, folder: "Ed: Campus Unrest," Reagan Gubernatorial Papers, RRPL.

327 *Governor Brown announced . . . "chosen it"*: NYT 5/15/66, "Berkeley Report an Issue on Coast"; LAT 5/22/66, "Reagan Hits Choice"; LAT 5/23/66, "Reagan Slanders UC"; "News Release, Citizens Committee to Elect Ronald Reagan Governor," with copy of telegram to Edward Carter, Chairman, UC Regents, 5/20/66, box C-34, RR '66 Campaign Subject Files, folder: "66 Ed: University of California 1 of 2," Reagan Gubernatorial Papers, RRPL.

328 *Reagan was on . . . "kick 'em out!"*: NYT 6/1/66, "Reagan Shuns Image of Goldwater in Coast Race."

328 *At the National Press . . . "to interfere . . ."*: LAT 6/17/66, "Reagan Chides Brown in Deft Debut at National Press Club."

328 *Two days later . . . "public hearings?"*: LAT 6/19/66, "Reagan Still Sticks to UC Sex Charge."

328 *Don Mulford*: Author interview with Clark Kerr.

328 *An Oakland native*: This paragraph and the next are based on 94-53953-12, 4/29/60; 94-53953-X1, 4/26/60; 94-53953-1, 7/18/60; 94-53953-1, 7/25/60; 94-53953-5, 2/27/62; 94-53953-15, 5/6/66; 94-53953-18, 7/23/68.

329 *If Hoover was*: Author interview with Marvin Buchanan, a former FBI agent on Mulford's staff.

329 *In 1961 . . . "Kerr and his group"*: 94-53953-2, 3/13/61; 94-53953-21.

329 *In 1963 . . . "housing ordinance, etc."*: 94-53953-7; author interview with Burney Threadgill, Jr.

329 *In the following years*: As noted previously in the text, Mulford gave the FBI statements that Hoover used against Kerr. In a subsequent letter to Hoover, Mulford took credit for leading the fight to fire Kerr, 94-53953-21.

329 *For Reagan's visit*: Sparrow letter to Reagan, 1/5/66, box C-29, 1966 Campaign, Governor's Personal Correspondence, folder: Letters of Particular Interest, M–Z, RRPL; author interview with Sparrow.

329 *Among those present*: Sparrow letter, ibid.; author interview with Sparrow.

329 *Several months after*: LAT 1/8/68, "Reagan's New Education Aide"; LAT 10/27/69, "Reagan Adviser."

330 *Angry and resentful*: On Sherriffs's feelings about Kerr, see "Alex C. Sherriffs, The University of California and the Free Speech Movement: Perspectives from a Faculty Member and Administrator, An Interview Conducted by James H. Rowland, 1978," Regional Oral History Office, Bancroft, 15, 51–54, 62, 63, 64; author interview with Kerr. For examples of Sherriffs's continued informing, see 100-55462-215, in which he informs on Acting Chancellor Earl Cheit and the law professor Robert Cole; 100-55462-1645, in which he informs on Acting Chancellor Martin Meyerson and Neil Smelser, a sociology professor and the new assistant in charge of student political activity, telling an agent he had been trying to obtain Smelser's personnel file; 100-444372-154, in which he informs on the VDC activist Steve Weissman and the math professor Steve Smale.

330 *Professor Hardin Jones*: This paragraph is based on Jones informer file, 134-deleted, and SA to SAC, 9/28/65, therein; 77-7764-48.

330 *Sparrow had contacted . . . to FBI agents*: 77-7764-50; 77-7764-51; author interview with Sparrow.

330 *Among other things*: 77-7764-64. The letter was from Kerr to the math professor John L. Kelley.

330 *Sparrow also had helped*: 77-7764-50; 77-7764-51.

330 *In an interview . . . "welfare"*: Author interview with Sparrow. Sherriffs did not return phone calls from the author prior to his death on April 29, 2002. Hardin Jones died in 1978.

330 *At Mulford's home*: 94-53953-16; Sparrow letter to Reagan, 1/5/66, box C-29, 1966 Campaign, Governor's Personal Correspondence, folder: Letters of Particular Interest, M–Z; author interview with Sparrow.

330 *Reagan listened*: 94-53953-16; Sparrow letter to Reagan, 1/5/66, and Reagan to Sparrow (Sparrow is incorrectly called Spaun), 11/30/66, box C-29, 1966 Campaign, Governor's Personal Correspondence, folder: Letters of Particular Interest, M–Z, RRPL; author interview with Sparrow.

330 *Reagan's operatives*: Author interviews with Stan Plog and Ken Holden. On BASICO and Reagan, see Stanley Plog, "More Than Just an Actor: The Early Campaigns of Ronald Reagan," an interview conducted by Stephen Stern in June 1981, Oral History Program, UCLA, hereafter "Plog oral history."

330 *Behavior Science Corporation*: *Governor Reagan*, 138, 139, 141, 142; *Reagan's America*, 294–97; Plog oral history, op. cit.

331 *Stanley Plog*: Author interview with Plog; "Flanders vs. McCarthy: A Study in the Technique and Theory of Analyzing Congressional Mail," doctoral thesis by Stanley Clement Plog, Harvard University, April 1961, copy in possession of author.

331 *Ken Holden . . . liberal views*: Author interviews with Plog and Holden.

331 *(Plog by now was writing*: Author interviews with Plog and Holden.

331 *They started . . . been "Plogged"*: Author interviews with Plog and Holden.

331 *Reagan's campaign hired*: *Reagan's America*, 294; *Governor Reagan*, 138; Plog oral history, op. cit., 3.

331 *He had declared*: *Reagan's America*, 294; Plog oral history, op. cit., 2–3.

331 *As Plog and Holden . . . prepared his speeches*: This paragraph is based on author interviews with Plog and Holden; Plog oral history, op. cit., 4, 5, 6.

331 *Plog, Holden, or*: This paragraph is based on author interviews with Plog and Holden; author e-mails with Holden; Plog oral history, op. cit., 5, 9.

331 *Like Reagan, Plog and Holden*: This paragraph is based on author interviews with Plog and Holden.

331 *The secret contacts*: The account of Behavior Science's contacts with Hardin Jones, Alex Sherriffs, and John Sparrow is based on the author's interviews with Plog and

Holden; Sparrow letter to Reagan, 1/5/66, and Reagan to Sparrow (Sparrow is incorrectly called Spaun), 11/30/66, box C-29, 1966 Campaign, Governor's Personal Correspondence, folder: Letters of Particular Interest, M–Z (this letter contains Sparrow's quote), RRPL; author interview with Sparrow.

332 *Hardin Jones and*: Author interviews with Plog and Holden.

332 *For example*: 100-34204-2112; 100-34204-2113. The cover letters, dated 10/7/66, enclose reports by Jones and Grendon about student orientation that September. One enclosure is a letter from Jones to Theodore Meyer, Chairman of the Board of Regents; Jones secretly sent a copy to the FBI.

332 *Likewise . . . "parental controls"*: Author interview with Holden.

332 *Hardin Jones . . . Holden said*: Author interview with Holden.

332 *At one point*: This paragraph and the next are based on the author's interview with Holden.

333 *Indeed, after the meeting*: Reagan to Mulford, 1966 Campaign Correspondence, box C-17, Reagan Gubernatorial Papers, RRPL.

333 *Reagan had announced*: LAT 8/21/66, "Reagan Outlines Plan to Fight Crime in State."

333 *The institute . . . "of California"*: SFC 8/21/66, "Reagan's Pledge"; LAT 8/21/66, "Reagan Outlines Plan."

333 *Reagan already had . . . "this effort"*: Reagan to Hoover, 8/19/66, in 100-382196-9.

333 *After reviewing*: Hoover to Reagan, 8/24/66, RR, in HQ 100-382196-9.

333 *There was, however*: LAT 6/6/66, "To Set the Record Straight."

334 *In Reagan's case . . . "mutual interest"*: 100-382196-9.

334 *In an interview*: Author interview with DeLoach.

334 *William F. Buckley, Jr.*: The description of Buckley's column is based on LAT 8/29/66, William F. Buckley, Jr., "When UC Opens for Fall Term, State Will Watch." On Buckley and the founding of the YAF, see NYT 10/18/64, "A G.O.P. Rebellion"; LAT 4/29/90, "Doing the Right Thing."

334 *Just after*: LAT 9/10/66, "Reagan Says He'd Name McCone for UC Inquiry."

334 *McCone had resigned*: WP 4/12/65, "CIA Chief's Job."

335 *Governor Brown*: This and the next two paragraphs on the McCone Commission are based on NYT 8/20/65, "McCone Heads Panel"; LAT 12/7/65, "Grim Statistics"; NYT 12/7/65, "Watts Riot Panel"; LAT 12/12/65, "Watts: The Findings." On rioters chanting "Burn, Baby, Burn!" see WP 8/15/65, "Arsonists Race"; LAT 8/22/65, "Viewpoint of Rioters."

335 *McCone also ran*: NYT 2/16/91, "John A. McCone"; John A. McCone papers, Bancroft, BANC MSS 95/20c.

335 *He had supported*: LAT 9/23/66, "McCone Gives UC Probe Conditions."

335 *. . . but after Reagan*: LAT 9/23/66, "McCone Gives UC Probe Conditions"; LAT 8/19/66, "McCone Named."

335 *He announced*: Reagan's remarks are from LAT 9/10/66, "Reagan Says He'd Name McCone for UC Inquiry"; NYT 9/10/66, "Reagan Proposes"; Transcript of Reagan Kick-Off Telecast, September 9, 1966, Citizens Committee to Elect Ronald Reagan Governor News Release, box C-30, 1966 Speeches and Campaign Statements, folder: "Book II (3)," Ronald Reagan Governor's Papers, RRPL.

336 *Brown denied*: WP 9/12/66, "Brown and Reagan Shake, Then Trade Charges on Air"; LAT 9/14/66, "Brown Offers Plan for Better Schools, Tax Cut."

336 *Kerr meanwhile sought*: This paragraph is based on LAT 9/17/66, "UC Regents Divided."

336 *Besides, Berkeley*: NYT 5/22/66, "Berkeley Rated over Harvard"; Kerr, vol. 1, 56–58; Kerr, vol. 2, 285.

336 *But Reagan . . . professors at Berkeley*: LAT 9/18/66, "Reagan Vows to Hold Taxes Down if Elected"; LAT 9/20/66, "Student Standards for Admission."

337 *Since his strange*: This paragraph is based on *The Electric Kool-Aid Acid Test*, 229–55; *The Haight-Ashbury*, 33, 35–36, 37–38, 39–48, 54; Ken Kesey & The Merry Pranksters, www.lysergia.com/MerryPranksters/MerryPranksters_main.htm, accessed 5/19/11; Trips Festival handbill, Prankster History Project, www.pranksterweb.org/tripsprogram.htm, accessed 5/19/11.

337 *On the evening*: This and the next two paragraphs are based on *The Electric Kool-Aid Acid Test*, 255–63, 313; SFC 1/20/66, "Cops Find Kesey"; SFC 2/13/66, "Kesey Letter."

338 *As word*: This paragraph is based on *Prime Green*, 150, 160; NYT 5/23/08, "On the Lam." On the New Journalism, see *The New Journalism*, edited by Tom Wolfe and E. W. Johnson; WP 6/30/73, "Wolfeing Down Good Writin'." On *The Electric Kool-Aid Acid Test*, see NYT 8/18/68, "The SAME Day: Heeeeeewack!!!"; NYT Best Seller List, nytbestsellerlist.com/book/X5800/THE-ELECTRIC-KOOL-AID-ACID-TEST/Tom-Wolfe, accessed 5/18/11.

338 *But not from*: This paragraph is based on *The FBI and I*, 249–51.

338 *They'd had little . . . "to save them"*: SFC 10/6/66, "LSD Fugitive Challenges Law in Bold Return."

338 *Elaborating later*: This sentence and Kesey's quotes in the next paragraph are from SFC 4/12/67, "Kesey Gives Judge the Word"; SFC 10/22/66, "A Jailed Kesey Talks."

338 *As Kesey envisioned*: SFC 10/6/66, "LSD Fugitive Challenges Law in Bold Return."

339 *Yet most remarkable . . . October 20*: SFC 10/6/66, "LSD Fugitive Challenges Law in Bold Return"; SFC 10/27/66, "LSD Novelist Held."

339 *Lynum was not . . . "enforcement community"*: *The FBI and I*, 249–51.

339 *About twenty-five minutes*: The anecdote about Kesey's capture is based on *The FBI and I*, 249–51; SFC 10/27/66, "LSD Novelist"; SFC 4/7/67, "How an FBI Agent."

339 *Kesey's marijuana*: This paragraph is based on SFC 6/24/67, "Kesey Begins"; SFC 7/1/67, "Kesey Thrives"; SFC 11/5/66, "Kesey Gets Lecture."

340 *An outraged mother*: On Atthowe's suit, see *Berkeley Citizen*, 10/14/65, "Woman Seeking U.C. Lists Linked to Reagan Governor Campaign"; OT 10/7/66, "U.C. Sued on Campus Information"; OT 10/8/66, "U.C. Bows to Demand"; OT 10/12/66, "Student Group List"; OT 11/1/66, headline unavailable; OT 11/2/67, "U.C. Student List Opened"; OT 11/3/66, "Wide Open"; OT 2/18/69, "Ruling Hits Secrecy"; LAT 11/3/66, "UC Groups Must Open Records"; SFC 10/8/66, "A Suit to Get UC Student Lists"; SFC 11/3/66, "UC Files Open to 'Researcher'"; DC 10/11/66, "Mother Continues Her Suit." On Atthowe working with the DA's office, see Chapter 19 on the VDC Air Force.

340 *Reagan had vowed*: This and the next two paragraphs are based on LAT 10/21/66, "Reagan Criticizes."

340 *On that Sunday*: The account of Kennedy's speech is based on NYT 10/24/66, "Excerpts from Kennedy Speech on Coast"; NYT 10/24/66, "Kennedy Deplores Racism of a 'Few' Negro Leaders"; LAT 10/24/66, "Robert Kennedy Warmly Applauded at UC Berkeley."

341 *Stokely Carmichael . . . "Black Power"*: LAT 10/19/66, "Reagan Urges Carmichael." On Carmichael and black power, see *In Struggle*; *Malcolm X: A Life of Reinvention*, 481–82.

341 *Born on June 21, 1941*: This paragraph and the next are based on NYT 8/5/66, "Black Power Prophet"; NYT 9/25/66, "The Story of Snick"; NYT 11/16/98, "Stokely Carmichael"; *In Struggle*, 162–66; The Martin Luther King, Jr. Research and Education

Institute, Stanford University, "Stokely Carmichael (b. 1941)," www.stanford.edu
/~ccarson/articles/left_1.htm, accessed 5/20/11.

342 *Over and over . . . nonviolent protests*: NYT 11/16/98, "Stokely Carmichael"; *At Canaan's Edge*, 109–10; Carmichael speech at Berkeley, 10/29/66, text, audio, and
photo at American Radio Works, americanradioworks.publicradio.org/features/black
speech/scarmichael.html, accessed 5/19/11.

342 *Then, in June 1966 . . . at his back*: LAT 6/7/66, "Meredith's Vow"; NYT 11/16/98,
"Stokely Carmichael."

342 *While Meredith*: NYT 6/7/66, "Rights Leaders"; NYT 11/16/98, "Stokely Carmichael."

342 *On June 16 . . . he declared*: NYT 6/17/66, "Mississippi Reduces"; *In Struggle*, 209–
10; *At Canaan's Edge*, 486.

342 *Soon young blacks*: *In Struggle*, 215–16; NYT 9/25/66, "The Story of Snick."

342 *Martin Luther King, Jr. . . . "economic power"*: WP 7/27/66, "Leaders Decry Black
Power Slogan"; NYT 11/16/98, "Stokely Carmichael."

342 *But potential violence . . . "'white blood will flow'"*: NYT 7/3/66, "Why the Cry for
Black Power."

343 *At Berkeley . . . "Negro problems"*: LAT 10/23/66, "UC Wants No Politics in Black
Power Parley."

343 *Reagan's campaign operatives*: The excerpts are from the memo, BASICO Staff to
Reagan, 10/12/66, Re: Berkeley, in Ronald Reagan Governor's Papers, RRPL, box
C-33, RR Campaign Subject Files, folder: "ED: Campus Unrest."

343 *On October 18 . . . "calmly and rationally"*: LAT 10/19/66, "Reagan Urges Carmichael Not to Speak at UC."

344 *But despite*: This paragraph is based on LAT 10/19/66, "Reagan Urges Carmichael
Not to Speak at UC"; LAT 10/21/66, "Reagan Criticizes UC for Permitting Bob
Kennedy Talk"; LAT 10/27/66, "Brown Says Reagan Seeks to Be President, Fears the
Press"; Citizens Committee to Elect Ronald Reagan Governor, News Release,
10/18/66, Ronald Reagan Governor's Papers, folder: 1966 Education: campus un-
rest, RRPL.

344 *In suit, tie*: The account of Carmichael's talk is based on LAT 10/30/66, "Carmichael Hits"; NYT 10/30/66, "Carmichael Asks"; WP 10/31/66, "Crowd Laps Up
Carmichael's Insults." The text, audio, and a photo are at American Radio Works,
americanradioworks.publicradio.org/features/blackspeech/scarmichael.html, accessed
5/19/11.

346 *Despite Reagan's . . . greater militancy*: *In Struggle*, 215–28; NYT 9/25/66, "The
Story of Snick"; LAT 6/4/67, "'Chuck Has Got Us'"; LAT 5/30/67, "Black Conference Demands."

346 *When two students*: NYT 8/6/67, "The Call of the Black Panthers"; *In Struggle*, 278;
The Shadow of the Panther, 95–97, 107–108.

346 *Both Reagan and . . . "political sense"*: LAT 10/31/66, "Brown, Reagan Denounce
Speech by Carmichael"; WP 10/31/66, "Crowd Laps Up Carmichael's Insults"; WP
10/31/66, "Reagan Discounts Backlash."

21: Landslide

347 *Mario Savio*: SFNCB 5/24/65, in 100-54060-211; author interviews with Suzanne
Goldberg and Cheryl Stevenson.

347 *Suzanne had long*: The background on Goldberg is from her FBI files, including
100-54266 1A(1); 100-54266-3; 100-54266-8; 100-54266-9; 100-54266-illegible,
1/28/65, before 100-54266-14; 100-154429-1; HQ 100-443731-1. These records show

the FBI investigated her academic, financial, family, and criminal background (she had none other than her arrest at the December 3, 1964, Sproul Hall sit-in). Additional background on Goldberg is from *The Free Speech Movement: Coming of Age in the 1960s*, 239n, 243, 247, 346, 369, 404, 462, 657; oral history interview of Suzanne Goldberg, by Lisa Rubens, July 17, 2000, Bancroft Library; author interviews with Suzanne Goldberg and Cheryl Stevenson.

347 *But though she was*: Suzanne discusses falling in love with Savio in "Mario, Personal and Political," in *The Free Speech Movement: Reflections on Berkeley in the 1960s*; oral history interview of Suzanne Goldberg, by Lisa Rubens, ibid.; author interview with Suzanne Goldberg.

348 *. . . until one day . . . "religious context"*: SFC 5/22/65, "Two Rebels"; OT 5/22/65, "Savio, Fiancee."

348 *It was a small . . . "make us happier"*: SFNCB 5/24/65, "The Savios Get Time Off," with photo, in 100-54060-211. On Thompson, see NYT 2/18/83, "Elsa Thompson." On Hoffman, see SFC 10/20/09, "Leftist Lawyer." Goldberg told the author in an interview that her parents "wanted nothing to do with" the wedding.

348 *An FBI agent . . . "both a mess"*: 100-54060-217.

348 *Savio had applied . . . existential crisis*: Application for Readmission and Declaration of Major, both signed by Savio, 5/6/65, Bancroft, Chancellor's Records, CU-149, box 72, folder 14.

348 *The university approved*: Ibid.

348 *But the couple*: This paragraph is based on "Mario, Personal and Political," in *The Free Speech Movement: Reflections on Berkeley in the 1960s*.

349 *In September 1965 . . . a year*: 100-54060-264; 100-54060-266.

349 *Savio had told*: "Mario, Personal and Political," in *The Free Speech Movement: Reflections on Berkeley in the 1960s*.

349 *Goldberg was pregnant . . . "make a decision"*: SFC 8/12/65, "The Savios to Go," in 100-54060-250; "Mario, Personal and Political," in *The Free Speech Movement: Reflections on Berkeley in the 1960s*.

349 *The FBI also . . . travel plans*: 100-54060-266.

349 *Other agents*: 100-54060-264; 100-54060-265.

349 *FBI headquarters alerted*: 100-54060-284; 100-54060-285; 100-54060-286.

349 *In a classified*: 100-54060-271.

349 *They were among*: The CIA collected the information under a program called "CHAOS" and processed it in a computer system called "HYDRA." See Church, book III, 448, 519, 687, 689, 691, 693, 694–95, 698–99.

349 *In January 1966*: 100-54060-284.

349 *A bureau agent*: 100-54060-265; 100-54060-268.

349 *The lookout system*: Author interview with Curtis O. Lynum. See the discussion of "stop" notices, Church, book III, 448, 519.

349 *Oxford must have been*: The account of Savio's stay at Oxford is based on Bullock to Stewart, 9/15/66; Savio to Berkeley registrar, 12/10/65; Registrar Clinton C. Gilliam to Savio, 12/20/65, all in Chancellor's Records, CU-149, box 72, Bancroft; "Mario, Personal and Political," in *The Free Speech Movement: Reflections on Berkeley in the 1960s*.

350 *On February 16, 1966 . . . Berkeley*: 100-54060-287.

350 *FBI agents*: This paragraph is based on 100-54060-287; 100-54060-289; 100-54060-290; 100-54060-291; 100-54060-292.

350 *All to no avail . . . his parents*: 100-54060-294; 100-54060-305; Savio to College of Letters and Science, 8/11/66, Bancroft, UC Berkeley, Chancellor's Records, CU-149, box 72, folder 14.

351 *On May 20, 1966 . . . detention list*: 100-54060-294; 100-54050-298; 100-54050-305.

351 *Savio had planned*: This paragraph is based on 100-54060-294; 100-54050-305; *BDG* 5/20/66, "Mario Savio Returns to Berkeley," in 100-54060-297; *OT* 5/22/66, "Mario Savio Seeks U.C. Readmission"; *SFC* 5/23/66, "Savio Applies," in 100-54060-295; *BDG* 5/23/66, "Savio Asks," in 100-54060-296; *LAT* 5/23/66, Table of Contents, "The World."

351 *A few weeks later*: This paragraph is based on *LAT* 7/2/66, "Rafferty Would"; *BDG* 7/2/66, "Rafferty Objects," in 100-54060-301; *SFC* 7/2/66, "Rafferty's Little Note."

351 *Savio had . . . the Steppenwolf*: *SFX* 7/10/66, "The 'New Mario Savio'"; Savio to College of Letters and Science, 8/11/66, Bancroft, UC Berkeley, Chancellor's Records, CU-149, box 72, folder 14; author interview with Rob Hurwitt.

351 *The bar*: Author interview with Rob Hurwitt. On Hesse's *Steppenwolf*, see *NYT* 3/16/47, "Herr Hesse and the Modern Neurosis."

351 *Max Scherr*: 100-38806-6; 100-38806-12; 100-38806-14; *SFC* 11/3/81, "Berkeley Barb Founder," in 100-38806-82; *LAT* 11/9/81, "Barb Publisher"; *Berkeley at War*, 94; author interview with Rob Hurwitt.

351 *He sold it*: The *Sunday Ramparts* 10/2/65, "Reviewing the Press," in 100-38806-33; *Secrets*, p. 29.

351 *The Steppenwolf's new*: Author interview with Rob Hurwitt.

352 *Located in*: The description of the bar is based on "Raw Material" by Suzanne Lipsett, in *Berkeley! A Literary Tribute*, 92–93; 100-54060-305, 100-38806-18; author interview with Rob Hurwitt.

352 *One night . . . Savio laughed*: Author interview with Rob Hurwitt.

352 *Hurwitt was friends with*: This paragraph and the next are based on author interview with Rob Hurwitt. On Smale's proof of the Poincaré conjecture, see *LAT* 4/19/82, "Young Mathematician Solves"; *NYT* 9/30/86, "One of Math's Major Problems."

352 *In the wake*: The description of the interview is from *SFX* 7/10/66, "The 'New Mario Savio.'" The description of Ludlow is from author interview with Lynn Ludlow.

353 *Several days . . . and possible detention*: 100-54060-305.

353 *Only a year earlier*: Heyns to Kerr, 7/11/66; Chancellor's Records, CU-149, box 72, folder 14, Bancroft.

354 *In a memorandum . . . "READMIT"*: Malm to Cheit, 6/20/66, Chancellor's Records, CU-149, box 72, folder 14, Bancroft.

354 *Chancellor Roger Heyns . . . student protesters*: *LAT* 12/11/66, "Berkeley Faces Threat"; *LAT* 12/9/66, "Chancellor Heyns" by William F. Buckley, Jr.; *LAT* 12/3/66, "Heyns Refuses."

354 *He began looking . . . Board of Regents*: Cunningham to Cheit, 6/29/66; Heyns to Kerr, 7/11/66, both in Chancellor's Records, CU-149, box 72, folder 14, Bancroft.

354 *Cunningham worked . . . especially Savio*: Author interview with John Sparrow.

354 *On June 29, 1966 . . . Kerr objected*: Cunningham to Cheit, 6/29/66; Heyns to Kerr, 7/11/66, both in Chancellor's Records, CU-149, box 72, folder 14, Bancroft.

354 *Savio finally applied . . . "Savio Seeks Readmission"*: *LAT* 8/13/66, "Savio Obtains"; *NYT* 8/14/66, "Savio Seeks"; *BDG* 8/12/66, "Mario Savio Asks."

354 *In support*: Savio to College of Letters and Science, 8/11/66, Chancellor's Records, CU-149, box 72, folder 14, Bancroft; author interview with Rob Hurwitt.

355 *On top of*: Ibid.

355 *He did not*: *Freedom's Orator*, 129, 227.

355 *Also, his son*: Author interview with Suzanne Goldberg. Parents can have children with Fragile X even if the parents do not have Fragile X themselves. On Fragile X syndrome, see National Institutes of Health, http://www.nichd.nih.gov/health/topics /fragile_x_syndrome.cfm.

355 "*He was very* . . .": "Mario, Personal and Political," in *The Free Speech Movement: Reflections on Berkeley in the 1960s.*

355 *Four days later:* This paragraph is based on Fretter to Savio, 8/18/66, and press release, 8/17/66, in Chancellor's Papers, CU-149, box 72, folder 14, Bancroft; *NYT* 8/18/66, "Savio Readmission Denied"; *LAT* 8/18/66, "UC Readmission of Savio Refused"; *WP* 8/18/66, "Berkeley Bars Rebel Leader"; *Chicago Tribune* 8/18/66, "Campus Rebel Files Too Late"; *SFC* 8/18/66, "UC Says No," in 100-54060-308; *SFX* 8/17/66, "Savio Bid," in 100-54060-309; *BDG* 8/17/66, "M. Savio's," in 100-54060-312.

356 *Savio promptly:* Fretter to Savio, 8/18/66, Chancellor's Records, CU-149, box 72, folder 14, Bancroft; *SFX* 8/19/66, "Savio Seeks Winter"; *BDG* 8/19/66, "Savio Files Again."

356 *Cunningham just . . . hypocrite:* Cunningham to Cheit, 6/29/66; Heyns to Kerr, 7/11/66; Cunningham to Cheit, 8/19/66; all in Chancellor's Records, CU-149, box 72, folder 14, Bancroft.

356 *But these incidents:* Heyns to Kerr, 7/11/66; Chancellor's Records, CU-149, box 72, folder 14, Bancroft.

356 *Speaking in Stockton:* SFC 9/15/66, "Reagan's View."

356 *On November 4, 1966:* This account of Savio's protest and its background is based on 100-54060-329; 100-54060-327; *DC* 11/4/65, "Campus Groups," in 100-54060-345; *DC* 11/7/65, "Savio Violates Rules," in 100-54060-346; *BDG* 11/5/66, "Savio Returns," in 100-54060-347; *OT* 11/5/66, "Savio Back," in 100-54060-331; *SFX* 11/5/66, "UC Leaflet," in 100-54060-332; *SFX* 11/6/66, "UC Officials Silent," in 100-54060-300; *SFX* 11/8/66, "UC Gives," in 100-54060-333; *LAT* 11/5/66, "Students May Strike"; *LAT* 11/21/66, "Fight over UC Rallies"; *Freedom's Orator,* 246–48. FBI informers attended CCO meetings at Westminster House, see 100-54060-352; 100-54060-353; 100-54060-355.

358 *That evening, Lynum:* 100-54060-329.

358 *Chancellor Heyns:* 100-54060-330; *SFX* 11/5/66, "UC Leaflet," in 100-54060-332; *SFX* 11/6/66, "UC Officials Silent."

358 *On the following . . . constitutionality of the rule:* SFC 11/9/66, "UC"; Boyd to Savio, 11/7/66, Chancellor's Records, CU-149, box 72, folder 14, Bancroft.

358 *University officials:* NYT 11/9/66, "Savio Readmission."

358 *On Tuesday:* This paragraph is based on *DC* 11/9/66, "Heyns: Won't Be Coerced," in 100-54060-343.

358 *Later on Election . . . distributing leaflets:* DC 11/9/66, "UC Says No," in 100-54060-342. By the end of the academic year, Heyns had dropped his proposal to ban rallies on the Sproul steps, *Freedom's Orator,* 248. For further discussion of Heyns's retreat, see "Berkeley's 'Little Free Speech Movement,'" 465–67, in *The Free Speech Movement: Reflections on Berkeley in the 1960s.*

358 *Savio accused . . . "internal protection":* SFC 11/9/66, "Savio Is Refused."

359 *If the administration:* BDG 11/9/97, "UC Denies," in 100-54060-338.

359 *As the returns:* NYT 11/9/66, "Reagan Elected"; *LAT* 11/9/66, "Reagan Triumphs."

359 *Brown was once: California Rising,* 251; *WP* 2/7/66, "Knowland Heads Paper."

359 *But after two terms: Governor Reagan,* 129–61; *California Rising,* 341–66.

359 *In contrast, Reagan:* This paragraph and the following one are based on *Ronald Reagan, His Life and Rise to the Presidency,* 141; *California Rising,* 341–66; *Reagan,* 113, 117; *Governor Reagan,* 157; NYT 11/9/66, "White Backlash." Reagan publicly denied white backlash existed or that it contributed to his election, saying, "I don't think so at all." *LAT* 11/9/66, "Government of All"; *LAT* 11/6/66, "California Vote"; *LAT* 1/21/67, "Kerr Fired."

359 *When Brown conceded:* The description of Reagan campaign headquarters is drawn from NYT 11/9/66, "Reagan Elected"; *LAT* 11/9/66, "Government of All."

359 *It was a landslide . . . national political figure*: NYT 11/10/66, "Reagan Emerging";
     LAT 11/9/66, "Reagan Triumphs."
359 *The next day*: 100-382196-11.
360 *Curtis Lynum*: 80-990-4.
360 *Three days after*: 80-579-11.
360 *Reagan replied*: 80-579-13.
360 *H. R. Haldeman*: This paragraph is based on WP 11/13/93, "H. R. Haldeman"; Hal-
     deman to Reagan, 6/20/66, Governor Reagan Papers, 1966 campaign corres-
     pondence, box C-10, RRPL; oral history interview with H. R. Haldeman, Regent,
     University of California, 1965–1967, 1968, by Dale E. Treleven, Oral History Pro-
     gram, University of California, Los Angeles, 1991; Regents of the University of
     California, UC History Digital Archives, sunsite.berkeley.edu/~ucalhist/general
     _history/overview/regents/biographies_h.html, accessed 7/5/11.
360 *The soiree*: The dinner party anecdote in this and the following paragraphs is based
     on *Ronald Reagan, His Life and Rise to the Presidency*, 142; Kerr, vol. 2, 295–96;
     author interview with Kerr.
360 *For Kerr, the board*: On the board meeting and the Smale raise, see Kerr, vol. 2, 295–
     96. On Smale's receipt of the Fields Medal, see *Stephen Smale, The Mathematician
     Who Broke the Dimension Barrier*; The International Mathematical Union, www
     .mathunion.org/general/prizes/fields/details/, accessed 7/5/11.
361 *Even worse, perhaps . . . angered Reagan*: NYT 8/27/66, "American Critical"; LAT
     8/27/66, "Moscow Alarmed"; Reagan to Congressman Hall, 10/19/66, box C-34, '66
     Campaign Subject Files, folder: "66 ED: Higher—Faculty," RRPL.
361 *His August 1966*: FBI officials had listed Smale on the Security Index before he
     went to Moscow, and as he traveled there to receive the Fields Medal and through-
     out Europe, agents tracked him with help from the CIA and security agencies in
     France, Italy, Greece, and Turkey. See Smale FBI file 100-401213.
361 *Kerr knew*: This paragraph is based on Kerr, vol. 2, 295–96.
362 *While the regents*: Mulford's FBI meeting is described in 100-382196-NR, 11/22/66.
362 *But Hoover quickly*: 100-382196-20.
362 *As governor . . . had of Kerr*: 116-460320-2.
363 *The process began*: The questionnaire is in 116-460320-1.
363 *From the start . . . sources there*: 116-460320-4.
363 *They directed . . . "the applicant"*: 116-460320-26.
363 *And they told*: 116-460320-2; 116-460320-3.
363 *Everyone whom agents*: 116-460320.
363 *But files*: This paragraph and the next are based on 116-460320-2; 116-460320-16;
     116-460320-26.
363 *But Wesley Grapp*: This paragraph is based on 116-460320-1; 116-460320-16, 2/3/67;
     116-460320-16, 2/9/67; 116-460320-24; 116-460320-25.
364 *When officials*: Author interview with Curtis O. Lynum.
364 *Hundreds of people*: Many Are the Crimes, 266–305; *The Federal Loyalty-Security
     Program*, 145, 174.
364 *They ordered Grapp*: 116-460320-16, Director to SAC LA, 2/9/67; 116-460320-25.
364 *Yet the bureau's*: 116-460320-16.
364 *Perhaps Reagan thought: Where*, 72–73.
364 *Phil Battaglia*: Author interview with Battaglia.
364 *Edwin Meese III*: Author interview with Meese.
364 *Assistant Director*: Author interview with DeLoach.
364 *But Grapp and*: Author interviews with Wesley Grapp and Curtis O. Lynum.
364 *Savio was leading*: The account of the navy protest and the meeting in Pauley Ball-

room is based on *SFC* 12/1/66, "Fracas at Student Union"; *Chicago Tribune* 12/1/66, "Melee Erupts"; *LAT* 12/1/66, "Classroom Strike"; *OT* 12/1/66, "New U.C. Uproar"; *OT* 12/1/66, "Trespassing and Battery Charges"; *OT* 12/1/66, "Birthday Party for Son Derailed"; *Chicago Tribune* 12/2/66, "Berkeley Hit Again."

365 *The strike plan . . . had been canceled*: *SFC* 12/2/66, "Presents Demands"; *NYT* 12/2/66, "5,000 Boycott Classes"; *Chicago Tribune* 12/2/66, "Berkeley Hit Again"; *WP* 12/2/66, "9000 Cut Classes."

365 *Chancellor Heyns . . . nonstudents like Savio*: *Chicago Tribune* 12/3/66, "Crack Down"; *LAT* 12/3/66, "Heyns Refuses."

365 *The latest Berkeley . . . bar of soap*: *LAT* 12/3/66, "Heyns Refuses"; *Chicago Tribune* 12/3/66, "Crack Down"; *LAT* 12/5/66, "GOP Unit"; *OT* 12/5/66, "Soap, Haircut."

366 *In Sacramento*: *LAT* 12/3/66, "Heyns Refuses."

366 *Reagan spoke*: Reagan's remarks are from *LAT* 12/3/66, "Reagan UC Edict."

366 *Meanwhile . . . "a lovely little handout"*: The account of the board meeting is from *LAT* 12/5/66, "UC Rebels"; *LAT* 12/7/66, "Students at UC Berkeley Vote."

366 *The protesters . . . focusing on finals*: *LAT* 12/6/66, "UC Faculty Backs Heyns' Handling"; *LAT* 12/7/66, "Strike at Berkeley"; *LAT* 12/8/66, "UC Students Return."

366 *As the week . . . "Yellow Submarine"*: *LAT* 12/8/66, "UC Students Return."

366 *Released that fall*: *LAT* 8/7/66, "New Beatles Album Best Yet." Quoted lyrics are from the album *Revolver*. Lennon was born on October 9, 1940; McCartney, on June 18, 1942. On the writing of the song, see www.beatlesinterviews.org/dba10sub .html.

367 *With the students*: Kerr, vol. 2, 297.

367 *But Savio had . . . "understand it"*: *LAT* 12/7/66, "Strike at Berkeley."

22: Fired with Enthusiasm

368 *Just before midnight*: This paragraph is based on *SFC* 10/24/66, "Reagan Picks"; *NYT* 1/2/67, "Reagan Sworn"; *NYT* 12/4/66, "Reagan Starts"; *NYT* 1/6/67, "The Inauguration"; *NYT* 1/6/67, "The Inauguration"; *SFC* 1/2/67, "Reagan Takes Oath"; *The Reagans: Portrait of a Marriage*, 99–100. On Junipero Serra, see Virtual Museum of the City of San Francisco, www.sfmuseum.org/bio/jserra.html, accessed 7/6/11. On the statue titled *Columbus' Last Appeal to Queen Isabella*, see California State Capital Museum, capitolmuseum.ca.gov/VirtualTour.aspx?Content1=1282& Content2=1410&Content3=1266, accessed 7/6/11.

368 *So began*: This paragraph is based on *NYT* 1/6/67, "The Inauguration"; *NYT* 12/27/66, "Benny"; *LAT* 1/7/67, "After the Swearing In"; *SFC* 1/6/67, "Splendid Sacramento Ball"; *The Reagans: Portrait of a Marriage*, 100.

368 *On the morning . . . "of God"*: *NYT* 1/6/67, "Reagan Pledges"; *LAT* 1/1/67, "Inaugural Glitter"; *LAT* 12/27/66, "Much Ado."

369 *Motorcycle officers*: *LAT* 1/6/67, "Reagans Given Roaring"; *Sacramento Bee* 1/5/66, "15,000 Cheer."

369 *Setting forth . . . "ethical standards"*: *LAT* 1/8/67, "Education"; *SFC* 1/6/67, "Inaugural Message"; *NYT* 1/6/67, "Reagan Pledges"; *LAT* 1/6/67, "Text of Reagan."

369 *Nine days later*: 100-446740-14.

369 *Reagan's plan . . . during his campaign*: Kerr, vol. 2, 298; *NYT* 1/7/67, "Gov. Reagan Proposes"; *DC* 1/19/67, "Regents Might Not Like It"; *Sacramento Bee* 1/14/67, "Unruh Says UC"; *SFC* 1/6/67, "Reagan's Freeze"; *SFC* 1/10/67, "Statewide Outcry"; author interview with Kerr. It was ninety-nine years since the passage of the 1868 Organic Act established the university.

369 *Kerr was appalled*: This paragraph and the next are based on *LAT* 1/5/66, "Reagan Proposes"; *LAT* 1/10/67, "Big Drop"; *LAT* 1/12/67, "Dumke Freezes"; *SFX* 1/9/67, "Reagan Denies"; *SFC* 1/10/67, "Reagan Hits Rumors"; *SFX* 1/9/67, "Kerr Going"; *SFX* 1/14/67, "Kerr Shuts"; *SFC* 1/14/67, "UC Halts"; *SFC* 1/15/67, "Students to Fight"; *SFX* 1/15/67, "Freeze Not"; *LAT* 1/18/67, "Reagan Lashes"; *NYT* 1/18/67, "Reagan Accuses"; *LAT* 1/9/67, "Reagan's Effigy"; *LAT* 1/15/67, "Reagan's Off"; *NYT* 1/15/67, "Education Reagan v. Kerr"; *Sacramento Bee* 1/18/67, "UC, College 'Freeze'"; Kerr, vol. 2, 291, 297–99; author interview with Kerr.

370 *Concerned . . . academic community's interests*: Kerr, vol. 2, 292; author interview with Kerr.

370 *Reagan agreed*: 100-446740-14.

370 *Finch told*: 100-446740-14.

370 *Lynum immediately . . . "the Berkeley situation"*: 100-446740-14.

370 *But the Boss*: The account of the bedroom meeting is from 100-446740-14; 100-151646-216; 100-151646-218, 1/17/67; author interviews with Curtis O. Lynum and Glenn Harter.

371 *Hoover seized . . . "campus agitation"*: Hoover's reaction is recorded by his notations on 100-151646-218, 1/17/67.

371 *As Cartha DeLoach*: Author interview with Cartha DeLoach.

371 *Still, Hoover feared . . . "an academic war"*: Hoover's reaction is recorded by his notations on 100-151646-218, 1/17/67.

372 *Just after high noon*: The account of the protest is based on *OT* 1/20/67, "Regents to Take"; *LAT* 1/20/67, "Reagan Calls"; 100-34204-2207; *DC* 1/19/67, "Rally to Greet Regents"; *DC* 1/19/67, "A Silent Vigil"; *DC* 1/20/67, "3000 Protest Tuition"; *DC* 1/19/67, "Regents Might Not Like It"; *SFX* 1/20/67, "Confusion Marks"; Kerr, vol. 2, 303; author interview with Kerr.

372 *Awaiting Reagan . . . a critic of Kerr*: Kerr, vol. 2, 299; *LAT* 1/15/67, "Reagan's Off to a Bad Start."

372 *All through the campaign*: Reagan's criticism of Kerr is recounted in the text. As Lyn Nofziger, the governor's press aide, wrote in his memoir, "During his campaign, Reagan made it clear that one of his objectives as governor would be to persuade the regents . . . to get rid of Kerr," *Nofziger*, 64.

373 *Then Phil Boyd . . . to step down*: Kerr, vol. 2, 293–94.

373 *Kerr could understand . . . "downhearted"*: Ibid., 300, 301; author interview with Kerr.

373 *But the stubborn*: This paragraph is based on Kerr, vol. 2, 293, 301, 313; author interview with Kerr.

373 *Still, he sought . . . with FBI agents*: Kerr, vol. 2, 292; 100-446740-14.

373 *As the date . . . "about a month"*: Kerr, vol. 2, 312; *LAT* 1/15/67, "Reagan's Off"; *SFX* 1/18/67, "Kerr Dismissal"; author interview with Kerr.

373 *Kerr grew anxious*: This and the next two paragraphs are from Kerr, vol. 2, 312–13; author interview with Kerr.

374 *Reagan emerged*: The account of the regents' meeting and firing of Kerr is from *LAT* 1/21/67, "Kerr Fired"; Kerr, vol. 2, 303–305; *Ronald Reagan: His Life and Rise to the Presidency*, 144–46; *Governor Reagan*, 276–77; 100-34204-2205.

374 *Lyn Nofziger*: Nofziger, 64.

374 *Reagan looked nervous*: This paragraph is based on *SFX* 1/21/67, "Reagan Nervous."

374 *Immediately after*: This paragraph is based on Kerr, vol. 2, 313; *Ronald Reagan: His Life and Rise to the Presidency*, 146.

374 *Reagan, meanwhile*: *LAT* 1/21/67, "Showdown."

374 *As he exited*: *SFX* 1/21/67, "Reagan Nervous"; *OT* 1/20/67, "Rain Puts."

375 *Only after*: Kerr, vol. 2, 303; *NYT* 1/21/67, "Kerr Ousted."

375 *The words fell*: This paragraph is based on Kerr, vol. 2, 304–305.
375 *At the press conference*: The account of the press conference is from *LAT* 1/21/67, "Kerr Fired"; *NYT* 1/21/67, "Kerr Ousted"; Kerr, vol. 2, 318–29.
375 *Even as he spoke*: Kerr, vol. 2, 309, 325.
375 *When the . . . to tears*: Ibid., 308.
375 *As* California Monthly: *California Monthly*, January–February 1967, quoted in Kerr, vol. 2, 329.
376 *Later, when he*: NYT 3/3/70, "Carnegie Chairman."
376 *Three days after . . . "many ways"*: LAT 1/24/67, "Meyer Statement."
376 *Kerr's dismissal . . . political football*: DC 1/23/61, "Radicals Applaud"; NYT 1/25/67, "Berkeley Faculty."
376 *Hundreds of professors*: LAT 2/12/67, "10,000 at Capitol"; WP 1/24/67, "Reagan's Plans"; LAT 1/24/67, "Teachers Union"; WP 1/22/67, "317 Teachers"; LAT 1/22/67, "Some UC Campuses."
376 *There were national . . . "hatchet job"*: LAT 1/22/67, "Timing Big Surprise"; LAT 2/15/67, "U.S. Professors."
376 *Nathan Pusey*: LAT 1/22/67, "U.S. Educators."
376 *Edwin Pauley*: SFX 1/21/67, "Unruh Fears."
376 *Hugh Burns*: SFC 1/25/67, "Legislators"; LAT 1/21/67, "Ouster"; OT 1/21/67, "Reaction Ranges."
376 *Don Mulford*: OT 1/21/67, "Reaction Ranges"; LAT 1/21/67, "Ouster."
376 *Savio cheered*: This paragraph is based on OT 1/21/67, "Reaction Ranges"; DC 1/23/67, "Radicals Applaud."
376 *A few days later . . . "long disillusionments"*: NYT 1/25/67, "An Apology to Kerr"; DC 1/25/67, "The Return."
377 *And a few days*: The critical letter quoted in this and the following three paragraphs is in DC 1/26/67, "Activists State Position on Kerr."
377 *Savio added*: WP 1/22/67, "317 Teachers."
377 *At first, Reagan . . . after the vote*: LAT 1/21/67, "Showdown"; NYT 1/21/67, "Reagan Voices Surprise."
378 *Reagan also*: LAT 1/25/67, "Reagan Defends"; LAT 1/31/67, "Kerr Tells."
378 *"The inference . . . involved"*: NYT 1/25/67, "Political Move."
378 *Several days later . . . to remove Kerr: Ronald Reagan: His Life and Rise to the Presidency*, 146–47; LAT 1/25/67, "Reagan Defends."
378 *Minutes after the board*: Author interview with Sparrow.
378 *Then Sparrow*: 100-151646-219.
378 *Three days later . . . "in this regard"*: 100-34204-2205.
378 *Not long after . . . "your men are around"*: 100-382196-29.
378 *Hoover replied . . . "working together"*: 100-382196-29.

23: Obey the Rules

379 *Reagan had made*: Chicago Tribune 5/16/66, "Reagan Shows"; LAT 1/7/73, "Changing University"; *Governor Reagan*, 271.
379 *From the start . . . spectacle*: LAT 1/7/73, "Changing University"; NYT 12/10/67, "Reagan Gives a Surprising Performance."
379 *He thrust: Ronald Reagan: His Life and Rise to the Presidency*, 153; LAT 8/29/71, "Reagan Claim"; LAT 4/28/69, "Regents' Veto Power"; LAT 7/18/70, "Regents Block Promotion of 2 Tied to Liberal, Radical Causes"; LAT 1/7/73, "Changing University."
       Alex Sherriffs's monitoring of students, professors, and administrators, and his serving as liaison to conservative professors and regents, is documented in Ronald

Reagan Governor's Papers at the Ronald Reagan Presidential Library. For example, see:

Governor's Office, Molly Sturgis Tuthill Series, GO box 169, folder: "Research File—Education—University of California, Regents, 1967–1968," undated memo re "Chancellor Roger Heyns";

Governor's Office, Molly Sturgis Tuthill Series, GO box 165, folder: "Research File—Education—RR Memos from ACS (1/6)," especially memos ACS to Reagan, Clark, Beck, 3/18/67, "Regents Meeting at Irvine March 14 and 15, 1968"; ACS to RR, Clark, Nofziger, 6/20/68, "Vietnam Commencement"; ACS to RR, Clark, Nofziger, 8/12/68, "President Hitch"; ACS to RR, Clark, Deaver, Meese, 10/10/68, "Telephone call from John Sparrow"; ACS to RR, Clark, Deaver, Meese, 10/11/68, "10-11-68 phone call with Glenn Campbell";

Governor's Office, Molly Sturgis Tuthill Series, GO box 165, folder: "Research File—Education—RR Memos from ACS (3/6)," especially memos ACS to RR, Meese, Ellingwood, et al., 10/14/69, "Meeting with faculty members"; ACS to RR, 2/3/70, "Appointment of Harry Edwards"; ACS to Reagan, 11/13/69, "Attached material"; ACS to Reagan, Meese, Ellingwood, "Attached article";

Governor's Office, Molly Sturgis Tuthill Series, GO box 165, folder: "Research File—Education—RR Memos from ACS (Alex Sherriffs) (4/6)," ACS to RR, 4/6/70 (Sparrow has sent Sherriffs a copy of Professor Charles Schwartz's letter to the editor published in *The Daily Californian* saying he wants all students to take a Hippocratic Oath appropriate for scientists; ACS forwards it to RR noting, "If ever 'McCarthyism' existed, it exists here." RR replies, "I agree");

Governor's Office, Molly Sturgis Tuthill Series, GO box 165, folder: "Research File—Education—RR Memos from ACS (Alex Sherriffs) (5/6)," ACS to RR, 10/13/70, "Meeting with responsible faculty"; ACS to Meese, 6/8/71, re the "disaster known as" the UC Berkeley Criminology School, referencing Jerome Skolnick, Caleb Foote, and Anthony Platt;

Governor's Office, Molly Sturgis Tuthill Series, GO box 165, folder: "Research File—Education—RR Memos from ACS (Alex Sherriffs) (3/6)," 10/10/69 letter from history professor, UC Santa Barbara, re UC administrators "are permitting the students and inferior teachers to set the standards"; ACS forwards the letter to RR, who replies, "I think it is time to arouse [*sic*] every Middlesex village and farm—RR.";

Governor's Office, Molly Sturgis Tuthill Series, GO box 165, folder: "Research File—Education—Campus Unrest—General 1/3," Hardin Jones supplies RR staff with copy of letter, 5/24/66, Professor Jacob J. Finkelstein to Professor Leon Henkin, Chairman of Committee on Academic Freedom, that states, "My final fear, then, is that the rightwing forces of the state of California are determined to move against the Berkeley campus in fury and in vengeance";

Series II, Education Unit, Subseries D: Higher Education, Boxes GO-69 and GO-70, which contain such folders as: "Faculty—Bad Guys (1)(2)"; "Faculty—Harry Edwards"; "Faculty—Jerry Farber"; "Faculty—Professor Herbert Marcuse"; "Faculty—Mike Tigar."

Correspondence Unit, box 1969-42, folder: "Alex Sherriffs, June," ACS to Mrs. Randolph A. Hearst, 6/30/60; Correspondence Unit, box 1968-28, folder: "August 16—Colleges, State and Special Schools," ACS to Hutchinson, 8/29/68, re Jerry Farber; ACS to Sagray re Professor Jack Kurzweil, 8/26/68; ACS to McGhecq re Professor Harry Edwards, 8/26/68.

379 *He cut*: LAT 9/29/74, "Governor and Academia"; *LAT* 3/1/67, "Tuition Plan"; *LAT*

9/11/67, "UC Split"; *LAT* 1/7/73, "Changing University." In the latter retrospective of Reagan's governorship and UC, William Trombley, the *Los Angeles Times* education reporter, wrote, "Generally speaking, Reagan has been granting UC and the State University and Colleges about 90% of their operating budget requests, compared to the 95% or more they received from former Gov. Brown. This seems a slight difference, but it means larger classes, higher student-faculty ratios, fewer dollars spent per student, heavier teaching loads, crowded libraries, dirty buildings and few, if any, new programs."

379 *Although some cuts*: *LAT* 1/7/73, "Changing University"; *LAT* 8/29/71, "Reagan Claim."

379 *He would claim*: *LAT* 8/29/71, "Reagan Claim."

379 *He complained*: NYT 10/25/70, "Ronald Reagan Is Giving"; *LAT* 3/2/67, "Higher Education"; *LAT* 3/1/67, "Tuition Plan"; *LAT* 1/7/73, "Changing University."

380 *Allen Ginsberg*: The description of the Be-In is based on *The Haight-Ashbury*, 17–122; *Do It!*, 56; *SFC* 1/15/67, "They Came . . . Saw"; *SFC* 1/15/67, "Suddenly, Out of a Clear"; *SFC* 1/16/67, "Human Be-In"; *SFC* 1/16/67, "The Tribes Gather"; About the Human Be-In, Allen Cohen, s91990482.onlinehome.us/allencohen/be-in.html, accessed 5/26/11.

380 *Word of the new*: On the burgeoning hippie scene in San Francisco and Berkeley, see WP 8/21/66, "The 'Golden Dream'"; WP 10/27/67, "The Acid Affair—XIII"; *LAT* 10/30/67, "Haight-Ashbury Revisited"; NYT 5/5/67, "Organized Hippies"; *LAT* 2/4/67, "State's Hippies"; *SFC* 1/22/67, "'They're Young Seekers'"; *SFC* 6/22/67, "Hippies Begin Their Summer of Love"; *LAT* 4/10/67, "Hippies Merely a Nuisance"; *LAT* 4/11/67, "Hippie Diggers"; NYT 8/19/67, "Hippie Regulars"; WP 8/21/66, "A New Drug Culture"; NYT 5/14/67, "The 'Hashbury' Is the Capital of the Hippies"; NYT 2/19/67, "Where the Action Is," by Herb Gold.

380 *The politico-psychedelic*: Regarding LSD dosage, Owsley is quoted as follows: "For most people, the proper dose is about 150 to 200 micrograms. When you get to 400, you just totally lose it. I don't care who you are. Kesey liked 400. He *wanted* to lose it." *Rolling Stone*, July 12–27, 2007, "Owsley Stanley: The King of LSD," by Robert Greenfield.

380 *Hunter Thompson*: NYT 5/14/67, "The 'Hashbury' Is the Capital of the Hippies."

380 *But as* the Ramparts: *Ramparts*, March 1967, "A Social History of the Hippies," by Warren Hinckle.

380 *To Joan Didion . . . "not holding"*: "Slouching Toward Bethlehem," in *We Tell Ourselves Stories in Order to Live*, 93, 67.

380 *Bobby Seale*: The account of Seale at Sproul is from *SFC* 5/11/67, "Black Panthers at UC"; *DC* 5/11/67, "Black Panthers Defend Negro."

381 *. . . a few days before*: The story of the Panthers' Sacramento visit is based on 105-165706-22; *LAT* 5/3/67, "Heavily Armed Negro Group Walks into Assembly Chamber"; NYT 5/3/67, "Armed Negroes Protest Gun Bill"; *LAT*, 5/10/67, "Day in Sacramento"; *LAT* 5/4/67, "Security Tightened at Capitol"; *LAT* 5/10/67, "Heavier Guard Set to Protect Reagan"; *The Shadow of the Panther*, 129–35.

381 *Reagan sent . . . "self determination . . ."*: *LAT* 5/4/67, "State Senate Given Reagan Cannon-Aid."

381 *One week later*: The description of King at Sproul Plaza is based on *DC* 5/18/67, "King—You Take It"; *DC* 5/18/67, "Vietnam Summer"; *OT* 5/18/67, "Dr. King: War Sparks Rioting"; *LAT* 5/18/67, "King Shies at '68 Boomlet"; NYT 6/11/67, "Martin Luther King Defines 'Black Power.'"

382 *King still*: King profile, King Online Encyclopedia, The Martin Luther King,

Jr., Research and Education Institute, Stanford University, mlk-kpp01.stanford.edu
/index.php/encyclopedia/encyclopedia/enc_martin_luther_king_jr_biography/, accessed 5/26/11.

382 *But though*: LAT 5/29/67, "Negro Clamor for Rights Poses Perils"; LAT 5/30/67,
"Black Conference Demands Speedier Freedom Movement."

382 *These tensions ignited . . . black residents*: "Report of the National Advisory Commission on Civil Disorders," 1968, also known as the Kerner Report (Pantheon Books,
1988), 1, 6, 32, 35–108. The report found that prior monetary estimates of damage
had been greatly exaggerated, 6.

382 *Reagan saw . . . "a plan"*: LAT 7/26/67, "Reagan Sees Plan Behind Violence."

382 *U.S. Department*: LAT 7/25/67, "Central Direction of Riots Doubted by U.S."

382 *A bipartisan*: "Report of the National Advisory Commission on Civil Disorders," op.
cit., 9.

382 *Rather*: Ibid., 1–24; NYT 3/1/68, "Panel on Civil Disorders Calls for Drastic Action
to Avoid 2-Society Nation"; WP 3/1/68, "Racism, Poverty Blamed for Riots."

382 *And though*: "Report of the National Advisory Commission on Civil Disorders," op.
cit., 6, 7, 334.

383 *There was*: Ibid., 18, 335.

383 *Mario Savio*: Savio's draft records were obtained by the author under the FOIA. He
was Selective Service no. 50-63-42-1094, and as of September 14, 1965, was classified 3-A, registrant with a child or children, so his service was deferred. On this kind
of deferment, see NYT 8/27/65, "New Husbands"; NYT 9/5/65, "Husbands' Status."

383 *But unless*: Selective Service System, "How the Draft Has Changed Since Vietnam," www.sss.gov/viet.htm, accessed 7/20/11. In February 1968, the draft was revised to eliminate deferments for certain categories of students in junior colleges
and graduate schools. See NYT 2/17/68, "Most Deferments to End for Graduate
Students"; NYT 2/17/68, "Text of 3 Documents on Deferment"; NYT 2/17/68, "Draft
Uncertainties"; NYT 2/17/68, "Educators Oppose Draft Rule."

383 *By now*: The number of troops as of June 30, 1967, is from *The Sixties: Years of Hope,
Days of Rage*, 220.

383 *Deferments*: Ibid.

383 *Some students*: The "How to Beat the Draft" flyer was described by Edwin Meese III,
Testimony of Edwin Meese, Investigative Hearings, Committee on Un-American
Activities, House of Representatives, 89th Congress, August 17 and 18, 1965, pp.
1096–97, and in author interview with Stew Albert.

383 *Other men burned*: For example, see LAT 1/9/67, "Draft Law Violators"; NYT 4/7/67,
"Draft Card Burner"; SFC 10/13/67, "Mass UC Draft Card Burn-In"; LAT 1/4/67,
"Man Arrested in Draft Case." Gitlin reports that more than 200,000 men were accused of draft violations, 25,000 indicted, 8,750 convicted, and 4,000 sentenced to
prison, *The Sixties*, 291.

383 *Berkeley's Country Joe*: Lyrics from "I-Feel-Like-I'm-Fixin'-to-Die Rag," copyright
1965 Joe McDonald. Copyright 1977, Alkatraz Corner Music, BMI.

384 *The most militant*: This paragraph is based on LAT 10/4/67, "Youths Refusing Draft";
LAT 10/17/67, "140 Foes of Draft Jailed"; SFC 10/14/67, "Heyns Says UC Teach-In
Will Be Held"; SFC 10/17/67, "125 Jailed in Oakland Sit In." On Stop the Draft
Week, see also *Berkeley at War* and *The Sixties*. The FBI assembled voluminous files
on Stop the Draft Week, though the case was prosecuted by the Alameda County
District Attorney's Office.

384 *Reagan disapproved*: This paragraph is based on SFC 10/15/67, "Writs Sought to
Halt UC Draft Meet."

384 *As they had . . . Pauley Ballroom*: LAT 10/17/67, "Court Bans UC Viet Teach-in."

384 *In defiance . . . required hospital treatment*: LAT 10/17/67, "Court Bans UC Viet Teach-in"; LAT 10/18/67, "Protest for Provocation's Sake"; LAT 10/18/67, "Police Wield Clubs in Oakland"; LAT 10/19/67, "Third Day of Oakland Antiwar"; LAT 10/29/67, "Crowd Controls Studied"; SFC 10/17/67, "Students Defy Court Ban"; SFC 10/18/67, "Many Are Injured—20 Arrested"; SFC 10/18/67, "Newsmen Hurt."

385 *Jack Weinberg*: SFC 10/20/67, "Victory for Anti-War Militants."

385 *Chief Charles Gain . . . news reporters*: LAT 10/19/67, "Third Day of Oakland Antiwar."

385 *"Wading in" . . . "bad taste"*: LAT 10/29/67, "Crowd Controls Studied."

385 *Reagan, however . . . "agencies"*: SFC 10/18/67, "Reagan's Reaction."

385 *The demonstrations on*: LAT 10/19/67, "Third Day of Oakland Antiwar"; SFC 10/20/67, "600 at Peaceful Picketing."

385 *But on Friday . . . assaulting an officer*: SFC 10/21/67, "2000 Police Called Up, 28 Arrests"; NYT 10/21/67, "Thousands in Oakland Stage Protest"; SFC 11/27/67, "The Story Behind the Oakland Riots."

385 *The clash*: The Sixties, 249–55.

385 *The next day*: This paragraph is based on LAT 10/22/67, "Pentagon Protest Erupts in Violence"; NYT 10/22/67, "Guards Repulse War Protesters at the Pentagon"; WP 10/24/67, "America's Youth Found Its Voice in the March"; WP 10/25/67, "Last of 682 Demonstrators Arraigned."

386 *The demonstration*: Armies of the Night, 94.

386 *Reagan was . . . "our country"*: SFC 10/25/67, "Reagan Condemns Draft Protests."

386 *He had called*: LAT 5/10/67, "Reagan to GOP."

386 *Now he*: NYT 10/26/67, "Reagan Says Declaration of War."

386 *Some days*: Author interviews with Burney Threadgill, Jr., and Bob Lamborn.

386 *The FBI still*: Church, book III, 26, 448–51, 470, 483–90.

386 *Jones and . . . "being circulated"*: 100-34204-2348; 100-34204-2287.

386 *But Stew Albert's*: SFC 2/18/67, "Police Spy on UC Student Groups," in 100-444372-NR, behind 100-444372-190. Stew and Joann Albert were later divorced; he married Judy Clavir, who became known as Judy Gumbo.

386 *Soon Jerry Rubin*: 100-34204-2278; DC 2/17/67, "Rubin Blasts," in 100-34204-2267; SFC 2/21/67, "Student Records," in 100-34204-2261; Berkeley Barb, 2/25/67, "Police State U," in 100-34204-2276; DC 2/22/67, "Ten Students a Day," in 100-34204-2297.

386 *Chancellor Heyns*: SFX 2/23/67, "UC Will Tighten," in 100-34204-2279; DC 2/27/67, "Approval Needed," in 100-34204-2292; 100-34204-2278.

386 *Or as Jones*: 100-34204-2278.

386 *In addition*: 100-151646-225; 100-151646-226; 100-34204-2342; 100-34204-2344; 100-34204-2311; 100-151646-234; author interview with Sparrow.

387 *But when . . . "at UCB"*: 100-34204-2215. According to Jones's memo, the reporter was John Vanek.

387 *Three days before*: This paragraph is based on 100-382196-41.

387 *Reagan kicked*: The summary of Reagan's tour is based on NYT 1/14/68, "California GOP"; Chicago Tribune 1/15/68, "Reagan Makes"; LAT 1/17/68, "Reagan Opens"; NYT 1/17/68, "Gov. Reagan Opens"; NYT 1/17/68, "The Proceedings"; Chicago Tribune 1/17/68, "Asks for Change"; Chicago Tribune 1/18/68, "People Losing Liberty"; LAT 1/18/68, "People Feel"; LAT 1/18/68, "Reagan Takes"; WP 1/18/68, "Conservatives to Back"; NYT 1/18/68, "Reagan Lays"; LAT 1/19/68, "U.S. Lags"; LAT 1/19/68, "Window on Washington"; Chicago Tribune 1/21/68, "Reagan Urges Bomb."

387 *At each stop*: NYT 1/21/68, "Reagan Finishing."

387 *Hoover's aides . . . "to the Director"*: 80-990-41; 100-382196-42; 100-382196-43; 100-382196-44.

387 *But as*: 100-151646-239.

387 *The day before . . . partisan politics*: 100-382196-44.
388 *At 10:00 a.m. . . . "maintained there"*: 100-382196-45; author interview with Edwin Meese III.
388 *After the meeting*: The summary of the rest of Reagan's tour is based on NYT 1/19/68, "Reagan Scornful"; *Chicago Tribune* 1/21/68, "Reagan Urges Bomb"; LAT 1/21/68, "Reagan Flays"; NYT 1/21/68, "Reagan Finishing"; WP 1/24/68, "Window on Washington."
388 *Several days . . . "for us"*: 100-382196-38; 100-382196-46.
389 *Demoted from*: LAT 1/8/68, "Reagan's New Education Aide"; UC Berkeley Directory of Officers and Students, Bancroft; "Convenient Myths About Today's Students," remarks of Alex Sherriffs, Commonwealth Club of San Francisco, May 19, 1967, in Ronald Reagan Governor's Papers, RRPL, Research Unit, box 45, folder: "University 1967 3 of 3."
389 *The psychology professor*: "Alex Sherriffs, Education Advisor to Ronald Reagan and State University Administrator," 1969–1982, interviews conducted by Gabrielle Morris and Sarah Sharp, Regional Oral History Office, Bancroft, 23.
389 *Meanwhile, he continued*: See, for example, 100-151646-214; 100-151646-221; 100-34204-1645; 100-34204-2311; 100-34204-2340.
389 *He never disclosed . . . he said*: Rowland interview with Sherriffs; Sparrow to Reagan, 11/5/66, and Reagan to Sparrow (Sparrow is incorrectly called Spaun), 11/30/66, 1966 Campaign Series, Governor's Personal Correspondence, RRPL, box C-29, folder: Letters of Particular Interest, M–Z; Reagan to Mulford, 8/17/66, 1966 Campaign Series, Campaign Correspondence, Ronald Reagan's Governor's Papers, RRPL, box C-16; author interview with Sparrow. The author made several attempts to speak with Sherriffs in the months before his death in April 2002 but neither he nor his representative responded.
389 *Sherriffs would later*: Rowland interview with Sherriffs, Bancroft, op. cit., 61.
389 *But as Reagan took*: Ibid., 65; LAT 1/8/68, "Reagan's New Education Aide."
389 *He exulted in*: Rowland interview with Sherriffs, in which he expresses his anger and contempt over what he saw as Kerr's liberal policies, his "duplicity," and his mistreatment of Chancellor Ed Strong, 51–52, 53, 57, 60, 62, 63, 65; LAT 12/20/67, "Reagan Names."
389 *On December 19, 1967*: LAT 1/8/68, "Reagan's New Education Aide."
389 *Sherriffs's office . . . "or get out"*: Sherriffs oral history by Morris and Sharp, Bancroft, op. cit., 3–6a, 23; LAT 10/27/69, "Reagan Adviser."
389 *Like Reagan . . . "on the campuses?"*: Sherriffs oral history by Morris and Sharp, 33.
389 *And like Reagan . . . "quite a bit"*: LAT 1/8/68, "Reagan's New Education Aide."
389 *Sherriffs quickly . . . on student unrest*: LAT 9/26/73, "Reagan Aide Named to Key College Post"; LAT 10/27/69, "Reagan Adviser." Sherriffs's job description is in Ronald Reagan Governor's Papers, Correspondence Unit, RRPL, box 1969-42, folder: "Alex Sherriffs Correspondence, August 1969." He describes his work in Sherriffs's oral history by Morris and Sharp, op. cit.
390 *Sherriffs . . . "spies tell me . . ."*: LAT 9/26/73, "Reagan Aide Named to Key College Post"; Sherriffs's campus intelligence gathering is detailed to some extent in the Reagan gubernatorial records cited in the third note to this chapter. The "my spies" quote is from Ronald Reagan Governor's Papers, Governor's Office Series, GO box 165, folder: "Research File—Education—RR Memos from ACS (Alex Sherriffs) (2/6)."
390 *Edwin Meese III*: LAT 5/4/86, "The Roots of Ed Meese," by Kate Coleman; LAT 12/22/66, "Prosecutor Appointed Reagan Clemency Aide"; *With Reagan*, 30; author interview with Edwin Meese III.
390 *Like Reagan*: This paragraph is drawn from Ronald Reagan Governor's Papers,

RRPL, GO box 1, "Cabinet Members—Biographies, Governor's Office, Cabinet Office Files—Administrative"; *LAT* 6/26/80, "California Cronies"; *WP* 3/15/81, "Deep Inside Ed Meese Runs a Law-and-Order Streak"; *LAT* 12/22/66, "Prosecutor Appointed Reagan Clemency Aide"; *With Reagan*, 28–32; author interview with Bob Lamborn.

390 *His great-grandfather*: This paragraph is based on *WP* 1/24/84, "Back in Law Enforcement"; *LA Daily Journal* 11/26/71, "Second Most Powerful Man in California Government"; *LAT* 5/4/86, "The Roots of Ed Meese," by Kate Coleman; *With Reagan*, 28–29; Summary of Meese's U.S. Army Reserve record, obtained by the author under the FOIA.

390 *Graduating from*: This paragraph and the next are based on *With Reagan*, 28–29; *LAT* 5/4/86, "The Roots of Ed Meese," by Kate Coleman; *LAT* 6/26/80, " 'California Cronies' Have Reagan's Ear," by Robert Scheer; *WP* 3/15/81, "Deep Inside Ed Meese Runs a Law-and-Order Streak"; *Ronald Reagan: His Life and Rise to the Presidency*, 187; *California Rising*, 306; *The Right Moment*, 86–88; Kerr, vol. 2, 212–13; author interview with Sparrow.

391 *Meese deployed . . . easier to dominate*: *LAT* 5/4/86, "The Roots of Ed Meese," by Kate Coleman.

391 *When he prosecuted*: Meese was born on December 2, 1931.

391 *He was a major . . . Chamber of Commerce*: Summary of Meese military records, op. cit.; *LAT* 12/22/66, "Prosecutor Appointed Reagan Clemency Aide"; *SFX* 5/12/67, "How Threat of Death Penalty Saved a Life."

391 *Suzanne Goldberg*: *LAT* 5/4/86, "The Roots of Ed Meese," by Kate Coleman.

391 *The Free Speech . . . protest after another*: Ibid.; *WP* 3/15/81, "Deep Inside Ed Meese Runs a Law-and-Order Streak"; *With Reagan*, 27–32; Meese Testimony, Investigative Hearings before the Committee on Un-American Activities, House of Representatives, 89th Congress, Second Session, August 16–19, 1966.

391 *He soon took*: *LA Daily Journal* 11/26/71, "Second Most Powerful Man in California Government"; *WP* 3/15/81, "Deep Inside Ed Meese Runs a Law-and-Order Streak"; *LAT* 12/22/66, "Prosecutor Appointed Reagan Clemency Aide"; Reagan Gubernatorial Papers, RRPL, GO box 1, "Cabinet Members—Biographies, Governor's Office, Cabinet Office Files—Administrative"; *With Reagan*, 27–32.

391 *Installing*: S.F. *Bay Guardian* 4/4/84, "Remembering Ed Meese."

391 *"We have . . ."*: Ronald Reagan Governor's Papers, RRPL, box 75, folder: "Governor's Office, Legal Affairs Unit, Campus Disturbances, Clippings, 5/5."

392 *In another report*: Ronald Reagan Governor's Papers, RRPL, box G0198, "Research File—Ronald Reagan—Executive Research 1967–1970, folder 1 of 2," Governor's Office, Molly Sturgis Tuthill Series.

392 *He noted that*: Ronald Reagan Governor's Papers, Governor's Office Series, RRPL, box 75, folder: "Governor's Office, Legal Affairs Unit, Campus Disturbances, Clippings, 5/5."

392 *Although it was*: Meese's effort is documented in Major General James H. Skeldon to Meese, 10/28/68, and Meese to Commanding General Stanley R. Larsen, 10/16/68, both in Reagan Gubernatorial Papers, Correspondence Unit, RRPL, box 1968/28, folder: "Colleges—October."

392 *And like Reagan's request*: The army lacked authority to collect such information on civilian political activity in the first place, Church, book III, 548, 787, 788, 789, 793, 794, 803, 804, 805, 806, 823; author interview with Christopher H. Pyle, professor of politics, Mount Holyoke College, and former U.S. Senate consultant. The Church committee noted, "It was only in January 1970, when a former Army intelligence officer, Christopher H. Pyle, wrote an article for the *Washington Monthly* exposing

the extent of Army's domestic program, that serious efforts to curb the Army's domestic activities were undertaken." The army curtailed its activities only at this point. Church, book III, 804–805. Pyle told the author the army had no legal authority to gather and distribute this information.

393 *And though*: The army spied on more than 100,000 civilians, including Martin Luther King, Jr., Joan Baez, and Benjamin Spock. Church, book III, ibid. Savio's FBI files show the bureau routinely sent reports on him to the army, too.

393 *Larsen was . . . "to General Ames"*: Skeldon and Meese letters, RRPL, op. cit.

393 *Glenn C. Ames: LAT* 3/1/68, "National Guard Ready."

393 *In an interview . . . "on the campus"*: Author interview with Edwin Meese III.

393 *One of them was*: Author interview with Bob Lamborn; *DC* 10/11/66, "Mother Continues Her Suit"; *DC* 11/1/66, "Political Names Verdict"; *DC* 11/3/66, "Housewife Gets List"; *LAT* 11/3/66, "UC Groups Must Open"; *LAT* 10/21/66, "UC Regent Will Ask"; *SFC* 10/12/66, "Privacy Ruling"; *SFC* 10/8/66, "A Suit to Get UC Student Lists"; *SFC* 11/3/66, "UC Files Opened to 'Researcher'"; *The Berkeley Citizen* 10/14/66, "Woman Seeking U.C. Lists Linked"; *OT* 10/7/66, "U.C. Sued"; *OT* 10/8/66, "U.C. Bows to Demand"; *OT* 10/12/66, "Student Group List"; *OT* 11/2/66, "U.C. Student List Opened"; *OT* 11/3/66, "Wide Open U.C. Records?"; *OT* 2/18/69, "Ruling Hits Secrecy"; *OT* 3/2/78, "U.S. Probes Eastbay Firm's"; *East Bay Voice,* July–August 1978, "Corporate Spies," by Seth Derish.

393 *Like Meese . . . local Republican clubs*: Atthowe birth certificate, copy obtained by author; *OT* 3/2/78, "U.S. Probes Eastbay Firm's"; Statement of Patricia M. Atthowe, Candidate for School Director No. 4, 3/11/65, contained in the library files of the *Oakland Tribune* newspaper.

394 *Atthowe was deeply*: She set out her views in a report she prepared with a cover styled like the cover page of a civil suit that read, "The People of the State of California, i.e., Parents, Taxpayers, Alumni, et al., Plaintiffs, Vs. The Regents of the University of California, a corporation; Roger W. Heyns, Chancellor of the University of California; Eldridge Cleaver, Minister of Information, Black Panther Party; Does one to three hundred, i.e., irresponsible and/or cowardly faculty, Defendants—Complaint and petition for academic responsibility and restoration of public trust," copy in Ronald Reagan Gubernatorial Papers, RRPL, box 76, folder: "Governor's Office, Legal Affairs Unit, Campus Disturbances, UC Berkeley 1/2."

394 *Her husband had helped*: 100-34204 sub C Section 3, which contains booking sheets for each arrestee.

394 *The protests so . . . "I do not"*: Atthowe to Brown, 12/3/65, Brown to Atthowe, 12/10/65, in Edmund G. Brown Papers, BANC MSS 68/90c, box 802, folder, "University of California, December 10–31," 1964, Bancroft.

394 *She was resolute*: This paragraph is based on *OT* 2/19/65, "Ad Response Leads Woman"; *OT* 4/13/65, "Patricia Atthowe"; *OT* 4/21/65, "Board of Education"; *OT* 5/13/65, "Dunstan, Corneille."

394 *In a speech*: This paragraph is based on the *BCU Bulletin*, November 1965 through February 1967, Bancroft. On the BCU, see also *Berkeley at War*, 56–57, 66–67, 88, 92, 111, 150, 152, 158.

394 *Throughout 1966*: Her work for the Reagan campaign is noted in *SFC* 11/3/66, "UC Files Opened to 'Researcher'"; *The Berkeley Citizen* 10/14/66, "Woman Seeking U.C. Lists Linked." Her work with the DA's office and her lawsuit for access to student records is noted in prior chapters.

395 *After his victory: OT* 5/6/68, "Disrupters Here Organized?"

395 *She elaborated . . . Legal Affairs Unit*: Ronald Reagan Governor's Papers, RRPL, box

76, folder: "Governor's Office, Legal Affairs Unit, Campus Disturbances, UC Berkeley 1/2."

395 *The following year*: This paragraph is based on WP 3/2/78, "House Probers Rebuffed"; plaintiff's interview of Charles Fox, 4/4/75, investigative report in *Synanon v. Hearst* litigation; plaintiff's interview of Harper Knowles, 5/9/75, investigative report in *Synanon v. Hearst* litigation; plaintiff's interview of Donald Francis Lynn, 12/30/74, investigative report in *Synanon v. Hearst* litigation; plaintiff's interview of Richard Combs, 3/3/75, investigative report in *Synanon v. Hearst* litigation; Harold L. Atthowe application for private investigator license, California Bureau of Private Investigators and Adjusters, which lists Donald F. Lynn as manager of Research West.

395 *Atthowe also hired*: Author interview with Bob Lamborn; Lamborn application for private investigator license, California Bureau of Collection and Investigative Services, 4/19/73.

395 *Born in 1923 . . . bite into it*: Summary of Lamborn Army Service Record, copy obtained by the author under the FOIA; SFC 5/5/04, "Robert Lamborn"; author interview with Bob Lamborn; author interview with Mike Lamborn.

395 *Returning to Berkeley . . . conservative politics*: Plaintiff's investigative report in *Synanon v. Hearst* litigation, 11/12/74; SFC 5/5/04, "Robert Lamborn"; author interviews with Bob Lamborn, Mike Lamborn, and Burney Threadgill, Jr.

395 *One afternoon . . . on campus*: Author interviews with Threadgill and Lamborn.

396 *Soon Lamborn . . . COINTELPRO operation*: Author interview with Bob Lamborn; "Lamborn on the Hill," 3/28/96, private writing, provided to the author by Bob Lamborn; "Lamborn Family Vineyards," www.winzone.com/Lamborn, accessed 5/26/02; "Our Story," www.lamborn.com/About-Us/Our-Story, accessed 5/28/11.

396 *Lamborn began . . . Western Research*: Author interviews with Bob Lamborn and Burney Threadgill, Jr.

396 *Ranks of women*: "Women Defend the Nation," The Cold War Museum, www.coldwar.org/articles/50s/women_civildefense.asp, accessed 5/28/11.

396 *As Lamborn*: Author interview with Bob Lamborn.

396 *Charles Fox*: Plaintiff's interview of Charles Fox, 4/4/75, investigative report in *Synanon v. Hearst* litigation.

396 *Perhaps out of*: Plaintiff's interview of Richard Combs, 3/3/75, investigative report in *Synanon v. Hearst* litigation.

396 *Harper Knowles . . . "did on campus"*: Plaintiff's interview of Harper Knowles, 5/9/75, investigative report in *Synanon v. Hearst* litigation.

396 *Moving the firm's . . . "Trust Department"*: Plaintiff's investigative report in *Synanon v. Hearst* litigation, 11/5/74.

396 *She merged*: Inter-Office Memorandum, 11/30/77, Lowell Bergman to Altmeyer, re Research West, Urban Policy Research Institute Collection, Southern California Library for Social Studies and Research, Los Angeles; Plaintiff's interview of Harper Knowles, 5/9/75, investigative report in *Synanon v. Hearst* litigation; *The Nation* 5/6/78, "The Intelligence Laundry," by Bill Wallace; author visit to 1419 Broadway.

396 *Atthowe took pains*: SFC 2/25/79, "House Probe of PG&E 'Spying'"; author interview with Bob Lamborn.

396 *The first came*: The account of Research West and the Synanon case is from the author's review of records in *Synanon Foundation, Inc., et al., v. William Randolph Hearst, Jr., et al.*, S.F. Superior Court cases 651-749 and 667-448; *LAT* 7/2/76, "Hearst Corp. to Pay"; *NYT* 7/2/76, "Hearst Corp. to Pay"; *NYT* 7/3/76, "Libel Suit Costs"; *NYT* 12/10/78, "A Changed Synanon"; *LAT* 7/3/82, "ABC Payoff: Unanswered Questions"; *S.F. Bay Guardian* 7/23/76, "The Adventures of Ed Montgomery";

S.F. Bay Guardian 7/30/76, "On the Synanon Trail"; *NYT* 3/4/97, "Charles Dederich"; *East Bay Voice*, July–August 1978, "Corporate Spies in East Bay," by Seth Derish.

Synanon was started in the late 1950s in Santa Monica by Charles Dederich, who had kicked booze with Alcoholics Anonymous but was unhappy with AA's refusal to accept drug addicts. At Synanon's core was a form of therapy he created called "The Game," involving lengthy, verbally violent encounter sessions. He was charismatic and the organization grew, attracting many nonresident adherents. Over the years, Synanon morphed into a social movement and a religion. It amassed real estate and other holdings estimated at $30 million, receiving corporate donations and operating several businesses. Synanon was credited with helping addicts, but in the late seventies Dederich reportedly required participation in mass vasectomies, spouse-swapping, and physical punishment. In 1980 he pleaded no contest to criminal charges of conspiracy to commit murder by putting a rattlesnake in the mailbox of a lawyer representing former members. *The Point Reyes Light*, a tiny Marin County weekly edited by David Mitchell, won the 1979 Pulitzer Prize for Public Service for investigative reporting about Synanon. See *LAT* 3/4/97, "Charles Dederich Sr."; *LAT* 10/17/01, "West Words"; *NYT* 9/4/80, "Synanon Founder"; *Sociological Analysis*, 1980, "The Social Development of the Synanon Cult," by Richard Ofshe.

397 *Atthowe's next brush*: The account of Atthowe, Research West, and the Moss hearing is from *SFC* 2/25/77, "House Probe of PGE 'Spying'"; *WP* 11/7/77, "Ga. Utility Kept Files on Critics"; *Sacramento Bee* 3/18/78, "Refusal on Activist Files"; *Sacramento Bee* 6/28/78, "Moss Panel Moves to Cite"; *SFC* 3/18/78, "Private Detectives Still Won't Give Records to Congress"; *WP* 3/18/78, "Detective Agency Chief Defies a Hill Subpoena"; *LAT* 8/25/83, "PDID Detective Mistrusted"; Research West's solicitation for "Business Conflicts Reports"; *NYT* 12/6/97, "John E. Moss, 84, Is Dead"; *LAT* 12/6/97, "John E. Moss"; "Contempt Proceedings Against Patricia Atthowe," Subcommittee on Oversight and Investigations of the Committee on Interstate and Foreign Commerce, U.S. House of Representatives, Ninety-fifth Congress, Second Session, March 3 and 17, 1978.

398 *Since then*: This paragraph is based on plaintiff's interview of Harper Knowles, 5/9/75, investigative report in *Synanon v. Hearst* litigation; author interviews with Bob Lamborn and Burney Threadgill, Jr. The FBI documents cited are 100-39577-NR, 4/18/69, before 100-39577-17; 100-39577-17; 100-39577-15.

398 *The CIA was legally*: The National Security Act of 1947, which created the CIA, provided in Section 403(d)(3): "That the Agency shall have no police, subpoena, law enforcement powers or internal security functions," Church, book III, 686.

398 *. . . but Lamborn said . . . "no legal jurisdiction"*: Author interview with Bob Lamborn.

398 *Harold E. Chipman*: Declaration of Lois A. Chipman, 6/10/82, in *Lois A. Chipman v. Harold E. Chipman*, Marin County Superior Court, No. 98958; *Dirty Work: The CIA in Western Europe*, 398; *Blond Ghost: Ted Shackley and the CIA's Crusades*, 197–201. Chipman died on June 2, 1988; his obituary said he was a retired army cryptographer, *WP* 6/5/88, "Death Notices."

398 *They were partners*: Declaration of Harold E. Chipman, 6/24/82, in *Lois A. Chipman v. Harold E. Chipman*, Marin County Superior Court, No. 98958; Declaration of Harold E. Chipman in answer to complaint, 11/9/81, *First Interstate Bank of California v. Market Analysis, Inc.*, Alameda County Superior Court, No. 548443-2 (stating he is president of MAI); Promissory Note, 12/31/81, attached to complaint in

Finkelstein v. Market Analysis, Inc., S.F. Municipal Court, No. 851082 (Atthowe signing as secretary of MAI).

398 *Chipman's wife . . . "almost anything"*: Declarations of Lois Chipman and Harold E. Chipman, op. cit.

398 *Chipman apparently*: His Checker cab is noted in *Lois A. Chipman v. Harold E. Chipman*, op. cit.; his alias is noted in *Soto v. Market Analysis, Inc.*, California Department of Industrial Relations, Division of Labor Standards Enforcement, No. 07-15518 NJK, 1982.

398 *In response to*: Delores M. Nelson, Information and Privacy Coordinator, CIA, to Seth Rosenfeld, 9/17/09.

399 *Research West meanwhile*: This paragraph is based on Research West solicitation for "Business Conflicts Reports," which it described as a "monthly confidential newsletter," 1978; another Atthowe solicitation, 6/1/78, "You are the victim"; author interview with Bob Lamborn; "Western Research/Research West," 1978, investigative report by Seth Derish.

399 *Mother's Cake . . . Mel's Drive-In*: The information on Mother's Cookies is based on records provided to the author by Peter Sheehan, attorney, Alameda County Legal Aid Society, 12/13/83; author interview with former secretary for Mother's Cookies.

399 *Research West's client list . . . also was a client*: Author interview with Bob Lamborn.

399 *Atthowe moved . . . $19,000*: Atthowe's rental agreement was described in *Tower II v. Research West*, Alameda County Superior Court, No. 548284-3, 1981. Her involvement with Market Analysis, Inc., was described in several lawsuits that named the firm: *T. David Hodgkinson v. Market Analysis, Inc., et al.*, S.F. Superior Court, No. 785155, 1982; *First Interstate Bank of California v. Market Analysis, Inc.*, Alameda County Superior Court, No. 548443-2, 1981; *Tower II v. Market Analysis, Inc.*, Alameda County Superior Court, No. 552949-4, 1981; *Finkelstein v. Market Analysis, Inc.*, San Francisco Municipal Court, No. 951082, 1983.

399 *But by 1981*: This paragraph is based on records in the following litigation, copies in the author's possession: *Security Pacific National Bank v. Research West and Richard K. Miller*, S.F. Superior Court, No. 781207, 1981; *Richard K. Miller v. Research West, et al.*, S.F. Superior Court, No. 799821, 1982; *T. David Hodgkinson v. Market Analysis, Inc., et al.*, S.F. Superior Court, No. 785155, 1982; *First Interstate Bank of California v. Market Analysis, Inc.*, Alameda County Superior Court, No. 548443-2, 1981; *First Interstate Bank of California v. Research West, et al.*, Alameda County Superior Court, No. 548442-3, 1981; *Tower II v. Market Analysis, Inc.*, Alameda County Superior Court, No. 552949-4, 1981; *Tower II v. Research West*, Alameda County Superior Court, No. 548284-3, 1981; *Watergate Co. v. Patricia Atthowe and Research West*, Alameda County Municipal Court, No. 385928, 1982; *Parkwood Apartments v. Julie and Jean Atthowe*, Alameda County Municipal Court, No. 379293, 1981; *Irene Sargent v. Patricia Atthowe*, Alameda County Municipal Court, No. 386796, 1982; *Eastman Kodak Co. v. Research West*, Alameda County Superior Court, No. 555481-2, 1982; *IBM v. Research West*, Alameda County Municipal Court, No. 379290, 1981; *Finkelstein v. Market Analysis, Inc.*, San Francisco Municipal Court, No. 951082, 1983. State and federal tax liens were on file with the California Secretary of State as of 1983; Research West's financial collapse was noted in *LAT* 8/25/83, "Detective Described." Patricia Atthowe and family members did not respond to the author's certified letters seeking comment.

400 *By then . . . "governor's office"*: Author interview with Bob Lamborn; "Lamborn on the Hill," 3/28/96.

400 *Meese confirmed*: Author interview with Edwin Meese III.

400 *Not long after . . . "Atthowe's reliability"*: Break-ins, Death Threats and the FBI: The Covert War Against the Central America Movement, by Ross Gelbspan, 82. See p. 237, n. 23, which attributes this to the notes of a November 10, 1983, interview with Richard K. Miller by Detective Wealer and Sergeant Szymanski of IAD of LAPD.

400 *Perhaps the strangest*: The account of John Rees is based on *Village Voice* 8/16/83, "The Spy Who Came Down on the Freeze," by Seth Rosenfeld. It is also based on these materials at the Tamiment Library and Robert F. Wagner Labor Archives, New York University, as part of the National Lawyers Guild Records TAM 191: SAIC Berger interview of Rees 6/29/78; FBI HQ main file 62-112345 and WFO main file 134-10260; Rees deposition in *IPS v. FBI*, U.S. District Court for the District of Columbia, Civil Action No. 74-316; Pat Richartz declaration, 11/5/76; affidavit of Sheila O'Donnell, 8/15/80; *Information Digest* issue of 2/21/69; Guild Investigative Group memo, 1/22/77; *Yipster Times*, n.d., "Private Spies Infiltrate Left," by Steve Conliff; *Boston Phoenix*, 8/23/77, "Information Digest: The New Blacklist," by Jeffrey Stein; *Baltimore Sun*, 9/25/77, "City Man Fed Data to FBI, Police." This account also draws on FBI memo 176-1410-78-334, DeLoach to Rosen, 9/27/68, "Disturbances Arising Out of Democratic National Convention Antiriot Laws," on file at the Urban Policy Research Institute Collection, Southern California Library for Social Studies and Research, Los Angeles, as well as author interviews with Stew Albert and John Rees.

   Further information for the Rees account came from various news articles. On Rees and Metalious: *SFC* 2/27/64, "Legal Fight on Metalious Will"; *SFC* 3/2/64, "Writer Turns Down Estate"; *NYT* 2/27/64, "Family of Grace"; *WP* 2/27/64, "Metalious Children"; *NYT* 2/28/64, "Funeral Is Ordered"; *NYT* 3/2/64, "Briton Renounces"; *LAT* 4/12/64, "Grace Metalious Left"; *WP* 6/27/64, "$127,000 Estate Left"; *NYT* 6/30/64, "Judge Upholds"; *NYT* 11/25/64, "Estate of Grace." On Metalious: *LAT* 2/26/64, "'Peyton Place' Writer"; *NYT* 2/26/64, "Grace Metalious Is Dead"; *WP* 2/26/64, "Grace Metalious"; *LAT* 10/1/64, "The Book Report." On Rees: *WP* 6/27/76, "John Rees"; *WP* 8/16/77, "When Left Reaches"; *WP* 11/7/77, "Ga. Utility Kept Files on Critics"; *Philadelphia Inquirer* 10/26/00, "Engaged in an Endless Pursuit"; *NYT* 6/25/07, "Trove of F.B.I. Files"; *Philadelphia Inquirer* 9/10/00, "Rumors Had Troopers Seeing Reds"; *The Age of Surveillance*, 446–51, 456n; *Break-ins, Death Threats and the FBI: The Covert War Against the Central America Movement*, by Ross Gelbspan; Political Research Associates 9/8/00, "The Maldon Institute," by Chip Berlet, www.publiceye.org/liberty/Rees/Rees.html, accessed 5/30/11.

401 *Rees—and HUAC*: On the Chicago Seven indictments, see *LAT* 3/21/69, "Eight Police, Eight Protesters Indicted"; *NYT* 3/21/69, "16 Indicted." Eight people were originally indicted: Abbie Hoffman, Jerry Rubin, David Dellinger, Tom Hayden, Rennie Davis, John Froines, Lee Weiner, and Bobby Seale. Seale's case was severed and the main case became known as the Chicago Seven trial. All seven were acquitted on conspiracy charges, *NYT* 2/19/70, "Chicago 7 Cleared of Plot." Five defendants were convicted of other riot-related charges, but they were reversed on appeal, *WP* 11/22/72, "'Chicago 7' Convictions Overturned." Riot charges against Seale were dismissed, *WP* 10/20/70, "Seale's Case." Contempt-of-court convictions against all defendants were reversed, *WP* 5/12/72, "New Contempt Trial." At retrial, Dellinger, Rubin, Hoffman, and attorney William Kunstler were convicted of contempt, but the court imposed no sentence, *WP* 12/7/73, "U.S. Judge Declines."

404 *Rees was also . . . "but very clever"*: Author interview with Bob Lamborn. Gelbspan also reports that Rees and Atthowe worked together, *Break-ins, Death Threats and the FBI*, 82. Sheila Rees could not be reached for comment.

404 *In one of those*: The Hayden anecdote is based on author interviews with Rees and Lamborn. Hayden told the author he didn't recall it.
404 *J. Edgar Hoover*: The Ferber anecdote is from 62-103031-252; 62-103031-254. On Ferber, see *WP* 4/10/85, "Mark Ferber, 55, Political Scientist."
404 *Over brunch*: The Lang anecdote is based on 62-103031-256, 1/21/69; 62-103031-256, 1/22/69. On Lang, see *NYT* 9/25/05, "Serge Lang, 78, a Gadfly." Hoover also approved anonymously telling Reagan that Richard Erle Healey, the son of CP leader Dorothy Healey, had a UCLA fellowship, even though he never was in the party. 62-116009-219, p. 1030; *LAT* 8/8/06, "Dorothy Healey"; *LAT* 2/16/69, "L.A.'s No. 1 Red."
405 *In an interview*: Author interview with Edwin Meese III.
405 *Meese even asked . . . "extremely cooperative"*: 62-112075-2.

24: A Key Activist

406 *Mario and Suzanne Savio*: 100-54060-424; *SFX* 4/28/67, "Mario Quits," in 100-54060-421; *DC* 5/2/67, "Mario Savio," in 100-54060-422; 100-54060-113.
406 *Savio had been struggling*: *DC* 5/2/67, "Mario Savio," in 100-54060-422.
406 *He had been convicted*: *OT* 3/1/67, "Mario Savio Gets," in 100-54060-407.
406 *That conviction*: *SFX* 4/28/67, "Mario Quits," in 100-54060-421.
406 *And, finally*: *DC* 2/22/67, "Savio Drops," in 100-54060-401; *DC* 2/27/67, "Savio Withdraws," in 100-54060-411.
406 *He was, moreover*: Suzanne Goldberg, "Mario, Personal and Political," in *The Free Speech Movement: Reflections on Berkeley in the 1960s*, 560–61; author interview with Suzanne Goldberg.
406 *Although Savio . . . doted on Stefan*: Suzanne Goldberg, "Mario, Personal and Political," 560–61.
406 *Recalling his own . . . "point of panic"*: *Freedom's Orator*, 256–57, in which author Robert Cohen quotes the 8/10/67 letter from Savio to Hollander.
406 *But the young couple*: Suzanne Goldberg, op. cit., 561; author interview with Goldberg. Stefan's disability is noted in *OT* 10/26/67, "Savio's Sentences Softened."
406 *. . . and as Suzanne recalled*: Suzanne Goldberg, op. cit., 561.
406 *On top of all this*: In *Freedom's Orator*, Robert Cohen discusses Savio's long-term depression, 24, 253, 256, 268–69.
406 *"Things were too ____ and go"*: *SFX* 4/28/67, "Mario Quits," in 100-54060-421; *DC* 5/2/67, "Mario Savio," in 100-54060-422.
407 *A few weeks after*: This paragraph is based on 100-54060-384; 100-54060-385; 100-54060-410; 100-54060-444.
407 *But it was wrong . . . merely mentioned*: 100-151646-214.
407 *Nonetheless, FBI officials*: 100-54060-384; 100-54060-385; 100-54060-410; 100-54060-444; 100-54060-561.
407 *There is no evidence*: Author's review of Savio's FBI records.
407 *And on the basis*: 100-443052-23; 100-54060-387.
407 *FBI agents also . . . "José Martí"*: 100-54060-413; 100-54060-420; 100-54060-581.
407 *Martí was*: *Jose Martí, an Introduction*, 2, 11. Author Oscar Montero writes, "Martí believed that the sovereignty of a nation guaranteed the rights of its citizens, but he mistrusted the flag-waving nationalism of the demagogue," p. 9. "Martí believed that race prejudice, whatever forms it might take, whatever excuse might be used to justify it, had no place in a democracy. Martí feared for the United States . . . ," p. 15. The Columbia University professor German Arciniegas wrote, "The theme of the Cuban hero's life and writing was freedom," *NYT* 2/7/54, "The Theme Was Freedom."

407 *Savio had listed*: Author interview with Stew Albert.

407 *For weeks*: This paragraph is based on 100-54060-424.

408 *The Savios had driven*: This Mexico anecdote is based on 100-54060-462; But note that in an interview, Suzanne Goldberg questioned the FBI report and recalled events differently. She said their car broke down near Ojai, California; that they had sufficient funds; and that Savio's father came to help them. She did not recall visiting the U.S. Consulate.

408 *For a while*: 100-54060-430, 100-54060-434, 100-54060-462, an FBI report summarizing information from the U.S. Consulate.

408 *FBI agents ended*: 100-54060-429.

408 *Savio was . . . "American education"*: SFX 7/6/67, "Savio, Wife Get," in 100-54060-432.

408 *Jail was*: This paragraph is based on *Freedom's Orator*, 254–56.

408 *When Suzanne visited . . . on probation.)*: OT 9/4/67, "Mrs. Savio Arrested," in 100-54060-90; DC date illegible, "Suzanne Savio on Probation," in 100-54060-96; DC LED 9/7/67, in 100-54060-97.

409 *At another point . . . "'a normal life'"*: 100-54060-443.

409 *At 6:00 p.m.*: This paragraph is based on DC 10/26/67, "Savio Released," in 100-54060-452; DC date illegible, "Judge Excuses Suzanne," in 100-54060-453; 100-54060-439; 100-54060-443; 100-54060-444; 100-54060-445; 100-54060-446; 100-54060-449. The FBI reported his release date as October 24, while the Associated Press reported it as October 25.

409 *On January 30, 1968*: This paragraph and the next are based on 100-54060-464. Besides Savio, the memo named fourteen Key Activists in various cities: Jerry Rubin, Robert Scheer, Sidney Peck, Tom Hayden, Dave Dellinger, Clark Kissinger, Carl Oglesby, Gregory A. Calvert, Linda M. Dannenberg, Steven E. Halliwell, Carl A. Davidson, Robert H. Pardun, Nicholas M. Egleson, Michael L. Spiegel. John Gerassi, an S.F. State professor, was soon added, 100-54060-17.

409 *The Church committee*: 100-54060-464; Church, book III, 516–18, 533. As of spring 1969, the FBI had designated fifty-five people as Key Activists, Church, book III, 518. As of fall 1971, they numbered seventy-three, Church, book III, 533.

409 *Agents assigned*: This paragraph is based on Church, book III, 516–18.

410 *In San Francisco*: This paragraph is based on 100-54060-524; 100-54060-526.

410 *It was all . . . any subpoena*: 100-54060-468; 100-54060-572; 100-54060-524; 100-54060-430; 100-54060-524. Savio's FBI files reflect no objection by any commercial institution to the FBI's requests for his private information.

410 *Although subsequent laws*: NYT 5/20/11, "Deal Reached on Extension of Patriot Act"; NYT 8/19/03, "Administration Plans Defense."

410 *Discovering that Savio*: The part about Savio and Berkeley Tanometer is from 100-54060-482.

411 *Agent Jones continued*: 100-54060-482; 100-54060-494.

411 *But despite . . . "day-to-day activities"*: 100-54060-468; 100-54060-494; 100-54060-526.

411 *Savio stood*: The account of Savio's speech and the views he expressed in this part are from *People's World* 3/30/68, "America's Choice," in 100-54060-486; BDG 3/11/68, "Mario Savio Courts," in 100-54060-518.

411 *The PFP slate*: *Berkeley at War*, 83; LAT 5/14/68, "Black Panther Official to Run."

411 *Robert Scheer . . . Free Speech Movement*: *Berkeley at War*, 83; LAT 12/11/67, "Antiwar Group Sets"; LAT 1/4/68, "Peace Party Wins Ballot."

412 *In the following . . . "the poor"*: DC date illegible, "Savio Condemns Democratic," in 100-54060-496; DC 4/9/68, "5000 Marchers Chant," in 100-54060-495; SFX 4/11/68, "'End Racism,'" in 100-54060-487; BDG 5/3/68, "Mario Proposes Robin Hood," in 100-54060-513; 100-54060-493; 100-54060-500; 100-54060-501.

412 *Martin Luther King, Jr. . . . Lorraine Motel*: BBC, "On This Day," news.bbc.co.uk /onthisday/hi/dates/stories/april/4/newsid_2453000/2453987.stm, accessed 6/1/11.

412 *Riots broke out*: LAT 4/8/68, "1,900 U.S. Troops Enter."

412 *In Oakland*: NYT 4/8/68, "Oakland Police Kill."

412 *Two days later*: DC 4/9/68, "5000 Marchers Chant," in 100-54060-495.

413 *Huey Newton was*: LAT 4/1/68, "Newton Murder Charge."

413 *Massing outside*: DC 4/9/68, "5000 Marchers Chant," in 100-54060-495. Newton was later convicted of voluntary manslaughter, NYT 11/2/68, "Judge Curbs."

413 *As Savio campaigned . . . pick him up*: 100-54060-481; 100-54060-485; 100-54060-497; 100-54060-501; 100-54060-503.

413 *All the while*: This paragraph is based on *Freedom's Orator*, 258–59.

413 *He was deeply*: Savio's comments are in *Berkeley Barb* 4/5–11/1968, "Savio Savvy," in 100-54060-525.

414 *The bureau*: The quoted memo is 100-54060-517.

414 *COINTELPRO-New Left*: This and the next two paragraphs are based on the discussion of COINTELPRO in Church, book III, 1–78. On Hoover's termination of COINTELPRO after the break-in of the FBI office in Media, Pennsylvania, exposed it, see Church, book III, 3, n. 1, and LAT, 3/8/06.

415 *On May 17, 1968*: This paragraph and the next are based on 100-54060-512.

415 *However, Charles Bates*: This paragraph and the next are based on 100-54060-514.

415 *On May 31, 1968*: 100-443052-43.

415 *According to the Church committee . . . their political activities*: Church, book II, 93–94.

415 *The Savios' joint*: 100-443052-43.

415 *Savio drew*: The FBI noted the tally in 100-54060-524. In the general election that November, Savio lost to the incumbent, the liberal Democrat Nick Petris, by 183,122 votes to 11,712, WSJ 6/4/69, "Leaders of Berkeley's 1964 Student Rebellion"; OT 11/6/68, "County Re-elects."

415 *Shortly after midnight*: NYT 6/5/68, "Kennedy Claims Victory"; NYT 6/5/68, "Kennedy Shot."

416 *Since his speech*: By early 1967, Kennedy had become critical of the war, called for new peace initiatives, and urged a halt to the bombing, NYT 2/25/67, "Kennedy Bids"; LAT 3/3/67, "Kennedy Urges Bombing Halt"; NYT 3/3/67, "Kennedy Asks Suspension." In February 1968, he broadened his dissent from President Johnson's policy, denying there was any likelihood of a U.S. military victory in Vietnam or that the war was in the best interests of the South Vietnamese people, NYT 2/9/68, "Kennedy Asserts." In March 1968, he declared his intention to run for president on a platform of de-escalation, LAT 3/17/68, "Kennedy Declares"; NYT 3/17/68, "Kennedy Challenges"; NYT 3/19/68, "Students Cheer"; NYT 3/24/68, "Political Activism"; NYT 4/3/68, "Kennedy Resumes"; LAT 5/17/68, "Kennedy Raps."

416 *His murder*: The Sixties, Years of Hope, Days of Rage, 310, 311.

416 *In Sacramento*: Reagan's letter is dated June 7, 1968, and is in Ronald Reagan Governor's Papers, RRPL, GO box 169, folder: "Research File—Education—University of California, Regents, 1967–68, 1 of 2," Governor's Office, Molly Sturgis Tuthill Series.

417 *About two weeks*: 100-54060-523.

417 *The June 21, 1968*: Church, book II, 165.

417 *The same day . . . state senator*: 100-54060-524.

417 *Savio did have . . . Jones's report*: 100-54060-524.

417 *His job*: 100-54060-534; *The Life and Times of Cody's Books*, 106.

417 *By now*: 100-443052-40; 100-54060, vol. 5. Robert Cohen also notes Savio's activism declined postelection, *Freedom's Orator*, 259.

417 *FBI officials finally*: 100-54060-527.

25: At Bayonet Point

418 *The strikers stood*: The account in the first two paragraphs is based on *DC* 1/29/69, "TWLF Changes Tactics"; *DC* 1/29/69, "Police Quell Campus Disorder"; *SFC* 1/29/69, "Violence at UC—Fights, Tear Gas"; 157-9295-NR, 1/28/69, 5:01 p.m., and 157-9295-NR, 1/28/69, 6:04 p.m., both after 157-9295-13; 157-9295-NR, 1/28/69, 1:38 p.m., after 157-9295-18; author interview with Manuel Delgado.

418 *It was January 28, 1969*: For discussions of the TWLF by two participants, one Asian, one Chicano, see *The Origins and Trajectory of Asian American Political Activism in the San Francisco Bay Area, 1968–1978*, by Harvey C. Dong, Dissertation for Doctor of Philosophy in Ethnic Studies in the Graduate Division, UC Berkeley, Fall 2002; *The Last Chicano, A Mexican American Experience*, by Manuel Ruben Delgado.

418 *Some TWLF leaders*: Author interviews with Manuel Delgado and Richard Aoki; "Campus Disorders in California: Origins and Development," box 221, folder "Demonstrations, Riots, Disorders," Edwin Meese III Collection, Hoover Institution, which notes that as a student at Pasadena City College in 1964 Nabors had initiated a Pasadena Free Speech Movement in response to the FSM at Berkeley.

418 *And whereas*: The TWLF was widely seen as the most violent strike on campus to date, based on reports of physical conflicts, property damage, and level of police force, 62-112228-47-114; *SFX* 2/23/69, "It's All Quiet"; author interview with Aoki.

418 *Hoover ordered*: The FBI's investigation of the TWLF is documented in several files, including 157-1202; 157-9295; 100-151646; 100-34204.

418 *But one of . . . radical organizations*: The author's conclusion that Aoki was an FBI informer has several bases. First, the former FBI agent Burney Threadgill, Jr., discussed Aoki's work as an informer in interviews with the author; second, Aoki's own suggestive statements to the author; third, he is named as an "informant" with the temporary code number "T-2" in 105-165706-22, a November 16, 1967, FBI report on the Black Panthers; fourth, this conclusion is consistent with other FBI records concerning Aoki. It is also based on the declaration of former FBI agent M. Wesley Swearingen, *Seth Rosenfeld v. Federal Bureau of Investigation and U.S. Department of Justice*, C 11-02131MEJ, U.S. District Court, Northern District of California, 2011; author interview with M. Wesley Swearingen.

419 *He had given*: Aoki's firearms contributions to the Black Panthers, his background, and his central role in the TWLF are described in the following text, as are Reagan's measures in response to the TWLF. On Aoki and his giving the Panthers guns, see *The Last Chicano; Seize the Time; Up Against the Wall; Huey*; Dolly Veale interview of Richard Aoki in *Legacy to Liberation*, 319–34; KPFA Apex interview of Aoki, by reporter Wayie Ly, July 2006, ramemorial.blogspot.com/2009/08/life-and-times-of-richard-aoki-in-his.html, accessed 6/4/11; *SFC* 4/26/09, "Campus Activist Richard Masato Aoki"; *OT*, "Former Black Panther," www.insidebayarea.com/oaklandtribune/ci_11953825, accessed 6/8/11; *Asian Week* 4/27–5/3/01, "Back in the Day," www.asianweek.com/2001_04_27/feature_richardaoki.html, accessed 6/8/11; *Berkeley Barb*, 2/14–21/69, "TWLF Leader Tells," accessed 6/8/11; *OT* 10/8/66, "The Struggle Wasn't Just Black and White," www.mindfully.org/Reform/2006/Black-Panthers-Led8oct06.htm, accessed 6/8/11; Richard Masato Aoki Memorial, ramemorial.blogspot.com/, accessed 6/8/11; East Bay Living History Project, Japanese American Citizens League of Berkeley, panel discussion with Richard Aoki, 9/18/03, DVD; *Aoki: A Documentary Film*, www.aokifilm.com/, accessed 6/8/11, and DVD.

419 *Richard Masato Aoki*: The description of Aoki is from speakers' comments at his memorial service at UC Berkeley on May 2, 2009, including Victoria Wong, who recalled the slicked-back hair, the sunglasses even at night, and that "he had swag-

ger up to the moon." Carl Mack recalled that he spoke "like a black man." Manuel Delgado also recalled that Aoki "sounded black" and had mystique, remarking, "I thought of him as a Japanese Samurai," *The Last Chicano*, 167. He told a friend that "if I were ever re-incarnated I wanted to come back as a Japanese like Richard Aoki," *The Last Chicano*, 168.

419 A *thirty-year-old*: Author interview with Aoki, in which he described his army service and said he earned a BA in sociology in 1968 and a master's degree in social work in 1970. He was born on November 20, 1938, in San Leandro, California, 62-112228-47-114, p. 199; Student Telephone Directory, Associated Students University of California, 1966–70, Bancroft.

419 *The double*: This paragraph is based on *SFC* 3/10/1909, "Aoki Engaged"; *SFC* 3/?/1909, "Archdeacon Does Not Approve"; *SFC* 3/12/1909, "Brother of Aoki Frowns"; *SFC* 3/15/1909, "Don't Want Aoki"; *SFC* 3/20/1909, "Throw Bricks at Japanese Suitor"; *SFC* 3/22/1909, "Say Miss Emery Will Regret it"; *SFC* 3/28/1909, "Miss Emery Weds"; *SFC* 5/9/1909, "Aoki's Brother Leaves Mission"; *SFC* 7/25/1909, "Baby Comes"; *SFC* 12/28/1909, "Mrs. Aoki Tires"; *SFC* 5/27/1910, "Gladys Emery Seeks"; *SFC* 6/8/1910, "Aoki Follows His Wife"; *SFC* 4/26/1909, "Campus Activist Richard Masato Aoki"; author interviews with Aoki, his cousin James Aoki, Harvey Dong.

419 *Shozo Aoki*: This paragraph is based on Aoki's Alameda County birth certificate; author interviews with Aoki and James Aoki; Dolly Veale interview of Richard Aoki, in *Legacy to Liberation*, 319–34; KPFA Apex interview with Aoki, by reporter Wayie Ly, July 2006, ramemorial.blogspot.com/2009/08/life-and-times-of-richard-aoki-in-his.html, accessed 6/4/11. On the Japanese internment, see *A People's History of the United States*, 416; Topaz Museum, *Topaz Times*, www.topazmuseum.org/index.html, accessed 6/4/11.

419 *The internment destroyed . . . others had been*: Author interview with Aoki; Veale interview with Aoki, op. cit.; KPFA Apex interview with Aoki, op. cit.

419 *Disillusioned*: Author interview with Aoki.

420 *It was part*: Author interview with Aoki; KPFA Apex interview with Aoki, op. cit.; *Oakland: The Story of a City*, 241. The U.S. Supreme Court struck down racial covenants in 1948, ibid., 204–206.

420 *Growing up . . . co-valedictorian*: This paragraph is based on KPFA Apex interview with Aoki, op. cit.; author interviews with Aoki and Earl Napper.

420 *Despite the stigma*: Author interview with Aoki; author interview with Dr. Naomi F. P. Southard, a minister at the Aokis' family church; KPFA Apex interview with Aoki, op. cit.

420 *At Berkeley High*: The part about Aoki being a good student at Berkeley High and having "career ambitions" is from KPFA Apex interview with Aoki, op. cit.; his presidency of the Stamp and Coin Club is noted in the Berkeley High yearbooks for 1955 and 1956, at the Berkeley Public Library.

420 *But he got into trouble*: Author interview with Aoki.

420 *Three days after*: Author interviews with Aoki and Aoki's high school friend Earl Napper; KPFA Apex interview with Aoki, op. cit.

420 *He had enlisted*: Author interview with Aoki.

420 *He gave friends*: In interviews with the author, his friends recalled a range of explanations. Earl Napper said Aoki simply told him, "A man's got to do what he's got to do." Oliver Petry, another high school friend, said Aoki wanted to "be trained to shoot guns." Harvey Dong, a close friend at UC Berkeley and a fellow activist, recalled that Aoki saw the army as a means of advancement. However, Mike Cheng, a neighbor of Aoki's, who with Ben Wang produced the documentary film *Aoki*, told the author that Aoki had recounted that he had a juvenile criminal record but a

judge said it would be wiped clean if he enlisted in the military. Aoki similarly told the author, "Well, my juvenile record was sealed; that was part of the condition for going into the service; I cut a deal."

420 *Aoki harbored*: Author interviews with Aoki and Mike Cheng; KPFA Apex interview with Aoki, op. cit.

420 *He served*: Author interview with James Aoki.

420 *Although he never*: Author interview with Aoki.

420 *"I got to play with . . ."*: KPFA Apex interview with Aoki, op. cit.

420 *In 1964, however*: Author interviews with Aoki and James Aoki.

420 *As Aoki told it*: "However, around the eighth year that I was in the service . . . I began to question the war in Vietnam. This happened in 1963 or so," KPFA Apex interview with Aoki, op. cit.; "I did have a fantasy of being the first Japanese American general in the history of the United States Army, but that kind of vanished in my . . . about the seventh year I was in the military, because I developed a moral opposition to the war in Vietnam," and "It was about my last year in the military as I was getting opposed to the war in Vietnam," both in author interview with Aoki. But note that he also said his doubts arose somewhat earlier: "Probably around 1960 or so I began to have questions about U.S. involvement in Vietnam. I developed opposition to the war . . . ," Veale interview with Aoki, op. cit.

420 *So it was only*: Author interview with Aoki. He told Veale he became involved with the VDC in 1964, Veale interview with Aoki, op. cit. But it was the following year; the VDC was not created until after Vietnam Day in May 1965.

420 *. . . began to explore . . . he told the author*: Author interview with Aoki. He also told Veale that this is when he met "representatives from all the political tendencies in Berkeley," Veale interview with Aoki, op. cit.

421 *In fact*: As noted above, the author's conclusion that Aoki was an FBI informer has several bases, including that he is named as an "informant" with the temporary code number "T-2" in 105-165706-22, a November 16, 1967, FBI report on the Black Panthers. The report states that Aoki, on May 1, 1967, told the FBI about his joining the Panthers. It appears that the FBI released this information to the author inadvertently. In response to his FOIA request, the FBI stated it had located 1,859 pages and released 1,352 pages, withholding 507 pages in full and many others in part. David M. Hardy, the head of the FBI's FOIA unit, stated in an October 1, 2010, letter to the author that there were no "main" files on Aoki. That is, the FBI had no files on Aoki himself, and the released records were instead references to Aoki in files on other subjects. This is strikingly at odds with Aoki's long involvement in radical causes of priority concern to the FBI, including the Socialist Workers Party and the Black Panther Party, and the FBI's procedures for maintaining informer files. Thus, as of this writing it appears that the FBI is withholding substantial information on Aoki and on the FBI's involvement in significant public matters. Aoki's involvement in left organizations in the years prior to his discharge from the army is documented in FBI files and described in the following text.

421 *He had been recruited . . . "he was a character"*: The account of Threadgill developing and using Aoki as an informer in this paragraph and the next is from author interview with Threadgill.

421 *Aoki's undercover activities*: Aoki's operation as an informer follows a pattern seen in that of three other internal security informers whose identities have been revealed.

Anthony Bachman was a grocery store clerk and rooming-house owner who became a paid FBI informer, joined the Socialist Workers Party, and in that guise delved into left-wing political activities in the San Francisco Bay Area. Between

1954 and 1975, he informed on groups including the Fair Play for Cuba Committee, the Bay Area Student Committee for the Abolition of the House Un-American Activities Committee, the California Labor School, the Meisenbach Defense Committee, CORE, the Bay Area Peace Action Council, the Student Mobilization Committee, NAACP, SLATE, and the YSA, in which he became an officer. He named hundreds of people in a twenty-two-year informer career outlined in the SWP's FBI Records lodged with the Wisconsin Historical Society Archives. See especially box 31, File SF 134-429, vols. 1–8a; 134-429-1 and 134-429-752 identify Bachman as informer SF-2011-S. William Tulio Divale was a UCLA student who infiltrated the W.E.B. Du Bois Club and the Communist Party in Southern California, and proceeded to inform on a plethora of political groups and people ranging from Students for a Democratic Society to the FSM and Mario Savio. His informer number was LA 4688-S and he signed his reports using the code name Wayne Dixon. Divale wrote a book about his exploits called *I Lived Inside the Campus Revolution*. The FBI released approximately 4,870 pages on Divale to the author, including his informer reports. On Divale, see also *LAT* 6/18/69, "Student Undercover Agent"; *LAT* 6/19/69, "Student Who Spied"; *LAT* 7/22/71, "FBI Informer Remembers."

Milan Melvin was a UC Berkeley student whom the FBI recruited as a paid informer in 1960. In the next few years he reported on the Communist Party and other groups, including SDS. He claimed the FBI offered to expunge his criminal record in return for his cooperation. He later married the singer Mimi Fariña, the sister of Joan Baez. He recounted his FBI activities in a memoir, *Highlights of a Lowlife*. See chapter 3, "Working for the FBI."

421 (*Aoki had what*: Veale interview with Aoki, op. cit.; *Secrecy and Power*, 249–50.
421 *The FBI was in*: According to a federal court finding, the FBI placed 1,300 informers in the SWP and YSA from 1960 to 1976, paying them a total of $1.7 million. During the sixties, one in ten members of the party was an informer. The judge ordered the FBI to disclose the files of some of the informers, but U.S. Attorney General Griffin Bell refused. The court found that the FBI had engaged in illegal and "patently unconstitutional" harassment of the groups, WP 8/26/86, "Socialists Win Damages"; WP 4/24/80, "FBI Harassment of 2 Socialist Groups Is Detailed."
422 *FBI records trace*: 62-HQ-60527-49573.
422 *On October 1, 1961*: 100-427226-352.
422 *The following spring*: 100-427226-487.
422 *By December 1962*: 100-427226-487.
422 *Aoki served as*: 100-440943-9; 100-440943-10; 100-427226-723.
422 *Although he was . . . get involved*: Author interview with Aoki; Veale interview with Aoki, op. cit., 325.
422 *The following year*: 100-444372-150; 105-151352-5.
422 *As a result*: KPFA Apex interview with Aoki, op. cit.
422 *When this author asked . . . "I think"*: Author interview with Aoki.
422 *There he met*: Author interview with Aoki.
422 *"We prowled . . ."*: The quote is from Veale interview with Aoki, op. cit.
422 *He also connected . . . socialist meeting*: Author interviews with Aoki and Seale.
422 *In the fall*: Author interview with Aoki; Veale interview with Aoki, op. cit., 324; Student Telephone Directory, Associated Students University of California, 1966–70, Bancroft.
422 *Meanwhile, Newton*: Seize the Time, 59–62; The Shadow of the Panther, 107–12; Up Against the Wall, 25, 33–34; Huey, Spirit of the Panther, 28–35.

422 *One night*: Author interview with Seale; *Huey, Spirit of the Panther*, 38. Aoki recalled it as scotch, Veale interview with Aoki, op. cit., 326.

423 *Aoki soon gave*: The excerpt is from *Seize the Time*, 72–73.

423 *Sometime after*: Ibid., 72, 77, 79; 105-165706-22, the November 16, 1967, report which states that Aoki, on May 1, 1967, told the FBI about his joining the Panthers; *Huey, Spirit of the Panther*, 20, 41.

423 *As Aoki said . . . "public image"*: Author interview with Aoki.

423 *Or as the historian . . . "worldwide scrutiny"*: *Up Against the Wall*, 56.

423 *The following spring*: *Seize the Time*, 148, 149; *Up Against the Wall*, xxv–xxvi, 53–56, 93.

423 *The action generated*: *Up Against the Wall*, xi, xvi.

423 *But though carrying*: *Up Against the Wall*, xv, xxvi; *The Shadow of the Panther*, *LAT* 5/3/67, "Heavily Armed Negro Group"; *LAT* 5/4/67, "Stronger Gun Laws Needed"; *NYT* 5/21/67, "A Gun Is Power"; *LAT* 7/29/67, "Day in Sacramento," which notes Mulford law was signed and bars carrying weapons in public except for law enforcement, military personnel, and other specified persons; *NYT* 11/21/68, "Panthers Inquiry Sought," which notes there had been at least four gun battles between Panthers and police in the San Francisco Bay Area in the prior thirteen months. Pearson writes, "While the Panthers stated that their aim was to prevent police from brutalizing black residents, the very act of their loading up in cars with openly displayed weapons was like a magnet that drew the police to them," *The Shadow of the Panther*, 113.

423 *In October 1967*: Newton was tried three times: he was convicted of voluntary manslaughter, the conviction was reversed, and retrials ended in deadlocked juries before the state finally dismissed charges. See *LAT* 10/29/67, "Oakland Officer Slain"; *NYT* 10/29/67, "Patrolman Killed"; *LAT* 4/1/68, "Newton Murder Charge"; *LAT* 9/9/68, "Newton Is Guilty"; *LAT* 5/30/70, "Huey Newton Wins Reversal"; *LAT* 12/16/71, "Newton Freed in Policeman's Death After Third Trial"; *NYT* 12/16/71, "Newton Is Cleared"; *Up Against the Wall*, 87–88, 113–14.

423 *In April 1968*: *NYT* 4/8/68, "Oakland Police Kill"; *LAT* 4/8/68, "Oakland Tense"; *NYT* 4/13/68, "Black Panthers Denounce."

423 *The Panthers denied*: The Panther leaders Eldridge Cleaver, David Hilliard, Warren Wells, and Charles Bursey were among those convicted, *NYT* 9/18/68, "Six Black Panthers Plead"; *NYT* 11/9/68, "6 Black Panthers Must Stand Trial"; *LAT* 8/29/69, "Panther Official Gets"; *NYT* 10/30/69, "Panther Is Given 15-year Sentence"; *NYT* 12/23/70, "Panther Trial"; *LAT* 6/13/71, "Panther Chief of Staff"; *NYT* 6/13/71, "Jury Finds Hilliard"; *NYT* 11/18/79, "Cleaver Pleads."

423 *Seale would later*: *Seize the Time*, 377, 382.

424 *Aoki confirmed*: Author interview with Aoki.

424 *By any reckoning*: On the "Black-Nationalist-Hate Groups" COINTELPRO, see Church, book III, 20–22. See also "The FBI's Covert Action Program to Destroy the Black Panther Party," ibid., 185–224, which notes *inter alia* that the FBI endeavored to disrupt the group, ruin its public image, and get members in trouble with local police. The committee notes that "some of the FBI's tactics against the BPP were clearly intended to foster violence, and many others could have reasonably been expected to cause violence," book III, 188. The FBI used informers to carry out COINTELPRO, book III, 40, 43, 201. Though the BPP was not among the FBI's initial targets when the "Black-Nationalist-Hate Groups" COINTELPRO began in 1967, it became "the primary focus of the program," book III, 188. The FBI's COINTELPRO actions were "far broader" than their formal description implied, as COINTELPRO existed on an "ad hoc" basis before the creation of the formal programs, and many COINTELPRO-type actions were not labeled as such, book III, 4, 5, 12. On the Panthers, guns, and trouble, see also *Up Against the Wall*; *The Shadow of the Panther*; *Huey, Spirit of the Panther*;

Seize the Time. On COINTELPRO against the Panthers, see *Racial Matters*, 293; *Rolling Stone* 9/9/76, "Revolution on Ice," by Lowell Bergman and David Weir.

424 *During the same period*: This paragraph is based on 105-165706-22; *Seize the Time*, 72–73, 77, 79.

424 *But at the time*: Victoria Wong, statement at Aoki Memorial, UC Berkeley, May 2, 2009, "We didn't know he was in the Panther Party"; author interviews with Aoki, Manuel Delgado, and LaNada War Jack (then known as LaNada Means). See also *Diverse Issues in Higher Education* 2/8/07, "Overshadowed."

424 *"I played it"*: Author interview with Aoki.

424 *In the spring . . . "out of control"*: LAT 5/19/68, "Reagan Says Nation."

424 *. . . that if the Paris*: Ibid.; LAT 5/24/68, "The Perils of Oversimplification"; NYT 5/24/68, "'I Am Not.'"

424 *. . . and that Democratic*: NYT 5/23/68, "Reagan Appeals."

424 *University administrators . . . "equal treatment"*: NYT 5/20/68, "Reagan Condemns."

424 *Everywhere he was*: NYT 5/24/68, "'I Am Not'"; NYT 8/6/68, "Reagan Officially."

424 *Although he lost*: NYT 8/1/68, "Nixon and Reagan Ask"; LAT 8/8/68, "GOP Names Nixon."

425 *So in September*: LAT 9/14/68, "Reagan Demands."

425 *It had been*: *Berkeley at War*, 83–84; *The Free Speech Movement: Reflections on Berkeley in the 1960s*, 496; NYT 10/20/68, "Berkeley Resists."

425 *The topic was*: LAT 9/12/68, "Black Panther Leader."

425 *Cleaver already . . . morally wrong*: NYT 5/2/98, "Eldridge Cleaver, Black Panther . . . Dead at 62"; LAT 11/29/68, "Eldridge Cleaver: A Black Militant Forged by Life"; LAT 9/21/68, "Limit on Cleaver."

425 *Critically acclaimed*: NYT 3/24/68, "To Mr. and Mrs. Yesterday"; NYT 5/2/98, "Eldridge Cleaver, Black Panther . . . Dead at 62"; NYT 12/29/96, "When Revolt"; NYT 11/26/68, "Cleaver Presses Bid."

425 *But that April*: NYT 4/8/68, "Oakland Police Kill."

425 *While free on bail*: NYT 10/4/68, "Berkeley Faculty Says Regents"; LAT 9/21/68, "Limit on Cleaver."

425 *Reagan denounced . . . "Fuck Reagan"*: NYT 5/2/98, "Eldridge Cleaver, Black Panther . . . Dead at 62"; NYT 10/8/68, "Cleaver to Give"; NYT 10/10/68, "Obscenities Hurled"; *Berkeley at War*, 83–84.

425 *In one speech . . . "marshmallows"*: NYT 10/3/68, "Cleaver Derides Reagan."

425 *Hoover heightened . . . "future diatribes"*: The COINTELPRO action is described in 100-44806-426, 11/13/68, Moore to Sullivan; 100-44806-426, 11/14/68, Director to SAC Sacramento, Scholarly Resources, COINTELPRO documents, Black Nationalist Hate Groups, Doe Library, UC Berkeley.

425 *University officials*: LAT 9/13/68, "UC Clarifies Status."

425 *But the regents*: LAT 9/21/68, "Limit on Cleaver."

425 *This prompted*: 62-112228-47-114; LAT 10/4/68, "UC Academic Senate Rejects"; NYT 10/4/68, "Berkeley Faculty Says"; NYT 10/24/68, "Students Seize Berkeley Office"; NYT 10/25/68, "Police Recapture."

425 *The next day*: 62-112228-47-114; NYT 10/24/68, "Students Seize Berkeley Office"; LAT 10/27/68, "New Cleaver Issue Eruptions"; *Berkeley at War*, 84.

425 *Edwin Meese III*: *Berkeley at War*, 84.

425 *But after all*: LAT 10/9/68, "Cleaver Omits Obscenities"; NYT 10/9/68, "Cleaver Lectures"; *From Free Speech to Steady State*, 1964–1974, Office of Public Information, UC Berkeley, www.oac.cdlib.org/view?docId=kt5k4012z6&query=cleaver& brand=oac4, accessed 6/6/11.

425 *in November 1968*: NYT 11/28/68, "Cleaver Is Sought."

425 *He took sanctuary*: NYT 7/16/69, "Cleaver Arrives"; *Berkeley at War*, 85.

426 *Leary's North African*: *Who the Hell Is Stew Albert?*, 116–25; NYT 10/21/70, "Timothy Leary."

426 *Reagan was still*: This paragraph is based on SFC 1/15/69, "Reagan Worried by Too Liberal Faculty"; SFC 1/18/69, "Pickets Miss Reagan with Eggs"; DC 1/20/69, "500 Protest Outside"; NYT 1/18/69, "Coast Regents Pick TV Official"; FBI HQ 62-112228-47, Section 4, p. 40; 100-34204-3099, vol. 30.

426 *By now Berkeley*: This paragraph is based on "Roger W. Heyns, Berkeley Chancellor, 1965–1971, The University in a Turbulent Society," an interview conducted by Harriet Nathan in 1986, Regional Oral History Office, the Bancroft Library, UC Berkeley, 54–56; LAT 1/2/69, "Campuses Move Ahead with Black Curriculum"; Heyns's 1/21/69 statement, contained in FBI HQ 62-11228-47-114, p. 46. The UC Berkeley demographic statistics cited in the text were supplied by the school's public information office to the FBI in 1969 and are reported in FBI HQ 62-11228-47-114, p. 5. Harvey C. Dong presents somewhat different numbers in his dissertation, but the outcome is essentially the same, with the three ethnic groups, Afro-American, Native American, and Chicano, plus a fourth labeled Latino, accounting for 6.2 percent of the student body as of 1970. By comparison, Dong writes, black, Chicano, and Native American people that year comprised about 19 percent of the state population. Asian Americans fared better, according to Dong. He writes that a study made before the TWLF strike noted that they accounted for about 7.4 percent of the student body, about twice their percentage of the state population. But the Asian American category combined different ethnicities, masking disparities such as the underrepresentation of Filipinos. See "The Origins and Trajectory of Asian American Political Activism in the San Francisco Bay Area, 1968–1978," Dissertation for Doctor of Philosophy in Ethnic Studies in the Graduate Division, UCB, Fall 2002, pp. 52–53.

426 *Students began . . . under consideration*: LAT 9/22/68, "Dark Clouds of Strife Hovering over Campuses; DC 1/15/69, "AASU Demands Black Studies Department"; DC 1/15/68, "Open Letter"; DC 1/17/69, "L and S Executive Committee Approves Afro-American Program, Not Department"; Heyns's statement in 62-11228-47-114, p. 46; AASU proposal in 62-11228-47-114, p. 98.

426 *Meanwhile, other students . . . "model minority"*: 100-452260-23, FBI report on Asian American Political Alliance, in TWLF cross-references; author interviews with Richard Aoki and Harvey Dong; "Asian American Movement 1968," aam1968. blogspot.com, accessed 6/6/11; *Columbia Spectator* online edition, 4/9/09, "Beyond the Face of APAAM," www.columbiaspectator.com/2009/04/09/beyond-face-apaam. On Yuji Ichioka, see SFC 9/12/02, "Yuji Ichioka, Asian American Studies Pioneer"; www.aasc.ucla.edu/yi/, accessed 6/6/11.

427 *The AAPA aligned*: 100-452260-23, FBI report on Asian American Political Alliance.

427 *At about the same*: This paragraph is based on *The Last Chicano*, 135–62; LAT 10/21/68, "Hitch Agrees to Some Demands of Mexican-American Students"; NYT 10/20/68, "Grape Issue Stirs Berkeley Crisis"; 100-151646-282, p. 36; author interview with Manuel Delgado.

427 *Racial tension*: NYT 12/11/68, "Protest on Coast Dispersed by Rain"; NYT 1/6/69, "Reagan Backs Officials"; DC 1/6/69, "S.F. State Slated for Opening Today"; DC 1/6/69, "Reagan: Bayonets at State if Needed"; WP 1/11/69, "Calif. Teachers Defy Firing Threat"; LAT 12/3/68, "S.F. State Opens."

427 *The most prominent*: Other protests related to ethnic programs on campus occurred at Brandeis University, Mass.; Swarthmore College, Pa.; University of Wisconsin, Madison; Queens College, N.Y.; University of Detroit, Mich.; and San Fernando Valley State College, San Mateo College, and USC, all in California, WP 1/11/69,

"California Teachers Defy"; NYT 2/17/69, "U. of Wisconsin Campus Quiet"; WP 1/24/69, "380 Seized at Coast College Rally"; NYT 12/17/68, "Hundreds of Police Patrol Campus"; LAT 12/17/68, "Black, Latin Student Groups."

427 *On January 5, 1969 . . . "must be applied"*: NYT 1/6/69, "Reagan Backs Officials"; WP 1/7/69, "Teachers Strike as College Reopens."

428 *Reagan's remarks*: LAT 1/8/69, "Strike Cuts Attendance at S.F. State Classes"; LAT 1/11/69, "Democrat Leader Seeks Rules to Insure 'No More Chicagos'"; WP 1/9/69, "Reagan: Colleges Must Stay Open."

428 *The governor's press*: LAT 1/8/69, "Guard Call Up Not Planned at College."

428 *Reagan himself noted*: NYT 1/11/69, "College Seeking to Oust Strikers."

428 *He had said . . . "constitutional rights"*: LAT 11/2/65, "Emergency Ambulance Fee Seems Cheapskate"; LAT 10/21/65, "Reagan Urges Johnson."

428 *He was alluding*: WP 8/21/58, "Ike Backing Race Ruling with Army"; NYT 10/1/62, "U.S. Troops Sent." Reagan would make a similar reference while campaigning for president in 1976, LAT 1/17/76, "Reagan Views Rights."

428 *By mid-January 1969*: This paragraph is based on DC 1/16/69, "People Get Ready"; DC 1/16/69, "Black Studies Program Approved"; DC 1/17/69, "L and S Executive Committee Approves Afro-American Program, Not Department"; DC 1/15/69, "Open Letter to the Campus."

428 *The AASU decided*: This paragraph is based on author interviews with Aoki and Delgado; The Last Chicano, 165–69.

429 *The discussions were*: This paragraph is based on The Last Chicano, 88, 130, 165–69.

429 *Despite their differences*: This paragraph is based on ibid., 169–70; Dong dissertation, op. cit.; author interview with Delgado.

429 *In contrast*: Author interviews with Aoki and Delgado.

429 *Charles Brown . . . in the navy*: "The Life and Times of Richard Aoki," The Richard Aoki Memorial Committee, May 2009.

429 *LaNada Means*: Author interview with Means; The Last Chicano, 168–69. She is now known by her tribal name and academic title, Dr. LaNada War Jack.

429 *Ysidro Macias*: The Last Chicano, 135.

429 *Manuel Delgado*: LAT 4/24/69, "Viewpoints at Odds in Aftermath of UC Strike."

429 *The cofounder*: This paragraph is based on The Last Chicano, 1, 42, 45, 46, 48, 54, 55, 57, 58, 60, 61, 69–77, 84–89, 91, 95, 96.

429 *Arriving for winter*: This paragraph and the next are based on ibid., 95, 96, 124–28, 146; author interview with Delgado.

430 *"The politically charged . . ."*: The Last Chicano, 146.

430 *Outside University Hall . . . as he drove off*: SFC 1/18/69, "Pickets Miss Reagan with Eggs"; DC 1/20/69, "500 Protest Outside"; NYT 1/18/69, "Coast Regents Pick TV Official"; FBI HQ 62-112228-47, Section 4, p. 40; 100-34204-3099, vol. 30.

430 *Reagan smiled*: DC 1/24/69, Letter to Editor, "Why?"

431 *Two days later . . . Third World applicants*: DC 1/20/69, "Third World Votes—Strike Wednesday"; OT 1/20/69, "Third World Front Slates U.C. Strike," as recounted in FBI HQ 62-112228-47-114, Section 4, pp. 40–44.

431 *Chancellor Heyns himself*: This paragraph and the next are based on Heyns's 1/21/69 statement, contained in 62-11228-47-114, p. 46; DC 1/22/69, "TWLF, Heyns, Prepare for Strike"; LAT 1/22/69, "Heyns Deplores Plans"; SFC 1/22/69, "UC's Reaction." Heyns voiced his personal frustration at the slow pace of reform in "Roger W. Heyns, Berkeley Chancellor, 1965–1971, The University in a Turbulent Society," an interview conducted by Harriet Nathan in 1986, Regional Oral History Office, Bancroft, 54, 55, 91.

431 *On the eve*: This paragraph is based on DC 1/22/69, "Picketing Today"; DC 1/22/69,

"Chicano Column: A Claim for the People" (Manuel Delgado wrote this column periodically in *The Daily Californian*, see *The Last Chicano*, 161); *LAT* 1/22/69, "Heyns Deplores Plans"; *SFC* 1/22/69, "UC's Reaction."

432 *The strike lurched . . . Sather Gate*: DC 1/23/69, "Unions Support TWLF"; DC 1/23/69, "Strike Effects Sporadic"; *SFC* 1/23/69, "A Quiet Strike at Berkeley Campus"; author interview with Manuel Delgado.

432 *Undercover intelligence . . . "fraternity types"*: 100-34204-3134, vol. 32.

432 *That night*: This paragraph and the next are from *SFC* 1/24/69, "Heyns Is 'Sure' of Arson at UC"; DC 1/23/69, "Late Bulletin: Wheeler Fire"; DC 1/24/69, "Heyns Orders Wheeler Open"; DC 1/24/69, "TWLF Deplores Burning"; *LAT* 1/24/69, "Protesting Groups on Berkeley Campus Deplore $300,000 Fire." On Wheeler's construction, see *The Campus Guide*, 77 et seq. Aoki's quotes are from the author's interview with him.

432 *The next day*: DC 1/24/69, "Cold Wind, Wheeler Fire Cut Down Strike Support"; *SFC* 1/24/69, "Heyns Is 'Sure' of Arson at UC."

432 *Despairing*: This and the next three paragraphs are based on *The Last Chicano*, 175–78; author interview with Delgado.

433 *As the strikers . . . hurried off to work*: DC 1/30/69, "Incidents Disrupt Classes"; DC 1/30/69, "1000 Students Stage March Around Campus"; *SFC* 1/30/69, "Path Cleared Through Pickets." Savio's poem was published on January 22, 1969, on the editorial page. On the FBI monitoring of his employment at Cody's Books, see 100-54060-538; 100-54060-540; 100-54060-541; 100-54060-542. On Savio at Cody's, see *Freedom's Orator*, 249, 250–51; *The Life and Times of Cody's Books*, 106.

434 *Within hours*: This paragraph and the next are based on DC 1/30/69, "Incidents Disrupt Classes"; DC 1/30/69, "1000 Students Stage March Around Campus"; *SFC* 1/30/69, "Path Cleared Through Pickets."

434 *This pattern . . . blocking a thoroughfare*: DC 1/31/69, "Strikers Rove Campus"; *SFC* 1/30/69, "Path Cleared Through Pickets"; *LAT* 1/29/69, "S.F. Bay Area Gets Snow, Dike Near Modesto Breaks"; *LAT* 2/6/69, "The State Water Resources Board."

434 *Aoki, speaking . . . "very successful"*: DC 1/31/69, "Strikers Proclaim Support."

434 *Support had*: DC 1/31/69, "ASUC Senate Finally Supports TWLF Strike."

434 *The Daily Californian*: DC 1/22/69, "Power"; DC 1/24/69, "Down the Spiral"; DC 1/30/69, "Say Nothing and Carry a Big Stick."

434 *In a letter*: DC 1/31/69, LED, "What Whites Can Learn."

435 *But many . . . "true WASP"*: DC 1/30/69, LEDS: "Strike for Communication, Not Violence," "Counter-Strike: Blue Armbands," "A True Wasp Responds."

435 *The picket lines*: *LAT* 1/31/69, "Police Break Up"; *LAT* 2/1/69, "Only Five Classes."

435 *Appearing before . . . "violates the law"*: DC 2/4/69, "Senate Hits Disruption"; *SFC* 2/4/69, "Heyns Assails Strikers."

435 *Dissatisfied . . . police resources*: SFX 2/2/69, "Angry Sheriff Warns UC on Disorders"; DC 2/3/69, "County Sheriff Demands"; DC 2/4/69, LED, "Heyns to Hitch."

435 *In the midst*: The account of the kidnap in this paragraph and the next is from *The Last Chicano*, 190; author interviews with Delgado and Aoki. Aoki confirmed this account of the Richard Rodriguez incident as true and said he suspected Rodriguez was "stirring dissension up within our ranks." Aoki added, "I was considered the hard of the hard."

435 *On Tuesday . . . Pepperland*: The account of the day's events is based on NYT 2/5/69, "20 at Berkeley Are Held in Clash"; *LAT* 2/5/69, "Berkeley Students Battle"; DC 2/5/69, "Strike Violence Grows, Police Invade Campus"; *SFC* 1/5/69, "Officers Charge Crowds." The Beatles' song "Yellow Submarine" was released in 1966, the

eponymous film in 1968. See *Time* 12/27/68, "New Magic in Animation"; Internet Movie Database, www.imdb.com/title/tt0063823/, accessed 6/7/11.

436 *Glenn Dyer*: Dyer's remarks are from Glenn Dyer, Division Chief, Alameda County Sheriff's Department, "Flexible Response," transcript of his presentation to Cable Splicer meeting, May 1970, in Appendix 3 to Annex E of Cable Splicer III records, in possession of author.

436 *In his Sacramento*: *Ronnie & Jesse*, 257; *Governor Reagan*, 291; *DC* 2/6/69, "Reagan Decision"; *NYT* 2/6/69, "Reagan Declares"; *LAT* 2/6/69, "Berkeley Emergency Declared by Reagan; Patrol Ordered In"; *DC* 2/7/69, "Berkeley Woes." The text of Reagan's proclamation is in 157-9295-NR, 2/6/69, after 157-9295-18.

436 *The extraordinary measure . . . indefinitely*: *SFC* 2/6/69, "Reagan Clears Way"; *DC* 2/6/69, "Reagan Decision"; *DC* 2/7/69, "Berkeley Woes Retold"; *LAT* 2/6/69, "Berkeley Emergency Declared by Reagan; Patrol Ordered In"; *NYT* 2/6/69, "Reagan Declares an Emergency in Berkeley Campus Disorders"; *LAT* 4/16/69, "Get Tougher with Dissidents, Reagan Advises Stanford"; *NYT* 5/31/69, "Angry Berkeley Sheriff." Meese writes, "I was given the responsibility of planning and coordinating this response," *With Reagan*, 32.

437 *At a press conference . . . "and intimidation"*: *DC* 2/6/69, "Reagan Decision"; *SFC* 2/6/69, "Reagan Clears Way"; *LAT* 2/6/69, "Berkeley Emergency Declared by Reagan; Patrol Ordered In." Chancellor Heyns said he and President Hitch joined Madigan in asking Reagan to declare the emergency, *SFC* 2/6/69, "Chancellor Heyns Regrets."

437 *Five days later*: The account of the Cable Splicer conference, and the description of the Cable Splicer program, are based on "Cable Splicer records," in the author's possession, including: "Command Post Exercise Directive Cable Splicer II (Control of Civil Disturbances—Military Support of Civil Authority)" with "inclosures," from Glenn C. Ames, Major General, Commanding, California State Military Department, 1/3/69; "After Action Report 1 May 1969, Command Post Exercise Cable Splicer II," Headquarters, State Military Forces, Military Department, State of California; "Governor Ronald Reagan's Speech, Governor's Orientation, 10 Feb. 1969"; transcribed statements of law-enforcement speakers, Cable Splicer III conference, May 1970. This account also draws on *LAT* 8/26/75, "Army Disclosing Its Role in Plans to Quell Urban Riots"; *DC* 9/24/76, "Secret Police-Military Plan Revealed."

438 *Reagan was present . . . deploy these forces*: The governor's powers to proclaim a state of extreme emergency and deploy state military and police forces are outlined in Ronald Reagan to All Sheriffs and Chiefs of Police, 4/4/68, with enclosures, "Emergency Assistance Procedures," and "Emergency Employment of Army Resources (ARNG), Disaster Preparedness (ANG), Policy Guidance on Use of Military Resources in Connection with Civil Disturbance or Impending Disorders," California ARNG Regulation 500-10, California ANG Regulation 355-8, 2/13/68; "Operational Plan for Major Disorders, Confidential, State of California, Office of the Governor, March 1968"; Charles Samson to Directors of Civil Defense and Disaster, re State Law Enforcement Mutual Aid Plan, 7/10/67, all in box 170, folder: "CDO/OES 1968," Edwin Meese III Collection, Hoover Institution.

438 *With him*: "Governor's Orientation Sign-in Roster," Cable Splicer documents, op. cit.; *DC* 9/24/76, "Secret Police-Military Plan Revealed."

438 *Reagan had hoped*: "Tentative Agenda, 10 Feb. 1969," and "Governor's Orientation, Agenda, 10 Feb. 1969," both in Cable Splicer documents, op. cit.

438 *So after everyone*: The quotes are from "Governor Ronald Reagan's Speech, Governor's Orientation, 10 Feb. 1969," transcript, in Cable Splicer documents, op. cit.

439 *President Johnson*: On Johnson and Nixon pressing Hoover for more intelligence on domestic dissent, see Church, book III, 488–500, 501–503.

439 *Hoover launched*: On STAG: 100-34204-3203, 3/4/69; 100-62751-2, 3/26/69; Church, book III, 505–10. On black campus groups: 100-34204-3131, 2/12/69, ordering the investigation of all black student groups on campus where there have been disruptions, even if those groups were not involved. By 1970, Hoover had expanded the inquiries to include every black campus organization in the country, "regardless of their past or present involvement in disorders," Church, book III, 527–28.

439 *In Berkeley*: 100-34204, vols. 31–34; 157-1202, vols. 1–4; 62-112228-47-114.

439 *Alex Sherriffs*: 62-112228-47-114, pp. 3, 19.

440 . . . San Francisco Examiner: 157-9295-6; 100-34204-3190.

440 . . . *Patricia Atthowe*: 100-62751-1, B-1, in which Don Lynn of Research West provides the film; 157-9295-19, 2/19/69 (Research West continued to have Western Research Foundation's permanent FBI code number, CSSF 33X); 157-3156-35; 157-3156-179.

440 *Professor Hardin Jones*: This paragraph is based on Hardin Jones's informer file, 134-deleted, serial 9, 7/31/68; 100-34204-2963, 9/18/68; 116-2036-28 (a letter from Jones that Hugh Burns provided to the FBI); *LAT* 10/3/69, "150 of Berkeley Faculty Favor Cleaver's Giving All 10 Talks." Hardin Jones and his wife, Helen Jones, later coauthored a book, *Sensual Drugs: Deprivation and Rehabilitation of the Mind.*

440 *Don Jones*: These informers' reports are contained in 100-34204.

440 *Yet nothing*: Forensic tests were inconclusive but officials called it arson, *DC* 2/17/69, "Wheeler Reports"; *SFC* 1/24/69, "Heyns Is 'Sure,'"; "Earl F. Cheit, Professor, Vice Chancellor, Dean, Vice President, Athletic Director, Advisor, Trustee, University of California, 1957–2002, 2002," an interview conducted by Germaine LaBerge in 1999 and 2001, Regional Oral History Office, Bancroft, 196; 100-151646-270 (UC Berkeley police on 1/23/69 requested "any possible" help from FBI with investigating the fire).

440 *February 13, 1969 . . . "police functions go"*: The account of the day's events is based on *DC* 2/13/69, "TA Union Membership"; *DC* 2/14/69, "Renewed Campus Violence"; *SFC* 2/14/69, "Big Clash at UC—36 Arrested"; *DC* 2/18/69, "Hallinan Says TA's Union"; *SFC* 2/8/69, "Campus Quiet—Black Legislator Assails Reagan."

441 *In the basement . . . "kid"*: The account of events in the basement is based on *DC* 2/19/69, "Sproul Beatings Reported"; *DC* 1/19/69, LED, "Beatings"; *SFC* 2/20/69, "UC Clerks Charge."

441 *In the next . . . "or provocation"*: *DC* 2/14/69, editorial, "Stay Away"; *DC* 2/18/69, LED, "Faculty Committee Asks"; *SFC* 2/15/69, "Doubts on Some Arrests at UC"; *DC* 2/14/69, "Local AFT Plans Picket Today"; *DC* 2/17/69, "Faculty Union Joins Strike"; *DC* 2/18/69, LED, "Campus Librarians' Union"; *DC* 2/19/69, "TAs Vote to Strike"; *DC* 2/19/69, "AFSCME Votes to Support AFT Strike."

441 *Madigan defended*: SFC 2/14/69, "Big Clash at UC—36 Arrested."

441 *As the next . . . cafeteria*: SFC 2/18/69, "Strikers Step Up UC Campus War"; DC 2/18/69, "Rain-Soaked Strikers March, Damage Cafeteria and Library."

441 *The next morning . . . acquitted*: Author interview with Aoki; *DC* 2/19/69, "Jim Nabors, Beaten, Arrested"; *SFC* 2/19/69, "Cops, Students"; *SFC* 2/19/69, "The Latest Arrests at UC," which notes Aoki was charged with interfering with an officer, Manuel Delgado for blocking a thoroughfare, and Jim Nabors for blocking and assault.

442 *There was more*: This paragraph and the next are based on *DC* 2/20/69, "Police, Strikers Clash Again"; *SFC* 2/20/69, "Thousands in Melee on Campus"; *LAT* 2/20/69, "5 Injured, 25 Arrested."

442 *When the regents*: This paragraph and the next are based on *SFC* 2/21/69, "National

Guard Alerted"; DC 2/21/69, "Violence Hits New High in Strike"; LAT 2/21/69, "Berkeley Erupts in Tear Gas War"; SFC 3/2/69, "The Week's News in Review, 'Keep It Cool,'" which says February 20 was the most violent day, as does 62-112228-47-114, p. 78. The San Francisco Examiner said the week's protests involved "the worst rioting in the university's 100-year history," SFX 2/23/69, "It's All Quiet."

442 *That night:* DC 2/21/69, "Violence Hits New High in Strike"; LAT 2/21/69, "Berkeley Erupts"; NYT 2/21/69, "Dismissal of Marcuse."

443 *At dawn . . . waited nearby:* DC 2/24/69, "Regents Ruling: Suspensions"; DC 2/24/69, "Police Stock Riot Guns, Heavy Rifles"; DC 2/24/69, "Rally and National Guard"; DC 2/25/69, "Mobilized National Guardsmen Describes [sic]"; SFC 2/22/69, "Berkeley Is Quiet but Tense"; 62-112228-47-114, pp. 79–80.

443 *Reagan's limousine . . . "whatever it takes":* SFC 2/22/69, "Berkeley Is Quiet but Tense"; SFC 2/22/69, "Reagan's Vow to End the Riots."

443 *Inside University Hall:* The account of the regents' meeting is based on SFC 2/22/69, "Rioters Will Be Suspended"; LAT 2/22/69, "UC Cracks Down on Rioters"; DC 2/24/69, "Regents Ruling."

443 *Across Oxford Street . . . rain:* SFX 2/23/69, "Optimism Develops at Cal"; SFC 2/22/69, "Berkeley Is Quiet but Tense"; DC 2/24/69, "Rally and National Guard."

443 *In the following days . . . "any means necessary":* DC 2/21/69, "Third World Liberation Front, A Commitment," commentary by Jim Nabors.

444 *The political-science . . . pursued their rights:* A transcript of Malcolm X's "By Any Means Necessary" speech, delivered in 1964, at the Audubon Ballroom in uptown Manhattan, is at www.blackpast.org/?q=1964-malcolm-x-s-speech -founding-rally-organization-afro-american-unity, accessed 6/8/11. The Panthers' adoption of the credo is noted in Up Against the Wall, 347. That Nabors was a political science student is noted in "Campus Disorders in California: Origins and Development," box 221, folder: "Demonstrations, Riots, Disorders," Edwin Meese III Collection, Hoover Institution.

444 *Nabors's allusion:* NYT 2/24/69, "Negro Parley Calls White Racism Biggest Issue" (National Conference of Black Social Workers adopts resolution saying it would deal with issues and problems of white racism "by any means necessary"); NYT 3/2/69, LED, Book Review, "Women, Revolution, Sexism, Etc., Etc." (Ellen Willis and seven other feminists write, "But we believe that feminism is revolutionary. Male chauvinism is not simply a 'discomfort' but an intolerable form of oppression that must be eliminated by any means necessary"); author interview with Stew Albert on growing militancy of the New Left.

444 *Reagan had said:* SFC 2/22/69, "Reagan's Vow to End the Riots."

444 *Professors and students . . . "their constituency":* DC 2/24/69, "Letters Condemn Police Brutality"; DC 2/25/69, LED, "Turning Violence On or Off"; DC 2/25/69, LED, "The Student as Political Pawn."

444 *There were more . . . violent clashes:* This and the next two paragraphs are based on DC 2/25/69, "Time Bomb Found in Dwinelle"; SFC 2/27/69, "Illegal but Quiet UC Rally"; SFC 2/28/69, "New UC Violence—Heyns Halts Talks."

444 *On February 28 . . . severely beaten:* 62-112228-47-114, p. 86; SFC 3/1/69, "Guardsmen Clear Campus, Streets."

444 *When police . . . Sproul Plaza:* SFC 3/1/69, "Guardsmen Clear Campus, Streets"; LAT 3/1/69, "Tear Gas Used to Disperse Mob"; 62-112228-47-114, p. 87.

444 *For the first time:* This paragraph and the next are based on SFC 3/1/69, "Guardsmen Clear Campus, Streets"; LAT 3/1/69, "Tear Gas Used to Disperse Mob"; 62-112228-47-114, p. 87.

444 *Vandals had poured:* SFC 3/5/69, "UC Senate OK's Ethnic Department."

444 *This was the . . . ethnic studies*: Heyns's remarks and the Academic Senate vote are based on SFC 3/5/69, "UC Senate OK's Ethnic Department"; NYT 3/5/69, "Student Demand Backed"; LAT 3/5/69, "Faculty at UC Berkeley Votes"; DC 3/5/69, "Senate Favors Ethnic Studies."

445 *The strike . . . Antonioni*: SFC 3/7/69, "UC Strike Leaders, Faculty Talk"; SFC 3/8/69, "Quiet Day"; 62-112228-47-114, pp. 87–90, 96; 157-9295-NR, 3/6/69, vol. 2, which states wiretap code number; 157-1202-285, vol. 4, which shows tap on BPP national HQ at 3106 Shattuck Avenue, Berkeley; author interview with Curtis O. Lynum. *Zabriskie Point*, cowritten by Sam Shepard, is about an apocalyptic encounter between a woman and a young man who has shot a police officer during a campus protest. See NYT 2/10/70, "Screen: Antonioni's 'Zabriskie Point.'"

445 *On March 14*: SFC 3/15/69, "Strike at UC Suspended to Aid Negotiations"; LAT 3/15/69, "Moratorium Ends Strike"; NYT 3/15/69, "Berkeley Strike Halted."

445 *Richard Aoki . . . end the strike*: Aoki's remarks are from the author's interview with him.

445 *Strike leaders*: Author interviews with Carlos Munoz, Ling-Chi Wang, Manuel Delgado, and Richard Aoki; NYT 11/23/69, "Black Studies"; The Sun Reporter 3/22/69, "Rigidity at UC"; Aoki statement in "The Life and Times of Richard Aoki," booklet published by the Richard Aoki Memorial Committee, May 2009; Dong dissertation, op. cit., which notes that the TWLF achieved a "degree of success" and that ethnic studies programs spread to other colleges.

445 *But there was much*: Aoki stated, "Anyway, to make a long story short, that long strike ended after three months when the University capitulated and granted us our Ethnic Studies department." See "The Life and Times of Richard Aoki," booklet published by the Richard Aoki Memorial Committee, May 2009. This is not an accurate description of how the strike ended. As noted in the text, the strikers had demanded a Third World College, which they never achieved. Nor did the strikers achieve other demands, such as student control of the ethnic studies department.

445 *Although the vast*: 62-112228-47-114, pp. 17, 78, 178; NYT 2/5/69, "20 at Berkeley"; LAT 2/6/69, "CHP Ordered to UC"; LAT 2/20/69, "5 Injured, 25 Arrested."

445 *Vandalism damages*: 62-112228-47-114, pp. 195–96.

445 *Police arrested*: 62-112228-47-114, p. 158. Arrest figures vary, with one total put at 150, Dong dissertation, op. cit., p. 71.

445 *The university disciplined*: 62-112228-47-114, p. 178.

445 *Aoki would later*: KPFA Apex interview of Aoki by reporter Wayie Ly, July 2006, ramemorial.blogspot.com/2009/08/life-and-times-of-richard-aoki-in-his.html, accessed 11/7/11.

445 *The FBI never . . . about him.)*: Author interview with Dr. John Fox, FBI staff historian; Second Declaration of David M. Hardy, Section Chief, Records/Information Dissemination Section, FBI, and Defendants' Supplemental Brief filed 1/30/12, both in *Seth Rosenfeld v. Federal Bureau of Investigation and U.S. Department of Justice*, C 11-02131MEJ.

446 *Aoki earned . . . as a radical*: SFC 4/26/09, "Campus Activist Richard Masato Aoki." The interviews are cited in the above entry for the key words "He had given," p. 740.

446 *In later years*: Coroner Investigator's Report on Aoki, Case No. 2009-00777.

446 *Aoki's fellow activists*: Richard Aoki memorial, May 2, 2009, Wheeler Hall, UC Berkeley, attended by author. See ramemorial.blogspot.com, accessed 6/10/11.

446 *As Agent Don Jones*: Jones's comments are in 62-112228-47-114, p. 2. Reagan's near-continuous charges that UC administrators were lax are noted in NYT 2/23/69, "After Two Years."

446   *"This is guerilla . . .":* LAT 2/21/69, "Must 'Eliminate.'" Reagan explained that by eliminate he did not actually mean "kill."

446   *But according to Jones . . . "riffraff":* 62-112228-47-114, pp. 16–18.

446   *However inflammatory:* WP 4/14/69, "Berkeley Campus Has Become Governor Reagan's San Juan Hill"; WP 4/22/69, "Hayakawa's Stand on Dissent."

446   *The state of . . . poised for action:* NYT 5/16/69, "Shotguns and Tear Gas"; LAT 5/20/69, "UC Demonstrators Routed."

26: People's Park

In addition to the sources cited in the following notes, this chapter generally draws on *Ramparts,* August 1969, "Dialectics of Confrontation," by Robert Scheer, with Nancy Bardacke, Rick Brown, and Art Goldberg; *Rolling Stone* 6/14/69, "The Battle of People's Park," by John Burks, John Grissim, Jr., and Langdon Winner; NYT 6/29/69, "People's Park—270′ × 450′ of Confrontation," by Winthrop Griffith; LAT 5/30/69, "Berkeley: Birth, Growth of 'War,'" by John Kendall and William Endicott; DC 4/22/69, "Would-be University Parking Lot Becomes 'Power to the People Park'"; DC 5/14/69, "Park to Become Fenced-in Field"; DC 5/14/69, "The Revolution Is Not a Dinner Party"; "The People's Park," Stanley Irwin Glick, Doctoral Dissertation, State University of New York at Stony Brook, 1984, hereafter "Glick dissertation"; "People's Park, 1969: A Confrontation Between Conflicting American Cultures," Michael D. Kolkind, University of Wisconsin–Eau Claire, 2007; *Neither Law nor Order: The People's Park and the People's Police,* by James Yandell; "The 'People's Park': A Report on a Confrontation at Berkeley, California," Office of the Governor, 7/1/69; *Berkeley at War: The 1960s,* by W. J. Rorabaugh; *The Sixties: Years of Hope, Days of Rage,* by Todd Gitlin; *Who the Hell Is Stew Albert?*; *Wholly Round,* by Rasa Gustaitis.

447   *The park was:* The first part of the chapter about the creation of People's Park and the university administration's reaction to it is based on *Ramparts,* August 1969, "Dialectics of Confrontation"; NYT 6/29/69, "People's Park—270′ × 450′ of Confrontation"; LAT 5/30/69, "Berkeley: Birth, Growth of 'War,'"; DC 4/22/69, "Would-be University Parking Lot Becomes 'Power to the People Park'"; DC 5/14/69, "Park to Become Fenced-in Field"; DC 5/14/69, "The Revolution Is Not a Dinner Party"; Glick dissertation; *Berkeley at War*; *The Sixties,* 353–61; *Who the Hell Is Stew Albert?,* 100–103; *Wholly Round,* 51–74.

450   *Sergeant R. E. Hull:* The quote is from UCPD Supplementary Report, 4/20/69.

450   *Savio, who had: Cody's Books*; author interview with Stew Albert.

450   *Chancellor Heyns:* This paragraph is based on Glick dissertation, 59–61; "The 'People's Park,'" Office of the Governor, 7/1/69, pp. 11–12; DC 4/28/69, "UC to Build Playing Field on Site of 'People's Park.'"

450   *That day, park supporters:* DC 4/28/69, "UC to Build Playing Field on Site of 'People's Park'"; a copy of the leaflet is in 100-34204-3334.

451   *In Sacramento:* This paragraph and the next are based on Emergency Planning Council minutes, May 9, 2009, box 176, folder: "Emergency Planning Council Meetings," Meese Collection, Hoover Institution. Meese's duties in handling protests are noted in *With Reagan,* 30–34.

452   *In the early-morning:* This paragraph is based on UCPD Supplementary Report of Sergeant R. E. Hull, 5/15/69; DC 5/16/68, "Police Seize Park"; *Neither Law nor Order,* 17–20; Glick dissertation, 90–91; "The 'People's Park,'" Office of the Governor, 7/1/69, p. 15.

452 *Within minutes*: UCPD Supplementary Report of Sergeant R. E. Hull, 5/15/69; *DC* 5/16/68, "Police Seize Park."

452 *One of the deputies*: Riche notes his arrival at People's Park in "Statement of Lawrence Lowell Riche," Alameda County District Attorney's Office, 6/12/69. Background on Riche is from Deposition of Lawrence L. Riche, 9/25/72, taken jointly in *Rundle v. Madigan*, C-70-224 RFP, U.S. District Court, Northern District of California, and *Francke v. State of California et al.*, No. 397,680, Alameda County Superior Court, hereafter "Riche deposition 9/25/72."

452 *Like nearly a sixth*: At least seven of the forty-four deputies were on probation. See Glenn Dyer, Answer to Interrogatories, 9/17/71, *Rundle v. Madigan*, No. C-70-334 RFP, U.S. District Court, Northern District of California; Deposition of Alameda County Sheriff Frank Madigan (hereafter "Madigan deposition"), 1/20/71, *Francke v. State of California et al.*; *SFC* 11/21/69, "Two Guards Quit." That Riche had never done riot duty and hoped to be a teacher is in Deposition of Lawrence L. Riche, 4/26/71, *Blanchard v. State of California et al.*, No. 393,210, Alameda County Superior Court (hereafter "Riche deposition 4/26/71"), 6, 22, 31.

452 *"We couldn't see . . .":* The quote is from Riche deposition 9/25/72, op. cit., 116, 117.

452 *Riche peered*: This paragraph is based on Supplementary Report of Sergeant R. E. Hull, 5/15/69; Glick dissertation, 90–91.

452 *Word that police*: This paragraph is based on *DC* 5/16/68, "Police Seize Park"; *DC* 5/16/69, "A Day of Violent Paradoxes"; UCPD Supplementary Report of Sgt. R. E. Hull, 5/15/69; UCPD, n.d., "People's Park Resume"; Glick dissertation, 91.

453 *"Now, we have . . .":* Siegel's quotes are from UCPD partial transcript of Siegel speech.

453 *Siegel would later*: *LAT* 5/30/69, "Berkeley: Birth, Growth of 'War.'"

453 *In any event*: *DC* 5/16/68, "Police Seize Park"; UCPD Supplementary Report of Sgt. R. E. Hull, 5/15/69; UCPD, n.d., "People's Park Resume"; Glick dissertation, 92–93.

453 *William Donovan Rundle, Jr. . . . "against injustice"*: Rundle's joining in the rally and march is from "Statement of William Donovan Rundle, Jr.," 9/25/69; FBI report of interview with Rundle, 9/30/69; FBI report of interview with Rundle's attorney, Ronald M. Greenberg, 9/29/69, all in U.S. Department of Justice civil rights file 144-11-656 released to me under the FOIA; author interview with Greenberg.

453 *It is clear . . . forces in Berkeley*: The poor preparation is detailed in the following text. Note also that former Deputy Riche would later testify before the federal grand jury investigating civil rights violations during the park protest, "It's my own opinion that we were ill-equipped," Riche, Grand Jury Testimony, U.S. District Court, Northern District of California, January 1970, 91. That Madigan remained in charge is in *NYT* 5/31/69, "Angry Berkeley Sheriff."

454 *For all their planning*: The flaws noted in this paragraph are detailed in the text. On the shortage of men, see also Glick dissertation, 93–95; "The 'People's Park,'" Office of the Governor, 7/1/69, pp. 18, 22. On insufficient supplies of tear gas, see also "The 'People's Park,'" Office of the Governor, 7/1/69, p. 18, which notes that at 1:20 p.m. outmanned police requested more gas; UCPD Incident Report Log, 5/15/69, p. 4, which notes that as of 1:41 p.m. some officers had run out of gas; 100-34204-3496, with enclosed SFPD report 5/17/69, which notes that as of 2:15 p.m. the sheriff's department had exhausted its reserve and purchased the last supply available in the Bay Area. On insufficient supplies of birdshot, see also *Allan H. Francke v. State of California et al.*, No. 397,680, Marin County Superior Court, 131–33, 177–78. Madigan notes that birdshot is generally considered not lethal, ibid., 175. Captain Dyer testified that the deputies were overwhelmed and turned to riot guns, Deposition of Glenn Dyer (hereafter "Dyer deposition"), 1/22/71, *Rundle v. Madigan*, U.S. District Court Northern District of California, No. C-70-334 RFP, 37–38, 42.

454 . . . *National Advisory Commission*: "Report of the National Advisory Commission on Civil Disorders," 1968, also known as the Kerner Report (Pantheon Books, 1988), 335.

454 *In an interview*: Author interview with Edwin Meese III.

454 *Chanting "We want the park!"*: Glick dissertation, 92.

454 *Although people were angry . . . young children*: Neither Law nor Order, 22–23.

454 *But at Haste*: "The 'People's Park,'" Office of the Governor, 7/1/69, pp. 17–18; *Neither Law nor Order*, 23; *Ramparts*, August 1969, "Dialectics of Confrontation"; *DC* 5/16/68, "Police Seize Park."

454 *One highway patrolman*: UCPD Supplementary Report of Sgt. R. E. Hull, 5/15/69; UCPD, n.d., "People's Park Resume"; UCPD "Chronology of Incidents of Violence or Disorder During the Peoples Park Problems." The wound was superficial, *LAT* 5/30/69, "Berkeley: Birth, Growth of 'War'"; "The 'People's Park,'" Office of the Governor, 7/1/69, p. 18.

454 *Trapped in the crowd*: Rundle statement, op. cit.

454 *Several blocks away . . . white vapor*: Deposition of Lawrence L. Riche, 4/26/71, *Blanchard v. State of California et al.*, No. 393, 210, 49–51, 52–64; Riche deposition 9/25/72, op. cit., 88–89, 124, 125; "Statement of Lawrence Lowell Riche," Alameda County District Attorney's Office, 6/12/69; Deposition of Glenn Dyer, 1/22/71, *Rundle v. Madigan*, U.S. District Court Northern District of California, No. C-70-334 RFP, 25–37. On Riche's gear, see Testimony of Lawrence L. Riche, 10/12/70, in *U.S. v. Riche*, U.S. District Court, Northern District of California, No. 70-88, pp. 3–4.

455 *Still caught . . . The Tempest*: Rundle statement, op. cit.

455 *Like Rundle*: Riche deposition 9/25/72, op. cit., 72, 73.

455 *Remarkably, in planning . . . officers should apply*: Madigan deposition, op. cit.: He states that at a planning meeting on May 14, 1969, the day before the confrontation, there was no discussion about the use of tear gas, 99; no discussion about the use of shotguns, 103; and no discussion about techniques for arresting people if the crowd became too large for common police methods, 101–102. Although Madigan was in charge of all officers at the scene, he testified that he attended no meetings at which the use of police force to enforce the law during the park disturbance was discussed, 103, or even the possibility that the crowds would become too big to easily handle, 104. Dyer testified that at Haste and Telegraph the deputies were overwhelmed by the size of the crowd and were totally unable to control it. Glenn Dyer, Answer to Interrogatories, 9/17/71, *Rundle v. Madigan*, No. C-70-334 RFP, U.S. District Court, Northern District of California, p. 11.

455 *Greatly outnumbered*: Glenn Dyer, Answer to Interrogatories, 9/17/71, *Rundle v. Madigan*, No. C-70-334 RFP, U.S. District Court, Northern District of California, p. 11; Glick dissertation, 94–95.

455 *. . . ordered to withdraw*: Dyer deposition, 38, 41.

455 *Thomas Houchins . . . riot guns*: Madigan deposition, op. cit., 110, 112, 145.

455 *Each deputy*: Dyer deposition, op. cit., 42–43; Riche deposition 4/26/71, op. cit., 68; *Ramparts*, August 1969, "Rampage."

455 *As discussed . . . be fired first*: Madigan deposition, op. cit., 174–77; Dyer deposition, op. cit., 46–47; Riche deposition 9/25/72, op. cit., 35.

455 *There simply*: Madigan deposition, op. cit., 131–33, 177–78.

456 *As Madigan . . . "not be used"*: Ibid., 174–77.

456 *At 1:15 p.m. . . . and yelling*: UCPD "Chronology of Incidents of Violence or Disorder During the Peoples Park Problems"; "Statement of Lawrence Lowell Riche," Alameda County District Attorney's Office, June 12, 1969, p. 8.

456 *Some people were*: Dyer deposition, op. cit., 55–56.
456 *Captain Glenn Dyer . . . held his fire*: Ibid., 47–48, 50, 56; Riche deposition 9/25/72, op. cit., 40; Riche deposition 4/26/71, op. cit., 88; Riche testimony, *U.S. v. Riche*, U.S. District Court, Northern District of California, 11/17/70, 18.
456 *The deputies pursued*: *Ramparts*, August 1969, "Rampage," 55.
456 *This cluster kept . . . parking lot on Haste Street*: "Statement of Lawrence Lowell Riche," Alameda County District Attorney's Office, 6/12/69, p. 9.
456 *. . . hitting uninvolved students*: Don Simpson, an undergraduate in electrical engineering and a bystander, was shot in the shoulder, according to a claim filed with Alameda County. In an interview with the author, Michael Beavers recalled other students also were hit.
456 *Michael W. Beavers . . . he recalled*: Author interview with Beavers.
456 *The pattern would*: *Neither Law nor Order*, 23–24, 40–41.
456 *Marching in single file*: "Statement of Lawrence Lowell Riche," Alameda County District Attorney's Office, 6/12/69, pp. 9–10.
456 *A small crowd . . . provoke the deputies*: *Ramparts*, August 1969, "Rampage," 55–57. Venn denied doing anything to cause him to be shot, 44-42153-3; Santucci told his superiors he shot a man who was fleeing after throwing a rock that hit him; that man was later identified as Venn, 44-42153-7; Santucci was indicted for shooting Venn and pleaded not guilty, 44-42513-28; the indictment was dismissed on 12/18/70, 44-42513-44.
456 *. . . as with many other*: Ibid., 55, 56, 59; *Neither Law nor Order*, 25, 26, 32, 34; *LAT* 5/30/69, "Berkeley: Birth, Growth of 'War'"; Statement of William Donovan Rundle, Jr., 9/25/69, op. cit.
456 *Several blocks away*: This paragraph is from RR white paper, 18–20.
456 *The upended car*: This paragraph is based on *Ramparts*, August 1969, "Rampage," 57; *LAT* 5/30/69, "Berkeley: Birth, Growth of 'War'"; *Neither Law nor Order*, 24–25.
457 *Vincent Ferrari*: This paragraph is based on *LAT* 5/30/69, "Berkeley: Birth, Growth of 'War.'"
457 *Scores of people*: *Ramparts*, August 1969, "Rampage"; "Statement of Lawrence Lowell Riche," Alameda County District Attorney's Office, 6/12/69, p. 10.
457 *Much of the avenue*: *Ramparts*, August 1969, "Rampage"; *Neither Law nor Order*, 31.
457 *By now some deputies*: There is no record of what kind of ammunition each officer had fired at this point. However, Dyer testified that he fired his two rounds of birdshot as warning shots; he was thus down to buckshot from the start. Simpson and Beavers already had been hit with buckshot.
457 *Perched on the roof . . . blood stains the shingles*: The account of the shooting of Rector and Blanchard is based on *Ramparts*, August 1969, "Rampage"; *LAT* 5/30/69, "Berkeley: Birth, Growth of 'War'"; *Neither Law nor Order*, 31–34; Glick dissertation, 100; *SFC* 2/9/71, "Blinded Man Testifies." Photos of the wounded Rector and Blanchard are online at www.peoplespark.org/69gall6.html, accessed 1/23/12.
457 *Riche looked toward*: Riche deposition, 4/26/71, op. cit., 94–107.
458 *A photo*: *People's Park*, 55; *Ramparts*, August 1969, "Rampage," 59.
458 *The deputies turned*: *Ramparts*, August 1969, "Rampage," 59.
458 *It was about 3:00 p.m.*: Ibid.
458 *. . . and some of them*: UCPD Incident Report Log, 5/15/69, p. 4.
458 *By now Madigan*: "Additional to Incident Report of May 4th, 1969," dated 9/11/69, UCPD records, states mutual aid was requested as of 1:29 p.m.
458 *Members of that . . . "use bird shot"*: 100-34204-3496, SFPD report 5/17/69.
458 *An army jeep*: This paragraph is based on *Neither Law nor Order*, 27–28; *LAT* 5/30/69, "Berkeley: Birth, Growth of 'War.'"

458 *Nearby at Berkeley High: Neither Law nor Order,* 28–30.
458 *Mario Savio:* Savio statement to Ronald M. Greenberg, attorney for William Rundle, Jr., and his private investigator, as summarized in legal papers and author interview with Greenberg. Suzanne Goldberg and Lynne Hollander told me they were not familiar with the matter.
458 *The squad of deputies:* This paragraph is based on *Ramparts,* August 1969, "Rampage"; author interviews with Ehrenberger and Francke.
459 *"I heard . . .":* Author interview with Francke.
459 *The deputies gathered . . . outstretched:* Riche deposition 9/25/72, op. cit., 70–71; Riche federal grand jury testimony, January 1970, 115; "Statement of Lawrence Lowell Riche," Alameda County District Attorney's Office, 6/12/69, 14–17; "Statement of William Donovan Rundle, Jr.," 9/25/69, op. cit.; author interview with Greenberg.
459 *Nearby, the overturned . . . check out the car:* "Statement of William Donovan Rundle, Jr.," 9/25/69, op. cit.; "Statement of Lawrence Lowell Riche," Alameda County District Attorney's Office, 6/12/69, 14; *LAT* 5/30/69, "Berkeley: Birth, Growth of 'War.'"
459 *Riche was ordered:* Riche deposition, 9/25/72, op. cit., 136; Riche federal grand jury testimony, January 1970, 130.
459 *As the deputies approached . . . stayed behind:* "Statement of William Donovan Rundle, Jr.," 9/25/69, op. cit.; author interview with Greenberg.
459 *Slowly he raised:* "Statement of William Donovan Rundle, Jr.," 9/25/69, op. cit.
459 *As he did:* FBI report of interview of Ronald M. Greenberg, 9/29/69, and U.S. DOJ attorney Jeffrey L. Smith memo of interview with Ronald M. Greenberg, 9/11/70, both in U.S. Department of Justice civil rights file 144-11-656 released to the author under the FOIA; author interview with Greenberg; *SFC* 9/2/70, "What Four Saw."
459 *Buckshot tore:* *SFC* 2/13/70, "Deputies Sued in Shootings"; author interview with Greenberg.
459 *Riche saw:* "Statement of Lawrence Lowell Riche," Alameda County District Attorney's Office, 6/12/69, 17. Riche stated that he neither arrested the man nor called for medical help, Riche federal grand jury testimony, January 1970, 138, 151.
459 *Witnesses would:* Witness statements in U.S. Department of Justice civil rights file 144-11-656, released to the author under the FOIA.
459 *But Riche claimed:* "Statement of Lawrence Lowell Riche," Alameda County District Attorney's Office, 6/12/69, 17.
459 *He claimed other:* Testimony of Lawrence L. Riche, 9/9/70, *U.S. v. Riche,* U.S. District Court, Northern District of California, 171, 173, 180, 190, 191; Riche deposition 9/25/72, op. cit., pp. 24, 57, 72, 74; Riche federal grand jury testimony, January 1970, 134–37.
459 *He had fired:* Riche federal grand jury testimony, January 1970, 137.
459 *Savio, too . . . for Rundle:* Savio statement to Greenberg, op. cit. Suzanne Goldberg and Lynne Hollander told me they were not familiar with the incident.
460 *Paramedics came:* "Statement of William Donovan Rundle, Jr.," 9/25/69, op. cit.
460 *A passerby:* FBI report 9/30/69 in U.S. Department of Justice civil rights file 144-11-656, released to the author under the FOIA.
460 *It was the:* Author interview with Greenberg.
460 *At least 169 people . . . in the back:* Figures for shootings and injuries on May 15, 1969, varied from source to source. The total injuries are from UCPD, n.d., "People's Park Resume." That nineteen required medical treatment is from "The 'People's Park,'" Office of the Governor, 7/1/69, p. 23. An FBI memo reported that at least sixty civilians were injured, 100-151646-331, p. 17. Todd Gitlin reported in *The Sixties,* 357, that by some accounts at least a hundred civilians were shot. No officer suffered

serious injury, *LAT* 5/30/69, "Berkeley: Birth, Growth of 'War'"; *NYT* 5/16/69, "Shotguns and Tear Gas." No officer was shot, *Ramparts*, August 1969, "Rampage," 42. Many civilians were shot in the back, *Neither Law nor Order*, 42–43.

460 *Police had arrested*: "The 'People's Park,'": Office of the Governor, 7/1/69, p. 23.

460 *By 6:00 p.m.*: "Statement of Lawrence Lowell Riche," Alameda County District Attorney's Office, 6/12/69.

460 *In Sacramento . . . of Sheriff Madigan*: SFC 5/16/69, "Reagan Calls Out the Guard"; "The 'People's Park,'" Office of the Governor, 7/1/69, p. 22; *NYT* 5/26/69, "Most Guardsmen"; 100-151646-331; Counterintelligence Spot Report, 5/15/69, U.S. Army Intelligence Corps, in 62-112228-47-illegible (states 2,500 troops at OAT).

460 *. . . a police helicopter . . . arrest*: DC 5/16/69, "A Day of Violent Paradoxes."

460 *The sun burned*: "The 'People's Park,'" Office of the Governor, 7/1/69, pp. 22, 25; *SFC* 5/17/69, "Less Violence as Troops Take Over."

461 *The National Guard*: This paragraph is based on *SFC* 5/17/69, "Less Violence as Troops Take Over"; *DC* 5/19/69, "Park Supporters Peacefully March in Protest Friday"; *DC* 5/26/69, p. 3, photo of armored personnel carrier stationed at the Berkeley marina; *SFC* 5/20/69, "Unlikely Soldiers in an Unlikely War"; *LAT* 6/3/69, "National Guard Pullout."

461 *At the regents' meeting*: This paragraph is from *DC* 5/19/69, "Regents Support UC Park Action."

461 *Even as he spoke*: This paragraph and the next are based on UCPD "Incident Report—Confrontation on People's Park," 5/16/69; *DC* 5/19/69, "Park Supporters Peacefully March in Protest Friday."

461 *Savio was deeply . . . civil rights movement*: 100-151646-331; *SFC* 5/17/69, "An Angry Call."

461 *On Saturday . . . Guard's withdrawal*: UCPD Supplementary Report, 5/17/69; UCPD Incident Report Log, 5/17/69.

462 *In a lookout post*: UCPD Supplementary Report, 5/17/69; UCPD Incident Report Log, 5/17/69.

462 *. . . one of which paraphrased*: "Monday, May 19th" Revolutionary Union flyer, in UCPD files.

462 *A phalanx of soldiers*: UCPD Supplementary Report, 5/17/69; UCPD Incident Report Log, 5/17/69.

462 *To many demonstrators . . . young women*: SFC 5/20/69, "Unlikely Soldiers in an Unlikely War"; DC 5/27/69, "National Guardsman Tells . . ."; *Neither Law nor Order*, 49 (soldiers flashing peace sign).

462 *But they still*: 100-34204-3399, with army records; 100-34204-33-illegible, 5/17/69; 100-151646-320; SFC 5/19/69, "Wigged Out Troopers in Berkeley."

462 *On campus, meanwhile*: UCPD Incident Report Log, 5/17/69; Glick dissertation, 126–27.

462 *Sunday also saw . . . turned them away*: SFC 5/19/69, "A Berkeley Runaround"; *NYT* 5/19/69, "6 Arrested on 4th Day"; UCPD "Chronology of Incidents of Violence or Disorder During the Peoples Park Problems."

462 *Tension mounted . . . bayonets bristling*: DC 5/20/69, "University Police Remove Six Slugs Fired Through University Window"; SFC 5/20/69, "Berkeley's Silent Citizens Speak Out"; DC 5/20/69, "Riot Victim Dies"; *LAT* 5/20/69, "UC Demonstrators Routed"; *Neither Law nor Order*, 50. An internal investigation by the SFPD determined that buckshot had penetrated a library window, and that it most likely was fired by the SFPD tactical squad on May 15, 1969, see 100-62751-126.

462 *That night, James Rector . . . use of deadly force*: DC 5/20/69, "Riot Victim Dies."

462 *Madigan had personally*: SFC 5/17/69, "Sheriff Defends Use of Shotguns"; SFC

5/17/69, "Berkeley Injury Confusion"; *SFX* 5/18/69, "Man-Killer Ammo"; *SFC* 5/21/69, "Buckshot Blamed"; Glick dissertation, 101–102. Madigan eventually admitted Rector was struck by police buckshot, *DC* 5/23/69, "482 Arrests in Peaceful March."

462 *Now doctors: SFC* 5/20/69, "Berkeley Riot Victim Dies"; *SFC* 5/21/69, "Buckshot Blamed."

462 *In anger . . . and children:* The account of the march and tear-gassing on Sproul Plaza is based on *DC* 5/21/69, "South Campus Area Cleared by Police as Memorial March Halted"; *LAT* 5/30/69, "Berkeley: Birth, Growth of 'War' "; *SFC* 5/23/69, "Tangled Events Leading to Gassing"; *SFC* 5/23/69, "Advice for Tear-Gassed Students"; *SFC* 5/23/69, "Reagan and the 'Dogs of War' "; *DC* 5/26/69, "Cranston Criticizes"; Civil Claim of Ilona Hancock filed with Alameda County; *Neither Law nor Order,* 52–57; Glick dissertation, 130–33.

463 *At a press conference: DC* 5/22/69, "Copter Gas Spray Defended"; *SFC* 5/22/69, "Guard Tells Why."

463 *At first a guard . . . use in Vietnam: SFC* 5/23/69, "Tangled Events Leading to Gassing"; *SFC* 5/23/69, "Advice for Tear-Gassed Students"; *DC* 5/23/69, "Tear Gas Techniques"; *DC* 5/22/69, "Faculty 'Unwilling to Teach' "; *SFC* 5/22/69, "Dispute over the Gas"; Glick dissertation, 137–40. Two years earlier, Ames sent Meese a report on CS gas that said, "The effects of CS are impressive. It produces immediate effects even in low concentrations," Willison to Meese, 10/31/67, with California ARNG Circular No. 350-19, in Meese Papers, Hoover Institution, box 227, folder: "Military: Emergency Operations Procedures—1967." On CS gas, see *Encyclopædia Britannica Online,* s.v. "CN," www.britannica.com/EBchecked/topic/122731/CN, accessed 11/9/11.

463 *The helicopter tear-gassing: SFC* 5/22/69, "Sit-In at Heyns' Residence"; *DC* 5/22/69, "Faculty 'Unwilling to Teach' "; Glick dissertation, 141–45.

463 *Paul Halvonik . . . "constitutional infringement": DC* 5/22/69, "ACLU Wants Sheriff Fired."

463 *Reagan was unfazed . . . "things will happen":* The anecdote about Reagan meeting with the professors is from *DC* 5/22/69, "Reagan, Faculty Trade Blasts"; *SFC* 5/22/69, "An Angry Reagan Debates"; *LAT* 5/22/69, "Reagan, Eight UC Professors in Shouting Match"; *Looking for the Future,* by Leon Wofsy, 48–49.

464 *Still, Berkeleyans defied:* The account of the march and the arrests downtown under Operation Box is from *DC* 5/23/69, "482 Arrests in Peaceful March"; *SFC* 5/24/69, "I Was a Prisoner at Santa Rita"; *Ramparts,* August 1969, "A Night at Santa Rita"; *Neither Law nor Order,* 58–63; author interview with Richard Kamler, arrested in Operation Box. Lieutenant Ralph Schillinger of the Berkeley Police Department identified the mass arrest as "Operation Box" in his remarks to the Cable Splicer III conference in May 1970. Transcript in author's possession.

465 *The abuse began:* The description of events at Santa Rita is from *SFC* 5/24/69, "I Was a Prisoner at Santa Rita"; *Ramparts,* August 1969, "A Night at Santa Rita"; *DC* 5/26/69, "Restraining Order Issued Against Sheriffs"; *Neither Law nor Order,* 64–71. The quotes are from these sources. The affidavits are attached to Complaint for Temporary Restraining Order and Injunction, *Stephen Thomas Murray et al. v. Frank Madigan,* No. 51398, U.S. District Court, Northern District of California, filed 5/22/70 by counsel Peter Haberfeld, James J. Brosnahan, Stanley Friedman, and Joseph Grodin. Author interviews with Peter Haberfeld and James J. Brosnahan.

466 *On May 25, U.S. District Court Judge:* This paragraph is based on 5/26/69, "Restraining Order Issued"; Order, *Stephen Thomas Murray et al. v. Frank Madigan,* op. cit., 5/29/69; author interviews with Peter Haberfeld and James J. Brosnahan.

466 *Reagan meanwhile relaxed*: This paragraph is based on *DC* 5/23/69, "Reagan Eases Curfew Rules"; *DC* 5/28/69, "War over Park Continues."

466 *Eventually, Alameda County*: *DC* 5/23/69, "482 Arrests in Peaceful March"; *SFC* 7/10/69, "The Park Trial Winds Up"; *LAT* 7/10/69, "The State" author interview with former Alameda County Assistant District Attorney William M. Baldwin.

466 *At a press conference . . . "Viet Cong"*: *SFC* 5/30/69, "Madigan Warns Marchers."

466 *The mass arrests . . . People's Park*: *DC* 5/23/69, "Referendum Proposals Win"; Glick dissertation, 154.

466 *Students at every*: *DC* 5/26/69, "Other Campuses Support Park."

466 *Seven thousand students*: *SFC* 5/27/69, "Huge March to Demand."

466 *More Berkeley faculty*: *DC* 5/22/69, editorial, "Murder's Sad Legacy."

466 *The campus's Academic*: *DC* 5/26/69, "Faculty Endorses Community Park Concept"; Glick dissertation, 158.

466 *Several professors*: *DC* 5/27/69, LED, "Ad Hoc Faculty."

466 *Inspired by*: This paragraph is based on *DC* 5/28/69, "Forum Today on Park Ecology"; *DC* 5/29/69, "A Peaceful Day"; "Smokey the Bear Sutra," by Gary Snyder, at www.sacred-texts.com/bud/bear.htm, accessed 7/28/11.

467 *At Winterland Auditorium*: *DC* 5/28/69, photo caption; *DC* 5/29/69, "Do You Think Rock Is Being Used"; *SFC* 5/29/69, "Benefit."

467 *. . . "rainbow spirals . . ."*: This phrase is from the lyrics to "That's It for the Other One," words and music by Jerry Garcia, Bob Weir, and Bill Kreutzmann of the Grateful Dead, at the Annotated Grateful Dead, artsites.ucsc.edu/GDead/agdl/gdhome.html, accessed 7/28/11.

467 *The Episcopal bishop*: *SFC* 5/28/69, "A Growing Opposition "; *SFC* 5/26/69, "Strong Attack on Reagan by Myers."

467 *Wallace Johnson . . . "his own Vietnam"*: *DC* 5/26/69, "Council: End of Curfew"; *DC* 5/3/69, "McCarthy Anti-Cops"; *SFC* 5/30/69, "McGovern Assails"; *DC* 5/23/69, "Berkeley: Reagan's Vietnam."

467 *Reagan steadfastly*: This paragraph is based on *SFC* 5/20/69, "Reagan Attacks Anarchy." See also *DC* 5/26/69, "Reagan Denounces Park Plans."

467 *At a Sacramento press conference*: This and the following three paragraphs are based on *SFC* 5/21/69, "Reagan Condemns Planned Violence"; *LAT* 5/21/69, "Reagan Charges Park Riots Were Planned."

468 *It was unknown*: On the FBI's COINTELPRO involving the Black Panthers and the United Slaves, see Church, book III, 189–95. The report says, "Because of the milieu of violence in which members of the Panthers often moved we have been unable to establish a direct link between any of the FBI's specific efforts to promote violence and particular acts of violence that occurred. We have been able to establish beyond doubt, however, that high officials of the FBI desired to promote violent confrontations between BPP members and members of other groups, and that those officials condoned tactics calculated to achieve that end," ibid., 189.

468 *A review of FBI . . . "property damage"*: These records include 100-151646-331 and 100-151646-347, comprehensive reports on People's Park; UCPD Supplementary Report of Sgt. R. E. Hull, 5/15/69; UCPD, n.d., "People's Park Resume"; UCPD "Chronology of Incidents of Violence or Disorder During the Peoples Park Problems"; UCPD Incident Report Log, 5/15/69. It is possible that some demonstrators, planning in advance for a confrontation, stockpiled rocks and other missiles, but these records do not document that or otherwise show that the missiles were not amassed during the confrontation. For example, a UCPD report states that protesters spontaneously smashed large concrete trash containers to make missiles. See UCPD Supplementary Report of Sgt. R. E. Hull, 5/15/69.

468 *According to*: 100-151646-331.
469 *The free-speech spokesman*: That Savio did not play a leadership role in the formation of People's Park or the ensuing protests is supported by FBI and police records;
contemporaneous press reports; author interview with Suzanne Goldberg.
469 *At a $100-a-plate . . . of his car*: DC 5/23/69, "Real Truth"; LAT 5/23/69, "Reagan
Asserts"; SFC 5/23/69, "The Conflicting Version."
469 *(This sounded sinister*: SFX 5/20/69, "UC Park Victim Described as 'Loner.'")
469 *To the glee . . . "name of dissent"*: DC 5/23/69, "Real Truth"; LAT 5/23/69, "Reagan
Asserts"; SFC 5/23/69, "The Conflicting Version."
469 *Several days later . . . "complete surrender . . ."*: LAT 5/28/69, "Guard to Stay in Berkeley"; DC 5/28/69, "War over Park Continues."
469 *Reagan successfully*: WP 7/11/69, "Conservative Tide"; NYT 7/27/69, "Democrats on
Coast"; NYT 8/11/69, "Reagan, Campus Critic"; NYT 8/23/69, "California Poll";
SFC 5/28/69, "Senate GOP Endorses Reagan Line"; SFC 5/28/69, "A Defender of
Reagan's Action."
469 *He refused . . . "on hand"*: SFC 5/24/69, "March"; SFC 5/28/69, "A Pledge to Control
Big March"; SFC 5/29/69, "New Plans for March Tomorrow"; DC 5/29/69, "March
to Park"; DC 5/30/69, "March Today"; DC 5/30/69, "25,000 March on People's
Park." (*The Daily Californian* for 5/30/69 was published under the name "The Independent Californian.")
469 *At a press conference . . . lethal ammunition*: SFC 5/30/69, "Madigan Warns Marchers"; NYT 5/31/69, "Angry Berkeley Sheriff."
469 *People's Park*: SFC 5/31/69, "Lennon and Joan Baez."
470 *Reverend Richard York*: The account of the march is based on DC 5/30/69, "March
Today"; DC 5/30/69, "25,000 March on People's Park"; SFC 5/31/69, "Parade in
Berkeley"; SFC 5/31/69, "Flower Power Rules the Day"; SFC 5/31/69, "The March"
(map); *Cody's Books*, 125–26; "A View from the Avenue," by Pat and Fred Cody, in
Experiment and Change in Berkeley, Essays on City Politics 1950–1975, 154–57; LAT
5/31/69, "Violence—a Fear"; LAT 5/31/69, "Thousands March"; NYT 5/31/69,
"Troops Keep Demonstrators"; WP 5/31/69, "Thousands March."
470 *Pat Cody*: Pat Cody's comments are from *Cody's Books*, 125–26.
470 *The march, however*: This paragraph and the next are based on DC 6/24/69, "Park
Decision Hit"; DC 6/24/69, "The Alternatives for the Regents"; NYT 5/31/69,
"Troops Keep Demonstrators"; WP 5/31/69, "Thousands March."
471 *A few days after*: The account of the rally is from DC 6/27/69, "A Radical Analysis of
the Park."
471 *He had been . . . bachelor's degree*: Savio would be readmitted in fall 1970, OT
9/19/70, "Student Protest Leader Savio Back," and BDG 9/19/70, "Mario Savio Will
Return." His having kept away from campus protests and focused on family is in
Freedom's Orator, 254, 255, 257, 259.
471 *Two FBI informers*: 100-54060-547; 100-54060-552.
471 *Savio did not*: Savio's views on drugs and the counterculture are discussed in *Freedom's Orator*, 265–67, 476–77, n. 164.
472 *"Some of the good . . ."* The text of Savio's talk was reprinted in DC 7/1/69, "Mario
Savio: 'Seize the Means of Leisure.'"
473 *While Reagan defended*: SFC 6/3/69, "The Governor's Statement"; SFC 6/11/69,
"Reagan's Defense of UC Attack."
473 *. . . the American Civil Liberties Union*: *Neither Law nor Order*; DC 5/19/69, "ACLU
Wants Reports About 'Police Excesses'"; DC 5/22/69, "ACLU Wants Sheriff Fired."
473 *Ramparts magazine*: *Ramparts*, August 1969, "Rampage."
473 *The Los Angeles Times*: LAT 5/30/69, "Berkeley: Birth, Growth of 'War.'"

474 *Sheriff Frank Madigan . . . in charge*: SFC 6/19/69, "Sheriff's Officer Who Shot Rector."

474 *ACLU officials feared*: Those concerns were articulated in James Pachl to Alameda County Grand Jury, 7/27/69.

474 *The results . . . meager discipline*: SFC 7/3/69, "Reprimand at Santa Rita Prison Farm"; DC 7/3/69, "Madigan Raps Cops for Terror at Santa Rita"; SFX 7/2/69, "Madigan Throws Book at Jailers"; SFC 1/15/70, "A Grand Jury Probe on Police and People's Park."

474 *The Alameda County Coroner . . . "sheriff's deputy"*: DC 7/15/69, "Rector Slaying Justifiable"; SFC 7/11/69, "Rector Inquest—Events Leading to the Shooting"; SFC 7/12/69, "Killer Unidentifiable—But Deputy Says He May Have Fired Shot"; SFC 7/12/69, "Staff of Coroner Picked Jury"; SFC 7/12/69, "Rector's Slaying Ruled Justifiable."

474 *By contrast*: This paragraph is based on SFC 11/8/69, "People's Park Report Blames All Concerned"; SFC 11/12/69, "Blame for All"; SFC 2/8/70, "This World"; SFX 11/12/69, "2 Bay Deputies Face Trial"; Alameda County Grand Jury Report, copy in author's possession.

475 *By now Reagan*: "The 'People's Park,'" Office of the Governor, 7/1/69, copy in author's possession.

475 *Reagan's office*: SFC 7/10/69, "Reagan Told Park Clash Was Planned."

475 *. . . but records indicate*: Testimony of Herbert E. Ellingwood, Legal Affairs Secretary, 7/16/69, Hearings, Permanent Subcommittee on Investigations, Committee on Government Operations, U.S. Senate, Part 22, p. 5029 et seq. Ellingwood worked under Meese.

475 *Meese made clear*: LAT 6/26/80, "'California Cronies' Have Reagan's Ear"; WP 3/15/81, "Deep Inside Ed Meese Runs a Law-and-Order Streak." Meese confirmed his opinion in an interview with the author.

475 *The study*: "The 'People's Park,'" Office of the Governor, 7/1/69, 16; SFC 11/19/69, "Siegel Is Acquitted." The California State Bar Committee of Bar Examiners later sought to block Siegel from being admitted to practice law, but the State Supreme Court reversed the decision. LAT 10/10/73, "High Court Orders Berkeley Riot Figure Admitted to Bar."

475 *The report repeated*: "The 'People's Park,'" 17, but the footnoted citations vaguely cite only "Reports by police at the scene."

476 *Back in June*: SFC 6/27/69, "Officer Who Ordered UC Gas Attack."

476 *This drew an angry . . . "public are concerned"*: Ames to Madigan, 7/11/69, Meese Papers, Hoover Institution, box 219, folder: "Demonstrations/Riots/Disorder."

476 *That, essentially*: Author interview with Edwin Meese III.

476 *As United States Attorney . . . fifty states*: The Judge Cecil Poole Project, Ninth Judicial Circuit Historical Society, www.njchs.org/project/index.html, accessed 7/28/11; NYT 11/16/97, "Cecil F. Poole."

476 *Poole had angered*: NYT 12/20/67, "U.S. Attorney Deplores"; LAT 9/29/68, "Sen. Murphy Cites," in which Murphy cited Poole's position on the arrests in raising an objection during hearings on Poole's nomination as a federal judge.

476 *Fiercely independent*: In an interview with the author, James J. Brosnahan, who was an assistant United States Attorney who worked with him, recalled Poole's independence.

476 *. . . he initiated*: LAT 1/15/70, "U.S. Begins Probe." Poole sought and obtained approval for the inquiry from U.S. Attorney General John Mitchell and presented the FBI's findings to a federal grand jury.

477 *From the start*: This paragraph and the next are based on Smith to Rosenberg,

8/8/69, contained in U.S. Department of Justice civil rights file 144-11-656, released to the author under the FOIA.

477 *These fears . . . fifty feet*: SFC 5/19/69, "Photo Stirs New Furor"; SFC 5/30/69, "'Doctored' Photo Charge by Sheriff"; *Ramparts*, August 1969, "Rampage."

477 *Nonetheless . . . to do so*: SFC 1/15/70, "A Grand Jury Probe on Police and People's Park."

477 *Poole presented*: NYT 2/3/70, "12 Riot Deputies Indicted"; LAT 2/8/70, "Deputies Indicted"; SFC 2/3/70, "12 Charged in Beatings, Shootings."

478 *They were among . . . School of Law*: LAT 2/3/70, "The State."

478 *The indictments charged*: NYT 2/3/70, "12 Riot Deputies Indicted"; LAT 2/8/70, "Deputies Indicted"; SFC 2/3/70, "12 Charged in Beatings, Shootings." A copy of the press release announcing the indictments is in Christopher Venn civil rights file, 44-43569-19.

478 *Madigan was appalled*: This paragraph is based on SFC 2/3/70, "12 Charged in Beatings, Shootings"; SFC 2/4/70, "Madigan's Anger at Indictments."

478 *Assemblyman Don Mulford*: SFC 2/18/70, "Mulford Hits Deputy Indictments."

478 *The Oakland Police Officers*: SFC 2/4/69, "Some Angry Reaction to Indictment."

478 *And the Alameda County Deputy Sheriffs'*: The letter-writing campaign is evident from correspondence in U.S. Department of Justice civil rights file 144-11-647 on James Rector and the prosecution of the deputies, released to the author under the FOIA. One memo notes DOJ has received "several thousand" form letters opposing the prosecutions, O'Connor to Leonard, 12/2/70, in DOJ civil rights file 144-11-647. See also SFC 2/4/70, "Madigan's Anger at Indictments."

478 *In an appeal*: L. W. Brown, Secretary, Deputy Sheriffs Association to Nixon, 10/20/70, in U.S. Department of Justice civil rights file 144-11-647, op. cit.

478 *The organization*: Robert J. Donovan to John Mitchell, telegram, 9/30/70, in U.S. Department of Justice civil rights file 144-11-647, op. cit.

479 *Declaring that he*: This paragraph is based on SFC 2/11/70, "Chaos Predicted if Prop 7 Fails."

479 *Two weeks later*: This paragraph is based on LAT 2/13/70, "Berkeley Police Lot Blasted"; LAT 2/14/70, "Two Officers Injured"; NYT 2/14/70, "2 Policemen Hurt in Blast on Coast"; NYT 2/17/70, "15 Seized and 10 Hurt Here"; LAT 2/17/70, "Chicago Seven Riot Erupts in Berkeley"; NYT 2/17/70, "Protest in Berkeley"; LAT 2/17/70, "Protest in Berkeley"; WP 2/17/70, "Contempt Sentences Protested"; NYT 2/18/70, "6 Hurt in Police Station Blast"; LAT 2/19/70, "S.F. Officer Injured by Time Bomb Dies"; LAT 2/22/70, "Demonstrations Follow Trial"; LAT 3/25/70, "$35,000 Reward Posted."

479 *In a letter*: Governor's office press release, 2/18/70, Meese Papers, Hoover Institution, box 219, folder: "Demonstrations/Riots/Disorders."

479 *Mitchell promptly*: Mitchell to Reagan, 2/20/70, teletype, Meese Papers, Hoover Institution, box 219, folder: "Demonstrations/Riots/Disorders."

480 *With the first*: This paragraph is based on Reagan to Mitchell, 4/28/70, Meese Papers, Hoover Institution, box 177, folder: "CDO/OES 1970." Mitchell addressed the California Peace Officers Association the following year, harshly criticizing antiwar protesters, WP 5/11/71, "Mitchell Warns on Protests"; NYT 5/11/70, "Mitchell Urges All Police."

480 *Jimi Hendrix*: Hendrix made the comments during his May 30, 1970, performance at the Berkeley Community Theatre, recorded on *Live at Berkeley*, the Jimi Hendrix Experience, CD, 2003.

480 *At their own*: The comments of Plummer, Houchins, Larson, and Ames in this paragraph and the next are from transcriptions of their talks at the Cable Splicer III conference, May 1970, copies in author's possession.

481 *The federal trial*: The description of Riche's trial in this paragraph and the next is based on SFC 8/30/70, "Deputy on Trial in 60 Riot Case"; SFC 8/31/70, "First Deputy's Trial in Berkeley Riots"; SFC 9/2/70, "What Four Saw at People's Park"; SFC 9/4/70, "What a Deputy Told"; SFC 9/9/70, "People's Park Likened to Vietnam"; SFC 9/10/70, "Deputy's Dramatic Testimony Through Mask"; SFC 9/16/70, "Ex Deputy's Case Goes to Jury."

481 *When Riche was . . . "riot that day"*: SFC 9/17/69, "An Acquittal in People's Park Case."

482 *One month later . . . a hung jury*: SFC 10/16/70, "Ex-Deputy Cleared"; SFX 11/20/70, "People's Park Deputy Again Splits Jury."

482 *With most*: This paragraph is based on Reagan to Mitchell, 10/20/70, in U.S. Department of Justice civil rights file 144-11-647 on James Rector and the prosecution of the deputies, released to the author under the FOIA.

482 *Replying ten days*: This paragraph is based on Mitchell to Reagan, 10/30/70, U.S. Department of Justice civil rights file 144-11-647.

482 *In an interview*: Author interview with Edwin Meese III.

482 *During a confidential*: This paragraph is based on O'Connor to file, 11/3/70, U.S. Department of Justice civil rights file 144-11-647.

483 *Several more trials*: On the trials see SFC 10/16/70, "The People's Park Deputy Acquitted"; SFC 10/20/70, "Judge Sets Retrial in Riot Shooting"; SFC 11/19/70, "People's Park Deputy's Third Trial"; SFC 11/20/70, "People's Park Deputy Again Splits Jury"; SFC 12/17/70, "Jury Frees Two of Three Deputies"; SFC 12/18/70, "A Hung Jury."

483 *Then, on December 18 . . . other three*: SFC 12/19/70, "A Move to Drop Deputy Charges"; SFX 12/18/70, "Deputy Cases Dismissed." Judge Weigel's irritation is noted in O'Connor to file, 12/21/70, in U.S. Department of Justice civil rights file 144-11-647, op. cit.

483 *The remaining prosecutions . . . deadlocked juries*: SFC 1/20/71, "Ex-Deputy Is Not Guilty"; SFC 2/19/71, "Deputies Acquitted in Riot Shootings."

483 *. . . the Justice Department . . . Browning said*: SFC 3/5/71, "People's Park Cases Dropped."

483 *No deputy was*: Ibid.

483 *With the federal prosecutions*: The following section about the civil litigation arising from police activities during the People's Park affair is based on the author's review of claims filed with Alameda County, state and federal court cases, news articles, and interviews with plaintiffs and attorneys. Some of the litigation received notice in the press. See, for example, SFC 1/17/70, "Suit by Passerby"; SFC 1/23/70, "Writer Sues"; SFC 2/13/70, "Deputies Sued"; SFC 2/20/70, "Shot Student Sues"; SFC 4/9/71, "A False Arrest Award"; SFC 5/15/73, "High Court Bans Suit."

483 *William Rundle, Jr.*: William Donovan Rundle, Jr., et al. v. Frank Madigan et al., No. C-70-334 RFP, U.S. District Court, Northern District of California.

483 *He had been*: Author interview with Ronald M. Greenberg.

483 *Greenberg alleged . . . like Rundle*: Rundle v. Madigan, op. cit., Memorandum of Points and Authorities in Opposition to Defendants' Motion for Summary Judgment and in Support of Plaintiffs' Request for Partial Summary Judgment, filed 12/3/71.

483 *Madigan and . . . Rundle's lawsuit*: The defense motion and its citation of the Reagan report on People's Park is noted in Rundle v. Madigan, op. cit., Memorandum of Points and Authorities.

483 *. . . but Judge Peckham ruled*: Ruling filed 11/20/72 in Rundle v. Madigan, op. cit.

483 *Greenberg uncovered . . . shooting*: Author interview with Ronald M. Greenberg.
484 *Agents never*: Author interview with Greenberg; statement of Steve Dane.
484 *His film*: Author review of film, courtesy of Ronald M. Greenberg.
484 *Greenberg was convinced*: Author interview with Ronald M. Greenberg.
484 *This never was*: Order of Dismissal Upon Settlement of Case, 4/10/74, in *Rundle v. Madigan*, op. cit.; author interview with Ronald M. Greenberg.
484 *This never . . . misconduct lawsuits*: The total is for 82 people who each got from $200 to more than $500,000. It may be far higher, as not all plaintiffs, or their lawyers, were available or recalled sums, and the county and state, in reply to public records act requests, said relevant records were lost or destroyed. The stated total draws on interviews of Richard Ehrenberger, Allan Francke, Mike Beavers, Ken Meade, Ronald M. Greenberg, Gloria Pass, Mike Syvanen, Fred Goss, Robert Givens, John Thorpe, and on *SFC* 8/9/72, "Payoff"; *SFC* 4/19/71, "A False Arrest."
484 *Governor Reagan and*: "The 'People's Park,'" Office of the Governor, 7/1/69, p. 27; Testimony of Herbert E. Ellingwood, Legal Affairs Secretary, 7/16/69, Hearings, Permanent Subcommittee on Investigations, Committee on Government Operations, U.S. Senate, Part 22, p. 5033.
484 *. . . the $764,000*: "The 'People's Park,'" Office of the Governor, 7/1/69, p. 27.
484 *Moreover, in criminal court*: As the prosecutor, O'Connor, noted in his motion for dismissal, only 20 percent of recent cases instituted by the department against police officers for violating civil rights of people involved in civil disturbances had resulted in convictions. The defense, by contrast, could prevail by convincing just one juror that there was enough of a reasonable doubt not to vote for conviction, *SFC* 2/18/71, "Jury Is Out in Trial of People's Park Deputies."
484 *Nor, for that*: *LAT* 3/3/70, "U.S. Civil Rights Chief"; *WP* 3/8/70, "Jerry Leonard—a Team Man"; *NYT* 5/16/70, "Energetic Rights Chief"; *LAT* 7/14/70, "Leonard Backs Pace."
484 *Even as Leonard*: Church, book III, 503, which notes that the list included the civil rights leaders Rev. Ralph Abernathy, Cesar Chavez, James Farmer, and Mrs. Coretta King.
485 *The CIA concluded*: Church, book III, 699–700.
485 *Hoover had been . . . "New Left Activities"*: Hoover began this nationwide operation on May 1, 1969, two weeks before the People's Park protest erupted. The opening document began, "The White House has requested the identity and background of the main college faculty members involved in New Left Activities, particularly those who have either promoted or participated in violence or confrontation with authorities," 100-446997-78-1.
485 *He had continued*: Church, book III, COINTELPRO: "The FBI's Covert Action Programs Against American Citizens," p. 3 et seq. The FBI terminated the program in 1971. However, a few isolated COINTELPRO-type actions were subsequently discovered, and in any event aggressive investigation "may be even more disruptive than covert action," Church, book III, 3, 12–14.
485 *Angela Davis*: Davis is identified as a COINTELPRO target in 100-439922-NR, 5/28/70; 100-439922-NR, 6/12/60; her firing is noted in *NYT* 9/20/69, "U.C.L.A. Teacher Is Ousted as Red."
485 *In July 1969 . . . fired her*: *WP* 9/29/69, "Firing of Red Stirs Furor"; *I Lived Inside the Campus Revolution*, 163–86. Note that Divale writes that he quit working as an FBI informer in June, the month before he wrote the letter accusing Davis, ibid., x, 143–61, 170. However, his FBI informer file shows that, while he was described as "former LA 4688-S," he provided information to the FBI at least through August 26, 1969. See 134-2702A-661. On the academic freedom controversy over Davis, see

NYT 7/2/70, "Ousted Red Teacher Sues"; NYT 9/23/72, "California Regents Reject"; NYT 9/24/72, "Miss Davis's Job"; NYT 10/7/69, "U.C.L.A. Students Are Urged"; NYT 10/9/69, "Political Test at U.C.L.A."; NYT 10/12/69, "Battle over Academic Freedom." In the midst of this academic freedom controversy, Davis was indicted for murder, kidnapping, and conspiracy for allegedly engineering an attempted courtroom escape in Marin County on August 7, 1970, in which a judge and several other people were killed. She was accused of plotting the breakout but denied the charges and was acquitted. The case had sparked an international movement to free her. See NYT 11/12/70, "Angela Davis Is Indicted"; NYT 6/6/70, "Davis Juror Reports."

485   *FBI officials*: Their goal is stated in 62-103031-291, 6/25/71. See also 62-103031-290, 6/30/71, with enclosed Informative Note, 7/16/71, and Cunningham to Hoover, 6/15/71, in 62-103031-291. On the high court's ruling, see *LAT* 10/10/72, "Supreme Court Rejects Firing."

485   *Hoover did not . . . "limited" investigations*: The phrase "This is a limited investigation" appears throughout FBI files on the People's Park civil rights investigations. See, for example, Rector and Blanchard civil rights 44-42514-18, 44-42514-27, 44-42514-52; Rundle civil rights 44-43569-no serial, 10/1/69, and 44-43569-no serial, 10/17/69, both in DOJ 144-11-656; Venn civil rights 44-42513-9 and 44-42513-19.

485   *This meant*: Author correspondence with Athan Theoharis and author interview with James J. Brosnahan, both of whom described a limited investigation as being less comprehensive than a full investigation. It is true that the FBI investigation was the basis for the grand jury indictments. However, the grand jury process is not an adversary proceeding—defense lawyers may neither make presentations nor cross-examine witnesses—and the standard of evidence required for an indictment is far less than the proof beyond a reasonable doubt required for conviction. This has led to the old saw that any competent prosecutor could convince a grand jury to indict a ham sandwich.

485   *Soon after*: The anecdote about Ellingwood's meeting with DeLoach is from 100-151646-348, 7/17/69.

Epilogue: The Aftermath

489   *On the morning*: NYT 5/3/72, "J. Edgar Hoover, 77, Dies"; WP 5/3/72, "J. Edgar Hoover Dies." On Hoover's demise, his office files, his memorial, and Miss Gandy, see also *The Boss*; *Secrecy and Power*; *J. Edgar Hoover: The Man and the Secrets*.

489   *Helen Gandy*: LAT 12/2/75, "Hoover Secretary Says"; NYT 12/2/75, "Secretary Says She Destroyed."

489   *Thirty-five*: WP 12/2/75, "Turmoil at FBI."

489   *Gandy would later*: LAT 12/2/75, "Hoover Secretary Says"; NYT 12/2/75, "Secretary Says She Destroyed."

489   *But some documents . . . settlement*: LAT 12/2/75, "Hoover Secretary Says"; WP 12/2/75, "Turmoil at FBI." Stew Albert and his wife, Judith Clavir (also known as Judy Gumbo), denied involvement in the Capitol bombing and never were charged. They later won a harassment suit against the FBI for breaking into and bugging their home, and used the proceeds to buy a new Audi with a vanity license plate reading, "CAPBOM," NYT 3/4/71, "2 Yippies Charge Harassment"; WP 4/29/78, "'74 N.Y. Break-Ins"; NYT 6/27/78, "Suit over F.B.I."; *Who the Hell Is Stew Albert?*, 191–96. On the Capitol bombing, see NYT 5/3/71, "Hearings Opened on Capitol Blast"; WP 10/17/75, "Arrest in Capitol Bombing."

489   *At 11:00 a.m. . . . sixteen attorneys general*: NYT 5/3/72, "J. Edgar Hoover, 77, Dies"; WP 5/3/72, "J. Edgar Hoover Dies."

489 *Politicians*: NYT 5/3/72, "J. Edgar Hoover, 77, Dies"; *J. Edgar Hoover: The Man and the Secrets*, 42.

489 *In Sacramento*: LAT 5/3/72, "Friends—and Critics—Pay Tribute."

489 *In September 1970 . . . "the Director"*: Miller's visit is in 100-382196-85. Felt visited Governor Reagan in 1967 while inspecting the Sacramento field office, 100-382196-32.

489 *A few months*: The anecdote about the Mardian-Hoover meeting is in 100-382196-NR, 11/25/70, before 100-382196-89. Mardian, a lawyer for Richard Nixon's reelection campaign, was convicted of conspiracy in the Watergate cover-up, but his conviction was reversed on the ground that he should have been tried separately from his six codefendants. He had supported Goldwater for president and Reagan for governor, NYT 7/22/06, "Robert Mardian, 82"; NYT 11/8/70, "Security Official Named"; NYT 11/13/70, "New Security Watcher."

490 *That July, Sinatra*: On Sinatra and the Reagans, see *Nancy Reagan: The Unauthorized Biography*, 185–90.

490 *while gambling*: The scuffle anecdote is from LAT 9/8/70, "Casino Boss Arrested"; *Chicago Tribune* 9/8/70, "Sinatra Draws Las Vegas Ire"; LAT 9/11/70, "Gun Count Won't Be."

490 *It was the latest . . . the Cal-Neva Lodge*: LAT 8/13/70, "Cal-Neva Lodge"; LAT 10/6/63, "Chicago Crime Ruler"; LAT 10/20/63, "Gaming Rule on Sinatra"; LAT 12/9/63, "Can't Allow Gangsters"; NYT 4/25/66, "Gambler Facing a Ban"; NYT 5/17/66, "Nevada Board Recommends"; *Nancy Reagan: The Unauthorized Biography*, 185–90; *The Sinatra Files*, 202–206. The latter says the FBI had, in turn, alerted the JFK, LBJ, and Nixon administrations to his mob associations, but does not mention the FBI warning, Reagan, ibid., 164–212.

490 *Hoover sought*: This paragraph is based on 80-579-54; 100-382196-NR, 3/22/71, after 100-382196-91; Informative Note, 3/18/71, 100-382196-NR, before 100-382196-92; 100-382196-92; 100-382196-94; 100-382196-96, 3/23/71.

490 *The director also loaned*: 100-382196-NR, 11/21/71, before 100-382196-102.

490 *Hoover kept*: LAT 1/3/71, "Hoover's Limousine."

490 *. . . such as Southern*: *The Director*, 11, 13, 15, 16, 17, 29, 35.

490 *And when Reagan . . . "OK—H."*: 100-382196-NR, 11/22/71, before 100-382196-102.

491 *The FBI had paid*: LAT 1/3/77, "Hoover's Limousine"; LAT 3/5/75, "Reagan's Auto."

491 *That spring*: WP 4/5/71, "Untouchable Hoover, FBI Under Fire"; NYT 4/2/71, "Dissidence Unit"; WP 4/8/71, "Justice Dept. Asks"; WP 4/9/71, "Senate Unit Asks."

491 *Senator Hale Boggs*: WP 4/6/71, "Boggs Demands Firing of Hoover."

491 *The Citizens Commission . . . glimpse of COINTELPRO*: WP 4/5/71, "Untouchable Hoover, FBI Under Fire"; WP 3/24/71, "Stolen Documents Describe"; WP 3/25/71, "Thieves Got over 1,000 FBI Papers"; WP 4/9/71, "Boggs' Wiretap Stand"; *The FBI: A Comprehensive Reference Guide*, 125–27.

491 *Reagan decided*: This paragraph is based on 100-382196-99, 5/10/71; 100-382196-100, 5/13/71 (Reagan's remarks).

491 *But first . . . "in this country"*: 80-138-18; 80-138-19; 80-138-20.

491 *Reagan incorporated . . . "the master"*: 80-138-19.

491 *In a note*: 100-382196-99, 5/13/71.

491 *Reagan was at . . . to the Capitol*: 80-579-55, 5/2/72; 80-579-55, 5/3/72.

491 *It was pouring*: The rotunda account is based on WP 5/4/72, "Throngs View"; WP 5/3/72, "J. Edgar Hoover Dies"; LAT 5/4/72, "Justice Dept.'s No. 2 Man"; *J. Edgar Hoover: The Man and the Secrets*, 41–42.

492 *Hoover had been*: The burial account is based on WP 5/5/72, "Nixon Eulogizes Hoover."

492 *. . . Tolson . . . three years later*: LAT 4/15/75, "Ex-Aide to J. Edgar Hoover Succumbs";

NYT 4/15/75, "Clyde Tolson, Former FBI Official"; WP 4/15/75, "FBI's Clyde A. Tolson."

492 *On February 27, 1973*: 80-579-56, 2/28/73.

492 *The governor was*: 161-2715-12, p. 1; 161-2715-13, p. 8.

492 *Carl Stern . . . their release*: WP 9/26/73, "TV Newsman Wins Access to FBI File"; LAT 12/7/73, "FBI's 3-Year Drive on New Left Told"; WP 3/8/74, "Hoover Ordered FBI to Plant Spies"; LAT 3/10/74, "Hoover Harassed Both Left, Right"; *FBI Files on Puerto Ricans*, COINTELPRO Chronology, www.pr-secretfiles.net/programs _chronology.html?detail=7, accessed 8/5/11.

492 *Senator Frank Church's*: LAT 4/8/84, "Frank Church"; NYT 4/8/84, "Frank Church of Idaho"; WP 4/8/84, "Frank Church Dies"; WP 2/19/84, "The CIA's Canadian Victims"; LAT 7/16/77, "New Data on CIA Drug Tests Found"; WP 11/21/75, "Summary of CIA Plots"; WP 4/27/76, "CIA Ignored Bans"; Church, book I, "Part XVII, Testing and Use of Chemical and Biological Agents by the Intelligence Community," 385–422; Church, book III, "Supplementary Detailed Staff Reports on Intelligence Activities and the Rights of Americans"; *A Season of Inquiry*; *Acid Dreams*; *The Search for the Manchurian Candidate*.

492 *On April 7, 1977 . . . outside the courthouse*: LAT 3/31/77, "FBI Officials May Face Trial"; WP 3/31/77, "Indictment Urged of FBI Agents"; LAT 4/7/77, "Ex-FBI Official Indicted"; LAT 4/8/77, "Ex-FBI Supervisor Indicted"; LAT 4/14/77, "FBI Agents Mass"; WP 4/15/77, "Kelley Urges Bell"; WP 4/18/77, "Indictment of Agent Shakes the FBI"; WP 4/30/77, "Carter Unveils Bill on Wiretaps."

492 *Now in private life*: LAT 12/20/74, "Reagan's Daily Radio Program."

492 *In a May 23, 1977 . . . against Kearney*: 100-382196-126; 100-382196-128.

493 *Justice officials*: This paragraph is based on LAT 4/11/78, "Gray, 2 Former High FBI Officials Indicted"; WP 10/16/80, "FBI 'Bag Jobs' Allowable, Court Told"; LAT 10/21/80, "Gray Approved"; WP 11/5/80, "Final Summations"; LAT 11/7/80, "Ex-FBI Officials Convicted in Break-ins"; LAT 12/15/80, "2 Ex-FBI Officials Fined."

493 *In one of . . . his counselor*: LAT 4/16/81, "2 FBI Men Pardoned by Reagan"; WP 4/16/81, "President Pardons 2 Ex-FBI Officials Guilty in Break-ins"; NYT 4/16/81, "President Pardons 2 Ex-FBI Officials in 1970's Break-ins."

493 *Reagan said*: NYT 4/16/81, "Reagan Statement About the Pardons."

493 *In a private*: Reagan to Miller, 4/28/81, President Reagan Records, RRPL, Felt/ Miller Pardon File, released in response to author's FOIA request, FOIA F04-113 and FOIA F05-117.

493 *Reagan's action*: This paragraph is based on NYT 4/16/81, "President Pardons 2 Ex-FBI Officials in 1970's Break-ins"; LAT 4/16/81, "2 FBI Men Pardoned by Reagan"; LAT 5/12/81, "Presidential Clemency—Who Gets It?"; LAT 5/12/81, "Reagan Criticized for Comments"; WP 4/17/81, "Attorney General Backs FBI"; President Reagan Records, RRPL, Felt/Miller Pardon File, released in response to author's FOIA request, FOIA F04-113 and FOIA F05-117.

494 *The pardons signaled . . . Soviet Union*: LAT 11/10/82, "Nuclear Freeze Spreads"; WP 11/13/82, "Magazine Articles Cited"; WP 11/11/82, "Reagan Again Says."

494 *As it became*: WP 10/5/82, "Reagan Coolly Received."

494 *He repeated . . . military superiority*: NYT 11/12/82, "Foreign Agents Linked"; NYT 11/13/82, "Sources Are Cited"; WP 11/13/82, "Magazine Articles Cited"; NYT 12/11/82, "President Says Freeze"; WP 12/11/82, "Reagan Again Says."

494 *The* Reader's Digest *. . . "considered reliable"*: *Atlanta Constitution*, 11/21/82, "Reagan Taps McDonald Source"; *Village Voice* 8/16/83, "The Spy Who Came Down on the Freeze," by Seth Rosenfeld.

494 *Though bureau officials*: NYT 11/13/82, "Sources Are Cited"; NYT 12/11/82, "President Says Freeze"; NYT 3/26/83, "FBI Rules Out Russian Control"; LAT 3/26/83, "Freeze Groups Not Red Dupes"; WP 3/26/83, "Soviet Role"; *Village Voice* 8/16/83, "The Spy Who Came Down on the Freeze," by Seth Rosenfeld.

494 *By then President*: LAT 5/29/83, "U.S. Spies: 'The Wraps Are Off.'"

494 *He had relaxed . . . prevent terrorist attacks*: LAT 3/7/83, "FBI Domestic Surveillance Rules Eased"; WP 3/8/83, "FBI Eases Rules"; WP 12/19/81, "Smith Backs New Rules"; LAT 1/14/85, "Safeguards Sought for Lawful Dissent."

495 *But it was*: This paragraph is based on WP 4/18/85, "Nicaragua Visitors Questioned"; WP 2/26/86, "FBI Spied on Peace Group"; WP 5/12/87, "FBI Probing Nicaragua Visitors"; WP 1/29/88, "FBI Took Broad View"; WP 11/15/88, "FBI to Limit Probes of Library Users."

495 *The FBI also mounted*: This paragraph is based on WP 1/28/88, "FBI Probed Foes"; WP 1/29/88, "FBI Took Broad View"; WP 1/30/88, "The CISPES Investigation"; NYT 2/18/88, "Law and Ideology"; WP 7/15/89, "Senate Panel Raps FBI Probe"; WP 2/24/88, "White House Didn't Prompt"; WP 9/15/88, "FBI Punishes 6 for 'Mistakes'"; WP 9/17/88, "FBI Willing to Purge"; WP 7/15/89, "Senate Panel Raps"; *Break-ins, Death Threats and the FBI*. Activists also complained of more than fifty break-ins at their homes and offices; FBI officials denied the bureau was involved in any break-ins, WP 2/21/87, "Hill Told of FBI Drive"; WP 12/5/86, "No Links Seen"; *Break-ins, Death Threats and the FBI*.

495 *President Reagan also curtailed*: LAT 5/29/83, "U.S. Spies: 'The Wraps Are Off'"; WP 4/22/83, "Administration Accused of Policy of Secrecy."

495 *At a congressional*: This paragraph is based on WP 4/22/83, "Administration Accused of Policy of Secrecy."

495 *On March 26, 1975*: This paragraph is based on LAT 3/27/75, "2 L.A. Buildings, Berkeley FBI Office Bombed"; WP 3/28/75, "3 Blasts Add"; author interview with Kerr. The FBI had moved to the Great Western Building from Wells Fargo.

496 *Within hours*: Alan Pifer, president of the Carnegie Foundation for the Advancement of Teaching, quoted in *Change*, March–April 1987, "Clark Kerr, The Master Builder"; NYT 10/7/67, "School Systems Termed." Starting in 1974, Kerr was chairman of its successor, the Carnegie Council on Policy Studies in Higher Education, LAT 1/21/74, "Kerr to Head Educational Council."

496 *But while highly*: LAT 10/22/73, "The Curiously Divided Life"; Kerr, vol. 2, 314.

496 *He was warned*: Kerr, vol. 2, 314, which notes that Kerr chose not to attend. On Cort Majors, see San Diego Hall of Champions, www.sdhoc.com/sport/football/cort-majors, accessed 8/7/11.

496 *He was asked*: LAT 10/22/73, "The Curiously Divided Life." Kerr chose not to attend.

496 *And when he resumed*: NYT 4/11/67, "Kerr Returning."

496 *Six years later*: LAT 10/22/73, "The Curiously Divided Life."

496 *Some students . . . completed his talk*: LAT 2/8/70, "Kerr Sees End"; WP 10/15/69, "Custard Pie"; Kerr, vol. 2, 276.

496 *Kerr and his family*: Author interview with Kerr.

496 *He became the . . . "fully exploited . . . "*: NYT 2/11/68, "Clark Kerr Takes"; NYT 12/17/68, "The Deadly Talks"; NYT 7/28/68, National Committee for a Political Settlement, full-page ad; Kerr, vol. 1, 14, 286–87.

496 *After his dismissal*: Author interview with Kerr; author review of Kerr FBI files.

496 *But in 1982*: WP 3/26/82, "U.S. Chooses Observers"; NYT 3/2/82, "Team of Observers."

496 *And in 1984*: NYT 12/25/84, "Postal Contract Includes"; LAT 11/15/84, "Clark Kerr to Arbitrate"; NYT 7/22/84, "Mail Unions Work."

497 *However . . . Health Education Centers: Change*, March–April 1987, "Clark Kerr, the
     Master Builder"; *LAT* 10/22/73, "The Curiously Divided Life"; *LAT* 3/18/68, "Kerr
     Reviews Major Issues"; *NYT* 12/2/03, "Clark Kerr"; *LAT* 12/2/03, "Clark Kerr";
     Carnegie Foundation for the Advancement of Teaching, "Foundation History,"
     www.carnegiefoundation.org/about-us/foundation-history, accessed 8/7/11.
497 *Kerr also criticized*: *NYT* 6/7/74, "Kerr, at New School, Deplores."
497 *And he warned*: *LAT* 4/17/74, "Clear Kerr Warns."
497 *On leaving Carnegie*: *LAT* 12/2/03, "Clark Kerr."
497 *He called on*: *NYT* 1/11/83, "About Education."
497 *He urged*: *LAT* 7/1/96, "Higher Education."
497 *Meanwhile, he produced*: Clark Kerr, *The Gold and the Blue: A Personal Memoir of
     the University of California, 1949–1967. Volume One: Academic Triumphs*; Clark
     Kerr, with the assistance of Marian L. Gade and Maureen Kawaoka, *The Gold and
     the Blue: A Personal Memoir of the University of California, 1949–1967. Volume Two:
     Political Turmoil.*
497 *And the Pennsylvania*: Kerr, vol. 2, 317.
497 *The Board of Regents*: *LAT* 5/31/74, "Regents Honor"; Kerr, vol. 2, 314–15.
497 *Kerr died in 2003*: *LAT* 12/2/03, "Clark Kerr"; *NYT* 12/2/03, "Clark Kerr."
497 *In the late 1970s*: The remainder of this paragraph is based on the author's interview
     with Kerr.
498 *Mario Savio*: *Freedom's Orator*, 242.
498 *Savio was twenty-seven*: *NYT* 7/12/70, "Where Are the Savios"; 100-54060-561,
     10/29/70.
498 *"It's not so . . ."*: *NYT* 7/12/70, "Where Are the Savios."
498 *But that September*: *NYT* 9/20/70, "1964 Protest Leader Returning to Berkeley"; *WP*
     9/20/70, "Mario Savio Plans Return."
498 *Asked about*: *LAT* 9/25/70, "Reagan Predicts"; *WP* 10/6/70, "Savio, Leader."
498 *There were signs*: This paragraph is based on *WP* 1/30/71, "Berkeley Radical"; *DC*
     1/29/71, "Savio in Mayoral Race," in 100-54060-568; *DC*, 2/23/71, LED, "Savios
     Tell of Cancelled Race."
498 *In May a source*: 157-984-99.
498 *An agent*: 100-54060-580.
498 *Savio had listed . . . "alias"*: 100-54060-581; 100-54060-582: author interview with
     Stew Albert.
498 *Savio had all . . . disintegrating*: *Freedom's Orator*, 268–74.
498 *In April 1972*: 100-443052-56; *OT* 4/4/72, "Mario Savio Sued."
498 *An FBI agent*: 100-443731-7.
498 *She was an*: *BDG* 4/5/72, "Mario Savio's Wife," in 100-54266-116.
498 *Goldberg would later*: *Freedom's Orator*, 269.
498 *For a while*: 100-54266-119.
499 *She won custody*: *NYT* 10/12/74, "Fruits of '64 Speech Revolt."
499 *Savio despaired . . . "place to stay"*: *SFC* 12/8/96, "Stirring Up a Generation," by
     Michael Taylor.
499 *Hoover died that*: *WP*, "The Watergate Story," Timeline, www.washingtonpost
     .com/wp-srv/onpolitics/watergate/chronology.htm#1972, accessed 8/7/11.
499 *The FBI continued*: 100-54060-591.
499 *Posing as*: 100-54060-591.
499 *For seven months . . . at UCLA*: 157-984-204; 157-984-199.
499 *Richard Schmoerlitz . . . "inside the system"*: *NYT* 10/12/74, "Fruits of '64 Speech
     Revolt."
499 *The FBI promptly*: 157-984-205.

499 *Savio had been overcome*: This paragraph is based on *Freedom's Orator*, 268–74.

499 *By early 1974*: This paragraph is based on NYT 10/12/74, "Fruits of '64 Speech Revolt."

500 *Still, he was*: This paragraph is based on LAT 5/31/74, "Activist of the '60s Assails the Police," in 157-984-206. On the SLA, see LAT 5/18/74, "SLA Hideout Stormed"; LAT 5/20/74, "Identification of 6th Body"; LAT 5/17/75, "SLA Shootout—Sorting the Myths, Facts."

500 *Savio was nearly*: 100-54060-597.

500 *That very day*: Senate Resolution 21, 1/21/75, Church, book II, 343.

500 *The committee soon revealed*: The FBI's campaign to destroy King is detailed in Church, book III, "Dr. Martin Luther King, Jr., Case Study," 79 et seq. On the audio tape and suicide note, see 158–61.

500 *The committee's findings . . . president's discretion*: *The FBI: A Comprehensive Reference Guide*, 159; *The Boss*, 432–33; WP 3/11/76, "FBI Gets Guidelines"; WP 8/21/77, "An Agenda for Rebuilding the FBI"; WP 11/10/77, "FBI Domestic Spying"; WP 11/27/77, "The Watchdog Must Wake Up"; WP 4/26/78, "Waiting Game on Charters"; LAT 8/13/75, "New Curbs on FBI Spying"; WP 8/14/75, "Levi Set to Curb FBI Acts"; LAT 12/11/75, "Levi Offers Guidelines"; WP 12/27/75, "Loophole Seen"; WP 12/30/75, "FBI Pondering Intelligence Role."

500 *The year Reagan . . . named Daniel*: SFC 12/8/96, "Stirring Up a Generation," by Michael Taylor; *Freedom's Orator*, 274; author interview with Lynne Hollander Savio.

500 *Savio finally*: NYT 11/8/66, "Mario Savio"; *Freedom's Orator*, 278.

501 *He taught*: LAT 3/12/90, "25 Years Later"; *Freedom's Orator*, 278. Robert Cohen writes that in 1980 Savio became involved in Barry Commoner's Citizen's Party but soon found it overly bureaucratic and quit, *Freedom's Orator*, 277–78.

501 *In 1984*: NYT 10/3/84, "Around the Nation."

501 *It was during*: On Kerr: WP 3/26/82, "U.S. Chooses Observers"; NYT 3/2/82, "Team of Observers." On Reagan and the Contras: NYT 2/27/87, "A Web of Maneuvers"; LAT 2/27/87, "Reagan Seen Aiding North"; WP 2/27/87, "Contra War"; NYT 3/5/87, "Reagan and Panel Differ"; NYT 3/2/87, "Memos Raise Questions"; The National Security Archive, "The Iran-Contra Affair 20 Years On," www.gwu.edu/~nsarchiv /NSAEBB/NSAEBB210/index.htm, accessed 8/8/11.

501 *Looking older . . . "another Vietnam"*: NYT 10/3/84, "Class Reunion," with photo. According to Robert Cohen, Savio became deeply concerned about U.S. policy in Central America and visited Nicaragua and El Salvador to see conditions there firsthand. He and Lynne Hollander Savio drafted a proposal for a version of Mississippi Freedom Summer in which American college volunteers would do community work in Nicaragua. He was unable to raise funds, however, and the project stalled, *Freedom's Orator*, 281–84.

501 *He wept*: WP 10/3/84, "Berkeley Marks 20th Anniversary."

501 *The following year . . . inspiration*: LA 4/17/85, "159 Protesting UC Ties to S. Africa."

501 *In 1990, Savio*: SFC 12/8/96, "Stirring Up a Generation," by Michael Taylor.

501 *He became*: *Freedom's Orator*, 286.

501 *In the ensuing*: LAT 12/3/94, "Mario Savio Back in Berkeley"; *Freedom's Orator*, 290–91.

501 *It was passed*: NYT 12/15/94, "Initiative on Aliens."

501 *He opposed*: LAT 11/12/96, "The Man Who Stopped the Machine"; *Freedom's Orator*, 293, 297.

501 *Passed by voters*: NYT 8/22/97, "California Anti-Preference Law"; NYT 11/4/97, "Court Declines."

501 *And he became*: *Freedom's Orator*, 299.

501 *The fee hike*: Ibid., 307.
501 *The latter effort . . . heartbeat*: Ibid., 284, 293, 309.
501 *Not long . . . fifty-three years old*: Ibid., 306; *SFX* 11/7/96, "Mario Savio Dies"; *LAT* 11/7/96, "Mario Savio"; *NYT* 11/8/96, "Mario Savio."
501 *University of California . . . library at Berkeley*: Steve Silberstein donated $3.5 million to the university, which announced that in addition to building the café the gift would be used to create a book fund in Savio's name and digitize archives on student movements. Silberstein was an economics student at Berkeley who graduated shortly before the Free Speech Movement occurred and was not involved in the protest. He later earned a master's degree in library science and founded Innovative Interfaces, which produces card catalog software used in libraries worldwide, *LAT* 4/30/98, "Berkeley Accepts Rebellious Past."
502 *Savio gave*: This paragraph and the next are based on Savio's talk about spiritual values, delivered at the commemoration of the FSM's thirtieth anniversary, held at UC Berkeley in December 1994. Titled "Their Values and Ours," it first appeared in *The Threepenny Review* in summer 1995 and is reprinted in *Freedom's Orator*.

Appendix: My Fight for the FBI Files

505 *This book began*: This account of my fight for the files is a revised and updated version of the author's article in *California Monthly*, September 2002, "The FBI at Cal."
505 *Back in 1977*: DC 4/1/77, "Newspaper Asks for FBI's Berkeley Files."
505 *The next year*: DC 5/28/82, "The FBI in Berkeley"; DC 5/28/82, "The Berkeley Files"; DC 6/1/82, "How the Feds Kept Track of the FSM"; DC 6/2/82, "FBI Supplied Governor"; DC 6/4/82, "Of Spies & Radicals"; DC 6/4/82, "FBI—'We Are Out of That Business Forever.'"
506 *The Freedom of Information Act*: On the FOIA, see *Litigation Under the Amended Federal Freedom of Information Act*, 1976 edition; *Litigation Under the Federal Open Government Laws 2010*; WP 10/14/65, "Information Freedom Bill Voted"; *LAT* 3/31/66, "Bill to Make Federal Data Accessible Gains"; *NYT* 7/5/66, "Johnson Supports Greater Access."
506 *The FOIA (pronounced foy-ah) . . . "an untrained observer"*: Judge Patel's order on fees is Memorandum and Order, 10/29/85, *Rosenfeld v. U.S. Department of Justice*, No. C-85-2247 MHP, U.S. District Court, Northern District of California.
506 *The FBI released*: Some history of the case is noted in Opinion, 3/29/91, *Rosenfeld v. U.S. Department of Justice*, Nos. C-85-1709 MHP and C-85-2247 MHP (Consolidated), U.S. District Court, Northern District of California.
507 *Ultimately, five federal judges*: This paragraph is based on Opinion, 3/29/91, *Rosenfeld v. U.S. Department of Justice*, ibid.
507 *Ten years had passed*: Memorandum and Order, 9/23/91, *Rosenfeld v. U.S. Department of Justice*, ibid.
507 *But in a 1995 decision*: Opinion, 6/12/95, No. 91-16538, *Rosenfeld v. U.S. Department of Justice*, U.S. Court of Appeals for the Ninth Circuit. Judges Mary M. Schroeder and William A. Norris joined in the opinion.
507 *Now, I thought . . . take the case*: SFC 6/9/11, "The 17-Year Legal Battle to Get the Campus Files."
507 *Nonetheless*: Petition for Writ of Certiorari, No. 95-804, *U.S. Department of Justice v. Rosenfeld*, U.S. Supreme Court, dismissed 1/26/96.
508 *Before the Supreme Court*: Order on Settlement, 5/22/96, *Rosenfeld v. U.S. Department of Justice*, Nos. C-85-1709 MHP, C-85-2247 MHP, and C-90-3576 MHP, U.S. District Court, Northern District of California. For a Justice Department view of

the Patel and Brunetti decisions, see its "FOIA Update," Vol. XII, No. 3, 1991, "Supreme Court Stays FOIA Disclosures," and Vol. XVI, No. 2, 1995, "*Rosenfeld* Decision issued by Ninth Circuit," both at www.justice.gov/oip/foi-upd.htm, accessed 9/12/11.

508 *In addition*: SFC 6/9/02, "The 17-Year Legal Battle"; Second Declaration of David M. Hardy, C-90-3576 MHP.

508 *The settlement . . . "forty years"*: Memorandum and Order, 2/18/92, *Rosenfeld v. U.S. Department of Justice*, C-90-3576 MHP, U.S. District Court, Northern District of California.

508 *Finally . . . Governor Reagan*: SFC 6/9/2002, "The Campus Files: Reagan, Hoover and the UC Red Scare," available at www.sfgate.com/campus/, accessed 9/7/11. Hoover's quote is in 62-103031-279.

508 *I was glad . . . and television*: WP 6/9/02, "FBI Tried for Years to Stifle Dissent, Records Show"; LAT 6/10/02, "FBI Tried to Quash Protests"; *San Jose Mercury News* 6/9/02, "Battle to Obtain Government Papers Ends." National Public Radio, CNN, and CBS were among the stations airing reports.

508 *The article also prompted*: For examples, see NYT 6/16/02, "The Bad Old Days at the F.B.I."; *Santa Rosa Press Democrat*, 6/22/02, "17-Year Battle"; *Albany Times Union*, 6/11/02, "A Case for Openness"; *San Jose Mercury News*, 6/15/02, "Preservation of Our Freedoms"; *Charlotte Observer*, 6/11/02, "Homeland Security"; *Cincinnati Post*, 6/12/02, "Our Secretive Government."

508 *Senator Patrick Leahy . . . "government accountability"*: SFC 6/23/02, "Feinstein Demands Answers"; SFC 11/17/02, "FBI Hasn't Answered"; Feinstein to Mueller, 6/18/02.

508 *The FBI sent two:* This and the next paragraph are based on Kalisch to Feinstein, 9/26/02; Mueller to Feinstein, 12/23/02.

509 *In July 2005 . . . "previous misconduct"*: The author's FOIA request was dated July 21, 2005. On November 20, 2006, the FBI released "Memorandum," 2/4/03, Deputy General Counsel Anne M. Gulyassy to General Counsel Kenneth L. Wainstein.

509 *I had hoped . . . February 2006:* The FBI's Kalisch told Feinstein that 17,400 of these pages had not been released sooner due to a "miscommunication." Kalisch to Feinstein, 9/26/02.

509 *At a hearing . . . reject my motion:* Defendants' Response, 11/9/06, *Rosenfeld v. U.S. Department of Justice*, Nos. C-90-3576 MHP, C-85-1709 MHP, and C-85-2247 MHP, U.S. District Court, Northern District of California.

509 *But after considering:* Order Re· Plaintiff's Challenges, 2/6/07, *Rosenfeld v. U.S. Department of Justice*, ibid.

509 *As a result . . . UC faculty members:* The additional releases are noted in Hardy to Wheaton, 8/6/07, 9/5/07, 9/7/07, 2/7/08, 9/19/08; 8/4/10; Hardy to Peter Wechsler, U.S. Department of Justice, 3/14/08; all regarding *Rosenfeld v. U.S. Department of Justice*, Nos. C-90-3576 MHP, C-85-1709 MHP, and C-85-2247 MHP, U.S. District Court, Northern District of California. The UC faculty members identified in these records as COINTELPRO targets are Angela Davis, UCLA (100-449698-922, 3/16/70; 100-71737-148, 12/16/69; 100-71737-164, 4/1/70); Keith Delroy Lowe, UC San Diego (100-449698-46-5, 9/6/68); Leon Letwin, UCLA (100-54554-1224, 10/22/64; 100-54554-1233, 11/5/64; 100-54554-1264, 1/20/65); and Herbert Marcuse, UC San Diego (100-449698-46-11, 11/8/68; 100-449698-43-3, 7/8/68). The records also show these State College faculty were COINTELPRO targets: Donald Freed, San Fernando Valley State College (100-71737-81, 1/6/69; 100-71737-148, 12/16/69); Eli Katz, San Diego State College (100-54554-1005, 1/10/63); and Robert Niemann, California State College at Los Angeles (100-71737-27, 7/31/68; 100-71737-50, 9/30/68; 100-71737-80, 1/2/69).

The released pages included "abstracts," FBI records briefly summarizing the internal and external bureau communications within "main" files. FBI officials used abstracts from 1921 to 1979, prior to computerization, to help manage their paper flow. I had requested copies for certain subjects starting in 1981, but the FBI had released none. Now the bureau said there were more than 10 million abstracts in two storage facilities, and no way to search them for those responsive to my request without making a manual review. Essentially, the FBI was trying to carve out a new exemption for public records too "burdensome" to search—a kind of "the dog ate my documents" exemption. Judge Laporte, however, ordered the FBI to provide further information and search for a sample of them. Eventually the bureau released 8,564 pages of abstracts. It turned out these 5"×8" sheets were organized just like the main files they summarize, with identical titles and serial numbers. One set of abstracts was housed at the Federal Records Center of the National Archives and Records Administration, in Suitland, Maryland. Most of the approximately 2,000 boxes containing them were labeled on the outside. Although the FBI asserted, in effect, that abstracts have no historical value, they provide a useful synopsis of bureau cases prior to computerization in the seventies, and where the corresponding main files have been destroyed they may be especially valuable. Yet for decades the FBI has failed to release copies of them, even when requesters specify "any and all records." See Second Declaration of David M. Hardy, 11/9/06; Declaration of Debra Anne O'Clair, 8/21/07; Order Re: Plaintiff's Challenges, 2/6/07; Order on Plaintiff's Renewed Challenge Regarding Abstract Cards as Modified, 10/23/07; all in *Rosenfeld v. U.S. Department of Justice*, Nos. C-90-3576 MHP, C-85-1709 MHP, and C-85-2247 MHP, U.S. District Court, Northern District of California. The released abstracts are noted in Hardy to Wheaton, 2/7/08.

509 *The settlement agreement . . . this request*: Exhibit A to Second Declaration of David M. Hardy, 11/9/06, all in *Rosenfeld v. U.S. Department of Justice*, Nos. C-90-3576 MHP, C-85-1709 MHP, and C-85-2247 MHP, U.S. District Court, Northern District of California.

509 *I tried to resolve*: Defendants' Response, 11/9/06, *Rosenfeld v. U.S. Department of Justice*, Nos. C-90-3576 MHP, C-85-1709 MHP, and C-85-2247 MHP, U.S. District Court, Northern District of California. The FBI noted correctly that the Settlement Agreement stated "any disputes arising under this new FOIA request shall be deemed a separate matter not covered by this agreement and shall not be considered part of the Rosenfeld I and Rosenfeld II litigation." But at the same time, the FBI sought to (and did) modify its obligations under other parts of the agreement, and the parties could have agreed to resolve the disputes over the Reagan request without requiring another lawsuit.

509 *I did . . . "claims unexhausted"*: Memorandum & Order, 8/22/08, *Rosenfeld v. U.S. Department of Justice*, C-07-03240 MHP, U.S. District Court, Northern District of California.

510 *Only after . . . released ninety-seven pages*: Complaint; First Amended Complaint; Defendants' Notice of Motion and Motion for Partial Summary Judgment, 6/2/08; Memorandum & Order, 8/22/08; all in *Rosenfeld v. U.S. Department of Justice*, C-07-03240 MHP, U.S. District Court, Northern District of California.

510 *There was yet*: Memorandum & Order, 8/22/08; Memorandum & Order, 9/1/10; Defendants' Notice of Motion and Motion for Partial Summary Judgment, 6/2/08; Second Declaration of David M. Hardy, 6/16/08; Defendants' Memorandum of Law in Opposition to Plaintiff's Cross-Motion for Partial Summary Judgment, 6/16/08; all in *Rosenfeld v. U.S. Department of Justice*, C-07-03240 MHP, U.S. District Court, Northern District of California.

510 *Eventually*: Seventh declaration of David M. Hardy, 10/1/10, *Rosenfeld v. U.S. Department of Justice*, C-07-03240 MHP, U.S. District Court, Northern District of California.

510 *Then there were*: This paragraph is based on Memorandum & Order, 9/1/10; Seventh Declaration of David M. Hardy, 10/1/10, both in *Rosenfeld v. U.S. Department of Justice*, C-07-03240 MHP, U.S. District Court, Northern District of California.

510 *The documents reveal*: This paragraph is based on 100-138754-188, 8/4/47, pp. 156–60, as processed and released to the author by letter dated May 2, 1996, and as released without redactions by letter dated July 24, 2009. The earlier version showed that the Reagans named Alexander Knox, Howard Da Silva and Larry Parks. The later version shows they also named Anne Revere, Karen Morley, Hume Cronyn, Dorothy Tree, Howland Chamberlain, Selena Royle, and Lloyd Gough.

510 *Yet it appeared*: The FBI had released information on Miller in 100-382196-7 in 1996, but later withheld it in a subsequent release that included that document and other records.

511 *This unwarranted secrecy*: Hardy to Rosenfeld, 12/7/09.

511 *The newly released*: On the FBI checking on Maureen Reagan, compare 100-382196-7; 77-81528-5; 77-81528-8, and 77-81528-10 as released in 1996 with versions released by letter dated July 24, 2009.

511 *The FBI still . . . law-enforcement information*: My attorney, David Greene, and I met with FBI officials and the Justice Department lawyer several times before court hearings and questioned deletions. On the FBI's warning Reagan about his son, compare the versions of 80-579-3 released in 1996; on July 24, 2009; and on September 3, 2010.

511 *However, Judge Patel . . . "statutory mandate . . ."*: Memorandum & Order, 9/1/10, *Rosenfeld v. U.S. Department of Justice*, C-07-03240 MHP, U.S. District Court, Northern District of California.

511 *Judge Patel also ruled*: Memorandum & Order, 9/1/10, ibid.

511 *Judge Patel assumed*: As senior judge, Patel had a reduced caseload.

511 *Benjamin Wolf Stein*: Seth Rosenfeld v. Federal Bureau of Investigation and U.S. Department of Justice, C11-02131MEJ.

511 *Reagan's long association*: The photo is discussed in 100-382196-38; 100-382196-46.

511 *During my fourth*: The FBI's search for, and locating of, the photo was described in communications from Assistant U.S. Attorney Ila C. Deiss to David Greene.

512 *In fact*: Hardy to Rosenfeld, 7/2/09.

Selected Bibliography

Ackerman, Kenneth D. *Young J. Edgar: Hoover, the Red Scare, and the Assault on Civil Liberties.* New York: Carroll and Graf, 2007.

Adler, Margot. *Heretic's Heart: A Journey Through Spirit and Revolution.* Boston: Beacon Press, 1997.

Agee, Philip. *Inside the Company: CIA Diary.* Toronto: Bantam Books, 1975.

Agee, Philip, and Louis Wolf, eds. *Dirty Work: The CIA in Western Europe.* Secaucus, N.J.: Lyle Stuart, 1978.

Albert, Judith Clavir, and Stewart Edward Albert. *The Sixties Papers: Documents of a Rebellious Decade.* New York: Praeger, 1984.

Albert, Stew. *Who the Hell Is Stew Albert?: A Memoir.* Los Angeles: Red Hen Press, 2004.

Albright, Joseph, and Marcia Kunstel. *Bombshell: The Secret Story of America's Unknown Atomic Spy Conspiracy.* New York: Times Books/Random House, 1997.

American Friends Service Committee. *The Draft? A Report Prepared for the Peace Education Division of the American Friends Service Committee.* New York: Hill and Wang, 1968.

Andersen, Christopher. *Citizen Jane: The Turbulent Life of Jane Fonda.* New York: Dell, 1990.

Anderson, Martin. *Revolution.* San Diego: Harcourt Brace Jovanovich, 1988.

Aptheker, Bettina F. *Intimate Politics: How I Grew Up Red, Fought for Free Speech and Became a Feminist Rebel.* Emeryville, CA: Seal Press, 2006.

Arax, Mark. *In My Father's Name: A Family, a Town, a Murder.* New York: Simon and Schuster, 1996.

Arkin, William M. *Code Names: Deciphering U.S. Military Plans, Programs, and Operations in the 9/11 World.* Hanover, NH: Steerforth Press, 2005.

Austin, Curtis J. *Up Against the Wall: Violence and the Making and Unmaking of the Black Panther Party.* Fayetteville: University of Arkansas Press, 2006.

Bagwell, Beth. *Oakland: The Story of a City.* Oakland: Oakland Heritage Alliance, 1996.

Bales, James D., ed. *J. Edgar Hoover Speaks Concerning Communism.* Washington, DC: The Capitol Hill Press, 1970.

Barger, Ralph "Sonny," with Keith and Kent Zimmerman. *Hell's Angel: The Life and Times of Sonny Barger and the Hell's Angels Motorcycle Club.* New York: William Morrow, 2000.

Barrett, Edward L., Jr. *The Tenney Committee: Legislative Investigation of Subversive Activities in California.* Ithaca, NY: Cornell University Press, 1951.

Barson, Michael, and Steven Heller. *Red Scared! The Commie Menace in Propaganda and Popular Culture.* San Francisco: Chronicle Books, 2001.

Bates, Tom. *Rads: The 1970 Bombing of the Army Math Research Center at the University of Wisconsin and Its Aftermath.* New York: HarperCollins, 1992.

Batterson, Steve. *Stephen Smale: The Mathematician Who Broke the Dimension Barrier.* Providence, RI: American Mathematical Society, 2000.

Baus, Herbert M., and William B. Ross. *Politics Battle Plan.* New York: Macmillan, 1968.

Billingsley, Kenneth Lloyd. *Hollywood Party: How Communism Seduced the American Film Industry in the 1930s and 1940s.* Roseville, CA: Prima Publishing, 2000.

Bird, Kai, and Martin J. Sherwin. *American Prometheus: The Triumph and Tragedy of J. Robert Oppenheimer.* New York: Alfred A. Knopf, 2005.

Blackstock, Nelson. *Cointelpro: The FBI's Secret War on Political Freedom.* New York: Vintage Books, 1976.

Blair, Betsy. *The Memory of All That: Love and Politics in New York, Hollywood and Paris.* New York: Alfred A. Knopf, 2003.

Bonanno, Bill. *Bound by Honor: A Mafioso's Story.* New York: St. Martin's Press, 1999.

Bonanno, Joseph, with Sergio Lalli. *A Man of Honor: The Autobiography of Joseph Bonanno.* New York: St. Martin's Press, 2003.

Bonanno, Rosalie, with Beverly Donofrio. *Mafia Marriage: An Unforgettable Look Inside the Godfather's Own House.* New York: St. Martin's Press, 2003.

Boyarsky, Bill. *The Rise of Ronald Reagan.* New York: Random House, 1968.

———. *Ronald Reagan: His Life and Rise to the Presidency.* New York: Random House, 1981.

Branch, Taylor. *At Canaan's Edge: America in the King Years, 1965–68.* New York: Simon and Schuster, 2006.

———. *Parting the Waters: America in the King Years, 1954–63.* New York: Simon and Schuster, 1988.

———. *Pillar of Fire: America in the King Years, 1963–65.* New York: Simon and Schuster, 1998.

Brown, Edmund G. (Pat). *Public Justice, Private Mercy: A Governor's Education on Death Row.* New York: Weidenfeld and Nicolson, 1989.

———. *Reagan and Reality: The Two Californias.* New York: Praeger, 1970.

Brown, Edmund G. (Pat), and Bill Brown. *Reagan: The Political Chameleon.* New York: Praeger, 1976.

Buckley, Jr., William F., ed. *The Committee and Its Critics: A Calm Review of the House Committee on Un-American Activities.* Chicago: Henry Regnery, 1962.

Buitrago, Ann Mari, and Leon Andrew Immerman. *Are You Now or Have You Ever Been in the FBI Files: How to Secure and Interpret Your FBI Files.* New York: Grove Press, 1981.

Burrough, Bryan. *Public Enemies: America's Greatest Crime Wave and the Birth of the FBI, 1933–34.* New York: The Penguin Press, 2004.

Cagin, Seth, and Philip Dray. *We Are Not Afraid: The Story of Goodman, Schwerner, and Chaney and the Civil Rights Campaign for Mississippi.* New York: Bantam Books, 1989.

Camus, Albert. *The Stranger.* New York: Vintage International, 1989.

Cannon, Lou. *Governor Reagan: His Rise to Power.* New York: PublicAffairs, 2003.

———. *President Reagan: The Role of a Lifetime.* New York: Simon and Schuster, 1991.

———. *Reagan.* New York: G. P. Putnam's Sons, 1982.

———. *Ronald Reagan: The Presidential Portfolio: A History Illustrated from the Collection of the Ronald Reagan Library and Museum.* New York: PublicAffairs, 2001.

———. *Ronnie & Jesse: A Political Odyssey—A Candid Biography of the Two Rival Political Champions, Ronald Reagan and Jesse Unruh.* New York: Doubleday, 1969.

Carson, Clayborne. *In Struggle: SNCC and the Black Awakening of the 1960s.* Cambridge, MA: Harvard University Press, 1981.

Carson, Clayborne, ed. *The Eyes on the Prize Civil Rights Reader: Documents, Speeches, and Firsthand Accounts from the Black Freedom Struggle, 1954–1990*. New York: Penguin Books, 1991.

Caute, David. *The Great Fear: The Anti-Communist Purge Under Truman and Eisenhower*. New York: Simon and Schuster, 1978.

Ceplair, Larry, and Steven Englund. *The Inquisition in Hollywood: Politics in the Film Community, 1930–1960*. New York: Anchor Press/Doubleday, 1980.

Charns, Alexander. *Cloak and Gavel: FBI Wiretaps, Bugs, Informers, and the Supreme Court*. Urbana, IL: University of Illinois Press, 1992.

Chevalier, Haakon. *Oppenheimer: The Story of a Friendship*. New York: George Braziller, 1965.

Cleaver, Eldridge. *Soul on Ice*. New York: Dell, 1968.

Coakley, J. Frank. *For the People: Sixty Years of Fighting for Law and Order*. Orinda, CA: Western Star Press, 1992.

Cody, Pat, and Fred Cody. *Cody's Books: The Life and Times of a Berkeley Bookstore, 1956–1977*. San Francisco: Chronicle Books, 1992.

Cogley, John. *Report on Blacklisting, I: Movies*. New York: The Fund for the Republic, 1956.

Cohen, Mitchell, and Dennis Hale, eds. *The New Student Left: An Anthology*. Boston: Beacon Press, 1968.

Cohen, Robert. *Freedom's Orator: Mario Savio and the Radical Legacy of the 1960s*. New York: Oxford University Press, 2009.

———. *When the Old Left Was Young: Student Radicals and America's First Mass Student Movement, 1929–1941*. New York: Oxford University Press, 1993.

Cohen, Robert, and Reginald E. Zelnik, eds. *The Free Speech Movement: Reflections on Berkeley in the 1960s*. Berkeley: University of California Press, 2002.

Colacello, Bob. *Ronnie & Nancy: Their Path to the White House—1911–1980*. New York: Warner Books, 2004.

Colby, William, and Peter Forbath. *Honorable Men: My Life in the CIA*. New York: Simon and Schuster, 1978.

Cole, David. *Enemy Aliens: Double Standards and Constitutional Freedoms in the War on Terrorism*. New York: The New Press, 2003.

Cole, David, and James X. Dempsey. *Terrorism and the Constitution: Sacrificing Civil Liberties in the Name of National Security*. New York: The New Press, 2002.

Colvig, Ray. *The Clark Kerr Memoirs Project: Turning Points and Ironies: Issues and Events—Berkeley, 1959–67*. Berkeley: Berkeley Public Policy Press, Institute of Governmental Studies, University of California, 2004.

Conlin, Joseph. *The Troubles: A Jaundiced Glance Back at the Movement of the '60s*. New York: Franklin Watts, 1982.

Conners, Bernard F. *Don't Embarrass the Bureau*. Indianapolis: Bobbs-Merrill, 1972.

Cook, Fred J. *The FBI Nobody Knows*. New York: Macmillan, 1964.

Copeland, Alan, and Nikki Arai, eds. *People's Park*. New York: Ballantine Books, 1969.

Corn, David. *Blond Ghost: Ted Shackley and the CIA's Crusades*. New York: Simon and Schuster, 1994.

Cunningham, David. *There's Something Happening Here: The New Left, the Klan, and FBI Counterintelligence*. Berkeley: University of California Press, 2004.

Dallek, Matthew. *The Right Moment: Ronald Reagan's First Victory and the Decisive Turning Point in American Politics*. New York: The Free Press, 2000.

Davidson, Sara. *Loose Change: Three Women of the Sixties*. New York: Doubleday, 1977.

Davis, Angela. *An Autobiography*. New York: International Publishers, 1988.

Deaver, Michael K. *A Different Drummer: My Thirty Years with Ronald Reagan*. New York: HarperCollins, 2001.

——. *Behind the Scenes: In Which the Author Talks About Ronald and Nancy Reagan . . . and Himself.* New York: William Morrow, 1987.

Delgado, Manuel Ruben. *The Last Chicano: A Mexican American Experience.* Bloomington, IN: AuthorHouse, 2009.

Delk, James D. *The Fighting Fortieth: In War and Peace.* Palm Springs: ETC Publications, 1998.

DeLoach, Cartha "Deke." *Hoover's FBI: The Inside Story by Hoover's Trusted Lieutenant.* Washington, DC: Regnery, 1995.

Demaris, Ovid. *The Director: An Oral Biography of J. Edgar Hoover.* New York: Harper's Magazine Press, 1975.

Diamond, Sigmund. *Compromised Campus: The Collaboration of Universities with the Intelligence Community, 1945–1955.* New York: Oxford University Press, 1992.

Diggins, John Patrick. *Ronald Reagan: Fate, Freedom, and the Making of History.* New York: W. W. Norton, 2007.

Divale, William Tulio, and James Joseph. *I Lived Inside the Campus Revolution.* New York: Cowles Book Co., 1970.

Donati, William. *Ida Lupino: A Biography.* Lexington, KY: The University Press of Kentucky, 1996.

Donner, Frank J. *The Age of Surveillance: The Aims and Methods of America's Political Intelligence System.* New York: Vintage Books, 1981.

——. *The Un-Americans.* New York: Ballantine Books, 1961.

Douglass, John Aubrey. *The California Idea and American Higher Education: 1850 to the 1960 Master Plan.* Stanford, CA: Stanford University Press, 2000.

Doyle, William. *An American Insurrection: The Battle of Oxford, Mississippi, 1962.* New York: Doubleday, 2001.

Draper, Hal. *Berkeley: The New Student Revolt.* Introduction by Mario Savio. New York: Grove Press, 1965.

D'Souza, Dinesh. *Ronald Reagan: How an Ordinary Man Became an Extraordinary Leader.* New York: Touchstone Books, 1997.

Dugger, Ronnie. *On Reagan: The Man & His Presidency.* New York: McGraw-Hill, 1983.

Edwards, Anne. *Early Reagan: The Rise to Power.* New York: William Morrow, 1987.

——. *The Reagans: Portrait of a Marriage.* New York: St. Martin's Press, 2003.

Edwards, Lee. *The Conservative Revolution: The Movement That Remade America.* New York: The Free Press, 1999.

——. *To Preserve and Protect: The Life of Edwin Meese III.* Washington, DC: Heritage Foundation, 2005.

——. *Reagan: A Political Biography.* San Diego: Viewpoint Books, 1967.

Eisen, Jonathan, ed. *Altamont: Death of Innocence in the Woodstock Nation.* New York: Avon Books, 1970.

Eliot, Marc. *Reagan: The Hollywood Years.* New York: Three Rivers Press, 2008.

Felt, W. Mark. *The FBI Pyramid: From the Inside.* New York: G. P. Putnam's Sons, 1979.

Felt, W. Mark, and John O'Connor. *A G-Man's Life: The FBI, Being "Deep Throat," and the Struggle for Honor in Washington.* New York: PublicAffairs, 2006.

Fraser, Ronald, ed. *1968: A Student Generation in Revolt: An International Oral History.* New York: Pantheon Books, 1988.

Freeman, Jo. *At Berkeley in the '60s: The Education of an Activist, 1961–1965.* Bloomington: Indiana University Press, 2004.

Fujino, Diane C. *Samurai Among Panthers: Richard Aoki on Race, Resistance and a Paradoxical Life.* Minneapolis: University of Minnesota Press, 2012.

Gardner, David P. *The California Oath Controversy.* Berkeley: University of California Press, 1967.

Garrow, David J. *Bearing the Cross: Martin Luther King, Jr., and the Southern Christian Leadership Conference.* New York: Vintage Books, 1988.

———. *The FBI and Martin Luther King, Jr.* New York: W. W. Norton, 1981.

Garry, Charles, and Art Goldberg. *Street-fighter in the Courtroom: The People's Advocate.* New York: E. P. Dutton, 1977.

Gentry, Curt. J. *Edgar Hoover: The Man and the Secrets.* New York: W. W. Norton, 1991.

———. *The Last Days of the Late, Great State of California.* New York: Ballantine Books, 1968.

Gilbert, Martin. *A History of the Twentieth Century: The Concise Edition of the Acclaimed World History.* New York: HarperCollins Perennial, 2001.

Gitlin, Todd. *The Sixties: Years of Hope, Days of Rage.* New York: Bantam Books, 1987.

Glick, Brian. *War at Home: Covert Action Against U.S. Activists and What We Can Do About It.* Boston: South End Press, 1989.

Goines, David Lance. *The Free Speech Movement: Coming of Age in the 1960s.* Berkeley: Ten Speed Press, 1993.

Goodman, Walter. *The Committee: The Extraordinary Career of the House Committee on Un-American Activities.* New York: Farrar, Straus and Giroux, 1968.

Grathwohl, Larry. *Bringing Down America: An FBI Informer with the Weathermen.* New Rochelle, NY: Arlington House Publishers, 1976.

Green, Constance McLaughlin. *The Secret City: A History of Race Relations in the Nation's Capital.* Princeton, NJ: Princeton University Press, 1967.

Guiles, Fred Lawrence. *Jane Fonda: The Actress in Her Time.* New York: Pinnacle Books, 1981.

Gustaitis, Rasa. *Wholly Round.* New York: Holt, Rinehart and Winston, 1973.

Guttenplan, D. D. *American Radical: The Life and Times of I. F. Stone.* New York: Farrar, Straus and Giroux, 2009.

Haines, Gerald K., and David A. Langbart. *Unlocking the Files of the FBI: A Guide to Its Records and Classification System.* Wilmington, DE: Scholarly Resources, 1993.

Halperin, Morton H., Jerry J. Berman, Robert L. Borosage, and Christine M. Marwick. *The Lawless State: The Crimes of the U.S. Intelligence Agencies: A Report by the Center for National Security Studies.* New York: Penguin Books, 1976.

Halstead, Fred. *Out Now: A Participant's Account of the American Movement Against the Vietnam War.* New York: Monad Press, 1978.

Harris, David. *Dreams Die Hard: Three Men's Journey Through the Sixties.* New York: St. Martin's/Marek, 1982.

Hayden, Tom. *Rebel: A Personal History of the 1960s.* Los Angeles: Red Hen Press, 2003.

———. *Reunion: A Memoir.* New York: Random House, 1988.

Haynes, John Earl, and Harvey Klehr. *Venona: Decoding Soviet Espionage in America.* New Haven: Yale University Press, 1999.

Hayward, Steven F. *The Age of Reagan: The Fall of the Old Liberal Order, 1964–1980.* Roseville, CA: Prima Publishing, 2001.

Heineman, Kenneth J. *Put Your Bodies Upon the Wheels: Student Revolt in the 1960s.* Chicago: Ivan R. Dee, 2001.

Heirich, Max. *The Beginning: Berkeley 1964.* New York: Columbia University Press, 1970.

———. *The Spiral of Conflict: Berkeley 1964.* New York: Columbia University Press, 1971.

Helfand, Harvey. *University of California, Berkeley: An Architectural Tour.* New York: Princeton Architectural Press, 2002.

Herken, Gregg. *Brotherhood of the Bomb: The Tangled Lives and Loyalties of Robert Oppenheimer, Ernest Lawrence and Edward Teller.* New York: Henry Holt, 2002.

Ho, Fred, ed. *Legacy to Liberation: Politics and Culture of Revolutionary Asian Pacific America.* Brooklyn, NY: Big Red Media; San Francisco, CA, and Edinburgh, Scotland: AK Press, 2000.

Hoover, J. Edgar. *A Study of Communism.* New York: Holt, Rinehart and Winston, 1962.

Horowitz, David. *Student: The Political Activities of the Berkeley Students.* New York: Ballantine Books, 1962.

Hougan, Jim. *Spooks: The Haunting of America—the Private Use of Secret Agents.* New York: William Morrow, 1978.

Jacobs, John. *A Rage for Justice: The Passion and Politics of Phillip Burton.* Berkeley: University of California Press, 1997.

Jacobs, Paul, and Saul Landau. *The New Radicals: A Report with Documents.* New York: Vintage Books, 1966.

Jayko, Margaret, ed. *FBI on Trial: The Victory in the Socialist Workers Party Suit Against Government Spying.* New York: Pathfinder, 1988.

Jeffreys-Jones, Rhodri. *The CIA and American Democracy.* New Haven: Yale University Press, 1989.

Jezer, Marty. *Abbie Hoffman: American Rebel.* New Brunswick, NJ: Rutgers University Press, 1993.

Johnson, Haynes. *The Age of Anxiety: McCarthyism to Terrorism.* Orlando, FL: James H. Silberman Books/Harcourt, 2005.

Johnson, Loch K. *America's Secret Power: The CIA in a Democratic Society.* New York: Oxford University Press, 1989.

———. *Bombs, Bugs, Drugs and Thugs: Intelligence and America's Quest for Security.* New York: New York University Press, 2000.

———. *A Season of Inquiry: The Senate Intelligence Investigation.* Lexington: University Press of Kentucky, 1985.

Jones, Hardin B., and Helen C. Jones. *Sensual Drugs: Deprivation and Rehabilitation of the Mind.* Cambridge, UK: Cambridge University Press, 1977.

Kelley, Kitty. *Nancy Reagan: The Unauthorized Biography.* New York: Pocket Star Books, 1991.

Kerr, Clark. *The Gold and the Blue: A Personal Memoir of the University of California, 1949–1967. Volume One: Academic Triumphs.* Berkeley: University of California Press, 2001.

———. *The Uses of the University: The Godkin Lectures at Harvard University, 1963.* Cambridge, MA: Harvard University Press, 1963.

Kerr, Clark, with the assistance of Marian L. Gade and Maureen Kawaoka. *The Gold and the Blue. Volume Two: Political Turmoil.* Berkeley: University of California Press, 2003.

Kerr, Clark, ed. *The Clark Kerr Memoirs Project: Documentary Supplements to "The Gold and the Blue."* Berkeley: Berkeley Public Policy Press, Institute of Governmental Studies, University of California, 2003.

Kessler, Ronald. *The Bureau: The Secret History of the FBI.* New York: St. Martin's Paperbacks, 2003.

———. *The FBI: Inside the World's Most Powerful Law Enforcement Agency.* New York: Pocket Books, 1993.

Kirkpatrick, Lyman B., Jr. *The Real CIA.* New York: Macmillan, 1968.

Klehr, Harvey, and Ronald Radosh. *The Amerasia Spy Case: Prelude to McCarthyism.* Chapel Hill: University of North Carolina Press, 1996.

Kleinknecht, William. *The Man Who Sold the World: Ronald Reagan and the Betrayal of Main Street America.* New York: Nation Books/Perseus, 2009.

Kuno, Donald W. *The Life and Times of an FBI Agent.* Minneapolis: University of Minnesota Printing Services, 1996.

Kuntz, Tom, and Phil Kuntz, eds. *The Sinatra Files: The Life of an American Icon Under Government Surveillance.* New York: Three Rivers Press, 2000.

Kurlansky, Mark. *1968: The Year That Rocked the World.* New York: Ballantine Books, 2004.

LaFrance, Danielle, ed. *Berkeley! A Literary Tribute.* Berkeley: Heyday Books, 1997.

Larrowe, Charles P. *Harry Bridges: The Rise and Fall of Radical Labor in the U.S.* New York: Lawrence Hill, 1972.

Lattin, Don. *The Harvard Psychedelic Club.* New York: HarperCollins, 2010.

Leamer, Laurence. *Make-Believe: The Story of Nancy and Ronald Reagan.* New York: Harper and Row, 1983.

Lee, Martin A., and Bruce Shlain. *Acid Dreams: The Complete Social History of LSD—the CIA, the Sixties, and Beyond.* New York: Grove Press, 1992.

Leslie, Jack. *Decathlon of Death.* Mill Valley, CA: Tarquin Books, 1979.

Lewis, Joseph. *What Makes Reagan Run? A Political Profile.* New York: McGraw-Hill, 1968.

Lipset, Seymour Martin, and Sheldon S. Wolin. *The Berkeley Student Revolt: Facts and Interpretations.* New York: Anchor Books, 1965.

Lovell, Mary S. *The Sisters: The Saga of the Mitford Family.* New York: W. W. Norton, 2001.

Lowenthal, Max. *The Federal Bureau of Investigation.* New York: Harvest Books/Harcourt Brace Jovanovich, 1950.

Lyford, Joseph P. *The Berkeley Archipelago.* Chicago: Regnery Gateway, 1982.

Lynum, Curtis O. *The FBI and I: One Family's Life in the FBI During the Hoover Years.* Bryn Mawr, PA: Dorrance, 1987.

———. *The FBI Wife.* Victoria, BC: Trafford Publishing, 2003.

Mackenzie, Angus. *Secrets: The CIA's War at Home.* Berkeley: University of California Press, 1997.

Marchetti, Victor, and John D. Marks. *The CIA and the Cult of Intelligence.* New York: Alfred A. Knopf, 1974.

Margolis, Jon. *The Last Innocent Year: America in 1964, the Beginning of the "Sixties."* New York: HarperCollins, 1999.

Markoff, John. *What the Dormouse Said: How the 60s Counterculture Shaped the Personal Computer Industry.* New York: Viking Penguin, 2005.

Marks, John. *The Search for the "Manchurian Candidate": The CIA and Mind Control.* New York: McGraw-Hill, 1980.

Marwick, Arthur. *The Sixties: Cultural Revolution in Britain, France, Italy, and the United States, 1958–1974.* Oxford: Oxford University Press, 1998.

Marx, Gary T. *Undercover: Police Surveillance in America.* Berkeley: University of California Press, 1988.

Mayer, Jane, and Doyle McManus. *Landslide: The Unmaking of the President, 1984–1988.* Boston: Houghton Mifflin, 1988.

McAdam, Doug. *Freedom Summer.* New York: Oxford University Press, 1988.

McConnell, William S., ed. *Great Speeches in History: The 1960s.* San Diego: Thomson-Gale/Greenhaven Press, 2003.

McGilligan, Patrick, and Paul Buhle. *Tender Comrades: A Backstory of the Hollywood Blacklist.* New York: St. Martin's Press, 1997.

Meese III, Edwin. *With Reagan: The Inside Story.* Washington, DC: Regnery Gateway, 1992.

Melvin, Milan, and Peter Laufer. *Highlights of a Lowlife: The Autobiography of Milan Melvin.* Bodega Bay, CA: Swan Isle Books, 2004.

Miller, James. *Democracy Is in the Streets: From Port Huron to the Siege of Chicago.* New York: Touchstone/Simon and Schuster, 1987.

Miller, Marion. *I Was a Spy: The Story of a Brave Housewife.* Indianapolis: Bobbs-Merrill, 1960.

Miller, Michael V., and Susan Gilmore, eds. *Revolution at Berkeley: The Crisis in American Education.* New York: Dell, 1965.

Mills, Nicolaus. *Like a Holy Crusade: Mississippi 1964—the Turning of the Civil Rights Movement in America.* Chicago: Ivan R. Dee, 1992.

Mitford, Jessica. *Poison Penmanship: The Gentle Art of Muckraking.* New York: Alfred A. Knopf, 1979.

Mitgang, Herbert. *Dangerous Dossiers: Exposing the Secret War Against America's Greatest Authors.* New York: Ballantine Books, 1988.

Moldea, Dan E. *Dark Victory: Ronald Reagan, MCA, and the Mob.* New York: Penguin Books, 1986.

Montgomery, Gayle B., and James W. Johnson. *One Step from the White House: The Rise and Fall of Senator William F. Knowland.* Berkeley and Los Angeles: University of California Press, 1998.

Morgan, Bill. *The Beat Generation in San Francisco: A Literary Guidebook.* San Francisco: City Lights Books, 2003.

Morris, Edmund. *Dutch: A Memoir of Ronald Reagan.* New York: Random House, 1999.

Murphy, George. *"Say . . . Didn't You Used to Be George Murphy?"* New York: Bartholomew House, 1970.

Nasaw, David. *The Chief: The Life of William Randolph Hearst.* Boston: Mariner Books/Houghton Mifflin, 2000.

Nathan, Harriet, and Stanley Scott, eds. *Experiment and Change in Berkeley: Essays on City Politics, 1950–1975.* Berkeley: Institute of Governmental Studies, University of California, 1978.

Navasky, Victor S. *Kennedy Justice.* New York: Atheneum, 1997.

——. *Naming Names.* New York: Penguin Books, 1981.

Nelson, Steve, James R. Barrett, and Rob Ruck. *Steve Nelson: American Radical.* Pittsburgh: University of Pittsburgh Press, 1981.

Newton, Jim. *Justice for All: Earl Warren and the Nation He Made.* New York: Riverhead Books, 2006.

Nisbet, Robert. *Teachers and Scholars: A Memoir of Berkeley in Depression and War.* New Brunswick, NJ: Transaction Publishers, 1992.

Nofziger, Lyn. *Nofziger.* Washington, DC: Regnery Gateway, 1992.

Oakland Museum of California. *What's Going On? California and the Vietnam Era,* Marcia A. Eymann and Charles Wollenberg, eds. Berkeley: University of California Press, 2004.

O'Neill, William L. *Coming Apart: An Informal History of America in the 1960s.* New York: Times Books, 1971.

O'Reilly, Kenneth. *Hoover and the Un-Americans: The FBI, HUAC, and the Red Menace.* Philadelphia: Temple University Press, 1983.

——. *Racial Matters: The FBI's Secret File on Black America, 1960–1972.* New York: The Free Press, 1989.

Packer, Herbert L. *Ex-Communist Witnesses: Four Studies in Fact Finding.* Stanford, CA: Stanford University Press, 1962.

Peck, Abe. *Uncovering the Sixties: The Life and Times of the Underground Press.* New York: Citadel Press, 1991.

Pearson, Hugh. *The Shadow of the Panther: Huey Newton and the Price of Black Power in America.* Reading, MA: Addison-Wesley, 1994.

Perlstein, Rick. *Before the Storm: Barry Goldwater and the Unmaking of the American Consensus.* New York: Hill and Wang, 2001.

Perry, Charles. *The Haight-Ashbury: A History.* New York: Wenner Books, 2005.
Powers, Richard Gid. *Secrecy and Power: The Life of J. Edgar Hoover.* New York: The Free Press, 1987.
Ransom, Harry Howe. *The Intelligence Establishment.* Cambridge, MA: Harvard University Press, 1970.
Rarick, Ethan. *The Life and Times of Pat Brown: California Rising.* Berkeley and Los Angeles: University of California Press, 2005.
Rawson, Tabor. *I Want to Live! The Analysis of a Murder.* (Based on the screenplay by Nelson Gidding and Don M. Mankiewicz and the original material by journalist Edward S. Montgomery.) New York: Signet Books, 1958.
Reagan, Maureen. *First Father, First Daughter: A Memoir.* Boston: Little, Brown, 1989.
Reagan, Michael, and Joe Hyams. *On the Outside Looking In: The Intimate Autobiography of the Eldest Son of President Ronald Reagan and Jane Wyman.* New York: Zebra Books/Kensington, 1988.
Reagan, Nancy, with William Novak. *My Turn: The Memoirs of Nancy Reagan.* New York: Random House, 1989.
Reagan, Ronald. *An American Life: The Autobiography.* New York: Simon and Schuster, 1990.
Reagan, Ronald, and Richard G. Hubler. *Where's the Rest of Me? The Ronald Reagan Story.* New York: Duell, Sloan and Pearce, 1965.
Rhodes, Richard. *The Making of the Atomic Bomb.* New York: Touchstone/Simon and Schuster, 1988.
Rips, Geoffrey. *The Campaign Against the Underground Press: PEN American Center Report.* San Francisco: City Lights Books, 1981.
Roberts, Gene, and Hank Klibanoff. *The Race Beat: The Press, the Civil Rights Struggle and the Awakening of a Nation.* New York: Vintage Books, 2006.
Robins, Natalie. *Alien Ink: The FBI's War on Freedom of Expression.* New York: William Morrow, 1992.
Romerstein, Herbert, and Eric Breindel. *The Venona Secrets: Exposing Soviet Espionage and America's Traitors.* Washington, DC: Regnery, 2000.
Rorabaugh, W. J. *Berkeley at War: The 1960s.* New York: Oxford University Press, 1989.
Rosen, Ruth. *The World Split Open: How the Modern Women's Movement Changed America.* New York: Penguin Books, 2000.
Rosovsky, Henry. *The University: An Owner's Manual.* New York: W. W. Norton, 1990.
Rossman, Michael. *On Learning and Social Change: Transcending the Totalitarian Classroom.* New York: Vintage Books, 1972.
———. *The Wedding Within the War.* New York: Anchor Books, 1971.
Rubin, Jerry. *Do It!* New York: Simon and Schuster, 1970.
———. *Growing (Up) at Thirty-Seven.* New York: Warner Books, 1976.
———. *We Are Everywhere.* New York: Harper and Row, 1971.
Schrecker, Ellen. *The Age of McCarthyism: A Brief History with Documents.* Boston: Bedford Books/St. Martin's Press, 1994.
———. *Many Are the Crimes: McCarthyism in America.* Boston: Little, Brown, 1998.
Schrecker, Ellen W. *No Ivory Tower: McCarthyism and the Universities.* New York: Oxford University Press, 1986.
Schuparra, Kurt. *Triumph of the Right: The Rise of the California Conservative Movement, 1945–1966.* Armonk, NY: M. E. Sharpe, 1998.
Seaborg, Glenn T., and Ray Colvig. *Chancellor at Berkeley.* Berkeley: Institute of Governmental Studies Press, University of California, 1994.
Seale, Bobby. *Seize the Time: The Story of the Black Panther Party and Huey P. Newton.* New York: Random House, 1968.

Searle, John R. *The Campus War: A Sympathetic Look at the University in Agony.* New York: World Publishing/Times Mirror, 1971.

Sherrill, Robert. *First Amendment Felon: The Story of Frank Wilkinson, His 132,000-Page FBI File, and His Epic Fight for Civil Rights and Civil Liberties.* New York: Nation Books, 2005.

Shinder, Jason, ed. *The Poem That Changed America: "Howl" Fifty Years Later.* New York: Farrar, Straus and Giroux, 2006.

Skinner, Kiron K., Annelise Anderson, and Martin Anderson, eds. *Reagan's Path to Victory: The Shaping of Ronald Reagan's Vision: Selected Writings.* New York: The Free Press, 2004.

Smith, G. Kerry, ed. *The Troubled Campus: Current Issues in Higher Education, 1970.* American Association for Higher Education, National Center for Higher Education. San Francisco: Jossey-Bass, 1970.

Spada, James. *Ronald Reagan: His Life in Pictures.* New York: St. Martin's Press, 2000.

Starr, Kevin. *The Dream Endures: California Enters the 1940s.* New York: Oxford University Press, 1997.

———. *Embattled Dreams: California in War and Peace, 1940–1950.* New York: Oxford University Press, 2002.

———. *Endangered Dreams: The Great Depression in California.* New York: Oxford University Press, 1996.

Stone, I. F. *The Killings at Kent State: How Murder Went Unpunished.* New York: New York Review Books/Vintage, 1970.

Stone, Robert. *Prime Green: Remembering the Sixties.* New York: HarperCollins, 2007.

Sullivan, William C., with Bill Brown. *The Bureau: My Thirty Years in Hoover's FBI.* New York: W. W. Norton, 1979.

Summers, Anthony. *The Secret Life of J. Edgar Hoover.* New York: Pocket Star Books, 1993.

Sussman, Peter Y., ed. *Decca: The Letters of Jessica Mitford.* New York: Alfred A. Knopf, 2006.

Swearingen, Wesley M. *FBI Secrets: An Agent's Exposé.* Boston: South End Press, 1995.

Talese, Gay. *Honor Thy Father.* New York: Ivy Books/Ballantine, 1992.

Taylor, Paul. *On the Ground in the Thirties.* Preface by Clark Kerr. Salt Lake City: Gibbs M. Smith, 1983.

Theoharis, Athan. *Chasing Spies: How the FBI Failed in Counterintelligence but Promoted the Politics of McCarthyism in the Cold War Years.* Chicago: Ivan R. Dee, 2002.

———. *J. Edgar Hoover, Sex, and Crime: A Historical Antidote.* Chicago: Ivan R. Dee, 1995.

———. *The Quest for Absolute Security: The Failed Relations Among U.S. Intelligence Agencies.* Chicago: Ivan R. Dee, 2007.

———. *Spying on Americans: Political Surveillance from Hoover to the Huston Plan.* Philadelphia: Temple University Press, 1978.

Theoharis, Athan, ed. *From the Secret Files of J. Edgar Hoover.* Chicago: Ivan R. Dee, 1991.

Theoharis, Athan G. *The FBI and American Democracy: A Brief Critical History.* Lawrence: University Press of Kansas, 2004.

Theoharis, Athan G., ed. *Beyond the Hiss Case: The FBI, Congress, and the Cold War.* Philadelphia: Temple University Press, 1982.

———. *A Culture of Secrecy: The Government Versus the People's Right to Know.* Lawrence: University Press of Kansas, 1988.

———. *The FBI: A Comprehensive Reference Guide.* Phoenix: Oryx Press, 1999.

Theoharis, Athan G., and John Stuart Cox. *The Boss: J. Edgar Hoover and the Great American Inquisition.* Philadelphia: Temple University Press, 1988.

Thompson, Hunter S. *Hell's Angels: A Strange and Terrible Saga.* New York: Ballantine Books, 1967.

Turner, William. *Rearview Mirror: Looking Back at the FBI, the CIA and Other Tails.* Granite Bay, CA: Penmarin Books, 2001.

Turner, William W. *Hoover's FBI: The Men and the Myth.* Los Angeles: Sherbourne Press, 1970.

Tussman, Joseph. *Experiment at Berkeley.* New York: Oxford University Press, 1969.

Unger, Harlow G. *American Profiles: Teachers and Educators.* New York: Facts on File, 1994.

Vaughn, Stephen. *Ronald Reagan in Hollywood: Movies and Politics.* Cambridge, UK: Cambridge University Press, 1994.

Viorst, Milton. *Fire in the Streets: America in the 1960s.* New York: Simon and Schuster, 1979.

Von Hoffman, Nicholas. *Citizen Cohn: The Life and Times of Roy Cohn.* Toronto: Bantam Books, 1988.

Watters, Pat, and Stephen Gillers, eds. *Investigating the FBI: A Book of the Committee for Public Justice.* Garden City, NY: Doubleday, 1973.

Weiner, Tim. *Legacy of Ashes: The History of the CIA.* New York: Doubleday, 2007.

Weinstein, Allen, and Alexander Vassiliev. *The Haunted Wood: Soviet Espionage in America—the Stalin Era.* New York: Modern Library, 2000.

Welch, Neil J., and David W. Marston. *Inside Hoover's FBI: The Top Field Chief Reports.* Garden City, NY: Doubleday, 1984.

Wiener, Jon. *Gimme Some Truth: The John Lennon FBI Files.* Berkeley: University of California Press, 1999.

Wills, Garry. *Certain Trumpets: The Nature of Leadership.* New York: Touchstone Books, 1994.

———. *John Wayne's America: The Politics of Celebrity.* New York: Simon and Schuster, 1997.

———. *Reagan's America: Innocents at Home.* New York: Doubleday, 1987.

Wise, David, and Thomas B. Ross. *The Invisible Government.* New York: Random House, 1964.

Wofsy, Leon. *Looking for the Future: A Personal Connection to Yesterday's Great Expectations, Today's Reality and Tomorrow's Hope.* Oakland, CA: I. W. Rose Press, 1995.

Wolfe, Tom. *The Electric Kool-Aid Acid Test.* New York: Bantam Books, 1968.

———. *Radical Chic & Mau-Mauing the Flak Catchers.* New York: Bantam Books, 1971.

Wolin, Sheldon S., and John H. Schaar. *The Berkeley Rebellion and Beyond.* New York: New York Review Books/Vintage, 1970.

Wollenberg, Charles. *Berkeley: A City in History.* Berkeley: University of California Press, 2008.

Woodward, Bob. *The Secret Man: The Story of Watergate's Deep Throat.* New York: Simon and Schuster, 2005.

Yapp, Nick. *Getty Images: 1960s.* London: Konemann/Getty Images, 1998.

Zaroulis, Nancy, and Gerald Sullivan. *Who Spoke Up? American Protest Against the War in Vietnam, 1963–1975.* New York: Holt, Rinehart and Winston, 1984.

Zinn, Howard. *A People's History of the United States: 1492–Present.* New York: Harper Perennial Modern Classics, 2005.

Documents, Interviews, and Other Sources

Selected FBI Documents

This is a book about a secret history of the sixties—about covert FBI activities and their connections to events and figures that have had far-reaching impact on America. The story could not have been told without the FBI files and the Freedom of Information Act that provided access to them—despite the concerted opposition of the FBI and the U.S. Department of Justice. The FBI records on the following subjects were among more than 300,000 pages of bureau files released to the author in response to his FOIA requests and five lawsuits he brought to enforce the act. Many of them were released for the first time as a result of these requests, and most were reprocessed to have fewer deletions. Reading them now makes clear why J. Edgar Hoover and his aides never intended that these records—and the activities they document—would become public.

"80" Files
Ad Hoc Committee to End Discrimination
Afro-American Students Union at UC Berkeley
American Documentary Films
American Federation of Teachers
American Legion
American Legion Contact Program
American Legion San Francisco
Anti-Imperialist Coalition
April Coalition
April 22 Coalition
Associated Students of University of California Berkeley (ASUC Berkeley)
Bay Area Student Committee for the Abolition of the House Un-American Activities Committee (BASCAHUAC)
Berkeley Black Caucus
Berkeley Civil Disturbances
Berkeley Coalition
Berkeley Democratic Caucus
Berkeley Free Press
Berkeley Tenants Union
Berkeley Tribe
Bob Meisenbach Defense Committee
Roy Brewer
Hugh M. Burns
California Senate Fact-Finding Subcommittee on Un-American Activities
Campus Draft Opposition

Center for Participant Education (CPE)
Frank Church
CINRAD (Communist Infiltration of the Radiation Lab, University of California, Berkeley)
Civil Rights Demonstrations—Sheraton Palace
Civil Rights Protests—Cadillac Motors
William Frederick Cody
COINTELPRO
Committee to Uphold the Right to Travel
Communes East Bay
Community for New Politics
Congress of Unrepresented People
Congress on Racial Equality (CORE)
The Daily Californian
Michael L. Delacour
John Henry Denton
William Tulio Divale
Dubois Club of America Bombing
Dubois Clubs of America
Educational Liberation Front
Herbert Ellingwood
Faculty Involvement in New Left Activities
Faculty Peace Committee
Filthy Speech Movement
Free Student Union
John George
John George for Congress Campaign
Suzanne Goldberg
Irving Wesley Hall
Ilona Harrington Hancock
House Committee on Un-American Activities (HCUA)
House Committee on Un-American Activities (HCUA) Hearing, San Francisco
Roger Heyns
Charles Hitch
Rob Hurwitt
International Days of Protest
International Liberation School
Don Jones
Hardin B. Jones
Eli Katz
John LeRoy Kelley
Clark Kerr
William Knowland
Harper Knowles
David Krech
Labor League of Hollywood Voters
Robert Lamborn
Loyalty Oaths at the University of California
John A. McCone
Florence Plotnick McDonald
Robert Meisenbach

Michael Meo
Theodore R. Meyer
Jessica Mitford
Motion Picture Alliance for the Preservation of American Ideals
Motion Picture Industry Council
Movement Against Political Suspensions
Don Mulford
George Murphy
National Americanism Commission of the American Legion
John Brian Neilands
John Francis Neylan
Edwin Wendell Pauley
Production of "Communist Target—Youth" Report and *Operation Abolition* Movie
Radical Research Committee of the American Legion
Radical Student Union
Max Rafferty
Maureen Reagan
Neil Reagan
Ronald Reagan
James Rector
Red Family
Research West
Responsibilities Program
Responsible Citizens Aroused
Ron Dellums for Congress Campaign
Jerry Clyde Rubin
Rubin for Mayor Campaign
Mario Savio
Max Scherr
Gustav Hobart Schultz
Peter Dale Scott
Screen Actors Guild
Alex C. Sherriffs
Daniel Mark Siegel
Roy E. Simpson
SLATE
Stephen Smale
Speaker Ban at the University of California
Robert Gordon Sproul
STAG (Student Agitation)
Stop the Draft Week
Edward W. Strong
Student Council, Fair Play for Cuba Committee
Student Mobilization Committee
Students Associated Against Totalitarianism
Students for Civil Liberties
Students for a Democratic Society at Berkeley (SDS at Berkeley)
Jack B. Tenney
Third World Liberation Front (TWLF)
Burney Threadgill, Jr.
Tocsin

Robert Treuhaft
University of California
University of California, Berkeley, Academic Senate
University of California Regents
Christopher Venn
Vietnam Day Committee
War Crimes Commission
Washington Video Productions
Burton David White
Jane Wyman
Young Americans for Freedom (YAF)
Young Democrats
Young Republicans
Youth International Party (YIPPIE)

Selected Interviews by Author

To paraphrase Victor Navasky, it would be a mistake to assume that FBI files provide answers rather than clues. So while FBI files form the core of this book, the author conducted more than 150 interviews during the course of research that spanned three decades. The interviewees represent the opposing sides in the conflicts centered on campus—from student radicals to university administrators to members of Governor Reagan's staff and FBI officials. Some interviews were brief but most were substantial and many were lengthy. Clark Kerr, for example, graciously granted me a series of interviews over the years that each lasted hours. Early on, Mario Savio examined some FBI records on the Free Speech Movement and shared his thoughts with me. Later, Suzanne Goldberg, his first wife, and Lynne Hollander Savio, his widow, separately met with me several times for detailed interviews that involved not only sharing their recollections but reviewing released FBI records. Burney Threadgill, Jr., a retired FBI special agent, spent many hours sitting with me, turning the pages and discussing bureau operations. So did Curtis O. Lynum, the retired special agent in charge of the San Francisco FBI office, even after commenting that I wasn't supposed to have these documents and asking me pointedly if my editor knew what I was doing. Wesley Grapp, the retired special agent in charge of the Los Angeles FBI office, and Cartha "Deke" DeLoach, who was one of Hoover's closest aides, also read certain records and spoke with me at length on the telephone. Edwin Meese III kindly reviewed some files and discussed them with me. Although many of the names listed below do not appear in the text, their comments and insights were nonetheless important to my understanding of events, and I am grateful to everyone who took the time to speak with me.

Gerald D. Adams
Todd Adams
Alan Adler
Steven Aftergood
Stew Albert
Tom Anderson
Anne Aoki
James Aoki
Richard Masato Aoki
Stephen Arian

Richard Atkinson
Ben Bagdikian
William M. Baldwin
Frank Bardacke
Karlyn Barker
William P. Beall
Michael Beavers
Chip Berlet
Robert Benya
Jack Berman

Eleanor Bertino
Joe Blum
William D. Boone
Taylor Branch
William Bratter
Judith Braun
James Brosnahan
Edmund G. "Pat" Brown
Marvin Buchanan
Mary Burgan
Ann Mari Buitrago
Robert Bulwa
Malcolm Burnstein
John Burton
Jerome C. Byrne
Peter Camejo
Stephen Carr
Clayborne Carson
Bill Carter
James Chanin
William Coblentz
Jerry Cohen
Kate Coleman
Wayne M. Collins
Ray Colvig
Shirlee Conte
George Dalen
Lucy Dalglish
Olivia de Havilland (by e-mail)
Manuel Ruben Delgado
Cartha "Deke" DeLoach
Jim Dempsey
Christopher Densmore
Jeremiah Denton
Seth Derish
Melvin Dixon
Harvey Dong
Colleen Draklich
Lawrence Duga
Fred Dutton
Don Edwards
Richard Ehrenberger
David Fechheimer
Dianne Feinstein
Bill Fleming
Dr. John Fox
Peter Franck
Allan Francke
Marian Gade
Victor Garlin
Arthur Gatti

Robert Givens
Paul Glusman
Suzanne Goldberg
Frederick Goss
Wesley Grapp
Ronald M. Greenberg
Peter Haberfeld
Irving Hall
Conn "Ringo" Hallinan
Terence Hallinan
Stuart Hanlon
Glenn Harter
Elinor Haas Heller
Tom Hayden (by e-mail)
Morris Hirsch
Alex Hoffman
Ken Holden
Rob Hurwitt
D. Lowell Jensen
Loch Johnson
Don Jones
Helen Jones
Sam Kagel
John Kelley
Clark Kerr
Clark E. Kerr
William Kerr
Donald Kuno
Bob Lamborn
Michael Lamborn
Serge Lang
Ernie Lazar
Patrick Leahy
Mary Ellen Leary
John Leggett
Lynn Ludlow
Jeff Lustig
Curtis O. Lynum
Kate Martin
Robert McClennan
"Country Joe" McDonald
Florence McDonald
Donald McLaughlin
John McManus
Stephen McNeil
Ken Meade
Francis Medaille
Edwin Meese III
Virgil Meibert
Bob Meisenbach
Barry Melton

Mary Mocine
Paul Montauk
Susan Montauk
Ed Montgomery
Bill Moyers
Carlos Munoz
Earl Napper
J. B. Neilands
Jeff Nesmith
James J. Newberry
Lyn Nofziger
Sheila O'Donnell
Thomas Orloff
James Pachl
Anthony L. Palumbo
Thomas Parkinson
Nancy Pelosi
Jay Peterzell
Barbara Petry
Oliver Petry
Stanley Plog
Wendy Preuit
Craig Pyes
Christopher H. Pyle
Lee Quarnstrom
LaRae Quy
John Rees
Pat Richartz
Michael Rossman
William M. Roth
Jerry Rubin
Thomas Salciccia
Bill Sato
Lynne Hollander Savio
Mario Savio

Diane Schroerluke
Bobby Seale
John Searle
Willis Shotwell
Dan Siegel
Stephen Smale
Mike Smith
David Sobel
Naomi P. F. Southard
John Sparrow
Syd Stapleton
Kevin Starr
Paul Staudohar
Cheryl Stevenson
Michael Syvanen
Athan Theoharis
John Thorpe
Burney Threadgill, Jr.
Dale Treleven
William W. Turner
Stephen Vaughn
Doug Wachter
Pam Wagner
Emmit Wallace
Ling-Chi Wang
David Ward
LaNada War Jack (LaNada Means)
Anne Weills
Steve Weissman
Burton White
Burton Wolfe
Charles Wollenberg
Ann Woolner
R. James Woolsey
Roger Young

Freedom of Information Act Lawsuits Brought by the Author

Seth Rosenfeld v. Federal Bureau of Investigation and U.S. Department of Justice,
    C 85-1709 MHP, U.S. District Court, Northern District of California, 1985
Seth Rosenfeld v. Federal Bureau of Investigation and U.S. Department of Justice,
    C 85-2247 MHP, U.S. District Court, Northern District of California, 1985
Seth Rosenfeld v. Federal Bureau of Investigation and U.S. Department of Justice,
    C 90-3576 MHP, U.S. District Court, Northern District of California, 1990
Seth Rosenfeld v. Federal Bureau of Investigation and U.S. Department of Justice,
    C 07-3240 MHP, U.S. District Court, Northern District of California, 2007
Seth Rosenfeld v. Federal Bureau of Investigation and U.S. Department of Justice,
    C 11-02131 MEJ, U.S. District Court, Northern District of California, 2011

Other Judicial Records

(Copies obtained through the respective court or agency unless otherwise noted)

Concerning Ronald Reagan
Michael D. Jeffers v. Screen Extras Guild, Civ. No. 21698, State Court of Appeal, California, 1955 (California State Archives, Office of the Secretary of State, Sacramento, California)

Concerning the 1960 protest at City Hall
People v. Robert Meisenbach, no. 57454, San Francisco Superior Court, 1960 (in Meisenbach FBI file 100-434714 EBF 72)

Concerning the Free Speech Movement
State of California v. Mario Savio, et al., nos. C-7468 to C-7547, Berkeley-Albany Municipal Court, 1965 (Alexander Meiklejohn Collection, BANC MSS 99/281, carton 34, Bancroft Library, University of California, Berkeley)

Concerning Ed Montgomery and the *San Francisco Examiner*
Synanon v. Hearst, no. 651-749, San Francisco Superior Court, 1972
Synanon v. Hearst, no. 667-448, San Francisco Superior Court, 1973
Montgomery v. Bay Guardian Co., Inc., no. 722-487, San Francisco Superior Court, 1977

Concerning Research West or its staff
Lois A. Chipman v. Harold E. Chipman, no. 98958, Marin County Superior Court, 1980
Soto v. Market Analysis, Inc., no. 07-15518 NJK, California Department of Industrial Relations, Division of Labor Standards Enforcement, 1982
Security Pacific National Bank v. Research West and Richard K. Miller, no. 781207, San Francisco Superior Court, 1981
Richard K. Miller v. Research West, et al., no. 799821, San Francisco Superior Court, 1982
T. David Hodgkinson v. Market Analysis, Inc., et al., no. 785155, San Francisco Superior Court, 1982
First Interstate Bank of California v. Market Analysis, Inc., no. 548443-2, Alameda County Superior Court, 1981
First Interstate Bank of California v. Research West, et al., no. 548442-3, Alameda County Superior Court, 1981
Tower II v. Market Analysis, Inc., no. 552949-4, Alameda County Superior Court, 1981
Tower II v. Research West, no. 548284-3, Alameda County Superior Court, 1981
Watergate Co. v. Patricia Atthowe and Research West, no. 385928, Alameda County Municipal Court, 1982
Parkwood Apartments v. Julie and Jean Atthowe, no. 379293, Alameda County Municipal Court, 1981
Irene Sargent v. Patricia Atthowe, no. 386796, Alameda County Municipal Court, 1982
Eastman Kodak Co. v. Research West, no. 555481-2, Alameda County Superior Court, 1982
IBM v. Research West, no. 379290, Alameda County Municipal Court, 1981
Finkelstein v. Market Analysis, Inc., no. 951082, San Francisco Municipal Court, 1983
Eisen v. Regents of University of California, 269 Cal. App. 2d 696, February 17, 1969
Mary Louise Lamborn v. Robert Lewis Lamborn, no. 391939, Alameda County Superior Court, 1969 (courtesy Ernie Lazar)
Patricia Atthowe v. Clark Kerr et al., no. C-363953, Alameda County Superior Court, 1966 (courtesy Ernie Lazar)

Concerning People's Park
Stephen Thomas Murray, et al. v. Frank Madigan, no. 51398, U.S. District Court, Northern District of California, 1970

U.S. v. Riche, CR 70-87, U.S. District Court, Northern District of California, 1970
U.S. v. Riche, CR 70-88, U.S. District Court, Northern District of California, 1970
U.S. v. Johnson and Riche, CR 70-89, U.S. District Court, Northern District of California, 1970
U.S. v. Santucci, CR 70-90, U.S. District Court, Northern District of California, 1970
U.S. v. Barker, Davis, Killian, Lynch, Nelson, O'Neill, Otey, Riche, Turner and Vien, CR 70-91, U.S. District Court, Northern District of California, 1970
U.S. v. Nelson, Riche and Turner, CR 70-92, U.S. District Court, Northern District of California, 1970
U.S. v. Nelson, CR 70- 93, U.S. District Court, Northern District of California, 1970
U.S. v. Otey and Riche, CR 70-94, U.S. District Court, Northern District of California, 1970
U.S. v. Riche and Vien, CR 70-95, U.S. District Court, Northern District of California, 1970
U.S. v. Otey, CR 70-96, U.S. District Court, Northern District of California, 1970
Akin v. Madigan, no. C-70 713 ACW, U.S. District Court, Northern District of California, 1970
Blanchard v. State of California, no. 393,210, Alameda County Superior Court, 1970
Francke v. State of California et al., no. 397,680, Alameda County Superior Court, 1970
Moor v. Madigan, no. C-70 333 RFP, U.S. District Court, Northern District of California, 1970
Porter v. Madigan, no. C-70 384 SC, U.S. District Court, Northern District of California, 1970
Rundle v. Madigan, no. C 70-334 RFP, U.S. District Court, Northern District of California, 1970
Scheer v. Madigan, no. C-70 155 RFP, U.S. District Court, Northern District of California, 1970

Concerning FBI domestic security operations
Socialist Workers Party v. Attorney General (Wisconsin Historical Society)
National Lawyers Guild v. Attorney General (Tamiment Library and Robert F. Wagner Labor Archives, New York University)

Hearings and Reports of the "Church Committee"
United States Senate. Hearings Before the Select Committee to Study Governmental Operations with Respect to Intelligence Activities: Volume 6: Federal Bureau of Investigation. Washington, DC: U.S. Government Printing Office, 1976.
United States Senate. Intelligence Activities and the Rights of Americans: Book II, Final Report of the Select Committee to Study Governmental Operations with Respect to Intelligence Activities. Washington, DC: U.S. Government Printing Office, 1976.
United States Senate. Supplementary Detailed Staff Reports on Intelligence Activities and the Rights of Americans: Book III, Final Report of the Select Committee to Study Governmental Operations with Respect to Intelligence Activities. Washington, DC: U.S. Government Printing Office, 1976.
United States Senate. Alleged Assassination Plots Involving Foreign Leaders, An Interim Report of the Select Committee to Study Governmental Operations with Respect to Intelligence Activities. Washington, DC: U.S. Government Printing Office, 1975.

Other Governmental Hearings and Reports
National Advisory Commission on Civil Disorders. The Kerner Report. New York: Bantam Books, 1968.

National Archives and Records Administration. *Federal Records Relating to Civil Rights in the Post-World War II Era: Reference Information Paper 113.* Washington, DC: National Archives and Records Administration, 2006.

United States Congress. *J. Edgar Hoover: Late Director, Federal Bureau of Investigation, Department of Justice—Memorial Tributes in the Congress of the United States and Various Articles and Editorials Relating to His Life and Work.* Washington, DC: U.S. Government Printing Office, 1974.

United States House of Representatives. *Contempt Proceedings Against Patricia Atthowe, Including Hearings and Related Documents: Before the Subcommittee on Oversight and Investigations of the Committee on Interstate and Foreign Commerce.* Washington, DC: U.S. Government Printing Office, 1978.

United States House of Representatives. *Communist Target—Youth: Communist Infiltration and Agitation Tactics, a report by J. Edgar Hoover, published by the House Committee on Un-American Activities.* Washington, DC: U.S. Government Printing Office, 1960.

U.S. House of Representatives. *The Northern California District of the Communist Party: Structure, Objectives, Leadership, Hearings Before the Committee on Un-American Activities, May 12–14, 1960, and June 10, 1960.* Washington, DC: U.S. Government Printing Office, 1960 (the HUAC hearings at San Francisco City Hall).

U.S. Senate. *Hearings Before the Subcommittee to Investigate the Administration of the Internal Security Act and Other Internal Security Laws of the Committee on the Judiciary, Washington, D.C., March 19, 1953* (Testimony of Richard E. Combs, Chief Counsel, California Senate Fact-finding Committee on Un-American Activities).

U.S. Senate. *Hearings Before the Permanent Subcommittee on Investigations, Committee on Government Operations, Part 22, July 16, 1969.* Washington, DC: U.S. Government Printing Office, 1969 (Testimony of Herbert E. Ellingwood, Legal Affairs Secretary, Office of Governor Ronald Reagan).

U.S. House of Representatives. *Hearings on H.R. 12047, H.R. 14925, H.R. 16175, H.R. 17140, and H.R. 17194—Bills to Make Punishable Assistance to Enemies of U.S. in Time of Undeclared War, House Committee on Un-American Activities, August 16–19, 1966.* Washington, DC: U.S. Government Printing Office, 1966 (Testimony of Edwin Meese III, Alameda County District Attorney's Office, and Remarks of Jerry Rubin).

U.S. House of Representatives. *Hearings Regarding the Communist Infiltration of the Motion Picture Industry, House Committee on Un-American Activities, October 20 and 23, 1947.* Washington, DC: U.S. Government Printing Office, 1947 (Testimony of Ronald Reagan, Screen Actors Guild, and H. A. Smith, HUAC investigator, and remarks of HUAC chairman J. Parnell Thomas).

California State Senate. *Sixth Report of the Senate Fact-Finding Committee on Un-American Activities.* Sacramento: State Senate, 1951.

California State Senate. *Thirteenth Report, Un-American Activities in California, 1965, Report of the Senate Factfinding Subcommittee on Un-American Activities.* Sacramento: State Senate, 1965.

California State Senate. *Thirteenth Report Supplement, Un-American Activities in California, 1966, Report of the Senate Factfinding Subcommittee on Un-American Activities.* Sacramento: State Senate, 1966.

Selected Manuscript and Archival Collections
The Bancroft Library, UC Berkeley

Free Speech Movement records, CU-309, University Archives. Part of this collection is online at the Free Speech Movement Digital Archive at www.lib.berkeley.edu /BANC/FSM

Free Speech Movement Participants' Papers, BANC MSS 99/162 c
Sproul Hall Incident Records: Participant Survey reports, 1964–1965, CU-560
Office of the President Records, University of California, CU-5
Office of the Chancellor Records, University of California, Berkeley, CU-149
Clark Kerr Personal and Professional Papers, CU-302
Edmund G. Brown Papers, BANC MSS 68/90 c
Social Protest Collection, BANC MSS 86/157 c, BANC FILM 2757
Wayne M. Collins Papers, BANC MSS 78/177 c
Malcolm Burnstein Papers, BANC MSS 99/294 c
Elsa Knight Thompson Papers, BANC MSS 2004/101 c
Meiklejohn Civil Liberties Institute Collections, BANC MSS 99/281 c
Hardin B. Jones Papers, BANC MSS 79/112 c
John A. McCone Papers, BANC MSS 95/20 c
People's Park clipping files, 1969, California Bureau of Criminal Identification and
    Investigation, CU-430
Mario Savio correspondence: Mississippi, to Cheri Stevenson, Berkeley, Calif., BANC
    MSS 2006/110
Max Heirich Papers relating to the Free Speech Movement, 1964-1971, BANC MSS
    2003/326 c

Hoover Institution Archives, Stanford University
Eric Bellquist Papers
Bill Boyarsky Papers
Kathryn R. Davis Papers
Hardin Blair Jones Papers
John H. Lawrence Papers
Edwin Meese III Papers
New Left Collection

California Historical Society, San Francisco
The American Civil Liberties Union of Northern California Records

Stanford University Library
Allen Ginsberg Papers, M0733, Department of Special Collections
King Online Encyclopedia, The Martin Luther King, Jr. Research and Education Insti-
    tute, Stanford University, mlk-kpp01.stanford.edu/index.php

California State Archives, Sacramento
California Un-American Activities Committee Records, 93-04-12, 93-04-16

Ronald Reagan Presidential Library, Simi Valley
Ronald Reagan Governor's Papers (also called Reagan Gubernatorial Papers)
Ronald Reagan Military Service Records
Mark Felt and Edward Miller Pardon File

Lyndon Baines Johnson Presidential Library, Austin
Recordings of Telephone Conversations—White House Series, Recordings and Tran-
    scripts of Conversations and Meetings

National Archives and Records Administration, Washington, D.C.
U.S. House of Representatives, Records of the House Un-American Activities Committee and House Internal Security Committee, Record Group 233
U.S. Department of Justice, Civil Rights Investigations, RG 60

Wisconsin Historical Society, Madison
Michael Fellner Papers
Socialist Worker Party Records
Stephen Vaughn Papers

American Friends Service Committee Archives, Philadelphia
Peace Caravan Records

Brooklyn College Archive and Special Collections
John J. Rooney Collection, Brooklyn College of the City University of New York, Accession No. 89-005

Southern California Library for Social Studies and Research, Los Angeles
Urban Policy Research Institute Papers

Mississippi Department of Archives & History, Jackson
Mississippi State Sovereignty Commission Records
Council of Federated Organizations Records

The Free Speech Movement Archives (FSM-A)
Digital Collection, www.fsm-a.org/

SLATE Digital Archives
http://slatearchives.org/

DataCenter, Oakland
Newspaper clipping files

Tamiment Library and Robert F. Wagner Labor Archives, New York University
Records of *National Lawyers Guild v. Attorney General*

Dissertations, Theses, and Scholarly Papers

Dong, Harvey L. 2002. *The Origins and Trajectory of Asian American Political Activism in the San Francisco Bay Area, 1968–1978*. Ph.D. diss., University of California, Berkeley.

Glad, Betty. 1989. "Reagan's Midlife Crisis and the Turn to the Right," *Political Psychology*, vol. 10, no. 4, pp. 593–624, International Society of Political Psychology, www.jstor.org/stable/3791330, accessed 8/9/11.

Glick, Stanley Irwin. 1984. *The People's Park*. Ph.D. diss., State University of New York at Stony Brook.

De Groot, Gerard J. 1996. "Ronald Reagan and Student Unrest in California, 1966–1970," *Pacific Historical Review*, vol. 65, no. 1, pp. 107–29, University of California Press, www.jstor.org/stable/3791330, accessed 2/14/12.

———. 1997. "'A Goddamned Electable Person': The 1966 California Gubernatorial Campaign of Ronald Reagan," *History, The Journal of the Historical Association*, vol. 82, no. 267, onlinelibrary.wiley.com/doi/10.1111/1468-229X.00044/pdf, accessed 2/14/12.
Howell, Jeffrey Brian. 2005. *The Undiscovered Country: The Civil Rights Movement in Holmes County, Mississippi, 1954–1968*, M.A. diss., Mississippi State University.
Kolkind, Michael D. 2007. *People's Park, 1969: A Confrontation Between Conflicting American Cultures*. McIntyre Library, University of Wisconsin, Eau Claire.
Ofshe, Richard. 1980. "The Social Development of the Synanon Cult: The Managerial Strategy of Organizational Transformation," *Sociology of Religion*, vol. 41, no. 2 Association for the Sociology of Religion, socrel.oxfordjournals.org/content/41/2/109 .abstract, accessed 9/23/11.
Plog, Stanley Clement. 1961. *Flanders vs. McCarthy: A Study in the Technique and Theory of Analyzing Congressional Mail*. Ph.D. diss., Harvard University.
Risen, Clay. 2009. "Spies Among Us," *The American Scholar*, the Phi Beta Kappa Society, http://theamericanscholar.org/spies-among-us/, accessed 1/20/12.

Selected Oral Histories

Burns, Hugh M. "Legislative and Political Concerns of the Senate Pro Tem, 1957–1970," an interview conducted by Amelia R. Fry, Gabrielle Morris, and James H. Rowland in 1981, *Governmental History Documentation Project: Goodwin Knight/Edmund Brown, Sr., Era*, Regional Oral History Office, Bancroft Library, University of California, Berkeley.
Byrne, Jerome C. An oral history interview conducted in 1993 by Dale E. Treleven, UCLA Oral History Program, California State Archives State Government Oral History Program.
Cunningham, Thomas J. "Southern California Campaign Chairman for Earl Warren, 1946," an interview conducted in 1972 by Amelia R. Fry in *Earl Warren Oral History Project*, Regional Oral History Office, Bancroft Library, University of California, Berkeley, 1976.
Dunckel, Earl B. "Ronald Reagan and the General Electric Theater, 1954–55," an interview conducted by Gabrielle Morris in 1982 in *Government History Documentation Project: Ronald Reagan Gubernatorial Era*, Regional Oral History Office, Bancroft Library, University of California, Berkeley, 1982.
Dutton, Frederick G. "Democratic Campaigns and Controversies, 1954–1966," an oral history conducted by Amelia R. Fry in 1977–78 in *Governmental History Documentation Project: Goodwin Knight/Edmund Brown, Sr., Era*, Regional Oral History Office, Bancroft Library, University of California, Berkeley, 1981.
Finch, Robert H. "Views from the Lieutenant Governor's Office, 1967–1969," an oral history conducted in 1981 by Harry P. Jeffrey, Jr., in *Government History Documentation Project: Ronald Reagan Gubernatorial Era*, Regional Oral History Office, Bancroft Library, University of California, Berkeley, 1983.
Goldberg, Suzanne. An oral history conducted by Lisa Rubens in July 2000, Free Speech Movement Oral History Project, Regional Oral History Office, Bancroft Library, University of California, Berkeley, 2000.
Grendon, Alexander. "Research with Hardin Jones at Donner Laboratory, 1956–1978," an oral history conducted by Sally Smith Hughes in 1979, History of Science and Technology Program, Bancroft Library, University of California, Berkeley, 1985.
Heyns, Roger W. "Berkeley Chancellor, 1965–1971: The University in a Turbulent Society," an interview conducted by Harriet Nathan in 1986, Regional Oral History Office, Bancroft Library, University of California, Berkeley, 1987.

Kerr, Clark. An oral history interview conducted by Janet Kerr-Tener in 1985, LBJ Library Oral History Collection, Lyndon Baines Johnson Library and Museum, Austin, Texas.

Mulford, David Donald. "Oral History Interview with David Donald Mulford, California State Assemblyman, 1957–1970," an interview conducted in 1988 and 1989 by Timothy P. Fong and Ann Lage, Regional Oral History Office, Bancroft Library, University of California, Berkeley.

Palumbo, Anthony L. "Law Enforcement, Emergency Planning, and the California National Guard, 1965–1974," an oral history conducted by Sarah Sharp in 1983 in *Law Enforcement and Criminal Justice in California, 1966–1974*, Regional Oral History Office, Bancroft Library, University of California, Berkeley, 1985.

Plog, Stanley. "More Than Just an Actor: The Early Campaigns of Ronald Reagan," an interview conducted by Stephen Stern in 1981 in *Government History Documentation Project: Ronald Reagan Era*, Oral History Program, Powell Library, University of California, Los Angeles, 1981.

Reagan, Neil. "Private Dimensions and Public Images: The Early Political Campaigns of Ronald Reagan," an interview conducted by Stephen Stern in 1981 in *Governmental History Documentation Project: Ronald Reagan Era*, Oral History Program, Powell Library, University of California, Los Angeles, 1981.

Reagan, Ronald. "On Becoming Governor," an oral history conducted by Sarah Sharp in 1979 in *Governor Reagan and His Cabinet: An Introduction*, Regional Oral History Office, Bancroft Library, University of California, Berkeley, 1986.

Reagan, Ronald. "Pragmatic Leadership: Ronald Reagan as President of the Screen Actors Guild," an interview conducted by Michael Tuchman in 1981, Oral History Program, Powell Library, University of California, Los Angeles, 1981.

Savio, Mario. "Mario Savio Discusses the FSM and Its Roots," date and interviewer unknown, courtesy Lynne Hollander and Michael Rossman, Moffitt Library, University of California, Berkeley, *The Pacifica Radio/UC Berkeley Social Activism Sound Recording Project: The Free Speech Movement and Its Legacy*, Tape 4, www.lib.berkeley.edu/MRC/pacificafsm.html#saviointerview, accessed 9/3/10.

Savio, Mario. "The Reminiscences of Mario Savio," an interview conducted by Bret Eynon, March 5, 1985, Columbia University Center for Oral History Collection, Columbia University, New York.

Sherriffs, Alex C. "The Governor's Office and Public Information, Education and Planning, 1967–1974: Interviews," an oral history conducted by Gabrielle Morris et al., Regional Oral History Office, Bancroft Library, University of California, Berkeley, 1984.

Sherriffs, Alex C. "The University of California and the Free Speech Movement: Perspectives from a Faculty Member and an Administrator," an oral history conducted in 1978 by James H. Rowland, Regional Oral History Office, Bancroft Library, University of California, Berkeley, 1980.

Strong, Edward W. "Philosopher, Professor, and Berkeley Chancellor, 1961–1965," an oral history conducted in 1988 by Harriet Nathan, Regional Oral History Office, Bancroft Library, University of California, Berkeley, 1992.

Trombley, William H. "Oral History Interview," conducted in 1994 by Dale E. Treleven, UCLA Oral History Program, for the California State Archives State Government Oral History Program.

Williams, Arleigh. "Dean of Students Arleigh Williams: The Free Speech Movement and the Six Years' War, 1964–1970," an oral history conducted in 1988 and 1989 by Germaine LaBerge, Regional Oral History Office, Bancroft Library, University of California, Berkeley, 1990.

Acknowledgments

The FBI files that are the basis of this book became available under the Freedom of Information Act only as a result of the extraordinary pro bono assistance of a small army of lawyers dedicated to open government. Thomas Steel, the San Francisco civil rights attorney, took my case in 1985, and over the next thirteen years brought three lawsuits with his superb staff of attorneys—David Golove, Emily Graham, Jeff Byrne, John Beattie, Elizabeth Pritzker, Kate Dyer, Gill Sperlein, Barbara Saavedra, Joe Matthews, Stuart Buckley, Jonathan Melrod, and Nanci Clarence—and assistants Janice Gonsalves, Farshid Arjam, Natalia Thurston, and Tim Carter. Thanks also to D. Milton Estes. The First Amendment Project of Oakland stepped in after Tom Steel's untimely passing and pursued these lawsuits, and a fourth, for the next fourteen years; my gratitude to executive director David Greene, senior counsel James Wheaton, attorneys Lowell Chow and Geoffrey King, and support staff Monica Aguilar-Barriga and Nicole Feliciano. Benjamin Wolf Stein of Oakland brought a fifth lawsuit that also produced essential information.

Mario Savio and Clark Kerr graciously granted me permission to obtain their FBI files, as did other participants. I am grateful to the federal judges who presided over my FOIA litigation, and I acknowledge the efforts of the staff at the FBI's Record/Information Dissemination Section.

At *The Daily Californian*, editor Jeffrey Rabin and reporter Don Hess made an initial FOIA request with help from attorney Don Jelinek. Editors Ken Weiss and Margaret Talbot provided me the opportunity to write about those files. Reporters David Newdorf and Mandalit del Barco helped break the news.

At the Center for Investigative Reporting, cofounders Lowell Bergman, Dan Noyes, and David Weir generously provided guidance from the start. Sharon Tiller and Laura Lent were always encouraging. Angus McKenzie shared his FOIA expertise and good spirits. Thanks also to Robert Rosenthal, CIR's executive director, and Christa Scharfenberg, its associate director.

At UC Berkeley's Graduate School of Journalism, my gratitude to deans Ben Bagdikian and Tom Goldstein, and to professors Thomas Leonard (university librarian), Alex Greenfeld, Robert Gunnison, and Rasa Gustaitis. At the school's Investigative Reporting Program, thanks to Marlena Telvick and, again, to Lowell Bergman, the director and the Logan Distinguished Professor in Investigative Reporting. At UC Berkeley's Institute of Governmental Studies, I am grateful to Susan Rasky, Peter Schrag, Ethan Rarick, Liz Wiener, and director Jack Citrin. Also at UC Berkeley, thanks to Michael Levy at the School of Law library and professors Harry Scheiber, Peter Dale Scott, and Kathleen Moran.

At the Institute for Justice and Journalism Program, then at the University of Southern California, I am grateful to Steve Montiel, Marc Cooper, and Bobby Kirkwood.

In 2002, the *San Francisco Chronicle* published my report about the FBI's efforts to oust UC president Clark Kerr, and I am especially indebted to publisher John Oppedahl; executive editor Phil Bronstein; assistant executive editor Narda Zacchino; editors Ken Conner, David Lewis, and Alison Biggar; and Jeanne Cooper and Joe Brown. A tip of my baseball cap to my other colleagues at the *Chronicle* and at the *San Francisco Examiner*: Michael Collier, Bob Egelko, Johnnie Miller, Richard Geiger, Judy Canter, Lois Jermyn, Susan Gilbert, Allen Matthews, John Diaz, Lois Kazakoff, Susan Sward, Peter Fagan, Kay Marie Jacobson, Ruth Rosen, Rob Hurwitt, Lynn Ludlow, Jose Antonio Vargas, Steve Cook, Sharon Rosenhause, Eric Brazil, Gerald Adams, David Armstrong, Lance Williams, Reynolds Holding, Elizabeth Fernandez, Paul Wilner, Gloria Orbegozo, Keay Davidson, April Chan, Mike Kepka, Raul Ramirez, Tim Reiterman, Jim Finefrock, Oscar Villalon, and Steve Proctor.

I am indebted to many archivists who, after all, hold the keys to our collective history. The staff at UC Berkeley's Bancroft Library fielded many requests and offered valuable suggestions; these include William Roberts, David Farrell, David Kessler, Iris Donovan, James Eason, Lori Hines, Baiba Strads, Lisa Rubens, Theresa Salazar, Susan Snyder, Jack Von Euw, Anthony Bliss, Lorna Kirwan, and Kathryn Neal.

At the Ronald Reagan Presidential Library, thanks to Michael Duggan, Michael Pinckney, Steve Branch, and Jennifer Mandel; at the John F. Kennedy Presidential Library, to Stephen Plotkin; at the Richard Nixon Presidential Library, to Gregory Cumming and Meghan Lee; at the Lyndon Baines Johnson Presidential Library, to Allen Fisher and Regina Greenwell; at the National Archives and Records Administration in Washington, D.C., and College Park, Maryland, to Martha Murphy, Marty McGann, James Mathis, Eugene Morris, Richard Peuser, Katherine Mollan, Jeffery Hartley, Fred Romanski, Susan Karren, William Greene, Tab Lewis, and Stephen Cooper; at NARA's San Bruno facility, to Robert Glass and Charles Miller; at the Hoover Institution, to Carol Leadenham; at the California Historical Society, to Mary Morganti; at the Wisconsin Historical Society, to Harry Miller; at the Miller Center of Public Affairs, University of Virginia, to Kent Germany; at the Screen Actors Guild, to Valerie Yaros; at the Tamiment Library and Robert F. Wagner Labor Archives in New York City, to Jan Hilley.

At the San Francisco Public Library's San Francisco History Center, thanks to Christina Moretta, Susan Goldstein, Wendy Kramer, Andrea Grimes, Jeff Thomas, and Tom Carey; at the Berkeley Public Library, to Isobel Schneider; at the Merritt College Library, to Judith Singer; at the Oakland Public Library History Room, to Dorothy Lazard; at the Oakland Museum of California, to Nathan Kerr; at the Southern California Library for Social Studies and Research in Los Angeles, to Raquel Chavez; at the Eudora Welty Library in Jackson, Mississippi, to Savannah Kelly; thanks also to the staff at the California State Archives in Sacramento.

At FSM-a, the Free Speech Movement Archives, thanks to Barbara Stack; at DataCenter, in Oakland, to Fred Goff and Bill Berkowitz; at Media Alliance, to Micha Peled, Erica Wudtke, Tracy Rosenberg, and Jeff Perlstein.

Jim Dempsey at the Center for Democracy & Technology; David Sobel and Lee Tien at the Electronic Frontier Foundation; Thomas Blanton and Nate Jones at the National Security Archive; Lucy Dalglish at the Reporters Committee for Freedom of the Press; Kate Martin at the Center for National Security Studies; Jay Peterzell, formerly at CNSS; Kel McClanahan at National Security Counselors; Harry Hammitt at Access Reports; and Sidney M. Wolfe at Public Citizen all variously shared their expertise on the FOIA and domestic surveillance.

Several people kindly made available personal or organizational records: Kate Coleman, Ernie Lazar, Anne Weills, Suzanne Goldberg, Lynne Hollander, Michael Fellner, Irving Hall, Patrick Hallinan, Ronald M. Greenberg, Roz Payne, Diane Schroerluke,

Jerome Cohen, and Wendy Preuit. Edwin Meese III and Joanne Drake granted access to certain records of Governor Reagan. Steve Clark, Rob Cahalane, and Chris Hoeppner opened Socialist Workers Party files; Alan Lessik, Stephen McNeill, and Don Davis at the American Friends Service Committee and Christopher Densmore at the Friends Historical Library at Swarthmore College shared records on the AFSC.

I received valued help and encouragement from friends and colleagues: Tracy Freedman, Jack Sirica, Coimbra Maher Sirica, Laurie Goodstein, John Simon, David Fechheimer, Dianne Roxas, Zachary Fechheimer and Sam Fechheimer, Betty Medsger, Susan Orenstein, Dan Moldea, Karen Schryver, Danelle Morton, David Cay Johnston, Amanda Chapman, Peter Laufer, Seth Derish, David Friend, Christopher Cox, Jerry Mitchell, John Fleming, John Markoff, Leslie Terzian Markoff, Jane Hundertmark, John Murphy, Amelia Smith, Corinne Cadon, G. Pascal Zachary, Wendy Miller, Dan Hubig, Karlyn Barker, Naomi Schneider, Peter Scheer, Leonard Sellers, Henry Weinstein, Kristen Bender, Veronica Martinez, Naomi Marcus, Bruce Brugmann, Kirsten Soares, David Corn, Alex Kline, and Beverly Kees.

Thanks also to Jim Wilhelm, James Chanin, Ken Meade, Dan Siegel, Stew Albert, Judy Gumbo Albert, Michael Rossman, Jack Weinberg, Burton White, Burton Wolfe, Esther Concepcion, Crystal Hishida Graff, Michael Balter, Michael Krinsky, Peter Franck, Elena Broslovsky, Alan Copeland, Arthur Gatti, Chip Berlet, David D. Cole, Alisa Giardinelli, Katherine Silkin, Maureen Kawaoka, Mary Mocine, Ralph Nader, Michael Caudell-Feagan, and, at the ACLU of Northern California, Dorothy Ehrlich, Elaine Elinson, Stella Richardson, and John Crew.

I acknowledge the scholars upon whose work I particularly relied: on the FBI, Athan Theoharis, Richard Gid Powers, Curt Gentry, and Ovid Demaris; on Ronald Reagan, Lou Cannon, Garry Wills, Anne Edwards, Stephen Vaughn, Marc Eliot, and Bill Boyarsky; on Mario Savio and the FSM, Robert Cohen, Reginald Zelnik, David Goines, and Max Heirich; on the University of California and the city of Berkeley, Charles Wollenberg, John Aubrey Douglass, Todd Gitlin, W. J. Rorabough, and Clark Kerr (with Marian Gade and Maureen Kawaoka); on the civil rights movement, Taylor Branch, Clayborne Carson, David Garrow, and Nicolaus Mills; on the Red Scare in Hollywood, Ellen Schrecker, Larry Ceplair, Steven Englund, and Victor Navasky; and on California, Kevin Starr.

I am also beholden to my journalistic predecessors whose contemporaneous accounts were indeed the first rough draft of history.

Retired FBI agents M. Wesley Swearingen, Burney Threadgill, Jr., Wesley Grapp, George Dalen, William Turner, Curtis O. Lynum, Donald Kuno, Glenn Harter, Bill Fleming, and Joe Davidson, and retired associate director Cartha DeLoach, discussed the bureau under J. Edgar Hoover, as did the FBI's historian, John Fox. My thanks to Mary Threadgill for her kindness.

Several research assistants did great work: Jennifer Dawson, Robin Urevich, Jessica Ravenna, Robert Shaffer, Jessie Brown, Zachary Slobig, Martha Reifschneider, Hien Ngoc Nguyen, and Christine Shearer.

Athan Theoharis generously took time from his own work to read drafts and share his knowledge, as did Russell Schoch, Marian Gade, Charles Wollenberg, Suzanne Goldberg, Lynne Hollander, and Clark E. Kerr.

Over the decades, my research received much-appreciated support from the Fund for Investigative Journalism, the Stern Family Fund, the Deer Creek Foundation, W. H. Ferry, and Steve Silberstein.

Alice Fried Martell, my agent, is a pleasure to work with and was always there for me with expertise and inspiration. Thanks also to her assistant, Stephanie Finman.

I am honored to have as my publisher Farrar, Straus and Giroux, who were unfailingly supportive and deftly guided the book from proposal to publication. I am especially grateful to Jonathan Galassi, Sarah Crichton, and Susan Goldfarb (who saw it through); Paul Elie (who shared his insights on narrative writing); John Glusman (who acquired the book); Chantal Clarke, Denise Oswald, Daniel Piepenbring, Karen Maine, and Jonathan Lippincott—all made the book better in innumerable ways. My sincere thanks as well to Amanda Schoonmaker, Jeff Seroy, Nick Courage, and Brian Gittis.

Heidi Benson, my partner and fellow writer, read drafts, scoured files, and lived among multiplying stacks of boxes, all while sharing her great good humor. Pusyphus the cat sprawled across the once-secret FBI files on my desk as I typed.

Seth Rosenfeld
San Francisco
June 1, 2012

Index

Abbott, Burton W., 108–109, 553n
Abernathy, Ralph, 665n
Abrams, Floyd, 495
Academy Awards (Oscars), 109, 127, 128, 137
Acid Tests, 320, 337
Actors' Lab Theatre (Hollywood), 136
Adams, Carolyn "Mountain Girl," 337
Adams, Sherman, 524n
Ad Hoc Committee to End Discrimination, 175, 689
Adler, Margo, 204
Adventures of Ozzie and Harriet, The (television show), 323
affirmative action, 501
Afro-American Students Union (AASU), 428–29, 431
Air Force, U.S., 118, 447
Alameda County, 384, 411, 413, 478, 482, 656n; Anti-Racket Council, 33; Communist Party in, 14–15; Coroner, 474; Court, 311, 340, 390, 408, 466, 664n, 665n; District Attorney's Office, 33, 63, 219, 310, 340, 395, 396, 432, 486, 628n, 634n, 635n; Mayors Conference, 478; Naval Air Station, 310; Sheriff's Office, 270, 312, 365, 393, 434, 441–43, 452, 473–75, 477, 481, 493
Alaska, 160, 199
Albert, Joann, 386, 629n
Albert, Stew, 317, 365, 386, 402, 406, 426, 432, 449, 475, 489
Alcoholics Anonymous, 634n
Alien and Sedition Laws (1789), 518n
Allied Commission on Reparations, 252
All Quiet on the Western Front (film), 146
Alpert, Richard (Baba Ram Dass), 305
Altamont Speedway Free Festival, 448
Altman, Robert, 459
American Association of University Professors, 52, 191

American Association of University Women, 107
American Bar Association, 252
American Broadcasting Company (ABC), 225
American Civil Liberties Union (ACLU), 58, 240, 474
American Federation of Teachers (AFT), 440, 441
American Friends Service Committee (AFSC), 47, 531n
Americanism Education League, 64, 239
American Legion, 21, 30, 37, 41, 64, 68, 80, 86, 95–97, 136, 395; "Americanism Committees," 56, 64, 135
American Life, An (Reagan), 122, 139, 554n
American Nazi Party, 265, 305
American Prometheus (Bird and Sherwin), 27
American Revolution, 80, 115, 295, 327
Americans for Democratic Action, 93, 562n
American Veterans Committee, 120, 125–26, 132, 363
American Way of Death, The (Mitford), 201
Ames, Gen. Glenn C., 393, 438, 463, 476, 481, 659n
Amherst College, 407
Amish, 45
anarchists, 17, 392, 414, 446, 467
Andersen, Hans Christian, 145
Angel Island detention center, 71
Anglican Church (Church of England), 26, 46, 402
Anna and the King of Siam (film), 140
Another Country (Baldwin), 245
Anthony Adverse (film), 139
anti-Communism, 37–39, 52, 66, 79, 93, 125, 129, 131, 145, 234, 263; of Reagan, 140, 150, 179, 292–93, 333, 364, 467; of regents, 189; *see also* HUAC; John Birch Society; McCarthy, Joseph; *Tocsin*
Antioch College, 68–70, 515n

anti-Semitism, 121
antiwar movement, 4, 37, 48, 379, 403, 422,
    432, 444, 451; civil disobedience in, 268,
    272, 275, 391; draft opposed by, 364–65, 384,
    385, 415; FBI surveillance of, 349, 409, 439,
    603n; Johnson and, 387, 437; Kennedy and,
    341; at People's Park, 467, 470; police clashes
    with, 401; see also Vietnam Day Committee
Antonioni, Michelangelo, 445
Aoki, Jitsuji, 419
Aoki, Richard Masato, 418–24, 429, 432–35,
    441, 445–46, 511, 640n
Aoki, Shozo, 419
Aoki, Toshiko, 420
Apalachin (New York), meeting of mob leaders
    in, 297
apartheid, 501
Aptheker, Bettina, 204, 205, 225, 253, 254, 257,
    258, 266, 269, 307, 309, 312–14, 319, 386,
    589n, 594n
Aptheker, Herbert, 204, 253, 258, 312
Aquinas, St. Thomas, 396
Arciniegas, German, 637n
Arens, Richard, 80, 93
Argentina, 272
Army, U.S., 79, 95, 160, 275, 276, 326, 404,
    420, 437, 452, 458, 471, 478, 507; Air Corps,
    118–19, 121, 395, 557n; Castle Field Army
    Base, 41; 14th Cavalry Regiment, 117; Green
    Berets, 261, 307; Indians killed by, 451;
    intelligence, 24, 56, 204, 274, 392, 407, 481,
    631–32n, 641n; in Korea, 429; in Little Rock,
    428; Ninth Division, 452; Oakland
    Induction Center, 384–85; Presidio Army
    Base, 118; Reserve, 391, 393; Sixth, 481;
    326th Glider Infantry, 199; Venona Project,
    27; in Vietnam, 309, 481, 642n; during
    World War II, 13, 24, 118, 199, 202, 310, 328,
    395; see also National Guard
Arnold, Gen. Henry H., 557n
Artman, Charlie, 244
Asian American Political Alliance (AAPA),
    426–29
Asian Americans, 420, 446n
assassinations/plots by CIA, 235–37, 492, 593n;
    of civil rights leaders, 199, 412, 430; of
    Kennedy brothers, 158, 175, 198, 213, 229,
    415, 416, 469; of Martin Luther King, 412; of
    Medgar Evers, 199
Associated Press, 86, 92, 508
Atchison, Topeka, and Santa Fe Railway
    System, 550n
Atlanta, 251, 272; Democratic National
    Convention in, 185

atomic bomb, 4, 13, 25–26, 169, 515n, 522n;
    foreign development of, 28; tests of, 158, 233,
    249; see also nuclear weapons
Atomic Energy Act (1946), 362
Atomic Energy Commission, 40, 56, 163, 235,
    252, 364
"atom smasher," 13
Atthowe, Harold L., 393
Atthowe, Patricia, 310, 340, 393–400, 440
Auerbach, Richard, 63–65, 67, 88–89, 94–97,
    101, 105–110, 127–28, 539n
Austin, Curtis, 423
Austin, J. L., 188
Avalon, Paul (de Loqueyssie), 121

baby boomers, 62, 73, 158, 448, 473, 497
Bachman, Anthony, 642–43n
Backus, Georgia, 560n
Baez, Joan, 217, 266, 384, 632n, 643
Baier, Theodore, 485–86
Baldwin, James, 259
"Ballad of a Thin Man" (Dylan), 307, 407
Band, the, 307
Bank of America, 454, 462, 464
Bardacke, Frank, 449, 450, 462, 471, 475
Barger, Ralph H. "Sonny," 281, 306
Baron, Arthur S., 583n
Basic Opportunity Grant Program, 497
Bates, Charles, 387, 415
Battaglia, Phil, 378
Battle of Algiers, The (film), 430
Battle of the Bulge, 258
Baumgardner, F. J., 232–33
Bay Area Peace Action Council, 643n
Beach Boys, 307
Bay Area Student Committee for the Abolition
    of the House Un-American Activities
    Committee (BASCHUAC), 550n, 643n
Beall, William, 280–81
Beatles, 307, 366, 436
beatniks, 4, 79, 246, 248, 268, 448
Beauvoir, Simone de, 54
Beaux-Arts-style architecture, 13
Beavers, Michael W., 456, 656n
Bechtel, Stephen D., 234
Bechtel family, 235
Behavior Science Corporation (BASICO),
    330–33, 343
Belisle, John A., Jr., 589n
Bell, Daniel, 472
Bell, Griffin, 643n
Bellflower School District, 32
Belmont, Alan H., 104–106, 554n

Benny, Jack, 121, 368
Bergman, Lowell, 506
Berkeley, George, 12, 13, 62, 206, 357, 518n
Berkeley, University of California at, 13;
Academic Senate, 67, 223, 224, 227, 357,
366, 425, 435, 444, 466, 533n; Campanile,
13, 56, 461; Chicano Center, 432; Cowell
Hospital, 175, 459, 463; Doe Library, xii,
436, 441, 462; Drama Department, 440;
Educational Opportunity Program, 426, 427,
431; Friends of SNCC, 175, 191, 340; Greek
Theatre, xii, 62, 222, 224, 231, 249, 309, 321,
340, 344, 356, 416; Institute of Industrial
Relations, 50; Institute on Labor, Education
and World Peace, 37; Inter-Fraternity
Council, 340, 376; Moses Hall, 415, 449;
Newman Hall, 194; Pauley Ballroom, 238,
365, 376, 384, 386, 431; Plymouth Student
Center, 94; Psychedelic Information Service,
386; radiation laboratories, xii, 13–14, 23, 25,
56, 60, 249, 284, 329, 514, 515n,; Sather
Gate, xii, 37, 192, 211, 242, 418, 430, 432–34,
436, 440, 444, 462; Sexual Freedom Forum,
285, 340; Sproul Hall, xii, 153, 155, 158, 193,
195, 205, 212, 215–27, 243, 255, 268, 274,
275, 279, 300, 343, 347, 356, 380–81, 384,
390, 391, 394, 406, 408, 409, 418, 425, 441,
452, 471, 500, 502; student activism at, *see*
Free Speech Movement; Vietnam Day
Committee; Student Placement Office, 354;
Wheeler Auditorium, 440, 445
Berkeley Barb, 365, 406, 413, 449
Berkeley Citizens United, 394
Berkeley City Council, 470, 472
Berkeley Free Church, 470
Berkeley City Breakfast Club, 282
Berkeley Co-op, 208, 505
Berkeley Community Theater, 307, 480, 663n
Berkeley Daily Gazette, 257, 270, 271, 317,
318, 448
Berkeley Draft Information Committee, 364–65
Berkeley High School, 80, 420; East Campus,
458
Berkeley Police Department, 63, 107, 274, 279,
281, 318–19, 433, 464, 468, 469, 479, 480
Berkeley Realty Board, 394
Berkeley Tanometer, 410
Berlin Wall, 331
Berman, Jack, 101–103
Berrigan, Daniel, 169, 399
Berrigan, Philip, 169
Best Years of Our Lives, The (film), 127
Beverly, Helen, 574n
Beverly Hillbillies, The (television show), 323

Biberman, Herbert, 140
Bible, 42, 166, 344, 382
Biddle, Francis, 72, 564n
Biltmore Hotel (Los Angeles), 128, 359;
Biltmore Bowl, 335
Bird, Kai, 26
Bissell, Richard, 190, 579n
Bisson, Thomas A., 34–35, 535n
Black, Hugo, 543n
black bag jobs, 14, 21–22, 26, 29, 138, 141, 202,
257, 489, 492–93, 524n, 666n
blacklisting, 8, 58, 130, 135, 136, 139–40,
145–46, 202, 292, 387, 399, 524n, 535n,
557n, 560n, 563n, 566n
Black Panthers, 4, 382, 422–25, 435, 440, 445,
490, 644n; Aoki and arming of, 419, 423–24,
511, 640n; Carmichael and, 345, 346; FBI
and, 392, 403, 414, 415, 424, 445, 468, 642n,
660n; Peace and Freedom Party and, 411,
413; and People's Park, 468, 470, 480;
Sacramento field trip of, 380–81, 423; in
shootouts with police, 412, 423, 425
Black Power, 341–44, 346, 411, 468
blacks, 144, 158, 200, 420–21, 423, 434–35, 439,
441, 476, 497, 650n; activists, 342, 346, 379,
444, 473, 491 (*see also* Black Panthers; Black
Power; civil rights movement); at Berkeley,
428–31, 435, 646n; farmers, 179, 181, 458; in
urban riots, 334, 335, 341, 344, 359, 382, 412,
494; wage discrimination against, 158–59,
412
Black Tom (New Jersey) munitions depot, 113
Black Watch Delicatessen (Hollywood), 136
Blair, Betsy, 136
Blanchard, Alan, 457, 475, 476, 478, 483
Bloody Thursday, 462, 465, 468–69, 473, 478,
483
Blum, Joe, 266
Board of Regents, University of California, 4,
13, 34, 51–52, 55, 62–63, 74, 206, 351, 425,
440–43, 497, 527n, 591n; ban on political
activity on campuses, 157, 189–92, 194–95,
211–12; faculty and, 216, 405, 536n; FBI and,
5, 7, 66–67, 76, 250–51, 258, 283–84,
287–88, 328–30, 334, 354, 362, 439–40, 485,
505, 507; Hearst family members on, 38, 397,
527–28n; Kerr fired by, 496; Kerr proffers
resignation to, 249–50; and loyalty oath, 38,
44, 51–52, 55, 67, 191, 224, 515n, 534n, 578n;
Pauley on, 237–41, 286, 334; and People's
Park, 448–49, 461, 470, 471; Reagan and, 7,
327–30, 336, 360–61, 366–67, 369–80,
389–90, 416, 426, 435, 461, 485, 486; and
Sproul Hall sit-in, 220–30

Body and Soul (film), 127
Boeing Aircraft, 95
Bogart, Humphrey, 559*n*
Boggs, Hale, 491
Bohemian Club (San Francisco), 190
Bohm, David Joseph, 410, 522*n*
Bohnen, Roman, 560*n*
Bolsheviks, 19
Bolton, Earl, 58
Bonanno, Joseph "Joe Bananas," 297–300, 511, 607–608*n*
Bonanno, Joseph, Jr., 297–99, 511
Bonanno, Salvatore, 297
Bond, Ward, 145
Borah, Woodrow Wilson, 542*n*
Boraxo, 471
Boss, The (Theoharis and Cox), 16, 17
Boston: antiwar movement in, 272; Colonial-era, 46; federal court ruling against Hoover in, 18
Bower, Mrs. Harold K., 98
Boyarsky, Bill, 374
Boyd, Bud, 109
Boyd, Phil, 373
Boyd, William, 358
Boy Scouts of America, 32, 329, 525*n*
Branch, Taylor, 568*n*, 576*n*
Brand, Stewart, 337
Brandeis University, 646*n*
Braun, Judith, 145
Brennan, Charles, 371, 387
Brewer, Roy M., 125, 131, 137, 562*n*
Bridges, Harry, 20, 37, 56, 83, 88, 292, 395
Bridges, Lloyd, 130, 510, 560*n*
Brigadoon (musical), 163
Britain: 18, 36, 113, 201, 233, 238, 272, 291, 349, 400, 402
Broder, David, 607*n*
Brodeur, Arthur G., 542*n*
Bromberg, Joseph Edward, 130, 524, 560*n*
Brosnahan, James J., 466
Boston, 400
brothels, *see* prostitution
Brother Rat (film), 117, 556*n*
Browder, Earl, 73
Brown, Charles, 426, 429
Brown, Edmund G. "Pat," 69, 185, 241, 309, 313, 346, 351, 371, 379, 580*n*, 587*n*; Board of Regents appointees of, 240, 258, 374; and Free Speech Movement, 194–95, 215, 220, 222, 225, 227–28, 258–59, 391, 394; Hoover's antagonism toward, 5–6, 65–67, 298, 304, 371; Kerr supported by, 215, 230, 237, 250, 287–88, 372; Nixon's campaign against, 293, 359, 360; Reagan's defeat of, 4, 359, 368;

Reagan's gubernatorial campaign against, 3–4, 296, 298, 301, 304, 322–24, 326–28, 334–36, 340, 343, 344, 351, 387; and Vietnam Day Committee, 275, 283
Brown, Toni, 448
Brown, Willie, 222, 432
Brown v. Board of Education (1954), 33, 60, 179
Brownell, Herbert, Jr., 35
Browning, Charles, Jr., 121
Browning, Gordon, 524*n*
Browning, James, 482–83
Bruce, Lenny, 242, 246
Brussels, antiwar demonstrations in, 282
Bryan, Charles S., Jr., 108
Bryan, Stephanie, 108
Bryan, William Jennings, 607*n*
Bryant, Bob, 108–109
Bryn Mawr College, 513
Buckley, William F., Jr., 316, 334
Buddhism, 306, 380, 430
Bullock, Alan Louis Charles, 349–50
Bundy, Edgar, 612*n*
Bureau of Narcotics, U.S., 525*n*
Burger, Warren, 492
Burke, Webb, 67
Burnett, Frances Hodgson, 569*n*
Burns, Hugh M., 36–43, 52, 140, 190, 192, 250, 284, 312, 357, 376, 381, 528*n*; *see also* California Senate, un-American activities committee
Bursey, Charles, 644*n*
Burton, John, 222, 306–307, 467
Burton, Phil, 81
Byrne, William L., Jr., 298–99

Cable Splicer program, 437–38, 451, 460, 464, 480
Caen, Herb, 96
Cahill, Thomas, 86
Cal Conservatives for Political Action, 243, 244
Caleca, Vincent, 169, 573*n*
California: Board of Equalization, 393; Constitution of, 40, 51, 55; Crime Commission, 108; Emergency Planning Council, 451, 653*n*; Emergency Relief Administration, 50; Employment Office, 354; Highway Patrol, 392, 434, 436, 439, 441, 444, 451, 452, 454, 456, 461, 464; Internal Revenue Service, 486; Justice Department, 403, 451; Military Department, 437, 438, 451, 481; Motor Vehicle Department, 32; National Guard, 437, 442, 460, 476;

Supreme Court, 55, 486, 535*n*, 662*n*; *see also specific counties and municipalities*
California, University of (UC): Associated Students (ASUC), 78, 372, 376, 384, 453; Berkeley, *see* Berkeley, University of California at; Board of Regents, *see* Board of Regents, University of California; Davis, 210, 525*n*; Hastings College of the Law, 40; Los Angeles (UCLA), *see* UCLA; Master Plan for Higher Education, 73–76, 211, 229, 336, 375, 429, 497, 535*n*, 543*n*; Personnel Security Questionnaires, 241, 363–64, 532*n*; Police Department, 450; Press, 542*n*; San Diego, 605*n*, 673*n*; Santa Barbara, 34, 468, 525*n*, 626*n*
California Apartment House Owners Association, 301
California Idea and American Higher Education, The (Douglass), 75
California State Assembly, 55, 328, 381, 403, 411, 447, 490; Public Morals Committee, 39; Un-American Activities Committee, 36–37, 39
California Institute of Technology, 235, 536*n*
California Labor School, 37, 643*n*
California Monthly, 375
California Plan (Burns Committee), 57
California State Senate, 38, 189, 250, 424, 527*n*, 530*n*; un-American activities committee, 5, 36–49, 53–58, 65, 189, 201, 230, 250–51, 283, 303, 312, 321–23, 325–27, 330, 362, 363, 371, 535*n*, 537*n*
California Teachers Association, 77
Cal-Neva Lodge (Lake Tahoe), 490
Calvary Baptist Church (Monrovia, California), 98
Calvert, Gregory A., 638*n*
Cambodia, bombing of, 480
Cambridge University, 15
Campbell, Fred, 258
Camus, Albert, 174
Canada, 229, 383; antiwar movement in, 272
Canaday, John, 357
Cannon, Lou, 146, 302, 554–55*n*, 565*n*
capital punishment, 78, 80, 390
Capitol, U.S., 489, 491, 493
Capone, Al, 20
Captain Video and His Video Rangers (television show), 161
Cardinal Hayes High School (Bronx, New York), 314
Carmichael, Stokely, 340–46, 353
Carnegie Commission on the Future of Higher Education, 496, 497

Carnovsky, Morris, 560*n*
Carson, Johnny, 225
Carter, Edward, 230,
Carvel, Elbert, 524*n*
Cassady, Neal, 277
Castro, Fidel, 85, 210, 235, 236, 262, 377, 430
Catcher in the Rye, The (Salinger), 245
Catch-22 (Heller), 245
Catholics, 83, 100, 137, 159–62, 168–70, 173, 174, 194, 234, 396; Irish, 113; missionaries, 450
Catholic University, 550*n*
Catholic Worker, 317
Caute, David, 557*n*
Center for Investigative Reporting, 506
Central High School (Washington, D.C.), 16
Central Intelligence Agency (CIA), 109, 233, 247, 286–87, 292, 485, 619*n*; assassination plots of, 235–37, 491, 593*n*; Bay of Pigs invasion, 190, 235; domestic surveillance by, 398, 494; FBI collaboration with, 5, 198, 298, 334, 349, 386, 404, 484, 505, 622*n*; Kerr and, 189–90, 229, 579*n*
Ceplair, Larry, 141, 564*n*
Chaikoff, Israel L., 542*n*
Chamberlain, Howland, 127, 675*n*
Champlin, Charles, 247
Chandler, Dorothy Buffum, 239, 373–74
Chandler, Merle, 221
Chandler, Otis, 373
Chaney, James, 178, 186, 213
CHAOS (CIA operation), 619*n*
Chaplin, Charlie, 217
Chapman, Abe "The Trigger," 42
Charles, Ray, 305
Chavez, Cesar, 427, 665*n*
Cheit, Earl, 354, 615*n*
Chen, Edward M., 511
Cheng, Mike, , 641*n*
Chessman, Caryl, 78
Chevalier, Haakon Maurice, 24–26, 36
Chez Panisse (Berkeley), 320
Chiang Kai-shek, 73
Chicago, 32, 113, 199, 291, 526*n*, 550*n*; antiwar protests in, 272; Democratic Convention in, 401, 430; Mafia in, 490; Police Department, 402
Chicago Seven, 401, 471, 479, 636*n*
Chicago Sun-Times, 236
Chicago Tribune, 257, 608*n*
Chicanos, 426–28, 430, 646*n*
Chico (California), 451
China, 34, 36; Communist, 28, 34, 70, 233, 276, 316; Nationalist, 34

Chipman, Harold E., 398, 634*n*
Chotin, Arthur, 482
Christian Brothers, 165
Christian Church (Disciples of Christ), 113, 114
Christianity, 28, 48, 162
Christopher, George, 85, 298, 326, 335
Church, Frank, 177, 292, 492, 515*n*; Senate
    committee chaired by, *see* Church
    committee
Church committee, 177, 203, 213, 236–37, 273,
    349, 409, 415, 417, 500, 515–516*nn*, 523*n*,
    541*n*, 581*n*, 603*n*, 631*n*, 698
Churchill, Winston, 11, 518*n*
Church League of America, 612*n*
Cicero, 418
Cimmet, Jerry, 481, 482
Cincinnati, 32, 262; FBI Field Office in, 98
Cincinnati, University of, 32
Citizen Kane (film), 251, 528*n*
Citizens Party, 411
City Lights bookstore (San Francisco), 246, 317
Civic Center Park (Berkeley), 268, 279
civil disobedience, 190, 194, 196, 211, 212, 254,
    259, 264, 335, 346, 353, 409; in antiwar
    movement, 268, 272, 275, 391; in civil rights
    movement, 197, 342, 382, 461; *see also*
    nonviolence
Civil Rights Act (1964), 183, 228, 300, 303, 428,
    577*n*
civil rights movement, 127, 172–87, 191, 205,
    217, 242, 246, 262, 264–65, 295, 344–36,
    382, 406, 408, 587*n*; allegations of
    Communist infiltration of, 203, 213, 257–58;
    civil disobedience in, 197, 342, 382, 461;
    Kennedy's response to, 340–41, 344; school
    integration, 33, 60, 173, 179; sit-ins, 3, 78,
    173, 206, 223, 274, 279, 341, 353, 390, 418;
    socialists in, 422, 424; voter registration, 158,
    178–87, 342, 345, 353, 477; *see also specific*
    organizations
Civil Service, U.S., 524*n*
Claremont Men's College, 535*n*
Clark, Albert, 275
Clark, Mark, 607*n*
Clark, Tom, 72
Clavir, Judy (Judy Gumbo), 489, 629*n*, 666*n*
Cleaver, Eldridge, 411, 412, 423, 425–26, 430,
    449, 632*n*, 644*n*
Cleaver, Kathleen, 411
Cleaver, Margaret, 114, 116
Cloak and Dagger (film), 130
Cloke, Kenneth, 589
Cloke, Susan, 589
Clorox Company, 395, 396

Coakley, Frank, 274–76, 278, 283, 321, 390,
    474, 486, 553*n*
Coalinga College, 301
Coast Guard, U.S., 429
Cobb, Lee J., 130, 510, 560*n*
Coblentz, William, 240, 241, 443
Cody, Pat and Fred, 470
Cody's bookstore (Berkeley), xii, 433, 450, 461,
    470, 471
Cohe, Celia Anne, 589*n*
Cohelan, Jeffrey, 308, 319
Cohen, Allen, 380
Cohen, Meyer "Mickey," 41, 42, 109
Cohen, Robert, 160, 570*n*, 576*n*, 671*n*
COINTELPRO, 213–14, 275, 313, 396, 414–15,
    424, 485, 491, 492, 509, 514, 583*n*, 585*n*,
    603*n*, 606*n*, 644*n*, 655*n*, 673*n*
Cold War, 4, 5, 27, 28, 62, 72, 78, 119, 158, 164,
    199, 235, 246, 260, 262–63, 396, 509, 511,
    518*n*, 521*n*
Cole, Robert, 615*n*
College of the Holy Names, 393
Collier's Weekly, 134
Coltrane, John, 246
Columbia Broadcasting System (CBS), 583*n*,
    673*n*
Columbia University, 226, 405, 637*n*
Columbus, Christopher, 368
Combs, Richard Ennis, 40–41, 49, 53, 57–59,
    63, 190, 230, 250, 251, 283–84, 326, 330,
    396, 528–30*nn*, 532*n*, 534–35*nn*, 537*n*, 538*n*
Committee in Solidarity with the People of El
    Salvador (CISPES), 495
Committee to Uphold the Right to Travel, 422
Commoner, Barry, 411, 671*n*
Communist Infiltration of the Motion Picture
    Industry (COMPIC), 119–20, 129, 137, 141,
    514, 557*n*, 562–63*nn*
Communist Labor Party, 18
Communists, 4, 11, 25, 26, 29–32, 68–69, 73,
    80–81, 84, 89, 95, 144, 189, 201–202, 214,
    241, 251, 269, 284, 291, 294, 332, 382, 390,
    407, 414, 518*n*, 523*n*, 529*n*, 533*n*, 563*n*, 582*n*;
    accusations against Kerr, 56–57, 63, 190–91;
    230, 231, 283–84; in Asia, 28, 34, 300; on
    college faculties, suspicions of, 7, 11, 14–15,
    23, 24, 28, 29, 31–38, 42, 44, 51–52, 57, 65,
    68–69, 73, 241, 268, 285, 287, 322, 326, 485,
    514, 522–23*n*, 535*n*, 590*n*; in Europe, 164;
    FBI surveillance of, 14, 15, 17–27, 30, 31,
    40–41, 56, 68, 72, 90–95, 121–23, 129, 146,
    213, 230, 293, 401, 407, 421 516*n*, 522*n*,
    523*n*, 526*n*, 536*n*, 558*n*, 643*n* (*see also*
    COINTELPRO; "Communist Target—

Youth"; domestic surveillance); in film industry, allegations of, 8, 28, 119–27, 132–41, 143, 145, 147, 291–92, 564*n*, 581*n*, 606*n* (*see also* COMPIC); Free Speech Movement and, 208, 210–11, 213–14, 225–28, 232–33, 253–55, 257–59, 264, 265, 313, 464; infiltration of civil rights movement by, allegations of, 177, 183, 203–204, 213, 265; line of, 32, 127, 266, 284; national committee of, 14; suspected, persecution of, *see* blacklisting; sympathizers with, 72, 79, 123, 136, 210, 252, 378; Vietnam Day Committee and, 267, 272–73, 301, 313; W.E.B. Du Bois Club, 203, 643*n*; during World War II, 119, 231; youth conferences and organizations of, 93, 204, 422; *see also* anti-Communism
"Communist Target—Youth," 92–94, 98–99, 103–106, 110–12, 149, 150, 198, 232, 233, 328, 405, 475, 548*n*, 550*n*
COMPIC, 119–20, 129, 137, 141, 514, 557*n*, 562*n*, 563*nn*
Compromised Campus (Diamond), 524*n*
Concerned Stalinists for Peace, 449
Conference of Studio Unions (CSU), 125–27, 558*n*, 576*n*
Congregational Church, 48
Congress, U.S., 20–22, 72, 129, 136, 166, 173, 257, 397, 411, 481, 511; civil rights legislation in, 303 (*see also* Civil Rights Act; Voting Rights Act); COINTELPRO found illegal by, 414, 485; and Hoover's death, 489, 492; Joint Committee on Atomic Energy, 233; Freedom of Information legislation in, 495, 506; prosecution for contempt of, 138, 140, 189, 398; Republican control of, 128; during Vietnam War, 262, 301, 308, 319; *see also* House of Representatives, U.S.; Senate, U.S.
Congressional Cemetery, 492
Congress of Racial Equality (CORE), 78, 80, 153, 175–76, 213, 341, 643*n*
Connor, Bull, 173
Connors, Chuck, 323
Constitution, U.S., 51, 55, 145, 214, 224, 294, 302, 365, 428, 506, 533*n*; First Amendment, 81, 228; Fifth Amendment, 81, 139; Fourteenth Amendment, 228
Conte, Richard, 559*n*
cooperatives, 48–49; *see also* Berkeley Co-op
Copenhagen, antiwar demonstration in, 282
Copley News Service, 553*n*
Cornell University, 347
Costanoan Indians, 450, 451
Costello, Frank, 42

Cott, Lawrence, 278
Council of Campus Organizations (CCO), 356, 621*n*
Council of Federated Organizations (COFO), 180, 182, 183
Country Joe and the Fish, 279, 383
Courage of Lassie (film), 127
Court of Appeals, U.S.: 278; Ninth Circuit, 5, 299, 233, 239, 278, 507–509, 516*n*, 672–73*n*
Cow Palace (San Francisco), 157, 248, 322–23, 327, 517*n*
Cowley, Malcolm, 247
Crane, Les, 225
Creedence Clearwater Revival, 467
Crocker, Charles, 271
Cronyn, Hume, 127, 675*n*
Crosby, Bing, 352
Crying of Lot 49, The (Pynchon), 242
Cuba, 85, 189, 235–36, 262, 407, 637*n*; American-owned factories in, 312; Bay of Pigs invasion, 190, 235; Missile Crisis, 235; *see also* Fair Play for Cuba Committee
Cunningham, Thomas, 354, 356
Customs Service, U.S., 80
cyclotron, 13

Daily Californian, 53–54, 58, 61, 78, 80–81, 84, 96, 243, 244, 255, 256, 281, 313, 316, 320, 372, 376, 387, 427, 428, 430, 433, 434, 441–44, 449, 505, 626*n*
Dalen, George, 144–45, 293
Dales, Jack, 129, 141, 560*n*
Dallas, FBI field office in, 198
Dallet, Joseph, 15
Dalziel, Mary Louise, 395
Dane, Steve, 484
Dannenberg, Linda M., 638*n*
Dark Ages, 472
Darwin, Charles, 84
Da Silva, Howard, 127, 560*n*, 675*n*
Daughters of the American Revolution (DAR), 80, 98
Davidson, Carl A., 638*n*
Davis, Angela, 485, 665*n*, 673*n*
Davis, Don, 429
Davis, Rennie, 636*n*
Death of a Salesman (Miller), 130
Death of God, The (Vahanian), 168
Death Valley Days (television show), 297, 471
de Bonnis, John, 472
Dederich, Charles, 648*n*
Defense Department, U.S., 95, 486; *see also* Pentagon

DeFore, Don, 323
DeFremery Park (Oakland), 305, 306
de Havilland, Olivia, 123–24, 137, 562n
De La Beckwith, Byron, 199
Delacour, Mike, 447–49, 462
Delgado, Manuel Ruben, 427, 429–35, 641n,
 648n, 650n
Dellinger, Dave, 636n, 638n
DeLoach, Cartha "Deke," 64–70, 73, 93, 98,
 107, 110, 112, 146–47, 149–50, 231, 241, 252,
 258, 301, 304, 334, 364, 371, 404–405,
 485–87, 692
Demaris, Ovid, 16, 147
Democratic Party, 19, 70, 80, 93, 137, 173,
 263, 269, 292, 353, 412; all-white, in South,
 184, 345; in California, 4, 5, 39, 240, 298,
 306–307, 359, 368, 416; in Congress, 80,
 120, 253, 319, 327; of FDR, 20, 119, 159;
 liberals in, 5, 187, 258, 308, 639n; National
 Committee, 238, 240, 360; National
 Conventions, 185, 401, 430, 607n;
 presidential candidates of, 59, 146, 157, 173,
 184–85, 187, 228–29, 261, 291, 296, 574n;
 Reagan and, 8, 113, 119, 146, 291, 301–303,
 371, 424, 467, 490; see also Young
 Democrats
Dennis v. United States (1951),
Deputy Sheriff's Association, 478
Detroit, 32; riot in, 382
Detroit, University of, 646n
Dewey, Thomas, 121
Diamond, Sigmund, 524n
Dickson, Edward, 55
Didion, Joan, 54–55, 380
direct action, 154–55, 158, 175, 176, 216
Director, The (Demaris), 16, 147
Disney, Walt, 36, 293
Disneyland (Anaheim), 310
District Court, U.S., Northern California, 299,
 463, 466, 516n, 555n
Divale, William Tulio, 485, 643n, 665n
Dixon (Illinois), 113; High School, 128
domestic intelligence, 19–21, 23, 27, 94, 214,
 237, 396, 485, 493, 509, 518n, 520n, 523n; see
 also COINTELPRO; spying, domestic
Domino Theory, 262, 314
Dong, Harvey, 641n, 646n
Donovan, Robert, 482
Dos Passos, John, 170
Douglass, Frederick, 205
Douglass, John Aubrey, 74, 75, 543n
Dow Chemical Company, 399
Draklich, Colleen, 42
Draper, Harold, 594n

drugs, 3, 4, 242, 351, 371, 380, 396–97, 440,
 446; arrests for possession and use of, 247,
 414, 447; see also LSD; marijuana
Du Bois, W.E.B., 424
Duncan, Donald, 307
Dunckel, Earl, 142, 143
Dunker, Clarence W., 91
Dupuis, Fred, 127–29
Durant, Henry, 12, 13
Dutch, A Memoir of Ronald Reagan (Morris),
 554n
Dutton, Frederick G., 258, 449
Dyer, Glenn, 436, 456, 654–56nn
Dylan, Bob, 168, 266, 307–308, 462, 610n

Eagle Rock High School, 32, 525n
Early Reagan (Edwards), 554n, 556n
East Bay Police Departments, Subversive
 Details of, 312
Eaton, Cyrus, 66
Ebsen, Buddy, 323
Economic Club of New York, 387
Edson, Clarence, 472, 478, 482
Edwards, Anne, 115, 554n
Egleson, Nicholas M., 638n
Ehrenberger, Richard, 458–59, 478, 482
Eichmann, Adolf, 154
Einstein, Albert, 85, 163
Einstein, Evelyn, 85
Eisenhower, Dwight D., 33, 60, 85, 172, 173,
 203, 229, 234, 235, 261, 262, 283, 303, 428,
 523n, 590n
Elder, Walter, 236
El Dorado Hotel (Sacramento), 368, 437, 440
Electric Kool-Aid Acid Test, The (Wolfe), 338
Elks Club, 39, 121
Ellerbush, Eugene, 410
Ellingwood, Herb, 485–86, 491, 510, 662n
Elliot, Marc, 141
Ellis, H. Rex, 121
Ellis, Mary Jo, 560n
El Salvador, 671n
Eltenton, George, 11–12, 24–26, 36, 56
Emerson, Ralph Waldo, 163
Emery, Helen Gladys, 419
Emery, John, 419
England, see Britain
Englund, Steven, 141, 564n
Enlightenment, 472
Episcopal Diocese of California, 419
Ergo (play), 440
Esquire magazine, 338
Ettelson, Lee, 108

Eureka College, 3, 114–17, 159, 327, 369, 388, 556n
Evers, Medgar, 199
Excepted Service, U.S., 524n
Executive Order 10450, 363

Face the Nation (television show), 494
Fairmont Hotel (San Francisco), 234, 271, 272, 307
Fair Play for Cuba Committee, 203, 643n
Fanon, Frantz, 424
Fariña, Mimi, 643n
Farish Street Baptist Church (Jackson, Mississippi), 182
Farmer, James, 213, 665n
Farmer, Virginia, 560n
fascism, 15, 21, 22, 36, 50, 71, 86, 119, 160, 169, 201, 224, 267, 363, 496, 554n
Faubus, Orval, 173, 428
FBI, The (television show), 147, 566n
FBI Story, The (film), 147
Federal Bureau of Investigation (FBI), 20, 42, 67, 186, 199, 259; Administrative Index (ADEX), 499, 542n; American Legion cooperation with, see American Legion; black bag jobs of, 21, 26, 138, 141, 202, 257, 489; Central Records System, 22; CINRAD, 23, 514, 557n; COMINFIL investigations, 177; "Communist Target—Youth" report, see "Communist Target—Youth"; COMPIC investigation, see COMPIC; Counter Intelligence Program, see COINTELPRO; Crime Records Division, 64, 147; Custodial Detention Program, 71–72; Domestic Intelligence Division, 105, 493 (see also domestic surveillance); "Faculty Involvement in New Left Activities" program, 485; field offices of, see FBI Field Office under specific cities; FOIA lawsuits against, xi, 4–5, 229–30, 233, 239, 446, 492, 505–12, 516nn, 581n, 605–606nn, 674n, 689; General Index, 29, 68; Government Relations office, 508; headquarters of, 184, 234, 246, 252, 319, 349, 362, 364, 370, 417, 485, 511; illegal break-ins conducted by, 11, 21, 29, 68, 124, 129, 145, 489, 493–94 (see also black bag jobs); informers of, see informers; Internal Security Section, 387; Key Activist Program, 409, 411, 414, 417, 638n; Mass Media Program, 107; National Academy, 53, 310; Permanent Symbol Numbers, 563n, 611n; "Project: Revolution in San Francisco," 89; Records Management

Division, 509; Reserve Index, 254, 287, 353, 407, 605n; Responsibilities Program, 28–35, 38, 57, 59, 240, 362, 399, 517n, 526n, 582n; Security Index, 71–73, 89, 200–201, 227, 254, 269, 287, 407, 413, 541nn, 542n, 582–83nn, 589n, 605n, 622n; STAG program, 439; "Subversive Activities at the University of California, Berkeley" report, 4, 287; surveillance and harassment of suspected subversives by, see specific groups, movements, and organizations; see also Hoover, J. Edgar
Federal Communications Commission (FCC), 274, 282
Feinstein, Dianne, 508n, 517n, 673n
Felt, Mark, 489, 493
feminists, 54, 444, 651n
Ferber, Mark F., 404
Ferlinghetti, Lawrence, 246, 307, 317
Ferrari, Vincent, 457
Fields, W. C., 40
Filipinos, 427, 646n
Filippone, John, 149, 567n
Filthy Speech Movement, 242–51, 255, 283, 285, 323, 324, 327, 328, 336, 354, 370, 595n
Finch, Robert, 6, 370, 372
Findley, Tim, 464, 465
Finley, Roland, 251
Firing Line (American Legion newsletter), 65
First Amendment Project, 509
First Father, First Daughter (Reagan), 149
Fisher, James, 194
Fishman, Irving, 80
Fitzgerald, F. Scott, 170
Fleming, Ian, 244, 245
Flemming, Elena, 594n
Flexner, Abraham, 207
Florez, Ernesto Tapia, 171
Floyd, Charles "Pretty Boy," 20
Folsom Prison, 425
Fontenrose, Joseph, 67
Foray, June, 560n
Ford, Gerald R., 506n
Ford, John, 137
Fort Ord, 420
Foster, John, 182
Foster, Preston, 137, 562n
Founding Fathers, 309, 494
Fowler, Glenn D., 310–11, 611n
Fox, Charles, 311, 396
Fox, George, 46
Fragile X Syndrome, 355, 620n
France, 26, 233, 622n
Franck, Peter, 278

Francke, Allan, 459, 478, 482
Franklin, Benjamin, 44
Franklin & Marshall College, 44
Fraternal Order of Eagles, 39
Frawley, Patrick, Jr., 312
Freed, Donald, 673n
Freud, Sigmund, 347
Freedom House (Mileston, Mississippi), 178–84
Freedom of Information Act (FOIA; 1966),
  397, 497, 506, 554–55n, 559n, 562nn, 567n,
  609n, 628n, 642n; Atthowe's denunciation
  of, 398; Hoover's view of, 508; information
  deleted from documents released under,
  299, 440; lawsuits to gain access to FBI
  records under, xi, 4–5, 229–30, 233, 239,
  446, 492, 505–12, 516nn, 581n, 605–606nn,
  674n, 689; Reagan's curtailment of, 495
Freedom Rides, 175, 341
Freedom Schools, 186
Freedom's Orator (Cohen), 160, 567n, 570n,
  576n, 637n, 661n
Free Speech Movement (FSM), 3, 4, 248, 262,
  295, 334, 343, 356, 364, 377, 408, 416, 444,
  491, 499, 581n, 672n; anniversary
  commemoration of, 501, 502; Atthowe's
  denunciation of, 394–95; Board of Regents
  response to, 251–52, 330; Council of
  Campus Organizations and, 356–58; FBI
  investigations and harassment of, 6, 7, 198,
  200, 203–204, 226–28, 232–33, 237, 240,
  241, 252–59, 265, 283, 304, 312–13, 395–96,
  415, 505, 507, 510, 515–17nn, 581n; Filthy
  Speech Movement and, 242–44, 255;
  Graduate Coordinating Council, 347;
  incidents precipitating, 153–71, 186–98,
  204–205, 210–11, 215, 220, 239, 263, 279,
  301, 372, 389, 416, 422, 500; nonexclusionary
  policy of, 303; Pasadena, 640n; Peace and
  Freedom Party and, 413, 415, 447; People's
  Park and, 449, 453, 470, 471, 475; Reagan's
  antagonism toward, 6, 7, 300–302, 370, 387,
  464; Sproul Hall rally of, 205–15, 453; Sproul
  Hall sit-in of, 216–27, 268, 274, 344, 391;
  Third World Liberation Front and, 418, 429;
  Vietnam Day Committee and, 262–66, 284
Free Speech Movement, The (Goines), 243,
  535n, 584n, 586n
Fresno (California), 5, 36, 39, 41–42, 301, 365;
  High School, 39
Fretter, William B., 355
Frey, John, 413, 423
Frog Jumping Jubilee, 451
Froines, John, 636n
Frye, Marquette, 335

Fund for the Improvement of Post-Secondary
  Education, 497

Gain, Charles, 385
gambling, 41–42, 297, 490
Gandhi, Mohandas K., 175, 197, 217
Gandy, Helen, 489
Garcia, Jerry, 339, 467
Garfield, John, 127, 134
Garfield Junior High School (Berkeley), 411
Garry, Charles, 102–104
Garson, Barbara, 589–90n, 594n
Garthwaite, Terry, 448
Garvey, Marcus, 424
Gatti, Arthur, 161–64, 167–69, 171, 413
Gee, Emma, 427
Gee, Neville, 532n
Gelbspan, Ross, 636n
General Dynamics, 447
General Electric (GE), 142, 179, 293, 549n
General Electric Theater (television show), 112,
  143, 148, 150, 293, 510
Geneva Accords, 267
George III, King of England, 340
George Washington University, 17
Georgia Power Company, 397
Gerassi, John, 415, 638n
Germany, 390; in World War I, 17; in World
  War II, 521n
Gerner, Henry, 99
Gestapo, 491, 535n, 554n
Giancana, Salvatore "Sam," 236, 490
Gibson, Jim, 345
Gibson, Julie, 560n
Gilbert, Jody, 560n
Gilbert, John Young, 525n
Ginsberg, Allen, 4, 242, 246, 247, 266–68, 276,
  278, 280, 305–307, 380, 500, 596n
Gipp, George, 131
Girl Scouts of the United States of America, 98
Gitlin, Todd, 385, 628n, 657n
Giubbini, Walter, 100–104, 110
Gleason, Ralph, 225, 308
Glenn, Claude D., 281
Glusman, Paul, 449, 462
Godel, Eda Toni, 590n
Goines, David, 208–209, 211, 244–45, 535n,
  584n, 586n
Goldberg, Art, 203, 205, 244, 449, 462, 475, 586n
Goldberg, Arthur, 309
Goldberg, Charles, 347
Goldberg, Jackie, 196, 217, 245, 499, 586n
Goldberg, Nettie, 347

Goldberg, Suzanne: *see* Savio, Suzanne
  Goldberg
Goldblatt, Lee F., 594*n*
Gold and the Blue, The (Kerr), 497
Golden Gate Park (San Francisco), 380
Goldfinger (film), 244
Golding, William, 245
Goldman, Emma, 17–18
Gold Rush, 12, 390
Goldwater, Barry, 136, 157, 174, 184, 228, 248,
  261, 294, 296, 301, 302, 322, 439, 568*n*,
  607*n*, 667*n*
Gone With the Wind (film), 123
Goodman, Andrew, 178, 186, 213
Goodman, Paul, 276
Goodrich, Marcus, 137
Gospels, 162
Göttingen University, 15
Gough, Lloyd, 127, 560*n*, 563*n*, 675*n*
Governor Reagan (Cannon), 146, 555*n*
Graff, Freddy, 560*n*
Graham, Barbara, 109
Graham, Bill, 467
Graham, Billy, 92; Crusade, 202
Grandmothers for Peace, 266, 306
Grant, Allan, 372, 374
Grapp, Wesley M., 239–41, 284, 286, 287, 360,
  363–64, 594*n*, 692*n*
Grateful Dead, 248, 337, 380, 467
Great Crash (1929), 20
Great Depression, 15, 20, 37, 46, 48, 54, 113, 208
Greater Los Angeles Press Club, 300
Great Surprise, The, 320
Greece, 622
Greenberg, Ronald M., 483–84, 657*n*
Greene, David, 509, 510, 675*nn*
Green Party, 411
Greensboro (North Carolina) lunch counter
  sit-ins, 78, 173
Greenwich Village (New York City), 168,
  245, 266
Gregory, Dick, 276–78
Groves, General Leslie, 38
Growing (Up) at 37 (Rubin), 600*n*
Growing Up Absurd (Goodman), 276
Guevara, Che, 262, 280
Guilty Bystander (film), 130
Gulf of Tonkin Resolution, 261–62
Gullahorn, Barbara, 262, 272, 600*n*
Guthrie, William, 118–19, 556–57*n*

Hafner, Richard, 187
Haines, Fred, 82–84, 543*n*

Haldeman, H. R., 360–62, 373
Hall, Irving, 93, 94
Hall, Theodore, 27
Hall, Thomas Charles, Jr., 525*n*
Halliburton Company, 549*n*
Hallinan, Conn "Ringo," 280, 590*n*, 594*n*
Hallinan, Matthew, 319
Hallinan, Terence, 319
Hallinan, Vincent, 83–84, 319, 612*n*
Halliwell, Steven E., 638*n*
Halvonik, Paul, 463
Hamilton, Steve, 365, 406
Hammer, Alvin, 560*n*
Harawitz, Eleanor, 590*n*
Hardy, David M., 642*n*
Harris, Joseph Amos, 594*n*
Harter, Glenn A., 3, 6, 7, 251, 370
Harvard University, 4, 15, 32, 62, 206, 226, 247,
  305, 331, 336, 340, 376
Harvard Crimson, 589*n*
Hawks, Howard, 127
Hayden, Sterling, 137
Hayden, Tom, 404, 409, 432, 471, 636*n*, 637*n*,
  638*n*
Hayward, Susan, 109
Healey, Dorothy, 637*n*
Healey, Richard Erle, 637*n*
Health, Education and Welfare (HEW), U.S.
  Department of, 231, 251, 591*n*
Health Education Centers, 497
Heanes, Herbert, 423
Hearst, Catherine Wood Campbell, 251, 284,
  330, 366, 397, 399
Hearst, George, 527*n*
Hearst, Phoebe Apperson, 62, 527*n*
Hearst, Randolph Apperson, 251, 528*n*
Hearst, William Randolph, 52, 251, 527–28*n*
Hearst Corporation, 84, 107, 251, 397,
  508, 528*n*
Heaven and Hell (Huxley), 261
Hellcats of the Navy (film), 142
Hell's Angels, 280–82, 301, 305–307, 338,
  451, 470
Hell's Angels (Thompson), 281
Heller, Elinor Haas, 240, 241
Heller, Joseph, 245
Helms, Richard, 236, 593*n*
Hemingway, Ernest, 170
Hendrix, Jimi, 495, 677*n*
Hepburn, Katharine, 126–27, 136
Herodotus, 170
Herrick Hospital (Berkeley), 462
Hershey, Gen. Lewis Blaine, 430
Hess, Steven, 607*n*

Hesse, Herman, 351
Heyns, Roger, 275, 309, 354–58, 365, 366, 384, 386, 426, 431–32, 434, 435, 440, 444–45, 448–50, 470, 602*n*, 621*n*,
Hicks, Louis, 57, 230
Highlights of a Lowlife (Melvin), 643*n*
Hill, David, Jr., 298, 607*n*
Hill, Gladwin, 387
Hilliard, David, 644*n*
Hillside Junior High School (Queens, New York), 162
Hinckle, Warren, 394
hippies, 4, 267, 322, 352, 379–80, 447, 450, 452, 454, 465, 470, 472
Hippocratic Oath, 626*n*
Hiroshima, 419; atomic bombing of, 11, 169
Hitch, Charles, 404, 427, 649*n*
Hitler, Adolf, 201, 285, 491
Hoblit, Harold, 201, 257, 461
Ho Chi Minh, 430
Hoffman, Abbie, 317, 636*n*
Hoffman, Alex, 257, 348
Hoffmann, Albert, 247
Holden, Ken, 331–33
Holland, Tom, 560*n*
Hollander, Lynne, *see* Savio, Lynne Hollander
Holliday, J. S., 12
Hollywood Independent Citizens Committee of the Arts, Sciences and Professions (HICCASP), 120, 132
Hollywood Legion Stadium, 125, 128
Hollywood Park horse-racing track, 42
Hollywood Reporter, The, 139
Hollywood Ten, 138, 140
Hollywood Writers' Mobilization, 37
Holocaust, 167
homosexuality, 22, 73, 312, 396, 521
Honor Thy Father (Talese), 297
Hood, John, 188
Hood, Richard B., 121, 129, 136
Hoover, Annie (JEH's mother), 16
Hoover, Dickerson (JEH's father), 16
Hoover, J. Edgar, 14–23, 26–36, 102–12, 164, 208, 247, 319, 328–29, 358, 419–21, 479, 485, 514–17*nn*, 522*n*, 525*n*, 526*nn*, 530*nn*, 550*nn*, 559*n*, 564*n*, 606*n*, 614*n*; activists targeted by, 253, 257, 258, 269–70, 312–14, 386, 407, 409, 413–15, 424, 425; American Legion support for, 56; and antiwar movement surveillance and harassment, 270–73, 275–76, 282, 286, 311–17, 409–10; ascent of, 18–20; biographies of, 16; birth of, 16; and Burns committee, 40–43, 59, 371, 530*n*; childhood and adolescence of, 16–17; Church

Committee criticism of, 177, 203, 409, 516*n*, 523*n*; CIA cooperation with, 349; and civil rights movement, 177, 178, 183–84, 186, 213, 265, 484, 585*n*, 650*n*; criticized by former agents, 201; death of, 489, 491–92, 499, 594*n*; and essay question inquiry, 63–73, 76, 198; film and television depictions of FBI controlled by, 147–50; Filthy Speech Movement denounced by, 246; Freedom of Information Act denounced by, 508; and Free Speech Movement investigation, 197, 203–204, 212, 220, 225–28, 232–34, 240, 241, 252–53, 255, 257–59, 265; HUAC and, 88–90, 92–100, 102–12, 198, 401, 547*n* (*see also* "Communist Target—Youth"); illegal surveillance advocated by, 11, 14, 15 (*see also* COINTELPRO; domestic intelligence; wiretaps); Kesey targeted by, 338, 339; Kerr vilified by, 229–31, 237, 250, 283, 285, 287–88, 395, 505, 506, 508, 511; in law school, 17; movie industry investigated by, 564*n* (*see also* COMPIC); and organized crime, 297–99, 582*n*; and Palmer raids, 17–19; Pauley provided information by, 239–41, 286–87, 443; Reagan and, 3–8, 128–30, 134, 137, 148–49, 291–92, 298–99, 301, 303–304, 333–34, 359–60, 370–72, 378, 387–88, 404–405, 409, 438, 439, 487, 490–91, 508, 511, 517*n*; during Roosevelt administration, 19–22, 203; rules and requirements for field agents imposed by, 144, 199–200, 269–70, 386, 524*n*, 582*n*; Senators and, 16; Soviet spying suspected by, 4, 11–12, 23, 26–27, 36; speech defect of, 30, 163; and Third World Liberation Front investigation, 418; Tolson's relationship with, 16, 19, 22, 489, 492, 521*n*; *see also* Federal Bureau of Investigation
Hopkins, Mark, 271
Hopper, Hedda, 304
Horne, Victoria, 560*n*
Horowitz, David, 172, 550*n*
Houchins, Thomas, 442, 455, 458, 474, 476, 480, 483
House of Representatives, U.S.: Appropriations Subcommittee, 253; Oversight and Investigations Subcommittee, 397; Un-American Activities Committee, *see* HUAC
Hoving, Thomas P. F., 470
Howard University, 341
"Howl" (Ginsberg), 246
HUAC 28, 56, 77–100, 191, 201, 312, 401, 513, 543*n*, 549*n*, 560*n*; FBI coordination with, 8,

56, 548n; film industry investigated by, 8, 128–30, 135–40, 559n; mission of, 77; protests against San Francisco city hall hearings, 4, 77–103, 108, 110, 112, 126, 150, 172–75, 188–89, 198, 205, 212, 217, 232, 310, 327, 421, 494, 517n; state versions of, 37 (*see also* California State Senate, un-American activities committee)
Hubbard family, 185
Hubler, Richard, 554n
Huichin tribe, 12, 368
Hull, R. E., 450, 452, 462
Human Be-In, 380
Humphrey, Hubert, 196, 228–29, 302, 307, 308
Huntington, Collis P., 271
Hurwitt, Rob, 225, 266, 274, 278–81, 307, 309, 318, 352, 568n, 587n
Hutchin, Mona, 207
Hutton, Bobby, 412, 423
Huxley, Aldous, 78, 247

I. F. Stone's Weekly, 263
IBM, 72, 222,
Ichioka, Yuji, 427
Ickes, Harold, 238
Iiyama, Patti, 210, 584n
I Lived Inside the Campus Revolution (Divale), 507, 643n
immigrants, 17–18, 56, 71, 113, 136, 159, 160, 169, 341, 390; illegal, 501
Immigration and Naturalization Service, U.S., 148, 349
Indians, *see* Native Americans; *specific tribes*
Information Digest, 402, 403
Informer, The (film), 137
informers, 15, 17, 18, 29, 69, 71, 84, 93, 96, 198, 200, 230, 304, 362, 407, 440, 468, 495, 507, 511, 557n, 562–63nn, 642–44nn, 665n (*see also* Aoki, Richard); American Legion members as, 30, 41; Burns committee and, 42; campus, 5, 55, 95, 250, 273–74, 310, 329–33, 386, 471, 507, 534n, 557n (*see also* Bachman, Anthony; Jones, Hardin Blair; Melvin, Milan; Rees, John Herbert; Sherriffs, Alex; Sparrow, John); in Communist Party, 56–57, 84, 230, 254, 293, 407; Hollywood, 120, 136, 139, 141 (*see also* Reagan, Ronald); police, 400, 494
Inquisition in Hollywood, The (Ceplair and Englund), 141
Institute for Policy Studies, 403
Intel Science Talent Search, 569n
Internal Revenue Service (IRS), 108, 142, 415

Internal Security Act (1950), 72, 518n, 528n, 541–42n
International Alliance of Theatrical and Stage Employees (IATSE), 125
International Association of Chiefs of Police, 65
International Longshore and Warehouse Union, 20, 417
International Mathematical Union Fields Medal, 361
Intrepid Trips, Inc., 277
Iowa Test of Basic Skills, 161
Irvin, Sam, 491
Irving, Carl, 187, 568n
Isabella, Queen of Spain, 368
Israel, 396, 452
Italian Federation, 467
Italy, 159, 349, 622n
Ivanov, Peter, 23–26, 36
I Want to Live! (film), 109
I Was a Spy (Miller), 293

J. Edgar Hoover, Sex and Crime (Theoharis), 521n
Jackson, Robert, 71
Jackson (Mississippi), 187, 342
Jackson Clarion-Ledger, 179, 184
Jackson State College, 480
James, Maria-Elena, 511
Japan, 248; antiwar protests in, 272; in World War II, 119, 163, 169, 198, 235, 419
Japanese Americans, 419–21, 423, 427, 641n, 642n
Jazz Workshop (New York), 247
Jefferson, Thomas, 133, 138
Jefferson Airplane, 320, 380, 467
Jensen, D. Lowell, 391, 475
Jesus, 164, 168, 170, 202, 430, 470
Jews, 54, 160, 341; German, 15
Jim Crow segregation, 16, 175, 177
John Birch Society, 96, 98, 283, 293, 298, 303–305, 336, 403, 606n
Johnny Belinda (film), 561n
Johnny Got His Gun (Trumbo), 37
Johnson, Leonard, 483
Johnson, Lyndon, 237, 264, 382, 388, 437, 439, 506, 590n, 591n, 667n; civil rights supported by, 183, 484; FBI background checks on potential appointees of, 229–31, 239, 252, 496; reelection campaign of, 157, 184–85, 228–29, 261, 296; and Vietnam War, 260–62, 268, 271, 273, 285, 286, 307–309, 348, 387, 639n

Johnson, Paul, 186
Johnson, Wallace, 467
Joint Anti-Fascist Refugee Committee, 132
Joint Chiefs of Staff, 271
Jolson Story, The (film), 127
Jones, Donald Edwin, 188–90, 202–204, 208, 211, 213, 219–20, 227, 253, 257, 265, 269–70, 273, 284–85, 327, 330, 332, 349–51, 353, 378, 380, 386, 387, 407, 409–11, 413, 417, 421, 439, 440, 446, 495
Jones, Everett Lee, 68–70
Jones, Hardin Blair, 248–51, 284–87, 329–33, 335, 378, 386, 396, 440, 605*n*, 650*n*
Jones, Harry, 68
Jones, Helen, 650*n*
Jones, Mary Elizabeth "Boots," 68–70
Joy of Cooking (rock band), 448, 449
Juke Girl (film), 127
Junior Chamber of Commerce, U.S., 391
Justice Department, U.S., 17–19, 26, 28, 71, 72, 100, 204, 237, 274, 299, 318, 382, 477–79, 482–85, 490–92, 509, 522*n*, 563*n*; Alien Enemy Bureau, 17; Bureau of Investigation, 19 (*see also* Federal Bureau of Investigation); Civil Rights Division, 482, 484

Kagel, Sam, 230, 591*n*
Kaiser, Henry J., 235
Kaiser Aluminum, 399
Kalisch, Eleni P., 673*n*
Kappa Sigma fraternity, 47
Katz, Eli, 683*n*
Kaufman, Robert Paul, 590*n*, 594*n*
KCBS radio station (San Francisco), 107, 273
Kearney, John, 492, 493
Kefauver, Estes, 74, 108
Keith, George H., 312
Kelley, George "Machine Gun," 20
Kelley, John L., 615*n*
Kelly, Gene, 136
Kennedy, John F., 173–74, 194, 258, 293, 476, 574*n*, 590*n*; assassination of, 158, 175, 198, 213, 229, 236; civil rights speech of, 340–41, 344, 346; and Cuban missile crisis, 235; Hoover and, 99, 203, 297, 523*n*; presidential campaign and election of, 146, 173, 291, 574*n*; and Vietnam War, 261, 262
Kennedy, Laurence, Jr., 374, 378
Kennedy, Robert F., 415–17, 430, 468, 523*n*, 617*n*, 639*n*
Kenney, Gen. George C., 557*n*
Kent, Arthur, 529*n*
Kent State University, 448, 480

Kerouac, Jack, 246–48, 277
Kerr, Caroline Clark (CK's mother), 44
Kerr, Catherine "Kay" Spaulding (CK's wife), 48, 62, 252
Kerr, Clark, 44–63, 249–59, 340, 391, 394, 472, 496–97, 532*nn*, 537*nn*, 538*n*, 542*n*, 576*n*, 579*n*, 591*n*; birth of, 45, 113; and Board of Regents, 249–52, 258, 361, 366, 372–75; and Burns committee, 52–54, 57–59, 321–22; campus expansion plan of, 448; at Carnegie Commission on the Future of Higher Education, 496, 497, 559*n*; as chancellor of UC Berkeley, 44, 54–62, 188, 515*n*; childhood of, 44–46; and CIA, 189–90, 579*n*; education of, 46–47, 159, 163; family background of, 44–45; FBI investigations of, 7–8, 11, 56–57, 63, 64, 88, 203–204, 254, 258, 259, 329–30, 354, 378, 392, 496, 505–508, 516*n*, 522*nn*; firing of, 372–80, 387, 443; and Free Speech Movement, 188–97, 209–17, 220–28, 251–52, 257–58, 357, 501; graduate studies of, 48, 49; Hoover's antipathy toward, 7–8, 64, 73, 97, 203, 204, 229–31, 237, 250, 259, 283, 285, 287–88, 291, 304, 362, 371–72, 505, 506, 508; inaugurated as president of University of California, 62–63; and loyalty oaths, 44, 51–52 55, 140, 430*n*, 534*n*; as "Machiavellian Quaker," 50, 249; marriage and family of, 48, 62; Master Plan for Higher Education, 73–76, 211, 229, 336, 375, 429, 497, 535*n*, 543*n*; multiversity vision of, 206–207; and panty raids, 60–61; in Peace Caravans, 47, 142, 143, 179, 531*n*; Quaker religion of, 46–48, 55, 161, 533*n*; Reagan's hostility toward, 7–8, 301, 323, 328, 332, 336, 360, 369–74, 377–78, 388–89, 392, 469, 517*n*; Savio's critique of, 206, 207, 376–77; Sherriffs and, 188–92, 194, 197, 204, 220, 228, 251, 330, 378, 389; and student involvement in HUAC protest, 87, 88, 95; and Vietnam Day Committee, 275, 282–88, 301, 309, 313, 320; during World War II, 50
Kerr, Samuel (CK's father), 44, 47
Kerr, William (CK's half brother), 531*n*
Kesey, Ken, 247–48, 277–78, 281, 305–308, 320, 337–39
KGO-TV, 339
Khrushchev, Nikita, 85, 99, 201
Kierkegaard, Søren, 254
Killian, Victor, 560*n*
King, Coretta Scott, 665*n*
King, Martin Luther, Jr., 158, 175, 213, 265, 342, 381–82, 412, 415, 430, 500, 585*n*, 632*n*, 665*n*

Kings Row (film), 118, 562*n*
Kinney, Douglas, 102
Kissinger, Clark, 638*n*
Kiwanis Club, 98
Kleindienst, Richard, 489
Knight, Goodwin, 251, 553*n*
Knowland, William F., 226, 359, 568*n*
Knowles, Harper, 56, 68, 278, 312, 395, 396
Knox, Alexander, 126, 128, 689*n*
Knute Rockne, All American (film), 117, 127
Kohler, Walter, Jr., 524*n*
Kollwitz, Käthe, 410
Korean War, 28, 30, 52, 72, 135, 142, 146, 429
KPFA radio station (Berkeley), 82, 260, 348,
  469, 543*n*, 599*n*
KQED radio station, 308
Kragen, Adrian, 95–96
Krassner, Paul, 262. 317
Kress stores, 78
Ku Klux Klan, 158, 178, 265, 305, 576*n*
Kuno, Donald, 105, 552*n*
Kunstler, William, 636*n*
Kurzweil, Jack, 590*n*

Labor League of Hollywood Voters, 139
Labor-Management Advisory Committee, 229
labor unions, *see* unions
Labor Youth League, 422
Ladar, Jerrold, 274
Ladd, Milton "Mickey," 541–42*n*
Lady Chatterley's Lover (Lawrence), 244
Lamborn, Robert, 395–400, 404
land grant colleges, 13, 207
Lang, Serge, 405
Lange, Dorothy, 49, 532*n*
Laporte, Elizabeth D., 509, 674*n*
Larsen, General Stanley R., 392–93, 481
Last Chicano, The (Delgado), 641*n*
Las Vegas, 142, 490
Latinos, 418, 646*n*
Lausche, Frank, 524*n*
Lawrence, D. H., 244
Lawrence, Ernest O.,13, 249
Lawrence, Mark, 560*n*
Lawson, John Howard, 124
Lazar, Ernie, 609*n*
League for Industrial Democracy, 532*n*
League of Nations, 47
Leahy, Patrick, 508
Leary, Timothy, 247, 372, 380, 426, 472
Lechner, John R., 64, 65
Leckie, A. B., 133

Lee, Canada, 560*n*
Leech, John, 529*n*
Lehigh University, 68
Lembke, Daryl, 457
Lennon, John, 366, 469, 623*n*
Leonard, Brother, 165
Leonard, Dick, 107, 273
Leonard, Jerris, 482, 484
Lerner, Michael, 343, 453
LeRoy, Mervyn, 137, 141, 147, 562*n*
Letwin, Leon, 673*n*
Levering, Harold, 55
Levering Act (1952), 55, 57, 535*n*
Lewis, Fulton, Jr., 65, 319, 553*n*, 614*n*
Lewis, John, 342
Library of Congress, 17
Life magazine, 253
Lilienthal, Philip E., 542*n*
Lima, Margaret, 590*n*, 594*n*
Lincoln, Abraham, 13, 84, 492, 533*n*
Lindsey, Robert, 554
Linkletter, Art, 239
Lions Club, 98
Lipsett, Suzanne, 352
Little Lord Fauntleroy (Burnett), 160, 569*n*
Little Rock school integration crisis, 173, 428
Lloyd, Norman, 560
Loading Zone, 372
Lockheed Aircraft, 95
Lomanitz, Giovanni Rossi, 14, 24, 522*n*
London, 61, 349, 350; antiwar demonstration
  in, 282; blitz, 134
London *Daily Mirror*, 400–401
Long Beach Naval Air Station, 310
longshoremen's union, 20, 292
Longshoremen's Hall (San Francisco), 337
Loqueyssie, Baron Paul Emile de (Paul
  Avalon), 121
Lord of the Flies (Golding), 245
Los Alamos National Laboratory, 14, 23, 27
Los Angeles, 39, 50, 55, 64, 66, 67, 69, 128, 148,
  189, 220, 228, 238, 251, 330, 335, 348, 359,
  364, 366, 374, 377, 408, 429, 453, 461, 483,
  499; American Veterans Committee of, 120;
  BASICO offices in, 330, 331; censorship in,
  32; Communist Party office in, 124; FBI
  field office, 39, 42, 48, 64, 68, 120–21,
  128–30, 145, 146, 148–50, 239, 284, 293,
  298, 302, 333, 350, 360, 363, 373, 493, 605*n*,
  608*n*; Police Department, 400, 500; San
  Pedro neighborhood, 95; Savio family in,
  171; Watts section, 334
Los Angeles Committee for a Democratic Far
  Eastern Policy, 120, 363, 561*n*

Los Angeles Herald Examiner, 65, 67
Los Angeles Rams football team, 238
Los Angeles State College, 146
Los Angeles Times, 49, 239, 247, 258, 278, 328,
    334, 335, 369, 373, 376, 381, 382, 457, 458,
    468, 500, 527*n*, 608*n*, 627*n*
Los Angeles Trade Technical School, 483
Lost Generation, 170
Lost Weekend, The (film), 134
Louisiana, 80, 491, 568
Louisiana State University, 550*n*
Lowe, Keith Delroy, 673*n*
Lowell High School (San Francisco), 234
Lowndes County (Alabama) Freedom
    Organization, 342, 346, 353
Loyal Order of Moose, 39
loyalty oaths, 40, 55, 63; Screen Actors
    Guild, 135, 140, 564*n*; university, 4, 38, 44,
    51, 55, 67, 73, 140, 187, 191, 224, 515*n*, 534*n*,
    578*n*
LSD, 243, 246–48, 306, 308, 321, 337–38, 380,
    426, 462, 492, 596*n*, 627*n*
Lucky's supermarket (Berkeley), 176–77
Ludden, Robert, 223, 321
Ludlow, Lynn, 352–53, 372
Lupino, Ida, 136, 562*n*
Lustig, Richard Jeffrey, 594*n*
Lutheran Church, 390
Lynch, James, 73
lynchings, 179, 420
Lynn, Donald, 63, 275, 310, 395, 396
Lynum, Curtis O., 3, 6–8, 198, 246, 268, 269,
    270, 329, 358, 387, 539*n*, 582*n*;
    counterintelligence efforts of, 311–13; and
    Free Speech Movement, 203, 212–14,
    226–28, 232–33, 241, 253–55; informers of,
    284–85; Kesey investigated by, 338–39; news
    stories planted by, 212–14, 315; Reagan and,
    3, 6–8, 360, 370–71; retirement of, 415; and
    Vietnam Day Committee, 265, 272–73,
    275–76, 282, 314, 317
Lyons, Arthur, 121

MacGregor, Helen, 33
Macias, Ysidro, 427, 429, 457
Mack, Carl, 641*n*
MacLeod, Celeste, 79, 82, 86
Madigan, Frank, 435–37, 439, 441–52, 454–56,
    458, 460, 462, 466, 469, 474–78, 483, 649*n*,
    654*n*, 655*n*, 659*n*
Mafia, 236, 297, 298, 490, 511, 667*n*
"Maggie's Farm" (Dylan), 462
Maguire, Mike, 82–86, 95, 101

Mailer, Norman, 78, 254, 260–62, 268, 306,
    385–86, 599*nn*
Majors, Cort, 496
Malcolm X, 423, 424, 444
Malm, F. T., 354
Manhattan College, 165, 167
Manhattan Project, 13, 27, 169
Maoists, 243
Mao Zedong, 28, 210, 377, 430
March on Washington (1963), 175
Marcuse, Herbert, 673*n*
Mardian, Robert, 489–90, 667*n*
marijuana, 220, 242, 243, 248, 266, 276, 277,
    321, 336–77, 339, 352, 390, 426, 430, 447,
    472, 500
Marine Corps, U.S., 79, 91, 191, 233
Market Analysis, Inc., 398, 399
Martí, José, 407, 498
Martin, Francis J., 493
Martin Van Buren High School (Queens, New
    York), 162
Mar Vista Elementary School (Venice,
    California), 499
Marx, Karl, 17, 164, 472
Marxists, 23, 203, 211, 213, 246, 318, 523*n*
Maryknoll order, 169
Marymount Junior College, 148
Mary Poppins (film), 244
Massachusetts, 146, 407, 408; colonial, 46
Massachusetts Institute of Technology (MIT),
    32, 190
Master Plan for Higher Education, *see*
    California, University of
Masters of Deceit (Hoover), 164
Matteawan State Hospital for the Criminally
    Insane (Beacon, New York), 314
Mayer, Charles, 93, 208
Mayer, Louis B., 138
Mayer, Ray, 560*n*
McCann-Erickson advertising agency, 121
McCarthy, Joseph, 28, 79, 187, 263, 331, 524*n*
McCartney, Paul, 366, 623*n*
McClennan, Robert, 319
McComb (Mississippi), 182, 184
McCone, John Alex, 233–39, 286–87, 298,
    334–36, 358, 517*n*, 593*nn*
McCone, Rosemary, 592*n*
McCone Commission, 335
McDonald, Joe, 266, 293; *see also* Country Joe
    and the Fish
McDonald, Larry, 403
McDonald, William J., 550*n*
McDowell, John, 128
McGowan, Felix, 169

McGrory, Mary, 234
McGuiness, James, 136, 562n
McGuire, John, 65
McHugh, Ray, 553n
McKneally, Martin, 64
McManus, John F., 304
McWilliams, Carey, 120
Means, LaNada (War Jack), 429
Medaille, Francis, 314–18, 449; see also
   O'Hanlon, Michael
Media (Pennsylvania), FBI field office in, 414,
   491, 492, 639n
Meehan, Emmett Sylvester, 393
Meehan, Henry P., 393
Meese, Edwin, III, 147, 434, 436, 442, 451,
   453, 481, 555n, 587n, 588n, 659n; in
   Alameda County district attorney's office,
   219–21, 274, 310–11, 326–27, 390–91, 395,
   396, 475, 478, 486, 611n; background of,
   390, 393; on Reagan's staff, 149, 299, 364,
   388, 390, 392–93, 395, 400, 404, 405, 409,
   425, 437, 438, 451, 453, 454, 460, 473, 476,
   482, 493, 631n
Meet the Press (television show), 303, 304
Meisenbach, Robert, 79–80, 82, 83, 85–86,
   90–92, 94, 96, 99, 172, 174, 212; Defense
   Committee, 643n; trial of, 99–111, 479, 550n
Mel's Drive-In (Berkeley), 175, 399, 575n
Melton, Barry, 279
Melville, Herman, 225
Melvin, Milan, 643n
Memphis, 342, 412
Menjou, Adolph, 131, 304
Mennonites, 45
Meredith, James, 342
Merritt College, 346, 422, 427, 461, 475
Merry Pranksters, 248, 277, 278, 306, 337
Metalious, Grace, 400–401
Methodist Church, 99
Metro-Goldwyn-Mayer (MGM), 136
Metropolitan Museum of Art (New York), 470
"Mexicali Rose" (Tenney), 40
Mexican-American Student Confederation
   (MASC), 427, 428
Mexican American studies, 431
Mexico, 170, 229, 272, 337, 338, 408, 542n,
   573n
Meyer, Theodore, 373–76
Meyerson, Martin, 249–50, 258, 615n
Meyerson, Mike, 246
Michener, James, 47
Michigan, University of, 354
Michigan State Police, 98
microphones, FBI surveillance with, 11, 14, 15,

21, 23, 24, 26, 69, 191, 201, 202, 239, 277,
   488, 500, 522n, 666n
Mileston (Mississippi), 179, 181, 182, 184
Milestone, Lewis, 146, 181
Military Academy, U.S., Board of Visitors of,
   590n
Milland, Ray, 134
Miller, Arthur, 130
Miller, Big Bill, 352, 365, 449
Miller, Edward S., 489, 493
Miller, John "Skins," 560n
Miller, Marion, 293, 510–11
Miller, Patricia, 560n
Miller, Richard K., 399–400
Miller, Tom, 212
Miller, Walter Herbert, 525n
Mills Building (San Francisco), 40
Mills College, 315
Minnesota Mining and Manufacturing
   Company (3M), 238
Minutemen, 317
Mississippi, 184, 195, 199, 264, 342, 458, 477,
   480, 484, 500, 576n; Carmichael in, 342;
   constitution of, 182; courts in, 186; Dylan in,
   308; Freedom Democratic Party, 184;
   Freedom Summer, 153, 178–87, 191, 203,
   205, 208, 209, 218, 225, 243, 248, 262,
   294–95, 427, 568n, 576n, 578n, 671n; murder
   of civil rights workers in, 178, 186, 213
Mississippi State University, 199, 342
Mitchell, David, 634n
Mitchell, John, 478–80, 482, 484, 662n
Mitford, Jessica, 86, 201–202, 221, 257, 403,
   461, 547n, 582n, 583n
MK-ULTRA, 247
Moby Dick (Melville), 225
Modesto Junior College, 91, 501
Monroe, Marilyn, 128
Montgomery, Ed, 77, 85–86, 90, 101, 102, 105,
   108–10, 212–15, 227, 258, 265, 273, 315–16,
   326, 394, 396–97, 440, 485, 551n, 553n,
   554nn, 585n, 586n
Montgomery, Robert, 126, 132, 588n, 614n
Montgomery bus boycott, 173
Moore, G. E., 174
Moothart, Perry, 250
Morgenthau, Robert, 296, 298
Morley, Karen, 127, 130, 560n, 675n
Morning Fog, The, 320
Morrill Land Grant College Act (1866), 13, 207
Morris, Albert, 102
Morris, Edmund, 554
Morse, Wayne, 173
Moses, 296

Moses, Robert, 178, 209, 262
Moss, John, 397–98
Mother's Cake & Cookie Company, 399
Motion Picture Alliance for the Preservation of American Ideals, 131, 562n
Mountain City Consolidated Copper Company, 108
movies, see titles of specific films
Movie Show magazine, 128
Moyers, Bill, 591n
Mueller, Robert S., III, 5, 508
Muir Beach (California), 337
Mulford, Don, 189, 225, 226, 230–32, 250, 282, 326, 328–31, 333, 362, 366, 376, 381, 394, 413, 478, 614n
Mulford Act, 250
Murphy, George, 132, 134, 137, 148, 149, 283, 293, 368, 476, 562n, 564n, 567n, 662n
Mystery Trend, 320

Nabors, Jim, 426, 443–44, 640n, 650n, 651n
Nader, Ralph, 397
Nagasaki, atomic bombing of, 11, 169
Naked and the Dead, The (Mailer), 260
Naming Names (Navasky), 130
Napper, Earl, 641n
Nation, The, 58, 86, 248
National Advisory Commission on Civil Disorders, 382, 454
National Archives and Records Administration, Federal Records Center, 674n
National Association for the Advancement of Colored People (NAACP), 523n, 643n
National Biscuit Company, 39, 528n
National Broadcasting Company (NBC), 303, 492
National Committee for Political Settlement in Vietnam, 496
National Coordinating Committee to End the War in Vietnam, 272
National Education Association, 495
National Goals, Inc., 401
National Inter-fraternity Council, 107
Nationalist Chinese, 34
National Labor Relations Board (NLRB), 20, 125
National Lawyers Guild, 403
National Presbyterian Church (Washington, D.C.), 492
National Press Club, 328
National Review, 316, 334
National Science Foundation, 165, 166
National Security Act (1947), 237, 634n

National Velvet (film), 127
Native Americans, 322, 382, 426, 431, 450–51, 646n
Native American Student Union, 429
Natural Resources Defense Council, 397
Naval Reserve, 360
Navasky, Victor, 130, 692n
Navy, U.S., 70, 95, 102, 238, 429; intelligence, 58, 204; ROTC, 364, 406, 434; in Vietnam War, 261; in World War II, 234, 239
Nazis, 14, 15, 25, 87, 119, 121, 154, 346; American, 265, 305; sympathizers, 121
Nelson, Gary, 475
Nelson, George "Baby Face," 20
Nelson, Ruth, 560n
Nelson, Steve, 14–15, 23–24, 26, 522n
Neshoba (Mississippi) County Fair, 186
Neubarth, Harry J., 100–101, 105
Newark (New Jersey), 401, 596n; riot in, 382
New Deal, 20, 128, 131, 293, 322, 411
New Journalism, 338
New Left, 4, 262, 332, 335, 409, 424, 485, 515n, 651n; FBI counterintelligence against, 414–15
New Left Forum, 452
New Mexico, Free University of, 515n
New Mexico State University, 452
Newport Folk Festival, 266, 307
Newport News (Virginia), 198
Newton, Huey, 346, 411, 413, 422
Newton, Jim, 526n
Newtonian mechanics, 165
Newton, Melvin, 422
New York City, 15, 120, 121, 138, 140, 242, 314–17, 387, 470, 479, 526n; antiwar demonstrations in, 272; City College of, 347; FBI field office in, 144, 294, 492, 589n, 606n; law department of, 525; Mafia in, 297; Savio family in, 159–60, 172, 350, 355, 408–409, 589n; Welfare Department, 88
New Yorker, The, 16, 242, 519n
New York Herald Tribune, 92, 258
New York Post, 68, 348
New York State, 340; American Legion in, 98; Assembly, 403; Police, 297; University of, 32, 34
New York Stock Exchange, 317
New York Times, 92, 164, 224, 246, 256, 257, 271, 297, 322, 342, 354, 355, 358, 370, 387, 494, 496, 498, 508, 588n; Book Review, 245
Neylan, John Francis, 52, 528n
Nicaragua, 495, 501, 671n
Nichols, Louis, 129
Niemann, Robert, 673n

Nigger (Gregory), 264
Nine Lives Are Not Enough (film), 127
Nixon, Richard M., 67, 133, 146, 173, 237, 252, 291, 293, 359, 360, 424, 439, 478, 495, 482, 484, 492, 499, 650*n*, 667*n*
Nobel Prize, 13, 165
Nofziger, Lyn, 374, 624*n*
Nolan, Dick, 108
nonviolence, 50, 153, 182, 217, 267, 384, 391, 417, 433; in civil rights movement, 78, 175, 185, 342, 382, 461; of Free Speech Movement, 197, 253, 418
Norris, William A., 672*n*
Noyes, Dan, 506
nuclear freeze movement, 493, 494
nuclear weapons, 11, 85, 99, 163, 166, 172, 217, 228, 229, 235, 241, 263, 264, 386; *see also* atomic bomb
Nuremberg trials, 25

Oakdale High School, 91
Oakland, 23, 200, 209, 274, 310, 316, 328, 390, 393, 399, 413, 432, 446, 452, 461, 509, 525*n*; American Legion in, 56; Atthowe in, 340, 393, 396, 440; civil defense conference in, 455; Communist Party office in, 14; FBI field office in, 25, 200, 201, 275, 278; Hell's Angels in, 281, 306; Humphrey's speech in, 196; Japanese in, 419–20; Pacific Gas and Electric in, 31, 525*n*; Panthers in, 346, 381, 412; riot in, 341; VDC demonstrations in, 278–82, 301, 305–308, 391; Warren as prosecutor in, 33
Oakland Airport, 366
Oakland Army Terminal, 270, 272, 274–75, 278, 282, 301, 309, 460
Oakland City College, 422, 424
Oakland Police Department (OPD), 274, 279–81, 384, 412–13, 420, 423, 425, 478
Oakland School Board, 394
Oakland Tribune, 62, 157, 187, 196, 226, 359, 394, 578*n*
Oberlin College, 262
Occidental College, 535*n*
Ochs, Phil, 168, 262, 266, 308
O'Connell, Daniel, 587*n*
"Ode to Allen Ginsberg" (Mailer), 306
Odets, Clifford, 136
Official and Confidential (Summers), 521*n*
Oglesby, Carl, 638*n*
O'Hanlon, Michael, 267, 270, 274, 279, 307, 314–15; *see also* Medaille, Francis
Ohlone peoples, 12

Oklahoma, University of, 32
Olczak, Stanley, 98
Olney, Warren, III, 59
O'Meara, Charles, 63
One Flew Over the Cuckoo's Nest (Kesey), 248, 278
O'Neill, Eugene, 121
Ono, Yoko, 469
On the Outside Looking In (Reagan), 299
On the Road (Kerouac), 260, 277
Operation Abolition (film), 94, 95, 97, 217, 543*n*
Oppenheimer, Frank, 15, 24
Oppenheimer, J. Robert, 11, 13–15, 23–27, 36, 41, 522–23*n*
Oppenheimer, Kitty, 15
Oppenheimer, Story of a Friendship (Chevalier), 26
Oracle (newspaper), 380
Orange Coast College, 267
Orations (Cicero), 418
Oregon State College, 395
Oscars, *see* Academy Awards
Osman, Robert, 182–84, 577*n*
Oswald, Lee Harvey, 198, 351
Overseas Press Club, 226
Oxford University, 349–50

Pacht, Jerome, 348
Pacific Gas & Electric Company, 31, 94, 399, 400, 525*n*
Pacific Telephone and Telegraph, 95, 410
pacifists, 50, 267, 276, 277, 384; *see also* nonviolence
Palmer, A. Mitchell, 17–19
Palmer Broadcasting, 116, 117
Palmer Method of cursive writing, 46
Palmer Raids, 17–19, 71
Palo Alto (California), 247, 277, 337
Parchman Penitentiary (Mississippi), 342
Pardun, Robert H., 638*n*
Parent-Teacher Associations, 95, 98
Parkinson, Thomas, 268
Parks, Larry, 127, 130, 560*n*, 675*n*
Parks, Rosa, 173
Pasadena, 310; City College, 640*n*; Firearms Range, 293
Patel, Marilyn Hall, 5, 299, 506–11, 675*n*
Patriot Act (2001), 410
Pauley, Edwin Wendell, 62, 66, 67, 189, 190, 237–41, 243, 250, 258, 284, 286–87, 334, 361, 366, 374, 376, 443, 594*n*
Pauley, George, 457

Pauley Petroleum Building (Los Angeles), 240, 286
Payne, Frederick, 524
Peace Caravans, 47, 142, 143, 179, 531*n*
Peace Corps, 262
Peace and Freedom Party, 411, 413, 447
Peak, Gen., 118
Pearl Harbor, Japanese attack on, 118, 198, 419
Pearson, Drew, 235
Pearson, Hugh, 644*n*
Peck, Gregory, 120, 134
Peck, Sidney, 638*n*
Peckham, Robert F., 463, 466, 483
Peet, Edward, 612*n*
Peet, George, 104
Pell Grant program, 497
Pennell, Larry, 147
Pennsylvania, 44, 46, 68, 128, 373, 492, 497
Pennsylvania, University of, 32
Pentagon, 254, 317, 385, 493
People's Park, xii, 447–87, 493, 515*n*, 664–66*nn*
People's World, 312
Peppino, Don, 164
Peralta, Luis Maria, 12
Peralta Community College, 446
Peter, Paul and Mary, 266
Petras, James, 590*n*
Petry, Oliver, 641*n*
Peyton Place (Metalious), 400
Pharris, Cecil, 103, 105
Phillips, Joseph Dexter, Jr., 34
Physicians for Social Responsibility, 495
Pieper, N.J.L. "Nat," 15, 23, 56
Pigott, Theiline, 592*n*
Pilgrims, 46
Pitts, Zasu, 204
Pius XI, Pope, 550*n*
Pius XII, Pope, 234
Plog, Stanley, 331, 333, 343
Plotkin, Homer, 146
Plummer, Charles, 464, 480
Poincaré, Henri, 352
Point Reyes Light, 634
Poland, German invasion of, 521*n*
Pomona (California), 110
Pomona College, 535*n*
Pool, Joe, 327
Poole, Cecil, 385, 476–78, 482, 662*n*
Popular Front, 119
Porter, Cole, 121
Porter, Dan, 458
Portland (Oregon), 337
Post, Louis, 18
Postal Service, U.S., 200, 496

Postman Always Rings Twice, The (film), 127
Powell, Charles, 156–57, 193
Powell, Lewis F., Jr., 252–53, 258, 491, 598*n*
Powers, Richard Gid, 17, 22
Prager, Stanley, 560*n*
Presbyterian Church, 16, 492
President Reagan (Cannon), 555*n*
President's Advisory Committee on Labor-Management Policy, 590*n*
President's Commission on National Goals, 590*n*
Presidio (San Francisco), 118, 392
Preuit, Wendy, 162–66
Princeton University, 4, 47
Prisoner of War (film), 142
Privacy Protection Study Commission, 404
Prival, Lucien, 560*n*
Progressive Citizens of America (PCA), 128, 136
Progressive Labor Party, 243, 267, 319, 516*n*
Progressive Party, 83
Prohibition, 20, 114
Project Prayer, 294
Proposition 6, 535*n*
Proposition 14, 158, 193, 264, 335
Proposition 187, 501
Proposition 209, 514
prostitution, 5, 41–42
Protestants, 16
Prussion, Karl, 84, 543*n*
Puerto Rico, University of, 525*n*
Pulitzer Prize, 108, 385
Puritans, 46
"Purple Haze" (Hendrix), 480
Pusey, Nathan, 376
Pyle, Christopher H., 631–32*n*
Pynchon, Thomas, 242

Quakers, 46–48, 50, 51, 55, 142, 195, 222, 533*n*; Friends Religious Society, 495
Quarnstrom, Lee, 277
Queens (New York), 160–62, 168, 173
Queens College, 167, 175, 226; Newman Club, 169, 170

Radio Directors Guild, 557*n*
Rafferty, Maxwell, 351, 357
Ramparts magazine, 272, 380, 415, 447, 449, 464, 473, 582*n*
Read, Jon, 449
Reader's Digest, 494

Reading (Pennsylvania), 44–46; Country Club, 45; High School, 44, 46
Reagan (Cannon), 555*n*
Reagan, Christine (RR's daughter), 561*n*
Reagan, The Hollywood Years (Elliot), 141, 561*n*
Reagan, John (RR's father), 113
Reagan, Maureen (RR's daughter), 8, 117, 148–49, 299, 511, 517*n*, 555*n*, 556*n*
Reagan, Michael (RR's son), 8, 118, 297–99, 511, 556*n*, 608
Reagan, Nancy Davis (RR's wife), 141, 142, 147, 292, 323, 327, 368, 388, 437, 490, 492, 511, 565*n*
Reagan, Neil "Moon" (RR's brother), 117, 121, 124, 148, 297, 510*n*, 555*n*, 557–59*nn*
Reagan, Nelle (RR's mother), 113
Reagan, Patricia Ann (RR's daughter), 565*n*
Reagan, Ronald, 111–50, 209, 232, 446, 453, 509, 512, 516*n*, 557–59*nn*, 562*nn*–66*nn*; acting career of, 113, 117–18, 134, 142, 184, 291, 556*n*; anti-Communism of, 140, 150, 179, 292–93, 333, 364, 467; autobiographies by, 113, 122, 139, 144, 554*n*, 558*n*; biographies of, 137, 141, 146, 149, 554–56*nn*, 561*n*; birth of, 113; Board of Regents and, 7, 327–30, 336, 360–61, 366–67, 369–80, 389–90, 416, 426, 435, 461, 485, 486; childhood and adolescence of, 113–14, 161, 163; children of, 117–18, 142, 148–49, 565*n*; at Eureka College, 3, 114–16, 159, 327, 369, 388, 556*n*; FBI background investigations of, 114, 116, 119–20, 147, 150, 362–64, 605*n*; as FBI informer, xi, 8, 112, 113, 115, 120–25, 127–30, 134, 135, 137–40, 145–47, 291, 298, 371, 388, 510, 511, 554*n*, 558*n*, 563*n*, 564*n*; as General Electric spokesman, 112, 142–44, 150, 179, 510; as governor of California, 6–8, 149, 359–64, 366–94, 400, 403–405, 407, 409, 416–17, 419, 425–28, 430–31, 435–40, 442–44, 451, 453–54, 460–64, 466–71, 473, 475–76, 478–80, 482–93, 496, 498, 508, 517*n*; gubernatorial campaign and election of, 3-4, 291–304, 322–44, 346, 356, 358–59 361, 363, 394–95, 411, 428, 517*n*; HUAC testimony of, 128, 131–33, 135; loyalty oaths and, 135, 140, 564*n*; marriage and divorce of Wyman and, 117, 134–35, 556*n*; marriage of Nancy and, 141–42; presidency of, 149, 291, 403, 494–95, 500; presidential candidacy of, 387, 424; Presidential Foundation, 149; radio career of, 116–17; at Screen Actors Guild, 113, 126–31, 135, 137, 142, 222, 283, 510, 560*n*; "A Time for Choosing" television

speech, 294–96; in World War II, 118–19, 122, 142, 383, 557*n*
Reagan, Ronald Prescott (RR's son), 565*n*
Reagan's America (Wills), 554*n*, 558*n*, 561*n*, 562*n*, 566*n*
Recall Ronald Reagan Campaign, 386
Rector, James Bennett, 457–58, 462, 469, 474–76, 478, 482, 483, 659*n*
Red Channels (pamphlet), 136
Red Guerrilla Family, 496
Red House Collective, 402
Redlands, University of, 535*n*
Red Scare, post–World War I, 17–19
Rees, John Herbert, 400–404, 494, 636*n*
Rees, Sheila, 402, 403
Reformed Church, 44
Republican Alliance, 301
Republican Party, 28, 70, 98, 128, 223, 267, 269, 293, 353, 389, 448, 562*n*; Board of Regents and, 373; in California, 33, 53, 133, 137, 175, 189, 200, 225, 274, 298, 331, 393, 395, 448, 467, 469; Congress controlled by, 128, 133; conservatives in, 234, 251, 293; governor's conference, 491; National Conventions, 33, 39, 157, 424; presidential candidates of, 157, 184, 387, 424; Reagan as gubernatorial candidate of, 302, 322, 326, 328, 333, 335, 340, 344, 359, 388; *see also* Young Republicans
Research West, 395–400, 404, 633*n*, 635*n*, 650*n*
Reserve Officers' Training Corps (ROTC), 16, 80, 267, 328, 390, 392, 419; Navy, 434; protests against, 365, 409
Revere, Anne, 127, 140, 560*n*, 675*n*
Revere, Paul, 127
Review of the News, The, 403
Rexroth, Kenneth, 262
Reynolds, Quentin, 133–34
Richartz, Pat, 402–403
Riche, Lawrence, 452, 454–57, 459–60, 465, 474, 475, 478, 481–84, 654*n*, 657*n*
Rifleman, The (television show), 323
riots, 280, 392, 401, 516*n*, 636*n*; campus, 195, 196, 257, 258, 301, 324, 372, 394, 436–37, 443, 651*n*; demonstrations against HUAC denounced as, 61, 85–86, 88–90, 92, 97, 99, 100, 102, 105, 108, 110–12, 212; People's Park, 451–52, 455–59, 468, 474–75, 479, 481–83; urban, 334, 335, 341, 344, 359, 382, 412, 494
Riskin, Myra, 590*n*
Roach, Hal, 118
Roberts, Gene, 342
Robeson, Paul, 120, 132, 187–88

Robinson, Edward G., 120, 126
Rockefeller Foundation, 34
Rockwell, George Lincoln, 265, 600*n*
Rockwell, Norman, 263, 265
Rodriguez, Richard, 435, 648*n*
Rogers, Roy, 294
Rogers, William P., 93–94
Rolling Stones, 225, 305
Rollins, Wade Cuthbert, Jr., 525*n*
Rollman, Justin A., 96
Roman Catholic Church, 83, 168, 177;
    Confraternity of Church Doctrine, 162, 164;
    Grand Cross of the Order of St. Sylvester,
    234; Los Angeles Archdiocese, 65; Vatican
    II, 168; Veritas Lectures, 169; *see also*
    Catholics
Romania, 203
Romano, Amelia, 560*n*
Rome, 349; antiwar demonstration in, 282
Romerstein, Herbert, 401
Romilly, Constancia "Dinky," 547*n*
Ronald Reagan in Hollywood (Vaughn), 554
Ronnie & Jesse (Cannon), 555*n*
Rooney, John J., 253, 257
Roosevelt, Franklin Delano (FDR), 19–22, 37,
    50, 71, 117, 119, 123, 128, 159, 173, 203, 303,
    520*n*, 521*n*, 523*n*, 541*n*; New Deal of, *see*
    New Deal
Roosevelt, James, 123, 124
Roosevelt Hotel, 120, 130
Rose Bowl, 310
Rosenberg, Julius and Ethel, 27
Rosenfeld, Edward Jerry, 594*n*
Rosenthal, Dan, 244
Rosovsky, Henry, 195
Rosselli, Johnny, 236
Rossen, Robert, 127
Rossman, Michael, 500
Rote, Harry, Jr., 91
Roth, William Matson, 240, 241, 258, 298, 443
Rousselot, John, 293, 303, 609*n*
Royle, Selena, 127, 130, 675*n*
Roysher, Martin, 210, 212
Rubin, Jerry, 262, 266, 267, 270–74, 305, 310,
    317, 319, 327, 365, 380, 385–86, 397, 403,
    406, 409, 479, 600*n*, 636*n*, 638*n*
Ruby, Jack, 351
Rule 17, 37, 59–60, 191
Rumford, Bryon, 158
Rumford Fair Housing Act, 158, 335, 359, 394
Rundle, William Donovan, Jr., xii, 453–55,
    459–60, 471, 478, 481–84, 654*n*, 657*n*
Ruskin, Shimen, 560*n*
Russell, Frank, 34

Russia, 23; Communist, *see* Soviet Union
    25–27, 36, 38, 99, 109, 120, 164, 172, 177,
    198, 199, 264, 390, 395; deportation of
    radical aliens to, 18; immigrants from, 17–18
Russian Revolution, 18
Rydin, R. G., 550*n*
Ryskind, Morrie, 304

Sacramento Memorial Auditorium, 368–69
Salaff, Stephen, 590*n*
Salinger, J. D., 245
Salinger, Pierre, 230
San Bernardino High School, 429
San Diego Patriotic Society, 294
San Diego State College, 525*n*, 673*n*
Sandinistas, 495, 501
Sandperl, Ira, 217
San Fernando Valley State College, 646*n*, 673*n*
San Francisco, 11, 23–25, 39, 40, 52, 100, 190,
    195, 200, 234, 240, 258, 262, 298, 307, 317,
    337, 339, 373, 417, 473, 479, 481, 500,
    506–507; antiwar leaflets dropped over, 310;
    Bar Association of, 253; Beat Generation in,
    246; bombing of Preparedness Day parade
    in, 113; California Department of Motor
    Vehicles in, 32; Cole Valley, 23; Communist
    Party in, 40, 88, 92, 190, 204, 232, 318;
    County Jail, 178; Department of Public
    Health; detainees in, 71; FBI field office in,
    3, 8, 15, 24, 56, 59, 63, 67, 68, 88, 89, 92, 100,
    101, 104–107, 109, 198–201, 212, 226, 232,
    251, 252, 265, 284, 310, 311, 314, 318, 319,
    329, 338, 370, 387, 407, 410, 415, 477, 539*n*;
    General Strike in, 56, 88, 89; Golden Gate
    Park, 380; Haight-Ashbury, 267, 337, 380,
    408, 479; Hell's Angels chapter in, 305;
    mayoral election in, 175; Nob Hill, 271;
    North Beach, 467; Presidio, 118, 392; public
    television station, 308; Republican Alliance
    in, 301–302; Republican National
    Convention in, 157, 322; sit-in at Sheraton
    Palace Hotel in, 177–78; Soviet consulate in,
    14, 23, 25; War Labor Board in, 230; Western
    Research Foundation office in, 56, 536*n*
San Francisco Airport, 220
San Francisco Bay Guardian, 507, 553*n*
San Francisco Chronicle, 58, 66, 85, 96, 109,
    202, 210, 225, 306, 308, 338, 339, 349, 384,
    419, 442, 461, 464, 477, 482, 508, 517*n*, 527*n*
San Francisco City Hall, protests ("youth
    riots") against HUAC hearings at, 4, 77–89,
    92–93, 108, 110, 112, 126, 150, 172, 175, 188,
    198, 205, 212, 217, 232, 310, 326

San Francisco Examiner, 38, 65, 77, 85, 90, 93, 101, 108, 190, 210, 212, 251, 265, 273, 283–84, 313, 315, 316, 326, 352, 372, 373, 394, 396, 440, 485, 506, 527*n*, 534*n*, 651*n*
San Francisco Giants baseball team, 100
San Francisco Hall of Justice, 100
San Francisco Medical Center, 466
San Francisco Mime Troupe, 262
San Francisco Police Department, 79, 95, 100, 105, 177, 246, 319, 458
San Francisco State College, 338, 415, 426, 427, 438
San Francisco State University, 86, 501, 729
San Francisco Superior Court, 97, 100, 104
San Francisco Symphony, 368
San Joaquin Valley, 40, 101; cotton pickers' strike in, 49, 283
San Jose, 79, 108, 337, 457, 462
San Jose Mercury-News, 554*n*, 555*n*
San Jose State College, 99, 306, 310
San Manuel Bueno, Martir (Unamuno), 168
San Mateo College, 646*n*
San Mateo County, 339, 385
San Quentin prison, 78, 553*n*
Santa Cruz (California), 337
Santa Fe Railroad, 270
Santana, 467
Santa Rita County Jail and Prison Farm, 222, 365, 408, 409, 464, 466, 474–78, 482, 483
Santucci, Louis, 441, 456, 656*n*
Sartre, Jean-Paul, 54
Saturday Evening Post, 263
Savio, Dora Berretti (MS's mother), 159–60, 348
Savio, Ferdinando (MS's great-grandfather), and family, 569*n*
Savio, Joseph (MS's father), 159–60, 164, 569*n*
Savio, Lynne Hollander (MS's second wife), 408, 500, 671*n*
Savio, Mario, 159–87, 231, 295, 296, 307, 347–59, 383, 406–15, 438, 567*n*, 568*nn*, 587*n*; in antiwar movement, 365–67; application for readmission to Berkeley of, 351–56, 358–59, 365; arrest, prosecution, and jail sentences of, 244, 249, 268, 269, 274, 321, 390, 408–409, 575*n*; birth of, 159, 160, 341; California State Senate candidacy of, 411–13, 415, 424, 447; Catholicism of, 161–62, 167–70; childhood of, 160–62, 570*n*; in civil rights movement, 173–87, 205, 248, 342, 477, 578*n*; in college in New York, 167–68; on Council of Campus Organizations, 356–58; death of, 501; enrollment at Berkeley of, 171, 172, 174; family background of, 159–60; FBI files on, 253–55, 407–11, 413–15, 417, 506,

514, 517*n*, 638*n*; and Filthy Speech Movement, 245, 255; in high school, 162–67; Kerr criticized by, 206, 207, 376–77; marriages and family of, 255, 347–50, 355, 357, 364–65, 406–407, 409, 498–501; in Mexico, 170–71, 408; at Oxford, 349–50; in People's Park actions, 450, 458–61, 468, 469, 471, 473, 475, 484, 661*n*; psychological difficulties of, 5, 160, 161, 167, 175, 256, 349–50, 355, 406, 408, 497–98, 570*n*; Reagan's antagonism toward, 6–8, 323, 468–69; speech defect of, 160, 162–63, 175, 210; Third World Liberation Front and, 418, 429, 433; *see also* Free Speech Movement
Savio, Nadav (MS's son), 498
Savio, Stefan (MS's son), 350, 355, 357, 364–65, 406, 409
Savio, Suzanne Goldberg (MS's first wife), 208–209, 216, 225, 255–56, 347–50, 355, 498, 570*n*, 598*n*
Savio, Thomas (MS's brother) 160, 348
Scaife, Richard Mellon, 399
Scarface (film), 127
Schary, Dore, 123, 136
Scheer, Robert, 266, 272, 278, 281, 319–20, 409, 411, 415, 447, 464–65, 475, 562*n*, 638*n*
Scherr, Max, 351
Schiff, Helen, 590*n*
Schillinger, Ralph, 659*n*
Schine, G. David, 79
Schlessinger, Wendy, 449
Schmoerlitz, Richard, 499
Schon, Leo, 105
Schroeder, Mary M., 672*n*
Schroy, Colonel, 275
Schumacher, Michael, 305, 609*n*
Schurmann, Franz, 276
Schwab's Pharmacy (Hollywood), 135
Schwartz, Charles, 626*n*
Schwerner, Michael, 178, 196, 213
Scott, Peter Dale, 432
Scottsdale (Arizona) Police Department, 297, 607*n*
Screen Actors Guild (SAG), 8, 113, 125–27, 129–33, 135, 137–39, 142, 145, 149, 222, 283, 294, 362, 368, 388, 510, 555*n*, 559*n*, 560*n*, 564*n*, 588*n*
Seabury, Paul, 93–94
Seale, Bobby, 346, 380–81, 411, 422–24, 636*n*
Searle, John, 312–13
Secrecy and Power, (Powers), 17
Secret Service, 204, 267, 402, 417, 498
segregation, 33, 173, 179, 186, 341; challenges to, *see* civil rights movement

Seize the Time (Seale), 423
Selective Service System, 91, 430, 567n, 628n
Senate, U.S., 79, 631n; Foreign Relations Committee, 292; Internal Security Subcommittee, 57, 528n, 537n; Judiciary Committee, 508; Select Committee on Intelligence, 495; Select Committee to Study Governmental Operations with Respect to Intelligence Activities, *see* Church committee
Sensual Drugs (Jones), 650n
Sentner, David, 65, 110
Serra, Junipero, 368
Service v. Dulles et al. (1957), 526n
Shakespeare, William, 455
Shakespeare & Company Bookstore (Berkeley), 507
Shapiro, Howard, 509
Shattuck Avenue Project, 176
Shaumleffel, Ralph, 85
Shaw, Artie, 138
Sheen, Fulton J., 137
Shell Development Company, 25
Shelley, John, 177
Shepard, Sam, 652n
Sheraton Palace Hotel (Berkeley), 177–78
Sherriffs, Alex, 187–88, 221, 263, 391, 535n, 568n, 578nn, 580n, 598n, 602nn, 626n; antipathy to student activism of, 188–92, 194, 197, 204, 391; disciplinary action against FSM urged by, 214–15, 220, 251; as FBI informer, 188–90, 203, 204, 210–12, 227–28, 253, 273, 284, 330, 378, 386, 389, 510; Reagan and, 329–30, 332, 333, 389, 416, 510, 625–626nn
Sherry, Arthur, 59
Sherwin, Martin J., 27
Short, Robin, 560n
Shoshone-Bannock tribe, 429
Shriners, 322
Shull, Gordon, 550n
Shupack, Bob, 165
Siegel, Dan, 453, 471, 475, 662n
Silberstein, Steve, 672n
Simon, Norton, 361
Simpson, Don, 656n
Simpson, Roy, 75
Sirica, Jack, 554n
Sirica, John, 554n
Sistrunk, Paul, 185, 186
sit-ins, 3, 78, 206, 223, 274, 279, 341, 353, 390, 418
Six Gallery (San Francisco), 246, 596n
Sixties, The (Gitlin), 385, 550n, 657n

SLATE, 78, 80, 81, 175, 188–90, 196, 203, 246, 643n
Smale, Stephen, 262, 266, 268, 270–72, 352, 361, 600n, 615n, 622n
Smelser, Neil, 257–58, 615n
Smith, Art, 560n
Smith, Gar, 413
Smith, H. Allen, 130–31, 136, 560n
Smith, Jeffrey L., 477
Smith, Mike, 365, 406
Smith, William French, 495
Smith Act (1940), 526n, 563n
Smith College, 142
"Smokey the Bear Sutra" (Snyder), 467
Snyder, Gary, 217, 278, 467
Socialists, English, 291
Socialist Workers Party (SWP), 254, 267, 414, 415, 421, 516n, 643nn; Oakland-Berkeley Branch of, 422
Society of Former Special Agents, 562n, 594n
Society of Friends, *see* Quakers
Sokolsky, George, 93, 553n
Sondergaard, Gale, 130, 139–40, 510, 560n
Sonoma State University, 501
Souers, Admiral Sidney F., 30
Soul on Ice (Cleaver), 425
Soul Students Advisory Council, 422
South Africa, 501
Southern Christian Leadership Conference, 495
Southern Pacific Railroad Company, 31, 525n
Soviet Union, 38, 120, 109, 198, 201, 421, 439, 491, 518n; and Cuban Missile Crisis, 235, 335; espionage of, 4, 11–12, 14, 22–28, 31, 36, 56, 62, 119, 490, 495; nuclear weapons and, 85, 163–64, 172, 233, 264, 494; repression in, 295, 361, 295; *Sputnik* launched by, 62, 74, 163; U.S. fear of aggression of, 99, 135, 140, 199, 301, 390 (*see also* Cold War); in World War II, 238, 305
Spain, 168; colonization of California by, 368
Spanish Civil War, 15
Sparrow, John, 221, 251, 329–30, 332, 333, 354, 378, 386, 626n
special agents in charge (SACs), 31–33; assistants to, 104, 130; of Cincinnati field office, 98; of Dallas field office, 198; of Jackson field office, 186; of Los Angeles field office, 64, 67, 121, 130, 136, 239, 360, 363; of Sacramento field office, 404, 405, 692n; of San Francisco field office, 3, 15, 56, 63, 88, 89, 105, 198, 212, 226, 284, 329, 352, 387, 415, 692n
Spider magazine, 245–46, 596n

Spider Woman, The (film), 139
Spiegel, Michael L., 638*n*
Spivak, Lawrence, 303
Spock, Benjamin, 188, 262, 263, 382
Sproul, Robert Gordon, 33, 124, 192
spying, 11–12, 115; domestic, 115, 190, 273, 293, 388–89, 393, 397–98, 414, 461, 491–92, 497, 507 (*see also* domestic intelligence)
Stalin, Joseph, 135, 201
Stalinism, 135, 449
Standard Oil Corporation, 95, 263, 399, 459
Stanford, Leland, 271
Stanford University, 48, 61, 86, 187, 247, 281, 338, 451
Stanley, Augustus Owsley, III, 248, 337, 380, 627*n*
Stansfield, John, 102
Stapleton, Sydney, 594*n*
Starobin, Bob, 205
Starr, Kevin, 40
Stassen, Harold, 238
State Department, U.S., 190, 199, 234, 263, 349, 422, 526*n*
Statler Hilton Hotel (Los Angeles), 302
Statue of Liberty, 113
Steel, Thomas, 506–509
Stein, Benjamin Wolf, 511
Steinberg, Alan B., 594*n*
Steinmetz, Harry, 525*n*
Stephen Smale (Batterson), 600*n*
Steppenwolf (Hesse), 351
Steppenwolf Bar (Berkeley), 351–52, 355, 406, 449
Stern, Carl, 492
Stern, Jan, 566*n*
Stevens, Wallace, 410
Stevens, Will, 108
Stevenson, Adlai, 59–60, 187, 224, 524*n*
Stevenson, Cheryl, 177, 179–80, 184–85, 187
Stewart, James, 147
Stockholm, antiwar demonstration in, 282
Stone, Harlan Fiske, 19, 28
Stone, I. F., 262, 263
Stone, Robert, 277, 281, 338
"Stone Free" (Hendrix), 480
"Strange New Cottage in Berkeley, A" (Ginsberg), 500
Stranger, The (Camus), 174
Stripling, Robert, 128, 132
Strong, Edward, 154–55, 191, 192, 195, 204–205, 212, 216, 220, 228, 580*n*
Student (Horowitz), 172, 543*n*, 550*n*
Student Civil Liberties Union, 189
Student Mobilization Committee, 643*n*

Student Non-Violent Coordinating Committee (SNCC), 178, 184, 209–10, 265, 342, 345; University Friends of, 175, 191, 340
Students for Civil Liberties, 78, 95, 205
Students for a Democratic Society (SDS), 272, 275, 343, 386, 404, 430, 490, 515*n*, 657*n*
Stukenbroeker, Fern, 285
Sullivan, Mark, 385
Sullivan, William C., 94, 105–106, 183
Summer of Love, 379, 380
Summers, Anthony, 521*n*
Super Market Institute, 291–92, 606*n*
Supreme Court, U.S., 21, 33, 60, 173, 179, 213, 244, 252, 485, 486, 491, 505, 507–508, 543*n*, 563*n*, 641*n*
Swarthmore College, 46–47, 159
Sweezy v. New Hampshire (1957), 526*n*
Symbionese Liberation Army (SLA), 500
Synanon, 396–97, 634*n*

Taft, William Howard, 271
Talbott, Floyd, 409
Talese, Gay, 297
"Talking Birmingham Jam" (Ochs), 168
Tamm, Quinn, 65
Tandy, Jessica, 127
Tau Kappa Epsilon fraternity, 116
Taxco (Mexico), 170–71, 184
Taylor, Elizabeth, 127
Taylor, Gen. Maxwell, 213, 271
Taylor, Paul, 49
Tchula (Mississippi), 180
teach-ins, 261–65, 272, 275–76, 337, 384, 467
Teapot Dome scandal, 19
tear gas, demonstrators attacked with, 279, 348, 418; at People's Park, 442, 444, 454–58, 461, 463, 468, 476, 483, 655*n*
telephones, tapping, *see* wiretaps
Telstar, 127
Temko, Allan, 461
Tempest, The (Shakespeare), 455, 459
Tennessee Valley Authority, 293
Tenney, Jack, 40, 51, 55, 124, 140, 530*n*, 533*n*
Tenney Committee, 40, 124, 564*n*
Thant, U, 224
Theoharis, Athan G., 16, 141, 521*n*, 541*n*, 564–65*n*, 582–83*n*
Thirdside Café (New York), 168
Third World Liberation Front (TWLF), 418, 424, 427, 429–31, 439, 515*n*; Steering Committee, 440
Third World Strike, 419, 454
Thomas, J. Parnell, 128–29, 131, 133

Thomas, Norman, 47, 532n
Thomas, Thompson, and Utterback Table of
  Sea Water Conductivity, 165
Thompson, Elsa Knight, 348
Thompson, Hunter S., 248, 281, 305, 306, 380
Thompson, J. Walter, Company, 360
Thompson, John J., 242, 243, 246, 248, 255
Thoreau, Henry David, 163, 194
Threadgill, Burney, Jr., 199–202, 380, 395–96,
  421, 582n, 583n
Tigar, Mike, 78, 81
Tikkun magazine, 453
Till, Emmett, 179
Time magazine, 76
Times-Mirror Company, 239
Tiny Tim, 168
Tocsin (anti-Communist weekly), 311–13, 396,
  611–12nn
Tokyo, 237; antiwar demonstration in, 282
Toledo (Ohio) Board of Education, 97
Toledo Blade, 97
Tolson, Clyde, 4, 16, 19, 22, 28, 32, 64, 66, 68,
  76, 96, 103–104, 106, 150, 184, 228, 405,
  490, 492, 522n
Toothman, Edward, 279, 281
Tornabene, Joel, 465, 478
Towle, Katherine, 155, 156, 191, 568n, 579nn
Tracy, Spencer, 136
trade unions, see unions
Tree, Dorothy, 127, 560n, 675n
Treuhaft, Robert, 201, 221, 588n
Trillin, Calvin, 242
Trips Festivals, 337, 338
Trombley, William, 376, 627n
Truman, Harry S, 29–30, 203, 237–38,
  518n, 523n
Trumbo, Dalton, 37, 124, 136
Truth About Communism, The (film), 394
Turnbow, Hartman, 181, 458, 576n
Turkey, 622n
Turner, Brian, 586n
Turner, William, 201, 473, 582n
Tussman, Joseph, 594n

UCLA, 468; Neuropsychiatric Institute, 499;
  Pauley Pavilion, 238; Writers' Congress, 36
Unamuno, Miguel de, 168
Unemployed Cooperative League, 48
Union of Concerned Scientists, 397
unions, 15, 20, 25, 40, 51, 56, 190, 201, 254,
  382, 533n; campus employees', 432, 440–41;
  film industry, 120, 292 (see also Screen
  Actors Guild)

Unitarian Church, 68
United Farm Workers, 427
United Fruit Corporation, 263
United Mine Workers Union (UMW), 20
United Nations, 60, 120, 135, 224; Charter, 271
United Press International (UPI), 107–108, 553n
United Reform Church of America, 402
Universal-International Studios, 137, 562n
Up Against the Wall (Austin), 423
Uruguay, 272
Uses of the University, The (Kerr), 206, 377

Vahanian, Gabriel, 268
Valachi, Joe, 297
Vale, Rena, 41, 529n
Van Deman, Gen. Ralph, 40,
Vandenberg Air Force Base, 447
Van der Ryn, Sim, 467
Vanek, John, 629n
Vaughn, Stephen L., 118, 554n, 556n
Veale, Dolly, 642n, 644n
Venice (California) Town Council, 499
Venn, Christopher D., 456, 477, 656n
Venona Project, 27
"Verse on the Prospect of Planting Arts and
  Learning in America" (Berkeley), 12
Veterans Administration Hospital (Menlo
  Park), 248
Vietnam Day Committee (VDC), xii, 262–88,
  301, 304–11, 313–20, 340, 360–61, 370, 389,
  447, 505; Aoki in, 420, 422; bombing of,
  318–20; FBI investigations and harassment
  of, 304, 310–11, 313–19, 394–96, 495;
  International Days of Protest, 272, 278, 282;
  Medaille (aka O'Hanlon) in, 314–17; Meese
  denounces, 326–27; Oakland march and
  rally of, 305–307, 391; Peace Commandos,
  309–11, 305; Peace Trip Dance sponsored
  by, 320–22, 324, 327–28, 337, 371; Stop the
  Draft Week, 384–85, 396, 449, 515n, 628n;
  teach-in, 261–65, 272, 275–76, 337; veterans
  of, 351–52, 365, 380, 402, 411, 415, 426, 489
Vietnam War, 228, 229, 233, 351, 383, 386,
  402, 452, 459, 463, 466, 467, 481, 501, 639n,
  642n; bombing of North Vietnam, 213, 262,
  341; Gulf of Tonkin incident, 261–62;
  opposition to, 341, 346, 348, 349, 361,
  364–65, 379, 380, 382, 387, 391, 401–403,
  409, 411, 415, 422, 432, 437, 496 (see also
  antiwar movement); Paris peace talks, 424;
  Tet Offensive, 452
Virgo, Peter, 560n
Voge, Herve, 11, 522n

Voge family, 56
"Voodoo Child (Slight Return)" (Hendrix), 480
voter registration, 158, 178, 182, 342, 345, 353, 477
Voting Rights Act (1965), 186

Wachter, Billie, 421
Wachter, Douglas, 78, 80–81, 86–87, 93, 397, 421
Wachter, Saul, 87, 421
Wadman, William, 53–54, 57–59, 63, 68, 203, 230, 251, 535n, 538n
Wagner, Pam, 70
Walker, Dorothy, 471
Walk in the Sun, A (film), 128
Wallace, Henry, 83, 128
Walrus Club, 532n
Walsh, Thomas, 103
Walter, Francis E., 94
Walter, Michael "Tiny," 281
Wang, Ben, 641n
War Labor Board, 50, 57, 230
Warner, Jack, 118, 119, 383, 557n
Warner Brothers, 20, 113, 117–19, 121, 364
Warren, Earl, 32–35, 37, 50, 52, 59, 303, 310, 525n, 543n, 602n
Warren Commission, 213
War Resisters League, 267
Washington, D.C., 8, 16, 17, 33, 57, 65, 68, 77, 129, 148, 166, 326, 402, 507, 511; antiwar protests in, 385; FBI headquarters in, 8, 68, 112, 285, 362, 485; Metropolitan Police Department, 148, 402, 403; National Press Club in, 328; Soviet embassy in, 24
Washington, University of, 50
Washington Monthly, 631n
Washington News, 132
Watergate Apartments (Washington, D.C.), 478
Watergate scandal, 360, 499, 542n, 554n, 667n
Waters, Alice, 320
Watkins v. United States (1957), 526n
Wayne, John, 131, 294, 304
Webster, William, 494
Weigel, Stanley A., 481–83
Weinberg, Jack, 153–56, 158, 193, 205, 209, 212, 214, 245, 266, 278, 385, 411, 432, 583n
Weinberg, Joseph, 23, 522nn, 530n
Weinberger, Caspar, 484
Weiner, Lee, 636n
Weir, Bob, 660n
Weir, David, 506
Weiss, Ken, 505

Weissman, Steve, 222, 225, 266, 272, 273, 278, 583n, 615n
Welch, Joseph, 79, 93
Welch, Robert, 303
Welles, Orson, 251, 528n
Wellman, David, 594n
Wells, Warren, 644n
Wells Fargo Building, 269, 495
"We Shall Not Be Moved" (protest song), 83, 104, 272
Wesley Foundation, 99
Western College for Women, 178
Western Research Foundation, 56, 278, 312, 395–97, 536n, 650n; see also Research West
Western Union Telegraph Company, 32, 525n
Westinghouse Science Talent Search, 164–65, 253, 410, 569n, 573n
Westmoreland, Gen. William, 430
West Virginia, University of, 525n
Wheaton, James, 509
Wheaton (Illinois), 612n
Wheeler, William, 68, 77, 80
Where's the Rest of Me? (Reagan), 113, 122, 144, 554nn
White, Burton, 83, 93, 101, 543n
White Citizens' Council, 180
White Album, The (Didion), 55
Whitehead, Don, 147
Whitman, Ernest, 560n
Whitman, Walt, 246
Whitmore, Earl, 385
Whitner's department store (Reading, Pennsylvania), 44
Whitney, Lynn, 560n
Whittier College, 535n
Whole Earth Catalog, 337
Wilcox, Clair, 46
Wilder, Billy, 134
Wilken, Claudia, 507
Wilkinson, Frank, 189, 191
Willard Junior High School (Berkeley), 108
Williams, Arleigh, 155, 191, 214–15
Williams, John, 404, 405
Willis, Edwin, 80
Willis, Ellen, 651n
Wills, Garry, 39, 554n, 558n, 561n, 562n
Wilson, Lyle, 553n
Wilson, William B., 18
Wilson (film), 128
Winchell, Walter, 553n
Winterland Auditorium (San Francisco), 467
wiretaps, 5, 12, 14, 21, 22, 109, 138, 201, 202, 402, 421, 491–93

Wisconsin, University of, 32, 646*n*
Wizard of Oz, The (film), 141
Wofsy, Leon, 227–28, 241, 464, 589–90*nn*, 594*n*
Wolfe, Burton H., 527*n*, 528*n*,
Wolfe, Maynard M., Jr., 97
Wolfe, Tom, 278, 337, 338
Wollenberg, Charles, 532*n*
Women's Republican Club (Wheeling, West Virginia), 28
Wong, Victoria, 640*n*
Wood, Ann Ginger, 594*n*
Wood, Sam, 137
Woodstock Festival, 450, 467
Woolsey, R. James, 237
Woolworth's, 78, 173
Wooster, College of, 550*n*
World War I, 17, 47
World War II, 4, 15, 20, 36–40, 50, 54, 114, 146, 159–60 203, 218, 231, 260, 328, 351, 360, 395; atomic bomb in, 11, 13, 163; black migration during, 390; enemy aliens arrested during, 198; fortunes made in arms industry during, 234, 235; German espionage during, 22; internment of Japanese Americans during, 419, 421; movies about, 128, 142; news coverage of, 134; prisoners of war during, 71; Reagan in, 118–19, 122, 142, 383, 557*n*; Soviet Union in, 27, 38, 238; veterans of, in FBI, 144, 199, 202, 239, 310
Wright, Guy, 313
Wyler, William, 127

Wyman, Jane, 6, 117, 118, 122, 124, 127, 134, 139, 141, 148–49, 297, 363, 510, 511, 555*n*, 556*nn*, 561*n*, 566*n*

Yale University, 4, 336, 390, 405
Yarus, Buddy, 560*n*
Yasgur, Max, 467
Yates v. United States (1957), 526*n*
Yearling, The (film), 134
"Yellow Submarine" (Lennon and McCartney), 366, 372, 436, 648*n*
Yippies, 317, 489
York, Richard, 470
Young Americans for Freedom (YAF), 267, 294, 307, 316, 334
Young Communist Movement, 204
Young Democrats, 196, 203, 307
Young Republicans, 158, 196, 207, 267, 316, 365
Young Socialist Alliance (YSA), 158, 386, 421, 422, 430, 516*n*, 581*n*
Young Socialists, 207
Yucca Flat (Nevada), 163

Zabriskie Point (film), 445, 652*n*
Zanger, Leonie Loeb, 35
Zapata, Emiliano, 171
Zelnik, Reginald, 409
Zimbalist, Efrem, Jr., 147
Zubilin, Vassili, 24

HILLSBORO PUBLIC LIBRARIES
Hillsboro, OR
Member of Washington County
COOPERATIVE LIBRARY SERVICES